Financial
Accounting
& Reporting

· ·

Financial Accounting & Reporting

••

Fifth edition

Barry Elliott and Jamie Elliott

FINANCIAL TIMES
Prentice Hall

An imprint of **Pearson Education**

Harlow, England · London · New York · Reading, Massachusetts · San Francisco · Toronto · Don Mills, Ontario · Sydney
Tokyo · Singapore · Hong Kong · Seoul · Taipei · Cape Town · Madrid · Mexico City · Amsterdam · Munich · Paris · Milan

Pearson Education Limited
Edinburgh Gate
Harlow
Essex CM20 2JE
England

and Associated Companies throughout the world

© Pearson Education Limited 2001

First published 1993
Second edition 1996
Third edition 1999
Fourth edition 2000
Fifth edition 2001

ISBN 0273-65156-0

British Library Cataloguing-in-Publication Data
A catalogue record for this book is available from the British Library

Library of Congress Cataloging-in-Publication Data
Elliott, Barry.
   Financial accounting & reporting / Barry Elliott and Jamie
Elliott. -- 5th ed.
      p.   cm.
   Includes bibliographical references and index.
   ISBN 0-13-015295-1
   1. Accounting   2. Financial statements.   I. Elliott, Jamie.
II. Title. III. Title: Financial accounting and reporting.
HF5635.E428   2001
657--dc21
                                                                                99-17038
                                                                                CIP

Typeset in 10/12 Monotype Ehrhardt by 42
Printed and bound in Great Britain by T.J. International Ltd., Padstow, Cornwall

Contents

Preface and acknowledgements

Our objective is to provide a balanced and comprehensive framework to enable students to acquire the requisite knowledge and skills to appraise current practice critically and to evaluate proposed changes from a theoretical base. To this end, the text contains:

- current standards and exposure drafts
- illustrations from published accounts
- a range of review questions
- exercises of varying difficulty
- outline solutions to selected exercises in an appendix at the end of the book
- extensive references.

We have assumed that readers will have an understanding of financial accounting to a foundation or first-year level, although the text and exercises have been designed on the basis that a brief revision is still helpful.

Lecturers are using the text selectively to support a range of teaching programmes for 2nd and Final Year undergraduate and postgraduate programmes. We have therefore attempted to provide subject coverage of sufficient breadth and depth to assist selective use.

The text has been adopted for financial accounting, reporting and analysis modules on:

- second year undergraduate courses for Accounting, Business Studies and Combined Studies;
- final year undergraduate courses for Accounting, Business Studies and Combined Studies;
- MBA courses;
- specialist MSc courses; and
- professional courses preparing students for professional accountancy examinations.

Changes to the fifth edition

Our emphasis has been on keeping the text current and responding to constructive comments from reviewers on both the content and the order of the chapters.

The principal changes from the fourth edition in the content are:

- Chapter 6 Financial reporting: statutes and standards includes FRSSE and Company Law – *The Strategic Framework*

- Chapter 7 Conceptual framework includes the *Statement of Principles* and FRED 21 *Accounting Policies*
- Chapter 8 Published accounts of listed companies includes the ASB Discussion Paper *Proposals for Change*
- Chapter 9 Preparation of published accounts includes Summary Financial Statements
- Chapter 11 Reduction of share capital includes proposed Company Law changes
- Chapter 12 Off balance sheet finance and capital instruments includes an overview of FRED 20 *Retirement Benefits*
- Chapter 13 includes FRS 16 *Current Tax* and FRED 19 *Deferred Tax* Taxation in company accounts
- Chapter 15 Fixed tangible assets – lessee includes the ASB Discussion Paper *Leases: Implementation of a New Approach*
- Chapters 25–30 have been updated.

The principal changes in the order of chapters have been:

- The consolidation chapters (including foreign currency) appear as a later section
- Tax and Pensions appear with liabilities
- Earnings per share appears in the Interpretation section (Part 5).

The content of financial reports continues to be subjected to discussion with a tension between preparers, stakeholders, auditors, academic accountants and standard setters; this is mirrored in the tension that exists between theory and practice.

- Preparers favour reporting transactions on a historical cost basis which is reliable but does not provide shareholders with relevant information to appraise past performance or to predict future earnings.
- Stakeholders favour forward looking reports relevant in estimating future dividend and capital growth and in understanding environmental and social impacts.
- Auditors favour reports that are verifiable so that the figures can be substantiated to avoid them being proved wrong at a later date.
- Academic accountants favour reports that reflect economic reality and are relevant in appraising management performance and in assessing the capacity of the company to adapt.
- Standard Setters lean towards the academic view and favour reporting according to the commercial substance of a transaction.

  In order to understand the tensions that exist, students need:

- the skill to prepare financial statements in accordance with the historical cost and current cost conventions, both of which appear in annual financial reports;
- an understanding of the main thrust of mandatory and voluntary standards;
- an understanding of the degree of flexibility available to the preparers and the impact of this on reported earnings and the balance sheet figures;
- an understanding of the limitations of these financial reports in portraying economic reality; and
- an exposure to source material and other published material in so far as time permits.

Teacher's Manual

A separate Teacher's Manual has been written to accompany this text. It contains fully worked solutions to all the exercises and is of a quality that allows them to be used as overhead transparencies. The Manual is available to lecturers on application to the publishers.

We are indebted to Catherine Newman, Laura Prime and Alison Stanford of Pearson Education for active support in keeping us largely to schedule and the attractively produced and presented text.

Finally we thank our wives, Di and Jacklin, for their continued good humoured support during the period of writing and revisions, and Giles Elliott for his critical comment at the commencement of the project. We alone remain responsible for any errors and for the thoughts and views that are expressed.

Acknowledgements

Financial Reporting is a dynamic area and we see it as extremely important that the text should reflect this and be kept current. Assistance has been generously given by colleagues and many others in the preparation and review of the text and assessment material. This 5th edition is very much a result of the authors, colleagues, reviewers and Pearson editorial and production staff working as a team and we are grateful to all concerned for their assistance in achieving this.

We owe particular thanks to:

Sally Aisbitt of the University of Teesside, who has updated her chapter 'International reporting & interpretation' which first appeared in the second edition;

Ron Altshul of the University of Sunderland, who has updated 'Taxation in company accounts'.

Steve Dungworth of De Montfort University, for 'Ethics for accountants' which first appeared in the third edition.

Ozer Erman of Kingston University, for 'Share capital, capital maintenance and distributable profits' and 'Capital Reductions' which first appeared in the second edition.

Walter Hamilton, formerly of Sandwell College, for 'Foreign currency translation' which first appeared in the third edition.

Martin Howes for inputs to financial analysis.

Thanks are owed to Iain Fleming of the University of Paisley and John Morley of the University of Brighton for painstaking and constructive review of selected chapters in the fourth edition.

Thanks are owed to: A.T. Benedict of the Southbank University, Keith Brown of de Montfort University, Kenneth N. Field of the University of Leeds, Ian Harrison, Chief Examiner of the Associated Examining Board, Sue McDermott of London Guildhall University, David Murphy of Manchester Metropolitan University, Bahadur Najak of the University of Durham, Graham Sara of Coventry University, Laura Spira of Oxford Brookes University, Ken Trunkfield, formerly of the University of Derby, and Martin Tuffy of the University of Brighton.

Thanks are also due to the following people and organisations: Alan Millichamp, M. Moorhouse of Rank Hovis McDougall plc, Andrew Strickland of Scrutton Bland Chartered Accountants, David Starr of Grant Thornton Chartered Accountants, the Accounting Standards Board, the Association of Chartered Certified Accountants, the Chartered Institute of Management Accountants, the Institute of Chartered Accountants of Scotland, Chartered Institute of Public Finance and Accountancy, Chartered Institute of Bankers and the Institute of Investment Management and Research.

We would also like to thank the authors of some of the end-of-chapter exercises. Some of these exercises have been inherited from a variety of institutions with which we have been associated, and we have unfortunately lost the identities of the originators of such material with the passage of time. We are sorry that we cannot acknowledge them by name and hope that will excuse us for using their material.

Barry and Jamie Elliott
June 2000

Parts of the Combined Code have been reproduced by kind permission of Gee Publishing Limited, © 1998 The London Stock Exchange Limited.

PART **1**

Income and asset value measurement systems

Accounting and reporting on a cash flow basis

1.1 Introduction

Accountants are communicators. Accountancy is the art of communicating financial information about a business entity to users such as shareholders and managers. The communication is generally in the form of financial statements that show in money terms the economic resources under the control of the management. The art lies in selecting the information that is relevant to the user and is reliable.

Shareholders require periodic information that the managers are accounting properly for the resources under their control. This information helps the shareholders to evaluate the performance of the managers. The performance measured by the accountant shows the extent to which the economic resources of the business have grown or diminished during the year.

The shareholders also require information to **predict future performance**. At present companies are not required to publish forecast financial statements on a regular basis and the shareholders use the report of past performance when making their prediction.

Managers require information in order **to control the business and make investment decisions**.

In this chapter we will consider both categories of user, and the extent to which cash flow accounting would satisfy their information needs under the following headings:

- Shareholders
- What skills does an accountant require in respect of external reports?
- Managers
- What skills does an accountant require in respect of internal reports?
- Procedural steps when reporting to internal users
- Illustration of operating cash flows
- Illustration continued with statement of financial position
- Treatment of fixed assets in the cash flow model
- What are the characteristics of these data that make them reliable
- Reports to external users

1.2 Shareholders

Shareholders are external users. As such, they are unable to obtain access to the same amount of detailed historical information as the managers, e.g. total administration costs are disclosed in the published profit and loss account, but not an analysis to show how the figure is made up. Shareholders are also unable to obtain associated information, e.g. budgeted sales and costs. Even though the shareholders own a company, their entitlement to information is restricted.

The information to which shareholders are entitled is restricted to that specified by statute, e.g. the Companies Acts, or by professional regulation, e.g. Statements of Standard Accounting Practice, or by market regulations, e.g. Stock Exchange requirements. This means that there may be a tension between the **amount** of information that a shareholder would like to receive and the amount that the directors are prepared to provide. For example, shareholders might consider that forecasts of future cash flows would be helpful in predicting future dividends, but the directors might be concerned that such forecasts would help competitors. As a result, this information is not disclosed.

There may also be a tension between the **quality** of information that shareholders would like to receive and that which directors are prepared to provide. For example, the shareholders might consider that judgements made by the directors in the valuation of long-term contracts should be fully explained, whereas the directors might prefer not to reveal this information given the high risk of error that often attaches to such estimates. In practice, companies tend to compromise: they do not reveal the judgements to the shareholders, but maintain confidence by relying on the auditor to give a clean audit report.

The financial reports presented to the shareholders are also used by other parties such as lenders and trade creditors, and they have come to be regarded as general-purpose reports. However, it may be difficult or impossible to satisfy the needs of all users. For example, users may have different time-scales – shareholders may be interested in the long-term trend of earnings over three years, whereas creditors may be interested in the likelihood of receiving cash within the next three months.

The information needs of the shareholders are regarded as the primary concern. The government perceives shareholders to be important because they provide companies with their economic resources. It is shareholders' needs that take priority in deciding on the nature and detailed content of the general-purpose reports.[1]

1.3 What skills does an accountant require in respect of external reports?

For external reporting purposes the accountant has a two-fold obligation:

● An obligation to ensure that the financial statements comply with statutory, professional and Stock Exchange requirements; this requires the accountant to possess **technical expertise**.
● An obligation to ensure that the financial statements present the substance of the commercial transactions the company has entered into; this requires the accountant to have **commercial awareness**.[2]

1.4 Managers

Managers are internal users. As such, they have access to detailed financial statements showing the current results, the extent to which these vary from the budgeted results and the future budgeted results. Examples of internal users are sole traders, partners and, in a company context, directors and managers.

There is no statutory restriction on the amount of information that an internal user may receive; the only restriction would be that imposed by the company's own policy. Frequently, companies operate a 'need to know' policy and only the directors see all the financial statements; employees, for example, would be most unlikely to receive information that would assist them in claiming a salary increase – unless, of course, it happened to be a time of recession, when information would be more freely provided by management as a means of containing claims for an increase.

1.5 What skills does an accountant require when preparing internal reports?

For the internal user, the accountant is able to tailor his or her reports. The accountant is required to produce financial statements that are specifically relevant to the user requesting them.

The accountant needs to be skilled in identifying the information that is needed and conveying its implication and meaning to the user. The user needs to be confident that the accountant understands the user's information needs and will satisfy them in a language that is understandable. The accountant must be a skilled communicator who is able to instil confidence in the user that the information is:

● relevant to the user's needs;[3]

● measured objectively;

● presented within a time-scale that permits decisions to be made with appropriate information;

● verifiable, in that it can be confirmed that the report represents the transactions that have taken place;

● reliable, in that it is as free from bias as is possible;

● a complete picture of material items; and

● a fair representation of the business transactions and events that have occurred or are being planned.

The accountant is a trained reporter of financial information. Just as for external reporting, the accountant needs commercial awareness. It is important, therefore, that he or she should not operate in isolation.

1.5.1 Accountant's reporting role

The accountant's role is to ensure that the information provided is useful for making decisions. For external users, the accountant achieves this by providing a general-purpose financial statement that complies with statute and is reliable. For internal users, this is done by interfacing with the user and establishing exactly what financial information is relevant to the decision that is to be made.

We now consider the steps required to provide relevant information for internal users.

1.6 Procedural steps when reporting to internal users

A number of user steps and accounting action steps can be identified within a financial decision model. These are shown in Figure 1.1.

Note that, although we refer to an accountant/user interface, this is not a single occurrence because the user and accountant interface at each of the user decision steps.

At **step 1**, the accountant attempts to ensure that the decision is based on the appropriate appraisal methodology. However, the accountant is providing a service to a user and, while the accountant may give guidance, the final decision about methodology rests with the user.

At **step 2**, the accountant needs to establish the information necessary to support the decision that is to be made.

At **step 3**, the accountant needs to ensure that the user **understands** the full impact and financial implications of the accountant's report taking into account the user's level of understanding and prior knowledge. This may be overlooked by the accountant, who feels that the task has been completed when the written report has been typed.

It is important to remember in following the model that the accountant is attempting to satisfy the information needs of the individual user rather than those of a 'user group'. It is tempting to divide users into groups with apparently common information needs, without recognising that a group contains individual users with different information needs. We return to this later in the chapter, but for the moment we continue by studying a situation where the directors of a company are considering a proposed capital investment project.

Let us assume that there are three companies in the retail industry: Retail A Ltd, Retail B Ltd and Retail C Ltd. The directors of each company are considering the purchase of a warehouse. We could assume initially that, because the companies are operating in the same industry and are faced with the same investment decision, they have identical information needs. However, enquiry might establish that the directors of each company have a completely different attitude to, or perception of, the primary business objective.

For example, it might be established that Retail A Ltd is a large company and under the Fisher/Hirshleifer separation theory the directors seek to maximise profits for the benefit of the equity investors; Retail B Ltd is a medium-sized company in which the directors seek to obtain a satisfactory return for the equity shareholders; and Retail C Ltd

---

Figure 1.1 General financial decision model to illustrate the user/accountant interface.

USER

User step 1 Identify decision and how it is to be made

User step 2 Establish with the accountant
the information necessary for decision-making

User step 3 Seek relevant data from the accountant

USER/ACCOUNTANT INTERFACE

Provide an understandable report to the user

Prepare report for user to allow him to make decision

Measure the relevant information

Identify the material information needed by the user

ACCOUNTANT

is a smaller company in which the directors seek to achieve a satisfactory return for a wider range of shareholders, including, perhaps, the employees as well as the equity shareholders.

The accountant needs to be aware that these differences may have a significant effect on the information required. Let us consider this diagrammatically in the situation where a capital investment decision is to be made, referring particularly to user step 2: 'Establish with the accountant the information necessary for decision making'.

We can see from Figure 1.2 that the accountant has identified that:

● the relevant financial data are the same for each of the users, i.e. cash flows; but
● the appraisal method selected, i.e. internal rate of return (IRR) and net present value (NPV), are different; and
● the appraisal criteria employed by each user, i.e. higher IRR and NPV, are different.

In practice, the user is likely to use more than one appraisal method, as each has advantages and disadvantages. However, we can see that, even when dealing with a single group of apparently homogeneous users, the accountant has first to identify the information needs of the particular user. Only then is the accountant able to identify the relevant financial data and the appropriate report. It is the **user's** needs that are predominant.

If the accountant's view of the appropriate appraisal method or criterion differs from the user's view, the accountant might decide to report from **both** views. This approach affords the opportunity to improve the user's understanding and encourages good practice.

The diagrams can be combined (Figure 1.3) to illustrate the complete process. The user is assumed to be Retail A Ltd, a company that has directors who are profit maximisers.

Figure 1.2 Impact of different user attitudes on the information needed in relation to a capital investment proposal.

	USER A	USER B	USER C
	Directors of Retail A Ltd	Directors of Retail B Ltd	Directors of Retail C Ltd
User attitude	PROFIT MAXIMISER for SHAREHOLDERS	PROFIT SATISFICER for SHAREHOLDERS	PROFIT SATISFICER for SHAREHOLDERS/STAFF
Relevant data to measure	CASH FLOWS	CASH FLOWS	CASH FLOWS
Appraisal method (decided on by user)	IRR	NPV	NPV
Appraisal criterion (decided on by user)	HIGHEST IRR	NPV but only if positive	NPV possibly even if negative

---

Figure 1.3 User/accountant interface where the user is a profit maximiser.

	General model **USER**	**Specific application for Retail A Ltd** **A PROFIT MAXIMISER**
Step 1	Decision to be made	Appraise which project warrants capital investment
Step 2	Information needed	Project with the highest IRR
Step 3	Seek relevant data	Report of IRR by project
	USER/ACCOUNTANT INTERFACE	**USER/ACCOUNTANT INTERFACE**
	Provide report	Submit report of project with highest IRR per £ invested
	Prepare report	Prepare report of highest IRR
	Measure	Measure the project cash flows
	Identify information needed by the user	User decision criterion is IRR
	ACCOUNTANT	**ACCOUNTANT**

The accountant is reactive when reporting to an internal user. We observe this characteristic in the Norman example set out in section 1.8. Because the cash flows are identified as relevant to the user, it is these flows that the accountant will record, measure and appraise.

The accountant can also be proactive, by giving the user advice and guidance in areas where the accountant has specific expertise, such as the appraisal method that is most appropriate to the circumstances.

1.7 Agency costs[4]

The information in Figure 1.2 assumes that the directors have made their investment decision based on the assumed preferences of the shareholders. However, in real life, the directors might also be influenced by how the decision impinges on their own position. If, for example, their remuneration is a fixed salary, they might select not the investment with the highest IRR, but the one that maintains their security of employment. The result might be suboptimal investment and financing decisions based on risk aversion and over-retention. To the extent that the potential cash flows have been reduced, there will be an agency cost to the shareholders. This agency cost is an opportunity cost – the amount that was forgone because the decision making was suboptimal – and, as such, it will not be recorded in the books of account and will not appear in the financial statements.

1.8 Illustration of periodic financial statements prepared under the cash flow concept to disclose realised operating cash flows

In the above example of Retail A, B and C, the investment decision for the acquisition of a warehouse was based on an appraisal of cash flows. This raises the question: 'Why not continue with the cash flow concept and report the financial changes that occur after the investment has been undertaken using that same concept?'

To do this, the company will record the consequent cash flows through a number of subsequent accounting periods; report the cash flows that occur in each financial period; and produce a balance sheet at the end of each of the financial periods. For illustration we follow this procedure in paras 1.8.1 and 1.8.2 for transactions entered into by Mr S. Norman.

1.8.1 Appraisal of the initial investment decision

Mr Norman is considering whether to start up a retail business by acquiring the lease of a shop for five years at a cost of £80,000.

Our first task has been set out in Figure 1.2 above. It is to establish the information that Mr Norman needs, so that we can decide what data it will be necessary to collect and measure. Let us assume that, as a result of a discussion with Mr Norman, it has been ascertained that he is a profit satisficer who is looking to achieve at least a 10% return, which represents the time value of money. This indicates that:

● the relevant data to be measured are **cash flows**, represented by the outflow of cash invested in the lease and the inflow of cash represented by the realised operating cash flows;

● the appropriate appraisal method is **NPV**; and

● the appraisal criterion is a **positive NPV** using the discount rate of 10%.

Let us further assume that the cash to be invested in the lease is £80,000 and that the realised operating cash flows over the life of the investment in the shop are as shown in Figure 1.4. This shows that there is a forecast of £30,000 annually for five years and a final receipt of £29,000 in 20X6 when he proposes to cease trading.

We already know that Mr Norman's investment criterion is a positive NPV using a discount factor of 10%. A calculation (Figure 1.5) shows that the investment easily satisfies that criterion.

1.8.2 Preparation of periodic financial statements under the cash flow concept

Having **predicted** the realised operating cash flows for the purpose of making the investment decision, we can assume that the owner of the business will wish to obtain **feedback**

Figure 1.4 Forecast of realised operating cash flows.

	Annually years 20X1–20X5	Cash in year 20X6 after shop closure
	£	£
Receipts from		
Customers	400,000	55,000
Payments for		
Trade creditors	(342,150)	(20,000)
Expense creditors	(21,600)	(3,000)
Rent	(6,250)	(3,000)
Total payments	(370,000)	(26,000)
Realised operating cash flows	30,000	29,000

Figure 1.5 NPV calculation using discount tables.

	£	£
Cost of lease		(80,000)
£30,000 annually for 5 years (30,000 × 3.79)	113,700	
£29,000 received in year 6 (29,000 × 0.564)	16,356	
		130,056
Positive net present value		50,056

to evaluate the correctness of the investment decision. He does this by reviewing the actual results on a regular **timely** basis and **comparing** these with the predicted forecast. Actual results should be reported quarterly, half-yearly or annually in the same format as used when making the decision in Figure 1.4. The actual results provide management with the feedback information required to audit the initial decision; it is a technique for achieving accountability. However, frequently, companies do not provide a report of actual cash flows to compare with the forecast cash flows, and fail to carry out an audit review.

In some cases, the transactions relating to the investment cannot be readily separated from other transactions, and the information necessary for the audit review of the investment cannot be made available. In other cases, the routine accounting procedures fail to collect such cash flow information because the reporting systems have not been designed to provide financial reports on a cash flow basis; rather, they have been designed to produce reports prepared on an accrual basis.

What would financial reports look like if they were prepared on a cash flow basis?

To illustrate cash flow period accounts, we will prepare half-yearly accounts for Mr Norman. To facilitate a comparison with the forecast that underpinned the investment decision, we will redraft the forecast annual statement on a half-yearly basis. The data for the first year given in Figure 1.4 have therefore been redrafted to provide a forecast for the half-year to 30 June, as shown in Figure 1.6.

Figure 1.6 Forecast of realised operating cash flows.

	Half-year to 30 June 20X1 £
Receipts from	
Customers	165,000
Payments for	
Trade creditors	(124,000)
Expense creditors	(18,000)
Rent	(6,250)
Total payments	(148,250)
Realised operating cash flows	16,750

Figure 1.7 Monthly sales, purchases and expenses for six months ended 30 June 20X1.

Month	Sales invoiced £	Cash received £	Purchases invoiced £	Cash paid £	Expenses invoiced £	Cash paid £
January	15,000	7,500	16,000		3,400	3,100
February	20,000	17,500	19,000	16,000	3,500	3,400
March	35,000	27,500	29,000	19,000	3,800	3,500
April	40,000	37,500	32,000	29,000	3,900	3,800
May	40,000	40,000	33,000	32,000	3,900	3,900
June	45,000	42,500	37,000	33,000	4,000	3,900
TOTAL	195,000	172,500	166,000	129,000	22,500	21,600

Note: The following items were included under the Expenses invoiced heading:

Expense creditors   – amount
Wages   – £3,100 per month paid in the month
Commission   – 2% of sales invoiced payable 1 month in arrears

We assume that, having applied the net present value appraisal technique to the cash flows and ascertained that the NPV was positive, Mr Norman proceeded to set up the business on 1 January 20X1. He introduced capital of £50,000, acquired a five-year lease for £80,000 and paid £6,250 in advance as rent to occupy the property to 31 December 20X1. He has decided to prepare financial statements at half-yearly intervals. The information given in Figure 1.7 concerns his trading for the half-year to 30 June 20X1.

Mr Norman was naturally eager to determine whether the business was achieving its forecast cash flows for the first six months of trading, so he produced the statement of realised operating cash flows (Figure 1.8) from the information provided in Figure 1.7. From this statement we can see that the business generated positive cash flows after the end of February. These are, of course, only the cash flows relating to the trading transactions.

The information in the 'Total' column of Figure 1.8 can be extracted to provide the financial statement for the six months ended 30 June 20X1, as shown in Figure 1.9.

The figure of £15,650 needs to be compared with the forecast cash flows used in the investment appraisal. This is a form of auditing. It allows the assumptions made on the

Figure 1.8 Monthly realised operating cash flows.

	Jan £	Feb £	Mar £	Apr £	May £	Jun £	Total £
Receipts							
Debtors	7,500	17,500	27,500	37,500	40,000	42,500	172,500
Less payments							
Trade creditors		16,000	19,000	29,000	32,000	33,000	129,000
Expense creditors	3,100	3,400	3,500	3,800	3,900	3,900	21,600
Rent	6,250						6,250
Realised	−1,850	−1,900	5,000	4,700	4,100	5,600	15,650

Figure 1.9 Realised operating cash flows for the six months ended 30 June 20X1.

		£
Receipts from		
Customers		172,500
Payments		
To trade creditors	(129,000)	
To expense creditors	(21,600)	
To rent	(6,250)	
		156,850
Realised operating cash flow		15,650

initial investment decision to be confirmed. The forecast/actual comparison (based on the information in Figures 1.6 and 1.9) is set out in Figure 1.10.

What are the characteristics of these data that make them relevant?

● The data are **objective**. There is no judgement involved in deciding the values to include in the financial statement, as each value or amount represents a verifiable cash transaction with a third party.

● The data are **consistent**. The statement incorporates the same cash flows within the periodic financial report of trading as the cash flows that were incorporated within the initial capital investment report. This permits a logical comparison and confirmation that the decision was realistic.

● The results have a **confirmatory** value by helping users confirm or correct their past assessments.

● The results have a **predictive** value, in that they provide a basis for revising the initial forecasts if necessary.[5]

● There is **no requirement for accounting standards** or disclosure of accounting policies that are necessary to regulate accrual accounting practices, e.g. Depreciation methods.

Figure 1.10 Forecast/actual comparison.

		Actual £	Forecast £
Receipts from			
Customers		172,500	165,000
Payments			
To trade creditors	(129,000)		(124,000)
To expense creditors	(21,600)		(18,000)
To rent	(6,250)		(6,250)
Total payments		(156,850)	(148,250)
Realised operating cash flow		15,650	16,750

1.9 Illustration of preparation of balance sheet under the cash flow concept

Although the information set out in Figure 1.10 permits us to compare and evaluate the initial decision, it does not provide a sufficiently sound basis for the following:

● Assessing the stewardship over the total cash funds that have been employed within the business.

● Signalling to management whether its working capital policies are appropriate.

1.9.1 Stewardship

To assess the stewardship over the total cash funds we need to:

(a) evaluate the effectiveness of the accounting system to make certain that all transactions are recorded;

(b) extend the cash flow statement to take account of the capital cash flows; and

(c) prepare a statement of financial position or balance sheet as at 30 June 20X1.

The additional information for (b) and (c) above is set out in Figures 1.11 and 1.12 respectively.

Figure 1.11 Cash flow statement to calculate the net cash balance.

	Jan £	Feb £	Mar £	Apr £	May £	Jun £	Total £
Operating cash	−1,850	−1,900	5,000	4,700	4,100	5,600	15,650
New capital	50,000						50,000
Lease payment	−80,000						−80,000
Cash balance	−31,850	−33,750	−28,750	−24,050	−19,950	−14,350	−14,350

Figure 1.12 Statement of financial position.

	Opening 1 Jan 20X1 £	Closing 30 Jun 20X1 £
Capital introduced	50,000	50,000
Net operating cash flow		15,650
	50,000	65,650
Lease		80,000
Net cash balance	50,000	−14,350
	50,000	65,650

The cash flow statement and statement of financial position, taken together, are a means of assessing stewardship. They identify the movement of **all** cash and derive a **net** balance figure. These statements are a normal feature of a sound system of internal control, but they have not been made available to external users.

1.9.2 Working capital policies

By 'working capital' we mean the current assets and current liabilities of the business. In addition to providing a means of making management accountable, cash flows are the raw data required by financial managers when making decisions on the management of working capital. One of the decisions would be to set the appropriate terms for credit policy. For example, Figure 1.11 shows that the business will have a £14,350 overdraft at 30 June 20X1. If this is not acceptable, management will review its working capital by reconsidering the credit given to customers, the credit taken from suppliers, stock holding levels and the timing of capital cash inflows and outflows.

If, in the example, it were possible to obtain 45 days' credit from suppliers, then the creditors at 30 June would rise from £37,000 to a new total of £53,500. This increase in trade credit of £16,500 means that half of the May purchases (£33,000/2) would not be paid for until July, which would convert the overdraft of £14,350 into a positive balance of £2,150. As a new business it might not be possible to obtain credit from all of the suppliers. In that case other steps would be considered, such as phasing the payment for the lease of the warehouse or introducing more capital.

An interesting research report[6] identified that for small firms survival and stability were the main objectives rather than profit maximisation. This, in turn, meant that cash flow indicators and managing cash flow were seen as crucial to survival. In addition, cash flow information was perceived as important to external bodies such as banks in evaluating performance.

1.10 Treatment of fixed assets in the cash flow model

The statement of financial position in Figure 1.12 does not take into account any **unrealised** cash flows. Such flows are deemed to occur as a result of any rise or fall in the realisable value of the lease. This could rise if, for example, the annual rent payable under the lease were to be substantially lower than the rate payable under a new lease entered into on 30 June 20X1. It could also fall with the passing of time, with six months having expired by 30 June 20X1. We need to consider this further and examine the possible treatment of fixed assets in the cash flow model.

Using the cash flow approach, we require an independent verification of the realisable value of the lease at 30 June 20X1. If the lease has fallen in value, the difference between the original outlay and the net realisable figure could be treated as a negative unrealised operating cash flow.

For example, if the independent estimate was that the realisable value was £74,000, then the statement of financial position would be prepared as in Figure 1.13. The fall of £6,000 in realisable value is an unrealised cash flow and, while it does not affect the calculation of the net cash balance, it does affect the statement of financial position.

The additional benefit of the statement of financial position, as revised, is that the owner is able clearly to identify the following:

Figure 1.13   Statement of financial position as at 30 June 20X1 (assuming that there were unrealised operating cash flows).

	£
Capital introduced	50,000
Net operating flow: **realised**	15,650
: **unrealised**	(6,000)
	59,650
Lease: **net realisable value**	74,000
Net cash balance	−14,350
	59,650

- The operating cash in-flows of £15,650 that have been realised from the business operations.
- The operating cash out-flow of £6,000 that has not been realised, but has arisen as a result of investing in the lease.
- The net cash balance of −£14,350.
- The statement provides a **stewardship-orientated** report: that is, it is a means of making the management accountable for the cash within its control.

1.11   What are the characteristics of these data that make them reliable?

We have already discussed some characteristics of cash flow reporting which indicate that the data in the financial statements are **relevant**, e.g. their predictive and confirmatory roles. We now introduce five more characteristics of cash flow statements which indicate that the information is also **reliable**, i.e. free from bias.[7] These are prudence, neutrality, completeness, faithful representation and freedom from material error.

1.11.1   Prudence characteristic

Revenue and profits are included in the cash flow statement only when they are realised. Realisation is deemed to occur when cash is received. In our Norman example, the £172,500 cash received from debtors represents the revenue for the half-year ended 30 June 20X1. This policy is described as prudent because it **does not anticipate** cash flows: cash flows are recorded only when they actually occur and not when they are reasonably certain of occurring. This is one of the factors that distinguishes cash flow from accrual accounting.

1.11.2   Neutrality characteristic

Financial statements are not neutral if, by their selection or presentation of information, they influence the making of a decision in order to achieve a predetermined result or outcome. With cash flow accounting, the information is not subject to management selection criteria.

Cash flow accounting avoids the tension that can arise between prudence and neutrality because, whilst neutrality involves freedom from deliberate or systematic bias, prudence is a potentially biased concept that seeks to ensure that, under conditions of uncertainty, gains and assets are not overstated and losses and liabilities are not understated.[8]

1.11.3 Completeness characteristic

The cash flows can be verified for completeness provided there are adequate internal control procedures in operation. In small and medium enterprises there can be a weakness if one person, typically the owner, has control over the accounting system and is able to under-record cash receipts.

1.11.4 Faithful representation characteristic

Cash flows can be depended upon by users to represent faithfully what they purport to represent provided, of course, that the completeness characteristic has been satisfied.

1.12 Reports to external users

1.12.1 Stewardship orientation

Cash flow accounting provides objective, consistent and prudent financial information about a business's transactions. It is stewardship orientated and offers a means of achieving accountability over cash resources and investment decisions.

1.12.2 Prediction orientation

External users are also interested in the ability of a company to pay dividends. It might be thought that the past and current cash flows are the best indicators of future cash flows and dividends. However, the cash flow might be misleading, in that a declining company might sell fixed assets and have a better **net cash position** than a growing company that buys fixed assets for future use. There is also no matching of cash inflows and outflows, in the sense that a benefit is matched with the sacrifice made to achieve it.

Consequently, it has been accepted accounting practice to view the profit and loss account prepared on the accrual accounting concept as a better predictor of future cash flows to an investor than the cash flow statements that we have illustrated in this chapter.

However, the operating cash flows arising from trading and the cash flows arising from the introduction of capital and the acquisition of fixed assets do become significant to investors if they threaten the company's ability to survive.

In the next chapter we revise the preparation of the same three statements using the **accrual accounting** model.

Summary

To review our understanding of this chapter, we should ask ourselves the following questions.

How useful is cash flow accounting for internal decision making?

Forecast cash flows are relevant for the appraisal of proposals for capital investment.

Actual cash flows are relevant for the confirmation of the decision for capital investment.

Cash flows are relevant for the management of working capital. Financial managers might have a variety of mathematical models for the efficient use of working capital, but cash flows are the raw data upon which they work.

How useful is cash flow accounting for making management accountable?

The cash flow statement is useful for confirming decisions and, together with the statement of financial position, provides a stewardship report. Lee states that 'Cash flow accounting appears to satisfy the need to supply owners and others with stewardship-orientated information as well as with decision-orientated information.'[9]

Lee further states that:

> By reducing judgements in this type of financial report, management can report factually on its stewardship function, whilst at the same time disclosing data of use in the decision making process. In other words, cash flow reporting eliminates the somewhat artificial segregation of stewardship and decision-making information.

This is exactly what we saw in our Norman example – the same realised operating cash flow information was used for both the investment decision and financial reporting. However, for stewardship purposes it was necessary to extend the cash flow to include **all** cash movements and to extend the statement of financial position to include the **unrealised** cash flows.

How useful is cash flow accounting for reporting to external users?

Cash flow information is relevant:

- as a basis for making internal management decisions in relation to both fixed assets and working capital; and
- for stewardship and accountability.

Cash flow information is reliable, being:

- objective;
- consistent;
- prudent; and
- neutral.

However, professional accounting practice requires reports to external users to be on an accrual accounting basis. This is because the accrual accounting profit figure is a better predictor for investors of the future cash flows likely to arise from the dividends paid to them by the business, and of any capital gain on disposal of their investment. It could also be argued that cash flows may not be a fair representation of the commercial substance of transactions e.g. if a business allowed a year's credit to all its customers there would be no income recorded.

Review questions

1 Explain why it is the user who should determine the information that the accountant collects, measures and reports, rather than the accountant who is the expert in financial information.

2 Yuji Ijiri rejects decision usefulness as the main purpose of accounting and puts in its place accountability. Ijiri sees the accounting relationship as a tripartite one, involving the accountor, the accountee, and the accountant … the decision useful approach is heavily biased in favour of the

accountee … with little concern for the accountor … in the central position Ijiri would put fairness.[10]

Discuss Ijiri's view in the context of cash flow accounting.

3 Discuss the extent to which you consider that accounts for a small businessperson who is carrying on business as a sole trader should be prepared on a cash flow basis.

4 Explain why your decision in question 3 might be different if the business entity were a medium-sized limited company.

5 'Realised operating cash flows are only of use for internal management purposes and are irrelevant to investors.' Discuss.

6 'While accountants may be free from bias in the measurement of economic information, they cannot be unbiased in identifying the economic information that they consider to be relevant.' Discuss.

7 Explain the effect on the statement of financial position in Figure 1.13 if the fixed asset consisted of expenditure on industry-specific machine tools rather than a lease.

8 'It is essential that the information in financial statements has a prudent characteristic if the financial statements are to be objective.' Discuss.

Exercises

An extract from the solution is provided in the appendix at the end of the text for exercises marked with an asterisk (*).

* *Question 1*

Jane Parker is going to set up a new business on 1 January 20X1. She estimates that her first six months in business will be as follows:

(i) She will put £150,000 into a bank account for the firm on 1 January 20X1.

(ii) On 1 January 20X1 she will buy machinery £30,000, motor vehicles £24,000 and premises £75,000, paying for them immediately.

(iii) All purchases will be effected on credit. She will buy £30,000 goods on 1 January and will pay for these in February. Other purchases will be: rest of January £48,000; February, March, April, May and June £60,000 each month. Other than the £30,000 worth bought in January, all other purchases will be paid for two months after purchase.

(iv) Sales (all on credit) will be £60,000 for January and £75,000 for each month after. Debtors will pay for the goods in the third month after purchase, i.e. £60,000 is received in May.

(v) She will make drawings of £1,200 per month.

(vi) Wages and salaries will be £2,250 per month and will be paid on the last day of each month.

(vii) General expenses will be £750 per month, payable in the month following that in which they are incurred.

(viii) Rates will be paid as follows: for the three months to 31 March 20X1 by cheque on 28 February 20X1; for the 12 months ended 31 March 20X2 by cheque on 31 July 20X1. Rates are £4,800 per annum.

(ix) She will introduce new capital of £82,500 on 1 April 20X1.

(x) Insurance covering the 12 months of 20X1 £2,100 will be paid for by cheque on 30 June 20X1.

(xi) All receipts and payments will be by cheque.

(xii) Stock in trade on 30 June 20X1 will be £30,000.

(xiii) The net realisable value of the vehicles is £19,200, machinery £27,000 and premises £75,000.

Required: Cash flow accounting

(i) **Draft a cash budget (includes bank) month by month for the period January to June, showing clearly the amount of bank balance or overdraft at the end of each month.**

(ii) **Draft an operating cash flow statement for the six-month period.**

(iii) **Assuming that Jane Parker sought your advice as to whether she should actually set up in business, state what further information you would require.**

* Question 2

Mr Norman set up a new business on 1 January 20X8. He invested £50,000 in the new business on that date. The following information is available.

1 Gross profit was 20% of sales. Monthly sales were as follows:

Month	Sales £	Month	Sales £
January	15,000	May	40,000
February	20,000	June	45,000
March	35,000	July	50,000
April	40,000		

2 50% of sales were for cash. Debtors (50% of sales) pay in month following sale.

3 The supplier allowed one month's credit.

4 Monthly payments were made for rent and rates £2,200 and wages £600.

5 On 1 January 20X8 the following payments were made: £80,000 for a five-year lease of business premises and £3,500 for insurances on the premises for the year. The realisable value of the lease was estimated to be £76,000 on 30 June 20X8 and £70,000 on 31 December 20X8.

6 Staff sales commission of 2% of sales was paid in the month following the sale.

Required:

(a) **A purchases budget for each of the first six months.**

(b) **A cash flow statement for the first six months.**

(c) **A statement of operating cash flows and financial position as at 30 June 20X8.**

(d) **Write a brief letter to the bank supporting a request for an overdraft.**

Question 3

Fred and Sally own a profitable business that deals in windsurfing equipment. They are the only UK agents to import 'Dryline' sails from Germany, and in addition to this they sell a variety of boards and miscellaneous equipment that they buy from other dealers in the UK.

Two years ago they diversified into custom-made boards built to individual customer requirements, each of which was supplied with a 'Dryline' sail. In order to build the boards they have had to take over larger premises, which consist of a shop front with a workshop at the rear, and employ two members of staff to help.

Demand is seasonal and Fred and Sally find that there is insufficient work during the winter months to pay rent for the increased accommodation and also wages to the extra two members of staff. The four of them could spend October to March in Lanzarote as windsurf instructors and close the UK operation down in this period. If they did, however, they would lose the 'Dryline' agency, as Dryline insists on a retail outlet in the UK for twelve months of the year. Dryline sails constitute 40% of their turnover and carry a 50% mark-up.

Trading has been static and the pattern is expected to continue as follows for 1 April 20X5 to 31 March 20X6:

Sales of boards and equipment (non-custom-built) with Dryline agency: 1 April–30 September £120,000; of this 30% was paid by credit card, which involved one month's delay in receiving cash and 4% deduction at source.

Sixty custom-built boards 1 April–30 September £60,000; of this 15% of the sales price was for the sail (a 'Dryline' 6 m² sail costs Fred and Sally £100, the average price for a sail of the same size and quality is £150 (cost to them)).

Purchasers of custom-built boards take an average of two months to pay and none pays by credit card.

Sales 1 October–31 March of boards and equipment (non-custom-built) £12,000, 30% by credit card as above.

Six custom-built boards were sold for a total of £6,000 and customers took an unexplainable average of three months to pay in the winter.

Purchases were made monthly and paid for two months in arrears.

The average mark-up on goods for resale excluding 'Dryline' sails was 25%. If they lose the agency, they expect that they will continue to sell the same number of sails, but at their average mark-up of 25%. The variable material cost of each custom-made board (excluding the sail) was £500.

Other costs were:
  Wages to employees £6,000 p.a. each (gross including insurance).
  Rent for premises £6,000 p.a. (six-monthly renewable lease) payable on the first day of each month.
  Other miscellaneous costs:
    1 April–30 September £3,000
    1 October–31 March   £900.

Bank balance on 1 April was £100.

Salary earnable in Lanzarote:
  Fred and Sally £1,500 each + living accommodation
  Two employees £1,500 each + living accommodation

All costs and income accruing evenly over time.

Required:
(i) Prepare a cash budget for 1 April 20X5 to 31 March 20X6 assuming that:
    (a) Fred and Sally close the business in the winter months.
    (b) They stay open all year.
(ii) What additional information would you require before you advised Fred and Sally of the best course of action to take?

References

1 *Statement of Principles for Financial Reporting*, ASB, 1999, para. 1.11.
2 *Ibid.*, para. 3.12.
3 J. Arnold, T. Hope and A.J. Southworth, *Financial Accounting*, Prentice Hall, 1994, p. 64.
4 G. Whittred and I. Zimmer, *Financial Accounting Incentive Effects and Economic Consequences*, Holt, Rinehart & Winston, 1992, p. 27.
5 ASB, *op. cit.*, para. 3.3.
6 R. Jarvis, J. Kitching, J. Curran and G. Lightfoot, The financial management of small firms: an alternative perspective, ACCA Research Report No 49.
7 *Ibid.*, para. 3.8.
8 ASB, *op. cit.*, para. 3.36.
9 T.A. Lee, *Income and Value Measurement. Theory and Practice* (3rd edition) Van Nostrand Reinhold (UK), 1985, p. 173.
10 D. Solomons, *Making Accounting Policy*, Oxford University Press, 1986, p. 79.

Accounting and reporting on an accrual accounting basis

2.1 Introduction

The Accounting Standards Board (ASB) has issued a revised draft Statement on the principles that underlie accounting and financial reporting. The intention is to specify a conceptual framework. The ASB has stated that it intends to use, wherever possible, the text issued by the International Accounting Standards Committee (IASC) entitled *Framework for the Preparation and Presentation of Financial Statements*. In this chapter, when we refer to the objectives of financial statements and the qualitative characteristics of financial information, we will be giving references to the ASB *Statement of Principles*.

In this chapter we consider the following:

● Historical cost convention

● Accrual accounting concept

● Mechanics of accrual accounting – adjusting cash receipts and payments

● Subjective judgements required in accrual accounting
  1 Adjusting cash receipts in accordance with IAS 18
  2 Adjusting cash receipts in accordance with UK accounting practice
  3 Adjusting cash payments in accordance with the matching principle

● Mechanics of accrual accounting – the balance sheet

● Reformatting the statement of financial position into a balance sheet

● Accounting for the sacrifice of fixed assets

● Reconciliation of cash flow and accrual accounting data

2.1.1 Objective of financial statements

The ASB has stated that the objective of financial statements is to provide information about the financial position, performance and capability of an enterprise that is useful to a wide range of users in making economic decisions.[1]

Common information needs for decision making

The ASB recognises that all the information needs of all users cannot be met by financial statements, but it takes the view that some needs are common to all users: in particular, they have some interest in the financial position, performance and adaptability of the enterprise as a whole. This leaves open the question of which user is the primary target; the ASB states that, as investors are providers of risk capital, financial statements that meet their needs would also meet the needs of other users.[2]

Stewardship role of financial statements

In addition to assisting in making economic decisions, financial statements also show the results of the stewardship of management: that is, the accountability of management for the resources entrusted to it. The ASB view[3] is that users who assess the stewardship do so in order to make economic decisions, e.g. whether to hold or sell shares in a particular company or change the management.

Decision makers need to assess ability to generate cash

The ASB considers that economic decisions also require an evaluation of an enterprise's ability to generate cash, and of the timing and certainty of its generation.[4] It believes that users are better able to make the evaluation if they are provided with information that focuses on the financial position, performance and cash flow of an enterprise.

2.1.2 Financial information to evaluate the ability to generate cash differs from financial information on actual cash flows

The ASB approach differs from the cash flow model used in Chapter 1, in that, in addition to the cash flows and statement of financial position, it includes within its definition of performance a reference to profit. It states that this information is required to assess changes in the economic resources that the enterprise is likely to control in the future. This is useful in predicting the capacity of the enterprise to generate cash flows from its existing resource base.[5]

2.1.3 Statements making up the financial statements published for external users

The ASB suggests that the financial statements published by a company for external users should consist of four primary statements:

● the profit and loss account;
● the statement of total recognised gains and losses;
● the balance sheet; and
● the cash flow statement.[6]

In this chapter we consider two of the conventions under which the profit and loss account and balance sheet are prepared: the historical cost convention; and the accrual accounting concept.

2.2 Historical cost convention

The historical cost convention results in an appropriate measure of the economic resource that has been withdrawn or replaced.

Under it, transactions are reported at the £ amount recorded at the date the transaction occurred. Financial statements produced under this convention provide a basis for determining the outcome of agency agreements with reasonable certainty and predictability because the data are relatively objective.[7]

By this we mean that various parties who deal with the enterprise, such as lenders, will know that the figures produced in any financial statements are objective and not manipulated by subjective judgements made by the directors. A typical example occurs when a lender attaches a covenant to a loan that the enterprise shall not exceed a specified level of gearing.

At an operational level, revenue and expense in the profit and loss account are stated at the £ amount that appears on the invoices. This amount is objective and verifiable. Because of this, the historical cost convention has strengths for stewardship purposes, but inflation-adjusted figures may well be more appropriate for decision usefulness.

2.3 Accrual accounting concept

The accrual concept dictates when transactions with third parties should be recognised and, in particular, determines the accounting periods in which they should be incorporated into the financial statements.[8] Under this concept the cash receipts from customers and payments to creditors are replaced by revenue and expenses respectively.

Revenue and expenses are derived by adjusting the realised operating cash flows to take account of business trading activity that has occurred during the accounting period, but has not been converted into cash receipts or payments by the end of the period.

2.3.1 Accrual accounting is a better indicator than cash flow accounting of ability to generate cash

The accounting profession generally supports the view expressed by the Financial Accounting Standards Board (FASB) in the USA that accrual accounting provides a better indication of an enterprise's present and continuing ability to generate favourable cash flows than information limited to the financial aspects of cash receipts and payments.[9]

The International Accounting Standards Committee (IASC) supported the FASB view in 1989 when it stated that financial statements prepared on an accrual basis inform users not only of past transactions involving the payment and receipt of cash, but also of obligations to pay cash in the future and of resources that represent cash to be received in the future, and that they provide the type of information about past transactions and other events that is most useful in making economic decisions.[10]

Having briefly considered why accrual accounting is more useful than cash flow accounting, we will briefly revise the preparation of financial statements under the accrual accounting convention.

2.4 Mechanics of accrual accounting – adjusting cash receipts and payments

We use the cash flows set out in Figure 1.7 on page 11. The derivation of the revenue and expenses for this example is set out in Figures 2.1 and 2.2. We assume that the enterprise has incomplete records, so that the revenue is arrived at by keeping a record of unpaid invoices and adding these to the cash receipts. Clearly, if the invoices are not adequately controlled, there will be no assurance that the £22,500 figure is correct. This is a relatively straightforward process at a mechanistic level. The uncertainty is not how to adjust the cash flow figures, but when to adjust them. This decision requires managers to make subjective judgements. We now look briefly at the nature of such judgements.

Figure 2.1 Derivation of revenue.

	£
Cash received	172,500
Invoices not paid (= Sales invoiced − Cash received)	22,500
Revenue = Total invoiced	195,000

Figure 2.2 Derivation of expense.

	Materials	Services
	£	£
Cash paid	129,000	21,600
Invoices not paid	37,000	900
Expense = Total invoiced	166,000	22,500

2.5 Subjective judgements required in accrual accounting 1 – adjusting cash receipts in accordance with IAS 18

In Figure 2.1 we assumed that revenue was derived simply by adding unpaid invoices to the cash receipts. In practice, however, this is influenced by the commercial facts underlying the transactions. For example, if the company is a milk producer, the point at which it should report the milk production as revenue will be influenced by the existence of a supply contract. If there is a contract with a buyer, the revenue might be recognised immediately on production.

So that financial statements are comparable, the IASC[11] has set out revenue recognition criteria in IAS 18 *Revenue* in an attempt to identify when performance was sufficient to warrant inclusion in the revenue for the period. It stated that:

> In a transaction involving the sale of goods, performance should be regarded as being achieved when the following conditions have been fulfilled:
> (a) the seller of the goods has transferred to the buyer the significant risks and rewards of ownership, in that all significant acts have been completed and the seller retains no continuing managerial involvement in, or effective control of, the goods transferred to a degree usually associated with ownership; and
> (b) no significant uncertainty exists regarding:
>   (i) the consideration that will be derived from the sale of the goods;
>   (ii) the associated costs incurred or to be incurred in producing or purchasing the goods;
>   (iii) the extent to which the goods are returned.

The criteria are simple in their intention, but difficult in their application. For instance, at what exact point in the sales cycle is there no significant uncertainty? The enterprise has to decide on the critical event that can support an assumption that revenue may be recognised.

To assist with these decisions, the standard provided an appendix with a number of examples. Figure 2.3 gives example of critical events, but you should refer to the standard itself for further information. It is interesting to note that companies registered in other parts of the world are more explicit than UK companies. The following is an extract from the accounts of Hwa Kay Thai Holdings Ltd, a company incorporated in Bermuda and listed on the Hong Kong Stock Exchange.

Revenue of the Group for the year is recognised on the following basis:

Dividend income from investments is recognised when the shareholders' right to receive payment has been established.

Sales of goods are recognised when goods are delivered and title has passed.

Income from restaurant operations is recognised when food and beverages are sold and services rendered.

Income from property management, infrastructure and other consultancy fee income are recognised when services are rendered.

Interest income is accrued on a time basis, by reference to the principal outstanding and at the interest rate applicable.

Rental income from properties under operating leases is recognised on a straight line basis over the terms of the respective leases.

In the UK, companies disclose the Accounting Policy for turnover; e.g. Galliford, a housebuilding and construction company, in its 1999 accounting policies, states:

Turnover comprises the value of contracting work executed during the year, legal completions of private housing, contracted development sales and other invoiced sales, and excludes value added tax.

Figure 2.3   Extracts from IAS 18 *Revenue Recognition* illustrating critical events.

Transaction	Critical event
Services	
Servicing fees included in the price of the product	Where the selling price of a product includes an identifiable amount for subsequent servicing for, say, a warranty period, it will normally be appropriate to defer the relevant portion of the selling price and to recognise it as revenue over the appropriate period
Sales of goods	
Shipment made giving the buyer right of return	Recognition of revenue in such circumstances will depend on the substance of the agreement. In the case of normal retail sales (e.g. chain store offering money back if not satisfied) it may be appropriate to recognise the sale but to make a suitable provision for returns based on previous experience. In other cases the substance of the agreement may amount to a sale on consignment, in which case the revenue should not be recognised until the goods are sold to a third party

The company also discloses its treatment of claims:

> Provision for claims against the group is made as soon as it is believed that a liability will arise, but claims and variations made by the group are not recognised in the profit and loss account until the outcome is reasonably certain.

2.6 Subjective judgements required in accrual accounting 2 – adjusting cash receipts in accordance with UK accounting practice

The ASB differs from the IASC, in that it has not issued a standard on revenue recognition. Instead, accountants rely on established practice that recognises revenue at four points in the selling process. These are outlined below.

2.6.1 Completion of production

In the case of the milk producer, revenue might be recognised on the completion of production subject to certain provisos – there is a ready market for the milk; the price is determinable and stable; and there are no outstanding marketing costs to be incurred.

2.6.2 Time of despatch

In the case of a furniture wholesaler, when the furniture has been despatched to the retailer, the most significant uncertainties have been eliminated. The outstanding uncertainties are that the retailer will default or return the furniture as being substandard. The risk of non-payment or return can normally be estimated with reasonable certainty based on experience.

2.6.3 After despatch but before payment is received

A video wholesaler may give the retailer an agreed period of, say, thirty days to examine the goods and return them if unsatisfactory. Revenue recognition might be deferred until the end of this period; alternatively, experience might indicate that it is reasonable to recognise the revenue before the expiry of thirty days.

2.6.4 After payment

In the sale of technical equipment, such as video recorders, retailers may be permitted a warranty period of, say, a year. In this case, the revenue may be recognised but a provision is created to meet estimated future costs likely to arise under the warranty. Again, history might indicate a reasonable level of provision.

From this we can see that, although the general principles are clear, each transaction needs to be assessed on its own merits in order to ascertain whether significant uncertainties exist at the balance sheet date.

Figure 2.4 Profit and loss account for the six months ended 30 June 20X1.

	Operating cash flow £	ADJUST cash flow £	Business activity £
Revenue from business activity	172,500	22,500	195,000
Less: Matching expenses			
Transactions for materials	129,000	37,000	166,000
Transactions for services	21,600	900	22,500
Transaction with landlord	6,250	(3,125)	3,125
OPERATING CASH FLOW from business activity	15,650		
Transactions NOT converted to cash or relating to a subsequent period		(12,275)	
PROFIT from business activity			3,375

2.7 Subjective judgements required in accrual accounting 3 – adjusting cash payments in accordance with the matching principle

We have seen that the enterprise needs to decide when to recognise the revenue. It then needs to decide when to include an item as an expense in the profit and loss account. This decision is based on an application of the matching principle.

The matching principle means that financial statements must include costs related to the achievement of the reported revenue. These include the internal transfers required to ensure that reductions in the assets held by a business are recorded at the same time as the revenues.[12]

The expense might be more or less than the cash paid. For example, in the Norman example, £37,000 was invoiced but not paid on materials, and £900 on services; £3,125 was prepaid on rent for the six months after June. The cash flow information therefore needs to be adjusted as in Figure 2.4.

2.8 Mechanics of accrual accounting – the balance sheet

The balance sheet or statement of financial position, as set out in Figure 1.12, needs to be amended following the change from cash flow to accrual accounting. It needs to include the £ amounts that have arisen from trading but have not been converted to cash, and the £ amounts of cash that have been received or paid but relate to a subsequent period. The adjusted statement of financial position is set out in Figure 2.5.

2.9 Reformatting the statement of financial position into a balance sheet

The item 'net amount of activities not converted to cash or relating to subsequent periods' is the net debtor/creditor balance. If we wished, the statement of financial

Figure 2.5 Statement of financial position adjusted to an accrual basis.

	£
Capital	50,000
Net operating cash flow: **realised**	15,650
Net operating cash flow: **to be realised next period**	(12,275)
	53,375
Lease	80,000
Net cash balance (refer to Figure 1.11)	(14,350)
Net amount of activities not converted to cash, or relating to subsequent periods	(12,275)
	53,375

position could be reframed into the customary balance sheet format, where items are classified as assets or liabilities. The ASB defines assets and liabilities in its *Statement of Principles*:

> 1 An item is an asset if it possesses the following characteristic:
> a right or other access to future economic benefits controlled by an entity as a result of past transactions or events.
> 2 An item is a liability if it possesses the following characteristic:
> an obligation to transfer economic benefits as a result of past transactions or events.[13]

The reframed balance sheet set out in Figure 2.6 is in accordance with these definitions. Note that the same amount of £3,375 results from calculating the difference in the opening and closing net assets in the balance sheets as from calculating the residual amount in the income statement. When the amount derived from both approaches is the same, the balance sheet and income statement are said to **articulate**. The income statement provides the detailed explanation for the difference in the net assets and the amount is the same because the same concepts have been applied to both statements.

2.10 Accounting for the sacrifice of fixed assets

The income statement and balance sheet have both been prepared using verifiable data that have arisen from transactions with third parties outside the business. However, in order to determine the full sacrifice of economic resources that a business has made to achieve its revenue, it is necessary also to take account of the use made of the fixed assets during the period in which the revenue arose.

In the Norman example, the fixed asset is the lease. The extent of the sacrifice is a matter of judgement by the management. This is influenced by the prudence principle, which regulates the matching principle. The prudence principle determines the extent to which transactions that have already been included in the accounting system should be recognised in the profit and loss account.[14]

Figure 2.6   Balance sheet as at 30 June.

		Reframed
	£	£
CAPITAL	50,000	50,000
Net operating cash flow: **realised**	15,650	
Net operating cash flow: **to be realised**	(12,275)	
NET INCOME		3,375
	53,375	53,375
FIXED ASSETS	80,000	80,000
NET CURRENT ASSETS		
Net amount of activities not converted to cash	(12,275)	
CURRENT ASSETS		
Trade debtors		22,500
Prepaid rent		3,125
CURRENT LIABILITIES		
Trade creditors		(37,000)
Expense creditors		(900)
Net cash balance	(14,350)	(14,350)
	53,375	53,375

2.10.1   Treatment of fixed assets in accrual accounting

Applying the matching principle, it is necessary to estimate how much of the initial outlay should be assumed to have been revenue expenditure, i.e. used in achieving the revenue of the accounting period. The provisions of FRS 15 on **depreciation** assist by defining depreciation and stating the duty of allocation, as follows:

> Depreciation is the measure of the cost or revalued amount of the economic benefits of the tangible fixed asset that have been consumed during the period. Consumption includes the wearing out, using up or other reduction in the useful economic life of a tangible fixed asset whether arising from use, effluxion of time or obsolescence through either changes in technology or demand for the goods and services produced by the asset.[15]

> The FRS further provides that the depreciable amount of a tangible asset should be allocated on a systematic basis over its useful economic life. The depreciation method should reflect as fairly as possible the pattern in which the asset's economic benefits are consumed by the entity. The depreciation charge for each period should be recognised as an expense in the profit and loss account unless it is permitted to be included in the carrying amount of another asset.[16]

> With regard to the depreciation method FRS 15 provides that a variety of methods can be used to allocate the depreciable amount of a tangible fixed asset on a systematic basis over its useful economic life and that the method chosen should result in a depreciation charge throughout the asset's useful economic life and not just towards the end of its useful economic life or when the asset is falling in value.[17]

This sounds a rather complex requirement. It is therefore surprising, when one looks at the financial statements of a multinational company such as BP plc, to find that depreciation on tangible assets other than mineral production is simply provided on a straight-line basis of an equal amount each year, calculated so as to write off the cost by equal instalments. This treatment is recognised in FRS 15 which states that where the pattern of consumption of an asset's economic benefits is uncertain, a straight-line method of depreciation is usually adopted.[18] The reason is that, in accrual accounting, the depreciation charged to the income statement is a measure of the amount of the economic benefits that have been consumed, rather than a measure of the fall in realisable value. In estimating the amount of service potential expired, a business is following the **going concern concept**.

2.10.2 Going concern concept

The going concern concept assumes that the business enterprise will continue in operational existence for the foreseeable future. This assumption introduces a constraint on the prudence concept by allowing the account balances to be reported on a depreciated cost basis rather than on a net realisable value basis.[19]

It is more relevant to use the loss of service potential than the change in realisable value because there is no intention to cease trading and to sell the fixed assets at the end of the accounting period.

In our Norman example, the procedure would be to assume that, in the case of the lease, the economic resource that has been consumed can be measured by the amortisation that has occurred due to the effluxion of time. The time covered by the accounts is half a year: this means that one-tenth of the lease has expired during the half-year. As a result, £8,000 is treated as revenue expenditure in the half-year to 30 June.

This additional revenue expenditure reduces the income in the income account and the asset figure in the balance sheet. The effects are incorporated into the two statements in Figures 2.7 and 2.8. The asset amounts and the income figure in the balance sheet are also affected by the exhaustion of part of the fixed assets, as set out in Figure 2.8.

Figure 2.7 Income statement for the six months ending 30 June.			
	Operating cash flow CURRENT period £	Adjust cash flow £	Business activity CURRENT period £
Revenue from business activity	172,500	22,500	195,000
Less			
Expenditure to support this activity:			
Transactions with suppliers	129,000	37,000	166,000
Transactions with service providers	21,600	900	22,500
Transactions with landlord	6,250	3,125	3,125
OPERATING CASH FLOW from activity	15,650		
TRANSACTIONS NOT CONVERTED TO CASH		(12,275)	
INCOME from business activity			3,375
Allocation of fixed asset cost to this period			8,000
INCOME			(4,625)

Figure 2.8   Balance sheet as at 30 June.

	Transaction cash flows	Notional flows	Reported
	£	£	£
CAPITAL	50,000		50,000
Net operating cash flow: **realised**	15,650		
Net operating cash flow: **to be realised**	(12,275)		
Net income before depreciation		3,375	
DEPRECIATION		(8,000)	
Net income after depreciation			(4,625)
	53,375		45,375
FIXED ASSETS	80,000	80,000	
Less depreciation		(8,000)	
Net book value			72,000
NET CURRENT ASSETS			
Net amount not converted to cash	(12,275)		
CURRENT ASSETS			
Trade debtors			22,500
Prepaid rent			3,125
CURRENT LIABILITIES			
Trade creditors			(37,000)
Expense creditors			(900)
Net cash balance	(14,350)		(14,350)
	53,375		45,375

It is current accounting practice to apply the same concepts to determining the entries in both the income statement and the balance sheet. The amortisation charged in the income statement at £8,000 is the same as the amount deducted from the fixed assets in the balance sheet. As a result, the two statements articulate: the income statement explains the reason for the reduction of £4,625 in the net assets.

How decision useful to the management is the income figure that has been derived after deducting a depreciation charge?

The loss of £4,625 indicates that the distribution of any amount would further deplete the financial capital of £50,000, which was invested in the company by Mr Norman on setting up the business. This is referred to as **capital maintenance**; the particular capital maintenance concept that has been applied is the **financial capital maintenance concept**.

2.10.3   Financial capital maintenance concept

The financial capital maintenance concept recognises a profit only after the original monetary investment has been maintained. This means that, as long as the cost of the assets representing the initial monetary investment is recovered against the profit, by way of a depreciation charge, the initial monetary investment is maintained.[20]

The concept has been described in slightly different terms in the IASC *Framework for the Presentation and Preparation of Financial Statements*:

> a profit is earned only if the financial or money amount of the net assets at the end of the period exceeds the financial or money amount of the net assets at the beginning of the period, after excluding any distributions to, and contributions from, owners during the period. Financial capital maintenance can be measured in either nominal monetary units [as we are doing in this chapter] or in units of constant purchasing power [as we will be doing in Chapter 4].[21]

2.10.4 Summary of views on accrual accounting

The profit (loss) is considered to be a guide when assessing the amount, timing and uncertainty of prospective cash flows as represented by future income amounts. The IASC, FASB and ASB clearly state that the accrual accounting concept is more useful in predicting future cash flows than cash flow accounting.

Academic research provides conflicting views. In 1986 research carried out in the USA indicated that the FASB view was inconsistent with its findings and that cash flow information was a better predictor of future operating cash flows;[22] research carried out in the UK, however, indicated that accrual accounting using the historical cost convention was 'a more relevant basis for decision making than cash flow measures'.[23]

2.11 Reconciliation of cash flow and accrual accounting data

The accounting profession attempted to provide users of financial statements with the benefits of both types of data, by requiring a cash flow statement to be prepared as well as the income statement and balance sheet prepared on an accrual basis.

From the income statement prepared on an accrual basis (as in Figure 2.7) an investor is able to obtain an indication of a business's present ability to generate favourable cash flows; from the balance sheet prepared on an accrual basis (as in Figure 2.8) an investor is able to obtain an indication of a business's continuing ability to generate favourable cash flows; from the cash flow statement (as in Figure 2.9) an investor is able to reconcile the income figure with the change in net cash balance.

Figure 2.9 reconciles the information produced in Chapter 1 under the cash flow basis with the information produced under the accrual basis. It could be expanded to provide information more clearly, as in Figure 2.10. Here we are using the information from Figures 1.9 and 1.12, but within a third statement rather than the income statement and balance sheet.

2.11.1 Published cash flow statement

FRS 1 *Cash Flow Statements*[24] specifies the standard headings under which cash flows should be classified. They are:

● cash inflow or outflow from operations;

● returns on investments and servicing of finance;

● taxation;

● capital expenditure and financial investments;

● acquisitions and disposals;

● equity dividends paid;

Figure 2.9 Reconciliation of income figure with net cash balance.

	£
Income per income statement	(4,625)
Add: unrealisable cash outflow	8,000
	3,375
Add: unrealised operating cash flows	12,275
Operating cash flow	15,650
Other sources:	
Capital	50,000
Total cash available	65,650
Applications	
Lease	(80,000)
Net cash balance	(14,350)

● management of liquid resources;

● financing.

To comply with FRS 1, the cash flows from Figure 2.10 would be set out as in Figure 2.11. FRS 1 is mentioned at this stage only to illustrate that cash flows can be reconciled to the accrual accounting data. There is further discussion of FRS 1 in Chapter 24.

Figure 2.10 Cash flow statement netting amounts that have not been converted to cash.

	£	£
Sales	195,000	
Debtors	(22,500)	172,500
Purchases	166,000	
Creditors	(37,000)	(129,000)
Expenses	22,500	
Creditors	(900)	(21,600)
Rent	3,125	
Prepaid	3,125	(6,250)
Net cash inflow from operating activities		15,650
Investing activities		
Lease		(80,000)
Financing		
Issue of capital		50,000
Decrease in cash		(14,350)

Figure 2.11 Cash flow statement in accordance with
FRS I *Cash Flow Statements*.

	£
Net cash inflow from operating activities	15,650
Investing activities	
Payment to acquire lease	(80,000)
Net cash outflow before financing	(64,350)
Financing	
Issue of capital	50,000
Decrease in cash	(14,350)
Reconciliation of operating loss to net cash	
inflow from operating activities	£
Operating profit/loss	(4,625)
Depreciation charges	8,000
Increase in debtors	(22,500)
Increase in prepayments	(3,125)
Increase in creditors	37,000
Increase in accruals	900
	15,650

Review questions

1 *The Corporate Report* identified seven user groups: investors, loan creditors, business contact, analysts acting for any of these, the government, employees and the public.
   Discuss which of the financial statements illustrated in Chapters 1 and 2 would be most useful to each of these seven groups if they could only receive one statement.

2 'Accrual accounting is preferable to cash flow accounting because the information is more relevant to all users of financial statements.' Discuss.

3 'Cash flow accounting and accrual accounting information are both required by a potential shareholder.' Discuss.

4 'Information contained in a profit and loss account and a balance sheet prepared under accrual accounting concepts is factual and objective.' Discuss.

5 'The asset measurement basis applied in accrual accounting can lead to financial difficulties when assets are due for replacement.' Discuss.

6 'Accountants preparing financial statements in the UK do not require a standard such as IAS 18 *Revenue*.'[25] Discuss.

7 Explain the revenue recognition principle and discuss the effect of alternative treatments on the reported results of a company.

8 The annual financial statements of companies are used by various parties for a wide variety of purposes. For each of the seven different 'user groups', explain their presumed interest with reference to the performance of the company and its financial position.

Exercises

An extract from the solution is provided in the appendix at the end of the text for exercises marked with an asterisk (*).

* ## Question I

Jane Parker is going to set up a new business on I January 20XI. She estimates that her first six months in business will be as follows:

(i) She will put £150,000 into the firm on I January 20XI.

(ii) On I January 20XI she will buy machinery £30,000, motor vehicles £24,000 and premises £75,000, paying for them immediately.

(iii) All purchases will be effected on credit. She will buy £30,000 goods on I January and she will pay for these in February. Other purchases will be: rest of January £48,000; February, March, April, May and June £60,000 each month. Other than the £30,000 worth bought in January, all other purchases will be paid for two months after purchase, i.e. £48,000 in March.

(iv) Sales (all on credit) will be £60,000 for January and £75,000 for each month after that. Debtors will pay for goods in the third month after purchase, i.e. £60,000 in April.

(v) Stock in trade on 30 June 20XI will be £30,000.

(vi) Wages and salaries will be £2,250 per month and will be paid on the last day of each month.

(vii) General expenses will be £750 per month, payable in the month following that in which they are incurred.

(viii) She will introduce new capital of £75,000 on I June 20XI. This will be paid into the business bank account immediately.

(ix) Insurance covering the 12 months of 20XI £26,400 will be paid for by cheque on 30 June 20XI.

(x) Rates will be paid as follows: for the three months to 31 March 19XI by cheque on 28 February 20X2 delay due to an oversight by Parker; for the 12 months ended 31 March 20X2 by cheque on 31 July 20XI. Rates are £8,000 per annum.

(xi) She will make drawings of £1,500 per month by cheque.

(xii) All receipts and payments are by cheque.

(xiii) Depreciate motor vehicles by 20% per annum and machinery by 10% per annum, using the straight-line depreciation method.

(xiv) She has been informed by her bank manager that he is prepared to offer an overdraft facility of £30,000 for the first year.

Required:

(a) **Draft a cash budget (for the firm) month by month for the period January to June, showing clearly the amount of bank balance at the end of each month.**

(b) **Draft the projected trading and profit and loss account for the first six months' trading, and a balance sheet as at 30 June 20XI.**

(c) **Advise Jane on the alternative courses of action that could be taken to cover any cash deficiency that exceeds the agreed overdraft limit.**

*   Question 2

Mr Norman is going to set up a new business on 1 January 20X8. He will invest £150,000 in the business on that date and has made the following estimates and policy decisions:

1   Forecast sales (in units) made at a selling price of £50 per unit are:

Month	Sales units	Month	Sales units
January	1,650	May	4,400
February	2,200	June	4,950
March	3,850	July	5,500
April	4,400		

2   50% of sales are for cash. Credit terms are payment in month following sale.

3   The units cost £40 each and the supplier is allowed one month's credit.

4   It is intended to hold stock at the end of each month sufficient to cover 25% of the following month's sales.

5   Administration £8,000 and wages £17,000 are paid monthly as they arise.

6   On 1 January 20X8, the following payments will be made: £80,000 for a five-year lease of the business premises and £350 for insurance for the year.

7   Staff sales commission of 2% of sales will be paid in the month following sale.

Required:
(a) A purchases budget for each of the first six months.
(b) A cash flow forecast for the first six months.
(c) A budgeted profit and loss account for the first six months' trading and a budgeted balance sheet as at 30 June 20X8.
(d) Advise Mr Norman on the investment of any excess cash.

Question 3

The Piano Warehouse Company Limited was established on 1 January 20X7 for the purpose of making pianos. Jeremy Holmes, the managing director, had twenty years' experience in the manufacture of pianos and was an acknowledged technical expert in the field. He had invested his life's savings of £15,000 in the company, and his decision to launch the company reflected his desire for complete independence.

Nevertheless, his commitment to the company represented a considerable financial gamble. He paid close attention to the management of its financial affairs and ensured that a careful record of all transactions was kept.

The company's activities during the year ended 31 December 20X7 were as follows:

(i)   Four pianos had been built and sold for a total sum of £8,000. Holmes calculated their cost of manufacture as follows:

Materials	£2,000
Labour	£2,800
Overhead costs	£800

(ii) Two pianos were 50% completed at 31 December 20X7. Madrigal Music Limited had agreed to buy them for a total of £4,500 and had made a down-payment amounting to 20% of the agreed sale price. Holmes estimated their costs of manufacture to 31 December 20X7 as follows:

Materials	£900
Labour	£800
Overhead costs	£100

(iii) Two pianos had been rebuilt and sold for a total of £3,000. Holmes paid £1,800 for them at an auction and had spent a further £400 on rebuilding them. The sale of these two pianos was made under a hire purchase agreement under which The Piano Warehouse Company received £1,000 on delivery and two payments over the next two years plus interest of 15% on the outstanding balance.

At the end of the company's first financial year, Jeremy Holmes was anxious that the company's net profit to 13 December 20X7 should be represented in the most accurate manner. There appeared to be several alternative bases on which the transactions for the year could be interpreted. It was clear to him that, in simple terms, the net profit for the year should be calculated by deducting expenses from revenues. As far as cash sales were concerned he saw no difficulty. But how should the pianos that were 50% completed be treated? Should the value of the work done up to 31 December 20X7 be included in the profit of that year, or should it be carried forward to the next year, when the work would be completed and the pianos sold? As regards the pianos sold under the hire purchase agreement, should profit be taken in 20X7 or spread over the years in which a proportion of the revenue is received?

Required:

(a) Prepare a profit and loss account for the year ended 31 December 20X7 on a basis that would reflect conventional accounting principles.

(b) Examine the problems implied in the timing of the recognition of revenues, illustrating your answer by the facts in the case of The Piano Warehouse.

(c) Discuss the significant accounting conventions that would be relevant to profit determination in this case, and discuss their limitations in this context.

(d) Advise the company on alternative accounting treatments that could increase the profit for the year.

* **Question 4**

Albert, a builder specialising in loft conversions, started up in business on 1 January 20X6.

During the first year of trading, Albert was so busy installing loft conversions that he did not prepare detailed accounts. However, he maintained transactions records and at 31 December 20X6 made a brief note of his financial position, which showed the following:

(a) There were workshop fixtures that had cost £4,000 when installed on 1 January 20X6 in Albert's workshop. The premises were leased for four years at a rental of £800 per annum. No premium had been paid for the lease. It was decided to write off the fixtures over the term of the lease.

(b) A stock of materials that had cost £8,300.

(c) Customers owed £17,180 for loft conversions that had been installed and accepted by the customers.

(d) Suppliers and subcontractors were owed £9,000.

(e) There was a bank overdraft of £960 and cash in hand of £360.

(f) Albert had withdrawn £9,600 for his living expenses during the year ended 31 December 20X6.

(g) Office expense creditors amounted to £1,280.

Albert felt depressed as he had just run into overdraft, and he felt that it was not worth producing financial accounts on 31 December 20X6. However, encouraged by the Inland Revenue, he decided that he would continue with the basic records and prepare final accounts at 31 December 20X7, when the position of the business should have improved.

On 31 December 20X7 Albert took the following records to his accountant:

(a) Cash and bank analysis 1 January 20X7 to 31 December 20X7

Cash receipts	£
Cash received from customers	137,240
Cash drawn from bank	51,500
Additional capital from Albert on 30 September 20X7	4,000
Cash payments	
(i) Supplies of materials, etc	78,060
(ii) Drawings by Albert	12,000
(iii) Selling expenses	8,720
(iv) Office expenses	12,400
(v) Salesmen's salaries	20,700
(vi) Into bank	60,120
Cash in hand at 31 December 20X7	560
Cheque payments	
(i) Selling expenses	11,680
(ii) Office expenses	8,200
(iii) Supplies of materials	7,200

(b) At 31 December 20X7, debtors, creditors and stock were:

Debtors	£17,980
Creditors	£4,140
Stock of materials, etc.	£10,980

The accountant obtained the following additional information at his interview with Albert:

(a) Bank charges of £120 appeared in the bank statements, but were not included in the cash analysis.

(b) A private account of £400 had been paid for Albert, but had been included as an office expense.

(c) Rent on office premises of £800 was paid and is included in office expenses £8,200 above.

Required:
(a) Prepare a balance sheet as at 1 January 20X7.
(b) Prepare a cash account and bank account for year ended 31 December 20X7 (any cash shortage is to be charged as an expense).
(c) Prepare a trading and profit and loss account for the year ended 31 December 20X7 and a balance sheet as at 31 December 20X7.
(d) Explain the effect on the profit and loss account and balance sheet if it is subsequently discovered that:
invoices from creditors at 31 December 20X7 totalling £1,000 had been overlooked; a payment of £2,000 that had been made in cash for school fees for Albert's son had been overlooked; and suppliers and contractors were owed £10,000 at 31 December 20X7 not £9,000.

(e) Explain briefly how the risk of creditors' invoices being overlooked at the year-end could be reduced.

References

1 *Statement of Principles for Financial Reporting*, ASB, 1999, para. 1.3.
2 *Ibid.*, para. 1.11.
3 *Ibid.*, para. 1.14(a).
4 *Ibid.*, para. 1.18.
5 *Ibid.*, para. 1.14(b).
6 *Ibid.*, para. 7.3.
7 M. Page, *British Accounting Review*, vol. 24(1), 1992, p. 80.
8 D. Chopping and L. Skerratt, *Applying GAAP 1997/8*, ICAEW, 1997, p. 7.
9 *Statement of Financial Accounting Concepts No. 1, Objectives of Financial Reporting by Business Enterprises*, Financial Accounting Standards Board, 1978.
10 *Framework for the Presentation and Preparation of Financial Statements*, IASC, 1989, para. 20.
11 *Revenue*, IAS 18, IASC, 1993, para. 23.
12 D. Chopping and L. Skerratt, *op. cit.*, p. 9.
13 ASB, 1999, *op. cit.*, Chapter 4 Principles.
14 D. Chopping and L. Skerratt, *op. cit.*, p. 10.
15 FRS 15 *Tangible Fixed Assets*, ASB, 1999, para. 2.
16 *Ibid.*, para. 77.
17 *Ibid.*, para. 81.
18 *Ibid.*, para. 81.
19 D. Chopping and L. Skerratt, *op. cit.*, p. 12.
20 J. Baillie, *Systems of Profit Measurement*, Gee & Co., 1985, p. 37.
21 *Framework for the Presentation and Preparation of Financial Statements*, IASC, 1989, para. 102.
22 R.M. Bowen, D. Burgstahler and L.A. Daley, 'Evidence on the relationships between earnings and various measures of cash flow', *Accounting Review*, October 1986, pp. 713–25.
23 J.I.G. Board and J.F.S. Day, 'The information content of cash flow figures', *Accounting and Business Research*, Winter 1989, pp. 3–11.
24 *Cash Flow Statements*, ASB 1991 Revised 1996.
25 D. Chopping and L. Skerratt, *op. cit.*, p. 55.

CHAPTER **3**

Income and asset value measurement

an economist's approach

3.1 Introduction

This chapter discusses the need for income measurement. It compares the methods of measurement adopted by the accountant with those of the economist, the reasons for the different approaches, the relationship of income to capital and the impact of the concept of value on these measures. The prime objective is to engender an understanding of the rule of income and capital within the commercial enterprise, and to prevent misunderstanding of what initially may appear to be a conflict of method between the two disciplines. In this chapter we consider the following:

● Role and objective of income measurement

● Accountant's view of income, capital and value

● Economist's view of income, capital and value

● Critical comment on the economist's measure

● Critical comment on the accountant's measure

● Income, capital and changing price levels

3.2 Role and objective of income measurement

Although accountancy has played a part in business reporting for centuries, it is only since the Companies Act 1929 that financial reporting has become income orientated. Prior to that Act an income statement was of minor importance. It was the balance sheet that mattered, providing a list of capital, assets and liabilities that revealed the financial soundness and solvency of the business.

According to some commentators,[1] this scenario may be attributed to the sources of capital funding. Until the late 1920s, as in present-day Germany, external capital finance in the UK was mainly in the hands of bankers, other lenders and trade creditors. As the main users of published financial statements, they focused on the company's ability to pay trade creditors and the interest on loans, and to meet the scheduled dates of loan repayment: they were interested in the short-term liquidity and longer-term solvency of the entity.

Thus the balance sheet was the prime document of interest. Perhaps in recognition of this, the English balance sheet, until recent times, tended to show liabilities on the left-hand side, thus making them the first part of the balance sheet read.

The gradual evolution of a sophisticated investment market, embracing a range of financial institutions, together with the growth in the number of individual investors, caused a reorientation of priorities. Investor protection and investor decision-making needs started to dominate the financial reporting scene, and the revenue statement replaced the balance sheet as the sovereign reporting document.

Consequently, attention became fixed on the income statement and on concepts of accounting for profit. Moreover, investor protection assumed a new meaning. It changed from simply protecting the **capital** that had **been invested** to protecting the **income information** used by investors when making an investment decision.

However, the sight of major companies experiencing severe liquidity problems over the past decade has revived interest in the balance sheet; while its light is perhaps not of the same intensity as that of the profit and loss account, it cannot be said to be totally subordinate to its accompanying statement of income.

The main objectives of income measurement are to provide:

● a means of control in a micro- and macroeconomic sense;

● a means of prediction;

● a basis for taxation.

We consider each of these below.

3.2.1 Income as a means of control

Assessment of stewardship performance

Managers are the stewards appointed by shareholders. Income, in the sense of net income or net profit, is the crystallisation of their accountability. Maximisation of income is seen as a major aim of the entrepreneurial entity, but the capacity of the business to pursue this aim may be subject to political and social constraints in the case of large public monopolies, and private semi-monopolies such as British Telecommunications plc.

Maximisation of net income is reflected in the earnings per share (EPS) figure, which is shown on the face of the published profit and loss account. The importance of this figure to the shareholders is evidenced by contracts that tie directors' remuneration to growth in EPS. A rising EPS may result in an increased salary or bonus for directors and upward movement in the market price of the underlying security. The effect on the market price is indicated by another extremely important statistic, which is influenced by the income statement: namely, the price/earnings (PE) ratio. The PE ratio reveals the numerical relationship between the share's current market price and the last reported EPS.

Actual performance versus predicted performance

This comparison enables the management and the investing public to use the lessons of the past to improve future performance. The public, as shareholders, may initiate a change in the company directorate if circumstances necessitate it. This may be one reason why management is generally loath to give a clear, quantified estimate of projected results – such an estimate is a potential measure of efficiency. The comparison of actual with projected results identifies apparent underachievement.

The macroeconomic concept

Good government is, of necessity, involved in managing the macroeconomic scene and as such is a user of the income measure. State policies need to be formulated concerning the allocation of economic resources and the regulation of firms and industries, as illustrated by the measures taken by Oftel and Ofwat to regulate the size of earnings by British Telecom and the water companies.

3.2.2 Income as a means of prediction

Dividend and retention policy

The payment of a dividend, its scale and that of any residual income after such dividend has been paid are influenced by the profit generated for the financial year. Other influences are also active, including the availability of cash resources within the entity, the opportunities for further internal investment, the dividend policies of capital-competing entities with comparable shares, the contemporary cost of capital and the current tempo of the capital market.

However, some question the soundness of using the profit generated for the year when making a decision to invest in an enterprise. Their view is that such a practice misunderstands the nature of income data, and that the appropriate information is the prospective cash flows. They regard the use of income figures from past periods as defective because, even if the future accrual accounting income could be forecast accurately, 'it is no more than an imperfect surrogate for future cash flows'.[2]

The counter-argument is that there is considerable resistance by both managers and accountants to the publication of future operating flows and dividend payments.[3] This means that, in the absence of relevant information, an investor needs to rely on a surrogate. The question then arises: which is the best surrogate?

In the short term, the best surrogate is the information that is currently available, i.e. income measured according to the accrual concept. In the longer term, management will be pressed by the shareholders to provide the actual forecast data on operating cash flows and dividend distribution, or to improve the surrogate information.

Suggestions for improving the surrogate information have included the provision of cash earnings per share. More fundamentally, Revsine has suggested that ideal information for investors would indicate the economic value of the business (and its assets) based on expected future cash flows. However, the Revsine suggestion itself requires information on future cash flows that it is not possible to obtain at this time.[4] Instead, he considered the use of replacement cost as a surrogate for the economic value of the business, and we return to this later in the chapter.

Future performance

While history is not a faultless indicator of future events and their financial results, it does have a role to play in assessing the level of future income. In this context, historic income is of assistance to existing investors, prospective investors and management.

Identifying maintainable profit by the analysis of matched costs

Subject to the requirement of enforced disclosure via the Companies Acts 1985 and 1989, as supplemented by *Standard Accounting Practice*, the measurement of income discloses items of income and expenditure necessarily of interest in assessing stewardship success and future prospects. In this respect, exceptional items, extraordinary items and other itemised costs and turnover are essential information.

3.2.3 Basis for taxation

The contemporary taxation philosophy, in spite of criticism from some economists, uses income measurement to measure the taxable capacity of a business entity.

However, the determination of income by the Inland Revenue is necessarily influenced by socioeconomic fiscal factors, among others, and thus accounting profit is subject to adjustment in order to achieve taxable profit. As a tax base, it has been continually eroded as the difference between accounting income and taxable income has grown.[5]

The Inland Revenue in the UK has tended to disallow expenses that are particularly susceptible to management judgement. For example, a uniform capital allowance is substituted for the subjective depreciation charge that is made by management, and certain provisions that appear as a charge in the profit and loss account are not accepted as an expense for tax purposes until the loss crystallises, e.g. a charge to increase the doubtful debts provision may not be allowed until the debt is recognised as bad.

3.3 Accountant's view of income, capital and value

Variations between accountants and economists in measuring income, capital and value are caused by their different views of these measures. In this section we introduce the accountant's view and, in the next, the economist's, in order to reconcile variations in methods of measurement.

3.3.1 The accountant's view

Income is an important part of accounting theory and practice, although until 1970, when a formal system of propagating standard accounting practice throughout the accountancy profession began, it received little attention in accountancy literature. The characteristics of measurement were basic and few, and tended to be of an intuitive, traditional nature, rather than being spelled out precisely and given mandatory status within the profession.

Accounting tradition of historical cost

The income statement is based on the actual costs of business transactions, i.e. the costs incurred in the currency and at the price levels pertaining at the time of the transactions.

Accounting income is said to be historical income, i.e. it is an *ex post* measure because it takes place after the event. The traditional profit and loss account is historical in two senses: because it concerns a past period, and because it utilises historical cost, being the cost of the transactions on which it is based. It follows that the balance sheet, being based on the residuals of transactions not yet dealt with in the profit and loss account, is also based on historical cost.

In practice, certain amendments may be made to historical cost in both profit and loss account and balance sheet, but historical cost still predominates in both statements. It is justified on a number of counts which, in principle, guard against the manipulation of data.

The main characteristics of historical cost accounting are as follows:

● **Objectivity**. It is a predominantly objective system, although it does exhibit aspects of subjectivity. Its nature is generally understood and it is invariably supported by independent documentary evidence, e.g. an invoice, statement, cheque, cheque counterfoil, receipt or voucher.

● **Factual**. As a basis of fact (with exceptions such as when amended in furtherance of revaluation), it is verifiable and to that extent is beyond dispute.

● **Profit or income concept**. Profit as a concept is generally well understood in a capital market economy, even if its precise measurement may be problematic. It constitutes the difference between revenue and expenditure or, in the economic sense, between opening and closing net assets.

Unfortunately, historical cost is not without its weaknesses. It is not always objective, owing to alternative definitions of revenue and costs and the need for estimates.

We saw in the preceding chapter that revenue could be determined according to a choice of criteria. There is also a choice of criteria for defining costs. For example, although inventories are valued at the lower of cost or net realisable value, the **cost** will differ depending upon the definition adopted, e.g. first-in-first-out, last-in-first-out or standard cost.

Estimation is needed in the case of inventory valuation, assessing possible bad debts, accruing expenses, providing for depreciation and determining the profit attributable to long-term contracts. So, although it is transaction based, there are aspects of historical cost reporting that do not result from an independently verifiable business transaction. This means that profit is not always a unique figure.

Assets are often subjected to revaluation. In an economy of changing price levels, the historical cost system has been compromised by a perceived need to restate the carrying value of those assets that comprise a large proportion of a company's capital employed; e.g. land and buildings. This practice is controversial, not least because it is said to imply that a balance sheet is a list of assets at market valuation, rather than a statement of unamortised costs not yet charged against revenue.

However, despite conventional accountancy income being partly the result of subjectivity, it is largely the product of the historical cost concept. A typical accounting policy specified in the published accounts of companies now reads as follows:

> The financial statements are prepared under the historical cost conventions as modified by the revaluation of certain fixed assets.

Nature of accounting income

Accounting income is defined in terms of the business entity. It is the excess of revenue from sales over direct and allocated indirect costs incurred in the achievement of such sales. Its measure results in a net figure. It is the numerical result of the matching and accruals concepts discussed in the preceding chapter.

We saw in the preceding chapter that accounting income is transaction based and therefore can be said to be factual, in as much as the revenue and costs have been realised and will be reflected in cash inflow and outflow, although not necessarily within the financial year.

We also saw that, under accrual accounting, the sales for a financial period are offset by the expenses incurred in generating such sales. Objectivity is a prime characteristic of accrual accounting, but the information cannot be entirely objective because of the need to break up the ongoing performance of the business entity into calendar periods or financial years for purposes of accountability reporting. The allocation of expenses between periods requires a prudent estimate of some costs, e.g. the provision for depreciation and bad debts attributable to each period.

Accounting income is presented in the form of the conventional profit and loss account or income statement. This income statement, in being based on actual transactions, is concerned with a past-defined period of time. Thus accounting profit is said to be historic income, i.e. an *ex post* measure because it is after the event.

Nature of accounting capital

The business enterprise requires the use of non-monetary assets, e.g. buildings, plant and machinery, office equipment, motor vehicles, stock of raw materials and work-in-progress. Such assets are not consumed in any one accounting period, but give service over a number of periods; therefore, the unconsumed portions of each asset are carried forward from period to period and appear in the balance sheet. This document itemises the unused asset balances at the date of the financial year-end. In addition to listing unexpired costs of non-monetary assets, the balance sheet also displays monetary assets such as debtor and cash balances, together with monetary liabilities, i.e. moneys owing to trade creditors, other creditors and lenders. Funds supplied by shareholders and retained income following the distribution of dividend are also shown. Retained profits are usually added to shareholders' capital, resulting in what is known as shareholders' funds. These represent the company's equity capital.

The net assets of the firm, i.e. that fund of unconsumed assets which exceeds moneys attributable to creditors and lenders, constitutes the company's net capital, which is the same as its equity capital. Thus the profit and loss account of a financial period can be seen as a linking statement between that period's opening and closing balance sheets: in other words, income may be linked with opening and closing capital. This linking may be expressed by formula, as follows:

$$Y_{0-1} = NA_1 - NA_0 + D_{0-1}$$

where Y_{0-1} = income for the period of time t_0 to t_1; NA_0 = net assets of the entity at point of time t_0; NA_1 = net assets of the entity at point of time t_1; D_{0-1} = dividends or distribution during period t_{0-1}.

Less formally: Y = income of financial year; NA_0 = net assets at beginning of financial year; NA_1 = net assets at end of financial year; D_{0-1} = dividends paid and proposed for the financial year. We can illustrate this as follows:

Income Y_{0-1} for the financial year t_{0-1} as compiled by the accountant was £1,200

Dividend D_{0-1} for the financial year t_{0-1} was £450

Net assets NA_0 at the beginning of the financial year were £6,000

Net assets NA_1 at the end of the financial year were £6,750

The income account can be linked with opening and closing balance sheets, namely:

$$Y_{0-1} = NA_1 - NA_0 + D_{0-1}$$
$$= £6,750 - £6,000 + £450$$
$$= £1,200 = Y_{0-1}$$

Thus Y has been computed by using the opening and closing capitals for the period.

In practice, however, the accountant would compute income Y by compiling a profit and loss account. So, of what use is this formula? For reasons to be discussed later, the economist finds use for the formula when it is amended to take account of what we call **present values**. Computed after the end of a financial year, it is the *ex post* measure of income.

Nature of traditional accounting value

As the values of assets still in service at the end of a financial period have been based on the unconsumed costs of such assets, they are the by-product of compiling the income financial statement. These values have been fixed not by direct measurement, but simply by an assessment of costs consumed in the process of generating period turnover. We can say, then, that the balance sheet figure of net assets is a residual valuation after measuring income.

However, it is not a value in the sense of worth or market value as a buying price or selling price; it is merely a **value of unconsumed costs of assets**. This is an important point that will be encountered again later.

3.4 Economist's view of income, capital and value

Let us now consider the economist's tradition of present value and the nature of economic income.

3.4.1 Economist's tradition of present value

Present value is a technique used in valuing a future money flow, or in measuring the money value of an existing capital stock in terms of a predicted cash flow *ad infinitum*.

Present value (PV) constitutes the nature of economic capital and, indirectly, economic income. Given the choice of receiving £100 now or £100 in one year's time, the rational person will opt to receive £100 now. This behaviour exhibits an intuitive appreciation of the fact that £100 today is worth more than £100 one year hence. Thus the mind has **discounted** the value of the future sum: £100 today is worth £100; but compared with today, i.e. **compared with present value**, a similar sum receivable in twelve months' time is worth less than £100. How much less is a matter of subjective evaluation, but compensation for the time element may be found by reference to interest: a person forgoing the spending of £1 today and spending it one year later may earn interest of, say, 10% per annum in compensation for the sacrifice undergone by deferring consumption.

So £1 today invested at 10% p.a. will be worth £1.10 one year later, £1.21 two years later, £1.331 three years later, and so on. This is the concept of compound interest. It may be calculated by the formula $(1 + r)^n$, where 1 = the sum invested; r = the rate of interest; n = the number of periods of investment (in our case years). So for £1 invested at 10% p.a. for four years:

$$(1 + r)^n = (1 + 0.10)^4$$
$$= (1.1)^4$$
$$= £1.4641$$

and for five years:

$$= (1.1)^5$$
$$= £1.6105, \text{ and so on}$$

Notice how the **future value** increases because of the compound interest element – it **varies** over time – whereas the investment of £1 remains constant. So, conversely, the sum of £1.10 received at the end of year one has a PV of £1, as does £1.21 received at the end of year two and £1.331 at the end of year three.

It has been found convenient to construct tables to ease the task of calculating present values. These show the cash flow, i.e. the future values, at a constant figure of £1 and allow the investment to vary. So:

$$PV = \frac{CF}{(1+r)^n}$$

where CF = anticipated cash flow; r = the discount (i.e. interest) rate. So the PV of a cash flow of £1 receivable at the end of one year at 10% p.a. is:

$$\frac{£1}{(1+r)^1} = £0.9091$$

and £1 at the end of two years:

$$\frac{£1}{(1+r)^2} = £0.8264$$

and so on over successive years. The appropriate present values for years three, four and five would be £0.7513, £0.6830, £0.6210 respectively.

£0.9091 invested today at 10% p.a. will produce £1 at the end of one year. The PV of £1 receivable at the end of two years is £0.8264 and so on.

Tables presenting data in this way are called 'PV tables'; while the earlier method compiles tables usually referred to as 'compound interest tables'. Both types of table are compound interest tables; only the presentation of the data has changed.

To illustrate the ease of computation using PV tables, we can compute the PV of £6,152 receivable at the end of year five, given a discount rate of 10%, as being £6,152 × £0.6210 = £3,820. Thus £3,820 will total £6,152 in five years given an interest rate of 10% p.a. So the PV of that cash flow of £6,152 is £3,820, because £3,820 would generate interest of £2,332 (i.e. 6,152 – 3,820) as compensation for losing use of the principal sum for five years. Future flows must be discounted to take cognisance of the time element separating cash flows. Only then are we able to compare like with like by reducing all future flows to the comparable loss of present value.

This concept of PV has a variety of applications in accountancy and will be encountered in many different areas requiring financial measurement, comparison and decision. It originated as an economist's device within the context of economic income and economic capital models, but in accountancy it assists in the making of valid comparisons and decisions. For example, two machines may each generate an income of £10,000 over three years. However, timing of the cash flows may vary between the machines. This is illustrated in Figure 3.1.

If we simply compare the profit-generating capacity of the machines over the three-year span, each produces a total profit of £10,000. But if we pay regard to the time element of the money flows, the machines are not so equal.

However, the technique has its faults. Future money flows are invariably the subject of **estimation** and thus the actual flow experienced may show variations from forecast. Also, the element of **interest**, which is crucial to the calculation of present values, is **subjective**. It may, for instance, be taken as the average prevailing rate operating within the economy or a rate peculiar to the firm and the element of risk involved in the particular decision. In this chapter we are concerned only with PV as a tool of the economist in evaluating economic income and economic capital.

3.4.2 Nature of economic income

Economics is concerned with the economy in general, raising questions such as: how does it function? how is wealth created? how is income generated? why is income generated?

Figure 3.1 Dissimilar cash flows.

Cash flows		
Machine A	Machine B	Receivable end of year
£	£	
1,000	5,000	1
2,000	4,000	2
7,000	1,000	3
10,000	10,000	

The economy as a whole is activated by income generation. The individual is motivated to generate income because of a need to satisfy personal wants by consuming goods and services. Thus the economist becomes concerned with the individual consumer's psychological state of personal **enjoyment and satisfaction**. This creates a need to treat the economy as a **behavioural entity**.

The behavioural aspect forms a substantial part of micro- and macroeconomic thought, emanating particularly from the microeconomic. We can say that the economist's version of income measurement is microeconomic orientated in contrast to the accountant's business entity orientation.

The origination of the economic measure of income commenced with Irving Fisher in 1930.[6] He saw income in terms of consumption, and consumption in terms of individual perception of personal enjoyment and satisfaction. His difficulty in formulating a standard measure of this personal psychological concept of income was overcome by equating this individual experience with the consumption of goods and services and assuming that the cost of such goods and services formed the measure.

Thus, he reasoned, consumption (C) equals income (Y); so $Y = C$. He excluded savings from income because savings were not consumed. There was no satisfaction derived from savings; enjoyment necessitated consumption, he argued. Money was worthless until spent; so growth of capital was ignored, but reductions in capital became part of income because such reductions had to be spent.

In Fisher's model, capital was a stock of wealth existing at a point in time, and as a stock it generated income. Eventually, he reconciled the value of capital with the value of income by employing the concept of present value. He assessed the PV of a future flow of income by **discounting** future flows using the discounted cash flow (DCF) technique. Fisher's model adopted the prevailing average market rate of interest as the discount factor.

Economists since Fisher have introduced savings as part of income. Sir John Hicks played a major role in this area.[7] He introduced the idea that income was the maximum consumption enjoyed by the individual without reducing the individual's capital stock, i.e. the amount a person could consume during a period of time that still left him or her with the same value of capital stock at the end of the period as at the beginning. Hicks also used the DCF technique in the valuation of capital.

If capital increases, the increase constitutes savings and grants the opportunity of consumption. The formula illustrating this was given in section 3.3, i.e. $Y_{0-1} = NA_1 - NA_0 + D_{0-1}$.

However, in the Hicksian model, $NA_1 - NA_0$, given as £6,750 and £6,000, respectively, in the aforementioned example, would have been discounted to achieve present values.

The same formula may be expressed in different forms. The economist is likely to show it as $Y - C + (K_1 - K_0)$ where C = consumption, having been substituted for dividend, and K_1 and K_0 have been substituted for NA_1 and NA_0 respectively.

Hicks's income model is often spoken of as an *ex ante* model because it is usually used for the measurement of **expected** income in advance of the time period concerned. Of course, because it specifically introduces the present value concept, present values replace the balance sheet values of net assets adopted by the accountant. Measuring income **before the event** enables the individual to estimate the level of consumption that may be achieved without depleting capital stock. Before-the-event computations of income necessitate predictions of future cash flows.

Suppose that an individual proprietor of a business anticipated that his investment in the enterprise would generate earnings over the next four years, as specified in Figure 3.2. Furthermore, such earnings would be retained by the business for the financing of new equipment with a view to increasing potential output.

Figure 3.2   Business cash flows for four years.

Years	Cash inflows
	£
1	26,000
2	29,000
3	35,000
4	41,000

We will assume that the expected rate of interest on capital employed in the business is 8% p.a.

The economic value of the business at K_0 (i.e. at the beginning of year one) will be based on the discounted cash flow of the future four years. Figure 3.3 shows that K_0 is £106,853, calculated as the present value of anticipated earnings of £131,000 spread over a four-year term.

The economic value of the business at K_1 (i.e. at the end of year one, which is the same as saying the beginning of year two) is calculated in Figure 3.4. This shows that K_1 is £115,403 calculated as the present value of anticipated earnings of £131,000 spread over a four-year term.

From this information we are able to calculate Y for the period Y_1, as in Figure 3.5. Note that C (consumption) is nil because, in this exercise, dividends representing consumption have not been payable for Y_1. In other words, income Y_1 is entirely in the form of projected capital growth, i.e. savings.

By year-end K_1, earnings of £26,000 will have been received; in projecting the capital at K_2 such earnings will have been reinvested and at the beginning of year K_2 will have a PV of £26,000. These earnings will no longer represent a **predicted** sum because they will have been **realised** and therefore will no longer be subjected to discounting.

Figure 3.3   Economic value at K_0.

	(a)	(b)	(c)
Year	Cash flow	$DCF = \dfrac{1}{(1+r)^n}$	PV $(a) \times (b)$
	£		£
K_1	26,000	$\dfrac{1}{(1.08)^1} = 0.9259$	24,073
K_2	29,000	$\dfrac{1}{(1.08)^2} = 0.8573$	24,862
K_3	35,000	$\dfrac{1}{(1.08)^3} = 0.7938$	27,783
K_4	41,000	$\dfrac{1}{(1.08)^4} = 0.7350$	30,135
	131,000		106,853

Figure 3.4 Economic value at K_1.

	(a)	(b)	(c)
Year	Cash flow	$DCF = \dfrac{-1}{(1+r)^n}$	$\dfrac{PV}{(a) \times (b)}$
	£		£
K_1	26,000	1.0000	26,000
K_2	29,000	$\dfrac{1}{(1+r)^1} = 0.9259$	26,851
K_3	35,000	$\dfrac{1}{(1+r)^2} = 0.8573$	30,006
K_4	41,000	$\dfrac{1}{(1+r)^3} = 0.7938$	32,546
	131,000		115,403

Figure 3.5 Calculation of Y for the period Y_1.

$$Y = C + (K_1 - K_0)$$
$$Y = 0 + (115,403 - 106,853)$$
$$= 0 + 8,550$$
$$= £8,550$$

The income of £8,550 represents an anticipated return of 8% p.a. on the economic capital at K_0 of £106,853 (8% of £106,853 is £8,548, the difference of £2 between this figure and the figure calculated above being caused by 'rounding'). As long as the expectations of future cash flows and the chosen interest rate do not change, then Y_1 will equal 8% of £106,853.

What will the anticipated income for the year Y_2 amount to?

Applying the principle explained above, the anticipated income for the year Y_2 will equal 8% of the capital at the end of K_1 amounting to £115,403 = £9,233. This is proved in Figure 3.6, which shows that K_2 is £124,636 calculated as the present value of anticipated earnings of £131,000 spread over a four-year term.

From this information we are able to calculate Y for the period Y_2 as in Figure 3.7. Note that capital value attributable to the end of the year K_2 is being assessed at the beginning of K_2. This means that the £26,000 due at the end of year K_1 will have been received and reinvested, earning interest of 8% p.a. Thus by the end of year K_2 it will be worth £28,080. The sum of £29,000 will be realised at the end of year K_2 so its present value at that time will be £29,000.

If the anticipated future cash flows change, the expected capital value at the successive points in time will also change. Accordingly, the actual value of capital may vary from that forecast by the *ex ante* model.

Figure 3.6 Economic value at K_2.

Year	(a) Cash flow	(b) $DCF = \dfrac{1}{(1+r)^n}$	(c) $PV = (a) \times (b)$
	£	£	£
K_1	26,000	1.08	28,080
K_2	29,000	1.0000	29,000
K_3	35,000	0.9259	32,407
K_4	41,000	0.8573	35,149
	131,000		124,636

Figure 3.7 Calculation of Y for the period Y_2.

$Y = C + (K_2 - K_1)$
$Y = 0 + (124,636 - 115,403)$
$\quad = 0 + 9,233$
$\quad = £9,233$

3.5 Critical comment on the economist's measure

While the income measure enables us to formulate theories regarding the behaviour of the economy, it has inherent shortcomings not only in the economic field, but particularly in the accountancy sphere.

● The calculation of economic capital, hence economic income, is subjective in terms of the present value factor, often referred to as the DCF element. The factor may be based on any one of a number of factors, such as opportunity cost, the current return on the firm's existing capital employed, the contemporary interest payable on a short-term loan such as a bank overdraft, the average going rate of interest payable in the economy at large, or a rate considered justified on the basis of the risk attached to a particular investment.

● Investors are not of one mind or one outlook. For example, they possess different risk and time preferences and will therefore employ different discount factors.

● The model constitutes a compound of unrealised and realised flows, i.e. profits. Because of the unrealised element, it has not been used as a base for computing tax or for declaring a dividend.

● The projected income is dependent upon the success of a planned financial strategy. Investment plans may change, or fail to attain target.

● Windfall gains cannot be foreseen, so they cannot be accommodated in the *ex ante* model. Our prognostic cash flows may therefore vary from the actual flows generated, e.g. an unexpected price movement.

● It is difficult to construct a satisfactory, meaningful balance sheet detailing the unused stock of net assets by determining the present values of individual assets. Income is invariably the consequence of deploying a group of assets working in unison.

3.6 Critical comment on the accountant's measure

3.6.1 Virtues of the accountant's measure

As with the economist's, the accountant's measure is not without its virtues. These are invariably aspects of the historical cost concept, such as objectivity, being transaction based and being generally understood.

3.6.2 Faults of the accountant's measure

Principles of historical cost and profit realisation

The historical cost and profit realisation concepts are firmly entrenched in the transaction basis of accountancy. However, in practice, the two concepts are not free of adjustments. Because of such adjustments, some commentators argue that the system produces a heterogeneous mix of values and realised income items.[8]

For example, in the case of asset values, certain assets such as land and buildings may have a carrying figure in the balance sheet based on a revaluation to market value, while other assets such as motor vehicles may still be based on a balance of unallocated cost. The balance sheet thus pretends on the one hand to be a list of resultant costs pending allocation over future periods, and on the other hand to be a statement of current values.

Prudence concept

This concept introduces caution into the recognition of assets and income for financial reporting purposes. The cardinal rule is that income should not be recorded or recognised within the system until it is realised, but unrealised losses should be recognised immediately.

However, not all unrealised profits are excluded. For example, practice is that attributable profit on long-term contracts still in progress at the financial year-end may be taken into account. As with fixed assets, rules are not applied uniformly.

Unrealised capital profits

Capital profits are ignored as income until they are realised, when, in the accounting period of sale, they are acknowledged by the reporting system. However, all the profit is recognised in one financial period when, in truth, the surplus was generated over successive periods by gradual growth, albeit unrealised until disposal of the asset. Thus a portion of what are now realised profits applies to prior periods. Not all of this profit should be attributed to the period of sale.

Going concern

The going concern concept is fundamental to accountancy and operates on the assumption that the business entity has an indefinite life. It is used to justify basing the periodic reports of asset values on carrying forward figures that represent unallocated costs, i.e. to justify the non-recognition of the realisable or disposal values of non-monetary assets and, in so doing, the associated unrealised profits/losses. Although the life of an entity is deemed indefinite, there is uncertainty, and accountants are reluctant to predict the future. When they are matching costs with revenue for the current accounting period, they follow the prudence concept of reasonable certainty.

In the long term, economic income and accountancy income are reconciled. The unrealised profits of the economic measure are eventually realised and, at that point, they will be recognised by the accountant's measure. In the short term, however, they give different results for each period.

3.7 Income, capital and changing price levels

A primary concern of income measurement to both economist and accountant is the maintenance of the capital stock, i.e. the maintenance of capital values. The assumption is that income can only arise **after** the capital stock has been maintained at the same amount as at the beginning of the accounting period.

However, this raises the question of how we should define the capital that we are attempting to maintain. There are a number of possible definitions:

● **Money capital**. Should we concern ourselves with maintaining the fund of capital resources initially injected by the entrepreneur into the new enterprise? This is indeed one of the aims of traditional, transaction-based accountancy.

● **Potential consumption capital**. Is it this that should be maintained, i.e. the economist's present value philosophy expressed via the discounted cash flow technique?

● **Operating capacity capital**. Should maintenance of productive capacity be the rule, i.e. capital measured in terms of tangible or physical assets? This measure would utilise the current cost accounting system.

Revsine attempted to construct an analytical bridge between replacement cost accounting that maintains the operating capacity, and the economic concepts of **income** and **value**, by demonstrating that the distributable operating flow component of economic income is equal to the current operating component of replacement cost income, and that the unexpected income component of economic income is equal to the unrealisable cost savings of replacement cost income.[9] This will become clearer when the replacement cost model is dealt with in the next chapter.

● **Financial capital**. Should capital be maintained in terms of a fund of general purchasing power (sometimes called 'real' capital)? In essence this is the consumer purchasing power (or general purchasing power) approach, but not in a strict sense as it can be measured in a variety of ways. The basic method uses a general price index. This concept is likely to satisfy the criteria of the proprietor/shareholders of the entity. The money capital and the financial capital concepts are variations of the same theme, the former being founded on the historic cost principle and the latter applying an adjustment mechanism to take account of changing price levels.

The money capital concept has remained the foundation stone of traditional accountancy reporting, but the operating and financial capital alternatives have played a controversial secondary role over the past twenty-five years.

Potential consumption capital is peculiar to economics in terms of measurement of the business entity's aggregate capital, although, as discussed on pages 49–52, it has a major role to play as a decision-making model in financial management.

3.7.1 Why are these varying methods of concern?

The problem tackled by these devices is that plague of the economy known as 'changing price levels', particularly the upward spiralling referred to as **inflation**. Throughout this chapter we have assumed that there is a stable monetary unit and that income, capital and value changes over time have been in response to operational activity and the interaction of supply and demand or changes in expectations.

Following the historic cost convention, capital maintenance has involved a comparison of opening and closing capital in each accounting period. It has been assumed that the purchasing power of money has remained constant over time.

If we take into account moving price levels, particularly the fall in the purchasing power of the monetary unit due to inflation, then our measure of **income** is affected if we insist upon **maintaining capital in real terms**.

3.7.2 Is it necessary to maintain capital in real terms?

Undoubtedly it is necessary if we wish to prevent an erosion of the operating capacity of the entity and thus its ability to maintain real levels of income. If we do not maintain the capacity of capital to generate the current level of profit, then the income measure, being the difference between opening and closing capitals, will be overstated or overvalued. This is because the capital measure is being understated or undervalued. In other words, there is a danger of dividends being paid out of real capital rather than out of real income. It follows that, if the need to retain profits is overlooked, the physical assets will be depleted.

In accountancy there is no theoretical difficulty in measuring the impact of changing price levels. There are, however, two practical difficulties:

● There are a number of methods, or mixes of methods, available and it has proved impossible to obtain consensus support for one method or compound of methods.

● There is a high element of subjectivity, which detracts from the objectivity of the information.

Subsequent chapters deal with moving prices and analyse the methods formulated, together with the difficulties that they in turn introduce into the financial reporting system.

Summary

In measuring income, capital and value, the accountant's approach varies from the sister discipline of the economist, yet both are trying to achieve similar objectives.

The accountant uses a traditional transaction-based model of computing income, capital being the residual of this model.

The economist's viewpoint is anchored in a behavioural philosophy that measures capital and deduces income to be the difference between the capital at commencement of a period and that at its end.

The objectives of income measurement are important because of the existence of a highly sophisticated capital market. These objectives involve the assessment of stewardship performance, dividend and retention policies, comparison of actual results with those predicted, assessment of future prospects, payment of taxation and disclosure of matched costs against revenue from sales.

The natures of income, capital and value must be appreciated if we are to understand and achieve measurement. The apparent conflict between the two measures can be seen as a consequence of the accountant's need for periodic reporting to shareholders. In the longer term, both methods tend to agree.

Present value as a concept is the foundation stone of the economist, while historical cost, adjusted for prudence, is that of the accountant. Present value demands a subjective discount rate and estimates that time may prove incorrect; historical cost ignores unrealised profits and in application is not always transaction based.

The economist's measure, of undoubted value in the world of micro- and macroeconomics, presents difficulty in the accountancy world of annual reports. The accountant's method, with its long track record of acceptance, ignores any generated profits, which caution and the concept of the going concern deem not to exist.

The economic trauma of changing price levels is a problem that both measures can embrace, but consensus support for a particular model of measurement has proved elusive.

Review questions

1 What is the purpose of measuring income?

2 Explain the nature of economic income.

3 The historical cost concept has withstood the test of time. Specify the reasons for this success, together with any aspects of historical cost that you consider are detrimental in the sphere of financial reporting.

4 What is meant by present value? Does it take account of inflation?

5 A company contemplates purchasing a machine that will generate an income of £25,000 per year over each of the next five years. A scrap value of £2,000 is anticipated on disposal. How much would you advise the company to pay for the asset?

6 Discuss the arguments for and against revaluing fixed assets and recognising the gain or loss.

7 To an accountant, net income is essentially a historical record of the past. To an economist, net income is essentially a speculation about the future. Examine the relative merits of these two approaches for financial reporting purposes.

8 Examine and contrast the concepts of profit that you consider to be relevant to:

(a) an economist;   (b) a speculator;

(c) a business executive;   (d) the managing director of a company;

(e) a shareholder in a private company;   (f) a shareholder in a large public company.

Exercises

An extract from the solution is provided in the appendix at the end of the text for exercises marked with an asterisk (*).

Question 1

(a) 'Measurement in financial statements', chapter 6 of the ASB's *Statement of Principles,* was published in 1999. Amongst the theoretical valuation systems considered is value in use – more commonly known as economic value.

Required:

Describe the Hicksian economic model of income and value, and assess its usefulness for financial reporting.

(b) Jim Bowater purchased a parcel of 30,000 ordinary shares in New Technologies plc for £36,000 on 1 January 20X5. Jim, an Australian on a four-year contract in the UK, has it in mind to sell the shares at the end of 20X7, just before he leaves for Australia. Based on the company's forecast growth and dividend policy, his broker has advised him that his shares are likely to fetch only £35,000 then.

In its annual report for the year ended 31 December 20X4 the company had forecast annual dividend pay outs as follows:

Year ended: 31 December 20X5, 25p per share
31 December 20X6, 20p per share
31 December 20X7, 20p per share

Required:
Using the Ideal Economic Model of income:
  (i) Compute Jim's economic income for each of the three years ending on the dates indicated above.
  (ii) Show that Jim's economic capital will be preserved at 1 January 20X5 level. Jim's cost of capital is 20%.

* Question 2

(a) Describe briefly the theory underlying Hicks's economic model of income and capital. What are its practical limitations?

(b) Spock purchased a space invader entertainment machine at the beginning of year one for £1,000. He expects to receive at annual intervals the following receipts: at the end of year one £400; end of year two £500; end of year three £600. At the end of year three he expects to sell the machine for £400.

Spock could receive a return of 10% in the next best investment.

The present value of £1 receivable at the end of a period discounted at 10% is as follows:

End of year one   £0.909
End of year two   £0.826
End of year three   £0.751

Required:
Calculate the ideal economic income, ignoring taxation and working to the nearest £.

Your answer should show that Spock's capital is maintained throughout the period and that his income is constant.

* Question 3

Jason commenced with £135,000 cash. He acquired an established shop on 1 January 20X1. He agreed to pay £130,000 for the fixed and current assets and the goodwill. The replacement cost of the shop premises was £100,000, stock £10,000 and debtors £4,000; the balance of the purchase price was for the goodwill. He paid legal costs of £5,000. No liabilities were taken over. Jason could have resold the business immediately for £135,000. Legal costs are to be expensed in 20X1.

Jason expected to draw £25,000 per year from the business for three years and to sell the shop at the end of 20X3 for £150,000.

At 31 December 20X1 the books showed the following tangible assets and liabilities:

Cost to the business before any drawings by Jason:		**He estimated that the net realisable values were:**
	£	£
Shop premises	100,000	85,000
Stock	15,500	20,000
Debtors	5,200	5,200
Cash	40,000	40,000
Creditors	5,000	5,000

Based on his experience of the first year's trading, he revised his estimates and expected to draw £35,000 per year for three years and sell the shop for £175,000 on 31 December 20X3.

Jason's opportunity cost of capital was 20%.

Required:
(a) Calculate the following income figures for 20X1:
  (i)   accounting income;
  (ii) income based on net realisable values;
  (iii) economic income ex ante;
  (iv) economic income ex post.
        State any assumptions made.
(b) Evaluate each of the four income figures as indicators of performance in 20X1 and as a guide to decisions about the future.

Question 4

The following information relates to Ozone Ltd at 1 January 20X0:

Expected net receipts for 20X0	£240,000
Expected net receipts for subsequent years	£400,000 p.a.
Cost of capital	10%

Further information becomes available at 31 December 20X0:

Expected future net receipts revised to	£440,000 p.a.
Actual net receipts for 20X0	£200,000

Additionally, a decision has been taken to begin a project on 31 December 20X0 at a cost of £40,000, with estimated net receipts at £20,000 p.a. for the next four years.

Information is also available concerning the company's net assets at the start and end of 20X0:

	1 Jan 20X0	31 Dec 20X0
	£	£
Net historical cost	2,920,000	2,800,000
Net replacement cost	3,800,000	2,600,000
Net realisable value	3,280,000	4,040,000

Required:

(a) **Using Hicks' concept of income:**
  (i) **calculate the budgeted income for the year;**
  (ii) **calculate the actual income for the year (two versions);**
  (iii) **reconcile the budgeted and actual outcomes with brief narrative explanations.**

(b) **Briefly assess the economist's contribution to accounting measurement of income and capital.**

References

1 T.A. Lee, *Income and Value Measurement: Theory and Practice* (3rd edition), Van Nostrand Reinhold (UK), 1985, p. 20.
2 D. Solomons, *Making Accounting Policy*, Oxford University Press, 1986, p. 132.
3 R.W. Scapens, *Accounting in an Inflationary Environment* (2nd edition), Macmillan, 1981, p. 125.
4 *Ibid.*, p. 127.
5 D. Solomons, *op. cit.*, p. 132.
6 I. Fisher, *The Theory of Interest*, Macmillan, 1930, pp. 171–181.
7 J.R. Hicks, *Value and Capital* (2nd edition), Clarendon Press, 1946.
8 T.A. Lee, *op. cit.*, pp. 52–54.
9 R.W. Scapens, *op. cit.*, p. 127.

Bibliography

American Institute of Certified Public Accountants, *Objectives of Financial Statements*, Report of the Study Group, 1973.
The Corporate Report, ASC, 1975, pp. 28–31.
N. Kaldor, 'The concept of income in economic theory', in R.H. Parker and G.C. Harcourt (eds), *Readings in the Concept and Measurement of Income*, Cambridge University Press, 1969.
T.A. Lee, 'The accounting entity concept, accounting standards and inflation accounting', *Accounting and Business Reseach*, Spring 1980, pp. 1–11.
J.R. Little, 'Income measurement: an introduction', *Student Newsletter*, June 1988.
D. Solomons, 'Economic and accounting concepts of income', in R.H Parker and G.C. Harcourt, *op. cit.*
R.R. Sterling, *Theory of the Measurement of Enterprise Income*, University of Kansas Press, 1970.

CHAPTER

Changing price levels
the developing approach

4.1 Introduction

In this chapter we discuss the impact of moving price levels on income and capital measurement and the concepts that have been suggested to incorporate these movements into the financial reports. These concepts are still undergoing development and have not yet achieved general support among practitioners in the field. In this chapter we consider the following:

- A review of the problems of historic cost accounting (HCA)
- Shifting price level accounting
- The concepts in principle
- The concepts illustrated for one year's transactions
- A critique of each model

4.2 Review of the problems of historical cost accounting (HCA)

The transaction-based historical cost concept was unchallenged in the UK until the 1939–45 war. Then price levels started to hedge upwards at an ever-increasing pace during the 1950s and reached an annual rate of increase of 20% in the mid-1970s. The historical cost base for financial reporting witnessed growing criticism. The inherent faults of the system were discussed in Chapter 3, but inflation exacerbates the problem in the following ways:

- Significant information concerning equity progress and wealth is not reported when current values and changes in value are ignored.
- Comparability of business entities, which is so necessary in the assessment of performance and growth, becomes distorted.
- The decision-making process, the formulation of plans and the setting of targets become intrinsically flawed owing to financial base data being out of date.
- Financial reports become confusing at best, misleading at worst, because the financial data evolve into a mismatch of differing historical cost levels as the monetary unit becomes unstable.
- Unrealised profits arising in individual accounting periods are increased as a result of inflation.

In order to combat these serious defects, current value accounting became the subject of a rolling output of research, enmeshed in ongoing controversy.

4.3 Shifting price level accounting

A number of versions of current value accounting (CVA) were eventually identified, but the current value postulate was said to suffer from the following disadvantages:

- It destroys the factual nature of HCA, which is transaction based: the factual characteristic is to all intents and purposes lost as transaction-based historic values are replaced by judgemental values.

- It is not as objective as HCA because it is less verifiable from auditable documentation.

- It entails recognition of unrealised profit, a practice that is anathema to the traditionalist.

- The claimed improvement in comparability between commercial entities is a myth because of the degree of subjectivity in measuring current value by each.

- The lack of a single accepted method of computing current values compounds the subjectivity aspect. One fault-laden system is being usurped by another that is also faulty.

In spite of these criticisms, the search for a system of financial reporting devoid of the defects of HCA and capable of coping with shifting price levels has produced a number of CVA models. Before discussing these concepts in detail, it is useful to contrast the viewpoints of the accountant and economist in terms of a simple numerical approach.

4.3.1 Accountant's numerical approach

Assume that Entrepreneur started business with capital of £3,000 in cash and decided to enter the data-processing equipment industry by buying and selling secondhand computers. He promptly acquired six machines, all examples of a standard and popular model, for £500 each and sold them for £900 each within the course of one calendar month. All transactions were on an immediate cash basis. At the end of the month's activities he possessed cash of £5,400, consisting of capital of £3,000 and profit of £2,400. During the next calendar month a similar trading pattern emerged with six machines purchased at £500 each and the same six machines sold for £900 each. The cash holding became £7,800. The balance sheets at the end of each month were as in Figure 4.1.

4.3.2 Economist's numerical approach

In principle, the economist's measure of income would be in sympathy with that of the accountant. The economic capital of £3,000 has been maintained, so any excess of this sum is income or profit. Unfortunately, however, an economic environment of shifting price levels will disturb the unanimity of the two disciplines. The economist will insist on taking account of moving price levels in measuring income and maintaining the entity's capital base.

Let us assume that our entrepreneur, having successfully completed his first month's trading as described earlier, then encounters a market of changing prices. Secondhand computers of identical model to those recently bought and sold are not available at £500 each and prices have risen by £200 per machine. Thus, at the end of month one, clutching the sum of £5,000, our dismayed proprietor must expend £4,200 in buying six machines at £700 each.

Figure 4.1 Balance sheet of Entrepreneur at the end of months 1 and 2 using the accountant's approach.

	Month 1	Month 2
	£	£
Fixed assets	nil	nil
Current assets:		
Cash	5,400	7,800
	5,400	7,800
Capital	3,000	3,000
Profit for month	2,400	2,400
Profit b/fwd	———	2,400
		4,800
	5,400	7,800

At this point the business achieves the same situation as prevailed in the stable prices model immediately following the second month's purchase but before sale of the equipment: that is, it possesses a stock of six machines plus one month's profit amounting to £2,400. However, before the second purchase this profit was represented by cash of £2,400. After purchase the cash has dwindled to £1,200 as part of the cash has been used to keep pace with inflation. The economist would insist on income measurement taking account of this additional inflated expenditure and recognising that the **real** profit is £1,200, not £2,400 as measured by the accountant's HCA system.

After purchase of the six machines at the prevailing inflated price levels, the balance sheet, on the basis of the economist's measure, would appear as in Figure 4.2. The value

Figure 4.2 Balance sheet of Entrepreneur at end of month 1.

	£	£
Fixed assets		nil
Current assets:		
Stock	4,200	
Cash	1,200	
		5,400
		5,400
Capital		3,000
Provision for changing price levels		
per **stock replacement reserve**		1,200
Adjusted real capital		4,200
Real profit		1,200
		5,400

of real capital is now £4,200 compared with an equivalent real value of £3,000 at the beginning of month one, when a different price level existed. In other words, £4,200 at the end of the month represents a maintained capital base that at the beginning of the month was measured at £3,000, as six machines now cost £4,200 when earlier they had cost £3,000. The pound sterling has fallen in value and it now takes £4,200 to accomplish the task of £3,000 before prices moved.

4.4 The concepts in principle

Several current income and value models have been proposed to replace or operate in tandem with the historical cost convention. However, in terms of basic characteristics, they may be reduced to the following three models:

● Current purchasing power (CPP) or general purchasing power (GPP).

● Current entry cost or replacement cost (RC).

● Current exit cost or net realisable value (NRV).

We discuss each of these models below.

4.4.1 Currrent purchasing power accounting (CPPA)

The CPP model measures income and value by adopting a price index system. Movements in price levels are gauged by reference to price changes in a group of goods and services in **general** use within the economy. The aggregate price value of this **basket** of commodities cum services is determined at a base point in time and indexed as 100. Subsequent changes in price are compared on a regular basis with this base period price and the change recorded. For example, the price level of our chosen range of goods and services may amount to £76 on 31 March 20X1, and show changes as follows:

£76 at 31 March 20X1
£79 at 30 April 20X1
£81 at 31 May 20X1
£84 at 30 June 20X1
and so on.

The change in price may be indexed with 31 March as the base:

20X1	Index	Calculation
31 March	100	i.e. £76
30 April	103.9	i.e. $\dfrac{79}{76} \times 100$
31 May	106.6	i.e. $\dfrac{81}{76} \times 100$
30 June	110.5	i.e. $\dfrac{84}{76} \times 100$

In the UK, an index system similar in construction to this is known as the Retail Price Index (RPI). It is a barometer of fluctuating price levels covering a miscellany of goods and services as used by the average household. Thus it is a **general** price index. It is amended from time to time to take account of new commodities entering the consumer's range of choice and needs. As a model, it is unique owing to the introduction of the concept of gains and losses in **purchasing power**.

4.4.2 Current entry or replacement cost accounting (RCA)

The replacement cost (RC) model assesses income and value by reference to entry costs or current replacement costs of materials and other assets utilised within the business entity. The valuation attempts to replace like with like and thus takes account of the quality and condition of the existing assets. A motor vehicle, for instance, may have been purchased brand new for £25,000 with an expected life of five years, an anticipated residual value of nil and a straight-line depreciation policy. Its HCA carrying value in the balance sheet at the end of its first year would be £25,000 less £5,000 = £20,000. However, if a similar new replacement vehicle cost £30,000 at the end of year one, then its gross RC would be £30,000; depreciation for one year based on this sum would be £6,000 and the net RC would be £24,000. Thus a holding gain of £4,000 has emerged in respect of the machine in use, and the machine with a carrying value of £20,000 would be revalued at £24,000.

4.4.3 Current exit cost or net realisable value accounting (NRVA)

The net realisable value (NRV) model is based on the economist's concept of opportunity cost. It is a model that has had strong academic support, most notably in Australia from Professor Ray Chambers who referred to this approach as Continuous Contemporary Accounting (CoCoA). If an asset cost £25,000 at the beginning of year one and at the end of that year it had a NRV of £21,000 after meeting selling expenses, it would be carried in the NRV balance sheet at £21,000. This amount represents the cash forgone by holding the asset, i.e. the opportunity of possessing cash of £21,000 has been sacrificed in favour of the asset. Depreciation for the year would be £25,000 less £21,000 = £4,000.

4.5 The concepts illustrated for one year's transactions

These three models may now be deployed as a simple illustration in conjunction with the traditional system. We assume the basic data are as in the preceding example of Entrepreneur.

The business commenced with capital in cash of £3,000, then acquired six items of stock for resale at £500 per item, but only 50% of the stock was sold, the sales taking place in the *middle* of the first month's trading, and the selling price being £900 per item. All transactions are on a cash basis and stock valuation is based on first-in-first-out (FIFO).

We will draft a revenue account for the first month of trading and a balance sheet as at the end of that month for each model. Data peculiar to each system are displayed in Figure 4.3. Accounts are shown in Figure 4.4.

Observe the following points in relation to each model.

Figure 4.3 Price movements.

CPPA or GPPA

General index at 1 January = 100

15 January = 112

31 January = 130

RCA

Replacement cost of stocks per item   at 15 January = £610

at 31 January = £700

NRVA

Net realisable value per item at 31 January = £900

Figure 4.4 Trading account for the month ended 31 January 20X1.

Profit and Loss Accounts for the Month ended 31 January 20X1

	HCA		CPPA		RCA		NRVA	
	£		CPP£		£		£	
Sales	2,700	W1	3,134	W5	2,700	W1	2,700	W1
Opening stock	—		—		—		—	
Purchases	3,000	W2	3,900	W6	3,000	W2	3,000	W2
Closing stock	(1,500)	W3	(1,950)	W7	(1,500)	W3	(1,500)	W3
COSA	na		na		330	W10	na	
Cost of sales	1,500		1,950		1,830		1,500	
Holding gain	na		na		na		1,200	W15
Profit	1,200		1,184		870		2,400	

Balance Sheet as at 31 January 20X1

	£		CPP£		£		£	
Current assets								
Stock	1,500	W3	1,950	W7	2,100	W11	2,700	W14
Cash	2,700	W4	2,700		2,700		2,700	
	4,200		4,650		4,800		5,400	
Capital	3,000		3,900	W8	3,000		3,000	
Holding gains								
On stock consumed	na		na		330	W12		
On stock in hand	na		na		600	W13		
Profit	1,200		1,184		870		2,400	
Loss on monetary items	na		(434)	W9	na		na	
	4,200		4,650		4,800		5,400	

na = not applicable

Figure 4.4 *(cont.)*

Workings (W)

HCA

W1 Sales: 900 × 3 = £2,700
W2 Purchases: 500 × 6 = £3,000
W3 Closing stock: 500 × 3 = £1,500
W4 Cash: 1 January 20X1 Capital   3,000
                   1 January 20X1 Purchases   (3,000)

                   1 January 20X1 Balance   nil
                   15 January 20X1 Sales
                        £900 × 3 =   £2,700

                   15 January 20X1 Balance   £2,700

CPPA   CPP£
W5 Sales   £2,700 × 130/112 =   3,134
W6 Purchases   £3,000 × 130/100 =   3,900
W7 Closing stock £1,500 × 130/100 =   1,950
W8 Capital   £3,000 × 130/100 =   3,900

W9 Balance of cash was nil until 15 January when sales generated £2,700. This sum was held until 31 January during which period cash, a monetary item, lost purchasing power. The loss of purchasing power is measured by applying the general index to the cash held.
£2,700 × 130/112 − £2,700 = CPP £434.

RCA

W10 Additional replacement cost of stock consumed as at the date of sale is measured as a cost of sales adjustment (COSA). COSA is calculated as follows:

        £610 × 3 = 1,830
 Less: £500 × 3 = 1,500

 COSA   £330

W11 Closing stock: 700 × 3 = £2,100
W12 Holding gains on stock consumed: as for W10
W13 Stock at replacement cost   = 700 × 3
                                       =   2,100
     Less: stock at cost   = 500 × 3
                                       =   1,500

     Holding gains on closing stock   £600

NRVA

W14 Closing stock at net realisable value = 900 × 3 = £2,700
W15 900 × 3 =   2,700
     500 × 3 =   1,500

     Holding gain   £1,200

4.5.1 CPPA

● All historical cost values are adjusted to a common index level for the month. In theory this can be the index applicable to any day of the financial period concerned. However, in practice it has been deemed preferable to use the last day of the period; thus the financial statements show the latest price level appertaining to the period.

● The application of a general price index as an adjusting factor results in the creation of an **alien** currency of **purchasing power**, which is used in place of sterling. Note, particularly, the impact on the entity's sales and capital compared with the other models. **Actual** sales shown on **invoices** will still read £2,700.

● Note the application of the concept of gain or loss on holding monetary items.

4.5.2 RCA

● Basically, only two adjustments are involved: the additional replacement cost of stock consumed and holding gains on closing stocks. However, in a more complex exercise an adjustment will be necessary regarding fixed assets and you will also encounter a gearing adjustment.

● Notice the concept of holding gains. This model introduces, in effect, unrealised profits in respect of closing stocks. The holding gain concerning stock consumed at the time of sale has been realised and deducted from what would have been a profit of £1,200. The statement is declaring **real** profits of £870.

4.5.3 NRVA

● This produces the same initial profit as HCA, namely £1,200, but a peculiarity of this system is that this realised profit is supplemented by **unrealised** profit generated by holding stocks. Under RCA accounting, such gains are shown in a separate account and are not treated as part of real income.

● This simple exercise has ignored the possibility of investment in fixed assets, thus depreciation is not involved. A reduction in the NRV of fixed assets at the end of a period compared with the beginning would be treated in a similar fashion to depreciation by being charged to the revenue account, and consequently profits would be reduced. An increase in the NRV of such assets would be included as part of the profit.

Observe the following comparative points.

● Only in the case of GPP is there a change in the measurement of sales. Remember that this system of measuring general inflation establishes, in effect, an alien or artificial currency described as 'general purchasing power'.

● The impact on net profits is drastic in terms of RCA and GPP when comparing these two measures with that of HCA. Appreciate the implications for the business if it were to become unaware of the influence of moving price levels and distributed all its profits as dividend. The maintenance of capital in terms of physical operating capacity would not take place. This would be tantamount, in **real** terms, to paying dividend out of capital.

● The economist introduces a separate concept of business profit by considering the holding gains of RCA and NRVA as part of revenue account profit.

● Only GPP changes the value of share capital.

● RCA and NRVA measure the impact of inflation on the individual firm, in terms of the change in price levels of its **raw materials and assets,** i.e. inflation peculiar to the company, whereas GPPA measures general inflation in the economy as a whole. GPPA may be meaningless in the case of an individual company. Consider a firm that carries a constant volume of stock valued at £100 in HCA terms. Now suppose that price levels double when measured by GPI, so that its stock is restated to £200 in a GPPA system. If, however, the cost of that **particular** stock has sustained a price change consisting of a five-fold increase, then under the NRVA model the value of the stock should be £500.

In the mid-1970s, when the accountancy profession was debating the problem of changing price level measurement, the general price level had climbed by some 23% over a period during which petroleum-based products had risen by 500%.

It can be said that the GPPA model is **shareholder orientated** because it shows whether the shareholder's funds are keeping pace with inflation by maintaining their purchasing power. In contrast, the RCA and NRVA models are **management orientated** because holding gains are identified and in consequence will be retained in order to maintain physical operating capital. Compare shareholders' funds in the four models. In these examples, such funds also consist of total assets.

4.6 Critique of each model

A critique of the various models may be formulated in terms of their characteristics and peculiarities as virtues and defects in application.

4.6.1 HCA

This model's virtues and defects have been discussed in Chapter 3 and earlier in this chapter.

4.6.2 RCA

Virtues

● Its **unit of measurement** is the monetary unit and consequently it is understood and accepted by the user of accountancy reports. In contrast, the GPP system employs an artificial unit based on arithmetic relationships, which is different and thus unfamiliar.

● It **identifies and isolates holding gains** from operating income. Thus it can prevent the inadvertent distribution of dividends in excess of operating profit. It satisfies the prudence criterion of the traditional accountant and **maintains the physical operating capacity** of the entity.

● It introduces **realistic current values** of assets in the balance sheet, thus making the balance sheet a 'value' statement and consequently more meaningful to the user. This contrasts sharply with the balance sheet as a list of unallocated carrying costs in the HCA system.

Defects

- It is a **subjective measure**, in that replacement costs are often necessarily based on estimates or assessments. It does not possess the factual characteristics of HCA. It is open to manipulation within constraints. Often it is based on index numbers which themselves may be based on a compound of prices of a mixture of similar commodities used as raw material or operating assets. This subjectivity is exacerbated in circumstances where rapid technological advance and innovation are involved in the potential new replacement asset, e.g. computers, printers.

- It **assumes replacement of assets** by being based on their replacement cost. Difficulties arise if such assets are not to be replaced by similar assets. Presumably, it will then be assumed that a replacement of equivalent value to the original will be deployed, however differently, as capital within the firm.

4.6.3 NRVA

Virtues

- It is a concept readily understood by the user. The value of any item invariably has two measures – a buying price and a selling price – and the twain do not usually meet. However, when considering the value of an **existing** possession, the owner instinctively considers its 'value' to be that in potential sale, i.e. NRV.

- It **avoids the need to estimate depreciation** and, in consequence, the attendant problems of assessing life-span and residual values. Depreciation is treated as the arithmetic difference between the NRV at the end of a financial period and the NRV at its beginning.

- It is **based on opportunity cost** and so can be said to be more meaningful. It is the **sacrificial** cost of possessing an asset, which, it can be argued, is more authentic in terms of being a true or real cost. If the asset were not possessed, its cash equivalent would exist instead and that cash would be deployed in other opportunities. Therefore, NRV = cash = opportunity = cost.

Defects

- It is a **subjective measure** and in this respect it possesses the same major fault as RCA. It can be said to be less prudent than RCA because NRV will tend to be higher in some cases than RCA. For example, when valuing finished stocks, a profit content will be involved.

- It is **not a realistic measure** as most assets, except finished goods, are possessed in order to be utilised, not sold. Therefore, NRV is irrelevant.

- It is **not always determinable**. The assets concerned may be highly specialist and there may be no ready market by which a value can be easily assessed. Consequently, any particular value may be fictitious or erroneous, containing too high a holding gain or, indeed, too low a holding loss.

- It **violates the concept of the going concern**, which demands that the accounts are drafted on the basis that there is no intention to liquidate the entity. Admittedly, this concept was formulated with HCA in view, but the acceptance of NRV implies the possibility of a cessation of trading.

4.6.4 GPP

Virtues

- It is an **objective measure** since it is still transaction based, as with HCA, and the possibility of subjectivity is constrained if a GPI is used that has been constructed by a central agency such as a government department. This applies in the UK, where the Retail Price Index is constructed by the Department of Employment.

- It is a **measure of shareholders' capital** and that capital's maintenance in terms of purchasing power units. Profit is the residual value after maintaining the money value of capital funds, taking account of changing price levels. Thus it is a measure readily understood by the shareholder/user of the accounts. It can prevent payment of a dividend out of real capital as measured by GPPA.

- It **introduces the concept of monetary items** as distinct from non-monetary items and the attendant concepts of gains and losses in holding net monetary liabilities compared with holding net monetary assets. Such gains and losses are experienced on a disturbing scale in times of inflation. They are **real** gains and losses. The **basic RCA and NRV models** do not recognise such 'surpluses' and 'deficits'.

Defects

- It is **HCA based but adjusted** to reflect general price movements. Thus it possesses the characteristics of HCA, good and bad, but with its values updated in the light of an arithmetic measure of general price changes. The major defect of becoming out of date is mitigated to a degree, but the impact of inflation on the entity's income and capital may be at variance with the rate of inflation affecting the economy in general.

- It may be **wrongly assumed that the GPP balance sheet is a current value statement**. It is not a current value document because of the defects discussed above; in particular, asset values may be subject to a different rate of inflation than that reflected by the GPI.

- It **creates an alien unit of measurement** still labelled by the £ sign. Thus we have the HCA £ and the GPP £. They are different pounds: one is the bona fide pound, the other is a synthetic unit. This may not be fully appreciated or understood by the user when faced with the financial accounts for the recent accounting period.

- Its **concept of profit is dangerous**. It pretends to cater for changing prices, but at the same time it fails to provide for the additional costs of replacing stocks sold or additional depreciation due to the escalating replacement cost of assets. The inflation encountered by the business entity will not be the same as that encountered by the whole economy. Thus the maintenance of the CPP of shareholders' capital via this concept of profit is not the maintenance of the entity's operating capital in physical terms, i.e. its capacity to produce the same volume of goods and services. The use of CPP profit as a basis for decision making without regard to RCA profit can have disastrous consequences.

Summary

The traditional HCA system reveals disturbing inadequacies in times of changing price levels, calling into question the value of financial reports using this system. Considerable resources and energy have been expended in searching for a substitute model able to counter the distortion and confusion caused by an unstable monetary unit.

Three basic models have been developed: RCA, NRVA and GPPA. Each has its merits and defects; each produces a different income value and a different capital value. However, it is important that inflation-adjusted values be computed in order to avoid a possible loss of entity resources and the collapse of the going concern.

Chapter 5 takes discussion of the problem a step further by dealing with contemporary accounting practice concerning changing price levels in particular and financial reporting in general.

Review questions

1   Specify the three current income and value models that have been proposed as alternatives to the traditional historical cost concept, and explain their basic characteristics.

2   'Historical cost accounting is the worst possible accounting convention, until one considers the alternatives.' Discuss this statement in relation to one of the following accounting conventions:
    ● current purchasing power accounting;
    ● replacement cost accounting.

3   It is generally agreed that financial statements prepared on the historical cost basis need to be adjusted so as to reflect the effect of price level changes. However, opinion is divided as to the choice of index to be used for the purpose. Typically, the choice is considered to be between a general price index (such as the Retail Price Index for the UK) and a specific price index.
    (a) Differentiate between the two indices.
    (b) State the case for and against the use of a specific price index for purposes outlined above.

4   Is there any one 'best' method of accountancy reporting? Express your opinion.

5   Explain the fundamental deficiencies associated with CPP and RCA solutions to the price level problem, and suggest how these might be overcome for the purposes of financial reporting.

6   Explain the limitations of historical cost accounting when prices are rising.

7   Explain why financial reports prepared under the historical cost convention are subject to the following major limitations:
    (a) stock on hand is undervalued;
    (b) the depreciation charge to the profit and loss account is understated;
    (c) gains and losses on net monetary assets are undisclosed;
    (d) balance sheet values are understated;
    (e) periodic comparisons are invalidated.

8   'Financial statements should reflect realistically the performance and position of an organisation, but most of the accountant's rules conflict directly with the concept of realism.' Discuss.

Exercises

An extract from the solution is provided in the appendix at the end of the text for exercises marked with an asterisk (*)

* **Question 1**

Aspirations Ltd commenced trading as wholesale suppliers of office equipment on 1 January 20X1, issuing ordinary shares of £1 each at par in exchange for cash. The shares were fully paid on issue, the number issued being 1,500,000.

The following financial statements, based on the historical cost concept, were compiled for 20X1.

Aspirations Ltd

Trading and Profit and Loss Account for the year ended 31 December 20X1

	£	£
Sales		868,425
Purchases	520,125	
Less: Stock 31 December 20X1	24,250	
Cost of sales		495,875
Gross profit		372,550
Expenses	95,750	
Depreciation	25,250	
		121,000
Net profit		251,550

Balance Sheet as at 31 December 20X1

	Cost	Depreciation	
Fixed assets	£	£	£
Freehold property	650,000	6,500	643,500
Office equipment	375,000	18,750	356,250
	1,025,000	25,250	999,750
Current assets			
Stocks		24,250	
Debtors		253,500	
Cash		1,090,300	
		1,368,050	
Less: Creditors payable within one year		116,250	
		1,251,800	
Less: Creditors payable in more than one year		500,000	751,800
Issued share capital			1,751,550
1,500,000 £1 ordinary shares			1,500,000
Profit and loss account			251,550
			1,751,550

The year 20X1 witnessed a surge of inflation and in consequence the directors became concerned about the validity of the revenue account and balance sheet as income and capital statements. Index numbers reflecting price changes were:

Specific index numbers reflecting replacement costs	1 January 20X1	31 December 20X1	Average for 20X1
Stock	115	150	130
Freehold property	110	165	127
Office equipment	125	155	145
General price index numbers	135	170	155

Regarding current exit costs

Stock is anticipated to sell at a profit of 75% of cost.

The value of assets at 31 December 20X1 was

	£
Freehold property	640,000
Office equipment	350,000

Initial purchases of stock were effected on 1 January 20X1 amounting to £34,375; the balance of purchases was evenly spread over the twelve-month period. The fixed assets were acquired on 1 January 20X1 and, together with the initial stock, were paid for in cash on that day.

Required:
Prepare the accounts adjusted for current values using each of the three proposed models of current value accounting: namely, the accounting methods known as replacement cost, general (or current) purchasing power and net realisable value.

* Question 2

The draft balance sheet of Rapport Ltd as at 31 March 20X8, together with the profit and loss account for the year ended on that date, are given below together with some supplementary information.

Balance Sheet of Rapport Ltd as at 31 March 20X8				
			20X8	20X7
			£	£
	Cost	Depreciation		
Fixed assets				
Land	30,000	—	30,000	30,000
Buildings	40,000	1,600	38,400	39,200
Plant and machinery	50,000	16,000	34,000	24,000
	120,000	17,600	102,400	93,200
Current assets				
Stock		28,000		18,000
Debtors		9,000		8,000
Cash		2,000		2,000
		39,000		28,000

Current liabilities

Bank overdraft	10,000	8,000
Creditors	8,000	8,000
	18,000	16,000
Net current assets	21,000	12,000
	123,400	105,200

Financed by

Ordinary share capital	60,000	60,000
Profit and loss reserves	63,400	45,200
	123,400	105,200

Profit and Loss of Rapport Ltd
for the year ended 31 March 20X8

	£	£
Sales		106,000
Opening stock	18,000	
Purchases	79,000	
	97,000	
Closing stock	28,000	69,000
Gross profit		37,000
Expenses	8,000	
Depreciation	10,800	18,800
Net profit		18,200

Supplementary information

1 The land and buildings were acquired on 1 April 20X6, the date Rapport Ltd was incorporated. Buildings are depreciated over fifty years on a straight-line basis.

2 The plant and machinery was acquired as follows:

on 1 April 20X6   £30,000
     1 April 20X7   £20,000

All machinery is depreciated at 20% per annum on a straight-line basis.

3 It can be assumed that all sales, purchases and expenses accrued evenly throughout the year. The stock at 31 March 20X7 was purchased on that date.

4 Given below are the movements on various price indices for the years in question:

	RPI	Land	Buildings	Machinery	Stock
At 1 April 20X6	80	90	170	140	100
At 1 April 20X7	88	110	200	150	120
At 1 April 20X8	94	150	240	170	150
Average for 20X7/8	92	130	220	160	140

Required:

(i) **Produce the balance sheet and profit and loss account of Rapport Ltd on a replacement cost basis.**

(ii) **Discuss the importance of the distinction between realised holding gains, unrealised holding gains, and operating gains.**

* **Question 3**

Using the information given in Question 2 above.

Required:

(i) **Produce the balance sheet and profit and loss account of Rapport Ltd on the basis of current purchasing power accounting.**

(ii) **Identify which economist's income measure is being used and discuss the usefulness of the measure of distributable profits.**

Bibliography

R.J. Chambers, *Accounting Evaluation and Economic Behaviour*, Prentice Hall, 1966.

R.J. Chambers, 'Second thoughts on continuous contemporary accounting', *Abacus*, September 1970.

R.A. Hill 'Economic income and value: the price level problem', *ACCA Students' Newsletter*, November 1987.

Tom Lee, *Income and Value Measurement, Theory and Practice* (3rd edition), Van Nostrand Reinhold (UK), 1985, Chapter 5.

'A quickfall: the elementary arithmetic of measuring real profit', *Management Accounting*, April 1980.

Accounting for Stewardship in a Period of Inflation, The Research Foundation of the ICAEW, 1968.

F. Sandilands (Chairman), *Inflation Accounting – Report of the Inflation Accounting Committee*, HMSO Cmnd 6225, 1975, pp. 139–155 and Chapter 9.

Accounting for Changes in the Purchasing Power of Money, SSAP 7, ASC, 1974.

D. Tweedie and G. Whittington, *Capital Maintenance Concepts*, ASC, 1985.

G. Whittington, 'Inflation Accounting: all the answers from Deloitte, Haskins and Sells', distinguished lecture series, Cardiff, 5 March 1981, reproduced in *Contemporary Issues in Accounting*, DHS, 1984.

Changing price levels

financial reporting practice

5.1 Introduction

This chapter introduces the steps that have been taken by the profession to deal with the problem of shifting price levels in financial reports. In this chapter we consider the following:

● Past practice: current purchasing power (CPP)

● Past practice: current cost accounting (CCA)

● The ASC Handbook

● Worked example

● Critique of CCA statements

● Future developments

● The ASB approach

The controversy has raged for over forty years without securing more than transitory consensus support for any particular technique. While the issue of reporting the impact of such changes on business income and capital was first mooted in 1949–50 in theses published by all the leading professional accountancy bodies (i.e. ICAEW, ICAS, ACCA, CIMA), little interest was roused. The ICAEW publication Recommendation on Accounting Principles No. 12 *Rising Price Levels in Relation to Accounts*, published in January 1949, was supplemented in May 1952 by Recommendation on Accounting Principles No. 15 *Accounting for Changes in the Purchasing Power of Money*, but still interest lay dormant. In the Netherlands, there was more interest in RCA, as there had been since the gathering inflation of the years after the First World War, and this was reflected in the accounts of several major undertakings, particularly Philips NV Ltd. However, the HCA concept reigned seemingly inviolable in the UK and discussion was mainly confined to academic circles, possibly because inflation was a modest 2.5% and was not considered to be of material consequence on a year-to-year basis.

5.2 Past practice: current purchasing power (CPP)

In the late 1960s and early 1970s the UK economy experienced considerable growth, and inflation reached record levels. As a result, accountancy reports were challenged, the adequacy of HCA was questioned and the true and fair view was subjected to doubt. Growing anxiety within the profession resulted in the issue of Statement of Standard

Accounting Practice No. 7 (SSAP 7) *Accounting for Changes in the Purchasing Power of Money* by the Accounting Standards Committee (ASC).[1]

SSAP 7 propagated the CPPA technique of adjusting for shifting price levels. As a document it fostered considerable support within and without the profession among compilers and users of financial statements. The statement mandated the following practice:

1 The continued use of the traditional HCA concept as the foundation of the annual report and account, in conjunction with 2 following.

2 The concomitant publication of supplementary CPPA-based financial statements disclosing adjustments to the HCA data as a result of inflation, three documents being involved:
   (i) a supplementary profit and loss account;
   (ii) a supplementary balance sheet; and
   (iii) a statement reconciling HCA profit with CPPA profit.

3 The use of the UK Index of Retail Prices as the unit of measurement in assessing price movements, this index being in effect the CPP unit of currency.

4 The identification of gains and losses of purchasing power in holding monetary items. Monetary items were defined as items whose value in terms of numbers of pounds sterling was fixed by custom or contract and whose value remained unchanged by moving prices. Such items consisted of financial carrying balances in the form of loan creditors, trade creditors, loan debtors, trade debtors and cash in hand and at the bank. In an environment of rising price levels, possessors of net monetary liabilities would gain purchasing power while holders of net monetary assets would lose purchasing power. This concept was introduced in Chapter 4 on page 70.

The government of the day immediately instituted a Commission of Enquiry into inflation accounting under the chairmanship of Frank Sandilands. Sandilands was a man of considerable experience within the insurance industry, which was likely to feel the brunt of changing values occasioned by an unstable unit of currency. At the inauguration of this committee, SSAP 7 became known as a **provisional** statement of standing accounting practice (i.e. PSAP No. 7).

SSAP 7 was overtaken by events. The original consensus support for the standard started to wither. This became an overwhelming rout when the Sandilands Committee rejected the CPPA concept as an inadequate model in the practical situation of financial reporting.

5.2.1 Sandilands Committee Report (September 1975)[2]

The committee was one of investigation and report. Its job was to formulate a thesis in support of concepts or ideas that could lead to an acceptable method of measuring and accountancy reporting during periods of shifting price levels. This it accomplished by rejecting the CPPA paradigm and substituting the current cost accounting (CCA) system in its place. It was hoped that when adopted by the accountancy profession it would result in meaningful financial data – real values – that were void of distortion and which kept pace with the changing value of money.

The report recommended the following:

1 Rejection of the NRVA concept, referred to in the report as 'continuously contemporary accounting', on the grounds that its supporters were invariably academics and there was no evidence of any business entity adopting this technique. The committee also believed that the merits of this current exit value accounting model did not include qualities required by users of financial reports.

2 Rejection of the RCA concept because 'some of the more rigid forms of RCA' were not suitable for general application by all companies. Furthermore, the committee said that the RCA's capital maintenance aspects would not meet the needs of users of accountancy data if strictly applied.

3 Rejection of the HCA and CPPA concepts operating in unison because this would necessitate the publication of two sets of accounts. It was felt that this situation would be misleading and cause confusion, especially when it was realised that CPP is an artificial unit of currency.

4 Rejection of the CPPA concept, even if used alone, because:
   (a) the deployment of a **general** index measure of inflation to arrive at inflation-adjusted figures would not reveal the **real** impact of shifting prices on **individual** companies; and
   (b) the concept of gains and losses on monetary items, a unique quality of the CPPA technique, was of no practical value to the going concern.

5 Acceptance of a system of current cost accounting (CCA)[3] based on the deprival value of an asset, i.e. a value based on the loss, direct and indirect, sustainable by an entity if it were to be deprived of the asset concerned. This method of valuation was later amended by SSAP 16 (see below). In effect, the CCA model became a compound of the concepts of RC, NRV and PV, with very heavy bias towards RC. The committee believed that, where RC could be estimated, it would represent the value of an asset to a business. In practice, specific index numbers peculiar to individual assets and classes of assets would be used in addition to pure RC.

The government, the former ASC and the accountancy profession in general accepted the report, despite some dismay among accountants that the CPPA model had been deposed. A new committee was instituted, as recommended, called the Inflation Accounting Steering Committee under the chairmanship of Douglas Morpeth. Meanwhile, the ASC advised companies that had adopted the CPPA system to continue the practice until the new committee was able to report, and those entities that had not implemented SSAP 7 to invent and apply their own version of CCA until mandated otherwise.

5.3   Past practice: current cost accounting (CCA)

The Morpeth Committee reported in November 1976 and rendered precise proposals for the adoption of a CCA system together with the abandonment of the HCA model of financial reporting. As Exposure Draft No. 18 (ED 18) it became the subject of acrimonious debate on the grounds of its complexity, particularly with regard to the valuation of capital assets and stocks, its non-recognition of monetary items, and its mandatory abandonment of the HCA system. It was withdrawn suddenly when it failed to obtain ratification by the members of ICAEW in open forum. Two years later, following publication of the *Interim Recommendations of the ASC* issued on the demise of ED 18 (the so-called Hyde Guidelines of November 1977), and after a replacement exposure draft (ED 24 of April 1979),[4] ASC published SSAP 16 *Current Cost Accounting*,[5] its definitive statement of application to financial reports.

5.3.1   SSAP 16 (March 1980)

This statement retained the CCA paradigm as the mainstay of financial reporting, but the model originally proposed by Sandilands, modified by Morpeth, simplified by Hyde, had been amended again in the light of the evolving, perceived needs of the practitioner and user of accounts. The amendments destroyed the simplicity of Hyde in the interests of greater accuracy and an improved true and fair perspective, but the statement was a welcome alternative to the cumbersome complexity of ED 18.

SSAP 16 stipulated the following:

1 Entities should provide CCA financial statements in the form of a revenue account and balance sheet. The revenue account was to be charged with depreciation computed by reference to current cost (CC) and also with a cost of sales adjustment (COSA) to reflect total CC of sales. The balance sheet was to show non-monetary assets in terms of CC. However, a choice of presentation of the data was offered, a choice that was specified and which, incidentally, caused distortion when comparing data between companies.

2 Refinements were introduced in the form of monetary working capital (MWC) and gearing adjustments. In reality, the gearing adjustment was a version of the purchasing power gain on holding net monetary liabilities and cash in times of an unstable currency, the very concept once advocated as part of the CPP model. Losses were to be ignored in the interests of simplicity.

The operation of the gearing calculation meant that the capital maintenance concept, i.e. the maintenance of the entity's operating capacity in terms of net assets, was being applied only to the shareholders' share of such assets. That proportion of the company's operating capability attributed to borrowings was treated as realised during the financial period concerned, and thus additional charges to revenue account over and above HC (i.e. the aggregate of extra depreciation, COSA and monetary working capital adjustment) could be reduced.

3 Current cost was to be based on value to the business, which was seen as a form of deprival value. This deprival value was defined by SSAP 16 as:
   (a) net current replacement cost; or, if a permanent diminution to below net current replacement cost has been recognised,
   (b) recoverable amount, defined as the greater of net realisable value of an asset and, where applicable, the amount recoverable from its further use.

This definition of CC in SSAP 16 is interesting. In effect it may, subject to criteria, be RC, or the greater of NRV and PV. Thus CCA as a system was a combination of RCA, NRVA and PVA, the latter being the economist's measure referred to in the present value theorem of Fisher and Hicks.

4 All entities listed on the Stock Exchange and others, subject to specified size criteria, were obliged to adopt the CCA system, although there were exceptions in respect of insurance companies and non-profit organisations.

SSAP 16's gearing adjustment came under increasing attack during the standard's three-year trial period. The arithmetical formula utilised by the document had been proposed with an eye to simplicity of calculation. Relentless debate and growing criticism led to a compromise in ED 35, which offered a choice of formulae and promised amendments to SSAP 16's presentation requirements. But it was too late and ED 35 was withdrawn. This was quickly followed by the standard's loss of mandatory status. It had existed two years longer than its proposed three-year trial period.

The general hostility towards SSAP 16 emanated from a compound of factors. There was a reduced interest in inflation as a topic due to more effective government control of a shifting price plateau. There were objections to the measurement models CCA and CPPA, individually and in combination, due to anxiety about their inherent subjectivity and the cost of operating such systems. There was also an increasing, flagrant non-compliance with the requirements of SSAP 16 by business in general. The influence of the HCA system was all-pervading within the accountancy profession: the model had its defects, but the usurping models appear to have possessed a greater number of faults.

5.4 The ASC Handbook[6]

A vacuum was created by the withdrawal of SSAP 16. Almost forty years of contentious debate had failed to obtain lasting consensus support for a model system of accounting to deal with shifting prices. The immediate reaction of the ASC was not to withdraw SSAP 16 as a document, but to cancel its ineffective mandatory application. The intent was to leave the standard in issue as an authoritative reference document of a CCA reporting system in the absence of a prescriptive model. But to leave a **standard** extant as a non-standard seemed to be administrative folly, so eventually SSAP 16 was withdrawn completely. It was replaced by *Accounting for the Effects of Changing Prices: A Handbook*, published by the ASC in 1986. This is now the authoritative reference document.

The *Handbook* specifies the constraints of the HCA method and then proceeds to formulate remedial concepts. In so doing it departs from the CCA v. CPP theme that has pervaded discussion in the past. An alternative to HCA does not necessarily lie in a straight choice between these two models, argues the *Handbook*. Instead of opting for a particular reporting technique, it includes consideration of the following three variables when selecting an accounting system:

● The basis to be adopted for valuing assets

● The capital maintenance concepts to be used

● The unit of measurement to be used

The basis to be adopted for valuing assets

The *Handbook* implies that the two principal asset valuation bases are historical cost and current cost. Under each of these bases the assets are valued at 'cost' less depreciation. CPP is regarded not as a basis of valuing assets, but as a means of adjusting non-monetary assets from £ sterling to units of constant purchasing power. CPP is a modification of the historic cost accounts, but it could equally be applied to current costs.

The *Handbook* regards current cost asset valuation basis as more relevant than the historical cost basis.

The capital maintenance concepts to be used

Two different approaches may be taken in measuring the capital of a company. The operating capital maintenance concept views capital in physical terms, while the financial capital maintenance concept views it in financial terms.

The **operating capital maintenance concept** is in principle the CCA approach. It is concerned with capital as productive capacity and sees capital maintenance as the retention of sufficient funds to maintain the business entity's physical operating capacity, i.e. its ability to produce a quantified volume of goods and services. Profit is the residual after making provision to maintain the physical operating capital.

The **financial capital maintenance concept** sees capital as a fund belonging to shareholders/proprietors. Profit is the difference between the capital funds at the beginning of a financial period and those at the end. If there have been any capital injections or withdrawals, the closing capital fund would be adjusted before calculating the profit.

The financial capital might be either money capital or real capital. Money capital is denoted in nominal units of purchasing power represented by £ sterling, i.e. the traditional historical cost system. Real capital is money capital that has been adjusted to maintain its general purchasing power, i.e. the CPP system.

The *Handbook* took the view that both the operating capital and financial capital maintenance concepts are useful: the former being appropriate for manufacturing companies and the latter for value-based companies whose operations are not dependent on the replacement of fixed assets.

The unit of measurement to be used

The principal alternatives are the £ sterling and units of constant purchasing power. Because there are three variables, there are eight possible combinations. Each combination produces an accounting system. These are listed in Figure 5.1.

The first two systems, historical cost (HCA) and historical cost adjusted to current purchasing power units (CPP) have been discussed in Chapter 4.

The second two systems see capital as productive capacity, but they use historical cost as the basis for reporting. There is an asymmetry in that historical cost records the original cost of obtaining resources, whereas the operating capital concept takes a current view of the company's position. This difference in the time-scale of the asset valuation basis and capital maintenance criteria means that accounting systems 3 and 4 are internally inconsistent and not valid systems.

The two current cost systems that use current purchasing power as the unit of measurement are regarded as too complex in practice. They might well produce data that are relevant and comparable, but this requires two restatement processes: first, restating from historical cost to current cost using specific indices; and then restating from current cost to constant purchasing power units. In addition to the additional cost, it was felt that the resulting figures might be more difficult to understand because of their complexity.

This leaves system 5, which is the real terms current cost accounting system (RTA) applying the financial capital maintenance concept, and system 7, which is the current cost accounting system (CCA) applying the operating capital maintenance system.

The *Handbook* expresses the opinion that the usefulness of financial statements would be considerably enhanced by the inclusion of financial data using current cost as the asset valuation method; operating or financial capital maintenance concept as appropriate;

Figure 5.1 Eight possible accounting systems.

Asset valuation basis	Capital maintenance concept	Unit of measurement	Accounting system
1 Historical cost	Financial	£ sterling	HCA
2 Historical cost	Financial	Constant purchasing power	CPP
3 Historical cost	Operating	£ sterling	
4 Historical cost	Operating	Constant purchasing power	
5 Current cost	Financial	£ sterling	RTA
6 Current cost	Financial	Constant purchasing power	
7 Current cost	Operating	£ sterling	CCA
8 Current cost	Operating	Constant purchasing power	

and £ sterling as the unit of measurement, i.e. it supports either the RTA or CCA systems. We will now describe the real terms current cost accounting system (RTA) in greater detail.

5.4.1 'Real terms' version of CCA

This is a method unique to the *Handbook* in its role as a propagating agent in that the model has not been an important part of the general debate on the shifting price syndrome. The CCA mode as enshrined in the late SSAP 16, the CCA system of general discussion, has always utilised the operating capital maintenance philosophy as its method of measuring profit. The 'real terms' model of the CCA paradigm adopts the financial measurement idea. In so doing it combines the characteristics of CCA and CPP. The now defunct ASC had introduced the real terms topic in the form of a financial statement showing shareholders' funds on a CPP footing compared with those same funds valued on a CCA basis. So the system is not new. However, what is new is that the *Handbook* has introduced the real terms data as an integral part of a formal system of financial reporting.

The method of measuring profit in real terms is as follows:

1 Calculate the shareholders' funds applicable to the commencement of the financial period using CCA asset values.

2 Restate the amount in terms of pounds sterling at the reporting date (i.e. by adjusting the amount at 1 by the relevant change in a **general price index** such as the RPI).

3 Compare 2 with the shareholders' funds applicable to the end of the year computed as CCA values.

The comparison at 3 will reveal whether or not the entity's real financial capital has been maintained. If the end of year figure is larger than the restated value applicable to the start of the year, then a 'real terms' profit has been generated. If the year-end figure is smaller, then the entity has suffered a real terms loss.

5.4.2 Presentation of inflation-adjusted information

The *Handbook* expressed the ASC's belief that inflation-adjusted data could be incorporated into a company's main accounts, but its appeal has apparently fallen on deaf accountants' ears. Such an approach is rarely witnessed in practice among UK enterprises, which are used to HCA accounting. Under these circumstances many entities prefer to provide information revealing the impact of price level changes in the form of accompanying notes to the accounts. The *Handbook* suggested that such notes should provide information in terms of earnings, assets and trends.

Earnings

An adjusted earnings statement is listed below showing:

● The difference between earnings attributable to ordinary shareholders on the basis used in the profit and loss account and those earnings stated after maintaining the operating or real financial capital of the enterprise.

● The adjustments for additional depreciation and additional cost of sales.

● Any further adjustments consistent with the capital maintenance concept adopted.

As mentioned above, the *Handbook* suggests that the type of capital maintenance concept adopted, i.e. operating or real financial, will be influenced by the nature of the entity's business and its perception of the users of its accounts.

Assets

The ASC considered it helpful for companies to disclose certain key pieces of data from its current cost balance sheet, such as the following:

● The gross and net current cost of fixed assets.

● The accumulated current cost depreciation.

● The current cost of stocks.

Alternatively, an abridged CCA balance sheet may be disclosed.

Trends

As supplementary information, it was suggested that it would be very informative if time series data were to be supplied on a CPPA basis: that is, where a company publishes five- or ten-year historical summaries, certain figures contained in those summaries were to be restated in CPPA terms. 'Certain figures' were described as those either adjusted for the effects of specific changing prices (e.g. CCA-adjusted earnings) or which require no adjustment (e.g. turnover and dividends).

5.4.3 Examples of reporting practice

In the 2nd edition our example was from the Scottish Power plc 1990 accounts. However, that company no longer produces Current Cost information and its 1997 accounts have been prepared under the historical cost convention. In Figure 5.2 we use extracts from the 1996 accounts of British Gas plc, a company that prepares its accounts in accordance with current cost principles. It is interesting to note that the historical cost profit of £156m becomes a £237m loss when changing price effects are taken into account. However, the Accounting Policy of Centrica has changed and the 1998 accounts are prepared under the historical cost convention i.e. with no current cost accounts and no revaluations.

Figure 5.2 British Gas plc.

Reconciliation of historical and current cost profits

	1996 £m
Current cost profit/(loss) on ordinary activities before taxation	(237)
Current cost adjustments:	
Cost of sales adjustment	(1)
Monetary working capital adjustment	5
Supplementary depreciation	471
Profit on sale of tangible fixed assets adjustment	40
Gearing adjustment	(122)
	393
Historical cost profit on ordinary activities before taxation	156

Accounting policies

The accounts have been prepared in accordance with applicable accounting standards and under current cost principles. Under these principles provision is made in the accounts (current cost adjustments) for the effects of specific price changes on the resources necessary to maintain the operating capability of the business.

Figure 5.2 (*cont.*)

The current cost adjustments comprise:

i) cost of sales adjustment (the difference between the current cost as at the date of sale and the historical cost of stocks sold, calculated by applying appropriate indices to average stocks);

ii) monetary working capital adjustment (the movement in monetary working capital attributed to changes in input prices during the year, calculated by applying appropriate indices to average monetary working capital);

iii) supplementary depreciation (the additional sum necessary to bring the aggregate of replacement expenditure and historical cost depreciation up to a full current cost depreciation charge based upon current cost asset values);

iv) profit on sale of tangible fixed assets adjustment (the difference between the current cost and historical cost profit or loss on sale);

v) gearing adjustment (a reduction in the effect of the current cost adjustments (i) to (iv) above in the profit and loss account to allow for the benefit to shareholders of financing the business partly by borrowings (after deducting liquid funds)).

5.5 Worked example

The HCA profit and loss account for Economica plc for the year ended 31 December 20X5, together with its HCA balance sheet as at 31 December 20X5, are set out in

Figure 5.3 Economica plc HCA Profit and Loss Account.

*Profit and Loss Account for the year ended
31 December 20X5, on the basis of HCA*

		20X5		20X4
		£000		£000
Turnover		42,500		38,250
Less: Cost of sales		(12,070)		(23,025)
Gross profit		30,430		15,225
Less: Distribution costs	2,460		2,210	
Less: Administrative expenses	1,620		1,540	
		(4,080)		(3,750)
Profit before interest and tax		26,350		11,475
Interest		(880)		(880)
Profit before tax		25,470		10,595
Tax		(8,470)		(4,250)
Profit after tax		17,000		6,345
Dividend		(5,000)		(4,000)
Retentions		12,000		2,345
Balance b/f		14,000		11,655
Balance c/f		26,000		14,000
EPS		34p		13p

Figure 5.4 Economica plc HCA Balance Sheet.

Balance Sheet as at 31 December 20X5, on the basis of HCA

	£000	20X5 £000	£000	20X4 £000
Fixed assets:				
Cost	85,000		85,000	
Depreciation	34,000		25,500	
		51,000		59,500
Current assets:				
Stock	25,500		17,000	
Debtors	34,000		23,375	
Cash and bank	17,000		1,875	
	76,500		42,250	
Current liabilities:				
Trade creditors	25,500		17,000	
Corporation tax	8,500		4,250	
Dividend proposed	5,000		4,000	
	39,000		25,250	
Net current assets	37,500		17,000	
Less: 8% debentures	11,000		11,000	
		26,500		6,000
		77,500		65,500
Share capital and reserves:				
Authorised and issued £1 ordinary shares		50,000		50,000
Share premium		1,500		1,500
Profit and loss account		26,000		14,000
		77,500		65,500

Figures 5.3 and 5.4. Corresponding data for the preceding year are also disclosed. Index data are set out in Figure 5.5.

From these we will prepare accounts on a CCA basis: (1) following the operating physical capital maintenance concept; and (2) following real terms financial capital maintenance.

Figure 5.5 Index data relating to Economica plc.

1 Index numbers as prepared by the Central Statistical Office for fixed assets:

1 January 20X2	100
1 January 20X5	165
1 January 20X6	185
Average for 20X4	147
Average for 20X5	167

All assets were acquired on 1 January 20X2. There were no further acquisitions or disposals during the four years ended 31 December 20X5.

Figure 5.5 (cont.)

2 Indices as prepared by the Central Statistical Office for stocks and monetary working capital adjustments were:

I October 20X4	115
31 December 20X4	125
15 November 20X4	120
I October 20X5	140
31 December 20X5	150
15 November 20X5	145
Average for 20X5	137.5

3 Three months' stock is carried.

4 Depreciation: historical cost based on 10% pa straight-line with residual value of nil:

	£HCA
20X4	8,500,000
20X5	8,500,000

5 General price index at I January 20X5 = 317.2
General price index at 31 December 20X5 = 333.2

First we shall convert the HCA balance sheet in Figure 5.4, as at 31 December 20X4, to the CCA basis, using the index data in Figure 5.5.

The **non-monetary items** comprise the fixed assets and stock. These are converted and the converted amounts are taken to the CC Balance Sheet and the increases taken to the Current Cost Reserve, as follows.

(W1) Fixed assets

	HCA £000	Index	CCA £000	Increase £000
Cost	85,000	$\times \dfrac{165}{100} =$	140,250	55,250
Depreciation	25,500	$\times \dfrac{165}{100} =$	42,075	16,575
	59,500		98,175	38,675

The CCA valuation at 31 December 20X4 shows a net increase in terms of numbers of pounds sterling of £38,675,000. The £59,500,000 in the HCA balance sheet will be replaced in the CCA balance sheet by £98,175,000.

(W2) Stocks

	HCA £000	Index	CCA £000	Increase £000
	17,000	$\times \dfrac{125}{120} =$	17,708	= 708

Note that Figure 5.5 specifies that three months' stocks are held. Thus on average they will have been purchased on 15 November 20X4, on the assumption that they have been acquired and consumed evenly throughout the calendar period. Hence the index at the time of purchase would have been 120. The £17,000,000 in the HCA Balance Sheet will be replaced in the CCA Balance Sheet by £17,708,000.

(W3) Current cost reserve

The total increase in CCA carrying values for non-monetary items is £39,383,000, which will be credited to CC reserves in the CC Balance Sheet in Figure 5.6. It comprises £38,675,000 on the fixed assets and £708,000 on the stock.

Note that monetary items do not change by virtue of inflation. Purchasing power will be lost or gained, but the carrying values in the CCA balance sheet will be identical to those in its HCA counterpart. We can now compile the CCA balance sheet as at 31 December 20X4 in Figure 5.6.

Having prepared the opening balance sheet, we can proceed with the CCA adjustments for 20X5.

Figure 5.6   Economica plc CCA Balance Sheet.

Economica plc CCA Balance Sheet as at 31 December 20X4

		£000	£000
Fixed assets:			
Cost			140,250
Depreciation			(42,075)
	(W1)		**98,175**
Current assets:			
Stock	(W2)	**17,708**	
Debtors		23,375	
Cash		1,875	
		42,958	
Current liabilities:			
Trade creditors		17,000	
Corporation tax		4,250	
Dividend proposed		4,000	
		25,250	
Net current assets		17,708	
Less: 8% debentures		(11,000)	
			6,708
			104,883
Share capital: authorised and issued £1 shares			50,000
Share premium			1,500
CC reserves	(W3)		**39,383**
Retained profit			14,000
			104,883

5.5.1 Cost of sales adjustment

We will compute the cost of sales adjustment by using the average method. The average purchase price index for 20X5 is 137.5. If price increases have moved at an even pace throughout the period, this implies that consumption occurred, on average, at 30 June, the mid-point of the financial year.

(W4) Cost of sales adjustment (COSA) using the average method

	HCA £000	Adjustment		CCA £000	Difference £000
Opening stock	17,000	$\times$	$\dfrac{137.5}{120}$ =	19,479	= 2,479
Purchases	—	—		—	—
	17,000			19,479	
Closing stock	(25,500)	$\times$	$\dfrac{137.5}{145}$ =	24,181	= 1,319
	(8,500)			(4,702)	3,798

The method is very practical in terms of simplicity and convenience. Other possible methods are:

● standard cost;
● recent invoice prices;
● LIFO/base stock; and
● the pricing of individual items.

In our example the impact of price changes on the cost of sales would be an increase of £3,798,000, causing a profit decrease of like amount and a Current Cost Reserve increase of like amount.

5.5.2 Depreciation

As assets are consumed throughout the year, the CCA depreciation charge should be based on average current costs. However, the *Handbook* claims that it is acceptable to use the year-end index if desired. The year-round figure would grant conformity with the cumulative depreciation in the balance sheet. A peculiarity of the more academically cor-rect averaging system is that it gives rise to backlog depreciation which, on first acquain-tance, may appear to constitute a contradiction in terms. (See W7.)

(W5) Depreciation adjustment: average method

	HCA £000	Adjustment		CCA £000	Difference £000
Depreciation	8,500	$\times$	$\dfrac{167}{100}$ =	14,195	= 5,695

5.5.3 Monetary working capital accounting (MWCA)

The objective is to transfer from the profit and loss account to CC Reserve the amount by which the need for monetary working capital (MWC) has increased due to rising price levels. The change in MWC from one balance sheet to the next will be the consequence of a combination of changes in volume and escalating price movements. Volume change may be segregated from the price change by using an average index.

(W6) Monetary working capital adjustment (MWCA)

	20X5 £000	20X4 £000		Change £000
Trade debtors	34,000	23,375		
Trade creditors	25,500	17,000		
MWC =	8,500	6,375	Overall change =	2,125

The MWC is now adjusted by the average index for the year.

This adjustment will reveal the change in volume

$$\left(8,500 \times \frac{137.5}{150}\right) - \left(6,375 \times \frac{137.5}{125}\right)$$

=	7792	– 7012	= Volume change	780
	So price change =			1,345

5.5.4 Non-monetary assets – holding gains are calculated for fixed assets and stock

(W7) Non-monetary assets

(i)	Holding gain on fixed assets		£000
	Revaluation at year-end		
	Fixed assets at 1 January 20X5 (as W1) at CCA revaluation		140,250
	CCA value at 31 December 20X5 = $140,250 \times \frac{185}{165}$ =		157,250
	Revaluation holding gain for 20X5 to CC Reserve in W8		**17,000**

This holding gain of £17,000,000 is transferred to CC reserves.

(ii)	Backlog depreciation on fixed assets	
	CCA aggregate depreciation at 31 December 20X5 for CC Balance Sheet	£000
	= **£HCA 34,000,000 × $\frac{185}{100}$ in CC Balance Sheet**	**62,900**
	Less: CCA aggregate depreciation at 1 January 20X5 (as per W1 and balance sheet at 1 January 20X5)	42,075
	Being CCA depreciation as revealed between opening and closing balance sheets	20,825
	But CCA depreciation charged in revenue accounts (i.e. £8,500,000 in £HCA plus additional depreciation of £5,695,000 per W5) =	14,195
	So total backlog depreciation to CC Reserve in W8	**6,630**

The CCA value of fixed assets at 31 December 20X5: £000

	£000
Gross CCA value (above)	157,250
Depreciation (above)	62,900
Net CCA carrying value in the CC Balance Sheet in W8	**94,350**

Note: This backlog depreciation may be validated as under:

	£000
Revaluation surplus or holding gain on fixed assets during financial year =	17,000
Prior years' depreciation on this holding gain (for years 20X2, 20X3 and 20X4), i.e. 3 years × (10% of £17,000,000) =	5,100
Difference between depreciation for 20X5 on year-end CCA values and average CCA values occuring during 20X5 = (10% of £157,250,000) – £14,195,000 =	1,530
Total backlog (displaying agreement with the earlier figure) =	6,630

This £6,630,000 is backlog depreciation for 20X5. Total backlog depreciation is not expensed (i.e. charged to revenue account) as an adjustment of HCA profit, but is charged against CCA reserves. The net effect is that the CC Reserve will increase by £10,370,000 i.e. £17,000,000 – £6,630,000.

(iii)   Stock valuation at year-end

CCA valuation at 31 December 20X5

£HCA000	£CCA000	£CCA000
= 25,500 × 150/145 = 26,379 = increase of		879

CCA valuation at 1 January 20X5 (per W2)

= 17,000 × 125/120 = 17,708 = increase of		708
Stockholding gain occuring during 20X5 to W8		**171**

5.5.5 CCA balance sheet before gearing adjustment

We may now compile the CCA balance sheet as at the end of the financial year (20X5), but at this stage the gearing adjustment has not been computed. The balance sheet is shown as W8.

(W8) Economica plc: CCA balance sheet as at 31 December 20X5

		20X5			*20X4*
Fixed assets	£000	£000		£000	£000
Cost	157,250 (W7)			140,250 (W1)	
Depreciation	62,900 (W7)			42,075 (W1)	
		94,350			98,175
Current assets					
Stock	26,379 (W7)			17,708 (W2)	
Debtors	34,000			23,375	
Cash	17,000			1,875	
	77,379			42,958	

Current liabilities

Trade creditors	25,500		17,000	
Corporation tax	8,500		4,250	
Dividend proposed	5,000		4,000	
	39,000		25,250	
Net current assets	38,379		17,708	
Less: 8% debentures	11,000		11,000	
		27,379		6,708
		121,729		104,883

Financed by

Share capital: authorised			
and issued £1 shares		50,000	50,000
Share premium		1,500	1,500
*CC reserves		55,067	39,383
** Retained profit		15,162	14,000
Shareholders' funds		121,729	104,883

*CC Reserves	£000	£000	
Opening balance		39,383	(Figure 5.6)
Holding gains			
Fixed assets	17,000	(W7) (i)	
Stock	171	(W7) (iii)	
		17,171	
COSA	3,798	(W4)	
MWCA	1,345	(W6)	
Less: backlog depreciation	(6,630)	(W7) (ii)	(1,487)
		55,067	

**Retained profit			
Opening balance		14,000	(Figure 5.3)
HCA profit for 20X5	12,000		
COSA	(3,798)	(W4)	
Extra depreciation	(5,695)	(W5)	
MWCA	(1,345)	(W6)	
		1,162	
CCA profit for 20X5		15,162	

The gearing adjustment must now be calculated, which will change the carrying figures of CC reserves and retained profit, but not the shareholders' funds as the adjustment is compensating. The gearing adjustment cannot be computed before the determination of the shareholders' interest because that figure is necessary in order to complete the gearing calculation.

Gearing adjustment

The CC operating profit of the business is quantified after making such retentions from the historical profit as are required in order to maintain the physical operating capacity of the entity. However, from a shareholder standpoint, there is no need to maintain in real terms the portion of the entity financed by loans that are fixed in monetary values. Thus, in calculating profit attributable to shareholders, that part of the CC adjustments relating to the proportion of the business financed by loans can be deducted:

$$\textbf{(W9) Gearing adjustment} = \frac{\text{Average net borrowings for year}}{\begin{array}{c}\text{Average net borrowings for year} + \text{Average}\\ \text{Shareholders' funds for year}\end{array}}$$
$$\times \text{Aggregate adjustments}$$

This formula is usually expressed as

$$\frac{L}{(L + S)} \times A$$

where L = loans (i.e. net borrowings); S = shareholders' interest or funds; A = adjustments (i.e. extra depreciation + COSA + MWCA). Note that $L/(L + S)$ is often expressed as a percentage of A (see example below re. 6.31%).

Net borrowings

This is the sum of all liabilities less current assets, excluding items included in MWC or utilised in computing COSA. In this instance it is as follows:

	Closing balance £000	Opening balance £000
Debentures	11,000	11,000
Corporation tax	8,500	4,250
Cash	(17,000)	(1,875)
Total net borrowings, the average of which equals L	2,500	13,375

$$\text{Average net borrowings} = \frac{2{,}500{,}000 + 13{,}375{,}000}{2} = £7{,}937{,}500$$

Note: in some circumstances (e.g. new issue of debentures occurring during the year) a weighted average will be used.

Net borrowings plus shareholders' funds

	Closing balance £000	Opening balance £000
Shareholders' funds in CC pounds (inclusive of proposed dividends)	126,729	108,883
Add: net borrowings	2,500	13,375
	129,229	122,258

Or, as shown in the *Handbook*:

	£000	£000
Fixed assets	94,350	98,175
Stock	26,379	17,708
MWC	8,500	6,375
	129,229	122,258

$$\text{Avergage } L + S = \frac{129,229,000 + 122,258,000}{2}$$

$$= 125,743,500$$

$$\text{So gearing} = \frac{L}{L+S} \times A$$

$$= \frac{£7,937,500}{125,743,500} \times \overset{\text{COSA}}{(3,798,000} + \overset{\text{MWCA}}{1,345,000} + \overset{\text{Extra depreciation}}{5,695,000)}$$

$$= 6.31\% \text{ of } £10,838,000 = £683,877, \text{ say } £684,000$$

Thus the CC adjustment of £10,838,000 charged against historical profit may be reduced by £684,000 due to a gain being derived from net borrowings during a period of inflation as shown in Figure 5.7.

There are a number of alternative methods of calculating the gearing adjustment. Only two are advocated in the *Handbook*, of which the method illustrated above is one. The alternative would adjust for that part of the total adjustments made to allow for the impact of price changes on the net operating assets, including the net surplus in the revaluation of assets arising during the period, that may be regarded as associated with items that are financed by net borrowings. **Total unrealised holding gains also need to be calculated if the financial capital maintenance concept is used.** The gains represent the amount by which the uplift of the opening HC balance sheet carrying figures to CC carrying figures differs from the equivalent uplift in the closing balance sheet carrying figures. For example:

(W10) Total unrealised holding gains to be used in Figure 5.9 (p. 97).

[Closing balance sheet at CC – Closing balance sheet at HC] – [Opening balance sheet at CC – Opening balance sheet at HC]
= (£121,729,000 – £77,500,000) – (£104,883,000 – £65,500,000) = £4,846,000
     (W8)   (Figure 5.4)   (Figure 5.6)   (Figure 5.4)

So, CC adjustments as above	**£10,838,000**
Total unrealised holding gains	**4,846,000**
	5,992,000 × 6.31% = **£378,095**
	say **£378,000**

The profit and loss account, balance sheet and reserve movements are set out in Figures 5.7, 5.8 and 5.9.

Figure 5.7   Economica plc CCA Profit and Loss Account.

Economica plc CCA Profit and Loss Account for year ended 31 December, 20X5
(i.e. under the operating capital maintenance concept)

		£000
Turnover		42,500
Cost of sales		(12,070)
Gross profit		30,430
Distribution costs		(2,460)
Administrative expenses		(1,620)
Historic cost operating profit		26,350
Current cost operating adjustments		**(10,838)**
Current cost operating profit		15,512
Interest payable	(880)	
Gearing adjustment	**684**	(196)
Current profit on ordinary activities before taxation		15,316
Tax on profit on ordinary activities		(8,470)
Current cost profit for the financial year		6,846
Proposed dividends		(5,000)
Current cost profit retained		1,846
EPS		13.7p

Analysis of Current Cost Operating Adjustments

		£000	£000
Cost of sales	W4		3,798
Monetary working capital	W6		1,345
Working capital			5,143
Depreciation	W5	5,695	
Fixed asset disposals		nil	
Fixed assets			5,695
			10,838

Figure 5.8   Economica plc CCA Balance Sheet.

Economica plc CCA Balance Sheet as at 31 December 20X5

20X4				20X5
£000	£000	*Fixed assets*	£000	£000
140,250		Tangible assets	157,250	
42,075		Depreciation	62,900	
	98,175			94,350
		Current assets		
17,708		Stock	26,379	
23,375		Debtors	34,000	
1,875		Cash	17,000	
42,958			77,379	
		Creditors: amounts falling due within one year:		
17,000		Trade creditors	25,500	
		Other creditors		
4,250		— corporation tax	8,500	
4,000		— proposed dividend	5,000	
25,250			39,000	
	17,708	*Net current assets*		38,379
		Creditors: amounts falling due after more than one year		
	(11,000)			(11,000)
	6,708			27,379
	104,883			121,729
	£000	*Capital and reserves*		£000
	50,000	Called-up share capital		50,000
	1,500	Share premium account		1,500
	53,383	Total of other reserves		70,229
	104,883			121,729

Analysis of 'Total of Other Reserves'

£000		£000
14,000	Profit and loss account	15,846
39,383	Current cost reserve	54,383
53,383		70,229

> ### Figure 5.8 (cont.)
>
> Movements on reserves
>
> (a) Profit and loss account: £000
>
>   Balance at 1 January 20X5   14,000 (from Figure 5.3)
>
>   Current cost retained profit   1,846 (from Figure 5.7)
>
>   Balance at 31 December 20X5   15,846
>
> (b) Current cost reserve:
>
> | | Total | Fixed assets | Stock | MWCA | Gearing |
> |---|---|---|---|---|---|
> | | £000 | £000 | £000 | £000 | £000 |
> | Balance as at 1 January 20X5 | 39,383 | 38,675 | 708 | | |
> | Movements during the year: | | | | | |
> | Unrealised holding gains in the year | 10,541 | 10,370 | 171 | | |
> | Gearing adjustment | (684) | | | | (684) |
> | MWCA | 1,345 | | | 1,345 | |
> | COSA | 3,798 | | 3,798 | | |
> | Balance as at 31 December 20X5 | 54,383 | 49,045 | 4,677 | 1,345 | (684) |

The GPP (or CPP) real terms financial capital

The real terms financial capital maintenance concept may be incorporated within the CCA system as in Figure 5.9 by calculating an inflation adjustment.

(W11) The general price index numbers to be used to calculate the inflation adjustment in Figure 5.9 are

General price index at 1 January 20X5   = 317.2

General price index at 31 December 20X5 = 333.2

Opening shareholders' funds at CC × Percentage change in GPI during the year =

$$104{,}883{,}000 \ \times \ \frac{333.2 - 317.2}{317.2} \ = \ £5{,}290{,}435$$

$$\text{say} \quad £5{,}290{,}000$$

5.6 Critique of CCA statements

Considerable effort and expense are involved in compiling and publishing CCA statements. Does their usefulness justify the cost? CCA statements have the following uses:

1 The operating capital maintenance statement reveals CCA profit. Such profit is devoid of fluctuations caused by inflationary price increases in raw materials and other stocks, and thus is more realistic than the alternative HCA profit.

Figure 5.9 Economica plc Real Terms Profit and Loss Account.

Economica plc CCA Profit and Loss Account Under the Real Terms System
for the year ended 31 December 20X5

	£000	£000
Historical cost profit after tax for the financial year		17,000
Add: Total unrealised holding gains arising during the year (see		
page 93 W10)	4,846	
Less: Realised holding gains previously recognised as unrealised	none	
	4,846	
Less: Inflation adjustment to CCA shareholders: funds (W11)	(5,290)	
Real holding gains		(444)
Total real gains		16,556
Deduct: proposed dividends		5,000
Amount retained		11,556

Real Terms System: Analysis of Reserves

20X4		20X5
£000		£000
53,383	Profit and loss account	64,939
—	Financial capital maintenance reserve	5,290
53,383		70,229

Movements on reserves

	Profit and loss account	*Financial capital maintenance reserve*
	£000	£000
Balances at 1 January 20X5	53,383	—
Amount retained	11,556	—
Inflation adjustment for year		5,290
Balances as at 31 December 20X5	64,939	5,290

2 Significant increases in a company's buying and selling prices will give the HCA profit a holding gains content. That is, the reported HCA profit will include gains consequent upon holding stocks during a period when the cost of buying such stocks increases. Conversely, if specific stock prices fall, HCA profit will be reduced as it takes account of losses sustained by holding stock while its price drops. Holding gains and losses are quite different from operating gains and losses. HCA profit does not distinguish between the two, whereas CCA profit does.

3 HCA profit might be adjusted to reflect the moving price level syndrome:
  (a) by use of the operating capital maintenance approach, which regards only the CCA **operating** profit as the authentic result for the period and which treats any holding gain or loss as a movement on reserves;

(b) by adoption of the real terms **financial** capital maintenance approach, which applies a general inflation measure via the RPI, combined with CCA information regarding holding gains.

Thus the statement can reveal information to satisfy the demands of the management of the entity itself – as distinct from the shareholder/proprietor, whose awareness of inflation may centre on the RPI. In this way the concern of operating management can be accommodated with the different interest of the shareholder. The HCA profit would fail on both these counts.

4 CC profit is important because:

(a) it quantifies cost of sales and depreciation after allowing for changing price levels; hence trading results, free of inflationary elements, grant a clear picture of entity activities and management performance;

(b) resources are maintained, having eliminated the possibility of paying dividend out of real capital;

(c) yardsticks for management performance are more comparable as a time series within the one entity and between entities, the distortion caused by moving prices having been alleviated.

5.7 Future developments

A mixed picture emerges when we try to foresee the future of changing price levels and financial reporting. First, accountancy has displayed a marked reluctance to abandon the HC concept in favour of a 'valuation accounting' approach such as CC. Secondly, the shifting price syndrome has retreated in recent years following the fall in the rate of inflation, which has fostered apathy among accountants. Thirdly, a mass of pressing problems has become manifest in the day to day world of financial reporting, e.g. the valuation of brands, the ongoing lack of consistency between companies in the treatment of goodwill, the conflict of accounting substance and legal form, and the emergence (perhaps delayed recognition of the effects) of forms of capital that blur the distinction between equity and debt finance, i.e. the so-called mezzanine security. These are just a few of the accounting issues that demand urgent attention, and which move accounting for inflation from the centre stage.

The 'value accounting' concept seems to be gaining some acceptance, if not without challenge, in other areas of accounting. For some time it has applied to leases per SSAP 21, but now it invades the realm of brands in that brand accounting necessitates a valuation often totally devoid of any HC input. Extensive research into the practicalities of financial reporting using PV is in progress in the USA. These factors may impact the inflation accounting debate and generate a consensus in favour of one role model, such as the CC system.

However, economic history does not suggest that instability of prices will be banished. In fact, recent monetary experience suggests that inflation is endemic in the modern industrial economy. Without doubt, if and when inflation commences to accelerate beyond manageable levels, the indexing cum revaluation of financial information will once again fuel debate.

There are also signs of needing to rehash company reports and accounts with a view to presenting more information and in a different format:

● The ASB has introduced changes to the format of the profit and loss account (a 'layered' concept) with the aim of assisting users in understanding/assessing company performance.

● City scandals involving major industrial corporations have raised questions regarding the intrinsic validity of the existing auditors' report and the adequacy of the financial reporting system.

● The Solomons Report of 1989 has raised the need to revamp the financial reporting system by improving the standard process via a UK conceptual framework (see Chapter 7). It also discussed the need to adopt a valuation base in the financial reporting of assets.

The pressure to make financial reporting more relevant may well lead eventually to a mandatory form of valuation accounting, involving adjustments for moving prices. We can assume that inflation accounting will develop and become an accounting form: an integral part of the annual report.

5.8 The ASB approach

The ASB has been wary of this topic. It is only too aware that standard setters in the past have been unsuccessful in obtaining a consensus on the price level adjusting model to be used in financial statements. Consequently, it has clearly decided to follow a gradualist approach and to require uniformity in the treatment of specific assets and liabilities where it is current practice to move away from historical costs.

The ASB view[7] was set out in a Discussion Paper, *The Role of Valuation in Financial Reporting*, issued in 1993. The ASB had three options when considering the existing sytem of modified historic costs:

● to remove the right to modify cost in the balance sheet;

● to introduce a coherent current value system immediately;

● to make *ad hoc* improvements to the present modified historic cost system.

Remove the right to modify cost in the balance sheet

This would mean pruning the system back to one rigorously based on the principles of historical costs, with current values shown by way of note.

This option has strong support from the profession not only in the UK,[8] e.g. 'in our view … the most significant advantage of historical cost over current value accounting … is that it is based on transactions which the company has undertaken and the cash flows that it has generated … this is an advantage not just in terms of reliability, but also in terms of relevance', but also in the USA,[9] e.g. 'a study showed that users were opposed to replacing the current historic cost based accounting model … because it provides them with a stable and consistent benchmark that they can rely on to establish historical trends'.

Although this would have brought UK practice into line with that of North America and some of the EU countries, it has been rejected by the ASB. This is no doubt on the basis that the Board wishes to see current values established in the UK in the longer term.

Introduce a coherent current value system immediately

This would mean developing the system into one more clearly founded on principles embracing current values. One such system, advocated by the ASB in chapter 6 of its *Statement of Accounting Principles*, is based on **value to the business**. The value to the business measurement model is eclectic in that it draws on various current value systems. The approach to establishing the value to the business of a specific asset is quite logical:

- If an asset is worth replacing, then use replacement cost (RC).
- If it is **not** worth replacing, then use:
  value in use (economic value) if it is worth keeping, **or**
  net realisable value (NRV) if it is **not** worth keeping.

However, the ASB did not see it as feasible to implement this system at that time because 'there is much work to be done to determine whether or not it is possible to devise a system that would be of economic relevance and acceptable to users and preparers of financial statements in terms of sufficient reliability without prohibitive cost'.[10]

Make ad hoc *improvements to the present modified historical cost system*

The Board favoured this option for removing anomalies, on the basis that practice should be evolutionary and should follow various ASB pronouncements (e.g. on the revaluation of properties and quoted investments) on an *ad hoc* basis. The *Statement of Accounting Principles* continues to envisage that a mixed measurement system will be used and it focuses on the mix of historical cost and current value to be adopted.[11]

It is influenced in choosing this option by the recognition that there are anxieties about the costs and benefits of moving to a full, current, value system, and by the belief that a considerable period of experimentation and learning would be needed before such a major change could be successfully introduced.[12]

Given the inability of the standard-setters to implement a uniform current value system in the past, it seems a sensible, pragmatic approach for the ASB to recognise that it would fail if it made a similar attempt now.

The historical cost based system and the current value based system have far more to commend them than the *ad hoc* option chosen by the ASB. However, as a short-term measure, it leaves the way open for the implementation in the longer term of its preferred value to the business model.

5.8.1   What changes might we see evolving from the gradualist approach of the ASB?

First, there will be the influence exerted by FRS 3 *Reporting Financial Performance*, with, for example, its requirement for a note of historical cost profits and losses. This will reconcile the reported profit on ordinary activities to the historical cost profit for the year, by adjusting for the difference between a historical cost depreciation charge and the actual depreciation charge calculated on revalued amounts.

Secondly, as indicated in the ASB's Discussion Paper *The Role of Valuation in Financial Reporting*, it might be useful to separate trading profit from operating gains in either the profit and loss account or the statement of total gains and losses.[13]

Summary

The HCA method is the central plank of the financial reporting system, yet its inherent defects are legion, particularly in times of inflation. The advantages of a system of measuring and reporting on the impact of shifting prices are almost universally accepted, yet agreement on the model to be applied evades the profession.

Currently, the ASC *Handbook* is an authoritative reference document of a CCA reporting system, but it lacks mandatory status. Some companies have followed the spirit of the *Handbook* and have published inflation-adjusted accounts, but not, unfortunately, with regularity.

The contemporary financial reporting scene is beset by problems such as the emergence of brand accounting, the debate on accounting for goodwill, the need for more informative revenue accounts and a sudden spate of financial scandals involving major industrial conglomerations. These have combined to raise questions regarding the adequacy of the annual accounts and the intrinsic validity of the auditors' report.

In assessing future prospects it would seem that more useful financial information is needed. This need will be met by changes in the reporting system, which are likely, sooner or later, to include some form of 'value accounting' as distinct from HC accounting. Such value accounting will probably embrace inflationary adjustments to enable comparability to be maintained, as far as possible, in a price-changing economic environment.

Review questions

1 What factors should be taken into account when designing a system of accounting for changing price levels?

2 Why has the HCA model survived in spite of its shortcomings in times of inflation?

3 Explain the features of the CPP model in contrast with those of the CCA paradigm.

4 'The problem with CPP accounting is in the choice of a suitable price index.' Would you agree with this statement? Give your reasons.

5 To what extent are CCA statements useful?

6 What is the operating capital maintenance concept?

7 What is the financial capital maintenance concept?

8 What is the real terms version of CCA?

Exercises

An extract from the solution is provided in the appendix at the end of the text for exercises marked with an asterisk (*).

* Question 1

Shower Ltd was incorporated towards the end of 20X2, but it did not start trading until 20X3. Its historical cost balance sheet at 1 January 20X3 was as follows:

	£
Share capital, £1 shares	2,000
Loan (interest free)	8,000
	£10,000
Fixed assets, at cost	6,000
Inventory, at cost (4,000) units	4,000
	£10,000

A summary of Shower Limited's bank account for 20X3 is given below:

		£	£
1 Jan 20X3	Opening balance		nil
30 Jun 20X3	Sales (8,000 units)		20,000
Less			
29 Jun 20X3	Purchase (6,000 units)	9,000	
	Sundry expenses	5,000	14,000
31 Dec 20X3	Closing balance		£6,000

All the company's transactions are on a cash basis.

The fixed assets are expected to last for five years and the company intends to depreciate its fixed assets on a straight-line basis. The fixed assets had a resale value of £2,000 at 31 December 20X3.

Notes

1 The closing stock is 2,000 units and the stock is sold on a first-in-first-out basis.

2 All prices remained constant from the date of incorporation to 1 January 20X3, but thereafter, various suitable price indices moved as follows:

		Specific indices	
	General price level	Inventory	Fixed assets
1 January 20X3	100	100	100
30 June 20X3	120	150	140
31 December 20X3	240	255	200

Required:
Produce balance sheets as at December 20X3 and income statements for the year ended on that date on the basis of:
(i)   historical cost;
(ii) current purchasing power (general price level);
(iii) replacement cost;
(iv) continuous contemporary accounting (NRVA).

* **Question 2**

Raiders plc prepares accounts annually to 31 March. The following figures, prepared on a conventional historical cost basis, are included in the company's accounts to 31 March 20X5.

1 In the profit and loss account:

	£000	£000
(i) Cost of goods sold:		
Stock at 1 April 20X4	9,600	
Purchases	39,200	
	48,800	
Stock at 31 March 20X5	11,300	37,500
(ii) Depreciation of equipment		8,640

2   In the balance sheet:

	£000	£000
(iii) Equipment at cost	57,600	
Less: Accumulated depreciation	16,440	41,160
(iv) Stock		11,300

The stock held on 31 March 20X4 and 31 March 20X5 was in each case purchased evenly during the last six months of the company's accounting year.

Equipment is depreciated at a rate of 15% per annum, using the straight-line method. Equipment owned on 31 March 20X5 was purchased as follows: on 1 April 20X2 at a cost of £16 million; on 1 April 20X3 at a cost of £20 million; and on 1 April 20X4 at a cost of £21.6 million.

The following indices are available:

	Current cost of stock	Current cost of equipment	Retail Price Index
1 April 20X2	109	145	313
1 April 20X3	120	162	328
30 September 20X3	128	170	339
31 December 20X3	133	175	343
31 March/1 April 20X4	138	180	345
30 September 20X4	150	191	355
31 December 20X4	156	196	360
31 March 20X5	162	200	364

Required:
(a)   Calculate the following current cost accounting figures:
  (i)   The cost of goods sold of Raiders plc for the year ended 31 March 20X5.
  (ii)   The balance sheet value of stock at 31 March 20X5.
  (iii)   The equipment depreciation charge for the year ended 31 March 20X5.
  (iv)   The net balance sheet value of equipment at 31 March 20X5.
(b)   Discuss the extent to which the figures you have calculated in (a) above (together with figures calculated on a similar basis for earlier years) provide information over and above that provided by the conventional historical cost profit and loss account and balance sheet figures.
(c)   Outline the main reasons why the Standards Setters have experienced so much difficulty in their attempts to develop an accounting standard on accounting for changing prices.

*   ## Question 3

The balance sheets of Parkway plc for 20X7 and 20X8 are given below, together with the profit and loss account for the year ended 30 June 20X8.

		Balance Sheet					
		20X8				20X7	
	£	£	£	£	£	£
Fixed assets	Cost	Depn	NBV	Cost	Depn	NBV
Freehold land	60,000	—	60,000	60,000	—	60,000
Buildings	40,000	8,000	32,000	40,000	7,200	32,800
Plant and machinery	30,000	16,000	14,000	30,000	10,000	20,000
Vehicles	40,000	20,000	20,000	40,000	12,000	28,000
	170,000	44,000	126,000	170,000	29,200	140,800

Current assets					
Stocks		80,000			70,000
Debtors		60,000			40,000
Short-term investments		50,000			—
Cash at bank and in hand		5,000			5,000
		195,000			115,000
Creditors: amounts falling due within one year					
Trade creditors		90,000			60,000
Bank overdraft		50,000			45,000
Taxation		28,000			15,000
Dividends		15,000			10,000
		183,000			130,000
Net current assets			12,000		(15,000)
			138,000		125,800
Financed by					
Ordinary share capital			80,000		80,000
Share premium			10,000		10,000
Retained profits			28,000		15,800
			118,000		105,800
Long-term loans			20,000		20,000
			138,000		125,800

Profit and Loss Account of Parkway for
the year ended 30 June 20X8

	£
Sales	738,000
Cost of sales	620,000
Gross profit	118,000

Notes

1 The freehold land and buildings were purchased on 1 July 20X0. The company policy is to depreciate buildings over fifty years and to provide no depreciation on land.

2 Depreciation on plant and machinery and motor vehicles is provided at the rate of 20% per annum on a straight-line basis.
3 Depreciation on buildings and plant and equipment has been included in administration expenses, while that on motor vehicles is included in distribution expenses.
4 The directors of Parkway plc have provided you with the following information relating to price rises:

	RPI	Stock	Land	Buildings	Plant	Vehicles
1 July 20X0	100	60	70	50	90	120
1 July 20X7	170	140	290	145	135	180
30 June 20X8	190	180	310	175	165	175
Average for year	180	160	300	163	145	177

Required:
(a) Making and stating any assumptions that are necessary, and giving reasons for those assumptions, calculate the monetary working capital adjustment for Parkway plc.
(b) Critically evaluate the usefulness of the monetary working capital adjustment.

Question 4

The historical cost accounts of Smith plc are as follows:

Smith plc Profit and Loss Account for the year ended 31 December 20X8

	£	£
Sales		2,000
Cost of sales:		
Opening stock 1 January 20X8	320	
Purchases	1,680	
	2,000	
Closing stock at 31 December 20X8	280	
		1,720
Gross profit		280
Depreciation	20	
Administration expenses	100	
		120
Net profit		160

Balance Sheet of Smith plc as at 31 December 20X8

	20X7	20X8
	£	£
Fixed assets		
Land and buildings at cost	1,360	1,360
Less aggregate depreciation	(160)	(180)
	1,200	1,180

Current assets				
Stock	320		280	
Debtors	80		160	
Cash at bank	40		120	
	440		560	
Creditors	200		140	
		240		420
		1,440		1,600
Ordinary share capital		800		800
Retained profit		640		800
		1,440		1,600

Notes

1 Land and buildings were acquired in 20X0 with the buildings component costing £800 and depreciated over 40 years.
2 Share capital was issued in 20X0.
3 Closing stocks were acquired in the last quarter of the year.
4 RPI numbers were:

Average for 20X0	120	20X8 last quarter	232
20X7 last quarter	216	Average for 20X8	228
At 31 December 20X7	220	At 31 December 20X8	236

Required:

(i) **Explain the basic concept of the CPP accounting system.**

(ii) **Prepare CPP accounts for Smith plc for the year ended 20X8.**
The following steps will assist in preparing the CPP accounts:
(a) **Restate the profit and loss account for the current year in terms of £CPP at the year-end.**
(b) **Restate the closing balance sheet in £CPP at year-end, but excluding monetary items, i.e. debtors, creditors, cash at bank.**
(c) **Restate the opening balance sheet in £CPP at year-end, but including monetary items, i.e. debtors, creditors and cash at bank, and showing equity as the balancing figure.**
(d) **Compare the opening and closing equity figures derived in (b) and (c) above to arrive at the total profit/loss for the year in CPP terms. Compare this figure with the CPP profit calculated in (a) above to determine the monetary gain or monetary loss.**
(e) **Reconcile monetary gains/loss in (d) with the increase/decrease in net monetary items during the year expressed in £CPP compared with the increase/decrease expressed in £HC.**

Question 5

The finance director of Toy plc has been asked by a shareholder to explain items that appear in the current cost profit and loss account for the year ended 31.8. 20X9 and the balance sheet as at that date:

		£		£
Historical cost profit				143,000
Cost of sales adjustment	(1)	10,000		
Additional depreciation	(2)	6,000		
Monetary working capital adjustment	(3)	2,500		18,500
Current cost operating profit before tax				124,500
Gearing adjustment	(4)			2,600
CCA Operating profit				127,100
Fixed assets at gross replacement cost		428,250		
Accumulated current cost depreciation	(5)	(95,650)		332,600
Net current assets				121,400
12% Debentures				(58,000)
				396,000
Issued share capital				250,000
Current cost reserve	(6)			75,000
Profit and Loss Account				71,000
				396,000

Required:

(a) **Explain what each of the items numbered 1–6 represents and the purpose of each.**

(b) **What do you consider to be the benefits to users of providing current cost information?**

References

1 *Accounting for changes in the purchasing power of money*, SSAP 7 (Provisional), ASC, May 1994.
2 *Inflation Accounting*, Report of the Inflation Accounting Committee, Cmnd 6225, HMSO, 1975 (The Sandilands Report).
3 H.C. Edey, 'Sandilands and the logic of current cost', *Accounting and Business Research*, Volume 9, No 35, Summer 1979, pp. 191–200.
4 *Current cost accounting*, ED 24, ASC, March 1979.
5 *Current cost accounting*, SSAP 16, ASC, March 1980.
6 Accounting Standards Committee, *Accounting for the effects of changing prices: A Handbook*, October 1986.
7 *The Role of Valuation in Financial Reporting*, ASB, 1993.
8 Ernst and Young, *UK GAAP* (4th edition), 1994, p. 91.
9 *The Information Needs of Investors and Creditors*, AICPA Special Committee on Financial Reporting.
10 *The Role of Valuation in Financial Reporting*, ASB, 1993, para. 31(ii).
11 *Statement of Accounting Principles*, ASB, December 1999, para. 6.4.
12 *The Role of Valuation in Financial Reporting*, ASB, 1993, para. 33.
13 D. Chopping and L. Skerratt, *Applying GAAP 1993/4*, ICAEW, 1993, p. 98.

Financial reporting

statutes and standards

6.1 Introduction

In this chapter we will consider the regulatory framework applicable to financial reporting. The framework is **evolutionary** and consists of numerous regulations: some are statutory, some mandatory and others statements of best practice.

Our primary objective is to consider the dominant role of accounting standards, looking at the need for them, their nature, effectiveness and future development. We also consider the role of legislation and the continuing growth of voluntary recommended practice.

Since the mid-1960s the accountancy profession has been embroiled with a growing mass of regulations governing the measurement, presentation and disclosure of financial information. The freedom for companies to publish financial data in any format simply to tell the story the directors wished to tell has been replaced by the need to conform to universal standards. By 1991 the Financial Reporting Council was commenting on the standard setting process in its first annual report that 'This is the most promising means of devising standards that are proof against accounting innovations which are **more to do with showing a company's position in a favourable light** than with providing the clearest statement of its affairs'. There is now a recognition that, for public listed companies, Financial Directors report to a capital market that is both more sophisticated and more global.

The initial engine of change was probably the Stock Exchange but companies are now subject to many different regulatory bodies. In this chapter we consider each of the constituents of the framework discussing:

● Need for Mandatory regulations

● UK Standards (SSAPs and FRSs and SORPs)

● International Accounting Standards (IASs) and EU Directives

● Stock Exchange rules

● Non-mandatory Statements of Best Practice

● Operating and Financial Review (OFR)

● The Combined Code

● Interim Reports

● Financial Reporting Standard for Smaller Enterprises (FRSSE)

6.2 Statutory legislation

Until 1981 the legislative demands and constraints concerning the form and content of published accounts of limited companies were relatively slight. Then the statutory situation underwent a radical change when the UK implemented the EC Fourth Directive in its own Companies Act 1981. This was followed the Companies Act 1985 which consolidated the Acts of 1947, 1948, 1967, 1980 and 1981 and set out the general rules and formats governing the content and form of published company accounts. The primary objective of these rules is to impose a legislative standardisation of presentation with a view to facilitating inter-company comparisons. In other words, they are an attempt to assist users to understand and evaluate company progress. The 1985 Act has now been amended and supplemented by the Companies Act 1989, which gave effect to the EC Seventh Directive concerning consolidated accounts and the EC Eighth Directive concerning auditors, and also introduced regulations relating to the small company and directors.

6.3 Mandatory regulations

Mandatory regulations take the form of Statements of Standard Accounting Practice (SSAPs) and Financial Reporting Standards (FRSs).

6.3.1 Role of accounting numbers in defining contractual entitlements

Contracting parties frequently define the rights between themselves in terms of accounting numbers.[1] For example, the remuneration of directors and managers might be expressed in terms of a salary plus a bonus based on an agreed performance measure, e.g. growth in earnings per share. However, if there is a risk that earnings will not grow at a rate that is acceptable to the directors and managers, there could be a temptation to improve the earnings for the period by taking measures that might not be in the interest of the shareholders.

Typical measures include: **deferral of expenditure**, e.g. development expenditure; **deferral of amortisation,** e.g. capitalising development expenditure that has been incurred; and **reclassifying** deteriorating assets from current to fixed to avoid the need to recognise a loss under the lower of cost and net realisable value rule applicable to current assets.

The introduction of a mandatory standard that changes management's ability to adopt such measures will **affect wealth distribution** within the firm. For example, if managers are unable to delay the amortisation of development expenditure, then performance related bonuses will be lower and there will effectively have been a transfer of wealth from managers to shareholders.

This effect of changes in mandatory standards on wealth distribution is a major reason why standards are required, and also why it is difficult to obtain a consensus. Each party considers the economic consequence, real or imagined, on their personal position.

6.3.2 Need for mandatory standards

Mandatory standards are needed to define the way in which accounting numbers are presented in financial statements, so that presentation is less subjective. It had been thought that the accountancy profession could obtain uniformity of disclosure by persuasion, but in reality, the profession found it difficult to resist management pressures.

During the 1960s the financial sector of the UK economy lost confidence in the accountancy profession when internationally known UK-based companies were seen to have published financial data that were materially incorrect. Shareholders would normally be unaware that this had occurred and it tends only to become public knowledge in restricted circumstances, e.g. when a third party has a **vested interest** in revealing the facts such as following or during a take-over battle, or, when a company falls into the hands of an administrator, inspector or liquidator, **whose duty it is to inquire and report** on shortcomings in the management of a company.

The two scandals that we discuss (GEC/AEI and Pergamon Press)[2] were both made public in the restricted circumstances referred to above, when financial reports were prepared from the same basic information but disclosed a materially different picture.

GEC take-over of AEI in 1967

The first calamity for the profession involved GEC Ltd in its take-over bid for AEI Ltd. Each entity had compiled financial reports, but their subjectivity together with their inconsistency in the treatment of the basic information created two widely differing sets of accounts.

AEI profit forecast for 1967 as determined by the old AEI directors

AEI Ltd produced a **profit forecast of £10 million** in November 1967 and recommended its shareholders to reject the GEC bid. The forecast had the blessing of the auditors, in as much as they said that it had been prepared on a fair and reasonable basis and in a manner consistent with the principles followed in preparing the annual accounts. The investing public would normally have been quite satisfied with the forecast figure and the process by which it was produced. Clearly, AEI would not subsequently have produced other information to show that the picture was materially different from that forecast.

However, GEC was successful with its bid and as a result it was GEC's directors who had control over the preparation of the AEI accounts for 1967.

AEI profit for 1967 as determined by the new AEI directors

Under the control of the directors of GEC the accounts of AEI were produced for 1967 showing **a loss of £4.5 million**. Unfortunately, this was from basic information that was largely the same as that used by AEI when producing its profit forecast.

There can be two reasons for the difference between the figures produced. Either the facts have changed or the judgements made by the directors have changed. In this case, it seems there was a change in the facts to the extent of a post-acquisition closure of an AEI factory; this explained £5 million of the £14.5 million difference between the forecast profit and the actual loss. The remaining £9.5 million arose because of differences in judgement. For example, the new directors took a different view of the value of stock and work-in-progress.

Pergamon Press

Audited accounts were produced by Pergamon Press Ltd for 1968 showing a profit of approximately £2 million. An independent investigation by Price Waterhouse suggested that this profit should be reduced by 75% because of a number of unacceptable valuations, e.g. there had been a failure to reduce certain stock to the lower of cost and net realisable value, and there had been a change in policy on the capitalisation of printing costs of back issues of scientific journals – they were treated as a cost of closing stock in 1968, but not as a cost of opening stock in 1968.

Public view of the accounting profession following these cases

It had long been recognised that accountancy is not an exact science, but it had not been appreciated just how much latitude there was for companies to produce vastly different results based on the same transactions. Given that the auditors were perfectly happy to sign that accounts showing either a £10 million profit or a £4.5 million loss were true and fair, the public felt the need for action if investors were to have any trust in the figures that were being published.

The difficulty was that each firm of accountants tended to rely on precedents within its own firm in deciding what was true and fair. This is fine until the public becomes aware that profits depend on the particular partner who happens to be responsible for the audit. The auditors were also under pressure to agree to practices that the directors wanted because there were no professional mandatory standards.

This was the scenario that galvanised the City press and the investing public. An embarrassed, disturbed profession announced in 1969, via the ICAEW, that there was a pressing need for the introduction of Statements of Standard Accounting Practice to supplement the legislation.

6.3.3 Creation of a standard-setting body

In this section we consider the ASSC, the ASC, the Dearing Committee, the Dearing Report and the ASB.

Accounting Standards Steering Committee (ASSC)

The Accounting Standards Steering Committee was formed by the ICAEW in 1970. The committee increased its membership to include other professional accounting bodies. The objectives of the ASSC were as follows:

● **Damage limitation** by narrowing the areas of difference in accounting practice that had been bringing the profession into disrepute.

● The **development of a consensus** by encouraging wider exposure and discussion of proposals for standards. This was a vital step because failure to carry directors or the profession would lead to non-compliance or rejection, as with SSAP 7 and SSAP 16 dealing with inflation.

● To **encourage disclosure** by requiring companies to disclose the accounting policies they have adopted, e.g. depreciation policy, and also to disclose when they have not followed the accounting policy laid down in an SSAP.

● To **improve standards** by developing a continuing programme.

Accounting Standards Committee (ASC)

By 1976 the ASSC included the Institute of Chartered Accountants in England and Wales, the Institute of Chartered Accountants of Scotland, the Institute of Chartered Accountants of Ireland, the Chartered Association of Certified Accountants, the Chartered Institute of Management Accountants and the Chartered Institute of Public Finance and Accountancy. The word 'steering' was omitted and the organisation became the Accounting Standards Committee. The procedure was for the ASC to prepare a draft standard; the draft was adopted if all six professional bodies were unanimous; each of the professional accounting bodies then issued the SSAP to its own members.

By 1982 it was felt that the professional accounting bodies had too great a control over the process. Consequently, the terms of reference of the ASC were widened, e.g. to consult representatives of finance, commerce, industry and government and other persons concerned with financial reporting; the membership was reduced to twenty, including five users of financial reports who were not required to be accountants; and government officials, e.g. representatives from the Department of Trade and Industry, could be co-opted as non-voting members,.

The process was also organised to give users full opportunity to make their inputs to the standard setting. The aims of the process were as follows:

● Topics that were to be the subject of a standard were made public.

● Consultation was encouraged by the issue of discussion documents.

● An exposure draft prepared by the ASC was published.

● A draft standard was prepared by the ASC, taking into account reactions to the discussion documents and exposure drafts.

The Dearing Committee[3]

Although the ASC had produced twenty-five standards by 1991, there was criticism that it was not adequately staffed, had no ground-plan and was reactive rather than proactive. However, it had operated as effectively as possible given its resources, and had indeed been ambitious in attempting to address areas where the profession was itself divided, e.g. inflation accounting.

The political climate changed in the 1980s with wider share ownership and the growing use of watchdog organisations to encourage self-regulation, e.g. Oftel in the telecommunications industry and Ofwat in the water industry. Changes in the way in which the accounting profession ensured conformity to universal standards were only to be expected.

The Dearing Committee was set up by the Consultation Committee of the Accountancy Bodies and was charged to review the standard-setting process in the light of future changes in the financial markets, i.e. recognising that financial statements are a prerequisite for a properly functioning capital market, and taking account of the current attitude of the state and public to the regulation of companies. The committee reported in 1988.

Dearing Report

The report contained a number of recommendations, including the following:

● It recommended the creation of a conceptual framework by developing work that had already taken place, e.g. FASB statements produced in the USA. The Solomons Report, which was produced with the benefit of knowing US developments, is discussed in a later section. It is a noticeable feature of the evolution of a conceptual framework that the ASB is eclectic in making use of material from a wide range of sources, e.g. the Corporate Report, the Trueblood Report or Study Group on Objectives of Financial Statements, FASB statements such as SFAC 1 and the IASC document *Framework for the Presentation and Preparation of Financial Statements*.[4]

● It recommended setting up a Financial Reporting Council with nine professional accountants, nine users, the ASB chairman and its own chairman. This Council would be responsible for giving the ASB guidance on priorities and advising the ASB on areas of public concern or controversy.

● It recommended the setting up of the Accounting Standards Board (ASB) with a salaried staff comprising accountants responsible for issuing standards. The procedure for formulating standards would be similar to that followed by the ASC.

However, the ASB would found its accounting standards on stated **principles** wherever possible, to avoid the prescription of detailed, legalistic rules. In addition, the ASB would operate an Urgent Issues Task Force to make pronouncements and to amend standards if the need suddenly arose.

● It recommended setting up a Review Panel reporting to the Council to examine departures from standards by large companies. This would allow the auditor to make reference for guidance where the directors proposed to depart from a standard and where the auditor disagreed with their proposed treatment or agreed and considered that the standard needed to be amended.

Accounting Standards Board (ASB)

The ASC ceased to exist on 1 August 1990 when it was replaced by the new Accounting Standards Board (ASB). The twenty-two extant SSAPs issued by the former ASC were adopted by the new Board.

The SSAPs issued by the former ASC are mandatory on all members of the six accountancy bodies, namely, the Institute of Chartered Accountants in England and Wales, the Institute of Chartered Accountants of Scotland, the Institute of Chartered Accountants of Ireland, the Chartered Association of Certified Accountants, the Chartered Institute of Management Accountants and the Chartered Institute of Public Finance and Accountancy. This mandatory authority has been strengthened by the Companies Act 1985 Pt VII as amended by the Companies Act 1989. The SSAPs themselves are now 'accounting standards' under section 256(1) Companies Act 1985.

6.3.4 Arguments in support of standards

We discuss four arguments in support of standards based on comparability, credibility, influence and discipline.

Comparability

Financial statements should allow a user to make predictions of future cash flows, make comparisons with other companies[5] and evaluate the management's performance.

In order to be able to make valid inter-company comparisons of performance, progress and trends, investment decision makers must be supplied with relevant and reliable data that have been standardised. Such comparisons would be distorted and valueless if companies were permitted to select accounting policies at random or, even worse, with the intention of disguising changes in performance and trends.

Credibility

The accountancy profession would lose all credibility if it permitted companies experiencing similar events to produce financial reports that disclosed markedly different results simply because they could select different accounting policies. Uniformity of subjective treatment is essential if financial reports are to disclose a true and fair view. However, the explanatory foreword to the ASC standards emphasised that the standards were not intended to be a comprehensive code of rigid rules, and that they do not supersede the exercise of informed judgement in determining what constitutes a true and fair view in each circumstance.

Influence

The process of formulating standards has encouraged a constructive appraisal of the policies being proposed for individual reporting problems and has stimulated the development of a conceptual framework. For example, the standard on leasing introduced the idea in UK standards of considering the commercial substance of a transaction rather than simply the legal position.

When the ASC was set up in the 1970s there was no clear statement of accounting principles other than the four fundamental concepts of SSAP 2. The immediate task was to bring some order into accounting practice. This is illustrated by the ASC report *A Conceptual Framework for Financial Accounting and Reporting: The Possibilities for an Agreed Structure* by R. MacVe in 1981, which considered that the possibility of an agreed body of accounting principles was remote at that time.

However, the process of setting standards has stimulated accounting thought and literature to the point where, by 1994, the ASB had produced its exposure drafts of *Statement of Accounting Principles*, which appeared in final form in December 1999.

Discipline

Companies left to their own devices without the need to observe standards will eventually be disciplined by the financial market. However, in the short term, investors in such entities may suffer loss. Mandatory standards will impose systematic ongoing regulation, which should prevent serious loss to the entity and those who rely on the annual accounts when making credit, loan and investment decisions.

There is a tension between the desire that standards should not be a comprehensive code of rigid rules and the desire to regulate accounting practices that are imaginatively devised by directors and their financial advisers to create a picture that they may consider true and fair – but which others may not. Directors are under pressure to maintain and improve the market valuation of their company's securities; they will attempt to influence any financial statistic that has an impact on the market valuation, e.g. the trend in the EPS figure, the net asset backing for the shares or the gearing ratios.

The Financial Reporting Council is aware of the need to impose discipline when it states in its annual review, November 1991, para. 2.4, that the high level of company failures in the current recession, some of which have been associated with obscure financial reporting, has damaged confidence in the high standard of reporting by the majority of companies.

6.3.5 ASB comments on the process of formulating standards

The ASB advises in its foreword to *Accounting Standards* 1991 paras 22–4, that:

> Topics that become the subject of FRSs are identified by the Board either from its own research or from external sources, including submissions from interested parties. An FRS is a financial reporting standard.
>
> When a topic is identified the Board commissions its staff to undertake a programme of research and consultation. This programme involves consideration of and consultation on the relevant conceptual issues, existing pronouncements and practice ... and the economic, legal and practical implications of the introduction of particular accounting requirements.
>
> When the issues have been identified and debated by the Board a discussion draft (DD) is normally produced and circulated to parties who have registered their interest to the Board. The purpose of this draft is to form a basis for discussion with parties particularly affected by or having knowledge of the issues

raised in the proposals. An exposure draft (FRED) of an FRS is then published to allow an opportunity for all interested parties to comment on the proposals and for the Board to gauge the appropriateness and level of acceptance of these proposals. A FRED is a financial reporting exposure draft.

There is a consultative process, but this should not lead us to expect that all FRSs will receive universal support.

If the experience with the ASC is a guide, then the publication of a standard will not automatically generate universal compliance. The very fact that a standard is required often indicates that the topic is contentious. The process of formulation attempts to address this, but we have seen examples where the disaffection with a standard has been so great that it has had to be revised, as with *Deferred Taxation* (SSAP 11) or withdrawn, as with the inflation standards (SSAPs 7 and 16).

The ASB has not always been unanimous when issuing an FRS. For example, a dissident view was expressed by Mr Bradfield on the issue of FRS 3 *Reporting Financial Performance* based on the fear that the FRS could frequently produce misleading measures of performance.[6]

A dissident view was also expressed by Mr Main, a Forte director and one of the ASB industry members, on the issue of FRS 7 *Fair Values in Acquisition Accounting*, based on the view that costs incurred in the immediate post-acquisition period to implement a business plan to reorganise on acquisition were an integral part of the investment appraisal process and, as such, should not be reported in the group's post-acquisition trading results. This view was supported by the chairman of the Hundred Group of Finance Directors, Mr Nigel Stapleton, who was also the chief financial officer of Reed Elsevier. Mr Stapleton's view was that the ASB had gone well beyond the accounting requirements of other countries and that the requirements of FRSs 6 and 7 would distort the profit and loss account.[7]

The ASB insisted that this complaint was without foundation and that it was determined to ensure that revenue expenses were charged to revenue.

However, the existence of dissident views reflects the differences of opinion that exist between members of the accountancy profession and management. This arises from the fact that the profession ultimately finds itself with audit responsibility, while management's primary concern is to oppose any measures that could reduce future earnings or management's flexibility to influence the year in which the profits are reported.

The ASB had a clear objective in FRS 3, FRS 6 and FRS 7: to reduce management's capacity to manipulate the reported earnings figure by enforcing the matching principle and also by requiring greater disclosure of changes occurring during the financial year. However, other issues are not quite so clear. For instance, there are disagreements as to the appropriate conceptual treatment of goodwill.

In 1995 the ASB adopted the procedure followed for a long time in the USA by the Financial Accounting Standards Board of holding public meetings as part of the consultation process.

6.3.6 Legal force of financial reporting standards

The force of reporting standards has increased. Opinions obtained in 1983 by the ASC from L. Hoffman QC and Miss Arden QC stated that compliance with accepted accounting principles was *prima facie* evidence that the accounts were true and fair. However, if there remained a strong body of professional opinion which consistently failed to apply an SSAP then the *prima facie* assumption was weakened.

We mentioned above that accounting standards have received statutory recognition in the Companies Act. In 1993 the ASB obtained another Opinion from Miss Arden QC, which strengthened its hand by stating that 'Whenever a standard is issued by the Board, then, irrespective of the lack in some quarters of support for it, the court would be bound to give special weight to the opinion of the Board in view of its status as the standard-setting body, the process of investigation, discussion and consultation that it will have undertaken before adopting the standard and the evolving nature of accounting standards.'[8]

This has given the ASB enormous confidence in dealing with controversial issues. Provided there is a process of investigation, discussion and consultation, the ASB should be able to enforce any standard that it issues. From a pragmatic point of view this should lead to greater uniformity, but it leaves unanswered the criticism that the conceptual framework is insufficiently robust to cope with really controversial issues.

It is an independent body, but the structure of standard-setting in the UK provides it with additional muscle to enforce compliance with standards – over and above the ultimate sanction of looking to the courts. Figure 6.1 illustrates the structure. The ASB does not stand alone in enforcing compliance. The Urgent Issues Task Force and the Financial Reporting Review Panel have assisting roles.

The Urgent Issues Task Force

The UITF's role is to issue Abstracts where a standard is in force but is not being appropriately interpreted. Abstracts can be very specific, e.g. UITF Abstract 4 gives guidance on the disclosure of long-term debtors within current assets; or very general, e.g. UITF Abstract 7 gives guidance on the level of disclosure required when a company makes use of the True and Fair Override. Abstracts that deal with specific technical disclosure might subsequently be subsumed within an FRS, e.g. UITF Abstract 2 dealing with restructuring costs was subsumed within FRS 3. If a company fails to comply with a UITF Abstract, it is required to give adequate disclosure of the fact in its financial statements.

The Financial Reporting Review Panel

The Financial Reporting Review Panel (FRRP) is completely independent of the ASB and the UITF. It has a barrister as chairman and twenty-two other members who are accountants, bankers and lawyers. Its role is to review material departures from accounting standards and, where financial statements are defective, to require the company to take appropriate remedial action. It operates under section 245B of the Companies Act 1985, which has given the courts power to order a company to rectify defective accounts.

Figure 6.1   Structure of standard-setting in the UK.

The FRRP cannot create standards. If a company has used an inappropriate accounting policy that contravenes a standard, the FRRP can act. If there is no standard and a company chooses the most favourable from two or more accounting policies, the FRRP cannot act.

The FRRP is responsible for overseeing some 2,500 companies. Clearly it cannot review every set of accounts. It becomes involved as a result of a complaint by an individual, a referral from the Stock Exchange, e.g. where accounts have been qualified by an auditor for non-compliance, or following media comment.

The FRRP prefers to deal with defects by agreement, although it has threatened applying to the courts. For example, in the accounts of Trafalgar House for the year ended 30 September 1991 certain fixed assets had been reclassified from current to fixed assets – these properties were then written down in value and the reduction charged to reserves, so avoiding the profit and loss account. The FRRP disagreed with this treatment and, following an apparent reluctance by the directors of Trafalgar House to accept their opinion, informed the directors that they were 'minded to make an application to the court ... requiring the directors of the company to prepare revised accounts'. The directors then agreed to make requisite changes to their 30 September 1992 accounts. As a result of the FRRP action the 1992 revised accounts saw a reported £122.5m profit turned into a £30m loss. This was clearly a significant intervention by the regulators.

The FRRP has a policing role. It obtains evidence to provide to the court to make a decision about whether accounts show a true and fair view. In practice, its opinion appears to be persuasive.

FRRP public statements

A research study[9] into companies that have been the subject of a public statement suggests that when a firm's performance comes under severe strain, even apparently well-governed firms can succumb to the pressure for creative accounting and that good governance alone is not a sufficient condition for ensuring high-quality financial reporting. The researchers compared these companies with a control group and a further interesting finding was that there were fewer Big Five auditors in the FRRP population – the researchers commented that this could be interpreted in different ways, e.g. it could be an indication that the Panel prefers to avoid confrontation with the large audit firms because of an increased risk of losing the case or a reflection of the fact that these audit firms are better at managing the politics of the investigation process and negotiating a resolution that does not lead to a public censure.

Government support

The ASB enjoys the support of the government, which has indicated that it will provide statutory backing for specific standards if necessary. This was evidenced when the Department of Trade and Industry, following an acknowledgement by the ASB[10] that it did not have the power to enforce compliance, confirmed[11] that it would legislate to adopt recommendations made by the ASB requiring companies to disclose terms of directors' share options along the lines suggested by the Cadbury Report.

6.3.7 Arguments against standards

We have so far discussed the arguments in support of standard-setting. However, there are also arguments against.

Adverse allocative effects

Adverse allocative effects could occur if standard-setters did not take account of the economic consequences flowing from the standards they issued.[12] For example, additional costs could be imposed on preparers, and suboptimal managerial decisions might be taken to avoid any reduction in earnings or net assets. Furthermore, the consequences might be felt by people who did not actually use the accounts, e.g. a leasing standard might depress the leasing industry, leading to the loss of employment by staff engaged in manufacturing assets supplied under lease, or in servicing the leasing industry.

Consensus-seeking

Consensus-seeking can lead to the issuing of standards that are over-influenced by those with easiest access to the standard-setters – particularly as the subject matter becomes more complex, e.g. capital instruments. It could be argued that the ASB is attempting to base its standards on the *Statement of Principles*, but there is a counter-argument that the *Statement of Principles* is too general to fulfil this role effectively.

Overload

Standard overload is not a new charge. However, it takes a number of conflicting forms, for example:

● There are too many standards.
● Standards are too detailed.
● Standards are not sufficiently detailed, so it is difficult to apply them appropriately.
● Standards are general-purpose, leaving a significant proportion of companies unassisted.
● Standards are general-purpose and fail to recognise the differences between large and small entities and interim and final accounts.
● There is more than one standard-setter, e.g. statutory criteria, ASB pronouncements, UITF announcements, Financial Review Panel pronouncements, International Accounting Standards relevant to multinationals reporting in more than one country, and Stock Exchange standards. Accountants are becoming so regulated that it is difficult to exercise professional judgement.

Uncertainty of application

Uncertainty of application can take two forms. First, undisclosed interpretations of standards may be handed down by the UITF and Financial Review Panel which are not disclosed to the general body of preparers and users. This leads to a body of precedent that is clearly significant, but of which only selected parties are aware. Secondly, as we have already mentioned, the standard may be too general and the ASB may hope that the **spirit** of the standard will be applied.

6.4 Statements of Standard Accounting Practice (SSAPs)

Below is a list of extant standards. Breaks in the numerical sequence are a consequence of standards being withdrawn and/or renumbered on reissue.

SSAP 2 *Disclosure of Accounting Policies*
Many accounting policies exist and those being applied must be identified in the annual accounts. The standard also refers to four of the major fundamental accounting concepts: going concern, accruals, consistency and prudence. The standard has sustained criticism because it omits other fundamental concepts of equal importance such as substance over form, which is discussed in greater depth in Chapter 7.

SSAP 4 *Accounting for Government Grants*
This is a relatively non-controversial standard concerning the treatment by a company of the receipt of grants from the government.

SSAP 5 *Accounting for Value Added Tax*
This requires that Value Added Tax should be excluded from turnover and many companies refer to this in their Accounting Policies. Discussed further in Chapter 13.

SSAP 9 *Stocks and Long-term Contracts*
This concerns the methods of valuing stocks and the treatment of attributable profit on long-term contracts in progress at the end of the financial year. Discussed further in Chapter 17.

SSAP 13 *Accounting for Research and Development*
This insists on the expensing of expenditure to the profit and loss account unless it satisfies criteria to be classified as development expenditure when it may be carried as an asset in the balance sheet. Discussed further in Chapter 16.

SSAP 15 *Accounting for Deferred Tax*
This attempts to reconcile accounting and taxable profits in an effort to achieve a matching of the tax expense with relevant income and expense. The standard in the UK requires the use of the partial provision method. It has been the subject of a Discussion Draft, *Accounting for Tax*, issued in March 1995 and it looks as though the UK will follow International Accounting Standards on provisioning. Discussed further in Chapter 13.

SSAP 17 *Accounting for Post-balance Sheet Events*
This recognises that information might become available after the end of the financial year and before the accounts are signed by the directors and auditors. It gives guidance on events that should result in an adjustment of the financial statements because they provide additional evidence relating to conditions existing at the balance sheet date, e.g. the insolvency of a debtor or the receipt of evidence that the previous estimate of accrued profit on a long-term contract was materially inaccurate. It also gives guidance on non-adjusting events, which are events that arise after the balance sheet date and concern conditions that did not exist at that time. These events will not lead to the financial statements being adjusted, but may need to be disclosed, e.g. closing a significant part of the trading activities if this was not anticipated at the year-end. Discussed further in Chapter 12.

SSAP 19 *Accounting for Investment Properties*
This deals with properties which have been completed and are held for investment purposes owned and occupied for the company's own purposes. Such properties are valued for balance sheet purposes at open market value and are not depreciated as a tangible fixed asset. Discussed further in Chapter 14.

SSAP 20 *Foreign Exchange Translation*

This gives guidance on the treatment of exchange differences arising on the translation of foreign subsidiaries. In particular, it indicates whether the difference should be taken to the profit and loss account or to reserves. Discussed further in Chapter 22.

SSAP 21 *Accounting for Leases and Hire Purchase Contracts*

This is a standard that addresses one aspect of off-balance-sheet finance by applying the concept of substance over form. It mandated the measurement and capitalisation of finance leases. Discussed further in Chapter 15.

SSAP 24 *Accounting for Pension Costs*

This requires the employer to recognise the expected cost of providing pensions on a systematic basis over the period during which the employer derives benefit from the employees' services. Discussed further in Chapter 12.

SSAP 25 *Segmental Reporting*

This mandates the publication of additional financial data. It is particularly important for investors following the tendency for individual companies to diversify. Discussed further in Chapter 25.

FRS 1 *Cash Flow Statements*

This sets out the headings under which a cash flows should be classified. Discussed further in Chapter 24.

FRS 2 *Accounting for Subsidiary Undertakings*

This superseded SSAP 14 on its issue in July 1992. It defines a subsidiary undertaking and concentrates on substance rather than the technicalities which allowed companies to treat what were in substance subsidiaries as not being subsidiaries. This prevented off-balance-sheet finance manipulation that had been prevalent. Discussed further in Chapter 19.

FRS 3 *Reporting Financial Performance*

This superseded SSAP 6 on its issue in October 1992. It was the ASB objective to present an information package to wean users and preparers away from their concentration on the profit for the year figure or in more common terms away from the 'bottom line'. The profit and loss account is analysed into continuing, discontinued and acquired activities and exceptional items disclosed on the face of the profit and loss account are limited to three items, namely, profit/loss on termination of an operation, costs of a fundamental restructuring and profit/loss on disposal of fixed assets. Discussed further in Chapter 8.

FRS 4 *Capital Instruments*

This deals with the accounting treatment of complex capital instruments. It requires instruments that have an obligation to transfer cash to be classified as liabilities. It also requires finance costs to be allocated to financial periods to achieve a constant rate on the net amount outstanding. Discussed further in Chapter 12.

FRS 5 *Reporting the Substance of Transactions*

This requires items to be included in the accounts if they satisfy the Statement of Principles definition of an element, i.e. an asset, liability, ownership interest, gain, loss, contribution from owners or distribution to owners. ASB intention is that items that are elements should be included in the accounts and that disclosure is not sufficient. Effect is to deal with off-balance-sheet finance. Discussed further in Chapter 12.

FRS 6 *Acquisitions and Mergers*
This sets out the criteria for merger accounting, e.g the relative size of the combining companies is not so disparate that one company dominates by virtue of its size. Discussed further in Chapter 19.

FRS 7 *Fair Values in Acquisition Accounting*
This explains how to arrive at fair values for assets and liabilities on the acquisition of a subsidiary. It takes the view that the fair value of the assets and liabilities is the value existing at the date of the acquisition. It no longer allows companies to make provisions for future operating losses that might occur in the subsidiary. Discussed further in Chapter 19.

FRS 8 *Related Party Transactions*
This explains the disclosure required when a company enters into transactions with related parties. It allows users to identify transactions that might not be at arm's length. Discussed further in Chapter 8.

FRS 9 *Associates and Joint Ventures*
This updates SSAP 1 and provides for the first time specific guidance on dealing with joint ventures. Discussed further in Chapter 21.

FRS 10 *Goodwill and Intangible Assets*
This deals with new rules for dealing with both goodwill and intangible assets. Discussed further in Chapter 16.

FRS 11 *Impairment of Fixed Assets and Goodwill*
The objective is to ensure that any impairment is measured and recognised on a consistent basis so that fixed assets and goodwill are not reported at more than their recoverable amount. Discussed further in Chapters 14 and 16.

FRS 12 *Provisions, Contingent Liabilities and Contingent Assets*
The objective is to ensure that appropriate recognition criteria and measurement bases are applied and that sufficient information is disclosed in the notes to the financial statements to enable users to understand their nature, timing and amount. Discussed further in Chapter 12.

FRS 13 *Derivatives and other Financial Instruments: Disclosures*
The objective is to disclose information about the impact of financial instruments on the entity's risk profile, how the risks arising from financial instruments might affect the entity's performance and financial condition, and how these risks are being managed. Discussed further in Chapter 26.

FRS 14 *Earnings per share*
The FRS prescribes the basis for calculating and presenting earnings per share and methods for determining the number of shares to be included in the earnings per share calculation. Discussed further in Chapter 23.

FRS 15 *Tangible Fixed Assets*

The objective is to ensure that uniform principles are applied to the initial measurement of tangible fixed assets, that revaluations are performed on a consistent basis, depreciation is calculated in a consistent manner and recognised as the economic benefits are consumed over the assets' useful economic lives and sufficient information is disclosed to enable users to understand the impact of accounting policies. Discussed further in Chapter 14.

FRS 16 *Current Tax*

The objective is to ensure that reporting entities recognise current taxes in a consistent and transparent manner. Discussed further in Chapter 13.

FRSSE *Financial Reporting Standard for Smaller Entities*

The objective is to ensure that smaller entities provide information about the financial position, performance and financial adaptability that is useful to users in assessing the stewardship of management and for making economic decisions, recognising that the balance between users' needs in respect of stewardship and economic decision-making for smaller entities is different from that for other reporting entities.

6.5 Statements of Recommended Practice (SORPs)

In addition to SSAPs, the former ASC issued SORPs. These statements were non-mandatory on members of the profession. Unlike SSAPs, which deal with topics of fundamental and major importance, SORPs are concerned with issues that do not concern the generality of companies. However, they were issued with a view to encouraging standardisation of the topics concerned.

Two types of SORP are extant: SORPs developed by the ASC; and SORPs developed and, after approval and franking by the ASC, issued by an 'industry' group. Such SORPs are referred to as franked SORPs.

The ASB announced a change of policy in 1990 in relation to SORPs in its Bulletin issue 4. The main aspects of this announcement are as follows:

● The ASB believes that SORPs continue to have a useful part to play in financial reporting.

● The ASB's central task is the formulation of standards, and thus its limited time and resources will restrict its involvement with SORPs.

● Because SORPs do not possess the statutory implications of accounting standards, the Board believes that it is not necessary for it to adopt extant SORPs.

● In future, SORPs will not be issued by the ASB. If necessary, an industry standard will be promulgated.

● Future SORPs will be developed by bodies recognised by the ASB.

● Franked SORPs are not to be issued by the ASB. Instead, the Board will append a 'negative assurance statement' to a SORP, i.e. a statement that will not approve it, but merely confirm that it contains no fundamental points of principle which are unacceptable in the context of current accounting practice and that it does not conflict with any extant or contemplated FRS.

In 1994 the ASB issued new arrangements for handling SORPs by setting up two specialist committees to advise it on proposals for SORPs put forward by specialist bodies.

Given the highly specialist nature of certain sectors, this was clearly essential. The first of the two committees is the Financial Sector and Other Special Industries Committee, which covers insurance, investment trusts, leasing and pension schemes; the second committee covers the public and not-for-profit sectors. In addition, the ASB stated that its approach will be to satisfy itself that any industry body developing a proposed SORP is balanced and representative, and conducts the development of its proposals with due process. Otherwise the policy set out in Bulletin 4 will continue.

Excluding franked SORPs, which by definition are the specialist concern of the individual industries concerned, there are two extant SORPs: SORP 1 *Pension Scheme Accounts* and SORP 2 *Accounting for Charities.*

Franked SORPs, on the other hand, are very broad and diverse. Here is a list of the extant ones, together with the issuing body:

● As issued by the Oil Industry Accounting Committee, the SORP deals with disclosures about oil and gas exploration and production activities; accounting for such activities; accounting for abandonment costs.

● As issued by the Local Authority (Scotland) Accounts Advisory Committee, this SORP concerns accounting practices for Scottish Local Authorities.

● As issued by Accounting Standards for Local Authorities Group, this SORP deals with the application of SSAPs to local authorities in England and Wales.

● As issued by the Committee of Vice Chancellors and principals, this SORP concerns accounting for universities.

This gives an idea of the vast need for accounting standards of one kind or another, especially when one realises that additional SORPs are required for other industries such as agriculture, banking, insurance and unit trusts.

6.6 International Accounting Standards (IASs)

The ASB makes standards to be applied to UK and Republic of Ireland group financial statements, including any overseas entities that are part of those financial statements. Accounting standards are not intended to apply to financial statements prepared overseas for local purposes.

The International Accounting Standards Committee (IASC), which came into existence in June 1973 in furtherance of an agreement by the accountancy bodies of Australia, Canada, France, Germany, Japan, Mexico, the Netherlands, the UK, Ireland and the USA, is active on the international scene. A revised agreement was signed in 1982.

The objectives of the IASC are set out in its constitution:

● To formulate and publish, in the public interest, accounting standards to be observed in the presentation of financial statements and to promote their world-wide acceptance and observance.

● To work generally for the improvement and harmonisation of regulations, accounting standards and procedures relating to the presentation of financial statements.

There is a growing closeness between the work of the IASC and national bodies such as the ASB. In formulating IAS on new subjects, the IASC 'endeavours not to make International Accounting Standards so complex that they cannot be applied effectively on a world-wide basis'. The ASB in its foreword to *Accounting Standards* states that: 'FRSs are formulated with due regard to international developments. The Board supports the IASC in its aim to harmonise international financial reporting. As part of this support an FRS contains a section explaining how it relates to the International Accounting Standard (IAS) dealing with the same topic. In most cases, compliance with an FRS automatically ensures compliance with the relevant IAS.'

At the twentieth anniversary of the IASC, the chairman of the Hundred Group of Finance Directors made the following comments:

> the purpose of an international standard must be to make access to capital markets as easy and straightforward as possible. It is not primarily to do with regulation, or prudence, or any of the various requirements that apply in individual countries for historical or cultural reasons. We should remember that there are many differences between markets, reporting and otherwise, which do not need to be harmonised, they simply need to be understood by people putting up new capital overseas.[13]

These comments emphasise that financial reports are seen by finance directors as an exercise in communication.

During the five years up to 1995 the ASB concentrated its energies on ending financial reporting abuses. It saw its role as one of enforcing national accounting treatments within the UK that were congruent with the underlying commercial nature of a transaction and represented its substance.

Following its success in attacking these abuses, the ASB became more outward-looking in 1995. In the UK, it began to work more closely with the Auditing Practices Board and, on the international scene, it has expressed a wish to make its views known to the International Accounting Standards Committee (IASC).

As far as auditing is concerned, it is recognised that, as FRSs become more complex, it is essential to ensure that auditors can verify their application – a good example of this was the agreed approach taken to Related Party Transactions.

On the international scene, the ASB has stated that it wishes to develop ideas ahead of the IASC, but not to go to standard until the IASC position is clear. The ultimate aim for the ASB is that compliance with UK standards means that a company can obtain a stock exchange listing anywhere in the world.

Why is the ASB suddenly more interested in the IASC?

The ASB has been influenced in its international stance by the agreement reached in 1995 between the IASC and the International Organisation of Securities Commissions (IOSCO) which resulted in a core set of international standards by 1999. If International Accounting Standards (IASs) became the international language, national standard-setters would be made redundant. It was as a protection against being marginalised that the ASB sought closer links with the IASC to ensure that national standards were not issued which deviated from subsequent IASC standards. Without links to the national bodies there is a risk that the IASC will become just an ivory tower.

6.7 EU directives

The EU has undertaken the harmonisation of company law within the Union. The Council of Ministers adopts a draft directive placed before it by the EU Commission. The member states then have a fixed time in which to incorporate the provisions of the directive into their own national legislation. Directives of particular importance to the accountancy profession have been the Fourth, Seventh and Eighth.

6.7.1 Fourth Directive

The Fourth Directive was drafted in 1971, adopted in 1978 and enacted in the UK via the Companies Act 1981 (now incorporated in the consolidating Companies Act 1985). It legalised a standard format for the profit and loss accounts and balance sheets of companies and introduced the override concept of true and fair. The true and fair concept says that, if the application of statute is likely to prejudice the true and fair view, the directors are obliged in law to waive the provisions of the Act in order to ensure that the accounts give a true and fair view. In the UK, the true and fair view has long been the dominant factor and it was given the force of law in the Companies Act 1947.

6.7.2 Seventh Directive

The Seventh Directive was issued in 1976, adopted in 1983 and enacted in the UK in the Companies Act 1989. It mainly concerns the preparation of consolidated accounts.

6.7.3 Eighth Directive

The Eighth Directive was issued in 1984 and member states had until 1988 to implement it. It concerns the regulation of auditors and was enacted in the UK in the Companies Act 1989.

Harmonisation is important. In recognition of this the IASC began its Comparability Improvement Project in 1987 with the aim of reducing or eliminating alternative accounting treatments. As a result, the IASC has revised a number of its accounting standards with effect from January 1995. For example, IAS 9 *Research and Development Costs* was revised so that the option of expensing development costs available under UK GAAP was removed, and, if development costs are eligible for deferral, they must be recognised as an asset and allocated on a systematic basis to future periods.

6.7.4 EU Financial Reporting Strategy: the way forward

It is recognised that action is required in the field of financial reporting to enhance comparability of financial statements in order to accelerate the completion of a single securities market. It is proposed that:

Before the end of 2000: the Commission will present a formal proposal requiring all listed EU companies to prepare their consolidated accounts in accordance with one single set of accounting standards, namely International Accounting Standards (IAS) to come into effect from 2005 at the latest.

Before the end of 2001: the Commission will bring forward a proposal to modernise the Accounting Directives so they can remain the basis for financial reporting for all limited liability companies.

6.8 The Stock Exchange

The Stock Exchange was probably the earliest promulgator of rules and regulations governing financial statements. Many of its requirements have been incorporated into statute and standards, although there are still additional demands that are not yet in the statute or standard. For example, the Stock Exchange requires interim accounts and for information to be published in the national press.

Any public company wishing to have its shares bought and sold on the Stock Exchange must first secure what is called a **quotation** or **listing** on the Exchange. Securing such a listing is not a formality. The protection of prospective shareholders is the prime objective of the Exchange and in furtherance of this objective a company wishing to be listed is subjected to a prolonged and deep investigation. The investigation looks at its history, the calibre of its management, its financial condition, its future prospects and its constitution. A successful applicant must then conform with the rules of the Stock Exchange. These rules are incorporated in the *Stock Exchange (Listing) Regulations and its Admission of Securities to Listing*.

The rules contain a section known as 'Continuing Obligations'. The objective is to control the flow of information that could be reasonably expected to have an immediate impact on the company's share price. This includes routine information such as profit and dividend announcements; and exceptional matters such as the appointment or resignation of directors. Strict observance of the obligations is a prime requisite for a fair and orderly securities market. The guiding principle is that price-sensitive information must be released in a way that ensures all users have simultaneous access to the same information.

With this aim in mind the Stock Exchange lays down regulations concerning the listed company's published accounts, preliminary profit statement and public pronouncements. However, with the London Stock Exchange proposing to turn itself into a commercial company, the government is planning to transfer its listing authority function to the FSA.[14]

6.8.1 Published accounts

The annual accounts and report must be sent to the shareholders within six months of the end of the financial year. The directors' report must contain, *inter alia*, the following information:

● significant departures from SSAPs and the reasons for them;
● explanation of material variations between actual profit and published profit forecast;
● analysis of geographical areas of turnover and contribution to trading profit from trading operations outside the UK. This is now also covered in SSAP 25;
● name of principal country in which each subsidiary operates;
● information regarding associated companies showing: principal country in which the associate operates; particulars of share and loan capitals of the associate; and the percentage of loan capital in which the listed company has an interest;
● a statement of outstanding bank loans and overdrafts and any other borrowings outstanding at the balance sheet date analysed over repayable time-spans, e.g. less than 1 year, 1–2 years;
● information regarding the capitalisation of interest; directors' shareholdings; members holding more than 5% of the issued capital; details of significant contracts; waived remuneration and waived dividends.

6.8.2 Interim information

Interim reports must be produced. These must be sent to members or inserted as advertisements in two national daily newspapers. Any preliminary profit announcement must be advertised. The ASB has issued 'best practice' Statements for both Interim Reports and Preliminary Announcements. These are discussed further in para 6.11 below.

6.8.3 Public announcements

Share-price-sensitive information must be notified to the Stock Exchange's Company Announcements Office as soon as practical. The latter also needs to be informed of matters such as proposed changes in capital structure.

6.9 Non-mandatory recommendations

The number of non-mandatory 'requirements' is growing. Initially there was only the professional bodies' guidance to their members. This has been extended with the ASB *Operating and Financial Review* document, the ASB *Interim Report* Statement and the Combined Code.

6.9.1 Professional bodies

Each of the accounting bodies issues recommendations to its members on topics of professional interest. For example, the Association of Certified Accountants issues guidance notes on technical matters relating to the presentation of financial statements, the preparation of accounts from incomplete records and the determination of realised profits and disclosure of distributable profits in the context of the Companies Acts.

6.9.2 The Operating and Financial Review

The *Operating and Financial Review* (OFR)[15] statement was issued by the ASB in 1993 to encourage the development of best practice. It is intended to have persuasive rather than mandatory force. The format is not prescriptive and directors are encouraged to develop the presentation of their OFR in a way that best complements the format of their annual accounts. It is not an accounting standard and is mainly for listed companies for which its use has been recommended by the Financial Reporting Council, the Hundred Group of Finance Directors and the London Stock Exchange.

The OFR is intended to provide a discussion and interpretation of the main factors and uncertainties of the business and the structure of its financing. While it is not a forecast, it should bring out those aspects of the year under review that are relevant to an assessment of future prospects, to provide a more consistent foundation for investment decisions. Companies are not required to disclose information that would allow competitors to damage their business.

Because the intention is to assist investors, the OFR should not be merely a numerical analysis. The emphasis is on providing a readily understood discussion that deals with both good and bad aspects of the business; that comments on trends, factors and uncertainties that have affected or will affect the results; and that explains the reasons for and the effect of changes in accounting policies.

The statement also offers detailed guidance to support these general principles. For example, a discussion of factors affecting future results could include capital expenditure and the likely benefits expected from it; a discussion of uncertainties affecting future results could include scarcity of raw materials, dependence on major suppliers, skill shortages and product liability.

The financial review part of the statement is intended to explain the capital structure of the business, its treasury policy and the dynamics of its financial position – its sources of liquidity and their application, including the implications of the financing requirements arising from its capital expenditure plans.

How successful has OFR been in encouraging companies to disclose risk?

The ASB recommended that companies identify **their principal risks** and comment on the **approach to managing these risks and, in qualitative terms, the nature of the potential impact on results**.

It is important, for example, to be aware of how a company manages financial risk. In the age of multinational accounting and economic cycles, important factors are the currencies in which borrowings are made, the use of financial instruments for hedging purposes and the current liquidity position. Risks relating to financial instruments have been the subject of FRS 13 because of the perceived high risks attached to financial instruments. The following is a brief extract from the 1999 accounts of BOC:

Management of financial risk
The board of directors sets the treasury policies and objectives of the Group which includes controls over the procedures used to manage currency, interest rate and credit risk.

Interest rate risk
In order to manage interest rate risk the Group maintains both floating rate and fixed rate debt. At present there is a 35:65 ratio (1998: 42:58) between floating rate and fixed rate net debt.

How successful has OFR been in informing investors of risk?

Although the reporting of risks attaching to financial instruments is being addressed, the reporting of business risks and how management is dealing with them is woefully lacking. The OFR has, in general, been treated as a PR document that is bland with little significant effort to highlight in advance the real sources of uncertainties that have the major impacts on returns. The previous OFR of every company that reports **unexpected** worsening of turnover, profits or liquidity should be examined to determine how these risks were presented in the annual report. Invariably there is little comment until after the event.

How could OFR be improved?

● Make mandatory and more prescriptive
In a research report *Operating and Financial Reviews: Views of Analysts and Institutional Investors*, some analysts believed the OFR would contain useful information, but that market forces would not be sufficient to get companies to produce high-quality reports on a voluntary basis; some believed that an entirely new set of audit skills was needed to audit an OFR properly.[16]

● Make subject to true and fair view
The view has been put forward (Zeff)[17] that whilst 'one of the widely applauded leadership steps the ASB has taken is the recommendation that companies include an operating and financial review in their annual reports there is a need for the OFR to be made mandatory and thus subject to the true and fair view'.

● Disclose business risks more fairly to smaller investors
At present, there is a Stock Exchange requirement that listed companies should disclose risks which are likely to have a material impact on earnings and which are unlikely to be anticipated by the general public. This does not mean that they appear in the OFR. Analysts rely instead on risk reporting by companies at company briefings and this information is not available to the smaller shareholder in a timely manner.

This is a clear indication that it is unrealistic to expect voluntary early disclosure of significant risk without some additional external pressure. This external pressure is now coming from the ICAEW's Financial Reporting Committee which in 1997 produced a discussion paper, *Financial Reporting of Risk – Proposals for a Statement of Business Risk*.

This paper proposes that there should be an additional report in which directors identify key risks, explain how they measure them and how they propose to deal with them. Such a report would allow investors to understand the uncertainties that their board faces, e.g. cheap foreign imports, difficulty in obtaining supplies of components and raw materials, effect of adverse publicity about products, expiry of patents for major products. There would, of course, need to be the normal relief from reporting commercially sensitive information, e.g. early negotiations to establish trading alliances where a company's major product is losing the protection of patents.

A Consultation Document from The Company Law Review Steering Committee issued in March 2000 proposes in para 5.79 that there should be a New Mandatory OFR containing:

● a review by the directors of the company's operations and finances modelled on current ASB guidance and best practice
● a discussion and analysis of the performance of the business and main trends and factors
    ● underlying the results and financial position, and
    ● likely to affect future performance.

The objective is to enable users to assess the strategies adopted by the business and the potential for successfully achieving them.

The Document further proposes that the OFR should include as mandatory items:

● A fair review of the company's business over the year, operating performance, its position at the year end and material post-year end events with details of:
    ● market changes
    ● new products
    ● changes in market positioning, turnover and margins
    ● new and discontinued products and services
    ● acquisitions and disposals.
● The company's purpose, strategy and principal drivers to allow users to see:
    ● the criteria by reference to which its success is evaluated
    ● the source from which it derives its success
    ● segmental performance against objectives
    ● competitive positioning.

The Document also proposes further disclosures of material for the following:

● An account of the company's key relationships with employees, customers, suppliers and others on which its success depends, with details of:
    ● employment policies and practices
    ● policies on creditor payment.
● Corporate governance – values and structures, with details of:
    ● company's structures for securing an effective working relationship between members, directors and senior management.
● Dynamics of business such as trends and uncertainties which may affect future performance or investment programmes with details of risks and opportunities:
    ● competition and customer/supplier dependency
    ● technological change
    ● financial risks
    ● environmental costs and liabilities
    ● investment in training, research and development, brands, intellectual property.

● Environmental policies and performance, including:
  ● compliance with regulations.

● Policies and performance on community, social, ethical and reputational issues.

● Receipts from, and returns to, shareholders covering distributions and distribution policy and share repurchases.

The above appears detailed but the Document is careful to emphasise that a substantial measure of discretion has been left for directors to determine how usefully to analyse and assess their business and deliberately avoids overprescription, with the risk that involves of rigidity and a 'cookbook' approach.

The proposals appear to follow existing ASB guidelines and best practice and will be welcomed by existing and potential investors.

6.10   The Combined Code[18]

6.10.1   The Cadbury Committee Report[19]

The process started in 1991 with the setting up by the Financial Reporting Council, the London Stock Exchange and the accounting profession of the Cadbury Committee to report on the financial aspects of corporate governance. A year later the committee produced the Cadbury Committee Report, which set out a voluntary Code of Best Practice based on openness, integrity and accountability.

Although the Code was voluntary, the board of directors were responsible for applying its provisions, stating whether the accounts comply with the Code, and explaining if they did not.

The Code made proposals in four areas relating to (1) the board of directors, (2) non-executive directors, (3) executive directors and (4) controls and reporting. The general thrust of the proposals was that there should be key safeguards. These were as follows:

● The board should retain control over important decisions such as major capital expenditure programmes, bank borrowings and material loans.

● Non-executive directors should be able to exert significant influence by virtue of number and experience.

● Audit committees consisting of non-executive directors should have clear terms of reference.

● The position of chairman should be separate from that of chief executive.

● Financial reporting and auditing systems should provide full disclosure at an appropriate time to affect decisions.

The Cadbury Committee Report made its points in a general terms. For example, in the area of Board of Directors, it proposed:

1.1 The board should meet regularly, retain full and effective control over the company and monitor the executive management.

1.2 There should be a clearly accepted division of responsibilities at the head of a company, which will ensure a balance of power and authority, such that no one individual has unfettered powers of decision. Where the chairman is also the chief executive, it is essential that there should be a strong and independent element on the board, with a recognised senior member.

1.3 The board should include non-executive directors of sufficient calibre and number for their views to carry significant weight in the board's decisions.

1.4 The board should have a formal schedule of matters specifically reserved to it for decision to ensure that the direction and control of the company is firmly in its hands.

1.5 There should be an agreed procedure for directors in the furtherance of their duties to take independent professional advice if necessary, at the company's expense.

1.6 All directors should have access to the advice and services of the company secretary, who is responsible to the board for ensuring that board procedures are followed and that applicable rules and regulations are complied with. Any question of the removal of the company secretary should be a matter for the board as a whole.

The Cadbury Committee Report of 1992 was followed by the Greenbury Report in 1995 and the Hampel Report in 1998. The Combined Code is derived from the Cadbury, Greenbury and Hampel Reports.

6.10.2 The structure of The Combined Code

The Code has made an interesting development by separating its proposals into 2 Parts:

● Part 1 containing *Principles of Good Governance*
● Part 2 containing *Codes of Best Practice*

Disclosure statement

The distinction between *Principles* and *Codes* is important because companies will be required to present their disclosure statement in two parts.

In the first part, the company will be required *to report on how it applies the Principles*. The Combined Code does not prescribe the form or content of this report and companies are encouraged to describe how they arrived at their approach.

In the second part, companies will be required *to confirm that they comply with the Code provisions* or to explain where they have not complied.

The 2 Sections of The Combined Code

Part 1 and Part 2 are divided into 2 Sections:

● Section 1 is applicable to listed companies
  ● Compliance will be enforced by the London Stock Exchange (LSE)
● Section 2 is applicable to institutional shareholders with regard to their voting, dialogue with companies and evaluation of a company's governance arrangements
  ● Compliance is not the responsibility of the LSE and the Committee have commended it to organisations representing institutional shareholders with the hope that at least the major institutions will voluntarily disclose to their clients and the public the extent to which they are able to give effect to these provisions.

We will consider in this chapter i.e. the Principles in Part 1 and the detailed Code Provisions in Part 2 relating to listed companies i.e concentrating on Section 1. We will consider institutional shareholders in Chapter 28.

6.10.3   Principles of good governance relating to listed companies

The Code deals with Principles under 4 headings:

A: Directors
B: Directors' Remuneration
C: Relations with shareholders
D: Accountability and Audit

Directors, Directors' Remuneration and Accountabilty and Audit featured in the Cadbury Report but Principles for Relations with shareholders is new.

We will briefly consider two of the headings A: Directors and D: Accountability and Audit.

6.10.4   Directors

We can see from 6.10.1 above that the content of Section A: *Directors* is largely based on the Cadbury Report. However, there is now the division into Principles and detailed Code Provisions.

Directors – Principles

There are 6 Principles relating to Directors, namely:

A1.   The Board
The board should lead and control effectively

At the start of each year, directors will need to consider the question of how this applies to their individual company. How regularly should the board meet (this will depend on factors such as the role of subcommittees)? How much authority has been delegated? How much and how frequently should information flow to and from the board, given the degree of delegation?

At the year-end, auditors need to form an opinion on whether the company has complied with the Code. In respect to point A1, they would review the frequency of meetings, degree of delegation and adequacy of information flows. However, effective compliance with point A1 requires more than this: the auditors would assess the board's overall response to the spirit of the Code, e.g. determining whether it has appointed high-calibre non-executive directors.

A2.   Chairman and CEO
These roles should be separate with the Chairman running the Board and the CEO running the company's business

The chief executive is responsible for implementing board decisions. The chairman is responsible for seeking a balanced board, ensuring that all relevant issues are put before it and all members participate. When the roles are not separated and there is no strong independent element on the board, difficulties can arise. For example, an analysis of forty-five companies that went into receivership in 1989 and 1990 indicated that over 60 per cent of them had a combined chairman and chief executive, and in most of these cases there was evidence of a single dominant character.

The Code has been strengthened since the Cadbury Committee which accepted the situation and proposed that, where the Chairman is also the Chief Executive, there should be a strong and independent element on the Board.

A3. Board Balance
> *The Board should include a balance of executive and non-executive directors so that no individual or small group can dominate the board.*

The effectiveness of non-executive directors can be significantly affected by the extent to which they receive briefings and the extent to which they contribute to work on sub-committees. It is the board's responsibility as a whole to ensure that they are able to make effective inputs.

The emphasis is on bringing in strong, independent voices. A key consideration with regard to independence is that they should not be tied into the company's performance financially, e.g. by holding share options or being pensionable by the company.

A4. Supply of information
> *The board should be supplied in a timely manner with information in a form and of a quality appropriate to enable it to discharge its duties.*

Just as with non-executive directors, the effectiveness of executive directors can be significantly affected by the extent to which they receive briefings and the extent to which they contribute to work on subcommittees

A5. Appointments to the Board
> *Appointments to the Board should be formal and transparent.*

A6. Re-election
> *All directors should submit themselves to re-election at regular intervals and at least every three years.*

Directors – Code Provisions

The Code Provisions relating to Principles A2–A6 include the following:

A2. Chairman and CEO
- Any decision to combine the roles should be publicly justified.

A3. Board Balance
- The non-executive directors should be not less than one third of the board and of sufficient calibre that their views carry significant weight.
- The majority should be independent of management and free from any relationship that would interfere with their independent judgement.
- Shareholders should be informed as to which of the non-executive directors are independent.

A4. Supply of information
- Directors should ensure that they obtain from management all the information that they consider timely and appropriate to be able to contribute at meetings.
- They should recognise that management may not voluntarily produce all the information that they need.

A5. Appointments to the Board
- Unless the board is small there should be a nominations committee.
- The majority of its members should be non-executive directors.
- The chairman should be either the Chairman of the company or a non-executive director.

A6. Re-election

- All directors should submit themselves to re-election at least every three years.
- All new director appointments should be subject to shareholder election at the first opportunity after their appointment.

We will now consider the Principle and Code Provisions relating to the Board. The Combined Code sets out in Part 1 the **Principle** relating to A1 (the Board) as follows:

A1. The Board

Every listed company should be headed by an effective board which should lead and control.

The Combined Code then sets out in Part 2 the **Code Provisions** (A1.1–A1.6) relating to this Principle as follows:

A1.1 The board should meet regularly.

At the start of each year, directors will need to consider the question of how this applies to their individual company. How regularly should the board meet (this will depend on factors such as the role of subcommittees)? How much authority has been delegated? How much and how frequently should information flow to and from the board, given the degree of delegation?

A1.2 The board should have a formal schedule of matters specifically reserved to it for decision.

Such items typically include approval of capital projects, degree of delegated powers, corporate strategy, treasury and risk management. Many of these items also featured in the ASB's *Operating and Financial Review* requirements discussed above.

A1.3 There should be a procedure for directors to take independent professional advice if necessary.

The procedure for obtaining such advice should be set out in the director's letter of engagement.

A1.4 All directors should have access to the advice and services of the company secretary.

The procedure for obtaining such advice should be set out in the director's letter of engagement.

A1.5 All directors should bring an independent judgement to bear on issues of strategy, performance, resources (including key appointments) and standards of conduct.

This requires all directors to ensure that they are properly briefed and to recognise that they have a responsibility for each of the elements in A1.5 ranging from long-term strategy, earnings, tangible and intangible assets and the business ethics and culture of the company.

A1.6 Every director should receive appropriate training.

This was a proposal of the Hampel Committee. It is necessary given the Principle that the company should be headed by an effective board which should lead and control, agree strategy, approve capital expenditure and operating budgets and be aware of when to seek professional advice.

The nature of the training will vary with circumstances. Some training may best be given on formal courses e.g. to understand the legal liabilities of a director and to understand financial data that should be presented at Board level. However, there are difficulties in that companies are of different size and subject to different risks which means that the training needs of directors are not uniform.

In a small company it may be that the company requires specialist training to supplement the formal e.g. identifying health and safety risks is one such area. The directors may be inhibited from pursuing this training need through ignorance or cash flow concerns about the action that might be needed to reduce the risks.

In a medium-sized company there might well be established procedures in place for dealing with health and safety risks, possibly with specialists employed within the company. Its training needs may be very different, for example the dominant strategy might be to float the company in say 2 to 3 years' time. This type of training need might be satisfied by the appointment of a non-executive director with experience of floating a company to hand-hold in the period up to flotation together with the appointment of a Finance Director for the two years prior to flotation.

In large companies there is greater ability to delegate responsibilities for instance by appointment of internal auditors to monitor the operation of internal control procedures and also to obtain expert advice. The need for this was recognised in the Cadbury Report which stipulated that there should be an agreed procedure for directors in the furtherance of their duties to take independent professional advice if necessary, at the company's expense.

6.10.5 Accountability and Audit

The Cadbury Committee Report

The Cadbury Committee Report proposals for **Reporting and Controls** were as follows:

4.1 It is the board's duty to present a balanced and understandable assessment of the company's position.

4.2 The board should ensure that an objective and professional relationship is maintained with the auditors.

4.3 The board should establish an audit committee of at least three non-executive directors with written terms of reference which deal clearly with its authority and duties.

4.4 The directors should explain their responsibility for preparing the accounts next to a statement by the auditors about their reporting responsibilities.

4.5 The directors should report on the effectiveness of the company's system of internal control.

4.6 The directors should report that the business is a going concern, with supporting assumptions or qualifications as necessary.

The Combined Code

The Combined Code deals with this area under the heading 'Accountability and Audit'. We will now consider the Principles and Code Provisions relating to Accountability and Audit. The Combined Code sets out in Part 1 the **Principles** and in Part 2 the **Provisions** as follows:

Accountability and Audit – Principles and Code Provisions

There are 3 Principles relating to Accountability and Audit, namely D1 Financial Reporting, D2 Internal Control and D3 Audit Committee and Auditors. We will consider each briefly:

D1. Financial Reporting
The board should present a balanced and understandable assessment of the company's position and prospects.

The ASB's *Operating and Financial Review* has provided the detail to support this requirement. The ASB has followed the same philosophy as the committee in requiring understandable narrative rather than a simple numerical analysis.

The Code Provisions set out in Part 2 relating to this Principle are as follows:

D1.1 The directors should explain their responsibility for preparing the accounts and there should be a statement by the auditors about their reporting responsibilities.

This requirement is intended to make clear to the users of the accounts that the directors alone are responsible for the preparation of the financial statements, and not the auditors. This is already standard practice..

D1.2 The board's responsibility to present a balanced and understandable assessment extends to interim and price-sensitive public reports and reports to regulators as well as information required to be presented by statutory requirements.

Interim Reports are considered further in 6.11 below.

D1.3 The directors should report that the business is a going concern, with supporting assumptions or qualifications as necessary.

A working group set up by the Institute of Chartered Accountants in England and Wales, the Institute of Chartered Accountants in Scotland and the Hundred Group of Finance Directors issued draft guidance in May 1993. However, this guidance required a view to be taken on future events, which gave rise to discussion about how long into the future it is reasonable to expect directors and auditors to look.

Auditors were worried that their liability could be unrealistically increased if they were required to confirm that a company would not fail at a future date. There was a need to balance the level of the auditor's risk with the level of shareholder expectation that an unqualified audit report meant that all was, and would continue to be, well.

After much discussion, the Auditing Practices Board issued SAS 130 *The Going Concern Basis in Financial Statements* in November 1994, which gave guidance to auditors. The ASB recognised that there was an audit duty to obtain audit evidence that a business was a going concern, and in SAS 130 it stated that:

● The audit of the going concern should be an active rather than a passive audit procedure which means that the auditor must carry out checks even if the company appears financially healthy at the balance sheet date. Prior to the issue of SAS 130 there were many auditors who carried out little audit investigation of viability if the present position looked financially sound. This is no longer acceptable.

● The going concern period should in general be for one year after the date of the balance sheet and, if it is actually less than a year, this should be highlighted within an unqualified audit opinion. During the exposure draft stage of SAS 130 representations were made that it was not feasible to set a specific period of one year for all companies and that the period should reflect the commercial reality. The compromise has been to require a statement from the directors if the period is actually less than one year.

● The adequacy of the means by which the directors have satisfied themselves that it is appropriate to adopt the going concern basis should be assessed. This would entail confirming that there is an adequate system of budgets and forecasts which produce reliable estimates.

The following is an extract from the Corporate Governance statement of the directors of Magnum Power plc in their May 1997 accounts:

Going Concern

The directors consider that, in preparing the financial statements, they have taken into account all information that could reasonably be expected to be available. On this basis, they consider that it is appropriate to prepare the financial statements on a going concern basis. Whilst the Group is better funded than at a similar juncture in the previous financial year, the directors have continued to assume that further orders will be awarded to the Group and/or that additional financial support can be obtained. There can be no guarantee that such additional financial support will be available when required by the Group. The financial statements do not include any adjustments which would result if further orders were not awarded to the Group or if such additional finical support were not available.

The auditors in their Auditors' Report consider and report on the adequacy of the disclosure as follows:

Going Concern

In forming our opinion, we have considered the adequacy of the disclosure relating to the basis of preparing the financial statements, and the future prospects of the Group. The Group's trading is still at an early stage and there remains a reasonable degree of uncertainty regarding future sales projections which is not uncommon for a business at the Group's stage of development. It is likely that the Group will require to secure additional finance within the next twelve months, to fund its continuing development. There can be no guarantee that such finance will become available when required by the Group. In view of the significance of these uncertainties, we consider that they should be drawn to your attention, but our opinion set out below is not qualified in this respect.

D2. Internal Control Principle
The board should maintain a sound system of internal control to safeguard shareholders' investment and the company's assets.

The Code Provisions relating to D2 include:

- They should, at least annually, review the effectiveness of the system of internal control, including financial, operational and compliance controls and risk management.
- They should periodically review the need for an internal audit function if they do not have one already.

The defining of directors' and auditors' responsibility in relation to internal control has been difficult. Following the Cadbury Report directors have included in the Statement of Directors Responsibilities an acknowledgement as, for example, in the following extract from the Body Shop International 1994 Annual Report:

'They are responsible for safeguarding the assets of the Company and hence for taking reasonable steps for the prevention and detection of fraud and other irregularities … The Board of Directors supports the principles of the Code of Best Practice and is committed to integrity and accountability in the stewardship of the Group's affairs'.

This is not very informative for the reader and gives no indication of the nature of the steps taken by the Company.

In 1997 the Hampel Report addressed this by concluding that the steps should include responsibility for monitoring non-financial and financial risks and controls. The

Hampel approach was not prescriptive and there was a need for guidance on how directors were to apply the Hampel reccomendations. Proposals for such guidance are contained in the Turnbull Commitee's report *'Internal Control: Guidance for Directors of Listed Companies incorporated in the United Kingdom'* published in April 1999.

The Turnbull Report emphasis is on *risk management* and it takes the view that it is the board of directors which should regularly assure itself that appropriate processes are functioning effectively to monitor risk i.e. that key risks have been identified, evaluated and managed, that the system of internal control has been effective and that any weaknesses have been addressed. The emphasis is on procedures that enable a company to respond to significant risks, Directors will be required to disclose in the Annual Report that such processes are in place and to report any material losses arising as a result of any weaknesses.

The extension of directors responsibilities to include monitoring non-financial risks might pose difficulties for non-executive directors whose expertise might lie in assessing financial risk and who might not be closely aware of controls appropriate as ethical, compliance, environmental and operational controls.

The role of external auditors

External auditors have been reluctant to give an opinion that a company has an effective internal control system because a system is peculiar to an individual company and typically varies in quality across a company making it difficult to give an overall opinion on 'the system'. The Turnbull Report proposal that directors should adopt a risk based approach means that the auditors can report on the process and action taken in respect of unacceptable levels of risk (as defined by the directors).

Future developments

Risk management is in an evolutionary stage and it will be interesting to see how it is exercised in practice. The Hampel and Turnbull Reports have set the scene and it is now for interested parties such as Directors, Auditors, Stakeholders to respond and for companies to develop the processes. At that point it will become clearer what constitutes Best Practice e.g. should the process of internal control be simply designed to limit risks that result in losses or should it also include identifying opportunities that have been missed. It is standard practice to carry out SWOT analysis within companies to identify Strengths, Weaknesses, Opportunities and Threats and it could well be that this could form the basis of risk management.

D3. Audit Committee and Auditors Principle
The board should establish formal and transparent arrangements for considering how they should apply the financial reporting and internal control principles and for maintaining an appropriate relationship with the company's auditors.

In some companies the auditors and board have become too close. The committee's view is that an audit committee comprising non-executive directors could assist in maintaining objectivity. The Cadbury Report had attached great importance to audit committees and outlined specimen terms of reference, including the appointment of auditors, fixing the level of their fees, the nature and scope of the audit, the external auditors' management letter and the executive action taken by the company, and the nature and scope of the internal audit function.

The Code Provisions relating to D3 include:

● The board should establish an audit committee made up of a majority of independent non-executive directors with written terms of reference setting out authority and duties.

● The audit committee should review the scope and results of the audit, its cost effectiveness and the independence and objectivity of the external auditors.

● Where the external auditors supply a substantial volume of non-audit services the committee need to keep under review the balance of maintenance of objectivity and value for money.

6.11 Interim reports following Cadbury

The Cadbury Committee recommended in 1992 that the ASB, in conjunction with the London Stock Exchange, should clarify the accounting principles that companies should follow in preparing Interim Reports. At the request of the ASB, the Financial Reporting Committee of the ICAEW published a consultative paper in 1993 which formed the basis for the ASB's 1996 Exposure Draft. The Exposure Draft was developed in consultation with the London Stock Exchange, The Hundred Group of Finance Directors, the Institute of Investment Management and Research, the National Association of Pension Funds, the Big Six accounting firms and the Auditing Practices Board.

There has also been significant academic research, e.g. *Financial Reporting 1993–4: A Survey of UK Reporting Practice* by Hussey and Woolfe published by the Institute of Chartered Accountants in England and Wales.[20]

As Sir David Tweedie commented 'Producing the ASB Statement has been very much a co-operative effort. It carries the commendation of the Financial Reporting Council, the Hundred Group and both the London and Irish Stock Exchanges. The authoritative backing of these bodies gives the Statement the best possible start in life and we greatly appreciate their support.'

In 1998 the ASB published its 'best practice' Statement on *Interim Reports*.[21] Like the Operating and Financial Review it is non-mandatory.

What is best practice?

● A shorter period for publishing.
The London Stock Exchange allowed 4 months to publish. The ASB propose that this should be reduced to 2 months.

● Use of the **discrete** method
The ASB does not support the **integral** approach which is sometimes followed. Under this approach the interim report is merely a proportion of the estimate of the full year's results.

Instead, it favours the **discrete** method which uses the same measurement and recognition bases and accounting policies as used in the annual accounts. Consequently, the Interim Report should show what actually happened in the period; e.g. seasonal businesses will disclose results which differ markedly between the first half and second half of the year.

What does the ASB recommend to appear in *Interim Reports*?

The Statement recommends that interim reports should contain:

(i) **A management commentary** to highlight and explain significant events and trends as required already by the London Stock Exchange but, in addition, to follow the end of year practice by disclosing turnover and profit by segment and the turnover and profits of discontinued operations and acquisitions.

(ii) **A summarised profit and loss account and balance sheet** with classifications consistent with the year-end accounts and supported by a **Statement of Total Recognised Gains and Losses**.

(iii) **A summarised cash flow statement** using FRS 1 *Cash Flow Statement* headings and reconciling operating profit to operating cash flow and cash in period to movement in net debt.

The Statement was much needed. Current practice varied widely and did not always show what actually happened in the period and did not provide investors with information that was either timely or relevant. The Statement should go a long way towards securing a general improvement in consistency, comparability and quality of interim reporting. It reflects a welcome and fruitful collaborative exercise.[22]

As a result of the Statement companies are encouraged to highlight and explain the most relevant and appropriate figures in their interim reports, to give a succinct but balanced picture with an emphasis on reporting trends and the impact of events and activities since the last full annual report.

The ASB has also addressed preliminary announcements and issued a 'best practice' Statement on *Preliminary Announcements* in 1997 aimed at improving the timeliness, quality, relevance and consistency of preliminary announcements whilst complying with the need for reliability.

Will there be further developments?[23]

The Securities and Exchange Commission in the US requires listed companies to publish quarterly reports and UK companies with US listing are already complying. A similar requirement will no doubt be made for UK listed companies to keep London abreast of best international practice. Although preliminary and interim results are highly price-sensitive, there has been no requirement for them to be audited or reviewed. In the US there is a suggestion that the quarterly reports should be reviewed and, if adopted, a review by the auditors of UK companies would seem to be a natural sequel.

Has the Cadbury Report resolved the problems of corporate governance?

Critics could argue with some justification that it is futile to rely on non-executive directors to monitor executive directors. Executive and non-executive directors are perceived to be playing musical chairs at each other's board of directors with little time or facility for any detailed role. For example, a minister of the Crown who acted as non-executive director for a company in the defence industry has gone on record that he was unaware of major business decisions made by the company. This only adds force to the view that they are engaged only for their contacts and not for any major corporate governance role. Even executive directors question whether it is feasible for part-time directors to make any valid comment on the work of the full-time professional directors, and successful entrepreneurs have been known to see them simply as a waste of money. However, there is clearly important progress being made by the ASB in developing voluntary 'best practice' statements such as *Interim Reports*.

An indication[24] that the ASB's best practice statement is taking effect is provided by a survey of interim reports comparing 1995 with 1999 which showed that 78% of companies now give cash flow information (1995: 61%) and there has been an increase in explanatory narrative sections, with 38% of companies exceeding 1,000 words (1995: 14%).

6.12 Evaluation of effectiveness of mandatory regulations

The events in the Sketchley plc take-over in 1990 suggest that mandatory regulations will not be effective.[25]

- In November 1989 Sketchley reported a fall in pre-tax profits for the half year ended 30 December 1989 from £7.2m to £5.4m.

- In February 1990 Godfrey Davis Holdings made a bid to take over Sketchley.

- In March 1990 Sketchley issued a defence document forecasting pre-tax profits for the year ended 31 March 1990 of £6m. Godfrey Davis Holdings withdrew in the light of these poor results.

- In March 1990, one week later, the Compass Group made a bid. Sketchley appointed a new management team and this second bid was defeated.

The new management team decided that the company had not made a profit of £6m for the year ended 31 March 1990 after all – they had made a loss of £2m.

This has a familiar ring. It is very like the AEI situation of 1967, almost 25 years before. The adjustments made are as follows:

	Sketchley plc 1990 Preliminary results	
(a)	Effect of more prudent accounting judgement (exercised by the new management team)	£000
	Reassessment of bad and doubtful debts	3,358
	Reassessment of stock provisions	2,770
	Write-off of fixed assets	773
		6,901
(b)	Provision for redundancy costs	554
(c)	Other items, including the effect of accounting policy changes	557
		8,012
	Profit before taxation, as forecast	6,000
	Loss before taxation, as reported	2,012

Of course, it is not too difficult to visualise the motivation of the old and new management teams. The old team would take as favourable a view as possible of the asset values in order to resist a bid. The new team would take as unfavourable a view as possible, so that their performance would appear that much better in the future. It is clear, however, that the adjustments only arose on the change of management control, and without such a change we would have been basing investment decisions on a set of accounts that showed a £6m profit rather than a £2m loss.

There is often mention of the expectation gap, whereby shareholders appear to have lost faith in financial statements. The situation just discussed does little to persuade them that they are wrong. After all, what is the point of a regulatory system that ensures that the accounts are true and fair until the very moment when such a requirement is really necessary?

The area of provisioning and the exercise of judgement has finally been addressed by the regulators with the issue in 1998 of FRS 12 Provisions, Contingent Liabilities and Contingent Assets.

6.13 Developments for small companies

Small firms play a major role in the UK economy and are seen to be the main job creators. Statistics published by the DTI (Small and Medium Enterprise (SME) Statistics for the United Kingdom, 1997, URN 98/92, July 1998) showed that in 1997 there were around 3.7 million businesses in the UK. Of these, 2.5 million were sole traders or partners without employees. There were 1.2 million companies on the Companies House register and, of these, around 12,000 (1%) were public companies (Companies in 1997/98 (The Companies Annual Report 1997–1998) The Stationery Office) with only about 2,450 listed on the Stock Exchange. Of the companies on the register, around 7,000 had more than 250 employees, 26,000 had between 50 and 250 employees, and around 1.01 million had nine or fewer employees.

Certain companies are relieved of statutory and mandatory requirements on account of their size.

6.13.1 Statutory requirements

Every year the directors are required to submit accounts to the shareholders and file a copy with the Registrar of Companies. In recognition of the cost implications and need for different levels of privacy, there is provision for small and medium-sized companies to file abbreviated accounts.

A small company satisfies two or more of the following conditions:

● Turnover does not exceed £2.8m.

● Assets do not exceed £1.4m.

● Average number of employees does not exceed 50.

The company is excused from filing a profit and loss account, and the directors' report and balance sheet need only be an abbreviated version disclosing major asset and liability headings. Its privacy is protected by excusing disclosure of directors' emoluments.

A medium-sized company satisfies two or more of the following conditions:

● Turnover does not exceed £11.2m.

● Assets do not exceed £5.6m.

● Average number of employees does not exceed 250.

It is excused far less than a small company: the major concession is that it need not disclose sales turnover and cost of sales, and the profit and loss account starts with the gross profit figure. This is to protect its competitive position.

6.13.2 Mandatory requirements

The approach by the standard-setters has generally been to require all companies to comply with SSAPs and FRSs. This can be justified on the grounds that compliance is necessary in order to present a true and fair view. Critics maintain that small companies might well never enter into transactions that fall within a standard, e.g. finance leasing, and that they should therefore be excused from compliance with the majority of standards. This is a weak position to take. After all, if a company actually does enter into a transaction for which a standard exists, it is difficult to see how it could be permitted to account for it in a non-standard way.

However, there is a legitimate interest in deregulation and a working party was set up by the CCAB at the request of the ASB to carry out a consultation exercise to assess whether companies should be excused from complying on the grounds of size or public interest.

From the consultations[26] there was a clear support for some relief from accounting standards to be based on size or a combination of size and public interest. The ASB accepted the recommendations of the CCAB Working Party and issued FRSSE[27] in November 1997. Recognising that there was concern as to the legality of setting different measurement and disclosure requirements, the ASB took legal advice which confirmed that smaller entities can properly be allowed exemptions or differing treatments in standards and UITFs provided such differences were justified **on rational grounds**.

How can rational grounds be established?

The test as to whether a decision is rational is based on obtaining answers to nine questions. If there are more negative responses that positive, there are rational grounds for a different treatment. The nine questions can be classified as follows:

Generic relevance

1 Is the standard essential practice for all entities?

2 Is the standard likely to be widely relevant to small entities?

Proprietary relevance

3 Would the treatment required by the standard be readily recognised by the proprietor or manager as corresponding to their understanding of the transaction?

Relevant measurement requirements

4 Is the treatment compatible with that used by the Inland Revenue in computing tax?

5 Are the measurement methods in a standard likely to be reasonably practical for small entities?

6 Is the accounting treatment the least cumbersome?

User relevance

7 Is the standard likely to meet information needs and legitimate expectations of the users of a small entity's accounts?

8 Does the standard provide disclosure likely to be meaningful and comprehensible to such a user?

Relevant to expand statutory provision

9 Do the requirements of the standard significantly augment the treatment required by statute?

How are individual standards dealt with in the FRSSE?

Standards have been dealt with in six ways as explained in (a) to (f) below:

(a) Adopted without change
   FRSSE adopted certain standards and UITFs without change, e.g. SSAP 17 *Accounting for Post Balance Sheet Events*, UITF 14 *Disclosure of Changes in Accounting Policy*.

(b) Not addressed

Certain standards were not addressed in the FRSSE, e.g. SSAP 5 *Accounting for Value Added Tax*, SSAP 25 *Segmental Reporting*, FRS 1 (Revised 1996) *Cash Flow Statements*, UITF 4 *Presentation of Long-term Debtors in Current Assets* and UITF 5, UITF 9–11, UITF 13, UITF 15–19, UITF 22; FRS 13 *Derivatives and other Financial Instruments Disclosures*; FRS 14 *Earnings per Share*.

(c) Statements relating to groups are cross referenced

If group accounts are to be prepared the FRSSE contains the cross-references required to FRS 2 *Accounting for Subsidiary Undertakings*, FRS 6 *Acquisitions and Mergers* and FRS 7 *Fair Values in Acquisition Accounting*.

(d) Disclosure requirements removed

Certain standards apply but the disclosure requirement is removed, e.g. FRS 10 *Accounting for Goodwill*.

(e) Disclosure requirements reduced

Certain standards apply but there is a reduced disclosure requirement, e.g.

● SSAP 9 *Stock and Long-term Contracts* applies but there is no requirement to sub-classify stock nor the disclose accounting policy.

● FRS 3 *Reporting Financial Performance* applies but:
  – no requirement to analyse the turnover, costs and results into continuing operations, acquisitions and discontinued operations;
  – no reference to the consequences of a decision to sell or terminate an operation and the provisions that may be recognised;
  – no reference to earnings per share;
  – no requirement for a note of historical cost profits and losses;
  – no requirement for a reconciliation of movements in shareholders' funds.

(f) Increased requirements

Certain standards are included with certain of the requirements reduced and other of the requirements increased, e.g., under FRS 8 *Related Party Disclosure* a new paragraph has been added, clarifying that the standard requires the disclosure of directors' personal guarantees for their company's borrowings.

How unanimous was the response to the consultation exercise?

As one would expect reactions were mixed with supporters both for excluding and for retaining a particular standard. For example, some commentators who represented the main users suggested that the cash flow statement should also be required from smaller entities. Their argument was that the management of cash is crucial in small, as well as large, businesses and that a cash flow statement provided a useful focus for discussions with management as well as a reference point for subsequent more detailed analysis.

The CCAB Working Party, however, accepted the arguments of those commentators who supported the exclusion of cash flow statements. Their arguments were:

● FRS 1 already exempts small entities from preparing a statement.

● For many small businesses in which transactions are straightforward, the cash flow statement adds little to what was already apparent from the balance sheet and profit and loss account.

● The gap between the period-end and the date of finalising the financial statements may be of such a length (up to ten months) as to limit the usefulness of any cash flow information.

● Managers in small businesses are well aware of the need to manage cash effectively. Their mechanisms for doing so may be informal but little would be added by a requirement for a cash flow statement in annual accounts prepared some months after period-end.

The ASB itself, whilst recognising that cash flow statements were not mandatory under FRS 1 for smaller entities, believed that a cash flow statement is an important aid to the understanding of an entity's financial position and performance and therefore included in the FRSSE a *Voluntary Disclosures* section which recommended that smaller entities present a simplified cash flow statement using the indirect method.

Does the FRSSE improve the information provided to users?

It is interesting to note that only one of the FRSs issued by the ASB, namely FRS 8 *Related Party Disclosure*, is deemed by the CCAB and ASB to have any relevance to smaller entities. It would seem reasonable to deduce from this that the ASB exists primarily to regulate the financial reporting of the 2,000 or so companies listed on the London Stock Exchange and has had little time to consider the million other companies that prepare and file accounts.

There are two clear adverse effects of this:

● The lack of adequate research by the ASB into the information needs of the users of accounts of smaller and medium sized companies means, according to some researchers,[28] that the FRSSE has been produced without proper regard to those needs.

● The exercise started from the wrong end of the scale, according to the Small Practitioners Association,[29] in that it started with the standards designed for large public companies and then went through the nine questions approach to decide which of these to include in the FRSSE. A more logical approach would have been to have carried out the research suggested by Dugdale, Hussey and Jarvis[30] and developed positive standards that satisfied identified user needs.

However, given the pressure to establish appropriate FRSs for listed companies and to maintain a presence in the international standard-setting scene, there seems little prospect that ASB resources could be stretched to embrace the needs of the one million non-listed companies.

One could reasonably ask questions such as:

● Why should non-listed companies require ten months to prepare and file accounts?

● Why should this be accepted by the CCAB working party as actual justification for not requiring a Cash Flow Statement?

● Is it feasible, or indeed even desirable, to expect the ASB to be concerned with non-listed company reporting given that almost 100% of the time since it was set up has been devoted to the reporting requirements of listed companies?

How will the FRSSE be kept up to date?

The ASB has set up an advisory committee, the Committee on Accounting for Smaller Entities, chaired by Professor Whittington, to assist in updating and revising the FRSSE periodically but any change in the FRSSE as a result of new standards, e.g. FRS 10, will be the subject of public consultation.

In December 1999 the ASB[31] issued FRSSE effective March 2000. This FRSSE supersedes the FRSSE issued in December 1998. Because it is revised periodically the FRSSE will lag behind the issue of individual FRSs, for instance the FRSSE in December 1999 considers FRSs up to FRS 15 and does not deal with FRS 16.

The requirements relating to FRS 11 *Impairment of Fixed assets and Goodwill* are that only the key principle that assets held above recoverable amount should be written down to recoverable amount and the conditions for recognising the reversal of write-downs are included in the FRSSE.

The basic principles remain unchanged:

● Smaller entities may properly be allowed exemptions or different treatment provided such differences are justified on rational grounds as discussed in para 6.13.2.

● The objective of the FRSSE is to ensure that the reporting entity provides information about the financial position, performance and financial adaptability of the entity that is useful to users in assessing the stewardship of management and for making economic decisions, recognising that the balance between users' needs in respect of stewardship and economic decision-making for smaller entities is different from that for other reporting entities.

● The financial statements should present a true and fair view which takes account of the substance of any arrangement or transaction i.e. after identifying whether the transaction has changed existing, or given rise to new, assets or liabilities.

Company Law Review

The Company Law Review Steering Group issued a Consultation Document in February 1999, *The Strategic Framework*, acknowledging that there appeared to be serious problems which required remedy arising from fact that the Companies Act:

● is structured around the needs of larger, publicly owned companies with a separation between the shareholders/investors and the directors with many provisions imposing duties on directors to provide protection for shareholders against abuses of directors' powers (Sec 5.2.3)

● is opaque and inaccessible to small business users and requires a thorough knowledge of the whole Act to understand what exemptions and adaptations are available (Sec 5.2.5)

● lays down regulatory requirements for the protection of the company's creditors that are overly burdensome and fail to serve the purposes for which they were designed (Sec 5.2.7)

● With regard to the work of the ASB, *The Strategic Framework* recognises that 'A considerable amount of piecemeal work has been done on improving approaches within the existing framework e.g. FRSSE'. It also recognises the view expressed by some directors of small companies that statutory accounts are a tiresome irrelevance but, whilst being open to consultation, reminds us that the Fourth Directive requires all limited companies to publish accounts and that any replacement of this requirement would require a change in EU law (Sec 5.2.14).

It has been interesting[32] to see the responses to the questions raised by *The Strategic Framework*. Selected questions with responses included:

Qn 9: Is it agreed that the difficulties met by small and closely-held companies in operating within the Act are serious and worthy of remedy?

Responses: The overwhelming majority supported the proposition, feeling that the present law was opaque, unwieldy, unnecessarily complex and burdensome and therefore ripe for review.

Qn 10(a): Is it agreed that it is not desirable to restrict access to limited liability?

Responses: A significant majority took the view that it was not desirable to restrict access to limited liability, arguing that limited liability status acted as a spur to entrepreneurship and innovation.

Qn 10(b): If not, then what restraints should be considered?

Responses: It was thought desirable by respondents to (b) to require a minimum capital threshold as a practical and useful measure to cause proprietors of small businesses to consider whether they needed to be incorporated.

Qn 11(a): Should the current accounting exemptions for small and medium-sized companies be removed or amended?

Responses: The vast majority took the view that some change was necessary but there was a wide divergence as to the nature of the change that was desirable. Responses ranged from complete exemption from preparing and filing accounts to replacing with alternative forms of financial information such as cash flow statements, ratios and graphical presentation, to requiring the same compliance as that required of large companies.

11(b): Do current exempt accounts provide proportionate, or any, protection to creditors, bearing in mind the cost of preparation?

Responses: The overwhelming view was that abbreviated accounts filed by small and medium-sized companies provided little or no protection to creditors.

6.13.3 How does UK approach compare with that in the developing world?

The United Nations Conference on Trade and Development (UNCTAD) has a working group of experts on international standards of accounting and reporting (ISAR) which plans to discuss the accounting needs of small and medium-sized enterprises in 2000. This is because such enterprises are regarded by governments in developing countries as important generators of employment and economic growth. Many countries have many businesses that keep no records and pay no taxes, but when they want to grow they come within regulations and are subject to additional costs and regulatory requirements.[33] As far as accounting requirements are concerned, it is suggested that a way forward would be to follow the system being developed in West Africa where the micro-business starts with simple cash accounting, and then progresses to accrual accounting and finally compliance with International Accounting Standards. In the developing world, it is felt that accounting hurdles are too high and a progressive system of accounting is required as seen in West Africa. Many small and medium-sized enterprises in the UK are halfway along the spectrum with accrual accounting and audited accounts but, as we have seen above, there are still calls in the UK for a reduction in the regulatory burden and many small enterprises are operating outside the formal system, keeping no records and paying no tax.

Summary

It is evident from cases such as AEI/GEC that management cannot be permitted to have total discretion in the way in which it presents financial information in its accounts and rules are needed to ensure uniformity in the reporting of similar commercial transactions. Decisions must then be made as to the nature of the rules and how they are to be enforced.

In the UK the standard setting bodies have tended to lean towards rules being framed as general principles and accepting the culture of voluntary compliance.

Although there is a preference on the part of the standard-setters to concentrate on general principles, there is a growing pressure from the preparers of the accounts for more detailed illustrations and explanations in how the standards are to be applied. This is apparent from FRS 4 with its Application Notes and the increasing number of Urgent Issue Task Force Abstracts.

With regard to voluntary compliance, The Combined Code supports the continuance of this approach but there is evidence that the government will require increasing mandatory compliance as seen with the proposal to make the OFR mandatory.

Review questions

1 Why is it necessary for financial reporting to be subject to (a) mandatory control and (b) statutory control?

2 How is it possible to make shareholders aware of the significance of the exercise of judgement by directors which can turn profits of £6m into losses of £2m?

3 Discuss the main arguments for dispensing with all SSAPs and FRSs.

4 'The effective working of the financial aspects of a market economy rests on the validity of the underlying premises of integrity in the conduct of business and reliability in the provision of information. Even though in the great majority of cases that presumption is wholly justified, there needs to be strong institutional underpinning.

That institutional framework has been shown to be inadequate. The last two to three years have accordingly seen a series of measures by the financial and business community to strengthen it. Amongst these has been the creation of the Financial Reporting Council and the bodies which it in turn established.'[34]

Discuss the above statement with particular reference to one of the following institutions: Accounting Standards Board, Financial Reporting Review Panel, Urgent Issues Task Force. Illustrate with reference to publications or decisions from the institution you have chosen to discuss.

5 To what extent do you think FRSs should take economic consequences into account? Discuss in relation to dissident views.

6 (a) Name four UITF Abstracts and explain why they were required.

(b) 'The principles involved in decisions which the UITF give in response to an approach by directors or auditors prior to finalising the accounts should be published and should be in the public domain.' Discuss.

7 (a) Name four companies that have been the subject of FRRP pronouncements and explain the reason for FRRP involvement.

(b) Shorter accounting standards are not a realistic option until both companies and the accountancy profession can be trusted to 'fully honour an approach limited to basic principles'. Discuss why companies and the accountancy profession cannot be so trusted.

8 Explain the main changes to *Interim Reports* following the ASB Statement of best practice.

9 Refer to the research data mentioned in reference 9 and discuss other possible reasons for there being fewer Big Five auditors in the FRRP firms.

10 'The most favoured way to reduce information overload was to have the company filter the available information set based on users' specifications of their needs'[36] Discuss how this can be achieved.

Exercises

Question 1

Constructive review of the regulators

Required:
(a) Obtain a copy of the Financial Reporting Council's Annual Review.
(b) Prepare a profile of the members of the Financial Reporting Council, the ASB, the UITF and the Financial Reporting Review Panel.
(c) Comment on the strengths and weaknesses revealed by the profile.
(d) Advise (with reasons) on changes that you consider would strengthen one or more of these bodies.

Question 2

The ASB stated in 1994 that:

> The size of its documents is a matter that the Board has constantly in mind. In essence the Board would like to publish short standards based on principle dealing with (say) 80 per cent of the issues. If many of the remaining, often peripheral and specialised, issues have to be dealt with it will disproportionately increase the length and complexity of our standards. How far the Board will be driven in that direction will depend on the willingness of the financial community to comply with the spirit of shorter standards and not to search for loopholes that will have to be plugged by the issue of further rules.[35]

Required:
(a) Discuss how the ASB has dealt with what it describes as 'the remaining, often peripheral and specialised, issues'.
(b) Obtain an interview with the tax partner of a local firm of accountants to seek their view on following the approach recommended by the ASB (i) in relation to tax advice and (ii) in relation to financial reporting practice.

Question 3

Enforcement of disclosure

Required:
(a) Identify the circumstances in which the Stock Exchange is used to obtain compliance with voluntary disclosures recommended by other committees' mandatory bodies.
(b) Ascertain how the Stock Exchange is able to police the adequacy of such disclosures.
(c) Discuss the acceptability of regulations contained in various codes of best practice being enforced by the Stock Exchange rather than the ASB or statute.

References

1 G. Whittred and I. Zimmer, *Financial Accounting Incentive Effects and Economic Consequences*, Holt, Rinehart & Winston, 1992, p. 8.

2 E.R. Farmer, *Making Sense of Company Reports*, Van Nostrand Reinhold, 1986, p. 16.

3 Dearing Report, *The Making of Accounting Standards*, CCAB, 1988.

4 *Framework for the Presentation and Preparation of Financial Statements*, IASC, 1989, para. 40.

5 *Ibid.*

6 FRS 3, *Financial Reporting Performance*, ASB, 1992.

7 *Accountancy Age*, 29 September 1994, p. 2.

8 Foreword to *Accounting Standards*, ASB, 1993, Appendix para. 10.

9 K. Peasnell, P. Pope and S. Young, 'Breaking the rules', *Accountancy International*, February 2000, p. 76.

10 UITF Abstract 10, *Disclosure of Directors' Share Options*, ASB, 1994.

11 *Accountancy Age*, 3 November 1994, p. 1.

12 M. Bromwich, *The Economics of Accounting Standard Setting*, Prentice Hall, 1985, p. 78.

13 *Certified Accountant*, August 1993, p. 13.

14 L. White, 'Exchanging roles', *Accountancy International*, March 2000, p. 46.

15 *Operating and Financial Review*, ASB, 1993.

16 P. Weetman, Bill Collins and E. Davie, *Operating and Financial Review: Views of Analysts and Institutional Investors*, ICAS, 1994.

17 S. Zeff, 'Good so far but difficult decisions ahead', *Accountancy*, October 1995, p. 96.

18 *The Combined Code*, Committee on Corporate Governance, Gee, 1998.

19 Cadbury Report, 1992.

20 R. Hussey and S. Woolfe, *Interim Statements and Preliminary Profit Announcements*, ICAEW Research Board, 1994.

21 *Interim Reports*, ASB, 1998.

22 Hannah King, 'What's the latest on interim reports?', *Accountancy*, October 1997, p. 88.

23 K. Bagshaw, *Preliminary Announcements: A Guide to Best Practice and Interim Reports: A Guide to Best Practice*, Accountancy Books, 1999.

24 *Progress in the Interim: Surveying Corporate Half Yearly Reporting*, Arthur Andersen, 1999.

25 *Student Financial Reporting*, ICAEW, 1991/2, p. 17.

26 A Consultative Document 'Exemptions from Standards on Grounds of Size or Public Interest', CCAB, November 1994; and A Paper 'Designed to fit – A Financial Reporting Standard for Smaller Entities', CCAB, December 1995.

27 *Financial Reporting Standard for Smaller Entities*, ASB, 1997.

28 D. Dugdale, J. Hussey and R. Jarvis, 'Can less mean more', *Certified Accountant*, November 1997, pp. 32–33.

29 'FRSSE: OK, not perfect', *Accountancy*, December 1997, p.11.

30 D. Dugdale, *et al.*, *op. cit.*

31 FRSSE, ASB, 1999.

32 *Responses to the Consultation Document published by the Company Law Review Steering Group, February 1999*, Dti, December 1999.

33 P. Walton, 'UN research into the accounting needs of SMMES', *Accounting and Business*, February 2000, p. 34.

34 *The State of Financial Reporting*, Financial Reporting Council Second Annual Review, November 1992.

35 *Ibid.*, 1994.

36 V. Beattie, *Business Reporting: The Inevitable Change?*, ICAS, 1999, p. 53.

Conceptual framework

7.1 Introduction

In the previous chapter we reviewed the standard-setting process and gave an overview of the statutory and mandatory rules that govern financial reporting. In this chapter we will discuss the rationale underlying such rules or standards and consider the developments that have occurred in the search for a conceptual framework for financial reporting in the UK. In this chapter we consider the following:

A – Development of conceptual framework up to 1992

● Definition of a conceptual framework
● Historical overview of the evolution of financial accounting theory
● *The Corporate Report – 1975*
● ICAS *Making Corporate Reports Valuable – 1988*
● *The Solomons Report – 1989*
● IASC *Framework for the Presentation and Preparation of Financial Statements – 1989*
● AICPA *Improving Business Reporting – A Customer Focus: Meeting the Information Needs of Investors and Creditors – 1994*

B – ASB; development of conceptual framework

● ASB *Statements of Principles for Financial Reporting – 1992/1999*

A – DEVELOPMENT OF A CONCEPTUAL FRAMEWORK UP TO 1992

7.2 Definition of a conceptual framework

Standard-setters in the UK have been operating in a professional environment where there has been no unique, agreed conceptual framework upon which to base new standards.

7.2.1 What exactly do we mean by a conceptual framework?

Many attempts have been made in the USA and the UK to define a conceptual framework. For example, the Financial Accounting Standards Board (FASB) in the USA stated in its *Scope and Implications of the Conceptual Framework Project* 1967 that

A conceptual framework is a constitution, a coherent system of interrelated objectives and fundamentals **that can lead to consistent standards** and that prescribes the nature, function and limits of financial accounting and financial statements.[1]

In general terms, then, it is a basic structure for organising one's thinking about what one is trying to do and how to go about it. It can answer questions such as:

● For whom and by whom are the accounts to be prepared?
● For what purposes are they wanted?
● What kind of accounting reports are suitable for these purposes?
● How do present accounts fit the bill?
● How could accounting practices be improved to make them more suitable?

In the UK, MacVe stated that a conceptual framework would 'provide **a consistent approach** for making decisions about choices of accounting practice and for setting accounting standards'.[2]

In the financial press, E. Stamp wrote in 1982 that a conceptual framework would consist of the following elements:

(a) general agreement on the overall objectives of financial reporting;

(b) general agreement on the nature and needs of the various users of financial reports;

(c) identification of a set of (ideally, mutually exclusive and collectively exhaustive) **criteria to be used in choosing between alternative solutions to standard-setting problems** and in assessing the quality and utility of financial reports.[3]

Each of these three definitions is looking for the establishment of a parameter of accounting objectives within which reference points might be fixed to give guidance in the standard-setting process. They are seeking a **mechanism to create general consistency** and avoid conflicting rules and practices. This is essential given the background, where the absence of standards allowed the preparers of financial statements to manipulate the results.

However, it would be wrong to imagine that financial reporting practices have evolved in a vacuum without any sort of accounting theory underlying them. A brief historical overview of the evolution of accounting theory will allow us to put financial reporting into context.

7.3 Historical overview of the evolution of financial accounting theory

Financial reporting constantly has to deal with problems arising from changing economic, political and commercial practices, e.g. how to take account of changing prices, changing government regulations such as grants and subsidies, and changing commercial practices such as franchising and leasing.

Because financial reporting is not a single activity carried out by one person or institution, there is the risk of inconsistency in reporting similar activities. If the annual financial reports are to be decision-useful for investors, who are regarded in the UK as the principal stakeholders, then there is a need for consistency or uniformity in reporting.

The way in which the profession has attempted to achieve consistency has varied over time. In the 1950s and 1960s it followed an **empirical inductive** approach. This resulted in the production of standards or reporting practices that were based on rationalising what happened in practice. Under this approach we saw the issue of standards such as SSAP 2, SSAP 3 and SSAP 9.

In the 1970s it followed a **deductive** approach. This resulted in the production of standards or reporting practices based on principles that had been deducted from assumptions – there was no need to refer to what actually happened in the real world. This was in part due to the fact that the deductive approach challenged established practices, e.g. the use of the historical cost model.

However, in recognition of the fact that financial reporting does occur in the real world, there has been a growing concern that theories are acceptable only if they are capable of being tested empirically, e.g. by identifying their impact on share prices, and if they satisfy cost/benefit criteria.

7.3.1   **Empirical inductive approach**

The empirical inductive approach looked at the practices that existed and attempted to generalise from them.

This tended to be how the technical departments of accounting firms operated. By rationalising what they did, they ensured that the firm avoided accepting different financial reporting practices for similar transactions, e.g. accepting unrealised profit appearing in the income statement of one client and not in another. The technical department's role was to advise partners and staff, i.e. it was a **defensive role** to avoid any potential charge from a user of the accounts that they had been misled.

Initially a technical circular was regarded as a private good and distribution was restricted to the firm's own staff. However, it then became recognised that it could benefit the firm if its practices were accepted as the industry benchmark, so that in the event of litigation it could rely on this fact.

When the technical advice ceased to be a private good, there was a perceived additional benefit to the firm if the nature of the practice could be changed from being a positive statement, i.e. this is how we report profits on uncompleted contracts, to a **normative** statement, i.e. this is how we report *and* this is how all other financial reporters *ought* to report.

Consequently, there has been a growing trend since the 1980s for firms to publish rationalisations for their financial reporting practices. It has been commercially prudent for them to do so. It has also been extremely helpful to academic accountants and their students.

Typical illustrations of the result of such empirical induction are the wide acceptance of the historical cost model and various concepts such as matching and realisation that we discussed in Chapter 2. In terms of standards, we have already mentioned that SSAP 2 and SSAP 9 evolved under this regime.

This approach has played an important role in the evolution of financial reporting practices and will continue to do so. After all, it is the preparers of the financial statements and their auditors who are first exposed to change, whether economic, political or commercial. They are the ones who have to think their way through each new problem that surfaces. This means that a financial reporting practice already exists by the time the problem comes to the attention of theoreticians.

The major reasons that it has been felt necessary to try other approaches are both pragmatic and theoretical.

Pragmatic reason

The main pragmatic reason is that the past procedure, whereby deduction was dependent upon generalisation from existing practice, has become untenable. The accelerating rate of economic, political and commercial change leaves too little time for effective and uniform practices to evolve.

Theoretical reasons

The theoretical reasons relate to the acceptability of the income determined under the traditional historic cost model. There are three principal reasons:

● **True income**. We have seen that economists had a view that financial reports should report a true income, which differed from the accountants' view.

● **User-defined income – public**. There is a view that there may be a number of relevant incomes depending upon differing user needs which may be regarded as public goods.

● **User-defined income – private**. There is a view that there may be a number of relevant incomes depending upon differing user needs which may be regarded as private rather than public goods.

It was thought that the limitations implicit in the empirical inductive approach could be overcome by the deductive approach.

7.3.2 Deductive approach

The deductive approach is not dependent on existing practice, which is often perceived as having been tainted because it has been determined by finance directors and auditors. However, the problem remains: from whose viewpoint is the deduction to be made?

Possible alternatives to the preparers and auditors of the accounts are economists and users. However, economists are widely perceived as promoting unrealistic models and users as having needs so diverse that they cannot be realistically satisfied in a single set of accounts. Consider the attempts made to define income. Economists have supported the concept of a true income, while users have indicated the need for a range of relevant incomes.

True income

We have already seen in Chapter 3 that there is a significant difference between the accountant's income and the economist's income applying the ideas of Fisher and Hicks.

User needs and multiple incomes

Multiple measures of income, derived from the general price level adjusted accounting model, the replacement cost accounting model and the exit price accounting model, were considered in Chapter 4. Each model provides information that is relevant for different purposes, e.g. replacement cost accounting produces an income figure that indicates how much is available for distribution while still maintaining the operating capacity of the entity.

These income figures were regarded as a public good, i.e. cost-free to the user, and were recommended in SSAP 7 and required for a trial period in SSAP 16. Latterly, it has been recognised that there is a cost implication to the production of information, i.e. that it is not a public good; that standards should be capable of being empirically tested; and that consideration should be given to the economic consequences of standards. This has resulted in a concern that standards should deal with substance rather than form, e.g. the treatment of leases introduced this concept quite specifically as part of SSAP 21.

It could be argued that the deductive approach to income, whether an economist's true income or a theoretician's multiple income, has a basic weakness in its dependence upon the viewpoint of only one user group – the investors. This weakness was recognised in the UK and the information needs of the other groups were spelt out in pronouncements such as *The Corporate Report*.[4]

The Corporate Report is discussed in greater detail below, but for all practical purposes, the rights of user groups other than investors have been 'spirited away'. In the UK it has become accepted dogma that investor needs are a surrogate for the needs of all other users. For example, Solomons, in *Guidelines for Financial Reporting Standards*, p. 32, states: 'As we have already noted that the needs of investors, creditors, employees and customers are not fundamentally different, it seems safe to look to the needs of present and potential investors as a guide ...'.[5] This assumption has also been accepted by the ASB, but there is little independent evidence to support it.

Where do we stand now?

We have seen that accounting theory was initially founded on generalisations from the accounting practices followed by practitioners. Then came the deductive approach of economists and theoreticians. The latter were not perceived to be realistic and empirical testing, e.g. by examining their economic consequence on share prices, is relied on to give them credibility.

The practitioners have now staked their claim to create accounting theory or a conceptual framework through the ASB. The advantage of this is that the conceptual framework will be based on consensus. This is illustrated by chapter 5 of the *Statement of Principles* relating to measurement, which has not attempted to make price level adjustment mandatory. Some would call this approach timid, but it is a healthy way forward. It recognises that on many issues genuine disagreements exist on what best portrays reality. What we need to encourage is experimentation.

This is the view put forward in *The Future Shape of Financial Reports*, 1989, by Arnold *et al.*:

> Change in financial reporting is bound to be evolutionary rather than revolutionary. Most of the important improvements in financial reporting in the last fifty years have had their origins in experimentation by practitioners (sometimes with ideas first developed in academic circles) rather than prescription by legislation or accounting standards; indeed legislation and accounting standards usually lag developments in practice by some years. This process has applied not only to relatively minor enhancements but also to much more fundamental changes such as the inclusion of consolidated accounts ... Most experiments would have to be outside the statutory reporting framework by way of supplementary statements ... Financial reporting practice is continually evolving and over the years many companies have been willing to experiment. We hope that this report will stimulate companies to look afresh at their reporting and initiate further experimentation based on some of our proposals.[6]

An experimentation approach is valid if companies can be relied on to produce reports that give a true and fair view. However, experience shows that this is not always the case; hence the standard-setters have been compelled to issue FRSs, not to legitimise evolving practice, but to combat malpractice. Companies cannot be relied on not to cheat. Consequently the ASB has progressed from consensus to regulatory standard-setting. For example, FRS 5 was issued to enforce reporting according to the substance of a transaction rather than some legalistic fiction; FRS 6 was issued to prevent companies applying merger accounting to business combinations that were clearly acquisitions in substance; FRS 7 was issued to prevent companies manipulating provisions when taking over another company with the primary object of creating higher profits in subsequent accounting periods by charging expenses of the later period against the carried forward provision.

7.4 The Corporate Report

Reports have been commissioned at various times on financial reporting. *The Corporate Report*, published by the ASC in 1975, has had a continuing influence.

7.4.1 Terms of reference of The Corporate Report

The terms of reference under which the report was formulated claimed that the purpose of the study was to 're-examine the scope and aims of published financial reports in the light of modern needs and conditions'. It was concerned with public accountability of economic entities of all kinds, but especially business enterprises. It attempted to establish a set of working concepts as a basis for financial reporting; and to identify the persons for whom published accounts should be prepared, and the information appropriate to their interests. It considered the most suitable means of measuring and reporting the economic position, performance and prospects of undertakings for the purpose and persons identified.

7.4.2 Philosophy of The Corporate Report

The basic philosophy was that reports should seek to satisfy the information needs of users. It was therefore necessary to identify user needs and, from these, to arrive at the fundamental objectives of corporate reports.

In the view of the ASC there was an implied responsibility for every economic entity whose size made it significant to report publicly. By 'economic entity', it meant every type of organisation in modern economic society, i.e. central government departments, local authorities, co-operatives, limited companies, unincorporated firms and non-profit-making entities such as trade unions and charities. By 'significant', it meant an economic entity where 'the organisation commands human or material resources on such a scale that the results of its activities have significant economic implications for a community as a whole'. Economic significance was assumed if the entity was a listed company, employed more than 500 staff, and had capital employed of more than £2 million or a turnover in excess of £5 million.

7.4.3 Fundamental objective of corporate reports

The fundamental objective of corporate reports was to communicate economic measurements of, and information about, resources and performance that would be useful to those users having a right to such information. To fulfil this objective, corporate reports had to possess the following qualitative characteristics: relevance, reliability, comparability, understandability, completeness, objectivity and timeliness.

7.4.4 Who were the users recognised by The Corporate Report?

The Corporate Report identified seven user groups as being entitled to receive accounting information and whose information needs should be satisfied by a financial report:

● Existing and potential equity investors.

● Existing and potential loan creditors.

● Existing, potential and past employees.

● Analysts/advisers, including financial analysts, financial journalists, economists, statisticians, researchers, trade unions, stockbrokers and others such as credit rating agencies.

● The business contact group, i.e. customers, trade creditors, suppliers, competitors, business rivals and parties interested in mergers and take-overs.

● The government, i.e. the tax authorities, regulatory departments and local authorities.

● The public, i.e. taxpayers, ratepayers, consumers and community groups and special interest groups, e.g. consumer and environmental groups.

7.4.5 What are the information needs of these users?

Shareholders might wish to evaluate the entity performance in order to predict future cash flows; loan creditors to assess its stability; trade creditors its liquidity; rivals its vulnerability; employees their relative importance in the production process; the government the amount of taxes that arises.

The report considered it impractical to seek to satisfy such diverse needs by a general-purpose financial report and suggested that there should be statements in addition to the profit and loss account, balance sheet and cash flow statement. The additional statements reflected the underlying intention of the report, which was to produce statements that would be useful for improving the social as well as the economic welfare of society. It saw a company as a combination of stakeholders rather than as simply a legal vehicle for shareholders.

7.4.6 Additional statements suggested by *The Corporate Report*

The additional statements were as follows:

1 **A statement of value added** showing the amounts paid to shareholders, lenders, employees and the state, and retained for reinvestment. This statement was subsequently produced by a number of companies, but no standard has been issued and its use is decreasing.

2 **An employment report** to disclose:
   (a) a staff profile, e.g. numbers employed, reasons for change, age and sex distribution;
   (b) staff conditions, e.g. frequency of accidents, hours worked, geographical location of sites, employment costs, amounts spent on training, adequacy of the pension funds to meet future obligations, the benefits earned by employees and their contribution;
   (c) likelihood of change, e.g. material closures or acquisition of plant.

3 **A statement of money exchange with government** to disclose the flow of money between the state and the company. At various times, substantial inducements have been provided by the government in the form of tax relief, grants and subsidies. At the same time, companies have become increasingly involved in the collection of tax for the government. The statement was intended to provide a comprehensive picture of the flows of money, e.g. PAYE, VAT, business rates, corporation tax and grants.

4 A statement of transactions in foreign currency to disclose direct cash flows between the UK and overseas countries. Investors take into account the geographical spread of assets, liabilities and turnover when assessing the business and exchange risk. Segmental information on turnover has been required by the Stock Exchange, and SSAP 25 *Segmental Reporting* has extended the disclosure requirements. This statement has consequently not been seen as a major improvement and is not widely used.

5 A statement of future prospects to show the **levels** of future profits, future employment and future investment. There are statutory requirements to disclose certain information, e.g. capital investment that has been contracted but not completed at the date of the balance sheet. Apart from such statutory requirements, there is major resistance from directors to quantifying future profits, employment or investment. This is discussed a little more fully when considering accountability.

6 A statement of corporate objectives to address medium-term strategic targets and show management policy. This statement is gradually assuming more importance as companies in the 1990s publicise their social and environmental policies. The statement is perceived by management as a vehicle for projecting the corporate image rather than for making them accountable to users. Future developments are therefore likely to remain in the social rather than the economic area.

7.4.7 Measurement base suggested by *The Corporate Report*

The report assessed various measurement bases (e.g. historical cost, current purchasing power, replacement cost, net realisable value, value to the firm) and supported the use of current values with a general price index adjustment. As we have seen in preceding chapters, this is still undecided.

7.4.8 Short-term effect of *The Corporate Report*

The report was a comprehensive treatise that reviewed users, purposes and measurement bases for financial reporting. Unfortunately, its immediate impact was not great because many felt that it went too far in identifying user groups beyond the shareholders and creditors; too far in the demand for additional statements; and too far in wishing to discard historic cost as the measurement base.

7.4.9 Long-term effect of *The Corporate Report*

Since its issue in 1975, the report has been seen as a seminal document. Its philosophy has influenced the development of the *Statements of Principles* that the ASB has produced as the conceptual framework in the UK.

7.5 ICAS *Making Corporate Reports Valuable*

In 1988, following a major research project by its Research Committee, the Institute of Chartered Accountants of Scotland (ICAS) published the *Making Corporate Reports Valuable* (MCRV)[7] report. The general objective of MCRV was to stimulate discussion that would lead to improvements in corporate reporting. The long-term purpose was that reports should be produced that would be better able to assist the user in gauging management performance and assessing an entity's prospects; reports that were more understandable, less daunting in presentation, more readable and with as little technical jargon as possible.

In pursuit of this goal the MCRV formulated the Research Committee's views on meeting the needs of management and investors. It considered company strategy and planning, the need for clear financial statements covering such areas as entity objectives, present financial wealth, changes in financial wealth, operations, distributable wealth, cash flow and segmental information.

The report criticised historic cost accounting and supported the use of a current value system. It also advocated the publication of projected results so that the user would have available the preceding year's figures, the current year's and the subsequent year's.

To its credit, the Research Committee demonstrated that its proposals could be applied in practice by preparing the financial statements of Melody plc and obtaining feedback from the preparers of the accounts. These were published in 1990 and are perhaps a prototype of what financial statements might look like in the future.

The balance sheet was described as a statement of assets and liabilities and was a value statement. Assets, including stock, were revalued in current terms, thus breaking away from the historical cost philosophy. The net assets at the end of the period were the financial wealth generated by operations plus any increase in the realisable value of financial wealth.

The profit and loss account was described as an operations statement and, by including stock at market value, produced a residual figure called financial wealth generated by operations.

The annual report also contained a statement of cash flow, a value added statement, a chairman's review, a directors' report and a document referred to as 'Management's discussions and analysis of financial conditions and results of operations' for the year under review, supplemented by the financial plans for the following year.

The auditors' report appears as the 'Report of the independent assessors'. It is addressed to the members, creditors and employees of Melody plc and is more informative than the traditional short-form report favoured in the UK.

Another statement that makes its debut spells out 'responsibility for the financial statements'. It informs the user that the ultimate responsibility lies with the directors, and in doing so it also explains the role of the independent assessors and the nature of their report.

MCRV is a useful addition to our experience of financial reporting and its influence will no doubt be felt as the standard-setters move towards dealing with the problem of an appropriate measurement base.

It might be useful at this point to list some of the key thoughts in MCRV.

Representation of position

● Accounts should aim to portray economic reality.

● Substance over form is emphasised.

● The investors need the same information as the management.

Income

● It is against excessive emphasis on the bottom line with a single earnings figure.

● It emphasises the balance sheet rather than accruals-based income. Income is seen as a reconciliation between consecutive balance sheets expressed in current values.

Capital maintenance

● It takes a proprietary view in seeking to maintain the owners' purchasing power using a consumer price index.

Measurement base

● It supports the use of net realisable values.

7.6   The Solomons Report

Professor David Solomons produced *Guidelines for Financial Reporting* (1989). In the report he commented on the existing standard-setting process and made proposals for an explicit conceptual framework.

7.6.1   Existing standard-setting process

1 Solomons commented on the haphazard manner in which standards had developed and the fact that consistency of standards was a matter of chance. Standards created to deal with contemporary phenomena have been compiled in isolation and often conflict one with another, e.g. SSAP 2's philosophy of prudence may be said to be violated by SSAP 9's requirement to accrue for attributable profit and by SSAP 13's capitalisation of development expenditure, which also over-emphasises the accrual concept.

2 He noted that, even so, there was a considerable degree of consistency, which indicated that the standard-setters must have been applying an implicit framework. The Solomons Report aimed to provide the ASC with an explicit framework, or at least part of one, that would reinforce the implicit framework where it was sound and replace it where it was defective.

3 He noted that the conceptual framework in the UK differed in three respects from those operating in the USA, namely:
   (a) it saw the primary role of financial reports and statements as the assessment of enterprise and managerial performance, and regarded the balance sheet as the primary financial statement; revenues and expenditures were seen as changes in balance sheet items;
   (b) it attached great importance to representational faithfulness;
   (c) it emphasised the need to recognise adequately the pervasiveness of uncertainty in financial statements.

4 He disagreed with the provisions of some of the existing standards, e.g. SSAP 15 *Deferred Tax*, SSAP 21 *Accounting for Leases* and SSAP 24 *Accounting for Pension Costs*.

5 He took a conservative view that 'every report on a company's earnings for the past year throws light on past performance and, by doing so, helps investors to update or revise their expectations about future earnings' (*Guidelines*, p. 33).

6 He was against excessive emphasis on the bottom line with a single earnings figure (p. 19).

7 He placed emphasis on the balance sheet rather than on accruals-based income. Income was seen as a reconciliation between consecutive balance sheets expressed in current values (p. 17).

7.6.2 Proposals for an explicit conceptual framework

While Solomons supported the idea of general purpose financial statements, he addressed some of the areas that appeared in *The Corporate Report*, for example:

- **User needs** together with the functions that reports serve
- The **qualitative characteristics** of reports
- The **measurement base**

Solomons argued strongly for a move from historical cost accounting to one based on value to the business and for the maintenance of real financial capital as opposed to nominal financial capital or operating capability.

7.6.3 Reaction to the Solomons Report

The report gave rise to a number of critical responses,[8,9,10] but also received support in *The Future Shape of Financial Reports*, one objective of which was to 'demonstrate, by reference to Solomons ... that it is possible to design a revised system which allows companies to report in a way which much more closely reflects economic reality and which is related more closely to the needs of the user'.[11]

7.7 IASC *Framework for the Presentation and Preparation of Financial Statements*[12]

This exposure draft deals with the following:

- The objective of financial statements.
- The qualitative characteristics that determine the usefulness of information in financial statements.
- The definition, recognition and measurement of elements from which financial statements are constructed.
- The concepts of capital, capital maintenance and profit.

The **objective** of financial statements is that they should provide information about the financial position, performance and changes in financial position of an enterprise that is useful to a wide range of potential users in making economic decisions.

The **qualitative characteristics** that determine the usefulness of information are **relevance** and **reliability**. Comparability is a qualitative characteristic that interacts with both relevance and reliability. Materiality provides a threshold or cut-off point rather than being a primary qualitative characteristic. The balance between cost and benefit is a persuasive constraint rather than a qualitative characteristic.

The **definition** of an element is given in paragraph 46:

Financial statements portray the financial effects of transactions and other events by grouping the effects into broad classes according to their economic characteristics. These broad classes are termed the **elements** of financial statements. The elements directly related to the measurement of financial position in the balance sheet are assets, liabilities and equity. The elements directly related to the measurement of performance in the profit and loss account are income and expense.

The exposure draft defines each of the elements. For example, an asset is defined in paragraph 53: 'The future economic benefit embodied in an asset is the potential to contribute, directly or indirectly, to the flow of cash and cash equivalents to the enterprise.'

It defines when an element is to be **recognised**. For example, in paragraph 87 it states that: 'An asset is recognised in the balance sheet when it is probable that the future economic benefits will flow to the enterprise and the asset has an attribute that can be measured reliably.'

Regarding **measurement**, it comments in paragraph 99 that:

The measurement attribute most commonly adopted by enterprises in preparing their financial statements is historical cost. This is usually combined with other measurement attributes, such as realisable value. For example, inventories are usually carried at the lower of cost and net realisable value, and marketable securities may be carried at market value, that is, their realisable value. Furthermore, many enterprises combine historical costs and current costs as a response to the inability of the historical cost model to deal with the effects of changing prices of non-monetary assets.

The document deals in a similar style with the other elements.

Finally, regarding the concepts of **capital**, **capital maintenance** and **profit**, the IASC comments that:

At the present time, it is not the intention of the Board of the IASC to prescribe a particular measurement model (i.e. historical cost, current cost, realisable value, present value) ... This intention will, however, be reviewed in the light of world developments.

Clearly, there will be no international standard until a national standard is developed within bodies such as the ASB and until consensus is obtained.

The exposure draft is an influential document and we can trace its impact on the *Statement of Principles* issued by the ASB.

7.8 AICPA *Improving Business Reporting – A Customer Focus: Meeting the Information Needs of Investors and Creditors*

This was a study carried out by AICPA over a three-year period and published in 1994.[13] It resulted in a number of interesting recommendations to improve business reporting. A major recommendation was that standard-setters should develop a comprehensive model of business reporting, focusing on factors that create longer-term value and including financial and non-financial measures to cope with rapid changes, e.g. in technology and competition.

The committee identified that users had a high interest in being able to identify:

● **trends,** e.g. from five-year summaries of key statistics, separate reporting of segments and core and non-core assets and liabilities information;

● **substance of transactions,** e.g. accounting for off-balance-sheet transactions, complex capital instruments and investments in unconsolidated entities;

● **significant risks** arising from uncertainties over the valuation of assets and liabilities.

The committee identified that the users had a lower interest in:

- variety of income theories;
- valuation of intangible assets;
- accounting for combinations.

The committee identified user interest in a number of non-financial areas:

- the corporate strategy in general terms;
- the strengths, weaknesses, opportunities and threats (SWOTs) to the company;
- performance measures that management use with an explanation of reasons for changes and trends;
- management plans and degree to which achieved;
- information about the directors, management and their remuneration package.

A review of the recommendations broadly supports the stance being taken by the ASB, with mandatory standards being introduced for the financial statements, e.g. FRS 5 *Reporting the Substance of Transactions* and voluntary disclosures for non-financial areas, e.g. *Operating and Financial Review*.

B – ASB; DEVELOPMENT OF CONCEPTUAL FRAMEWORK

7.9 ASB *Statement of Principles for Financial Reporting 1992–1999*

7.9.1 Exposure Draft – 1995

The ASB issued a draft document of a Statement of Principles in 1992 followed by an Exposure Draft in 1995. In its introduction to the Exposure Draft[14] the ASB stated that the purpose and status of the *Statement of Principles* was:

- to assist the Board in the development of future accounting standards and in its review of existing accounting standards;
- to assist the Board by providing a basis for reducing the number of alternative accounting treatments permitted by law and accounting standards;
- to assist preparers of financial statements in applying accounting standards and in dealing with topics that do not form the subject of an accounting standard;
- to assist auditors in forming an opinion as to whether financial statements conform with accounting standards;
- to assist users of financial statements in interpreting the information contained in financial statements prepared in conformity with accounting standards;
- to provide those who are interested in the work of the Board with information about its approach to the formulation of accounting standards.

7.9.2 ASB Progress Paper '*Statement of Principles for Financial Reporting – the way ahead*'[15]

The Exposure Draft was not well received and in July 1996 the ASB issued a Progress Paper to clarify misunderstandings concerning the *Statement of Principles* Exposure Draft. In the Progress Paper it emphasised that

- the *Statement* was not intended to be a mandatory accounting standard but to provide a theoretical base on which mandatory standards could be developed;
- concepts such as true and fair, accruals and going concern would remain a fundamental part of the financial reporting system; and
- a system of current cost accounting was not on the ASB agenda.

The Progress Paper explained that, in the ASB's view, many traditional accounting principles were devised for manufacturing companies and were not effective in coping with more complex financial reporting issues such as intangible assets, joint ventures and financial instruments; further, there was the risk that the ASB would not be able to participate credibly internationally unless it moved closer to the conceptual frameworks of other leading standard-setters e.g. the International Accounting Standards Committee and the US Financial Accounting Standards Board.

The ASB consequently set itself the following major objectives:

- To exclude from the balance sheet items that were neither assets nor liabilities. For example, matching would continue to be applied in the profit and loss account, but balances carried forward in the balance sheet as assets and liabilities would be subjected to a test of their authenticity, and losses could not be carried forward as assets because they do not provide future economic benefits.
- To make 'off-balance-sheet' assets and liabilities more visible by requiring their inclusion in the balance sheet wherever possible. For example, financial instruments that do not entail initial cash investments, e.g. interest rate swaps, are commonly not recorded when they are acquired. The ASB's proposals would lead to more of such transactions being recorded and brought onto the balance sheet.
- To ensure that all gains and losses are reported prominently to avoid any being overlooked: for example, as required within the statement of total recognised gains and losses. The suggestion is that gains and losses on those assets and liabilities that are held on a continuing basis, primarily in order to enable the entity's operations to be carried out, should be reported in the statement of recognised gains and losses and not in the profit and loss account, and that all other gains and losses should be reported in the profit and loss account.
- To focus performance reporting on the components of income, not just the bottom line: for example, as required within the statement of total recognised gains and losses and the layered approach of FRS3.
- To employ current values if historical costs are inappropriate: e.g., by addressing measurement and providing a rationale for how various measures might be viewed.

It is the ASB's view that a statement of principles is designed to:

- provide a coherent frame of reference and definitions that ensure consistency of standards;
- minimise the need to reinvent fundamental concepts for every project; and
- assist preparers, auditors and others to assess alternatives when reporting treatment is not clear from statutes or standards.

The ASB also states that the main role of the *Statement of Principles* is in the standard-setting process but that it is not a mandatory standard and that there are other factors taken into account when setting standards. These other factors include:

● legal requirements

● cost-benefit considerations

● industry-specific issues

● the desirability of evolutionary change

● implementation issues

The *Statement* is therefore intended to play an important role, but it is neither mandatory nor intended to frustrate evolutionary changes, e.g. the appropriate financial reporting of derivatives and other financial instruments.

As Sir David Tweedie, Chairman of the ASB commented, 'The Board has developed its *Statement of Principles* in parallel with its development of accounting standards ... It is in effect the Board's compass for when we navigate uncharted waters in the years ahead. This is essential reading for those who want to know where the Board is coming from, and where it is aiming to go.'

7.9.3 *Statement of Principles* 1999[16]

The Statement contains eight chapters dealing with key issues. Each of the chapters is commented on below.

7.9.4 Chapter 1: 'The objective of financial statements'

The *Statement of Principles* follows the IASC *Framework* in the identification of user groups. Both the ASB and IASC have followed *The Corporate Report* except for the omission of any reference to the analysts/advisers, presumably on the basis that the analysts/advisers will be acting as agents for one of the other user groups.

The statement identifies the investor group as the primary group for whom the financial statements are being prepared. It then states the information needs of each group as follows:

● **Investors**. These need information to:
  – assess the stewardship of management e.g. in safeguarding the entity's resources and using them properly, efficiently and profitably;
  – take decisions about management e.g. assessing need for new management;
  – take decisions about their investment or potential investment e.g. deciding whether to hold, buy or sell shares and assessing the ability to pay dividends.

● **Lenders**. These need information to:
  – determine whether their loans and interest will be paid on time;
  – decide whether to lend and on what terms.

● **Suppliers**. These need information to:
  – decide whether to sell to the entity;
  – determine whether they will be paid on time;
  – determine longer-term stability if the company is a major customer.

● **Employees**. These need information to:
  – assess the stability and profitability of the company;
  – assess the ability to provide remuneration, retirement benefits and employment opportunities.

- **Customers**. These need information to:
  - assess the probability of the continued existence of the company taking account of their own degree of dependence on the company e.g. for future provision of specialised replacement parts and servicing product warranties.
- **Government and other agencies**. These need information to:
  - be aware of the commercial activities of the company;
  - regulate these activities;
  - raise revenue;
  - produce national statistics.
- **Public**. Members of the public need information to:
  - determine the effect on the local economy of the company's activities e.g. employment opportunities, use of local suppliers;
  - assess recent developments in the company's prosperity and changes in its activities.

The information needs of which group are to be dominant?

Seven groups are identified, but there is only one set of financial statements. Although they are described as general-purpose statements, a decision has to be made about which group's needs take precedence.

The *Statement of Principles* identifies the **investor group** as the defining class of user i.e. the primary group for whom the financial statements are being prepared.

It takes the view that financial statements 'are able to focus on the common interest of users'. The common interest is described as: 'all potential users are interested, to a varying degree, in the financial performance and financial position of the entity as a whole'.

This means that it is a prerequisite that the information must be relevant to the investor group. This suggests that any need of the other groups that is not also a need of the investors will not be met by the financial statements.

The 1995 Exposure Draft stated that: 'Awarding primacy to investors does not imply that other users are to be ignored. The information prepared for investors is useful as a frame of reference for other users, against which they can evaluate more specific information that they may obtain in their dealings with the enterprise.'

It is important, therefore, for all of the other users to be aware that this is one of the principles. If they require specific disclosures that might be relevant to them, they will need to take their own steps to obtain them, particularly where there is a conflict of interest. For example, if a closure is being planned by the directors, it may be in the investors' interest for the news to be delayed as long as possible to minimise the cost to the company; employees, suppliers, customers and the public must not expect any assistance from the financial statements – their information needs are not the primary concern.

What information should be provided to satisfy the information needs?

The *Statement* proposes that information is required in four areas: financial performance, financial position, generation and use of cash, and financial adaptability.

Financial performance

Financial performance is defined as the return an entity obtains from the resources it controls. This return is available from the profit and loss account and provides a means to assess past management performance, how effectively resources have been utilised and the capacity to generate cash flows.

Financial position

Financial position is available from an examination of the balance sheet and includes

- the economic resources controlled by an entity i.e. assets and liabilities
- financial structure i.e. capital gearing indicating how profits will be divided between the different sources of finance and the capacity for raising additional finance in the future
- liquidity and solvency i.e. current and liquid ratios
- capacity to adapt to changes – see below under **Financial adaptability**.

Generation and use of cash

Information is available from the cash flow statement which shows cash flows from operating, investment and financing activities providing a perspective that is largely free from allocation and valuation issues. This information is useful in assessing and reviewing previous assessments of cash flows.

Financial adaptability

This is an entity's ability to alter the amount and timing of its cash flows. It is desirable in order to be able to cope with difficult periods e.g. when losses are incurred and to take advantage of unexpected investment opportunities. It is dependent on factors such as the ability, at short notice, to:

- raise new capital
- repay capital or debt
- obtain cash from disposal of assets without disrupting continuing business i.e. realise readily marketable securities that might have been built up as a liquid reserve
- achieve a rapid improvement in net cash flows from operations.

7.9.5 Chapter 2: 'The reporting entity'

This chapter focuses on identifying when an entity should report and which activities to include in the report.

When an entity should report

The principle is that an entity should prepare and publish financial statements if:

- there is a legitimate demand for the information i.e. it is both decision-useful and benefits exceed the cost of producing the information; and
- it is a cohesive economic unit i.e. a unit under a central control that can be held accountable for its activities.

Which activities to include

The principle is that those activities should be included that are within the direct control of the entity e.g. assets and liabilities which are reported in its own balance sheet or indirect control e.g. assets and liabilities of a subsidiary of the entity which are reported in the consolidated balance sheet.

Control is defined as (a) the ability to deploy the resources and (b) the ability to benefit (or to suffer) from their deployment. Indirect control by an investor can be difficult to determine. The test is not to apply a theoretical level of influence e.g. holding $x\%$ of shares but to review the relationship that exists between the investor and investee in practice, such as the investor having the power to veto the investee's financial and operating policies and benefit from its net assets.

7.9.6 Chapter 3: 'The qualitative characteristics of financial information'

The *Statement of Principles* is based on the IASC *Framework* and contains the same four principal qualitative characteristics relating to the content of information and how the information is presented. The two primary characteristics relating to content are the need to be relevant and reliable; the two relating to presentation are the need to be understandable and comparable. The characteristics appear diagrammatically as follows:

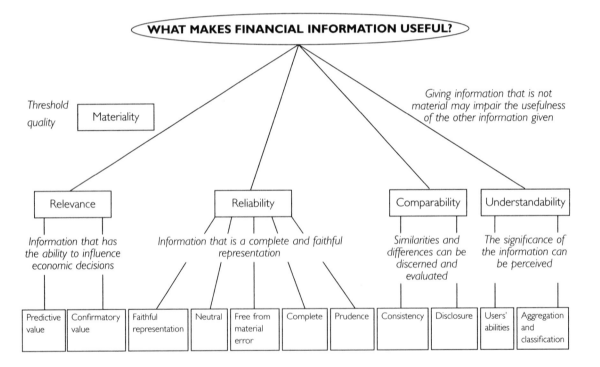

From the diagram we can see that for information content to be **relevant** it must have:

● the ability to influence the economic decisions of users;

● predictive value i.e. help users to evaluate or assess past, present or future events; or

● confirmatory value i.e. help users to confirm their past evaluations.

For information to be **reliable** it must be:

● free from material error i.e. transactions have been accurately recorded and reported;

● a faithful representation i.e. reflecting the commercial substance of transactions;

● neutral i.e. not presented in a way to achieve a predetermined result;

● prudent i.e. not creating hidden reserves or excessive provisions, deliberately understating assets or gains, or deliberately overstating liabilities or losses;

● complete i.e. the information is complete subject to a materiality test.

To be useful, the financial information also needs to be **comparable** over time and between companies and **understandable**.

It satisfies the criteria for understandability if it is capable of being understood by a user with a reasonable knowledge of business activities and accounting, and a willingness to study the information with reasonable diligence. However, the trade-off between relevance and reliability comes into play with the requirement that complex information that is relevant to economic decision-making should not be omitted because some users find it too difficult to understand. There is no absolute answer where there is the possibility of a trade-off and it is recognised by the ASB that the relative importance of the characteristics in different cases is a matter of judgement.

The chapter also introduces the idea of **materiality** as a threshold quality and any item that is not material does not require to be considered further. The statement recognises that no information can be useful if it is not also material by introducing the idea of a threshold quality which it describes as follows: An item of information is material to the financial statements if its misstatement or omission might reasonably be expected to influence the economic decisions of users of those financial statements, including their assessment of management's stewardship.[17]

First, this means that it is justified not to report immaterial items which would impose unnecessary costs on preparers and impede decision-makers by obscuring material information with excessive detail.

Secondly, it means that the important consideration is not user expectation (e.g. they might expect turnover to be accurate to within 1%) but the effect on decision-making (e.g. there might only be an effect if turnover were to be more that 10% over- or understated in which case, only errors exceeding 10% are material).

It also states that 'Materiality depends on the size of the item or error judged in the particular circumstances of its omission or misstatement'. The need to exercise judgement means that the preparer needs to have a benchmark.

A Discussion Paper issued in January 1995 by the Financial Reporting & Auditing Group of the ICAEW entitled 'Materiality in Financial Reporting FRAG 1/95' identified that there are few instances where an actual figure is given by statute or standard-setters e.g. FRS 6 para 76 refers to a material minority and indicates that this is defined as 10%.

The Paper also referred to a rule of thumb used in the USA:

> The staff of the US Securities and Exchange Commission have an informal rule of thumb that errors of more than 10% are material, those between 5% and 10% may be material and those under 5% are usually not material. These percentages are applied to gross profit, net income, equity and any specific line in the financial statements that is potentially misstated.

The ASB has moved away from setting percentage benchmarks and there is now a need for more explicit guidance on the application of the materiality threshold.

7.9.7 Chapter 4: 'The elements of financial statements'

This chapter gives guidance on the items that *could* appear in financial statements. These are described as **elements** and have the following essential features:

- **Assets**. These are rights to future economic benefits controlled by an entity as a result of past transactions or events.
- **Liabilities**. These are obligations of an entity to transfer future economic benefits as a result of past transactions or events i.e. ownership is not essential.
- **Ownership interest**. This is the residual amount found by deducting all liabilities from assets which belong to the owners of the entity.
- **Gains**. These are increases in ownership interest not resulting from contributions by the owners.
- **Losses**. These are decreases in ownership interest not resulting from distributions to the owners.
- **Contributions by the owners**. These are increases in ownership interest resulting from transfers from owners in their capacity as owners.
- **Distributions to owners**. These are decreases in ownership interest resulting from transfers to owners in their capacity as owners.

These definitions have been used as the basis for developing standards e.g. FRS 5 states that the substance of a transaction means identifying whether the transaction has given rise to new assets or liabilities, defined as above.

7.9.8   Chapter 5: 'Recognition in financial statements'

The objective of financial statements is to disclose in the balance sheet and the profit and loss account the effect on the assets and liabilities of **transactions** e.g. purchase of stock on credit and the effect of **events** e.g. accidental destruction of a vehicle by fire. This implies that transactions are recorded under the double entry principle with an appropriate debit and credit made to the element that has been affected e.g. the asset element (stock) and the liability element (creditors) are debited and credited to recognise stock bought on credit. Events are also recorded under the double entry principle e.g. the asset element (vehicle) is derecognised and credited because it is no longer able to provide future economic benefits and the loss element resulting from the fire damage is debited to the profit and loss account. The emphasis is on determining the effect on the assets and liabilities e.g. the increase in the asset element (stock), the increase in the liability element (creditors) and the reduction in the asset element (vehicle).

This emphasis has a particular significance for application of the matching concept in preparing the profit and loss account. The traditional approach to allocating expenditure across accounting periods has been to identify the costs that should be matched against the revenue in the profit and loss account and carry the balance into the balance sheet i.e. the allocation is driven by the need to match costs to revenue. The *Statement of Principles* approach is different in that it identifies the amount of the expenditure to be recognised as an asset and the balance is transferred to the profit and loss account i.e. the question is 'Should this expenditure be recognised as an asset (capitalised) and, if so, should any part of it be derecognised (written off as a loss element)?'

This means that the allocation process now requires an assessment as to whether an asset exists at the balance sheet date by applying the following test:

1 If the future economic benefits are eliminated at a single point in time, it is at that point that the loss is recognised and the expenditure derecognised i.e. the debit balance is transferred to the profit and loss account.

2 If the future economic benefits are eliminated over several accounting periods – typically because they are being consumed over a period of time – the cost of the

asset that comprises the future economic benefits will be recognised as a loss in the performance statement over those accounting periods i.e. written off as a loss element as their future economic benefit reduces.

The result of this approach should not lead to changes in the accounts as currently prepared but it does emphasise that matching cost and revenue is not the main driver of recognition i.e. the question is not 'How much expenditure should we match with the revenue reported in the profit and loss account?' but rather 'Are there future economic benefits arising from the expenditure to justify inclusion in the balance sheet?' and, if not, derecognise it i.e. write it off.

Dealing with uncertainty

There is almost always some uncertainty as to when to recognise an event or transaction e.g. when is asset element off raw material stock to be disclosed as the asset element work-in-progress? Is it when a stock requisition is issued, when the storekeeper isolates it in the stock to be issued bay, when it is issued onto the workshop floor, when it begins to be worked on?

The *Statement of Principles* states that the principle to be applied if a transaction has created or added to an existing asset or liability is to recognise it if:

1 sufficient evidence exists that the new asset or liability has been created or that there has been an addition to an existing asset or liability; and

2 the new asset or liability or the addition to the existing asset or liability can be measured at a monetary amount with sufficient reliability.

The use of the word sufficient reflects the uncertainty that surrounds the decision when to recognise and the *Statement* states: 'In the business environment, uncertainty usually exists in a continuum, so the recognition process involves selecting the point on the continuum at which uncertainty becomes acceptable'.[18]

Before that point it may be appropriate to disclose by way of note to the accounts e.g. a contingent liability that is possible (less than 50% chance of crystallising into a liability) but not probable (more than 50% chance of crystallising).

Sufficient reliability

Prudence requires more persuasive evidence of the measurement for the recognition of items that result in an increase in ownership interest than for the recognition of items that do not. However, the exercise of prudence does not allow for the omission of assets or gains where there is sufficient evidence of occurrence and reliability of measurement, or for the inclusion of liabilities or losses where there is not. This would amount to the deliberate understatement of assets or gains, or the deliberate overstatement of liabilities or losses.

Reporting gains and losses

Chapter 5 does not address the disclosure treatment of gains and losses. This is covered within specific FRSs e.g. FRS 3 Reporting Financial Performance. A change in assets or liabilities might arise from three classes of past event: transactions, contracts for future performance, and other events such as a change in market price.

If the change in an asset is offset by a change in liability, there will be no gain or loss. If the change in asset is not offset by a change in liability, there will be a gain or loss. If there is a gain or loss a decision is required as to whether it should be recognised in the profit and loss account or in the statement of total recognised gains and losses.

Recognition in profit and loss account

For a gain to be recognised in the profit and loss account, it must have been earned and realised. **Earned** means that no material transaction, contract or other event must occur before the change in the assets or liabilities will have occurred; **realised** means that the conversion into cash or cash equivalents must either have occurred or be reasonably assured.

Profit, as stated in the profit and loss account, is used as a prime measure of performance. Consequently, prudence requires particularly good evidence for the recognition of gains.

It is important to note that in this chapter the ASB is following a **balance sheet orientated** approach to measure gains and losses. The conventional profit and loss account approach would identify the **transactions** that had been undertaken and **allocate** these to financial accounting periods.

7.9.9 Chapter 6: 'Measurement in financial statements'

The majority of listed companies in the UK use the mixed measurement system whereby some assets and liabilities are measured using historical cost and some are measured using a current value basis. The *Statement of Principles* envisages that this will continue to be the practice and states that the aim is to select the basis that:

● Provides information about financial performance and financial position that is useful in evaluating the reporting entity's cash-generation abilities and in assessing its financial adaptability.

● The carrying values are sufficiently reliable and, if the historical cost and current value are equally reliable, the better measure is the one that is the most relevant.
  – Current values may frequently be no less reliable than historical cost figures given the level of estimation that is required in historical cost figures e.g. determining provisions for bad debts, stock provisions, product warranties.

● Reflects what the asset and liability represents e.g. the relevance of short-term investments to an entity will be the specific future cash flows and these are best represented by current values.

ASB view on need for a current value basis of measurement

The *Statement* makes the distinction[19] between return *on* capital i.e. requiring the calculation of accounting profit and return *of* capital i.e. requiring the measurement of capital and testing for capital maintenance. The *Statement* makes the point that the financial capital maintenance concept is not satisfactory when *significant* general or specific price changes have occurred.

ASB gradualist approach

The underlying support of the ASB for a gradualist move towards the use of current values is reflected in 'Although the objective of financial statements and the qualitative characteristics of financial information, in particular relevance and reliability may not change ... as markets develop, measurement bases that were once thought unreliable may become reliable. Similarly, as access to markets develops, so a measurement basis that was once thought insufficiently relevant may become the most relevant measure available'.[20]

Determining current value

Current value systems could be defined as replacement cost (entry value), net realisable value (exit value) or value in use (discounted present value of future cash flows). The approach of the *Statement* is to identify the value to the business by selecting from these three alternatives the measure that is most relevant in the circumstances. This measure is referred to as deprival value and represents the loss that the entity would suffer if it were deprived of the asset.

The value to the business is determined by considering whether the company would replace the asset. If the answer is yes, then use replacement cost; if the answer is *no* but the asset is worth keeping, then use value in use; and if *no* and the asset is not worth keeping, then use net realisable value. This can be shown diagrammatically as follows:

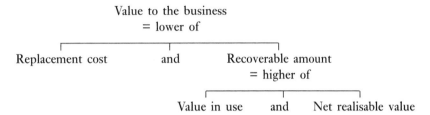

How will value to the business be implemented?

The profession experienced difficulties when it attempted to implement SSAP 7 and SSAP 16 and various *Guidelines* and *Handbook* recommendations. It was not alone in this e.g. New Zealand attempted to introduce a mandatory requirement for supplementary current cost information in 1982 but had to make it voluntary in 1986.

This reflected practice in the US, where a proposal for voluntary disclosure of current cost information was issued in 1986 in *Financial Reporting and Changing Prices*, FAS 1.

The ASB is acutely aware of such previous difficulties and is being pragmatic by following an incremental approach to the question of measurement stating that 'practice should develop by evolving in the direction of greater use of current values consistent with the constraints of reliability and cost'. This seems a sensible position for the ASB to take. Its underlying views were clear when it stated that 'a real terms capital maintenance system improves the relevance of information because it shows current operating margins as well as the extent to which holding gains and losses reflect the effect of general inflation, so that users of real terms financial statements are able to select the particular information they require'.[21]

Policing the mixed measurement system

Many companies have adopted the modified historical cost basis and revalued their fixed assets on a selective basis. However, this piecemeal approach allowed companies to cherry-pick the assets they wish to revalue on a selective basis at times when market values have risen. The ASB have addressed this in FRS 15 *Tangible Fixed Assets* issued in 1999.

7.9.10   Chapter 7: 'Presentation of financial information'

Chapter 7 states that the objective of the presentation adopted is to communicate clearly and effectively and in a simple and straightforward manner as is possible without loss of relevance or reliability and without significantly increasing the length of the financial statements.

The point about length is well made given the length of current annual reports and accounts e.g. Stagecoach Holdings plc extends to 69 pages, Sea Containers Ltd 76 pages and Hugo Boss 115 pages.

The *Statement* analyses the way in which information should be presented in financial statements to meet the objectives set out in chapter 1. It covers the requirement for items to be aggregated and classified and outlines good presentation practices in the statement of financial performance, balance sheet, cash flow statement and accompanying information e.g:

Statement of financial performance

Good presentation involves:

● Recognising only gains and losses.

● Classifying items by function e.g. production, selling, administrative and nature e.g. interest payable.

● Showing separately amounts that are affected in different ways by economic or commercial conditions e.g. continuing, acquired and discontinued operations, segmental geographical information.

● Showing separately:
  – items unusual in amount or incidence
  – expenses that are not operating expenses e.g. financing costs and taxation
  – expenses that relate primarily to future periods e.g. research expenditure.

Balance sheet

Good presentation involves:

● Recognising only assets, liabilities and ownership interest.

● Classifying assets so that users can assess the nature, amounts and liquidity of available resources.

● Classifying assets and liabilities so that users can assess the nature, amounts and timing of obligations that require or may require liquid resources for settlement.

● Classifying assets by function e.g. show fixed assets and current assets separately.

Accompanying information

Typical information includes chairman's statement, directors' report, operating and financial review, highlights and summary indicators.

The *Statement* states that the more complex an entity and its transactions become, the more users need an objective and comprehensive analysis and explanation of the main features underlying the entity's financial performance and financial position.

Good presentation involves discussion of:

● The main factors underlying financial performance, including the principal risks, uncertainties and trends in main business areas and how entity is responding.

● The strategies adopted for capital structure and treasury policy.

● The activities and expenditure (other than capital expenditure) that are investment in the future.

It is interesting to note the *Statement* view that highlights and summary indicators, such as amounts and ratios that attempt to distil key information, cannot on their own adequately describe or provide a basis for meaningful analysis or prudent decision-making. It does, however, state 'That having been said, well-presented highlights and summary indicators are useful to users who require only very basic information, such as the amount of sales or dividends'. The ASB will be giving further consideration to this view that there is a need for a really brief report.

7.9.11   Chapter 8: 'Accounting for interests in other entities'

Interest in other entities can have a material effect on the company's own financial performance and financial position and need to be fully reflected in the financial statements e.g. an extract from the 1998 Annual Report an Accounts of Stagecoach plc shows:

	Company balance sheet	*Consolidated balance sheet*
Tangible fixed assets	£0.7m	1,548.4m
Investments	£734.3m	51.4m

In deciding whether to include the assets in the consolidated balance sheet a key factor is the degree of influence exerted over the activities and resources of the investee:

● If the degree of influence allows control of the operating and financial policies, the financial statements are aggregated.

● If the investor has joint control or significant influence, the investor's share of the gains and losses are recognised in the consolidated profit and loss account and reflected in the carrying value of the investment.

However, there is no clear agreement on the treatment of interest in other entities and further developments can be expected.

7.10   Accounting policies[22]

Four fundamental concepts – going concern, accruals, consistency and prudence – were defined in SSAP 2 *Disclosure of Accounting Policies* which was issued in 1971. The ASB now considers it the appropriate time to withdraw SSAP 2 and bring its concepts into line with the *Statement of Principles* by issuing FRED 21 *Accounting Policies*.

7.10.1   How does FRED 21 differ from SSAP 2?

There are two major types of difference, namely in their role and in their approach to the four concepts.

Their role

Their roles are different, in that SSAP 2 was referred to when companies were devising accounting policies, whereas the objective of FRED 21 is to ensure that entities adopt or select the accounting policies most appropriate to their particular circumstances to give a true and fair view and disclose estimation techniques.

Selecting the most appropriate policies

FRED 21 spells out the criteria and constraints when selecting appropriate accounting policies. The criteria are qualitative characteristics of financial information from the

Statement of Principles i.e. relevance, reliability, comparability and understandability. The constraints are the need to balance the criteria and the need to balance the cost of providing information with the likely benefits of the information to users.

Disclosing estimation techniques

Estimation techniques are the methods and estimates adopted to arrive at a monetary value e.g. depreciation methods, discounting methods, bad debt provisioning.

There is an interesting proposal that if there are alternative estimation techniques that are equally relevant, then the directors will have to calculate the effect of all acceptable estimation techniques in order to assess whether they are material. The ASB's intention is to compel companies to measure the range of values that could be used. One commentator[23] has observed that this may well be a short step away from requiring the disclosure of that range so that users can assess the impact of different estimation techniques on financial statements.

Their approach to the four concepts

Their approach is different because we now have the *Statement of Principles*. We will briefly consider each of the four concepts.

Going concern

The *Statement of Principles*[24] states that financial statements are usually prepared – and measures are usually arrived at – on the basis that the reporting entity is a going concern because measures based on break-up values tend not to be relevant to users seeking to assess the entity's cash-generation ability and financial adaptability. FRED 21 follows this approach, stating that the information provided by financial statements is usually more relevant if prepared on the hypothesis that the entity is to continue in operational existence for the foreseeable future.[25]

Accruals

The concept has retained a status equal to that of going concern and FRED 21 states that the non-cash effects of transactions and other events should be reflected as far as possible in the period in which they occur.[26] However, FRED 21 follows the balance sheet approach which considers whether there has been an increase in assets or an increase in liabilities rather than matching revenues and costs with the residual appearing in the balance sheet. It takes the view that the accruals concept goes to the heart of the definitions of assets, liabilities, gains, losses and changes to shareholders' fund and that both going concern and accruals concepts play an important role on the recognition of these items.

Consistency

This is described as a desirable quality but subsidiary to comparability. FRED 21 states that, like the *Statement*, it sees comparability as a more desirable objective than consistency and that consistency should not be allowed to prevent improvements in accounting.[27]

Prudence

FRED 21 treats prudence as one aspect of the overall objective of reliability. Just as in the *Statement*, the aim is to avoid the misuse of the prudence concept that has occurred since SSAP 2 was issued. The misuse arose mainly because finance directors applied the concept artificially to smooth income by the deliberate understatement of assets and the deliberate overstatement of liabilities. Its original justification had been that it prevented the overstatement of assets and the understatement of liabilities, but its use as a smoothing device became widespread and justifies the ASB's current approach.

Realisation was seen in SSAP 2 as a necessary condition if the profit and loss account was to be prudent. FRED 21 no longer requires this realisation test to be satisfied, opting instead for recognition when profit can be reliably measured because markets have developed, so that it is often possible to be reasonably certain that a gain exists, and to measure it with sufficient reliability, even if no disposal has occurred.

We can see from the above that the going concern and accruals concepts have retained their force but consistency and prudence are merely desirable qualities that can be superseded at any time by a more desirable quality e.g. comparability.

Summary

Directors and accountants are constrained by a mass of rules and regulations which govern the measurement, presentation and disclosure of financial information. Regulations are derived from three major sources: the legislature in the form of statutes, the accountancy profession in the form of standards, and the Stock Exchange in the form of Listing Rules.

There have been a number of reports relating to financial reporting in the UK and other countries. The preparation and presentation of financial statements continue to evolve. Steps are being taken to provide a conceptual framework and there is growing international agreement on the setting of standards.

User needs have been accepted as paramount; qualitative characteristics of information have been specified; the elements of financial statements have been defined precisely; the presentation of financial information has been prescribed; and comparability between companies is seen as desirable.

However, the intention remains to produce financial statements that present a true and fair view. This is not achieved by detailed rules and regulations, and the exercise of judgement will continue to be needed. This opens the way for creative accounting practices that bring financial reporting and the accounting profession into disrepute. Strenuous efforts will continue to be needed from the auditors, the ASB, the Review Panel and the Financial Reporting Council to contain the use of unacceptable practices. The regulatory bodies show that they have every intention of accepting the challenge.

The question of the measurement base that should be used has yet to be settled. Solomons suggested the use of value to the business and this has received support in *The Future Shape of Financial Reports*. The measurement question still remains a major area of financial reporting that needs to be addressed.

The *Statement of Principles* sees the objective of financial statements as providing information about the financial position, performance and financial adaptability of an enterprise that is useful to a wide range of users in making economic decisions. It recognises that they are limited because they largely show the financial effects of past events and do not necessarily show non-financial information. On the question of measurement the view has been expressed that

historical cost has the merit of familiarity and (to some extent) objectivity; current values have the advantage of greater relevance to users of the accounts who wish to assess the current state or recent performance of the business, but they may sometimes be unreliable or too expensive to provide. It concludes that practice should develop by evolving in the direction of greater use of current values to the extent that this is consistent with the constraints of reliability, cost and acceptability to the financial community.[28]

There are critics[29] who argue that the concern with recording current asset values rather than historical costs means that

the essential division between the ASB and its critics is one between those who are more concerned about where they want to be and those who want to be very clear about where they are now. It is a division between those who see the purpose of financial statements as taking economic decisions about the future, and those who see it as a basis for making management accountable and for distributing the rewards among the stakeholders.

Finally, it is interesting to give some thought to extracts from two publications which indicate that there is still a long way to go in the evolution of financial reporting, and that there is little room for complacency.

The first is from *The Future Shape of Financial Reports*:

As Solomons and *Making Corporate Reports Valuable* discussed in detail, the then system of financial reporting in the UK fails to satisfy the purpose of providing information to shareholders, lenders and others to appraise past performance in order to form expectations about an organisation's future performance in five main respects:

1 ... measures of performance ... are based on original or historical costs ...
2 Much emphasis is placed on a single measure of earnings per share ...
3 ... insufficient attention is paid to changes in an enterprise's cash or liquidity position ...
4 The present system is essentially backward looking ...
5 Emphasis is often placed on the legal form rather than on the economic substance of transactions ...

We have seen that some of these five limitations are being addressed, but not all, e.g. the provision of projected figures.

The second extract is from *Making Corporate Reports Valuable*:

The present balance sheet almost defies comprehension. Assets are shown at depreciated historical cost, at amounts representing current valuations and at the results of revaluations of earlier periods (probably also depreciated); that is there is no consistency whatsoever in valuation practice. The sum total of the assets, therefore, is meaningless and combining it with the liabilities to show the entity's financial position does not in practice achieve anything worthwhile.[30]

The ASB has taken steps to deal with the frequency of revaluations but the criticism still holds in that there will continue to be financial statements produced incorporating mixed measurement bases.

The point made by some critics remains unresolved: 'Accountability and the ASB's decision usefulness are not compatible. Forward-looking decisions require forecasts of future cash flows, which in the economic model are what determines the values of assets. These values are too subjective to form the basis of accountability. The definition of assets and the recognition rules restrict assets to economic benefits the enterprise controls as a result of past events and that are measurable with sufficient reliability. But economic decision-making requires examination of all sources of future cash flows, not just a restricted sub-set of them.'[31]

The need for a conceptual framework is being addressed around the world. The UK is not alone in its search. In the USA, Australia, Canada and the IASC, the approach has been the same as that now followed by the ASB, i.e. commencing with a consideration of the objectives of financial statements, qualitative characteristics of financial information, definition of the elements, and when these are to be recognised in the financial statements. There is a general agreement on these areas.

Review questions

1 (a) Name the user groups and information needs of the user groups identified by *The Corporate Report*, the IASC *Framework for the Presentation and Preparation of Financial Statements* and the ASB *Statement of Principles*.
   (b) Discuss the effect of *The Corporate Report* on current financial reporting practice.

2 Compare and contrast the regulatory framework and the conceptual framework. Evaluate the ASB's attempt to find a conceptual framework.

3 Give a brief synopsis of the ICAS *Making Corporate Reports Valuable* and the Solomons Report.

4 R. MacVe in *A Conceptual Framework for Financial Accounting and Reporting: The Possibility for an Agreed Structure* suggested that the search for a conceptual framework was a political process. Discuss the effect that this thinking has had and will have on the standard-setting.

5 (a) In 1999, the ASB published the *Statement of Principles*. Explain what you consider to be the purpose and status of the *Statement*.
   (b) Chapter 4 of the *Statement* identifies and defines what the ASB believes to be the elements that make up financial statements. Define any four of the elements and explain how, in your opinion, the identification and definition of the elements of financial statements would enhance financial reporting.
   (c) Chapter 5 of the *Statement* states that matching is not regarded as the driver of the recognition process. Explain what is meant by this and its probable effect in practice.

6 The evidence suggests that the simple percentage rule has not worked ... its simplicity and rigidity leave it open to abuse! Discuss.[32]

7 'The replacement of accrual accounting with cash flow accounting would avoid the need for a conceptual framework.' Discuss.[33]

8 Financial accounting theory has accumulated a vast literature. A cynic might be inclined to say that the vastness of the literature is in sharp contrast to its impact on practice.
   (a) Describe the different approaches that have evolved in the development of accounting theory.
   (b) Assess its impact on standard-setting.
   (c) Discuss the contribution of accounting theory to the understanding of accounting practice, and suggest contributions that it might make in the future.

Exercises

An extract from the solution is provided in the appendix at the end of the text for exercises marked with an asterisk (*).

* **Question I**

The following information is available in relation to MCRV Ltd for the year ending 31 December 20X8:

(a) Statement of assets and liabilities as at 31 December. This statement at the start of the year is assumed to contain valuations at net realisable value throughout:
   (i) Fixed assets are estimated by the directors on the basis of an orderly disposal in a secondhand market.
   (ii) The NRV of raw materials was assumed by the directors to be the same as their purchase price.
   (iii) The NRV of finished goods was estimated as selling price less the estimated costs of disposal in the normal course of business.
(b) A summary of the cash book.
(c) The non-cash transactions during the year are as shown in the journal entries.

Statement of Assets and Liabilities as at 31 December

		20X7		20X8
		£		£
Fixed assets		200		270
Current assets				
Stock		50		66
Debtors		30		40
Cash		10		76
		290		452
Less:				
Current liabilities				
Creditors	35		30	
Long-term loans	60		70	
		95		100
		195		352

Cash Transactions during the year ended 31 December 20X8

		£		£
Cash received during 20X8:				
Credit customers				190
Long-term loans				30
				220
Cash paid during 20X8:				
Credit suppliers		85		
Fixed assets		30		
Salaries		30		
Loan interest		9		
				154
				66

Journal Entries for Non-cash Transactions for the year ended
31 December 20X8

	Dr	Cr
	£	£
Debtors	200	
Sales		200
Credit sales for 20X8		
Stock	80	
Creditors		80
Credit purchases for 20X8		
Cost of goods sold	70	
Stock		70
Goods used for sale		
Stock	6	
Cost of goods sold		6
Uplift in closing stock from cost to		
net realisable value		

Required:
(a) Prepare an operations statement for the year ended 31 December 20X8 to show wealth created by operations.
(b) Prepare a statement of changes in wealth, in the following format:
> **Increase in wealth due to operations**
> **Increase in value of fixed assets**
> **Decrease in value of long-term loans**   _____
> **Realisable increase in net assets**   ===========
(c) Explain circumstances in which there can be a decrease in the value of long-term loans.
(d) Explain how the percentage return on capital employed, current ratio and acid test ratio based on the historical cost concept would differ from those calculated using the concept applied in the above question.
(Adapted from extract in Melody plc annual report (ICAS))

Question 2

The following extract is from *Conceptual Framework for Financial Accounting and Reporting: Elements of Financial Statements and Their Measurement*, FASB 3, December 1976.

> The benefits of achieving agreement on a conceptual framework for financial accounting and reporting manifest themselves in several ways. Among other things, a conceptual framework can (1) guide the body responsible for establishing accounting standards, (2) provide a frame of reference for resolving accounting questions in the absence of a specific promulgated standard, (3) determine bounds for judgement in preparing financial statements, (4) increase financial statement users' understanding of and confidence in financial statements, and (5) enhance comparability.

Required:

(a) **Define a conceptual framework.**

(b) **Critically examine why the benefits provided in the above statements are likely to flow from the development of a conceptual framework for accounting.**

Question 3

The following extract is from 'Comments of Leonard Spacek', in R.T. Sprouse and M. Moonitz, *A Tentative Set of Broad Accounting Principles for Business Enterprises*, Accounting Research Study No. 3, AICPA, New York, 1962, reproduced in A. Belkaoui, *Accounting Theory*, Harcourt Brace Jovanovich.

> A discussion of assets, liabilities, revenue and costs is premature and meaningless until the basic principles that will result in a fair presentation of the facts in the form of financial accounting and financial reporting are determined. This fairness of accounting and reporting must be for and to people, and these people represent the various segments of our society.

Required:

(a) **Explain the term 'fair' as used in UK financial reports.**

(b) **Discuss the extent to which the ASB conceptual framework satisfies the above definition.**

Question 4

The Financial Reporting Council's November 1991 publication *The State of Financial Reporting: A Review* had a section on the work of the Accounting Standards Board which stated that 'We have devoted much of our energies during the first year to the demanding task of developing a clear Statement of Principles from which our work on individual standards will derive.'

Required:

(a) **Discuss why the *Statement of Principles* was not finalised until 1999 – eight years after the 1991 comment by the FRC.**

(a) **Summarise why the Accounting Standards Board (ASB) placed such emphasis on developing a clear *Statement of Principles*.**

(b) **Outline the principal matters to be dealt with in any three of the eight chapters of the *Statement of Principles* 1999.**

References

1 *The Scope and Implications of the Conceptual Framework Project*, Stanford, Conn., FASB, 1967.
2 R. MacVe, *A Conceptual Framework for Financial Accounting and Reporting*, ICAEW, 1981.
3 E. Stamp, 'A conceptual framework', *Accountancy*, March 1982.
4 ASC, *The Corporate Report*, 1975.
5 D. Solomons, *Guidelines for Financial Reporting Standards*, ICAEW, 1989.
6 J. Arnold *et al.*, *The Future Shape of Financial Reports*, ICAEW, 1991.
7 ICAS, *Making Corporate Reports Valuable*, 1988.
8 T. Lee, 'In criticism of the Solomons Guidelines', *The Accountant's Magazine*, March 1989.
9 R. MacVe, 'In criticism of the Solomons Guidelines', *Accountancy*, March 1989, p. 20; *Accountancy*, April 1989, p. 26.
10 D. Solomons, 'The Solomons Guidelines: A reply to the critics', *Accountancy*, August 1989.
11 J. Arnold *et al.*, *The Future Shape of Financial Reports*, ICAEW, 1991, p. 32.
12 IASC *Framework for the Presentation and Preparation of Financial Statements*, 1989.

13 *Improving Business Reporting – A Customer Focus. Meeting the Information Needs of Investors and Creditors*, AICPA, 1994.

14 *Statement of Principles for Financial Reporting*, ASB, 1995.

15 ASB Progress Paper *Statement of Principles for Financial Reporting – the way ahead.*

16 *Statement of Principles for Financial Reporting*, ASB, 1999.

17 *Ibid.*, para. 3.27.

18 *Ibid.*, para. 5.10.

19 *Ibid.*, para. 6.41.

20 *Ibid.*, para. 6.24.

21 *Statement of Principles for Financial Reporting*, ASB, 1995, para 5.37.

22 *Accounting Policies*, ASB, 1999.

23 H. Lunt, 'The Fab Four's solo careers', *Accountancy*, March 2000, p. 75.

24 *Statement of Principals for Financial Reporting*, ASB, 1999, para. 6. 30.

25 FRED 21, *Accounting Policies*, ASB, 1999, para. 16(a).

26 *Ibid.*, para. 16(b).

27 *Ibid.*, Appendix 4, para. 12.

28 A. Lennard, 'The peg on which our standards hang', *Accountancy*, January 1996, p. 80.

29 S. Fearnley and M. Page, 'Why the ASB has lost its bearings', *Accountancy*, April 1996, p. 94.

30 ICAS, *Making Corporate Reports Valuable*, 1988, p. 35.

31 S. Fearnley and M. Page, *op. cit.*

32 J. Blakemore and B. Pain, Materiality in Accounting, *ACCA Students' Newsletter*, May 1998, pp. 34–36.

33 R. Skinner, *Accountancy*, January 1990, p. 25.

PART **2**

Regulatory framework – an attempt to achieve uniformity

Published accounts of listed public companies

8.1 Introduction

Each company listed on the Stock Exchange publishes its annual report and accounts. This document is sent to each of the shareholders of the company as a stewardship report by the directors on their handling of the company's affairs for the **past year**; for this reason it contains financial statements on the growth that has been achieved during the year and on the financial position at the end of the year, together with an explanation of any material unexpected changes that occurred. It is also used by existing and potential investors as an aid in predicting **cash flows of future years**; for this reason it contains a narrative report identifying major changes that are likely to occur.

In this chapter we consider the information contained in the published accounts and the way it is presented. We will use The Body Shop International plc annual report and notes on accounts for the year ended 28 February 1998 as an illustration. We will consider the following:

- A public company's financial calendar
- Information appearing in a director's report
- Operating and Financial Review
- Criteria for information appearing in profit and loss account and balance sheet
- What information is required to be disclosed in Format 1 and Format 2?
- Does it really matter under which heading a cost is classified in the profit and loss account provided it is not omitted?
- Effect of SSAP 25 *Segmental Reporting* and FRS 3 on presentation
- The balance sheet formats and accounting rules for asset valuation
- Disclosure of accounting policies

8.2 A public company's financial calendar for providing shareholders with information

The ownership and management of a public company whose shares are listed on the Stock Exchange are separate. The owners or shareholders are provided with regular information for stewardship accountability and to allow them to make investment decisions. Each company follows its own financial calendar. For example, the financial calendar for The Body Shop in 1998 appears in Figure 8.1, with our comments in italics.

Figure 8.1   Financial calendar for The Body Shop International plc.

28 February 1998   **End of the company's financial year**

The profit and loss account will be made up for the year ended 28 February 1998 and a balance sheet prepared. The auditors will carry out their audit work with a view to signing the audit report on 13 May 1998.

The profit for the year will have been announced in accordance with Stock Exchange requirements as soon as possible after draft accounts have been agreed with the auditor so that all investors learn of the profit for the year at the same time in an attempt to avoid one investor having an advantage over another – the hope is that insider trading can be eliminated.

22 May 1998   **Publication of 1998 Annual Report and Accounts**

The auditors will sign a report that they have audited the accounts and will give their opinion as to whether or not those accounts give a true and fair view of the state of affairs of the company.

The annual report and accounts will be issued by the company.

22 May 1998   **Record date for final dividend**

The company closes its share register and for practical purposes it has to have a cut-off date when it effectively says that the dividend will be paid to the person named on the register at that date.

19 June 1998   **Annual general meeting**

The meeting at which the shareholders vote to

*1 Receive the **directors' report** and the **audited accounts** for the year ended 28 February 1998.*

2 Declare a dividend.

3 Reappoint the auditors and authorise the directors to fix their salary.

10 July 1998   **Payment of final dividend**

22 October 1998   **Announcement of the interim results for the six months ended 31 August 1998**

The interim report contains numerical data, e.g. net turnover, profit attributable to shareholders and narrative information, e.g. any special factors that influenced the profit. The information is normally unaudited.

6 November 1998   **Record date for the interim dividend**

6 January 1999   **Payment of the interim dividend**

8.2.1   What information appears in an annual report?

An annual report contains a number of separate reports and statements. These may be required:

● By statute:
  Directors' report; Profit and loss account; Balance sheet and Auditors' report

- By ASB mandatory FRS:
  Cash flow statement

- By ASB recommendation:
  Operating and financial review

- By Stock Exchange listing requirement:
  Compliance with the *Combined Code*

8.3 Information appearing in a directors' report

- The Companies Act 1985 states that each year the directors are to prepare a report that gives information about the business's activities to allow the shareholders to assess the asset backing of their shares; to make shareholders aware of material movements in the ownership of the issued share capital; to indicate the company's activities in the community; and to recommend a dividend.

- Information about the business's *activities* includes:
  details about the principal activities during the year and any significant changes;
  a fair review of the development of the business of the company during the year and of its position at the end of the year,[1] e.g. comment on the development of new markets, comment on any significant rationalisation involving discontinuing segments of the business, etc.;
  likely future developments;
  research and development activity undertaken during the year;
  significant changes in the fixed assets of the company during the year;
  any important events affecting the company which have occurred since the end of the financial year.

- Information allowing the shareholders to assess **asset backing** includes:
  a note of the amount if the market value of land and buildings differs materially from the book values; this gives shareholders a view of the asset backing in determining the value of their shares.

- Information making shareholders aware of **material movements in the ownership of the issued share capital** includes:
  share interests that exceed 3% of the nominal capital of the company;
  the purchase of own shares;
  shares of the company in which directors have an interest.

- Information indicating the company's **activities in the community** includes:
  charitable and political donations;
  policy in respect of applications for employment by disabled applicants;
  action taken in respect of employee reports and consultation.

- Regarding a dividend, the directors recommend how much should be distributed by way of dividend and how much they propose to carry to reserves (section 235).

The information in the report requires a number of judgements to be made, e.g. a **fair** review, **significant** changes and any **important** events. Because it involves judgement and opinion (which is not easily verified), the directors' report is not audited. However, the information should be sufficient in quantity and quality to satisfy the reasonable expectations of the readers to whom it is addressed. The auditors have a statutory duty to carry out such investigations as are necessary for them to form an opinion about whether or not the information contained in the directors' report is **consistent** with the financial statements on which they are reporting.[2]

8.3.1 What does a directors' report look like?

The paragraph headings from The Body Shop International plc 1999 annual report are set out in Figure 8.2 as an illustration of the type of information contained in a published set of accounts. The extract in Figure 8.3 indicates the culture of a company in respect of employee and commercial issues, and illustrates how the report has become almost an index for other sources of financial information.

Figure 8.2   Directors' report.

Principal activities	Review of the business	Results and dividends
Annual general meeting	Directors	Fixed assets
Supplier payment policy	Share capital	Substantial shareholdings
Disabled employees	Employee involvement	Research and development
Donations	Auditors	Corporate Governance
Year 2000		

Note: Corporate Governance is covered in a report by considering such items as:
● Board of Directors and Board Committees
   – the Audit Committee
   – the Remuneration and Nominations Committee
● Internal Financial Control
● Going concern
● Auditors review.

Figure 8.3   Extract from The Body Shop International plc 1999 directors' report.

The directors submit their report and accounts for the 52 weeks ended 27 February 1999.

Principal activities

The Group originates, produces and sells skin and hair care products and related items through its own shops and franchised outlets.

Group Review of the Business and Future Developments

A review of the Group's business during the year is contained in the Chief Executive's Statement on pages 7 to 10 and in the Operating and Financial Review on pages 13 to 21.

Supplier payment policy

The Company's Trading Charter states that the relationship between the Company and its suppliers should be commercially viable, mutually beneficial and based on trust and respect … It is Company policy to pay suppliers in accordance with terms that have been mutually agreed in advance.

Disabled employees

Applications for employment by disabled persons are given full and fair consideration for all vacancies, having regard to their particular aptitudes and abilities. In the event of an employee becoming disabled, every effort is made to retain them in order that their employment with the Group may continue. It is the policy of the Group that training, career development and promotion opportunities should be available to all employees.

Figure 8.3 (*cont.*)

Donations

The Group has continued its policy of contributing to the community in a variety of ways. These include encouraging employees and franchisees to involve themselves in community projects, as well as campaigns to increase public awareness of human rights, environmental and animal protection issues.

8.3.2 Company Law reform

The directors' report contains backward looking qualitative information with some items which relate to an assessment of the business from a business perspective, such as the fair review requirement, but many others which appear for public policy purposes such as political and charitable donations and the employment of the disabled. The Consultative Document [March 2000, para 5.102] states that it is envisaged that the directors' report, with its jumble of disclosures, will disappear and that the items currently appearing in the directors' report could be reported elsewhere, e.g. in:

● a new OFR e.g. important events including post balance sheet events;

● a supplementary statement e.g. political and charitable gifts;

● notes to the accounts e.g. asset values and directors' interests;

● note to the performance statement e.g. amount recommended for dividend;

● a return filed with Companies House.

8.3.3 Chief Executive's Report

The directors' report was supported by statements from the Co-Chairs and the Chief Executive. A brief extract from The Body Shop International 1999 annual report illustrates the type of information provided:

From the Co-Chairs Gordon and Anita Roddick

We are happy to report that the direction we devised for The Body Shop is taking shape under the leadership of Patrick Gournay. Patrick has brought with him a culture of strong leadership, vision and accountability which has been unanimously welcomed in the Company.

This period has been the most difficult in the history of The Body Shop and also the most important. We are proud of our values and how they have shaped the responsibility and care with which we are making this transition... The team that he is building up shares our concerns, love and understanding of the Company...

From the Chief Executive

1999 Trading Results

During this period of fundamental change at The Body Shop, our 1999 trading results are in line with expectations... Group turnover was 4% higher at £303.7

million, but operating profit fell from £38.1 to £24.6 million excluding exceptional and restructuring costs...after exceptional and restructuring costs of £21.1 million, pre-tax profits fell from £38 million to £3.4 million.

Strategic update

In January, we announced our plan to implement significant changes to the business in order to focus our resources on the retail end of our business...

Manufacturing and supply chain

We are reorganising our supply chain on a regional basis in order to increase our flexibility and speed to market...As part of our strategy, we have decided to sell our two manufacturing plants at Littlehampton to a third party... Our plan is for the two Littlehampton plants, under new ownership, to supply our UK and European operations.

Outlook

We are on schedule to meet the targets that we have set ourselves to reshape the business and reposition The Body Shop as a world class retailer.

8.4 Operating and financial review

The operating and financial review statement was described in Chapter 6. The Body Shop International 1999 annual report disclosed the following financial review extracts:

Turnover

Group turnover for the year increased by 4% to £303.7 million, of which 60% relates to international markets. Of the total turnover, 53% (1998: 60%) represented wholesale sales to franchisees and 47% (1998: 40%) was achieved in retail sales through company-owned stores, mail order and The Body Shop Direct. The change in mix reflects the higher proportion of company-owned stores, with retail sales of £143.4 million being 22% higher than in the previous year.

Operating performance

Gross profit was 1% lower at £176.0 million (1998: £177.2 million) influenced by our efforts to reduce system inventory and eliminate obsolete stock. The £1.2 million difference reflects an increase in retail gross profit of £10.8 million, given the increased number of company-owned stores, offset by a decrease of £12.0 million due to other factors. Of these the main components were lower wholesale sales, partly due to de-stocking by head franchisees (£4.6 million); reduced wholesale margins due primarily to increased sales discounts and price support to certain markets (£4.7 million); and increased stock write-offs (£3.9 million).

Shareholders' return

The loss attributable to shareholders amounted to £4.6 million, compared with a profit of £22.8 million in the previous year... Our normal policy is to increase dividends in line with the growth of earnings per share. However, in the light of the 1999 trading result, the directors have proposed an unchanged final dividend...

8.5 Criteria for information appearing in a published profit and loss account and balance sheet

There are four criteria to consider:

● The financial statements are required to present a true and fair view of the profits and of the assets and liabilities.

● The information is required to comply with fundamental accounting concepts.

● The format in which it is presented is prescribed.

● Sensitive information is required to be disclosed by way of notes to the accounts.

We comment on each of these in turn.

8.5.1 True and fair requirement

The Companies Act 1985 requires financial statements to give a true and fair view of the profit or loss for the financial year and the state of affairs at the end of the year via the profit and loss account and balance sheet respectively.[3]

True and fair is a legal concept and can be authoritatively decided only by a court. However, the courts have never attempted to define 'true and fair'. A legal opinion was obtained by the ASC which included the following statement:

> It is however important to observe that the application of the concept involves judgement in questions of degree. The information contained in the accounts must be accurate and comprehensive to within acceptable limits. What is acceptable and how is this to be achieved? Reasonable businessmen and accountants may differ over the degree of accuracy or comprehensiveness which in particular cases the accounts should attain. Equally, there may sometimes be room for differences over the method to adopt in order to give a true and fair view, cases in which there may be more than one true and fair view of the same financial position. Again, because true and fair involves questions of degree, we think that cost-effectiveness must play a part in deciding the amount of information which is sufficient to make accounts true and fair.
>
> Accounts will not be true and fair unless the information they contain is sufficient in quantity and quality to satisfy the reasonable expectations of the readers to whom they are addressed.[4]

A further counsel's opinion was obtained by the ASB in 1991[5] and published in its foreword to Accounting Standards. It advised that accounting standards are an authoritative source of accounting practice and it is now the norm for financial statements to comply with them. In consequence the court may take accounting standards into consideration when forming an opinion on whether the financial statements give a true and fair view.

Many continental countries viewed the concept of the true and fair view with suspicion, since it ran counter to their legal systems. In Germany the true and fair override provision has not been directly implemented and laws are interpreted according to their function and objectives. It appears that the role of true and fair in the European context is to act as a protection against over-regulation.[6]

8.5.2 The fundamental accounting concepts underlying the published profit and loss account and balance sheet

The Companies Act 1985 requires compliance with the fundamental accounting principles of accruals, prudence, going concern and consistency that were discussed in Chapters 1 and 2.[7]

There may well be a conflict between the prudence concept, which is an **excluding concept** in that it excludes a transaction unless there is reasonable certainty that cash flows will materialise, and the accruals concept, which is an **inclusive concept** in that it includes a transaction unless the profit is unrealised. The Companies Act gives no guidance on how to resolve the conflict, but SSAP 2 states that, where the accruals concept is inconsistent with the prudence concept, the latter prevails.[8] However, refer back to Chapter 7, para. 10 for the position following the implementation of FRED 21.

8.5.3 The prescribed formats

The Companies Act 1985 allows a company a choice from four formats of profit and loss account.[9] Two of the formats are the choice of using the vertical or horizontal layout. The other two choices, however, allow for the analysis of costs in different ways: according to **type of expenditure**, e.g. raw materials, wages and depreciation, or according to **type of operation**, e.g. cost of sales, distribution costs and administration expenses.

The formats are as follows:

Format 1: Vertical with costs analysed according to type of operation.
Format 2: Vertical with costs analysed according to type of expenditure.
Format 3: Horizontal with costs analysed according to type of operation.
Format 4: Horizontal with costs analysed according to type of expenditure.

Public companies tend in general to use either Format 1, the vertical presentation with costs analysed according to the type of operation, or Format 2 with the costs analysed according to the type of expenditure.

8.5.4 Disclosure of sensitive information by way of note to the accounts

Directors are required to submit an annual report to the shareholders both to account to the shareholders for their **stewardship** of the shareholders' economic resources and to provide information that will assist the shareholders to make **predictions** as to future cash flows without giving competitors information from which they might benefit. In addition, where there is a growing belief that a number of other stakeholders are interested in the activities of a company, e.g. employees, the directors must make a report to those stakeholders.

For stewardship, prediction and other stakeholders, some information may be regarded as being of particular interest. We have described this as **sensitive information**.

Information that is sensitive when accounting for stewardship purposes

The Companies Act requires the company to disclose information that permits the shareholders to see both how much the directors are taking out of the company directors' share options, Related Party disclosures, and how much auditors are taking out of the company.

How much the directors are taking out of the company

Shareholders must be confident that the directors are not bleeding the company by voting themselves excessive salaries and expense allowances.[10] The remuneration paid to a director will depend on the provisions of the articles of association and of any service agreement between the company and director. However, the remuneration may be made up in many ways and the Companies Act requires disclosure of:

● emoluments;
● pension payments;
● compensation for loss of office;
● aggregate consideration paid to or receivable by third parties for the service of any person as a director of the company.

How much are directors making from share options?

There is now a requirement to disclose share options held by directors.

An abbreviated extract from The Body Shop shows for one of the directors, J Reid:

Options held at 1.3.1998	Granted in year	Exercised in year	Lapsed in year	Options held at 27.2.1999	Exercise price	Earliest date exercisable	Expiry date
589,063	—	—	—	589,063	1.28	14.06.00	14.06.05
13,732	—	—	13,732	—	1.42	01.10.03	31.03.04
	18,750	—	—	18,750	1.04	17.07.05	17.01.06

There is also a statement of performance criteria attaching to options. This states:

At 27 February 1999 a total of 4,808,263 options were exercisable by Directors under performance criteria as follows:

(a) Under the 1991 and 1995 schemes, options granted are subject to the condition that growth in the Company's normalised earnings per share over any three consecutive financial years ... exceeds the growth in the Retail Price Index by at least 4% per annum.

(b) Options which are granted to a value in excess of four times salary are subject to an additional performance condition. This requires the growth in the Company's earnings per share over five consecutive years to have been such as would place it in the top quartile of the FTSE 100 companies, ranked by reference to growth in earnings per share during the same period.

Related party transactions

Financial reports are presumed to record transactions carried out on an arm's-length basis between independent parties. This has two implications. The first is that the transfer of resources has been recorded at fair value; the second is that predictions can be made with confidence that any future transfer of resource will occur on the same basis. This presumption is not correct however when one of the parties has the ability to control or influence the financial and operating policies of the other, or the parties are subject to common control or influence.

Related party classifications

Doubtless great ingenuity will be shown by parties who wish to avoid related party disclosure. One approach will be to avoid classification as a related party. Consequently the ASB in FRS 8 *Related Party Transactions* set out a list of relationships that are related, while recognising that each situation will need to be assessed.

Parties are related when during the financial year:

● One party has direct or indirect control of the other party
● The parties are subject to common control

● One party has influence over the financial and operating polices of the other party to an extent that the other party might be inhibited from pursuing at all times its own separate interests

● The parties, in entering a transaction, are subject to influence from the same source to such an extent that one of the parties has subordinated its own separate interests

Relationship that is always related

Related parties of a company issuing a financial report include:

● parent, subsidiary and fellow subsidiary companies

● associates and joint ventures
  ● Note that transactions between parent, subsidiary and associated companies within the same group are now a common feature of business. We will discuss the treatment on intragroup transactions in Chapter 12-14.

● directors of the company and the parent company
  ● Transactions between companies with common director pose a problem. Financial scandals in recent years have featured dominant, powerful chief executives who were also involved with a related party, e.g. Robert Maxwell, the MGM Group and Maxwell Communications.

● pension funds for the benefit of employees of the company or of any entity that is a related party of the reporting entity.

Relationships in which related party is presumed

There is a presumption, unless it can be demonstrated that neither party has influenced the financial and operating policies of the other in such a way as to inhibit the pursuit of separate interest, where one party is:

● in a senior position having authority or responsibility for directing or controlling the major activities and resources of the reporting entity i.e. in a position of key management

● a person owning or able to exercise control over 20% or more of the voting rights of the reporting entity, whether directly or through nominees

● each person acting in concert in such a way as to be able to exercise control or influence over the reporting entity

● an entity managing or managed by the reporting entity under a management contract

● Members of the close family of any person who is realated party

The need to prepare such a list of actual and presumed related relationships indicates the problem that the ASB faced when related parties are determined to avoid disclosure. The ASB would prefer a broad approach setting out principles, but it is well aware that related parties who wish to avoid disclosure will look for loopholes. It therefore follows a legalistic approach to frustrate attempts to structure relationships to fall outside the definition of related party.

Related party transactions

Just as parties will attempt to avoid being classified as related parties, so they will structure transactions to avoid their classification as related transactions. FRS 8 therefore lists many examples, including purchase or sale of intangible and tangible assets; providing or receiving services; agency arrangements; leasing arrangements; licence agreements; loan and share financing; and contingent arrangements such as guarantees and provisions of collateral security.

Related party disclosures

Where there is a transaction between related parties it would be helpful to have the following information:

● The names of the parties

● A description of the relationship between them

● The amounts involved

● Any other information needed to make the effect of transaction understandable

● Amounts due at the balance sheet date

● Amounts written off in the period in respect of debts between the parties

Illustrations of Related party disclosures

There is disclosure required where the transaction has not been on normal commercial terms. This is not to imply that it is detrimental to the company but expenses and liquidity in future periods could be affected if commercial terms became necessary e.g.

An extract from 1998 Annual Report & Accounts of Leicester City plc reports as follows:

'The following loans from Directors and their related parties, on which no interest was charged and for which there are no repayment terms, existed during the year:

	Balance at 24.10.97	Maximum amount outstanding during the year	Balance at 31.7.98
	£	£	£
J M Elsom (Director)	10,000	10,000	10,000
Capital Construction (GB) Limited	250,000	250,000	250,000

R.W. Parker (a director of Leicester City plc) is a director of Capital Construction (GB) Ltd'

There is also disclosure required when terms are normal commercial terms e.g.

An extract from the 1998 Report & Accounts of Sheffield United plc reports as follows:

'During the year the group received secretarial and associated services from Townsend Estate Management Limited totalling £7,000. Mr I Townsend or his wife are materially interested as either a director or shareholder in this company. These services have been provided on normal commercial terms.'

Related party disclosure puts users on notice. In the introduction to FRED 8 *Related Party Disclosures*, David Tweedie, the ASB Chairman said,

'in the nature of things, the requirement to disclose related party transactions can never be a complete safeguard against deliberate dishonesty'.

Nevertheless the disclosure of all material related party transactions and the name of the party controlling the reporting entity will be a useful step forward. Users of accounts will be put on notice of the existence of transactions of this kind and given information about them.

How much the auditors are taking out of the company

Shareholders need to form a view on the amount of work that has been undertaken and to be confident that the audit opinion is **independent**. Until 1989, the disclosed figure represented the amount of remuneration and expenses paid for the conduct of the audit. It did not include fees for non-audit work. By non-audit work we mean any fees paid for accounting services, such as where the client has experienced problems in producing the draft accounts and needs assistance; or fees paid for tax advice or for management consultancy services. In The Body Shop International 1999 accounts, non-audit fees were £600,000.

Because auditors receive substantial payments for the audit work alone, e.g. £300,000 was disclosed in the 1999 accounts for The Body Shop, there may be some concern about the extent to which an auditor can be independent. The profession is aware of the possibility of a credibility gap and has its own rules of professional conduct which state in relation to fees that: 'It is undesirable that a practice should derive too great a part of its professional income from one client or group of connected clients. A practice, therefore, should endeavour to ensure that the recurring fee paid by one client or group of connected clients does not exceed 15% of the gross fees of the practice.'[11]

Information that is sensitive when producing financial statements to assist shareholders to predict future cash flows

At the operating level, shareholders need to be aware of the **accrual adjustments** that are subject to the judgement of the directors. These include the depreciation charge for the year, exceptional write down of a current asset, e.g. a stock write-down, a debtor write down, and the creation of a provision for, say, warranty claims.

At the profit before tax level, shareholders need to be aware of income arising from moneys invested outside the business and expenditure incurred to service borrowings.

Information that is sensitive for other stakeholders

We could place the disclosure relating to staff into this category. Directors are required to provide information on staff in categories determined by the directors, having regard to the manner in which the company's activies are organised.

One suggested form of presentation is as shown in Figure 8.4,[12] where the analysis follows the layout of the profit and loss account; alternatively, the analysis could be by geographical area, principal activity, principal product or full- or part-time with a disclosure of full-time equivalents where there are a substantial number of part-time staff.

This information is useful in the context of reporting to the employees. However, there is no standard form of presenting it, and it is not completely adequate for the prediction of cash flows. Staff cost information is not analysed into the expense headings that are used in the profit and loss account, so, although the total cost is given, this is not necessarily broken down into cost of sales, distribution costs and administrative expenses.

8.6 What information is required to be disclosed in Format I and Format 2?

An illustration of a profit and loss account using the two formats is set out in Figure 8.5. Note that in both formats the same amount is disclosed for profit on ordinary activities before tax and the two statements are identical after that point.

Figure 8.4   Staff costs.

	£
Employee costs during the year amounted to:	
Wages and salaries	
Social security costs	
Other pension costs	_____
	========

The average weekly number of persons employed during the
year was as follows

	Number employed	*Full-time equivalent*
Production		
Distribution		
Sales		
Research and development		
Administration	_____	_____
	========	========

Figure 8.5 Illustration of Formats 1 and 2.

Format 1 **Costs analysed by type of operation**		**Format 2** **Costs analysed by type of expenditure**	
	£000		£000
Turnover	1,000	Turnover	1,000
Cost of sales	400		
Gross profit	600		
Distribution costs	120		
Administrative expenses	70		
	410		
		Change in stocks of finished stocks and work-in-progress	(20)
		Own work capitalised	(125)
		Raw materials and consumables	140
		Other external charges	280
		Staff costs	170
		Depreciation	110
		Exceptional amounts written off current assets	35
Other operating income	20	Other operating income	(20)

Trading profit	430		430
Income from shares	15		15
Interest receivable	12		12
	457		457
Amounts written off			
investments	9		9
Interest payable	17		17
Profit on ordinary			
activities before tax	**431**		**431**
Tax on profit on			
ordinary activities	130		130
Profit after tax	301		301
Extraordinary income	0		
Extraordinary charges	0		
Profit for financial year	301		
Dividends paid or proposed	90		90
Amount transferred to			
reserves	211		211

The Hanson Annual Report 1999 illustrated the Format 2 presentation as follows:

Note 3 Costs and overheads

	Continuing	Acquisitions
Changes in stock of finished goods	(5.5)	2.5
Raw materials	297	20.7
Employment costs	376.7	35.0
Depreciation and depletion	118.6	6.1
Depreciation of finance lease	4.8	—
Amortisation of goodwill	4.0	5.2
Other operating charges	692.7	49.7
	1,488.3	119.2
Acquisitions	119.2	
	1,607.5	

8.6.1 Classification of operating expenses and other income in Format 1

A company needs to classify all of the operating expenses of the business into one of three categories – cost of sales, distribution and selling costs and administrative expenses – and identify other operating income in order to arrive at its trading profit. We comment briefly on each of the three cost categories and other income to explain how a company might classify its trading transactions. This will also indicate how the same transaction might be classified differently by different companies.

Cost of sales

Expenditure classified under this heading will typically include direct costs, overheads, depreciation and amortisation, and adjustments.

● **Direct costs** include:
   direct materials purchased;
   other external charges that comprise production costs from external sources, e.g. equipment rental, subcontract costs;
   direct labour.

● **Overheads** include:
   variable production overheads;
   fixed production overheads.

● **Depreciation and amortisation** include:
   depreciation of fixed assets used in production;
   exceptional amounts written off stock;
   research costs;
   development costs.

● **Adjustments** include:
   Change between the opening and closing stock. If closing stock is less than opening stock, the reduction must have been sold and the cost of sales will be increased by the amount that the stock has fallen. Conversely, if closing stock is more than opening stock, the amount by which it has increased will not be included as a cost of the current period's sales.
   Capitalisation of own work as a fixed asset. Any amount of the costs listed above that have been incurred in the construction of fixed assets for retention by the company will not appear as an expense in the profit and loss account: it will be capitalised. Any amount capitalised in this way would be treated for accounting purposes as a fixed asset and depreciated.
   Capitalisation of own work as a deferred asset. Any amount of the costs listed above that needs to be deferred to a future accounting period because the benefits of the expenditure can be reasonably matched with revenue expected in a future period, e.g. development expenditure capitalised under SSAP 13, would be treated for accounting purposes as a deferred asset and expensed by matching with the revenue as it arose in the future accounting periods. SSAP 13 is considered in detail in Chapter 20.
   Treatment of variances from standard. Where a company uses a standard costing system, the variances can either be transferred in total to the profit and loss account or be allocated to the cost of sales and the stock. Any variance allocated to the stock will have an impact on the results of a subsequent period. (This aspect is considered in Chapter 17.)

Why cost of sales figures may not be comparable between companies

The cost of sales figure is derived under the accrual accounting concept. This means that (a) the cash flows have been adjusted by the management in order to arrive at the expense that management considers to be associated with the sales achieved; and (b) additional adjustments may have been made to increase the cost of sales if the net realisable value of the closing stock is less than cost.

Clearly, when management adjust the cash flow figures they are exercising their judgement, and it is impossible to ensure that the management of two companies faced with the same economic activity would arrive at the same adjustment.

We will now consider some of the reasons for differences in calculating the cost of sales.

Differences in cost of sales arising from the treatment of direct costs

Different companies may assume different physical flows when calculating the cost of direct materials used in production. This will affect the stock valuation. One company may assume a first-in-first-out (FIFO) flow, where the cost of sales is charged for raw materials used in production as if they were issued on the basis that the first items purchased were the first items used in production. Another company may use a weighted average basis. This is illustrated for a company that started trading on 1 January 20X1 without any opening stock and sold 40,000 items on 31 March 20X1 for £4 per item as in Figure 8.6.

FIFO stock is 20,000 items at a cost of £3 per item, assuming that the purchases made on 1 January 20X1 and 1 February 20X1 were sold first. Weighted average stock is 20,000 items at a cost of £2 per item, being the total cost of £120,000 divided by the total number of items of 60,000 at the date of the sale.

The effect on the gross profit percentage would be as shown in Figure 8.7. This demonstrates that, even from a **single** difference in accounting treatment, the gross profit could be materially different in both absolute and percentage terms.

Companies are required to disclose their stock valuation policy, but the level of detail provided varies. Hence we are not able to quantify the effect of differences in stock valuation policies. For example, compare the accounting policy of The Body Shop International plc in Figure 8.8 with that of CALA plc in Figure 8.9. In the latter case, we are not even aware of the definition of cost that the company is actually using.

Figure 8.6 Effect on cost of sales of using FIFO and weighted average.

	Items	£	FIFO £	Weighted average £
Raw materials purchased				
On 1 Jan 20X1 at £1 per item	20,000	20,000		
On 1 Feb 20X1 at £2 per item	20,000	40,000		
On 1 Mar 20X1 at £3 per item	20,000	60,000		
On 1 Mar 20X1 in stock	60,000	120,000	120,000	120,000
On 31 Mar 20X1 in stock	20,000		60,000	40,000
Cost of sales	40,000		60,000	80,000

Figure 8.7 Effect of physical stock flow assumptions on the percentage gross profit.

	Items	FIFO £	Weighted average £
Sales	40,000	160,000	160,000
Cost of sales	40,000	60,000	80,000
		100,000	80,000
Gross profit %		62.5%	50%

Figure 8.8   The Body Shop International plc accounting policy for stock – 1999.

Stocks are valued at the lower of cost and net realisable value.

Costs are calculated as follows:
Raw materials – cost of purchase on first-in, first-out basis.
Work-in-progress and finished goods – cost of raw materials and labour together with attributable overhead.

Net realisable value is based on estimated selling price less further costs to completion and disposal.

Figure 8.9   CALA plc accounting policy for stock – 1999.

Stocks are valued at the lower of cost and net realisable value.

While we can carry out academic exercises as in Figure 8.7 and we are aware of the effect of different stock valuation policies on the level of profits, there is no way in real life that we can be certain of being able to carry out such an exercise.

Differences in cost of sales arising from the choice of depreciation policy
The charge made for depreciation might vary because of:

● different methods, e.g. straight-line or reducing balance;

● different assumptions on productive use, e.g. different assessments of the economic life of an asset;

● different carrying values, e.g. at cost or at revaluation;

● different assumptions of total cost to be expensed, e.g. different assumptions about the residual value of an asset.

Differences in cost of sales arising from management attitudes
Losses might be anticipated and measured at a different rate. For example, when assessing the likelihood of the net realisable value of stock falling below the cost figure, the management decision will be influenced by the optimism with which they view the future of the economy, the industry and the company.

Differences in cost of sales arising from the capability of the accounting system to provide data
Accounting systems within companies differ, e.g. costs that are collected by one company may well not be collected by another company. For example, in its 1994 accounts, The Body Shop International plc mentioned costs that had been incurred in research and development:

> The Directors, senior managers and technical staff, together with the research department, are all involved in the continuous search for raw materials and the

examination of their potential use in our products. The cost of this activity is spread over a number of departments of the Group and although substantial **it is not practicable to produce a meaningful figure**.

By not having the information collected, the company is not able to consider its capitalisation, although it might be that it could not be capitalised anyway. In its 1997 and 1998 accounts it was interesting to see that the reference to it not being practicable no longer appears.

Distribution costs

These are costs incurred after the production of the finished article and up to and including transfer of the goods to the customer.

Expenditure classified under this heading will typically include the following:

● **Warehousing** costs – costs associated with the operation of the premises, e.g. rent, rates, insurance, utilities, depreciation, repairs and maintenance; wage costs, e.g. gross wages, national insurance and pension contributions of warehouse staff.

● **Promotion** costs – advertising, trade shows.

● **Selling** costs – salaries, commissions, national insurance and pension contributions of sales staff; costs associated with the premises, e.g. rent, rates; cash discounts on sales; travelling and entertainment.

● **Transport** costs – costs associated with the operation of the premises, e.g. rent, rates, insurance, utilities, depreciation, repairs, maintenance; wage costs, e.g. gross wages, national insurance, pension contributions of transport staff; vehicle costs, e.g. running, maintenance, depreciation.

Administrative expenses

These are all those operating costs that have not been classified as either cost of sales or distribution costs.

Expenditure classified under this heading will typically include:

● **Administration** – salaries, commissions, national insurance, pension contributions of administration staff; costs associated with the premises, e.g. rent, rates; amounts written off the debtors that appear in the balance sheet under current assets; and professional fees.

Other operating income

Under this heading a company discloses material income derived from ordinary activities of the business that have not been included in the sales turnover figure. If the amounts are not material, they would not be separately disclosed, but included within the sales turnover figure.

Income classified under this heading will typically include the following:

● **Income derived from intangible assets**, e.g. royalties, commissions.

● **Income derived from third-party use of fixed tangible assets** that are surplus to the current productive needs of the company.

● **Income received from employees**, e.g. canteen, recreation fees.

8.6.2 What costs and income are brought into account after calculating the trading profit in order to arrive at the profit on ordinary activities before tax?

We have explained the four categories of cost and other income that are taken into account when calculating the trading profit. In order to arrive at the profit on ordinary activities before tax, income from investments and loans is required to be disclosed separately and not included with the other income – unless, of course, the investment or loan income is not material and is included within the other operating income for convenience.

8.7 Does it really matter under which heading a cost is classified in the profit and loss account provided it is not omitted?

This depends on how readers of the accounts use the gross profit and trading profit figures. An examination of annual reports indicates that directors usually make little reference to the gross profit figure and instead draw attention to the **trading profit (or operating profit)** figure.

Trading profit is used to calculate the return on capital employed, as illustrated by the extract from the financial highlights of the BOC Group annual report for 1999:

> Return on capital for 1999 was 13.1% defined as operating profit before exceptional items as a percentage of average capital employed.

8.8 Effect of SSAP 25 *Segmental Reporting*[13] and FRS 3 *Reporting Financial Performance*

8.8.1 Segmental Reporting

Although the Companies Act 1967 introduced some requirements for the disclosure of segmental information, an accounting standard on the topic was not issued until June 1990 when SSAP 25 *Segmental Reporting* was issued. The objective of segmental reporting is to assist users of accounts to evaluate the different business segments and geographical regions of a group and how they affect the overall results of that group. SSAP 25 sets out how these different segments should be defined and the information which should be disclosed.

SSAP 25 gives guidance on the sorts of factors that directors should take into account when defining segments, e.g. the nature of the products or services, how the groups activities are organised. These factors help to determine whether a segment is distinguishable, but it must also be a significant segment to require disclosure and a significance test will measure if any of the turnover, results or net assets account for more than 10% of the group's total. SSAP 25 also states that turnover, results (before minority interest and tax) and net assets should be disclosed for both business and geographic segments.

8.8.2 FRS 3 – the ASB's intention

The ASB issued FRS 3 in 1992, proposing major changes in the profit and loss account and for items passing through reserves.[14] The intention was to move away from the idea that the performance of complex organisations could be summarised in a single number, such as profit before tax or earnings per share.

Instead the Board adopted what it describes as an 'information set' approach. The 'information set' consists of a **range** of important components of performance, from which individual users will draw their own conclusions on past performance and future cash flows. It will be for users to identify particular components that they consider of significance in their own varying circumstances. The aim of this approach is to encourage 'a more mature understanding and analysis of financial performance'.

8.8.3 Changes in the format of the profit and loss account arising from FRS 3

The changes to the Format 1 layout required under the Companies Act 1985 are as follows:

● Operating profit is analysed further into three components: the results of continuing operations, of newly acquired operations and of discontinued operations.

● There is further detail of certain exceptional items in arriving at the profit on ordinary activities before interest, again included under the appropriate heading of continuing or discontinued operations.

The exceptional items that are required to be disclosed on the face of the profit and loss account are as follows:

● Profits or losses on the sale or termination of an operation.

● Costs of a fundamental reorganisation or restructuring having a material effect on the nature and focus of the reporting entity's operations.

● Profits or losses on the disposal of fixed assets.

Other exceptional items should be credited or charged in arriving at the profit or loss on ordinary activities before taxation under statutory headings to which they relate. Exceptional items are events that fall within the ordinary activities of the business which need to be disclosed by way of note by virtue of their size or incidence. Ordinary activities are any activities which are undertaken by a reporting entity as part of its business and include the effects on the reporting entity of any event in the various environments in which it operates, including the political, regulatory, economic and geographical environments, irrespective of the frequency or unusual nature of these events. As well as the profit and loss account entry, the exceptional item might be of such materiality that a separate note will be necessary in order to give a true and fair view.

There has also been a change in the definition of extraordinary items. They are defined under the standard as 'material items possessing a high degree of abnormality which arises from events or transactions that fall outside the ordinary activities of the reporting entity and which are not expected to recur. They do not include exceptional items nor do they include prior period items merely because they relate to a prior period.' This implies that only events such as natural disasters will fall within the definition. As far as the layout is concerned, there will still be a caption for extraordinary items, but there will rarely be anything to report against it.

An illustration is provided from the 1998 accounts of Reckitt & Colman in Figures 8.10 and 8.11 on pages 207 and 208.

Figure 8.10 Group profit and loss account – Reckitt & Colman as at 2 January 1999.

	1998	1997 restated
	£m	£m
Turnover		
Continuing operations	2,140.3	2,196.6
Aquisitions	62.1	—
Total turnover	2,202.4	2,196.6
Cost of sales	(948.1)	(941.0)
Gross profit	1,254.3	1,255.6
Net operating expenses	(966.1)	(901.3)
Operating profit		
Excluding acquisitions and Year 2000 costs	311.8	354.3
Acquisitions	7.9	—
Year 2000 cost	(31.5)	—
Total operating profit	288.2	354.3
Non-operating items		
(Loss)/Profit on disposal of business	7.0	2.3
Profit on disposal of tangible fixed assets	1.0	0.9
Profit on ordinary activities before interest	282.2	357.5
Interest payable less receivable	(36.0)	(36.5)
Coupon on convertible capital bonds	(18.4)	(18.5)
Profit on ordinary activities before tax	227.8	302.5

Definition of discontinued operations

FRS 3 requires the turnover and operating profit to be analysed between continuing, acquisitions and discontinued operations. In para. 4 it sets out the conditions that must be satisfied if operations that have been sold or terminated are to be disclosed as discontinued. All of these conditions must be satisfied.

● The sale or termination is completed either in the period or before the earlier of three months after the commencement of the subsequent period and the date on which the financial statements are approved.

● If a termination, the former activities have ceased permanently.

● The sale or termination has a material effect on the nature and focus of the reporting entity's operations and represents a material reduction in its operating facilities, resulting either from its withdrawal from a particular market (whether class of business or geographical) or from a material reduction in turnover in the reporting entity's continuing markets.

● The assets, liabilities, results of operations and activities are clearly distinguishable physically, operationally and for financial reporting purposes.

If any of the conditions is not satisfied, the operations must be treated as continuing. The intention is to prevent companies deciding that they would quite like to treat any loss-

Figure 8.11 Segmental analysis – Reckitt & Colman as at 2 January 1999.

Turnover and profit – by product group

	Turnover		Operating Profit		Operating Margin	
	1998	1997	1998	1997	1998	1997
	£m	£m	£m	£m	%	%
Household	1,722.2	1,747.8	215.5	257.2	12.5	14.7
Pharmaceutical	273.4	260.7	69.7	70.3	25.5	27.0
Food	206.8	188.1	34.5	26.8	16.7	14.2
	2,202.4	2,196.6	319.7	354.3	14.5	16.1
Year 2000 costs	—	—	(31.5)	—	—	—
	2,202.4	2,196.6	288.2	354.3	13.1	16.1

Capital employed – by product group

	1998	1997
	£m	£m
Household	1,436.5	1,428.7
Pharmaceutical	62.7	61.4
Food	62.2	47.0
	1561.4	1,537.1

making operations as discontinued and then change their mind when they return to profitability. This allows shareholders to assess future cash flows on the basis of a clear change in the operation rather than changes made only to improve the appearance of the current year's management performance.

Although the conditions appear straightforward, there are already uncertainties of interpretation. There is no definition of 'ceased permanently' and the meaning of 'material effect on the nature and focus' will not be obvious in all circumstances and will depend upon agreement between the auditors and the management. If the regulator disagrees with the treatment, presumably there will be a UITF or, more likely, discussion behind the scenes that will leave the wider public not much the wiser.

The FRS format only requires a separate analysis into continuing and discontinued operations down to the operating profit level. This led one of the ASB members to dissent from the standard because the effect of taxation and minority interest on the gain or loss on disposal is not highlighted. Taxation on the profits on a disposal of a subsidiary is based on sales proceeds and the cost of the investment which means that in the group situation the accounting and taxable profits could often be materially different where there has been a disposal. The dissenting view was that a user would benefit from the profit before tax, profit after tax, minorities and EPS being analysed into continuing and discontinued operations.

Accounting treatment if a decision is made to terminate an operation

If a decision has been made to sell or terminate an operation, a provision should be made to reflect:

● the direct costs of the sale or termination;

● any operating losses of the operation to be sold or terminated after taking into account any future operating profits or profits on the sale of the assets.

Unless the operation in question qualifies as a discontinued operation in the period, the provision should be made under continuing operations. In a later period, if the operation does qualify as a discontinued operation, the provision should be used to offset the results of the operation in the discontinued category. This is to ensure that the profits from continuing operations are not massaged by making a provision under the discontinued classification when there has not actually been discontinuance.

8.8.4 Changes in the primary statements

A primary statement called 'statement of total recognised gains and losses' should be presented with the same prominence as the other primary statements. The components should be the gains and losses that are recognised in the period in so far as they are attributable to shareholders. This will take the profit for the year and adjust it for unrealised gains and losses, currency translation differences and prior period adjustments (see Figure 8.12).

FRS 3 placed greater emphasis on the components of income rather than the bottom line. The statement was introduced in 1992 largely to put the reporting of financial performance on the all-inclusive basis favoured by users, who were concerned that gains and losses were sometimes masked or obscured by reserve accounting, which permits items to bypass the profit and loss account.

Not all items in Figure 8.12 will of course always appear for every company.

Why have a statement of total recognised gains and losses?

The reason for the statement is that a number of gains and losses are either permitted or required by law or accounting standards to be dealt with directly through reserves. This means that financial statements would be incomplete if they stopped at the retained profit for the year figure without giving the shareholders information about other changes in their equity. The statement includes all gains and losses for the period and not just those that have passed through the profit and loss account. In order to avoid double counting, if a gain has been passed through the Statement of Total Recognised Gains and Losses, it is not subsequently passed through the profit and loss account, e.g. if a fixed asset is revalued and the unrealised gain passed through the Statement of Total Recognised Gains and Losses in

Figure 8.12   Illustration of the statement of total recognised gains and losses.

	£m
Profit for the financial year	29
Unrealised surplus on revaluation of properties	4
Unrealised (loss)/gain on trade investments	(3)
	30
Currency translation difference	(2)
Total recognised gains and losses relating to the year	28
Prior period adjustments	(10)
Total gains and losses recognised since last annual report	18

20×1, any profit arising from a sale in 20×2 and credited to the profit and loss account will be restricted to the difference between the sales price and the revaluation figure.

Does the requirement for the statement of total recognised gains and losses reflect the views of standard-setters in other parts of the world?

The G4 + 1 Group comprising standard-setters from Australia, Canada, New Zealand, UK and the USA and the IASC has published a paper on the reporting of financial performance[15] in which the approach favoured by the substantial majority of the working party was to reduce the complexity which supplementary statements may cause by proposing a *single performance statement* with three major components:

  (i) operating activities;

 (ii) financing and other treasury activities;

(iii) other gains and losses.

The contents of other gains and losses broadly corresponding to the UK Statement of Total Recognised Gains and Losses which is clear confirmation that there is common support for the **all-inclusive basis** of reporting.

    This has been issued as a Discussion Paper.[16] The format of an inclusive financial report would be as follows:

Statement of financial performance

	£000	£000
Revenues		1,000
Cost of sales		(700)
Other expenses		(100)
Operating income		200
Financing and other Treasury activities		
Interest on debt	(50)	
Gains and losses on financial instruments	15	(35)
Operating and financing income before tax		165
Taxation on income		(63)
Operating and financing income after tax		102
Other financial gains and losses		
Profit on disposal of discontinued operations		
Profit on sale of properties in continuing operations	25	
Revaluation of long term assets	15	
Exchange difference on foreign currency net debt	(10)	
	30	
Tax	(12)	
		18
Total		120

This format discloses the realised gains and losses on disposal that appear after operating profit under FRS 3, para. 20, within the Other financial gains and losses section. The revaluation and exchange differences that are reported in the Statement of Total Recognised Gains and Losses are also disclosed in this section.

The intention is that gains and losses should only be reported once in the period in which they arise and that the single performance statement would provide users with all the information on gains and losses of a period in one statement. The users would then be able to select those aspects of the financial performance that they perceive as most relevant to their needs.

FRS 3 will clearly need to be reviewed by the ASB with a view to combining the profit and loss account and the Statement of Total Recognised Gains and Losses into a single statement.

8.8.5 Discussion of changes in the notes to the accounts

Note of historical cost profits and losses

A note of historical cost profits and losses may be required where there is a material difference between the result as disclosed in the profit and loss account and the result on an unmodified historical cost basis. The note should include a reconciliation of the reported profit on ordinary activities before taxation to the equivalent historical cost amount, and should show the retained profit for the financial year reported on the historical cost basis.

Two reasons for requiring such a note are that it improves comparability between companies, which might be following different policies on the timing and scale of revaluations, and it allows a user to assess the profit or loss on the sale of revalued assets based on their historical cost (see Figure 8.13). This is necessary because 60% of larger companies revalued fixed assets in their balance sheets.

Figure 8.13 Illustration of a note of historical cost profits and losses (from the illustration in FRS 3).

	£m
Reported profit on ordinary activities before taxation	45
Realisation of property revaluation gains of previous years	9
Difference between a historical cost depreciation charge and the actual depreciation charge calculated on the revalued amount	5
Historical cost profit on ordinary activities before taxation	59
Historical cost profit for the year retained after taxation, minority interests, extraordinary items and dividends	35

Reconciliation of movements in total shareholders funds

A note should be presented reconciling the opening and closing totals of shareholders' funds of the period (see Figure 8.14). Although the profit and loss account, with its realised gains, and the statement of total recognised gains and losses, with its unrealised gains, reflect the year's performance, other changes in shareholders' funds can be important in understanding the change in the financial position, e.g. goodwill written off.

8.9 The balance sheet

We now explain the prescribed formats for balance sheet presentation, the accounting rules that govern the values at which the various assets are included and the explanatory notes that are required to accompany the balance sheet.

Figure 8.14 Illustration of a note of reconciliation of movements in shareholders' funds.

	£m
Profit for the financial year	29
Dividends	(8)
	21
Other recognised gains and losses relating to the year	(1)
New share capital subscribed	20
Goodwill written off	(25)
New addition to shareholders' funds	15
Opening shareholders' funds	365
Closing shareholders' funds	380

8.9.1 The prescribed formats

The Companies Act 1985 specifies two formats. Format 1 is a vertical presentation, while Format 2 is a horizontal presentation of balances.

Format 1 contains the following items:

A. Called-up share capital
B. Fixed assets
    I. Intangible assets
    II. Tangible assets
    III. Investments
C. Current assets
    I. Stocks
    II. Debtors
    III. Investments
    IV. Cash at bank and in hand
D. Prepayments and accrued income
E. Creditors: amounts falling due within one year
F. Net current assets
G. Total assets less current liabilities
H. Creditors: amounts falling due after more than one year
I. Provisions for liabilities and charges
J. Accruals and deferred income
K. Capital and reserves
L. Minority interests

Format 2 requires the same basic disclosure, except that it does not require the amount of the net current assets to be disclosed.

8.9.2 The accounting rules for asset valuation

The Companies Act 1985 provides two sets of accounting rules. These are the historic cost accounting rules and the alternative accounting rules.

The historical cost accounting rules are set out below, referenced to the balance sheet headings used in Format 1.

Balance sheet heading	Historical cost accounting rules
B. Fixed assets	Fixed assets are to be shown at their purchase price or production cost less depreciation.
C. Current assets	Current assets are to be stated at the lower of their net realisable value and their purchase price or production cost.

The alternative accounting rules are set out below, again referenced to the balance sheet headings used in Format 1.

Balance sheet heading	Alternative accounting rules
B. Fixed assets	Intangible fixed assets, other than goodwill, may be included at their current cost. Tangible fixed assets may be included at their market value as at the date of their last valuation or at their current cost.
C. Current assets	Stock may be included at current cost.

The Act does not define current cost and the meaning would depend on whatever accounting standard or guidance happens to be operative at the date the accounts are prepared. In practice, the majority companies tend to use the historic cost accounting rules modified by the use of the alternative accounting rules as and when all or some of the fixed assets are revalued.

8.9.3 What are the explanatory notes that accompany a balance sheet?

The notes are of three types: notes giving greater detail of the make-up of items that appear in the balance sheet; notes providing additional information; and notes drawing attention to related party transactions.

Notes giving greater detail of the make-up of balance sheet figures

Each of the alpha headings A–L and each of the subheadings I–III may have additional detail disclosed by way of a note to the accounts. Some items may have a note of their detailed make-up. For example, stock of £38.6m in the balance sheet may have a note as follows:

	£m
Raw materials	11.2
Work-in-progress	1.5
Finished goods	25.9
	38.6

Fixed assets normally have a fixed asset schedule as shown in Figure 8.15. From this the net book value as at 27 February 1999 is read off the total column for inclusion in the balance sheet.

Notes giving additional information

These are notes intended to assist in predicting future cash flows. They give information on matters such as capital commitments that have been contracted for but not provided in the accounts, and capital commitments that have been authorised but not contracted

Figure 8.15   Body Shop plc – Fixed asset company movements.

	Freehold property £m	Short-term leaseholds £m	Plant/ equipment £m	Total £m
Cost				
At 1 March 1998	0.5	42.0	48.2	90.7
Additions	—	0.2	6.0	6.2
Disposals	—	(0.1)	(3.4)	(3.5)
At 27 February 1999	**0.5**	**42.1**	**50.8**	**93.4**
Accumulated depreciation				
At 1 March 1998	0.1	11.5	28.4	40.0
Charge for year	0.1	1.2	6.0	7.3
Accelerated depreciation	—	1.3	0.2	1.5
Disposals	—	(0.1)	(2.3)	(2.4)
At 27 February 1999	**0.2**	**13.9**	**32.3**	**46.4**
Net book value				
At 27 February 1999	**0.3**	**28.2**	**18.5**	**47.0**
At 28 February 1998	0.4	30.5	19.8	50.7

for; future commitments, e.g. share options that have been granted; and contingent liabilities, e.g. guarantees given by the company in respect of overdraft facilities arranged by subsidiary companies or customers.

Notes drawing attention to existence of related party transactions

Related party relationships may mean that financial statements include transactions that have not been entered into on an arm's-length basis, which would be the normal assumption made by a user. The objective of FRS 8 *Related Party Disclosures*[17] was to ensure that disclosure drew attention to the fact that the reported financial position and results may have been affected by the existence of related parties and material transactions with them. Disclosure is required of the person controlling the reporting entity and of related party transactions such as purchase or sale of goods, property or other assets; rendering or receiving services; agency arrangements; leasing arrangements; transfer of research and development; licence agreements; provision of finance and management contracts. As Sir David Tweedie states in the introduction to FRS 8 'In financial matters it is not enough to look at the puppets; users need to see the strings and know who is pulling them.'

FRS 8 defines such a related party relationship as existing where one party has direct or indirect control of the other party, or the parties are subject to common control, or one party has such influence over the financial and operating policies of the other party that the other party might be inhibited from pursuing its own separate interests, or the parties entering into a transaction are subject to such influence from the same source that one party has subordinated its own separate interests.

Although related parties include companies in the same group and associated companies, because information has already been required, e.g. under FRS 2 and FRS 9, the principal impact will be on directors and their close families, pension funds, key management and those controlling 20% or more of the voting rights.

8.10 Disclosure of accounting policies

The Companies Act requires a company to state the accounting **policies** adopted by the company in determining the amounts shown in the balance sheet and the profit or loss of the company.[18]

8.10.1 What is the difference between accounting principles or concepts, accounting bases and accounting policies?

Accounting principles

All companies are required to comply with the broad accounting principles of going concern, consistency, accrual accounting and prudence. If they fail to comply, they must disclose, quantify and justify the departure from the principle.

Accounting bases

These are the methods that have been developed for applying the accounting principles. They are intended to restrict the subjectivity by identifying a range of acceptable methods. For example, assets may be valued according to the historic cost convention or the alternative accounting rules.

Bases have been established for a number of assets, e.g. goodwill, depreciation, consolidation methods.

Accounting policies

Accounting policies are chosen by a company as being the most appropriate to the company's circumstances and best able to produce a true and fair view. They typically disclose the accounting policies followed for the basis of accounting, i.e. historic or alternative accounting rules, and asset valuation, e.g. of stocks, stating whether it uses FIFO or other methods; fixed assets, stating whether depreciation is straight-line or other methods; and research and development, stating whether it has been capitalised or not. An example from the accounts of The Body Shop International plc is shown in Figure 8.16.

Figure 8.16 Extract from the annual report of The Body Shop International plc.

The financial statements have been prepared under the historical cost convention and in accordance with applicable accounting standards.

Research and development

Research and development expenditure is charged to the profit and loss account in the year in which it is incurred.

Depreciation

Depreciation is provided to write off the cost, less estimated residual values, of all tangible fixed assets, except freehold land, over their expected useful lives.

However, as discussed in Chapter 7, accounting policies will fall within the Standard that comes out of FRED 21 rather than SSAP 2.

8.10.2 How do users know the effect of changes in accounting policy?

Accounting policies are required by the Companies Act 1985 to be applied consistently from one financial period to another. It is only permissible to change an accounting policy if the directors consider that there are special reasons for a change.

When a change occurs there are three disclosure requirements:

- The Companies Act requires disclosures of particulars of the departure.

- FRS 3 requires an amendment to the comparative figures of the previous financial period as a prior period adjustment.

- UITF 14 Disclosure of Changes in Accounting Policies requires the effect of the change on the current period to be disclosed.

This has significantly reduced the opportunity for management to confuse users when making accounting changes with the effect on both the previous year and the current year being disclosed.

Summary

The published accounts of a listed company are intended to provide shareholders with a report to assess stewardship and management performance and the means to predict future cash flows. In order to assess stewardship and management performance, there have been statutory requirements for standardised presentation, using formats initially prescribed by EU directives and incorporated into the UK Companies Act, which allow shareholders to make comparisons between companies. There have also been mandatory requirements for the disclosure of accounting policies, which allow shareholders to make comparisons between years. As regards future cash flows, these are normally perceived to be influenced by past profits, the asset base as shown by the balance sheet and **significant changes**. In order to assist shareholders to predict future cash flows with an understanding of the risks involved, more information has been required by the ASB or statute.

This has taken two forms:

- more quantitative information in the accounts, e.g. segmental analysis, and the impact of changes on the operation, e.g. a breakdown of turnover, costs and profits for both new and discontinued operations; and

- more qualitative information, e.g. the operating and financial review, related party disclosures, effect of changes in accounting policy.

Review questions

1 Explain why two companies carrying out identical trading transactions could produce different gross profit figures.

2 A Format 1 profit and loss account contains the following profit figures:
   Gross profit
   Trading profit
   Profit on ordinary activities before tax
   Profit on ordinary activities after tax
   Profit for the year

Explain when you would use each profit figure for analysis purposes, e.g. trading profit is used in the percentage return on capital employed.

3 Classify the following items into cost of sales, distribution costs, administrative expenses, other operating income or item to be disclosed after trading profit:

(a) Personnel department costs

(b) Computer department costs

(c) Cost accounting department costs

(d) Financial accounting department costs

(e) Bad debts

(f) Provisions for warranty claims

(g) Interest on funds borrowed to finance an increase in working capital

(h) Interest on funds borrowed to finance an increase in fixed production assets

4 'Companies should begin to move to greater disclosure of:

● Days training per year for categories of staff.

● Expenditure on training, both in total and differentiated between categories of employees. This could be supplemented with information regarding the spread of expenditure during the year. This is most likely to be best presented in diagrammatic form.

● Career and development policy, both vertically and horizontally. A short statement setting out the relevance of the approach to the future of the company and how management plan to deal with it should be provided and could, over time, be extended to include information on staff turnover rates, average length of service, costs of recruitment, voluntary payments on termination of employment and number of professionally qualified staff.[19]

(a) Discuss the extent to which this information would assist the investor to:

(i) assess stewardship performance;

(ii) predict future cash flows.

(b) Discuss the extent to which the annual report should contain the information suggested in the CIMA publication and the reasons for its inclusion.

5 What are the fundamental objectives of corporate reports?[20]

6 'A single set of multi-purpose financial statements are unable to satisfy the needs of shareholders for both a stewardship report and a report to assist the prediction of future cash flows.' Discuss.

7 Discuss the relevance of the information in the Statement of Total Recognised Gains and Losses to an investor. Explain the advantages and disadvantages of combining the profit and loss account and Statement into a single report.

8 Describe the content of an OFR statement and discuss whether it should be made mandatory, more prescriptive and audited.

Exercises
....

An extract from the solution is provided in the appendix at the end of the text for exercises marked with an asterisk (*).

* ## Question 1

The following trial balance was extracted from the books of Old plc on 31 December 20X1.

	£000	£000
Sales		12,050
Returns outwards		313
Provision for depreciation		
plant		738
vehicles		375
Rent receivable		100
Trade creditors		738
Debentures		250
Issued share capital – ordinary £1 shares		3,125
– preference shares		625
Share premium		250
Profit and loss account balance		875
Stock	825	
Purchases	6,263	
Returns inwards	350	
Carriage inwards	13	
Carriage outwards	125	
Salesmen's salaries	800	
Administrative wages and salaries	738	
Plant (includes £362,000 acquired in 20X1)	1,562	
Motor vehicles	1,125	
Goodwill	1,062	
Distribution expenses	290	
Administrative expenses	286	
Directors' remuneration	375	
Trade debtors	3,875	
Cash at bank and in hand	1,750	
	19,439	19,439

Note of information not taken into the trial balance data:

(a) Provide for:
    (i) An audit fee of £38,000.
    (ii) Depreciation of plant at 20% straight-line.
    (iii) Depreciation of vehicles at 25% reducing balance.
    (iv) Amortise the goodwill over six years.
    (v) Corporation tax of £562,000.
    (vi) Debenture interest of £25,000.
    (vii) A preference dividend of 8%.
    (viii) An ordinary dividend of 10p per share.

(b) Closing stock was valued at £1,125,000 at the lower of cost and net realisable value.

(c) Administrative expenses were prepaid by £12,000.

Required:
(a) Prepare a profit and loss account for internal use for the year ended 31 December 20X1.
(b) Prepare a profit and loss account for the year ended 31 December 20X1 and a balance sheet as at that date in Format 1 style of presentation.

* **Question 2**

UKAY plc has prepared its draft trial balance to 30 June 20X1, which is shown below.

The authorised share capital is 4,000,000 9% preference shares of £1 each and 18,000,000 ordinary shares of 50p each.

Trial balance at 30 June 20X1

	£000	£000
Freehold land	2,880	
Freehold buildings (cost £4,680)	4,126	
Plant and machinery (cost £3,096)	1,858	
Fixtures and fittings (cost £864)	691	
Goodwill	480	
Trade debtors	7,263	
Trade creditors		2,591
Stock	11,794	
Bank balance	11,561	
Income tax on loan interest	151	
Development grant received		85
Profit on sale of freehold land		536
Sales		381,600
Cost of sales	318,979	
Administration expenses	9,000	
Distribution costs	35,100	
Directors' emoluments	562	
Bad debts	157	
Auditors' remuneration	112	
Hire of plant and machinery	2,400	
Loan interest paid net	454	
Dividends paid during the year – preference	162	
– ordinary	426	
9% loan		7,200
Share capital – preference shares		3,600
– ordinary shares		5,400
Profit and loss account		6,364
Revaluation account		780
	408,156	408,156

The following information is available:

1   The depreciation policy of the company is to provide depreciation at the following rates:

Plant and machinery	20% on cost
Fixtures and fittings	10% on cost
Buildings	2% on cost

In addition, it has been decided to create a Reserve of 10% on the cost of plant and machinery to allow for the increased cost of replacement. (Depreciation for 20X1 has not been provided in the draft trial balance.) Charge all depreciation to cost of sales.

2   Acquisitions of fixed assets during the year were:

Plant   £173,000   Fixtures   £144,000

3   Government grants of £85,000 have been received in respect of plant purchased during the year and are shown in the trial balance.

4   During the year freehold land which cost £720,000 was sold for £2,036,000. It was valued in last year's balance sheet at £1,500,000. The revaluation surplus had been credited to revaluation reserve.

5   Stock shown in the trial balance (£11,794,000) consists of:

Raw materials	£1,872,000
Work-in-progress	£6,660,000
Finished goods	£3,262,000

6   Trade debtors and creditors are all payable and due within the next financial year. The loan is unsecured and repayable in ten years' time.

7   During the year a fire took place at one of the company's depots, involving losses of £200,000. These losses have been written off to cost of sales shown in the trial balance. Since the end of the financial year a settlement of £150,000 has been agreed with the company's insurers.

8   It is agreed that £500,000 of the finished goods stock is obsolete and should be written off. However, since the end of the financial year an offer has been received from another company to buy this stock for £300,000, subject to certain modifications being made at an estimated cost to UKAY plc of £50,000. This has now been agreed.

9   A contract has been entered into, with a building contractor, to extend the company's premises. The contract price is £5,000,000 and the work is scheduled to start in December 20X1.

10 A final ordinary dividend of 3p per share is proposed, together with the balance of the preference dividend.

11 The corporation tax charge in the profit and loss account is to be that based on the net profit for the year, at a rate of 35%.

12 Goodwill is to be amortised over 5 years.

Required:
**(a) Prepare the company's profit and loss account for the year to 30 June 20X1 and a balance sheet as at that date, complying with the Companies Act 1985 and relevant accounting standards in so far as the information given permits.
(All calculations to nearest £000.)**
(b) Prepare the tangible fixed asset schedule for the notes to the accounts.

Question 3

Basalt plc is a wholesaler. The following is its trial balance as at 31 December 20X0.

	Dr £000	Cr £000
Ordinary share capital: £1 shares		300
Share premium		20
General reserve		16
Profit and loss account as at 1 January 20X0		55
Stock as at 1 January 20X0	66	
Sales		962
Purchases	500	
Administrative expenses	10	
Distribution expenses	6	
Plant and machinery – cost	220	
Plant and machinery – provision for depreciation		49
Returns outwards		25
Returns inwards	27	
Carriage inwards	9	
Warehouse wages	101	
Salesmen's salaries	64	
Administrative wages and salaries	60	
Hire of motor vehicles	19	
Directors' remuneration	30	
Rent receivable		7
Trade debtors	326	
Cash at bank	62	
Trade creditors		66
	1,500	1,500

The following additional information is supplied:
 (i) Depreciate plant and machinery 20% on straight-line basis.
 (ii) Stock at 31 December 20X0 is £90,000.
 (iii) Accrue auditors' remuneration £2,000.
 (iv) Corporation tax for the year will be £58,000 payable October 20X1.
 (v) There is a proposed ordinary dividend of £75,000 for the year.
 (vi) It is estimated that 7/11 of the plant and machinery is used in connection with distribution, with the remainder for administration. The motor vehicle costs should be assigned to distribution.

Required:
(a) Prepare a profit and loss account and balance sheet in a form that complies with the Companies Act 1985. No notes to the accounts are required.
(b) Briefly explain what you would expect to find in the following sections of an annual report:
   (i) Directors' report.
   (ii) Chairman's report.
   (iii) Auditors' report.

Question 4

Pinot Ltd trades as a wine wholesaler with a large warehouse in the East Midlands. The trainee accountant at Pinot Ltd has produced the following draft accounts for the year ended 31 December 20X6.

Profit and loss account

	£
Sales	1,628,000
Less: Cost of sales	1,100,000
Gross profit	528,000
Debenture interest paid	9,000
Distribution costs	32,800
Audit fees	7,000
Amortisation of goodwill	2,500
Corporation tax liability on profits	165,000
Interim dividend	18,000
Dividend received from Diat P'or plc	(6,000)
Bank interest	3,000
Over provision of corporation tax in prior years	(4,250)
Depreciation	
Land and buildings	3,000
Plant and machinery	10,000
Fixtures and fittings	6,750
Administrative expenses	206,300
Net profit	74,900

Draft balance sheet at 31 December 20X6

	£		£
Bank balance	12,700	Stock	156,350
10% debentures 20X9	180,000	Debtors	179,830
Ordinary share capital		Land and buildings	238,000
50p nominal value	250,000	Plant and machinery	74,000
Trade creditors	32,830	Fixtures and fittings	20,250
Corporation tax			
creditor	165,000	Goodwill	40,000
Profit and loss account	172,900	Investments at cost	130,000
Revaluation reserve	25,000		
	838,430		838,430

The following information is relevant:

1   The directors maintain that the investments in Diat P'or plc will be held by the company on a continuing basis and that the current market value of the investments at the balance sheet date was £135,000. However, since the balance sheet date there has been a substantial fall in market prices and these investments are now valued at £90,000.

2   The authorised share capital of Pinot Limited is 600,000 ordinary shares.

3   The directors propose to pay a final dividend of 7.2p per share.

4   During the year the company paid shareholders the proposed 20X5 final dividend of £30,000. This transaction has already been recorded in the accounts.

5   The company incurred £150,000 in restructuring costs during the year. These have been debited to the administrative expenses account. The trainee accountant subsequently informs you that tax relief of £45,000 will be given on these costs and that this relief has not yet been accounted for in the records.

6   The company employs an average of ten staff, 60% of whom work in the wine purchasing and importing department, 30% in the distribution department and the remainder in the accounts department. Staff costs total £75,000.

7   The company has three directors. The managing director earns £18,000 while the purchasing and distribution directors earn £14,000 each. In addition the directors receive bonuses and pensions of £1,800 each. All staff costs have been debited to the profit and loss account.

8   The directors propose to decrease the bad debt provision by £1,500 as a result of the improved credit control in the company in recent months.

9   Depreciation policy is as follows:

Land and buildings:	No depreciation on land. Buildings are depreciated over 25 years on a straight-line basis. This is to be charged to cost of sales.
Plant and machinery:	10% on cost, charge to cost of sales
Fixtures and fittings:	25% reducing balance, charge to administration.

10 The directors have provided information on a potential lawsuit. A customer is suing them for allegedly tampering with the imported wine by injecting an illegal substance to improve the colour of the wine. The managing director informs you that this lawsuit is just 'sour grapes' by a jealous customer and provides evidence from the company solicitor which indicates that there is only a small possibility that the claim for £8,000 will succeed.

11 Purchased goodwill was acquired in 20X3 when the directors decided to capitalise and amortise it over its useful economic life of 20 years.

12 Plant and machinery of £80,000 was purchased during the year to add to the £20,000 plant already owned. Fixtures and fittings, acquired 2 years ago with a net book value of £13,500 were disposed of. Accumulated depreciation of fixtures and fittings at 1 January 20X6 was £37,500.

13 Land was revalued by £25,000 by Messrs Moneybags, Chartered Surveyors, on an open market value basis, to £175,000. The revaluation surplus was credited to the revaluation reserve. There is no change in the value of the buildings.

14 Gross profit is stated after charging £15,000 relating to obsolete cases of wine that have 'gone off'. Since that time an offer has been received by the company for its obsolete wine stock of £8,000, provided the company does additional vinification on the wine at a cost of £2,000 to bring it up to the buyer's requirements. A cash discount of 5% is allowed for early settlement and it is anticipated that the buyer will take advantage of this discount.

15 Costs of £10,000 relating to special plant and machinery have been included in cost of sales in error. This was not spotted until after the production of the draft accounts.

Required:
(a) Prepare a profit and loss account for the year ended 31 December 20X6 and a balance sheet at that date for presentation to the members of Pinot Ltd in accordance with the requirements of the Companies Act and relevant accounting standards.
(b) Produce detailed notes to the profit and loss account and balance sheet of Pinot Limited for the year ended 31 December 20X6.

Question 5

Phoenix plc trial balance at 30 June 20X7 was as follows:

	£000	£000
Freehold premises	2,400	
Plant and machinery	1,800	540
Furniture and fittings	620	360
Stock at 30 June 20X7	1,468	
Sales		6,465
Administrative expenses	1,126	
Ordinary shares of £1 each		4,500
Trade investments	365	
Revaluation reserve		600
Development cost	415	
Share premium		500
Personal ledger balances	947	566
Cost of goods sold	4,165	
Distribution costs	669	
Over-provision for tax		26
Dividend received		80
Interim dividend paid	200	
Profit and loss account		488
Disposal of warehouse		225
Cash and bank balances	175	

The following information is available:

1 Freehold premises acquired for £1.8 million were revalued in 20X4, recognising a gain of £600,000. These include a warehouse, which cost £120,000, was revalued at £150,000 and was sold in June 20X7 for £225,000. Phoenix does not depreciate freehold premises.

2 Phoenix wishes to report Plant and Machinery at open market value which is estimated to be £1,960,000 on 1 July 20X6.

3 Company policy is to depreciate its assets on the straight-line method at annual rates as follows:
   Plant and machinery   10%
   Furniture and fittings   5%

4 Until this year the company's policy has been to capitalise development costs, to the extent permitted by relevant accounting standard. The company has decided to write off all such expenses, including £124,000 incurred in the year.

5 During the year the company has issued one million shares of £1 at £1.20 each

6 Included within administrative expenses are the following:
   Staff salary (including £125,000 to directors)   £468,000
   Directors' fees   £96,000
   Audit fees and expenses   £86,000

7 Corporation tax for the year is estimated at £122,000.

8 Directors propose a final dividend of 4p per share.

Required:
(a) In respect of the year ended 30 June 20X7:
   the profit and loss account;
   the statement of total recognised gains and losses;
   the note on historical cost profit and loss;
   the reconciliation of shareholders' funds.
(b) The balance sheet as at 30 June 20X7.
(c) The statement of movement of tangible fixed assets.

Question 6 Related party scenarios

(a) In 20X3 Arthur is a large loan creditor of X Ltd and receives interest at 20% p.a. on this loan. He also has a 24% shareholding in X Ltd. Until 20X1 he was a director of the company and left after a disagreement. The remaining 76% of the shares are held by the remaining directors. Is Arthur a related party to X Ltd?

(b) Brenda joined Y Ltd, an insurance broking company, on 1 January 20X0 on a low salary but high commission basis. She brought clients with her that generated 30% of the company's 20X0 turnover. Is Brenda a related party to Y Ltd?

(c) Carrie is a director and major shareholder of Z Ltd. Her husband, Donald, is employed in the company on administrative duties for which he is paid a salary of £25,000 p.a. Her daughter, Emma, is a business consultant running her own business. In 20X0 Emma carried out various consultancy exercises for the company for which she was paid £85,000. Are Donald or Emma related parties to Z Ltd?

(d) Fred is a director of V Ltd. V Ltd is a major customer of W Ltd. In 20X0 Fred also became a director of W Ltd. Are related party disclosures required in either V Ltd or W Ltd?

Required:
Discuss whether parties are related in the above situations.

Question 7

Maxpool plc, a listed company, owned 60% of the shares in Ching Ltd. Bay plc, a listed company, owned the remaining 40% of the £1 ordinary shares in Ching Ltd. The holdings of shares were acquired on 1 January 20X0.

On 30 November 20X0 Ching Ltd sold a factory outlet site to Bay plc at a price determined by an independent surveyor.

On 1 March 20X1 Maxpool plc purchased a further 30% of the £1 ordinary shares of Ching Ltd from Bay plc and purchased 25% of the ordinary shares of Bay plc.

On 30 June 20X1 Ching Ltd sold the whole of its fleet of vehicles to Bay plc at a price determined by a vehicle auctioneer.

Required:
Explain the implications of the above transactions for the determination of related party relationships and disclosure of such transactions in the financial statements of (a) Maxpool Group plc, (b) Ching Ltd and (c) Bay plc for the years ending 31 December 20X0 and 31 December 20X1.

(ACCA)

References

1 Companies Act 1985, section 235.
2 B. Johnson and M. Patient, *Accounting Provisions of the Companies Act 1985*, Farringdon Publishing, 1985, p. 296.
3 Companies Act 1985, section 228.
4 K. Wild and A. Guida, *Touche Ross Manual of Financial Reporting and Accounting* (3rd edition), Butterworth, 1990, p. 433.
5 K. Wild and C. Goodhead, *Touche Ross Financial Reporting Manual* (4th edition), Butterworth, 1994, p. 5.
6 'Differing views on true and fair', *Certified Accountant*, October 1994, p. 12.
7 Companies Act 1985, Schedule 4, paras 9–15.
8 SSAP 2, *Disclosure of Accounting Policies*, ASC, 1971, para. 14.
9 Companies Act 1985, Schedule 4, para. 8.
10 Ernst and Young, *UK GAAP* (2nd edition), Longman, 1990, p. 1109.
11 *Statement on Professional Independence*, CACA, 1944.
12 Arthur Andersen, *Accounting and Reporting Requirements* (3rd edition), Arthur Andersen, 1990, p. 187.
13 SSAP 25, *Segmented Reporting*, ASB, June 1990.
14 FRS 3, *Reporting Financial Performance*, ASB, October 1992.
15 L. Todd Johnson and A. Lennard, *Reporting Financial Performance: Current Developments and Future Directions*, ASB, 1997.
16 *Reporting Financial Performance: Proposals for Change*, Discussion Paper, ASB, June 1999.
17 FRS 8, *Related Party Disclosures*, ASB, October 1995.
18 Companies Act 1985, Schedule 4, paras 11, 36.
19 CIMA, *Corporate Reporting – The Management Interface*, CIMA, 1990, p. 27.
20 V. Beatty and M. Jones, 'Company reporting: the US leads the way', *Certified Accountant*, March 1994, p. 50.

CHAPTER 9

Preparation of published accounts

9.1 Introduction

In this chapter we illustrate the preparation of a profit and loss account and balance sheet using Format 1 from trial balance to published accounts. We then take into account the effects of FRS 3. We follow a progressive stage approach to the problem.

Stage 1 is the preparation of the internal profit and loss account from the trial balance data. Stage 2 is the preparation of a profit and loss account in Format 1. Stage 3 is the preparation of a balance sheet in Format 1 style. The aim is that you should be able to prepare a set of accounts that conform to the prescribed formats and that you should also understand how a company arrives at the figures that appear in the published financial statements that it presents to its shareholders.

9.2 Stage 1: preparation of the internal profit and loss account from a trial balance

In this chapter we use Format 1, i.e. the vertical format, with costs analysed according to the type of operation.[1]

The data given in Figure 9.1 are available for Illustrious plc for the year ended 31 December 20X1. The following information has not yet been taken into account in the amounts shown in the trial balance.

- Stock at cost at 31 December 20X1 was £22,875,000. Stock at net realisable value at 31 December 20X1 was £3,000,000. The cost of this stock was £4,000,000. The reduction to net realisable value was necessitated because the customer who would normally have taken the products assembled from these stock items had gone into liquidation.

- Depreciation is to be provided as follows:
    2% on freehold buildings using the straight-line method;
    10% on equipment using the reducing balance method;
    25% on motor vehicles using reducing balance.

- £2,300,000 was prepaid for repairs and £5,175,000 has accrued for wages.

Figure 9.1 Trial balance of Illustrious plc as at 31 December 20X1.

	£000	£000
Bank interest	1,150	
Bank overdraft		8,625
Cash in hand	4,600	
Debentures		63,250
Debtors	28,750	
Depreciation – equipment		3,450
– motor vehicles		9,200
Directors' remuneration	1,150	
Dividends	1,725	
Equipment	14,950	
Fees – audit	1,150	
Freehold land	57,500	
Freehold buildings	57,500	
Hire charges	300	
Interest on debentures	6,325	
Issued share capital		17,250
Lighting and power	920	
Miscellaneous expenses	275	
Motor expenses	9,200	
Motor vehicles	20,700	
Post, telephone, courier	1,840	
Profit and loss account		57,500
Provision for corporation tax		5,750
Purchases	258,750	
Rates and insurance	3,450	
Repairs and maintenance	2,760	
Salaries and wages	18,055	
Tax – corporation	5,750	
Sales		345,000
Stock at 1 Jan 20X1	43,125	
Trade creditors		29,900
	539,925	539,925

A profit and loss account prepared for internal purposes is set out in Figure 9.2. We have arranged the expenses in the profit and loss account in descending monetary value. This is not a prescribed method and companies may organise the items in a number of ways, such as alphabetical sequence or grouping by function, e.g. establishment, administration, selling, distribution and financial expenses.

Figure 9.2 Profit and loss account of Illustrious plc for the year ended 31 December 20X1.

	£000	£000
Sales		345,000
Less:		
Opening stock	43,125	
Purchases	258,750	
	301,875	
Closing stock	25,875	
Cost of sales		276,000
Gross profit		69,000
Less: Expenses:		
Salaries and wages	23,230	
Motor expenses	9,200	
Debenture interest	6,325	
Depreciation	5,175	
Rates and insurance	3,450	
Post, telephone, courier	1,840	
Fees – audit	1,150	
Bank interest	1,150	
Directors' remuneration	1,150	
Lighting and power	920	
Repairs and maintenance	460	
Hire charges	300	
Miscellaneous expenses	275	
		54,625
Profit before tax		14,375
Tax		5,750
Profit after tax		8,625
Dividends		1,725
Amount transferred to reserves		6,900

9.3 Stage 2: preparation of the profit and loss account of Illustrious plc in Format 1 style

The information contained in the internal profit and loss account in Figure 9.2 needs to be redrafted into the format required by the Companies Act. In addition, specific information that would not necessarily appear within the format information needs to be disclosed. First we redraft using Format 1 with its vertical presentation and costs analysed according to type of operations, as set out in Figure 9.3.

Figure 9.3 Illustrious plc profit and loss account redrafted into Format I style.

Profit and loss account of Illustrious plc
for the year ended 31 December 20X1

	£000
Turnover	345,000.00
Cost of sales	293,422.50
Gross profit	51,577.50
Distribution, selling and marketing costs	25,041.25
Administrative expenses	4,686.25
Operating profit	21,850.00
Interest payable	7,475.00
Profit on ordinary activities before tax	14,375.00
Tax	5,750.00
Profit on ordinary activities after tax	8,625.00
Dividends	1,725.00
Amount transferred to reserves	6,900.00

			Cost of sales	Distribution costs	Administration expenses
		£000	£000	£000	£000
Cost of sales		276,000	276,000		
Salaries and wages	NI	23,230	12,075	10,580	575
Motor expenses		9,200		9,200	
Depreciation	N2	5,175	1,150	3,450	575
Rates and insurance	N3	3,450	1,725	862.5	862.5
Post, telephone, courier	N3	1,840	920	460	460
Fees – audit		1,150			1,150
Directors' salaries	N4	1,150	575		575
Lighting and power	N3	920	460	230	230
Repairs and maintenance	N3	460	230	115	115
Hire charges	N3	300	150	75	75
Miscellaneous expenses	N3	275	137.5	68.75	68.75
		323,150	293,422.5	25,041.25	4,686.25

Interest will be disclosed after the trading profit:

	£000
Debenture interest	6,325
Bank interest	1,150
	7,475

9.3.1 How did we arrive at the figures for cost of sales, distribution costs and administrative expenses?

In order to analyse the costs, we need to consider each item in the detailed profit and loss account. Each item will be allocated to a classification or apportioned if it relates to more than one of the classifications. This requires the company to make a number of assumptions about the basis for allocating and apportioning. The process is illustrated in Figure 9.4.

From the assumptions that have been made, it is clear that the figures appearing under each of the cost classifications may be apportioned differently in different companies.

Figure 9.4   Assumptions made in analysing the costs.

N1 An analysis of salaries and wages

		Cost of sales	Distribution costs	Administration expenses
	£000	£000	£000	£000
Factory assembly staff	11,500	11,500		
Inspectors	575	575		
Warehouse staff	4,600		4,600	
Accounts department	575			575
Drivers	3,680		3,680	
Salespersons' salaries	2,300		2,300	
	23,230	12,075	10,580	575

N2 An analysis of depreciation

Freehold buildings	1,150	575	287.5	287.5
Equipment	1,150	575	287.5	287.5
Motor vehicles	2,875		2,875	
	5,175	1,150	3,450	575

N3 An apportionment of operating expenses

It is assumed that the following expenses can be apportioned on the basis of the space occupied by the activity, as follows:

	£000	£000	£000	£000
Rates and insurance	3,450	1,725	862.5	862.5
Post, telephone, courier	1,840	920	460	460
Lighting and power	920	460	230	230
Repairs and maintenance	460	230	115	115
Hire charges	300	150	75	75
Miscellaneous expenses	275	137.5	68.75	68.75

N4 An allocation of directors' salaries

It is assumed that the directors spend half their time on production and half on administration.

Figure 9.5   Illustrious plc disclosure note accompanying the profit and loss account.

Profit on ordinary activities before tax is stated after charging:

	£000
Depreciation and amortisation	5,175
Auditors' remuneration	1,150
Hire of equipment	300
Exceptional loss on stock	1,000

9.3.2   What information would be disclosed by way of note to the profit and loss account?

We have mentioned that sensitive information is required to be disclosed in the notes to the profit and loss account. The usual practice is to have a note referenced to the profit on ordinary activities before tax. For Illustrious plc the note would read as in Figure 9.5, with additional information regarding the loss on the stock. This treatment – the inclusion of the expense in its cost type heading with more detail in the notes – complies with FRS 3, which does not allow for the highlighting of exceptional items. These should be disclosed separately either by way of note or on the face of the profit and loss account if that degree of prominence is necessary in order to give a true and fair view.[2]

9.4   Stage 3: preparation of the balance sheet in Format 1 style

The balance sheet in Figure 9.6 follows the headings set out in section 8.9.1 above.

Figure 9.6   Illustrious plc balance sheet and disclosure notes.

Disclosure notes to show make up of balance sheet items

Note 1 Tangible fixed asset movements

Tangible fixed assets	Freehold property £000	Equipment £000	Motor vehicles £000	Total £000
Cost				
At 1 January 20X1	115,000	14,950	20,700	150,650
Additions				
Disposals				
At 31 December 20X1	115,000	4,950	20,700	50,650
Accumulated depreciation				
At 1 January 20X1		3,450	9,200	12,650
Charge for year	1,150	1,150	2,875	5,175
At 31 December 20X1	1,150	4,600	12,075	17,825
Net book value				
At 31 December 20X1	113,850	10,350	8,625	132,825
At 31 December 20X0	115,000	11,500	11,500	138,000

Figure 9.6 (cont.)

Balance sheet of Illustrious plc as at 31 December 20X1

	£000	£000
Fixed assets		
Tangible assets Note 1		132,825
Current assets		
Stocks	25,875	
Debtors	28,750	
Cash at bank and in hand	4,600	
Prepayments	2,300	
	61,525	
Creditors: amounts failing due within one year		
Creditors	29,900	
Provision for corporation tax	5,750	
Accrued charges	5,175	
Bank overdraft	8,625	
	49,450	
Net current assets		12,075
Total assets less current liabilities		144,900
Creditors: amounts falling due after more than one year		
Debentures		63,250
		81,650
Capital and reserves		
Share capital		17,250
Profit and loss account		64,400
		81,650

9.5 Preparation of accounts in Format 1 and FRS 3 format

By way of illustration, assume you are the chief accountant of Lewes Road Wines plc, a wholesale distributor currently operating from a single warehouse/office complex in Brighton. Until June 20X2 the company had a plant at Dover, where wine that was imported in bulk was bottled prior to its sale to retail outlets. The profitability of this activity had declined and the plant had closed.

One of your unqualified assistants has prepared the following draft for the published profit and loss account for the year to 31 December 20X2, which he has given to you together with his notes and workings in Figure 9.7

Figure 9.7   Lewes Road Wines plc profit and loss account (1).

Profit and loss account for the year ended 31 December 20X2

		£000
Turnover (Note 1)		1,288
Cost of sales (Note 2)		744
Gross profit		544
Distribution costs (Note 3)	232	
Administration costs (Note 4)	142	
		374
Operating profit		170
Other operating income (Note 5)		286
Profit on ordinary activities before interest		456
Interest receivable		4
		460
Interest payable		33
Profit on ordinary activities before taxation		427
Tax on profit on ordinary activities (Note 6)		103
Profit on ordinary activities after taxation		324
Proposed dividend		45
Retained profit for the year		279
Retained profits brought forward		274
Retained profits carried forward		553

Notes and workings

1 Turnover includes £175,000 in respect of bottling plant revenue.

2 *Cost of sales*

Wine purchased (including duty and carriage in)	536
Labour	72
Bottles, etc	150
Stock variation (all wine)	(14)
	744

£72,000 (at cost) of wine had to be discarded during the year owing to contamination at source.

Labour costs included £10,000 for wages at the bottling plant and £30,000 in respect of redundancy payments to former employees at the Dover works.

3 *Distribution costs*

Carriage	120
Sales department salaries	51
Bad debts	61
	232

£55,000 represented the bad debt incurred following the collapse of a chain of cut price wine shops.

Figure 9.7 (cont.)

4	*Administrative expenses*	
	Salaries (£10,000 in respect of Dover)	78
	Premises costs (£1,000 in respect of Dover)	19
	Other overheads (£2,000 in respect of Dover)	21
	Cost relating to the closure of the Dover plant	24
		142
5	*Other operating income*	
	Profit on revaluing Brighton premises	100
	Profit on sale of Dover premises	212
	Loss on sale of bottling equipment	(26)
		286
6	*Taxation*	
	Corporation tax due on 20X2 operating profit	44
	Corporation tax on the capital gain on sale of	
	Dover premises	56
	Under provision for taxation in 20X1	3
		103

There was an error on the previous year closing stock calculation resulting in an understatement of stock by £100,000.

You need now to redraft the profit and loss account so that it complies with the Companies Act 1985 and generally accepted accounting principles. Corporation tax is 30%. In approaching this task you need to consider the provisions of FRS 3 relating to the treatment of discontinued operations, exceptional items and prior period adjustments.

Discontinued operations

Applying the layered treatment of FRS 3 and para. 14, which requires the results of continuing and discontinued operations to be disclosed separately, it is necessary to identify the turnover, cost of sales and expenses that relate to the discontinued bottling operation in arriving at the operating profit.

Exceptional items

Exceptional items that require disclosure on the face of the profit and loss account are set out in para. 20 of FRS 3. They include losses arising on termination of an operation and profit on sale of fixed assets.

Revaluation

The revaluation surplus, being unrealised, cannot appear in the profit and loss account. It should, however, appear in the Statement of Total Recognised Gains and Losses.

Prior period adjustments

Paragraph 29 of FRS 3 requires prior period adjustments to be accounted for by restating the comparative figures and adjusting the opening balance of reserves for the cumulative effect. Note that this means that it is also necessary to take the tax effect into account.

The detailed workings and profit and loss account are given in Figure 9.8.

Figure 9.8   Lewes Road Wines plc profit and loss account (2).

Profit and loss account for the year ended 31 December 20X2

	Continuing operations £000	Discontinued operations £000	Total £000
Turnover	1,113	175	1,288
Cost of sales	654	160	814
Gross profit	459	15	474
Administrative costs	(105)	(13)	(118)
Distribution costs	(232)	—	(232)
Operating profit	122	2	124
Profit on property sale		212	212
Loss on disposal of discontinued activity		(80)	(80)
Profit on ordinary activities before interest	122	134	256
Interest receivable			4
			260
Interest payable			33
Profit on ordinary activities before taxation			227
Taxation			73
Profit on ordinary activities after taxation			154
Proposed dividend			45
Retained profit for the year			109
Retained profits b/f:			
As previously reported		274	
Prior year adjustment		100	
Tax thereon		(30)	344
Retained profits carried forward			453

Notes

Exceptional items

Cost of sales includes £72,000 in respect of wine that had to be discarded during the year owing to contamination at source.

Sales costs includes £55,000 in respect of a bad debt incurred following the collapse of a chain of cut price wine shops.

Figure 9.8 (cont.)

Workings

Cost of sales	Bottling	Other	Total
Per draft – labour	40	32	72
bottles, etc.	150		150
stock		(14)	(14)
wine		536	536
Prior year item		100	100
Loss on sale	(30)		(30)
	160	654	814

Administration expenses			
Per draft – salaries	10	68	78
premises	1	18	19
other	2	19	21
closure	24		24
Loss on sale	(24)		(24)
	13	105	118

Loss on closure	
Administration	24
Redundancy	30
Bottling equipment	—
	80

Statement of total recognised gains and losses

Profit for the financial year	154	[Figure 9.8 Profit after tax]
Unrealised surplus on revaluation	100	[Figure 9.7 Note 5 premises revalued]
Total recognised gains	254	
Prior year adjustment	70	[Figure 9.8 adjusting profit brought
	324	forward]

9.6 Additional information value of FRS 3

Changes in the operation

The additional disclosure of the effect of discontinued or acquired operations is intended to assist the user to assess more readily the current performance and to predict future maintainable profits. However, care is required when comparing current performance with that of previous years. The provisions of FRS 3 are vague relating to the treatment of acquisitions and, although the contribution from an acquisition is included as part of continuing operations, FRS 3 indicates that it is shown as a separate item of that constituent part; in the second and subsequent years it will not be shown as a separate item.

The contribution from acquisitions, the making of comparisons and the usefulness of the information can be problematical depending on when an acquisition occurs. If it was made in the first week of an accounting year, virtually a whole year will be reported as a contribution from acquisitions. But if it was made in the last week of the previous accounting period, the second period will include the results as part of continuing operations and, as the amount of the contribution for the few days in the period of acquisition will not be material, it will never be reported as an acquisition. This could have a material effect on users' perception of current and future growth rates. This indicates the need always to look behind ratios and percentage changes.[3]

Effect on comparisons of different bases of accounting

Some companies, e.g. Coats Viyella, prepare accounts under the historical cost convention. The majority of companies however prepare their accounts under the historical cost convention but as modified by the revaluation of fixed assets.

In order to facilitate comparisons a note is required of the profit calculated on a historical cost basis, i.e. eliminating the effect of revaluations on the reported profit. A note would provide the following information:

	£
Reported profit on ordinary activities before tax	x
Realisation of fixed asset revaluation gains of previous years	y
Difference between depreciation charge based on historical cost and that based on revalued amounts	z
Historical cost profit on ordinary activities before tax	$x + y + z$
Historical cost retained after tax and dividends	$(x + y + z) -$ tax $-$ dividend

Where there has been a disposal of a previously revalued property there can be a significant difference in the profit before tax as shown in the extract from the Annual report and accounts of Associated British Ports Holdings plc:

Note of Group historical cost profits and losses for the year ended 31 December 1998

	£m	£m
Profit on ordinary activities before tax	32.8	110.6
Realisation of property revaluation (deficits)/surplus of previous years	(36.7)	0.6
Historical cost (loss)/profit on ordinary activities before taxation	(3.9)	111.2
Taxation on profit on ordinary activities	(27.2)	(26.5)
	(31.1)	84.7
Dividends	(39.4)	(37.2)
Historical cost (loss)/profit for the year retained after taxation and dividends	(70.5)	47.5

Changes in shareholders' funds

Shareholders' funds may be changed as a result of profit or loss from trading, revaluation of fixed assets, goodwill write-offs against reserves, and prior year adjustments to the opening shareholders' funds brought forward. FRS 3 requires a statement to explain to the shareholders how their funds have changed. A statement would be built up as follows:

Reconciliation of movements in shareholders' funds for the year ended 31.12.20X9

Step 1 – identify realised profits/losses that have been retained:

Profit for financial year	a
Dividends	b
Realised and retained	$a - b$

Step 2 – identify asset changes arising from unrealised revaluations:

Other recognised gains/losses [net unrealised gains less unrealised losses]	c

Step 3 – identify share capital movements

Add new share capital raised/deduct share capital repaid	d

Step 4 – identify changes in goodwill other than by way of amortisation

Deduct goodwill written off against reserves		(e)
Net additions to shareholders' funds		$(a - b) + c + d - e$
Opening shareholders' funds	f	
Less prior period adjustments	(g)	$f - g$
Closing shareholders' funds		$[(a - b) + c + d - e] + (f - g)]$

9.7 Summary Financial Statements

In this chapter we have explained how disclosure requirements have been increasing, e.g. FRS 3 additional information in order to assist informed users such as financial analysts. However, recognising that there was a the risk of the informed layperson being over-whelmed with detail and/or recognising the cost of sending out Annual Reports running to 60 or more pages, the Companies Act 1989 allowed listed companies to offer a Summary Financial Statement to shareholders.

The Bass plc Summary Financial Statements for 1999 is a typical example. It contains:

● Financial highlights, e.g. a bar chart of 5 years' operating profit, adjusted earnings per share and dividend per share; the £ figures and % change for turnover, operating profit, adjusted earnings per share and dividend per share and the increase in property values.

● Chairman's Review commenting on how well the company has been achieving its strategy in relation to hotels, leisure retail and branded drinks; revaluation of properties; about the staff; Bass in the Community and current trading.

● Brands – eight colour pages on brands.

● Summary Financial Statement.

● Summary directors' report – two pages including photographs of the directors.

● Investors' information, with information on redemption of share, ISAs, share price information.

● Financial calendar – dates of year end, AGM, payment of final and interim dividends.

The Bass plc Summary Financial Statement for 1999 appears as follows:

Profit and loss

	1999 £m	1998 £m	1997 £m
Adjusted earnings per share	62.3p	57.4p	55.5p
Dividend per share	32.3	30.0p	27.5p
Turnover	4,686	4,609	5,254
Costs	(3,878)	(3,890)	(4,473)
Share of associates' profit	16	39	20
Operating profit	824	758	801
Exceptional items: major	(110)	183	(237)
Other	(2)	(10)	—
Interest	(140)	(97)	(87)
Profit before tax	572	834	477
Tax	(177)	(179)	(212)
Profit after tax	395	655	265
Minority interests	(8)	(5)	(15)
Earnings	387	650	250
Dividends	(277)	(240)	(244)
Retained for reinvestment	110	410	6

Net worth

	1999 £m	1998 £m	1997 £m
Fixed assets	6,335	5,576	5,027
Current assets	1,405	1,396	1,631
Short-term creditors	(1,803)	(1,989)	(1,470)
Net current (liabilities)/assets	(398)	(593)	161
Total assets less current liabilities	5,937	4,983	5,188
Long-term creditors	(2,231)	(2,012)	(1,180)
Provisions	(266)	(272)	(123)
Minority interests	(127)	(122)	(116)
Net assets	3,313	2,577	3,769
Shareholders' funds	3,313	2,577	3,769

Cash flow

	1999 £m	1998 £m	1997 £m
Operations	986	938	1,051
Net capital expenditure	(501)	(587)	(91)
Trade loans	32	27	29
Dividends from associates	10	3	—
Operating cash flow	527	381	481

Interest	(130)	(105)	(91)
Dividends	(250)	(250)	(206)
Taxation	(174)	(152)	(165)
Normal cash flow	(27)	(126)	19
Major disposals/(acquisitions)	—	489	385
Net cash flow	(27)	363	404
Return of capital	(30)	(801)	—
Net debt acquired	(5)	(901)	(3)
Net debt	(1,995)	(1,950)	(555)

9.7.1 ICAEW Review of Summary Financial Statements[4]

This review by the ICAEW Working Party indicated that summary statements were not widely used but that companies that had used the format had received favourable shareholder response. The Chairman of the Working Party commented in his own company's (B.A.T. Industries plc) 1995 accounts that the various new accounting regulations made the full Report and Accounts even harder to understand than hitherto.[5]

However, just as the full Report and Accounts has become overloaded with more and more reports, e.g. Corporate Governance, Operating and Financial Review, Remuneration Committee report, there is the risk that Summary Financial Statements will go down the same route and become more complex.

The relatively low rate of adoption by companies of the summary format, the risk of the summary reports becoming more complex and the cost of supplying full reports to all shareholders have prompted the ASB to address the problem.

9.7.2 ASB response to need for clarity for lay user

The ASB has taken the view that the option allowed by the Companies Act for companies to offer Summary Financial Statements should be given greater emphasis. It also recognises that, for some shareholders, even the Summary Financial Statements such as those of Bass above might be too detailed and it issued a Discussion Paper[6] in which it proposed that companies should be allowed to offer such shareholders an even shorter and simpler narrative financial review.

The detailed content of Summary Financial Statements has been incorporated in a Statutory Instrument[7] and there would need to be an amendment to Company Law. Any proposed amendment could be considered by the Company Law Review.

The ASB's Chairman has commented that for many private shareholders, accounting has always been something of a mysterious black art and even the informed layperson may get lost in the welter of detail of a full Annual Report and Accounts.

There is a contrasting view[8] that the reduction of results and financial position of a highly complex organisation might encourage the misguided view that these can be encapsulated in simple headline measures such as EPS and Gearing. One can understand this concern given that this has actually been the ASB's own stance when promoting the needs for greater transparency and explanation.

The reality is, of course, that many shareholders appear not to be interested in anything other than a general narrative and highlights. This would seem to indicate that for these shareholders it would be sufficient for Bass to offer:

● Financial highlights, e.g. a bar chart of 5 years' operating profit, adjusted earnings per share and dividend per share; the £ figures and % change for turnover, operating profit, adjusted earnings per share and dividend per share and the increase in property values.

● Chairman's Review commenting on how well the company has been achieving its strategy in relation to hotels, leisure retail and branded drinks; revaluation of properties; about the staff; Bass in the Community and current trading.

● Investors' information with information on redemption of share, ISAs, share price information.

● Financial calendar – dates of year end, AGM, payment of final and interim dividends.

The effect of this would be to reduce an Annual Report and Accounts of 61 pages down to a maximum of six pages.

Summary

A public company that is listed on the Stock Exchange is required to present an annual report and accounts to its shareholders.

The annual report consists of a number of statements. In Chapters 8 and 9 we have considered the following statements: the directors' report; the Operating and Financial Review; the profit and loss account; the Statement of Total Recognised Gains and Losses; the Reconciliation to the historical cost profit; the balance sheet and the Reconciliation of movements in shareholders' funds. We have seen the following:

● There is more than one format for presenting the profit and loss account and even companies operating in the same industry sector might choose a different format.

● Even where companies use the same format, they may classify costs into different cost categories.

● The additional information disclosed, e.g. staff costs, cannot necessarily be related to the categories of operations into which the company has classified its costs in its profit and loss account.

● There is no obvious, overriding rationale for the disclosure of information; it has grown in an *ad hoc* fashion with disclosure required:
  − for stewardship accounting, e.g. the disclosure of directors' remuneration;
  − for the shareholders as principal stakeholders, e.g. trading profit;
  − for interested stakeholders, e.g. an analysis of employees and details of staff costs;
  − on political grounds, e.g. the disclosure of political donations;
  − for the community as an interested stakeholder, e.g. company policy on the employment of disabled applicants.

● The balance sheet can be prepared under historical cost accounting rules **or** alternative accounting rules or a mixture of historical and alternative accounting rules.

● The Companies Act has not defined the costs to be used in the alternative accounting model.

Perhaps we have reached a stage where the purpose of the annual report needs to be reappraised and given a clearer focus.

Review questions

··

1 The directors of Ufool Ltd are aware that a sizeable number of shareholders, although still a minority, are extremely unhappy with current dividend levels and are agitating for larger distributions.

They have raised several points with the directors, who have turned to you as their trusty financial and accounting adviser for assistance. The points put forward by these shareholders are as follows:

(i) Although the annual accounts disclose that £150,000 profit was available for distribution, it is disclosed elsewhere in these accounts that £520,000 of the loan stock had been repaid. The shareholders assert that this repayment was an attempt to lower the true profit and that, if it were written back, more profit would be available for distribution.

(ii) Despite this year's relatively low profit, there is a very large balance of retained profits brought forward from preceding years. A significant proportion of these retained profits from preceding years should be used to pay a larger dividend this year.

(iii) It is unfair to have kept the dividend rate at 10% over the past few years when the average dividend yield on the Stock Exchange has risen from 12% to 18%. The company's dividend rate should follow this average.

(iv) The return on capital employed for the company is 20% and this high rate of profitability accurately reflects the ability of the company to pay far higher dividend levels.

(v) As profit figures can so easily be manipulated by the company's accountants, the £150,000 is more than likely to be a significant underestimate of the real profit, so more profit could be distributed if different accounting bases were used.

Comment on each of the above assertions to enable the board of directors to refute them convincingly.

2 It is said that Format 1 extends the management accounting concept of responsibility accounting to published financial statements. Explain what this means.

3 Under FRS 3 more disclosure is required than under the Companies Act. Explain the major additional disclosures and discuss how they can be justified.

4 When preparing accounts under Format 1, how would a bad debt that was materially larger than normal be disclosed?

5 Explain the conditions set out in FRS 3 for determining whether operations have been discontinued and the problems that might arise in applying them.

6 'Annual accounts have been put into such a straitjacket by the EU directives' overemphasis on uniform disclosure that there will be a growing pressure by national bodies to introduce changes unilaterally, e.g. the FRS 3 requirements, which will again lead to diversity in the quality of disclosure. This is both healthy and necessary.' Discuss.

7 Explain the relevance to the user of accounts if expenses are classified as 'administrative expenses' rather than as 'cost of sales'.

8 'The regulators are correct in their thinking that voluntary disclosures, e.g. OFR , Interim Reports, Cadbury *Code of Best Practice* are more helpful to shareholders than disclosures made under mandatory, more closely defined formats.' Discuss.

9 'The regulators are avoiding the need for uniform disclosure by adopting a policy of setting up committees, e.g. Cadbury, Greenbury, Hampel, whose recommendations are presented as

voluntary but which are enforced in practice by the Stock Exchange – but without any uniform disclosure format.' Discuss.

10 FRS 3 *Reporting Financial Performance* requires the publication of :

(i) The Statement of total recognised gains and losses;

(ii) The Note of Historical Cost profit or loss;

(iii) The Reconciliation of movements in shareholders' funds.

Explain the need for the publishing of these statements, identifying the circumstances in which they have to be published, and identify the items you would include in each of the statements.

Exercises

An extract from the solution is provided in the appendix at the end of the text for exercises marked with an asterisk (*).

* Question 1

Springtime Ltd is a trading company buying and selling as wholesalers fashionable summer clothes. The following balances have been extracted from the books as at 31 March 20X4:

	£000
Auditor's remuneration	30
Corporation tax based on the accounting profit:	
For the year to 31 March 20X4	3,200
Overprovision for the year to 31 March 20X3	200
Delivery expenses (including £300,000 overseas)	1,200
Dividends: final (proposed – to be paid 1 August 20X4)	200
interim (paid on 1 October 20X3)	100
Fixed assets at cost:	
Delivery vans	200
Office cars	40
Stores equipment	5,000
Franked investment income (amount received from listed companies)	1,200
Office expenses	800
Overseas' operations: closure costs of entire operations	350
Purchases	24,000
Sales (net of value added tax)	35,000
Stock at cost:	
At 1 April 20X3	5,000
At 31 March 20X4	6,000
Storeroom costs	1,000
Wages and salaries:	
Delivery staff	700
Directors' emoluments	400
Office staff	100
Storeroom staff	400

Notes:

1   Depreciation is provided at the following annual rates on a straight-line basis: delivery vans 20%;
    office cars 25%; stores 1%.
2   The following taxation rates may be assumed: corporation tax 35%; income tax 25%.
3   The franked investment income arises from investments held in fixed asset investments.
4   It has been decided to transfer an amount of £150,000 to the deferred taxation account.
5   The overseas operations consisted of exports. In 20X3/X4 these amounted to £5,000,000
    (sales) with purchases of £4,000,000. Related costs included £100,000 in storeroom staff and
    £15,000 for office staff.
6   Directors' emoluments include:

Chairperson	100,000	
Managing director	125,000	
Finance director	75,000	
Sales director	75,000	
Export director	25,000	(resigned 31 December 20X3)
	£400,000	

Required:

**(a) Produce a profit and loss account suitable for publication and complying as far as
possible with company law and generally accepted accounting practice.**

**(b) Comment on how FRS 3 has improved the quality of information available to
users of accounts.**

**(c) Give two reasons why information contained in the accounting policies notes is of
importance to users of accounts.**

* Question 2

Olive plc, incorporated with an authorised capital consisting of one million ordinary shares of £1
each, employs 646 persons, of whom 428 work at the factory and the rest at the head office. The
trial balance extracted from its books as at 30 September 20X4 is as follows:

	£000	£000
Land and Building (cost £600,000)	520	—
Plant and machinery (cost £840,000)	680	—
Proceeds on disposal of plant and machinery	—	180
Fixtures and equipment (cost £120,000)	94	—
Sales	—	3,460
Carriage inwards	162	—
Share premium account	—	150
Advertising	112	—
Stock in trade on 1 Oct 20X3	211	—
Heating and lighting	80	—
Prepayments	115	—
Salaries	820	—
Trade Investments at cost	248	—
Dividend received (net) on 9 Sept 20X4	—	45
Directors' emoluments	180	—
Pension cost	100	—

Audit fees and expense	65	—
Profit and loss account balance b/f	—	601
Sales commission	92	—
Stationery	28	—
Development cost	425	—
Formation expenses	120	—
Debtors and creditors	584	296
Interim dividend paid on 4 Mar 20X4	60	—
12% Debentures issued on 1 Apr 20X4	—	500
Debenture interest paid on 1 Jul 20X4	15	—
Purchases	925	—
Corporation tax on year to 30 Sept 20X3	—	128
Other administration expenses	128	—
Bad debts	158	—
Cash and bank balance	38	—
Ordinary shares of £1 fully called	—	600
	5,960	5,960

You are informed as follows:

(a) As at 1 October 20X3 land and buildings were revalued at £900,000. A third of the cost as well as all the valuation is regarded as attributable to the land. Directors have decided to report this asset at valuation.

(b) New fixtures were acquired on 1 January 20X4 for £40,000; a machine acquired on 1 October 20X1 for £240,000 was disposed of on 1 July 20X4 for £180,000, being replaced on the same date by another acquired for £320,000.

(c) Depreciation for the year is to be calculated on the straight-line basis as follows:

Buildings: 2% p.a.
Plant and machinery: 10% p.a.
Fixtures and equipment: 10% p.a.

(d) Stock in trade, including raw materials and work-in-progress on 30 September 20X4, has been valued at cost at £364,000.

(e) Prepayments are made up as follows:

	£000
Amount paid in advance for a machine	60
Amount paid in advance for purchasing raw materials	40
Prepaid rent	15
	£115

(f) In March 20X3 a customer had filed legal action claiming damages at £240,000. When accounts for the year ended 30 September 20X3 were finalised, a provision of £90,000 was made in respect of this claim. This claim was settled out of court in April 20X4 at £150,000 and the amount of the underprovision adjusted against the profit balance brought forward from previous years.

(g) The following allocations have been agreed upon:

	Factory	Administration
Depreciation of building	60%	40%
Salaries other than to directors	55%	45%
Heating and lighting	80%	20%

(h) Pension cost of the company is calculated at 10% of the emoluments and salaries.

(i) Corporation tax on 20X3 profit has been agreed at £140,000 and that for 20X4 estimated at £185,000. Corporation tax rate is 35% and the basic rate of income tax 25%.

(j) Directors propose a final dividend of 20% and wish to write off the formation expenses as far as possible without reducing the amount of profits available for distribution.

Required:

Prepare for publication:

(a) The profit and loss account of the company for the year ended 30 September 20X4, and

(b) the balance sheet as at that date along with as many notes (other than the one on accounting policy) as can be provided on the basis of the information made available.

Question 3

Cryptic plc extracted its trial balance on 30 June 20X5 as follows:

	£000	£000
Land and building at cost	750	—
Plant and machinery at cost	480	—
Accumulated depreciation on plant and machinery at 30 Jun 20X5	—	400
Depreciation on machinery	80	—
Furniture, tools and equipment at cost	380	—
Accumulated depreciation on furniture, etc. at 30 Jun 20X4	—	95
Debtors and creditors	475	360
Stock of raw materials at 30 Jun 20X4	112	—
Work-in-progress at factory cost at 30 Jun 20X4	76	—
Finished goods at cost at 30 Jun 20X4	264	—
Sales including VAT	—	2,875
Purchases of raw materials including VAT	1,380	—
Share premium account	—	150
Advertising	65	—
Deferred taxation	—	185
Salaries	360	—
Rent	120	—
Profit and loss account balance at 30 Jun 20X4	—	226
Factory power	48	—
Trade investments at cost	240	—
Overprovision for tax for the year ended 30 Jun 20X4	—	21
Electricity	36	—

Stationery	12	—
Dividend received (net)	—	24
Interim dividend paid on 15 April 20X5	60	—
Other administration expenses	468	—
Disposal of furniture	—	64
Value added tax account	165	—
Ordinary shares of 50p each	—	1,000
12% Preference shares of £1 each	—	200
Cash and bank balance	29	—
	5,600	5,600

The following information is relevant:

(a) The company discontinued a major activity during the year and replaced it with another. All fixed assets involved in the discontinued activity were redeployed for the new one. The following expenses incurred in this respect, however, are included in 'Other administration expenses':

	£000
Cancellation of contracts re. terminated activity	165
Fundamental reorganisation arising as a result	145

(b) On 1 January 20X4 the company acquired new land and buildings for £150,000. The remainder of land and building, acquired 9 years earlier, have NOT been depreciated until this year. The company has decided to depreciate the building, on the straight-line method, assuming that one-third of the cost relates to land and that the buildings have an estimated economic life of 50 years.

(c) Plant and machinery, acquired on 1 July 20X0, have been depreciated at 10% per annum on the straight-line method. The estimate of useful economic life had to be revised this year when it was realised that if the market share is to be maintained at current levels, the company has to replace all its machinery by 1 July 20X6. The balance in the 'Accumulated provision for depreciation' account on 1 July 20X4 was amended to reflect the revised estimate of useful economic life and the impact of the revision adjusted against the profit and loss balance brought forward from prior years.

(d) Furniture acquired for £80,000 on 1 January 20X3 was disposed of for £64,000 on 1 April 20X5. Furniture, tools and equipment are depreciated at 5% p.a. on cost.

(e) Results of the stocktaking at year-end are as follows:

Stock of raw materials at cost including VAT	£197,800
Work-in-progress at factory cost	£54,000
Finished goods at cost	£364,000

(f) The company allocates its expenditure as follows:

	Production cost	Factory overhead	Distribution cost	Administrative expenses
Salaries and wages	65%	15%	5%	15%
Rent	—	60%	15%	25%
Electricity	—	10%	20%	70%
Depreciation of building	—	40%	10%	50%

(g) The directors wish to make a provision for audit fees of £18,000 and estimate the corporation tax for the year at £65,000. £11,000 should be transferred from the deferred tax account. The directors propose to pay the preference dividend and a final dividend of 3p per share for ordinary shares.

(h) The following analysis has been made:

	New activity	Discontinued activity
Sales excluding VAT	£165,000	£215,000
Cost of sales	£98,000	£155,000
Distribution cost	£16,500	£48,500
Administrative expenses	£22,500	£38,500

(i) Assume that VAT applicable to all purchases and sales is 15%, the basic rate of income tax is 25% and the corporation tax rate is 35%.

Required:
(a) Advise the company on the accounting treatment in respect of information stated in (b) above.
(b) In respect of the information stated in (c) above, state whether a company is permitted to revise its estimate of the useful economic life of a fixed asset and comment on the appropriateness of the accounting treatment adopted.
(c) Set out a statement of movement of tangible fixed assets in the year to 30 June 20X5.
(d) Set out for publication the profit and loss account for the year ended 30 June 20X5, the balance sheet as at that date and any notes other than that on accounting policy, in accordance with the Companies Act 1985 and relevant standards.

Question 4

Fresno Group plc have prepared their financial statements for the year ended 31 January 20X4. However, the financial accountant of Fresno Group plc had difficulty in preparing the statements required by FRS 3 *Reporting Financial Performance* and approached you for help in preparing those statements. The accountant furnished you with the following information:

(i)

Fresno Group plc profit and loss account extract for year ended
31 January 20X4

	£m
Operating profit – continuing operations	290
Profit on sale of property in continuing operations	10
Profit on ordinary activities before taxation	300
Tax on ordinary activities	(90)
Profit after taxation	210
Dividends	(15)
Retained profit for year	195

The accountant did not provide for the loss on any discontinued operations in the profit and loss account. (However, you may assume that the taxation provision incorporated the effects of any provision for discontinued operations.)

(ii) The shareholders' funds at the beginning of the financial year were as follows:

	£m
Share capital – £1 ordinary shares	350
Share premium	55
Revaluation reserve	215
Profit and loss reserve	775
	1,395

(iii) Fresno Group plc regularly revalues its fixed assets, and at 31 January 20X4 a revaluation surplus of £375m had been credited to the revaluation reserve. During the financial year, a property had been sold on which a revaluation surplus of £54m had been credited to reserves. Further, if the company had charged depreciation on a historical cost basis rather than the revalued amounts, the depreciation charge in the profit and loss account for fixed assets would have been £7m. The current year's charge for depreciation was £16m.

(iv) The group has a policy of writing off goodwill on the acquisition of subsidiaries over ten years. The goodwill charge for the period amounted to £250m. In order to facilitate the purchase of subsidiaries, the company had issued £1 ordinary shares of nominal value £150m and share premium of £450m. All subsidiaries are currently 100% owned by the group.

(v) During the financial year to 31 January 20X4, the company had made a decision to close a 100% owned subsidiary, Reno plc. However, the closure did not take place until May 20X4. Fresno Group plc estimated that as at 31 January 20X4 the operating loss for the period 1 February 20X4 to 31 May 20X4 would be £30m and that in addition redundancy costs, stock and plant write-downs would amount to £15m. In the event, the operating loss for the period 1 February 20X4 to 31 May 20X4 was £65m, but the redundancy costs, stock and plant write downs amounted to only £12m.

(vi) The following information relates to Reno plc for the period 1 February 20X4 to 31 May 20X4.

	£m
Turnover	175
Cost of sales	(195)
Gross loss	(20)
Administrative expenses	(15)
Selling expenses	(30)
Operating loss before taxation	(65)

Required:
(a) Prepare the following statements in accordance with current statutory requirements and FRS 3 *Reporting Financial Performance* for Fresno Group plc for the year ending 31 January 20X4.
   (i) Statement of total recognised gains and losses.
  (ii) Reconciliation of movements in shareholders' funds.
 (iii) Analysis of movements on reserves.
 (iv) Note of historical cost profits and losses.

(b) **Explain the reasons why the ASB required companies to produce the information in (i)–(iv) above.**

(c) **Appraise the information prepared in (a)(i)–(a)(iv) above.**

(d) **Explain to the accountant:**

 (i) **How the decision to close the subsidiary, Reno plc, affects the financial statements of Fresno Group plc for the year ended 31 January 20X4.**

 (ii) **How the subsidiary, Reno plc, should be dealt with in the financial statements of Fresno Group plc for the year ended 31 January 20X5.**

Question 5

The following is the draft trading and profit and loss account of Parnell Ltd for the year ending 31 December 1997:

	£m	£m
Turnover		563
Cost of sales		310
		253
Distribution costs	45	
Administrative expenses	78	
		123
Profit on ordinary activities before tax		130
Tax on profit on ordinary activities		45
Profit on ordinary activities after taxation – all retained		85
Profit brought forward at 1 January 1997		101
Profit carried forward at 31 December 1997		186

You are given the following additional information, which is reflected in the above trading and profit and loss account only to the extent stated:

1. Distribution costs include a bad debt of £15 million which arose on the insolvency of a major customer. There is no prospect of recovering any of this debt. Bad debts have never been material in the past.

2. The company has traditionally consisted of a manufacturing division and a distribution division. On 31 December 1997, the entire distribution division was sold for £50 million; its book value at the time of sale was £40 million. The surplus on disposal was credited to administrative expenses. (Ignore any related corporation tax.)

3. During 1997, the distribution division made sales of £100 million and had a cost of sales of £30 million. There will be no reduction in stated distribution costs of administration expenses as a result of this disposal.

4. The company owns offices which it purchased on 1 January 1995 for £500 million, comprising £200 million for land and £300 million for buildings. No depreciation was charged in 1995 or 1996, but the company now considers that such a charge should be introduced. The buildings were expected to have a life of 50 years at the date of purchase, and the company uses the straight-line basis for calculating depreciation, assuming a zero residual value. No taxation consequences result from this change.

5. During 1997, part of the manufacturing division was restructured at a cost of £20 million to take advantage of modern production techniques. The restructuring was not fundamental and will **not** have a material effect on the nature and focus of the company's operations. This cost is included under administration expenses in the profit and loss account.

Required:

(a) State the objective of FRS3 entitled 'Reporting Financial Performance'.

(b) State how each of the items 1–5 above must be accounted for in order to comply with the requirements of FRS3.

(c) Redraft the trading and profit and loss account of Parnell Ltd for 1997, taking into account the additional information so as to comply, as far as possible, with relevant standard accounting practice. Show clearly any adjustments you make. Notes to the accounts are not required.

(The Chartered Institute of Bankers)

References

1 Companies Act 1985, 4 Sch. Formats, 4A Sch. 17, 21.
2 FRS 3, para. 19.
3 M. Stead, *How to Use Company Accounts for Successful Investment Decisions*, Pitman, 1995, p. 155.
4 *Summary Financial Statements – The Way Forward*, ICAEW, 1996.
5 M. Davies, R. Paterson and A. Wilson, *UK GAAP* 5th Edition, Macmillan, p 32.
6 Discussion Paper, *Year-end Financial Reports: Improving Communication*, ASB, 2000.
7 The Companies (Summary Financial Statement) Regulations 1995, SI 1995/2092.
8 M. Davies, R. Paterson and A. Wilson, UK GAAP 5th Edition, Macmillan, p 33.

PART 3

Balance sheet – liability and asset measurement and disclosure

CHAPTER 10

Share capital, capital maintenance and distributable profits

10.1 Introduction

In this chapter, we consider the constituents of total shareholders' funds and the nature of distributable and non-distributable reserves. We then analyse the role of the capital maintenance concept in the protection of creditors, before discussing the effectiveness of the protection offered by the Companies Act 1985 in respect of both private and public companies.

10.2 Total shareholders' funds: an overview

Total shareholders' funds consist of the issued share capital stated at nominal value, non-distributable and distributable reserves. Here we comment briefly on the main constituents of total shareholders' funds. We go on to deal with them in greater detail in subsequent sections.

10.2.1 Right to issue shares

Companies incorporated under the Companies Act 1985 are able to raise capital by the issue of shares and debentures. There are two main categories of company: private limited companies and public limited companies. Public limited companies are designated by the letters **plc** and have the right to issue shares and debentures to the public. Private limited companies are often family companies; they are not allowed to seek share capital by invitations to the public. The shareholders of both categories have the benefit of limited personal indemnity, i.e. their liability to creditors is limited to the amount they agreed to pay the company for their shares. Debentures are dealt with in Chapter 17.

10.2.2 Types of share

Broadly, there are two types of share: ordinary and preference.

Ordinary shares

Ordinary shares, often referred to as equity shares, carry the main risk and are entitled to the residual profit after paying any fixed interest or fixed dividend to investors who have invested on the basis of a fixed return. Distributions from the residual profit are made in the form of dividends, which are normally expressed as pence per share.

Preference shares

Preference shares usually have a fixed rate of dividend, which is expressed as a percentage of the nominal value of the share. The dividend is paid before any distribution to the ordinary shareholders. The specific rights attaching to a preference share can vary widely.

10.2.3 Non-distributable reserves

There are two types of **statutory** non-distributable reserve: share premium and capital redemption reserve. These are considered in greater detail below. In addition to the statutory non-distributable reserves, a company might have restrictions on distribution within its memorandum and articles, stipulating that capital profits are non-distributable as dividends.

10.2.4 Distributable reserves

Distributable reserves are normally represented by the balance on the profit and loss account that appears in the balance sheet and belong to the ordinary shareholders. However, as we shall see, there may be circumstances where credits that have been made to the profit and loss account are not actually distributable, usually because they do not satisfy the **realisation** concept.

Although the balance sheet profit and loss account figure contains the cumulative residual distributable profits, it is the earnings per share (EPS), based on the post-tax earnings for the year as disclosed in the profit and loss account, that forms the basis for the market valuation of the shares, applying the price/earnings ratio.

When deciding whether to issue shares, the directors will therefore probably consider the impact on the EPS figure. If the EPS increases, the share price can normally be expected also to increase.

10.3 Total shareholders' funds: more detailed explanation

Figure 10.1 is an example of total shareholders' funds as they would appear in a balance sheet.

Figure 10.1 Total shareholders' funds.	
Share capital	£
Ordinary shares of 25p each	100,000
7% Cumulative preference shares of 50p each	25,000
9% Non-cumulative preference shares of £1 each	20,000
6% Redeemable preference shares of £1 each	85,000
10% Convertible preference shares of 10p each	62,000
7% Participating preference shares of 1p each	40,000
Non-distributable reserves	
Share premium	50,000
Capital redemption reserve	15,000
Distributable reserves	
Profit and loss account balance	102,000
Total shareholders' funds	499,000

10.3.1 Issue of ordinary shares

A company may issue ordinary shares in a number of circumstances. Issues may be made:

● to raise funds;

● as consideration for an acquisition;

● to avoid paying out cash funds to shareholders;

● to reward directors and employees.

Issues to raise funds

An offer for subscription

In the past, offers for subscription were often made by manufacturers seeking funds to expand capacity. However, with the development of capital markets, the funds might equally well be intended for an investment trust to acquire and hold shares.

For example, Murray Emerging Economics Trust plc issued an offer for subscription on 29 November 1994 for 65 million ordinary shares of 25p each at an issue price of 100p per share payable in full on application. The funds were to be used to invest in a diversified portfolio of listed securities in emerging and frontier markets world-wide for long-term capital growth.

Warrants

Murray Emerging Economics Trust plc stated in its offer document that the company would have 'a simple capital structure comprising Ordinary shares and Warrants. The Ordinary Shares will be offered (with Warrants attached on a 1 for 5 basis) at a price of 100p per share.'

A warrant entitles the new shareholder to subscribe for shares at a future date at a predetermined price. For example, the Murray offer document states 'A registered holder of a Warrant shall have the right to subscribe for cash on 28 February in any of the years 1997 to 2004 for one Ordinary Share of 25p at the price of 100p.' If the market price rises, the shareholder executes the warrant and profits by the difference between the market price and the subscription price. Warrants can be bought and sold on the Stock Exchange just like the shares.

From the company's point of view, the consideration for the shares might not be received until 2004.

A placing

A placing occurs when shares are offered to one or more selected institutions. For example, Molins, the tobacco and packaging machinery group, placed 2.46 million shares in 1994 at 498p per share to help finance the acquisition of a Nottingham-based maker of specialist packaging machinery for £28m. The costs of a placing are lower than for an offer for subscription.

Rights issue to existing shareholders

In 1994, Laird Group, the manufacturer of automotive components, launched a surprise £68m rights issue to fund a heavy programme of capital expenditure and acquisitions amounting to some £80m by the end of 1995 (*Financial Times*, 23 November 1994). Laird's 1 for 5 rights issue was priced at 295p, representing a 17% discount to the current market price.

Issues as consideration on an acquisition

Queens Moat Houses plc, the hotel and restaurant chain, in its 1992 accounts stated that 'Under the terms of an acquisition of a subsidiary undertaking in prior years, the company agreed to issue by instalments, as deferred consideration to the vendor, ordinary shares in the company on a pre-determined basis.'

Issues to shareholders that avoid paying out cash from the company's funds

An issue in lieu of dividends

Glaxo plc's 1993 accounts state 'On 13th November 1992, 913,110 ordinary shares were issued fully paid at a price of £7.99 to shareholders who elected to take shares in lieu of cash in respect of the final dividend.'

Issues to directors and employees that avoid paying out cash in the form of salary from the company's funds

Executive and employee share option schemes

Glaxo plc's 1993 accounts state that 19,611,256 ordinary shares were issued during the year resulting from the exercise of options under the Glaxo Group Share Option Scheme for an aggregate consideration of £68,716,298. Shares with a market value in excess of 700p were issued for 350p. Executives and employees could therefore buy for £68,716,298 and sell for twice that amount.

10.3.2 Issue of preference shares

The following illustrate some of the ways in which specific rights can vary.

Cumulative preference shares

Dividends not paid in respect of any one year because of a lack of profits are accumulated for payment in some future year when distributable profits are sufficient.

Non-cumulative preference shares

Dividends not paid in any one year because of a lack of distributable profits are permanently forgone.

Participating preference shares

These shares carry the right to participate in a distribution of additional profits over and above the fixed rate of dividend after the ordinary shareholders have received an agreed percentage. The participation rights are based on a precise formula.

Redeemable preference shares

These shares may be redeemed by the company at an agreed future date and at an agreed price.

Convertible preference shares

These shares may be converted into ordinary shares at a future date on agreed terms. The conversion is usually at the preference shareholder's discretion.

There can be a mix of rights, e.g. Dixon plc in its 1994 accounts contained 5% dividend convertible cumulative redeemable preference shares with a note that stated 'Subject to certain conditions, preference shares are convertible at the shareholders' option into fully paid Ordinary shares of the Company on 31 October in any years 1994–2002 on the basis of 26.667 Ordinary shares for every 100 Preference shares. The Company will be entitled after 1 January 2003, and will be obliged on 31 December 2007, to redeem at 100p per share any outstanding.'

10.4 Accounting entries on issue of shares

10.4.1 Shares issued at nominal value

If shares are issued at nominal value, the company simply debits the cash account with the amount received and credits the ordinary share capital or preference share capital, as appropriate, with the **nominal value** of the shares.

10.4.2 Shares issued at a premium

After a company has been trading, a market price is created for its shares and, on any subsequent issue, the company would set an issue price close to the full market price. On receipt of consideration for the shares, the company again debits the cash account with the amount received and credits the ordinary share capital or preference share capital, as appropriate, with the **nominal value** of the shares.

Assuming that the market price exceeds the nominal value, a premium element will be credited to a share premium account. The share premium is classified as a **non-distributable reserve** to indicate that it is not repayable to the shareholders who have subscribed for their shares: it remains a part of the company's permanent capital.

The accounting treatment for recording the issue of shares is straightforward. For example, the journal entries to record the issue of 1,000 £1 ordinary shares at a market price of £2.50 per share payable in the following instalments:

on application on 1 January 20X1   25p
on issue   on 31 January 20X1 £1.75 including the premium
on first call on 31 January 20X2   25p
on final call on 31 January 20X4   25p

would be as follows:

1 Jan 20X1	Dr	Cr
	£	£
Cash account	250	
Application account		250

31 Jan 20X1	Dr	Cr
	£	£
Cash account	1,750	
Issue account		1,750

31 Jan 20X1	Dr	Cr
	£	£
Application account	250	
Issue account	1,750	
Share capital account		500
Share premium		1,500

The first and final call would be debited to cash account and credited to share capital account on receipt of the date of the calls.

There is another statutory non-distributable reserve. The **capital redemption reserve** is created when shares are redeemed. Typically it arises when redeemable preference shares are redeemed. The accounting entries are to credit cash and debit the redeemable preference shares to record the payment, and to credit capital redemption reserve and debit profit and loss account balance to record the transfer from distributable to non-distributable reserves.

10.5 Creditor protection: capital maintenance concept

We have seen in earlier chapters that the Companies Act 1985 contains detailed provisions to protect shareholders, e.g. legislation relating to the presentation and disclosure of information in financial statements. To protect **creditors**, the Act has rules relating to the use of the **total shareholders' funds** which determine how much is distributable.

As a general rule, the issued share capital is not repayable to the shareholders and the reserves are classified into two categories: distributable and non-distributable. The directors have discretion as to the amount of the distributable profits that they recommend for distribution as a dividend to shareholders. However, they have no discretion as to the treatment of the non-distributable funds. There is a statutory requirement for the company to retain within the company net assets equal to the non-distributable reserves. This requirement is to safeguard the interests of creditors and is known as **capital maintenance**.

10.6 Creditor protection: why capital maintenance rules are necessary

It is helpful at this point to review the position of unincorporated businesses in relation to capital maintenance.

10.6.1 Unincorporated business

An unincorporated business such as a sole trader or partnership is not required to maintain any specified amount of capital within the business to safeguard the interests of its creditors. The owners are free to decide whether to introduce or withdraw capital. However, they remain personally liable for the liabilities incurred by the business, and the creditors can have recourse to the personal assets of the owners if the business assets are inadequate to meet their claims in full.

When granting credit to an unincorporated business the creditors may well be influenced by the personal wealth and apparent standing of the owners and not merely by the assets of the business as disclosed in its financial statements. This is why in an unincorporated business there is no external reason for the capital and the profits to be kept separate.

In partnerships, there are frequently internal agreements that require each partner to maintain his or her capital at an agreed level. Such agreements are strictly a matter of contract between the owners and do not prejudice the rights of the business creditors.

Sometimes owners attempt to influence creditors unfairly, by maintaining a lifestyle in excess of what they can afford, or to frustrate their legal rights as creditors by putting their private assets beyond their reach, e.g. by transferring their property to relatives or trusts. These subterfuges become apparent only when the creditors seek to enforce their claim against the private assets. Banks are able to protect themselves by seeking adequate security, e.g. a charge on the owners' property.

10.6.2 Incorporated limited liability company

Because of limited liability, the rights of creditors against the private assets of the owners, i.e. the shareholders of the company, are restricted to any amount unpaid on their shares. Once the shareholders have paid the company for their shares, they are not personally liable for the company's debts. Creditors are restricted to making claims against the assets of the company.

Hence the legislature considered it necessary to ensure that the shareholders did not make such distributions to themselves that assets needed to meet creditors' claims were put beyond creditors' reach. This was achieved by setting out statutory rules.

10.7 Creditor protection: how to quantify the amounts available to meet creditors' claims

Creditors are exposed to two types of risk: the business risk that a company will operate unsuccessfully and will be unable to pay them; and the risk that a company will operate successfully, but will pay its shareholders rather than its creditors.

The legislature has never intended trade creditors to be protected against ordinary business risks, e.g. the risk of the debtor company incurring either trading losses or losses that might arise from a fall in the value of the assets following changes in market conditions.

The Companies Act 1985 requires the amount available to meet creditors' claims to be calculated by reference to the company's annual financial statements. There are two possible approaches:

● The **direct** approach requires the **asset** side of the balance sheet to contain assets with a realisable value sufficient to cover all outstanding liabilities.

● The **indirect** approach requires the **liability** side of the balance sheet to classify reserves into distributable and non-distributable, i.e. not available to the shareholders by way of dividend distributions.[1]

The Act follows the indirect approach by specifying capital maintenance in terms of the total shareholders' funds. It thus avoids the thorny problem of asset valuation, which would have led straight back to the arguments considered in Chapter 4 concerning the use of historic cost, realisable values and replacement costs.

However, this has not stopped certain creditors taking steps to protect themselves by following the direct approach, e.g. it is bank practice to obtain a mortgage debenture over the assets of the company. The effect of this is to disadvantage the trade creditors. The statutory restrictions preventing shareholders from reducing capital accounts on the liability side are weakened when management grants certain parties priority rights against some or all of the company's assets.

We will now consider total shareholders' funds and capital maintenance in more detail, starting with share capital. Two aspects of share capital are relevant to creditor protection: minimum capital requirements and reduction of capital. Reduction of capital is dealt with in the next chapter.

10.8   Issued share capital: minimum share capital

The creditors of public companies are protected by the requirements that there should be a minimum share capital and that capital should be reduced only under controlled conditions.

The minimum share capital requirement for a public company is currently set at £50,000, although this can be increased by the Secretary of State for Trade and Industry.[2] A company is not permitted to commence trading unless it has issued this amount. However, given the size of many public companies, it is questionable whether this figure is adequate.

The minimum share capital requirement refers to the nominal value of the share capital. In the UK, the law requires each class of share to have a stated nominal value. This value is used for identification and also for capital maintenance. The law ensures that a company receives an amount that is at least equal to the nominal value of the shares issued, less a controlled level of commission, by prohibiting the issue of shares at a discount and by limiting any underwriting commissions on an issue. This is intended to avoid a material discount being granted in the guise of commission. However, the requirement is concerned more with safeguarding the relative rights of existing shareholders than with protecting creditors.

There is effectively no minimum capital requirement for private companies. We can see many instances of such companies having an issued and paid-up capital of only two £1 shares, which cannot conceivably be regarded as adequate creditor protection. The lack of adequate protection for the creditors of private companies is considered again later in the chapter.

10.9   Distributable profits: general considerations

We have considered capital maintenance and undistributable reserves. However, it is not sufficient to attempt to maintain the permanent capital accounts of companies unless there are clear rules on the amount that they can distribute to their shareholders as profit. Without such rules, they may make distributions to their shareholders out of capital. The question of what can legitimately be distributed as profit is an integral part of the concept of capital maintenance in company accounts.

10.9.1   The position before 1980

Before the Companies Act 1980 – now part of the 1985 Act – the position of distributable profits rested largely on case law from the early 1900s. The judgments in those cases were sometimes contradictory and confusing, and often did not coincide with an accountant's view of what constituted distributable profits. This was due to the fact that until 1980 statutes stated only that dividends must not be paid out of capital, and Table A also mentioned that 'dividends must only be paid out of profits'. However, these requirements begged questions as to the nature of profit and capital, rather than providing any clear guidance.

Two questions of general importance should be addressed:

● Should distributable profits include only realised profits, or might they also include unrealised gains?

● Should distributions also include realised capital profits, e.g. arising from the sale of fixed assets?

Realised profits and unrealised gains

Historically, the accounting profession has considered that only realised profits should be distributed. This is because realisation implies the availability of liquid assets, i.e. cash, for distribution. Unrealised profits are not represented by any cash receipt and depend on the subjective views of valuers. This is a good practical view and is reflected in the preparation of profit and loss accounts today.

Furthermore, legally, any accumulated realised losses of previous years could have been ignored in deciding the amount of distributable profits of the year in which a distribution was to be made.

Realised revenue profits and realised capital profits

Differentiation between these two is the result of accountants classifying assets into fixed and current. The accountant's view is that normal trading activities create current assets of a revenue nature, whereas fixed assets are of a capital nature. Moreover, any proceeds from the sale of fixed assets are also of a capital nature.

If only realised profits were to be distributed, it was not clear whether this meant only revenue profits, or whether capital profits should also be included. In some companies the latter were taken to a capital reserve, while in others they were taken to the profit and loss account. The now defunct SSAP 6 recommended that the profit and loss account should include all realised profits, which in turn influenced distribution policies. The legal situation was that realised capital profits could be distributed, provided there remained a surplus of assets over liabilities.

10.9.2   Present position

The issue of what constituted distributable profits was clarified by the Companies Act 1980. It is surprising that it took successive governments such a long time to clarify the situation. However, if the EC had not issued its Second Directive, it would probably have taken much longer. In the following sections we will describe the present rules for private and public companies.

10.10   Distributable profits: general rule for private companies

The definition of distributable profits under the Companies Act 1985 is:

> Accumulated, realised profits, so far as not previously utilised by distribution or capitalisation, less its accumulated, realised losses, as far as not previously written off in a reduction or reorganisation of capital.

This means the following:

● Unrealised profits cannot be distributed.

● There is no difference between realised revenue and realised capital profits.

● All accumulated net realised profits (i.e. realised profits less realised losses) on the balance sheet date must be considered.

EXAMPLE ● An analysis of the shareholders' funds section of a company's balance sheet as at the end of its latest financial year is set out in Figure 10.2.

Figure 10.2 Shareholders' funds.

	£000	£000
Share capital		2,000
Share premium		600
Capital redemption reserve		200
Permanent capital at beginning of year		2,800
Unrealised: gains	100	
: losses	(200)	
		(100)
Permanent capital at end of the year		2,700
Realised: current year's profits	500	
: current year's losses	(100)	
	400	
: previous year's b/f	1,200	
		1,600
Net assets of company		4,300

The distributable profit of this private company on the balance sheet date is simply its accumulated net realised profit, i.e. £1,600,000. No account need be taken of any accumulated net unrealised gains or losses. This means that there could be a reduction in the permanent capital of the company of £100,000 if the maximum amount is distributed. Its net assets after such a distribution are shown in Figure 10.3.

10.11 Distributable profits: general rule for public companies

According to the Companies Act, the undistributable reserves of a public company are its share capital, share premium, capital redemption reserve and also 'the excess of accumulated unrealised profits over accumulated unrealised losses at the time of the intended distribution and … any reserves not allowed to be distributed under the Act or by the company's own Memorandum or Articles of Association'.

Figure 10.3 Net assets after distribution of profits.

	£000	£000
Share capital		2,000
Share premium		600
Capital redemption reserve		200
Permanent capital at beginning of year		2,800
Unrealised: gains	100	
: losses	(200)	
		(100)
Permanent capital at end of the year – net assets		2,700

This means that, when dealing with a public company, the distributable profits have to be reduced by any net unrealised loss. In our example above, the distributable profits would be £1,500,000 if the company were a public company. We arrive at this by applying the wording of the Act that its net assets will not be less than:

	£000
Share capital	2,000
Share premium	600
Capital redemption reserve	200
Excess of unrealised profits over unrealised losses	No excess
	2,800

The net accumulated unrealised loss figure of £100,000 in the above example would be unusual in practice, since any net deficiency on the revaluation of an asset would normally be taken to the profit and loss account and may be deemed to have implications for distribution policy.

10.11.1 Investment companies

The Act allows for the special nature of some businesses in the calculation of distributable profits. There are additional rules for investment companies in calculating their distributable profits. For a company to be classified as an investment company, it must invest its funds mainly in securities with the aim of spreading investment risk and giving its members the benefit of the results of managing its funds.

Such a company has the option of applying one of two rules in calculating its distributable profits. These are either:

● the rules that apply to public companies in general, but excluding any realised capital profits, e.g. from the disposal of investments; or

● the company's accumulated realised revenue less its accumulated realised and unrealised revenue losses, provided that its assets are at least one and a half times its liabilities both before and after such a distribution.

The reasoning behind these special rules seems to be to allow investment companies to pass the dividends they receive to their shareholders, irrespective of any changes in the values of their investments, which are subject to market fluctuations. However, the asset cover ratio of liabilities can easily be manipulated by the company simply paying creditors, whereby the ratio is improved, or borrowing, whereby it is reduced.

EXAMPLE ● Figure 10.4 provides an analysis of the shareholders' funds and liabilities of an investment company.

> ### Figure 10.4 Shareholders' funds and liabilities of an investment company.
>
> | | £000 |
> |---|---|
> | Share capital | 2,000 |
> | Capital profits (losses): | |
> | Realised | 400 |
> | Unrealised | (900) |
> | Revenue profits (losses): | |
> | Realised | 700 |
> | Unrealised | (100) |
> | Shareholders' funds, i.e. net assets | 2,100 |
> | Liabilities | 1,000 |
> | Total assets | 3,100 |

Distributable profits of the company are:

● Under the general rule:

	£000
Realised revenue profits	700
Less: Excess of unrealised losses over unrealised profits ($£900,000 + £100,000 - £0$)	(1,000)
Nil distributable	(300)

or, applying the net asset maintenance rule:

	£000
Share capital	2,000
Excess of unrealised profits over unrealised losses	No excess
Other undistributable profits:	
Realised capital profit	400
	2,400

Under this option the company cannot distribute any profits unless net assets can be maintained at £2,400,000, whereas its net assets at the balance sheet date are £2,100,000.

● Under the second (investment company) rule:

	£000
Realised revenue profits	700
Less: Realised or unrealised revenue losses	(100)
Distributable profit	600

Subject to asset cover ratio of liabilities:

$$\text{Before distribution} \quad \frac{3,100,000}{1,000,000} = 3.1 \text{ times}$$

$$\text{After distribution} \quad \frac{3,100,000 - 600,000}{1,000,000} = 2.5 \text{ times}$$

In both cases the asset cover ratio of liabilities is more than 1.5 times and therefore the company can distribute £600,000 profit to its shareholders.

10.12 Distributable profits: how to arrive at the amount using relevant accounts

The Companies Act stipulates that distributable profits of a company must be based on **relevant accounts**. These would normally be the audited annual accounts, which have been prepared according to the requirements of the Act to give a true and fair view of the company's financial affairs. In the case of a qualified audit report, the auditor is required to prepare a written statement stating whether such a qualification is material in determining a company's distributable profit. Interim dividends are allowed to be paid provided they can be justified on the basis of the latest annual accounts, otherwise interim accounts will have to be prepared that would justify such a distribution.

10.13 Distributable profits: realisation principle applies

Realisation is central to the determination of profits which can be legally distributed to shareholders in either cash or non-cash form. The Companies Act provides that 'only profits realised at the balance sheet date shall be included in the profit and loss account'.

10.13.1 Retained profit figure may not consist only of realised profits

It is not always the case that the retained profit on a balance sheet consists only of realised profits and is therefore wholly distributable. The overriding requirement that accounts should give a true and fair view can lead to a mismatch between profits that are reported in order to present a true and fair view and profits that are distributable within the legal definition of the Companies Act.

An example is the calculation of the depreciation charge on revalued assets. The true and fair requirement as set out in FRS 15 is that the depreciation charge should be calculated on the carrying value of the asset in the balance sheet. If it were revalued from £100 to £200, the depreciation would be based on the £200. However, the legal requirement is that it should be based on the cost figure of £100.

In general, however, the retained balance may be regarded as realised and distributable.

10.13.2 Companies Act definition of realised

On the key question of whether a profit is realised or not, the Act simply says that realised profits or realised losses are:

such profits or losses of the company as fall to be treated as realised in accordance with principles generally accepted, at the time when the accounts are prepared, with respect to the determination for accounting purposes of realised profits or losses. (Schedule 4, para. 91)

Hence the Act does not lay down detailed rules on what is and what is not a realised profit; indeed, it does not even refer specifically to 'accounting principles'. Nevertheless, it would seem reasonable for decisions on realisation to be based on **generally accepted accounting principles** at the time, subject to the court's decision in cases of dispute.

The Companies Act includes only a few specific provisions about whether certain events are to be treated as realised or unrealised. We consider two such provisions: development costs and fixed asset revaluations.

Development costs

The Act provides that (product) development costs can be treated as a **realised** loss unless directors can justify treating it differently by special circumstances. An ICAEW Technical Release (TR 481)[3] states that, if the accounts have been prepared according to the requirements of the Companies Act and professional accounting and reporting standards, any consequent profit or loss is to be taken as realised unless a standard specifically states that an item is unrealised.

This seems to imply that, if the development costs have been accounted for in accordance with the requirements of SSAP 13, the amount taken to the profit and loss account is the realised part of the total cost.

Fixed asset revaluations

The Act provides that any diminution in the value of a fixed asset arising as a result of revaluations of **all** fixed assets (whether including goodwill or not) is an **unrealised** loss. This seems to imply that the revaluation of an **individual** asset would amount to a **realised** loss. In practice, the Act allows such a loss to be regarded as unrealised, provided directors can satisfy themselves (without an actual revaluation of all assets) that the aggregate value of assets is not less than their book value.

Revenue recognition has been widely discussed, but the question of deductible expenses has received less attention. Indeed, there is an assumption that they are easily ascertainable by applying some broad rules.

Cost and expense recognition

The measurement of realised profit involves (a) recognition of realised revenue and (b) deduction of appropriate costs and expenses. Accounting literature has regarded the recognition of revenue as the key element, but the identification of appropriate costs to be deducted is not necessarily simple and clear-cut.

The present position, as stated in SSAP 2, is that revenues and costs are 'matched with one another as far as this relationship can be established or justifiably assumed'; and revenues 'are matched with associated costs and expenses by including in the same account the costs incurred in earning them (so far as these are material and identifiable)'. This is provided that such an accrual concept is consistent with the prudence concept; otherwise prudence prevails, whereby provision is made for all known expenses and losses, even if their amounts are not known with certainty. This position will need to be reviewed after FRED 21 has been implemented.

As in the case of realised revenue, the explanation of appropriate costs and expenses requires clarification and redefinition for present-day conditions. Depreciation is an obvious example. According to FRS 15 the depreciation charge in the profit and loss account should be based on the carrying value of a fixed asset. However, the Companies Act only requires a deduction of depreciation based on its historical cost for the purpose of determining the amount of the profit. The Act regards any excess depreciation charge over its historic figure as part of realised profit.

There is some professional guidance: for example, TR 481 states that those costs and expenses which are required by existing SSAPs (and FRSs) to be taken to the profit and loss account are the appropriate costs and expenses for calculating realised profit. However, not all costs and expenses are, or can be, covered by SSAPs and FRSs.

Summary

Creditors of companies are not expected to be protected against ordinary business risks as these are taken care of by the financial markets in other ways, e.g. through rates of interest charged and insurance against bad debts. However, they are entitled to depend on non-erosion of the permanent capital by shareholders paying themselves out of the capital. Such protection is provided by the Companies Act 1985, although its effectiveness is questionable.

Because of the limited liability of shareholders, the legislature provided creditors with some protection by requiring a minimum capital and introducing rules governing capital reduction and the use of share premium and capital redemption reserves.

In the case of public companies, the minimum share capital is £50,000, which cannot be reduced. However, this is far too low a figure to provide any reasonable level of protection for creditors.

In the case of private companies, there is no minimum share capital requirement and, in any case, the Companies Act allows these companies to reduce their permanent capital. The provision of the Act concerning the declaration of solvency seems to provide good protection for the creditors. However, the main problem for the creditors of small private companies is that the directors and shareholders are the same group of people, and can pay themselves salaries instead of dividends. Hence, by paying themselves excessive salaries, they could reduce the permanent capital of their companies.

In the case of distributions, the Act lays down rules for determining the amount that can be distributed as dividend without reducing the permanent capital. The rules are more stringent for public companies than for private, but despite the improved situation under the Companies Act 1985, its rules may still lead to a reduction in permanent capital and still involve recognition and measurement problems in calculating distributable profits.

Review questions

1 What is the relevance of dividend cover if dividends are paid out of distributable profits?

2 How do industries differ in the levels of distributable profits?

3 What is the significance of high distributable profits to an existing/potential investor/loan creditor/creditor?

4 Why is the distributable profits figure not apparent from the accounts?

5 Give four examples of reasons why the retained profit figure might not equal distributable profits.

6 Is there any relationship between non-distributable reserves and total assets?

7 How can distributable profits become non-distributable?

8 In what circumstances can non-distributable reserves become distributable?

9 The Companies Act requires capitalised development costs to be deducted from realised profits unless circumstances justify the policy of capitalisation. Discuss (a) why you think the Act contains this provision and (b) what you consider would provide adequate justification for deferring the charge to the current year's profit and loss account.

10 (a) The regional electricity companies and the National Grid argued strongly against the ASB proposal to require full provisioning for deferred tax on its revision of SSAP 15. Explain why these companies would have been so strongly opposed.

  (b) Full provisioning for deferred tax would result in increased tax charges on earnings and large deferred tax liabilities, neither of which are likely to materialise. Explain (i) why they are unlikely to materialise, and (ii) how to reduce the impact while still following the principle of full provisioning.

  (c) It has been stated that 'by reducing distributable reserves the proposals directly affect not only annual dividends but also the apparent gearing position and balance sheet strength of companies. These proposals would do serious damage to the strength of an important sector of the economy.'[4] Discuss whether the effect on distributable profit is an acceptable reason for not providing in full for deferred tax.

Exercises

An extract from the solution is provided in the appendix at the end of the text for exercises marked with an asterisk (*).

* ## Question 1

(a) Define the term 'distribution', and state what items the Companies Act 1985 excludes from its definition of a distribution.

(b) Explain the need for the introduction of statutory rules concerning the distribution of a company's profits.

(c) State the Companies Act 1985 requirements regarding distributions by both public and private limited companies.

(d) State what other principal non-legal limitations the directors of a company would take into account when deciding on a distribution policy.

(e) You have draft balance sheets of two companies as follows:

	Company A £000	*Company B* £000
Fixed assets		
Property at valuation	90	90
Investment at cost	10	10
Net current assets (liabilities)	60	(20)
	160	80

	Company A	Company B
	£000	£000
Share capital	10	10
Share premium	20	20
Revaluation reserve	40	50
Profit and loss account	90	—
	160	80

You also ascertain the following:

1 Additional depreciation charged to the profit and loss account to date as a result of revaluations is £5,000 for company A and £10,000 for company B.

2 The fixed asset investments of both company A and company B have subsequent to the year-end proved to be worthless.

3 A court case has commenced against company B for £20,000. The directors have not come to a conclusion on the accounting treatment of this case, but they believe the loss after tax would be £13,000.

4 Company B had sold a plot of land at its revalued amount. However, the net gain of £15,000 over the original cost was still shown in the revaluation reserve and not in the profit and loss account.

Required:
State with clear reasoning the maximum dividends that could be paid by companies A and B respectively:
(a) treating them as private companies;
(b) treating them as public limited companies.

Question 2

V.R. Confident Ltd
Profit and loss account for the year ended 30 November 20X2

	£000
Net profit for the year, before taxation	604
Corporation tax, at 33%	290
	314

Balance sheet as on 30 November 20X2

		£000
Ordinary share capital		800
6% preference share capital		300
Share premium		200
Capital redemption reserve		400
Asset revaluation reserve		250
General reserve		160
Profit and loss account:		
Balance brought forward	(288)	
Current year	314	26
		2,136

Notes

(a) One-half of the asset revaluation reserve represents an increase in the value of a freehold property which was sold during the year to 30 November 20X2 (at the revalued amount). This sale was not recorded in the accounts. A tax liability of £35,000 is expected in connection with the disposal.

(b) The £300,000 depreciation charge to the profit and loss account was based on revalued figures. This charge would have been £240,000 if it had been based on the original cost of fixed assets.

(c) Some of the stock-in-trade, which appeared on the draft balance sheet at cost, was later sold for £90,000 below this figure.

(d) The draft balance sheet of company includes £500,000 research and development expenditure under fixed assets.

(e) Since the preparation of the draft accounts, one of the debtors of the company has gone into liquidation and is not expected to pay more than 50p in the £1 to its creditors. This debtor owed £120,000 to V.R.C. Ltd on 30 November 20X2.

Required:
(a) Explain briefly the provisions of Companies Act 1985 relating to profits that a company can distribute as dividends.
(b) Calculate the maximum amount of dividends that the directors of V.R.C. Ltd may propose to pay to ordinary shareholders within the legal requirements and in conformity with the relevant Statements of Standard Accounting Practice. Also state whether your answer would be different if V.R. Confident Ltd were a public limited company (plc).

* ## Question 3

The following are details of three separate companies' summarised balance sheets at 31 March 20X7.

	Alpha plc £000	Beta plc £000	Gamma Ltd £000
Fixed assets	5,000	760	1,000
Current assets	1,800	360	600
Current liabilities	(1,400)	(320)	(400)
	5,400	800	1,200
Share capital	400	600	4,000
Reserves: revaluation	2,200	(400)	—
Realised capital profit	1,600	—	—
Brought forward realised revenue profit (loss)	800	1,000	(3,200)
Current year realised revenue profit (loss)	400	(400)	400
	5,400	800	1,200

Alpha's property, previously included in the financial statements at original cost of £1,800,000, was revalued on 1 April 20X6 at £4 million. The revalued amount is included in the figures above, subject to the full amount being written off equally over the next 50 years from 1 April 20X6. Prior to this date, no depreciation had been provided on property. At 31 March 20X7, no transfer had been made between revaluation reserve and realised revenue profit.

Required:
(a) Compare briefly the bases for calculating the maximum distribution under the provisions of the Companies Act 1985 in respect of public and private companies.
(b) Calculate the maximum distribution that Alpha, Beta and Gamma could each make under the Companies Act 1985.

References

1 Companies Act 1985, section 264, para. 3.
2 *Ibid.*, section 118.
3 TR 481, *Determination of Realised Profits and Disclosure of Distribution Profits*, ICAEW, 1982.
4 E. Anstee, Group Finance Director, Eastern Group, *Accountancy Age*, 17 August 1995, p. 9.

Reduction of share capital

11.1   Introduction

In this chapter, we consider restrictions on the reduction of share capital and the accounting treatment of the share premium and the capital redemption reserve. We outline the legal requirements under the Companies Act 1985 for the redemption of shares by public and private companies, and for fundamental changes in a company's capital structure.

11.2   Capital: restrictions on reduction of capital

Once the shares have been issued and paid up, the share capital account is credited with the nominal value of such shares and this value forms part of the capital to be maintained. The intention is that this amount should not be reduced. However, there might be commercially sound reasons for a company to reduce its capital. The Companies Act therefore has provision for share capital to be reduced, subject to the consent of the court, in three ways.

1   Writing off part of capital which has already been lost and is not represented by assets

This situation normally occurs when a company has accumulated trading losses which prevent it from making dividend payments under the rules relating to distributable profits. The general approach is to credit the profit and loss account in order to eliminate any debit balance, and to debit share capital and non-distributable reserves. This has the effect of eliminating current losses, thus making future profits distributable. The debit balance on profit and loss account is transferred to a capital reduction account, and this account is credited with amounts transferred from the share capital and reserves.

The consent of the creditors may be required by order of the court. The rules governing a reduction of capital are that no reduction can be made unless it is authorised by the articles of association of the company, is approved by a special resolution of the shareholders and secures the consent of the court. The rights of the creditors are thus protected directly or indirectly through the court.

2   Repayment of part of paid-up capital to shareholders or cancellation of unpaid share capital

This can occur when a company wishes to reduce its unwanted liquid resources. The accounting entries for the repayment are to credit cash and debit share capital. The consent of the creditors is required.

3 Redemption of shares

This is discussed in section 16.4 below.

11.3 Non-distributable reserves: share premium

Prior to the Companies Act 1948, if a company issued shares at a premium, the premium could be distributed to the shareholders. However, it came to be recognised that the premium represented a capital receipt and should be treated in the same way as the nominal value of the shares. Consequently, the Companies Act now requires any premium to be taken to a separate share premium account as a non-distributable reserve. For example, if a company issued 100 £1 shares (nominal value) at a premium of £2.50 per share, the capital receipt of £350 would be recorded as follows:

	£	£
Cash	350	
Share capital		100
Share premium		250

Although both the proceeds from the nominal value of the shares and the premium element are regarded as capital receipts, the company has more flexibility in using its shares premium account. For example, it can be used to:

1 issue fully paid bonus shares;

2 write off preliminary expenses (i.e. company formation costs);

3 write off any share or debenture issue expenses or any discounts on the issue of debentures;

4 write off any premiums (payable) on redemption or purchase of own shares, provided the shares being redeemed or purchased were themselves issued at a premium and that adequate funds exist in the share premium account.

Let us consider each of these uses in terms of their impact on creditor protection. The capitalisation of the reserve indicated by (1) maintains the creditors' protection, since the share premium is reclassified as share capital, i.e.:

	£	£
Share premium	250	
Share capital		250

However, uses (2)–(4) reduce their protection, even though no direct payment has been made to any of the shareholders. To illustrate this, let us assume that the company's balance sheet includes the following items:

	£
Share capital	100
Share premium	250
Permanent capital	350

Further, assume that the company issues one 10% debenture (nominal value £100) for £90 cash and decides, applying (3) above, to write off the discount against the share premium account. The entries in the company's books would be:

	£	£
Cash	90	
Debentures discount	10	
10% Debentures		100
Share premium	10	
Debenture discount		10

The balance sheet items following these transactions would be:

	£
Share capital	100
Share premium	240
Permanent capital	340
10% Debentures	100
	440

Because the rules permit the discount to be classified as a capital item, the permanent capital available for the protection of capital has been depleted to the extent of the discount. The same would apply to uses (2) and (4). This did not matter unduly when the amount of discount on debentures was immaterial, but we have seen many examples in recent years of financial instruments being issued at material discounts, e.g. deep discounting.

11.4 Non-distributable reserves: capital redemption reserve

Until the beginning of the twentieth century, companies were not allowed to buy back their own shares after they had been issued. Shareholders could convert their investment into cash only by selling their shares to a third party either privately or via the Stock Exchange. This meant that the share capital base of the company could not be depleted by a return of capital, so the level of protection afforded to the creditors was unchanged by share transfers between existing and new shareholders.

However, commercial considerations caused a relaxation in the rules to accommodate shareholders who wanted to be reasonably certain of recovering the capital amount that they originally invested. To attract their investment, companies were permitted to issue **redeemable preference shares**.

When redeemable preference shares were redeemed, the company was required either to replace them with other shares or to make a transfer from distributable reserves to non-distributable reserves in order to maintain the permanent capital. The non-distributable reserve was called a capital redemption reserve and there were restrictions on how it could be used.

The accounting entries were to credit cash and debit the redeemable preference share account on redemption, and to credit a capital redemption reserve and debit the profit and loss account with an equal amount.

This right to redeem preference shares was later extended by the Companies Act 1981 to permit companies to purchase their own ordinary shares.

11.4.1 Purchase of own shares

The Companies Act now permits a company to effect **market** or **off-market** purchases of its own ordinary shares. Market purchases are those shares purchased from a recognised Stock Exchange and off-market purchases are all other shares. Market purchases must be authorised by the articles of association and an **ordinary resolution** of the shareholders setting out terms such as the price to be paid and the timing of the purchase. An example is found in the Ladbroke Group plc accounts for 1990 with the following note:

> Purchase of own shares. Shareholders' approval is being sought at the annual general meeting to renew the general authority for the company to make market purchases of its own ordinary shares for cancellation ... There is no present intention to purchase shares and, if granted, the authority would only be exercised if an improvement in earnings per share was expected to result.

Off-market purchases offer a greater opportunity for abuse by the directors and there are accordingly more stringent legal requirements, such as the need for a **specific purchase contract** which requires a **special resolution** of the shareholders.

In this chapter we will not distinguish between redemption and purchase of own shares, since the same accounting considerations apply to both.

11.4.2 Companies Act requirements

The Companies Act states that:

- No redemption can take place unless the shares are fully paid up. This is to protect creditors who regard any uncalled capital as part of the capital base of the company.

- No redemption can take place which would result in there being no shareholders. This would in effect be a winding-up or liquidation of the company and other rules would then apply.

- All redeemed shares are to be cancelled. This is to prevent the directors attempting to manipulate the market so as to create an artificial price for the shares.

Different rules apply to the redemption of shares by public companies and by private companies. We will consider each in turn.

11.5 Capital: redemption of shares by a public company

Although a public company is now permitted to redeem shares so that an individual shareholder can liquidate a shareholding, it is required to maintain the same overall level of permanent capital for the protection of the creditors. This can be achieved in two different ways.

Firstly, redemption can be made **out of the distributable profits** of a company. In this case the Act requires the transfer of an amount equal to the nominal value of the redeemed shares from distributable profits to a capital redemption reserve.

A capital redemption reserve may only be used for issuing fully paid bonus shares to the shareholders. In other words, it is like share capital in its permanence. Such a transfer from distributable profits is described as a capitalisation, which means that profits have been capitalised and the permanent capital has been maintained.

Furthermore, if the shares are redeemed at a premium, i.e. at a price above their nominal value, any such premium cannot be carried forward in the accounts, but must be written off against distributable profits.

Figure 11.1 Balance sheet before and after redemption.

Balance sheet before redemption		Purchase	W/off premium	Transfer to CRR	Balance sheet
	£	£	£	£	£
Share capital	100	(50)			50
Capital redemption reserve (CRR)				50	50
Share premium	240				240
Permanent capital	340				340
P&L account	160		(100)	(50)	10
	500				350
Cash	200	(150)			50
Other assets	300				300
Premium on redemption	—	100	(100)		—
	500				350

For example, a company buys 50 of its own £1 shares at a premium of £2 each, i.e. it makes a capital repayment of £150. The accounting entries are shown in Figure 16.1.

Secondly, shares may be redeemed **out of the proceeds of a new share issue**. In practice, a redemption may be made partly out of profits and partly out of the proceeds of a new issue. The accounting requirements are as follows:

1 An amount equal to the excess of nominal value of redeemed shares over the total proceeds of any new issue is to be transferred from distributable profits to capital redemption reserve, i.e. they become classified as an undistributable reserve.

2 Any premium on redemption may be written off against distributable profits. However, if the company wishes to reduce the impact on its distributable profits, it may set off the premium on redemption against the share premium account, i.e. an undistributable reserve. However, this is subject to certain constraints. The amount of set-off is restricted to the lowest of:
   (a) any share premium originally received on the issue of the shares that are now being redeemed; or
   (b) the amount standing to the credit of the share premium account, including any premium received on the newly issues shares; or
   (c) the total proceeds of the new issue.

EXAMPLE ● Ozer plc had issued class B shares at a premium of £1 each, i.e. at £2 per share in 20X1. In 20X4 the company issued 20 class A shares of £1 each at a premium of £1 each, receiving a total capital receipt of £40. It then redeemed 50 class B shares of £1 each at a premium of £3 for a total capital repayment of £200, i.e. there was a premium on redemption of £150.

Management would normally propose writing off the premium on redemption of £150 against the share premium account to avoid reducing the distributable profits. However, the outcomes of the above criteria are as follows:

● Share premium originally received on the issue of the class B shares which are now being redeemed: £50.

● Amount standing to the credit of the share premium account, including any premium received on the newly issued shares (see earlier illustration in Figure 11.1): £240 + £20 = £260.

● Total proceeds of the new issue: £40.

We can see that the maximum that can be written off the share premium is £40. The remaining £110 has to be written off the distributable profits.

It then remains to determine the amount required to be transferrred to the capital redemption reserve account. This is calculated as follows:

	£
Nominal value of shares redeemed	50
Less: Total proceeds of the new issue	(40)
Required transfer from distributable profits	10

The balance sheet items before and after the issue of the class A shares and the redemption of the class B shares are shown in Figure 11.2.

We can see from the revised balance sheet that, in spite of the legal requirements, the permanent capital of the company has not been maintained. It has actually been reduced by £40 from £340 to £300. This means that part of the redemption has been made out of capital. It could be maintained by the transfer to capital redemption reserve of £30, which is the difference in the nominal value of shares redeemed (£50) and issued (£20), and by the premium chargeable to share premium account not being more than

Figure 11.2 Balance sheet before and after issue and redemption of shares.

Balance sheet before redemption		New issue	Purchase	W/off premium	Transfer to CRR	Balance sheet
	£	£	£	£	£	£
Share capital:						
Class A	50	20				70
Class B	50		(50)			—
Capital redemption reserve					10	10
Share premium	240	20		(40)		220
Permanent capital	340					300
P&L account	160			(110)	(10)	40
	500					340
Cash	200	40	(200)			40
Other assets	300					300
Premium on redemption			150	(150)		—
	500					340

the premium received from the new issue, i.e. £20. Nevertheless, as the law stands, on redemption the capital of a public company may be reduced or increased rather than being maintained. It is the reduction in capital that is important to the creditors.

11.6 Capital: redemption of shares by a private company

The Companies Act explicitly accepts that private companies may reduce their permanent capital in order to keep control within the same family or group of people.

This can arise when a shareholder dies or decides to leave the company and the other shareholders are not in a position to buy the shares. In such cases, if the company buys the shares, the control remains with the remaining shareholders. However, the legislature recognised that a counterbalance was required to provide additional protection for the creditors. Consequently, the rights of the creditors are protected by requiring the directors to make a declaration of solvency.

The company must declare that it will still be able to pay its creditors after the redemption and that it will continue to be able to do so for a year after the date of the redemption. The declaration is also required to be agreed and reported upon by the company's auditors. Furthermore, the company must publicise the intended redemption in order to inform the creditors who may object to such a redemption through the courts.

It is perhaps ironic that private companies are required to make a declaration of solvency in relation to an intentional reduction of capital, whereas public companies are not required to do so, although a reduction might also have occurred in their case. The creditors of a private company may actually be in a stronger position than those of a public company.

The accounting requirements for private companies are that any reduction in their permanent capital should not exceed the **permissible capital payment** as defined by the Act. This payment is the excess of the total amount paid on redemption of shares over the distributable profits of a company and the proceeds of any new share issue specifically made for the purposes of redemption. The accounting entries needed to confine the reduction in permanent capital to the permissible capital payment are as follows:

● If the nominal value of shares redeemed exceeds the permissible capital payment, an amount equal to the excess must be transferred from distributable profits to the capital redemption reserve account.

● If the nominal value of shares redeemed is less than the permissible capital payment, an amount equal to this plus the proceeds of any new share issue may be used to reduce any undistributable reserves. Undistributable reserves for this purpose include any unrealised gain, share premium, capital redemption reserve and share capital.

The general effect is that, in limiting the reduction in permanent capital to the permissible amount, a private company first utilises its distributable profit before reducing any undistributable reserves. The following two examples show the nature of adjustments needed for this purpose.

EXAMPLE ● A private company redeems 50 of its shares of £1 each at a premium of £3 per share, i.e. for £200. It does not issue any new shares. Its balance sheet is shown in Figure 16.3.

Figure 11.3   Balance sheet before and after redemption at a premium.

Balance sheet before redemption	£	Redemption of shares £	Write-off redemption premium £	Transfer to CRR £	Balance sheet after redemption £
Share capital	100	(50)			50
Capital redemption reserve				10	10
Share premium	240				240
Permanent capital	340				300
P&L account	160		(150)	(10)	—
	500				300
Cash	260	(200)			60
Other assets	240				240
Premium on redemption	—	150	(150)		—
	500				300

Calculation of permissible capital payment:	£
Amount payable on redemption	200
Less: Distributable profits	(160)
Permissible capital payment	40
Transfer to capital redemption reserve:	
Nominal value of shares redeemed	50
Less: Permissible capital payment	(40)
Capital redemption reserve	10

In this case the nominal value of shares redeemed is more than the permissible capital payment. A transfer is made from distributable profits to the capital redemption reserve to limit the reduction to the permissible capital amount of £40.

EXAMPLE ● private company redeems 50 of its class B shares of £1 each at a premium of £5 per share, i.e. for £300. It also issues 20 class A shares of £1 each at a premium of £2 per share, i.e. for £60, to help finance the redemption. Its balance sheet is shown in Figure 11.4.

In this case the nominal value of redeemed shares is less than the permissible capital payment and therefore the permanent capital (i.e. undistributable reserves) can be reduced by the difference. However, as the newly issued shares have already increased the permanent capital, the total reduction in undistributable reserves includes the new issue too. The result is a reduction of £80 in the original permanent capital, which is the permissible capital payment in this case.

Figure 11.4 Balance sheet before and after issue and redemption of shares at a premium.

Balance sheet before redemption	£	Issue of A shares £	Redemption of B shares £	Transfer from P&L a/c £	Transfer from permanent capital £	Balance sheet £
Share capital:						
Class A	50	20				70
Class B	50		(50)			—
Share premium	240	40			(90)	190
Permanent capital	340					260
P&L account	160			(160)		—
	500					260
Cash	260	60	(300)			20
Other assets	240					240
Premium on redemption	—		250	(160)	(90)	—
	500					260

Calculation of permissible capital payment:		
Amount payable on redemption		300
Less: Distributable profits	160	
Less: New issue proceeds	60	
		(220)
Permissible capital payment		80
Required transfer in the accounts:		
Nominal value of shares redeemed		50
Less: Permissible capital payment		(80)
Allowed reduction in permanent capital:		(30)
Also: New issue proceeds because it has increased the permanent capital		(60)
Total allowed reduction in permanent capital		(90)

11.7 Distributable profits: effect of accumulated trading losses

A company's distributable profits made in the current year are affected by its accumulated profit or loss position. We have seen that existing losses must be made good before a distribution can be made. However, a company might have experienced significant losses which require a fundamental change to its capital structure.

11.7.1 Elimination that affects only the ordinary shareholders

The Companies Act 1985, section 135, allows a company to reduce its capital where it has incurred losses and the share capital is no longer represented by available assets. This provides the statutory authority for a company that has suffered losses, but now believes that it has overcome the problems and will be profitable, to adjust its capital to reflect the current level of asset backing.

One of the results of doing this is that future profits become available for distribution rather than being required to be set off against the accumulated losses. It is a material change for the shareholders, who will be able to receive a dividend from future profits without losses being required to be made good first. Consequently, authority for the reduction must be contained in the articles of association, there must be a special resolution with a majority of at least 75% of the members voting in favour of the proposal and court approval must be obtained.

11.7.2 Accounting treatment for a capital reduction to eliminate accumulated trading losses

The accounting treatment is straightforward. A capital reduction account is opened. It is debited with the accumulated losses and credited with the amount written off the share capital.

For example, assume that the capital and reserves of Hopeless Ltd were as follows at 31 December 20X1:

	£
200,000 ordinary shares of £1 each	200,000
Profit and loss account	(180,000)

The directors estimate that the company will return to profitability in 20X2, achieving profits of £4,000 per annum thereafter. Without a capital reduction, the profits from 20X2 must be used to reduce the accumulated losses. This means that the company would be unable to pay a dividend for forty-five years if it continued at that level of profitability and ignoring tax. Perhaps even more importantly, it would not be attractive for shareholders to put additional capital into the company because they would not be able to obtain any dividend for some years.

The directors therefore obtained a special resolution and court approval to reduce the £1 ordinary shares to ordinary shares of 10p each. The accounting entries would be:

	Dr £	Cr £
Capital reduction account	180,000	
Profit and loss account:		180,000
Transfer of debit balance		
Share capital	180,000	
Capital reduction account:		180,000
Reduction of share capital		

11.7.3 Accounting treatment for a capital reduction to eliminate accumulated trading losses and loss of value on fixed assets

Companies often take the opportunity to revalue all of their assets at the same time as they eliminate the accumulated trading losses. Any loss on revaluation is then treated in the same way as the accumulated losses and transferred to the capital reduction account.

For example, assume that the capital and reserves and assets of Hopeless Ltd were as follows at 31 December 20X1:

	£	£
200,000 ordinary shares of £1 each		200,000
Profit and loss account		(180,000)
		20,000
Fixed assets		
Plant and machinery		15,000
Current assets		
Cash	17,000	
Current liabilities		
Creditors	12,000	
Net current assets		5,000
		20,000

The plant and machinery is revalued at £5,000 and it is resolved to reduce the share capital to ordinary shares of 5p each. The accounting entries would be:

	Dr £	Cr £
Capital reduction account	190,000	
Profit and loss account		180,000
Plant and machinery:		10,000
Transfer of accumulated losses and loss on revaluation		
Share capital	190,000	
Capital reduction account:		190,000
Reduction of share capital to 200,000 shares of 5p each		

The balance sheet after the capital reduction shows that the share capital fairly reflects the underlying asset values:

	£	£
200,000 ordinary shares of 5p each		10,000
		10,000
Fixed assets		
Plant and machinery		5,000
Current assets		
Cash	17,000	
Current liabilities		
Creditors	12,000	5,000
		10,000

An interesting illustration appears in the 1996 accounts of T&N plc. T&N plc is one of the world's leading suppliers of high technology automotive components and industrial materials. In 1996 the company achieved operating profits of £178m on a turnover of £2,038m. The company is amongst many defendants named in court actions brought in the United States relating to alleged asbestos-related diseases resulting from exposure to asbestos products. The company made a provision of £515m in respect of asbestos-related claims. This resulted in a debit balance on profit and loss account in the 1996 balance sheet of £259.6m and the company shareholders and Court approved a reduction in the issued share capital by the cancellation of 60p per £1 Ordinary share. The capital reduction was to take effect after 31 December 1996 and the accounts contain a proforma statement amended as follows:

	Called up share capital	Share premium	Special reserve (iii)	Revaluation reserves	Goodwill write off reserve	Associates reserves	P & L	Equity shareholders funds
As at 31.12.1996	532.2	0.2	—	21.6	(181.1)	5.0	(259.6)	118.3
Capital reduction (i)	(319.3)	—	319.3	—	—	—	—	—
Eliminate deficit on Holding company P&L Account (ii)	—	—	(262.5)	—	5.3	—	257.2	—
After capital reduction	212.9	0.2	56.8	21.6	(175.8)	5.0	(2.4)	118.3

(i) Reduction in the nominal value of each ordinary share from £1 to 40p.

(ii) Application of special reserve to eliminate the deficit on the holding company's profit and loss account, including goodwill previously written off.

(iii) The special reserve is not distributable.

Following a capital reduction there is a natural concern for shareholders as to the level of future dividends. T&N addressed any such concerns by the following note which indicated that the large asbestos-related provision in 1996 and the resulting capital reduction was to have no effect on the income shareholders could expect from their shares compared to previous years. It read:

As a result of the capital reduction the company is only able to declare dividends out of profits arising after January 1997. Accordingly, there will be no final dividend for the year ended 31 December 1996. Subject to there being sufficient profits available, however, the directors intend to declare a special first 1997 dividend of 3p per share in lieu of the final 1996 dividend with the result that the shareholders will receive the same dividend as in 1996.

Clearly the provision of £515m will have an impact on the rate of growth the company is able to achieve after 1996 but at least the dividends are being maintained.

11.7.4 Elimination that affects the ordinary shareholders and other stakeholders

In the Hopeless Ltd example, the ordinary shareholders alone bore the losses. The Companies Act, sections 425–427, provides a procedure for a reconstruction that involves a compromise between shareholders and creditors, with an amendment of the rights of the latter.

Such a reconstruction requires the support of 75% of each class of creditor whose rights are being compromised, 75% of each class of shareholder and the permission of the court. Once it has been approved by the court, it is binding on all parties. The court seeks to ensure that there is reasonable evidence of commercial viability and that anticipated profits are sufficient to service the proposed new capital structure.

Assuming in the Hopeless Ltd example that the creditors agree to bear £5,000 of the losses, the accounting entries would be as follows:

	£	£
Share capital	185,000	
Creditors	5,000	
Capital reduction account:		190,000
Reduction of share capital to 200,000 shares of 7.5p each		

Reconstruction schemes can be complex, but the underlying evaluation by each party will be the same. Each will assess the scheme to see how it affects their individual position.

Trade creditors

In their decision to accept £5,000 less than the book value of their debt, the trade creditors of Hopeless Ltd would be influenced by their prospects of receiving payment if Hopeless were to cease trading immediately, the effect on their results without Hopeless as a continuing customer, and the likelihood that they would continue to receive orders from Hopeless following reconstruction.

Loan creditors

Loan creditors would take into account the expected value of any security they possess and a comparison of the opportunities for investing any loan capital returned in the event of liquidation with the value of their capital and interest entitlement in the reconstructed company.

Preference shareholders

Preference shareholders would likewise compare prospects for capital and income following a liquidation of the company with prospects for income and capital from the company as a going concern following a reconstruction.

In practice, the formulation of a scheme will involve more than just the accountant except in the case of very small companies. A merchant bank, major shareholders and major debenture holders will undoubtedly be concerned. Each vested interest will be asked for its opinion on specific proposals: unfavourable reactions will necessitate a rethink by the accountant. The process will continue until a consensus begins to emerge.

Each stakeholder's position needs to be considered separately. For example, any attempt to reduce the nominal value of all classes of shares and debentures on a proportionate basis would be unfair and unacceptable. This is because a reduction in the nominal values of preference shares or debentures has a different effect from a reduction in the nominal value of ordinary shares. In the former cases, the dividends and interest receivable will be reduced; in the latter case, the reduction in nominal value of the ordinary shares will have no effect on dividends as holders of ordinary shares are entitled to the residue of profit, whatever the nominal value of their shares.

Total support may well be unachievable. The objective is to maintain the company as a going concern. In attempting to achieve this, each party will continually be comparing its advantages under the scheme with its prospects in a liquidation.

Illustration of a capital reconstruction

XYZ plc has been making trading losses, which have resulted in a substantial debit balance on the profit and loss account. The balance sheet of XYZ plc as at 31 December 20X3 was as follows:

		£000
Ordinary share capital (1 shares)		1,000
Less: Accumulated losses	Note 1	(800)
		200
10% Debentures (£1)		600
Net assets at book value	Note 2	800

Notes:

1 The company is changing its product and markets and expects to make £150,000 profit before interest and tax every year from 1 January 20X4.

2 (a) The estimated break-up or liquidation value of the assets at 31 December 20X3 was £650,000.

(b) The going concern value of assets at 31 December 19X3 was £700,000.

The directors are faced with a decision to liquidate or reconstruct. Having satisfied themselves that the company is returning to profitability, they propose the following reconstruction scheme:

● Write off losses and reduce asset values to £700,000.

● Cancel all existing ordinary shares and debentures.

● Issue 1,200,000 new ordinary shares of 25p each and 400,000 12.5% debentures of £1 each as follows:
  – the existing shareholders are to be issued with 800,000 ordinary 25p shares;
  – the existing debenture holders are to be issued with 400,000 ordinary 25p shares and the new debentures.

The stakeholders, i.e. the ordinary shareholders and debenture holders, have first to decide whether the company has a reasonable chance of achieving the estimated profit for 20X4. The company might carry out a sensitivity analysis to show the effect on dividends and interest over a range of profit levels.

Next, stakeholders must consider whether allowing the company to continue provides a better return than that available from the liquidation of the company. Assuming that it does, they assess the effect of allowing the company to continue without any reconstruction of capital and with a reconstruction of capital.

The accountant writes up the reconstruction accounts and produces a balance sheet after the reconstruction has been effected. The accountant will produce the following information:

Effect of liquidating		*Debenture holders*	*Ordinary shareholders*
	£	£	£
Assets realised	650,000		
Less: Prior claim	(600,000)	600,000	
Less: Ordinary shareholders	(50,000)	—	50,000
	—	600,000	50,000

This shows that the ordinary shareholders would lose almost all of their capital, whereas the debenture holders would be in a much stronger position. This is important because it might influence the amount of inducement that the debenture holders require to accept any variation of their rights.

Company continues without reconstruction

	£	Debenture holders £	Ordinary shareholders £
Expected annual income:			
Expected operating profit	150,000		
Less: Debenture interest	(60,000)	60,000	
Less: Ordinary dividend	(90,000)		90,000
Annual income	—	60,000	90,000

However, as far as the ordinary shareholders are concerned, no dividend will be allowed to be paid until the debit balance of £800,000 has been eliminated, i.e. there will be no dividend for more than nine years (for simplicity the illustration ignores tax effects).

Company continues with a reconstruction

	£	Debenture holders £	Ordinary shareholders £
Expected annual income:			
Expected operating profit	150,000		
Less: Debenture interest	(50,000)	50,000	
(12.5% on £400,000)			
Less: Dividend on shares	(33,000)	33,000	
Less: Ordinary dividend	(67,000)		67,000
Annual income	—	83,000	67,000

How will debenture holders react to the scheme?

At first glance, debenture holders appear to be doing reasonably well: the £83,000 provides a return of 14% on the amount that they would have received in a liquidation (83,000/600,000 × 100), which exceeds the 10% currently available, and it is £23,000 more than the £60,000 currently received. However, their exposure to risk has increased because £33,000 is dependent upon the level of profits. They will consider their position in relation to the ordinary shareholders.

For the ordinary shareholders the return should be calculated on the amount that they would have received on liquidation, i.e. 130% (67,000/50,000 × 100). In addition to receiving a return of 130%, they would hold two-thirds of the share capital, which would give them control of the company.

A final consideration for the debenture holders would be their position if the company were to fail after a reconstruction. In such a case, the old debenture holders would be materially disadvantaged as their prior claim will have been reduced from £600,000 to £400,000.

Accounting for the reconstruction

The reconstruction account will record the changes in the book values as follows:

Reconstruction account

	£000		£000
Profit and loss account	800	Ordinary share capital	1,000
Assets (losses written off)	100	10% Debentures (old debentures cancelled)	600
Ordinary share capital (25p shares)	300		
12.5% Debentures (new issue of debentures)	400		
	1,600		1,600

The post-reconstruction balance sheet will be as follows:

	£
Ordinary share capital (25p)	300,000
12.5% Debentures of £1	400,000
	700,000

11.8 Proposals for changes to Company Law

The Company Law Steering Group was appointed by the Government to look into the question of any changes that may be needed to the Company Law 'for a competitive economy'. In October 1999, it published a number of consultation documents. One of these is on the formation of companies and the maintenance of their capital. The Review Group makes some important proposals for changes regarding the documents that the companies should produce (on their formation), and also regarding the question of their capital maintenance (for the protection of their creditors).

11.8.1 Company formation

Here it is proposed to replace the Memorandum of Association and Articles of Association with two different documents and to make it easier for companies to alter some of the contents of these. At present, the Memorandum acts as a declaration by a company to the outside world of its name, place, share capital, limitation of members' liability and its objects; whereas the Articles are the internal rules of a company, e.g. meetings etc. It is proposed to replace these with (a) the Registration Form, which will have roughly the same information as on the Memorandum, but it will be easier for companies to change some of its contents; and (b) the Company Constitution, which will, generally, resemble the Articles.

Two major changes proposed in relation to the contents of these new documents are that (a) the objects clauses (i.e. the nature of trade of a company), and (b) authorised share capital of companies should be abolished. Historically, object clauses of companies have created many problems and the legal requirement as to the contents of the objects clause was simplified in recent legislation. The present proposal of abolishing it completely will mean that companies will be able to undertake any lawful trade. The only problem here seems to be the Second Directive of the European Commission ('the

Directive') which requires every public company to have an objects clause. So, unless the Directive can be changed, the proposal will only apply to private companies. The second proposal is to abolish the requirement for companies to have an authorised share capital. This will make it easier for companies to increase or reduce their intended capital.

Another proposal is to allow a company to be formed by one person. At present only private companies are allowed to have one member. This is to be extended to cover all types of companies, private as well as public ones.

11.8.2 Capital maintenance

A major proposal here is to allow companies to issue share of no par value (NPV shares) i.e. shares without nominal values. This will affect the way a share issue is recorded and the permanent capital of a company is maintained.

Shares with no par value

At present any kind of shares issued by UK companies are required to have a nominal value. It seems difficult to defend this requirement today. There seem to be two main arguments for it, namely that (a) the total (nominal) value of share capital of a company can be known and therefore can be maintained, and (b) dividend by a company can be based on the (nominal) value of its shares. But the starting point of these arguments seems to be wrong. Nominal values of shares have no real financial meaning, as they are usually the result of an arbitrary value put on them in the past. What is more, in accounting, the net proceeds of a share issue are artificially divided between share capital and share premium accounts as a result of a legal requirement. This is so even though this receipt is the result of one single financial transaction (a capital receipt on sale of a stake in the company). This would not have mattered if share capital and share premium accounts were treated in the same way by the Companies Act, but they are not. So the amount (i.e. nominal value) in the share capital account can not be an appropriate base in measuring the capital to be maintained by a company. Secondly, basing any dividends on such unrealistic figures can only be misleading. Dividends can easily be based on 'per share'.

In 1952, a committee appointed by the government recommended the introduction of shares of no par value, but the then government failed to legislate for it. The current report by the Steering Group also states that creditors of a company attach more importance to other indicators (e.g. asset values and cash flows) than share capital. But today it is not possible for the UK government to allow all companies to issue NPV shares as the Directive requires public companies to have nominal values for their shares. So the proposal to allow such shares will only apply to private companies. This will lead to different rules of writing-up and maintaining the share capital accounts of private and public companies. The Review Group expresses its wish for the Directive to be changed so that all companies can be allowed to issue NPV shares, but this may not be an easy task in practice.

Minimum capital and share issue

At present, there is no requirement for private companies to have a minimum amount of share capital and no change is proposed in this. When these companies issue NPV shares, the whole of net proceeds will be taken to one account called 'subscribed share capital'. This subscribed share capital will only be allowed to be reduced by the expenses of a new share issue or any discounts or commissions paid on them, provided the new shares are of the same class as the existing ones.

Public companies are at present required to have a minimum share capital of £50,000. Whether this amount is adequate for a public company has been questionable from its inception. The Steering Group does not make any proposal for this but seeks further consultation.

Accounting for the issue of shares by public companies will not change, as they have to have nominal values for their shares. Nominal values will continue to be credited to share capital account and any excess of net receipt over this value to share premium account.

At present, no company is allowed to give discounts or commissions on the issue of shares (except for underwriting or placing an issue) as this will amount to a reduction of share capital. It is proposed to maintain this requirement for public companies but to abolish it for private ones as it will have no meaning for NPV shares.

As there will be no authorised share capital, it will be easier for the directors to issue more shares, to subdivide existing shares and to cancel unissued shares.

Share premium

Public companies will continue to have a share premium account which, at present, can be used for the following purposes:

(a) issue bonus shares;

(b) write off formation expenses;

(c) write off expenses, commissions and discounts on issue of shares or debentures;

(d) provide for premium on redemption of debentures.

It is proposed to:

(a) allow this as it does not reduce capital;

(b) disallow this as it reduces capital;

(c) allow only for the shares of the same class (which has created share premium);

(d) disallow as debentures are of different class.

Reduction of share capital

There are two major proposals here, namely to reduce the power of courts in these cases and to require a solvency declaration by all companies before a reduction can be affected.

At present a company can reduce its share capital for three purposes, namely to:

● eliminate or reduce the part which has not been called up;

● pay back part which is in excess of it needs;

● write off lost capital (i.e. accumulated losses).

Currently, in all these cases, the court's consent is required to protect the interests of creditors.

It is proposed to retain the purposes for which share capital can be reduced, but to eliminate the need for court approval for private companies completely and, in the case of public companies, to allow their creditors the right to challenge the intended reduction through the courts. It is also proposed that the directors of all companies, whether private or public, would issue a formal solvency statement stating that the company will be able to pay its debts during a year after the reduction or on winding up in that year. If the company has auditors, their opinion on the solvency statement would also be needed.

Redemption of shares

At present, a public company is allowed to buy back its own shares or redeem them out of the proceeds of a new share issue or out of its distributable profits. To the extent that this is not possible, there must be a transfer from distributable profits to an account called capital redemption reserve which becomes part of the permanent capital of the company and which can only be used to issue bonus shares. It is proposed to maintain this requirement for public companies.

Private companies are at present allowed to reduce their capital to the extent of their 'permissible capital payment'. It is proposed to drop the notion of permissible capital payment and to allow these companies to reduce their capital, provided any redemption is first met from a new share issue or distributable profits and that a solvency statement – as mentioned above – is issued by the directors. There will be no need for a capital redemption reserve account for them.

At the moment, all shares redeemed by any type of company are required to be cancelled on redemption. There are other current proposals by the Department of Trade to allow companies to retain (i.e. not to cancel) these shares but to hold them as part of their treasury activities to the extent that they do not exceed 10% of the issued capital. The Steering Group proposes that this should also be introduced into the new legislation.

When shares are redeemed at a premium, this premium is required to be written off against the distributable profits. But companies are also given the option to utilise their share premium account to the extent of the lower of: (a) premium received on the issue of shares now being redeemed, and (b) balance existing on the share premium account. It is argued by the Steering Group that this enables a company to avoid a situation whereby a redemption may cause its capital to increase, and therefore this option should be maintained for public companies. On the other hand, it can be demonstrated that this provision may cause a company's permanent capital to decrease. It is surprising that this possibility has been missed out by the Review Group after so many years. This problem will not arise for private companies with NPV shares, as they will have no share premium account.

This demonstrates how easy and straightforward the situation would have been if public companies could also have NPV shares; any excess of the payment for a redemption over the net proceeds of a new issue would have caused an equivalent transfer from distributable profits to the subscribed capital (or to a redemption account) thereby maintaining the permanent capital exactly as it was.

11.8.3 Distributable profits

It is intended to maintain the substance of provisions relating to distributable profits.

The Steering Group concedes that there are problems relating to the definition of 'realised profits' and to the valuation of assets and liabilities for this purpose. It also states that there is a need to look at accounting standards in this context. As these are complex accounting matters, it will be interesting to see how they can be adequately covered by legislation. These questions on distributable profits are being considered by a working group (Group G) of the Steering Group, which is expected to produce its own proposals.

11.8.4 Comments on the proposed changes

The proposed abolition of authorised capital and the elimination of the need to obtain court approval for a reduction in issued capital will make it less onerous and less expensive for all companies to increase or reduce their issued capital.

For creditors of private companies, the only protection will be a forecast (solvency declaration by directors) that the company will be able to pay its debts in the short term. Small family-run companies could always, effectively, reduce their capital through their remuneration. Creditors of these companies had to depend on the character and personal guarantees of their owners. The proposed changes should not materially alter the position of the creditors of these companies. But the position of creditors of large private companies will be less secure than that of creditors of public companies.

For creditors of public companies there will not be a material change, as these companies will still be required to maintain their permanent capital through transfers from distributable to undistributable reserves, on any capital reduction. But the problem of the flexibility of the use of share premium will remain, which may still lead to an erosion of capital.

Review questions

1 How can distributable profits become non-distributable?

2 In what circumstances can non-distributable become distributable?

3 Why do companies reorganise when they have accumulated realised losses?

4 What does the court consider in those circumstances?

5 The directors of Edac plc are considering purchasing some or all of the company's preference shares (nominal value £1 per share) on the open market during the year ending 30 June 20X1. Edac plc's share premium account balance at purchase date will be £320,000.

Three completely independent scenarios are under consideration.

Scenario A

● 80,000 of the shares are to be bought back at a premium of 40p per share. There will be no accompanying new share issue.

● Legally distributable profits at buy-back date are estimated to be £376,000.

● The preference shares had originally been issued at par.

Scenario B

● 120,000 of the shares are to be bought back at a premium of 25p per share. There will be no accompanying new share issue.

● Legally distributable profits at buyback date are estimated to be £205,900.

● The preference shares had originally been issued at 115p per share.

Scenario C

● As Scenario B, except that partial financing is to be provided by an issue of 90,000 ordinary shares of £1 per share at 110p per share.

   (a) For each scenario A, B and C, calculate and identify the amounts which Edac plc would appropriate from distributable profits in connection with the buy-back. Assume that the share premium account would be utilised to the full extent permitted under the Companies Act 1985.

   (b) Assume now that Edac plc is a private limited company (Edac Ltd) and that it has distributable profits which are estimated at £15,000 (not £205,000). Recalculate the figures for scenario C as follows:

(i) Show the permissible capital payment.

(ii) Compare the nominal value of bought-back shares with the aggregate of the new share proceeds and the permissible capital payment. Show the surplus or deficit which arises from this.

(c) Say how Edac Ltd would be most likely to deal with the balance in (b)(ii).

Your answers should show your calculations and contain a brief written explanation.

6 The Woolwich repurchased 1.79 million shares at a cost of around £221m.[1]
Discuss possible reasons for the buy-back of shares.

Exercises

An outline solution is provided in the appendix at the end of the text for exercises marked with an asterisk (*).

Question 1

(a) Company law defines 'share premium' and attempts to protect it from reduction.

(i) Define 'share premium'.

(ii) State the circumstances in which company law requires a company to place an amount in the share premium account.

(iii) State why and how company law seeks to protect any balance placed in the share premium account.

(b) State whether each of the following are realised or unrealised profits (or losses) for the purpose of calculating distributable profits:

(i) Depreciation charged on a revalued fixed asset.

(ii) Development expenditure in the profit and loss account which was previously capitalised in the balance sheet.

(iii) The share of profits from an associated company to an investing company which does not prepare consolidated financial statements.

(iv) The profit on the disposal of a fixed asset which had been revalued in a previous year.

(v) A provision for libel damages in a forthcoming court case.

(vi) Surpluses arising on revaluation of assets before sale.

(vii) A charge to the profit and loss account is a provision for bad debts.

Question 2

You are the auditor of Smith Family Ltd, which is a family owned private company. One of the members, Otto Smith Senior, who is also a director, wishes to retire from business and would like to dispose of his holding of 200,000 Ordinary £1 shares. These had originally been purchased at a premium of 20 pence per share. Independent valuations of the company suggested that a reasonable price for his holding would be £300,000.

The remaining family members are happy with this proposal and are considering financing the purchase as follows:

either (i) from internal resources;

or (ii) partly from internal resources and partly by the issue of 50,000 ordinary £1 shares at a premium of £1 per share to Otto Smith Junior.

The summarised balance sheet of Smith Family Ltd at 31 July 20X7 (before the proposed buyback) shows:

Net assets

Cash	400,000
Other sundry assets	850,000
	1,250,000

Financed by:

Ordinary £1 shares	1,000,000
Share premium	100,000
Profit and loss account	150,000
	1,250,000

The directors have approached you for advice.

Required:

Draft a report to the Directors of Smith Family Ltd which:

(a) outlines the power of a private limited company to purchase its own shares;

(b) explains the procedure which must be followed;

(c) describes the special rules allowing the purchase of the shares;

(d) includes for both financing options the necessary Journal Entries, the Balance Sheets after the purchase of the shares, and an explanation of the changes to the Balance Sheet.

(Chartered Institute of Public Finance and Accounting)

* **Question 3**

The draft balance sheet of Telin plc at 30 September 20X5 was as follows:

	£000		£000
Ordinary shares of £1 each, fully paid	12,000	Product development costs	1,400
12% Preference shares of £1 each, fully paid	8,000	Sundry assets	32,170
Share premium	4,000	Cash and bank	5,450
Retained (distributable) profits	4,600		
Creditors	10,420		
	39,020		39,020

Preference shares of the company were originally issued at a premium of 2p per share. The directors of the company decided to redeem these shares at the end of October 20X5 at a premium of 5p per share. They also decided to write off the balances on development costs and discount on debentures (see below).

All write-offs and other transactions are to be entered into the accounts according to the provisions of Companies Acts and in a manner financially advantageous to the company and to its shareholders.

The following transactions took place during October 20X5:

(a) On 4 October the company issued for cash 2,400,000 10% debentures of £1 each at a discount of 2½%.

(b) On 6 October the balances on development costs and discount of debentures were written off.

(c) On 12 October the company issued for cash 6,000,000 ordinary shares at a premium of 10p per share. This was a specific issue to help redeem preference shares.

(d) On 29 October the company redeemed the 12% preference shares at a premium of 5p per share and included in the payments to shareholders one month's dividend for October.

(e) On 30 October the company made a bonus issue, to all ordinary shareholders, of one fully paid ordinary share for every twenty shares held.

(f) During October the company made a net profit of £275,000 from its normal trading operations. This was reflected in the cash balance at the end of the month.

Required:
(a) Write up the ledger accounts of Telin plc to record the transactions for October 20X5.
(b) Prepare the company's balance sheet as at 31 October 20X5.
(c) Briefly explain accounting entries which arise as a result of redemption of preference shares.

Question 4

The following is the balance sheet of Alpha Ltd as on 30 June 20X8:

	£000	£000	£000
Fixed assets	Cost	*Accumulated*	
Tangible assets		*depreciation*	
Freehold property	46	5	41
Plant	85	6	79
	131	11	120
Investments			
Shares in subsidiary company		90	
Loans		40	130
Current assets			
Stock		132	
Debtors		106	
		238	
Creditors: amounts falling due within one year			
Trade creditors		282	
Bank overdraft		58	
		340	
Net current liabilities			(102)
Total assets *less* liabilities			148

Capital and reserves

250,000 8½% Cumulative redeemable preference shares of £1 each fully paid	250
100,000 ordinary shares of £1 each 75p paid	75
	325
Profit and loss account	(177)
	148

The following information is relevant:

1 There are contingent liabilities in respect of (i) a guarantee given to bankers to cover a loan of £30,000 made to the subsidiary and (ii) uncalled capital of 10p per share on the holding of 100,000 shares of £1 each in the subsidiary.

2 The arrears of preference dividend amount to £106,250.

3 The following capital reconstruction scheme, to take effect as from 1 July 20X8, has been duly approved and authorised:

   (i) the unpaid capital on the ordinary shares to be called up;

   (ii) the ordinary shares thereupon to be reduced to shares of 25p each fully paid up by cancelling 75p per share and then each fully paid share of 25p to be subdivided into five shares of 5p each fully paid;

   (iii) the holders to surrender three of such 5p shares out of every five held for reissue as set out below;

   (iv) the 8½% cumulative preference shares together with all arrears of dividend to be surrendered and cancelled on the basis that the holder of every 50 preference shares will pay to Alpha a sum of £30 in cash, and will be issued with:

     1 one £40 convertible 7¾% note of £40 each, and

     2 60 fully paid ordinary shares of 5p each (being a redistribution of shares surrendered by the ordinary shareholders and referred to in (iii) above);

   (v) the unpaid capital on the shares in the subsidiary to be called up and paid by the parent company whose guarantee to the bank should be cancelled;

   (vi) the freehold property to be revalued at £55,000;

   (vii) the adverse balance on profit and loss account to be written off, £55,000 to be written off the shares in the subsidiary and the sums made available by the scheme to be used to write down the plant.

Required:
(a) Prepare a capital reduction and reorganisation account.
(b) Prepare the balance sheet of the company as it would appear immediately after completion of the scheme.

* **Question 5**

A summary of the balance sheet of Doxin plc, as at 31 December 20X0, is given below:

	£000		£000
800,000 Ordinary shares of		Assets other than bank (at	
£1 each	800,000	book values)	1,500,000
300,000 6% preference shares			
£1 each	300,000	Bank	200,000
General reserves	200,000		
Creditors	400,000		
	1,700,000		1,700,000

During 20X1, the company:

(i) Issued 200,000 ordinary shares of £1 each at a premium of 10p per share (a specific issue to redeem preference shares).

(ii) Redeemed all preference shares at a premium of 5%. These were originally issued at 25% premium.

(iii) Issued 4,000 7% debentures of £100 each at '90'.

(iv) Used share premium, if any, to issue fully paid bonus shares to members.

(v) Made a net loss of £500,000 by end of year which affected the bank account.

Required:

(a) Show the effect of each of the above items in the form of a moving balance sheet (i.e. additions/deductions from original figures) and to draft the balance sheet of 31 December 20X1.

(b) Consider to what extent the interests of the creditors of the company are being protected.

References

1 S. Perrin, 'Buyback favours', *Accountancy*, February 2000, p. 34.

Off balance sheet finance and capital instruments

12.1 Introduction

Accountants have traditionally followed an objective, transaction-based book-keeping system for recording financial data and an accrual, conservative-based system for classifying into income and capital and reporting to users and financial analysts.

However, since the 1950s there has been a growth in the use of off-balance-sheet finance and complex capital instruments. The financial analyst can no longer rely on the residual balances that appear in the traditional balance sheet when assessing risks and returns.

The traditional balance sheet is undergoing conceptual change. To understand this change we need to consider the evolving treatment in the primary financial statements of the various forms of loan capital and the changing needs of financial analysts. In this chapter we consider:

- Primary financial statements: their interrelationship
- Reasons that companies borrow
- Capital gearing and its implications
- Off-balance-sheet finance
- Substance over form
- FRS 5 *Reporting the Substance of Transactions*
- FRS 5 Application Notes
- FRS 4 *Capital Instruments*
- FRS 4 Application Notes
- Why companies take steps to strengthen their balance sheet
- SSAP 17 *Post balance sheet events*
- FRS 12 *Provisions, Contingent Liabilities and Contingent Assets*
- *Retirement benefits*

12.2 Primary financial statements: their interrelationship

12.2.1 Profit and loss account

At a mechanistic level, the historical profit and loss account is an integral feature of the book-keeping system, in that receipts and payments of a revenue nature are transferred to this account.

At a conceptual level, it is an integral part of the financial reporting system, in that the matching, accruals and prudence concepts are applied to the receipts and payments transaction balances in order to arrive at the reported profit or loss for the period.

12.2.2 Balance sheet

At a mechanistic level, the historical cost balance sheet simply contains all those monetary balances remaining within the ledger after revenue and expenses have been transferred to the profit and loss account. It is a form of second trial balance representing the balances of residual data at the end of the financial year as liabilities or assets.

Liabilities are expenses incurred and expected as a consequence of activities not yet finalised by cash transaction with creditors and other third parties; assets constitute expenditure whose economic benefits have not been fully utilised.

These **residual** values are a direct result of the accruals, or matching, concept.

12.3 Primary financial statements: changes in their interrelationship

12.3.1 Importance of the profit and loss account

Although the profit and loss account and balance sheet were presented in tandem, the profit and loss account used to be considered more important than the balance sheet. It was seen as having a dynamic quality, in that it reported the change in wealth that had occurred during the year with details of costs, taxation, earnings and dividends.

In contrast, the balance sheet's static quality revealed only the left-over balances arising from the double entry book-keeping system.

12.3.2 Emerging importance of the balance sheet

This picture was irrevocably altered by the emergence of capital-hungry joint stock companies. Equity capital, which was the traditional source of finance, was unable to satisfy total demand and loan capital became important. Later, other financial institutions such as insurance companies, merchant banks and pension funds entered the field. The balance sheet came to be viewed in a new light.

Equity or ordinary shareholders were the risk carriers of the limited company. Risk-averse investors seeking greater security of investment income at the expense of capital growth were able to invest in preference shares.

Risk-averse investors seeking greater security of both investment income and investment capital became loan creditors; however, they demanded greater security, and evidence of such security, before parting with money.

While all investors looked to the profit and loss account as a means of assessing the borrower's ability to service the interest and dividend payments, the loan creditors, as a further precaution, looked to the balance sheet to determine the safety of the principal sum secured on the net assets available in the event of foreclosure or liquidation.

12.4 Reasons that companies borrow

Companies borrow money for many reasons:

● **Temporary cash flow problems.** Cash may be needed as a consequence of temporary cash flow problems, and early repayment might be foreseen.

● **Lower cost.** Prevailing interest rates may be attractively low.

● **Fiscal advantages.** Loan interest might attract tax relief for the borrower; such relief is not available for dividend payments.

● **Income gearing.** A fixed rate of loan interest may be less than the anticipated return obtainable by the company in employing the loan funds. The excess will benefit shareholders via earning per share and increased dividends and, perhaps, capital growth.

● **Timing.** When there is a lack of buoyancy in the capital market, a company might satisfy a medium-term capital requirement by borrowing with a view to redeeming the debt and making a share issue when market conditions are favourable.

● **Dilution of voting power.** Shareholders and management might be reluctant to issue shares if this would dilute the control of the existing shareholders. They might also consider that an increase in the number of shares would increase the risk of a take-over bid.

● **Earnings per share considerations.** The anticipated return on any proposed new share capital, although desirable in absolute terms, might be insufficient to prevent a fall in EPS. A resultant fall in the market value per share might be unacceptable.

In practice, capital gearing decisions will be influenced by a mixture of motives.

12.5 Capital gearing and its implications

Capital gearing is an attempt to measure the risk to the equity shareholders arising from a company's capital structure. It is the arithmetic relationship between borrowed capital and total capital employed. There is no single definition or standard description, but companies operating with a low proportion of borrowed capital as compared with equity capital are described as **low geared**.

The usual arithmetical model compares long-term debt with equity funds. However, it is customary to include within long-term debt any form of long-term capital demanding fixed servicing costs. Hence, preference shares are included because they receive a priority payment of fixed dividend before any distribution to the ordinary shareholders, thus increasing the risk that the latter will receive little or nothing.

The measurement usually takes the form of a ratio, which we illustrate using two definitions of gearing. The first definition excludes bank overdraft, the second includes it.

Overdraft excluded

$$\text{Company Y:} \quad \frac{\text{Debentures + Preference shares}}{\text{Debentures + Preference shares + Equity}}$$

Year 2	Year 1
£m	£m
$\dfrac{£10 + £20}{£10 + £20 + £50}$	$\dfrac{£5 + £20}{£5 + £20 + £30}$
37.5%	45.5%

$$\text{Company Z:} \quad \frac{£2 + £6}{£2 + £6 + £80} \qquad \frac{£0 + £10}{£10 + £72}$$

$$9.1\% \qquad\qquad 12.2\%$$

$$\text{Industry average:} \quad 25\% \qquad\qquad 27\%$$

Company Y is shown in year 2 to be more highly geared than the industry's average. However, a reduction has occurred in the gearing from 45.5% to 37.5% because the increase in borrowing of £5m has been more than offset by a growth in equity of £20m.

Company Z is shown in year 2 to be lower geared than the industry's average. It too has experienced a reduction in gearing due to a change in its capital structure. The change arises from the redemption of £4m preference shares, the issue of £2m debentures and an increase of £8m in equity shares. Notice the gearing of each company as a proportion of the industry average:

	Year 2	Year 1
Company Y	150%	168.5%
Company Z	36.4%	45.2%

In general, 'long-term debt' means borrowed funds (and preference shares) assumed to be repayable after one year. However, where companies make a habit of maintaining a bank overdraft, it can be argued that such funding is in effect long or medium term and should be treated as such when assessing risk.

Overdraft included

$$\frac{\text{Debentures + Preference shares + Overdraft}}{\text{Debentures + Preference shares + Overdraft + Equity}}$$

$$£000 \text{ (Year 2)} \qquad\qquad £000 \text{ (Year 1)}$$

$$\text{Company Y:} \quad \frac{£10 + £20 + £5}{£10 + £20 + £5 + £50} \qquad \frac{£5 + £20 + £7}{£5 + £20 + £7 + £30}$$

$$41.2\% \qquad\qquad 51.6\%$$

$$\text{Company Z:} \quad \frac{£2 + £6 + £3}{£2 + £6 + £3 + £80} \qquad \frac{£0 + £10 + £4}{£10 + £4 + £72}$$

$$12.1\% \qquad\qquad 16.3\%$$

$$\text{Industry average:} \quad 31\% \qquad\qquad 36\%$$

The measure of risk is increased for both entities:

	Year 2	Year 1
Company Y	132.9%	143.3%
Company Z	39.0%	45.3%

In comparison with the industry's average, the gearing of Y is higher for both years and the gearing of Z is lower.

12.5.1 Implication of gearing

The risk to the ordinary shareholders in the above example is higher with company Y than with company Z. The fixed dividend of preference shareholders and the fixed interest of loan creditors remains constant irrespective of the level of profits. This leads to fluctuations in the amount of profits attributable to equity. In times of high profits, the return will be generous; in periods of low profits, the return may be low or non-existent. This volatility is a measure of the risk inherent in an equity shareholding arising from the level of loan finance; it influences dividend yield and the market price of the equity shares.

12.5.2 Interest cover

Interest cover is calculated from the profit and loss account. It indicates the extent to which profits before interest and tax cover the interest charges shown in the profit and loss account. It can be adapted to take account of fixed dividends on preference shares. An illustration for companies Y and Z shows:

$$\frac{\text{Profit before interest and tax}}{\text{Interest}}$$

Company Y	Company Z	Industry average	Company Y	Company Z	Industry average
$\dfrac{£27}{4}$	$\dfrac{£18}{3}$		$\dfrac{£21}{£5}$	$\dfrac{£14}{4}$	
6.75 times	6 times	4 times	4.2 times	3.5 times	4.5 times

The interest cover ratios suggest that, while Y is more highly geared than Z, it has a marginally greater safety factor (6.75 times compared with 6; 4.2 times compared with 3.5). It has a considerably greater cover than the industry. However, if profits suffered a severe decline, the relative interest cover ratios could change drastically.

An analysis of the capital structure indicates an entity's ability to discharge its obligations in respect of interest and principal on long-term borrowings. This information is of value to all types of provider of funds, e.g. bankers, debenture holders, preference and ordinary shareholders.

It is primarily the balance sheet that provides the capital structure information; it thus performs a key role in financial decision-making. But is its information adequate?

12.6 Off-balance-sheet finance

Off-balance-sheet finance is the descriptive phrase for all financing arrangements where strict recognition of the legal aspects of the individual contract results in the exclusion of liabilities and associated assets from the balance sheet.

The impact of such transactions is to understate resources (assets) and obligations (liabilities) to the detriment of the true and fair view.[1] The analyst cannot assess the value of capital employed or the real gearing ratio, and attempts to determine risk are nullified.

This can happen as an innocent side-effect of the transaction-based book-keeping system. For example, when a company undertakes the long-term hire of a machine by payment of annual rentals, the rental is recorded in the profit and loss account, but the machine, because it is not owned by the hirer, will not be shown in the hirer's balance sheet.

If the facility to hire did not exist, the asset could still be used and a similar cash outflow pattern incurred by purchasing it with the aid of a loan. A hiring agreement, if perceived in terms of its **accounting substance** rather than its **legal form**, has the same effect as entering into a loan agreement to acquire the machine.

The exclusion of a liability and its associated asset undermines the use of the balance sheet as a vehicle for assessing risk by means of the gearing ratio.

The true and fair view can also be compromised by deliberate design. The problem of off-balance-sheet finance became exacerbated by attempts to camouflage the substance of transactions by relying on a strictly legal distinction. For example, loan capital arrangements were concealed from shareholders and other creditors by a legal subterfuge to which management and lenders were party, and with which the auditors colluded.

12.7 Substance over form

SSAP 21 *Accounting for Leases and Hire Purchase Contracts*[2] was the first formal imposition of the principle of accounting for substance over legal form, aiming to ensure that the legal characteristics of a financial agreement did not obscure its commercial impact. In particular, it was intended to prevent the inherent gearing implications of the traditional balance sheet being circumvented and, consequently, the true and fair view being jeopardised.

The standard's aim has generally been achieved, but total elimination of leasing as a vehicle for generating off balance sheet finance has proved difficult. For instance, some companies have manipulated an escape from the '90% clause' of the standard, which distinguishes a finance lease from an operating lease.

The explosive growth of additional and complex forms of financial arrangements during the 1980s focused attention on the need to increase the disclosure and awareness of such arrangements and led to the issue of FRS 5 *Reporting the Substance of Transactions*.[3]

12.8 FRS 5 *Reporting the Substance of Transactions*

FRS 5 was formulated to ensure that financial statements reveal the substance of the transactions undertaken by an entity, rather than merely representing their legal aspects. The standard sets about its task by defining assets and liabilities as follows:

● **Assets**: rights or other access to future economic benefits controlled by an entity as a result of past transactions or events.

● **Liabilities**: an entity's obligations to transfer economic benefits as a result of past transactions or events.

The definitions emphasise **economic benefits controlled** (assets) and **economic benefits transferable** (liabilities). Thus the issues of legal ownership of, or title to, assets and the possession of legal responsibilities for liabilities are necessarily evaded in the quest for an identification of substance inherent within the individual transaction. The definitions are not new; they are the same as those proposed in the ASB's *Statement of Principles*.

12.8.1 Applying the definitions

This involves the consideration of key factors in analysing the commercial implications of an individual transaction. The standard specifies the following key factors:

1 **Substance** must first be identified by determining whether the transaction has given rise to new assets or liabilities for the reporting entity and whether it has changed the entity's existing assets and liabilities.

2 **Rights** or other access to benefits (i.e. possession of an asset) must be evidenced by the entity's exposure to risks inherent in the benefits, taking into account the likelihood of those risks having a commercial effect in practice.

3 **Obligations** to transfer benefits (i.e. acceptance of a liability) must be evidenced by the existence of some circumstance by which the entity is unable to avoid, legally or commercially, an outflow of benefits.

4 **Options, guarantees or conditional provisions** incorporated in a transaction should have their commercial effect assessed within the context of all the aspects and implications of the transaction in order to determine what assets and liabilities exist.[4]

12.8.2 Recognition in the balance sheet

Having applied the definition to determine the existence of an asset or liability, it is then necessary to decide whether to include the asset or liability in the balance sheet. This decision necessitates:

● sufficient evidence being extant of the item (including, where appropriate, evidence that a future inflow or outflow of benefit will occur); and

● that monetary evaluation of the item is measurable with sufficient reliability.[5]

12.8.3 Transactions in assets previously recorded

Transactions in assets previously recorded are also dealt with by FRS 5 because they may be affected by future transactions, perhaps deliberately so in order to avoid continued recognition. The standard mandates that the substance of the new transaction needs to be identified as specified in factor (1) (section 17.8.1) above to determine if:

● the asset should continue to be reported at its current amount;

● its value should be altered to take account of the change; or

● it should cease to be recognised and a disposal should be recorded.

Continued recognition should be maintained at the current carrying amount if the new transaction does not result in any significant change in either:

● the entity's rights or other access to benefits relating to that asset; or

● its exposure to the risks inherent in those benefits.[6]

Discontinued recognition should be effected where transfers to other parties involve:[7]

● all significant rights or other access to benefits relating to that asset, and

● all significant exposure to risks inherent in those benefits.

It is interesting to note that the *Conceptual Framework* is applied in the standard, since general principles are expounded to assist the determination of base characteristics and recognition of assets and liabilities. However, the standard also assists by including in its application notes specific kinds of off balance sheet finance.

12.9 FRS 5 application notes

The application notes illustrate the appropriate treatment for transactions such as consignment stocks, sale and repurchase agreements, and debt factoring.

12.9.1 Consignment stocks

Consignment stocks are a regular feature of some trades, whereby transfers from one party to another are arranged so that legal title is retained by the consignor, but the economic risks and benefits move to the consignee. Determining the absolute commercial impact of the transaction requires consideration of the rights of each party to have the stock returned to the consignor. The agreement may contain an absolute right of return of the stocks to the consignor, but in practice penalty provisions may effectively neutralise the right so that stocks are never returned.

EXAMPLE ● Producer P plc supplies leisure caravans to caravan dealer C Ltd on the following terms:

1 Each party has the option to have the caravans returned to the producer.

2 C Ltd pays a rental charge of 1% per month of the cost price of the caravan as consideration for exhibiting the caravan in its display compound.

3 Eventual sale of a caravan necessitates C Ltd remitting to P plc the lower of:
   (a) the ex-factory price of the caravan when first delivered to C Ltd, or
   (b) the current ex-factory price of the caravan, less all rentals paid to date.

4 If the caravans remain unsold for six months, C Ltd must pay for each unsold caravan on the terms specified above.

To some extent the risks and rewards of ownership are shared between both parties. However, in practice we must decide in favour of one party because it is not acceptable to show the caravans partly on each balance sheet.

The factors in favour of treating the consigned goods as stock of P plc are:

● P plc's right to demand the return of the vans.

● C Ltd's ability to return the vans to P plc.

● P plc is deriving a rental income per caravan for six months or until the time of sale, whichever occurs first.

The factors in favour of treating the goods as the stock of C Ltd are:

● C Ltd's obligation to pay for unsold vans at the end of six months.

● The payment of a monthly rental charge. This may be considered as interest on the amount outstanding.

● C Ltd's payment need not exceed the ex-works price existing at the time of supply.

However, if C Ltd has an **unrestricted** right to return the caravans before the six months have elapsed it can, in theory, avoid the promise to pay for the caravans. Indeed, providing the ex-works cost has not increased beyond the rental (i.e. 1% per month), the company can recover the sum of the rental.

On balance the factors seem to favour treating the transaction as a sale to C Ltd, so its balance sheet would carry the caravans as stock and P plc would carry them as a liability.

Consider also the option of return held by C Ltd. This may not be unrestricted. Disputes may develop if the exhibited caravans suffer wear and tear considered excessive by P plc; or other restrictions may be considered inherent in the various clauses. Thus substance over form is not always easy to identify or isolate. In practice, a decision may be delayed to observe how the terms actually operated, on the basis that what actually transpired constitutes the substance.

12.9.2 Sale and repurchase agreements

Sale and repurchase agreements appear in a variety of guises. The essential ingredient is that the original holder or purported vendor of the asset does not relinquish physical control: it retains access to the economic benefits and carries exposure to the commercial risks. In short, the characteristics of a normal sale are absent. FRS 5 deems that such a transaction be treated as non-sale, the asset in question remaining in the balance sheet of the purported vendor.

EXAMPLE ● A company specialising in building domestic houses sells a proportion of its landholding to a merchant bank for £750,000 on 25 March 20X5, agreeing to repurchase the land for £940,800 on 24 March 20X7. The land remains under the control and supervision of the vendor.

FRS 5 deems this contract to be a financing arrangement. The risks and rewards of ownership have not been transferred to the bank. Money has been borrowed on the security of the land. The bank is to receive a fixed sum of £190,800 at the end of a two-year term. This equates to 12% per annum compound interest. The balance sheet should retain the land as an asset, the cash inflow of £750,000 being displayed as a loan, redeemed two years later by its repayment at £750,000 plus accrued interest of £190,800.

In deciding whether it is a sale or a finance agreement, consider which party enjoys the benefits and suffers the risk between sale and repurchase. In the simplest version of this kind of contract, this will usually be indicated by the prices at which the two transactions are arranged. If the prices are market prices current at the date of each transaction, risks and rewards of ownership rest with the buyer for the period between the two transactions. But if the later price displays any arithmetic linking with the former, this suggests a relationship of principal and interest between the two dates. Thus benefits and risk reside with the original entity-seller, who is in effect a borrower; the original entity-buyer is in effect a lender.

12.9.3 Debt factoring

Factoring is a means of accelerating the cash inflow by selling debtors to a third party. Sales ledger administration and protection from bad debts may be involved. Is the transaction really a sale in substance, or merely a borrowing arrangement with collateral in the form of accounts receivable? Once again, identification of substance will necessitate consideration of the overall terms of the factoring contract as the factor may be supplying a variety of services. We may safely dispense with the benefits of ownership and concentrate on the risks: there is no likelihood of any improvement in benefit in relation to debtors, apart perhaps from a reduction in finance costs as a side-effect of earlier cash inflow.

FRS 5 specifies three accounting treatments for factored debts: derecognition, a linked presentation and a separate presentation.

Derecognition

This is the treatment whereby the carrying value of the transferred debtors is removed entirely from the balance sheet, i.e. the debts are derecognised. Proceeds received from the factor will be debited to cash account and credited to debtors, the imbalance on the latter being seen as a discount and transferred to the profit and loss account as a finance cost. Any other factoring costs should be identified separately and classified as administration charges.

Derecognition can be applied only if all the significant benefits and risks in respect of the debts are transferred to the factor. Three conditions must exist:

● The transaction is one of arm's-length price for an outright sale.

● The transaction is for a fixed amount and there is no recourse to the seller, implicit or explicit, in the event of loss caused by non-payment or slow payment.

● The seller derives no benefit and carries no risk if the debts outperform or underperform expectations.

Linked presentation

This is the treatment whereby the funds received from the factor are deducted from the debtor's gross carrying value, the gross, deduction and net figures all being shown in the balance sheet. For example, S assigns debts to F and receives 80% of the gross amount of debts assigned at any time. F charges interest of 15% p.a. on a daily basis. F provides protection from bad debts for a charge of 1% of the gross value of all debts factored. S continues to administer the sales ledger and to handle all aspects of debt collection. Any debt not recovered after 90 days becomes the responsibility of F. F pays for all debts assigned, less any advances and credit protection charges, 90 days after purchase.

The commercial effect of this factoring arrangement is that, although the debts have been legally transferred to F, S continues to carry significant benefits and risks; the risk of slow payment is carried by S at a cost of a daily rate of interest charged by F. Assuming a gross debt of £1,200 outstanding for 90 days and that each month is of 30 days, S's balance sheet would be:

| | As at the end of month: | | |
	1	2	3
Current assets:			
Stock	x	x	x
Debts factored without recourse:			
Gross debts (after providing for credit protection fee and accrued interest)	1,176	1,164	1,152
Less: Non-returnable proceeds	960	960	960
	216	204	192

Linked protection is a novel but rather ambiguous accounting treatment. There are alternative treatments, but these have been rejected by FRS 5. Showing the non-returnable proceeds as a liability on the balance sheet would be nonsense because non-returnability means that the proceeds cannot be a liability. Showing net debts factored only – namely, 216, 204 and 192 – would not show that the entity retains significant benefits and risks associated with the asset because of the failure to reveal the gross figure.

The method was formulated by the ASB in response to representation from banks in relation to securitisation (see below), but the method is not confined to a particular type of asset. The standard does not envisage that situations requiring linked presentation will occur often, and it sets extremely strict criteria for its adoption. The conditions may be summarised as follows:

● The finance relates to a specific item (or group of similar items).
● If a loan is involved, it is secured on that item only.
● The provider of finance has no recourse to other assets.
● There is no obligation to repay the finance.
● The entity is not able to acquire the asset by repayment of the finance.
● If funds generated by the item are insufficient to repay the finance, this does not constitute default by the company.
● The provider of finance has given a written undertaking that repayment will be sought from the asset concerned only, without recourse to other assets.

Partial linked presentation may be adopted where a financing agreement meets the conditions only in part. This situation necessitates dividing the finance into two components: that component meeting all the conditions will be linked; the other component will be treated as a liability on the balance sheet.

12.9.4 Securitised assets

Securitising is a process of raising finance from external sources by offering security in the form of a specific block of assets. Domestic household mortgages have been the most commonly securitised assets in the UK. Other **receivables**, such as credit card balances, hire purchase loans and trade debts, are sometimes securitised, and non-monetary assets such as property and stocks.

Figure 12.1 illustrates the processing structure of a securitisation deal. The originating company (1) makes a loan to (2) a mortgage company and then sells the loan to (3)

Figure 12.1 Processing structure of a securitised loan.

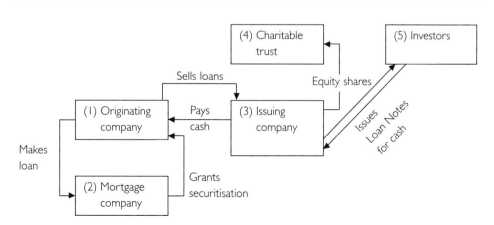

another company, which pays cash in return for the loan documents. This company usually has shareholders in the form of (4) a charitable trust. If it is not a charitable trust, it is likely to be a company friendly to the originating company (1). Company (3) is invariably thinly capitalised and, if its shares are issued to a third party, it often avoids classification as a subsidiary of the originating company (1). In addition, the major financial and operating policies of (3) the issuer are usually predetermined by agreements which constitute the securitisation, such that neither (4) the owner of its share capital nor (1) the originator has any significant discretion over its management. The issuer (3) issues loan notes to (5) the investment market in order to finance the loans. The loan notes will carry coupon rates related to the rate of interest receivable on the mortgage.

Entries in the originating company's balance sheet

Whether or not the mortgage appears as an asset and the sale proceeds as a liability depends upon two main issues:

● Has the sale of the mortgages involved the transfer of all significant benefits and risks to the issuing company? If not, the originator must show the mortgages as an asset and the sale proceeds as a loan received.

● Is the issuing company a subsidiary or quasi-subsidiary of the originating company? If it is, consolidating the issuing company's accounts with those of the originator will mean that transactions between the two companies are self-cancelling. Thus the assets and liabilities on the issuer's balance sheet will appear on the consolidated balance sheet of the originator, possibly as a linked presentation if the issuing company is a quasi-subsidiary.

The way the transaction is structured via a company issuing loan notes to the investment market is meant to remove the asset and loan from the originator's balance sheet. Success in achieving this depends on the transfer of benefit and risks associated with granting a securitised loan. The outcome of the benefit/risks analysis determines the accounting treatment, i.e. derecognition, linked presentation or separate presentation, whereby the gross value of the securitised asset is included with the assets in the balance sheet and the proceeds of the sale of loans with the creditors.

12.9.5 Loan transfers

A loan transfer occurs when one lender transfers an advance to a different lender. In addition to the balance sheet aspects of recognition and disclosure, there may be a profit or loss to be considered through the profit and loss account.

Loans are inherently applicable to the named parties in the individual contract. Consequently, such loans cannot be bought and sold in the same fashion as tangible assets. The whole process is a specialist area. Three types of arrangement may be identified: novation, assignment and subparticipation.

Novation

Novation means that a new contract with a new lender replaces the original contract, which is then cancelled. In effect, one creditor is substituted for another. The loan is removed from the balance sheet of the original lender and so are any residual obligations in favour of the borrower. Aspects of off-balance-sheet finance do not arise unless intervening side-arrangements have been contracted.

Assignment

Assignment means that rights to principal sum and interest, but not obligations, are transferred to a third party known as the assignee. There are two types of assignment:

● Statutory assignment may relate to the whole of the loan and must be given in writing to the borrower and other obligors (such as a guarantor).

● Equitable assignment may relate to only part of a loan and does not require notice being given to the borrower.

Under both types of assignment the borrower's rights under the original contract must not be prejudiced. Assignments may retain residual rights and obligations regarding other parties.

Subparticipation

Subparticipation means that rights and obligations are not transferred. The lender enters into a non-recourse, back-to-back agreement with a third party, the subparticipant. This subparticipant deposits a money amount, equal to the whole or a portion of the loan, with the lender in exchange for a share of the cash flows emanating from the borrower. The transaction raises the question of whether or not the deposit and the loan can be offset in the balance sheet to reveal only the net effect via a single asset caption.

What is the accounting treatment for loan transfers under FRS 5?

FRS 5 describes two critical tests to apply to determine the correct treatment for loan transfers:

1 Whether the original lender has access to significant benefits and exposure to risks regarding the loan or part transferred.

2 Whether the lender has a liability to repay the transfer.

If the original lender does not have access to the benefits in (1) and does not have a liability in (2), derecognition can be applied; otherwise linked presentation or separate presentation is appropriate.

The standard specifies the benefits and risks relating to loans and calls for specific disclosures when a linked presentation is adopted. Benefits are the future cash flows from payments of principal and interest. Risks include bad debts, slow payment and a change in the interest rate paid by the borrower which is not matched by a change in the rate paid to the transferee.

Disclosures where there is linked presentation are as follows:

● The main terms of the agreement.

● The gross amount of loans transferred and outstanding at the balance sheet date.

● The profit or loss recognised in the period, appropriately analysed.

● The directors of the entity must state explicitly in each set of financial statements using linked presentation that the entity is not obliged to support any losses, nor does it intend to do so.

● The provider of finance must give a written undertaking that repayment of the finance will be sought only to the extent that sufficient funds are generated by the specific item it has financed, and that it will not seek recourse otherwise.

12.10 FRS 4 *Capital Instruments*[8]

The introduction to FRS 4 draws attention to the rampant growth in the number, variety and complexity of capital instruments since the mid-1980s. A significant feature of such instruments has been the combination of equity and debt in a form of hybrid instrument, such as debt carrying the option of ultimate conversion into equity. This has led to an indistinct definition of shareholders' funds, which can confuse analysts and other users of the two primary financial statements. For example:

● Use of the gearing ratio to measure risk is jeopardised by the blurring of equity and debt.

● The proportion of total capital employed financed by shareholders becomes difficult to assess when debt is categorised with shares.

● Excluding the cost of servicing debt from the interest in the profit and loss account may mislead as to the cost of capital.

These factors may mean that the financial statements fail to give a true and fair view, and may cause a loss of confidence in the accountancy profession.

12.10.1 Aim of FRS 4

The prime aim of FRS 4 is to counter the growing confusion by standardising the definition of capital instruments and their presentation. Its stated threefold objective is to ensure the following:

● Financial statements provide a clear, coherent and consistent treatment of capital instruments, particularly in the classification of instruments as debt or equity.

● Costs associated with capital instruments are allocated to accounting periods on a fair basis over the period the instrument is in issue.

● Financial statements provide relevant information concerning the nature and amount of the entity's sources of finance and the associated costs, commitments and potential commitments.

12.10.2 Scope of FRS 4

The FRS is applicable to all reporting entities, irrespective of size or nature of ownership, which issue capital instruments and whose financial statements are intended to give a true and fair view.

It defines capital instruments as 'all instruments that are issued by reporting entities as a means of raising finance', and includes shares, debentures, loans and other debt instruments and options and warrants that give the holder the right to subscribe for or obtain capital instruments. It requires capital instruments to be categorised as shareholders' funds or liabilities. It provides that capital instruments are reportable as liabilities if they contain an obligation or contingent obligation to transfer economic benefits, and as shareholders' funds if they do not contain an obligation to transfer benefits.

12.10.3 Hybrid capital instruments and split accounting

The classification of capital instruments necessitates identification of the existence or non-existence of any **obligation to transfer economic benefits**. Instruments are described as hybrid when there is an element of equity, such as convertible debt. It could be argued that the instrument should be split into its component parts, but FRS 4, with certain exceptions, rejects this approach and insists that if obligation exists in any form then the instrument should be classified as debt. For example, convertible debt must be reported as a liability on the assumption that the debt will never be converted.

When is split accounting permissible?

Split accounting, such as the splitting of convertible debt into debt and the option to acquire shares, is permissible only if the constitutent parts of a hybrid instrument are able to be transferred, cancelled or redeemed independently of each other. Otherwise, the instrument must be classified as a single instrument.

12.10.4 Accounting treatment of debt instruments

There are two aspects to consider: the balance sheet treatment and the profit and loss account treatment.

The initial carrying value of the debt appearing in the balance sheet immediately following the issue should be the net proceeds, usually cash, received on issue less any issue costs attributable to the instrument. Such issue costs should be deferred and treated as a deduction from the carrying value of the debt. If the net proceeds received are not in cash form (being of non-monetary assets), an assessment of fair values of such assets will be necessary.

The carrying value of the debt appearing at subsequent accounting dates should be increased by finance costs attributable to the period less any portion of such costs remitted to the lender. Any accrued finance costs payable in the succeeding period may be excluded from the carrying value and treated as an accrued expense.

The finance costs will be debited in the profit and loss account. The finance cost of debt is the total payments to be incurred over the life-span of that debt less the initial carrying value. Such costs should be allocated to the profit and loss account over the life-term at a constant rate of interest based on the outstanding carrying value per period. If a debt is settled before maturity, any profit or loss should be reflected immediately in the profit and loss account – unless the substance of the settlement transaction fails to generate any change in liabilities and assets.

Illustration of the allocation of finance costs and the determination of carrying value

On 1 January 20X6 a company issued a debt instrument of £1,000,000 spanning a four-year term. It received from the lender £950,000, being the face value of the debt less a discount of £50,000. Interest was payable yearly in arrears at 8% per annum on the principal sum of £1,000,000. The principal sum was to be repaid on 31 December 20X9. The cost of issuing the instrument was £60,000.

To determine the yearly finance costs and year-end carrying value it is necessary to compute:

● the aggregate finance cost;
● the implicit rate of interest carried by the instrument;
● the finance charge per annum; and
● the carrying value at successive year-ends.

Figure 12.2 Allocation of finance costs and determination of carrying value.

	(i)		(ii) Finance charge to P&L a/c		(iii) Carrying value in balance sheet
	Cash flows £000		£000		£000
At 1 Jan 20X6	(890)	(1,000 – 50 – 60)	—		890
At 31 Dec 20X6	80	(8% × 100)	103.2	(11.59% × 890)	913.2
At 31 Dec 20X7	80	(8% × 100)	105.8	(11.59% × 913.2)	939.2
At 31 Dec 20X8	80	(8% × 100)	108.8	(11.59% × 939)	967.8
At 31 Dec 20X9	1,080	(8% × 100)	112.2	(11.59% × 967.8)	—
Net cash flow	430		= Cost	430	

Aggregate finance cost

This is the difference between the total future payments of interest plus principal, less the net proceeds received less costs of the issue, i.e. £430,000 in column (i) of Figure 12.2.

Implicit rate of interest carried by the instrument

This can be computed by using the net present value (NPV) formula:

$$\sum_{t=1}^{t=n} \frac{At}{(1+r)^t} - I = 0$$

where A is forecast net cash flow in year A, t time (in years), n the life-span of the debt in years, r the company's annual rate of discount and I the initial net proceeds less the cost of issue. Note that the application of this formula can be quite time-consuming. A reasonable method of assessment is by interpolation of the interest rate.

The aggregate formula given above may be disaggregated for calculation purposes:

$$\sum_{t=1}^{t=n} \frac{A1}{(1+r)^1} + \frac{A2}{(1+r)^2} + \frac{A3}{(1+r)^3} + \frac{A4}{(1+r)^4} - I = 0$$

Using the data concerning the debt and assuming (allowing for discount and costs) an implicit constant rate of, say, 11%:

$$\Sigma = \frac{80,000}{(1.11)^1} + \frac{80,000}{(1.11)^2} + \frac{80,000}{(1.11)^3} + \frac{1,080,000}{(1.11)^4} - 890,000 = 0$$

$$= 72,072 + 64,930 + 58,495 + 711,429 - 890,000 = +16,926$$

The chosen implicit rate of 11% is too low. We now choose a higher rate, say 12%:

$$\Sigma = \frac{80,000}{(1.12)^1} + \frac{80,000}{(1.12)^2} + \frac{80,000}{(1.12)^3} + \frac{1,080,000}{(1.12)^4} - 890,000 = 0$$

$$= 71,429 + 63,776 + 56,942 + 686,360 - 890,000 = -11,493$$

This rate is too high, resulting in a negative net present value. Interpolation will enable us to arrive at an implicit rate:

$$11\% + \left[\frac{16,926}{16,926+11,493} \times 12\% - 11\% \right]$$

$$= 11\% + 0.59\% = 11.59\%$$

Figure 17.2 shows the entries for each year 20X6–20X9.

This is a trial and error method of determining the implicit interest rate. In this example the choice of rates, 11% and 12%, constituted a change of only 1%. It would be possible to choose, say, 11% and then 14%, generating a 3% gap within which to interpolate. This wider margin would result in a less accurate implicit rate and an aggregate interest charge at variance with the desired £430,000 of column (ii). The aim is to choose interest rates as close as possible to either side of the monetary zero, so that the exact implicit rate may be computed.

The object is to determine an NPV of zero monetary units, i.e. to identify the discount rate that will enable the aggregate future discounted net flows to equate to the initial net proceeds from the debt instrument. In the above illustration, a discount (interest) rate of 11.59% enables £430,000 to be charged to the profit and loss account after allowing for payment of all interest, costs and repayment of the face value of the instrument.

12.11 FRS 4 application notes

There are various capital instruments. Some are explained in FRS 4 and we consider them below.

Auction market preferred shares (AMPS)

These are shares whereby a fixed rate of annual dividend is determined by an auction process involving a panel of investors. The investor, invariably an investing institution, bidding to accept the lowest rate of dividend will succeed in obtaining the shares. If the auction process fails – perhaps owing to a lack of bids – the original anticipated dividend will be increased to a rate prescribed by formula. This increase is known as a default rate.

AMPS are shares in receipt of dividends payable from distributable profits. They can be redeemed only out of such profits or out of the proceeds of a fresh issue of shares. Thus because redemption rights and amounts are restricted, and dividend rights limited, there is no obligation to transfer economic benefits. These shares are non-equity shares reportable as shareholders' funds, the finance cost being the dividend rights accruing per period.

Participating preference shares

These are shares with preferential rights to dividend of a fixed amount but which, in addition, carry an entitlement to extra dividend based on a proportion of the dividends paid to equity shares. The shares' participation in profits is restricted and they carry priority rights against other classes of share: they are non–equity shares and must be classed as such in shareholders' funds.

The important aspect to appreciate in classifying AMPS and participating preference shares (and, indeed, other shares carrying preferential rights) is that:

● they must be classified as shareholders' funds in accordance with the Companies Act and FRS 4 rules; and

● within shareholders' funds, they must be subclassified as non-equity. They are obviously not debt, thus not liabilities.

However, when considering an entity's capital structure and computing the gearing ratio, both should be included with debt for comparison with equity in order to measure the element of risk carried by the equity shareholders.

Perpetual debt

This arises when the capital instrument conveys no right or obligation on the part of the issuer to repay the principal sum of the debt. Interest is often at a fixed rate or at a fixed margin above a benchmark, such as the banks' base rate. An example of perpetual debt is irredeemable debentures. Invariably such debt is a marketable commodity bought and sold on the international stock exchange, so that the individual investor is able to recoup the market value of the loan at will.

There is an argument that, because such debt is irredeemable, it need not be recorded on the balance sheet of the issuing company. However, this would make the gearing measure misleading.

The standard mandates the reporting of the debt on successive balance sheets. The annual servicing charge must be shown in the profit and loss account. Because such interest will not reduce the carrying amount of the debt, the debt should continue to be reported at the amount of the net proceeds received. The substance of the original transaction must continue to take precedence over its legal form.

Repackaged perpetual debt

This is debt that often carries an abnormally high rate of fixed interest for a set number of years. This interest then reduces to zero or to a nominal rate. The debt is irredeemable, but its value, after the expiry of the primary period of high interest, is negligible. In substance the high servicing cost has redeemed the loan. In practice, an arrangement ensues whereby the debt is transferred to a friendly third party, which arranges with the issuing entity to redeem the loan for a token amount.

EXAMPLE ● This example necessitates the use of the NPV formula, and the trial and error process, in computing the annual finance charge. As most practical versions of repackaged perpetual debt cover extensive periods of time (perhaps ten years or more), the example features an unusually short life-span and very high interest rate in order to reduce the arithmetic workload in computing the percentage finance charge. These unrealistic theoretical features do not dilute the validity of the exercise.

PPD Ltd borrowed £1,000 on 1 January 20X6. The debt is said to be irredeemable. An interest rate of 40% per annum (i.e. £400 per year) is payable for four years. The debt incurs no further interest after the lapse of the four-year span.

The finance charge to be shown in the profit and loss account, together with the carrying value of the debt instrument in successive balance sheets, are computed as follows.

Calculating using a 20% p.a. rate (variables as defined in section 17.11 above):

$$\sum_{t=1}^{t=n} \frac{At}{(1+r)^t} - I = 0$$

$$\Sigma = \frac{400}{(1.2)^1} + \frac{400}{(1.2)^2} + \frac{400}{(1.2)^3} + \frac{400}{(1.2)^4} - 1,000 = +35$$

Recalculating using 22% p.a.:

$$\Sigma = \frac{400}{(1.22)^1} + \frac{400}{(1.22)^2} + \frac{400}{(1.22)^3} + \frac{400}{(1.22)^4} - 100{,}000 = -2$$

For the amount of –£2 involved it hardly seems worth interpolating. For simplicity the illustration only deals in small figures, but in practice millions of pounds may be involved and interpolation would be essential.

Interpolation:

$$20\% + \left(\frac{35}{37} \times 2\%\right) = 21.89\%$$

Figure 12.3 shows the entries for each year.

Figure 12.3   Repackaged perpetual debt.

	(i)	(ii)	(iii)
		Finance charge	Carrying value in
	Cash flows	to P&L a/c	balance sheet
	£	£	£
At 1 Jan year 1	(1,000)		1,000
At 31 Dec year 1	400	219	819
At 31 Dec year 2	400	179	598
At 31 Dec year 3	400	131	329
At 31 Dec year 4	400	71[a]	—
Net cash flow	600 = Cost	600	

[a] Reduced by rounding error of £1.

FRS 4 provides that repackaged perpetual debt is a liability and must appear on the balance sheet until the zero or notional rate of interest emerges. Meanwhile, in the profit and loss account the finance charge is calculated at a constant rate on the amount outstanding.

Stepped interest bonds

Stepped interest bonds are bonds with a varying pattern of yearly interest, usually stepped upwards, so that low rates in the early years are compensated by high rates in the later years of the loan.

EXAMPLE ● SIB Ltd borrowed £1,000 on 1 January 20X5. It was arranged that interest of 7% in 20X6 would be stepped up by 2% over successive years, making 9%, 11%, 13% and 15% over years 20X6, 20X7, 20X8 and 20X9 respectively. The rates were to apply to the principal sum borrowed.

Solution using the NPV formula (variables as defined in section 17.11 above):

$$\sum_{t=1}^{t=n} \frac{A}{(1+r)^2} - \text{Investment} = 0$$

Trying first 10% then 11% produced the following:

$$\text{At 10\%: } \frac{70}{(1.1)^1} + \frac{90}{(1.1)^2} + \frac{110}{(1.1)^3} + \frac{130}{(1.1)^4} + \frac{1,150}{(1.1)^5} - 1,000$$

NPV = +£24

$$\text{At 11\%: } \frac{70}{(1.11)^1} + \frac{90}{(1.11)^2} + \frac{110}{(1.11)^3} + \frac{130}{(1.11)^4} + \frac{1,150}{(1.11)^5} - 1,000$$

NPV = –£16

By interpolation:

$$10\% + \left(\frac{24}{40} \text{ of } 1\% \right) = 10.6\%$$

Figure 12.4 shows the finance charge and carrying value per year throughout the time-span of the loan.

Figure 12.4 Stepped interest bonds.

	(i) Cash flows £		(ii) Finance charge to P&L a/c £	(iii) Carrying value in balance sheet £
At 1 Jan 20X5	(1,000)			1,000
At 31 Dec 20X5	70	(7% × 1,000)	106 (10.6% × 1,000)	1,036
At 31 Dec 20X6	90	(9% × 1,000)	110 (10.6% × 1,036)	1,056
At 31 Dec 20X7	110	(11% × 1,000)	112 (10.8% × 1,056)	1,058
At 31 Dec 20X8	130	(13% × 1,000)	112 (10.6% × 1,058)	1,040
At 31 Dec 20X9	150	(15% × 1,000)	110 (+ cash 1,000)	—
Net cash flow	550	= Cost	550	

Deep discount bonds

Deep discount bonds are another version of variable rate capital instrument. They are usually issued at a discount against their face value and on redemption this face value sum is paid. In the meantime a low annual coupon rate of interest is payable on the bond. In some cases the instruments are free of annual interest and are often referred to as zero coupon bonds. The total cost to the borrower is that of discount on issue plus any yearly interest payment. In accordance with FRS 4, the costs should be spread by using constant rate on the carrying value of the bond. The discount must not be treated as an asset.

The illustration in Figure 17.2, showing the calculation of finance charges and carrying values, is identical to that of a deep discount bond.

Index-linked loans

These agreements may utilise a fixed formula for computing the servicing cost rather than carry a specific interest rate. A base rate may be part of the formula, such as LIBOR + 3%. Alternatively, index linking may be applied in conjunction with the annual interest rate to calculate the redemption principal sum.

A cardinal feature of index-linked borrowings is that finance costs contingent upon uncertain events, such as movements in a price index, should be adjusted to reflect those events only after they have occurred. The carrying value at each balance sheet date will need to be recomputed to reflect changes that have taken place during the accounting period concerned. The change between opening and closing carrying values will be treated as an increase or decrease in finance costs per period (FRS 4, para. 31).

EXAMPLE ● ILL Ltd issued an index-linked bond for £1,000 on 1 January 20X5. The bond was to bear interest at 5% p.a. for five years. At the end of the five-year term, the principal sum was to be repaid in accordance with a price index. The index movements measured at the end of years 1 to 5 were 108, 111, 117, 124 and 131 respectively. The index at 1 January 20X5 was 100.

We need to compute the finance charge chargeable to the profit and loss account, the carrying value in each successive year's balance sheet (see Figure 12.5) and the redemption principal payable at the end of 20X9.

Figure 12.5 Index-linked bonds.

	(i) Cash flow £	Index	(ii) Finance charge in P&L a/c £	(iii) Carrying value in balance sheet £
At 1 Jan 20X5	(1,000)	100	(1,000)	
At 3 Dec 20X5	50 (5% × 1,000)	108	130 (1,080 – 1,000 + 50)	1,080
At 31 Dec 20X6	50 (5% × 1,000)	111	80 (1,110 – 1,080 + 50)	1,110
At 31 Dec 20X7	50 (5% × 1,000)	117	110 (1,170 – 1,110 + 50)	1,170
At 31 Dec 20X8	50 (5% × 1,000)	124	120 (1,240 – 1,170 + 50)	1,240
At 31 Dec 20X9	50 (5% × 1,000)	131	120 (1,310 – 1,240 + 50)	—
			Cost = 560	

The redemption principal at 31 December 20X9 will be:

$$1,000 \times \frac{131}{100} = £1,310$$

The total sum payable on that day will be £1,360 inclusive of £50 interest.

Subordinated debt

This is debt under which the lender's rights rank lower than the rights of other creditors of the issuing entity. This usually means that repayment of the subordinated debt is subject to specified conditions aimed at protecting other creditors. Such conditions vary considerably: they might embrace all other creditors, or just other loan creditors, or perhaps only one or two types of loan creditor. The aim is to ensure that repayment of the subordinated stock is subjected to prohibition until the priority creditors have been reimbursed.

The accounting treatment of FRS 4 demands that subordinated debt be classified as a liability, which of course it is, but that in addition the balance sheet should disclose by way of note the nature of the subordination.

Convertible loan stock

This is debt that carries the right of convertibility into shares at some specified future date. It can take many forms, e.g. it may carry a fixed interest rate, a stepped rate or a zero rate, and conversion may be optional or mandatory. Compensation to the lender lies in a compound of obligations by the issuer, e.g. in the interest rate, the conversion terms and the discount at issue (if any). The fundamental characteristic of such stock is its **convertibility into shares**, invariably ordinary shares, but sometimes preference shares. Because the stock carries a **shareholder content**, it is a hybrid instrument. It should not be split between shareholder funds and liabilities unless its constituent parts are able to be transferred independently of each other. In practice, most convertible instruments will be non-splitting. The payment of interest is an obligation and, as an obligation equates with liability, the instrument should be classified as a liability. Although the conversion is for the future and, if optional, may not occur, the obligation to pay interest exists.

EXAMPLE ● CLS Ltd issued £1,000 of 10% convertible loan stock on 1 January 20X5. The stock was convertible into ordinary shares on 31 December 20X5 at the rate of five £1 ordinary shares for every £10 of convertible loan stock. Alternatively the lender would receive cash to the nominal value of the loan stock held. The market price of the shares on 31 December 20X9 was £2.50 per share. All the stock was converted.

The finance charge and carrying value of the stock over each of the five years is shown in Figure 12.6. Note the following:

● The finance charge is identical to the fixed interest payable per annum because it is a constant rate on the amount of the loan outstanding. If stepped interest had been involved and/or a discount on issue, the finance charge would have necessitated use of the NPV formula.

Figure 12.6 Convertible loan stock.

	(i) Cash flow	(ii) Finance charge P&L a/c	(iii) Balance sheet carrying value		
			Convertible liability	Issued capital nominal	Share premium
	£	£	£	£	£
At 1 Jan 20X5	(1,000)		1,000		
At 31 Dec 20X5	100	100	1,000		
At 31 Dec 20X6	100	100	1,000		
At 31 Dec 20X7	100	100	1,000		
At 31 Dec 20X8	100	100	—	500	500
		Cost 400			

- The proceeds of the shares issued on conversion are deemed to be the carrying value of the instrument at the date of conversion. Consequently, no gain or loss can arise in conversion. The market value is irrelevant in terms of accounting treatment, even though it is the motivating factor inducing conversion, i.e. shares worth an aggregate of £1,250 (500 × £2.50) as against a cash option on redemption of £1,000.

- The issue of 500 shares at a market value of £1,250 does not merit recognition of £250 loss because such loss was not incurred. The proceeds for the shares were, in effect, received in advance, i.e. on the issue date of the loan stock.

- Then again, such a loss could not be estimated throughout the life of the loan and spread (via the NPV formula) as part of the finance cost because convertibility was not certain. This lack of certainty is due to the volatility of share prices.

- If the share price had fallen to £2 or below, the conversion would probably not have taken place. Redemption would have been for cash of £1,000. At a price of £2.50 the lenders have gained £250 profit, but it is realisable only by selling the shares at the market price.

Illustration of convertible carrying zero interest and mandatory conversion

CLS plc issued £1,000 of convertible loan stock on 1 January 20X5. The instrument does not pay a coupon rate and is mandatorily convertible into ordinary shares at 31 December 20X9 at a rate of seven £1 ordinary shares for every £10 of loan stock.

Since no interest is payable, there is no obligation to transfer economic benefits. Hence the constituent element of conversion is the dominant characteristic – there is no liability element. **The lender is induced** to lend on the basis of compensatory conversion rights attached to the instrument, i.e. an attractive exchange of debt for shares compared with the share price at the time of the loan issue. The benefit to the company is that capital has been obtained by loan rather than shares, so that dilution of shareholders' interest has been postponed. The loan money is tantamount to the purchase of a fully paid warrant to acquire shares at a specified future date. In **substance** the transaction is one of shares in the **form** of debt.

Under FRS 4 this capital instrument should be classified as shareholders' funds, sub-analysed as equity interest. On 1 January 20X5 the equity interest should be recorded at an increase of £1,000, i.e. the net proceeds of the loan issue. FRS 4 is silent regarding which reserve in shareholders' funds should be credited with the proceeds. It might be considered prudent to include them in a separate capital reserve. Bearing in mind that conversion is mandatory, the equity interest concerned, £1,000, will be reclassified from capital reserve to:

	£
Ordinary shares of £1, at issue	+700
Share premium	+300

12.11.1 What other disclosures are required for capital instruments?

FRS 4 lays down a number of detailed requirements regarding disclosure, but its main concern is categorisation in the balance sheet. This consists of the threefold analysis of shareholders' funds, minority interests and liabilities. Within each category a sub-analysis is mandated as follows:

Category	Sub-analysed
Shareholders' funds	Equity interests
	Non-equity interests
Minority interests in subsidiaries	Equity interests in subsidiaries
	Non-equity interests in subsidiaries
Liabilities	Convertible liabilities
	Non-convertible liabilities

The object of the disclosure is to enable risk associated with gearing to be more readily assessed.

12.12 Balance sheet as valuation document

Another evolutionary feature of the modern balance sheet is its increasing tendency to be perceived as a valuation document. The traditional balance sheet was seen as a form of second trial balance, i.e. a statement listing economic benefits still to come, unused expenditures of earlier accounting periods, prepayments, obligations not yet discharged, unsettled accounts, and accruals.

The main motives for the change in perception are to report the financial strengths of an entity and to allow an assessment of risk by extracting appropriate ratios, such as gearing and net asset cover. We have already discussed the gearing ratio and will now discuss net asset cover.

12.12.1 Net asset cover

Net asset cover compares the current market price of a company's equity share with the value of underlying net assets attributable to that share as revealed by the entity's most recent published balance sheet.

EXAMPLE ● Each of NAC plc's 25p fully paid ordinary shares has a current middle market price of 80p on 31 January 20X7. Its summarised balance sheet as at 31 December 20X6 is shown in Figure 12.7.

Figure 12.7 Balance sheet to determine net asset cover.

	£	£
Fixed assets		1,100
Current assets	300	
Less: Current liabilities	(100)	
Net current assets		200
Total assets less current liabilities		1,300
10% Debentures		200
		1,100
Capital and reserves:		
Ordinary shares of 25p fully paid		600
6% Preference shares of £1 fully paid		200
Reserves		300
		1,100

Two methods – the micro and macro – may be used to compute the net asset cover, but the formula is:

$$\frac{\text{Net assets per equity share}}{\text{Current market price per equity share}}$$

NAC plc's net assets attributable to the equity shares are £900. The computations of net asset cover are, then:

(i) Micro method: $\dfrac{£900/2400}{80\text{p}} = 47:1$ or 47%

(ii) Macro method: $\dfrac{£900}{80\text{p} \times 2400} = 47:1$ or 47%

What does the ratio reveal?

In NAC's case, the ratio reveals that the current market price per share of 80p is represented by assets of 37.5p, i.e. the price is covered by 47% in the form of net assets. Thus, it may be argued, if the company is forced into liquidation, the equity holders will receive some 47% of the current market price. It pretends to reveal the extent of the **safety net** underpinning the current share price by assuming the following:

● The net asset carrying value in the balance sheet is a current market price value and all assets in the balance sheet will be saleable, even in a piecemeal situation.

● The aggregate values will be received after allowing for liquidation expenses.

● The share price is inclined to be static.

In order to differentiate the quality or realisability of individual assets, assets such as goodwill, copyright and patents were often deducted in arriving at the net assets applicable to each ordinary share. In other words, the safety net was seen to consist only of tangible assets; but not all city analysts applied such rules.

Is the ratio any use?

Yes, as long as we appreciate that the inherent assumptions may be questionable and that it is a very rough measurement of risk in a capital market where share prices are volatile and where balance sheet data may not be representative of market values. Fundamentally, it is a basis for comparison between like companies in the same industry. It is subjective and considerable care must be applied in the assessment using this ratio.

In spite of its shortcomings, management perceives that the balance sheet is used as a risk measure. Management attention is therefore often given to strengthening the balance sheet. For example, assets may be revalued to improve the apparent asset cover.

12.13 Why companies take steps to strengthen their balance sheet

One of several reasons is management's belief that the gearing ratio is important, and that it can be improved by increasing equity reserves as a consequence of revaluing existing assets in the balance sheet. The revaluation can have an effect on the gearing ratio and earnings per share (EPS).

12.13.1 Gearing ratio improved

In addition to revaluing the book values of assets appearing in the balance sheet, companies may introduce assets into the balance sheet. For example, brand accounting is a system of asset creation designed to bolster the net worth of the entity, and was adopted by a number of major companies during the late 1980s. It caused major concern throughout the accountancy profession because it violated the transaction basis of traditional accountancy reporting; valuation was extremely subjective and it was thought that a brand was too ephemeral to be recorded as an asset.

12.13.2 EPS improved

Earnings per share may be improved by the method chosen to eliminate assets. For example, a company may wish to create reserves, perhaps for use in a capitalisation issue, but more often for the purpose of writing off rather than amortising goodwill. If amortisation can be avoided, profits will be higher than otherwise and EPS may avoid a decline; hence the share price might be maintained.

12.13.3 Commercial pressures to revalue

Pressure on management to strengthen the balance sheet is often associated with a perceived commercial benefit from doing so. Strengthening might be undertaken to frustrate a potential take-over, either real or anticipated. A company experiencing or expecting a hostile bid may revalue its assets to improve the interpretation of its balance sheet and so influence its equity share price. The management may feel that the current price is too low and consequently attractive to a would-be predator. Thus revaluation becomes part of an attempt to make shareholders believe that the current share price does not reflect the true worth of the entity; hence the bidder's offer price is not adequate.

Strengthening might also be undertaken to support a potential takeover bid. A predator might try to improve its own balance sheet to encourage shareholders of the target company to accept its offer. Such an offer invariably embraces an exchange of shares between target company shareholders and the bidder.

We saw in earlier chapters that there have been proposals to reflect current values in the balance sheet by implementing a coherent price-level model to adjust the historic carrying amounts. To date, these proposals have not been adopted and historic values, with some modification, still appear in the balance sheet.

12.14 Definitions cannot remove uncertainty: SSAP 17 and FRS 12

We have seen that the ASB has issued standards to help determine the nature of a transaction, by defining assets and liabilities and requiring the substance of commercial transactions to be reflected in the accounts. However, there are times when the nature of the transaction is clear, but the events have not crystallised to the extent that the effect on the accounts is certain. There has to be an estimate and this requires the directors to exercise judgement.

The ASC had already issued standards in two areas: SSAP 17 *Accounting for Post Balance Sheet Events* and SSAP 18 *Accounting for Contingencies*, both issued in 1980. SSAP 18 has now been superseded by FRS 12.

12.14.1 SSAP 17 Accounting for Post Balance Sheet Events

SSAP 17 requires financial statements to reflect the conditions that existed at the balance sheet date. There is a period of perhaps two months after the year-end before the accounts are signed by the directors and auditors, and information that becomes available during that period should be appraised to determine whether the accounts need to be adjusted.

Adjusting events

If information becomes available during this period that gives further evidence of the conditions that existed **at the balance sheet date**, it is described as an **adjusting event** and, if it is **material**, will require changes in the amounts to be included in the financial statements. Examples are the subsequent determination of the purchase price or proceeds of sale of fixed assets sold before the year-end, and a valuation of property that provides evidence of a permanent diminution in value. The standard also deals with the valuation of stock in assessing its value at the balance sheet date. It states that there is a presumption that the sale proceeds of stock realised after the balance sheet date represent the realisable value at the balance sheet date, unless there is objective evidence that he decline occurred as a result of conditions which did not exist at the balance sheet date.

Non-adjusting events

Non-adjusting events are post balance sheet events which concern conditions that did not exist at the balance sheet date, but which are **so material** that non-disclosure would affect the ability of the users of financial statements to reach a proper understanding of the financial position. These events are required to be disclosed by way of note. The following is an extract from the 1999 Annual Report of Manchester United:

> **Post balance sheet events**
> Since the year end the football registrations of Massimo Taibi (from AC Venezia), Mikael Silvestre (from Inter Milan) and Quinton Fortune (from Athletico Madrid) have been acquired for a total cost, including related expenses, of £11.3 million.

Other examples given in SSAP 17, para. 31, include the purchase or sale of fixed assets, opening new trading activities and closing existing activities.

12.14.2 FRS 12 Provisions, Contingent Liabilities and Contingent Assets[9]

The ASB published FRS 12 in September 1998. The FRS was based on FRED 14 *Provisions and Contingencies* and superseded SSAP 18 *Accounting for Contingencies*. The key objective of FRS 12 is to ensure that appropriate recognition criteria and measurement bases are applied and that sufficient information is disclosed in the notes to enable users to understand their nature, timing and amount.

The FRS sets out a useful **decision tree** for determining whether an event requires the creation of a provision, the disclosure of a contingent liability or no action.

Decision tree

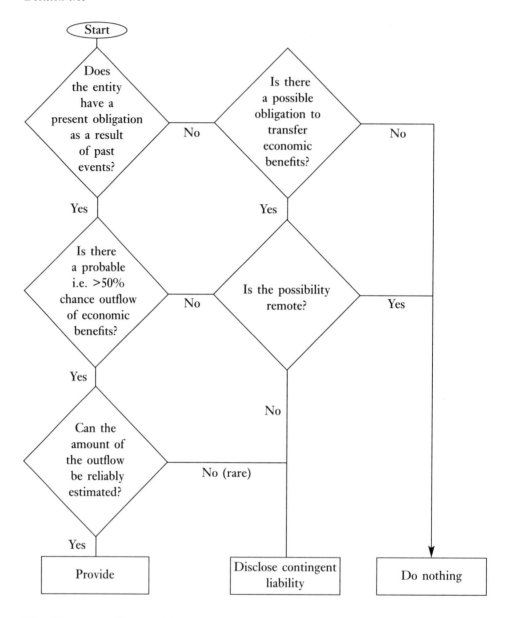

We will now consider provisions, contingent liabilities and contingent assets.

12.14.3 Provisions

The FRS is mainly concerned with provisions which it defines as 'Liabilities in respect of which the amount or timing of the expenditure that will be undertaken is uncertain'.

In particular it targets 'big bath' provisions that companies have been able to make. These are the type of provisions that it has been tempting for directors to make in order to smooth profits without any reasonable certainty that the provision would actually be required in subsequent periods. Sir David Tweedie has said:

A main focus of FRED 14 is 'big-bath' provisions. Those who use them sometimes pray in aid the concept of prudence. All too often however the provision is wildly excessive and conveniently finds its way back to the profit and loss account in a later period. The misleading practice needs to be stopped and FRED 14 proposes that in future provisions should only be allowed when the company has an unavoidable obligation – an **intention** which may or may not be fulfilled will **not be enough**. Users of accounts can't be expected to be mind readers.

12.14.4 What are the general principles that FRS 12 applies to the *recognition* of a provision?

The general principles are that a provision should be recognised when:[10]

(a) an entity has a **present obligation** (legal or constructive) **as a result of past events**;

(b) it is **probable** that a transfer of **economic benefits will be required to settle the obligation**;

(c) **a reliable estimate** can be made of the amount of the obligation.

Provisions by their nature relate to the future. This means that there is a need for estimation and FRS 12 comments[11] that **the use of estimates is an essential part of the preparation of financial statements and does not undermine their reliability**.

The FRS addresses the uncertainties arising in respect of present obligation, past event, probable transfer of economic benefits and reliable estimates when deciding whether to recognise a provision.

Present obligation

The test to be applied is whether it is more likely than not i.e. more than a 50% chance of occurring. For example, if involved in a disputed lawsuit, the company is required to take account of all available evidence including that of experts and of post balance sheet events to decide if there is a greater than 50% chance that the lawsuit will be decided against the company.

Where it is more likely that no present obligation exists at the balance sheet date, the company discloses a contingent liability, unless the possibility of a transfer of economic resources is remote.

Past event[12]

A past event that leads to a present obligation is called an **obligating event**. This is a new term with which to become familiar. This means that the company has no realistic alternative to settling the obligation. The FRS defines no alternative as being only where the settlement of the obligation can be enforced by law or in the case of a constructive obligation, where the event creates valid expectations in other parties that the company will discharge the obligation.

The FRS stresses that it is only those obligations arising from past events existing independently of a company's future actions that are recognised as provisions e.g. clean-up costs for unlawful environmental damage that has occurred require a provision; environmental damage that is not unlawful but is likely to become so and involve clean-up costs will not be provided for until legislation is virtually certain to be enacted as drafted.

Probable transfer of economic benefits[13]

The FRS defines probable as meaning that the event is more likely than not to occur. Where it is not probable the company discloses a contingent liability unless the possibility is remote.

12.14.5 What are the general principles that FRS 12 applies to the *measurement* of a provision?

FRS 12 states[14] that the amount recognised as a provision should the *best estimate* of the expenditure required to settle the present obligation at the balance sheet date.

Best estimate is defined as the amount that a company would rationally pay to settle the obligation or to transfer it to a third party. The estimates of outcome and financial effect are determined by the judgement of management supplemented by experience of similar transactions and reports from independent experts. Management deal with the uncertainties as to the amount to be provided in a number of ways:

● A class obligation exists
 – where the provision involves a large population of items such as a warranty provision statistical analysis of expected values should be used to determine the amount of the provision.

● A single obligation exists
 – where a single obligation is being measured the individual most likely outcome may be the best estimate;
 – however, there may be other outcomes that are significantly higher or lower indicating that expected values should be determined.

Management must avoid creation of excessive provisions based on a prudent view:

● Uncertainty does not justify the creation of excessive provisions[15]
 – if the projected costs of a particular adverse outcome are estimated on a prudent basis that outcome should not then be deliberately treated as more probable than is realistically the case.

The FRS states[16] that **where the effect of the time value of money is material, the amount of a provision should be the present value of the expenditures expected to be required to settle the obligation.**

Present value is arrived at by:

● using pre-tax cash flows and a discount rate that will, after deduction of tax, give the required post-tax rate of return;

● where the estimated cash flows required to meet the obligation have not been risk-adjusted, at a discount rate adjusted for the risks specific to the obligation;

● where the estimated future cash outflow has been risk-adjusted, a risk-free rate should be used;

● if the cash flows to be discounted are expressed in current prices, a real discount rate should be used;

● if the cash flows are in terms of expected future prices, a nominal discount rate should be used;

● as the settlement date approaches, the carrying value of the provision should be increased.

12.14.6 Application of criteria illustrated

Scenario 1

An offshore oil exploration company is required by its licence to remove the rig and restore the seabed. Management have estimated that 85% of the eventual cost will be incurred in removing the rig and 15% through the extraction of oil. The company's practice on similar projects has been to account for the decommissioning costs using the 'unit of production' method whereby the amount required for decommissioning was built up year by year, in line with production levels, to reach the amount of the expected costs by the time production ceased.

Decision process

1 Is there a present obligation as a result of a past event?
The construction of the rig has created a legal obligation under the licence to remove the rig and restore the seabed.

2 Is there a probable transfer of economic benefits?
This is probable.

3 Can the amount of the outflow be reasonably estimated?
A best estimate can be made by management based on past experience and expert advice.

4 Conclusion
A provision should be created of 85% of the eventual future costs of removal and restoration.
This provision should be discounted if the effect of the time value of money is material.
A provision for the 15% relating to restoration should be created when oil production commences.
The unit of production method is not acceptable in that the decomissioning costs relate to damage already done.

Scenario 2

A company has a private jet costing £24m. Air regulations required it to be overhauled every four years. An overhaul cost £1.6m. The company policy has been to create a provision for depreciation of £2m on a straightline basis over 12 years and an annual provision of £400,000 to meet the cost of the required overhaul every 4 years.

Decision process

1 Is there a present obligation as a result of a past obligating event?
There is no present obligation. The company could avoid the cost of the overhaul by, for example, selling the aircraft.

2 Conclusion
No provision for cost of overhaul can be recognised. Instead of a provision being recognised, the depreciation of the aircraft takes account of the future incidence of maintenance costs i.e. an amount equivalent to the expected maintenance costs is depreciated over 4 years.

12.14.7 Disclosures

Specific disclosures,[17] for each material class of provision, should be given as to the amount recognised at the year-end and about any movements in the year e.g.

- **Increases in provisions** – any new provisions; any increases to existing provisions; and, where provisions are carried at present value, any change in value arising from the passage of time or from any movement in the discount rate.

- **Reductions in provisions** – any amounts utilised during the period; management are required to review provisions at each balance sheet date and
  - adjust to reflect the current best estimates; and
  - if it is no longer probable that a transfer of economic benefits will be required to settle the obligation, the provision should be reversed.

Disclosures need not be given in cases where to do so would be seriously prejudicial to the company's interests.

In practice, this would mean that:

- **A provision for future operating losses** should not be recognised (unless under a contractual obligation) **because there is no obligation at the date of the balance sheet**. However, where a contract becomes onerous i.e. where it becomes more costly to fulfil or avoid a contract than the associated revenues the company could derive from it and cannot be avoided, then a provision should be made.

    This can be contrasted to cases where a company supplies a product as a loss leader to gain a foothold in the market. In the latter case, the company may cease production at any time. Accordingly, no provision should be recognised as no obligation exists.

- **A provision for restructuring** should only be recognised when there is a commitment supported by
  (a) a detailed formal plan for the restructuring identifying at least:
      (i) the business or part of the business concerned;
      (ii) the principal locations affected;
      (iii) details of the approximate number of employees who will receive compensation payments;
      (iv) the expenditure that will be undertaken; and
      (v) when the plan will be implemented; and
  (b) has raised a valid expectation in those affected that it will carry out the restructuring by implementing its restructuring plans or announcing its main features to those affected by it.

- **A provision for restructuring should not be created merely on the intention to restructure**. For example, a management or board decision to restructure taken before the balance sheet date does not give rise to a constructive obligation at the balance sheet date unless the company has, before the balance sheet date:
  - started to implement the restructuring plan e.g. dismantling plant or selling assets;
  - announced the main features of the plan with sufficient detail to raise the valid expectation of those affected that the restructuring will actually take place.

- **A provision for restructuring** should only include the direct expenditures arising from the restructuring which are necessarily entailed and not associated with the ongoing activities of the company. For example, the following costs which relate to the future conduct of the business are not included:
  - retraining costs; relocation costs; marketing costs; investment in new systems and distribution networks.

● **A provision for environmental liabilities** should be recognised at the time and to the extent that the entity becomes obliged, legally or constructively, to rectify environmental damage or to perform restorative work on the environment. This means that a provision should be set up only for the entity's costs to meet its *legal* obligations. It could be argued that any provision for any additional expenditure on environmental issues is a public relations decision and should be written off.

● **A provision for decomissioning costs** should be recognised to the extent that decomissioning costs relate to damage already done or goods and services already received.

The last point may require a change of accounting policy in the way in which companies provide for restoration costs. Gold Mines of Sardinia Ltd, an Australian company listed on the Alternative Issues Market in the UK, stated in its accounting policies in the 1997 accounts:

> *Restoration costs*
> Restoration costs that are expected to be incurred are provided for as a part of the exploration, evaluation, development, construction or production phases that give rise to the need for restoration. Accordingly, these costs are recognised gradually over the life of the facility as these phases occur. The costs include obligations relating to reclamation, waste site closure, plant closure, platform removal and other costs associated with the restoration of the site. These estimates of the restoration obligations are based on anticipated technology and **legal** requirements and future costs, which have been **discounted to their present value**.

It would appear that the company is applying the units of production method in respect of restoration costs.

12.14.8 The use of provisions

Only expenditures that relate to the original provision are to be set against it because to set expenditures against a provision that was originally recognised for another purpose would conceal the impact of two different events.

12.14.9 Tax treatment moves closer to accounting practice

The Revenue now accepts that provisions made under FRS 12 are tax-deductible except where there remain specific tax rules to the contrary. The change has arisen because it is recognised that under FRS 12 provisions are only made where a business expects to pay out money in the future and has taken that *probable* expense into account when calculating its profits.

12.14.10 Contingent liabilities

FRS 12 deals with provisions and contingent liabilities within the same FRS because the ASB regards all provisions as contingent because they are uncertain in timing and amount. For the purposes of the accounts, it distinguishes between provisions and contingent liabilities in that:

● Provisions are a present obligation requiring a probable transfer of economic benefits that can be reliably estimated – a provision can therefore be recognised as a liability.

● Contingent liabilities fail to satisfy these criteria e.g. lack of a reliable estimate of the amount; not probable that there will be a transfer of economic benefits; yet to be confirmed that there is actually an obligation – a contingent liability cannot therefore be recognised in the accounts but may be disclosed by way of note to the accounts or not disclosed if an outflow of economic benefits is remote.

Where the occurrence of a contingent liability becomes sufficiently probable, it falls within the criteria for recognition as a provision as detailed above and should be accounted for accordingly and recognised as a liability in the accounts.

Where the likelihood of a contingent liability is possible, but not probable and not remote, disclosure should be made, for each class of contingent liability, where practicable, of:

(a) an estimate of its financial effect, taking into account the inherent risks and uncertainties and, where material, the time value of money;

(b) an indication of the uncertainties relating to the amount or timing of any outflow; and

(c) the possibility of any reimbursement

For example, an extract from the 1998 Annual Report of Manchester United plc informs as follows:

> *Contingent liabilities*
> The terms of the current four year contract between FA Premier League Limited and BskyB which commenced in the 1997/98 football season, includes the advance receipt of monies, in 1996/97, which may only be retained upon fulfilment of the terms of the contract in the future. There is uncertainty as to whether the contract may be challenged by the Office of Fair Trading. The maximum amount that could be repayable by the Group is £2,6250,000 (1997 – £3,500,000).

12.14.11 Contingent asset

A contingent asset is a possible asset that arises from past events whose existence will be confirmed only by the occurrence of one or more uncertain future events not wholly within the entity's control.

Recognition as an asset is only allowed if the asset is *virtually certain* i.e. and therefore by definition no longer contingent.

Disclosure by way of note is required if an inflow of economic benefits is *probable*. The disclosure would include a brief description of the nature of the contingent asset at the balance sheet date and, where practicable, an estimate of their financial effect taking into account the inherent risks and uncertainties and, where material, the time value of money.

No disclosure is required where the chance of occurrence is anything less than probable. For the purposes of FRS 12, probable is defined as more likely than not i.e. more than a 50% chance.

12.15 Accounting for pension costs

12.15.1 Background

As people become more and more aware of the need for provision for their old age, their expectation that their employers will offer a pension scheme has increased and what was a 'fringe benefit' for only certain categories of staff has been broadened across the workforce. This has been encouraged by government with favourable tax treatment of both employers' and employees' contributions to pension schemes.

The provision of pensions for employees as part of an overall remuneration package has led to the related costs being a material part of the accounts. The very nature of such arrangements means that the commitment is a long-term one that may well involve estimates. The way the related costs are allocated between accounting periods and are reported in the financial statements needs careful consideration to ensure that a fair view of the position is shown.

This is because of the 'matching principle' by which we endeavour to include costs in the accounts for the period which gain benefit. Employers gain benefit from employees during their working life, not after they have retired and are receiving a pension!

At present we have an accounting standard, SSAP 24 *Accounting for Pension Costs* which covers the required treatment. This is currently under review and it is probable that it will soon be replaced. The ASB has issued an exposure draft (FRED 20 *Retirement Benefits*) which is to lead to a new standard to replace SSAP 24. It is, however, controversial and, while the changes it proposes are likely to be implemented, it is by no means certain that its adoption will be automatic.

Before considering the accounting treatment, we need to consider the methods used to provide pensions; we therefore need to consider the types of scheme commonly used.

12.15.2 Types of scheme

(a) Ex gratia arrangements

These are not schemes at all but are circumstances where an employer agrees to grant a pension to be paid for out of the resources of the firm. Consequently these are arrangements where pensions have not been funded but decisions are made on an *ad hoc* or case-by-case basis, sometimes arising out of custom and practice. No contractual obligation to grant or pay a pension exists.

(b) Defined contribution schemes

These are schemes in which the employer undertakes to make certain contributions each year, usually a stated percentage of salary. These contributions are usually supplemented by contributions from the employee. The money is then invested and, on retirement, the employee gains the pension benefits that can be purchased from the resulting funds.

Such schemes have uncertain benefits but fixed, pre-determined costs. Schemes of this sort were very common among smaller employers within the UK but fell from fashion. The use recently of transferable personal plans has led to a resurgence of this type of plan for smaller employers.

(c) Defined benefit schemes

These now form the majority of schemes in the UK. Under these, the employees will, on retirement, receive a pension based on length of service and salary, usually final salary or an average of the last few (usually three) years' salary.

This means that the benefits to the employee, and hence the cost to the employer, are uncertain. They are funded in the same basic way as defined contribution schemes but the level of contribution requires regular review to ensure that the fund will be adequate to meet the pension commitments. While this type of scheme remains the most common in the UK, the uncertainty of future costs has led to some employers (including some very large companies) changing to defined contribution schemes.

The current position

At present SSAP 24 *Accounting for Pension Costs* covers the accounting treatment of costs relating to pension schemes. We need to divide the consideration of this into the treatment in the profit and loss account and the balance sheet.

Profit and loss account

Here the accounting treatment will vary depending on which type of scheme is in force.

In the case of 'ex gratia arrangements' the capital cost of any un-funded ex gratia arrangements should be charged in the profit and loss account on the period when they are granted. This is because any benefit gained by the employer ceases the moment the employee retires. The capital cost can be determined by reference to the cost of purchasing an annuity for a person of that age and sex at that time.

For 'defined contribution schemes' the amount of contributions payable within each accounting period should be charged in the profit and loss account for that period.

For 'defined benefit schemes' both the costs and the fund value are computed on an actuarial basis. The valuation needs to give an estimate of the costs of providing the benefits over the remaining service lives of the relevant employees. This should be done in such a way as to produce a pension cost that is a level percentage of both current and future pensionable payroll.

Both the accounting standard and the actuarial professional bodies give guidelines on the assumptions and methods to be employed in the valuation and require that these guidelines be followed.

If a valuation gives rise to a variation in the regular costs, it should normally be allocated over the remaining service lives of the employees. Should, however, such a variation arise out of a surplus or deficit arising from a significant reduction in pensionable employees, it should be recognised when it arises unless such treatment would be inconsistent with the prudence concept and involve the anticipating of income (or cost reduction). This last point could arise where a surplus gives rise to a 'contribution holiday'.

Should a deficit arise out of some major event falling outside the actuarial assumptions then prudence might dictate earlier recognition rather than allocation over future service lives. An example of this might be a major change in numbers of employees or the age/gender balance of the workforce. Similarly, where a refund arises which is subject to tax deduction, it may be recognised on receipt.

Balance sheet

This has a much simpler approach and is based purely on the accruals principle for all three types of arrangement.

The difference between cumulative pensions costs charged in the profit and loss account and monies paid either as pensions or as contributions to a scheme or fund should be shown as either a prepayment or a provision.

As such, this means that the figure on the balance sheet is simply a balancing one representing the difference between the amounts charged against profits and the amounts paid into the fund.

This means that SSAP 24, like so many standards, is 'profit driven' and strives to achieve a meaningful figure for profit at the expense of placing a meaningless one on the balance sheet!

Notes to the accounts

The standard requires that considerable disclosure be made in the notes to the accounts. In the case of a defined contribution scheme, these are fairly simple:

● the nature of the scheme (i.e. defined contribution);

● the accounting policy;

● the pension cost charge for the period;

● any outstanding or prepaid contributions at the balance sheet date.

For a defined benefit or ex gratia scheme, more detail is required:

● The nature of the scheme (i.e. defined benefit).

● Whether it is funded or unfunded.

● The accounting policy and, if different, the funding policy.

● Whether the pension cost and provision (or asset) are assessed in accordance with the advice of a professional qualified actuary and, if so, the date of the most recent formal actuarial valuation or later formal review used for this purpose. If the actuary is an employee or officer of the reporting company, or of the group of which it is a member, this fact should be disclosed.

● The pension cost charge for the period together with explanations of significant changes in the charge compared to that in the previous accounting period.

● Any provisions or prepayments in the balance sheet resulting from a difference between the amounts recognised as cost and the amounts funded or paid directly.

● The amount of any deficiency on a current funding level basis, indicating the action, if any, being taken to deal with it in the current and future accounting periods.

● An outline of the results of the most recent formal actuarial valuation or later formal review of the scheme on an ongoing basis. This should include disclosure of:
   (a) the actuarial method used and a brief description of the main actuarial assumptions;
   (b) the market value of scheme assets at the date of their valuation or review;
   (c) the level of funding expressed in percentage terms;
   (d) comments on any material actuarial surplus or deficiency indicated by (c) above;
   (e) any commitment to make additional payments over a limited number of years;
   (f) the accounting treatment adopted in respect of a refund made where a credit appears in the financial statements in relation to it;
   (g) details of the expected effects on future costs of any material changes in the group's and/or company's pension arrangements.

Where a company or group has more than one pension scheme, disclosure should be made on a combined basis, unless disclosure of information about individual schemes is needed for a proper understanding of the accounts. For the purposes of the notes above, however, a current funding level basis deficiency in one scheme should not be set off against a surplus in another.

12.15.3   Financial Reporting Exposure Draft 20 *Retirement Benefits*[18]

The ASB's proposals are to make radical changes to the accounting treatment and to tidy up some anomalies that have arisen over periods of time.

Considering the anomalies, firstly the FRED proposes that all post-retirement benefits be covered. There was doubt about this in the SSAP and it had been addressed by the Urgent Issues Task Force. The main area here concerns provision of health care insurance for retired former employees, but other benefits can arise. The FRED is unequivocal and is designed to cover all eventualities.

The radical changes proposed are in valuing the assets of the scheme and in measuring its liabilities.

In the first place, scheme assets will be valued on a market values basis rather than the actuarial basis employed under the existing standard.

Scheme liabilities will be measured by computing the potential pensions and discounting them at a market rate (the yield on an AA Corporate Bond). This is in contrast to the present system which employs the expected rate of return on scheme assets.

The profit and loss account charge will be the current costs of servicing the scheme; actuarial gains and losses arising from the valuation of the assets and liabilities of the scheme will be reported in the statement of total recognised gains and losses. This will be shown immediately rather than, as at present, allocated over the future working lives of the workforce.

This will give, on the balance sheet, the meaningful figure of the pension scheme as the recoverable surplus or deficit at balance sheet date, arguably the most meaningful figure to offer accounts users.

The FRED, published in November 1999, has attracted some powerful critics. The change of valuation model and the immediate recognition of gains/losses are thought to lead to more volatility in the financial statements. As this will be restricted to the statement of total recognised gains and losses, this will leave the profit and loss account (and the all-important earnings per share), if anything, more stable than at present while giving users an indication of the strength or weakness of the pension scheme and an indication of the future cash flows.

12.15.4 International comparisons

The current IAS is International Accounting Standard 19 *Employee Benefits*.

The valuation models in FRED 20 are said by the ASB to be broadly in agreement with the IAS but require immediate recognition of actuarial gains/losses, which contrasts with the requirements of the IAS which is closer to the SSAP 24 treatment.

The change from actuarial to market value models will bring UK practice closer to that of the US where standards are tightly defined and follow market values throughout.

12.15.5 Conclusion

Accounting for post-retirement benefits will always be difficult. The accountant has had to rely on the work of an actuary that is only too often not clearly understood! Pension costs and the future liabilities are often a material part of the accounts and moves (such as FRED 20) to make them more transparent must be welcomed. However, some companies will be nervous about disclosing significant surpluses which may attract unwelcome attention from predators and employees (past and present) seeking improved benefits!

Summary
••••••••••••••

Traditional book-keeping resulted in the production of a balance sheet that was simply a list of unused and unpaid balances on account at the close of the financial year. It was intrinsically a document confirming the veracity of the double entry system, but it revealed the capital structure of the reporting entity. Hence it became a document for measuring the risk encountered by the providers of capital.

Unfortunately the transaction-based nature of book-keeping created a balance sheet incapable of keeping pace with a developing financial market of highly sophisticated transactions. By operating within the legal niceties, management was able to keep future benefits and obligations off the balance sheet. It was also possible for capital instruments of one kind to masquerade as those of another – sometimes by accident, but often by design. This dilution in the effectiveness of the balance sheet had to be remedied.

The ASB has addressed the problem from first principles by requiring consideration to be given to the definitions of assets and liabilities; to the accounting substance of a transaction over its legal form; to the elimination of off-balance-sheet finance; and to the standardisation of accounting treatment in respect of items such as leases and capital instruments.

As a consequence, the former balance sheet paradigm has been changed beyond recognition. It is rapidly becoming the primary reporting vehicle. In so doing it is tending to be seen as a valuation document and as a definitive statement of assets used and liabilities incurred by the reporting entity. This has also influenced the approach taken to retirement benefits in FRED 20.

This will create an ongoing pressure on the regulators and companies to produce a relevant valuation document. The process of change is unlikely to be painless and considerable controversy will doubtless arise about whether a transaction falls within the ASB definition of an asset or liability; whether it should be recognised; and how it should be disclosed. This will remain an important developing area of regulation and the ASB is to be congratulated on its approach, which requires accountants to exercise their professional judgement.

Review questions

1 Some members of the board of directors of a company deliberating over a possible source of new capital believe that irredeemable debentures carrying a fixed annual coupon rate would suffice. They also believe that the going concern concept of the balance sheet would obviate the need to include the debt thereon: the entity is a going concern and there is no intention to repay the debt; therefore disclosure is unwarranted. Discuss.

2 A company is obliged to reveal, in note form, a quantitative assessment of the dilution of future earnings per share on the assumption that convertible stock in issue will experience total conversion into ordinary shares at the earliest possible date. Why should this philosophy not apply to the balance sheet and thus enable such stock to be classified as equity? Discuss.

3 In 20X6 Alpha plc made the decision to close a loss-making department in 20X7. The company proposed to make a provision for the future costs of termination in the 20X6 profit and loss account. Its argument was that a liability existed in 20X6 which should be recognised in 20X6. The auditor objected to recognising a liability, but agreed to recognition if it could be shown that the management decision was irrevocable. Discuss whether a liability exists and should be recognised in the 20X6 balance sheet.

4 Explain the following terms and the circumstances in which each is appropriate: (a) derecognised, (b) partially derecognised, and (c) linked presentation.

5 As a sales incentive, a computer manufacturer offers to buy back its computers after three years at 25% of the original selling price, so providing the customer with a guaranteed residual value which would be exercised if he or she were unable to achieve a higher price in the second-hand market.

Discuss whether derecognition, partial recognition or linked presentation is the appropriate disclosure treatment.

6 A boat manufacturer, Swann plc, supplies its dealers on a consignment basis, which allows either Swann plc or a dealer to require a boat to be returned. Each dealer has to arrange insurance for the boats held on consignment.

When a boat is sold to a customer, the dealer pays Swann plc the lower of:

● the delivery price of the boat as at the date it was first supplied, or
● the current delivery price less the insurance premiums paid to date of sale.

If a boat is unsold after three months, the dealer has to pay on the same terms.

Discuss, with reasons, whether boats held by the dealers on consignment should appear as stock in the balance sheet of Swann plc or the dealer.

7 Discuss the problems of interpreting financial reports when there are post balance sheet events, and the extent to which you consider SSAP 17 should be amended. Illustrate your decisions with practical examples as appropriate.

8 D plc has a balance on its debtors' account of £100,000. Previous experience would anticipate bad debts to a maximum of 3%. The company adopts a policy of factoring its debts. Explain how the transaction would be dealt with in the books of D plc under each of the following independent sets of circumstances:

(i) The factoring agreement involves a sole payment of £95,000 to complete the transaction. No further payments are to be made or received by either party to the agreement.

(ii) The debtors are transferred to the factoring entity on receipt of £93,000. The agreement provides for further payments, which will vary on the basis of timing and receipts from debtors. Interest is chargeable by the factor on a daily basis, based on the outstanding amount at the close of the day's transactions. The factor also has recourse to D plc for the first £10,000 of any loss.

9 Mining, nuclear and oil companies have normally provided an amount each year over the life of an enterprise to provide for decommissioning costs. Explain why the ASB considered this to be an inappropriate treatment and how these companies would be affected by FRS 12 *Provisions, Contingent Liabilities and Contingent Assets*.

Exercises

An extract from the solution is provided in the appendix at the end of the text for exercises marked with an asterisk (*).

* Question 1

On 1 April year 1, a deep discount bond was issued by DDB plc. It had a face value of £2.5 million covering a five-year term. The lenders were granted a discount of 5%. The coupon rate was 10% on the principal sum of £2.5 million, payable annually in arrears. The principal sum was repayable in cash on 31 March year 5. Issuing costs amounted to £150,000.

Required:
Compute the finance charge per annum and the carrying value of the loan to be reported in each year's profit and loss account and balance sheet respectively.

* Question 2

On 1 October year 1, RPS plc issued one million £1 5% redeemable preference shares. Issue costs of £50,000 were incurred. The anticipated date for dividend payments was 30 September every year. The company's share premium account amounted to £100,000 on 30 September year 1.

Required:
Show the accounting treatment of the total finance costs (i.e. issue costs and dividend) throughout the life-span of the capital instrument (take care: the instrument is non-equity shareholders' funds) and the balance sheet extracts.

Question 3

(a) Post balance sheet events are those events, both favourable and unfavourable, which occur between the balance sheet date and the date on which the financial statements are approved by the board of directors.

Required:
Set out the treatment of post balance sheet events as laid down by SSAP 17. Explain why this treatment is required by that SSAP in order to ensure that financial statements show a true and fair view and give appropriate information to the shareholders and other legitimate users.

(b) You are the financial accountant of Tooting Engineering Ltd (a substantial private company). You are responsible for preparing the company's financial statements and are at present finalising those for the year ended 31 December 20X6 for presentation to the board. The following items are material:

   (i) You have recently discovered that during September and October 20X6, while you were away sick, the cashier took advantage of the weakened internal controls to defraud the company of £8,000.

   (ii) At a board meeting on 3 February 20X7 the directors agreed to purchase the business of Mr N. M. Patel (a small engineering business) for £45,000.

   (iii) On 18 January 20X7 the company made a 1 for 4 rights issue to existing ordinary shareholders. This involved the issue of 20,000 £1 ordinary shares for a consideration of £25,000.

   (iv) A customer, General Products Ltd, owed Tooting Engineering Ltd £16,000 on 31 December 20X6. This company had always been considered a good credit risk until on 15 February 20X7 it went into voluntary liquidation. Of the £16,000 debt, £12,000 is still outstanding and General Products Ltd is expected to pay approximately 25p in the £ on this £12,000.

Required:
Explain how you will treat items (i)–(iv) above in the financial statements and give a brief explanation of why you are adopting your proposed treatment.

Question 4

As the financial controller of SEAS Ltd, you are responsible for preparing the company's financial statements and are at present finalising these for the year ended 31 March 20X8 for presentation to the board of directors. The following items are material:

   (i) Costs of £250,000 arose from the closure of the company's factory in Garratt, which manufactured coffins. Owing to a declining market, the company has withdrawn from this type of business prior to the year-end.

   (ii) You discover that during February 20X8, whilst you were away skiing, the cashier took advantage of the weakness in internal control to defraud the company of £30,000.

   (iii) During the year ended 31 March 20X8, stocks of obsolete electrical components had to be written down by £250,000 owing to foreign competitors producing them more cheaply.

(iv) At a board meeting held on 30 April 20X8, the directors signed an agreement to purchase the business of Mr Hacker (a small computer manufacturer) for the sum of £100,000.

(v) £300,000 of development expenditure, which had been capitalised in previous years, was written off during the year ended 31 March 20X8. This became necessary due to foreign competitors' price cutting, which cast doubt on the recovery of costs from future revenue.

(vi) Dynatron Ltd, a customer, owed the company £50,000 on 31 March 20X8. However, on 15 May 20X8 it went into creditors' voluntary liquidation. Of the £50,000, £40,000 is still outstanding and the liquidator of Dynatron is expected to pay approximately 25p in the £ to unsecured creditors.

(vii) On 30 April 20X8, the company made a 1 for 4 rights issue to the ordinary shareholders, which involved the issue of 50,000 £1 ordinary shares for a sum of £62,500.

Required
Explain how you will treat the above financial statements, and give a brief explanation of why you are adopting your proposed treatment.

Question 5

October 20X1, Little Raven plc issued 50,000 debentures, with a par value of £100 each, to investors at £80 each. The debentures are redeemable at par on 30 September 20X6 and have a coupon rate of 6%, which was significantly below the market rate of interest for such debentures issued at par. In accounting for these debentures to date, Little Raven plc has simply accounted for the cash flows involved, namely:

● On issue: Debenture 'liability' included in the balance sheet at £4,000,000.

● Profit and loss accounts: Interest charged in years ended 30 September 20X2, 20X3 and 20X4 (published accounts) and 30 September 20X5 (draft accounts) – £300,000 each year (being 6% on £5,000,000).

The new finance director, who sees the likelihood that further similar debenture issues will be made, considers that the accounting policy adopted to date is not appropriate. He has asked you to suggest a more appropriate treatment.

Little Raven plc intends to acquire subsidiaries in 19X6.

Profit and loss accounts for the years ended 30 September 20X4 and 20X5 are as follows:

	y/e 30 Sept 20X5 (Draft) £000	y/e 30 Sept 20X4 (Actual) £000
Turnover	6,700	6,300
Cost of sales	(3,025)	(2,900)
Gross profit	3,675	3,400
Overheads	(600)	(550)
Interest payable – debenture	(300)	(300)
– others	(75)	(50)
Profit for the financial year	2,700	2,500
Retained profits brought forward	4,300	1,800
Retained profit carried forward	7,000	4,300

Extracts from the balance sheet are:

	at 30 Sept 20X5 (Draft) £000	at 30 Sept 20X4 (Actual) £000
Share capital	2,250	2,250
Share premium	550	550
Profit and loss account	7,000	4,300
	9,800	7,100
6% Debentures	4,000	4,000
	13,800	11,100

Required:

(a) Outline the considerations involved in deciding how to account for the issue, the interest cost and the carrying value in respect of debenture issues such as that made by Little Raven plc. Consider the alternative treatments in respect of the profit and loss account and refer briefly to the appropriate balance sheet disclosures for the debentures. Conclude in terms of the requirements of FRS 4 (on accounting for capital instruments) in this regard.

(b) Detail an alternative set of entries in the books of Little Raven plc for the issue of the debentures and subsequently; under this alternative the discount on the issue should be dealt with under the requirements of FRS 4. The constant rate of interest for the allocation of interest cost is given to you as 11.476%. Draw up a revised profit and loss account for the year ended 30 September 20X5 – together with comparatives – taking account of the alternative accounting treatment.

(c) List the requirements of FRS 7 *Fair Values in Acquisition Accounting* in respect of determining the fair values of identifiable assets and liabilities acquired, and briefly discuss the need for an accounting standard in this regard.

References

1 K.V. Peasnell and R.A. Yaansah, *Off-Balance Sheet Financing*, ACCA, 1988.
2 SSAP 21, *Accounting for Leases and Hire Purchase Contracts*, ASC, 1984.
3 FRS 5, *Reporting the Substance of Transactions*, ASB 1994.
4 *Ibid.*, paras 16–18.
5 *Ibid.*, para. 20.
6 *Ibid.*, para. 21.
7 *Ibid.*, para. 22.
8 FRS 4, *Capital Instruments*, ASB, 1993.
9 FRS 12, *Provisions, Contingent Liabilities and Contingent Assets*, ASB, 1998.
10 *Ibid.*, para. 14
11 *Ibid.*, para. 25
12 *Ibid.*, para. 17
13 *Ibid.*, para. 23
14 *Ibid.*, para. 36
15 *Ibid.*, para. 43
16 *Ibid.*, para. 45
17 *Ibid.*, para. 89
18 FRED 20, *Retirement Benefits*, ASB, 1999.

Taxation in company accounts

13.1 Introduction

Limited companies and, indeed, all corporate bodies are treated for tax purposes as legally separate from their proprietors. Thus, a limited company is itself liable to pay tax on its profits. This tax is known as **corporation tax**. The shareholders are only accountable for tax on the income they receive by way of any dividends distributed by the company. If the shareholder is an individual, then **income tax** will become due on the dividend received.

This is in contrast to the position in a partnership, where each partner is then individually liable for the tax on that share of the pre-tax profit that has been allocated. Note that this is different from the treatment of an employee, who is charged tax on the amount of salary paid. A partner is taxed on the profit and not simply on drawings.

In this chapter we consider the different types of company taxation and their accounting treatment. In addition, we consider the major changes to the UK corporation tax system that took place in April 1999.

13.2 Corporation tax

Corporation tax is calculated under rules set by Parliament each year in the Finance Act. The Finance Act may alter the existing rules; it also sets the rate of tax payable. Because of this annual review of the rules, circumstances may change year by year, which makes comparability difficult and forecasting uncertain.

A further complication is that although the tax payable is **based** on the accounting profits as disclosed in the profit and loss account, the tax rules may differ from the accounting rules which apply prudence to income recognition. For example, the tax rules do not accept that all the expenses which are recognised by the accountant under SSAP 2 accrual and prudence concepts are deductible when arriving at the taxable profit.

The accounting profit may therefore be lower or higher than the taxable profit. For example, the Companies Acts require that the formation expenses of a company, which are the costs of establishing it on incorporation, must be written off in its first accounting period; the rules of corporation tax, however, state that it is a capital expense and cannot be deducted from the profit for tax purposes. The expenses may therefore reduce the reported accounting profit but the taxable profit will be higher. This means that more tax will be assessed as payable than one would assume from an inspection of the published profit and loss account.

Similarly, although most businesses would consider that entertaining suppliers and other business associates was a normal commercial trading expense, it is not allowed as a deduction for tax purposes.

A more complicated situation arises in the case of depreciation. Because the directors have the choice of method of depreciation to use, the legislators have decided to require all companies to use the same method when calculating taxable profits. If one thinks about this, then it would seem to be the equitable practice. Each company is allowed to deduct a uniform percentage from its profits in respect of the depreciation that has arisen from the wear and tear and diminution in value of fixed assets. The substituted depreciation that the tax rules allow is known as a **capital allowance**. The capital allowance is calculated in the same way as depreciation; the only difference is that the rates are those set out in the Finance Acts. At the time of writing, most commercial fixed assets (excluding land and buildings) qualify for a capital allowance of 25% calculated on the reducing balance method. There are restricted allowances, called industrial buildings allowances, for certain categories of buildings used in manufacturing.

Just as the depreciation that is charged by the company under accrual accounting concepts is substituted by a capital allowance, profits or losses arising on the sale of fixed assets are not used for tax purposes and a substituted balancing charge or balancing allowance is given. The profit or loss on disposal in the accounts is the difference between the book value and sales proceeds; the balancing allowance is the difference between the cost less capital allowances allowed to date minus the sales proceeds. If the sales proceeds are less than the written down balance after capital allowances there will be a balancing allowance; if the sales proceeds are more than the written down value after capital allowances there will be a balancing charge.

Profits and losses on disposal arise as corrections of the inevitable errors that have arisen in estimating depreciation accurately; balancing charges arise for the same basic reason, i.e. it is impossible to be certain that the capital allowances exactly measure the diminution in value that has occurred.

Thus, the calculation of the corporate tax liability of a company (known as the tax computation) may appear as in Figure 13.1. These are only examples of the adjustments

Figure 13.1   MITHRAS plc.

Corporation tax computation for the year to 31 March 2000		£
Net profit on ordinary activities before tax		110,000
ADD BACK to the accounting profit:	£	
Formation expenses	1,200	
Entertaining	4,983	
Depreciation expense	35,000	
		41,183
		151,183
DEDUCT Substitute amounts allowed by the tax rules:		
Capital allowances		40,000
		111,183
Corporation tax at 20% as set by the Finance Act		22,237

Figure 13.2   Tax charge on profit and loss account.

	£	£
Profit on ordinary activities before tax		110,000
Tax on profit on ordinary activities		22,237
Profit on ordinary activities after tax		87,763

---

that may be made to the accounting profit for tax purposes. They are intended to demonstrate solely the principles involved. The tax liability of £22,236.00 (disclosed in the accounts as shown in Figure 13.2) will be payable to the Inland Revenue nine months after the end of the accounting period in January 20X1. It must, therefore, appear on the balance sheet at 31 March 2000 as a current liability under the heading 'Other creditors including taxation and social security'.

Mithras was a simple company with trading income only. Had it had a more complex income structure it might have more items comprising its tax charge which would have to be disclosed either on the face of the profit and loss account or in the notes to that account. Other items could include, for example, foreign taxes paid on overseas earnings and tax suffered on investment income.

Accountants have guidance on how to disclose tax information in the published accounts. Accounting for taxation in the accounts of an entity subject to corporation tax is governed by FRS 16 *Current Tax*. The intention is that the user of the accounts should be able to see the significance of tax when predicting the future performance of the company.

There is guidance on the information that must be shown by way of note. For example, the note to the accounts must show an analysis of the charge to taxation shown in the profit and loss account. This may be illustrated by the following extract from the accounts of Greenalls Group plc for 1997–98, set out in Figure 13.3.

You will observe that Note 7 shows the breakdown of the charge against profits between corporation tax on the trading income; an adjustment in respect of the preceding year; and a credit relating to an exceptional item. It is usual to have an adjustment because it is rare for a company to be able to state its ultimate tax liability accurately when the accounts are prepared. It still has to agree with the Inland Revenue on exactly which expenses are allowable.

Figure 13.3   Greenalls Group plc: note on taxation.

Notes to the accounts accompanying the accounts as at 30.9.1998

7   Taxation on profits on ordinary activities

	1996–97 £m.	1997–98 £m.
Taxation on profits for the year		
UK corporation tax @ 31% (1996–97 32%)	33.8	31.74
Adjustment for previous years	(0.2)	(0.05)
Credit relating to exceptional items	(2.3)	—
	31.3	31.69

13.3   Corporation tax systems

The distinguished tax theoretician Professor G.S.A. Wheatcroft described '...writing a ... book on tax is like painting a picture of the sunset; as fast as a chapter is in draft the law has changed'. Fortunately this only applies to one chapter of this book.

There are three possible systems of company taxation (classical, imputation and split rate).[1] In the classical system, a company pays tax on its profits, and then the shareholders suffer a second tax liability when their share of the profits is distributed to them. In effect, the dividend income of the shareholder is regarded as a second and separate source of income from that of the profits of the company. It can be argued that this double taxation is inequitable when compared to the taxation system on unincorporated bodies (such as partnerships) where the rate of taxation suffered overall is unaltered if profits are withdrawn from the business or not. It is suggested that the classical system discourages the distribution of profits to shareholders since the second tranche of taxation only becomes payable on payment of the dividend, although some argue that the effect of the burden of double taxation on the economy is less serious than it might seem.[2]

In an imputation system, the dividend is regarded merely as a flow of the profits on each sale to the individual shareholders, there being considered to be merely one source of income which could either be retained in the company or distributed to the shareholders. It is this principle of the flow of net profits from particular sales to individual shareholders that has justified the repayment of the imputed tax credit to shareholders with low income or to non-taxable shareholders (such as charities and pension funds), even though that tax credit has represented a reduction in the overall tax revenue of the nation state because the imputed tax credit represented also an advance payment of the company's own corporation tax liability. If the dividend had not been distributed to the low income or non taxable shareholder who was entitled to repayment, the tax revenue collected would have been higher overall.

In a partial imputation system only part of the underlying corporation tax paid is treated as a tax credit. **The United Kingdom has an imputation system.**

13.3.1   Advance corporation tax – The system until 5 April 1999

As stated previously, under this system a company pays corporation tax on its income. When that company pays a dividend to its shareholders it is distributing some of its taxed income among the proprietors. In this system the tax paid by the company is 'imputed' to the shareholders who therefore receive a dividend which has already been taxed.

This means that, from the paying company's point of view, the concept of gross dividends does not exist. From the paying company's point of view, the amount of dividends paid and proposed shown in the profit and loss account will equal the cash that the company will have paid or will pay to the shareholders in the case of proposed dividends.

However, from the shareholder's point of view, the cash received from the company is treated as a net payment after deduction of tax. The shareholders will have received, with the cash dividend, a note of a tax credit, which is regarded as equal to basic rate income tax on the total of the dividend plus the tax credit. For example:

	£
Dividend being the cash paid by the company and disclosed in the company's profit and loss account	400
Tax credit calculated assuming a basic rate of income tax of 20% applied to the 'gross' dividend of £500 (being the rate until 5 April 1999)	100
Gross dividend	500

The ACT calculation (as shown above) has been based on a basic tax rate of 20% for dividends paid, being the basic rate of income tax on investment income until 5 April 1999. The concession of a lower rate of basic income tax on dividends was introduced as from 1 April 1993 as a signal of the then governmental intent to reduce the basic rate of income tax down from the rate at that time of 25% to 20% in due course.

This meant that an individual shareholder, who only paid basic rate income tax, had no further liability in that the assumption is that the basic rate tax has been paid by the company. A non-taxpayer could have claimed back the tax credit of £100 from the Inland Revenue (except for pension funds in respect of dividends paid on or after 2 July 1997).

This last point about the reclaim of the tax credit had a strong influence on the introduction of the second stage of imputation tax. The position was that while shareholders were able to recover tax credits immediately on receipt of the dividend, the companies paying the dividend would not have had to pay their corporation tax until nine months after the end of the accounting period. As you may imagine, the result of this lack of synchronisation between the recovery of the tax and the payment of the tax would have an adverse effect on the government's cash flow. The government consequently introduced measures to counter this by the introduction of **advance corporation tax** (ACT). Statute required that when a company paid a dividend it was required to make a payment to the Inland Revenue equal to the total tax credit associated with that dividend. This payment was called 'advance corporation tax' because it was a payment on account of the corporation's tax liability that would be paid on the profits of the accounting period. When the company eventually made its payment of the corporation tax liability, it was allowed to reduce the amount paid by the amount paid as ACT. The net amount of corporation tax that was paid after offsetting the ACT is known as **mainstream corporation tax**. The total amount of corporation tax is no greater than that assessed on the taxable profits of the company; there is merely a change in the timing of the amount of tax paid by paying it in two parts – the ACT element and the mainstream corporation tax element.

ACT was accounted for quarterly and paid to the Inland Revenue on the 14th of the month following the end of the calendar quarter. Thus if a dividend was paid during the three months to 31 March, the ACT payable on that dividend had to be paid to the Inland Revenue on 14 April. The date of the payment of the dividend was the crucial factor for ACT purposes, not the date the dividend was declared. This was because the shareholder was only able to claim a refund after payment of the dividend. This meant that the declaration of a proposed dividend gave rise to a potential liability for ACT which did not actually crystallise until after the dividend was actually paid.

As mentioned above, the ACT paid by the company was recovered by deducting the amount paid from the corporation tax liability. This could be illustrated by looking at the Mithras example above (although treating the example as if the accounts were for the year ended 31 March 1999 rather than 31 March 2000):

	£
Profit after taxation	87,763
Dividends paid	40,000
Retained profits for the period	47,763

The dividend of £40,000 that was paid in cash would have given rise to an ACT payment by the company of £10,000. This would have been offset against the £22,236.60 of corporation tax giving a net current liability (the mainstream corporation tax) of £12,236.60.

What would be the position if the company had declared a dividend but had not paid it out to the shareholders by the date of the balance sheet? In this case the offset would not have been possible because the £10,000 of ACT could only be offset against the corporation tax in the accounting period during which the tax was actually paid.

The offset of ACT against corporation tax is effectively restricted to the ACT rate multiplied by the company's profits chargeable to corporation tax. A further refinement was that for offset purposes the ACT rate was multiplied by the UK profit – this does not include profits generated overseas. In the case of Mithras, for example, the offset was limited to the chargeable profits of £111,183 multiplied by 20%, i.e. £22,237. Should a distribution have exceeded the chargeable profits for that period, then the ACT cannot be recovered immediately. Under tax law, such unrelieved ACT can be carried back against corporation tax payments in the preceding six years or forward against future liabilities indefinitely. In this example, say that only £40,000 of Mithras's total profits represented UK income. This would reduce the offset limit to £8,000 (£40,000 multiplied by 20%) and result in unrelieved ACT of £2,000. Therefore, the mix of UK versus overseas income had potential implications on the level of unrelieved ACT.

Unrecovered ACT will appear in the balance sheet as an asset. At this point the accountant must consider the prudence concept. In order for it to remain as such on the balance sheet it must be reasonably certain and foreseeable that it will be recoverable at a future date. If the ACT can be reasonably seen as recoverable then it should be shown on the balance sheet as a deferred asset. If, for any reason, it seems improbable that there will be sufficient future tax liabilities to 'cover' the ACT, then it must be written off as irrecoverable.

13.3.2 Corporation tax – The system from 6 April 1999

The system altered radically as from 6 April 1999, although a company continues to pay corporation tax on its income and when that company pays a dividend to its shareholders it is still considered to be distributing some of its taxed income among the proprietors. In this revised system the tax payable by the company is 'imputed' to the shareholders who therefore receive a dividend which has already been taxed. This means that, from the paying company's point of view, the concept of gross dividends continues not to exist. From the paying company's point of view, the amount of dividends paid and proposed shown in the profit and loss account will equal the cash that the company will have paid or will pay to the shareholders in the case of proposed dividends.

However, from the shareholder's point of view, the cash received from the company is treated as a net payment after deduction of tax. The shareholders will receive, with the cash dividend, a note of a tax credit, which is regarded as equal to basic rate income tax on the total of the dividend plus the tax credit. For example:

	£
Dividend being the cash paid by the company and disclosed in the company's profit and loss account	400.00
Imputed tax credit of 1/9 of dividend paid (being the rate from 6 April 1999)	44.44
Gross dividend	444.44

The imputed tax credit calculation (as shown above) has been based on a basic tax rate of 10% for dividends paid, being the basic rate of income tax on investment income from 6 April 1999. This means that an individual shareholder, who only pays basic rate income tax, has no further liability in that the assumption is that the basic rate tax has been paid by the company. A non-taxpayer can no longer obtain a repayment of tax.

The rate of 10% imputed tax credit will be the lowest band rate of corporation tax on profits from 1 April 2001.

The essential difference from the previous system up to 5 April 1999 is that the dividend paying company makes absolutely no deduction from the dividend **nor is any payment made by the company to the Inland Revenue**. The addition of 1/9 of the dividend paid as an imputed tax credit is purely nominal. A tax credit of 1/9th of the dividend will be deemed to be attached to that dividend (in effect an income tax rate of 10%). That credit is notional in that no payment of the 10% will be paid to the Inland Revenue.[3]

Large companies (those with taxable profits of £1,500,000) will start paying a proportion of their corporation tax liability in quarterly instalments starting within the year of account rather than paying their mainstream corporation tax liability nine months thereafter. Previously only those companies that paid dividends would have been required to hand over any corporation tax until nine months after the year end. The payment of taxation is no longer associated with dividends. Smaller companies will continue to pay their corporation tax nine months after the year end.

As there will no longer be payments of advance corporation tax (ACT) from 6 April 1999, there will no longer be unrecovered ACT arising that cannot be offset against the balance of the corporation tax that had been due nine months after the year end under the old system (described in 9.3.1). Such unrelieved ACT still an asset in April 1999 will be carried forward against future taxation liabilities indefinitely (in a system known as 'Shadow ACT').

The payment of taxation is no longer associated with dividends.

It has been argued by the Treasury that the imputation system encouraged the payment of dividends, and consequently discourages firms from reinvesting earnings. Since 1985, both investment and the ratio of dividend payments to GDP have soared in Britain relative to the USA, but it is not obvious that such trends are largely attributable to tax policy.[4] It is suggested that the proposed changes in the corporation tax system will tend to discourage companies from paying 'excessive' dividends because the major pressure for dividends has come from the pension fund investors who could reclaim the tax paid, and that the decrease in cash flow to the company caused by the start of quarterly corporation tax payments might tend to assist company directors in resisting dividend increases to compensate for this loss.

13.4 Investment income

When a company received a dividend from another UK company it would of course carry with it a tax credit. Under the imputation system there would be no further tax liability; such dividends were not subject to corporation tax. Under the system up to 5 April 1999, it was important to recognise that under the Companies Act format for the presentation of the profit and loss account, dividends received as investment income were disclosed as a constituent part of the profits before tax. For this reason the amounts of dividends received had to be 'grossed up' by adding back the tax credit to the cash received. The tax charge disclosed in the profit and loss account was then increased by the amount of the tax credit. **For example, if another company had received the whole of the dividend of £400, the entries in the profit and loss account would have been as in Figure 13.4** for the year to 5 April 1999. FRS 16 states that dividends do not need to be 'grossed up' with the inputed tax credit (of 1/9 of the dividend) from 6 April 1999, on the grounds that the inputed tax credit cannot be reclaimed even if losses are made in the receiving company.

Figure 13.4 Profit and loss account entries for investment income.

Profit and loss account for investment income

	To 5 April 1999		From 6 April 1999	
	£	£	£	£
Profits on ordinary activities before tax, say		1,000		1,000
Tax:				
On profits on ordinary activities	210		200	
		210		200
		790		800
Profit and loss account after receipt of the dividend				
Profit on ordinary activities before tax – say		1,000		1,000
Investment income (Gross Dividend)		500		400
Profit before tax		1,500		1,400
Tax				
On profits on ordinary activities	210		200	
Tax credit on investment income	100		—	
		310		200
		1,190		1,200

13.5 Investment income other than dividends from shares

Certain forms of income are subject to the deduction of income tax at source. Examples of these are debenture interest from debentures held by the company and royalties from licences granted by the company. Tax suffered by being deducted from such income before being paid to the company is treated as a payment on account of corporation tax and relieved in that way.

Just as with income, certain forms of expense are also subject to the deduction of income tax at source. Examples of these are debenture interest paid by the company on debentures issued by the company and royalties on licences granted to the company. This income tax is accounted for to the Inland Revenue quarterly. Tax deducted from payments must be treated as part of the related expense and passed over to the Inland Revenue.

As far as the published accounts are concerned, all items of income and expenditure which are subject to the deduction of tax at source should appear gross (i.e. before deduction of tax) in the profit and loss account.

13.6 Deferred tax

The profit on which tax is paid may differ from that shown in the published profit and loss account. This is caused by two separate factors.

One factor that we looked at above is that certain items of expenditure may not be legitimate deductions from profit for tax purposes. For example, we saw that formation expenses and entertainment expenses were not allowable as a deduction for tax purposes and were required to be added back to the accounting profit. These differences are referred to as **permanent** differences because they will not be allowed at a different time and will be permanently disallowed, even in future accounting periods.

The other factor is that there are some other expenses that are legitimate deductions in arriving at the taxable profit but are allowed as a deduction for tax purposes at a later date. These are simply differences of **timing** in that tax relief and charges to profit and loss account occur in different accounting periods. The accounting profit is prepared on an accruals basis but the taxable profit requires certain of the items to be dealt with on a cash basis. Examples of this could include accrued interest payable, properly included in the profit and loss account under the accruals concept but not eligible for tax relief until actually paid, thus giving tax relief in a later period.

The most significant timing difference, however, is in the treatment of depreciation. The depreciation charge made in the profit and loss account must be added back in the tax computation and replaced by capital allowances. The substituted capital allowance calculated in accordance with the tax rules is rarely the same amount as the depreciation charge computed in accordance with FRS 15 *Tangible Fixed Assets*.

The classic effect of this is for corporation tax to be payable on a lower figure than the accounting profit in the earlier years of an asset's life because the capital allowances usually exceed depreciation in the earlier years of an asset's life. In later accounting periods, the capital allowances will be lower than the depreciation charges and the taxable profit will then be higher than the accounting profit that appears in the published profit and loss account.

The process whereby the company pays tax on a profit that is lower than the reported profit in the early years and on a profit that is higher than reported profit in later years is known as **reversal**. Given the knowledge that, ultimately, these timing differences will reverse, the accruals concept requires that consideration be given to making provision for the future liability in those early years in which the tax payable is calculated on a lower figure. The provision that is made is known as a **deferred tax provision**.

As you might expect, there has been a history of disagreement within the accounting profession over the method to use to calculate the provision. There have been, historically, two methods of calculating the provision for this future liability – the **deferral** method and the **liability** method.

The deferral method, which had been traditionally favoured in the USA, involves the calculation each year of the tax effects of the timing differences that have arisen in that year. The tax effect is then debited or credited to the profit and loss account as part of the tax charge; the double entry is effected by making an entry to the deferred tax account. This deferral method of calculating the tax effect ignores the effect of changing tax rates on the timing differences that arose in earlier periods. This means that the total provision may consist of differences calculated at the rate of tax in force in the year when the entry was made to the provision.

The liability method requires the calculation of the total amount of potential liability each year at current rates of tax, increasing or reducing the provision accordingly. This means that the company keeps a record of the timing differences and then recalculates at the end of each new accounting period using the rate of corporation tax in force as at the date of the current balance sheet.

To illustrate the two methods we will take the example of a single asset, costing £10,000, depreciated at 10% straight line, but subject to capital allowances of 25% on the reducing balance method, and show the workings in Figure 13.5. This shows, that, if there were no other adjustments, for the first four years the profits subject to tax would be lower than those shown in the accounts, but afterwards the situation would reverse.

Figure 13.5 Timing differences.

		ACCOUNTS (depreciation) £	TAX (allowances) £	DIFFERENCE (timing) £	TAX rate
1.1.19X3	Cost of asset	10,000	10,000	—	
31.12.19X3	Depreciation/capital allowances	1,000	2,500	1,500	25%
		9,000	7,500	1,500	
31.12.19X4	Depreciation/capital allowances	1,000	1,875	875	25%
		8,000	5,625	2,375	
31.12.19X5	Depreciation/capital allowances	1,000	1,406	406	25%
		7,000	4,219	2,781	
31.12.19X6	Depreciation/capital allowances	1,000	1,055	55	24%
		6,000	3,164	2,836	
31.12.19X7	Depreciation/capital allowances	1,000	791	(209)	24%
		5,000	2,373	2,627	

The deferral method would charge to the profit and loss account each year the variation multiplied by the current tax rate, i.e. 19X3 at 25% on £1,500 giving £375.00, and 19X6 at 24% on £55 giving £13.20. This is in accordance with the accrual concept which matches the tax expense against the income that gave rise to it. Under this method the deferred tax provision will be credited with £375 in 19X3 and this amount will not be altered in 19X6 when the tax rate changes to 24%.

For example, the calculation for the five years would be as in Figure 13.6. The liability method would make a charge so that the total balance on deferred tax equalled the cumulative variation multiplied by the current tax rate. The intention is that the balance sheet liability should be stated at a figure which represents the tax effect as at the end of each new accounting period. This means that there would be an adjustment made in

Figure 13.6 Deferred tax provision using deferred method.

Year ended	Timing difference £	Basic rate %	Deferred tax charge in year £	Deferred tax provision Deferral method £
31.12.19X3	1,500	25%	375.00	375.00
31.12.19X4	875	25%	218.75	593.75
31.12.19X5	406	25%	101.50	695.25
31.12.19X6	55	24%	13.20	708.45
31.12.19X7	(209)	24%	(50.16)	658.29

Figure 13.7 Deferred tax provision using liability method.

Year ended	Timing difference £	Basic rate %	Deferred tax charge in year £	Deferred tax provision Deferral method £	Rate in 19X4	Deferred tax charge Liability method £
31.12.19X3	1,500	25%	375.00	375.00	24%	360.00
31.12.19X4	875	25%	218.75	593.75	24%	210.00
31.12.19X5	406	25%	101.50	695.25	24%	97.44
31.12.19X6	55	24%	13.20	708.45	24%	13.20
				708.45		680.64

19X6 to recalculate the tax effect of the timing difference that was provided for in earlier years. For example, the provision for 19X3 would be recalculated at 24%, giving a figure of £360 instead of the £375 that was calculated and charged in 19X3. The decrease in the expected liability will be reflected in the amount charged against the profit and loss account in 19X6. The £15 will in effect be credited to the 19X6 profit and loss account.

The effect on the charge to the 19X6 profit and loss account (Figures 13.6 and 13.7) is that there will be a charge of £13.20 using the deferral method and a **credit** of £14.61 using the liability method. The £14.61 is the reduction in the amount provided from £695.25 at the end of 19X5 to the £680.64 that is required at the end of 19X6.

13.7 Critique on the development of deferred tax accounting

The history of the accounting standards for deferred taxation has been a mixed and somewhat controversial one and is worth examining.

Accounting for deferred tax in the UK predates the issue of accounting standards. Prior to the issue of standards, companies applied an accounting practice known as 'tax equalisation accounting', whereby they recognised that accounting periods should each be allocated an amount of income tax expense that bears a 'normal relationship to the income shown in the income statement', and to let reported income taxes follow reported income has been the objective of accounting for income taxes ever since.[5] There is also an economic consequence that flows from the practice of tax equalisation in that the trend of reported after-tax income is smoothed, and there is less likelihood of pressure for a cash dividend distribution based on the crediting of the tax benefit of capital investment expenditure to the early years of the fixed assets.

In tax equalisation accounting practice, it was usual to follow the liability method. However, when, in 1973, ED 11 was issued there was an increasing trend among UK companies to have their shares quoted on the US stock exchanges, coupled with a desire for international harmonisation of accounting standards, and the ASC, in the exposure draft, chose the deferral method and required full provision.

Because the deferral method was not widely used in the UK, there was a considerable debate which reflected the lack of agreement with the deferral method. As one might expect, given the lack of consensus, the standard-setting bodies followed a course of allowing both methods. Therefore, when SSAP 11 was issued, companies were given the choice of the liability or the deferral method.

There followed a period of very high rates of capital allowances and, with a naive belief that this situation would continue and allow permanent deferral, companies complained that to provide full provision was unrealistic and so in 1977 ED 19 introduced the concept of **partial provision** in which deferred tax is only provided in respect of timing differences that are likely to be reversed. This means that, in the preceding example, there would only be an additional tax charge of £375 in 19X3 and a credit to a deferred tax provision if it could be seen with reasonable certainty that the situation would arise as in 19X7 where the depreciation charge would exceed the capital allowances for the year. The argument was that if the company continued with the replacement of fixed assets, and if the capital allowances were reasonably certain to exceed the depreciation in the foreseeable future, it was unrealistic to make charges against the profit and create provisions that would not crystallise. This would merely lead to the appearance of an ever-increasing provision on the balance sheet.

The current position under SSAP 15 *Accounting for Deferred Tax* (which superseded SSAP 11) may be summarised as follows.

- Provision for deferred tax should be computed under the **liability method** in which the potential liability is computed at the corporation tax rate at which it is estimated that the tax will be paid. This is normally the rate ruling at the balance sheet date applied to all items within the provision.

- Tax deferred or accelerated should only be accounted for **to the extent that a liability or asset will crystallise**. Thus a liability might be considered permanently deferred by virtue of the company's plans for continued investment in fixed assets. It ceases to be a timing difference for all practical purposes and becomes reclassified as a notional permanent difference.

- The decisions as to whether or not to provide must be based on **reasoned assumptions** each time accounts are prepared; a prudent view should be taken.

- Debit balances of deferred tax should only be carried forward if their recovery without replacement can be foreseen.

- Recoverable ACT may be offset against the deferred tax provisions.

- The total amount of unprovided deferred tax should be disclosed by way of a note so that the shareholder can see the potential liability if the assumptions were to be ill-founded.

Under the liability method the focus is on the balance sheet (the objective being to compute the deferred tax liabilities), whereas the deferral method places the focus on the profit and loss account (the objective being to show the annual effect that has arisen in the year of account).[6] Such an emphasis on the balance sheet, at the possible expense of the profit and loss account, is the trend that the ASB has adopted in its *Draft Statement of Principles*.[7]

It is clear that under the full provision method, provision is made for the tax consequences of all gains and losses that have been recognised in the published accounts at the balance sheet date and that are expected to enter into the determination of taxable profit at some stage. The ASB Discussion Paper of March 1995 *Accounting for Taxation* proposed that the liability method of accounting for deferred tax continued to be used but that the method should revert to the making of the full provision, i.e. no more partial provision should be permitted. The Board argued that making provision for deferred tax without taking account of when it will be paid overstates the liability to tax and proposed for discussion a method of discounting the deferred tax (which would also mitigate the effects of future transactions such as the replacement of fixed assets as referred to above). The Discussion Paper, in recommending the liability method, follows the change in the USA to this method in SFAS 96. The Board stated its belief that, in principle, deferred tax should be discounted but took the view that, in the interest of comparison between reporting entities, discounting should be either required or prohibited but not merely permitted so as to give a choice to the preparer of the accounts. Before the ASB managed to come to a conclusion on the matter of deferred taxation, the IASC modified IAS 12 in October 1996 with effect for accounting periods beginning on or after 1 January 1998. The modified IAS 12 bans the deferral method and provides that full provision should be made for deferred taxation without any discounting. Research has indicated that European Union harmonisation for deferred tax has been inadequate.[8]

The foreword to Accounting Standards published in June 1993 by the ASB states that 'FRSs are formulated with due regard to international developments ... the Board supports the IASC in its aim to harmonise ... where the requirements of an accounting standard and an IAS differ, the accounting standard should be followed.'

Professor Andrew Lennard, Assistant Technical Director of the ASB, confirmed during a lecture on 17 March 1999 that this was a matter where there was a divergence of view between the ASB and international regulators, where the ASB was unhappy to account in full for deferred tax where there was no discounting for long delays until the anticipated payment; indeed he expressed his exasperation with the topic in stating that 'he wished deferred tax accounting would go away'.[9]

Applying the full provision method is more consistent with both international practice and the ASB's *Draft Statement of Principles (as modified in March 1999)*. However, a criticism of the full provision method in the past was that it could, if the company had a continuous capital expenditure programme, lead to a build-up of large liabilities that may fall due only far into the future, if at all. The ASB produced the long delayed FRED 19 in August 1999. It was noted that most respondents to the Discussion Paper supported continuation of the partial provision method, but accepted that the partial provision method would become less well understood as more companies adopted the International Standard IAS 12. The ASB noted that deferred tax is not one of the areas where a good case can be made for taking a stand against the direction of international opinion.

The Board pointed out that a feature of the UK tax system is that there can be a significant delay between the recognition of certain items in tax computations and their recognition in the accounts, and that a problem of the full provision method is that it fails to take account of when the deferred tax liability will actually be paid. It has been suggested, FRED 19 states, that discounting of the delayed tax liability could remedy the problem (of these timing differences) but there was a divergence of views as to whether there was a conceptual justification for discounting and whether the benefits of the complicated discounting calculations outweigh the costs. The majority of the Board supported discounting, but the Board decided that they would invite views on discounting before coming to a conclusion. However, although discounting appears an attractive method for allowing for the delay in payment of the liability, it has been pointed out that in some cases where capital expenditure is uneven, an unexpected effect of discounting both the initial and final cash flow effects could be to turn an eventual liability into an initial asset. It will be interesting to see how the ASB deals with such an unexpected result.[10]

The ASB has not yet proceeded to production of FRS 19, although the consultation period ended in November 1999.

The significance for investors in British companies of a move to full provision for deferred taxation should not be underestimated. As Nick Ellis, the retiring financial director of BAA pointed out in his financial review for the year ended 31 March 1995, a move to a full provision would increase the normal rate of taxation from 23.9% to around 35% and reduce reserves by between £300 million and £600 million.

An example of the importance of the topic of deferred tax can be shown during the period from 13 March 1984 to 31 March 1986 when the capital allowances on plant were dropped in stages from 100% to 25%. British banks had assumed that the high levels of capital allowances would continue and had made inadequate provision for deferred tax in line with SSAP 15. As the banks were unable to increase their capital expenditure fourfold to compensate, there were a series of rights issues to fund the resulting depletion in capital.

Terry Smith pointed out in Table 17.2 of his *Accounting for Growth* (2nd edition)[11] that according to the companies' own figures their estimated EPS would fall as follows if full provision for deferred tax were made:

British Airways	36.4%	
Severn Trent	25.3%	
British Gas	20.5%	(Based on CCA earnings of 15.1p per share adjusted to exclude restructuring costs)
TI Group	13.8%	

In his Table 17.3 Smith lists companies which expected an EPS fall of over 10% and more than 10% of shareholders' funds in unprovided deferred tax:

	Estimated impact on historic gearing of full provision	
	From	*To*
	%	%
British Airways	148	214
BP	67	78
British Gas	56	68

He points out in his Table 17.4 that the five companies he lists without any exposure to an increase in deferred tax charge include some of the UK's most successful and, in financial terms, conservative large companies:

	Tax Rate – %
General Electric	32
Marks & Spencer	32
Reuters	32
GUS	33
Wolesey	33

13.7.1 Illustration of three methods for accounting for deferred tax

Under the **partial provision** and liability method advocated by SSAP 15, the profit and loss account and balance sheet entries reflect the liability that is expected to crystallise; the difference between the full provision and the partial provision is treated by way of a note, i.e. similar to a contingent liability with the likelihood of the contingency becoming a liability being reassessed each year-end. In the ASB Discussion Document *Accounting for Tax* published in 1995, the ASB explores accounting for tax from first principles and discusses three methods in the first stage of its project to replace SSAP 15 with a new FRS. The three methods are: flow-through, under which no provision is made for deferred tax; full provision, under which deferred tax is provided in full; and partial provision, under which deferred tax is only provided to the extent that it is likely to crystallise taking into account the tax effects of future transactions.

A comparative illustration of the flow-through, full provision and partial provision methods are given below based on the following data (assuming a 33% tax rate):

	Profit before tax and depreciation £000	Depreciation £000	Capital allowances £000
19X5	800	25	125
19X6	900	50	25
19X7	950	75	25
19X8	1,050	50	175

Tax charge:	19X5	19X6	19X7	19X8
	£000	£000	£000	£000
Accounting profit	800	900	950	1,050
Capital allowances	125	25	25	175
Taxable profit	675	875	925	875
Tax payable @ 33%	223	289	305	289

Flow-through method – assuming nil provision for deferred tax and deducting tax payable

Entries in the profit and loss account are as follows:

	19X5 £000	19X6 £000	19X7 £000	19X8 £000
Accounting profit	775	850	875	1,000
Tax	223	289	305	289
Deferred tax	—	—	—	—
Profit after tax	552	561	570	711

Full provision method

Calculation of deferred tax on difference between capital allowances and depreciation:

Year	Capital allowances £000	Depreciation £000	Difference £000	Tax on difference in profit & loss a/c £000	Provision in balance sheet £000
19X5	125	25	100	33	33
19X6	25	50	(25)	(8)	25
19X7	25	75	(50)	(16)	9
19X8	175	50	125	41	50

Entries in profit and loss account and balance sheet:

	19X5 £000	19X6 £000	19X7 £000	19X8 £000
Accounting profit	775	850	875	1,000
Tax payable	223	289	305	289
Deferred tax	33	(8)	(16)	41
Total tax @ 33%	256	281	289	330
Profit after tax	519	569	586	670
Provision in Balance sheet	33	25	9	50

If the £50,000 provision in 19X9 is not expected to reverse because the company proposes to maintain its capital investment spending programme indefinitely, the liability could be discounted to reduce the amount that appears in the balance sheet as a provision. The reason for discounting is that the liability would not crystallise with the current capital investment plan.

Partial provision method

Calculation to ensure that the provision in the balance sheet is the expected tax liability:

The approach is to estimate in 19X5 the amount of the provision of £33,000 that is likely to crystallise into a liability. This is assumed to happen when the depreciation charge in succeeding years exceeds the capital allowances (known as *reversing timing differences*) for those years. This may be presented in tabular form as follows:

Capital allowance > depreciation *(Originating)* £000	Depreciation > capital allowances *(Reversing)* £000	Cumulative *(Cumulative reversing differences)* £000
100	—	—
	25	25
	50	**75**
125	—	—

From this it can be seen that, although a full provision in 19X5 would be £33,000, only £24,000 is estimated to become a liability, i.e. 33% of the cumulative amount of £75,000.

Entries in profit and loss account and balance sheet:

	19X5 £000	19X6 £000	19X7 £000	19X8 £000
Accounting profit	775	850	875	1,000
Tax payable	223	289	305	289
Deferred tax	**24**	**(8)**	**(16)**	—
Total tax in P & L A/c @ 33%	247	281	289	289
Profit after tax	528	569	586	711
Provision in balance sheet	**24**	**16**	—	—

This assumes that the effect of the capital expenditure in 19X8 will not reverse.

13.7.2 What are the arguments that support not providing for deferred tax?

There are some who give weight to the legal concept that deferred tax is not a legal liability until it accrues and that it should not therefore appear in the balance sheet. They maintain that deferred tax should not appear in the financial statements and recommend that financial statements should:

● Present the income tax expense for the year equal to the amount of income taxes that has been levied based on the income tax return for the year.

● Accrue as a receivable any income refunds that are due from taxing authorities or, as a payable, any unpaid current or past income taxes.

● Disclose in the notes to the financial statements differences between the income tax bases of assets and liabilities and the amounts at which they appear in the balance sheet.[12]

The argument is that the process of accounting for deferred tax is confusing what **did** happen to a company, i.e. the agreed tax payable for the year, and what **did not** happen to the company, which is the tax that would have been payable if the adjustments required by the tax law for timing differences had not occurred. It is felt that the shareholder should be provided with details of the tax charge levied on the profits for the year and an explanation of factors that might lead to a different rate of tax charge appearing in future financial statements. The argument against adjusting the tax charge for deferred tax and the creation of a deferred tax provision holds that shareholders are accustomed to giving consideration to many other imponderables concerning the amount, timing and uncertainty of future cash receipts and payments, and the treatment of tax should be considered in the same way. This view has received support from others,[13] who have held that tax attaches to taxable income and not to the reported accounting income and that there is no legal requirement for the tax to bear any relationship to the reported accounting income. Others have argued that 'deferred tax means income smoothing'[14] – although it could be argued just as validly that deferred tax means the fullest possible use of accrual accounting.

However, the legal argument runs counter to the substance-over-form criteria that give weight to the economic aspects of the event rather than the strict legal aspects. It is an interesting fact that substance over form has achieved a growing importance during the 1980s and the legal arguments are receiving less recognition.

13.8 Disclosure of the accounting policy for deferred tax

Under SSAP 2 the accounting policy for depreciation and deferred tax must be disclosed. For illustration the accounting policy of The EMI Group plc is set out as follows:

Accounting policies

Deferred taxation is calculated using the liability method in respect of timing differences arising primarily from the difference between the accounting and tax treatments of depreciation. Provision is made, or recovery anticipated, where timing differences are expected to reverse without replacement in the foreseeable future.

The company discloses the deferred tax provision in the notes to the accounts, as follows:

Note 22. Deferred taxation

	31.3.1999 £m.	31.3.1998 £m.
Excess of accumulated taxation allowances over depreciation provided against fixed assets	14.1	14.2
Other timing differences	19.5	19.6
Advance corporation tax*	—	(9.3)
	33.6	24.5

*Following the abolition of ACT, it is no longer appropriate to offset ACT against deferred tax.

In this example, the other timing differences relate to items where tax is payable on a receipts and payments basis, e.g. the receipt or payment of interest on a loan, whereas the accounts are prepared on an accrual basis.

The ASB Discussion Paper of March 1995 *Accounting for Taxation* states that disclosures relating to tax should aim to give the reader more insight into the tax affairs of the reporting entity than at present. In particular, a simple reconciliation between the actual tax and expected tax (the profit before tax multiplied by the United Kingdom tax rate) should be provided.

13.9 Interpretation

The pre-tax profit is frequently the figure used when calculating ratios to assess the management performance, e.g. return on capital employed. However, the post-tax profit is an important figure when assessing the ability of a company to make dividend distributions.

The accounting profession has attempted to develop a system for allocating tax that achieves a greater degree of uniformity and explains the differences between the taxable income and the reported income.

The policy chosen by EMI plc is a common one – it is a company with a significant capital expenditure. It can therefore assume with reasonable confidence that capital allowances will exceed depreciation for the foreseeable future. Consequently, the tax relief will continue without the company being called upon to pay the Revenue authorities.

If, however, one was looking at the accounts of a weaker company, one might well consider that such a policy might be less than prudent and, were one to be doubtful that the entity was a going concern, then it would be important to remember that on liquidation a liability will, in all probability, crystallise.

It is necessary to remember that although the deferred tax is included in the balance sheet, there is still some uncertainty over its ultimate value because the tax rates that will be in force in the future are unknown and the level of earnings that the firms will experience in future years is unknown.

13.10 Value added tax

VAT is one other tax that affects most companies and for which there is an accounting standard (SSAP 5 *Accounting for Value Added Tax*). This standard was issued in 1974 when the introduction of value added tax was imminent and there was considerable worry within the business community on its accounting treatment. We can now look back, having lived with VAT for well over two decades, and wonder, perhaps, why an SSAP was needed. VAT is essentially a tax on consumers collected by traders and is accounted for in a similar way to PAYE income tax, which is a tax on employees collected by employers.

13.10.1 The effects of the standard

These vary depending on the status of the accounting entity under the VAT legislation. The term 'trader' appears in the legislation and is the terminology for a business entity. The 'traders' or companies, as we would normally refer to them, are classified under the following headings.

(a) Registered trader

Accounts should only include figures net of VAT.

This means that the VAT on the sales will be deducted from the invoice amount. The VAT will be payable to the government and the net amount of the sales invoice will appear in the profit and loss account in arriving at the sales turnover figure. The VAT on purchases will be deducted from the purchase invoice. The VAT will then be reclaimed from the government and the net amount of the purchases invoice will appear in the profit and loss account in arriving at the purchases figure.

The only exception to the use of net of VAT amounts is when the input tax is not recoverable, e.g. on entertaining and on 'private' motor cars.

(b) Non-registered or exempt trader

For a company that is classified as non-registered or exempt, the VAT that it has to pay on its purchases and expenses is not reclaimable from the government. Because the company cannot recover the VAT, it means that the expense that appears in the profit and loss account must be inclusive of VAT. It is treated as part of each item of expenditure and the costs treated accordingly. It will be included, where relevant, with each item of expense (including capital expenditure) rather than being shown as a separate item.

(c) Partially exempt trader

This entity can only recover a proportion of input VAT, and the proportion of non-recoverable VAT should be treated as part of the costs on the same lines as the exempt trader. The VAT rules are complex but, for the purpose of understanding the figures that appear in published accounts of public companies, treatment as a registered trader would normally apply.

Summary
....

The major change that will have an impact on reported post-tax profits will be any decision to change from the partial provisioning approach applying in the UK in 1999 to the full provisioning method which is favoured by the IASC.

This will have varying effects on the trend of reported profits, with those companies that have heavy investment programmes seeing the deferred tax charged to the profit and loss account significantly increased and the earnings per share correspondingly reduced.

From April 1999, the UK corporation tax system has changed radically. Advance Corporation Tax (ACT) is no longer paid to the Inland Revenue when a company pays a dividend. Also, all but smaller companies will pay their corporation tax liability in quarterly instalments starting within the year of account rather than paying their mainstream corporation tax liability nine months after the year end.

Review questions
....

1 Why doesn't the charge to taxation in a company's accounts equal the profit multiplied by the current rate of corporation tax?

2 (a) Explain clearly how advance corporation tax arose and its effect on the profit and loss account and the year-end balance sheet figures. (Use a simple example to illustrate.)

(b) Explain how the corporation tax system changed as from April 1999.

(c) Deferred tax accounting is an income-smoothing device and distorts the true and fair view. Explain the impact of deferred tax on reported income and justify its continued use.

3 How are the dividends received and paid shown in the accounts?

4 Distinguish between the treatment for taxation of dividends received and debenture interest received.

5 Distinguish between (a) the deferral and the liability methods of company deferred tax; and (b) the flow-through and full provision methods

6 Why must unprovided deferred tax be shown by way of a note to the accounts?

7 Under SSAP 15 *Accounting for Deferred Tax* what criteria does a deferred tax provision need to satisfy in order to be accepted as a liability in the balance sheet?

8 Explain the effect of SSAP 5 *Accounting for Value Added Tax*.

Exercises

An extract from the solution is provided in the appendix at the end of the text for exercises marked with an asterisk (*)

Question 1

In your capacity as chief assistant to the financial controller, your managing director has asked you to consider the following letter received from a substantial shareholder who holds 4% of the company's voting shares:

> 'I note that whilst the current rate of corporation tax for last year was at 33% for companies making profits in excess of £1,500,000, your company is showing a tax charge for the year (on profits of £3,621,000) of only 24%. I asked a friend with a knowledge of these matters if he could explain this apparent discrepancy to me, but he was unable to do so. He informed me that the usual reason for such a discrepancy lay in the deferral of a tax liability because of significant capital expenditure, but that there was no reference to deferred taxation in the accounts. I would be obliged if you could explain this to me in a letter before the Annual General Meeting.'

You are aware that the reason for the low rate of taxation is indeed because of the significant excess of capital allowances for corporation tax over depreciation in the accounts, and that your financial controller convinced the auditors that it was reasonable to make no provision for deferred tax because of the plans for significant capital expenditure over the next ten years.

Required:

The managing director has asked that you write a report to him, in which:

(a) You explain the reason for any discrepancy to him and justify to him the use of a methodology in the preparation of the accounts which caused the above apparent discrepancy (which justification will not be shown to any shareholders);

(b) You draft a reply to the shareholder for him, which letter should explain and justify the reason for any discrepancy in the most general of terms.

* **Question 2**

A fixed asset (a machine) was purchased by Adjourn plc on 1 July 19X2 at a cost of £25,000.

The company prepares its annual accounts to 31 March in each year. The policy of the company is to depreciate such assets at the rate of 15% straight line (with depreciation being charged pro rata on a time apportionment basis in the year of purchase). The company was granted capital allowances at 25% per annum on the reducing balance method (such capital allowances are apportioned pro rata on a time apportionment basis in the year of purchase).

The rate of corporation tax has been as follows:

Year ended 31 Mar 19X3 26%
          31 Mar 19X4 25%
          31 Mar 19X5 25%
          31 Mar 19X6 24%
          31 Mar 19X7 24%

Required:
(a) Calculate the deferred tax provision using both the deferral method and the liability method.
(b) Explain why the liability method is considered by commentators to place the emphasis on the balance sheet, whereas the deferral method is considered to place the emphasis on the profit and loss account.

Question 3

(a) Discuss briefly the rationale for deferred taxation, and consider the nature of the policy choices available to the standard setters.

Dastardly plc is a highly profitable company engaged in the production of peccadillos. On 31 December 19X4 the net book value of fixed assets (entirely plant and machinery) per the published accounts was £8,750,000 compared with the tax written down value of £8,000,0000. Previously the company has been in breach of SSAP 15 as no deferred taxation has been hitherto provided.

The company has produced a budget indication of likely capital expenditure over the next few years, and from this the following information regarding depreciation and capital allowances has been derived:

Year ended 31 December	Capital allowances £000	Depreciation £000
1995	1,600	1,400
1996	1,750	1,600
1997	1,100	1,670

From 1998 onwards it is expected that capital allowances will be well in excess of depreciation.

(b) Assuming a corporation tax rate of 33%, determine the deferred tax charge or credit for each of the four years up to 31 December 1997 on the basis of the above forecast. Also determine the deferred tax liability or asset for inclusion on the balance sheet at each year end:

(1) on a full provision basis;

(2) on a basis which accords with the requirements of SSAP 15.

(c) Assume the anticipated expenditure on capital items gave rise to the following pattern of timing differences:

Year ended 31 December	Capital allowances	Depreciation
	£000	£000
1995	1,100	1,670
1996	1,600	1,400
1997	1,750	1,600

Given that all other facts remain unaltered, recalculate the relevant deferred tax/charge credit for the profit and loss account for the next four years, as well as the balance sheet liability/asset for each year-end on a partial provision basis.

(University of Portsmouth)

References

1   OECD, *Theoretical and Empirical Aspects of Corporate Taxation*, Paris, 1974: van den Temple, *Corporation Tax and Individual Income Tax in the EEC*, EEC Commission, Brussels, 1974.

2   G.H. Partington, and R.H. Chenhall, *Dividends, Distortion and Double Taxation*, Abacus, June 1983.

3   R. Altshul, 'Act now', *Accountancy Age*, 5 February 1998, p. 19.

4   William Gale, 'What can America Learn from the British Tax System?', *Fiscal Studies*, Vol. 18, No. 4, November 1997.

5   P. Rosenfield and W.C. Dent, 'Deferred income taxes', in R. Bloom and P.T. Elgers (eds), *Accounting Theory and Practice*, Harcourt Brace Jovanovich, 1987, p. 545.

6   J.T. Parkes, 'A Guide to FASB's Overhaul of Income Tax Accounting', *Journal of Accounting*, Vol. 165, April 1988.

7   Ron Paterson, 'Accountancy column: In support of the profit and loss account', *The Financial Times*, 16 September 1993.

8   L.G. Van der Tas, 'Evidence of EC Financial Reporting Harmonisation: the case of deferred taxation', *European Accounting Review*, 1992, 213.

9   Andrew C. Lennard during a guest lecture at Sunderland Business School.

10 M. Metcalf, 'Alchemical accounting', *Accountancy*, November 1999, p. 100.

11 Terry Smith, *Accounting for Growth: Sripping the Camouflage from Company Accounts*, (2nd edition), Random House, 1996.

12 *Ibid.*, p. 546.

13 R.J. Chambers, *Tax Allocation and Financial Reporting*, Abacus, 1968.

14 Prof. D.R. Middleton, Letters to the Editor, *The Financial Times*, 29 September 1994.

CHAPTER **14**

Tangible fixed assets and depreciation

14.1 Introduction

In this chapter we consider tangible fixed assets. It is helpful to consider the importance of fixed assets relative to intangible fixed assets, stocks and debtors. This will, of course, vary with the nature of the industry as shown if we consider the pharmaceutical and brewing industries.

The relative importance of the different categories of asset within the two industries based on average industry profile has been compiled from IPA UK Industrial Performance Analysis 1996/97 (ICC Business Publications Ltd 1996 – ISSN 0262 3684) based on 83 pharmaceutical manufacturers and developers and 55 brewers and appears on Figure 14.1.

For fixed tangible assets the accounting treatment is based on the accruals or matching concepts, under which expenditure is capitalised until it is charged as depreciation against revenue in the period in which benefit is gained from its use. Thus, if an item is purchased that has an economic life of two years, so that it will be used over two

Figure 14.1 Ratio of assets to total assets for 1994/95 for 83 pharmaceutical manufacturers and developers and 55 brewers.

1994/95 Averages (£'000s)
Pharmaceutical manufacturers and developers (83 companies)

	Tangible fixed assets	Intangible fixed assets	Stock	Trade debtors	Total assets
Average (£'000)	82,375	31,246	23,471	35,452	243,667
% of total assets	33.8%	12.8%	9.6%	14.5%	

1994/95 Averages (£'000s)
Brewers (55 companies)

	Tangible fixed assets	Intangible fixed assets	Stock	Trade debtors	Total assets
Average (£'000)	202,284	123	8,410	11,525	258,256
% of total assets	78.3%	0%	3.3%	4.5%	

accounting periods to help earn profit for the enterprise, then the cost of that asset should be apportioned in some way between the two accounting periods.

However, this does not take into account the problems surrounding fixed asset accounting and depreciation, which have so far given rise to four statements of standard accounting practice. We will consider these problems in this chapter covering:

- FRS 11 – What is a fixed asset?
- FRS 15 – What is depreciation and the constituents in the depreciation formula?
- Determining the cost and valuation of fixed assets
- How is the economic life of an asset determined?
- Residual value
- Calculation of depreciation
- Disclosure requirements
- SSAP 4 – Government grants
- SSAP 19 – Investment properties
- Effect of depreciation on the interpretation of accounts

14.2 What is a fixed asset?

There are two definitions, one in the Companies Act 1985 which is supplemented by that in FRS 11 *Impairment of Fixed Assets and Goodwill.*

The Companies Act defines fixed assets as those which are intended for use on a continuing basis in the company's activities and any assets which are not intended for such use are taken to be current assets.[1]

FRS 11 supplements this by defining tangible fixed assets as 'assets that have a physical substance and are held for use in the production or supply of goods or services, for rental to others, or for administrative purposes on a continuing basis in the reporting entity's activities'.[2]

Certain assets fall very clearly into these definitions e.g. production plant and machinery, equipment owned by a plant hire company, the building that houses the accounts department, a computer used by that department.

14.2.1 Problems that may arise

Problems may arise in relation to the interpretation of the definition and in relation to the application of the materiality concept.

The definitions give rise to some areas of practical difficulty. For example, an asset that has previously been employed in the business but whose use has now ceased should no longer be treated as a fixed asset, even if it still has a value and the enterprise is endeavouring to sell it. Under both definitions the asset should not be treated as fixed.

Differing accounting treatments arise if there are different assessments of materiality. This may result in the same expenditure being reported as an asset in the balance sheet of one company and as an expense in the profit and loss account of another company. In the accounts of a self-employed carpenter, a kit of handtools that, with careful maintenance, will last many years will, quite rightly, be shown as a fixed asset. Similar assets used by the maintenance department in a large factory will, in all probability, be treated as 'loose tools' and written off as acquired.

Many enterprises have *de minimis* policies, whereby only items exceeding a certain value are treated as fixed assets; items below the cut-off amount will be expensed through the profit and loss account.

14.3 What is depreciation?

FRS 15 defines depreciation as:

> the measure of the cost or revalued amount of the economic benefits of the tangible asset that have been consumed during the period. Consumption includes the wearing out, using up or other reduction in the useful economic life of a tangible fixed asset whether arising from use, effluxion of time or obsolescence through either changes in technology or demand for the goods and services produced by the asset.[3]

Note that this definition places an emphasis on the consumption in a particular accounting period rather than an average over the asset's life. We will consider two aspects of the definition: the measure of wearing out; and the useful economic life.

14.3.1 Measure of wearing out

Depreciation is a measure of wearing out that is calculated annually and charged as an expense against profits. Under the 'matching concept', the cost of the asset is allocated over its productive life.

It is important to make clear what depreciation is **not**:

● It is not 'saving up for a new one'; it is not setting funds aside for the replacement of the existing asset at the end of its life; it is the matching of cost to revenue. The effect is to reduce the profit available for distribution, but this is not accompanied by the setting aside of cash of an equal amount to ensure that liquid funds are available at the end of the asset's life.

● It is not 'a way of showing the real value of assets on the balance sheet' by reducing the cost figure to realisable value.

We emphasise what depreciation is not because both of these ideas are commonly held by non-accountant users of accounts; it is as well to realise this possible misconception when interpreting accounts for non-accountants.

Depreciation is currently conceived as a charge for funds **already expended**, and thus it cannot be considered as the setting aside of funds to meet future expenditure. If we consider it in terms of capital maintenance, then we can see that it results in the maintenance of the initial invested monetary capital of the company. It is concerned with the allocation of that expenditure over a period of time, without having regard for the **value** of the asset at any intermediate period of its life.

Where an asset has been revalued the depreciation is, however, based on the revalued amount. This ensures that capital maintenance continues in monetary terms.

14.3.2 Useful economic life

FRS 15 para. 2 defines this as: 'The period over which the entity expects to derive economic benefits from the asset. In estimating useful economic life regard should be had to reasonably expected technological changes that will have an effect on the asset's life.'

The FRED definition is based on the premise that almost all assets have a finite useful economic life. This may be true in principle, but it is incredibly difficult in real life to arrive at an average economic life that can be applied to even a single class of assets, e.g. plant. This is evidenced by the accounting policy in the ICI 1999 accounts which states:

> *Depreciation* – The Group's policy is to write-off the book value of each tangible fixed asset to its residual value evenly over its estimated remaining life. Reviews are made annually of the estimated remaining lives of individual productive assets, taking account of commercial and technological obsolescence as well as normal wear and tear. Under this policy it becomes impractical to calculate average asset lives exactly; however, the total lives approximate to 33 years for buildings and 16 years for plant and equipment. Depreciation of assets qualifying for grant is calculated on their full cost.

In addition to the practical difficulty of estimating economic lives, there are also exceptions where nil depreciation is charged. Two common exceptions found in the accounts of UK companies relate to freehold land and certain types of property.

14.3.3 Freehold land

Freehold land (but not the buildings thereon) is considered to have an infinite life unless it is held simply for the extraction of minerals, etc. Thus land held for the purpose of, say, mining coal or quarrying gravel will be dealt with for accounting purposes as a coal or gravel deposit. Consequently, although the land may have an infinite life, the deposits will have an economic life only as long as they can be profitably extracted. If the cost of extraction exceeds the potential profit from extraction and sale, the economic life of the quarry has ended. When assessing depreciation for a commercial company, we are concerned only with these private costs and benefits, and not with public costs and benefits which might lead to the quarry being kept open.

An example of the reporting of mineral deposits appears in the 1996 accounts of Redland plc, where the accounting policies contain the following statement:

> Depreciation is provided on mineral bearing land to reflect the diminution in economic values as a result of mineral extraction. As a result no provision is made where the remaining life is judged to be in excess of 20 years since the amount is not material. No depreciation is provided on other freehold land.

14.3.4 Certain types of property

Prior to FRS 15, it was relatively common for companies not to charge depreciation on certain types of property. This was particularly true of companies in the brewing industry and others with a large property portfolio. The reason frequently cited was that the values of the property were maintained through refurbishment and repairs.[4]

An example is provided by this extract from the accounts of Whitbread plc for the year ended 1 March 1997. An extract from the accounting policy reads:

While it is the group's policy to depreciate fixed assets, the nature of the retail trade requires that, in order to protect that trade, retail premises are maintained to such a state of repair that their residual value is at least equal to their book amounts based on prices prevailing at the date of acquisition or subsequent valuation.

Depreciation charges are omitted as being immaterial in such cases but the companies are still required to conduct regular impairment reviews.

FRS 15 recognises[5] that there has been a growing trend towards the non-depreciation of certain tangible fixed assets, particularly property where it has been argued by companies that maintenance is carried out regularly, thereby extending the economic life or maintaining the residual value. The ASB response has been to state their belief that the estimate of a tangible fixed asset's useful economic life cannot be extended limitlessly through maintenance, refurbishment, overhaul or replacement of components of the asset because the physical life cannot be indefinite.

The Board view[6] is that the only grounds for not charging depreciation are that the depreciation charge and related accumulated depreciation are not material owing to a long estimated remaining useful life or high residual value.

This would appear to allow companies to continue not to provide for depreciation on grounds of immateriality or to adopt a long economic life of more than 50 years. There is, however, a sting in FRS 15's tail for companies that follow that path – it requires them to carry out an annual impairment review. This can be onerous and expensive. Consequently, companies will probably follow the example of PizzaExpress Plc in its 1999 Annual Report, where it states its accounting policy as follows:

Tangible fixed assets
Until 1 July 1998 no amortisation was provided on freehold and long leasehold properties because they were kept in a continual state of sound repair and the directors considered their lives and residual values were such that the amortisation would be insignificant. In accordance with FRS 15, 'Tangible fixed assets', it is now the Group's policy to amortise prospectively the cost of freehold and long leasehold properties over the lesser of 50 years or the outstanding term of the lease.

14.4 What are the constituents in the depreciation formula?

In order to calculate depreciation it is necessary to determine three factors:

● Cost (or revalued amount if the company is following a revaluation policy).
● Economic life.
● Residual value.

A simple example is the calculation of the depreciation charge for a company that has acquired an asset on 1 January 20X1 for £1,000 with an estimated economic life of four years and an estimated residual value of £200. Applying a straight-line depreciation policy, the charge would be £200 per year using the formula

$$\frac{\text{Cost} - \text{Estimated residual value}}{\text{Estimated economic life}} = \frac{£1,000 - £200}{4} = £200 \text{ per annum}$$

We can see that the charge of £200 is influenced in all cases by the definition of cost; the estimate of the residual value; the estimate of the economic life; and the management decision on depreciation policy.

In addition, if the cost were to be revalued at the end of the second year to £900, then the depreciation for 20X3 and 20X4 would be recalculated using the revised valuation figure. Assuming that the residual value remained unchanged, the depreciation for 20X3 would be:

$$\frac{\text{Revalued asset} - \text{Estimated residual value}}{\text{Estimated economic life}} = \frac{£900 - £200}{2} = £350 \text{ per annum}$$

14.5 Determination of the cost of fixed assets

The Companies Act 1985 states that, subject to any provisions for depreciation or diminution in value, all fixed assets shall be included at their purchase price or production cost.[7] Guidance is available on the definition of production cost in both the Companies Act and FRS 15 para. 6.

14.5.1 Guidance in the Companies Act

Production cost is defined as including:

> the price of the raw materials and consumables used and the costs incurred by the company which are directly attributable to the production cost of that asset. In addition, the production cost may include the following to the extent that they relate to the period of production:
>
> (a) a reasonable proportion of the costs incurred by the company indirectly attributable to the production of the asset; and
>
> (b) interest on the capital borrowed to finance the production of that asset.[8]

The Act also defines purchase price as 'the actual price paid and any expenses incidental to the acquisition'.

14.5.2 Guidance in FRS 15 *Tangible Fixed Assets*

FRS 15 provides additional guidance to cover items that may be included in production cost. An asset that is purchased and simply installed in, say, a factory presents little problem. There the cost will include, *inter alia*:

● the invoice price of the asset;

● any delivery costs (including, for imported assets, duty, etc.); and

● installation or erection costs, including site preparation.

Difficulty arises when major projects to build fixed assets are undertaken, particularly if the company's own labour or resources are employed in actual construction or project management. In these circumstances, the FRS provides that only costs attributable to bringing the asset into working condition for its intended use should be included.
Directly attributable costs are defined as:

(a) the direct labour costs of own employees (e.g. site workers, in-house architects)

(b) incremental costs that would have been avoided if the tangible fixed asset were not acquired ie administration and general overheads would be excluded.

Examples of directly attributable costs include cost of site preparation and clearance, initial delivery and handling costs, installation costs, professional fees, estimated cost of dismantling and removing the asset and restoring the site, to the extent that it is recognised under FRS 12 Provisions, Contingent Liabilities and Contingent Assets.

There are restrictions on the time over which costs may be capitalised, namely:

● The capitalisation of costs should not begin until there is reasonable probability that the project will be undertaken, or has been undertaken, and is expected to be successfully completed.

● When the construction of a fixed asset is completed in parts and each part is capable of being used commercially while construction continues on the other parts, capitalisation of costs on each part should cease when it is completed.

● When costs are incurred in commissioning a fixed asset, capitalisation of costs should cease when the fixed asset is substantially complete and ready for use even if it has not yet been brought into use.

In addition to the rules relating to the commencement and cessation of expenditure capitalisation, there are a number of other considerations. We deal briefly with three of these: how to treat cost over-runs; how to treat assets that are purchased from another member of a group; and how to treat borrowing costs incurred in connection with the fixed asset construction.

14.5.3 Treatment of cost over-runs

The material factor is the reason for the over-run. If the over-run arose from circumstances outside the planning or control of the company, such as a nationally agreed pay rise, then the expenditure is capitalised. If, however, the costs arose from inefficiencies, such as failure to ensure that materials were on site at the planned date, then these should not be included in the production cost of a fixed asset; they should be expensed through the profit and loss account of the period in which the inefficiency occurred.

14.5.4 Treatment of intragroup sales

In consolidated financial statements, the cost of a fixed asset should not include any intragroup profit or loss. This is intended to prevent a group creating unrealised profits in the consolidated profit and loss account. In selling and buying between subsidiary companies, the assets will be recorded in their individual company accounts at whatever transfer price they agree between themselves. It is only at group level that the price is adjusted to the net book value as at the date of the transfer.

14.5.5 Treatment of borrowing costs

The capitalisation of borrowing costs is addressed by an international standard. This standard does not insist on capitalisation of borrowing costs; rather it requires the company that has incurred borrowing costs to adopt, and consistently apply, a policy of capitalisation or non-capitalisation, to establish criteria if it decides on a capitalisation policy, and to disclose the amount of borrowing costs that have been capitalised during the current accounting period.

Views differ on the appropriate accounting treatment. Some regard borrowing costs as part of the cost of the asset; others regard them as costs that are charged to income regardless of how borrowing is applied. The significant borrowing costs incurred by companies make their accounting treatment an important consideration in the preparation of financial statements.[9]

The arguments in favour of capitalisation are based on the reality that, when a major project is undertaken which takes a substantial time to complete, borrowing will occur and will form a real part of the overall cost of the asset; if such costs are not capitalised, the earnings will be distorted during the production period. Problems will also occur if accounts are compared with companies that have acquired similar assets 'ready-made', where the supplier will have undoubtedly taken into account financing costs when determining the selling price.

However, it can be argued that capitalising financing costs during construction and then treating the continuing financing costs as a normal trading expense is illogical, and that the allocation of total borrowing costs between 'trading' and 'project' may be arbitrary. These arguments can be closely debated.

This is recognised by FRS 15, which proposes that the practice be allowed, but only if the reporting entity employs a consistent policy. There are specific requirements if it is company policy to capitalise borrowing costs, FRS 15 para. 19 *'Where an entity adopts a policy of capitalising finance costs, finance costs that are directly attributable to the construction of tangible fixed assets should be capitalised as part of the cost of those assets. The total amount of finance costs capitalised during a period should not exceed the total amount of finance costs incurred during that period.'* However, comparability is frustrated by allowing companies to choose whether or not to capitalise borrowing costs.

14.5.6 No unique cost

There is not a unique, correct cost. The determination of cost is influenced by a number of factors, such as the time when expenditures are to commence and cease being capitalised; the reason for the costs arising; and the company policy on the capitalisation of borrowing costs. Management decisions in each of these areas will have a direct impact on the asset figure that appears in the balance sheet and the profit for the year.

14.6 Determination of the valuation on the revaluation of fixed assets

It has become commonplace for accounts, otherwise prepared under the historical cost convention, to include some assets (usually interests in land and buildings) at valuation. This could provide useful information for the users of the accounts, in terms of both the current replacement cost of the fixed assets and the current replacement cost of at least the fixed asset content of the balance sheet when calculating the capital employed. However, in practice the information is not as useful as it could be because:

● the same balance sheet may contain a mixture of two accounting conventions at the expense of the integrity of both;

● it has also been possible for a company to revalue individual assets at will.

This is shown by the following extracts from the 1999 accounts of Galliford plc:

> *Accounting policy*
>
> The financial statements are prepared under the historical cost convention, as modified by the revaluation of certain freehold properties, and in accordance with applicable accounting standards.

Extract from note 9 of the 1999 accounts

Note 9 Land and buildings

	£000
Cost or valuation at 1 July 1998	2,088
Disposals	(1)
Additions	287
	2,374
Comprising:	
Cost	1,556
As valued 1978	548
As valued 1987	270
	2,374
Depreciation	390
Net book value at 30 June 1999	1,984

There is a mix of costs and valuations and the valuations are selective and at different dates. The company does however provide information of the position if historical cost convention had not been modified:

Land and buildings would have been included at the following amounts, but for certain revaluations in 1978 and 1987:

Cost	2,046
Aggregate depreciation	389
	1,657

FRS 15 proposes that the practice of revaluation should be allowed to continue, but with some restrictions:

● The accounting policy of whether or not to carry assets at valuation rather than cost must be applied consistently by class of asset.

● The valuation should be prepared by a qualified valuer (usually an external valuer) on an existing use basis although investment properties should be on an open market valuation.

● When the valuation is carried out by an officer or employee of the company, the basis of the valuation should be reviewed externally.

● Where an asset is revalued, all assets of the same class should be revalued.

● Depreciation provisions should be based on the revalued amount, so that the profit and loss account and balance sheet articulate. This avoids the process known as split depreciation, whereby the charge to the profit and loss account is based on a figure other than the carrying amount of the asset in the balance sheet.

14.6.1 Reporting gains and losses on revaluation

Revaluation gains should be recognised in the statement of total recognised gains and losses unless they represent the reversal of losses previously recognised in the profit and loss account. Revaluation losses that are due to the consumption of economic benefits should be recognised in the profit and loss account. An example of this could be the revaluation of mineral deposits in a mine following a geological survey.

Gains or losses on disposal should be similarly treated. Thus a gain or loss, which is fundamentally a final adjustment to depreciation, will pass through the profit and loss account whilst a gain resulting from holding an asset will simply appear in the Statement of total recognised gains and losses.

A number of companies already strictly apply the historical cost convention in their accounts, e.g. The Body Shop International, and, following the increased regulation of revaluation, it could well be that companies will follow the example of the Rank Group and revert to accounting for land and buildings on a historical cost basis. Companies will need to balance the effect of revaluation, e.g. valuation fees and, higher depreciation charges, in the profit and loss account and lower return on capital employed ratio against the increased relevance of information based on current values. Decisions will be influenced by a board assessment of relative importance, for example, if a company is likely to be the subject of a take-over or to need to raise additional finance, there could be merit in revaluing its assets.

14.7 How is the useful economic life of an asset determined?

FRS 15 defines useful economic life as 'the period over which the entity expects to derive economic benefits from that asset'. This is not necessarily the total life expectancy of the asset. Most assets become less economically and technologically efficient as they grow older. For this reason, assets may well cease to have an economic life long before their working life is over. It is the responsibility of the preparers of accounts to estimate the economic life of all assets.

It is conventional for enterprises to consider the economic lives of assets by class or category, e.g. buildings; plant; office equipment; or motor vehicles. However, this is not necessarily appropriate, since the level of activity demanded by different users may differ. For example, compare two motor cars owned by a business: one is used by the national sales manager, covering 100,000 miles per annum visiting clients; the other is used by the accountant to drive from home to work and occasionally the bank, covering perhaps one-tenth of the mileage.

FRS 15 takes this argument a stage further by stating that it might be appropriate to break down certain assets into their component parts. It gives the example of an aircraft where the engines may well have a shorter life-span than their airframe, which will continue flying (with the aid of replacement engines) long after the original engines have reached the end of their useful lives.

In practice, the useful economic life would be determined by reference to factors such as repair costs, the cost and availability of replacements, and the comparative cash flows of existing and alternative assets. The problem of optimal replacement lives is a normal financial management problem; its significance in financial reporting is that the assumptions used within the financial management decision may provide evidence of the expected economic life.

14.7.1 Other factors affecting the economic life figure

We can see that there are technical factors affecting the estimated economic life figure. In addition, other factors have prompted companies to set estimated lives that have no relationship to the active productive life of the asset. One such factor is the wish of management to take into account the effect of inflation.[10] This led some companies to reduce the estimated economic life, so that a higher charge was made against profits during the early period of the asset's life to compensate for the inflationary effect on the cost of replacement. The total charge will be the same, but the timing is advanced. This does not result in the retention of funds necessary to replace; but it does reflect the fact that there is at present no coherent policy for dealing with inflation in the published accounts – consequently, companies resort to *ad hoc* measures that frustrate efforts to make accounts uniform and comparable. *Ad hoc* measures such as these have prompted changes in the standards.

14.8 Residual value

FRS 15 defines residual value as:

> the net realisable value of an asset at the end of its useful economic life. Residual values are based on prices prevailing at the date of acquisition (or revaluation), and do not take account of expected future price changes.

This definition is not without its critics. While most would accept that it is proper when preparing accounts under the historical cost convention to ignore the potential effects of future inflation, it has been suggested that basing residual values on current prices without considering expected changes in technology or in the position of supply and demand will lead to inaccuracies in the regular charges to profit and loss. This highlights a weakness in the FRS, which requires economic lives to be reviewed regularly, but does not require similar reviews of residual values.

Besides inflation, residual values can be affected by changes in technology and market conditions. For example, during the period 1980–90 the cost of small business computers fell dramatically in both real and monetary terms, with a considerable impact on the residual (or second-hand) value of existing equipment.

14.9 Calculation of depreciation

Having determined the key factors in the computation, we are left with the problem of how to allocate that cost between accounting periods. For example, with an asset having an economic life of five years:

Asset cost	£11,000
Residual value	£ 1,000
Depreciable amount	£10,000

How should the depreciable amount be charged to the profit and loss account over the five years? FRS 15 tells us that it should be allocated on a systematic basis and the depreciation method used should reflect as fairly as possible the pattern in which the asset's economic benefits are consumed. The two most popular methods are **straight-line**, in which the depreciation is charged evenly over the useful life, and **reducing balance**, where depreciation is calculated annually on the net written-down amount. In the case above, the calculations would be as in Figure 14.2.

Note that, although the reducing balance is generally expressed in terms of a percentage, this percentage is arrived at by inserting the economic life into the formula as n; the 38% reflects the expected economic life of five years. As we change the life, so we change the percentage that is applied. The normal rate applied to vehicles is 25% reducing balance; if we apply that to the cost and residual value in our example, we can see that we would be assuming an economic life of eight years. It is a useful test when using reducing balance percentages to refer back to the underlying assumptions.

We can see that the end result is the same. Thus, £10,000 has been charged against profits, but with a dramatically different pattern of profit and loss charges. The charge for straight-line depreciation in the first year is less than half that for reducing balance.

14.9.1 Arguments in favour of the straight-line method

The method is simple to calculate. However, in these days of calculators and computers this seems a particularly facile argument, particularly when one considers the materiality of the figures.

Figure 14.2 Effect of different depreciation methods.

	Straight-line (£2,000) £	Reducing balance (38%) £	Difference £
Cost	11,000	11,000	
Depreciation for year 1	2,000	4,180	2,180
Net book value ('NBV')	9,000	6,820	
Depreciation for year 2	2,000	2,592	592
NBV	7,000	4,228	
Depreciation for year 3	2,000	1,606	(394)
NBV	5,000	2,622	
Depreciation for year 4	2,000	996	(1,004)
NBV	3,000	1,626	
Depreciation for year 5	2,000	618	(1,382)
Residual value	1,000	1,008	

The reducing balance formula was $1 - \sqrt[n]{(\text{Residual value/Cost})}$

14.9.2 Arguments in favour of the reducing balance method

First, the charge reflects the efficiency and maintenance costs of the asset. When new, an asset is operating at its maximum efficiency, which falls as it nears the end of its life. This may be countered by the comment that in year 1 there may be 'teething troubles' with new equipment, which, while probably covered by a supplier's guarantee, will hamper efficiency.

Secondly, the pattern of reducing balance depreciation gives a net book amount that approximates to second-hand values. For example, with motor cars the initial fall in value is very high.

14.9.3 Other methods of depreciating

Besides straight-line and reducing balance, there are a number of other methods of depreciating, such as sum of the digits, the machine-hour and the annuity method. We will consider these briefly.

Sum of the digits method

A compromise between straight-line and reducing balance that is popular in the USA is the sum of the digits method. The calculation based on the information in Figure 14.2 is now shown in Figure 14.3. This has the advantage that, unlike reducing balance, it is simple to obtain the exact residual amount (zero if appropriate), while giving the pattern of high initial charge shown by the reducing balance approach.

Machine-hour method

The machine-hour system is based on an estimate of the asset's service potential. The economic life is measured not in accounting periods but in working hours, and the depre-

Figure 14.3 Sum of the digits method.

		£
Cost		11,000
Depreciation for year 1	£10,000 × 5/15	3,333
Net book value ('NBV')		7,667
Depreciation for year 2	£10,000 × 4/15	2,667
NBV		5,000
Depreciation for year 3	£10,000 × 3/15	2,000
NBV		3,000
Depreciation for year 4	£10,000 × 2/15	1,333
NBV		1,667
Depreciation for year 5	£10,000 × 1/15	667
Residual value		1,000

ciation is allocated in the proportion of the actual hours worked to the potential total hours available. This method is commonly employed in aviation, where aircraft are depreciated on the basis of flying hours.

Annuity method

Although rarely employed, the annuity method is theoretically most attractive.[11] The asset, or rather the amount of capital representing the asset, is regarded as being capable of earning a fixed rate of interest. The sacrifice incurred in using the asset within the business is therefore twofold: the loss arising from the exhaustion of the service potential of the asset; and the interest forgone by using the funds invested in the business to purchase the fixed asset. With the help of annuity tables, a calculation shows what equal amounts of depreciation, written off over the estimated life of the asset, will reduce the book value to nil, after debiting interest to the asset account on the diminishing amount of funds that are assumed to be invested in the business at that time, as represented by the value of the asset.

Figure 14.4 contains an illustration based on the treatment of a five-year lease which cost the company a premium of £10,000 on 1 January 20X1.

An extract from the annuity tables to obtain the factor for year 5 and assuming a rate of interest of 10% would show:

Year	Annuity $A_{\overline{n}|}^{-1}$
1	1.1000
2	0.5762
3	0.4021
4	0.3155
5	0.2638

The interest debited to the asset account is credited to the interest account, whence it is subsequently transferred to the credit of the profit and loss account; the depreciation is credited to the asset account, and debited to the depreciation account, which account is transferred to the debit of the profit and loss account each year.

The charge for depreciation increases each year, while the credit for interest gradually falls as the book value of the asset decreases; the result on profits is seen to be an

Figure 14.4 Annuity method.

Year	Cost/WDV b/f £	Interest credited £	Depreciation charged £	WDV c/f £	Net P&L £
1	10,000	1,000	2,638	8,632	1,638
2	8,362	836	2,638	6,560	1,802
3	6,560	656	2,638	4,578	1,982
4	4,578	458	2,638	2,398	2,180
5	2,398	240	2,638	—	2,398
		3,190	13,190		10,000

increasing net charge in respect of the asset. However, when the interest earned by the assets, representing the preceding amounts written off, is taken into consideration, this method tends to give an equal real charge each year.

A variation on this system involves the investment of a sum equal to the net charge in fixed interest securities or an endowment policy, so as to build up a fund that will generate cash to replace the asset at the end of its life.

This last system has significant weaknesses. It is based on the misconception that depreciation is 'saving up for a new one', whereas in reality depreciation is charging against profits funds already expended. It is also dangerous in a time of inflation, since it may lead management not to maintain the capital of the enterprise adequately, so that it is able to replace the assets at their new (inflated) prices.

The annuity method, with its increasing net charge to profit and loss, does tend to take inflationary factors into account, but it must be noted that the *total* net profit and loss charge only adds up to the cost of the asset.

14.9.4 Which method should be used?

The answer to this seemingly simple question is 'it depends'. On the matter of depreciation FRS 15 is designed primarily to force a fair charge for the use of assets into the profit and loss account each year, so that the earnings reflect a true and fair view. It is regarded as defective by a number of companies, which consider the charge inadequate in times of inflation. We have seen that some companies reduced the economic life in order to generate a higher earlier charge; other companies, such as GEC,[12] adopted a practice of charging supplementary depreciation on assets without changing the balance sheet carrying value. This practice was disallowed by the ASC, which required the company either to revalue the assets so that the profit and loss account and balance sheet articulated after the charge, or to treat the supplementary charge as an appropriation rather than an expense. Treating the supplementary charge as an appropriation has an impact on the EPS figure and the return on capital figure.

Straight-line is most suitable for assets such as leases which have a definite fixed life. It is also considered most appropriate for assets with a short working life, although with motor cars the reducing balance method is usually employed to match second-hand values. Extraction industries (mining, oil wells, quarries, etc.) usually employ a variation on the machine-hour system, where depreciation is based on the amount extracted as a proportion of the estimated reserves.

14.9.5   What are substitute methods of depreciation?

The accounting policy of Scottish Power in its 1999 accounts states:

Tangible fixed assets – Infrastructure accounting
The depreciation charge for water infrastructure assets is the estimated level of annualised expenditure required to maintain the operating capability of the network and is based on the asset management plan agreed with the water industry regulator as part of the price regulation process... The method of accounting for water infrastructure renewals has been revised following the introduction of FRS 12 'Provisions, contingent liabilities and contingent assets' and the infrastructure renewals accounting basis as set out in FRS 15 'Tangible fixed assets'. ... The change of accounting policy has no effect on the profit and loss account other than to reclassify the renewals charge as depreciation.

FRS 15 accepts this approach under what it terms *Renewals Accounting*. It considers that *Renewals Accounting* is a substitute method of calculating the depreciation of infrastructure assets and proposes that the annual level of expenditure required to maintain the operating capacity of the infrastructure assets is treated as a depreciation provision and deducted from the carrying value of the asset; when the actual expenditure takes place it is capitalised.

14.9.6   Impairment of fixed assets

FRS 11 *Impairment of Fixed Assets and Goodwill*[13] was issued by the ASB in July 1998 based on FRED 15 issued in June 1997. FRS 11 deals with the problems of the measurement, recognition and presentation of material reductions in value of fixed assets both tangible and intangible.

Fixed assets will be required to be reviewed for impairment only if there is some indication that impairment has occurred, e.g. slump in property market or expected future losses.

The ASB's aim is to ensure that fixed assets are recorded **at no more than recoverable amount**. This is defined as being the higher of net realisable value and value in use. Value in use is defined as the **present value** of future cash flows obtainable from the asset's continued use using a **discount rate** that is equivalent to the rate of return that the market would expect on an equally risky investment.

There could be a temptation to assume high growth rates when estimating future cash flows. FRS 11 adopts the FRED 15 approach which provided (para. 51) that:

In the periods following an impairment review, the cash flows achieved should be compared with those forecast. If the actual cash flows are so much less than those forecast that use of the actual cash flows could have required recognition of an impairment in previous periods, the original impairment calculation should be re-performed using the actual cash flows. Any impairment identified should be recognised in the current period unless the impairment has reversed.

14.9.7   ASB Paper, *Discounting in Financial Reporting*, 1997[14]

Discounting has been already been used for leases, pensions and capital instruments. Although there has been concern that discounting is being introduced piecemeal into financial statements, the view of the ASB appears to be to apply discounting on a case by case basis. In general, discounting is not required for current assets and current liabilities because the period of the cash flows is unlikely to see a material change in amounts realised. For long-term assets and liabilities however the effect of discounting can be significant.

The ASB view is that discounting should take account of the risk attaching to the cash flows by adjusting the cash flows or by adjusting the discount rate. For the impairment of fixed assets test, it favours the use of risk-adjusted discount rates from the market.

14.10 FRS 11 – Impairment of Tangible Fixed Assets

14.10.1 FRS 11 approach

FRS 11 sets out the principles and methodology for accounting for impairments of fixed assets and goodwill. Where possible, individual fixed assets should be tested for impairment. However, where cash flows do not arise from the use of a single fixed asset, impairment is measured for the smallest group of assets which generates income that is largely independent of the company's other income streams. This smallest group is referred to as an Income-Generating Unit (IGU).

Impairment of a fixed asset, or IGU (if fixed assets are grouped), occurs when:

● the carrying amount of a fixed asset or IGU is greater than its recoverable amount; where
  ● carrying amount is the depreciated historical cost (or depreciated revalued amount);
  ● recoverable amount is the higher of net realisable value and value in use; where
    – net realisable value is the amount at which an asset could be disposed of, less any direct selling costs, and
    – value in use is the present value of the future cash flows obtainable as a result of an asset's continued use, including those resulting from its ultimate disposal.

When impairment occurs a **revised carrying amount** is calculated for the balance sheet as follows:

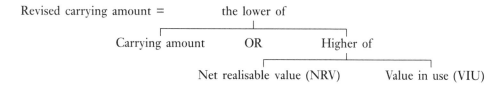

Note that it is only necessary to calculate value in use if:

Depreciated historical cost > Value in use > Net realisable value

The revised carrying amount is then depreciated over the remaining useful economic life.

14.10.2 Dividing activities into IGUs

In order to carry out an impairment review it is necessary to decide how to divide activities into IGUs. There is no single answer to this – it is extremely judgmental, e.g. if the company has multi-retail sites, the cost of preparing detailed cash flow forecasts for each site could favour grouping.

The risk of grouping is that poor performing operations might be concealed within an IGU and it would be necessary to consider if there were any commercial reasons for breaking an IGU into smaller constituents, e.g. if a location was experiencing its own unique difficulties such as local competition or inability to obtain planning permission to expand to a more profitable size.

14.10.3   Indications of impairment

A review for impairment is required when there is an indication that an impairment has actually occurred. The following are indicators of impairment:

● External indicators
  – a fall in the market value of the asset
  – material adverse changes in regulatory environment
  – material adverse changes in markets
  – material long-term increases in market rates of return used for discounting.

● Internal indicators
  – material changes in operations
  – major reorganisation
  – loss of key personnel
  – loss or net cash outflow from operating activities if this is expected to continue or is a continuation of a loss-making situation.

If there is such an indication, it is necessary to determine the depreciated historical cost if a single fixed asset or the net assets employed if an IGU and compare this with the net realisable value and value in use.

14.10.4   Value in use calculation

Value in use is arrived at by estimating and discounting the income stream. In some cases a detailed calculation of value in use will not be necessary if a simple estimate is sufficient to demonstrate that either value in use is higher than carrying value, in which case there is no impairment, or value in use is lower than net realisable value, in which case impairment is measured by reference to net realisable value.

The **income streams**:

● are likely to follow the way in which management monitors and makes decisions about continuing or closing the different lines of business;

● may often be identified by reference to major products or services (FRS 11 para. 29);

● should be based on reasonable and supportable assumptions;

● should be consistent with the most up-to-date budgets and plans that have been formally approved by management:
  – if for a period beyond that covered by formal budgets and plans should, unless there are exceptional circumstances, assume a steady or declining growth rate (FRS 11 para. 36);

● should be projected cash flows unadjusted for risk, discounted at a rate of return expected from a similarly risky investment or should be projected risk-adjusted pre-tax cash flows discounted at a risk-free rate.

The **discount rate** should be:

● calculated on a pre-tax basis

- an estimate of the rate that the market would expect on an equally risky investment excluding the effects of any risk for which the cash flows have been adjusted (FRS 11 para. 41):
  - increased to reflect higher risk if the cash flow forecasts assume a rate of growth that exceeds the long-term average growth rate for more than five years (FRS 11 para. 43);
  - reduced to a risk-free rate if the cash flows have been adjusted for risk (FRS 11 para. 45).

14.10.5   Treatment of impairment losses

If the depreciated historical cost (or net assets employed) exceeds the higher of net realisable value and value in use, then an impairment loss has occurred. The accounting treatment of such a loss is as follows:

Asset not previously revalued

An impairment loss should be recognised in the profit and loss account in the year in which the impairment arises.

Asset previously revalued

The reason for the impairment is important. If the impairment loss arises from damage, or other deterioration, the fall in value is similar to depreciation and must be charged to the profit as an operating cost. If however the impairment loss arises from a general change in prices, e.g. a fall in property prices, this would be reflected in the statement of total recognised gains and losses up to the amount of any previously recognised gain on revaluation. Any excess impairment (below depreciated historical cost) would be charged to the profit and loss account.

Allocation of impairment losses

Where an impairment loss arises the loss should be set against the specific fixed asset to which it relates. Where the loss cannot be identified as relating to a specific fixed asset, it should be apportioned within the IGU to reduce the most subjective values first, as follows:

- first, to reduce any goodwill within the IGU;
- secondly, to reduce any identifiable intangibles, but not below their readily ascertainable market values; and
- finally to the unit's tangible assets, allocated on suitable basis, but likewise not below their readily ascertainable market values.

Restoration of past impairment losses

Past impairment losses in respect of a tangible fixed asset may be restored where the recoverable amount increases due to an improvement in economic conditions or a change in use of the asset. Such a restoration should be reflected in the profit and loss account to the extent of the original impairment previously charged to the profit and loss account, adjusting for depreciation which would have been charged otherwise in the intervening period.

14.10.6   Illustration of data required for an impairment review

Pronto plc has a product line producing wooden models of athletes for export. The carrying amount of the net assets employed on the line as at 31 December 1999 was £96,500 comprising net assets of £94,500 directly attributable to the line and net assets of £2,000 apportioned from Head Office assets. The scrap value of the net assets at 31 December 2002 is estimated to be £5,000.

There is an indication that the export market will be adversely affected in 2002 by competition from plastic toy manufacturers. This means that the net assets employed to produce this product might have been impaired.

The finance director estimated the net realisable value of the net assets at 31 December 1999 to be £70,000. The value in use is now calculated to check if it is higher or lower than £70,000. If it is higher it will become the revised carrying amount; if lower the net realisable value will be the revised carrying amount.

Pronto plc has prepared budgets for the years ended 31 December 2000, 2001 and 2002. The assumptions underlying the budgets are as follows:

Unit costs and revenue:

	£
Selling price	10.00
Buying in cost	(4.00)
Production cost: material, labour, overhead	(0.75)
Head office overheads apportioned	(0.25)
Cash inflow per model	5.00

Estimated sales volumes:

	1999	2000	2001	2002
Estimated at 31 December 1998	6,000	8,000	11,000	14,000
Revised estimate at 31 December 1999	—	8,000	11,000	4,000

Determining the discount rate to be used:

	2000	2001	2002
The rate obtainable elsewhere at the same level of risk is	10%	10%	10%
The expected rates of inflation are estimated to be	10%	8%	6%

The real cost of capital to be applied to the income streams is as follows:

	Money cost of capital		Inflation rate		Real cost of capital		%
20X0	(1.10)	×	(1.10) −1	=	0.21	i.e.	21.0
20X1	(1.10)	×	(1.08) −1	=	0.188	i.e.	18.8
20X2	(1.10)	×	(1.06) −1	=	0.166	i.e.	16.6

The discount factors to be applied to each year are then re-calculated using real cost of capital discount rates as follows:

20X0 $1/1.21 = 0.826$
20X1 $(1/1.21)(1/1.188) = 0.696$
20X2 $(1/1.21)(1/1.188)(1/1.166) = 0.597$

Alternatively, cash flows could be adjusted to reflect the rates of inflation expected for each type of income and expense e.g. a different rate would be applied to material imported from a country with a weakening currency and local labour rates.

14.10.7 Illustrating calculation of value in use

Before calculating value in use, it is necessary to ensure that the assumptions underlying the budgets are reasonable e.g. Is the selling price likely to be affected by competition in 2002 in addition to loss of market? Is the selling price in 2001 likely to be affected? Is the estimate of scrap value reasonably accurate? How sensitive is value in use to the scrap value? Is it valid to assume that the cash flows will occur at year ends? How accurate is the real cost of capital? How reasonable are the inflation rate estimates? Will components making up the income stream e.g. sales, materials, labour be subject to different rates of inflation?

Assuming that no adjustment is required to be budgeted figures provided above, the estimated income streams are discounted using normal DCF approach as follows:

	20X0	20X1	20X2
Sales (models)	8,000	11,000	4,000
Income per model	£5	£5	£5
Income stream (£)	40,000	55,000	20,000
Estimated scrap proceeds			5,000
Cash flows to be discounted	40,000	55,000	25,000
Discounted (using real cost of capital factors)	0.826	0.696	0.597
Present value	33,040	38,280	14,925

Value in use = £86,245

14.10.8 Illustration determining the *revised* carrying amount

If the carrying amount at the balance sheet date exceeds net realisable value and value in use, it is revised to an amount which is the higher of net realisable value and value in use. For Pronto plc:

	£
Carrying amount as at 31 December 1999	96,500
Net realisable value	70,000
Value in use	86,245
Revised carrying amount	**86,245**

14.11 Disclosure requirements

14.11.1 SSAPs

SSAP 2[15] requires the policy adopted by the enterprise to be disclosed. This should enable readers of accounts to compare the policies of different companies and make the necessary adjustments. The relevant note in the 1993/4 accounts of Seeboard plc is reproduced below:

Tangible fixed assets and depreciation

Tangible fixed assets are stated in the historical cost accounts. In the current cost accounts, the values of tangible fixed assets are derived by applying appropriate indices to historical cost figures.

The charge for depreciation is calculated to write off assets over their estimated useful lives. Freehold land is not depreciated. The lives of each major class of asset are:

Network, network buildings, and capital contributions	40 years, at 3% for 20 years followed by 2% for the remaining 20 years
Other buildings	Up to 60 years
Fixtures, equipment and vehicles	Up to 10 years

With the exception of the references to current cost accounts, this note is fairly typical in that, while information is given, the use of the phrase 'up to ... years' makes it very difficult for the accounts user to know how prudent the preparers have been. However, this note does give a great deal of information, particularly about the main trading asset, the network, at a time when it is not unusual, particularly with private companies, to meet a phrase such as 'The fixed assets are depreciated over their expected useful lives', which tells the reader nothing at all!

14.11.2 Statutory disclosure requirements

The Companies Act 1985 requires that movements on fixed assets be disclosed by way of a note to the balance sheet. The style employed by British Sky Broadcasting Group Plc in its 1999 accounts is almost universally employed for this:

Tangible fixed assets
The movements in the year were as follows:

	Freehold land and buildings	Leasehold improvements	Equipment, fixtures and fittings	Total
	£m	£m	£m	£m
Group				
Cost				
Beginning of year	22.5	65.6	216.4	304.5
Additions	4.2	7.5	64.5	76.2
Disposals	—	—	(0.7)	(0.7)
End of year	**26.7**	**73.1**	**280.2**	**380.0**
Depreciation				
Beginning of year	2.6	28.0	98.5	129.1
Charge	0.7	3.7	28.1	32.5
Disposals	—	—	(0.6)	(0.6)
End of year	**3.3**	**31.7**	**126.0**	**161.0**
Net book value				
Beginning of year	19.9	37.6	117.9	175.4
End of year	**23.4**	**41.4**	**154.2**	**219.0**

Additionally, the net book amount of interests in land and buildings must be split between freehold, long and short leasehold interests.

In the directors' report there is a requirement that significant movements in fixed assets be reported and that directors express an opinion on whether or not the value of interests in land and buildings varies materially from the net book amount.

14.12 Government grants towards the cost of fixed assets

The accounting treatment of government grants is covered by SSAP 4, which, while primarily concerned with grants made by government (both central and local, encompassing EU agencies and a wide range of so-called quangos) to enterprise, should also be followed in the case of grants received from other sources.[16]

The basis of the standard is the accruals concept, which requires the matching of cost and revenue so as to recognise both in the profit and loss accounts of the periods to which they relate. This should, of course, be tempered with the prudence concept, which requires that revenue is not anticipated. Therefore, in the light of the complex conditions usually attached to grants, credit should not be taken until receipt is assured.

Similarly, there may be a right to recover the grant wholly or partially in the event of a breach of conditions, and on that basis these conditions should be regularly reviewed and, if necessary, provision made.

Should the tax treatment of a grant differ from the accounting treatment, then the effect of this would be accounted for in accordance with SSAP 15 *Accounting for Deferred Taxation.*

SSAP 4

Government grants should be recognised in the profit and loss account so as to match the expenditure towards which they are intended to contribute. If this is retrospective, they should be recognised in the period in which they became receivable.

Grants in respect of fixed assets should be recognised over the useful economic lives of those assets, thus matching the depreciation or amortisation.

On the balance sheet, any portion of a grant that has been deferred (e.g. a grant in respect of a fixed asset where economic life has not yet ended) should be shown as deferred income.

Any potential liability to repay grants should be disclosed in accordance with FRS 12 *Provisions, Contingent Liabilities and Contingent Assets.* This could arise if the company failed to satisfy any conditions attaching to the grant, e.g. to create more employment opportunities.

The revision to the standard dropped an alternative approach of deducting the value of any grant received from the cost of the asset. The reason for withdrawing this previously popular, simpler approach was that it seemed to contravene the Companies Act 1985.

14.13 Investment properties

While FRS 15 requires all fixed assets to be subjected to a systematic depreciation charge, this was considered inappropriate for properties held as fixed assets but not employed in the normal activities of the enterprise, rather being held as investments. For such properties a more relevant treatment is to take account of the current market value of the property. The accounting treatment is set out in SSAP 19 *Accounting for Investment Properties.*[17]

Such properties may be held either as a main activity (e.g. by a property investment company) or by a company whose main activity is not the holding of such properties. In each case the accounting treatment is similar.

Definition of an investment property

For the purposes of the statement, an investment property is an interest in land or buildings:

- in respect of which construction work and development have been completed;
- which is held for its investment potential, any rental income being negotiated at arm's length.

The following are exceptions to the definition:

- A property owned and occupied by a company for its own purposes is not an investment property.
- A property let to and occupied by another group company is not an investment property for the purposes of its own accounts or the group accounts.

Additionally, the standard does not apply to charities.

SSAP 19

Under SSAP 19 *Accounting for Investment Properties*:

- Unless the property is a lease with an unexpired term of twenty years or less, no depreciation should be charged.
- Instead, investment properties should be shown in the balance sheet at their open market value.
- Changes in value should be reflected in an investment revaluation reserve rather than through the profit and loss account.

Valuation

The following should be disclosed:

- The names or qualifications of the valuers.
- Whether or not they are employees of the company or group.
- The basis of valuation adopted.

While the standard does not insist on the valuation being carried out by independent, qualified valuers, it states in the explanatory note that where investment properties represent a substantial proportion of the total assets of a major enterprise, then the valuation should be carried out:

- annually by persons holding a recognised professional qualification and having recent post-qualification experience in the location and category of the properties concerned; and
- at least every five years by an external valuer.

14.14 Effect of depreciation on the interpretation of the accounts

A number of difficulties exist when attempting to carry out inter-firm comparisons using the external information that is available to a shareholder.

14.14.1 Effect of inflation on the carrying value of the asset

The most serious difficulty is the effect of inflation, which makes the charges based on historical cost inadequate. Companies have followed various practices to take account of inflation; these have ranged from revaluation to reducing the estimated economic life to increasing the charge in the profit and loss account by making a supplementary charge. None of these is an acceptable surrogate for index adjustment using specific asset indices on a systematic annual basis: this is the only way to ensure uniformity and comparability of the cost/valuation figure upon which the depreciation charge is based.

The method that is currently acceptable under FRS 15 is to revalue the assets. This is a partial answer, but it results in lack of comparability of ratios such as gearing.

14.14.2 Effect of revaluation on ratios

The rules of double entry require that when an asset is revalued the 'profit' (or, exceptionally, 'loss') must be credited somewhere. As it is not a 'realised' profit, it would not be appropriate to credit the profit and loss account, so a 'revaluation reserve' must be created. As the asset is depreciated, this reserve may be realised to profit and loss; similarly, when an asset is ultimately disposed of, any residue relevant to that asset may be taken into profit.

One significant by-product of revaluing assets is the effect on gearing. The revaluation reserve, while not distributable, forms part of the shareholders' funds and thus improves the debt/equity ratio. Care must therefore be taken in looking at the revaluation policies and reserves when comparing the gearing of companies.

The problem is compounded because the carrying value may be amended at random periods and on a selective category of asset.

14.14.3 Choice of depreciation method

There are a number of acceptable depreciation methods that may give rise to very different patterns of debits against the profits of individual years.

14.14.4 Inherent imprecision in estimating economic life

One of the greatest difficulties with depreciation is that it is inherently imprecise. The amount of depreciation depends on the estimate of the economic life of assets, which is affected not only by the durability and workload of the asset, but also by external factors beyond the control of management. Such factors may be technological, commercial or economic. Here are some examples:

● The production by a competitor of a new product rendering yours obsolete, e.g. watches with battery-powered movements replacing those with mechanical movements.

● The production by a competitor of a product at a price lower than your production costs, e.g. imported goods from countries where costs are lower.

● Changes in the economic climate which reduce demand for your product.

This means that the interpreter of accounts must pay particular attention to depreciation policies, looking closely at the market where the enterprise's business operates. However, this understanding is not helped by the lack of requirement to disclose specific rates of depreciation and the basis of computation of residual values. Without such information the potential effects of differences between policies adopted by competing enterprises cannot be accurately assessed.

14.14.5 Mixed values in the balance sheet

The effect of depreciation on the balance sheet is also some cause for concern. The net book amount shown for fixed assets is the result of deducting accumulated depreciation from cost (or valuation); it is not intended to be (although many non-accountants assume it is) an estimate of the value of the underlying assets. The valuation of a business based on the balance sheet extremely difficult. Not only may the valuer be faced with a mixture of **cost** and **valuation**.

14.14.6 Different policies may be applied within the same sector

Intercompany comparisons are even more difficult. Two enterprises following the historical cost convention may own identical assets, which, as they were purchased at different times, may well appear as dramatically different figures in the accounts. This is particularly true of interests in land and buildings.

14.14.7 Effect on the return on capital employed

There is an effect not only on the net asset value, but also on the return on capital employed. To make a fair assessment of return on capital it is necessary to know the current replacement cost of the underlying assets, but under present conventions, up-to-date valuations are required only for investment properties.

14.14.8 Effect on EPS

FRS 15 is concerned to ensure that the earnings of an enterprise reflect a fair charge for the use of the assets by the enterprise. This should ensure an accurate calculation of earnings per share. But there is a weakness here. If assets have increased in value without revaluations, then depreciation will be based on the historical cost.

Summary

Before FRS 11 and FRS 15 there were significant problems in relation to the accounting treatment of tangible fixed assets such as the determination of a cost figure and the adjustment for inflation; companies providing nil depreciation on certain types of asset; revaluations being made selectively and not maintained current.

With FRS 11 and FRS 15 the ASB has made the accounts more consistent and comparable. These FRSs have resolved some of these problems, principally requiring companies to provide for depreciation and if they have a policy of revaluation to keep such valuations reasonably current and applied to all assets within a class i.e. removing the ability to cherry pick which assets to revalue.

However, certain difficulties remain for the user of the accounts in that different management policies on the method of depreciation, which can have a major impact on the profit for the year; there are subjective assessments of economic life that may be reviewed each year with an impact on profits; and inconsistencies such as the presence of modified historical costs and historical costs in the same balance sheet. In addition, with pure historical cost accounting, where fixed asset carrying values are based on original cost, no pretence is made that fixed asset net book amounts have any relevance to today's values. The investor is expected to know that the depreciation charge is arithmetical in character and will not wholly provide the finance for tomorrow's assets or ensure maintenance of the business's operational base. To give recognition to these factors requires the investor to grapple with the effects of lost purchasing power through inflation; the effect of changes in supply and demand on replacement prices; technological change and its implication for the company's competitiveness; and external factors such as exchange rates. To calculate the effect of these variables necessitates not only considerable mental agility, but also far more information than is contained in a set of accounts.[18] This is an area that needs to be revisited by the standard-setters.

Review questions

1 Define a 'fixed asset' and explain how materiality affects the concept of 'fixed assets'.

2 Define depreciation. Explain what assets need not be depreciated and list the main methods of calculating depreciation.

3 What is meant by the phrases 'useful economic life' and 'residual value'?

4 Define 'cost' in connection with fixed assets.

5 What effect does revaluing assets have on gearing?

6 How should grants received towards expenditure on fixed assets be treated?

7 Define an investment property and explain what investment properties must be depreciated.

8 'Split depreciation should have been encouraged instead of prohibited.' Discuss.

9 'Depreciation should mean that a company has sufficient resources to replace assets at the end of their economic lives.' Discuss.

Exercises

An extract from the solution is provided in the appendix at the end of the text for exercises marked with an asterisk (*).

Question 1

(a)
Discuss why SSAP 19 *Accounting for Investment Properties* was produced.

(b) Universal Entrepreneurs plc has the following items on its fixed asset list:

   (i) £1,000,000 – the right to extract sandstone from a particular quarry. Geologists predict that extraction at the present rate may be continued for ten years.

   (ii) £5,000,000 – a freehold property, let to a subsidiary on a full repairing lease negotiated on arm's-length terms for fifteen years. The building is a new one, erected on a green field site at a cost of £4,000,000.

   (iii) A fleet of motor cars used by company employees. These have been purchased under a contract which provides a guaranteed part exchange value of 60% cost after two years' use.

   (iv) A company helicopter with an estimated life of 150,000 flying hours.

   (v) A nineteen-year lease on a property let out at arms-length rent to another company.

Required:
Advise the company on the depreciation policy it ought to adopt for each of the above assets.

(c) The company is considering revaluing its interests in land and buildings, which comprise freehold and leasehold properties, all used by the company or its subsidiaries.

Required:

Discuss the consequences of this on the depreciation policy of the company and any special instructions that need to be given to the valuer.

Question 2

Mercury

You have been given the task, by one of the partners of the firm of accountants for which you work, of assisting in the preparation of a trend statement for a client.

Mercury has been in existence for four years. Figures for the three preceding years are known but those for the fourth year need to be calculated. Unfortunately, the supporting workings for the preceding years' figures cannot be found and the client's own ledger accounts and workings are not available.

One item in particular, plant, is causing difficulty and the following figures have been given to you:

12 months ended 31 March	20X6	20X7	20X8	20X9
	£	£	£	£
(A) Plant at cost	80,000	80,000	90,000	?
(B) Accumulated depreciation	(16,000)	(28,800)	(28,080)	?
(C) Net (written down value)	64,000	51,200	61,920	?

The only other information available is that disposals have taken place at the beginning of the financial years concerned:

	Date of		Original	Sales
	Disposal	Original acquisition	cost	proceeds
	12 months ended 31 March		£	£
First disposal	20X8	20X6	15,000	8,000
Second disposal	20X8	20X6	30,000	21,000

Plant sold was replaced on the same day by new plant. The cost of the plant which replaced the first disposal is not known but the replacement for the second disposal is known to have cost £50,000.

Required:

(a) Identify the method of providing for depreciation on plant employed by the client, stating how you have arrived at your conclusion.

(b) Reconstruct a working schedule to support the figures shown at line (B) for each of the years ended 31 March 20X6, 20X7 and 20X8. Extend your workings to cover year ended 31 March 20X9.

(c) Produce the figures that should be included in the blank spaces on the trend statement at lines (A), (B) and (C) for year ended 31 March 20X9.

(d) Calculate the profit or loss arising on each of the two disposals.

* Question 3

In the year to 31 December 20X9, Amy bought a new fixed asset and made the following payments in relation to it:

	£	£
Cost as per suppliers list	12,000	
Less: Agreed discount	1,000	11,000
Delivery charge		100
Erection charge		200
Maintenance charge		300
Additional component to increase capacity		400
Replacement parts		250

Required:

(a) **State and justify the cost figure which should be used as the basis for depreciation.**

(b) **What does depreciation do, and why is it necessary?**

(c) **Briefly explain, without numerical illustration, how the straight-line and reducing balance methods of depreciation work. What different assumptions does each method make?**

(d) **Explain the term 'objectivity' as used by accountants. To what extent is depreciation objective?**

(e) **It is common practice in published accounts in Germany to use the reducing balance method for a fixed asset in the early years of its life, and then to change to the straight-line method as soon as this would give a higher annual charge. What do you think of this practice? Refer to relevant accounting conventions in your answer.**

(ACCA)

* Question 4

The finance director of the Small Machine Parts Ltd company is considering the acquisition of a lease of a small workshop in a warehouse complex that is being redeveloped by City Redevelopers Ltd at a steady rate over a number of years. City Redevelopers are granting such leases for five years on payment of a premium of £20,000.

The accountant has obtained estimates of the likely maintenance costs and disposal value of the lease during its five-year life. He has produced the following table and suggested to the finance director that the annual average cost should be used in the financial accounts to represent the depreciation charge in the profit and loss account.

Table prepared to calculate the annual average cost

Years of life	1	2	3	4	5
	£	£	£	£	£
Purchase price	20,000	20,000	20,000	20,000	20,000
Maintenance/repairs					
Year 2		1,000	1,000	1,000	1,000
3			1,500	1,500	1,500
4				1,850	1,850
5					2,000
	20,000	21,000	22,500	24,350	26,350
Resale value	11,500	10,000	8,010	5,350	350
Net cost	8,500	11,000	14,490	19,000	26,000
Annual average cost	8,500	5,500	4,830	4,750	5,200

The finance director, however, was considering whether to calculate the depreciation chargeable using the annuity method with interest at 15%.

Required:

(a) Calculate the entries that would appear in the profit and loss account of Small Machine Parts Ltd for each of the five years of the life of the lease for the amortisation charge, the interest element in the depreciation charge and the income from secondary assets using the ANNUITY METHOD. Calculate the net profit for each of the five years assuming that the operating cash flow is estimated to be £25,000 per year.

(b) Discuss briefly which of the two methods you would recommend.
The present value at 15% of £1 per annum for five years is £3.35214.
The present value at 15% of £1 received at the end of year 5 is £0.49717.
Ignore taxation.

(ACCA)

Question 5

(a) The following are extracts from the accounting policies' section of two different sets of accounts:

Greene King plc

Depreciation
Freehold and leasehold properties with 25 years or more to run (other than production premises) are repaired and refurbished such that their values are not impaired by the passage of time. In the opinion of the directors any depreciation would accordingly be immaterial and none has therefore been provided. Leasehold properties with fewer than 25 years to run are depreciated over the remainder of their lease.

The BOC Group plc 1999 Report and Accounts

Tangible fixed assets
No depreciation is charged on freehold land … Depreciation is charged on all other fixed assets on the straight-line basis over the effective lives except for certain tonnage plants where depreciation is calculated on an annuity basis over the life of the contract.

Required:

(i) Compare the two accounting policies quoted above, especially the treatment of buildings. Comment on the different methods of depreciation used. How applicable are they in each set of circumstances?

(ii) Discuss the purpose(s) of the depreciation charge in the profit and loss account.

(b) Simple Ltd has just purchased a roasting/salting machine to produce roasted walnuts. The finance director asks for your advice on how the company should calculate the depreciation on this machine. Details are as follows:

Cost of machine	£800,000
Residual value	£104,000
Estimated life	4 years
Annual profits	£2,000,000
Annual turnover from machine	£850,000

Required:

(a) Calculate the annual depreciation charge using the straight-line method and the reducing balance method. Assume that an annual rate of 40% is applicable for the reducing balance method.

(b) Comment upon the validity of each method, taking into account the type of business and the effect each method has on annual profits. Are there any other methods which would be more applicable?

References

1 Companies Act 1985 Sec, 262 (1).
2 FRS 11, *Impairment of Fixed Assets and Goodwill*, ASB, 1998, para. 2.
3 FRS 15, *Tangible Fixed Assets*, ASB, 1999, para. 2.
4 N.C.L. MacDonald, *Depreciation and Revaluations of Fixed Assets Financial Reporting*, ICAEW 1986–7, p. 25.
5 FRS 15, *Tangible Fixed Assets*, ASB, 1999, Appendix 4, para 4.8.
6 *Ibid.*, Appendix 4, para. 52.
7 Companies Act 1985, Schedule 4, para. 17.
8 *Ibid.*, para. 26.
9 FRS 15, *Tangible Fixed Assets*, ASB, 1999, paras 6–14.
10 P.R. Kirkman, *Accounting under Inflationary Conditions*, Prentice Hall, 1978, chapter 5.
11 W.T. Baxter, *Depreciation*, Sweet & Maxwell, 1978.
12 *Certified Accountant*, June 1986, p. 37.
13 FRS 11, *Impairment of Fixed Assets and Goodwill*, ASB, 1998.
14 *Discounting in Financial Reporting*, ASB, 1997.
15 SSAP 2, *Disclosure of Accounting Policies*, ASC, November 1971.
16 SSAP 4, *Accounting for Government Grants*, ASC, July 1990.
17 SSAP 19, *Accounting for Investment Properties*, ASC, November 1981.
18 N.C.L. MacDonald, *op. cit.*, pp. 3–4.

Fixed tangible assets (not owned) – lessee

15.1 Introduction

This chapter introduces the accounting principles and policies that apply to lease agreements from the viewpoint of the lessee. We are interested in developing a wider understanding of leasing and leasing-related issues, so that you can understand how they should be represented in the financial statements and why a company might favour a particular type of lease agreement.

In this chapter we consider the following:

- Leasing – an introduction
- SSAP 21 (and its international equivalents) – the controversy
- SSAP 21 – classification of a lease
- SSAP 21 – accounting for leases by lessees
- Leasing – a form of off-balance-sheet financing
- Materiality in relation to SSAP 21
- FRS 3 – *Reporting the Substance of Transactions*
- FRS 5 – The Private Finance Initiative

We must understand not only what a lease is and the mechanical adjustments required to account for any given leasing agreement in the financial statements, but also the economic consequences of the accounting treatment that is applied and the impact of these economic consequences on company behaviour.

15.2 Leasing – an introduction

In this section we consider the nature of the lease; historical developments in leasing; reasons for its popularity; and why it was necessary to introduce SSAP 21.

15.2.1 What is a lease?

SSAP 21 *Accounting for Leases and Hire Purchase Contracts* provides the following two definitions:

> A **lease** is a contract between a lessor and a lessee for the hire of a specific asset. The lessor retains ownership of the asset but conveys the right to use of the asset to the lessee for an agreed period of time in return for the payment of specific rentals.

In practice, there might well be more than two parties involved in a lease. For example, on leasing a car the parties involved are the motor dealer, the finance company and the company using the car.

> A hire purchase contract is a contract for the hire of an asset which contains a provision giving the hirer an option to acquire legal title to the asset upon the fulfilment of certain conditions stated in the contract.

As with leasing, there would probably be three parties involved.

The main difference between a lease and a hire purchase contract (also known as a lease purchase) can be expressed in terms of the legal ownership and eventual possession of the asset. In the case of a lease, the legal ownership of the asset remains with the lessor throughout the agreement, and possession of the asset returns to the lessor after the lease is completed. In a hire purchase contract, the legal ownership eventually lies with the hirer and possession continues once all the agreed payments have been made.

15.2.2 Historical developments in leasing

The growth in the leasing industry until the advent of SSAP 21, and indeed after its introduction, was staggering.[1] Statistics produced by the Finance and Leasing Association, whose members account for 80% of all leasing in the UK, show that the cost of assets acquired for leasing each year rose from £288m in 1973 to £2,894m in 1983 to £10,200m in 1991 (after the introduction of SSAP 21).[2] In fact, it was estimated that in 1985 the value of leased equipment represented over 20% of capital expenditure in the UK.[3]

15.2.3 Why did leasing become popular?

There were two major reasons: the tax advantage to the lessor; and the commercial advantage to the lessee.

Tax advantage

The government is responsible for the initial stimulus to the leasing industry. In 1972, first-year allowances (FYA) on equipment were increased to 100%. These allowances could be offset against taxable profits, which reduced a company's tax bill.

Companies, especially in the manufacturing sector, which had sustained tax losses in preceding years could not utilise the tax benefits of FYAs. This resulted in lessors claiming the FYAs and then leasing out equipment to these other companies at a reduced rental, thus enabling both lessors and lessees to benefit from a leasing agreement.

The leasing industry flourished even more in times of high interest rates. In these periods, lessors can achieve even greater cash flow benefits by deferring tax payments. Consequently, lessors are even more committed to leasing.

Many of these tax advantages were removed by the Finance Act 1984. This implemented a gradual reduction in the corporation tax rate and a gradual removal of FYAs.

Commercial advantage

Despite the Finance Act 1984, there are still a number of advantages associated with leases. These are attributable in part to the ability to spread cash payments over the lease period instead of making a one-off lump sum payment. They include the following:

● **Cash flow management**. If cash is used to purchase fixed assets, it is not available for the normal operating activities of a company.

- **Conservation of capital.** Lines of credit are kept open and may be used for purposes where finance might not be available easily (e.g. financing working capital).

- **Continuity.** The lease agreement is itself a line of credit that cannot easily be withdrawn or terminated due to external factors, in contrast to an overdraft that can be called in by the lender.

- **Flexibility of the asset base.** The asset base can be more easily expanded and contracted. In addition, the lease payments can be structured to match the income pattern of the lessee.

- **Off-balance-sheet financing.** Leasing provides the lessee with the possibility of off-balance-sheet financing,[4,5] whereby a company has the use of an economic resource that does not appear in the balance sheet, with the corresponding omission of the liability.

15.2.4   Why was SSAP 21 necessary?

As with many of the standards, action was required because there was no uniformity in the treatment and disclosure of leasing transactions. The need became urgent following the massive growth in the leasing industry and the growth in off-balance-sheet financing. In the former case, leasing had become a material economic resource; in the latter case, the accounting treatment of the lease transaction was seen to distort the financial reports of a company so that they did not represent a true and fair view of its commercial activities.

However, for the first time attention was paid to the economic consequences of introducing a standard, the ASC expressing a concern that the standard might have undesirable economic consequences.[6] The inclusion of the lease obligation might affect the lessee company's gearing adversely and, indeed, cause it to exceed its legal borrowing powers under the memorandum and articles. The memorandum and articles might, for example, have a stipulation that the total borrowings should not exceed the total shareholders' funds. In the event, the commercial reasons for leasing and the capacity of the leasing industry to structure lease agreements to circumvent the standard have prevented a reduction in lease activity. Evidence of lessors varying the term of the lease agreements is supported by Cranfield[7] and Abdel-Khalik et al.[8]

Macdonald[9] made the point that most transactions will be undertaken with a commercial purpose; some may be undertaken, or undertaken in a particular form, so as to change materially the accounting message communicated by the accounts; even those commercially motivated may be accounted for in one way rather than another so as to improve the accounting message. Macdonald also observed that, while it might be thought that the overriding requirement of the true and fair view could cope with such pressures, this was prevented by the lack of auditor independence, the inadequacy of qualified reports as opposed to revised accounts, and the absence of a codified conceptual framework with which to constrain auditor judgement.

A standard was necessary to ensure uniform reporting and to prevent the accounting message being manipulated.

15.3   SSAP 21 (and its international equivalent) – the controversy

This section considers the development of SSAP 21, its main thrust and why it was so controversial. It also discusses how the accounting and legal professions differ in their approach to the reporting of lease transactions.

15.3.1   Development of SSAP 21

SSAP 21 proved to be an extremely controversial accounting standard. The extent of the controversy is demonstrated by the amount of time that elapsed before it was issued.

SSAP 21 was issued in August 1984 to supersede ED 29 *Accounting for Leases and Hire Purchase Contracts*, which was issued in October 1981. ED 29 itself was the result of about five years' discussion and debate.[10]

Despite the controversy associated with legislating for leasing, accounting standards and pronouncements similar to SSAP 21 were appearing all over the world. For example, in the USA there was Financial Accounting Standard 13 (SFAS 13),[11] which was effective for leases entered into on or after 1 January 1977, and internationally we saw International Accounting Standard 17 (IAS 17),[12] issued in September 1982 and effective for accounting periods beginning on or after 1 January 1984 and subsequently revised in November 1997.

15.3.2   What is the main thrust of SSAP 21?

First, SSAP 21 distinguishes between two types of lease – finance and operating – and recommends different accounting treatment for each. In brief, the definitions were as follows:

● **Finance lease**. A lease that transfers substantially all the risks and rewards of ownership of an asset to the lessee.

● **Operating lease**. A lease similar to a short-term hire of an asset, with no suggestion of transferral of risks and rewards of ownership to the lessee.

The accounting treatment and definition of each lease will be explored in greater depth in sections 19.4 and 19.5

Secondly, the standard requires finance leases to be capitalised in the lessee's accounts. This means that the leased item should be recorded as an asset in the balance sheet, and the obligation for future payments should be recorded as a liability in the balance sheet. It is not permissible for the leased asset and lease obligation to be left out of the balance sheet. In the case of operating leases, the lessee is required only to expense the annual payments as a rental through the profit and loss account.

The Accounting Standards Committee's concern about off-balance-sheet financing and the need for capitalisation is emphasised in the foreword to SSAP 21:

> Why is a capitalisation requirement necessary? When a company is leasing a substantial amount of assets instead of buying them, the effect is that, unless the leased assets and obligations are capitalised, potentially large liabilities build up off balance sheet; equally, the leased assets employed are not reflected on the balance sheet. These omissions may mislead users of a company's accounts – both external users and the company's own management.

It went on to make another interesting point:

> Capitalisation of assets held under finance leases results in a company's assets and obligations being more readily apparent than if leased assets and obligations are not recognised.[13]

The implication of this is that a disclosure by way of note is not sufficient. Hence the need to record the asset and obligation in the balance sheet.

15.3.3 Why was SSAP 21 so controversial?

The proposal to classify leases into finance and operating leases, and to capitalise those which are classified as finance leases, appears to be a feasible solution to the accounting problems that surround leasing agreements. So, why did the ASC encounter so much controversy in its attempt to stop the practice of charging all lease payments to the profit and loss account?

The whole debate centres on one accounting policy: **substance over form**. Although this is not cited as a fundamental accounting concept in SSAP 2 *Disclosure of Accounting Policies*, it is defined in IAS 1.[14] Paragraph 9 states that in:

> the selection and application by management of the appropriate accounting policies and the preparation of financial statements ... transactions and other events should be accounted for and presented in accordance with their substance and financial reality and not merely with their legal form.

The real sticking point was that SSAP 21[15] (and ED 29[16] before it) invoked a substance over form approach to accounting treatment that was completely different to the traditional approach, which has strict regard to legal ownership. The ASC argued that in reality there were two separate transactions taking place. In one transaction, the company was borrowing funds to be repaid over a period. In the other, it was making a payment to the supplier for the use of an asset.

The correct accounting treatment for the borrowing transaction, based on its substance, was to include in the lessee's balance sheet a liability representing the obligation to meet the lease payments, and the correct accounting treatment for the asset acquisition transaction, based on its substance, was to include an asset representing the asset supplied under the lease.

Although SSAP 21 does not mention substance over form explicitly, it does state in the foreword that:

> It is sometimes argued that leased assets should not be recognised on a company's balance sheet as the company does not have legal title to the asset ... SSAP 21 ... recognises that whether an asset is owned, leased or held under a hire purchase contract, it represents an economic source which is needed in the business and which the accounts ought to reflect in a consistent manner.

In addition, IAS 17, para. 5, states categorically that 'whether a lease is a finance lease or not depends on the substance of the transaction rather than the form of the contract'.

15.3.4 How do the accounting and legal professions differ in their approach to the reporting of lease transactions?

The accounting profession sees itself as a service industry that prepares financial reports in a dynamic environment, in which the user is looking for reports that reflect commercial reality. Consequently, the profession needs to be sensitive and responsive to changes in commercial practice. This is demonstrated in a technical release (TR 603) issued by the ICAEW in December 1985, which advised members to consider the economic substance of a transaction and not just the legal form.

There was still some opposition within the accounting profession to the inclusion of a finance lease in the balance sheet as an 'asset'. The opposition rested on the fact that the item that was the subject of the lease agreement did not satisfy the existing criterion for classification as an asset because it was not 'owned' by the lessee. To accommodate this, the definition of an asset has been modified from 'ownership' to 'the right to use the item for substantially the whole of its useful economic life'.

The legal profession, on the other hand, concentrates on the strict legal interpretation of a transaction. The whole concept of substance over form is contrary to their normal practice.

It is interesting to reflect that, whereas an equity investor might prefer the economic resources to be included in the balance sheet under the substance over form principle, this is not necessarily true for a loan creditor. The equity shareholder is interested in resources available for creating earnings; the lender is interested in the assets available as security.

15.4   SSAP 21 – classification of a lease

As discussed earlier in the chapter, SSAP 21 provides definitions for classifying leases as finance or operating leases, then prescribes the accounting and disclosure requirements applicable to the lessor and the lessee for each type of lease.

The crucial decision in accounting for leases is whether a transaction represents a finance or an operating lease. We have already offered brief definitions of each type of lease, but SSAP 21 gives a fuller definition:

> A **finance lease** is a lease that transfers substantially all the risk and rewards of ownership of an asset to the lessee. It should be presumed that such a transfer of risks and rewards occurs if at the inception of the lease the present value of the minimum lease payments, including any initial payments, amounts to substantially all (normally 90% or more) of the fair value of the asset. The present value should be calculated by using the interest rate implicit in the lease. If the fair value of the asset is not determinable, an estimate thereof should be used.
>
> An **operating lease** is a lease other than a finance lease.

Welcome to one of the biggest problems in the application of lease accounting – determining how to categorise a lease transaction on the basis of these definitions![17]

The two ways to determine lease type are by applying either a financial terms test or a contractual terms test. In the financial terms test, a calculation is made of the present value of all lease payments to see if the 90% barrier is passed. In the contractual terms test, the terms and conditions applicable to the leasing agreement are considered. Typical terms and conditions that suggest a finance lease include the lessee bearing any losses associated with cancellation, the lessee having an option to renew a lease on completion, and the lessee receiving a residual value based on market value.

More specifically, note that there are three possible elements to the minimum lease payment:

I   the minimum payments over the remaining part of the lease period;

II   any residual amount guaranteed by the lessee (or related party);

III any residual amount guaranteed by any other party.

The normal treatment is for any amount guaranteed by the lessee to be included in the minimum lease calculation for the purpose of the 90% criteria test. Guaranteed amounts are dealt with extensively in SSAP 21 but we will deal briefly with the **classification** aspect (i.e. whether or not a lease is a finance lease). Briefly, lessees use elements I and II for the purposes of the 90% test.

TimCross plc enters into a lease agreement for which the implicit rate is computed and then the lease is classified using the 90% test:

- Fair value of leased asset   = £20,000
- Term of lease   = 5 years
- Annual lease payments   = £4,000
- Estimated residual value   = £6,000
- Guaranteed final amount (by lessee)   = £4,000

Step 1

The implicit rate is computed so that the DCF value of the five annual payments (of £4000) and the estimated residual amount (of £6,000) equals the fair value of the leased asset (£20,000). If the fair value is not known then an estimate should be used.

Step 2

To classify the lease, we need to consider the relationship between the estimated residual value and the guaranteed final amount carefully because it affects the 90% test. To classify the lease we need to calculate the present value (using the implicit rate calculated in step 1) of the five annual payments (of £4,000) and the guaranteed final amount (£4,000) rather than the residual value. In this example the present value of the minimum lease payments is £18,810, which exceeds 90% of the fair value (£20,000).

IAS 17 includes a helpful flow chart, prepared by the IAS secretariat, which represents examples of some possible positions that would normally be classified as a finance lease (Figure 15.1).

Figure 15.1   IAS 17 aid to categorising operating and finance leases.

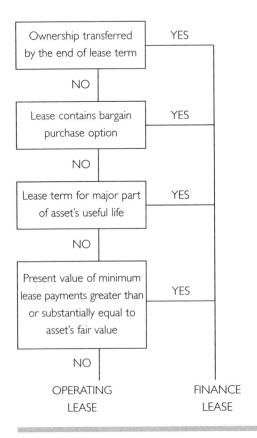

15.5 SSAP 21 – accounting for leases by lessees

15.5.1 Accounting requirements for operating leases

The treatment of operating leases conforms to the legal interpretation and corresponds to the lease accounting practice that existed pre-SSAP 21. No asset or obligation is shown in the balance sheet; the operating lease rentals payable are charged to the profit and loss account on a straight-line basis.

15.5.2 Disclosure requirements for operating leases

SSAP 21 requires that the total of operating lease rentals charged as an expense in the profit and loss account should be disclosed, and these rentals should be broken down in respect of hire of plant and machinery and other operating leases. Disclosure is required of the payments that a lessee is committed to make during the next year, in the second to fifth years inclusive, and over five years.

EXAMPLE ● OPERATING LEASE Clifford plc is a manufacturing company. It negotiates a lease to begin on 1 January 20X1 with the following terms:

Term of lease	4 years
Estimated useful life of machine	9 years
Age of machine on inception of lease	4 years
Purchase price of new machine	£75,000
Annual payments	£8,000

This is an operating lease as it applies only to a part of the asset's useful life, and the present value of the lease payments does not constitute 90% of the fair value.

The amount of the annual rental paid – £8,000 p.a. – will be charged to the profit and loss account and disclosed with hire of plant and machinery. There will also be a disclosure of the ongoing commitment with a note that £8,000 is payable within 1 year and £24,000 within 2 to 5 years.

15.5.3 Accounting requirements for finance leases

We follow a step approach to illustrate the accounting entries in both the balance sheet and the profit and loss account.

When a lessee begins a finance lease, both the leased asset and the related lease obligations need to be shown in the balance sheet.

Balance sheet steps for a finance lease

Step 1 The leased asset should be capitalised in the fixed asset account (and recorded separately) at the present value of lease payments or its fair value.

Step 2 The annual depreciation charge for the leased asset should be calculated by depreciating over the shorter of the estimated useful life of the asset or the lease period.

Step 3 The net book value of the leased asset should be reduced by the annual depreciation charge.

Step 4 The finance lease obligation is a liability which should be recorded in the borrowings element of creditors. At the inception of a lease agreement, the value of the leased asset and the leased liability will be the same.

Step 5 (a) The finance charge for the finance lease should be calculated as the difference between the total of the minimum lease payments and the fair value of the asset (or the present value of these lease payments if fair value is unknown), i.e. it represents the charge made by the lessor for the credit that is being extended to the lessee.

(b) The finance charge should be allocated to the accounting periods over the term of the lease. Three methods for allocating finance charges are used in practice:

- **Actuarial method.** This applies a constant periodic rate of charge to the balance of the leasing obligation. The rate of return applicable can be calculated by applying present value tables to annual lease payments.
- **Sum of digits method.** This method ('Rule of 78') is much easier to apply than the actuarial method. The finance charge is apportioned to accounting periods on a reducing scale.
- **Straight-line method.** This spreads the finance charge equally over the period of the lease.

Step 6 The finance lease obligation should be reduced by the difference between the lease payment and the finance charge. This means that first the lease payment is used to repay the finance charge, and then the balance of the lease payment is used to reduce the book value of the obligation.

Profit and loss account steps for a finance lease

Step 1 The annual depreciation charge should be recorded.

Step 2 The finance charge allocated to the current period should be recorded.

EXAMPLE ● FINANCE LEASE Clifford plc negotiates another lease to commence on 1 January 20X1 with the following terms:

Term of lease	3 years
Purchase price of new machine	£16,500
Annual payments (payable in advance)	£6,000
Clifford plc's borrowing rate	15%

Finance charges are allocated using the sum of digits method.

Categorise the transaction
First we need to decide whether the lease is an operating or a finance lease. We do this by applying the test to the financial terms as follows:

- Calculate the fair value:
  Fair value of asset = £16,500
- Calculate the present value of minimum lease payments:

$$£6,000 + \frac{£6,000}{1.15} + \frac{£6,000}{(1.15)^2} = £15,754$$

- Compare the fair value and the present value. It is a finance lease because PV of the lease payments account is approximately 95% of the fair value of the asset, which passes SSAP 21's 90% rule.

Balance sheet steps for a finance lease

Step 1 Capitalise lease at fair value:
Asset value = £16,500

Step 2 Calculate depreciation (using straight-line method):
£16,500/3 = £5,500

Step 3 Reduce the asset:

Balance sheet (extract) as at		*31 Dec 20X1*	*31 Dec 20X2*	*31 Dec 20X3*
ASSET	Opening value	16,500	11,000	5,500
(Right to	Depreciation	5,500	5,500	5,500
use asset)	Closing value	11,000	5,500	—

Or if we keep the asset at cost as in published accounts:

ASSET	Cost	16,500	16,500	16,500
(Right to	Depreciation	5,000	11,000	16,500
use asset)	Net book value	11,000	5,500	—

Step 4 Obligation on inception of finance lease:
Liability = £16,500

Step 5 Finance charge:

Total payments	3 × £6,000	= £18,000
Asset value		= £16,500
		£1,500

Finance charge
Allocated using sum of digits:

Year 1 = 2/(1 + 2) × £1,500 = (£1,000)
Year 2 = 1/(1 + 2) × £1,500 = (£500)

Note that the allocation is only over two periods because the instalments are being made in advance. If the instalments were being made in arrears, the liability would continue over three years and the allocation would be over three years.

Step 6 Reduce the obligation:

Balance sheet (extract) as at		*31 Dec 20X1*	*31 Dec 20X2*	*31 Dec 20X3*
Liability	Opening value	16,500	11,500	6,000
(Obligation	Lease payment	6,000	6,000	6,000
under finance		10,500	5,500	—
lease)	Finance charge	1,000	500	—
	Closing value	11,500	6,000	—

Note that the closing balance on the asset represents unexpired service potential and the closing balance on the liability represents the capital amount outstanding at the balance sheet date.

Profit and loss account steps for a finance lease

Step 1 A depreciation charge is made on the basis of use. The charge would be calculated in accordance with existing company policy relating to the depreciation of that type of asset.

Step 2 A finance charge is levied on the basis of the amount of financing outstanding.

Both then appear in the profit and loss account as expenses of the period:

	P&L account (extract) for year ending		
	31 Dec 20X1	*31 Dec 20X2*	*31 Dec 20X3*
Depreciation	5,500	5,500	5,500
Finance charge	1,000	500	—
Total	6,500	6,000	5,500

In the Clifford example, we used the sum of the digits method to allocate the finance charge over the period of the repayment. In the following example, we will illustrate the actuarial method of allocating the finance charge.

EXAMPLE 3 – FINANCE LEASE Witts plc negotiates a four-year lease for a fixed asset with a cost price of £35,000. The annual lease payments are £10,000 payable in advance. The cost of borrowing for Witts plc is 15%.

First we need to determine whether this is a finance lease. Then we need to calculate the implicit interest rate and allocate the total finance charge over the period of the repayments using the actuarial method.

● Categorise the transaction to determine whether it is a finance lease.

Fair value of asset	= £35,000
PV of future lease payments:	
£10,000 + (10,000 × $a_{\overline{3}|15}$)	
£10,000 + (10,000 × 2.283)	= £32,830

The PV of the minimum lease payments amounts to 93.8% of the fair value of the asset. It is therefore categorised as a finance lease.

● Calculate the 'interest rate implicit in the lease'.

Fair value = Lease payments discounted at the implicit interest rate

£35,000 = £10,000 + (10,000 × $a_{\overline{3}|i}$)

$a_{\overline{3}|i}$ = £25,000/10,000 = 2.5

i = 9.7%

● Allocate the finance charge using the actuarial method.

Figure 15.2 shows that the finance charge is levied on the obligation during the period at 9.7%, which is the implicit rate calculated above.

Figure 15.2	Finance charge allocation using actuarial method.				
Period	Obligation (start) £	Rentals paid £	Obligation (during) £	Finance 9.7% £	Obligation (end) £
Year 1	35,000	10,000	25,000	2,425	27,425
Year 2	27,425	10,000	17,425	1,690	19,115
Year 3	19,115	10,000	9,115	885	10,000
Year 4	10,000	10,000	—	—	—

15.5.4 Disclosure requirements for finance leases

SSAP 21 requires that assets subject to finance leases should be identified separately and stated in terms of gross amount and accumulated depreciation. This can be achieved either by separate entries in the fixed asset schedule or by integrating owned and leased assets in this schedule and disclosing the breakdown in the notes to the accounts.

The obligations relating to finance leases can also be treated in two different ways. The leasing obligation should be shown either separately from other liabilities in the balance sheet or integrated into 'creditors due within one year' and 'creditors due after one year' and disclosed separately in the notes to the accounts.

The notes to the accounts should also analyse the leasing obligations in terms of the timing of the payments. The analysis of the amounts payable should be broken down into those obligations falling due within one year, two to five years, and more than five years.

Note that Figure 19.2 also provides the information required for the balance sheet. For example, at the end of year 1 the table shows, in the final column, a total obligation of £27,425. This can be further subdivided into its non-current and current components by using the next item in the final column, which represents the amount outstanding at the end of year 2. This amount of £19,115 represents the non-current element, and the difference of £8,310 represents the current liability element at the end of year 1.

This method of calculating the current liability from the table produces a different current figure each year. For example, the current liability at the end of year 2 is £9,115, being £19,115 – £10,000. This has been discussed in *External Financial Reporting*, where the point was made that the current liability should be the present value of the payment that is to be made at the end of the next period, i.e. £10,000 discounted at 9.7%, which gives a present value for the current liability of £9,115 for inclusion in the balance sheet each year until the liability is discharged.[18] We use the conventional approach in working illustrations and exercises, but you should bear this point in mind.

EXAMPLE ● DISCLOSURE REQUIREMENTS IN THE LESSEE'S ACCOUNTS It is interesting to refer to the disclosures found in published accounts as illustrated by the Greenalls Group accounts here:

Extract from the Greenalls Group plc – Annual Report and Accounts 1999

Accounting Policies

Leasing

Assets which are subject to finance leases are capitalised and the related depreciation charged to the profit and loss account. Lease payments are treated as consisting of interest and capital, interest being charged to the profit and loss account over the term of the lease on an actuarial basis. Rental payments in respect of operating leases are charged to the profit and loss account on a straight line basis.

Notes to the Accounts

2 *Costs of sales and other operating expenses*

	1999 £000	1998 £000
Costs and expenses include the following:		
Depreciation of leased tangible assets	1,611	1,720
Operating leases – plant and machinery	4,101	4,268
– land and buildings	14,832	9,040

6 *Interest payable*

	1999 £000	1998 £000
Finance lease charges	3,461	3,527

10 *Tangible fixed assets*

The net book value of tangible fixed assets includes an amount of £54,028,000 (1998 – £54,857,000) in respect of assets held under finance leases of which £50,920,000 (1998 – £51,749,000) relates to hotels.

14 *Creditors: amounts falling due within one year (extract)*

	1999 £000	1998 £000
Net obligations under finance leases	933	1,564

15 *Creditors: amounts falling due after more than one year (extract)*

	1999 £000	1998 £000
Hotel finance lease obligations	48,010	44,952
Other finance lease	1,251	3,222

(The repayment schedule of the total borrowings is then disaggregated.)

21 *Commitments under Operating Lease for the next financial year (extract)*

	Group 1999 £000	1998 £000
Other operating lease ending:		
Within one year	1,050	559
Between one and five years	2,279	2,813
After five years	632	83
	3,961	3,455

15.6 Leasing – a form of off-balance-sheet financing

Prior to SSAP 21, one of the major attractions of leasing agreements for the lessee was the off-balance-sheet nature of the transaction. However, the introduction of SSAP 21 required the capitalisation of finance leases and removed part of the benefit of off-balance-sheet financing.

The capitalisation of finance leases effectively means that all such transactions will affect the lessee's gearing, return on assets and return on investment. Consequently, SSAP 21 substantially alters some of the key accounting ratios which are used to analyse a set of financial statements.

Operating leases, on the other hand, are not required to be capitalised. This means that operating leases still act as a form of off balance sheet financing.[19] Hence they are extremely attractive to many lessees. Indeed, leasing agreements are increasingly being structured specifically to be classified as operating leases, even though they appear to be more financial in nature.[20,21]

An important conclusion is that some of the key ratios used in financial analysis become distorted and unreliable in instances where operating leases form a major part of a company's financing.[22]

To illustrate the effect of leasing on the financial structure of a company, we present a buy versus leasing example.

EXAMPLE ● RATIO ANALYSIS OF BUY VERSUS LEASE DECISION Kallend Tiepins plc requires one extra machine for the production of tiepins. The MD of Kallend Tiepins plc is aware that the gearing ratio and the return on capital employed ratio will change depending on whether the company buys or leases (operating lease) this machinery. The relevant information is as follows.

The machinery costs £100,000, but it will improve the operating profit by 10% p.a. The current position, the position if the machinery is bought and the position if the machinery is leased are as follows:

It is clear that the impact of a leasing decision on the financial ratios of a company can be substantial.[23] Although this is a very simple illustration, it does show that the buy versus lease decision has far-reaching consequences in the financial analysis of a company.

	Current £	Buy £	Lease £
Operating profit	40,000	44,000	44,000
Equity capital	200,000	200,000	200,000
Long-term debt	100,000	200,000	100,000
Total capital employed	300,000	400,000	300,000
Gearing ratio	0.5:1	1:1	0.5:1
ROCE	13.33%	11%	14.66%

15.7 Materiality in relation to SSAP 21

The guidance notes on SSAP 21 state that 'the standard need not be applied to immaterial items', where the relevant criterion 'is the size of the lease in the context of the size of the lessee or lessor'. More specifically, the guidance notes also state:

> In deciding whether or not a lease is material, regard should be had to the effect which treating the lease according to the main requirements of the standard (e.g. capitalising it) would have on the financial statements as a whole. Thus, it may be necessary to consider the whole effect of (in this example) capitalisation on (a) total fixed assets, (b) total borrowings and obligations, (c) the gearing ratio and (d) the profit or loss for the year (as a result of the difference between charging the total of depreciation plus financial charge). If capitalisation of the lease would not have a material effect on any of these items, the lease need not be capitalised.

15.8   FRS 5 – Reporting the substance of transactions[24]

The main principle underlying FRS 5[25] is that transactions should be accounted for on the basis of their economic substance rather than their legal form. In relation to leases, FRS 5 states that 'the general principles of the FRS will also be relevant in ensuring that leases are classified as finance or operating leases in accordance with their substance'. However, to reduce the conflict between FRS 5 and existing standards, the standard with the more specific provisions should be applied. Consequently SSAP 21 remains the relevant accounting standard for dealing with straightforward leases but FRS 5 is the relevant accounting standard for dealing with more complex leases or for leases which form part of a series of transactions.

One particular instance in which FRS 5 tends to be more specific than SSAP 21 is for sale and leaseback arrangements in which the original owner sells an asset but continues to use it by leasing it back. The main issue with sale and leaseback transactions is whether the 'lessee' can derecognise the asset, show any profit or loss on the sale in the P&L account, and treat the lease as an operating lease. The classification will depend on whether substantially all the risks and rewards of asset ownership have, in reality, passed to the buyer. To determine the nature of the transaction, one must consider a series of qualitative tests. Was the sale at market price and are the lease rentals at a market rate? What happens if the value of the leased asset changes? Is the lease term equivalent to the useful economic life of the asset? Does the lessor lease assets as a normal part of business?

The main difference between the requirements of FRS 5 and SSAP 21 is that FRS 5 is much stricter concerning the required accounting treatment of the leased asset. In particular, economic substance requires that the leased asset should remain on the lessee's balance sheet.

One example of this treatment is evident in Associated Nursing Services plc 1997 annual report (as a result of adverse comment by the Financial Reporting Review Panel):

> In accordance with SSAP 21 and FRS 5 the assets subject to these sale and leaseback transactions have been retained on the Group's balance sheet and the proceeds of sale are included within creditors as liabilities under sale and leaseback arrangements. The rent payable by the Group throughout the term of the lease is apportioned first as a partial repayment of the related liabilities, and, secondly, as interest charged to profits.

There are a number of other examples of companies applying FRS 5 to classify leases. Vaux Group increased its 1994 balance sheet debt by £26.1m and fixed assets by £24m when it applied FRS 5 to sale and leaseback agreements for two hotels (with an option to repurchase).[26] First Choice Holidays reclassified operating leases on two aircraft and one engine as finance leases, increasing the group's assets by £55.2m.[27]

15.9   FRS 5 – The Private Finance Initiative

An exposure draft proposes an amendment to FRS 5 to take account of transactions subject to the evolving Private Finance Initiative (PFI).[28] The fundamental accounting issue is whether a party to a PFI contract has an asset of the property used to fulfil the contract. The exposure draft sets out the main features of a PFI contract, considers whether SSAP 21 or FRS 5 should be applied to the contract, and explains how the relevant standard should be applied.

Definition (para F1)

Under a PFI contract, the private sector is responsible for supplying services that traditionally have been provided by the public sector. It is integral to most PFI contracts that the operator designs, builds, finances and operates a property in order to provide the contracted service. Examples of such properties are roads, bridges, hospitals, prisons, information technology systems and educational establishments.

The main features of a PFI contract in brief are (para F2):

● A contract to provide services is awarded by the purchaser (a public sector entity) to the operator (a private sector entity).

● A property, which is legally owned by the purchaser or leased to the operator, will usually be necessary to perform the contract.

● The PFI contract will specify arrangements for the property at the end of the contract term.

● As a public sector body, the purchaser is required to demonstrate both that the involvement of the private sector offers value for money when compared with alternative ways of providing the services and that there has been a transfer of risk from the public to the private sector.

The exposure draft uses a flow chart to determine whether FRS 5 or SSAP 21 should be used to determine the accounting treatment of the relevant asset. The determination is as follows:

● SSAP 21 should be applied if (a) the contract **can** be separated into property and service elements, and (b) the payments for the property **do not** vary with factors such as usage or the operator's costs.

● FRS 5 should be applied in either of the following cases:

   ● the contract **can not** be separated into property and service elements;

   ● (a) the contract **can** be separated into property and service elements, and (b) the payments for the property **do** vary with factors such as usage or the operator's costs.

If FRS 5 should be applied, the benefits and risks of the property and any non-separable services attributable to each party needs to be assessed. This assessment will determine whether the purchaser or the operator recognises the asset of property. The key aspect is that the ASB is insistent that someone recognises the obligation.

15.10   Accounting for leases – a new approach

As discussed earlier in this chapter, SSAP 21 makes a distinction between finance leases and operating leases. However, an international group has questioned this distinction. Standard setters from the UK, Australia, Canada, New Zealand, the USA and the IASC (an extension of the G4 + 1 group) issued a Special Report[29] which concluded that non-cancellable operating leases should be treated in the same way as finance leases. The similar treatment is based on the premise that the rights and obligations created under a lease contract meet the definitions of an asset and liability of a conceptual framework. This approach is consistent with the ASB's draft Statement of Principles. The G4 + 1 group issued a discussion paper in 1999.

W. McGregor[30] explained that:

> A lease contract conveys a right to a lessee to use the leased property; in the language of the conceptual frameworks, the lessee controls the future economic benefits embodied in the leased property for the period of the lease term. Similarly, the lease contract establishes an obligation on the lessee to sacrifice future economic benefits to an external party in payment for the use of the leased property.

This approach addresses one of the main problems with the current accounting treatment, namely, the potential for framing a finance lease as an operating lease and not having to capitalise the lease contract on the lessee's balance sheet.

The ASB published a Discussion Paper[31] presenting the Position Paper developed by the G4 + 1 standard setters. The main thrust of the paper is that operating leases which are not currently included in the balance sheet would give rise to assets and liabilities reported at the fair value of the rights and obligations conveyed in the lease, e.g. where a lease is only for a small part of an asset's economic life, only that part would be reflected in the lessee's balance sheet. The ASB has said that a persuasive factor in adopting the main principles of the paper is the common and growing practice of analysts recasting financial statements by capitalising operating leases.

Summary

The initial upturn in leasing activity in the 1970s was attributable to the economy and tax requirements rather than the popularity of lease transactions *per se*. High interest rates, a high inflation rate, 100% first-year tax allowances and a sequence of annual losses in the manufacturing industry made leasing transactions extremely attractive to both the lessors and the lessees.

Once the leasing industry was firmly established, the amount of leasing activity continued to increase, even when many of the original benefits were no longer applicable. The Finance Act 1984 had removed the major tax advantages of leases, but by then many other benefits of leasing as a form of finance had been discovered.

Off-balance-sheet financing was considered a particular advantage of lease financing. SSAP 21 recognised this and attempted to introduce stricter accounting policies and requirements. However, although SSAP 21 introduced the concept of 'substance over form', the hazy distinction between finance and operating leases still allows companies to structure lease agreements to achieve either type of lease. This is important because, while stricter accounting requirements apply to finance leases, operating leases can still be used as a form of off-balance-sheet accounting.

We do not know the real extent to which SSAP 21 is either observed or ignored. However, it is true to say that creative accountants and finance companies are able to circumvent SSAP 21 by using structured leases. FRS 5 should reduce the scope for this practice. Also the IASC have revised IAS 17[32] to require enhanced disclosures by lessees, including disclosure of rental expenses, sublease rentals, and a description of leasing arrangements.

Review questions

1 Can the legal position on leases be ignored now that substance over form is used for financial reporting? Discuss.

2 Look at the 'Extract from the Greenalls Group plc' at the end of section 19.5. Consider this information in conjunction with the following information :

	1999	1998
	£000	£000
Operating profit	133,382	209,104
Fixed assets	1,665,921	1,892,883
Current assets	158,024	183,134

(a) Consider the effects of both operating leases and finance leases on the 'return on capital employed'.

(b) Consider the importance of the categorisation of lease transactions into operating lease or finance lease decisions when carrying out financial ratio analysis in general. What ratios might be affected?

(c) Discuss the effects of renegotiating/reclassifying all operating leases into finance leases. What effect might it have for Greenalls? For which industries might this classification have a significant impact on the financial ratios?

3 Explain the major provisions of SSAP 21 *Accounting for Leases*.

4 The favourite off balance financing trick used to be leasing. Using any illustrative numerical examples you may wish to:

(a) Define the term 'off-balance-sheet financing' and state why it is popular with companies.

(b) Illustrate what is meant by the above quotation in the context of leases and discuss the accounting treatments and disclosures required by SSAP 21 which have limited the usefulness of leasing as an off balance sheet financing technique.

(c) Suggest two other off-balance-sheet financing techniques and discuss the effect that each technique has on balance sheet assets and liabilities, and on the profit and loss account.

5 What effect will FRS 5 have on accounting for leases?

6 Private Finance Initiative contracts were discussed in 15.9. Using the exposure draft[33] described in that section (and any subsequent accounting releases) find out more details on the following:

(a) In what situations will the contract have separable service elements?

(b) What are the indications that the property is either an asset of the purchaser or the operator?

7 Cable & Wireless plc had the following accounting policy in its 1997 accounts:

> Where assets are financed by leasing agreements that give rights approximating to ownership, the assets are treated as if purchased outright. The amount capitalised is the present value of the minimum lease payments payable during the lease term. ... Lease payments are split between capital and interest elements using the annuity method. ... Depreciation on the relevant assets and interest are charged to operating profit.

Explain the following terms: 'rights approximating to ownership', 'the minimum lease payments' and 'the annuity method'.

Exercises

An extract from the solution is provided in the appendix at the end of the text for exercises marked with an asterisk (*).

* *Question 1*

On 1 January 20X8, Grabbit plc entered into an agreement to lease a widgeting machine for general use in the business. The agreement, which may not be terminated by either party to it, runs for six years and provides for Grabbit to make an annual rental payment of £92,500 on 31 December each year. The cost of the machine to the lessor was £350,000, and it has no residual value. The machine has a useful economic life of eight years and Grabbit depreciates its fixed assets using the straight-line method.

Required:

(a) Show how Grabbit plc will account for the above transaction in its balance sheet at 31 December 20X8, and in its profit and loss account for the year then ended, if it capitalises the leased asset in accordance with the principles laid down in SSAP 21.

(b) Explain why the ASC considered accounting for leases to be an area in need of standardisation and discuss the rationale behind the approach adopted in the standard.

(c) Off-balance-sheet financing is still a topical area. Explain why this is the case and discuss the ASC's recent attempt at dealing with the problem in the context of window dressing.

* Question 2

(a) When accounting for hire purchase transactions and finance leases, accountants prefer to overlook legal form in favour of commercial substance.

Required:
Discuss the above statement in the light of the requirements of SSAP 21 Accounting for Leases and Hire Purchase Contracts.

(b) State briefly how you would distinguish between a finance lease and an operating lease.

(c) Smarty plc finalises its accounts annually on 31 March. It depreciates its machinery at 20% per annum on cost and adopts the 'Rule of 78' for allocating finance charges among different accounting periods. On 1 August 20X7 it acquired machinery on a finance lease on the following agreement:

(i) a lease rent of £500 per month is payable for 36 months commencing from the date of acquisition;

(ii) cost of repairs and insurance are to be met by the lessee;

(iii) on completion of the primary period the lease may be extended for a further period of three years, at the lessee's option, for a peppercorn rent.

The cash price of the machine is £15,000.

Required:

(a) Set out how all ledger accounts reflecting these transactions will appear in each of the four accounting periods 20X7/8, 20X8/9, 20X9/0 and 20X0/1.

(b) Show the profit and loss account entries for the year ended 31 March 20X8 and balance sheet extracts as at that date.

Question 3

The Mission Company Ltd, whose year end is 31 December, has acquired two items of machinery on leases, the conditions of which are as follows:

Item Y: Ten annual instalments of £20,000 each, the first payable on 1 January 20X0. The machine was completely installed and first operated on 1 January 20X0 and its purchase price on that date was £160,000. The machine has an estimated useful life of ten years, at the end of which it will be of no value.

Item Z: Ten annual instalments of £30,000 each, the first payable on 1 January 20X2. The machine was completely installed and first operated on 1 January 20X2 and its purchase price on that date was £234,000. The machine has an estimated useful life of twelve years, at the end of which it will be of no value.

The Mission Company Ltd accounts for finance charges on finance leases by allocating them over the period of the lease on the sum of the digits method.

Depreciation is charged on a straight-line basis. Ignore taxation.

Required:

(a) **Calculate and state the charges to the profit and loss account for 20X6 and 20X7 if the leases were treated as operating leases.**

(b) **Calculate and state the charge to the profit and loss account for 20X6 and 20X7 if the leases were treated as financial leases and capitalised using the sum of the digits method for the finance charges.**

(c) **Show how items Y and Z should be incorporated in the balance sheet, and notes thereto, at 31 December 19X7, if capitalised.**

Question 4

X Ltd entered into a lease agreement on the following terms:

Cost of leased asset	£100,000
Lease term	5 years
Rentals six-monthly in advance	£12,000
Anticipated residual on disposal of the assets at end of lease term	£10,000
Lessee's interest in residual value	97%
Economic life	8 years
Inception date	1 January 20X4
Lessee's financial year-end	31 December
Implicit rate of interest is applied half-yearly	4.3535%

Required:

(a) **Show the profit and loss account entries for the year ended 31 December 20X4 and balance sheet extracts as at that date.**

(b) **Show the profit and loss account entries for the year ended 31 December 20X7 and balance sheet extracts as at that date.**

References

1 C. Drury and S. Braund, 'A survey of UK leasing practice', *Management Accounting*, April 1989, pp. 40–43.
2 N. Cope, 'Big ticket to ride out the recession', *Accountancy*, December 1992, pp. 55–57.
3 R. Perera, 'To buy or not to buy – how to decide', *Certified Accountant*, December 1986.
4 G. Allum *et al.*, 'Fleet focus: to lease or not to lease', *Australian Accountant*, September 1989, pp. 31–58.
5 R.L. Benke and C.P. Baril, 'The lease vs. purchase decision', *Management Accounting*, March 1990, pp. 42–46.
6 B. Underdown and P. Taylor, *Accounting Theory and Policy Making*, Heinemann, 1985, p. 273.
7 Cranfield School of Management, *Financial Leasing Report*, Bedford, 1979.

8 Abdel-Khalik *et al.*, 'The Economic Effects on Lessees of FASB Statement No. 13', *Accounting for Leases*, FASB, 1981.

9 G. Macdonald, in J. Freedman and M. Power (eds), *Law and Accountancy*, Paul Chapman Publishing, 1992, p. 76.

10 R. Owens, 'Why SSAP 21 isn't the answer', *Accountancy*, January 1984, pp. 49–51.

11 SFAS 13, *Accounting for Leases*, FASB, November 1976.

12 IAS 17, *Accounting for Leases*, IASC, September 1982.

13 J.H. Davison, Chairman, Accounting Standards Committee, foreword, SSAP 21, *Accounting for Leases and Hire Purchase Contracts*, 1984.

14 IAS 1, *Disclosure of Accounting Policies*, IASC, 1984.

15 N. Hyndman and R. Kirk, 'The latest accounting standards', *Management Accounting*, December 1989, pp. 20–22.

16 R. Speyer, 'What ED 29 means to the lessee', *Accountancy*, January 1982, pp. 112–115.

17 G. Macmillan, 'Lease accounting update', *Australian Accountant*, March 1986, pp. 36–39.

18 R. Main, *External Financial Reporting*, B. Carsberg and S. Dev (eds), Prentice Hall, 1984.

19 R.H. Gamble 'Off-balance-sheet diet: greens on the side', *Corporate Cashflow*, August 1990, pp. 28–32.

20 R.L. Benke and C.P. Baril, 'The lease vs. purchase decision', *Management Accounting*, March 1990, pp. 42–46.

21 N. Woodhams and P. Fletcher, 'Operating leases to take bigger market share with changing standards', *Rydge's (Australia)*, September 1985, pp. 100–110.

22 C.H. Volk, 'The risks of operating leases', *Journal of Commercial Bank Lending*, May 1988, pp. 47–52.

23 Chee-Seong Tah, 'Lease or buy?', *Accountancy*, December 1992, pp. 58–59.

24 FRS 5, *Reporting the Substance of Transactions*, ASB, March 1995.

25 I. Sharp, 'A question of substance', *Accountancy*, December 1994, p. 138.

26 'Brewer applies FRS5 just in case', *Accountancy*, March 1995, p. 104.

27 'Leased assets reach balance sheet', *Accountancy*, March 1995, p. 104.

28 Amendment to FRS 5 'Reporting the Substance of Transactions', *The Private Finance Initiative* (exposure draft), ASB, December 1997.

29 'G4+1', *'Accounting for Leases – A New Approach'*, July 1996.

30 W. McGregor, 'Lease accounting: righting the wrongs', *Accountancy*, September 1996, p. 96.

31 *Leases: Implementation of a New Approach*, Discussion Paper, ASB, December 1999.

32 IAS 17 (revised), *Accounting for Leases*, IASC, November 1997.

33 Amendment to FRS 5 'Reporting the Substance of Transactions', *The Private Finance Initiative* (exposure draft), ASB, December 1997.

CHAPTER 16

R&D; goodwill and intangible assets; brands

16.1 Introduction

In this chapter we consider the accounting treatments of the following:

- Research and development
- Goodwill and intangible assets
- Brands

16.2 Accounting treatment for research and development

In the UK, the accounting treatment for R&D may differ depending on whether the expenditure relates to research expenditure or development expenditure. Broadly speaking, the research expenditure must always be charged to the profit and loss account, and the option to capitalise development expenditure is available only if a strict set of criteria are met. In this section, we will consider why there is pressure to write off research and development expenditure, the accounting requirements for R&D, and how development costs are defined.

16.2.1 Why is there a pressure to write off R&D expenditure?

The Companies Act refers in the balance sheet to costs, rather than to projects or invest-ment in research. However, many readers will think of research and development (R&D) as an investment rather than as a cost. They may well perceive it as a strategic investment that is essential if we are to be competitive in world markets. This applies particularly to an advanced technical industry such as chemicals, where a sustained high level of R&D investment is required.

The 'R&D Scoreboard' is prepared for the DTI by Company Reporting and the *Financial Times*[1] analysed the results for figures published in annual reports up to 31 May 1999. It was reported that the UK has the next to lowest ratio of R&D to sales of any large industrialised country. According to the figures, average R&D-to-sales fig-ures for individual countries were:

	1998	1999
Sweden	7.4%	7.2%
Switzerland	6.3%	6.4%
Japan	4.8%	4.7%

Germany	4.3%	4.2%
US	4.9%	5.7%
France	4.0%	4.0%
UK	2.5%	2.9%
Italy	2.0%	1.8%

In the table of 'Top 50 International Companies by R&D Expenditure', only one UK company features. An extract, which includes a comparison with each of the top US, German and Japanese companies, is shown below:

Position	Company	Country	1998/9 R&D Expenditure (£m)	R&D-to-sales (%)
1	General Motors	USA	4,748,167	5.1
3	Daimler/Chrysler	Germany	3,508,363	3.8
8	Hitachi	Japan	2,722,200	6.1
36	Glaxo Wellcome	UK	1,163,000	14.6

One publication mentioned that the recognition of R&D as an asset had appeared in a report from the House of Lords Select Committee on Science and Technology, stating that 'R&D has to be regarded as an investment which leads to growth, not a cost'.[2,3] Unfortunately, two constraints militate against companies incurring high levels of expenditure. First, there is a commercial constraint: it is felt that a company which pursues a commitment to R&D is vulnerable to take-over bids. It is perhaps an irony that the threat comes from companies that have not had such a commitment. There is presumably an attraction for the company with the lower R&D commitment to mount a take-over with the prospect of a short-term increase in its earnings per share merely by reducing R&D by, say, 25%. That would show an immediate increase in disclosed trading profit.

So why do companies write off all of their research and development costs to the profit and loss account in the year in which the cost arises? As far as the company is concerned, one may hypothesise that directors have been pleased to take the expense in a year when they know its impact rather than carry it forward. They are aware of profit levels in the year in which the R&D arises and could find it embarrassing to take the loss in a subsequent year when profits were lower or the company even reported a trading loss.

This brings us to our second constraint: the difficulty of being reasonably certain that the intended economic benefits of R&D activities will flow to the enterprise. Because of this uncertainty, the accounting profession has traditionally considered it more prudent to write off the investment in research as a cost rather than report it as an asset in the balance sheet.

ED 14, the initial exposure draft issued in 1975, was influenced by the prudence concept, and required companies to write off all R&D expenditure in the year in which it arose. This was changed in the following year by the proposal in ED 17 that companies should be required to capitalise development costs.

The standard that eventually appeared was different again. A compromise was arrived at in SSAP 13, which permitted, rather than required, a company to capitalise development costs, provided stringent conditions were met. Companies were permitted the choice of treatment provided there was disclosure in the notes to the accounts. The Companies Act also permitted capitalisation, but only in special circumstances.

Directors wanted the capacity to choose the accounting treatment on a variety of grounds. Some felt that it would give their competitors an advantage if the build-up of a large development cost flagged the fact that a new product was about to be launched. Others rated a strong balance sheet higher than commercial secrecy and wanted to be able to include the asset on the balance sheet. Neither of these reasons has any basis in accounting principles, but the accounting profession was subject to the constraints of consensus standard-setting.

In its *Statement of Intent: Comparability of Financial Statements*, the IASC is moving away from these constraints.[4] It is proposing that the choice should be removed and that, if development costs meet the conditions for capitalisation, they must be capitalised and depreciated. This is the approach that has since been adopted by IAS 9[5] and IAS 38.[6]

There has been some research on both analysts'[7] and accountants'[8] reactions to R&D expenditure. Nixon[9] found that 'Two important dimensions of the corporate reporting accountants' perspective emerge: first, disclosure is seen as more important than the accounting treatment of R&D expenditure and, second, the financial statements are not viewed as the primary channel of communication for information on R&D'.

16.2.2   How are development costs defined?

SSAP 13 has given a definition of development costs and also sets out the conditions that need to be met in order to capitalise.

Development costs are defined in SSAP 13 as costs relating to the development of the company's use of knowledge acquired through research to produce new or substantially improved materials, devices, products, processes, systems or services before commercial production begins.

Examples of activities that are typically development are the evaluation of product or process alternatives; the design, construction and testing of preproduction prototypes and models; the design of tools, jigs, moulds and dies involving new technology; and the design, construction and operation of a pilot plant that is not of an economically feasible scale for commercial production.

The types of cost that are included within this classification are those incurred in R&D activities relating to salaries and wages; the costs of materials and services consumed; the depreciation of property, plant and equipment to the extent that they are used for R&D activities; overhead costs related to R&D activities: and other related costs such as the amortisation of patents and licences.

The standard also defines pure and applied research. Pure research is experimental or theoretical work undertaken primarily to acquire new scientific or technical knowledge for its own sake, rather than directed towards any specific aim or application. Applied research is original or critical investigation undertaken in order to gain new scientific or technical knowledge and directed towards a specific practical aim or objective.

Neither pure nor applied research may be capitalised under existing standards and legislation. This conflicts with the view put forward by the select committee that research is an investment.

Activities that are related to research and to development but are not classified as either include engineering follow-through in an early phase of commercial production; quality control during commercial production, including routine testing of products; troubleshooting in connection with breakdowns during commercial production; routine efforts to refine, enrich or otherwise improve on the qualities of an existing product;

adaptation of an existing capability to a particular requirement or customer's need as part of a continuing commercial activity; seasonal or other periodic design changes to existing products; routine design of tools, jigs, moulds and dies; and activities, including design and construction engineering, related to the construction, relocation, rearrangement or start-up of facilities or equipment other than facilities whose sole use is for a particular R&D development project.

The conditions that SSAP 13 requires to be met for development costs to be capitalised are as follows:

● There is a clearly defined project. Without this it would be difficult to ensure appropriate matching of revenue and expense. There would be a temptation in a poor year for a company to decide that costs should be classified as development and inappropriately carried forward.

● The expenditure on the project is separately identifiable. This relates to the first point. The amount carried forward needs to be verifiable.

● The outcome of the project has been assessed with reasonable certainty as to its technical feasibility and commercial viability. This requires a level of confidence that the future benefits and costs are not so uncertain that it is impossible to assess whether the project will be commercially successful.

● Revenue will exceed costs. This requires that there should be a matching of revenues and expenses and the recognition of a causal relationship between the development costs and the increased future benefits arising from subsequent sales.

● Adequate resources can reasonably be expected to be available to allow the project to be completed, including any consequential increases in working capital. This is an assessment of the financial structure of the company. It looks at solvency, liquidity and financing capability.

If the development costs, together with any further development costs, related production costs and selling and administrative costs directly incurred in marketing the product, are not probably recoverable from related future revenues, then the part that is not recovered should be written off as an expense in the profit and loss account.

To illustrate, Racal's R&D policy and the amount charged to the profit and loss account is included below:

Racal Electronics plc Annual Reports and Accounts 1999

Accounting policies
Research and Development – Private venture research and development expenditure is written off in the year in which it is incurred. Uninvoiced research and development fully funded by customers is carried forward as work in progress.

Operating profit arrived at after:

	1999 £m
Research and development:	
Continuing operations	44.0
Discontinued operations	5.9

16.3 Introduction to goodwill and intangible assets

The discussion of goodwill and intangibles proceeds as follows:

● the current position is considered briefly;

● historical developments are considered;

● goodwill and intangibles are introduced along with an illustration of their accounting treatment;

● the economic consequences of accounting for goodwill are discussed;

● the amortisation of goodwill is discussed;

● the main requirements of FRS 10 are set out and evaluated.

16.4 Introduction to the current position

The question of what is the appropriate accounting treatment for both goodwill and intangible assets has posed problems for the accounting standard-setting bodies for many years. In particular, accounting for goodwill has been continually under discussion for about twenty-five years. A number of exposure drafts and standards have been issued to address the problems associated with it. Each successive attempt to tackle goodwill received criticism from the profession, management or academic accountants. The latest accounting standard to deal with goodwill (FRS 10[10]) has tackled the associated problem of accounting for other intangibles within the same standard.

The stated objective of FRS 10 is to ensure that:

(a) capitalised goodwill and intangible assets are charged in the profit and loss account in the periods in which they are depleted; and
(b) sufficient information is disclosed in the financial statements to enable users to determine the impact of goodwill and intangible assets on the financial position and performance of the reporting entity. (para. 1)

In the summary to FRS 10, it states that:

Purchased goodwill and intangible assets should be capitalised as assets. Internally generated goodwill should not be capitalised and internally developed intangible assets should be capitalised only where they have a readily ascertainable market value (para. d).

In addition, capitalised assets are subject to amortisation and/or impairment review. These requirements are explained in more detail later in the chapter.

However, as with its predecessors, FRS 10 has not received unanimous support. Although FRS 10 has been greeted by some as the ultimate solution, Paterson[11] contests this view:

The publication of FRS 10 … was hailed as the culmination of a long debate within the accounting profession. However, I find it hard to regard this standard as having brought the debate to a real conclusion. I have little doubt that it will in due course be replaced by a further standard, and indeed FRS 10's own useful life may be found to be quite limited.

Although FRS 10 applies to both goodwill and intangible assets, they are differentiated and the requirements are stated separately within the accounting standard. Although some of the required accounting treatments apply to both goodwill and intangible assets,

Paterson[12] argues that the attempt to cater for both in a single standard has some severe drawbacks:

> I am also concerned that this issue [goodwill] has dominated the ASB's thinking, with the result that both negative goodwill and the wider issue of intangibles have received less attention than they deserve.

16.5 Historical developments

The accounting treatment of goodwill has been under consideration since the early 1970s. Since then the standard-setters have produced a series of discussion papers, exposure drafts and accounting standards, culminating in FRS 10. Some of the key publications include:

● ED 30[13]
● EC Seventh Directive[14]
● SSAP 22[15]
● ED 44[16]
● SSAP 22 revised[17]
● ED 47[18]
● Corfield Report[19]
● ASB Discussion Paper[20]
● ASB Working Paper[21]
● FRED 12[22]
● FRS 10[23]

In 1993 the ASB issued a discussion paper *Goodwill and Intangible Assets*, in which it suggested a restrictive approach to reporting intangible assets and in which it set out six possible treatments for goodwill.

It stated that internally generated intangibles should not be recognised in the balance sheet; intangibles acquired on the acquisition of another business should be subsumed within the goodwill arising on acquisition. This was far too general a treatment to provide either a true and fair view or the commercial substance of the transaction. The reasoning was no doubt the ASB's concern that companies would use the availability of separating intangibles from goodwill in order to change materially the accounting message communicated to the shareholders by a process of arbitrage.

The ASB did not recommend any single treatment in its discussion paper concerning goodwill, but, as a way of focusing the debate, the Board indicated support for capitalisation and predetermined life amortisation and separate write-off reserve.

In 1995 the ASB issued a working paper *Goodwill and Intangible Assets*, in which it stated that the approach to intangibles had been reconsidered. The revised proposal was that **internally generated** intangibles may be recognised, but only when there is a specific accounting standard, e.g. SSAP 13 *Accounting for Research and Development*,[24] allowing their recognition or when they have a **reliable market value** obtainable from frequent transactions in a **homogeneous population** of identical assets.[25] Also the ASB agreed that where goodwill has an indefinitely long life, this longevity should be mirrored in the accounting treatment.

Following these publications, the ASB released FRED 12 and then FRS 10. FRS 10 broadly follows FRED 12.[26,27] In the next two sections we introduce intangible assets followed by goodwill.

16.6   Intangible assets

16.6.1   Introduction to Intangible assets

FRS 10 defines **intangible assets** and describes some categories of intangible assets:

- 'Non-financial fixed assets that do not have physical substance but are identifiable and controlled by the legal entity through custody or legal rights' (para. 2) Therefore, they fall within the definition of an asset when the reporting entity controls the access to the future economic benefits that it represents.

- 'Licences, quotas, patents, copyrights, franchises and trade marks are examples of categories that may be treated as separate classes of intangible assets' (para. 2)

The real debate concerning intangibles begins with the issue of initial recognition – can an intangible asset be separately identified? Then, even if it can be separately identified, how should it be measured? There are a number of principal methods which have been used to value intangibles,[28] but opponents argue that in general these valuations are not sufficiently reliable to allow their inclusion in the financial statements.

Once an intangible asset has been recognised in the financial statements, further difficulties arise. How should this asset be amortised (depreciated)? What is the useful economic life of the asset? Is the useful life infinite? How should any reductions in value be measured and/or treated in the accounts?

16.6.1   Intangible assets: extracts of accounting policies from company accounts

In recent years, companies have applied a range of different accounting policies to the treatment of intangible assets in their financial statements. This variety of accounting treatment is illustrated by the following extracts from the accounts of Bass plc, Reckitt & Colman plc, The EMI Group, Racal Electronics plc and Charterhouse Communications plc. Although companies disclose their accounting treatment in their statement of accounting policies, this does not give us information on the motives influencing this choice; nor does it allow us to assess the value, or indeed the continued existence, of an asset.

For example, Bass plc does not include intangible assets in either its 1997, 1998 or 1999 balance sheets, as stated in its accounting policies.

Its 1997 accounting policies stated:

Fixed assets and depreciation
Intangible assets – No value is attributed to trademarks, concessions, patents and similar rights and assets, including hotel franchises and management contracts.

As readers of the accounts, we were unable to assess readily whether this policy was one of convenience, which would result in the understatement of assets and the creation of secret reserves, or whether it indicated that these assets did, indeed, have no value; or whether the company is applying the prudence concept and it is difficult to attach values to the intangible assets with any reasonable certainty. In practice, it may be very difficult to establish a link between the cost incurred and the value created for intangibles – the economic benefits associated with an asset depend on how successfully the appropriate market can be developed. Moreover, a reliable measurement of the cost of intangibles is often impossible because of the problems involved in establishing a separate cost figure. This is often the case when there is not an active market in a particular intangible to indicate a market value.

Following the issue of FRS 10 the 1998 and 1999 Bass plc Annual Report Accounting Policy reads as follows:

Intangible assets

On acquisition of a business, no value is attributed to intangible assets which cannot be separately identified or reliably measured. No value is attributed to internally generated intangible assets.

This policy will apply from 1998 but there is no indication as to pre-FRS 10 position relating to the intangible assets described in the Bass 1997 Accounting Policy.

Reckitt & Colman offers a different treatment from Bass. It includes trademarks in the balance sheet at their purchase cost and does not provide any annual systematic amortisation because in the company's view their useful economic life is unlimited. The intangible asset is written down only if there is evidence of an impairment in value.

The Reckitt & Colman Annual Report 1998 accounting policies read as follows:

Intangible assets and goodwill

Trademarks are not amortised, as it is considered that their useful economic lives are not limited. Their carrying value is reviewed annually by the directors to determine whether there has been any impairment in value and any such reductions in value are taken to the profit and loss account.

Cost	Trademarks £m
At beginning of financial year	1,143.0
Additions during year	64.6
Disposals during the year	(6.2)
Exchange adjustments	(5.4)
At 2 January 1999	1,196.0

Following the issue of FRS 10, the 1998 Reckitt and Colman Annual Report Accounting Policy was unchanged except that the wording 'permanent diminution' was changed to 'impairment'.

The EMI Group's policy partly followed the Bass treatment and partly followed the Reckitt & Colman treatment. For example, in its 1997 Accounts the company has written off some copyrights and capitalised other copyrights (at their purchase cost), which it amortises only if the royalties indicate that the book value is not supported by the level of royalties. Notable recent signings include the Spice Girls and George Michael.

The EMI Group's Annual Report 1997

Accounting policies

Music Publishing Copyrights purchased prior to 1 April 1989 were written off against shareholders' funds on acquisition. Copyrights acquired as a result of the acquisition of a business, on or after 1 April 1989, are treated as intangible assets in the Group balance sheet. The capitalised amount of such copyrights, being their purchase cost, is subject to amortisation only to the extent that the royalty income generated by the total music publishing portfolio is insufficient to support its book value. All costs attributable to copyrights obtained in the normal course of trade, and not as a result of the acquisition of a business, are written off as incurred.

In its 1999 Annual Report, EMI has changed its accounting policy due to the FRS 10 rigorous impairment review requirement. Its Accounting Policy reads as follows:

Music copyrights

Music publishing copyrights purchased prior to 1 April 1989 were written off against shareholders' funds on acquisition. Copyrights acquired as a result of acquisitions on or after 1 April 1989 have previously been capitalised as intangible assets in the Group balance sheet, but amortised only to the extent that royalty income generated by the total music publishing copyrights portfolio was insufficient to support its book value.

On adoption of FRS 10, our accounting policy for copyrights had to change because we could not perform the detailed annual impairment review required by FRS 10 to support an indefinite useful economic life. Consequently, copyrights are now amortised by equal annual amounts over up to 20 years, other than in exceptional circumstances when sufficient ongoing impairment tests can be performed to support a useful economic life of over 20 years. Where a useful economic life of up to 20 years has been adopted, copyrights are reviewed for impairment at the end of the first full financial year following acquisition and in other periods if events or changes in circumstances indicate that the carrying value may not be recoverable.

The comparatives for the year ended 31 March 1998 and opening balances have been restated, via prior period adjustment, to reflect the accumulated amortisation at 31 March 1997 and the charge for the year ended 31 March 1998 arising from this change in accounting policy.

Racal follows a policy of amortising the historical cost of intangible assets which it holds in the form of 'know-how' over the useful economic life of the know-how. This is illustrated in their annual accounts.

Racal Electronics plc Annual Reports and Accounts 1999

Accounting policies

Know-how – Payments made to acquire manufacturing licences for specific products are amortised against profits over a period of 3 to 5 years being the period of utilisation of such manufacturing knowledge.

Charterhouse Communications includes newly acquired publishing rights in its financial statements. Note that the intangible assets dwarf the tangible assets.

Charterhouse Communications plc Annual Reports and Accounts 1998

Accounting policies

Intangible Fixed Assets – Publishing rights and titles are stated at cost in these financial statements. On an annual basis, the directors consider the fair value of these assets on the basis of cash flow projections. Amortisation is not provided as there has been no permanent diminution in their value.

Balance Sheet at 31 May 1998

Fixed assets	£000
Intangible assets	6,501
Tangible assets	92
Investments	—
	6,593

16.7   Goodwill

16.7.1   Introduction to goodwill

FRS 10 defines purchased goodwill as 'the difference between the cost of an acquired entity and the aggregate of the fair values of an entity's identifiable assets and liabilities'. Fair values (according to FRS 6 and 7) have been explained in an earlier chapter and their effect on goodwill is considered in section 20.7.4.

16.7.2   Goowill may be positive or negative

Goodwill is positive if the agreed value of the business based on future cash flows is greater than the aggregate of the fair value of the identifiable assets and liabilities. It is negative if the agreed value of the business based on future cash flows is lower than the aggregate of the fair value of the identifiable assets and liabilities.

16.7.3   Goodwill may also be realised or unrealised

Goodwill is realised if it is arrived at as a result of an actual transfer of the business for consideration. It is unrealised if an actual transfer of the business has not occurred, but the directors have estimated a value for the business as a whole and the separable net assets. If there has been an actual transfer, the difference is referred to as **purchased** goodwill. If there has not been an actual transfer, the estimated difference is referred to as non-purchased or **inherent** goodwill.

Purchased goodwill is based on a transaction with a third party at arm's length; the difference is objective and verifiable. Non-purchased goodwill has not arisen from a transaction with a third party at arm's length; the difference is subjective.

For financial reporting purposes, it is normal accounting practice that only purchased goodwill should be recognised in the accounts.

We illustrate the calculation of goodwill using the CW Group.

EXAMPLE ● Assume that on 31 December 20X1 Cooper Woosnam plc (CW plc) purchases all of the assets and liabilities of Worthington Windsurfers plc (WW plc) for £300,000. (Note CW is *not* acquiring the shares in WW plc.) The separate balance sheets as at 31 December 20X1 immediately prior to the purchase are shown below:

	CW plc £000	WW plc £000	Fair value estimate £000
Fixed assets			
Goodwill			
Plant and machinery	1,000	110	150
Net current assets	1,050	90	90
	2,050	200	240
Long-term creditors	450	40	40
	1,600	160	200
Capital and reserves			
Share capital	900	150	150
Share premium account	300	—	—
Profit and loss account	400	10	10
Revaluation reserve			40
	1,600	160	200

A revaluation reserve will arise only if the fair values are actually incorporated into the books of WW plc. It will not appear in the books of CW plc.

The purchased goodwill is calculated as:

Valuable consideration paid – Fair value (estimate) of identifiable assets and liabilities

= £300,000 – £200,000

= £100,000

The goodwill will appear as an intangible asset in the accounts of CW plc as follows:

	CW plc £000	
Fixed assets		
Goodwill	100	
Plant and machinery	1,150	
Net current assets	840	(1,050 – 300 + 90)
	2,090	
Long-term creditors	(490)	
	1,600	
Capital and reserves		
Share capital	900	
Share premium account	300	
Profit and loss account	400	
	1,600	

Note that the £300,000 is an arm's-length payment and is verifiable. However, even though goodwill arises as a result of an arm's-length transaction, the fair values attached to the separable assets are subjective. In this example, an increase of £40,000 is made to the plant; it is an estimate made by the directors of CW plc. The result of the increase in the fair value over the book value is that a lower goodwill figure is calculated than would have appeared using book values. This means that there is scope for the directors of CW plc to adjust the purchased goodwill figure by revising the fair value estimates.

We often meet goodwill in the context of a take-over of one company by another. We illustrate this using the same data for both companies, but now assuming that CW plc acquires all of the issued shares of WW plc instead of the individual assets and liabilities.

EXAMPLE ● Assume that on 31 December 20X1 Cooper Woosnam plc (CW plc) purchases all the equity shares in Worthington Windsurfers plc (WW plc) for £300,000 for a cash consideration from page 495. The separate balance sheets as at 31 December 20X1 immediately after the acquisition of the shares are shown below:

The purchased goodwill is calculated exactly as in example 1:

Valuable consideration paid – Fair value (estimate) of identifiable assets and liabilities

= £300,000 – £200,000 = £100,000

	CW plc £000	WW plc £000	Fair value estimate £000
Fixed assets			
Plant and machinery	1,000	110	150
Investment in WW plc	300		
Net current assets	750	90	90
	2,050	200	240
Long-term creditors	450	40	40
	1,600	160	200
Capital and reserves			
Share capital	900	150	150
Share premium account	300	—	—
Profit and loss account	400	10	10
Revaluation reserve	—	—	40
	1,600	160	200

We have discussed the possibility for directors to make goodwill larger or smaller by adjusting the fair value of the assets and liabilities. In the past it has also been possible for the directors to increase the goodwill figure by providing for reorganisation costs that might arise on integrating the new subsidiary into the group.

If CW plc acquires the shares of WW plc, the goodwill appears in the consolidated accounts and not in the balance sheet of CW plc. The consolidated balance sheet immediately after the acquisition of the shares would be as follows:

CW consolidated balance sheet
£000

Fixed assets	
Goodwill	100
Plant and machinery	1,150
Investment in WW plc	—
Net current assets	840
	2,090
Long-term creditors	490
	1,600
Capital and reserves	
Share capital	900
Share premium account	300
Profit and loss account	400
	1,600

This meant that there was scope for the directors of CW plc to adjust the purchased goodwill figure, e.g. by revising the fair value estimates as in Example 1 or by making a provision for reorganisation costs. However FRS 7 was introduced to prevent abuse by overprovisioning.

Another illustration of the fair value exercise is included for Floral Street plc's acquisition of Devereux Litho Limited (as disclosed in the 1996 annual report):

	Net book value	Fair value adjustments	Fair value
	£	£	£
Tangible fixed assets	231,843	(121,301)	110,542
Stock	49,782	(49,782)	0
Debtors	214,819	(50,000)	164,819
Liabilities	(644,993)	(29,970)	(694,963)
Net Assets acquired	(168,549)	(251,053)	(419,602)
Goodwill	551,556	251,053	802,609
Consideration paid	383,007	0	383,007

16.7.4 Implication of FRS 7 *Fair Values in Acquisition Accounting*

On making an acquisition it became customary for the acquiring company to reduce the apparent value of the net assets that were being acquired by creating provisions as at the date of the acquisition. These were described as provisions for future losses and provisions for the cost of reorganising a company following acquisition. As a result the goodwill figure was increased. We have already seen that there was no requirement for the goodwill amount to be amortised through the profit and loss account of future years. This is illustrated in the following example.

EXAMPLE ● Pushy plc, which was making a consistent profit of £50m per year, acquired all of the shares in Slow plc, which was making a consistent profit of £8m per year. The acquisition was made for a cash consideration of £40m on 1 January 20X7. The balance sheets of the two companies as at 1 January 20X7 were as follows:

	Pushy plc £m	Slow plc book values £m	Slow plc fair values £m
Fixed assets	100	20	18
Net current assets	80	15	14
	180	35	32
Share capital	50	20	
Reserves	130	15	
	180	35	

The initial calculation of the goodwill figure was as follows:

	£m
Cost of shares in Slow plc	40
Less: Fair value of net assets	(32)
Goodwill	8

At this point, the creative genius of the directors came into play. If the company estimated that the costs of reorganisation were going to be £12m, the position would change:

	£m	£m
Cost of shares in Slow plc		40
Less: Fair value of net assets	32	
Less: Provision for cost of reorganisation	(12)	(20)
Goodwill		20

In any of the years following the acquisition, the provision could be used to soak up expenses, and the profits of the combined group would be inflated as follows:

Pre FRS 7 and FRS 10

	Normal profits	Reorganisation costs incurred	Reorganisation provision released	Profits reported
	£m	£m	£m	£m
20X7	50 + 8	(10)	10	58
20X8	50 + 8	(10)	10	58

The reported profit would be increased above normal profit of 58 if the fair value provision made exceeded the reorganisation costs incurred.

Post FRS 7 and FRS 10

There are two differences:

● Reorganisation provisions are not allowed
● Goodwill is required to be amortised (now left unchanged at £8m)

	Normal profits	Reorganisation costs incurred	Re-organisation provision released (no provision created)	Goodwill amortised assume 20 years	Profits reported
	£m	£m	£m	£m	£m
20X7	50 + 8	(10)		(0.4)	47.6
20X8	50 + 8	(10)		(0.4)	47.6

The effect of this was to charge expenses incurred in the period following the acquisition to the goodwill account, i.e. capitalise the expenses. Some will argue that this is entirely appropriate because the reorganisation costs are actually in the nature of capital outlay. The finance director of Reed-Elsevier and chairman of the 100 Group of UK Finance Directors took this view when he stated that there needed to be a distinction between revenue and capital items; that while provisioning against future losses should not be permissible, restructuring costs were a capital item and should be treated as such.

However, the investment community believed that companies were abusing the opportunity to create provisions by overprovisioning at the time of an acquisition to bolster subsequent years' accounts. The ASB took a similar view and issued FRS 7 *Fair Values in Acquisition*, which stated that the identifiable assets and liabilities to be recognised in the fair value/goodwill calculation should be those of the acquired entity that **existed** at the date of the acquisition. Provisions for reorganisation costs **expected** to be incurred as a result of the acquisition are not permitted because they were not liabilities of the acquired company at the date of acquisition.

In other words, the ASB considers management intent an insufficient basis for recognising changes to an entity's assets and liabilities. This is a different approach from that taken in the USA and in international accounting standards. No doubt, in taking this strong line, the ASB was influenced less by the niceties of theory than by the need to counteract the abuses that were occurring unchecked prior to FRS 7. Companies have only themselves to blame.

16.7.5 Accounting for purchased goodwill

The source of most disagreement in the goodwill debate has centred on which of two accounting treatments should be used to account for purchased goodwill. The two methods are:

● Goodwill should be treated as an asset and written off over its expected useful life through the profit and loss account.

● Goodwill should not be treated as an asset, but should be written off against reserves in the year of acquisition.

Prior to the publication of FRS 10, SSAP 22 allowed a choice of the two different methods with the preferred method being immediate write-off. **Under FRS 10 this choice has been removed and the purchased goodwill should be capitalised as an asset and amortised over its useful life and/or subject to an impairment review.**

We can illustrate the two treatments with the CW Group, whose balance sheets as at 31 December 20X1, the date of acquisition, are shown in Figure 16.1

As can be seen from the figure, if the policy of immediate write-off against reserve is followed, the reserve (in this case the profit and loss balance) is reduced by the value of the purchased goodwill. This means that the original value of £400,000 is reduced by £100,000 to a value of £300,000.

Figure 16.1 Comparison of immediate write-off with amortisation of goodwill.

	CW plc £000	WW plc £000	Fair value £000	Write off immediately £000	Amortise over life £000
			Consolidated CW Group		
Fixed assets					
Goodwill				—	100
Plant and machinery	1,000	110	150	1,150	1,150
Investment in WW plc	300				
Net current assets	750	90	90	840	840
	2,050	200	240	1,990	2,090
Long-term creditors	(450)	(40)	(40)	(490)	(490)
	1,600	160	200	1,500	1,600
Capital and reserves					
Share capital	900	150	150	900	900
Share premium account	300	—	—	300	300
Profit and loss account	400	10	10	300	400
Revaluation reserve			40		
	1,600	160	200	1,500	1,600

If the policy is to capitalise and amortise, goodwill is held as an intangible asset of £100,000 in the balance sheet and amortised through the profit and loss account over its useful economic life. Assuming that the directors of CW plc decide to amortise the goodwill over twenty years, the goodwill diminishes by £5,000 each year.

Following these accounting policies, at 31 December 20X2 the balance sheet will record goodwill at £95,000 (£100,000 – £5,000), and 'other income and expenses' of £5,000 will be charged to the profit and loss account. Note that this method has an impact on the earnings and therefore on the EPS in the twenty years following the acquisition.

Each of these methods attracts a degree of criticism. The most important explanation, then, for the general criticism of capitalisation and amortisation of purchased goodwill is the effect it has on reported earnings and EPS. An annual amortisation charge to the profit and loss account will naturally lower the reported earnings and the resultant EPS figure.

Immediate write-off is criticised because it results in the understatement of balance sheet totals. But, given the choice, past practice has shown that UK companies prefer a weakened balance sheet to the threat of a reduction in the all-important EPS.

The potential effect of the amortisation versus immediate write-off decision on financial statements is demonstrated by WPP's 1998 report and accounts. In the notes to the accounts, WPP adjusts its UK financial statements to take account of US accounting practices.

	1998 £m
Net income before dividends under UK GAAP	140.3
US GAAP adjustments:	
Amortisation of goodwill and other intangibles	(38.2)
Executive compensation	(2.6)
Net income as adjusted for US GAAP	99.5

The WPP accounts demonstrate that the adjustment for US GAAP (notably the capitalisation and amortisation of goodwill) has decreased the earnings per share from 19.1p to 13.5p. This is clearly a significant change – a reduction of almost 30%.

16.8 Economic consequences of each method

We have seen that amortisation has an effect on future EPS, while immediate write-off has an effect on the balance sheet structure. Writing off goodwill against reserves acts to distort some of the primary ratios, since it reduces the shareholders' reserves and therefore the capital employed as well. This has important effects on inter-firm comparison. As an example, let us compare WPP's UK accounts with its US-adjusted accounts. If we concentrate purely on the goodwill adjustments, what is the effect on the return on capital employed (ROCE) ratio as per the above? In brief, the profit in the US is decreased by the annual amortisation charge and the capital employed is increased by the capitalised value of goodwill (which had been written off in the UK). This will reduce the US ROCE. For comparability, the accounts need to be adjusted so that they use exactly the same goodwill policy.

Gearing ratios are also affected by writing off goodwill against reserves. These ratios include:

$$\text{Gearing ratio} = \frac{\text{Total liability} - \text{Current liability}}{\text{Capital employed}}$$

The gearing ratio measures the proportion of capital employed which has been raised by fixed interest debt. A highly geared company has a high proportion of borrowings, while a company with low gearing relies more on shareholders' funds and equity. The gearing ratio is interpreted in different ways by different users: shareholders might seek higher ratios because this will increase the EPS; creditors might prefer lower ratios as this means that there are fewer secured claims against the company's assets.

We have discussed the choices available for dealing with goodwill and have demonstrated the effect of each on the accounts. We will now discuss more fully the arguments relating to amortisation and immediate write-off.

16.9 Arguments relating to amortisation versus immediate write-off

To appreciate the subtleties of the goodwill debate fully, we examine capitalisation and amortisation and immediate write-off in turn. The issues relating to capitalisation and amortisation will be examined in more depth when considering FRS 10 in a later section.

16.9.1 Capitalisation and amortisation

Period of amortisation

When amortising goodwill, the useful economic life must be determined. How can this be done when the goodwill figure is made up of elements with completely different life expectancies? For example, with how much accuracy and consistency can you estimate the useful economic life of the following examples of goodwill?

> 'customer awareness, reputation for quality, marketing and distribution skills, technical know-how, established business connections, management ability, level of workforce training and the like'.[29]

Method of amortisation

Once the useful economic life is determined, how should goodwill be amortised? As for depreciation of fixed assets, the straight-line method is the easiest to calculate.

Annual review

How can one confirm that the carrying amount and the amortisation period remain appropriate? How can one identify diminutions in value or reductions in useful life?

Double counting

Opponents of the amortisation method claim that the annual amortisation charge creates a 'double charge' in the profit and loss account. It is argued that goodwill-creating and goodwill-maintaining expenses, such as training, advertising, promotion and technical support, are already charged to the profit and loss account.[30]

Advocates of amortisation argue that the goodwill-related expenses, such as training expenses that arise after the date of acquisition, result in the development of non-purchased or inherent goodwill. These expenses are therefore distinct from the purchased goodwill. Consequently, the amortisation charges and the goodwill-related expenses are not deemed to constitute double counting.

Competitive advantage

It is argued that immediate write-off grants a competitive advantage to UK and Irish companies over their international competitors. Whereas the majority of international companies capitalise and amortise purchased goodwill, UK and Irish companies have written off purchased goodwill. This might make it easier for these companies to acquire foreign companies. However, in an efficient capital market the accounting treatment adopted by a company should not affect its market valuation. Hence, foreign enterprises should not be disadvantaged just because UK and Irish companies use immediate write-off. However, the resistance of UK companies to following the Continental practice must be due to their perception of an economic benefit from the immediate write-off policy. The whole area of efficient capital markets is addressed in more detail below, in relation to earnings per share.

International comparability

In an attempt to standardise the accounting treatments employed internationally, the International Accounting Standards Committee (IASC) has revised IAS 22.[31] This standard now requires goodwill to be capitalised and amortised over a maximum of twenty years.[32]

Effect on reported earnings

The fact that amortisation reduces the EPS figure is not in question. The real uncertainty surrounds the economic consequence, i.e. share price reaction. Will users of financial statements interpret this reduction adversely, or will they attribute the drop in EPS to the implementation of amortisation for goodwill?

The conclusion of users will depend on whether or not there is an efficient capital market. An efficient capital market will correctly evaluate accounting information and set the market value of a business. Analysts should be able to explain any changes in EPS figures in terms of the annual amortisation charge. Since an amortisation policy does not change the cash flows or the ability to make distributions, the share price should reflect this fact and remain unchanged.

16.9.2 Immediate write-off against reserves

Effect on shareholders' funds

One of the main problems of writing off goodwill against reserves was that acquisitive companies displayed negligible shareholders' funds in their balance sheet. If goodwill was continually written off, these companies could feasibly have negative values for shareholders' funds.

What did it mean when a company had just made an acquisition of real value and was generating good profits, yet the totals in the shareholders' funds were decreasing?

What possible explanations were there for writing-off goodwill against reserves? One explanation was that it achieved consistency of treatment with non-purchased goodwill.

The extract from WPP's annual report 1997 in Figure 16.2 showed that WPP had a negative value for goodwill write-off reserve of £1,160.4m. But what did this mean? What

Figure 16.2 Negative goodwill in WPP 1997 Accounts.

	1997 £m	1998 £m
Called up share capital	73.6	76.6
Share premium account	421.6	562.9
Goodwill write-off reserve	(1,160.4)	—
Other reserves	78.4	28.5
Profit and loss account	561.6	(480.3)
Equity share owners' funds	(25.2)	187.7

could the company do with this figure? How was the user to distinguish between a 'good' and a 'bad' negative reserve? Was the accounting profession really considering the user when allowing such reporting practices? What did a negative share owners' funds of −£25.2m mean? In the 1998 Annual Report, the negative goodwill write-off reserve has been debited to the profit and loss account in the balance sheet.

Appropriate reserve against which to eliminate goodwill

Even though SSAP 22 recommended the immediate write-off of goodwill against reserves, it did not specify which reserve should be used for the write-off. This 'flexibility' resulted in a varied practice across different companies.

Distortion of primary ratios

We saw above that writing off goodwill against reserves acted to distort some of the primary ratios. Given that these ratios are the key to interpreting a set of financial statements, what effect did the reduction in reserves (due to goodwill write-off) have on user interpretation? To what extent did goodwill change these ratios?

One of the consequences of immediate write-off was that it was difficult to analyse and evaluate a company's balance sheet position. What was a 'strong' and what was a 'weak' balance sheet?

Consistency between purchased and non-purchased goodwill

One of the reasons that SSAP 22 favoured the immediate write-off of goodwill against reserves was that it provided a consistency of treatment between purchased and non-purchased goodwill. However, how did this argument reconcile with the assertion that goodwill was more similar to other intangible assets (e.g. franchise rights, trademarks) which were recorded in the balance sheet?

16.10 FRS 10

16.10.1 Summary of FRS 10

In 1997, the ASB published FRS 10, which superseded SSAP 22. We consider some of its requirements here. In addition some responses to a working paper concerning specific aspects of goodwill and intangibles are included in this section.[33]

Goodwill

● Positive purchased should be capitalised and classified as an asset on the balance sheet.
● Internally generated goodwill should not be capitalised.

Intangible assets

● Separately purchased intangibles should be capitalised as an asset on the balance sheet.
● If the value of an intangible asset acquired as part of the acquisition of a business can be measured reliably on initial recognition then it should be capitalised separately from goodwill.
● Internally developed intangibles may be capitalised if they have a readily ascertainable market value.

Cadbury Scwheppes support this separation of goodwill and other intangibles:

We strongly believe that any attempt to subsume all intangibles in goodwill is nothing less than a cop out. The modern business environment is very different from that which existed twenty or thirty years ago and it is clear that accounting, like many other activities, must move with the times. Many intangibles are far more significant to certain types of business than tangible assets (e.g. a drinks franchise business) and not to recognise them is to present an incomplete picture.[34]

Their view is understandable given the significance of intangible assets in their 1999 accounts:

	£m
Intangible assets	1,656
Goodwill	69
	1,725
Shareholders' funds	2,240

Recent standards by the IASC include IAS 38[35] and IAS 22 (revised).[36] On initial inspection it appears that the IASC have expanded the potential for capitalising internally generated intangible assets. Capitalisation is permitted whenever costs can be measured reliably rather than when the assets are traded on an active market. However, IAS 38 specifically excludes the cost of generating brands, mastheads and similar assets.

Amortisation

● Purchased goodwill and intangible assets with a limited useful economic life should be amortised on a systematic basis over that period. The rebuttable assumption is that this period is twenty years or less. These intangible assets should only be subject to an impairment review in the year following acquisition and if specific circumstances indicate that the carrying value may not be recoverable.

Kalamazoo questions capitalisation and amortisation with regard to intellectual property rights (IPR) of software products:

This practice could potentially result in a discrepancy in the treatment of IPR in computer software companies, with acquired software products being capitalised as assets but internal R&D written off … in fact the estimated useful life of a software product is notoriously difficult to predict and it is regarded as prudent by the industry to write off such expenditure in the year in which it is incurred. If this logic were consistently applied to acquired software products the buyer would be expected to write off the entire value of IPR acquired to the P&L account in the year of acquisition.[37]

Impairment

● FRS 11[38] provides that intangible assets with an indefinite useful economic life should not be amortised but should be subject to impairment review at the end of each reporting period. The procedures for carrying out an impairment review were originally published in an exposure draft (FRED 15).

Although there has been an accounting standard on impairment in the USA since 1995, impairment reviews have received mixed reactions in the UK over recent years. Unilever's comments were:

We continue to believe that it (impairment testing) will be a costly and impractical exercise in many cases, and will inevitably involve a considerable element of subjective judgement.[39]

Guinness responded:

> Having been involved in the field testing for the new impairment review procedures we are pleased to have been able to conclude that they:
> (a) required relatively limited expertise and effort;
> (b) were straightforward to apply and required only data that is readily at head office;
> (c) gave credible results that corresponded with management expectations;
> (d) called for no more subjective judgement than that necessary when evaluating an acquisition or producing the Group's Financial and Strategic Plan.[40]

16.10.2 The impairment review

According to Sir David Tweedie, ASB Chairman on introducing FRS 11:

> There has been a need for more consistency in the way in which companies recognise and measure impairment losses. FRS 11 will improve comparability and transparency and it will introduce a welcome note of reality in the valuation of fixed assets. It will no longer be possible to pretend that long-standing losses with no realistic hope of recovery are temporary. FRS 11 also completes the package of requirements for goodwill and intangible assets. Companies with goodwill and assets with indefinite lives now have the equipment they need to perform impairment reviews instead of charging arbitrary amounts of depreciation against the profit and loss account.[41]

The ASB argues that FRS 11 'puts forward a coherent and consistent approach for measuring and recognising impairments of fixed assets and goodwill'.[42] The main aspects of the proposals are:

● In general, an impairment review only needs to be carried out if there is an indication that impairment has taken place. Examples include expected future losses; a significant adverse change in either the business or its market (e.g. entry of a competing product); physical damage; a significant adverse change in the legal or other regulatory environment; a significant decrease in market value; a forthcoming reorganisation; or, loss of key employees.

● Although it is preferable to test individual assets for impairment, it might be possible only to test groups of assets. In this case, the impairment should be carried out on the smallest group of assets (income generating unit) which produce a largely independent income stream.

● Impairment is measured by comparing the carrying value of the assets with the recoverable amount. The recoverable amount is the higher of the selling price (net realisable value) and the value in use.

● 'Value in use' is computed by discounting the asset or income-generating unit's expected cash flows at a rate of return that the market would expect from an equally risky asset. This rate of return is a post-tax interest rate which might equate to the implicit rate implicit in market transactions of similar assets or the weighted average cost of capital (WACC) of a listed company (with similar risk profile).

● The rules for restoring past impairment losses for intangible assets and goodwill are strict. It is possible to recognise reversals if both the initial impairment and the subsequent reversal were due to external factors. However, the restrictions do not allow the recognition of internally generated goodwill.

Although these proposals do provide some guidance for tackling impairment, it is unclear whether they will deliver the 'coherent and consistent approach' suggested by the ASB. For instance, the 'value in use' depends on how the income generating units are determined, the assumptions underlying the expected cash flows, and the discount rate selected.

16.10.3 Negative goodwill

Negative goodwill should be recognised in the profit and loss account over the period in which non-monetary assets are depreciated or sold. Any negative goodwill in excess of non-monetary assets acquired should be recognised in the profit and loss account in the periods expected to be benefited. The amount of the release should be separately disclosed in the profit and loss account.

16.10.4 What happens to goodwill previously written-off to reserves?

Perhaps one of the biggest difficulties both users and preparers will face is the accounting treatment of goodwill previously written-off to reserves. Although FRS 10 states that ideally this goodwill should be reinstated, it recognises that 'this will not always be practicable in all circumstances, and therefore does not require reinstatement' (para. 68). In other words, FRS 10 allows flexibility and choice in the treatment of goodwill associated with 'old' acquisitions. This means that balance sheets in the future might consist of some capitalised purchased goodwill and some purchased goodwill written off to reserves.

It remains to be seen quite how the transitional arrangements are applied in practice. The arrangements for both goodwill and other intangibles are summarised as follows:

● Goodwill previously written-off to reserves can remain eliminated. However, it must be offset against the profit and loss account or another appropriate reserve, not shown as a separate goodwill reserve. Also, it must be taken into account if the related business is disposed of.

● Goodwill previously written-off to reserves can be reinstated as an asset. It can be reinstated in totality or excluding either pre-FRS 7 goodwill or pre-1989 goodwill where there is insufficient information.

● Any capitalised internally developed intangible assets which do not meet the new recognition criteria should be written off by making a prior year adjustment.

● Any impairment losses on capitalised goodwill or intangible assets that are due to the initial implementation of the new standard should be reported as a current year loss.

For example, consider the impact of restatement of goodwill previously written-off to reserves on a company such as The GGT Group. At 1996 the goodwill reserve was –£242,957,000 and the earnings were £4,691,000. If the total goodwill was reinstated as an asset and amortised over twenty years there would be an annual amortisation charge of over £12m. Earnings would need to increase by 250% and be maintained at that level for the next 20 years to break even.

The rate of growth in earnings is therefore an important factor. The WPP Group, for example, had £1,160 negative goodwill reserve in 1997 and profit after tax of £116m indicating that it would take 50% of the annual profit if goodwill were amortised over 20 years. However WPP Group profits have increased by over 70% in 3 years.

16.11   Brand accounting

Brand accounting refers to the practice of representing a specific type of intangible asset – brand names – as a fixed asset in the balance sheet and typically not amortising them but subjecting them to regular review.

Prior to FRS 10, brand accounting emerged for two main reasons.

● For acquisitive companies it could be attributed to the accounting treatment required for measuring and reporting goodwill. The London Business School carried out research into the 'brands phenomenon' and found that 'a major aim of brand valuation has been to repair or pre-empt equity depletion caused by UK goodwill accounting rules'.[43, 44]

● Non-acquisitive companies do not incur costs for acquiring goodwill, so their reserves are not eroded by writing off purchased goodwill. However, these companies may have incurred promotional costs in creating home-grown brands and it would strengthen the balance sheet if they were permitted to include a valuation of these brands.[45]

Justifications for brand accounting

We now consider some other justifications that have been put forward for the inclusion of brands as a separate asset in the balance sheet.

Effect on shareholders' funds

Immediate goodwill write-off results in a fall in net tangible assets as disclosed by the balance sheet, even though the market capitalisation of a company increases. One way to maintain the asset base and avoid such a depletion of companies' reserves is to divide the purchased goodwill into two parts: the amount attributable to brands and the remaining amount attributable to pure goodwill.[46] For instance, WPP have capitalised two corporate brand names (J. Walter Thompson; Hill and Knowlton) which were originally valued in 1988 at £350m (and remain at that amount in the balance sheet). Without this capitalisation, the share owners' funds of £187.7m in the 1998 accounts would be reduced by £350m to a negative figure of (£162.3m).

Effect on borrowing powers

The borrowing powers of public companies may be expressed in terms of multiples of net assets. In its articles of association there may be strict rules regarding the multiple that the company must not exceed. In addition, borrowing agreements and Stock Exchange listing agreements are generally dependent on net assets.

Effect on ratios

Immediate goodwill write-off distorts the gearing ratios, but the inclusion of brands as intangible assets minimised this distortion by providing a more realistic value for shareholders' funds. Guinness plc provided information on its gearing ratio in its five-year financial summary:

	31 December				
Gearing ratio	*1992*	*1993*	*1994*	*1995*	*1996*
including cost of acquired brands	56%	49%	35%	28%	34%
excluding cost of acquired brands	140%	111%	63%	49%	58%

Effect on management decisions

It is claimed that including brands on the balance sheet leads to more informed and improved management decision-making. The quality of internal decisions is related to the quality of information available to management.[47] As brands represent one of the most important assets of a company, management should be aware of the success or failure of each individual brand. Knowledge about the performance of brands ensures that management reacts accordingly to maintain or improve competitive advantage.

There is also evidence[48] that companies with valuable brand names are not including these in their balance sheets and are not, therefore, taking account of the assets for insurance purposes.

Summary

As business has become more complex and industrial processes more sophisticated, the amount paid to develop or acquire an intangible asset has become significant in comparison to the fixed asset base of some companies. Under FRS 10 internally generated intangible assets may be capitalised if they have a readily ascertainable market value. Under FRS 10 purchased goodwill and intangibles should be capitalised in the balance sheet. Once capitalised, FRS 10 requires that these assets either be amortised or subject to a regular impairment review, depending on their useful economic life.

Review questions

1   Here is an extract from Reckitt & Colman's 1998 accounts:

	1998	1997
Fixed assets	£m	£m
Intangible assets	1,219.0	1,135.0
Tangible assets	401.2	404.5
	1,620.2	1,539.5

(a) Discuss the impact of trademarks (intangible assets) in relation to total fixed assets.

(b) Determine which financial ratios are affected by the inclusion of intangible assets in the balance sheet. What are your views on the validity of these ratios, given that the total fixed assets figure could contain some extremely subjective values?

2   Here is some further information from Reckitt & Colman's accounts:

	1998	1997
Profit for the financial year:	£165.3m	£215.8m
Earnings per ordinary share :	40.6p	53.1p

Discuss the effects on the EPS figure if intangible fixed assets were required to be amortised against earnings over their useful economic life – where directors must justify periods over twenty years.

Using the information provided above and in question 1, estimate the modified EPS figure for amortisation periods of: (a) twenty years; (b) forty years.

3   FRS 11 addresses the impairment of fixed assets and intangibles. In relation to intangibles:

(a) What indications can there be that a review for impairment is required?

(b) Once there are indications of impairment, how is impairment measured?

4   How is 'value in use' calculated for an impairment review? What are the areas of subjectivity?

5 Discuss the suggestion that the requirement for companies to write off research investment rather than showing it as an asset exposes companies to short-term pressure from acquisitive companies that are damaging to the country's interest.

6 Discuss the advantages and disadvantages of the proposal that there should be a separate category of asset in the balance sheet clearly identified as 'research investment – outcome uncertain'.

7 Discuss the accounting treatment in the accounts of the franchisee and franchisor of the following items:

(a) An administration charge made by the franchisor.

(b) A training charge made by the franchisor.

(c) The cost of initial stocks supplied by the franchisor.

(d) Plant and machinery supplied by the franchisor.

(e) Know-how supplied at a cost by the franchisor.

(f) The use of a patent held by the franchisor.

(g) A contribution made by the franchisee to a central advertising pool held and operated by the franchisor on behalf of all the franchisees to cover costs such as television advertising.

8 Discuss the information you would expect to find in the financial report of The Body Shop plc in relation to franchising.

9 In connection with SSAP 13 Accounting for Research and Development:

(a) Define 'applied research' and 'development'.

(b) Why is it considered necessary to distinguish between applied research and development expenditure, and how does this distinction affect the accounting treatment?

(c) State whether the following are included within the SSAP 13 definition of research and development, and give your reasons:

(i) Market research.

(ii) Testing of preproduction prototypes.

(iii) Operational research.

(iv) Testing in search of process alternatives.

10 Describe the problems encountered when accounting for:

(a) tangible fixed assets;

(b) leasing (in lessees' accounts);

(c) research and development;

and outline the recommended accounting treatment given in the relevant Statements of Standard Accounting Practice (SSAPs) or Financial Reporting Standards (FRSs). How effective are the SSAPs/FRSs in limiting the use of different accounting treatments of the above areas?

11 As discussed in this chapter, the immediate write-off of goodwill against reserves can reduce dramatically both shareholders' funds and capital employed. Identify the financial ratios that are affected by these accounting changes in shareholders' funds and capital employed. Discuss the possible economic consequences of the resultant changes in these financial ratios.

12 Critically evaluate the basis of the following assertion:

I am sceptical that it (the impairment test) will work reliably in practice, given the complexity and subjectivity that lie within the calculation. (Paterson[49])

13 Consider the transitional arrangements relating to the possible restatement of goodwill previously written-off to reserves. In particular:

● How will preparers decide whether or not to restate goodwill previously written-off to reserves?

● What are the options available to preparers?

● How will users interpret and compare financial statements?

● Will there be uniformity of treatment?

● In practice, will companies write off previously capitalised internally developed intangible assets which do not meet the new recognition criteria?

Exercises

An extract from the solution is provided in the appendix at the end of the text for exercises marked with an asterisk (*).

Question 1

Environmental Engineering plc is engaged in the development of an environmentally friendly personal transport vehicle. This will run on an electric motor powered by solar cells, supplemented by passenger effort in the form of pedal assistance.

At the end of the current accounting period, the following costs have been attributed to the project:

(a) A grant of £500,000 to the Polytechnic of the South Coast Faculty of Solar Engineering to encourage their research.

(b) Costs of £1,200,000 expended on the development of the necessary solar cells prior to the decision to incorporate them in a vehicle.

(c) Costs of £5,000,000 expended on designing the vehicle and its motors, and the planned promotional and advertising campaign for its launch on the market in twelve months' time.

Required:
  (i) Explain, with reasons, which of the above items could be considered for treatment as deferred revenue expenditure, quoting any relevant Statements of Standard Accounting Practice.
 (ii) Set out the criteria under which any items can be so treated.
(iii) Advise on the accounting treatment that will be afforded to any such items after the product has been launched.

Question 2

As chief accountant at Italin plc, you have been given the following information by the director of research:

Project Luca

	£000
Costs to date (pure research 25%, applied research 75%)	200
Costs to develop product (to be incurred in the year to 30 September 20X1)	300
Expected future sales per annum for 20X2–X7	1,000

Fixed assets purchased in 20X1 for the project:

Cost	2,500
Estimated useful life	7 years
Residual value	400

(These assets will be disposed of at their residual value at the end of their estimated useful lives.)

The board of directors considers that this project is similar to the other projects that the company undertakes, and is confident of a successful outcome. The company has enough finances to complete the development and enough capacity to produce the new product.

Required:
Prepare a report for the board, outlining the principles involved in accounting for research and development, and showing what accounting entries will be made in the company's accounts for each of the years ending 30 September 20X1–20X7 inclusive. Indicate what factors need to be taken into account when assessing each research and development project for accounting purposes, and what disclosure is needed for research and development in the company's published accounts.

* Question 3

Oxlag plc, a manufacturer of pharmaceutical products, has the following research and development projects on hand at 31 January 20X2:

(a) A general survey into the long-term effects of its sleeping pill Chalcedon upon human resistance to infections. At the year-end the research is still at a basic stage and no worthwhile results with any particular applications have been obtained.

(b) A development for Meebach plc in which the company will produce market research data relating to Meebach's range of drugs.

(c) An enhancement of an existing drug, Euboia, which will enable additional uses to be made of the drug and which will consequently boost sales. This project was completed successfully on 30 April 19X2, with the expectation that all future sales of the enhanced drug would greatly exceed the costs of the new development.

(d) A scientific enquiry with the aim of identifying new strains of antibiotics for future use. Several possible substances have been identified, but research is not sufficiently advanced to permit patents and copyrights to be obtained at the present time.

The following costs have been brought forward at 1 February 20X1:

Project	A	B	C	D
			£000	
Specialised laboratory				
Cost	—	—	500	—
Depreciation	—	—	25	—
Specialised equipment				
Cost	—	—	75	50
Depreciation	—	—	15	10
Capitalised development costs	—	—	200	—
Market research costs	—	250	—	—

The following costs were incurred during the year:

Project	A	B	C	D
			£000	
Research costs	25	—	265	78
Market research costs	—	75	—	—
Specialised equipment cost	50	—	—	50

Depreciation on specialised laboratories and special equipment is provided by the straight-line method and the assets have an estimated useful life of 25 and 5 years respectively. A full year's depreciation is provided on assets purchased during the year.

Required:

(i) **Write up the research and development, fixed asset and market research accounts to reflect the above transactions in the year ended 31 January 20X2.**

(ii) **Calculate the amount to be charged as research costs in the profit and loss account of Oxlag plc for the year ended 31 January 20X2.**

(iii) **State on what basis the company should amortise any capitalised development costs and what disclosures the company should make in respect of amounts written off in the year to 31 January 20X3.**

(iv) **Calculate the amounts to be disclosed in the balance sheet in respect of fixed assets, deferred development costs and work-in-progress.**

(v) **State what disclosures you would make in the accounts for the year ended 31 January 20X2 in respect of the new improved drug developed under project C, assuming sales begin on 1 May 20X2, and show strong growth to the date of signing the accounts, 14 July 20X2, with the expectation that the new drug will provide 25% of the company's pretax profits in the year to 31 January 20X3.**

Question 4

(a) Briefly examine the case for and against treating goodwill in accounts differently from other assets.

(b) The consolidated balance sheet, as at 31 December 20X8, of Selma plc and its subsidiaries, reports the value of goodwill as £400,000, arrived at as follows:

	Notes	Balance 31 Dec 20X7	Cost in 20X8	Expenses in 20X8	Balance 31 Dec 20X8
Ora Nectar	(i)	—	£150,000	£50,000	£100,000
Wilma Ltd	(ii)	£200,000	£160,000	£60,000	£300,000

Notes:

(i) A canned orange juice, named Ora Nectar, launched in 20X8, was distributed free to schoolchildren during their short breaks. The cost incurred in the process is estimated to benefit Selma plc's sales during the next three years.

(ii) Selma plc acquired a 100% stake in Wilma Ltd on 1 January 20X6, paying £1,200,000. Aggregate fair value of separable net assets of Wilma Ltd on that date was valued at £900,000. The group adopted a policy of amortising the goodwill over an estimated useful life of six years. During 20X8, Selma plc incurred £160,000 on a campaign calculated to revamp the image of Wilma Ltd and it is estimated that as a direct result of this campaign the economic life of goodwill in Wilma Ltd was prolonged by a further two years.

£110,000 written-off goodwill in 20X8 was charged against the capital reserve arising from consolidation that resulted from the acquisition of another subsidiary.

Required:

Critically comment on Selma plc's accounting for goodwill.

Question 5

Financial Reporting Standard FRS 10 addresses the accounting for goodwill and intangible assets. Accounting for goodwill has been a contentious issue in the UK for several years and FRS 10 *Goodwill and Intangible Assets* attempts to eliminate the problems associated with SSAP 22 *Accounting for goodwill.*

Required:

(a) Describe the requirements of FRS 10 regarding the initial recognition and measurement of goodwill and intangible assets.

(b) Explain the proposed approach set out by FRS 10 for the amortisation of positive goodwill and intangible assets.

(c) Territory plc acquired 80% of the ordinary share capital of Yukon plc on 31 May 20X6. The balance sheet of Yukon plc at 31 May 20X6 was:

Yukon plc – Balance sheet at 31 May 20X6

	£000
Fixed assets	
Intangible assets	6,020
Tangible assets	38,300
	44,320
Current assets	
Stocks	21,600
Debtors	23,200
Cash	8,800
	53,600
Creditors: amounts falling due	
within one year	24,000
Net current assets	29,600
Total assets less current liabilities	73,920
Creditors: amounts falling due after	
more than one year	12,100
Provision for liabilities and charges	886
Accruals and deferred income	
Deferred government grants	2,700
	58,234
Capital reserves	
Called up share capital	10,000
(ordinary shares of £1)	
Share premium account	5,570
Profit and loss account	42,664
	58,234

Additional information relating to the above balance sheet

(i) The intangible assets of Yukon plc were brand names currently utilised by the company. The directors felt that they were worth £7 million but there was no readily ascertainable market value at the balance sheet date, nor any information to verify the directors' estimated value.

(ii) The provisional market value of the land and buildings was £20 million at 31 May 20X6. This valuation had again been determined by the directors. A valuers' report received on 31 November 20X6 stated the market value of land and buildings to be £23 million as at 31 May

20X6. The depreciated replacement cost of the remainder of the tangible fixed assets was £18 million at 31 May 20X6, net of government grants.

(iii) The replacement cost of stocks was estimated at £25 million and its net realisable value was deemed to be £20 million. Debtors and creditors due within one year are stated at the amounts expected to be received and paid.

(iv) 'Creditors amounts falling due after more than one year' was a long-term loan with a bank. The initial loan on 1 June 20X5 was £11 million at a fixed interest rate of 10% per annum. The total amount of the interest is to be paid at the end of the loan period on 31 May 20X9. The current bank lending rate is 7% per annum.

(v) The provision for liabilities and charges relates to costs of reorganisation of Yukon plc. This provision had been set up by the directors of Yukon plc prior to the offer by Territory plc and the reorganisation would have taken place even if Territory plc had not purchased the shares of Yukon plc. Additionally Territory plc wishes to set up a provision for future losses of £10 million which it feels will be incurred by rationalising the group.

(vi) The offer made to all of the shareholders of Yukon plc was 2.5 £1 ordinary shares of Territory plc at the market price of £2.25 per share plus £1 cash, per Yukon plc ordinary share.

(vii) Goodwill is to be dealt with in accordance with FRS 10. The estimated useful economic life is deemed to be 10 years. The directors of Yukon plc informed Territory plc that as at 31 May 20X7, the brand names were worthless as the products to which they related had recently been withdrawn from sale because they were deemed to be a health hazard.

(viii) A full year's charge for amortisation of goodwill is included in the group profit and loss account of Territory plc in the year of purchase.

Required:
Calculate the amortisation of goodwill in the Group Profit and Loss Account of Territory plc for accounting periods ending on 31 May 20X6 and 31 May 20X7.

* **Question 6**

Chambers plc imports household equipment from Germany. On 1 January 20X1, the company acquired 60% of the issued shares of Court Ltd, which owns a retail shop selling washing machines and tumble dryers. Chambers supplies goods to various customers, including Court, for resale to the general public.

The balance sheets of the two companies at 31 December 20X3 were as follows:

| | Chambers plc | | Court Ltd | |
	£000	£000	£000	£000
Fixed assets				
Tangible fixed assets:				
Freehold property, at cost	300		100	
Plant and equipment, at net book value	240		40	
		540		140
Investment in subsidiary, at cost		300		—
		840		140

	Chambers plc		Court Ltd	
	£000	£000	£000	£000
Current assets				
Stock of goods for resale, at cost	1,100		540	
Debtors	1,250		420	
Cash at bank	610		—	
	2,960		960	
Creditors due within one year				
Bank overdraft	—		100	
Other creditors	800		400	
	800		500	
Net current assets		2,160		460
Total assets less current liabilities		3,000		600
Creditors due after one year				
10% Debenture stock		—		100
		3,000		500
Capital and reserves				
Called-up share capital		400		50
Share premium account		600		100
Profit and loss account		2,000		350
		3,000		500

The following information is relevant:

(a) The balance on Court's profit and loss account at 1 January 20X1 was £150,000.

(b) When Chambers plc acquired its interest in Court, it valued that company's freehold property at £200,000, and this valuation has been reflected in subsequent consolidated balance sheets. Other assets of Court were taken at book value.

(c) Included in Court's stock at 31 December 20X3 are items which had cost that company £60,000. These had been bought from Chambers, whose selling prices are set by marking up the cost price of goods by 50%.

(d) Included in Chambers' debtors is a balance due from Court of £20,000. Court's 'other creditors' includes a balance of £10,000 due to Chambers. On 30 December 20X3, a cheque for £10,000 had been sent by Court to Chambers, which received and banked it on 3 January 20X4.

(e) Chambers follows the policy of writing off goodwill arising on consolidation using the straight-line method over ten years from the date of acquisition of its subsidiary.

Required:
(a) Prepare a consolidated balance sheet for Chambers plc and its subsidiary as at 31 December 20X3.
(b) With reference to users, explain the rationale of the parent company method of consolidation and compare it with the entity approach.
(c) Why has the question of goodwill in consolidated accounts caused so much discussion among accountants?

Question 7

The Brands Debate.

Prior to FRS 10, the depletion of equity reserves caused by the accounting treatment for purchased goodwill resulted in some companies capitalising brands on their balance sheets. This practice was started by Rank Hovis McDougall (RHM) – a company which has since been taken over. Martin Moorhouse, the group chief accountant at RHM, claimed that:

> ... putting brands on the balance sheet forced a company to look to their value as well as to profits. It served as a reminder to management of the value of the assets for which they were responsible and that at the end of the day those companies which were prepared to recognise brands on the balance sheet could be better and stronger for it.[50]

There were many opponents to the capitalisation of brands. A London Business School research study found that brand accounting involves too many risks and uncertainties and too much subjective judgement. In short, the conclusion was that 'the present flexible position, far from being neutral, is potentially corrosive to the whole basis of financial reporting and that to allow brands – whether acquired or home-grown – to continue to be included in the balance sheet would be highly unwise'.[51]

Required:
Consider the arguments for and against brand accounting. In particular, consider the issues of brand valuation; the separability of brands; purchased vs home-grown brands; and the maintenance/substitution argument.[52,53,54,55,56]

References

1 'The R&D Scoreboard', *Financial Times*, 25 June 1999.
2 B. Nixon and A. Lonie, 'Accounting for R&D: the need for change', *Accountancy*, February 1990, p. 91.
3 B. Nixon, 'R&D disclosure: SSAP 13 and after', *Accountancy*, February 1991, pp. 72–73.
4 *Statement of Intent: Comparability of Financial Statements*, IASC, 1990.
5 IAS 9 (revised), *Research and Development Costs*, IASC, December 1993.
6 IAS 39 *Intangible Assets*, IASC, September 1998.
7 A. Goodacre and J. McGrath, 'An experimental study of analysts' reactions to corporate R&D expenditure', *British Accounting Review*, 1997, 29, 155–179.
8 B. Nixon, 'The accounting treatment of research and development expenditure: Views of UK company accountants', *European Accounting Review*, vol. 6, no. 2, 265–277.
9 *Ibid.*
10 FRS 10, *Goodwill and Intangible Assets*, ASB, December 1997.
11 R. Paterson, 'Will FRS 10 hit the target?', *Accountancy*, February 1998, 74–75.
12 *Ibid.*
13 ED 30, *Accounting for Goodwill*, ASC, October 1982.
14 EC Seventh Directive, 1983.
15 SSAP 22, *Accounting for Goodwill*, ASC, December 1984.
16 ED 44, *Accounting for Goodwill*, ASC, September 1988.
17 SSAP 22, *Accounting for Goodwill (Revised)*, ASC, July 1989.
18 ED 47, *Accounting for Goodwill*, ASC, February 1990.
19 Sir Kenneth Corfield, *Intangible Assets: Their Value and How to Report It*, Coopers and Lybrand, Deloitte, 1990.
20 *Goodwill and Intangible Assets*, ASB Discussion Paper, 1993.
21 *Goodwill and Intangible Assets*, ASB Working Paper, 1995.

26 J. Brown, 'Accounting for goodwill and intangible assets', *Accountancy*, July 1996, p. 97.

27 S. Kennedy, 'Intangible aspects of goodwill', *Accountancy*, August 1996, p. 122.

28 M. Mullen, 'How to value intangibles', *Accountancy*, November 1993, p. 92.

29 ED 47, para. 4.

30 Price Waterhouse, *The Goodwill Debate – Forming a View*, Price Waterhouse, 1990.

31 IAS 22 (revised), *Business Combinations*, December 1993.

28 M. Mullen, 'How to value intangibles', *Accountancy*, November 1993, p. 92.

29 ED 47, para. 4.

30 Price Waterhouse, *The Goodwill Debate – Forming a View*, Price Waterhouse, 1990.

31 IAS 22 (revised), *Business Combinations*, December 1993.

32 M. Keegan and H. King, 'Together but different', *Accountancy International Edition*, October 1996, 64.

33 *Responses to Working Paper 'Goodwill and Intangible Assets'*, ASB, London 1995.

34 Cadbury Schweppes, Extracts from *Responses to Working Paper 'Goodwill and Intangible Assets'*, ASB, London 1995, p. 36.

35 IAS 38, *Intangible Assets*, IASC, September 1998.

36 IAS 22 (revised), *Business Combinations*, IASC, September 1998.

37 Kalamazoo, Extracts from *Responses to Working Paper 'Goodwill and Intangible Assets'*, ASB, London 1995, pp. 208–209.

38 FRS 11, *Impairment of Fixed Assets and Goodwill*, ASB, July 1998.

39 Unilever, Extracts from *Responses to Working Paper 'Goodwill and Intangible Assets'*, ASB, London 1995, pp. 348–349.

40 Guinness plc, Extracts from *Responses to Working Paper 'Goodwill and Intangible Assets'*, ASB, London 1995, pp. 164–167.

41 Sir D Tweedie, FRS 11, *Impairment of Fixed Assets and Goodwill*, ASB, 1998.

42 *Ibid*.

43 P. Barwise, C. Higson, A. Likierman and P. Marsh, *Accounting for Brands*, ICAEW, June 1989.

44 M. Cooper and A. Carey, 'Brand valuation in the balance', *Accountancy*, June 1989.

45 A. Pizzey, 'Healing the rift', *Certified Accountant*, October 1990.

46 'Finance directors say yes to brand valuation', *Accountancy*, January 1990, p. 12.

47 M. Moorhouse, 'Brands debate: wake up to the real world', *Accountancy*, July 1990, p. 30.

48 M. Gerry, 'Companies ignore value of brands', *Accountancy Age*, March 2000, p. 4.

49 R. Paterson, 'Will FRS 10 hit the target?', *Accountancy*, February 1998, 74–75.

50 M. Moorhouse, *op. cit.*

51 P. Barwise, *et al.*, *op. cit.*

52 D. Tonkin and B. Robertson, 'Brand names in a conceptual framework', *Accountancy*, March 1991, p. 28.

53 'Finance directors say yes to brand valuation', *op. cit.*

54 I. Cameron-Smith and F. Mattiussi, 'Intangible valuations – the expert view', *Accountancy*, March 1989, pp. 25-26.

55 S. Srikanthan *et al.*, 'Marketing: the unrecognised asset', *Management Accounting*, May 1987, pp. 38–42.

56 T. Arnold and M. Sherer, 'Valuation of brands: the RHM approach', *The Accountants' Magazine*, March 1989, p. 43.

CHAPTER 17

Stocks and work-in-progress

17.1 Introduction

This chapter explains the accounting principles involved in the valuation of stocks and work-in-progress, and how this impacts not only on balance sheet valuation, but also on the computation of annual profit.

We attempt to combine mechanics with a theoretical understanding of the accounting principles and illustrate this with practical examples showing how the interpretation of financial statements can be affected by differing treatments. In this chapter we consider:

- Stock defined and the controversy
- SSAP 9 and legal requirements
- Stock and work-in-progress valuation
- Stock control
- Creative accounting
- Audit of year-end physical stocktake
- Published accounts

17.2 Stock defined

SSAP 9 (Revised) *Stocks and Long-term Contracts* provides the following definition of stocks:[1]

> Stocks comprise the following categories:
>
> (a) goods or other assets purchased for resale;
> (b) consumable stores;
> (c) raw materials and components purchased for incorporation into products for sale;
> (d) products and services in intermediate stages of completion;
> (e) finished goods.

The valuation of stocks involves:[2]

> (a) the establishment of physical existence and ownership;
> (b) the determination of unit costs;
> (c) the calculation of provisions to reduce cost to net realisable value, if necessary.

The resulting evaluation is then disclosed in the published accounts in accordance with legal requirements.

These definitions appear to be very precise. We shall see, however, that although SSAP 9 was introduced to bring some uniformity into financial statements, there are many areas where professional judgement must be exercised. Sometimes this may distort the financial statements to such an extent that we must question whether they do represent a 'true and fair' view.

17.3 The controversy

The valuation of stocks and work-in-progress has been a controversial issue in accounting for many years. The stock value is a crucial element not only in the computation of profit, but also in the valuation of assets for balance sheet purposes.

Figure 17.1 presents information relating to Coats Viyella plc. It shows that the stock is material in relation to total assets and pre-tax profits. In relation to the profits we can see that an error of 10% in the 1998 stocks value (£38m) would potentially cause the profits for the group to change from a pre-tax profit to a pre-tax loss. As stock is usually a multiple rather than a fraction of profit, stock errors may have a disproportionate effect on the accounts. It is therefore crucial in determining earnings per share, net asset backing for shares and the current ratio. Consequently, the basis of valuation should be consistent, so as to avoid manipulation of profits between accounting periods, and comply with generally accepted accounting principles, so that profits are comparable between different companies.

Unfortunately, there are many examples of manipulation of stock values in order to create a more favourable impression. By increasing the value of stock at the year end, profit and current assets are automatically increased (and vice versa). Of course, closing stock of one year becomes opening stock of the next, so profit is thereby reduced. But such manipulation provides opportunities for profit-smoothing and may be advantageous in certain circumstances, e.g. if the company is under threat of take-over.

Figure 17.2 illustrates the point. Simply by increasing the value of stock in year 1 by £10,000, profit (and current assets) is increased by a similar amount. Even if the two values are identical in year 2, such manipulation allows profit to be 'smoothed' and £10,000 profit switched from year 2 to year 1.

According to normal accrual accounting principles, profit is determined by matching costs with related revenues. If it is unlikely that the revenue will in fact be received, prudence dictates that the irrecoverable amount should be written off immediately against current revenue.

It follows that stock should be valued at cost less any irrecoverable amount. But what is cost? Companies have used a variety of methods of determining costs, and these are

Figure 17.1 Coats Viyella plc.		
	1997	*1998*
Pre-tax profits (£m)	33.3	35.5
Stock (£m)	450.2	377.3
Total assets (£m)	1,805.3	1,661.4

Figure 17.2 Stock values manipulated to smooth income.

		Year 1		Year 1 With stock inflated
Sales		100,000		100,000
Opening stock	—		—	
Purchases	65,000		65,000	
Less: Closing stock	5,000		15,000	
COST OF SALES		60,000		50,000
		40,000		50,000

		Year 2		Year 2 With stock inflated
SALES		150,000		150,000
Opening stock	5,000		15,000	
Purchases	100,000		100,000	
	105,000		115,000	
Less: Closing stock	15,000		15,000	
COST OF SALES		90,000		100,000
PROFIT		60,000		50,000

explored later in the chapter. There have been a number of disputes relating to the valuation of stocks which affected profits (e.g. the AEI/GEC merger of 1967).[3] Naturally, such circumstances tend to come to light with a change of management, but it was considered important that a definitive statement of accounting practice be issued in an attempt to standardise treatment.

17.4 SSAP 9 and legal requirements

The first attempt by the profession to achieve uniformity came in 1972 with the issue of ED 6. Its purpose was to set out a defined practice of accounting for stocks and work-in-progress, provide rules for valuation and set out precise definitions of cost.

After the appropriate discussion period, SSAP 9 (original) *Stocks and Work in Progress* was issued in May 1975. Its introduction stated:

No area of accounting has produced wider differences in practice than the computation of the amount at which stocks and work in progress are stated in financial accounts. This Statement of Standard Accounting Practice seeks to define the practices, to narrow the differences and variations in those practices and to ensure adequate disclosure in the accounts.

SSAP 9 has been added to since 1975, and was revised in September 1988. Although the main substance of the original standard remained, the major revision concerned the accounting provisions relating to long-term contracts (dealt with in the next chapter).

The revised standard, now renamed SSAP 9 *Stocks and Long-term Contracts*, provides that the amount at which stocks are stated in periodic financial statements should be the total of the lower of cost and net realisable value of the separate items of stock or of groups of similar items. This is emphasised in the Companies Act 1985 (Schedule 4, para. 22), which requires that under the historical cost rules 'the amount to be included in respect of any current asset shall be its purchase price or production cost' or net realisable value if lower (para. 23(1)). The standard also emphasises the need to match costs against revenue, and it aims, like other standards, to achieve greater uniformity in the measurement of income as well as improving the disclosure of stock valuation methods. It includes an appendix for general guidance on practical considerations, although in the end it relies on management to choose the most appropriate method of stock valuation for the production processes used and the company's environment. Legal requirements in the Companies Act 1985 allow various methods of valuation, including FIFO, LIFO and weighted average or any similar method (see below). In selecting the most suitable method, management 'must exercise judgement to ensure that the methods chosen provide the fairest practical approximation to cost'.[4]

SSAP 9 does not recommend the use of base stock or LIFO because they often result in stocks being stated in the balance sheet at amounts that bear little relation to recent cost levels. This is one of several areas of conflict between SSAP 9 and the Companies Act 1985. In practice, companies exercise the wider choice available under the Companies Act.

Clearly, therefore, even though there are legal requirements and an SSAP in existence, the valuation of stocks and work-in-progress can provide areas of subjectivity and choice to management, and no definitive method is legally enforced. We will return to this theme many times in the following sections of this chapter.

17.5 Stock valuation

The valuation rule outlined in SSAP 9 is difficult to apply because of uncertainties about what is meant by cost and what is meant by net realisable value.

17.5.1 What is meant by cost?

There are a variety of methods of arriving at a 'cost' figure. Some are approved by SSAP 9, others are most certainly not, and this has caused controversy since SSAP 9 was first issued.

Methods acceptable under SSAP 9

The acceptable methods of stock valuation include FIFO, AVCO and standard cost.

First in–first out (FIFO)
Stock is valued at the most recent 'cost', since the cost of oldest stock is charged out first, whether or not this accords with the actual physical flow (Figure 17.3).

Average cost (ACVO)
Stock is valued at a 'weighted average cost', i.e. the unit cost is weighted by the number of items carried at each 'cost'. This is popular in manufacturing and in organisations holding a large volume of stock at fluctuating 'costs'. The practical problem of actually

Figure 17.3 First in–first out method (FIFO).

Date	Receipts Quantity	Receipts Rate	Receipts £	Issues Quantity	Issues Rate	Issues £	Balance Quantity	Balance Rate	Balance £
January	10	15	150				10		150
February				8	15	120	2		30
March	10	17	170				12		200
April	20	20	400				32		600
May				2	15	30			
				10	17	170			
				12	20	240			
				Cost of goods sold		560			
				Stock			8	20	160

recording and calculating the weighted average cost has been overcome by the use of sophisticated computer software (Figure 17.4).

Standard cost

In many cases this is the only way to value manufactured goods in a high-volume/turnover environment. However, the standard is acceptable only if it approximates to actual cost. This means that variances need to be reviewed to see if they affect the standard cost and for stock evaluation.

SSAP 9 recognises that an acceptable method of arriving at cost is the use of selling price, less an estimated profit margin. This method is only acceptable if it can be demonstrated that the method gives a reasonable approximation of the actual cost. It is the method employed by major retailers, e.g. Tesco 1999 accounts state in accounting policies:

> Stocks comprise goods held for resale and development properties and are valued at the lower of cost and net realisable value. Stocks in stores are calculated at retail price and reduced by appropriate margins to the lower of cost and net realisable value.

Figure 17.4 Average cost method (AVCO).

Date	Receipts Quantity	Receipts Rate	Receipts £	Issues Quantity	Issues Rate	Issues £	Balance Quantity	Balance Rate	Balance £
January	10	15	150				10		150
February				8	15	120	2		30
March	10	17	170				12		200
April	20	20	400				32		600
May				24	18.75	450			600
				Cost of goods sold		570			
				Stock			8	18.75	150

and Somerfield 1997 accounting policy states:

> Stock is valued at the lower of cost or net realisable value. Cost represents invoiced cost or selling price less the relevant profit margin to reduce it to estimated cost, including an appropriate element of overheads. Stock at warehouses is valued at weighted average cost and stock at stores on a first-in-first-out basis.

SSAP 9 does not recommend any specific method. This is a decision for each organisation based upon sound professional advice and the organisation's unique operating conditions.

Methods rejected by SSAP 9

These include LIFO, base stock and replacement cost.

Last in–first out (LIFO)

The cost of the stock most recently received is charged out first at the most recent 'cost'. The practical upshot is that the stock value is based upon an 'old cost', which may bear little relationship to the current 'cost' (Figure 17.5).

Base stock

The stock is valued at some predetermined value based upon the 'cost' at a specified time (Figure 21.6). This is an attractive idea for commodities which rapidly change cost owing to seasonal factors (e.g. fresh food), market forces (e.g. gold, oil, steel) or the influence of either on supply (coffee, tea, cocoa). The main difficulty is the choice of the 'base point', which leaves great scope for subjective manipulation and may not give a 'reliable' profit calculation for the purposes of performance evaluation.

An example was provided in the accounts of the Cookson Group for 1990, whose accounting policy is stated as follows:

> Certain stocks of the Group's metals and minerals companies are valued in the profit and loss account on the base stock or, for certain overseas companies, the last in first out (LIFO) method. As market prices of the materials involved can fluctuate widely over a period, and because these companies are processors and not traders, the effects of such variations in stock values are not operating profits or

Figure 17.5 Last in–first out method (LIFO).

Date	Receipts Quantity	Receipts Rate	Receipts £	Issues Quantity	Issues Rate	Issues £	Balance Quantity	Balance Rate	Balance £
January	10	15	150				10		150
February				8	15	120	2		30
March	10	17	170				12		200
April	20	20	400				32		600
May				20	20	400			
				4	17	68			
				Cost of goods sold		588			
				Stock			8		132

May closing balance = $[(2 \times 15) + (6 \times 17)]$

Figure 17.6   Base stock method.

Stocks	1990	1989
Included in current assets at the lower of cost and net realisable value		
Raw materials	95.9	123.5
Work-in-progress	32.6	38.1
Finished goods	91.1	116.0
Valuation for the balance sheet	219.6	277.6
Included in reserves and minorities		
Amount required to reduce £54.1m (1989 £71.1m) of stocks to their base and LIFO value	(7.5)	(18.3)
Valuation for the profit and loss	212.1	259.3

losses. The use of the base stock and LIFO methods, together with covering arrangements for quantities in excess of base stock levels, **causes the profit and loss account to be charged with the current cost of the materials consumed**. The directors believe that this method of accounting is more appropriate for these stocks than that required by SSAP 9. All stocks are stated in the balance sheet at the lower of cost over net realisable value on the FIFO method. The difference between the base stock or LIFO valuations, where these methods are used, and the FIFO valuation is included in reserves.

The 1996 accounts indicate a different treatment. The note to the accounts states:

> The Group's precious metal fabrication operations utilise significant amounts of precious metals, primarily gold, held on consignment terms. The terms provide, inter alia, that the consignor retains title to the metal and both parties have the right of return over the metal without penalty.

The accounting policy in the 1999 Accounts addresses FRS 5 *Substance of Transactions* and states:

> Stocks held under consignment are reviewed regularly in order to assess whether the substance of the arrangements is such that those stocks constitute assets which should be reflected in the Group balance sheet.

The effect of the consignment arrangement is the same as in 1990, i.e. it **causes the profit and loss account to be charged with the current cost of the materials consumed** without a stockholding to be dealt with under SSAP 9.

Replacement cost

The stock is valued at the current cost of the individual item rather than the actual cost (i.e. the cost to the organisation of replacing the item rather than the actual cost at the time of manufacture or purchase). This is an attractive idea since the 'value' of stock could be seen as the cost at which a similar item could be currently acquired. The problem again is in arriving at a 'reliable' profit figure for the purposes of performance evaluation. Wild fluctuation of profit could occur simply because of such factors as the time of the year, the vagaries of the world weather system or the manipulation of market forces. Let us take three examples, involving wheat, oil and silver.

Wheat. Assume that the price of wheat is £1,000 per tonne, but if the Russian harvest fails (again) this could go to £1,500 per tonne. What value should a major bread manufacturer attach to its raw material? If it chooses 'replacement cost' (i.e. £1,500), then it 'creates' £500/tonne 'profit'. If it chooses £1,000/tonne, then this may not be the price paid for the wheat at the time of purchase.

Oil. When the Gulf Crisis of 1990 began, the cost of oil moved from around $13 per barrel to a high of around $29 per barrel in a short time. If oil companies had used replacement cost, this would have created huge fictitious profits. This might have resulted in higher tax payments and shareholders demanding dividends from a profit that existed only on paper. When the Gulf Crisis settled down to a quiet period (before the 1991 military action), the market price of oil dropped almost as dramatically as it had risen. This might have led to fictitious losses for companies in the following financial year with an ensuing loss of business confidence.

Silver. In the early 1980s a Texan millionaire named Bunker Hunt attempted to make a 'killing' on the silver market by buying silver to force up the price and then selling at the high price to make a substantial profit. This led to remarkable scenes in the UK, with long lines of people outside jewellers wanting to sell items at much higher prices than their 'real' cost. Companies using silver as a raw material (e.g. jewellers, mirror manufacturers and electronics companies, which use silver as a conductive element) would have been badly affected had they used replacement cost in a similar way to the preceding two cases. The 'price' of silver in effect doubled in a short time, but the Federal Authorities in the USA stepped in and the plan was defeated.

Although LIFO, base stock and replacement cost do not have SSAP 9 approval, they are still used in practice. For example, LIFO is commonly used by UK companies with US subsidiaries, since LIFO is the main method of stock valuation in the USA.

Procedure to ascertain cost

Having decided upon the accounting policy of the company, there remains the problem of ascertaining the cost. In a retail environment, the 'cost' is the price the organisation had to pay to acquire the goods, and it is readily established by reference to the purchase invoice from the supplier. However, in a manufacturing organisation the concept of cost is not as simple. Should we use prime cost, or production cost, or total cost? SSAP 9 attempts to help by defining cost as the expenditure 'incurred in the normal course of business in bringing the product or service to its present location and condition'.

In a manufacturing organisation each expenditure is taken to include three constituents: direct materials, direct labour and appropriate overhead.

Direct materials
These include not only the costs of raw materials and component parts, but also the costs of insurance, handling (special packaging) and any import duties. An additional problem is waste and scrap. For instance, if a process inputs 100 tonnes at £45 per tonne, yet outputs only 90 tonnes, the output's stock value **must** be £4,500 (£45 × 100) and not £4,050 (90 × £45). (This assumes the 10 tonnes loss is a normal, regular part of the process.) An adjustment may be made for the residual value of the scrap/waste material, if any. The treatment of component parts will be the same, provided they form part of the finished product.

Direct labour
This is the cost of the actual production in the form of gross pay and those incidental costs of employing the direct workers (employer's national insurance contributions,

additional pension contributions, etc.). The labour costs will be spread over the goods production.

Appropriate overhead

It is here that the major difficulties arise in calculating the true cost of the product for stock valuation purposes. Normal practice is to classify overheads into five types and decide whether to include them in stock. The five types are as follows:

● Direct overheads – subcontract work, royalties.

● Indirect overheads – the cost of running the factory and supporting the direct workers; and the depreciation of capital items used in production.

● Administration overheads – the office costs and salaries of senior management.

● Selling and distribution overheads – advertising, delivery costs, packaging, salaries of sales personnel and depreciation of capital items used in the sales function.

● Finance overheads – the cost of borrowing and servicing debt.

We will look at each of these in turn, to demonstrate the difficulties that the accountant experiences.

Direct overheads. These should normally be included as part of 'cost'. But imagine a situation where some subcontract work has been carried out on *some* of our products because of a capacity problem (i.e. the factory could normally do the work, but due to a short-term problem some of the work has been subcontracted at a higher price/cost). In theory, those items subject to the subcontract work should have a higher stock value than 'normal' items. However, in practice, the difficulty of identifying such 'subcontracted' items is so great that many companies do not include such non-routine subcontract work in the stock value as a direct overhead. For example, if a factory produces 1,000,000 drills per month and 1,000 of them have to be sent out because of a machine breakdown, since all the drills are identical it would be very costly and time consuming to treat the 1,000 drills differently from the other 999,000. Hence the subcontract work would *not* form part of the overhead for stock valuation purposes (in such an organisation, the standard cost approach would be used when valuing stock). On the other hand, in a customised car firm producing 20 vehicles per month, special subcontract work would form part of the stock value because it is readily identifiable to individual units of stock.

To summarise, any regular, routine direct overhead will be included in the stock valuation, but a non-routine cost could present difficulties, especially in a high-volume/turnover organisation.

Indirect overheads. These always form part of the stock valuation, as such expenses are incurred in support of production. They include factory rent and rates, factory power and depreciation of plant and machinery; in fact, any indirect factory-related cost, including the warehouse costs of storing completed goods, will be included in the value of stock.

Administration overheads. This overhead is in respect of the whole business, so only that portion easily identifiable to production should form part of the stock valuation. For instance, the costs of the personnel or wages department could be apportioned to production on a head-count basis and that element would be included in the stock valuation. Any production-specific administration costs (welfare costs, canteen costs, etc.) would also be included in the stock valuation. If the expense cannot be identified as forming part of the production function, it will not form part of the stock valuation.

Selling and distribution overheads. These costs will not normally be included in the stock valuation as they are incurred after production has taken place. However, if the goods are on a 'sale or return' basis and are on the premises of the customer but remain the supplier's property, the delivery and packing costs will be included in the stock value of goods held on a customer's premises.

An additional difficulty concerns the modern technique of 'just-in-time' (JIT) stocking. Here, the customer does not keep large stocks, but simply 'calls off' stock from the supplier and is invoiced for the items delivered. There is an argument for the stock still in the hands of the supplier to bear more of this overhead within its valuation, since the only selling and distribution overhead to be charged/incurred is delivery. The goods have in fact been sold, but ownership has not yet changed hands. As JIT becomes more popular, this problem may give accountants and auditors much scope for debate.

Finance overheads. Normally these overheads would never be included within the stock valuation because they are not normally identifiable with production. In a job-costing context, however, it might be possible to use some of this overhead in stock valuation. Let us take the case of an engineering firm being requested to produce a turbine engine, which requires parts/components to be imported. It is logical for the financial charges for these imports (e.g. exchange fees or fees for letters of credit) to be included in the stock valuation.

Thus it can be seen that the identification of the overheads to be included in stock valuation is far from straightforward. In many cases it depends upon the judgement of the accountant and the unique operating conditions of the organisation.

In addition to the problem of deciding **whether** the five types of overhead should be included, there is the problem of deciding **how much** of the total overhead to include in the stock valuation at the year-end. SSAP 9 stipulates the use of 'normal activity' when making this decision on overheads. The vast majority of overheads are 'fixed', i.e. do not vary with activity, and it is customary to share these out over a normal or expected output. If this expected output is not reached, it is not acceptable to allow the actual production to bear the full overhead for stock purposes. A numerical example will illustrate this:

Overhead for the year	£200,000
Planned activity	10,000 units
Closing stock	3,000 units
Direct costs	£2 per unit
Actual activity	6,000 units

Stock value based on actual activity

Direct costs	$3,000 \times £2$	£6,000
Overhead	$\dfrac{3,000}{6,000} \times £200,000$	£100,000
Closing stock value		£106,000

Stock value based on planned or normal activity

Direct cost	$3,000 \times £2$	£6,000
Overhead	$\dfrac{3,000}{10,000} \times £200,000$	£60,000
Closing stock value		£66,000

Comparing the value of stock based upon actual activity with the value based upon planned or normal activity, we have a £40,000 difference. This could be regarded as increasing the current year's profit by carrying forward expenditure of £40,000 to set against the following year's profit.

The problem occurs because of the organisation's failure to meet expected output level (6,000 actual versus 10,000 planned). By adopting the **actual activity basis**, the organisation makes a profit out of failure. This cannot be an acceptable position when evaluating performance. Therefore, SSAP 9 stipulates **the planned or normal activity model** for stock valuation. The failure to meet planned output could be due to a variety of sources (e.g. strikes, poor weather, industrial conditions); the cause, however, is classed as abnormal or non-routine, and all such costs should be excluded from the valuation of stocks.

17.5.2 What is meant by net realisable value?

Section 21.5.1 attempted to identify the problems of arriving at the **true** meaning of cost for the purpose of stock valuation. Net realisable value is an alternative method of stock valuation if 'cost' does not reflect the true value of the stock. Prudence dictates that net realisable value will be used if it is lower than the 'cost' of the stock (however that may be calculated). These occasions will vary among organisations, but can be summarised as follows:

● There is a permanent fall in the market price of stock. Short-term fluctuations should not cause net realisable value to be implemented.

● The organisation is attempting to dispose of high stock levels or excessively priced stock to improve its liquidity position (quick ratio/acid test ratio) or reduce its stock holding costs. Such high stock volumes or values are primarily a result of poor management decision-making.

● The stock is physically deteriorating or is of an age where the market is reluctant to accept it. This is a common feature of the food industry, especially with the use of 'sell by' dates in the retail environment.

● Stock suffers obsolescence through some unplanned development. (Good management should never be surprised by obsolescence.) This development could be technical in nature, or due to the development of different marketing concepts within the organisation or a change in market needs.

● The management could decide to sell the goods at 'below cost' for sound marketing reasons. The concept of a 'loss leader' is well known in supermarkets, but organisations also sell below cost when trying to penetrate a new market or as a defence mechanism when attacked.

Such decisions are important and the change to net realisable value should not be undertaken without considerable forethought and planning. Obsolescence should be a decision based upon sound market intelligence and not a managerial 'whim'. The auditors of companies always examine such decisions to ensure they were made for sound business reasons. The opportunities for fraud in such 'price cutting' operations validate this level of external control.

Realisable value is, of course, the price the organisation receives for its stock from the market. However, getting this stock to market may involve additional expense and effort in repackaging, advertising, delivery and even repairing of damaged stock. This additional cost must be deducted from the realisable value to arrive at the net realisable value.

A numerical example will demonstrate this concept:

Item	Cost value	Net realisable value	Stock value
1 No. 876	£7,000	£9,000	£7,000
2 No. 997	£12,000	£12,500	£12,000
3 No. 1822	£8,000	£4,000	£4,000
4 No. 2076	£14,000	£8,000	£8,000
5 No. 4732	£27,000	£33,000	£27,000
	(a) £68,000	(b) £66,500	(c) £58,000

The stock value chosen for the accounts is (c) £58,000, although each item is assessed individually.

17.6 Work-in-progress

Stock classified as work-in-progress (WIP) is mainly found in manufacturing organisations and is simply the production that has not been completed by the end of the accounting period.

The valuation of WIP must follow the same SSAP 9 rules and be the lower of cost or net realisable value. We again face the difficulty of deciding what to include in cost. The three basic classes of cost – direct materials, direct labour and appropriate overhead – will still form the basis of ascertaining cost.

17.6.1 Direct materials

It is necessary to decide what proportion of the total materials have been used in WIP. The proportion will vary with different types of organisation, as the following two examples illustrate:

● If the item is complex or materially significant (e.g. a custom-made car or a piece of specialised machinery), the WIP calculation will be based on actual recorded materials and components used to date.

● If, however, we are dealing with mass production, it may not be possible to identify each individual item within WIP. In such cases, the accountant will make a judgement and define the WIP as being $x\%$ complete in regard to raw materials and components. For example, a drill manufacturer with 1 million tools per week in WIP may decide that in respect of raw materials they are 100% complete; WIP then gets the full materials cost of 1 million tools.

In both cases **consistency** is vital so that, however WIP is valued, the same method will always be used.

17.6.2 Direct labour

Again, it is necessary to decide how much direct labour the items in WIP have actually used. As with direct materials, there are two broad approaches:

● Where the item of WIP is complex or materially significant, the actual time 'booked' or recorded will form part of the WIP valuation.

● In a mass production situation, such precision may not be possible and an accounting judgement may have to be made as to the average percentage completion in respect of direct labour. In the example of the drill manufacturer, it could be that, on average, WIP is 80% complete in respect of direct labour.

17.6.3 Appropriate overhead

The same two approaches as for direct labour can be adopted:

● With a complex or materially significant item, it should be possible to allocate the overhead actually incurred. This could be an actual charge (e.g. subcontract work) or an application of the appropriate overhead recovery rate (ORR). For example, if we use a direct labour hour recovery rate and we have an ORR of £10/direct labour hour and the recorded labour time on the WIP item is twelve hours, then the overhead charge for WIP purposes is £120.

● With mass production items, the accountant must either use an overhead recovery rate approach or simply decide that, in respect of overheads, WIP is $y\%$ complete.

The above approaches must always be sanctioned by the firm's auditors to ensure that a true and fair view is achieved. The approach must also be consistent provided the basic product does not vary.

EXAMPLE I ● A company produces drills. The costs of a completed drill are:

	£	
Direct materials	2.00	
Direct labour	6.00	
Appropriate overhead	10.00	
Total cost	18.00	(for finished goods stock value purposes)

The company accountant takes the view that for WIP purposes the following applies:

Direct material	100% complete
Direct labour	80% complete
Appropriate overhead	30% complete

Therefore, for one WIP drill:

Direct material	£2.00 × 100% =	£2.00
Direct labour	£6.00 × 80% =	£4.80
Appropriate overhead	£10.00 × 30% =	£3.00
WIP value		£9.80

If the company has 100,000 drills in WIP, the value is:

100,000 × £9.80 = £980,000

This is a very simplistic view, but the principle can be adapted to cover more complex issues. For instance, there could be 200 different types of drill, but the same calculation can be done on each. Of course, sophisticated software makes the accountant's job mechanically easier.

This technique is particularly useful in processing industries, such as petroleum, brewing, dairy products or paint manufacture, where it might be impossible to identify WIP items precisely. The role of the auditor in validating such practices is paramount.

EXAMPLE 2 ● A custom-car company making sports cars has the following costs in respect of No. 821/C, an unfinished car, at the end of the month:

Materials charged to job 821/C	£2,100
Labour 120 hours @ £4	£480
Overhead £22/DLH × 120 hours	£2,640
WIP value of 821/C	£5,220

This is an accurate WIP value provided *all* the costs have been accurately recorded and charged. The amount of work involved is not great as the information is required by a normal job cost system. An added advantage is that the figure can be formally audited and proven. Work-in-progress valuation has its difficulties, but they are not insurmountable, given the skill of an accountant and a good working knowledge of the production process.

17.7 Stock control

The way in which stocks are physically controlled should not be overlooked. Discrepancies are generally of two types: disappearance through theft and improper accounting.[5] Management will, of course, be responsible for adequate systems of internal control, but losses may still occur through theft or lack of proper controls and recording. Inadequate systems of accounting may also cause discrepancies between the physical and book stocks, with consequent correcting adjustments at the year-end.

Many companies are developing in-house computer systems or using bought-in packages to account for their stocks. Such systems are generally adequate for normal recording purposes, but they are still vulnerable to year-end discrepancies arising from errors in establishing the physical stock on hand at the year-end, and problems connected with the paperwork and the physical movement of stocks.

A major cause of discrepancy between physical and book stock is the 'cut-off' date. In matching sales with cost of sales, it may be difficult to identify exactly into which period of account certain stock movements should be placed, especially when the annual stocktake lasts many days or occurs at a date other than the last day of the financial year. It is customary to make an adjustment to the stock figure, as shown in Figure 17.7. This depends on an accurate record of movements between the stocktake date and the financial year-end.

Figure 17.7 Adjusted stock figure.

	£
Stock on 7 January 20X1	XXX
Less: Purchases	(XXX)
Add: Sales	XXX
Stock at 31 December 20X0	XXX

Auditors have a special responsibility in relation to stock control. They should look carefully at the stocktaking procedures and satisfy themselves that the accounting arrangements are satisfactory. For example, in September 1987 Harris Queensway announced a stock reduction of some £15m in projected profit caused by write-downs in its furniture division. It blamed this on the inadequacy of control systems to 'identify ranges that were selling and ensure their replacement'. Interestingly, at the preceding AGM, no hint of the overvaluation was given and the auditors insisted that 'the company had no problem from the accounting point of view'.[6]

In many cases the auditor will be present at the stocktake. Even with this apparent safeguard, however, it is widely accepted that sometimes an accurate physical stocktake is almost impossible. The value of stocks should nevertheless be based on the best information available; and the resulting disclosed figure should be acceptable and provide a true and fair view on a going concern basis.

17.8 Creative accounting

No area of accounting provides more opportunities for subjectivity and creative accounting than the valuation of stocks and work-in-progress. This section summarises the major methods employed.

17.8.1 Year-end manipulations

Cut-off procedures at the year-end can be manipulated to affect stock levels and therefore profits. Purchase and sales invoices may be suppressed in order to affect the make-up of cost of sales/sales. Sometimes straightforward and blatantly false accounting may take place, particularly where there is a lack of auditor involvement. It is difficult for an auditor to question values of stocks in specialised industries, where inflated values may be used to value near-obsolete stock. Window-dressing may take place by manipulating the manufacturing process towards the end of the financial year. Speeding up or slowing down could well influence the amount of physical stock at the year-end. Likewise, finished goods might be dispatched before satisfying quality checks in order to increase sales.

17.8.2 Net realisable value (NRV)

Although the determination of net realisable value is dealt with extensively in the appendix to SSAP 9, the extent to which provisions can be made to reduce cost to NRV is highly subjective and open to manipulation. A provision is an effective smoothing device and allows overcautious write-downs to be made in profitable years and consequent write-backs in unprofitable ones.

17.8.3 Overheads

The treatment of overheads has been dealt with extensively in section 21.5.1 and is probably the area that gives the greatest scope for manipulation. Including overhead in the stock valuation has the effect of deferring the overhead's impact and so boosting profits. The Companies Act 1985 allows expenses incidental to the acquisition or production cost of an asset to be included in its cost. We have seen that this includes not only directly attributable production overheads, but also those which are indirectly attributable to production and interest on borrowed capital. SSAP 9 provides guidelines on the classification of overheads to achieve an appropriate allocation, but in practice it is difficult to make these distinctions and auditors will find it difficult to challenge management on such matters.

The statement suggests that the allocation of overheads included in the valuation needs to be based on the company's normal level of activity. The cost of unused capacity should be written off in the current year. The auditor will insist that allocation should be based on normal activity levels, but if the company underproduces, the overhead per unit increases and can therefore lead to higher year-end values. The creative accountant will be looking for ways to manipulate these year-end values, so that in bad times costs are carried forward to more profitable accounting periods.

17.8.4 Other methods of creative accounting

A simple manipulation is to show more or less stock than actually exists. If the commodity is messy and indistinguishable, the auditor may not have either the expertise or the will to verify measurements taken by the client's own employees. This lack of auditor measuring knowledge and involvement allowed one of the biggest frauds ever to take place, which became known as 'the great salad oil swindle'.[7]

Another obvious ploy is to include, in the stock valuation, obsolete or 'dead' stock. Of course, such stock should be written off. However, management may be 'optimistic' that it can be sold, particularly in times of economic recession. In high-tech industries, unrealistic values may be placed on stocks that in times of rapid development become obsolete quickly.

17.9 Audit of the year-end physical stocktake

The problems of accounting for stock and work-in-progress are highlighted at the company's year-end. This is when the closing stock figure to be shown in both the profit and loss account and balance sheet is calculated. In practice, the company will assess the final stock figure by physically counting all stock held by the company for trade. The year-end stocktake is therefore an important accounting procedure, one in which the auditors are especially interested.

The auditor generally attends the stocktake to verify both the physical quantities and the procedure of collating those quantities. At the stocktake, values are rarely assigned to stock items, so the problems facing the auditor relate to: the identification of stock items; their ownership; and their physical condition.

17.9.1 Identification of stock items

The auditor will visit many companies in the course of a year and will spend a considerable time looking at accounting records. However, it is important for the auditor also to become familiar with each company's products by visiting the shopfloor or production facilities during the audit. This makes identification of individual stock items easier at the year-end. Distinguishing between two similar items can be crucial where there are large differences in value. For example, steel-coated brass rods look identical to steel rods, but their value to the company will be very different. It is important that they are not confused at stocktake because, once recorded on the stock sheets, values are assigned, production carries on, and the error cannot be traced.

Figure 17.8 Treatment of stock items.		
	In stock	*Loading bay*
Sales		
If invoiced to customer	Delete from stock	Stock not counted
If credited (i.e. returned)	Include	Include
If not invoiced/credited	Include unless accounting entry falls into this year	Include
Purchases		
If invoiced to company	Include in stock	Include in stock
If credited (i.e. to be returned)	Delete stock	Delete stock
If invoiced/credited	Include unless accounting entry falls into next year	Include

17.9.2 Ownership of stock items

The year-end cut-off point is important to the final stock figure, but the business activities continue regardless of the year-end, and some account has to be taken of this. Hence the auditor must be aware that the recording of accounting transactions may not coincide with the physical flow of stock. Stock may be in one of two locations: included as part of stock; or in the loading bay area awaiting dispatch or receipt. Its treatment will depend on several factors (Figure 17.8). The auditor must be aware of all these possibilities and must be able to trace a sample of each stock entry through to the accounting records, so that:

● if purchase is recorded, but not sale, the item must be in stock;

● if sale is recorded, purchase must also be recorded and the item should not be in stock.

17.9.3 Physical condition of stock items

Stock in premium condition has a higher value than damaged stock. The auditor must ensure that the condition of stock is recorded at stocktake, so that the correct value is assigned to it. Items that are damaged or have been in stock for a long period will be written down to their net realisable value (which may be nil) as long as adequate details are given by the stocktaker. Once again, this is a problem of identification, so the auditor must be able to distinguish between, for instance, rolls of first quality and faulty fabric. Similarly, items that have been in stock for several stocktakes may have little value, and further enquiries about their status should be made at the time of stocktake.

17.10 Published accounts

Disclosure requirements in the Companies Act 1985 and SSAP 9 have already been indicated. The standard requires the accounting policies that have been applied to be stated and applied consistently from year to year. Stocks should be subclassified in the balance sheet or in the notes to the financial statements so as to indicate the amounts held in each of the main categories in the standard balance sheet formats. Extensive disclosure requirements are required for long-term contracts. But will the ultimate user of those financial statements be confident that the information disclosed is reliable, relevant and useful? We have already indicated many areas of subjectivity and creative accounting, but are such possibilities material?

In 1982 Westwick and Shaw examined the accounts of 125 companies with respect to stock valuation and its likely impact on reported profit.[8] The results showed that the effect on profit before tax of a 1% error in closing stock valuation ranged from a low of 0.18% to a high of 25.9% (in one case) with a median of 2.26%. The industries most vulnerable to such errors were household goods, textiles, mechanical engineering, contracting and construction.

Clearly, the existence of such variations has repercussions for such measures as ROCE, EPS and the current ratio. The research also showed that, in a sample of audit managers, 85% were of the opinion that the difference between a pessimistic and an optimistic valuation of the same stock could be more than 6%.

SSAP 9 has since been strengthened and these results may not be so indicative of the present situation. However, using the same principle, let us take a random selection of eight companies' recent annual accounts, apply a 5% increase in the closing stock valuation and calculate the effect on EPS (taxation is simply taken at 35% on the change in stock).

Figure 17.9 shows that, in absolute terms, the difference in pre-tax profits could be as much as £57.7m and the percentage change ranges from 2.7% to 24%. Of particular

Figure 17.9 Impact of a 5% change in closing stock.

Company:	1	2	3	4	5	6	7	8
	£m	£m	£m	£m	£m	£m	£m	£m
Actual stock	390.0	428.0	1,154.0	509.0	509.0	280.0	360.0	232.0
Actual pre-tax profit	80.1	105.6	479.0	252.5	358.4	186.3	518.2	436.2
Change in pre-tax profit	19.5	21.4	57.7	25.2	25.5	14.0	18.0	11.6
Impact of a 5% Change in Closing Stock (%)								
(i) Pre-tax profit	24.0	20.0	12.0	10.0	7.0	7.5	3.5	2.7
(ii) Post-tax profit	22.0	27.0	12.0	8.8	6.8	6.3	3.4	2.5
(iii) Current assets	2.6	2.3	2.8	3.1	2.8	1.8	2.9	1.4
(iv) Current assets								
Less: Current liabilities	4.9	4.6	14.1	14.0	48.8	8.2	2.2	3.8
(v) Earnings per share	27.0	25.0	12.0	9.3	8.4	6.9	3.4	3.4

KEY COMPANIES:

1 Electrical retailer

2 Textile, etc., manufacturer

3 Brewing, public houses, etc.

4 Retailer – diversified

5 Pharmaceutical and retail chemist

6 Industrial paints and fibres

7 Food retailer

8 Food retailer

note is the change in EPS, which tends to be the major stock market indicator of performance. In the case of the electrical retailer (company 1), a 5% error in stock valuation could affect EPS by as much as 27%. The stocks of such a company could well be vulnerable to such factors as changes in fashion, technology and economic recession.

Summary

Examples of differences in stock valuation are not uncommon.[9] For example, in 1984, Fidelity, the electronic equipment manufacturer, was purchased for £13.4m.[10] This price was largely based on the 1983/4 profit figure of £400,000. Subsequently, it was maintained that this 'profit' should actually be a loss of £1.3m – a difference of £1.7m. Much of this difference was attributable to stock discrepancies. The claim was contested, but it does illustrate that a disparity can occur when important figures are left to 'professional judgement'.

Another case involved the selling of British Wheelset by British Steel, just before privatisation in 1988, at a price of £16.9m.[11] It was claimed that the accounts 'were not drawn up on a consistent basis in accordance with generally accepted accounting practice'. If certain stock provisions had been made, these would have resulted in a £5m (30%) difference in the purchase price.

Other areas that cause difficulties to the user of published information are the capitalisation of interest and the reporting of write-downs on acquisition. Post-acquisition profits can be influenced by excessive write-downs of stocks on acquisition, which has the effect of increasing goodwill. These written-down stocks can eventually be sold at higher prices, thus improving post-acquisition profits.

Although legal requirements and SSAP 9 have improved the reporting requirements, many areas of subjective judgement can have substantial effects on the reporting of financial information.

Review questions

1 Discuss why some form of theoretical pricing model is required for stock valuation purposes.

2 Discuss the acceptability of the following methods of stock valuation: LIFO; base stock; replacement cost.

3 Discuss the application of individual judgement in stock valuation, e.g. changing the basis of overhead absorption.

4 Explain the criteria to be applied when selecting the method to be used for allocating costs.

5 Discuss the effect on work-in-progress and finished good valuation if the net realisable value of the raw material is lower than cost at the balance sheet date.

Exercises

An extract from the solution is provided in the appendix at the end of the text for exercises marked with an asterisk (*).

Question 1

Sunhats Ltd manufactures patent hats. It carries stocks of these and sells to wholesalers and retailers via a number of salespeople. The following expenses are charged in the profit and loss account:

Wages of: Storemen and Factory foremen

Salaries of: Production manager, Personnel officer, Buyer, Salespeople, Sales manager, Accountant, Company secretary

Other: Directors' fees, Rent and rates, Electric power, Repairs, Depreciation, Carriage outwards, Advertising, Bad debts, Interest on bank overdraft, Development expenditure for new type of hat.

Required:
Which of these expenses can reasonably be included in the valuation of stock?

* Question 2

Purchases of a certain product during July are:

July		
1	100 units @	10.00
12	100 units @	9.80
15	50 units @	9.60
20	100 units @	9.40

Units sold during the month were:

July		
10	80 units	
14	100 units	
30	90 units	

Required: Assuming no opening inventories,
(i) **Determine the cost of goods sold for July under three different valuation methods.**
(ii) **Discuss the advantages and/or disadvantages of each of these methods.**
(iii) **A physical stocktake revealed a shortage of five units. Show how you would bring this into account.**

* Question 3

Alpha Ltd makes one standard article. You have been given the following information:

1 The stock sheets at the year-end show the following items:

Raw materials:
100 tons of steel:
Cost £140 per ton
Present price £130 per ton

40 semi-finished units
Cost of materials £50 per unit
Labour cost to date £100 per unit
Selling price £500 per unit (completed)

Finished goods:
100 finished units:
Cost of materials £50 per unit
Labour cost £150 per unit
Selling price £500 per unit

10 damaged finished units:
Cost to rectify the damage £200 per unit
Selling price £500 per unit (when rectified)

2 Manufacturing overheads are 100% of labour cost.

Selling and distribution expenses are £60 per unit (mainly salespeople's commission and freight charges).

Required:
From the information in notes 1 and 2, state the amounts to be included in the balance sheet of Alpha Ltd in respect of stock. State also the principles you have applied.

Question 4

Beta Ltd commenced business on 1 January and is making up its first year's accounts. The company uses standard costs. The company stocks a variety of raw materials and components for use in its manufacturing business. The accounting records show the following:

	Standard cost of purchases £	Price variance £	Adverse (favourable) variances Usage variance £
July	10,000	800	(400)
August	12,000	1,100	100
September	9,000	700	(300)
October	8,000	900	200
November	12,000	1,000	300
December	10,000	800	(200)
Cumulative figures for whole year	110,000	8,700	(600)

Raw materials control account balance at year-end is £30,000 (at standard cost).

Required:
The company's draft balance sheet includes 'Stocks, at the lower of cost and net realisable value £80,000'. This includes raw materials £30,000: do you consider this to be acceptable? If so, why? If not, state what you consider to be an acceptable figure. (Note: for the purpose of this exercise, you may assume that the raw materials will realise more than cost.)

References

1 SSAP 9 (Revised) *Stocks and Long-term Contracts*, ASC, September 1988.
2 'A guide to accounting standards – valuation of stocks and work-in-progress', *Accountants Digest*, Summer 1984.
3 M. Jones, 'Cooking the accounts', *Certified Accountant*, July 1988, p. 39.
4 SSAP 9, Appendix 1, para. 12.
5 T.S. Dudick, 'How to avoid the common pitfalls in accounting for inventory', *The Practical Accountant*, January/February 1975, p. 65.
6 *Certified Accountant*, October 1987, p. 7.
7 E. Woolf, 'Auditing the stocks – part II', *Accountancy*, May 1976, pp. 108–110.
8 C. Westwick and D. Shaw, 'Subjectivity and reported profit', *Accountancy*, June 1982, pp. 129–131.
9 E. Woolf, *op. cit.*, parts I and II.
10 K. Bhattacharya, 'More or less true, quite fair', *Accountancy*, December 1988, p. 126.
11 R. Northedge, 'Steel attacked over wheelset valuation', *Daily Telegraph*, 2 January 1991, p. 19.

CHAPTER 18

Long-term contracts

18.1 Introduction

SSAP 9 (revised) defines a long-term contract as:

> A contract entered into for the design, manufacture or construction of a single substantial asset or the provision of a service where the time taken to substantially complete the contract is such that the contract activity falls into different accounting periods. A contract that is accounted for as long-term will usually extend for a period exceeding one year...[1]

The important and controversial areas in the treatment of contracts concern the fact that the activity normally falls into different accounting periods and is expected to 'extend for a period exceeding one year'. Given this, how should we deal with the determination and timing of profit in accordance with the matching concept and 'value' long-term contracts in the balance sheet?

The justification for recognising profit as the contract progresses is contained in the explanatory note preceding SSAP (revised):

> Owing to the length of time taken to complete such contracts, to defer recording turnover and taking profit into account until completion may result in the profit and loss account reflecting not so much a fair view of the results of the activity of the company during the year but rather the results relating to contracts that have been completed in the year. It is therefore appropriate to take credit for ascertainable turnover and profit while contracts are in progress.[2]

Ever since the Companies Act 1981 stipulated that only 'realised' profits were to be included in profit for the year, the profession has been concerned about the legality of taking profit in accordance with SSAP 9. In addition, the Companies Act 1985 states that the amount to be included in the current assets (including uncompleted long-term contracts) is the lower of purchase price or production cost and net realisable value. In these circumstances, there was much debate centred on the legal position of SSAP 9 and the accounting procedures necessary for presenting and disclosing relevant and reliable information to users.

18.2 Recognition of profit

Turning to the first problem: recognition of profit. Legally, the profit and loss account should give a 'true and fair view' of the profit or loss for the financial year (section 228(2)

Companies Act 1985). In the application of the matching principle it has always been generally accepted that a prudently calculated 'attributable profit' be included in the profit and loss account for the period under review. The objective, as always, was to give a 'true and fair' view of the results of activities during the period. SSAP 9 states that this attributable profit should be calculated on a prudent basis and, as a prerequisite, that the outcome of the contract can be assessed with reasonable certainty. Only then should profit be taken. Extensive guidelines are given in the appendix to SSAP 9 but the overriding principle is that no profit should be taken until the outcome of the contract can reasonably be foreseen. The profit to be recognised should prudently reflect the amount of work performed to date, and the method used to calculate such profit should be consistently applied. Inevitably, the recognition of attributable profit leaves much scope for the exercise of professional judgement, but there are generally accepted methods, e.g. the following:

(a) Attributable profit

$$= \frac{\text{Value of work certified to date}}{\text{Total contract price}} \times \text{Total estimated contract profit}$$

(b) **or**

$$= \frac{\text{Cost of work completed}}{\text{Estimated total costs}} \times \text{Total estimated contract profit}$$

(c) **or** (more prudently)

$$= \frac{\text{Cash received}}{\text{Total contract price}} \times \text{Total estimated contract profit}$$

SSAP 9 states that attributable profit is

that part of the total profit currently estimated to arise over the duration of the contract ... that fairly reflects the profit attributable to that part of the work performed at the accounting date.[3]

This definition appears to favour approach (b) above, but it is emphasised that there are a number of ways of calculating 'attributable profit', all theoretically acceptable and not inconsistent with SSAP 9. If we accept that attributable profit is calculated, how then should this be reflected in the financial statements? Prior to 1988, there was a process of 'accumulating costs'. An account would be opened for each contract and into this account would be charged all costs (not only direct but also attributable overheads) **plus the attributable profit**. The resulting balance would then appear in the balance sheet as work-in-progress (net of any foreseeable losses and progress payments received or receivable). The accounting treatment resulted in attributable profit being introduced directly into the profit and loss account and likewise included in the work-in-progress valuation. This practice appeared to conflict with legal requirements in the Companies Act 1985. The usual way out of the dilemma was to include a statement in the notes to the accounts.

This situation was clearly unacceptable and after several years of debate the ASC developed the revised SSAP 9 to deal with this and at the same time bring UK accounting practice into line with International Standards (IAS 2 and IAS 11).

18.3 Integrated approach

In general terms, the accounting requirements of SSAP 9 (revised) provide that the value of work completed by the year end should be included in turnover, against which the cost incurred in achieving that turnover should be charged as 'cost of sales'. This integrated approach radically changed the way in which long-term contracts were reported. The effect is that all attributable profit is removed from the balance sheet figure by treating all amounts recoverable on contracts as turnover and contract costs as cost of sales.

An example of the accounting entries at this point may help understanding:

(a) Contract price	1,600,000
(b) Costs to date	796,000
(c) Estimated costs to complete the contract	484,000
(d) Value of work satisfactorily completed	800,000
(e) Amount taken as cost of sales	760,000
(f) Cash received	752,000

Tabular format

	£000	
Recorded as turnover (being value of work done)	800	(A)
Cumulative payments on account	752	(B)
Classified as amounts recoverable	48	(C)
Total costs incurred	796	(D)
Transferred to cost of sales	760	(E)
Classified as long-term contract balances	36	(F)
Gross profit	40	(A–E)

Ledger account format

Contract account

(D) Costs incurred	796	(E) Cost of sales	760
		(F) Balance c/f	36
	796		796

Sales account

(A) Value of work completed – P/L a/c	800	(A) Debtor	800

Debtor account (contractee)

(A) Sales value of work	800	(B) Cash	752
		(C) Balance c/f	48
	800		800

Profit and loss account (extract)

	£000
Turnover	800
Cost of sales	760
Gross profit	40

Notes:

1 A provision for foreseeable losses is unnecessary since estimated costs to complete (£484) plus actual cost to date (£796) is substantially less than the contract price (£1,600).

2 An alternative approach would be to calculate the 'attributable profit' on one of the bases previously outlined, viz:

$$\frac{\text{Work certified}}{\text{Contract price}} \times \text{Total estimated contracted profit}$$

$$= \frac{800}{1,600} \times £320$$

$$= £160,000$$

This calculation assumes that future costs are guaranteed as predicted and no unforeseen events will take place. This increase in reported profit, £120,000, may of course influence such areas as tax liabilities, dividend potential, EPS and other performance measures. The profit declared, £160,000 may prove to be overoptimistic if we take into account such matters as cost increases and the vagaries of long-term operations. Prudence dictates, therefore, that the lower profit figure, £40,000, be used for reporting purposes at the intermediate stage of the project. This approach defers profit taking to the later stages when contract profitability is more certain and may be vital when the contract is of a fixed price nature, e.g. governmental contracts. The more prudent practice also complies with the realisation concept whereby profits should only be taken when truly realised. (Consider the difficulties involved in calculating profits in respect of the Channel Tunnel project and the potential dangers of using the 'profit' for dividend payments.)

In addition to the general accounting principles involved in long-term contracts the example should in Figure 18.1 is given in Appendix 3 of SSAP 9 to illustrate the financial statement presentation in a variety of circumstances. The following list refers to Figure 18.1.

Figure 18.1 Example as given in SSAP 9.

	Project number					Balance sheet total	Profit and loss account
	1	2	3	4	5		
Recorded as turnover – being value of work done	145	520	380	200	55		1,300
Cumulative payments on account	(100)	(600)	(400)	(150)	(80)		
Classified as amounts recoverable on contracts	45			50		95 DR	
Balance (excess) of payments on account		(80)	(20)		(25)		
Applied as an offset against long-term contract balances – see below		60	20		15		
Residue classified as payments on account		(20)	—		(10)	(30)CR	
Total costs incurred	110	510	450	250	100		
Transferred to cost of sales	(110)	(450)	(350)	(250)	(55)		(1,215)
	—	60	100	—	45		
Provision/accrual for foreseeable losses				(40)	(30)		(70)
charged to cost of sales		60	100		15		
Classified as provision/accrual for losses				(40)		(40)CR	
Balance (excess) of payments on account applied as offset against long-term contract balances		(60)	(20)		(15)		
Classified as long-term contract balances		—	80		—	80DR	
Gross profit on long-term contracts	35	70	30	(90)	(30)		15

Project

1 If turnover exceeds payments on account the 'amount recoverable on contracts' (45) is disclosed separately within debtors.

2 If payments on account are greater than turnover to date, the excess (80) is first offset against any debit balance on the contract included in stocks (60) and then any residual (20) is classified as payments on account – creditors.

3 Again, there are excess payments on account (20) which are offset against the debit balance on the contract (100). The residual amount (80) is classified as long-term contract balances.

4 Turnover exceeds payments on account and the excess (50) will be shown as 'amounts recoverable on contracts'. Turnover will be shown as 200, while against this will be recorded cost of sales (250) and a provision for a foreseeable loss (40) leaving a loss on this contract (90). The provision will appear in the balance sheet within 'creditors' or 'provisions for liabilities and charges' as appropriate.

5 The provision for the foreseeable loss (30) is deducted from the contract balance (45), so reducing it to net realisable value (15). The excess of payments on account (25) is first offset against the balance on the contract balance (now 15) and the residual (10) is classified as payment on account – creditors.

The effect of these various transactions on the profit and loss account and balance sheet can be summarised as follows:

Profit and loss account		£
Turnover		1300
Cost of sales	1215	
(provision for losses)	70	1285
Gross profit		15
Balance sheet		
Provision for foreseeable losses		40
Creditors – payments on account		30
Debtors – amounts recoverable on contracts		95
Long-term contract balances		80

The objective of this revised approach for recording and presenting the accounting information is to give an integrated presentation of long-term contract activity in the financial statements. The conflict with the Companies Act 1985 is also eliminated. There are of course still areas which involve the exercise of professional judgement. The John Laing plc 1999 accounts stated the following accounting policy for long-term contracts:

> Profits on long-term contracts are calculated in accordance with standard accounting practice and do not therefore relate directly to turnover. Profit on current contracts is only taken at a stage near enough to completion for that profit to be reasonably certain. Provision is made for all losses incurred to the accounting date together with any further losses that are foreseen in bringing contracts to completion.
>
> Amounts recoverable on contracts which are included in debtors are stated at cost, plus attributable profit to the extent that this is reasonably certain after making provision for contingencies, less any losses incurred or foreseen in bringing contracts to completion, and less amounts received as progress payments. Cost for

this purpose includes valuations of all work done by subcontractors, whether certified or not, and all overheads other than those relating to the general administration of the relevant companies. For any contracts where receipts exceed the book value of work done, the excess is included in creditors as payments on account.

However, overall, the aim is to give a true and fair view of the profit or loss for the accounting period and of the financial position at the end of the accounting period.

Review questions

1 Discuss the point in a contract's life when it becomes appropriate to recognise profit and the feasibility of specifying a common point, e.g. when contract is 25% complete.

2 'Profit on a contract is not realised until completion of the contract.' Discuss.

3 'Profit on a contract that is not completed is an unrealised holding gain.' Discuss.

4 'There should be one specified method for calculating attributable profit.' Discuss.

Exercises

Question 1

MACTAR have a series of contracts to resurface sections of motorways in England and Wales. The scale of the contract means several years' work and each motorway section is regarded as a separate contract.

Required:
From the following information, calculate for each contract the amount of profit (or loss) you would show for the year and show how these contracts would appear in the balance sheet with all appropriate notes.

M1	£m
Contract	3.0
Costs to date	2.1
Estimated cost to complete	0.3
Certified value of work completed to date	1.8
Payments applied for to date	1.75
Payment received to date	1.5

M6	£m
Contract sum	2.0
Costs to date	0.3
Estimated cost to complete	1.1
Certified value of materials delivered	0.1
Payments applied for to date	0.1
Payments received to date	—

M62	£m
Contract sum	2.5
Costs to date	2.3
Estimated costs to complete	0.8
Certified value of work completed to date	1.3
Payments applied for to date	1.0
Payments received to date	0.75

This contract has had **major** difficulties due to difficult terrain, and the contract only allows for a 10% increase in contract sum for such events.

* ## Question 2

At 31 October 20X0, Lytax Ltd was engaged in various contracts including five long-term contracts, details of which are given below:

	1 £000	2 £000	3 £000	4 £000	5 £000
Contract price	1,100	950	1,400	1,300	1,200
At 31 October					
Cumulative costs incurred	664	535	810	640	1,070
Estimated further costs to completion	106	75	680	800	165
Estimated cost of post-completion guarantee rectification work	30	10	45	20	5
Cumulative costs incurred transferred to cost of sales	580	470	646	525	900
Progress payments:					
Cumulative receipts	615	680	615	385	722
Invoiced					
– awaiting receipt	60	40	25	200	34
– retained by contractee	75	80	60	65	84

It is not expected that any contractees will default on their payments.

Up to 31 October 20X9, the following amounts have been included in the turnover and cost of sales figures:

	1 £000	2 £000	3 £000	4 £000	5 £000
Cumulative turnover	560	340	517	400	610
Cumulative costs incurred transferred to cost of sales	460	245	517	400	610
Foreseeable loss transferred to cost of sales	—	—	—	70	—

It is the accounting policy of Lytax Ltd to arrive at contract turnover by adjusting contract cost of sales (including foreseeable losses) by the amount of contract profit or loss to be regarded as recognised, separately for each contract.

Required:
Show how these items will appear in the balance sheet of Lytax Ltd with all appropriate notes. Show all workings in tabular form.

* Question 3

During its financial year ended 30 June 20X7 Beavers Ltd, an engineering company, has worked on several contracts. Information relating to one of them is given below:

Contract X201

Date commenced	1 July 20X6
Original estimate of completion date	30 September 20X7
Contract price	£240,000
Proportion of work certified as satisfactorily	
completed (and invoiced) up to 30 June 20X7	£180,000
Progress payments from Dam Ltd	£150,000

Costs up to 30 June 20X7

Wages	£91,000
Materials sent to site	£36,000
Other contract costs	£18,000
Proportion of Head Office costs	£6,000
Plant and equipment transferred to the site	
(at book value on 1 July 20X6)	£9,000

The plant and equipment is expected to have a book value of about £1,000 when the contract is completed.

Stock of materials at site 30 June 20X7	£3,000
Expected additional costs to complete the contract:	
Wages	£10,000
Materials (including stock at 30 June 20X7)	£12,000
Other (including Head Office costs)	£8,000

At 30 June 20X7 it is estimated that work to a cost value of £19,000 has been completed, but not included in the certifications.

If the contract is completed one month earlier than originally scheduled, an extra £10,000 will be paid to the contractors. At the end of June 20X7 there seemed to be a 'good chance' that this would happen.

Required:
(a) Show the account for the contract in the books of Beavers Ltd, up to 30 June 20X7 (including any transfer to the profit and loss account which you think is appropriate).
(b) Show the balance sheet entries.
(c) Circulate the profit (or loss) to be recognised in the 20X6–X7 accounts.

Question 4

Newbild Ltd commenced work on the construction of a block of flats on 1 July 20X0.

During the period ended 31 March 20X1 contract expenditure was as follows:

	£
Materials issued from stores	13,407
Materials delivered direct to site	73,078
Wages	39,498
Administration expenses	3,742
Site expenses	4,693

On 31 March 20X1 there were outstanding amounts for wages £396 and site expenses £122, and the stock of materials on site amounted to £5,467.

The following information is also relevant:

1 On 1 July 20X0 plant was purchased for exclusive use on site at a cost of £15,320. It was estimated that it would be used for two years after which it would have a residual value of £5,000.

2 By 31 March 20X1 Newbild Ltd had received £114,580, being the amount of work certified by the architects up to 31 March 20X1 less a 15% retention.

3 The total contract price is £780,000. The company estimates that additional costs to complete the project will be £490,000. From costing records it is estimated that the costs of rectification and guarantee work will be 2.5% of the contract price.

Required:
(a) Prepare the contract account for the period, together with a statement showing your calculation of the profit to be taken to the company's profit and loss account on 31 March 20X1. Assume for the purpose of the question that the contract is sufficiently advanced to allow for the taking of profit.
(b) Give the values which you think should be included in the figures of turnover and cost of sales, in the profit and loss account, and those to be included in debtors and work in progress in the balance sheet in respect of this contract.

Question 5

Good Progress Ltd entered into a contract on 1.1.20X0 at a contract price of £1,000,000 and an estimated total profit of £250,000. The contract was due for completion on 31.12.20X4.

The following information was available.

As at 31.12.20X0:

The contract was 25% complete and an architect's certificate was issued for £25,000.

As at 31.12.20X1

The contract was 40% complete and an architect's certificate was issued for £40,000.

Required:
Prepare the profit and loss account entries for the years ended 31 December 20X0 and 20X1 and the balance sheet entries as at those dates.

References

1 SSAP 9, *Stocks and Long-term Contracts*, ASC 1988, para. 22.
2 SSAP 9, ASC 1988, para. 7.
3 SSAP 9, ACS 1988, para. 23.

PART 4

Consolidated accounts

Accounting for groups at the date of acquisition

19.1 Introduction

A group is a business combination that exists when there are two or more companies that act as an economic entity controlled by a single management. This definition does not extend to companies established by the same individuals, e.g. a husband and wife who own two or more companies. The creation of a business combination is variously referred to as a take-over, an acquisition or a merger. We include within the term 'business combination' all types of merger, including vertical, horizontal and conglomerate.

In this chapter we will be considering:

A – Business combinations: reasons for and financial reporting requirements
- reasons for business combinations
- defining a group
- when a parent is exempt or permitted to omit a subsidiary from group accounts

B – Acquiring shares for cash at book values
- accounting for an Investment in a subsidiary in parent company accounts – no goodwill
- preparing consolidated accounts at date of acquisition – no goodwill
- accounting for an investment in a subsidiary in parent company accounts – with goodwill
- preparing consolidated accounts at date of acquisition – with goodwill

C – Acquiring shares for cash where fair values of assets and liabilities differ from book values
- FRS 7 *Fair Values in Acquisition Accounting* definition of fair values
- preparing consolidated accounts incorporating fair values
- applying FRS 7 to specific assets and liabilities

D – Minority interests
- FRS 2 *Accounting for Subsidiary Undertakings* treatment
- proportional consolidation
- proprietary and entity goodwill

E – Investment acquired by issue of shares
- accounting in parent company balance sheet
- accounting in parent company balance sheet where merger relief is available
- preparing consolidated accounts where consideration is in shares

F – Merger accounting
  ● Companies Act criteria for merger accounting
  ● FRS 6 *Acquisitions and Mergers* criteria for merger accounting
  ● Preparing merger accounts

A – BUSINESS COMBINATIONS: REASONS FOR AND FINANCIAL REPORTING REQUIREMENTS

19.2   Business combinations: why they occur

In simple terms, the ownership of the shares of the acquired company allows the new owner to control the net assets of that company. Why should one company wish to gain ownership and control of the net assets of another company?

19.2.1   Motives for business combinations

Many studies have looked at the reasons for business combinations. Figure 19.1 lists some of the motives that have been identified from a number of different sources.[1-4]

Foster[5] cites an interesting survey carried out by Baker, Miller and Rampsberger,[6] which illustrates that merger motives depend on the type of merger. Chief executives of a sample of companies involved in merger activity were asked to rank motives for horizontal mergers (in which the two companies have identical products) and conglomerate mergers (in which the two companies have no buyer/seller relationship, no products in common, and no other relationship). The ranking is shown in Figure 19.2.

Although researchers agree on the list of motives for mergers, there is no general agreement about the importance of each motive.

On the merger of Guinness plc with Grand Metropolitan to form Diageo the directors gave their reasons for the merger in the circular to Guinness Shareholders as follows:

> The directors of both Guinness and GrandMet believe that the Merger represents a significant opportunity to create a major new force in branded food and drinks which will operate on a truly international scale. Guinness will gain an increased interest in North America, the world's largest consumer market, through Pilsbury and Burger King. GrandMet will benefit from Guinness's successful spirits business in emerging markets. Both groups will benefit from the complementary nature of their respective spirits operations and the scope for cost savings as a result of the Merger.

They also told the shareholders that the step change in scale would provide the Merged Group with five valuable benefits which, together, would establish a platform for sustained future growth. The valuable benefits were:

● A complementary and broad product range from combined spirits and wines business allowing the Group to offer an expanded product range.

● Greater geographic breadth with the critical mass to exploit the opportunities for growth.

● Enhanced marketing capability from shared use of high calibre and experienced management team, translating into superior brand management, innovative new product and brand development and world class marketing.

● Greater cost efficiency generating operating cost savings of some £175m per annum by the third year.
● Financial capacity to develop the businesses both organically and by acquisition.

Figure 19.1   Motives for business combinations.

Production-based motives

● Synergies, e.g. economies of scale
● Accelerate growth or reduce risks and costs, e.g. acquiring a research department or new technology
● Acquire expanded capacity at a lower cost than buying new

Commercial-based motives for horizontal combinations between firms with similar products operating in the same or different markets

● Gain market share in the same industry, i.e. horizontal combinations
● Eliminate competition
● Acquire brands

Commercial-based motives for vertical combinations between firms in which a buyer/seller relationship could exist

● Acquire new sources of supply
● Acquire broader customer base

Financial-based motives for horizontal and vertical combinations

● Obtaining high profile image in the eyes of bankers, investors and suppliers, i.e. credit becomes cheaper

Financial-based motives for conglomerate combinations between two firms that have no buyer/seller relationship, no technical and distributional relationship and do not deal in similar products

● Acquire complementary resources to smooth earnings and balance cyclicality

Financial-based motives for any combination

● Utilise financial strengths of acquired company, e.g. tax credits, borrowing capacity
● Undervalued assets of the acquired company can be disposed of at a profit, i.e. asset stripping
● Underperforming parts of the acquired company can be disposed of and the proceeds used to defray the cost of the acquisition

Political-based motives

● Avoid being taken over, i.e. a defensive measure
● Avoid cultural problems associated with cross-border trade
● Enhance management salaries from the increased size of the combined business
● Ego, fashion and other 'irrational' reasons

Figure 19.2   Ranking motives for business combinations.

Horizontal combinations

1 To effect more rapid growth
2 To gain economies of sale
3 To increase market share
4 To expand geographical mix
5 To increase market value of seasonal sales
6 To expand/improve product mix

Conglomerate combinations

1 To effect more rapid growth
2 To spread risk through diversification
3 To increase market value of stock
4 To expand/improve the profit
5 To counter cycle of stock
6 To enhance power/prestige of firm

However, whether a merger achieves its objectives is another issue (within months there were rumours that Diageo would sell Burger King operation as a management buyout) and beyond the scope of this text. We will concentrate on the financial reporting requirements when a combination exists.

19.3   Business combinations: financial reporting requirements

The Companies Act 1985 (as amended by the Companies Act 1989) provides that accounts, known as **consolidated accounts** or **group accounts**, are to be prepared by the management of the acquiring company and presented to the shareholders of the acquiring company. Such consolidated accounts are required to present a **true and fair view** of the **combined profit (loss) of the entity and of the combined assets and liabilities** at the end of the year.[7]

There are also professional regulations emanating from the standard-setting authority. These are the Financial Reporting Standards issued by the ASB, e.g. FRS 2.

19.3.1   Why is it necessary to define when a group exists?

Groups are required to consolidate the results of members of the group to produce group accounts. It is therefore necessary to define when a company is to be regarded as a member of the group.

19.3.2   Why is an exact definition important?

If each of the member companies has a healthy profit and a strong balance sheet, the controlling company will have little incentive to avoid consolidation. However, if a member of the group makes losses or has a weak balance sheet, e.g. an excessive level of gearing, there is an obvious attraction in omitting the loss or weak asset/liability position of that member from the consolidation.

To prevent groups being able to manipulate the consolidated picture by including or excluding the results of a company, regulations have been introduced to define when a group relationship exists.

Definition of a group

A group exists if a dominant company, known as the **parent** undertaking or holding company, **controls** another company known as the **subsidiary** undertaking. For example, if Strong plc controls Weak plc, then Strong plc is the parent undertaking, Weak plc is the subsidiary undertaking, and together they comprise the Strong Group. FRS 2 *Accounting for Subsidiary Undertakings* defines control (para. 6) as 'the ability of an undertaking to direct the financial and operating policies of another undertaking with a view to gaining economic benefits from its activities'.

How is the existence of control determined?

The Companies Act 1985 stipulates that control exists in the following circumstances:[8]

1 Strong plc has **direct voting control** arising from its ownership of more than 50% of the voting shares.

2 Strong plc holds less than 50% of the voting shares but has organised affairs to achieve **indirect voting control**, e.g. by virtue of an agreement with the other shareholders or by virtue of the right to appoint the majority of the directors.

3 Strong plc holds no voting shares but has organised affairs so that it has the **right to exercise dominant influence** over the operating and financial policies of Weak plc, e.g. by a clause to this effect in the memorandum or articles of association or by a contract entered into by Weak plc granting this influence.

4 Strong plc **actually exercises dominant influence** over the operating and financial policies of Weak plc, by virtue of arrangements mentioned in (3) above, and it has an **equity interest that exceeds 20%** of the voting power but is less than 50%.

5 Strong plc has more than 20% of the equity shares in Weak plc and both companies are **managed on a unified basis**, e.g. when the management of Strong plc treat the two companies as a single entity.

19.4 Business combinations: when a parent or holding company is exempt from preparing consolidated accounts; may omit; or must omit the results of a subsidiary from the consolidated accounts

19.4.1 FRS 2 exempts a parent in some circumstances from preparing consolidated accounts

This exemption applies, for example, if:

● the company is small or medium-size;

● the parent is a wholly-owned subsidiary whose immediate parent is incorporated in a European Community country;

● the parent is a majority-owned subsidiary and a request has not been made by 5% of the total shares or more than 50% of the total minority holdings. This recognises that it is unlikely that the minority shareholders would normally be interested in consolidated accounts;

● all the subsidiaries are permitted or required to be excluded from the consolidation. This would be a highly unusual position.

19.4.2 Subsidiaries in fact but not in name

Managements have been able to avoid including the results of subsidiaries by technically arranging the legal form of the investment so that the investee company fell outside the definition of a subsidiary.

The Companies Act 1989 removed some of the ways in which one company could control another but avoid consolidating the results. For example, prior to the Companies Act 1989, the definition of a group was that Strong plc should hold more than 50% of the **ordinary** shares. This meant that Strong plc could control Weak plc by issuing voting shares that were not ordinary shares but gave effective control. The change from holding more than 50% of the ordinary shares to holding more than 50% of the voting power has removed this possibility.

19.4.3   Subsidiaries in name but not included in the group accounts

Another form of manipulation was for the holding company to accept that the investee was a subsidiary, but then find grounds for excluding it anyway.

There may be good reasons why the consolidation of the two sets of accounts would not give a true and fair view of the group and so there are still statutory grounds for requiring or allowing the exclusion of a subsidiary from the consolidated accounts. The grounds are set out in the Companies Act 1985 as follows.[9]

When a subsidiary must be excluded

The Companies Act provides that a subsidiary must be excluded where the activities of the subsidiary are so different that consolidated accounts would not give a true and fair view.

The ASB were unhappy with this as a ground for exclusion and have effectively prevented it from being used in practice by making it a condition that exclusion is only permitted where to include the subsidiary would result in the failure of the consolidated accounts to give a true and fair view. It also expressed the view that it could not envisage any situations where this condition could be satisfied.

It could be argued that by making this condition the ASB are usurping the role of the legislature in that the Companies Act exclusion is for all practical purposes overridden.

However, the ASB approach could be justified on the grounds that, with the issue of SSAP 25 *Segmental Reporting*, it is now possible for the parent to provide explanatory segmental information dealing with the subsidiary whose activities were different.

When a subsidiary may be excluded under the Companies Act

There is a permissive statutory right to omit the subsidiary in the following circumstances:

● The results of the subsidiary cannot be obtained without **disproportionate expense or undue delay**.

● There is a **severe, long-term restriction** that substantially hinders the exercise of the rights of the parent company over the assets or management of the subsidiary.

● The investment in the subsidiary is held exclusively with a **view to resale** and the results have not previously been consolidated. The latter condition is to prevent a parent company omitting a subsidiary that has started to make a loss in the year the loss arises by deciding to dispose of its shares in the subsidiary.

● The results of the subsidiary are **immaterial** in the context of the group. The requirement to view the position in the context of the group is to dissuade parent companies from setting up a series of subsidiaries that are immaterial when taken singly but material when taken together. The right only exists if the combined totals are immaterial.

What view did the ASB take of these permissive statutory rights?

● FRS 2 *Accounting for Subsidiary Undertakings*, issued by the ASB in 1992, does not permit subsidiaries to be excluded merely because the results of the subsidiary cannot be obtained without **disproportionate expense or undue delay**. The reason for restricting this permissive right is that the two reasons are subjective and it is too easy for a company to raise the excuse of **disproportionate expense or undue delay** if it did not wish to include the subsidiary e.g. because its results were poor.

● FRS 2 went further than the Companies Act by requiring, rather than permitting, the exclusion in the case of **severe long-term restrictions**. Where excluded, such subsidiaries are required to be treated as **fixed asset** investment and carried at a fixed amount. The fixed amount is to be calculated using the equity method and frozen at the amount calculated at the date the severe restrictions came into effect. If however the parent still exercises significant influence over it then this amount will be revised each year to bring into account its proportion of any profits or losses.

● FRS 2 also requires exclusion when the group's interest is held **exclusively with a view to a subsequent resale** and stipulates that such subsidiaries should be treated as **current assets** and carried at the lower of cost and net realisable value.

● FRS 2 and the Companies Act have the same approach to exclusion on grounds of **immateriality**.

B – ACQUIRING SHARES FOR CASH AT BOOK VALUES

19.5 Parent company: treatment of investment in a subsidiary acquired for cash and no goodwill

How is the investment in a subsidiary dealt with when all the shares are acquired for cash, or when the parent company issues shares equal to the net asset value of the subsidiary? We consider the parent company first and then the subsidiary company.

19.5.1 Accounting in the parent company

When a company acquires shares in another company, an immediate asset is recorded and there is a right to receive future dividends.

The asset

At the date of the acquisition, a non-current asset is created in the books of the investing company; this will give rise to a reduction in the **net current assets** if the consideration is in cash, or an increase in the share capital if the consideration is in shares.

Future dividends

The investing company effectively owns the earnings generated by the subsidiary. These earnings might be passed through to the holding company as dividends. The proportion of the earnings passed through will depend on the financial position of the subsidiary and the nature of the industry. For example, a subsidiary in the pharmaceutical industry might plough back a high proportion of its earnings; a subsidiary in the property industry, collecting rentals on properties, might pass all its earnings through to the holding company as a dividend.

Although the holding company can require the subsidiary to declare a dividend that would distribute all of the earnings, it has to have regard to the normal commercial facts, e.g. the need to replace and support development in the subsidiary.

Balance sheet entry for the investment when acquired for cash

Assume that Strong plc, the parent company, acquires shares in Weak plc, the subsidiary, which has a total issued capital of 5,000 £1 shares, for cash at a cost of £1.50 per share on 1 January 20X1 from existing shareholders. Figure 19.3 shows the balance sheet effect of acquiring different numbers of shares:

● The shares are reported as an Investment in shares in subsidiary and classified as a fixed asset valued at cost in the balance sheet of Strong plc.

● The net current assets of Strong plc are reduced by the payment made to the shareholders of Weak plc.

● The accounting for the transaction is not dependent on the number of shares acquired. Regardless of the number of shares acquired, there will be a new fixed asset entitled Investment in subsidiary and a reduction in the net current assets.

In practice, the price of a share might differ according to the number of shares acquired, e.g. a 5% interest would be valued on a dividend basis, while a 60% interest would be valued on an earnings basis: the price has been kept constant for illustration only, on the basis that the shares were acquired in the open market at the quoted market price.

Will any of the balance sheet ratios for Strong plc be different after recording the investment?

Any ratio that uses the **net current asset** figure or the **current asset** figure will be different, e.g. the current ratio, the working capital turnover ratio. Any ratio that uses total assets or net assets of Strong plc will be unaffected by the acquisition of shares in Weak plc.

Figure 19.3 Balance sheet entries of Strong plc as at the date of acquisition if Strong plc acquires various percentages of the 5,000 shares in Weak plc for cash.

	Before buying shares	After buying 5% of Weak	After buying 20% of Weak	After buying 60% of Weak	After buying 100% of Weak
	£	£	£	£	£
Fixed assets	12,250	12,250	12,250	12,250	12,250
Investment in Weak plc		375	1,500	4,500	7,500
Net current assets/(liabilities)	2,750	2,375	1,250	(1,750)	(4,750)
Net assets	15,000	15,000	15,000	15,000	15,000
Ordinary share capital	8,750	8,750	8,750	8,750	8,750
Profit and loss balance	6,250	6,250	6,250	6,250	6,250
Net capital employed	15,000	15,000	15,000	15,000	15,000

19.5.2 Accounting in the subsidiary company

There is often uncertainty about whether a takeover affects the accounts of the company that has been taken over. It depends on who sold the shares to the holding company and who received the consideration.

Assuming that Strong acquired shares in Weak for cash, (a) by purchasing the shares in the market from Big and Tiny who hold all the issued shares in Weak and (b) by acquiring new shares from Weak to give it more than 50% of the total shares in issue, i.e. Strong holds more shares than those held by Big and Tiny combined, the effect is as follows:

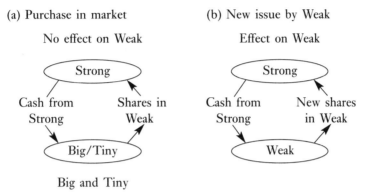

Note that if Strong purchases all the Weak shares from the two existing shareholders then Weak becomes a wholly owned subsidiary of Strong. If however it acquires a new issue of shares from Weak then Big and Tiny remain as shareholders of Weak and Big and Tiny will appear as a minority interest in the Strong Group accounts.

If Strong plc acquired the shares directly from Weak plc by way of a new issue, Weak plc will receive the payment of cash and increase its issued share capital. If Strong plc acquired the shares on the stock market from an existing shareholder, the shareholder will receive the cash and no transaction will be recorded in the financial records of Weak plc.

Assuming that the shares acquired by Strong plc were obtained from existing shareholders of Weak plc, the balance sheet of Weak plc would appear as in Figure 19.4. The

Figure 19.4 Balance sheet entries of Weak plc after the acquisition by Strong plc of various percentages of the shares held by existing Weak plc shareholders.

	Before buying shares	After buying 5% of Weak	After buying 20% of Weak	After buying 60% of Weak	After buying 100% of Weak
	£	£	£	£	£
Fixed assets	5,500	5,500	5,500	5,500	5,500
Net current assets	2,000	2,000	2,000	2,000	2,000
	7,500	7,500	7,500	7,500	7,500
Ordinary share capital	5,000	5,000	5,000	5,000	5,000
Profit and loss balance	2,500	2,500	2,500	2,500	2,500
	7,500	7,500	7,500	7,500	7,500

transfer of shares from one shareholder to another has no effect on the assets, liabilities and capital of the company that originally issued the shares. Weak plc will merely amend its register of members to record that the shares have been transferred to Strong plc.

What does a comparison of the amount paid by Strong plc and the Weak plc balance sheet show us?

Assuming that Strong plc acquired all of the shares in Weak plc, a comparison of the amount that Strong plc paid for the shares and the balance sheet of Weak plc at the date of acquisition reveals the following:

- Strong plc paid £7,500 for the 5,000 shares in Weak plc.
- The 5,000 shares in Weak plc are entitled to its reserves of £2,500.
- The shares and reserves of Weak plc are represented by net assets with a book value of £7,500 (consisting of fixed assets of £5,500 and net current assets of £2,000).
- The £7,500 Investment in Weak plc on the Strong plc balance sheet is represented by the £7,500 net assets on the Weak plc balance sheet.

19.6   Consolidated accounts: acquisition accounting

We will now explain the preparation of consolidated accounts for Strong plc and its wholly owned subsidiary, Weak plc, as at the date of acquisition.

By 'wholly owned', we mean that the parent company holds 100% of the voting shares of the subsidiary. Let us assume that Strong plc acquired all of the issued share capital of Weak plc on 1 January 20X1, paying £1.50 in cash for each £1 share, i.e. it is paying the net asset value for the shares. The balance sheets of Strong plc and Weak plc immediately after the acquisition are shown in Figure 19.5.

19.6.1   Step 1 in the consolidation process: aggregate all balances

Figure 19.6 shows the position after aggregating all of the assets and liabilities of the two companies that make up the Strong Group.

The aggregation seems to indicate that the Group has combined total net assets of £22,500. This cannot be true because the combined fixed assets of £17,750 and negative

Figure 19.5   Balance sheets of Strong and Weak immediately after acquisition.

	Strong plc £	Weak plc £
Fixed assets	12,250	5,500
Investment in Weak plc	7,500	
Net current assets/(liabilities)	(4,750)	2,000
	15,000	7,500
Ordinary share capital	8,750	5,000
Profit and loss balance	6,250	2,500
	15,000	7,500

Figure 19.6 Aggregate the assets and liabilities as at 1 January 20X1.

	Strong plc £	Weak plc £	Aggregate the two £
Fixed assets	12,250	5,500	17,750
Investment in Weak plc	7,500		7,500
Net current assets/(liabilities)	(4,750)	2,000	(2,750)
Total net assets	15,000	7,500	22,500
Ordinary share capital	8,750	5,000	13,750
Profit and loss balance	6,250	2,500	8,750
	15,000	7,500	22,500

net current assets of (£2,750) only total £15,000. The difference is the investment in Weak plc that appears in the balance sheet of Strong plc. We saw above that the investment is represented by the net assets in Weak plc, which are in turn represented by the shares and reserves in Weak plc. If we aggregate the amount paid for the shares in Weak plc *and* those same net assets, we are clearly double counting.

19.6.2 Step 2 in the consolidation process: eliminate shareholders' funds of the subsidiary

On consolidation, therefore, it is necessary to set the cost of the shares in the books of Strong plc (made to acquire the net assets of Weak plc) against the shares and reserves in the books of Weak plc (which represent the net assets of Weak plc); this is referred to as **elimination on consolidation**.

No entries are made in the books of the individual companies. The elimination will only appear in the consolidation working papers, as shown in Figure 19.7. Note that the reserves and the issued share capital of Weak plc have been eliminated on consolidation. This will always occur on consolidation, so that whenever one looks at a set of consolidated accounts, only the issued share capital and reserves of the parent company appear.

The consolidated balance sheet of the Strong Group as at 1 January 20X1 is shown in Figure 19.8. Note again that the share capital and reserves are those of the parent company only.

Figure 19.7 Elimination entries in the consolidated working papers as at 1 January 20X1.

	Strong plc £	Weak plc £	Aggregate £	Eliminate Dr/(Cr) £	Group £
Fixed assets	12,250	5,500	17,750		17,750
Investment in Weak plc	7,500		7,500	(7,500)	—
Net current assets/(liabilities)	(4,750)	2,000	(2,750)		(2,750)
	15,000	7,500	22,500		15,000
Ordinary share capital	8,750	5,000	13,750		8,750
Profit and loss balance	6,250	2,500	8,750	2,500	6,250
	15,000	7,500	22,500	0	15,000

Figure 19.7 (cont.)

Supporting the consolidation working papers by ledger accounts:

Investment in Weak plc

	£			£
I Jan 20X1 Bank	7,500	I Jan 20X1	Share capital of Weak plc	5,000
			Reserves of Weak plc	2,500
	7,500			7,500

Share capital of Weak plc

	£			£
I Jan 20X1 Investment in		I Jan 20X1	Balance	5,000
Weak plc	5,000			
	5,000			5,000

Reserves of Weak plc

	£			£
I Jan 20X1 Investment in		I Jan 20X1	Balance	2,500
Weak plc	2,500			
	2,500			2,500

Consolidated reserves in consolidated balance sheet

	£			£
		I Jan 20X1	Strong plc	6,250

Alternatively, the balances on the investment in Weak, share capital of Weak and reserves of Weak could be transferred to a cost of control account:

Cost of control account

	£			£
I Jan 20X1 Investment in		I Jan 20X1	Share capital of Weak plc	5,000
Weak plc	7,500		Reserves of Weak plc	2,500
	7,500			7,500

Figure 19.8 Consolidated balance sheet of Strong Group as at I January 20X1.

	£	Explanatory Notes
Fixed assets	17,750	Includes both parent and subsidiary
Net current assets	(2,750)	Includes both parent and subsidiary
	15,000	
Ordinary share capital	8,750	Parent shares only
Profit and loss balance	6,250	Parent reserves only
	15,000	

19.7 Parent company: treatment of positive and negative goodwill

How is the investment in a subsidiary dealt with when the shares are acquired for a cash consideration that is more or less than the net asset value of the shares?

The acquiring company is often prepared to pay a **premium** to obtain control of the other company. The amount of the premium will, of course, be influenced by the motive for the acquisition. This premium is **positive goodwill**.

For example, Galen Holdings plc, which is an integrated pharmaceutical company manufacturing and supplying ethical pharmaceutical products, reported two acquisitions, Bartholomew Rhodes Ltd and ICTI Inc., in the note to the Cash Flow Statement in their 1999 Annual Report and Accounts. This showed:

	£000
Net assets acquired	318
Goodwill	35,543
Consideration	35,861
Consideration satisfied by:	
Cash	23,433
Related costs of acquisition	276
Deferred consideration (payable January 2000)	1,823
Contingent consideration	10,329
	35,861

The commercial reason for the goodwill of £35,543,000 was explained as follows:

> The major therapeutic categories of prescription medicines we sell are analgesics, gastrointestinal, respiratory, cardiovascular and antibiotics and good progress has been made in all categories. The Bartholomew Rhodes acquisition has provided products in the analgesic, respiratory and cardiovascular categories and will further strengthen our business in the future.

The rationale for the acquisition of ICTI Inc. was also spelt out.

Sometimes the shares of the acquiree company do not achieve their net asset value. Perhaps the trading record is unattractive or the assets are specialist and not easily realised separately. There is then a **discount** on acquisition, or **negative goodwill**.

Let us assume that Strong plc has acquired all of the issued share capital of Weak plc on 1 January 20X1, paying £2.00 in cash for each £1 share. The effect on the balance sheets of Strong plc and Weak plc as at 1 January 20X1 would then be as in Figure 19.9.

For the holding company, the only change occurs in the carrying value of the investment and the net current assets arising from the payment of a price of £2 per share on 5,000 shares rather than £1.50. There is no accounting effect for the subsidiary.

19.8 Consolidated accounts: treatment of positive goodwill

We will now explain the preparation of consolidated accounts for Strong plc and its wholly owned subsidiary, Weak plc, as at the date of acquisition, where the cash consideration is more than the net asset value of the subsidiary.

Figure 19.9   Balance sheets as at 1 January 20X1.

	Strong plc £1.50 per £1 share	Strong plc £2.00 per £1 share	Weak plc at both prices
	£	£	£
Fixed assets	12,250	12,250	5,500
Investment in Weak plc	7,500	10,000	
Net current assets/(liabilities)	(4,750)	(7,250)	2,000
	15,000	15,000	7,500
Ordinary share capital	8,750	8,750	5,000
Profit and loss balance	6,250	6,250	2,500
	15,000	15,000	7,500

Figure 19.10   Elimination entries in the consolidated working papers where a premium has been paid on acquisition.

	Strong plc	Weak plc	Aggregate	Eliminate Dr/(Cr)	Group
	£	£	£	£	£
Fixed assets	12,250	5,500	17,750		17,750
Investment in Weak plc	10,000		10,000	(7,500)	2,500
Net current assets/(liabilities)	(7,250)	2,000	(5,250)		(5,250)
	15,000	7,500	22,500		15,000
Ordinary share capital	8,750	5,000	13,750	5,000	8,750
Profit and loss balance	6,250	2,500	8,750	2,500	6,250
	15,000	7,500	22,500	0	15,000

Supporting the consolidation workings papers by ledger accounts:

Investment in Weak plc

		£			£
1 Jan 20X1	Bank	10,000	1 Jan 20X1	Share capital of Weak plc	5,000
				Reserves of Weak plc	2,500
				Balance c/d	**2,500**
		10,000			10,000
1 Jan 20X1	Balance b/d	2,500			

Share capital of Weak plc

		£			£
1 Jan 20X1	Investment in Weak plc	5,000	1 Jan 20X1	Balance	5,000
		5,000			5,000

Figure 19.10 (cont.)

Reserves of Weak plc

	£			£
I Jan 20XI Investment in		I Jan 20XI Balance		2,500
Weak plc	2,500			
	2,500			2,500

Alternatively, using a cost of control account:

Cost of control account/goodwill account

	£		£
I Jan 20XI Investment in		I Jan 20XI Share capital of Weak plc	5,000
Weak plc	10,000	Reserves of Weak plc	2,500
		Balance c/d	**2,500**
	10,000		10,000
Balance b/d	**2,500**		

Consolidated reserves in consolidated balance sheet

	£		£
		I Jan 20XI Strong plc	6,250

We still need to eliminate the share capital and reserves of the subsidiary against the amount of £10,000 paid to acquire them. However, the amount paid exceeded the net asset value of £7,500. The difference is classified as an intangible asset called **goodwill**. The elimination appears in the consolidation working papers as shown in Figure 19.10.

The consolidated balance sheet will have an additional debit balance of £2,500. This debit balance is variously described as **premium on acquisition** or **cost of control** or **goodwill**. The consolidated balance sheet is shown in Figure 19.11.

The accounting treatment of goodwill is covered in FRS 10 *Goodwill and Intangible Assets* which makes the presumption that the useful economic life of goodwill will not exceed 20 years i.e. that goodwill will be amortised over a period not exceeding 20 years. This is considered in more detail in Chapter 16.

Figure 19.11 Consolidated balance sheet of Strong Group as at I January 20XI.

	£	Explanatory notes
Fixed assets		
Intangible – goodwill	**2,500**	Excess of payment over net assets acquired
Tangible	17,750	
Net current assets/(liabilities)	(5,250)	Increased by payment for cost of control
	15,000	
Ordinary share capital	8,750	
Profit and loss balance	6,250	
	15,000	

C – ACQUIRING SHARES FOR CASH WHERE FAIR VALUES OF ASSETS AND LIABILITIES DIFFER FROM BOOK VALUES

19.9   Consolidated accounts: effects of fair values

If the fair value of the net assets of the parent company and subsidiary differ from their book values at the date of acquisition, it might be expected that the net assets of the holding company and subsidiary would be dealt with in a similar fashion when preparing a set of consolidated accounts. This is not so.

Parent company net asset values

The values that appear in the books of the parent company will continue to be the values that are included in the consolidated working papers and consolidated accounts, i.e. they will be included at their **existing net book values**.

Subsidiary company net asset values.

In the acquiring company's consolidated accounts, the separable net tangible and net intangible assets acquired are recorded at fair value, as at the date of acquisition. Any difference between the fair value and the book value will be reflected in the goodwill calculation.

19.9.1   What do we mean by fair value?

The fair value is the value that willing parties would agree to if the transaction were at arm's length. The FRS gives more detailed guidance in relation to individual items.[10] The valuations for particular types of asset and liability are as follows:

● **Tangible fixed assets.** Fair value should be based on **market value**, if assets similar in type and condition are bought and sold on the open market; or depreciated replacement cost, reflecting the acquired business's normal buying process and the sources of supply and prices available to it. The fair value should **not exceed the recoverable amount** of the asset, which is defined as the greater of the net realisable value and, where appropriate, the value in use.

● **Intangible assets.** Where an intangible asset is recognised, its fair value should be based on its **replacement cost**, which is normally its estimated market value.

● **Stocks and work-in-progress.** Stocks and work-in-progress should be valued at the **lower** of net realisable value and replacement cost, which is the current cost of bringing the stocks to their present location and condition.

● **Quoted investments.** These should be valued at **market price** adjusted if necessary for unusual price fluctuations or for the size of the holding.

● **Monetary assets and liabilities.** Fair value should take into account the amounts expected to be received or paid and their **timing**. Fair value should be determined by reference to market prices, where available, by reference to the current price at which the business could acquire similar assets or enter into similar obligations, or by **discounting to present value**.

● **Contingencies**. These should be measured at fair values where these can be determined. For this purpose, reasonable **estimates of the expected outcome** may be made.

The following example from the 1999 Annual Report and Accounts of Galen Holdings plc, note 27, illustrates the re-statement of book values to fair values:

	Book value	Fair value adjustment	Fair value	ICTI Inc.	Other	Total
	£000	£000	£000	£000	£000	£000
Tangible fixed assets	—	—		170	11	181
Stock	604	(300)	304	—	—	304
Debtors	1,191	—	1,191	399	23	1,613
Cash	(218)	—	(218)	209	3	(6)
Creditors	(1,802)	—	(1,802)	(211)	(13)	(2,026)
Taxation	301	—	301	—	—	301
Lease obligations	—	—	—	(49)	—	(49)
Net assets acquired	76	(300)	(224)	518	24	318
Goodwill						35,543
Consideration						35,861

The fair value adjustment to stock reflects a write-down to estimated realisable value.

19.9.2 What is the effect on the fair values if the acquirer intends to incur additional liabilities after the date of the acquisition?

In determining fair values, the ASB has adopted an overriding principle that events occurring after the acquisition that resulted in the recognition of additional liabilities or the impairment of existing assets do not affect the fair values as at the date of acquisition. The effect of such adjustment to the liabilities or assets should be reflected in the accounts of the acquirer of that period and not treated as pre-acquisition. This means that identifiable liabilities are limited to obligations of the acquired entity that **existed at the date of acquisition**.

Note that there is a difference between additional liabilities which the acquirer might wish to enter into after acquisition and establishing a higher figure for liabilities as more information becomes available about the position **as at the date of acquisition**.

In practice, it may not always be possible for the acquirer to establish absolutely accurate fair values for the individual assets and liabilities as at the date of the acquisition e.g. the provision for bad debts is an estimate and debtors might realise a materially different figure in the period following the acquisition. If the fair value of the assets acquired is amended downwards then this means that the goodwill figure should be amended upwards. FRS 7 allows for this by providing that, if it has not been possible to complete the investigation for determining fair values by the date on which the first post-acquisition financial statements are approved, provisional valuations should be made and that these should be amended, if necessary, in the next financial statements **with a corresponding adjustment to goodwill**.

19.10 Preparing consolidated accounts where fair value differs from book values of subsidiary's net assets

Let us assume that the fair value of Weak plc's fixed assets is £5,750 and that the fair value of the net current assets is the same as the book value of £2,000. Let us further assume that all of the Weak plc shares were acquired for a cash payment of £2.00 per share.

The fair value of the fixed assets is £250 more than the book value and the amount paid for the goodwill is going to be reduced by this amount of £250, as shown in Figure 19.12, where the goodwill of £2,500 arising from the use of book values is reduced to £2,250 on the introduction of the fair value for the subsidiary's assets.

The consolidated balance sheet and the Weak plc balance sheet are shown in Figure 19.13. Note particularly that the consolidated balance sheet has a mixture of valuations, as follows:

● The parent company's net assets are brought in at their **net book value**.

● The subsidiary's net assets are brought in at their **fair value**.

Figure 19.12 Elimination entries in the consolidated working papers where a premium has been paid on acquisition and the subsidiary's assets adjusted to fair values.

	Strong plc	Weak plc	Aggregate	Eliminate Dr/(Cr)	Group
	£	£	£	£	£
Fixed assets	12,250	5,500	17,750	250	18,000
Investment in Weak plc	10,000		10,000	(7,750)	2,250
Net current assets/(liabilities)	(7,250)	2,000	(5,250)		(5,250)
	15,000	7,500	22,500		15,000
Ordinary share capital	8,750	5,000	13,750	5,000	8,750
Profit and loss balance	6,250	2,500	8,750	2,500	6,250
	15,000	7,500	22,500	0	15,000

Supporting the consolidation workings papers by ledger accounts:

Fixed assets of Weak plc			
	£		£
1 Jan 20X1 Balance	5,500	1 Jan 20X1 **Balance c/d**	**5,750**
1 Jan 20X1 Investment in			
Weak plc	250		
	5,750		5,750

Investment in Weak plc			
	£		£
1 Jan 20X1 Bank	10,000	1 Jan 20X1 Share capital of Weak plc	5,000
		1 Jan 20X1 Reserves of Weak plc	2,500
		1 Jan 20X1 Fixed assets of Weak plc	250
		Balance c/d	**2,250**
	10,000		10,000
1 Jan 20X1 Balance b/d	2,250		

Figure 19.12 (cont.)

Share capital of Weak plc

		£			£
1 Jan 20X1	Investment in		1 Jan 20X1	Balance	5,000
	Weak plc	5,000			
		5,000			5,000

Reserves of Weak plc

		£			£
1 Jan 20X1	Investment in		1 Jan 20X1	Balance	2,500
	Weak plc	2,500			
		2,500			2,500

Alternatively, using a cost of control account:

Cost of control account

		£			£
1 Jan 20X1	Investment in		1 Jan 20X1	Share capital of Weak plc	5,000
	Weak plc	10,000		Reserves of Weak plc	2,500
				Fixed assets	250
				Balance c/d	**2,250**
		10,000			10,000
	Balance b/d	**2,250**			

Consolidated reserves in consolidated balance sheet

	£			£
		1 Jan 20X1	Strong plc	6,250

Figure 19.13 Consolidated balance sheet of Strong Group as at 1 January 20X1.

	Based on book value £	Based on fair value £	Weak plc before and after the consolidation £
Fixed assets			
Intangible – goodwill	**2,500**	**2,250**	
Tangible	17,750	**18,000**	5,500
Net current assets/(liabilities)	(5,250)	(5,250)	2,000
	15,000	15,000	7,500
Ordinary share capital	8,750	8,750	5,000
Profit and loss balance	6,250	6,250	2,500
	15,000	15,000	7,500

The Weak plc balance sheet has been reproduced to emphasise that the book value in the company-only accounts of Weak plc does not need to be changed to reflect the fair value used in the consolidated accounts. This needs to be watched for carefully when preparing the consolidated accounts: if the subsidiary does not change the book value in its own accounts, it will be necessary to make an adjustment each year in the consolidated working papers, not only to change the carrying value of the asset, but also to change any **depreciation charge** that has been calculated in the subsidiary. This means that for consolidation purposes the profit in the subsidiary will be overstated by the difference in depreciation charge using book value rather than fair value, assuming that the fair value exceeds the book value. It might be group policy for the subsidiary company to revise its assets and liabilities to fair values, which reduces the risk of errors on consolidating.

19.11 Applying FRS 7 to specific situations

The approach taken by FRS is that the identifiable assets and liabilities to be **recognised** should be those of the acquired entity that **existed** at the date of acquisition, **measured** at fair values that reflect the **conditions at the date of acquisition**.

Tangible fixed assets

It is important not to be influenced by the intention of the acquirer. For example, assume that National Kennels plc acquired all the issued shares in Brighton Kennel Ltd on 1 January 20X0; that they sold certain of the Brighton Kennel Ltd equipment (which duplicated their existing equipment) on 2 January 20X0 for £69,000 and calculated a goodwill figure of £100,000 with the equipment included in the calculation at its net realisable value of £69,000.

Although the directors were proposing to treat the figure of £69,000 as the fair value of the equipment for the purpose of calculating the goodwill, this would not satisfy the FRS 7 criteria. The following additional information was provided by the directors:

Net book value	£216,000
Depreciated replacement cost	£270,000
Net realisable value	£69,000
Value in use:	
Present value of the future cash flows (assuming the equipment had not been sold)	£200,000

Although the initial thought would be to use the figure of £69,000, the correct fair value is the deprival value i.e. the lower of the depreciated replacement cost and the recoverable amount (being the higher of net realisable value and the value in use). The fair value using the deprival value approach is £200,000. The effect on the accounts for the year ended 31 December 20X0 would be:

Goodwill reduced by £131,000 to a negative figure of (£31,000).
Equipment increased by £131,000.
Negative goodwill to be released immediately to the Statement of Total Recognised Gains and Losses (FRS 10 para. 49) on the sale of the equipment.
A loss on sale of equipment charged to the profit and loss account of £131,000.

In many acquisition situations it is the practice to identify assets that are regarded as surplus to requirements by the acquirer e.g. assets that do not fit into the core business of the acquirer or where the production needs are already being adequately serviced. It would not be acceptable under FRS 7 to value these at net realisable value and a deprival value approach would need to be taken.

Contingencies

Contingent assets and liabilities are different in that under normal reporting practices they may not be recognised in the balance sheet. For the fair value exercise they will need to be estimated and included.

It could also be argued that as no provision would be allowed under FRS 12 because the contingency was not probable i.e.less than 50% likely, then it should not be included in the fair value exercise. The reasoning is that if it crystallised in the post-acquisition period this would have been due to a change of circumstances after the date of acquisition which changed the status from possible to probable.

However, it needs to be recognised that companies will not be neutral in there treatment of contingent items. This arises because of the FRS 7 para. 25 rule restricting the period within which fair values may be revised after the date of acquisition:

> Any necessary adjustments to provisional fair values and the corresponding adjustment to purchased goodwill should be incorporated in the financial statements for the first full financial year following the acquisition. Thereafter, any adjustments, except for the correction of fundamental errors, which should be accounted for as prior period adjustments, should be recognised as profits or losses when they are identified.

Assume that there is a negligence claim for £200,000 and the assessment is that it is possible but not probable to crystallise. As it is not probable, it will not have been provided for in the acquiree company's accounts. It would therefore seem to be prudent to include an estimate. In the fair value exercise this is achieved by increasing the goodwill with accounting entries as follows:

Dr Goodwill	£200,000
Cr Contingent Liability	£200,000

However, if the contingent liability does not crystallise in two years' time, after the date when Goodwill is required to be revised, the contingent liability is recognised as a profit and credited to the profit and loss account. The net result, assuming that goodwill is being amortised over 20 years, will be an annual charge to the P & L account in the year of acquisition and the following two years of £10,000 i.e. a total charge of £30,000 but a credit of £200,000 in the third year – a highly attractive outcome for any finance director!

D – MINORITY INTERESTS

19.12 Treatment of minority interests in consolidated accounts

We have prepared the consolidated balance sheet so far on the basis that Weak plc is a wholly owned subsidiary of Strong plc. We have included all of the assets and liabilities of the subsidiary company in the consolidated balance sheet because they were **all owned** by the holding company. But what happens if the holding company acquires less than 100% of the issued shares and therefore owns less than 100% of the net assets?

19.12.1 Conventional practice where the parent company owns less than 100% of the net assets of the subsidiary

The conventional consolidation practice is to **include all resources that are under the control** of the directors of the holding company, i.e. include all net assets just as we did when they were all owned by the holding company. The shares and reserves that have been acquired by the parent company are still eliminated against the investment. The shares and reserves that have not been acquired need to be transferred to a separate liability heading to indicate the amount that does not belong to the holding company. This separate liability is called **minority interest**.

Let us assume that Strong plc acquired 60% of the voting shares at a price of £2 per share. The balance sheet of Strong plc immediately after the acquisition is shown in Figure 19.14.

Step 1 in the consolidation process

Aggregate all balances as in Figure 19.15.

Figure 19.14 Balance sheet of Strong plc as at the date of acquisition of 60% of the shares in Weak plc for cash.

	£
Fixed assets	12,250
Investment in subsidiary	6,000
Net current assets/(liabilities)	(3,250)
	15,000
Ordinary share capital	8,750
Profit and loss balance	6,250
	15,000

Figure 19.15 Aggregated assets and liabilities as at 1 January 20X1.

	Strong plc £	Weak plc £	Aggregate £
Fixed assets	12,250	5,500	17,750
Investment in Weak plc	6,000		6,000
Net current assets/(liabilities)	(3,250)	2,000	(1,250)
Total net assets	15,000	7,500	22,500
Ordinary share capital	8,750	5,000	13,750
Profit and loss balance	6,250	2,500	8,750
	15,000	7,500	22,500

Step 2 in the consolidation process

Eliminate shareholders' funds of the subsidiary against the investment in subsidiary, as in Figure 19.16. The net assets are correctly stated at £18,000, but the share capital and reserves need to be adjusted to show the minority interest of 40% under a separate heading.

Step 3 in the consolidation process

Eliminate shareholders' funds of the subsidiary that belong to the minority shareholders. This is simply a transfer from the share capital and reserves of Weak plc to a separate account known as **minority interest**. The consolidation worksheet would be as in Figure 19.17. The minority shareholders are entitled to 40% of the net assets of £7,500, which is the £3,000 calculated in Figure 19.17. The consolidated balance sheet will be as in Figure 19.18.

Figure 19.16 Entries in the consolidated working papers eliminating the investment.

	Strong plc	Weak plc	Aggregate	Eliminate Dr/(Cr)	Group
	£	£	£	£	£
Fixed assets	12,250	5,500	17,750		17,750
Investment in Weak plc	6,000		6,000	(4,500)	**1,500**
Net current assets	(3,250)	2,000	(1,250)	_____	(1,250)
	15,000	7,500	22,500		18,000
Ordinary share capital	8,750	5,000	13,750	3,000	10,750
Profit and loss balance	6,250	2,500	8,750	1,500	7,250
	15,000	7,500	22,500	0	18,000

Supporting the consolidation workings papers by ledger accounts:

Investment in Weak plc			
	£		£
1 Jan 20X1 Bank	6,000	1 Jan 20X1 Share capital of Weak plc	3,000
		Reserves of Weak plc	1,500
		Balance c/d	**1,500**
	6,000		6,000
1 Jan 20X1 Balance b/d	1,500		

Share capital of Weak plc			
	£		£
1 Jan 20X1 Investment in Weak plc	3,000	1 Jan 20X1 Balance	5,000

Reserves of Weak plc			
	£		£
1 Jan 20X1 Investment in Weak plc	1,500	1 Jan 20X1 Balance	2,500

Figure 19.17   Entries in the consolidated working papers recording the minority interest.

	Strong plc	Weak plc	Aggregate	Eliminate Dr/(Cr)	Group
	£	£	£	£	£
Fixed assets	12,250	5,500	17,750		17,750
Investment in Weak plc	6,000		6,000	(4,500)	1,500
Net current assets	(3,250)	2,000	(1,250)		(1,250)
	15,000	7,500	22,500		18,000
Ordinary share capital	8,750	5,000	13,750	3,000	
				2,000	8,750
Profit and loss balance	6,250	2,500	8,750	1,500	
				1,000	6,250
Minority interest				**(3,000)**	**3,000**
	15,000	7,500	22,500	0	18,000

Supporting the consolidation workings papers by ledger accounts:

Investment in Weak plc

		£			£
I Jan 20XI	Bank	6,000	I Jan 20XI	Share capital of Weak plc	3,000
				Reserves of Weak plc	1,500
				Balance c/d	**1,500**
		6,000			6,000
I Jan 20XI	Balance b/d	1,500			

Share capital of Weak plc

		£			£
I Jan 20XI	Investment in Weak plc	3,000	I Jan 20XI	Balance	5,000
I Jan 20XI	**Minority interest**	**2,000**			
		5,000			5,000

Reserves of Weak plc

		£			£
I Jan 20XI	Investment in Weak plc	1,500	I Jan 20XI	Balance	2,500
I Jan 20XI	**Minority interest**	**1,000**			
		2,500			2,500

Figure 19.17 (cont.)

Alternatively, using a cost of control account:

Cost of control account

		£			£
I Jan 20X1	Investment in		I Jan 20X1	Share capital of Weak plc	3,000
	Weak plc	6,000		Reserves of Weak plc	1,500
				Balance c/d	**1,500**
		6,000			6,000
	Balance b/d	**1,500**			

Minority interest

		£			£
I Jan 20X1	Balance c/d	3,000	I Jan 20X1	Share capital	2,000
			I Jan 20X1	Reserves	1,000
		3,000			3,000
			I Jan 20X1	Balance b/d	3,000

Consolidated reserves in consolidated balance sheet

	£			£
		I Jan 20X1	Strong plc	6,250

Figure 19.18 Consolidated balance sheet of Strong Group as at 1 January 20X1 including goodwill.

	£
Fixed assets	
Intangible – goodwill	**1,500**
Tangible	17,750
Net current assets/(liabilities)	(1,250)
	18,000
Ordinary share capital	8,750
Profit and loss balance	6,250
Minority interest	**3,000**
	18,000

How are fair value adjustments treated when there is a minority interest?

The **control concept** requires all of the net assets of the subsidiary to be revalued to fair value and the minority interest to be stated as a percentage of this fair value. The minority shareholders are regarded as internal to the group and are stated at fair value.

The alternative would be to include mixed values in the consolidated balance sheet i.e. the subsidiary's net assets being included as a mix of parent % of fair value and minority % of book value. The control concept forbids this treatment.

19.12.2 Alternative consolidation treatment of minority shareholders where the holding company owns less than 100% of the issued shares of the subsidiary

An alternative consolidation practice that is not used in the UK for controlled subsidiaries is **proportional consolidation**. This involves deducting from all the balances appearing in the accounts of the subsidiary the proportion that does not belong to the holding company. In the Strong example, this would involve deducting 40% from each of the items in the Weak plc balance sheet. This is illustrated in Figure 12.19.

The proportional consolidation technique was rejected in the EC Seventh Directive on the grounds that including, for example, 60% of the value of a factory and 60% of its sales gives an incomplete and possibly misleading picture of the resources available to the group and the performance achieved.[11] However, the technique has been used in the oil and gas and construction industries where joint ventures are often entered into for specific projects.[12] It is also used when consolidating partnership interests into a set of consolidated accounts. FRS 9 *Associates and Joint Ventures* issued in 1997 proposed that joint ventures, whether corporate or non-corporate, be accounted for under the expanded equity method as for associates and should not be proportionately consolidated.[13]

The assets and liabilities in the illustration in Figure 19.19 do not show proportional consolidation to its best effect. Where there are significant minority holdings it could be argued that a proportional presentation is useful when presented in addition to the full consolidation because it shows the specific items in which the minority has an interest and their relative size e.g. the following extract from the 1998 Annual Report of Rodamco N.V.

Figure 19.19 Elimination entries in the consolidated working papers following proportional consolidation process.

	Strong plc £	Weak plc 100% £	Weak plc 60% £	Aggregate £	Eliminate Dr/(Cr) £	Group £
Fixed assets	12,250	5,500	3,300	15,550		15,550
Investment in Weak plc	6,000			6,000	(4,500)	1,500
Net current assets	(3,250)	2,000	1,200	(2,050)	____	(2,050)
	15,000	7,500	4,500	19,500		15,000
Ordinary shares	8,750	5,000	3,000	11,750	3,000	8,750
Profit and loss	6,250	2,500	1,500	7,750	1,500	6,250
	15,000	7,500	4,500	19,500	0	15,000

Consolidated balance sheet (fl.x million)

	28.2.1998 Proportionally consolidated	28.2.1998 Fully consolidated	28.2.1997 Proportionally consolidated
Assets			
Land and buildings			
Property	8,791	11,731	8,675
Renovation projects	872	1,002	430
Financial investments			
Shares in property companies	362	460	286
Participating interest in property companies	197	253	—
Mortgage notes receivable	210	272	190
Investments in group companies and participating interests			
Participating interest in loans to group Companies	60	60	12
Total investments	10,492	13,778	9,593
Accounts receivable	372	454	439
Other assets			
Liquid funds	689	966	923
Total assets	11,553	15,198	10,955
Liabilities			
Provisions	214	266	200
Long term debts			
Loans	1,021	1,021	951
Mortgages	945	1,190	652
Accounts payable	404	499	322
Total liabilities	2,584	2,976	2,125
Minority interest		3,253	
Shareholders' equity	8,969	8,969	8,830

This shows that more than 75% of the assets, all the loans and more than 90% of the mortgages appear in the subsidiaries' accounts.

19.12.3 Conventional consolidation measurement of the proprietary goodwill arising on consolidation when a minority interest exists

Whereas the net assets were treated applying the **control concept**, the goodwill is treated applying the **ownership concept**. Dealings in the shares of the subsidiary are regarded as external to the group with the goodwill figure of £1,500 in Figure 19.18 and represents the premium that Strong plc paid in order to **gain a controlling *ownership* interest** in Weak plc. It does not represent the goodwill of the whole entity but the 60% held by Strong plc.

Consolidated accounts prepared to provide information to the parent company shareholders are applying the **proprietary** or **parent** method. The minority interest is regarded as a type of liability as far as the parent company shareholders are concerned.

19.12.4 Alternative consolidation measurement of the entity goodwill arising on consolidation

Proprietary goodwill is the figure that you will actually find in published accounts, i.e. the cost of control. However, there is an argument that if the goodwill is introduced into the balance sheet, it should be stated at the **entity value** of 100% representing the goodwill attaching to the **economic unit** as a whole and not the 60% that attaches to the interest of the controlling shareholders' interest.

If the entity value were to be used it would be arrived at by grossing up the 60% value of £1,500 to its 100% value of £2,500. This would increase the assets in the consolidated balance sheet by £1,000 representing the amount of goodwill assumed to be attaching to the minority shareholders' interest; the minority interest would need to be correspondingly increased to give them credit for their interest in the total goodwill of £2,500.

However, the entity approach is not followed in practice and FRS 2, para. 38, specifically states that no goodwill should be attributed to the minority interest.

The argument against using £2,500 as the goodwill value in the balance sheet is that, while Strong plc might be prepared to pay a premium of £1,500 in order to **control** Weak plc, there is no certainty that it would increase this figure pro rata in relation to the number of additional shares acquired, i.e. it is a payment to gain control over the assets of the company and not to purchase a separately identifiable asset.

19.13 Consolidated accounts: treatment of negative goodwill

If the acquirer pays less than the net asset value, this gain is classified as a capital reserve in the consolidated balance sheet and is described as a **capital reserve arising on acquisition** or **negative goodwill**.

Assuming that Strong plc paid £1 per share for all 5,000 shares, the consolidated working papers would be as in Figure 19.20 and the consolidated balance sheet as in Figure 19.21.

Figure 19.20 Elimination entries in the consolidated working papers where there is negative goodwill.

	Strong plc	Weak plc	Aggregate	Eliminate Dr/(Cr)	Group
	£	£	£	£	£
Fixed assets	12,250	5,500	17,750		17,750
Investment in Weak plc	5,000		5,000	(7,500)	(2,500)
Net current assets	(2,250)	2,000	(250)		(250)
	15,000	7,500	22,500		15,000
Ordinary share capital	8,750	5,000	13,750	5,000	8,750
Profit and loss balance	6,250	2,500	8,750	2,500	6,250
	15,000	7,500	22,500	0	15,000

Figure 19.20 (cont.)

Supporting the consolidation workings papers by ledger account format:

Investment in Weak plc

	£			£
1 Jan 20X1 Bank	5,000	1 Jan 20X1	Share capital of Weak plc	5,000
			Reserves of Weak plc	2,500
1 Jan 20X1 Balance c/d	**2,500**			
	7,500			7,500
		1 Jan 20X1	Balance b/d	2,500

Share capital of Weak plc

	£			£
1 Jan 20X1 Investment in		1 Jan 20X1	Balance	5,000
Weak plc	5,000			
	5,000			5,000

Reserves of Weak plc

	£			£
1 Jan 20X1 Investment in		1 Jan 20X1	Balance	2,500
Weak plc	2,500			
	2,500			2,500

Consolidated reserves in consolidated balance sheet

	£			£
		1 Jan 20X1	Strong plc	6,250

Figure 19.21   Consolidated balance sheet of Strong Group as at 1 January 20X1.

	£	*Explanatory notes*
Fixed assets		
Tangible	17,750	
Net current assets/(liabilities)	(250)	
	17,500	
Ordinary share capital	8,750	
Profit and loss balance	6,250	
Capital reserve	**2,500**	Difference between cost of £5,000 and
	17,500	net assets of £7,500

E – INVESTMENT ACQUIRED BY ISSUE OF SHARES

19.14 Parent company share-for-share exchange

When a company takes over another company it can satisfy the consideration in a number of ways. It can offer payment in full in cash; it can offer ordinary shares in the parent company in exchange for the shares in the subsidiary; or it can offer a complex package consisting of a mixture of cash, ordinary shares and other financial instruments such as debentures, convertible bonds and deferred shares.

We consider the position where the parent company issues ordinary shares in the holding company as consideration for all of the issued ordinary shares of the subsidiary.

19.14.1 How many shares will the holding company issue?

First, we need to know the value of a Strong plc share and the agreed value of a Weak plc share. Let us assume that a Strong plc share is valued at £2 per share and a Weak plc share at its net asset value of £1.50 per share. This means that the consideration of £7,500 would be satisfied by the issue of 3,750 shares in Strong plc with a par value of £3,750 and a share premium of £3,750.

19.14.2 Balance sheet entry for the investment when acquired with a share-for-share exchange

The transaction will appear in the balance sheet as at the date of purchase as in Figure 19.22. We can see the following:

● The investment is shown as a fixed asset valued at cost with cost defined as the fair value of the consideration given.
● The net assets of Strong plc are **not reduced** as a result of the takeover of Weak plc.
● The share capital and share premium are increased; the purchase of the shares is still recorded as an investment in shares at cost in the balance sheet of Strong plc; and the accounting for the investment is not dependent on the number of shares acquired.
● The balance sheet of the subsidiary is unaffected by the exchange of shares.

Figure 19.22 Balance sheet entries of Strong plc as at the date of acquisition if Strong plc acquires 100% of the shares in Weak plc with a share-for-share exchange.

	Strong plc		Weak plc
	Before buying shares	After buying 100% of shares of Weak	Before and after
	£	£	£
Fixed assets	12,250	12,250	5,500
Investment in Weak plc		7,500	
Net current assets	2,750	2,750	2,000
	15,000	22,500	7,500
Ordinary share capital	8,750	8,750	5,000
New shares		**3,750**	
Share premium		**3,750**	
Profit and loss balance	6,250	6,250	2,500
	15,000	22,500	7,500

19.14.3   Which ratio will be different after recording the investment?

Any ratio that uses the total or net asset figure will be different, e.g. return on capital employed or capital turnover, and any ratio that uses total shareholder funds will be different, e.g. the balance sheet gearing ratio.

19.15   Consolidated accounts: acquisition accounting method after share exchange

We will explain the preparation of consolidated accounts for Strong plc and its wholly-owned subsidiary, Weak plc, as at the date of acquisition.

Assuming that the consideration was £1.50 per share, the consolidated working papers would be as in Figure 19.23 and the consolidated balance sheet as in Figure 19.24. Supporting the consolidation working papers by ledger accounts is virtually as illustrated in Figure 19.7.

Figure 19.23   Elimination entries in the consolidated working papers where this is a share-for-share exchange.

	Strong plc £	Weak plc £	Aggregate £	Eliminate Dr/(Cr) £	Group £
Fixed assets	12,250	5,500	17,750		17,750
Investment in Weak plc	7,500		7,500	(7,500)	—
Net current assets	2,750	2,000	4,750		4,750
	22,500	7,500	30,000		22,500
Ordinary share capital	8,750	5,000	13,750	5,000	8,750
New shares	3,750		3,750		3,750
Share premium	3,750		3,750		3,750
Profit and loss balance	6,250	2,500	8,750	2,500	6,250
	22,500	7,500	30,000	0	22,500

Figure 19.24   Consolidated balance sheet of Strong Group as at 1 January 20X1.

	£	Explanatory notes
Fixed assets		
Tangible	17,750	Assets of parent and subsidiary
Net current assets	4,750	Assets of parent and subsidiary
	22,500	
Ordinary share capital	12,500	Old and new shares of parent
Share premium	3,750	Premium on new shares
Profit and loss balance	6,250	Parent only
	22,500	

Note that after the issue of shares:

● The net assets of the two companies remain unchanged. The fixed assets and net current assets of Strong remain at £12,250 and £2,750 and the fixed assets and net current assets of Weak remain at £5,500 and £2,000. When the fixed assets and net current assets are combined as a group the total fixed assets are the combined total of £17,750 and the net current assets the combined total of £4,750.
● There is a share premium account of £3,750 in the Strong balance sheet.
● The profit and loss balance of the group is only £6,250 not £6,250 + £2,500.

This means that, whereas before the acquisition Strong could have paid out a dividend of £6,250 and Weak a dividend of £2,500, after the acquisition Strong is still only able to pay a total dividend of £6,250.

19.16 Parent company treatment of share-for-share exchange with merger relief

It is illogical for dividends to be restricted because of the acquisition when no assets have left the group, e.g. in Figure 19.23 above the fixed assets and net current assets still remained at a total of £22,500. The Companies Act 1985 therefore allowed the use of **merger relief**.

Merger relief is available under section 131 Companies Act 1985 where an issuing company has, by an arrangement which includes the exchange of shares, acquired at least a 90% equity holding in another company.

Merger relief relates **not** to the consolidated accounts, but to the company-only accounts of the parent company. It allows the parent company to value the investment in its balance sheet at the fair value of the shares issued but to record any premium on the shares issued in a merger reserve account rather than a share premium account.

It would perhaps be better to describe the relief as a share premium relief rather than merger relief in that it is relieving the parent from opening a share premium account.

The example used in Figure 19.22 is amended to show, in Figure 19.25, the investment in Strong plc's balance sheet on the assumption that merger relief is available. Note that the investment is carried in the balance sheet at the **fair value of the shares issued** (to comply with FRS 4 Capital Instruments) and there is no share premium account.

Why is it important for the premium to be called merger reserve rather than share premium account?

The reason is that a share premium account is a capital reserve and may not be distributed as a dividend.

How is Strong able to use the merger reserve to make a distribution of a dividend to Strong shareholders?

The merger reserve is initially classified as unrealised profits and may not be used by Strong to make dividend payments until reclassified as realised profits. The reserve will become realised as dividends are paid by Weak to Strong out of the £2,500 pre-acquisition dividends that existed in Weak as at the date of the acquisition.

Figure 19.25 Balance sheet entries of Strong plc as at the date of acquisition if Strong plc acquires 100% of the shares in Weak plc with a share-for-share exchange.

	Before buying shares £	Acquisition accounting no merger relief	Acquisition accounting with merger relief
Fixed assets	12,250	12,250	12,250
Investment in Weak		7,500	7,500
Net current assets	2,750	2,750	2,750
	15,000	22,500	22,500
Ordinary share capital	8,750	8,750	8,750
New shares		3,750	3,750
Share premium account		3,750	—
Merger reserve		—	3,750
Profit and loss balance	6,250	6,250	6,250
	15,000	22,500	22,500

The accounting entries in Strong following a dividend payment from Weak to Strong, assuming that the whole amount of £2,500 is passed up as a dividend would be:

	£	£
Dr Cash		2,500
Cr Profit and loss account		2,500

The payment of cash from Weak to Strong means that the investment of £7,500 has been impaired and it should be written down by £2,500 in recognition of the fact that the net assets backing the investment have been reduced by £2,500. The journal entry to record this is:

	£	£
Dr Profit and loss account	2,500	
Cr Investment in Weak		2,500

But then, the attraction of the merger relief takes effect – for every £1 written off the investment £1 can be transferred from the merger reserve to the profit and loss account. This means that the £2,500 has been reclassified as realised profit and has been made available to Strong to distribute as a dividend to the Strong shareholders.

In practice, it is more likely that the Weak pre-acquisition reserves of £2,500 would be distributed over a period and the reclassification from unrealised to realised would occur progressively as dividends were passed up to the parent.

F – MERGER ACCOUNTING

19.17 Explanation of the merger accounting method

The method that we have used so far in this chapter to produce the consolidated balance sheet as at the date of acquisition is known as **acquisition accounting**. It assumes that the holding company has depleted its net assets to acquire the net assets represented by the share capital and reserves of the subsidiary as at the date of acquisition.

We have seen that merger relief is available in the accounts of the **parent** company when the consideration has been satisfied by the issue of shares in the parent so that the net assets of the parent have not been depleted.

There is an alternative method, known as **merger accounting**, which is available when the shares of a subsidiary are acquired by a share-for-share exchange and no assets leave the group.

There are a number of advantages to the parent from using merger accounting, two of which are:

● The full year's profit of the acquired company are brought into the consolidated profit and loss account although the acquisition might not have actually taken place until the last day of the accounting period. This allows a company to achieve apparent earnings growth in the current financial year by acquiring the shares in a profitable company and merging the profits at the year end.

● The pre-acquisition profits of the subsidiary are not capitalised and remain available for distribution as a dividend to the Strong shareholders. The effect is the same as that achieved by applying the merger relief provisions described above.

Given these advantages, it would clearly be to the benefit of Strong to treat every acquisition as a merger accounted for using merger accounting. To avoid companies doing this the Companies Act and later the ASB have set down criteria that must be satisfied before merger accounting can be applied.

19.17.1 Companies Act criteria

We have been assuming so far that a dominant, acquiring company wins control of another company. If it pays cash to gain control, the net current assets of the parent company are depleted.

However, there may be a mutual agreement between two companies to merge or pool their resources as equal partners, with a view to trading as a combined group. This might be accompanied by an agreement to exchange shares, so that the resources of the combined group are the aggregate of the individual company's resources, i.e. no assets will have left the group.

Criteria have been established by the Companies Act and professional standards to regulate when merger accounting may be used. The criteria set out in the Companies Act are as follows:[14]

● At least 90% in nominal value of the equity shares of the subsidiary are held by the parent or its subsidiaries.

● The shares were obtained as a result of an arrangement involving the issue of equity by the parent or its subsidiaries.

● The fair value of non-equity consideration given by the parent and its subsidiaries did not exceed 10% of the nominal value of the equity shares issued.

It is important to note that, because the last criterion uses 10% of the **nominal** value of the equity shares rather than 10% of the **fair** value of the equity shares when there is a mixture of equity and non-equity consideration, it is a difficult criterion to satisfy whenever there is a mixture.

19.17.2 FRS 6 *Acquisitions and Mergers* criteria

The ASB has defined a merger in FRS 6 *Acquisitions and Mergers* as:

> A business combination that results in the creation of a new reporting entity formed from the combining parties, in which the shareholders of the combining parties come together in a partnership for the mutual sharing of the risks and benefits of the combined entity, and in which no party to the combination in substance obtains control over any other, or is otherwise seen to be dominant, whether by virtue of the proportion of its shareholders' rights in the combined entity, the influence of its directors or otherwise.[15]

It has also set out in FRS 6 the following additional points:[16]

- No party to the combination is portrayed as either acquirer or acquired, either by its own board or management or by that of another party to the combination.

- All parties to the combination, as represented by the boards of directors or their appointees, participate in establishing the management structure for the combined entity and in selecting the management personnel, and such decisions are made on the basis of a consensus between the parties to the combination rather than purely by exercise of voting rights.

- The relative sizes of the combining entities are not so disparate that one party dominates the combined entity by virtue of its relative size.

  (It is interesting to consider this criterion in more detail. There would be a presumption that one party was dominant if it was more than 50% larger than the other party. The test for being 50% larger is to look at the shareholdings. If, for example, there were two shareholders, Arnold and Bennett, in the parent company and two shareholders, Edward and Rutherford, in the subsidiary then the test would be to look at their respective holdings in the parent company after the combination. If Arnold and Bennett jointly held 240 shares in the parent, then Edward and Rutherford would need to jointly own more than 180 shares to satisfy this relative size criteria.

  If the group could produce evidence that the parties were working collaboratively together the presumption of a dominant party could be avoided.)

- Under the terms of the combination or related arrangements, the consideration received by equity shareholders of each party to the combination, in relation to their equity shareholding, comprises primarily equity shares in the combined entity.

- No equity shareholders of any of the combined entities retain any material interest in the future performance of only part of the combined entity.

19.18 Consolidated accounts: merger accounting method

We will now explain the preparation of consolidated accounts for Strong plc and its wholly-owned subsidiary, Weak plc, as at the date of acquisition using merger accounting.

The aim of merger accounting is to present the group accounts as if the companies that have combined have always been operating as a single group. The meaning of this is as follows:

● The shares issued by Strong plc would be issued at their nominal value and no share premium would be taken into account in the company-only accounts or in the consolidated accounts, assuming that merger relief is available.

● The Investment in Weak plc would be carried in the Strong plc balance sheet at the nominal value of the shares issued, which means that there will be no goodwill on consolidation using the merger accounting method.

● The book values of the assets and liabilities of the subsidiary are included in the consolidation, even though the fair values might be different.

● There is an aggregation of the book values of net assets.

● The reserves of Weak plc are not treated as being pre-acquisition, but are aggregated with those of Strong plc in the consolidated balance sheet.

● Adjustments are kept to a minimum and would include only adjustments required to adopt uniform accounting policies within the group.

The example used in Figure 19.23 is reworked using the merger accounting method, as shown in Figures 19.26 and 19.27. Note the following:

● The tangible assets are at the same figure because the acquisition example had assumed that the book value and fair value of the subsidiary were the same; if the fair value of the subsidiary's fixed assets were to be £5,750, then the acquisition accounting balance sheet would have tangible assets of £18,000 whereas the merger accounting balance sheet would remain at £17,750.

● There is no share premium in the merger accounting method.

● The difference between the nominal value of the shares issued and the nominal value of the shares acquired is treated as:

 – a **capital reserve** if the issued nominal value is lower than the acquired nominal value; and

 – a reduction in one of the consolidated reserves if the issued nominal value is higher than the acquired nominal value. Normal practice is to apply it first against the most restricted categories of reserve.

● The available reserves in the merger accounting method are the total of the reserves of both companies. The pre-acquisition profits of the subsidiary are not capitalised as in the acquisition method.

. 19.18.1 Which method is preferred by management?

Management has generally favoured the merger accounting method because the reserves are not capitalised and no goodwill figure needs to be amortised against future profits. However, the FRS 6 provisions are so stringent that most business combinations that have been accounted for as mergers would not meet the criteria laid down by FRS 6. It is therefore likely that merger accounting will be a rare occurrence as most business combinations will have to be regarded as acquisitions.[17]

Figure 19.26 Elimination entries in the consolidated working papers where there is a share-for-share exchange.

	Strong plc	Weak plc	Aggregate	Eliminate Dr/(Cr)	Group
	£	£	£	£	£
Fixed assets	12,250	5,500	17,750		17,750
Investment in Weak plc	3,750		3,750	(3,750)	
Net current assets	2,750	2,000	4,750		4,750
	18,750	7,500	26,250		22,500
Ordinary share capital	12,500	5,000	17,500	3,750	12,500
Capital reserve				(a)	1,250
Profit and loss balance	6,250	2,500	8,750		8,750
	18,750	7,500	26,250	0	22,500

Supporting the consolidation working papers by ledger accounts:

Investment in Weak plc

	£		£
I Jan 20X1 Share capital	3,750	I Jan 20X1 Share capital of Weak plc	3,750
	3,750		3,750

Share Capital of Weak plc

	£		£
I Jan 20X1 Investment in Weak plc	3,750	I Jan 20X1 Balance	5,000
I Jan 20X1 Capital reserve	1,250 (a)		
	5,000		5,000

Reserves of Weak plc

	£		£
I Jan 20X1 Consolidated reserves	2,500	I Jan 20X1 Balance	2,500
	2,500		2,500

Capital reserve

	£		£
		I Jan 20X1 Share capital of Weak plc	1,250

Consolidated reserves in consolidated balance sheet

	£		£
I Jan 20X1 Balance c/d	8,750	I Jan 20X1 Strong plc	6,250
		I Jan 20X1 Weak plc	2,500
	8,750		8,750

Figure 19.27 Consolidated balance sheet of Strong Group as at 1 January 20X1.

Consolidated balance sheet of Strong Group as at 1 January 20X1 using acquisition accounting	£	Consolidated balance sheet of Strong Group as at 1 January 20X1 using merger accounting	£
Fixed assets		Fixed assets	
Tangible	17,750	Tangible	17,750
Net current assets	4,750	Net current assets	4,750
	22,500		22,500
Ordinary share capital	12,500	Ordinary shares	12,500
Share premium	3,750		
		Capital reserve	**1,250**
Profit and loss a/c	6,250	**Profit and loss a/c**	**8,750**
	22,500		22,500

19.18.2 Which method is used by other countries?

There is a need for international convergence on the method for accounting for business combinations.[18] At present, countries with more permissive regulations for treating business combinations as a merger are perceived as having an unfair advantage when they compete in making take-over bids. The perception is that their profits are overstated comparatively because there is no goodwill to amortise and pre-acquisition profits of acquired companies have not been required to be capitalised.

National standards vary. The US standards are, for example, more permissive in allowing merger accounting than Canadian standards. Canadian companies are extremely critical of this because of the interrelationship of the US and Canadian economies which means that US and Canadian companies compete in business combinations. US standards are also different from those applied in Australia, New Zealand, the UK and the IASC itself.

The existence of different standards for accounting for business combinations has become of increasing importance because cross-border deals account for more than 25% of business combinations. There is a need for convergence at a simultaneous moment to avoid individual countries feeling that they are losing competitive advantage. This is being actively sought by the G4 +1 Group which has produced a position paper, *Recommendations for Achieving Convergence on the Methods of Accounting for Business Combinations*.

Practical application

The position paper takes the view that an acquirer can be identified in virtually all business combinations and that, consequently, the acquisition accounting method should be used. It further takes the view that the situations where an acquirer cannot be identified are so rare and it is so difficult to establish separate criteria that it is preferable to apply acquisition accounting to all mergers – even if this means designating an acquirer by arbitrary means.

Conceptual acceptability

The position paper takes the view that it is conceptually deficient to retain the cost basis of the subsidiary when assets and liabilities are combined. The decision–usefulness of the information that results from merger accounting is also questioned.

Although there is a pressure at international level to require all acquisitions to be treated using acquisition accounting and we may in the future see this become mandatory, it would be unfortunate for private companies, many of which use merger accounting for its convenience and its cost effectiveness in that:

● there is no requirement to apply FRS 7 *Fair Values in Acquisition Accounting* and incurring the cost of determining fair values for each of the assets and liabilities;

● as assets are combined at book values and shares at nominal value, there is no goodwill and hence no requirement to apply FRS 10 *Goodwill and Intangible Assets* or to carry out impairment tests that may arise under FRS 11 *Impairment of Fixed Assets and Goodwill*.

Summary
. . . .

When one company acquires a controlling interest in another and the combination is treated as an acquisition, the investment in the subsidiary is recorded in the acquirer's balance sheet at the fair value of the net assets acquired and the consideration is shown at this fair value.

On consolidation, the fair value of the net assets of the subsidiary is included in the consolidated balance sheet and any difference between the fair value of the net assets and consideration is treated is positive or negative goodwill and dealt with in accordance with FRS 10 *Goodwill and Intangible Assets*.

Companies used to be able to deflate the fair value of net assets taken over by creating a provision for costs that might be incurred in the future to improve the performance of the subsidiary or restructure it. This had two adverse effects, namely, goodwill was increased and written off against reserves and so bypassed the profit and loss account of future periods, and restructuring costs were charged against the provision created on acquisition and also bypassed the profit and loss account.

The first adverse effect has been eliminated by the defining of fair values under FRS 7 *Fair Values in Acquisition Accounting* and requiring goodwill to be capitalised and amortised under FRS 10 *Goodwill and Intangible Assets*. The second adverse effect has been eliminated by the issue of FRS 6 *Acquisitions and Mergers*, making the practice of creating provisions for restructuring costs unacceptable.

When one company acquires a controlling interest in another and the combination is treated as a merger, the investment in the subsidiary is recorded in the acquirer's balance sheet at the nominal value of the shares issued and the consideration is shown at this nominal value.

On consolidation, the book value of the net assets of the subsidiary is included in the consolidated balance sheet and any difference between the nominal value of shares issued and acquired is treated as a reserve. No goodwill arises.

In the UK an attempt has been made by the ASB in FRS 6 to set stringent criteria to force companies to account for the substance of the combination. In practice, however, it is relatively simple for a company to satisfy the majority of the criteria e.g. to demonstrate that no party is portrayed as either acquirer or acquired.

The ASB measures have made it a little more difficult for companies to enjoy the benefits of merger accounting for combinations that are to all intents and purposes acquisitions, and more difficult to deflate artificially the net assets acquired in order to avoid charges being made to profit and loss accounts of future years. The two FRSs have gone a long way to removing the capacity of companies to achieve earnings growth by technical compliance that failed to reflect the commercial reality of a combination.

Review questions

1 'The Seventh Directive basically requires consolidated accounts to be prepared using the technique of acquisition accounting on a fair value basis.'[19]

  (a) Explain the terms 'acquisition accounting' and 'on a fair value basis'.

  (b) Explain why a fair value basis is required.

2 'The amounts recorded by each subsidiary against the individual headings for assets and liabilities must be incorporated in full in the consolidated accounts … even if the parent does not own all of the capital of the subsidiary and is not therefore entitled to all of its assets.'[20]

  (a) Explain why assets that are not owned by a parent company are included in the consolidated balance sheet.

  (b) Discuss how the subsidiary balances could be consolidated if it were wished to include only the amount of the assets that were owned by the parent.

3 How would you describe 'the difference between the cost of the investment to the parent and the value of the subsidiary's net assets at the time the investment is purchased'[21] if:

  (a) the difference is positive;

  (b) the difference is negative.

4 A merger exists if 'the shareholders must achieve a continuing mutual sharing in the risks and benefits of the combining undertakings'.[22] Discuss the extent to which the criteria set out in the Companies Act follows this statement.

5 'An implicit assumption is that the consolidated accounts represent merely a change in the scope of the accounts, showing the combined results of the companies, as if separate streams were put side by side and taken together, nothing added and nothing taken away.'[23] Explain the method of consolidation that is being described.

6 (a) Explain the major differences in the consolidated balance sheet between consolidations prepared using the proprietary acquisition method and the entity acquisition method.

  (b) Explain why conventional consolidation follows the proprietary acquisition method.

7 When a company becomes a subsidiary there is no required change to the book values of assets and liabilities in its books, even though the book values will be restated to fair values in the consolidated accounts. This means that there may be two different values for the same asset: one in the subsidiary's own balance sheet and the other in the consolidated accounts. Discuss how it is possible to have two different values for the same asset and for both to be true and fair.

8 Discuss arguments for and against each of the following consolidation models:

Treatment of items on consolidation under the three models

	Proprietary	*Entity*	*Parent*
Net assets of holding company	100%	100%	100%
Net assets of subsidiary	% owned	100%	100%
Goodwill on consolidation	% owned	100%	% owned
Post-acquisition subsidiary profits	% owned	100%	100%
Minority interest	None	% net assets plus % goodwill	% net assets

9 Explain why in conventional acquisition accounting the pre-acquisition reserves of the subsidiary are eliminated on consolidation and not combined with the reserves of the acquiring company.

Exercises
···················

An extract from the solution is provided in the appendix at the end of the text for exercises marked with an asterisk (*).

Questions 1–5

Use for each question the balance sheets of Parent Ltd and Daughter Ltd as at 1 January 20X1 which were as follows:

	Parent Ltd £	*Daughter Ltd* £
Ordinary shares of £1 each	40,500	9,000
Retained profits	4,500	1,800
	45,000	10,800
Net assets	45,000	10,800

*   ## Question 1

On 1 January 20X1 Parent Ltd acquired all the ordinary shares in Daughter Ltd. The purchase consideration was satisfied by the issue of 5,400 new ordinary shares in Parent Ltd. The fair value of a £1 ordinary share in Parent Ltd was £2. The fair value of the net assets in Daughter Ltd was their book value.

Required:
Prepare the balance sheet of Parent Ltd and the Consolidated Balance Sheet as at 1 January 20X1, after the transaction.

* ### Question 2

On 1 January 20X1 Parent Ltd acquired all the ordinary shares in Daughter Ltd. The purchase consideration was satisfied by the issue of 5,400 new ordinary shares in Parent Ltd. The fair value of a £1 ordinary share in Parent Ltd was £3. The fair value of the net assets in Daughter Ltd was their book value.

Required:
Prepare the balance sheet of Parent Ltd and the Consolidated Balance Sheet as at 1 January 20X1, after the transaction.

* ### Question 3

On 1 January 20X1 Parent Ltd acquired all the ordinary shares in Daughter Ltd. The purchase consideration was satisfied by the issue of 5,400 new ordinary shares in Parent Ltd. The fair value of a £1 ordinary share in Parent Ltd was £3. The fair value of the net assets in Daughter Ltd was £12,000.

Required:
Prepare the balance sheet of Parent Ltd and the Consolidated Balance Sheet as at 1 January 20X1, after the transaction.

* ### Question 4

On 1 January 20X1 Parent Ltd acquired all the ordinary shares in Daughter Ltd for £6,000 cash. The fair value of the net assets in Daughter Ltd was their book value.

Required:
Prepare the balance sheet of Parent Ltd and the Consolidated Balance Sheet as at 1 January 20X1, after the transaction.

Question 5

On 1 January 20X1 Parent Ltd acquired 75% of the ordinary shares in Daughter Ltd. The purchase consideration was satisfied by the issue of 4,500 new ordinary shares in Parent Ltd. The fair value of a £1 ordinary share in Parent Ltd was £2 and the fair value of the net assets in Daughter Ltd was their book value.

Required:
Prepare the balance sheet of Parent Ltd and the Consolidated Balance Sheet as at 1 January 20X1, after the transaction.

* ### Question 6

The directors and shareholders of Y Ltd have agreed to accept an offer by B plc for the whole of Y Ltd's ordinary share capital. The offer comprises two newly issued ordinary shares (nominal value £0.20) of B plc for every five ordinary shares (nominal value £0.50) of Y Ltd. At the offer date the ordinary shares of B plc each had a stock market value of £3.00.

The summarised balance sheets of both companies immediately prior to the offer being effected on 1 January 20X5 are given below:

Balance sheets as at 1 January 20X5

	B plc		Y Ltd	
	£m	£m	£m	£m
Fixed assets				14.6
Current assets	29.7		12.3	
Current liabilities	19.5		9.9	
		10.2		2.4
Net assets		85.0		17.0
Retained profits		65.0		7.0
Ordinary share capital		20.0		10.0
		85.0		17.0

The book value of Y Ltd's assets at 1 January 20X5 approximated to their fair value. Y Ltd is a major supplier of B plc. On 1 January 20X5, B plc had £4.8 million of stock purchased from Y Ltd. This stock had cost Y Ltd £4.3 million to produce. In addition, at 1 January 20X5, B plc owed Y Ltd £3.2 million for goods supplied. (The 3.2 million is included in the current liabilities of B Ltd and the current assets of Y Ltd and must be eliminated from both on consolidation.)

Required:
Prepare, on an acquisition accounting basis, the opening balance sheet of the new group as at 1 January 20X5.

* ## Question 7

Using the information in Question 6,

Required:
(a) Prepare, on a merger accounting basis, the opening balance sheet of the new group as at 1 January 20X5.
(b) Outline in general terms, without reference to the above example, the factors that would influence a management decision on whether to use the merger or the acquisition basis for the consolidation of a new subsidiary.

* ## Question 8

Expansion plc, whose ordinary shares of £1 are quoted on the Stock Exchange at £4 each, has just made an offer for the whole of the ordinary share capital of Stagnant Ltd. This offer, on the basis of 1 for 1, was accepted and completed on 31 December 20X7.

At this date the summarised balance sheets of the two companies were:

	Expansion plc £	Stagnant plc £
2,000,000 ordinary shares of £1		2,000,000
3,000,000 ordinary shares of £1	3,000,000	
Reserves	4,000,000	2,000,000
Current liabilities	5,000,000	3,000,000
	£12,000,000	£7,000,000

	£	£
Fixed assets at net book value	6,000,000	1,000,000
Current assets	6,000,000	6,000,000
	£12,000,000	£7,000,000
Fair value of assets at 31 Dec 20X7		
Fixed	7,000,000	1,500,000
Current	6,000,000	6,500,000

Required:

Prepare a consolidated balance as at the date of acquisition:

(a) on a merger accounting basis;

(b) on an acquisition accounting basis.

* Question 9

Sitwell plc acquired 10,800 ordinary shares of £10 each ex div. in Standease plc, on 31 March 20X8, paying a consideration of £2 per share in cash and allotting as many of its ordinary shares of £10 each as would be necessary, taking into consideration the fair value of their respective net assets. The balance sheets of the two businesses immediately prior to the acquisition were as follows:

		Sitwell plc £		Standease plc £
Ordinary shares of £10 each		250,000		120,000
Reserves		30,000		75,400
		£280,000		£195,400
Machinery at cost		320,000		240,000
Less: provision for depreciation		(160,000)		(80,000)
		160,000		160,000
Stock in trade at cost	94,500		49,800	
Trade debtors	55,500		32,200	
Cash and bank balance	46,200		12,800	
Less: Trade creditors	(33,200)		(38,400)	
Tax payable	(18,000)		(12,000)	
Dividend payable	(25,000)		(9,000)	
		120,000		35,400
		£280,000		£195,400

It was agreed at the time of acquisition that:

(i) Standease plc would revise its basis of valuing stock in trade from average cost (hitherto adopted) to FIFO (the basis used by Sitwell plc). The stock with Standease plc, on 31 March 20X8, on the revised basis, amounts to £62,400.

(ii) For determining the fair value of the two businesses, machinery would be valued at its net current replacement cost. It has been ascertained that at current market prices the replacement of the machinery at Sitwell plc and Standease plc would cost £480,000 and £360,000 respectively.

Required:

(a) **Set out the conditions under which FRS 6 *Acquisitions and Mergers* requires the business combination to be accounted for as a merger, and state whether this method could be applied to this business combination.**

(b) **Prepare the draft balance sheet for the group immediately following the acquisition, using the merger method.**

Question 10

You are the finance director of X plc. At a recent board meeting it was decided to open negotiations with Z plc with a view to combining the two companies. The balance sheets of the two companies are set out below:

	X plc £m	Z plc £m
Fixed assets	15	30
Net current assets	18	9
	33	39
10% Debentures	4	6
	29	33
Ordinary shares of 50p each	10	
Ordinary shares of £1 each		8
Share premium	4	5
Profit and loss account	15	20
	29	33

It is agreed that the fair value of the fixed assets of Z plc is £36m. The terms of the proposed merger are that X plc would issue 15m new ordinary shares in exchange for the whole of the share capital of Z plc. The current market prices of the shares of the two companies for the purpose of the combination are: X plc = £3 per share; Z plc = £5 per share.

Required:

Your managing director has asked you to prepare for the next board meeting:

(a) **two consolidated balance sheets showing the effect of the combination using:**
   (i) **acquisition accounting;**
   (ii) **merger accounting;**

(b) **a brief report explaining for the board of directors:**
   (i) **Acquisition and merger accounting and the differences between them;**
   (ii) **The conditions to be satisfied if merger accounting is to be used;**
   (iii) **Whether the companies may choose either method, assuming the conditions in (ii) are satisfied.** *(CIPFA)*

(c) **recommend to the board which method to use.**

Question 11

The following accounts are the consolidated balance sheet and parent company balance sheet for Alpha Ltd as at 30 June 20X2.

		Consolidated balance sheet £		Parent company £
Ordinary shares		140,000		140,000
Capital reserve		92,400		92,400
Profit and loss account		79,884		35,280
Minority interest		12,320		—
		324,604		267,680
Fixed assets				
Freehold premises		127,400		84,000
Plant and machinery		62,720		50,400
Goodwill		85,680		—
Investment in subsidiary (50,400 shares)				151,200
Current assets				
Stock	121,604		71,120	
Debtors	70,420		46,760	
Dividend receivable	—		5,040	
Cash at bank	24,360		—	
	216,384		122,920	
Current liabilities				
Creditors	128,660		69,720	
Corporation tax	27,160		20,720	
Bank overdraft	—		39,200	
Proposed dividend	11,760		11,200	
	167,580		140,840	
Working capital		48,804		(17,920)
		£324,604		£267,680

Notes:

(i) There was only one subsidiary company called Beta Ltd.

(ii) There were no capital reserves in the subsidiary.

(iii) Alpha produced stock for sale to the subsidiary at a cost of £3,360 in May 20X2. The stock was invoiced to the subsidiary at £4,200 and was still on hand at the subsidiary's warehouse on 30 June 20X2. The invoice had not been settled at 30 June 20X2.

(iv) The profit and loss of the subsidiary had a credit balance of £16,800 at the date of acquisition.

(v) There was a right of set-off between overdrafts and bank balances.

Required:
(a) Prepare the balance sheet as at 30 June 20X2 of the subsidiary company from the information given above.
(b) Discuss briefly the main reasons for the publication of consolidated accounts.

Question 12 Browncoats Ltd

Greycoats plc acquired all of the shares in Browncoats Ltd on 1 April 20X0 for a cash consideration.

The following items have yet to have fair values attributed to them:

(a) There was a bank loan of £100,000 outstanding on which interest was payable at 15% per annum. It was due to be repaid by Browncoats Ltd at the end of four years. The current interest rate on similar loans is 8%.

(b) There were trade debts of £200,000 representing retention on a contract which would not be released for three years. The current interest rate is 7%.

(c) There was a contingent claim of £75,000 against a supplier for the supply of defective stock. The likeliest outcome was that Browncoats would recover the full amount of the claim.

Required:

(a) State any additional information that you would require in order to determine fair values

(b) Calculate the fair values for each item.

(c) Calculate the effect of each fair value adjustment on the profit and loss account and balance sheet in financial periods following the acquisition for items (i) and (ii). Assume that goodwill is amortised over a 20-year period.

References

1 D.J. Ravenscraft, 'An industrial organisation perspective', in L.E. Browne and E.S. Rosengren (eds), *The Merger Room*, Proceedings of a conference sponsored by Federal Reserve Bank of Boston, October 1987.

2 M. Foley and J. Chesworth, 'The fundamentals of a sound acquisition strategy', *Acquisitions Monthly*, September 1991.

3 F. Trautwein, 'Merger motives and merger prescriptions', *Strategic Management Journal*, Vol. 11, 1990, pp. 283–295.

4 G.A. Walter and J.B. Barney, 'Research notes and communications management objectives in mergers and acquisitions', *Strategic Management Journal*, Vol. 11, 1990, pp. 79–86.

5 G. Foster, *Financial Statement Analysis*, Prentice Hall, 1990.

6 H.K. Baker, T.O. Miller and B.J. Rampsberger, 'A typology of merger motives', *Akron Business and Economic Review*, Winter 1981.

7 Companies Act 1985, section 227.

8 *Ibid.*, section 258.

9 *Ibid.*, section 229.

10 FRS 7, *Fair Values in Acquisition Accounting*, ASB, 1994, paras 9–15.

11 S.M. McKinnon, *The Seventh Directive Consolidated Accounts in the EEC*, Kluwer, 1984, p. 76.

12 K. Wild and A. Guida, *Touche Ross Manual of Financial Reporting and Accounting* (3rd edition), Butterworth, 1990, p. 209.

13 FRS 9, *Associates and Joint Ventures*, ASB, 1997, para. 26.

14 Companies Act 1989, Schedule 2, para. 10.

15 FRS 6, *Acquisitions and Mergers*, ASB, 1994, para. 2.

16 FRS 6, *Acquisitions and Mergers*, ASB, 1994, paras 6–12.

17 Ernst and Young, *UK GAAP*, Macmillan (4th edition), 1994, p. 254.

18 T. Johnson, 'Levelling the playing field', *Accountancy*, February 1999, p. 82.

19 S.M. McKinnon, *op. cit.*, p. 321.

20 *Ibid.*, p. 76.

21 *Ibid.*, p. 65.

22 *Ibid.*, p. 329.

23 P.A. Taylor, *Consolidated Financial Reporting*, Paul Chapman Publishing, 1996, p. 38.

CHAPTER 20

Accounting for fixed asset investments

20.1 Introduction

An investment may be classified as either a fixed asset or a current asset. In this chapter we will consider the accounting treatment for fixed asset investments in both the investing company accounts and the consolidated accounts if the investment is in a subsidiary or an associate. This will include both the historical cost convention and the alternative accounting rules. We will also deal with questions relating to share capital, dividends and reserves.

20.2 Accounting treatment of the investment in the books of the investing company at the date of acquisition

We will continue with the Strong plc example from Chapter 19, but we will assume that on 1 January 20X1 Strong plc has undertaken four investments for cash by acquiring shares on the Stock Exchange in four identical companies. The companies are Five plc, Twenty plc, Sixty plc and Hundred plc, and Strong plc acquired a holding of 5%, 20%, 60% and 100%, respectively, as set out in Figure 20.1. Note that each of the investments appears **at cost** in the books of the investing company.

There are **no accounting entries** in the books of the investee companies arising from the transaction between Strong plc and the shareholders of the investee company. The balance sheets of the investee companies as at 1 January 20X1 are set out in Figure 20.2 to show the position before and after Strong plc has acquired its shareholdings.

20.3 Categories of fixed asset investments

Fixed asset investments are categorised according to the degree of **influence** that the investor is able to exercise over the investee company, as shown in Figure 20.3.

The ability to pass resolutions is one of the important factors in assessing the nature of the control that is exercisable. The size of the shareholding has a bearing on the type of resolution that can be passed. There are three types of resolution: ordinary, extraordinary and special.

Figure 20.1 Balance sheet of Strong plc as at 1 January 20X1, the date of acquisition by Strong plc at a market price of £2 per share.

	Before buying shares	After buying 5% of Five plc	After buying 20% of Twenty plc	After buying 60% of Sixty plc	After buying 100% of Hundred plc
		£	£	£	£
Fixed assets	12,250	12,250	12,250	12,250	12,250
Investment in:					
Five plc		500	500	500	500
Twenty plc			2,000	2,000	2,000
Sixty plc				6,000	6,000
Hundred plc					10,000
Net current assets	2,750	2,250	250	(5,750)	(15,750)
	15,000	15,000	15,000	15,000	15,000
Share capital	8,750	8,750	8,750	8,750	8,750
Profit and loss account	6,250	6,250	6,250	6,250	6,250
Shareholders' funds	15,000	15,000	15,000	15,000	15,000

20.3.1 Ordinary resolutions

An ordinary resolution is passed by a simple majority of votes cast on the resolution. It is required to adopt the accounts that are put before the annual general meeting, approve the dividends that have been recommended by the directors and appoint a director.

Figure 20.2 Balance sheet of each of the investee companies as at 1 January 20X1 after the acquisition by Strong plc of various percentages of shares held by existing shareholders.

	Each company before share transfer	Five plc after Strong buys 5%	Twenty plc after Strong buys 20%	Sixty plc after Strong buys 60%	Hundred plc after Strong buys 100%
	£	£	£	£	£
Fixed assets	5,500	5,500	5,500	5,500	5,500
Net current assets	2,000	2,000	2,000	2,000	2,000
Net assets	7,500	7,500	7,500	7,500	7,500
Ordinary share capital	5,000	5,000	5,000	5,000	5,000
Profit and loss balance	2,500	2,500	2,500	2,500	2,500
	7,500	7,500	7,500	7,500	7,500

Figure 20.3 Categorise the investments.

Nature of influence exercised by the investing company	Accounting category given to the investment	Shareholding in investee
1 Complete control with ability to pass ordinary, extraordinary and special resolutions	1 Investment in subsidiary	More than 75%
2 Control with ability to pass ordinary resolutions	2 Investment in subsidiary	More than 50% up to 74%
3 Significant influence exercised over operating and financial policy	3 Investment in associate	20% or more up to 50%
4 Interest held on a long-term basis for the purpose of securing a contribution to its activities by the exercise of control or influence[a]	4 Participating interest	20% or more up to 50%
5 An undertaking jointly managed by the parent and undertakings that are not consolidated provided the undertaking is unincorporated	5 Joint venture proportionally consolidated	Not stated
6 No influence but a material interest based on shareholding %	6 Significant investment	10% or more up to 20%
7 No influence but a material interest based on relative size of investment to total assets of the investor company, i.e. more than 10%	7 Significant investment	
8 No influence and not material	8 Other investments	Under 10%

[a]Companies Act 1985, section 260.

20.3.2 Extraordinary and special resolutions

An **extraordinary resolution** is passed by a majority of not less than three-quarters of such members as are entitled to vote. It is required to:

● wind up a company voluntarily when, because of its liabilities, it cannot continue trading;[1]
● vary class rights.[2]

A **special resolution** is passed by a majority of not less than three-quarters of such members as are entitled to vote at a meeting of which twenty-one days' notice has been given. It is required in a number of circumstances, such as:

● to change the objects of a company;[3]

● to allow a private company to re-register as a public company;[4]

● to reduce share capital if so authorised by the company's articles;[5]

● to resolve that the company be wound up by the court;[6]

● to resolve that the company be voluntarily wound up.[7]

20.4 Carrying value of investments at the end of the financial year in the books of the investing company under the historical cost convention

Fixed assets are included at their purchase price, which will normally only include relatively minor dealing costs and stamp duty, but in the context of a contested takeover of a public company, the incidental costs may be very significant.[8] This applies to each accounting category of investment mentioned in Figure 20.3.

Just as for tangible fixed assets, provision **must** be made for any impairment under FRS 11 *Impairment of Fixed Assets and Goodwill,* para. 6. If the value subsequently increases, the provision must be written back.

The accounts of Strong plc and the four investee companies are set out in Figures 20.4 and 20.5. They are prepared using the historical cost convention and assuming that the investee companies have paid no dividends. Note that, in the balance sheet of the investing company (Strong plc), the investments are carried at cost and the only increase in shareholders' funds recorded is the £360 transferred from its profit and loss account in Figure 20.4.

No accounting entries are made in the profit and loss account of Strong plc in respect of the profits of the investee companies because the investee companies have not distributed any of their profits to Strong plc through dividends.

You will recall that at the date of acquisition the carrying value of the investment was equal to the net assets of the investee plus the premium paid as the cost of control. The carrying value is shown in Figure 20.6. However, after a year's trading, this will no longer be the case because the net assets of the investee company will have changed. They will have increased if the investee has made a profit, and a proportion will belong to the investing company.

If the investor company continues to carry the investment as its cost as at 1 January 20X1, it will not reflect the increase of £1,080 that has occurred during 20X1. However, under the historic cost convention, the realisation concept prevents the investor company from increasing the investment to reflect the profit made by the investee until there has been a dividend distribution by the investee company, i.e. until funds are transferred.

Figure 20.4   Profit and loss accounts assuming that each investee company has identical results.

Profit and loss accounts of Strong plc, Five plc, Twenty plc, Sixty plc and Hundred plc for the year ended 31 December 20X1

	Strong plc £	Each investee £
Turnover	9,000	4,500
Cost of sales	4,500	2,250
Gross profit	4,500	2,250
Distribution costs	(900)	(450)
Administrative expenses	(720)	(360)
Trading profit	2,880	1,440
Investment income from:		
Subsidiaries		
Associates		

	Strong plc £	Each investee £
Other investments		
Profit before tax	2,880	1,440
Tax	720	360
Profit after tax	2,160	1,080
Extraordinary items	0	0
Profit for the year	2,160	1,080
Dividends	1,800	—
Transferred to reserves	360	1,080

Figure 20.5   Balance sheets assuming that each investee company has an identical position.

Balance sheets of Strong plc, Five plc, Twenty plc, Sixty plc, and Hundred plc as at 31 December 20X1

	Strong plc		Investee companies	
	As at 1 Jan 20X1 Date shares were acquired £	As at 31 Dec 20X1 One year after shares were bought £	As at 1 Jan 20X1 £	As at 31 Dec 20X1 £
Fixed assets (net book value)	12,250	11,025	5,500	4,950
Investment in:				
Five plc	500	500		
Twenty plc	2,000	2,000		
Sixty plc	6,000	6,000		

Figure 20.5 *(cont.)*

Hundred plc	10,000	10,000		
Net current assets/(liabilities)	(15,750)	(14,165)	2,000	3,630
Net assets	15,000	15,360	7,500	8,580
Share capital	8,750	8,750	5,000	5,000
Profit and loss account	6,250	6,610	2,500 (+1,080)	3,580
Shareholders' funds	15,000	15,360	7,500	8,580

Figure 20.6 Carrying value at 1 January 20X1.

	£	£
Cost of 5,000 shares at £2 per share		10,000
Represented by:		
Net assets of investee company		
as represented by: shares	5,000	
: reserves	2,500	
		7,500
Cost of control		2,500
		10,000

20.5 Carrying value of investments at the end of the financial year in the books of the investing company under the alternative accounting rules

The Companies Act 1985 permits a company to apply alternative accounting rules. If these alternative accounting rules were to be applied, the carrying figure would be determined not by its cost, but by a market valuation.

20.5.1 How to value fixed asset investments under the alternative accounting rules

Under the alternative accounting rules, fixed asset investments may be included either at a market value determined as at the date of their last valuation or at a value determined on any basis which appears to the directors to be appropriate in the circumstances of the company, provided details are given of the basis and reasons for adopting it.[9]

20.5.2 Valuing a wholly owned subsidiary under the alternative accounting rules

One method is to value investments in subsidiaries and investments in associates at the amounts of the net assets shown in the historic cost balance sheets of the subsidiaries and associates. This maintains the reserves in the parent company at the same amount as the reserves in the subsidiary and associate.[10]

If this were applied to the investment in Hundred plc, the effect on the balance sheet of Strong plc would be to increase the investment to £11,080, which reflects the net assets of Hundred plc as at 31 December 20X1 and the cost of control as at 1 January

Figure 20.7 Alternative accounting valuation of shares in Hundred plc, which is a wholly owned subsidiary.

	£	£
Cost of 5,000 shares at £2 per share at 1 Jan 20X1		10,000
Add: Increase in net assets during 20X1		**1,080**
		11,080
Represented by:		
Net assets of investee company at 31 Dec 20X1		
which are presented by: shares	5,000	
: reserves	3,580	
		8,580
Cost of control remains at the initial figure		2,500
		11,080

20X1, as shown in Figure 20.7. The increase in the investment is an **unrealised gain** and may not be taken to the profit and loss account. Instead, an amount equal to the £1,080 that has been debited to the investment account is credited to a **revaluation reserve**.

20.5.3 Valuing a partly owned subsidiary and associated undertaking under the alternative accounting rules

The investments in Sixty plc and Twenty plc could be dealt with similarly. The investment in Sixty plc, the partly owned subsidiary, would be increased by £648, which is 60% of the increase of £1,080 in its net assets; the investment in Twenty plc, the associated company, would be increased by £216, which is 20% of the increase in its net assets.

The revaluation reserve would be credited in total with £1,944, consisting of the increases in the net assets of the two subsidiary companies and the associated company, i.e. £1,080 in Hundred plc; £648 in Sixty plc and £216 in Twenty plc.

The investment in Five plc would be maintained at cost or market value. We are assuming that the market value has remained at the amount paid by Strong plc on 1 January 20X1.

20.5.4 Balance sheet entries under the alternative accounting rules

The balance sheet of Strong plc would be as set out in Figure 20.8. We can see that using the alternative accounting rules enables the balance sheet values of the investments to be **amended** to continue to reflect the underlying net asset value of the investment.

The underlying net assets are allocated to the shares held so that the investment equals the value of the net assets that are **owned by** Strong plc in the two subsidiary companies and the associated company.

The alternative accounting rules do not mean that the investments show the value of the net assets that are **controlled by** Strong plc in these companies. In order to disclose this value as at 31 December 20X1, it is necessary to prepare a consolidated balance sheet.

Figure 20.8 Balance sheets under alternative accounting rules.

Balance sheet of Strong plc as at 31 December 20X1

	Historic cost convention		Alternative accounting rules
	As at 1 Jan 20X1 £	As at 31 Dec 20X1 £	As at 31 Dec 20X1 £
Fixed assets	12,250	11,025	11,025
Investment in:			
Five plc	500	500	500
Twenty plc	2,000	2,000	2,216
Sixty plc	6,000	6,000	6,648
Hundred plc	10,000	10,000	11,080
Net current assets/(liabilities)	(15,750)	(14,165)	(14,165)
Net assets	15,000	15,360	17,304
Share capital	8,750	8,750	8,750
Profit and loss account	6,250	6,610	6,610
Revaluation reserve			**1,944**
Shareholders' funds	15,000	15,360	17,304

20.6 Preparation of a consolidated balance sheet at the end of the financial year to account for an investment in a subsidiary

A consolidated balance sheet will incorporate all of the assets and liabilities of the subsidiaries, i.e. it will show the net assets **controlled** by Strong plc. In order to complete the consolidated balance sheet it will be necessary to calculate:

● the **cost of control** that was paid for the investment in Sixty plc and the investment in Hundred plc;
● the **minority interest** in Sixty plc;
● the **consolidated reserves**.

20.6.1 Cost of control

The cost of control over the two subsidiaries is £4,000, as set out in Figure 20.9. In both cases the cost of control will be the figure computed as at the date of acquisition on 1 January 20X1.

The ledger account will not appear in the nominal ledger of any of the individual companies. It is purely a memorandum record to support the entries in the consolidated accounts. This memorandum record is normally referred to as the **consolidation working papers**. The ledger accounts for the minority interest and consolidated reserves will likewise be a memorandum.

Figure 20.9   Cost of control at 1 January 20X1.

On investment in Hundred plc:	£	£	£
Cost of 5,000 shares at £2 per share		10,000	
Less: Net assets of investee company			
represented by : shares	5,000		
: reserves	2,500		
		7,500	
Cost of control			2,500
On investment in Sixty plc:			
Cost of 3,000 shares at £2 per share		6,000	
Less: Net assets of investee company			
represented by : shares	3,000		
: reserves	1,500		
		4,500	
Cost of control			1,500
Total cost of control over Hundred plc and Sixty plc			4,000

If a ledger account format is used to record the consolidation adjustments in the consolidation working papers, the ledger account would be as follows:

Cost of control account

	£		£
1 Jan 20X1 Investment in Hundred	10,000	1 Jan 20X1 Shares in Hundred	5,000
		1 Jan 20X1 Reserves in Hundred	2,500
1 Jan 20X1 Investment in Sixty	6,000	1 Jan 20X1 Shares in Sixty	3,000
		1 Jan 20X1 Reserves in Sixty	1,500
		1 Jan 20X1 Balance c/d	4,000
	16,000		16,000

20.6.2 Minority interest

The minority interest is calculated in Figure 20.10 as £3,432. Alternatively, we can approach it from the net assets that belong to the minority shareholders. This would, of course, be the same amount, i.e. 40% of the net assets of £8,580 shown in Figure 20.5. Note that the cost of control is calculated as at the date of acquisition, i.e. 1 January 20X1, but the minority interest is calculated as at the date of the balance sheet, i.e. 31 December 20X1.

20.6.3 Consolidated reserves

The consolidated reserves will consist of the reserves of the parent company plus the parent company's proportion of the profits of the subsidiaries that have arisen **since the date the parent company acquired control**. The calculation is set out in Figure 20.11.

Figure 20.10 Minority interest in Sixty plc.

	£
Shares at 31 December 20X1 40% of 5,000 shares	2,000
Reserves at 31 December 20X1 40% of £3,580	1,432
	3,432

Minority Interest			
	£		£
31 Dec 20X1 Balance c/d	3,432	31 Dec 20X1 Shares in Sixty plc	2,000
		31 Dec 20X1 Reserves in Sixty plc	1,432
	3,432		3,432

Figure 20.11 Consolidated reserves calculated as at 31 December 20X1.

	£	£
Reserves of Strong plc as at 31 Dec 20X1		6,610
Reserves of Hundred plc as at 31 Dec 20X1	(Figure 20.5) 3,580	
Less: Reserves at 1 Jan 20X1 (pre-acquisition)	2,500	
Profits accrued since control was acquired	1,080	
Strong plc has a 100% interest of this amount		1,080
Reserves of Sixty plc as at 31 Dec 20X1	(Figure 20.5) 3,580	
Less: Reserves at 1 Jan 20X1 (pre-acquisition)	2,500	
Profits accrued since control was acquired	1,080	
Strong plc has a 60% interest of this amount		648
Consolidated reserves		8,338

The ledger account format would be as follows:

Consolidated reserves			
	£		£
31 Dec 20X1 Balance c/d	8,338	31 Dec 20X1 Strong plc reserves	6,610
		31 Dec 20X1 Hundred plc reserves	1,080
		31 Dec 20X1 Sixty plc reserves	648
	8,338		8,338

A consolidation worksheet (Figure 20.12) will be prepared to eliminate the investments and substitute the assets and liabilities of the two subsidiary companies. The illustration is based on the investments being carried at historic cost. Note that the consolidated balance sheet will include:

Figure 20.12 Consolidated worksheet as at 31 December 20X1.

	Strong plc £	Sixty plc £	Hundred plc £	Aggregate £	Adjust Dr/(Cr)	Consolidated balance sheet £
Fixed assets	11,025	4,950	4,950	20,925		20,925
Investment in:						
Five plc	500			500		500
Twenty plc	2,000			2,000		2,000
Sixty plc	6,000			6,000	(4,500)ᵃ	1,500
Hundred plc	10,000			10,000	(7,500)ᵇ	2,500
Net current assets	(14,165)	3,630	3,630	(6,905)		(6,905)
Net assets	15,360	8,580	8,580	32,520		20,520
Share capital	8,750	5,000	5,000	18,750	3,000ᵃ 5,000ᵇ 2,000ᶜ	8,750
Profit and loss account	6,610	3,580	3,580	13,770	1,500ᵃ 2,500ᵇ 1,432ᶜ	8,338
Minority interest					(2,000)ᶜ (1,432)ᶜ	3,432
	15,360	8,580	8,580	32,520	0	20,520

Notes cross-referenced to the worksheet and Figure 20.5:

(a) £3,000 is 60% of the issued share capital of Sixty plc
   £1,500 is 60% of the reserves of Sixty plc as at 1 Jan 20X1

(b) £5,000 is 100% of the issued share capital of Hundred plc
   £2,500 is 100% of the reserves of Hundred plc as at 1 Jan 20X1

(c) £2,000 is 40% of the issued share capital of Sixty plc
   £1,432 is 40% of the reserves of Sixty plc as at 31 Dec 20X1

● **all** of the fixed assets and net current assets of Hundred plc that are **100% owned**;

● **all** of the fixed assets and net current assets of Sixty plc that are only **60% owned** but are **controlled** by the directors of Strong plc via the 60% shareholding, which gives it the ability to pass ordinary resolutions.

In the consolidated balance sheet, the fixed assets and net current assets of Sixty plc that are not owned by Strong plc are represented by the **minority interest**.

20.7 Preparation of a consolidated balance sheet at the end of the financial year to account for an investment in an associate

As we have seen, subsidiaries are dealt with by aggregating their assets and liabilities with those of the parent company on the basis that the parent has control over them. Associates are dealt with differently. They are dealt with by **equity accounting** because the investing company has significant influence, but it does not have control over the operating and financial policy.

The intention is that shareholders in the investing company should be able to see the net assets that underlie the investment in the associate. To provide them with this information in the consolidated balance sheet, equity accounting follows the procedure that we described above for valuing an investment under the alternative accounting rules in the company-only accounts of the investing company.

The investment in associate is therefore adjusted in proportion to the shares held for the increase in the net assets of the associate that has occurred during the year. The rationale is ownership and not control.

Equity accounting is sometimes referred to as **one line consolidation** because the only change is to the investment in associate, which is adjusted to reflect the net asset backing. The individual assets and liabilities underlying the investment in the books of the investee company are not themselves aggregated with those of the holding company and subsidiaries.

The balance sheet valuation at 31 December 20X1 is set out in Figure 20.13. The £216 will be added to the consolidated reserves of £8,338. The consolidated balance sheet will be as in Figure 20.14. Note the use of the term 'stakeholders'. The net assets represent the investment by stakeholders rather than just the shareholders of the holding company because the minority shareholders' interest is also included.

Figure 20.13 Investment in associate accounted for using the equity method for the consolidated balance sheet (in accordance with FRS 9[11]).

	£
Group share of net assets at 1 Jan 20X1 20% of £7,500	1,500
Premium paid on acquisition	500
Cost at 1 Jan 20X1	2,000
Increase in net assets during 20X1 20% of £1,080	216
Carrying value as at 31 Dec 20X1	2,216

There will be an increase of £216 in the assets and in the reserves

FRS9[12] requires goodwill arising on the investor's acquisition, less any amortisation or write-down, to be separately disclosed.

Figure 20.14   Consolidated balance sheet as at 31 December 20X1.

	£	Explanatory notes
Fixed assets		
Intangible	4,000	Cost of control of Hundred and Sixty
Tangible	20,925	Assets of Strong, Hundred and Sixty
Investment in:		
Five plc	500	At cost as at 1 Jan 20X1
Twenty plc	2,216	Valued using the equity method, i.e. cost as at 1 Jan 20X1 plus proportion of net asset increase in 20X1
Net current assets (liabilities)	(6,905)	Net current assets of Strong, Hundred, Sixty plc
Net assets	20,736	
Share capital	8,750	Share capital of Strong plc
Profit and loss account	8,554	(a) Reserves of Strong plc
		(b) Strong's proportion of the post-acquisition reserves of: Hundred and Sixty and Twenty
Minority interest	3,432	Interest in Sixty plc
Stakeholders' funds	20,736	

There is an argument that the consolidated accounts should include only the net assets that are owned by the holding company, not all the assets under its control. If this argument were accepted, the consolidated accounts would be prepared on a **proportional** basis. Only the proportion of assets and liabilities relating to the shares held would be included. The effect on Figure 20.12 would be to reduce the fixed assets in Sixty plc to £2,970 (60% of £4,950) and the net current assets to £2,178 (60% of £3,630). The difference of £3,432 (40% of £4,950 + 40% of £3,630) would be contra'ed against the minority interest. The net assets appearing in the consolidated balance sheet would be owned by the holding company shareholders; the assets belonging to the minority shareholders would be excluded; and the consolidated balance sheet would be prepared to show the **proprietors'** interest rather than the stakeholders' interest.

There is no uniquely correct choice. The two statements are prepared under different definitions and the choice would be determined by assessing which definition produced the more decision-useful information. The normal procedure would be for the ASB to obtain views from interested parties in response to a discussion document or exposure draft on the topic. As a result of such consultation, the ASB, in the summary to FRS 2 *Accounting for Subsidiary Undertakings*, provides that minority interests should be reported separately in the consolidated balance sheet.

The traditional consolidated balance sheet is entity based, in that it includes all net assets of all stakeholders; the proportional consolidated balance sheet is proprietor based, in that it includes only the net assets of the proprietors of the group, i.e. the parent company shareholders.

20.8   How are shareholders' funds measured?

20.8.1   Parent company accounts under the historical cost convention

In the balance sheet of Strong plc, using the historical cost convention, we have seen in Figure 20.5 that the shareholders' funds at 31 December 20X1 are represented by **net assets of £15,360**. This includes the investments that are carried at cost and the profit of £360 realised by the holding company.

20.8.2   Parent company accounts under the alternative accounting rules

In the balance sheet of Strong plc, using the alternative accounting rules, we saw in Figure 20.8 that the shareholders' funds were represented by **net assets of £17,304**. The investments that appeared in the balance sheet were revalued under those rules. They were carried at cost if there was no influence, e.g. Five plc, and at cost plus the increase in the net assets applicable to the shares owned by the investing company if there was influence, e.g. Twenty, Sixty and Hundred plcs.

20.8.3   Consolidated accounts

In the consolidated balance sheet we saw in Figure 20.14 that the **net assets are stated at £20,736**. The investments in subsidiaries have been replaced by the assets and liabilities of the subsidiaries. In the consolidated balance sheet, the net assets of £3,432 that belong to the minority are also included – they are added to the assets of £17,304 that are owned by the shareholders of Strong plc to produce £20,736. They represent the **net assets that are controlled by Strong plc and owned by the stakeholders.**

20.9   How does a dividend distribution by a subsidiary affect the balance sheet of the investing company, the investee company and the group?

Simple logic tells us that if one company distributes a dividend to another company, the net current assets and the profit and loss balances in both companies will change. For example, a dividend paid by Sixty plc of £1,000 at 31 December 20X1 will be as shown in Figure 20.15 in the company-only accounts of Strong and Sixty.

We would expect the consolidated balance sheet to be £400 lower because that is the amount of the dividend that has gone outside the group, i.e. the net assets should fall from £20,736 to £20,336. We can confirm this when we prepare the consolidated balance sheet as in Figure 20.16. The consolidated reserve remains **unchanged** at £8,554 because it has merely moved from the net current assets of the investee to the net current assets of the investor. This indicates that intragroup dividends have no effect on the **group consolidated reserves** and that dividends **distributed outside** the group will reduce the net capital employed by the group. Of course, the reserves of the individual companies will change, as shown in Figure 20.15.

Figure 20.15   Balance sheets of Strong plc and Sixty plc as at 31 December 20X1.

	Strong £	£	Strong after dividend £	Sixty £	£	Sixty after dividend £
Fixed assets	11,025		11,025	4,950		4,950
Investment in:						
Five plc	500		500			
Twenty plc	2,000		2,000			
Sixty plc	6,000		6,000			
Hundred plc	10,000		10,000			
Net current assets/ (liabilities)	(14,165)	600	(13,565)	3,630	(1,000)	2,630
Net assets	15,360		15,960	8,580		7,580
Share capital	8,750		8,750	5,000		5,000
Profit and loss account	6,610	600	7,210	3,580	(1,000)	2,580
Shareholders' funds	15,360		15,960	8,580		7,580

Figure 20.16   Consolidated balance sheet as at 31 December 20X1.

	£	Explanatory notes
Fixed assets		
Intangible	4,000	Cost of control of Hundred and Sixty
Tangible	20,925	Assets of Strong, Hundred and Sixty
Investment in:		
Five plc	500	At cost as at 1 Jan 20X1
Twenty plc	2,216	Valued using the equity method, i.e. cost as at 1 Jan 20X1 plus proportion of net asset increase in 20X1
Net current assets (liabilities)	**(7,305)**	**Net current liabilities of Strong, Hundred and Sixty plc. The £400 paid outside the group increases (6,905) in Figure 20.14**
Net assets	20,336	
Share capital	8,750	Share capital of Strong plc
Profit and loss account	8,554	(a) Reserves of Strong plc (b) Strong's proportion of the post-acquisition reserves of: Hundred and Sixty and Twenty
Minority interest	**3,032**	**Interest in Sixty plc reduced by the £400 received as a dividend**
Stakeholders' funds	20,336	

20.10 In what circumstances will the consolidated reserves be adjusted in respect of intragroup transactions?

We have seen that the consolidated reserves are not adjusted by the payment of a dividend by a subsidiary. This is because the profits **realised** by the group have not been reduced or increased. However, certain intragroup transactions do require adjustment because they give rise to **unrealised** profits as far as the group is concerned. An example is the sale of stock from one member of the group to another member.

20.10.1 Intragroup sales

If goods sold by one member of the group to another member are sold to a third party outside the group by the end of the accounting period, any profit added on the intragroup sale will have been realised.

For example, assume that on 1 January 20X1 Strong plc sold goods for which it had paid £200 to Hundred plc for £250 and that the stock was sold for £375 to a customer of Hundred plc before 31 December 20X1.

The intragroup profit made by Strong plc is £50 and the profit made by Hundred plc is £125. The group will have realised a profit of £175, being the difference between the cost to Strong plc of £200 and the selling price to Hundred's customer of £375.

However, if the stock remains in the possession of the group member, the profit on sale is **unrealised** as far as the group is concerned. The profit recorded in the company-only accounts of the selling member of the group needs to be eliminated from the **consolidated reserves**. If it were not eliminated, it would be a simple matter for the group to increase its reported consolidated profits merely by selling stock internally.

For example, assume that on 1 January 20X1 Strong plc sold goods for which it had paid £200 to Hundred plc for £250 and that the stock is still held by Hundred plc as at 31 December 20X1. No adjustments are required to the company-only accounts of either Strong plc or Hundred plc. The sale will be reported in the profit and loss account of Strong plc, the profit of £50 will appear in its profits for the year and the stock will appear in the balance sheet of Hundred plc at £250.

The consolidated balance sheet will, however, need to be adjusted, as shown in Figure 20.17.

If the sale had been made **by** a partly owned subsidiary, FRS 2 provides that:

> to the extent that they are reflected in the book value of assets to be included in the consolidation, profits or losses on any intragroup transactions should be eliminated in full. The elimination of profits or losses relating to intragroup transactions should be set against the interests held by the group and minority interest in respective proportion to their holdings in the undertaking whose individual financial statements recorded the eliminated profit or loss.[13]

For example, if Sixty plc had sold goods costing £200 to Strong plc for £250 on 1 January 20X1 and the goods were still held by Strong plc at 31 December 20X1, then the stock would be reduced by £50, the consolidated reserves by £30 and the **minority interest by £20**.

In requiring the whole of the unrealised profit to be eliminated FRS 2 is following the **control concept** and regarding the transaction with the minority as being internal to the group and therefore to be fully eliminated. The **ownership concept** would have required only the parent % of the unrealised profit to be eliminated.

Figure 20.17 Consolidated balance sheet adjusted for unrealised profit.

Consolidated balance sheet as at 31 December 20X1
Adjusted for unrealised profit on intragroup sales

	£	*Explanatory notes*
Fixed assets		
Intangible	4,000	Cost of control of Hundred and Sixty
Tangible	20,925	Assets of Strong, Hundred and Sixty
Investment in:		
Five plc	500	At cost as at 1 Jan 20X1
Twenty plc	2,216	Valued using the equity method, i.e. cost as at 1 Jan 20X1 plus proportion of net asset increase in 20X1
Net current assets (liabilities)	(7,355)	Net current assets of Strong, Hundred, Sixty plc
(7,305 – £50)		**less unrealised profit of £50 in stock**
Net capital employed	20,286	
Share capital	8,750	Share capital of Strong plc
Profit and loss account	**8,504**	(a) Reserves of Strong plc
(£8,554 – £50)		(b) Strong's proportion of the post-acquisition reserves of: Hundred and Sixty and Twenty **less £50 unrealised profit on intragroup sales**
Minority interest	3,032	Interest in Sixty plc
Stakeholders' funds	20,286	

20.11

20.11 Why have the consolidated reserves increased during the year since acquisition?

The consolidated reserves as at 1 January 20X1 were £6,250, as shown in Figure 20.8. The consolidated reserves as at 31 December 20X1 were £8,504, as shown in Figure 20.17. In order to explain the change we need to prepare a consolidated profit and loss account. This is covered in the next chapter in Figure 21.5.

Summary

We have considered the accounting treatment for investments in associates and subsidiaries using the historical cost convention and the alternative accounting rules allowed under the Companies Act. Under the alternative accounting rules, we have seen that the carrying value of the investment in the investee company's balance sheet is adjusted to reflect the underlying net assets as disclosed in the subsidiary or associated company's own accounts.

On consolidation, the investments in associates are valued at their proportion of the net assets of the subsidiary plus any goodwill. In the next chapter we consider further the ASB proposals to amend the disclosure requirements for associates.

On consolidation, the net assets of subsidiaries are substituted for the investment accounts and any difference is treated as positive or negative goodwill and dealt with in accordance with group accounting policy; a minority interest is created for that proportion of the net assets that is not owned by the investee; and only post-acquisition reserves are included within the consolidated profit and loss account.

Review questions

1 On 1 January 20X1 Investor plc acquired 75% of the ordinary shares of Investee plc. When asked to explain what the company received for the outlay on this investment, the directors said that they had received '75% of the goodwill and 75% of the net assets of Investee plc valued at fair value'.

(a) State how the investment would be described in the balance sheet of Investor plc as at the date of acquisition, i.e. at cost under the historical cost convention or at valuation under the alternative accounting rules.

(b) If a consolidated balance sheet were to be prepared as at 1 January 20X1, state the consolidation process that would result in the consolidated accounts containing '75% of the goodwill and 75% of the net assets of Investee plc valued at fair value'.

(c) If a consolidated balance sheet were to be prepared as at 1 January 20X1, state the consolidation process that would result in the consolidated accounts containing '75% of the goodwill and 100% of the net assets of Investee plc valued at fair value'.

(d) If a consolidated balance sheet were to be prepared as at 1 January 20X1, state the consolidation process that would result in the consolidated accounts containing '100% of the goodwill and 100% of the net assets of Investee plc valued at fair value'.

(e) If a consolidated balance sheet were to be prepared as at 1 January 20X1, state the consolidation process that would result in the consolidated accounts containing '0% of the goodwill and 100% of the net assets of Investee plc valued at book value'.

2 Decide whether the following are true or false:

(a) '75% of the goodwill and 75% of the net assets of Investee plc valued at fair value at the date of acquisition' = 75% of the share capital and reserves of Investee plc as disclosed by its balance sheet at the date of acquisition.

(b) '0% of the goodwill and 100% of the net assets of Investee plc valued at book value at the date of acquisition' = the share capital and reserves of Investee plc as disclosed by its balance sheet at the date of acquisition.

(c) A minority interest will appear in each of the consolidated balance sheets prepared in question 1 above.

3 On 1 January 20X1 Hopeful plc acquired 25% of the ordinary shares of Hopeless plc. On 31 December 20X1 Hopeful plc was deciding whether to include its investment in the consolidated accounts at either:

(i) '25% of the goodwill and 25% of the net assets of Hopeless plc at fair valuation as at 1 January 20X1'; or

(ii) '25% of the goodwill and 25% of the net assets of Hopeless plc at fair valuation as at
1 January 20X1' + '25% of the change in net assets of Hopeless from 1 January 20X1 to
31 December 20X1'.

Explain:
(a) the circumstances in which Hopeful plc would use (i);
(b) why choice (ii) is available.

4 Investments are treated in the consolidated balance sheet according to the percentage of voting
rights acquired by the shareholding, e.g:

Shareholding	In the consolidating balance sheet
Less than 20%	At cost
More than 20% less than 50%	At cost + % of change in net assets
More than 50%	Investment replaced with net assets

(a) Explain the circumstances in which the investing company might wish to manipulate the
treatment in the consolidated balance sheet by adjusting its shareholding, e.g. reducing its
holding from 20% to 19.5%.

(b) Explain the qualitative criterion that controls the choice of accounting treatment for
shareholdings of less than 50%.

5 In the text we illustrated the elimination of unrealised profit on sale where the sale was made by
a holding company to a wholly owned subsidiary by eliminating 100% of the unrealised profit
(cost to Strong plc was £200; sale to Hundred plc was £250; unrealised profit eliminated was
£50). This is standard UK practice for all intragroup unrealised profits, whether from a holding
company to a subsidiary or vice versa.

However, alternative treatments may be academically justifiable[13] in the following situations:

(a) Sale was made by Strong plc to Sixty plc, a 60% owned subsidiary.
(b) Sale was made by Sixty plc to Strong plc.
(c) Sale was made by Hundred plc to Sixty plc.
(d) Sale was made by Sixty plc to Hundred plc.

Discuss possible alternative treatments of the £50 intragroup profit in each of these situations.

Exercises

An extract from the solution is provided in the appendix at the end of the text for exercises marked
with an asterisk (*).

Question 1

The accountancy profession has developed a range of techniques to measure and present the effects
of one company owning shares in another company.

Required:
**Briefly describe each of these techniques and how the resulting information might
best be presented.**

Question 2

(a) What criteria should you use when determining whether to include an investment under fixed
or current assets in a balance sheet?

(b) What information does the Companies Act 1985 require to be disclosed for each subheading under the main heading 'Investments'? Explain why this information might be relevant to a reader of the accounts.

(c) What information must be disclosed where the investment exceeds 10%, but is less than 20% of the allotted share capital of the investee? Explain why this information might be relevant to a reader of the accounts.

* ## Question 3

The following are the balance sheets of Parent Ltd and its subsidiary Son Ltd.

	Parent Ltd £	Son Ltd £
Ordinary share capital	160,000	80,000
Reserves	12,000	11,000
Profit and loss	15,000	14,000
Creditors	30,000	16,000
Bills payable to Parent Ltd	—	16,000
	217,000	137,000
Plant	60,000	54,000
Fixtures		10,000
Investment in Son Ltd (60,000 shares at cost)	80,000	
Current assets		
Debtors: Son Ltd	4,000	—
Others	20,000	36,000
Bills receivable from Son Ltd	8,000	
Stock	24,000	28,000
Cash at bank	21,000	9,000
	217,000	137,000

1 On 1 January 20X5 Parent Ltd acquired the shares in Son Ltd. At that date the balances on Son Ltd general reserve was £7,000 and the balance on the profit and loss account was £6,000.

2 The stock held by Son Ltd includes stock purchased from Parent Ltd for £7,200. Parent Ltd had made a profit of 50% on cost.

3 At the date of acquisition the plant in Son Ltd, which had a book value of £60,000, was valued at £70,000. Depreciation is 10% straight line. The fixtures were valued at book value.

Required:
Prepare a consolidated balance sheet as at 31 December 20X5.

Question 4

The balance sheets of Tay plc and Avon plc as at 31 December 20X6 contained the following information:

	Tay £m	Avon £m
Fixed assets at book value	12.6	3.8
Net current assets	7.9	1.2
	20.5	5.0
Financed by:		
Share capital (£1 ordinary shares)	10.0	2.0
Retained profit at 1 January 20X6	8.3	2.5
Profit for 20X6	2.2	0.5
	20.5	5.0

The following additional information is provided:

1 Tay purchased 1.6 million shares in Avon on 1 January 20X6. The purchase consideration consisted of 1.2 million shares in Tay which were valued at £6.50 each at the acquisition date. This transaction has not yet been entered in the books of Tay and is not reflected in the above balance sheet.

2 The fair value of Avon's fixed assets at 1 January 20X6 was £4.8 million. Avon neither purchased nor sold any fixed assets during 20X6 and depreciation is to be ignored. There were no material differences between the book value and fair value of Avon's net current assets at the date of acquisition.

3 The directors of Tay estimated, at the date of acquisition, that costs of £0.7 million will need to be incurred in 20X7 to re-organise the activities of Avon so as to maximise the benefits arising from the amalgamation. The directors are of the opinion that that these re-organisations costs should be treated as part of the purchase price.

4 The policy of Tay is to write off goodwill over ten years.

Required:
(a) State the objective of FRS 7, entitled *Fair Value Accounting*. Advise the management of Tay plc concerning the appropriate accounting treatment of fixed asset values at the acquisition date, and planned future re-organisation costs, in order to comply with this objective.
(b) The consolidated balance sheet of Tay plc and its subsidiary at 31 December 20X6 in accordance with company policy and standard accounting practice.

(Chartered Institute of Bankers)

* Question 5

Summer Wine Ltd was formed some years ago to bottle and distribute Holmfirth water for making true Yorkshire tea. It has expanded its activities by acquiring two other local concerns, Clegg Ltd and Compo Ltd.

Summer Wine Ltd purchased 1,000,000 ordinary shares in Clegg Ltd on 1 April 20X3 for £900,000. At that date the balance in the profit and loss account of Clegg Ltd stood at £50,000 (debit) and the balance on the general reserve was nil. The 600,000 ordinary shares in Compo Ltd were acquired on 1 October 20X6 at a cost of £600,000. It may be assumed that profit accrued evenly over the year.

The following balances have been extracted from the books of Summer Wine Ltd, Clegg Ltd and Compo Ltd as at 31 March 20X7:

	Summer Wine Ltd		Clegg Ltd		Compo Ltd	
	£000	£000	£000	£000	£000	£000
Ordinary share capital		3,000		1,000		1,000
(£1 shares)						
Profit and loss		240		190		50
account 1 Apr. 20X6						
General reserve		960				100
Trading profit for year		370		130		100
Fixed assets at cost	4,000		1,400		1,300	
Accumulated depreciation		2,000		180		156
Stock	760		80		32	
Debtors	960		540		70	
Creditors		800		320		36
Bank	120			200	40	
Interim dividend paid	30					
Investment in subsidiaries	1,500					
	7,370	7,370	2,020	2,020	1,442	1,442

You are also able to ascertain the following information:

(i) The directors propose to pay the following final dividends:

Summer Wine	£36,000
Clegg	£10,000
Compo	£10,000

(ii) Both Compo Ltd and Clegg Ltd supply goods to Summer Wine Ltd on a regular basis. At the current year end, the closing stock of Summer Wine contains items supplied by both companies. These are as follows:

Clegg Ltd	£340,000
Compo Ltd	£52,000

Compo Ltd supplies goods to Summer Wine at cost plus 30%. Clegg Ltd makes a gross profit of 25% of cost on all normal sales. However, sales to Summer Wine are invoiced less a bulk discount of 15% of selling price. It is group policy to exclude all profit on intercompany transactions.

(iii) Summer Wine has made no payment to Clegg Ltd for the goods supplied by Clegg Ltd which remain unsold by Summer Wine at 31 March 20X7.

(iv) In the accounts, realised and unrealised reserves should be shown separately. The group has currently made no transfers between the two.

Required:
(a) Prepare the consolidated balance sheet of the Summer Wine Group as at 31 March 20X7.
(b) Various techniques exist to present the ownership by a company of shares in another company. Briefly describe each of these techniques, when it is permissible for use and its effect on the financial reports.

Question 6

The first topic covered by an accounting standard was how best to present in the investor company's financial statements the economic effects of an investment in another company that was less than that required for normal consolidation procedures.

Combination Ltd operates a hotel marina. Expansion Ltd, a manufacturing company, holds 30% of the ordinary shares of Combination Ltd.

The separate summarised accounts for the year to 31 October 20X8 of Combination Ltd and Expansion Ltd are:

	Combination Ltd £000	Expansion Ltd £000
Balance sheet at 31 October 20X8		
Issued share capital, ordinary shares of £1	1,000	2,000
Reserves and unappropriated profits	2,000	1,500
Long-term debt	8,700	2,000
Current liabilities	300	2,500
	12,000	8,000
Fixed assets	11,200	4,000
Investment in Combination Ltd	—	900
Current assets	800	3,100
	12,000	8,000
Profit and loss account		
Profit for the year after tax	3,000	950
Share of profits of Combination Ltd	—	900
Dividends paid	(2,000)	(1,500)
Retained earnings	1,000	350

Required:

Prepare alternative presentations for the annual accounts of Expansion Ltd based upon:

  (i) a consolidation procedure bringing in the proportionate share of the assets, liabilities and profits of Combination Ltd;

 (ii) an expanded equity method whereby the proportionate share of total assets, liabilities and profits is shown on the face of the accounts but not aggregated;

(iii) an expanded equity method whereby the proportionate share of assets, liabilities and profits is shown separately but also aggregated with the appropriate items from the investor accounts.

Question 7 Carr Plc

Carr plc has invested in a number of companies. The directors usually acquire the entire share capital of a company in which Carr invests, but this did not prove possible in the case of an investment in Saunders Ltd. The directors are uncertain concerning the appropriate accounting treatment of Saunders Ltd and the following information is made available as at 31 December 20X6:

	Carr Group (excluding Saunders) £000	Saunders £000
Assets		
4 million shares in Saunders Ltd	23,500	—
Sundry net assets	126,500	20,000
	150,000	20,000
Financed by:		
Share capital (ordinary shares of £1 each)	40,000	5,000
Retained profit at 1 January 20X5	100,000	11,000
Profit for 20X5	6,400	2,000
Profit for 20X6	3,600	3,000
Less: proposed dividend for 20X6	—	(1,000)
	150,000	20,000

Carr plc purchased the shares in Saunders Ltd on 1 January 20X5. No credit has been taken in the accounts of Carr for the dividend proposed by Saunders Ltd in respect of 20X6.

Required:

(a) **Three separate balance sheets of the Carr Group at 31 December 20X6, incorporating the results of Saunders Ltd, on the assumption that Saunders Ltd is accounted for:**

   (i) As a pure investment.

   (ii) As an associated company, using equity accounting.

   (iii) As a subsidiary, using acquisition basis.

(b) **State the circumstances in which each of the three methods should be used. Advise the directors which of the above methods appears to be appropriate, based on the information provided, to comply with standard accounting practice.** *(Chartered Institute of Bankers)*

References

1 Insolvency Act 1986, section 84.
2 Companies Act 1985, section 125.
3 *Ibid.*, section 4.
4 *Ibid.*, section 43.
5 *Ibid.*, section 135.
6 Insolvency Act 1986, section 22.
7 *Ibid.*, section 84.
8 Ernst and Young, *UK GAAP* (5th edition), Longman, 1997, p. 720.
9 Companies Act 1985, Schedule 4, para. 31.
10 K. Wild and A. Guida, *Touche Ross Manual of Financial Reporting and Accounting* (3rd edition), Butterworth, 1990, p. 161.
11 FRS 9, *Associates and Joint Ventures*, ASB, 1997, para. 26.
12 *Ibid.*, para. 27.
13 FRS 2, *Accounting for Subsidiary Undertakinga*, ASB, 1992, para. 39.

CHAPTER 21

Consolidated profit and loss account

21.1 Introduction

The profit and loss account of the parent company in its company-only accounts is subject to the realisation concept. Entries are made in the profit and loss account in respect of investments only if there is a gain evidenced by a cash flow, such as the receipt of a dividend, or if there is a loss evidenced by a permanent diminution in the investment's value which is recognised under the prudence concept.

A shareholder of the parent company is made aware of unrealised changes in the value of the net assets **owned by the parent** only if it chooses to value its investments in subsidiaries and associates using the alternative accounting rules described in the preceding chapter. Under either the historical cost convention or the alternative accounting rules, however, it would be unable to ascertain the level of profits achieved by the subsidiaries and associates from an inspection of the parent's company-only accounts.

The role of the consolidated profit and loss account is to show the shareholders of the parent company the full amount of profits achieved by the parent; the full amount of the profits achieved by the subsidiaries; and the parent's proportion of the profits achieved by the associates.

If there have been any intragroup transactions, such as sales by the parent to a subsidiary, these will need to be eliminated. Although each company can report profits made from other group companies in its company-only accounts, they must be cancelled on consolidation if they have not been realised as far as the group is concerned. In this chapter we consider the following:

- Format of the consolidated profit and loss account
- A step approach to preparing a consolidated profit and loss account for wholly and partly owned subsidiaries
- Subconsolidation stages where there is more than one subsidiary and an associate
- FRS 9 *Associates and Joint Ventures*.

21.2 Format of the consolidated profit and loss account

The format of the company consolidated profit and loss account is set out in Figure 21.1 in a sectional format that highlights the structure of the statement and the nature of the information it contains.

Figure 21.1   Sectional (FRS 9) format of a consolidated profit and loss account.

First section
Trading activities of whole group

Group turnover	[Parent + subsidiary – intragroup sales]
Cost of sales	[Parent + subsidiary – intragroup purchases]
Gross profit	[Parent + subsidiary – intragroup]
Distribution costs	[Parent + subsidiary]
Administrative expenses	[Parent + subsidiary]
Other operating income	[Parent + subsidiary]
Group operating profit	[Parent + subsidiary]

Share of operating profit in
    Joint ventures   [Proportion of Joint Venture]
    Associates   [Proportion of Associate]

Interest:
    Interest receivable   [Parent + subsidiary]
        [+ Proportion of Associate]
    Interest payable   [Parent + subsidiary]
    Interest payable   [Proportion of Associate]

Profit on ordinary
activities before tax   [Parent + subsidiary + proportion of associate and joint venture]
Tax on profits on ordinary
activities   [Parent + subsidiary + proportion of associate and joint venture]
Profit on ordinary
activities after tax   [Parent + subsidiary + proportion of associate and joint venture]

Second section
**Amount of profit in the subsidiaries that does not belong to the shareholders
of the parent company**

Minority interest in partly-owned subsidiaries   [Minority interest]

Third section
**Extraordinary items that are attributable to the shareholders
of the parent company**

Extraordinary items [under the provision of   [Parent + subsidiary – minority +
FRS 3 it is extremely unlikely that there will   proportion of associate]
be an entry under this heading]

Fourth section
**Profit that has been realised and is available to the shareholders
of the parent company**

Profit for the year. This is the parent company's profit plus the profit of wholly owned subsidiaries plus the parent company's share of the profits of partly owned subsidiaries plus the parent company's share of the profit of associated companies.

Fifth section
Amount of dividends declared by the parent company only

This section includes the interim and final dividends declared by the parent company for the financial year. The dividends include both proposed and paid dividends.

Sixth section
Amount retained out of the profit for the year for reinvestment

Amount transferred to reserves is the amount of the profit for the year that is not to be distributed as dividend by the parent. It is ploughed back into the business.

21.3 A step approach to preparing a consolidated profit and loss account for wholly and partly owned subsidiaries

The consolidated profit and loss account can be prepared in a series of steps. For a group with subsidiaries we follow the five steps shown in Figure 21.2. If there are also associates, then there are three additional steps, as shown in Figure 21.3.

21.4 Subconsolidation stages where there is more than one subsidiary and an associate

Where there is more than one subsidiary and an associate, the consolidation is built up by aggregating one company at a time. The steps explained in Figure 21.3 will be applied to each company as it is aggregated.

We will now prepare the consolidated accounts for Strong plc using subconsolidating stages:

Figure 21.2 Five steps to consolidate subsidiary companies.

Steps 1 and 2 to arrive at profit on ordinary activities after tax

Aggregate the profit and loss accounts of the parent company and the subsidiary companies on a line-by-line basis.

Eliminate intragroup transactions such as intragroup sales; unrealised profit on intragroup sales; dividends paid by subsidiary companies to parent company.

Step 3 to arrive at the profit before extraordinary items

Deduct the minority interest for partly owned subsidiaries.

Step 4 to arrive at the profit for the financial year

Calculate the extraordinary profits and losses of the parent company plus the extraordinary profits and losses of wholly owned subsidiaries plus the parent company's share of the extraordinary gains and losses of partly owned subsidiaries.

Step 5 to arrive at the retained profit for the year

Disclose the dividends declared by the parent company.

Figure 21.3 Additional three steps to consolidate associated companies.

Step 6 to arrive at the profit on ordinary activities before tax figure

Add the parent company's share of operating profit of associates and joint ventures.

Step 7 to arrive at the profit on ordinary activities after tax figure

Add the parent company's share of the tax on the profit on ordinary activities of associates and joint ventures.

Step 8 to arrive at the profit for the financial year

Add the parent company's share of the extraordinary gains and losses of the associates and joint ventures to the figure already calculated in Step 4.

- Stage 1: consolidate the wholly owned subsidiary.
- Stage 2: consolidate the partly owned subsidiary.
- Stage 3: consolidate the associate.

We take the profit and loss information from Figure 20.4 and assume that:

- Strong plc has sold goods that cost £200 to Hundred plc for £250 and the goods are still in stock at 31 December 20X1.
- Hundred plc paid a dividend of £1,000 to Strong plc on 31 December 20X1.

The subconsolidation worksheet for stage 1 is set out in Figure 21.4. The amount transferred to reserves in the consolidated profit and loss account is £1,390 because the unrealised profit has been deducted from the aggregate total.

Figure 21.4 Stage 1: subconsolidating the wholly owned subsidiary.

Profit and loss accounts of Strong plc and Hundred plc
for the year ended 31 December 20X1 – subconsolidation worksheet

	Strong plc £	Hundred plc £	Aggregate £	Eliminate Dr/(Cr) £	Group P&L account £
Turnover	9,000	4,500	13,500	250 a	13,250
Cost of sales	4,500	2,250	6,750	(250) a	
				50 b	6,550
Gross profit	4,500	2,250	6,750		6,700
Distribution costs	(900)	(450)	(1,350)		(1,350)
Administrative expenses	(720)	(360)	(1,080)		(1,080)
Operating profit	2,880	1,440	4,320		4,270
Investment income from:					
Subsidiaries	1,000		1,000	1,000 c	
Associates					
Other investments					
Profit before tax	3,880	1,440	5,320		4,270
Tax	720	360	1,080		1,080
Profit after tax	3,160	1,080	4,240		3,190
Extraordinary items	0	0	0		0
Profit for the year	3,160	1,080	4,240		3,190
Dividends	1,800	1,000	2,800	(1,000) c	1,800
Transferred to reserves	1,360	80	1,440		1,390
Consolidated balance sheet entry to stock				(50) b	
				0	

Figure 21.4 (cont.)

Notes cross-referenced to the worksheet:

(a) The intragroup sales are eliminated.

(b) The unrealised profit on sale is eliminated from the profit and loss account. The corresponding credit entry will be to stock in the balance sheet so that the closing stock is reduced by £50.

(c) The dividend paid by the subsidiary to the holding company is cancelled against the income from subsidiary companies.

The subconsolidation worksheet for stage 2 is set out in Figure 21.5, and that for stage 3 in Figure 21.6.

Figure 21.5 Stage 2: subconsolidating the partly owned subsidiary.

Profit and loss accounts of Strong/Hundred and Sixty plc
for the year ended 31 December 20X1 – subconsolidation worksheet

	Strong/ Hundred plc	Sixty plc	Aggregate	Eliminate Dr/(Cr)	Group P&L account
	£	£	£	£	£
Turnover	13,250	4,500	17,750		17,750
Cost of sales	6,550	2,250	8,800		8,800
Gross profit	6,700	2,250	8,950		8,950
Distribution costs	(1,350)	(450)	(1,800)		(1,800)
Administrative expenses	(1,080)	(360)	(1,440)		(1,440)
Operating profit	4,270	1,440	5,710		5,710
Investment income from:					
Subsidiaries					
Associates					
Other investments					
Profit before tax	4,270	1,440	5,710		5,710
Tax	1,080	360	1,440		1,440
Profit after tax	3,190	1,080	4,270		4,270
Minority interest				432 [d]	432
Profit before extraordinary items					3,838
Extraordinary items	0	0	0	0	0
Profit for the year	3,190	1,080	4,270		3,838
Dividends	1,800	—	1,800		1,800
Transferred to reserves	1,390	1,080	2,470		2,038
Consolidated balance sheet entry					
Minority interest				(432) [d]	
				0	

Figure 21.5 (cont.)

Notes cross-referenced to the worksheet in Figure 21.5:

(d) The minority shareholders are entitled to 40% of the profit of Sixty plc, i.e. 40% of £1,080. This is transferred to the minority interest in the consolidated balance sheet.

Figure 21.6 Stage 3: subconsolidating the associate.

Profit and loss accounts of Strong/Hundred/Sixty and Twenty plc
for the year ended 31 December 20X1 – subconsolidation worksheet

	Strong/ Hundred/ Sixty £	Twenty plc adjustments	Group P&L account £
Group turnover	17,750		17,750
Cost of sales	8,800		8,800
Gross profit	8,950		8,950
Distribution costs	(1,800)		(1,800)
Administrative expenses	(1,440)		(1,440)
Group operating profit	5,710		5,710
Share of operating profit in:			
Associate company		20% of £1,440	288
			5,998
Tax on profit*	1,440		
Associate company tax		20% of £360	(1,512)
Profit after tax	4,270		4,486
Minority interest	432		432
Profit before extraordinary items	3,838		4,054
Extraordinary items	0	20% of £0	0
Profit for the year	3,838		4,054
Dividends	1,800		1,800
Transferred to reserves	2,038		2,254
*Tax relates to the following:	Parent and subsidiaries		1,440
	Associates		72

The consolidated profit and loss account of the Strong Group is now complete. We have aggregated Hundred plc and Sixty plc and accounted on an equity accounting basis for Twenty plc. The consolidated profit and loss account in Format 1 Companies Act 1985 style is set out in Figure 21.7.

Figure 21.7 Consolidated profit and loss account of the Strong Group for the year ended 31 December 20X1.

	£
Turnover	17,750
Cost of sales	8,800
Gross profit	8,950
Distribution costs	(1,800)
Administrative expenses	(1,440)
Operating profit	5,710
Share of operating profits in associated company	288
Profit on ordinary activities before tax	5,998
Tax	(1,512)
Profit on ordinary activities after tax	4,486
Minority interest	432
Profit before extraordinary items	4,054
Extraordinary items	0
Profit for the year	4,054
Dividends	1,800
Transferred to reserves	2,254

21.5 ASB review of accounting for associates

The mechanics that we have illustrated in Figure 21.6 to account for the results of an associate were first used by the Royal Dutch Shell group in 1964. Prior to that the only entry in the profit and loss account would have been any dividend receivable from the associate.

In 1971 the ASC issued SSAP 1 *Accounting for Associated Companies*, which required all companies with investments that gave them significant influence to apply the same approach, provided their intention was to retain the investment for the long term. It would have been inappropriate for a company to acquire short-term investments and include a share of the profits in their profit and loss account; in such a case, dividend receivable should be brought into the accounts.

The treatment we have illustrated in Chapters 19 and 20 is a modified form of consolidation. It does not aggregate each of the assets, liabilities, income and expenses of the associate in the same way as subsidiaries are treated. Instead, it uses **equity accounting**, under which the investing company incorporates the investing company's share of the pre-tax profits, tax and post-tax profits of the associate in the consolidated profit and loss account, and adjusts the carrying value of the investment in the consolidated balance sheet by the investing company's proportion of undistributed retained profit. However, it was not until the Companies Act 1989 that there was a statutory requirement to equity account for associates.

21.5.1   Why is it important to establish whether an investee is an associate?

Associate status is established by the existence of the ability to exercise significant influence. This is important because, although an investing company is happy to recognise associate status as long as the associate is profitable, if the investee becomes unprofitable, there is a natural eagerness to cease recognising it as an associate in order to avoid the investing company's share of any losses being brought into the profit and loss account.

21.5.2   Accounting for Associates under FRS 9 *Associates and Joint Ventures*[1]

SSAP 1 *Accounting for Associated Companies* set out various relationships that could indicate the ability to exercise significant influence.[2] These ranged from quantitative, such as the existence of a 20% holding, to qualitative, such as participation in the financial, operating and dividend policy decisions of the investee. FRED 11 *Associates and Joint Ventures*, issued by the ASB in 1996[3], broadly followed the basis set out in SSAP 1. SSAP 1 was replaced (for listed companies) by the issue of FRS 9 in 1997.

Definition of an associate

Companies legislation provides that an entity holding 20% or more of the voting rights should be presumed to exercise significant influence. The Companies Act does not define significant influence. FRS 9 gives more detailed guidance and definitions. It is not a mechanistic test under FRS 9 and the presumption is rebutted if the investor does not satisfy the FRS 9 criteria. A significant influence is normally exercised by the investor having a director on the board of the investee, but the key aspect is that there is a formal or informal understanding which allows the investor to participate in policy decisions. We will comment briefly on the FRS 9 definitions.

An associate is an entity (other than a subsidiary) in which another entity holds a **participating interest** and over whose operating and financial policies the investor exercises a **significant influence**.

A participating interest is a beneficial interest in shares held on a **long-term**, continuing basis to secure a benefit for the investor by the exercise of **control** or **influence** arising from holding those shares.

A significant influence exists when:

● there is **active involvement** by the investor in strategic decisions of the investee, such as changes in markets and product, changes in scale of the business, and dividend policy; and

● the investor's strategic interest determines the policies implemented by the investee.

To account for associates FRS 9 requires that:

● in consolidated financial statements an investor should use the equity method; and

● in the investor's individual accounts investments in joint ventures should be treated as fixed asset investments and shown either at cost, less any amounts written off, or at valuation.

21.5.3   Accounting for Joint Ventures under FRS 9 *Associates and Joint Ventures*

Definition of a joint venture

FRS 9 defines a joint venture as an entity that, as a result of a contractual relationship, is jointly controlled by the reporting entity and other venturers, i.e. none of the venturers individually controls it. This means that decisions on financial and operating policy essential to the activities, economic performance and financial position of that venture require each venturer's consent.

To account for joint ventures FRS 9 requires that:

● in consolidated financial statements an investor should use the **gross equity method**; and

● in the investor's individual accounts investments in joint ventures should be treated as fixed asset investments and shown either at cost, less any amounts written off, or at valuation.

Gross equity method

This is a new method which is a form of equity method under which the investor's share of the aggregate gross assets and liabilities underlying the net amount included for the investment is shown on the face of the balance sheet and, in the profit and loss account, **the investor's share of the investee's turnover is noted**.

The requirement to note the **turnover** was to respond to the objections of companies that equity accounting understated their turnover and companies such as British Aerospace had already adopted the practice of disclosing *'Sales, including share of joint venture sales'* and deducting the *'Share of joint venture sales'* to arrive at the statutory turnover figure.

When is it considered appropriate by the ASB to use proportional consolidation?

Prior to FRS 9 companies such as construction companies set up unincorporated partnerships when carrying out certain joint ventures e.g. assume that on 1 January 19X6 two construction companies, Tarcam plc and Liang plc enter into a partnership to tender for the construction by 31 December 19X9 of a new bridge over the River Thames. When they prepared their prepare their accounts at 31 December 19X6 each company would account for the contract on a proportional consolidation basis.

However, because FRS 9 has defined a joint venture as 'an entity that, as a result of a contractual relationship, is jointly controlled' and defined an entity as 'a body corporate, partnership, **or unincorporated association**' such partnership arrangements as that between Tarcam plc and Liang plc now fall within the FRS and Companies Act requirements. The Companies Act does not permit proportional consolidation and the ASB has therefore accommodated the pre FRS 9 proportional consolidation treatment by creating a new animal, the Joint Arrangement that is Not an Entity (a JANE).

It defines a JANE as 'A contractual arrangement under which the participants engage in joint activities that do not create an entity **because it would not be carrying on a trade or business of its own'**.

FRS 9 para. 8 gives the following additional information, namely, that 'For a joint arrangement to amount to an entity, it must carry on a trade or business, meaning a trade or business **of its own and not just part of its participants' trades or businesses'**.

This means that if the arrangement falls within the definition of an entity, it will be accounted for as a joint venture by equity accounting. If it does not fall within the definition of an entity i.e. it is a JANE it will be accounted for by proportional consolidation.

An illustration of approach to deciding if a joint arrangement is a Joint Venture or a JANE

Proportional consolidation would be appropriate for joint arrangements such as cost-sharing arrangements or one-off construction projects when each participant would include in their individual and consolidated accounts its share of the assets, liabilities and cash flows arising from the arrangement.

However, it can be difficult at first to understand how the decision is made to classify as a Joint Venture or JANE. The following illustration with Tarcam plc (a construction company) and Stagebus plc (a coach operator) explains the conceptual approach to classifying a joint arrangement:

● Assume that Tarcam plc entered into a contract with Stagebus plc to build **and operate** a toll bridge over the River Thames.

● The test is whether this arrangement falls within the definition of **an entity**

● This means determining whether the joint arrangement is carrying on a **different trade of its own**

● The joint arrangement is to trade as a toll bridge operator

● This is different from the participants' trades of construction and coach operator

● The joint arrangement is an entity

● It is therefore a joint venture and accounted for using equity accounting.

21.5.4 FRS 9 Disclosure requirement

Under SSAP 1 there had been disclosure of the net tangible assets underlying the investment in the consolidated balance sheet and the investor's proportion of the associate pretax profits, tax and post-tax profits. FRS 9 *Associates and Joint Ventures* proposes additional disclosures. Where the investor's interest is substantial, i.e. where it exceeds 15% of the investor's gross assets, gross liabilities, turnover or results, then the following information should be disclosed for an associate (for a joint venture turnover is not required):

● turnover for the associates;

● fixed assets;

● current assets;

● liabilities due within one year;

● liabilities due after more than one year.

Where the interest exceeds 25%, there is additional disclosure. A note should name the associate or joint venture and give its share of profit before tax, taxation and profit after tax.

The likely effect of FRS 9

The significant influence test may be more difficult to satisfy than the 20% rule
It will probably be more difficult for investors to establish associate status for an investment. It will prevent investors who have failed to achieve a take-over from bringing in a

proportion of the investee profits under the guise of accounting for an associate. There will be greater confidence that any profits brought into the consolidated accounts from associates will be accessible as cash flows, at least in the long term, and there will be greater transparency with regard to the implication for the investor of loans and liabilities incurred by the associate; after all, if an investor is unable to have a say in determining whether a dividend is paid or not, what justification could there be for including a share of the profit?

Failing the significant influence test may lead to re-classification of investments

The ASB in FRS 9 do not regard the 20% presumption as sufficient and companies should go back and review investments that had been classified as an associate pre-FRS 9 by testing for significant influence e.g. checking if there is investor Board representation on the investee's Board.

Users will be more able to assess associate position and performance

The requirement to disclose the share of associates' operating profit and interest payable rather than simply share of profit before tax means that it will be possible to identify aspects such as interest cover e.g. a pre-tax share of profits of £1,000 in an associate where there is a 25% holding might have arisen from an associate with £4,000 operating profit i.e. with no gearing or from an associate with operating profits of £10m less Interest payable of £9.999m i.e. a dangerously highly geared company. This means a user is more able to assess the risk attached to an investment in an associate.

However, it will be easier for companies to argue that they should not equity account for an investment that becomes loss-making on the grounds of lack of significant influence.[4]

Summary

The profit and loss accounts of individual companies are subject to the realisation concept. Investment income is recognised only when it is declared by the investee company and reasonably certain to be realised in the form of cash.

Where subsidiaries do not pass all of their profit up as a dividend, the shareholders of the parent company are unable to form a view of management performance. They are unable to ascertain from the parent company accounts the profits that are attributable to investments in companies over which their directors have influence or control.

The consolidated profit and loss account provides them with the means to see the overall performance of the group.

The balance sheets of individual companies are constrained by the asset recognition criteria that assets must belong to the company. The shareholders of the parent company are unable to form a view from the accounts of the parent company of the net assets that are controlled by the management of the parent company. The alternative accounting rules allow the company to increase the investment value to reflect the underlying net asset values of the shares owned. But they do not allow the company to include all of the net assets of investee companies unless they have a 100% shareholding.

The consolidated balance sheet provides them with the means to see all assets and liabilities **controlled** by the parent company, even though they might not satisfy the strict ownership criteria applied to the individual company balance sheet.

The ASB has issued FRS 9 to improve the information given about associates and joint ventures, particularly where they are significant, by following a layered approach applying the 15% and 25% thresholds that satisfies user needs and recognises cost implication for preparers.

Review questions

1 If instead of selling stock intragroup, Strong plc had sold a fixed asset which it held at £200 book value to Hundred plc for £250 on 1 January 20X1, what additional matters would need to be considered and adjusted for at 31 December 20X1 in:

 (a) the consolidated profit and loss account; and

 (b) the consolidated balance sheet?

 Illustrate the numerical effect, making any assumptions you consider necessary.

2 Some items in a consolidated profit and loss account relate to the combined entities and some items relate to the shareholders of the parent company. The consolidated profit and loss account has therefore been described as two-tiered.[5]

 (a) Explain why it is constructed with this two-tier approach.

 (b) How would you describe the consolidation process that produced a consolidated profit and loss account in which all items relate to the shareholders of the parent company?

 (c) How would you describe the consolidation process that produced a consolidated profit and loss account in which all items relate to the combined entities?

3 The Shortfall Group has been discussing the question of security for loans and overdraft with the group's bankers. The bankers have suggested the following types of security:

 (a) Guarantees from the directors.

 (b) A guarantee from the parent company to secure a loan to a subsidiary.

 (c) A guarantee from each of the companies in the group for a loan to one of the other companies.

 (d) A guarantee from each company in the group for loans to all other companies in the group.

 (e) A guarantee from each company in the group for loans to all other companies in the group with a debenture from each company.

 Explain the rights of the bank against the assets shown in the consolidated balance sheet in each of the above arrangements.

4 In the early days of group accounting (up until about 1929), the consolidation and equity methods were regarded as alternative accounting treatments for investments in subsidiaries and for the profits/losses generated by them. Since then the consolidation method has prevailed in this field.

 (a) Outline the similarities, and differences, between the two methods.

 (b) Explain the conventional present-day uses of the two methods.

 (c) Argue for or against the general use of the equity method, in accounting for investments in subsidiaries.

5 'Equity accounting should only be allowed if the investor is certain to obtain access to his share of the investee's cash flows within a period of time set by the ASB, e.g. within five years.' Discuss.

6 'Proportional consolidation would be a more informative form of presentation for associates than equity accounting supported by summarised financial statements.' Discuss and explain why the ASB has not permitted this treatment

7 'Equity accounting is a confused concept. It is not consistent with the requirement that consolidated accounts should only contain assets and liabilities that are under the **control** of the management of the investor.' Discuss with particular consideration of the justification for revising the investment in associates in the consolidated accounts to reflect underlying net asset backing.

8 It has been stated by Allan Cook, ASB Technical Director in the preface to the Exposure Draft *Associates and Joint Ventures* that 'Companies are increasingly seeking alliances to pool their resources as a means of sharing risk and gaining access to new markets. It is therefore important for users of financial statements to have clear information about such alliances and their effect on the company's financial position and performance.' Explain (a) how FRS 9 provides such information; and (b) likely effects on financial position and performance of associate and joint venture alliances.

9 'Return on capital employed based on a comparison of the consolidated operating profit with the net capital employed disclosed in the consolidated balance sheet is a meaningless figure because it is only the asset values of the subsidiaries that have been restated at fair values as at the date of acquisition.' Discuss and explain how the position could be improved.

10 The Hanson Annual Report 1996 contains the following note:

The following joint ventures which are the principal joint ventures in the group, have been proportionately included in the consolidated accounts:

Coal mining

Narama mine	Australia	50%
Warkworth mine	Australia	44%
Black Beauty Coal Mine	USA	33%

Gas fields

Schooner	UK	5%
Johnston	UK	5%
Welland	UK	11%

Discuss the effect that FRS 9 *Associates and Joint Ventures* may have on the Hanson Annual Report 1998.

Exercises

An extract from the solution is provided in the appendix at the end of the text for exercises marked with an asterisk (*).

Question 1

The profit and loss accounts of Try plc and Hard plc for the year ended 31 December 20X5 are as follows:

	Try plc	*Hard plc*
	£	£
Profit before tax	80,000	56,000
Tax	42,000	28,600
	38,000	27,400
Proposed dividend	20,000	
	18,000	27,400

Try plc acquired 75% of the equity shares of Hard plc on 1 January 20X3.

Required:
Prepare a consolidated profit and loss account for the year ended 31 December 20X5.

Questions 2–5

The following profit and loss accounts and balance sheets of Mother plc and Daughter plc as at 31 December 20X6 are to be used for questions 2 to 5:

	Mother plc £000	Daughter plc £000
Profit before tax	300	100
(includes dividends received from Daughter plc)		
Tax	(120)	(30)
Profit after tax	180	70
Transfer to general reserves	(30)	(20)
Dividends	(50)	(20)
Retained	100	30
Balance brought forward at 1 Jan 20X6	50	10
	150	40
Balance sheets		
Fixed assets	300	150
Investment in Daughter plc	200	
Net current assets	280	110
	780	260
Share capital	500	200
General reserve	130	20
Profit and loss account	150	40
	780	260

* ## Question 2

Required:
(a) Prepare a consolidated profit and loss account and consolidated balance sheet as at 31 December 20X6 on the assumption that Mother plc acquired all of the shares in Daughter plc on its incorporation on 1 January 20X2.
(b) Explain accounting treatment.

* ## Question 3

Required:
(a) Prepare a consolidated profit and loss account and consolidated balance sheet as at 31 December 20X6 on the assumption that Mother plc acquired 80% of the shares in Daughter plc on its incorporation on 1 January 20X2.
(b) Explain accounting treatment.

* ## Question 4

Required:

(a) **Prepare a consolidated profit and loss account and consolidated balance sheet as at 31 December 20X6 on the assumption that Mother plc acquired all of the shares in Daughter plc on 1 January 20X4, at which date the Daughter plc accounts showed credit balances on the general reserve of £15,000 and on the profit and loss account of £5,000, and corresponding net assets of £220,000.**

(b) **Explain accounting treatment.**

* ## Question 5

Required:

(a) **Prepare a consolidated profit and loss account and consolidated balance sheet as at 31 December 20X6 on the assumption that Mother plc acquired 80% of the shares in Daughter plc on 1 January 20X4, at which date the Daughter plc accounts showed credit balances on the general reserve of £15,000 and on the profit and loss account of £5,000, and corresponding net assets of £220,000.**

(b) **Explain accounting treatment.**

* ## Question 6

(a) On 1 October 19X0 LA plc acquired 60% of the issued share capital of TS plc, at a cost of £2.90 per share.

The trial balances of the two companies at 30 September 20X1 (their accounting year-end) are as follows:

	LA plc £	TS plc £
Debit balances:		
Fixed assets, at cost	450,000	100,000
Debtors	126,000	110,000
Shares in TS plc, at cost	62,640	—
Stock and work in progress	96,000	57,000
Cost of sales	988,000	500,000
Current account with TS plc	28,400	—
Distribution costs	108,000	47,000
Administration expenses	72,000	33,000
Cash in hand	2,360	2,400
Cash at bank	42,000	26,000
	£1,975,400	875,400
Credit balances:		
Ordinary shares of £1 each, fully paid	180,000	36,000
General reserve, balance at 1 Oct. 19X0	234,000	54,700
Profit and loss, balance at 1 Oct. 19X0	68,400	23,400
Current account with LA plc	—	27,200
Sales	1,318,000	659,000
Provision for depreciation, at 1 Oct. 19X0	67,000	32,400
Creditors	108,000	42,700
	£1,975,400	£875,400

Additional information:

1 TS plc's purchases include £36,000 of goods which were bought from LA plc. This stock was transferred at cost plus a mark-up of 20%. On 30 September 20X1 the stock of TS plc included £6,000 of these goods at transfer price.

2 On 29 September 20X1 TS plc had sent a cheque for £1,200 to LA plc; this was not received by LA plc until 3 October 20X1.

3 Depreciation for the year is to be charged as follows:

> LA plc   £23,000
> TS plc   £10,000

4 Dividends proposed are as follows:

> LA plc   £18,000
> TS plc   £13,000

5 Corporation tax on profits for the year are to be provided as follows:

> LA plc   £55,000
> TS plc   £35,000

6 LA plc and TS plc have not made any issues or redemptions of shares during the year.

7 LA plc has not yet made any necessary adjustment for goodwill or capital reserve on acquisition arising from its acquisition of shares in TS plc. The directors have requested the auditors to advise on appropriate policy.

Required:
Prepare for the LA Group the consolidated profit and loss account for the year ended 30 September 20X1 and a balance sheet at that date and advise on treatment of goodwill.

(b) In (a) above the shares in the subsidiary were acquired at the beginning of the financial year. If the acquisition had taken place part way through the year, it would have affected the preparation of the consolidated profit and loss account and balance sheet.

Required:
State how the final accounts which you have prepared in answer to (a) above would have been different. Give reasons for the differences. (Figures are not required.)

(c) Published accounts often contain a great deal of detail regarding the accounting policies adopted by a company. However, they make no reference to the fundamental concepts assumed to be incorporated.

Required:
State the fundamental concepts which are specified in SSAP 2 *Disclosure of Accounting Policies* and explain what action must be taken by the accountant if accounts are prepared in breach of any of these fundamental concepts.

(CIMA, November 1990)

Question 7

Dolphin plc owns 33.33% of the share capital of Bears Ltd. The shares (200,000) were purchased five years ago for £300,000. At that time, the balance sheet of Bears Ltd was as follows:

Net assets (at fair value)	£750,000

Represented by:

Share capital (ordinary £1 shares)	600,000
Reserves	150,000
	£750,000

The current balance sheets of the two companies as at 31 December 20X7 are as follows:

	Dolphin plc £	Bears Ltd £
Net assets	1,000,000	1,500,000
Investment in Bears Ltd	300,000	—
	1,300,000	1,500,000

Represented by:

	Dolphin plc £	Bears Ltd £
Share capital (ordinary £1 shares)	900,000	600,000
Reserves	400,000	900,000
	1,300,000	1,500,000

Profit and loss accounts for the year ended 31 December 20X7 are:

	Dolphin plc £	Bears Ltd £
Operating profit	120,000	180,000
Dividend received from Bears Ltd	10,000	—
	130,000	180,000
Dividend paid	60,000	30,000
Retained profit, added to reserves	70,000	150,000

Required:
Prepare a consolidated profit and loss account and balance sheet as at 31 December 20X7.

Question 8

The following are the summarised profit and loss accounts and balance sheets of Ball plc, which had already consolidated with a subsidiary, Bin plc, and Sun plc another subsidiary.

Profit and loss accounts for year ended 30 June 20X6

	Ball plc £000	Sun plc £000
Operating profit	150	90
Taxation	(30)	(20)
Preference dividend paid	(25)	(12)
Ordinary dividend payable	(30)	(20)
	65	38

Balance sheets as at 30 June 19X6

Tangible fixed assets	3,000	1,100
Investment in Sun plc	800	
Current assets	500	250
Current liabilities including dividends payable	(300)	(100)
	4,000	1,250
£1 Ordinary shares	2,000	600
£1 Preference shares	500	200
Share premium	500	30
Profit and loss	1,000	420
	4,000	1,250

The following information is available:

1 Profits and losses accrue evenly throughout the year.

2 It is policy of the group to retain the goodwill as an asset and carry out impairment reviews.

3 Ball plc acquired 80% of the ordinary shares of Sun plc in 20X3 when the balance on Sun plc's profit and loss account was £300,000 and the balance on share premium was £30,000.

4 No dividends from Sun plc have been accrued by Ball plc.

5 No fixed assets were bought or sold during the year and no shares have been issued since the acquisition in 20X3.

Required:

(a) Show how Ball plc's investment in Sun plc would appear in the consolidated accounts of Ball plc as at 30 June 20X6 assuming that Ball plc lost control over Sun plc on 31 March 20X6 because of severe long-term restrictions but retained significant influence.

(b) What difference would it make to the accounts in (a) if:
  (i) Ball plc had not retained significant influence;
  (ii) The investment in Sun plc was held exclusively for resale.

Question 9

On 1 January 20X5 Tinker Ltd bought 6,300 of the shares of Tailor Ltd. The total issued share capital of Tailor was then, and remains, 7,000 fully paid shares of £1 nominal value.

Tinker's summarised accounts for 20X5 are as follows:

Tinker Ltd and its subsidiary Tailor Ltd

	Parent company's accounts £		Consolidated group accounts £
Profit and loss account:			
Trading profit		8,400	10,200
Dividend from subsidiary		900	—
		9,300	10,200
Dividend on share capital		4,000	4,000
		5,300	6,200
Brought forward		22,700	22,700
Carried forward		28,000	28,900
Balance sheet:			
Plant and equipment (cost)		184,900	207,900
Depreciation		32,000	44,000
		152,900	163,900
Investment in subsidiary (cost)		9,100	—
Stock (cost) – Note 1	63,000		70,000
Debtors	23,000		25,000
Southern Bank	16,000		16,000
	102,000		111,000
Eastern Bank	—	6,000	
Creditors	56,000	58,000	
		46,000	64,000	47,000
		208,000	210,900
Ordinary share capital			
(£1 shares fully paid)		180,000	180,000
Reserves – Note 2		28,000	29,700
Minority interest		—	1,200
		208,000	210,900

Notes:

1 It is known that at 31 December 20X5 Tinker had in stock goods invoiced to it by Tailor during 20X5 for £1,200, the cost of which to Tailor was £900. An appropriate adjustment has been made for this (so far as it affects the parent company) in the group accounts.

2 The group reserves at 31 December 20X5 were as follows:

	£
Profit retained	28,900
Capital reserve on consolidation attributable to interest of parent company	800
	29,700

Required:
Prepare summarised accounts for Tailor Ltd for 20X5 in the same form.

Question 10

H Ltd has one subsidiary, S Ltd. The company has held a controlling interest for several years. The latest financial statements for the two companies and the consolidated financial statements for the H Group are as shown below:

Profit and loss accounts for the year ended 30 September 20X4

	H Ltd £000	S Ltd £000	H Group £000
Turnover	4,000	2,200	5,700
Cost of sales	(1,100)	(960)	(1,605)
	2,900	1,240	4,095
Administration	(420)	(130)	(550)
Distribution	(170)	(95)	(265)
Dividends receivable	180	—	—
Profit before tax	2,490	1,015	3,280
Corporation tax	(620)	(335)	(955)
Profit after tax	1,870	680	2,325
Minority interest	—	—	(170)
	1,870	680	2,155
Dividends	(250)	(240)	(250)
	1,620	440	1,905
Balance brought forward	2,700	1,020	2,335
Balance carried forward	4,320	1,460	4,240

Balance sheets at 30 September 20X4

	H Ltd £000	H Ltd £000	S Ltd £000	S Ltd £000	H Group £000	H Group £000
Fixed assets:						
Tangible	7,053		2,196		9,249	
Investment in S Ltd	1,700	8,753	—	2,196	—	9,249
Current assets:						
Stocks	410		420		785	
Debtors	400		220		595	
Dividend receivable	135		—		—	
Bank	27	972	19	659	46	1,426
Current liabilities						
Creditors	(100)		(80)		(155)	
Proposed dividend	(200)		(180)		(200)	
Dividend to minority	—		—		(45)	
Taxation	(605)	(905)	(375)	(635)	(980)	(1,380)
		8,820		2,220		9,295

	H Ltd £000	S Ltd £000	H Group £000
Share capital	4,500	760	4,500
Profit and loss	4,320	1,460	4,240
	8,820	2,220	8,740
Minority interest	—	—	555
	8,820	2,220	9,295

Goodwill of £410,000 was written off at the date of acquisition.

Required:

(a) Calculate the percentage of S Ltd which is owned by H Ltd.

(b) Calculate the value of sales made between the two companies during the year.

(c) Calculate the amount of unrealised profit which had been included in the stock figure as a result of intercompany trading and which had to be cancelled on consolidation.

(d) Calculate the value of intercompany debtors and creditors cancelled on consolidation.

(e) Calculate the balance on S Ltd's profit and loss account when H Ltd acquired its stake in the company.

(CIMA)

Question 11

Nile plc acquired investments in Aswan plc as follows on 1 June 20X8:

(i)   720,000 Ordinary shares paid for by a one for one swap of ordinary shares

(ii) £180,000 5% debentures at par paid for in cash

(iii) 240,000 6% Preference shares at par paid for in cash

The profit and loss accounts of the two companies for the year to 31 August 20X8 were as follows:

	Nile plc £000	Aswan plc £000
Turnover	7,950	5,800
Cost of sales	(5,300)	(4,250)
Gross profit	2,650	1,550
Administration expense	(450)	(260)
(Selling and Distribution costs	(360)	(250)
Operating profit	1,840	1,040
Interest expense	(30)	(15)
Dividends receivable	130	—
Interest received/receivable	13	—
Profit before tax	1,953	1,025
Corporation tax	(643)	(355)
Profit after tax	1,310	670
Dividends proposed	(310)	(120)
Retained profit for year	1,000	550
Retained profit b/f	400	300
Retained profit c/f	1,400	850

Additional Information

1   Aswan plc has had the following capital structure for the past five years to 31 August 20X8:
    800,000 issued Ordinary shares of £1 each
    400,000 6% Preference shares of £1 each
    £300,000 5% Debentures (20X9)

2   Included in Aswan's turnover are sales of £450,000 made in Nile plc in the period following the combination. Aswan made a profit of £150,000 on the sale. Half of these goods were still held in stock by Nile plc at the year end.

3   Aswan's proposed dividend includes the full preference dividend for the year.

4   Nile's interest received/receivable item includes a full year's debenture interest received from Aswan plc on the last day of the year.

5   It has been ascertained that the combination meets alll the merger accounting requirements of FRS 6 and Companies Act 1985.

Required:
Prepare a consolidated profit and loss account for the Nile Group for the year ended 31 August 20X8.

References

1   FRS 9, *Associates and Joint Ventures*, ASB, 1997.
2   SSAP 1, *Accounting for Associated Companies*, ASC, 1982, para. 13.
3   FRED 11, *Associates and Joint Ventures*, ASB, 1996.
4   Ernst and Young, *UK GAAP* (4th edition), Macmillan, 1994, p. 389.
5   P.A. Taylor, *Consolidated Financial Reporting*, Paul Chapman Publishing, 1996, p. 181.

CHAPTER 22

Foreign currency translation

22.1 The problem

A basic concept of traditional historical cost accounting is that transactions are recorded at cost. It would seem, therefore, that recording transactions that have been entered into in a foreign currency is quite straightforward, namely, convert the foreign currency into its local counterpart such as French francs to £ sterling and record the sterling equivalent in the books. Thus the purchase of goods from a French supplier costing 2,000 francs when the exchange rate was, say, 10 francs to the pound would reveal a cost of £200.

However, in practice, a period of credit is invariably involved so that by the time the debt is settled the exchange rate may have changed, causing the notion of cost to be perceived differently. For example, the debt of 2,000 francs may be discharged at a later date when the rate of exchange had changed to 8 francs to the pound. Consequently an invoice cost of 2,000 francs formerly converted to £200 would result in expenditure of £250 (2,000/8), an additional cost on settlement of £50 representing a loss caused by a changing exchange rate.

22.2 The background

For some twenty years following the 1939–1945 conflict fixed exchange rates between countries dominated international trade so that the problem outlined above was not of critical concern because changes in the fixed exchange rates were rare. But since the late 1960s there have been significant changes. There has been a massive growth in international trade, transnational conglomerates have developed and floating exchange rates have been substituted for fixed exchange rates. Changes now occur on a daily basis so that fluctuations in cost between contract date and settlement date are usual rather than exceptional. For example,[1] companies making up accounts as at 31 December each year would translate at end of year rates. Rates for the three year-ends 1995–1997 for the US$, German mark and Japanese Yen would show that the rate of exchange of £1 sterling fluctuated against the US$ and strengthened against both the German mark and the Japanese Yen as follows:

Date	US dollar	% change	German mark	% change	Yen	% change
31.12.1995	1.56		2.20		160	
31.12.1996	1.70	+9%	2.64	+20%	198	+24%
31.12.1997	1.65	–3%	2.96	+12%	213	+8%

These end of year figures might not, of course, indicate a uniform trend, e.g. the Yen at 30 September 1997 was 195 to the £. In addition, there has been substantial foreign equity investment over a broad geographical spread, e.g. The BOC Group listed in their 1997 accounts over 100 subsidiaries in over 50 countries.

22.3 The need for standardisation

The growth of foreign trade and foreign equity investment and the significant effect that exchange differences can potentially have on results necessitates the standardisation of the accounting treatment of foreign exchange conversion and translation. For example, the 1996 accounts of Kalon plc reported a profit for the year of £11.2m in its profit and loss account whereas the Statement of Total Gains and Losses showed:

	£000
Profit for year	11,171
Currency translation differences on the net investment in foreign subsidiaries	(21,354)
Total gains and losses recognised since last annual report	(10,183)

We will consider accounting treatment in both individual companies and consolidated accounts.

22.4 Accounting treatment in the individual company

We will illustrate the accounting treatment for exchange gains and losses for:

(i) the purchase of goods;

(ii) the purchase of fixed assets;

(iii) long-term loans;

(iv) obtaining a foreign loan to finance foreign company investment.

22.4.1 Treatment of exchange gains or losses arising on the purchase of goods

There are three critical events that may typically occur in the purchase/payment cycle. These are the receipt and recording of the purchase invoice, the payment and recording of cash paid in part or full settlement and the extraction of creditor balances at the balance sheet date if the invoice has not already been settled in full.

We will illustrate the decisions required at each of these critical events for the following transaction between UK Ltd and France SA.

Assume France SA manufactures an electric car which is imported by UK Ltd at a unit cost of 200,000 francs and sold for £25,000. UK Ltd plans to import and sell 100 cars per year and budgets for the years ended 30 June 20X0 and 20X1, assuming a rate of exchange of 10 francs to the £, for a unit gross profit of £5,000 and a total gross profit of £500,000. The contract is denominated in francs, which means that from the UK Ltd's point of view it is a foreign currency transaction with the risk of a loss or a gain if the exchange rate should vary from FF10 to the £. If the contract had specified payment in £ sterling it would have been a foreign currency transaction from the French supplier's point of view and France SA would have been exposed to the risk of exchange rate movements.

We will now consider the treatment of the purchase of one car on 30 April 20X0 to determine the effect of changes in the exchange rate on the financial year ended 30 June 20X0 and 20X1.

The invoice for 200,000 francs was received and recorded on 30 April 20X0. Payment was required in two equal instalments on 31 May and 31 August 20X0. Creditor balances were extracted at the financial year-end which was 30 June and 31 July for UK Ltd and France SA respectively.

Calculate the necessary accounting data in the books of each company at each of these three critical events.

Exchange rates were as follows:

	Francs to the £		*Francs to the £*
30 April	10	31 July	13.5
31 May	12	31 August	11
30 June	12.5		

The entries would be as follows:

In the books of UK Ltd			**In the books of France SA**

At purchase/invoice date:

Purchases	Trade creditor	Memo		Sales	Trade debtor
£		Francs (a)	£	Francs	Francs
30 April 20,000	30 April Purchases 200,000	20,000 (b)	30 April 200,000	30 April 200,000	

At date of 1st instalment:

	31 May Cash	(100,000)	(8,333) (c)	31 May Cash (100,000)	
	Exchange gain		(1,667) (d)		
	31 May Balance	100,000	10,000	31 May Bal 100,000	

(a) Memorandum record: UK Ltd will keep a memorandum record of the liability in francs e.g. FF200,000 and an accounting creditors ledger entry in sterling e.g. £20,000 in the UK Ltd books.

(b) Purchases: FF2,000,000/10 = £20,000

(c) Cash payment: FF100,000/12 = £8,333

(d) Exchange difference: There is an exchange gain of £1,667 (£10,000 – £8,333). This is **realised** as a result of the **conversion** of francs into £ sterling. It will therefore be posted to a Gains/Losses on Exchange Account and transferred to the Profit and Loss Account at 30 June 20X0.

At UK Ltd balance sheet date:

Purchases	Trade creditor	Memo		Sales	Trade debtor
£		Francs (a)	£	Francs	Francs
30 June Transfer to Trading (20,000) (e) Account	30 June Deduct Exchange gain		(2,000) (g)		
30 June Balance nil	30 June Balance 100,000		8,000 (f)	30 June Balance 200,000	30 June Balance 100,000

(e) Trading Account: purchases account balance is transferred to the trading account at the year-end.

(f) Balance sheet creditor figure: The FF balance is translated at closing rate
(FF100,000/12.5) = £8,000

(g) Exchange gain: This is the difference in the Creditor balance from £10,000 at 31 May to £8,000 at 30 June.

Accruals principle

The application of the accruals principle means that the company should recognise the change in value that has occurred during the current period and not wait until the foreign monetary liability has been turned into cash before recognising the change in value.[2] The closing rate is an objective measure set by the market. It is the exchange rate for spot transactions at the balance sheet date, being the mean between the buying and selling rates at the close of business on that day.[3] It could be argued, in theory, that the appropriate rate to use is that expected at the date of the contractual payment on 31 August. However, in practice, the rate current at the balance sheet date is regarded as an acceptable surrogate.

The exchange gain of £2,000 is classified as **realised** as a result of the **translation** of the debtor balance from francs to £ sterling. It is transferred to the profit and loss account, together with the **conversion** exchange gain of £1,667, as a total of £3,667 for the year. It has arisen from the strengthening of sterling since the date of entering into the contract.

Prudence principle

The effect of applying the accruals principle on reported profits can be significant. For UK Ltd the budgeted gross profit of £5,000 per car has been increased by £3,667, i.e. a 73% increase! This would, of course, have been a 73% decrease if sterling had weakened to the same extent during this period.

Assume France SA manufactures an electric car which is imported by UK Ltd at a unit cost of 200,000 francs and sold for £25,000. UK Ltd plans to import and sell 100 cars per year and budgets for the years ended 30 June 20X0 and 20X1, assuming a rate of exchange of 10 francs to the £, for a unit gross profit of £5,000 and a total gross profit of £500,000. The contract is denominated in francs which means that from the UK Ltd's point of view it is a foreign currency transaction with the risk of a loss or a gain if the exchange rate should vary from FF10 to the £. If the contract had specified payment in £ sterling it would have been a foreign currency transaction from the French supplier's point of view and France SA would have been exposed to the risk of exchange rate movements.

We will now consider the treatment of the purchase of 1 car on 30 April 20X0 to determine the effect of changes in the exchange rate on the financial year ended 30 June 20X0 and 20X1.

The invoice for 200,000 francs was received and recorded on 30 April 20X0. Payment was required in two equal instalments on 31 May and 31 August 20X0. Creditor balances were extracted at the financial year-end which was 30 June and 31 July for UK Ltd and France SA respectively.

Calculate the necessary accounting data in the books of each company at each of these three critical events.

Exchange rates were as follows:

	Francs to the £		Francs to the £
30 April	10	31 July	13.5
31 May	12	31 August	11
30 June	12.5		

It could be argued that, as any change in the rate of exchange could reverse as in section 22.2 above with the fluctuation of the Japanese Yen to the £ in 1997, any gain arising from a reduction in the foreign liability should not be recognised in the current period on the grounds that the amount of the eventual sterling payment cannot be assessed with reasonable certainty. It has been suggested[4] that the best solution is a compromise that takes something from both methods e.g. value the monetary assets and liabilities at closing rate, but defer the transfer of any gain to the profit and loss account which is the approach taken in France:

At France SA balance sheet date:

Purchases £	Trade creditor	Memo Francs (a)	£	Sales Francs	Trade debtor Francs
31 July	31 July			31 July Transfer to Trading A/c (200,000)	31 July
Balance nil	Balance	100,000	8,000 (i)	Balance nil	Balance 100,000 (j)

(i) It is not necessary to re-calculate a balance in the books of UK Ltd because 31 July is neither a payment or a year-end date for UK Ltd.

(j) A balance is required in the books of France SA for the purposes of its balance sheet.

At date of 2nd instalment:

Purchases £	Trade creditor	Memo Francs (a)	£	Sales Francs	Trade debtor Francs
	31 August Cash	100,000	(9,091) (k)		31 August Cash (100,000)
	Exchange loss		1,091 (l)		
	31 August Balance		nil		31 August Balance nil

(k) Cash payment: FF100,000/11 = £9,091

(l) Exchange loss: The difference between balance in books at 31 July and amount paid on 31 August (£9,091 – £8,000) = £1,091. This loss is **realised** and will therefore be posted to a gains/losses on exchange account and transferred to the Profit and Loss Account at 30 June 20X1. The gross profit of £5,000 per car is reduced by £1,091 i.e. a difference of 22%.

It can be seen from this illustration that the balances maintained in the foreign company's books do not entail gains or losses on exchange because the company, France SA, receives in total 200,000 francs irrespective of the changes in the exchange rate. The gains or losses in UK Ltd are a consequence of the contract being denominated in francs. If the contract had provided for payment in £ sterling, the supplier, France SA, would have borne the gains and losses and UK Ltd would have only recorded the sterling liability of £20,000 and two payments of £10,000 on 31 May and 31 August.

Accounting policies

A typical example of a foreign currency accounting policy appears in European Colour plc 1997 accounts which state

Transactions during the year and amounts receivable and payable at the year end denominated in foreign currencies are translated into sterling at the rates of exchange applicable at the date of the transaction and at the year end respectively. Resulting exchange differences are charged or credited to the profit and loss account.

22.4.2 How can fluctuations in reported profits arising from fluctuations in exchange rates be prevented?

Companies are able to enter into forward contracts to obtain the currency they require in the future at a specified rate.[5] This is known as hedging the transaction. For example, UK Ltd would enter into a contract to purchase 100,000 French francs on 31 May and 31 August 20X0 at a rate specified at the invoice date on 30 April 20X0. Assuming that the market expects sterling to strengthen against the franc, the forward rate will be at a higher rate of, say, 10.5 francs to the £.

● Calculate the necessary accounting data in the books of each company.
  The simplest method is to translate the invoice at the forward rate i.e. 200,000 francs @ 10.5 produces an invoice figure for the accounts of £19,048. The effect is that no exchange gain or loss would be recognised on the forward contract in either year. The risk of either an exchange gain or loss has been removed **at a cost of £952** per car representing a forward rate which has been quoted at a discount of 0.5 francs to the £ on the spot rate.

● Require payment in a stable currency
  The problem is exacerbated when one currency is hard and the other soft. This implies that the exchange rate will be unstable. Companies might decide therefore to request payment in a third currency that is regarded as more stable, e.g. the contract with France SA could be denominated in US$. This can also arise when there is international recognition of an international commodity being traded in an international hard currency, e.g. oil is generally contracted in US$ irrespective of the domicile of the contracting parties.

22.4.3 Treatment of exchange gains or losses arising on the purchase of fixed assets

The creditor account has the same entries as for the purchase of goods above. The main difference is that a fixed asset account is debited instead of the purchases account. Just as with the goods, the fixed asset is recorded at £20,000 and the gains and losses on exchange dealt with as **realised** through the profit and loss account. The depreciation charge is based on the £20,000, e.g. assuming a life of eight years with £4,000 residual value, there would be an annual charge of £2,000. The depreciation charge is not affected by exchange gains and losses.

It is important to note the following two points relating to:

(a) the realisation of exchange gains and losses; and

(b) the amounts attributable to purchases and fixed assets.

(a) Realisation of exchange gains and losses

Gains or losses arising from **conversion** at the date of payment, i.e. £1,667, are clearly realised and dealt with in the profit and loss account. The gains or losses arising from **translation** of creditors at the balance sheet date, i.e. £2,000, are also regarded as realised. At 30 June 20X0 it is not known that there will be an exchange loss on conversion in August causing a loss of £1,091 to appear in the year ended 30 June 20X1. It is normal practice to assume that the rate current at the balance sheet date on 30 June 20X0 is a reasonable estimate of the rate that will be applicable at the date of conversion on 31 August 20X0, i.e. the accruals principle applies.

Should gains or losses on translation be accepted as realised?

Such gains have not been realised in the form of cash, so what is the justification? Three justifications that could be made are:

● *The short-term nature* of the items concerned. This meant that there was a belief that the gain of £2,000 would be realised within 60 days of the year-end. It is, of course, true that exchange rates can vary and that the assumed gain may not be achieved or may even become negative. However, an estimate of foreign currency debt in terms of the reporting country currency must be determined for balance sheet purposes in order to assess total moneys due to creditors and the best objective evidence available on which to base a valuation of that debt at 30 June 20X0 is the rate current at that date. SSAP 17 *Accounting for Post Balance Sheet Events* specifies (para. 31 (item g)) that changes in rates of foreign exchange is an example of a non-adjusting event. This means that even though the exchange rate on 31 July shows a loss the balance sheet as at 30 June 20X0 does not require retrospective adjustment.

● *Symmetry of treatment* requires the translation difference to be treated the same way as the conversion difference. If, for example, there had been a translation loss at the balance sheet date, prudence would have required its recognition as realised. Symmetry requires that 'unrealised' translation gains and losses receive the same accounting treatment.

● SSAP 2 *Disclosure of Accounting Policies* lends support to this treatment of translation differences[6] stating that realisation is assumed when 'in the form of either cash or of other assets ... whether the amount is known with certainty or is a best estimate in the light of information available'.

(b) Carrying value of assets and recorded amounts for expenses

The rate of exchange used for making the entry into the books is the rate current at the date the contract was entered into. Exchange rate changes after the contract date do not affect the amount of either the expense or the asset.

(c) Preventing fluctuations

Just as in section 22.4.1 above, where we discussed how to prevent fluctuations by hedging, the transaction can be hedged **at a cost of £952** and the fixed asset brought into the books at **£19,048**.

22.4.4   Treatment of long-term loans

The two previous examples dealt with the treatment of conversion and translation gains and losses on exchange arising from transactions with short-term trade creditors.

Long-term loans are also **monetary items** within the meaning of SSAP 20 and gains and losses on translating long-term debt must therefore be dealt with in the same symmetrical fashion, i.e. by transfer to the profit and loss account, thus impacting on earnings and earnings per share. However, because of the long-term characteristic of the debt an increased risk is inherent in the assessment of any exchange difference and SSAP 20 *Foreign Currency Translation* brings such risks to our attention in two respects:

Prudence

This requires that where a gain is involved 'it is necessary to consider on the grounds of prudence whether the amount of the gain ... to be recognised in the profit and loss account should be restricted in the exceptional cases where there are doubts as to the convertibility or marketability of the currency in question'.[7]

Realised profits

Under the Companies Act 1985 all gains taken through the profit and loss account are regarded as having been realised and this includes all exchange gains. However, where para. 50 of SSAP 20 has been applied, this 'may result in unrealised exchange gains on unsettled long-term monetary items being taken to the profit and loss account'. This situation may appear to be in conflict with the requirement of the Companies Act 1985 but 'the need to show a true and fair view of results ... is considered to constitute a special reason for departure from the principle' (under para. 51 Sch. 4 Companies Act 1985).[8] Where this SSAP 20 'special circumstances' true and fair view overrider of the Companies Act is applied, additional disclosures are required. These involve a fourfold statement explaining:

● the normal requirements of the Companies Act;

● a description of the treatment adopted;

● reasons for the adoption of such treatment; and

● the effect of that treatment and, if necessary, an explanation why that effect cannot be quantified.[9]

Another point to consider in respect of realised profits is the distribution, via dividends, of such profits. If such a distribution requires gains arising on unsettled long-term monetary items to be included to cover the distribution, extra consideration of that dividend is vital. This would include a review of the possible legal implications of pursuing such a dividend policy.

Illustration

On 1 September 20X8 Sandwell Ltd purchased machinery from a French company, Bretagne SA, for 3,000,000 francs funded by a loan of this amount in francs from a French bank. The following information is available:

(a) The terms of the loan were:

(i) Repayments of principal were to be remitted in equal instalments of 600,000 francs on 31 August each year commencing on 31 August Year 2.

(ii) Interest of 12% per annum is payable in arrears on 31 August each year.

(b) The depreciation charge was based on an estimated economic life of ten years and no residual value. Sandwell depreciation policy was to use the straight-line method.

(c) Sandwell Ltd makes up its accounts to 31 March each year.

(d) Spot rates for the franc were:

	Francs to £
1 September Year 1	12.0
31 March Year 2	10.5
31 August Year 2	9.0
31 March Year 3	9.3
31 August Year 3	9.5
Average for year to 31 August Year 2	10.10
Average for year to 31 August Year 3	9.90

Requirements
Show loan, interest, asset, depreciation and profit and loss account entries for the financial years ended 31 August Years 2 and 3.

Loan account		£		Interest account		£
1 Sept Year 1	Cash [FF3m/12]	250,000				
31 Mar Year 2	P & L A/c Loss on translation	35,714 (a)	31 Mar Year 2	P & L A/c charge Interest accrued c/f		20,000 (b)
		285,714				20,000

(a) Loss on translation: [(FF3m/10.5) − £250,000] *(b) Interest:[12% of (FF3m/10.5) × (7/12)] = £20,000*

Loan account		£		Interest account		£
1 Apr Year 2	Balance	285,714	1 Apr Year 2	Balance b/f		20,000
31 Aug Year 2	Cash 1st instalment	(66,667) (c)	31 Aug Year 2	Cash interest		(40,000) (d)
31 Mar Year 3		219,047	31 Mar Year 3	Balance for P & L		20,000
	P & L A/c Loss on translation	39,018 (e)		Interest accrued c/f P & L A/c charge is		18,065 (f)
		258,065				38,065
1 Apr Year 3	Balance	258,065	1 Apr Year 3	Balance b/f		18,065

(c) Cash: (FF600,000/9) = £66,667
(e) The loss on translation is calculated as
  [(FF2.4m/9.3) − £219,047]

(d) Interest: 12% of (FF3m/9) = £40,000
(f) The interest accrued is calculated as
  [12% of (FF2.4m/9.3) × (7/12 months)]

Asset account		£		Depreciation account		£
1 Sep Year 1	Cash [FF3m/12]	250,000 (g)	31 Mar Year 2	P & L A/c		14,583 (h)
			31 Mar Year 3	P & L A/c		25,000 (i)
			31 Mar Year 3	Accumulated balance		39,583

(g) Cash: (FF3m/12) = £250,000

(h) Depreciation: (10% of £250,000) × (7/12) = £14,583
(i) Depreciation: (10% of £250,000) = £25,000

Profit and loss account – year ended 31 March Year 2	£	Profit and loss account – year ended 31 March Year 3	£
Depreciation	14,583	Depreciation	25,000
Interest on loan	20,000	Interest on loan	38,065
Loss on translation	35,714	Loss on translation	39,018

Illustration where transaction is hedged with a forward contract

We will show the loan and interest accounts for Sandwell Ltd as at 31 August Year 2 on the assumption that on 28 February Year 2 Sandwell entered into a forward contract with its local bank for the purchase of francs at 10.8 francs to the £ in order to meet its loan and interest payments due on 31 August Year 2.

The effect of the hedge is that the asset and initial entry in the loan account remain unaffected but, because the hedging agreement was entered into before 31 March Year 2, the translation balance is affected in respect of the instalment now hedged by a forward rate of 10.8 francs. Similarly, the interest account is affected by the forward rate at the accrual stage. The entries are as follows:

	Loan account			Interest	
		£			£
1 Sept Year 1	Cash [3m/12]	250,000			
31 Mar Year 2	P & L A/c		31 Mar Year 2	P & L A/c charge	
	Loss on translation	34,127		Interest accrued c/f	19,444
		284,127			19,444

The loss on translation is calculated as
(FF2.4m/10.5) = 228,571
(FF0.6m/10.8) = 55,556
284,127 − 250,000 = *34,127*

The interest accrued is calculated as
[12% of (FF3m/10.8) × (7/12 months)]

	Loan account			Interest	
		£			£
1 Apr Year 2	Balance b/f	284,127	1 Apr Year 2	Balance b/f	19,444
31 Aug Year 2	Cash 1st instalment		31 Aug Year 2	Cash	
	[FF600,000/10.8]	55,556		[12% of (FF3m/10.8)]	(33,333)
31 Aug Year 2	Balance c/f	228,571	31 Aug Year 2	Balance c/f	13,889

A comparison of position with and without hedging shows:

Profit and loss account without hedge		*Profit and loss account with hedge*	
		- for year ended 31 March Year 2	
	£		£
Depreciation	14,583	Depreciation	14,583
Interest on loan	20,000	Interest on loan	19,444
Loss on translation	35,714	Loss on translation	34,127

Accounting policies where there are matched forward contracts

Companies include in their accounting policies their treatment of the gains and losses described above. An example that is pleasantly clear and precise appeared in the Holiday Chemicals Holdings 1996 accounts – the foreign currency policy stated:

> In the accounts of individual undertakings, transactions denominated in foreign currencies are recorded at actual rates at the dates of the transaction. Monetary assets and liabilities denominated in foreign currencies at the year end are reported at the rates of exchange prevailing at the balance sheet date or, where appropriate, at the rate of exchange of a matched forward exchange contract. Any gains or losses arising from a change in exchange rates subsequent to the date of the transaction is included in the profit and loss account.

22.4.4 Foreign equity investments financed by foreign loans

An investment in foreign equity will usually be deemed to be a fixed asset, i.e. a non-monetary item. Non-monetary items, as seen above in the treatment of fixed assets, are not normally re-translated at the year-end and as a consequence no exchange difference arises. However, where a foreign investment is financed by a foreign loan, it would seem foolhardy to permit the profit and loss to bear an exchange loss arising from re-translating the loan when that loss is countered by an exchange gain in the equity investment concerned. The exchange risk, the liability, is in that case being hedged by the investment, the asset.

To facilitate the offsetting of a loss on a loan with a gain on an investment and vice-versa, it is necessary to breach the general rule that non-monetary items should not be amended by subsequent exchange rate movements. It is SSAP 20 which authorises this adjustment but it, and the offsetting process, are **not compulsory**.

SSAP 20 provides[10] that where a company has used foreign currency borrowings to finance, or provide a hedge against, its foreign equity investments and the conditions set out in this paragraph apply, the equity investments **may** be denominated in the appropriate foreign currencies and the carrying amounts translated at the end of each accounting period at closing rates for inclusion in the investing company's financial statements. Where investments are treated in this way, any exchange differences arising should be taken to reserves and the exchange gains or losses on the foreign currency borrowings should be off-set, as a reserve movement, against these exchange differences. The conditions which **must** apply are as follows:

(a) in any accounting period, exchange gains or losses arising on the borrowings may be off-set only to the extent of exchange differences arising on the equity investments;

(b) the foreign currency borrowings, whose exchange gains or losses are used in the offset process, should not exceed, in the aggregate, the total amount of cash that the investments are expected to be able to generate, whether from profits or otherwise; and

(c) the accounting treatment adopted should be applied consistently from period to period.

Illustration of foreign equity investments financed by foreign loans

On 1 July 20X8 Severn plc acquired a loan from a French company of 6,000,000 francs and, on the same day, invested 4,000,000 francs in the equity of a French company. Severn plc's year-end was 31 December 20X8. The exchange rates were:

	Francs to £
31 July	10
31 December	8

The changes in the loan, investment, reserves and profit and loss account are considered applying two assumptions:

(a) that Severn plc chose to offset exchange losses arising on translating the loan against the gain on the investment; and

(b) that Severn plc chose not to offset any loss on the loan against the gain on the investment.

(a) Applying offset

Loan account

		Francs	Rate	£
31 July	Cash borrowed	6,000,000	10	600,000
	Loss to reserves			100,000
	Loss to P & L A/C			50,000
31 Dec.	Balance	6,000,000	8	750,000

Investment account

		Francs	Rate	£
31 July	Cash invested	4,000,000	10	400,000
	Gain			100,000
31 Dec.	Balance			500,000

Reserves:

		£
31 Dec.	Increase from investment	100,000
	Decrease from loan	(100,000)
	Balance	nil

Note that the transfer of the loss to reserves cannot exceed the change in the investment account.

Profit and loss account:

	£
31 Dec. Loss on loan	50,000

(b) Not applying offset

Loan account

	£
	600,000
Loss to profit and loss account	150,000
	750,000

Investment account

	£
	400,000
	—
	400,000

Reserves:

	—
	—

Profit and loss account:

	£
Less on loan	150,000

Accounting policies where borrowings hedge a foreign equity investment

An example of a Foreign Currency accounting policy appears in Lonhro 1997 accounts:

> Exchange differences relating to borrowings which have been used to finance or provide a hedge against foreign equity investments are taken to reserves to the extent that they are matched by exchange movements on those investments.

22.4.5 Summary

The accounting treatment, known as the temporal method, is in harmony with the historical cost concept, namely:

● the cost of a non-monetary asset is established at the date of acquisition by translating the foreign currency amount on the invoice into local currency by adopting the spot exchange rate (or the forward rate if hedged) applicable at that date;

● the associated monetary liability is established using the same rate;

● the carrying value of non-monetary items remains unchanged by subsequent fluctuations in the exchange rates;

● the carrying value of the liability is dealt with differently in that it is changed for exchange differences arising from actual conversion of local currency or translation of local currency into the currency denominated under the contract.

22.5 The group situation

Here we are concerned with the impact and treatment of foreign exchange transactions on the consolidated accounts as distinct from the accounts of the individual company. Although individual group companies will employ the temporal method, it is not applicable to group accounts where there are independent foreign subsidiaries or branches. The result could be misleading and could, indeed, destroy the true and fair view relationships of the data. This is because the individual foreign subsidiary has acquired and financed its assets by using its own local currency, i.e. its own functional or operating currency. This means that:

● the historical cost in its own accounts will be recorded in its own currency;
● there will be no intention or need to translate, in its own books, into the currency of the parent;
● the assets concerned will remain with the subsidiary;
● the liabilities will be settled in local currency;
● no loss or gain will be suffered by the parent on settlement;
● there are no cash flow implications for the group as a consequence of any exchange differences arising on translating the accounts of a foreign subsidiary for consolidation purposes;
● the parent company's major interest is in the annual dividend received from the subsidiary;
● any exchange differences are not generally of a cash flow nature and, consequently, are not realisable, which prevents them being charged or credited to the consolidated profit and loss account.

The parent company is interested in the net worth of the subsidiary rather than the individual assets and liabilities. SSAP 20 *Foreign Currency Translation* has, therefore, stipulated that the closing rate method, rather than the temporal method, should be used when consolidating independent foreign subsidiaries. Because the closing rate is applied to the net worth, it must also be applied to the elements of the balance sheet if it is to balance.[11] The closing rate method provides that:

● the foreign assets and the foreign liabilities should be translated into the parent's currency using the exchange rate operating at the balance sheet date (hence the term 'closing rate' definition SSAP 20).[12] Amounts in the foreign subsidiaries' profit and loss accounts are also translatable at the closing rate but, although SSAP 20[13] makes a strong case for the adoption of the closing rate, it does permit the alternative of using the average rate for the profit and loss account if its use 'reflects more fairly the profits and losses and cash flows as they arise to the group';
● exchange differences are transferred to reserves including, where the average is applied to the profit and loss account, any differences between use of that average and the use of the closing rate.

This achieves the prime objective of SSAP 20 in using the closing rate, namely, the retention on translation of the relationships between revenue, expenses, individual assets and individual liabilities that exist in the foreign entity's local currency financial statements. The temporal method would apply different rates to different assets and liabilities and distort the relationships and ratios.

22.5.1 Illustrating the rationale for use of closing rate method for group accounts

Assume that a UK based company acquired a fixed asset from a French supplier for FF260,000 on 31 May, settlement was due on 31 July and the UK company's financial year ended on 30 June. Depreciation is charged commencing with the year following acquisition. For the purpose of the illustration we will only deal with the asset and associated liability in the profit and loss account and balance sheet extracts.

Exchange rate movements were:

	FF to £		FF to £		FF to £
31 May	10:1	30 June	9:1	31 July	8:1

In the UK company's books the following accounts and balance sheet would occur using the temporal method:

Year ended 30 June 20X1

Fixed asset account

		£
31 May X1	Creditor [FF260,000/10]	26,000

Balance sheet extract as at 30 June 20X1

	£
Fixed asset	26,000
less depreciation	—
	26,000

Creditor account

		£
31 May X1	Fixed asset [FF260,000/10]	26,000
30 June X1	Loss on exchange FF260,000/9 =	2,889
		28,889

Represented by:

	£
Capital	—
Profit and loss account	(2,889)
Creditor	28,889
	26,000

Profit and loss account for year ended 30 June 20X1

	£
Loss on exchange	2,889
Depreciation	—
Loss for year	2,889

Year ended 30 June 20X2

Provision for depreciation

		£
30 June X2	Profit and loss account [(FF260,000/10)/10]	2,600

Profit and loss account for year ended 30 June 20X2

	£
Loss on exchange	3,611
Depreciation	2,600
Loss for year	6,211
Balance b/f	2,889
Balance c/f	9,100

Fixed account account

		£
1 July X1	Balance [FF260,000/10]	26,000

Balance sheet extract as at 30 June 20X2

	£
Fixed asset	26,000
less depreciation	2,600
	23,400

Creditor account

		£
1 July X1	Balance [FF260,000/9]	28,889
31 July X1	Loss on exchange [FF260,000/8 – 28,889]	3,611
		32,500
31 July X1	Cash [FF260,000/8]	(32,500)

Represented by:

	£
Capital	—
Profit and loss account	(9,100)
Bank overdraft	32,500
	23,400

The position would be quite different if the French subsidiary were to acquire an identical asset. The accounts and balance sheet entries would be as follows:

Year ended 30 June 20X1

Profit and loss account for year ended 30 June 20X1

	FF
Loss on exchange – not relevant	
Depreciation	—
Loss/profit for year	—

Fixed asset account			*Balance sheet extract as at 30 June 20X1*	
		FF		FF
31 May X1 Creditor		260,000	Fixed asset	260,000
30 June X1 Balance c/d		260,000	less depreciation	—
				260,000
			Represented by:	
			Capital	—
Creditor account			Profit and loss account	—
30 June X1 Fixed asset		260,000	Creditor	260,000
30 June X1 Balance c/d		260,000		260,000

Year ended 30 June 20X2

Provision for depreciation			*Profit and loss account for year ended 30 June 20X2*	
		FF		FF
30 June X2 Profit and loss account		26,000	Loss on exchange – not relevant	
			Depreciation	26,000
			Loss/profit for year	(26,000)

Fixed asset account			*Balance sheet extract as at 30 June 20X2*	
		FF		FF
1 July X1 Creditor		260,000	Fixed asset	260,000
30 June X2 Balance c/d		260,000	less depreciation	26,000
				234,000
			Represented by:	
			Capital	—
Creditor account			Profit and loss account	—
1 July X1 Fixed asset		260,000	Creditor	260,000
30 June X2 Balance c/d		260,000		234,000
31 July X2 Less cash		(260,000)		

Observe that when the UK company is involved in buying the asset. The result is:

- a foreign exchange transaction materialises with a flow of sterling from the UK to the French supplier;
- this is reflected in the accounts at 30 June **20X1 when a potential loss of £2,889 is classified as realised** and charged to the profit and loss account because the loss is anticipated on the basis of the spot rate on 30 June;
- the spot rate is the best indication existing at the balance sheet date of the amount that will become payable to the creditor;
- the fixed asset is shown in the balance sheet at 30 June 20X1 at its historical cost of £26,000 applying the historical cost concept;
- the fixed asset is still shown in the balance sheet at 30 June 20X2 at its historical cost of £26,000, applying the historical cost concept subject to the depreciation provision, giving a net book value of £23,400;
- but that during the interim, between the balance sheet dates, the creditor's account has been settled with **the UK company incurring a loss of £3,611** due to the weakening of sterling against the franc;
- **the total loss on exchange of £6,500** over the two years occurred as a consequence of the changes in spot rates between contract date and settlement date;
- **the total cash paid to the French supplier in settlement of the invoice for £26,000 was £32,500.**

Now contrast this with the circumstances where a French subsidiary buys the fixed asset from a French supplier, the asset concerned to be retained and used by the French subsidiary. The result is:

- a transaction which is not of a foreign nature;
- it is, therefore, without foreign exchange gain or loss exposure;
- it deals with the transaction in its own books using its own domestic currency of francs;
- it still adopts the historical cost concept but based on francs.

Then consider the problem when the French subsidiary's accounts are to be consolidated with the UK parent. This means that:

- subsidiary's financial data must be aggregated with that of the parent;
- this will require the translation of French francs into £ sterling.

If the temporal method were applied, the result would be to treat the transactions of the French subsidiary as if they had been carried out by the UK company. This would create a loss on exchange of £6,500. However, **the group is not exposed to exchange gains or losses of £6,500 because in reality there will be no flow of funds between parent and subsidiary**.

In order to avoid this unrealistic assumption, the closing rate method is adopted when translating the subsidiary's French franc accounts into £ sterling. There is an additional benefit in that, after translation, all amounts will retain their same inter-relationships, e.g. all ratios will be unchanged.

22.5.2 Foreign consolidation illustrated – excluding treatment of capital and reserves

Continuing with the abbreviated example above, the items in the balance sheet and profit and loss account are translated at the closing rate, as follows:

Year ended 30 June 20X1

French subsidiary accounts:		*Group accounts:*	
Balance sheet as at 30 June 19X1		Rate of	
	FF	exchange	£
Fixed assets @ cost	260,000	9	28,889
Represented by:			
Capital	—		
Profit and loss account	—		
Creditor	260,000	9	28,889
	260,000		28,889

Year ended 30 June 20X2

French subsidiary accounts:		*Group accounts:*	
		Rate of	
	FF	exchange	£
Profit and loss account extract			
Depreciation	26,000	8	3,250
Loss for year	26,000	8	3,250
Balance b/f	—		—
	26,000		3,250

Balance sheet as at 30 June 19X2			
	FF		£
Fixed assets @ cost	260,000	8	32,500
Less Depreciation	26,000	8	(3,250)
	234,000		29,250
Represented by:			
Capital	—		
Profit and loss account	(26,000)	8	(3,250)
Balance b/f	—		
	(26,000)		
Creditor	260,000	8	32,500
	234,000		29,250

Note that:

● the closing rate method maintains in the consolidated accounts the arithmetical relationship that existed in the foreign subsidiary's accounts;

● there is no difference on exchange as a consequence of the foreign subsidiary's transactions occurring within its own currency realm.

Will there be any differences if closing rate is used?

Invariably, yes. They have not appeared in the illustration above because the illustration specifically excluded the treatment of capital and reserves in order to emphasise that the closing rate (a) retains data relationships and (b) the lack of exchange differences involving cash flows.

How will differences arise when the closing rate is used?

Capital and reserves represents the net assets or net worth. The net assets value in sterling will have been calculated by using the exchange rate at the end of the year, e.g. FF9:£1 at the end of year 1. In the following year, these net assets will normally still be part of the balance sheet – however, they will be restated using the closing rate applicable at the end of year 2, e.g. FF8:£1. This means that the 'opening balance' net assets will require amendment unless the rate of exchange at the end of year 2 is the same as the rate at the end of year 1. The difference transpires as a consequence of translation purely for the purpose of consolidating the French results with the parent's. The difference does not involve cash flows and it is, consequently, unrealised. It must therefore be transferred to consolidated reserves, as a credit if a gain and a debit if a loss, and not taken to the profit and loss account.

22.5.3 Illustration of use of average rate in translating the profit and loss account items

SSAP 20 permits a company to translate using the average rate.[14] Before discussing the rationale for this, we will illustrate the impact on the accounts taking Year 2 above as an example. Assume that the average exchange spot rate for year 2 was FF12 to the £. The resulting consolidated statements are:

Year ended 30 June 20X2

French subsidiary accounts: *Group accounts:*

	FF	Rate of exchange	£
Profit and loss account extract			
Depreciation	26,000	12	2,167
Loss for year	26,000		2,167
Balance b/f	—		—
	26,000		2,167

Balance sheet as at 30 June 20X2

	FF	Rate of exchange	£
Fixed assets @ cost	260,000	8	32,500
Less Depreciation	26,000	8	3,250
	234,000		29,250
Represented by:			
Capital	—		—
Reserves		[(FF26,000/8) – (FF26,000/12)]	(1,083)
Profit and loss account	(26,000)	12	(2,167)
Balance b/f	—		—
	(26,000)		(3,250)
Creditor	260,000	8	32,500
	234,000		29,250

Treatment of exchange difference when the average rate is used to translate the profit and loss account

Note that the total loss of £3,250 is the same as when the closing rate is used to translate the profit and loss account. However, by using the average rate, the company has separated the total into a realised loss of £2,167 which appears in the profit and loss account and an unrealised loss of £1,083 that is a reserve movement in the consolidated balance sheet.

When is the average rate appropriate for translating the profit and loss account?

Standard accounting practice favours the use of the closing rate because it retains the underlying financial relationships. However, the average rate is permitted where the pattern of trade in the foreign subsidiary (e.g. it may be seasonal) justifies using average rather than closing rate to achieve greater fairness in representation. It also has the advantage that interim accounts do not have to be restated in that the annual profit will be equal to the total of the profits reported in the interim accounts.

How is the average rate calculated?

This can cause problems. A definitive definition of an average does not exist but its calculation is likely to involve some form of weighting. The quality of the average will also be influenced by the level of detail available from the foreign subsidiary's management accounting records. Because the average is related to each subsidiary's own individual trading patterns, it is possible for fellow subsidiaries operating in the same foreign currency and country to calculate and apply different average rates.

The consistency concept requires that, if the average rate method is chosen, it must be consistently applied from year to year. This is to avoid companies using average when it results in a realised gain and closing rate when the average rate would result in a realised loss, i.e. to prevent manipulation of data.

22.5.4 Foreign consolidation illustrated – *including* treatment of capital and reserves

In the above example we have assumed that the primary intention of SSAP 20 has been for the translated amounts included within the consolidated accounts to be the same as in the foreign currency accounts. This is appropriate when the foreign subsidiary is independent of the parent. The rationale where the foreign subsidiary is independent is that the investment by the parent is in the net worth – this is described as the net investment approach.

Net investment approach

SSAP 20 explains that the application of the closing rate recognises that:

● the investment of a holding company is in the net worth of its foreign subsidiary rather than a direct investment in the individual assets and liabilities of that enterprise;

● this enterprise will normally have net current assets and fixed assets which may be financed partly by local currency borrowings;

● its day to day operations will not normally be dependent on the reporting currency of the investing company;

● the net investment will remain extant until the foreign subsidiary is liquidated or the investment otherwise disposed of, although it may well look forward to a stream of dividends from realised profits.

The net investment is the net worth or net asset value – this is represented by the capital and reserves in the foreign subsidiary. At the end of each year the parent translates the net investment at the spot rate prevailing at the balance sheet date. If the spot rate is different from that at the beginning of the year there will be an exchange difference. This exchange difference is unrealised and will be taken to reserves.

Treatment as a net investment translated at the closing rate is dependent upon the foreign subsidiary being independent. SSAP 20 states[15] that 'in the UK and Ireland foreign operations are normally carried out through foreign enterprises which operate as separate or quasi-separate entities rather than as a direct extension of the trade of the investing company'. The presumption is that the foreign enterprise is independent. If it were not independent, the temporal method would be used to translate the foreign financial statements rather than the closing rate.

How can we establish that the foreign subsidiary is not independent?

This can only be determined by an analysis of the operating affairs of the foreign entity. If the analysis reveals a close interlinking between the two companies to the extent that the results of the foreign enterprise may be regarded as being more dependent on the economic environment of the investing company than on its own reporting currency, then the foreign statements should be included in the consolidated accounts as if all of its transactions had been entered into by the investing company itself in its own domestic currency. This means that the trading operations of the foreign entity are deemed to constitute a *de facto* direct extension of the trade of the investing company and the temporal method is the appropriate means of translation.

Key factors need to be analysed in reaching a decision.

What are the key factors in determining lack of independence?

The key factors stated in SSAP 20 are:[16]

● the extent to which the cash flows of the enterprise have a direct impact upon those of the investing company;
● the extent to which the functioning of the enterprise is dependent directly upon the investing company;
● the currency in which the majority of the trading transactions are denominated;
● the major currency to which the operation is exposed in its financing structure.

Examples of dependency are where the foreign enterprise:

● acts as a selling agency receiving stocks of goods from the investing company and remitting the proceeds back to the investing company;
● produces a raw material or manufactures parts or sub-assemblies which are then shipped to the investing company for inclusion in its own products;
● is located overseas for tax, exchange control or similar reasons to act as a means of raising finance for other companies in the group.

However, in practice, the directors of the parent company may find it difficult to assess where there is a degree of marginal dominance.

22.5.5 **Illustration of consolidation using closing rate method – Dec Cruises plc**

Dec Cruises plc is preparing its consolidated accounts for the year ended 30 June Year 6. Dec Cruises plc acquired 75% of the ordinary shares in Seine Jaunts SA in Year 1 for £12,000,000 when the issued share capital of Seine Jaunts SA was FF100,000,000 and there was a credit balance on its profit and loss account of FF16,000,000.

Exchange rates were as follows:

	FF : £
Spot rates	
At date investment was acquired	8 : 1
At dates fixed assets were acquired:	
FF223,700,000 purchased in Year 3/4	8.5 : 1

FF27,000,000 purchased in Year 5/6	11.3 : 1
At 30 June Year 5	11.0 : 1
At 30 June Year 6	11.5 : 1
Average for year 5/6	11.2 : 1
At date of payment of interim dividend by Seine Jaunts SA in Year 5/6	11.1 : 1

We will follow a step approach to the net investment/closing rate method:

Step 1: Calculate the goodwill

		£000
Cost of investment by Dec Cruises plc		12,000
Less value of net assets in Seine Jaunts SA attributable to parent		
at date of acquisition	£000	
FF100,000,000 @ FF8 : £1	12,500	
FF16,000,000 @ FF8 : £1	2,000	
75% of	14,500	
		10,875
Goodwill		*1,125*

The value of goodwill is calculated as at date of acquisition and this value will not vary even though exchange rates change in subsequent years. Pre-FRS 10, most companies would have written off the £1,125,000 against reserves. Post-FRS 10, goodwill is to be amortised over its economic life. We are assuming for this illustration that the goodwill has been re-instated at 30 June Year 6 as an intangible asset on the balance sheet.

Step 2: Translate the foreign subsidiary's net assets in its balance sheet

	Dec Cruises	Seine Jaunts	Translation rate	Translated	Consolidated balance sheet
	(1)	(2)	(3)	(4)	(5)
	£000	FF000	FF : £	£000	£000
Fixed asset at cost	189,500	250,700	CR 11.5	21,800	211,300
Less depreciation at cost	74,930	40,700	CR 11.5	3,539	78,469
	114,570	210,000		18,261	132,831
Investment in Seine Jaunts	12,000				*1,125* [from Step 1]
Current assets					
Stocks at cost	25,470	33,000	CR 11.5	2,869	28,339
Trade debtors	7,810	18,700	CR 11.5	1,626	9,436
Dividend receivable	1,304				
Bank	316	4,350	CR 11.5	378	694
	34,900	56,050		4,873	38,469
Current liabilities					
Trade creditors	(7,470)	(30,170)	CR 11.5	(2,623)	(10,093)
Dividend proposed	(8,000)	(20,000)	CR 11.5	(1,739)	(8,000)
Minority interest dividend					
[25% of £1,739,000]					(435)
	(15,470)	(50,170)		(4,362)	(18,528)
Net current assets	19,430	5,880		511	19,941
	146,000	215,880		18,772	153,897
Long-term loans	(14,000)	(25,880)	CR 11.5	(2,250)	(16,250)
Net assets	132,000	190,000		16,522	137,647

Step 3: Calculate the minority interest

The minority shareholders are entitled to 25% of the net assets shown in the Seine Jaunts SA sterling balance sheet in Step 2 above, namely, 25% of £16,522,000 = **£4,131,000**.

Step 4: Translate the share capital and pre-acquisition reserves (Col 2 below) in Seine Jaunts SA balance sheet

The appropriate rate is the rate as at date of acquisition – the result will, of course, be the same as for the calculation of goodwill in Step 1.

	Dec Cruises	Currency Balance sheet	Translation rate	Translated balance sheet	Consolidated balance sheet
	(1)	(2)	(3)	(4)	(5)
	£000	FF000	FF : £	£000	£000
Ordinary shares £1	80,000				80,000
Ordinary shares FF10		100,000	@ 8.0	12,500	
Profit and loss pre-acquisition		16,000	@ 8.0	2,000	

Step 5: Calculate the balancing figure in Column 4

Profit and loss account	52,000				
Profit and loss post-acquisition		74,000	as a balancing figure 2,022		
					53,516
Minority interest (Step 2)	—	—		—	4,131
	132,000	190,000		16,522	137,647

Step 6: Calculate the consolidated post-acquisition reserves in Column 5

These will be the parent reserves of **£52,000** plus the parent's 75% interest in the subsidiary's post-acquisition reserves of **£2,022,000** i.e. £1,516,000 giving a total of **£53,516,000.**

Step 7: Prepare consolidated profit and loss account

	Dec Cruises	Seine Jaunts	Translation rate	Translated	Consolidated profit & loss account
	£000	FF000	FF : £	£000	£000
Operating profit before tax	64,730	82,700	CR 11.5	7,191	71,921
Dividends received	676				cancelled out
Dividends receivable	1,304				cancelled out
Profit before tax	66,710	82,700	CR 11.5	7,191	71,921
Tax	13,710	31,700	CR 11.5	2,756	16,466
Profit after tax	53,000	51,000	CR 11.5	4,435	55,455
Less minority interest				25% of 4,435	1,109
					54,346
Dividend paid	4,000	10,000	CR 11.1	901	4,000
Dividend proposed	8,000	20,000	CR 11.5	1,739	8,000
Retained for year	41,000	21,000		1,795	42,346

Step 8: Reconciliation of residual balance in subsidiary's translated balance sheet

The sterling reserves figure of £1,516,000 of Seine Jaunts SA calculated in Step 6 above can be reconciled as follows under the following four headings:

1 Effect of changes in rate on net assets at beginning of year:

	£000
Net assets of subsidiary at 30 June Year 5	
[FF190m – Retained profit of FF21m]	
= FF169m @ FF11 to £1	15,363
Net assets of Seine Jaunts SA as at date of acquisition	
[FF116m @ closing rate on that date FF8 to £1]	14,500
Gains since acquisition to 30 June Year 5	
– this automatically includes retained profits	863

Note that the assets have increased by FF74m since acquisition but this has been largely offset by the weakening of the FF against the £ from 8 to 11. Next adjust for any gain or loss through holding the net assets of FF169m during the year ended 30 June Year 6. This is calculated by restating the FF169m @ FF11.5 to £1, the weaker rate at 30 June Year 6:

Net assets at 1 July Year 5	15,363	
FF169m @ FF11.5 to £1	14,696	
Loss on exchange through holding these assets		(667)
Effect of changes in rate is a gain of		196

2 Profit for current year

Retained profit for year ended 30 June Year 6 from Step 7 above	1,795

3 Restate remittances not already translated at the closing rate

Adjustment in respect of remittance as the profit and loss has been translated at closing rate of FF11.5 except for interim dividend when the actual rate was used		
FF10m @ FF11.1 to £1	901	
FF10m @ FF11.5 to £1	870	
		31

4 Restate profit and loss items at closing rate if already at average rate

In this example we have used the closing rate to translate the profit and loss account. If we had used the average rate, the reconciliation statement would have included the difference between translating at average and translating at closing rate as an additional item.

Residual balance in balance sheet of Seine Jaunts SA	2,022
Less: Minority interest 25% is included in total minority interest in Step 3	506
Dec Cruises plc 75% interest to appear in the consolidated balance sheet	1,516

22.5.5 Illustration of consolidation using temporal method – Dec Cruises plc

Step 1: Calculate the goodwill

The goodwill is calculated at £1,125,000 as for the net investment/closing rate method:

	£000
	12,000

Cost of investment by Dec Cruises plc

Less value of net assets in Seine Jaunts SA attributable to parent

at date of acquisition	£000	
FF100,000,000 @ FF8 : £1	12,500	
FF16,000,000 @ FF8 : £1	2,000	
75% of	14,500	

	10,875
Goodwill	1,125

Step 2: Translate the foreign subsidiary's net assets in its balance sheet

The main difference between the net investment/closing rate method and temporal method is that the fixed assets and depreciation provisions are translated at the rates (AR) applying at the date of acquisition:

	Dec Cruises	Seine Jaunts	Translation rate	Translated	Consolidated balance sheet
	(1)	(2)	(3)	(4)	(5)
	£000	FF000	FF : £	£000	£000
Fixed asset at cost	189,500	223,700	AR 8.5	26,318	
		27,000	AR 11.3	2,389	218,207
Less depreciation at cost	74,930	38,000	AR 8.5	(4,471)	—
		2,700	AR 11.3	(239)	(79,640)
Net Book Value – temporal	114,570	210,000		23,997	138,567
Less: Net Book Value – closing rate	114,570			18,261	132,831
Increase in fixed assets	—			5,736	5,736
Net assets per closing rate were (Step 2)				16,522	137,647
Net assets per temporal method increased to				22,258	143,383

Step 3: Calculate the Minority Interest

The minority shareholders are entitled to 25% of the net assets shown in the Seine Jaunts SA sterling balance sheet. This will be increased from the 25% of £16,522,000 = £4,131,000 in Step 3 of the closing rate method to 25% of (£16,522,000 + £5,736,000) = **£5,565,000**.

Step 4: Translate the share capital and pre-acquisition reserves in Seine Jaunts SA balance sheet

Just as for the net investment/closing rate method, the appropriate rate is that at date of acquisition

	Dec Cruises	Currency balance sheet	Translation rate	Translated balance sheet	Consolidated balance sheet
	£000	FF000	FF : £	£000	£000
Ordinary shares £1	80,000				80,000
Ordinary shares FF10		100,000	@ 8.0	12,500	
Profit and loss pre-acquisition		16,000	@ 8.0	2,000	

Step 5: Calculate the balancing figure in the Seine £000 column

Profit and loss account	52,000			
Profit and loss post-acquisition		74,000 as a balancing figure 7,758		
				57,818
Minority interest	—	—	—	5,565
Net assets (see Step 2 above)	132,000	190,000	22,258	143,383

Step 6: Calculate the consolidated post-acquisition reserves

These will be the parent reserves of £52,000 plus the parent's 75% interest in the subsidiary's post-acquisition reserves of £7,758,000 i.e. £5,818,000 giving a total of £57,818,000.

Step 7: Prepare consolidated profit and loss account

A necessary task in the practical application of the temporal method is the need to keep a formal record of the spot rates applicable to the various transactions. Some companies maintain a daily record of the spot rates of all the foreign subsidiaries within the group.

In the Dec Cruises illustration, we need to deal with depreciation separately in the profit and loss account because we need to translate at the historical spot rate, i.e. the acquisition rate (AR).

	Dec Cruises	Seine Jaunts	Translation rate	Translated	Consolidated profit & loss account
	£000	FF000	FF : £	£000	£000
Operating profit before deprn.	83,680	107,770	AR 11.2	9,622	93,302
Depreciation	(18,950)	(22,370)	AR 8.5	(2,632)	
	—	(2,700)	AR 11.3	(239)	(21,821)
Profit before tax	64,730	82,700		6,751	71,481
Dividends received	676				cancelled out
Dividends receivable	1,304				cancelled out
Profit before tax	66,710	82,700		6,751	71,481
Tax	13,710	31,700	AR 11.2	2,830	16,540
Profit after tax	53,000	51,000		3,921	54,941
Less minority interest				25% of 3,921	980
				25% of £51	13 See Step 8
					53,948
Dividend paid	4,000	10,000	AR 11.1	901	4,000
Dividend proposed	8,000	20,000	AR 11.5	1,739	8,000
Retained for year	41,000	21,000		1,281	41,948

Step 8: Reconciliation of residual balance in subsidiary's translated balance sheet

Under the temporal method the difference on exchange should be treated as part of reported operating profits. Under the closing rate method it would be transferred to reserves. The difference on exchange is calculated as follows:

	FF000		Rate	£000
Net assets of subsidiary at 30 June Year 5:				
Fixed assets				
At 30 June Year 6	250,700			
Less purchases year ended 30 June Year 6	27,000			
		223,700	8.5	26,318
Depreciation				
At 30 June Year 6	40,700			
Less depreciation year ended 30 June Year 6	25,070			
		15,630	8.5	(1,839)
		208,070		24,479
Stock at 30 June Year 5				
Assuming same level as at 30 June Year 6		33,000	11.0	3,000
		241,070		27,479
Net monetary liabilities				
Balancing figure		(72,070)	11.0	(6,552)
Net assets [FF190m – FF21m retained profit] =		169,000		*20,927*
Equity interest at 30 June Year 6 per translated balance sheet see Step 2 above (rounded)				22,259
Net assets at 30 June Year 5 as above				*20,927*
Growth in net assets during year ended 30 June Year 6				1,332
Less profit for year ended 30 June Year 6 (see Step 7 above)				1,281
Exchange difference assuming no new capital movements during year				51

22.6 The hyper-inflationary economy

A foreign subsidiary operating within a hyper-inflationary economy may have such a material impact on the consolidated financial statements that the quality of the true and fair view may be jeopardised. Here are two of the factors of paramount influence in this situation:

(i) the foreign currency carrying amounts of assets and liabilities and the day-to-day transaction values of expenses and revenue may reflect increases that are considerably higher than those experienced in previous financial periods, thus destroying meaningful comparison;

(ii) the exchange spot rate of the foreign local currency is very likely to depreciate against the harder currency of the parent entity country as it reflects the different inflation rates between the two countries. Under the net investment/closing rate method the exchange losses will be taken to reserves and so by-pass the consolidated profit and loss account.

SSAP 20 suggests[17] that the local currency financial statements should be adjusted where possible to reflect current price levels before the translation process is undertaken. However, the standard omits to give guidance as to just how this should be done. The problem has been addressed by the Urgent Issues Task Force[18] which accepts two methods of eliminating or, perhaps, only alleviating financial distortions. These methods are:

(i) adjustment of the local currency accounting statements to reflect the domestic current price levels before proceeding with the translation – any gain or loss on the holding of net monetary assets or liabilities taken to the profit and loss account; or

(ii) designating a relatively stable currency as the functional currency into which the foreign subsidiary's accounts should be translated, using the temporal method, before translating into the monetary unit of the parent company – exchange differences to be passed through the consolidated profit and loss account. This requires two decisions: (a) a decision to pre-translate and (b) the choice of a functional currency.

(a) When to pre-translate?

The UITF suggest that pre-translation is considered necessary to businesses operating within economies suffering a cumulative inflation rate, over a three-year span, approaching or exceeding 100%. This might actually be taken as a definition of hyperinflation – although some might regard this as being a modest level of inflation.

(b) How is a functional currency selected?

The functional currency will depend on the prevailing circumstances, e.g. the hard currency of the US$ may suit some operational environments, such as South America, or, indeed, the oil producing areas where the US$ already operates.

22.7 The advent of the Euro: costs and implications[19]

In 1998 the first countries substituting the Euro for their national currency will be chosen from Germany, France, Italy, Spain, Austria, Belgium, Luxembourg, Finland, Ireland, Netherlands and Portugal. The UK will not be among those countries but has expressed the intention of joining in due course. Even though the UK remains out there will be substantial strategic effects on UK business, e.g. pricing transparency across Europe may lead to changes in pricing policy, labour cost transparency may lead to relocation of activities and financial costs may come down as exchange risks and the need for hedging will be reduced.

The UK businesses which are potentially affected are those which:

● have subsidiaries, parents, joint ventures or strategic alliances in EMU countries;
● buy or sell to enterprises or individuals from EMU countries;
● have loans or liquid assets in EMU currencies;
● are in competition with enterprises from EMU countries.

There is a detailed checklist prepared by *Federation Européen des Experts Comptables*.[20] The checklist recommends companies, *inter alia*, to 'Take advice on accounting for the gains and losses arising from converting/translating EMU curencies to the Euro, e.g. is the gain/loss realised or unrealised?'

In the UK finance directors will look to the ASB as one of the sources of such advice. For the purposes of this chapter, therefore, we propose to concentrate on the financial reporting aspects and ASB draft proposals for dealing with EMU and the Euro.

The Urgent Issues Task Force has issued a draft Abstract[21] concerning the accounting issues arising from the advent of the Economic Monetary Union (EMU) and the proposed introduction of the single currency, the Euro. The Abstract para. 1 comments that the advent of the EMU will necessitate significant expenditure by many business entities to adapt their operations and information systems to accommodate the single currency. This will be the case irrespective of whether a Member State participates in the EMU, as, all those in, or trading with, participating Member States are potentially affected.

The Abstract identifies **costs**, the **consequences with accounting implications**, the **issues** involved and the consensus reached by the Task Force in specifying the necessary **accounting treatment**. We will consider each of these aspects:

Costs

There will be a variety of costs incurred which may include: administrative planning; staff planning; provision of information to customers; modification to software and adaptation of hardware, e.g. vending machines, cash registers and banks' automatic telling machines.

Consequences with accounting implications

Apart from the additional costs, it will be necessary to consider foreign exchange differences. These will be of two types:

● differences that have arisen on balances denominated in participating currencies will become permanent;
● the exchange risk between currency units of participating Member States will disappear.

Issues

The UITF considered three issues:

1 Should costs sustained be expensed or capitalised as an asset?
2 What will be the impact on those cumulative foreign exchange differences between participating Member States that have arisen in pre-Euro periods?
3 What will be the impact on hedging instruments existing at the date the Euro is introduced, in respect of future transactions between participating Member States?

1 Should costs sustained be expensed or capitalised as an asset?
The UITF approached this question by considering it in relation to the ASB's definition of an asset in FRS 5 *Reporting the Substance of Transactions*, namely, 'assets are rights or other access to future economic benefits controlled by an entity as a result of past transactions or events'.

Applying the asset definition, it concluded that costs should be:–

expensed if:

● those costs fail to generate an asset, e.g. staff training costs and giving advice to customers;
● those costs are incurred simply to maintain an asset's originally assessed standard of performance;

capitalised if:

● expenditure adapts existing assets so that there is a clear enhancement of its service potential.

The UITF also addressed the question of provisions. It approached this question by considering it in relation to the ASB's definition of a liability, namely 'liabilities are an entity's obligation to transfer economic benefits as a result of past transactions or events'. It also introduced FRS 12's proviso concerning provisions that they should only be recognised when an entity 'has a legal or constructive obligation to transfer economic benefits as a result of past events' and accepting that 'the mere intention or even necessity to undertake expenditure related to the future would not be sufficient to give rise to an obligation'. This means that only expenditure incurred during the year and commitments at the balance sheet date in respect of preparing for the changeover to the Euro should be disclosed in the financial statements.

2 Cumulative foreign exchange differences

As we have seen in our discussions concerning the net investment/closing rate method of translation, differences on exchange in respect of independent foreign subsidiaries are treated as movements on reserve. Under the terms of FRS 3 *Reporting Financial Performance* para. 27 financial statements must show such gains or losses on exchange, appearing as a reserve, by recognition through the statement of total recognised gains and losses. After the introduction of the Euro such cumulative differences should remain on reserves – they should not be transferred to the profit and loss account as this would be tantamount of recognising them twice, a process that is prohibited by FRS 3.

3 Hedging instruments

There is no standard dealing with anticipatory hedging. The UITF concluded that it is appropriate to follow a policy of deferment, i.e. a policy whereby gains or losses are recognised in the revenue account in the same future financial period as the related income or expense subject to hedging. This means that there will be immediate effect as at the date of the introduction of the Euro.

Review questions

1 Explain the difference between conversion and translation exchange differences.

2 Summarise the procedures when translating foreign currency transactions at the individual company stage for both trade purchase and fixed asset purchase.

3 Explain how forward contracts affect the amount and accounting treatment of exchange gains and losses.

4 Explain how and why foreign currency loans may be used to hedge equity investments.

5 Greenall 1997 accounts include the following accounting policy relating to foreign currencies 'Assets and liabilities denominated in foreign currencies are translated at exchange rates ruling at the balance sheet date. The exchange differences arising, together with exchange differences on trading transactions, are dealt with in the profit and loss account.'

 Explain why the differences (a) on assets and liabilities and (b) on trading transactions are dealt with in the profit and loss account rather than through reserves.

6 Explain how it can be established that the foreign subsidiary is not independent and why this is relevant for financial reporting.

7 It has been argued that the use of the closing rate method of translating subsidiary financial statements produces accounting statements that give the impression that exchange rates are stable. Explain the basis for this view, discuss the validity of the argument and present an acceptable alternative method of translation.

8 Explain how a foreign subsidiary operating within a hyper-inflationary economy may have such a material impact on the consolidated financial statements that the quality of the true and fair view may be jeopardised.

9 Discuss, in relation to financial statements, the ASB view of **costs**, the **consequences with accounting implications** and the **issues** arising on the introduction of the Euro.

10 Explain the reason for the italicised policy from the Accounting Policies of Holiday Chemical Holdings 1996 accounts:

> In the accounts of individual undertakings, transactions denominated in foreign currencies are recorded at *actual exchange rates as at the date of the transaction.*
>
> Monetary assets and liabilities denominated in foreign currencies at the year end are reported *at the rates of exchange prevailing at the balance sheet date* or, where appropriate, *at the rate of exchange of a matched forward contract.* Any gain or loss arising from a change in the exchange rates subsequent to the date of the transaction *is included in the profit and loss account.*
>
> For the purposes of balance sheet consolidation *the closing rate method is used* under which translation gains or losses are shown as a movement on reserves.
>
> Profit and loss accounts of overseas subsidiary undertakings are translated *at the average exchange rate.*
>
> Exchange differences on foreign currency investment loans, to the extent that they offset exchange differences on related investments in overseas operations, are also *taken to reserves* and separately reported with *any excess being charged or credited to the profit and loss account* as appropriate.
>
> Gains or losses on forward exchange contracts in existence at the year end not matched against monetary assets or liabilities are accounted *for on the date of maturity of the contract.*

Exercises

An extract from the solution is provided in the appendix at the end of the text for exercises marked with an asterisk (*).

Question I

The directors of Pragmatic Ltd have sought your advice on the following issues which relate to events that took place in the accounting year ended 31 December 20X5.

(i) During the year ended 31 December 20X5, the company made a bulk purchase of raw materials from an Austrian supplier on credit terms. The transaction took place on 1 October 20X5 and was worth 1,000,000 Austrian Schillings. Payment was to be made in Schillings in two equal instalments on 1 December 20X5 and 1 February 20X6.

(ii) On 1 June 20X5, Pragmatic Ltd purchased a 10% equity interest in a Danish company for 1,335,000 Danish Kroner. As a hedge against future exchange rate fluctuations, it financed the cost of this investment by taking out a German Deutschmark denominated loan on the same date for 345,000 Deutschmarks.

You also obtained the following information relating to exchange rates against the pound:

	Austrian Schilling	Danish Krone	German Deutschmark
I January 20X5	16.0	9.0	2.31
I June 20X5	16.2	8.9	2.30
I October 20X5	16.0	8.9	2.30
I December 20X5	16.3	9.0	2.28
31 December 20X5	16.2	8.8	2.29
Average for Year	16.3	8.9	2.30

Required:

Prepare a report to the board of directors, explaining, in accordance with best accounting practice as embodied in the Companies Acts and Accounting Standards, how the transactions numbered (i) and (ii) should be treated in the financial statements for the year ended 31 December 20X5. Your report should include the relevant figures to be included in the accounts as well as an explanation and justification of the accounting treatment.

(CIPFA 1996)

* Question 2

The draft financial statements of Smith Ltd for 20X3 below incorporated the transactions listed in the Notes below at rates of exchange on the dates of the transactions.

Profit and Loss Account for year ended 31 December 20X3

		£000
Turnover		3,000
Cost of goods sold		2,076
Gross profit		924
Distribution costs	366	
Administration expenses	118	484
		440
Less interest payable and similar charges		20
		420
Taxation on profit on ordinary activities		184
		236
Dividends		200
Retained profit for year		36

Balance sheet as at 31 December 20X3		
Fixed assets		£000
Land and buildings		800
Plant and machinery		1200
Current assets		
Stock	700	
Debtors	818	
Bank balance	190	
	1,708	
Creditors: due within 1 year:		
Trade creditors	330	
Other creditors	360	
Tax and dividends	385	
	1,075	
Net current assets		633
		2,633
Creditors: due after more than 1 year		
Debenture loans		1,134
		1,499
Capital reserves		
Share capital		1,000
Profit and loss account		499
		1,499

Notes:

1 Plant and machinery includes a machine purchased from a Swiss company for SFR 1,008,000 in October 20X3 when the exchange rate was £1 = SFR 2.8. At 31.12.20X3 the rate was £1 = SFR 3.0. The amount due is included in other creditors.

2 Sales and debtors figures include:

(a) amount in respect of goods sold to a German company for DM 31,200 in November 20X3 when the rate was £1 = DM 4.0. At 31 December 20X3 the exchange rate was £1 = DM 3.9;

(b) amount receivable from a Swedish company for sales in September 20X3 for Kr 68,400 at the rate £1 = Kr 9.5. A forward rate of £1 = Kr 10 has been agreed. At 31 December 20X3 the rate was £1 = Kr 9.0.

3 Cost of sales, creditors and stock figures include an amount relating to the purchase of material for $20,240 from a US company in November 20X3 when the exchange rate was £1 = $2.3. At 31 December 20X3 the rate was £1 = $2.2.

4 Smith Ltd raised finance in the form of a five year loan from a Belgian Bank in December 20X3 (denominated in Belgian Francs) for BF69,210,600 at 10% interest when the rate of exchange was £1 = BF 61. The full amount was outstanding at 31 December 20X3 when the rate was £1 = BF 62.

Required:
(a) A re-drafted profit and loss account and balance sheet as at 31 December 20X3 to incorporate provisions of SSAP 20.
(b) A summary of SSAP 20 provisions applied and a brief comment on their effect in the case of Smith Ltd.

* Question 3

Kish plc is a manufacturing company specializing in ballet shoes. The directors reviewed their strategy and consequently acquired a 100% interest in a German company, Johannsen-Lisa. The German company manufactures tap dancing shoes.

Kish plc acquired its 100% interest on 1 January 20X1 for £1,000,000, at which time the reserves of Johannsen-Lisa were DM 3,487,500.

The balance sheet of Johannsen-Lisa as at 31 December 20X1 was as follows:

	DM000	DM000
Fixed assets		
Plant at cost		12,400
Depreciation		5,232
		7,168
Current assets		
Stock	5,715	
Debtors	7,944	
	13,659	
Creditors: amounts falling due within one year		
Creditors	7,459	
Net current assets		6,200
		13,368

Capital and reserves

7,750,000 shares of 1 DM each	7,750
Reserves	5,618
	13,368

The rates of exchange have been as follows:

DM to £

4.75	1 January 20X1
4.25	Average for 20X1
4.00	31 December 20X1

Required:

Translate the balance sheet of Johannsen-Lisa as at 31 December 20X1 using the closing rate. Translate the profit and loss account reserves for the year ended 31 December 20X1 using the average rate, and calculate the exchange difference between the opening equity and the closing balance sheet equity.

Question 4

Set out below is the balance sheet for Cuchulain, at 31 December 20X5. Cuchulain is a subsidiary of Conchubar plc, a UK company with numerous overseas operations and subsidiaries. Cuchulain operates in Inguba where the currency is the Emer.

	20X5
	Emer 000s
Fixed assets – cost	6,400
– depreciation	(2,700)
	3,700
Stock (cost)	2,950
Debtors	4,100
Creditors (including overdraft)	(3,350)
Proposed dividend	(500)
	6,900
Share capital	
4,000,000 shares at 1 Emer	4,000
Retained profits	2,900
	6,900

The following Information is also available:

1 Conchubar acquired an 80% interest in Cuchulain on 31 December 20X4, at which time the retained earnings of Cuchulain were 1,800,000. The cost of the acquisition was £550,000.

2 Rates of exchange have been as follows:

	Exchange rate
Date	£1 = Emers
1 January 20X4	12
Average 20X4	10.5
31 December 20X4	10
Average 20X5	8.5
31 December 20X5	8

Required:
Translate the balance sheet into sterling using the closing rate method (with the average rate for profit and loss account) and outline, with supporting calculations, the effect that consolidation of Cuchulain would have on the group accounts of Conchubar plc.

* Question 5

Set out below are the transactions of April Inc, a subsidiary company of June Ltd, during 20X7. April was incorporated at the beginning of 20X7 to operate in Germany. The exchange rates ruling during 20X7 between sterling and the Deutschmark are also given.

Date of transaction	Exchange rate	Transactions	D000s
1 January 20X7	D3 : £ 1	Initial share capital issued	4,000
		Bank loan raised	1,000
		Fixed assets purchased	3,000
		Stock purchased	1,000
		Cash at bank	1,000
Average during 20X7	D4 : £ 1	Sales/Purchases/Other transactions	
31 October 20X7	D4.5 : £ 1	Stock purchased	2,000
31 December 20X7	D5 : £ 1	Interest on loan paid	100

Profit and loss account for the year ended 31 December 20X7

	D000s	D000s
Sales		12,000
Opening stock	1,000	
Purchases	8,000	
Closing stock	(2,000)	
Cost of sales		7,000
Depreciation		300
Other expenses		1,600
Interest		100
Total expenses		9,000
Profit before tax		3,000
Tax		1,500
Net profit		1,500

Balance sheet as at 31 December 20X7

Fixed assets	3,000	
Less depreciation	(300)	2,700
Current assets		
Stock	2,000	
Debtors	3,000	
Bank	1,300	6,300
Current liabilities		
Creditors	1,000	
Tax	1,500	(2,500)

Long term loan	(1,000)
Net assets	5,500
Share capital	4,000
Profit and loss account	1,500
	5,500

Required:

(a) Translate the accounts for April for 20X7 into sterling, using:
   (i) the temporal method and
   (ii) the closing rate method.

(b) Analyse the exchange gain or loss that arises in part (a).

Question 6

Expansion plc purchased the whole of the share capital of a Hong Kong company Wong Electrics Ltd. on 1 January 20X7. The agreed price of £90,000 was paid in cash. Fixed assets and stocks were revalued for the purpose of the acquisition and the valuations have been included in the balance sheet on 1 January 20X7.

Wong Electrics Ltd – Balance sheet as at 1 January 20X7

	HK$
Ordinary share capital	150,000
Revaluation reserve	60,000
Revenue reserve	195,000
	405,000
Fixed assets	
Premises	420,000
Machinery	150,000
	570,000
Net current assets	60,000
	630,000
Less long term loan	225,000
	405,000

The summarised accounts for 20X7 of Expansion and Wong Electrics Ltd. are as follows:

	Expansion		Wong Electrics	
	£000	£000	HK$000	HK$000
Summarised profit and loss accounts				
Operating profit before depreciation		144		75
Less depreciation – premises	4		6	
– machinery	32	36	18	24
		108		51
Less taxation		42		15
Retained profit for 20X7		66		36
Add retained profits brought forward		205		195
Retained profits carried forward		271		231
Summarised balance sheets				
Ordinary share capital		400		150
Revaluation reserve		—		60
Retained profit		271		231
		671		441

Fixed assets				
Premises	586		420	
Less depreciation	80	506	6	414
Machinery	220		150	
Less depreciation	100	120	18	132
		626		546
Investment in subsidiary		90		—
Net current assets		205		120
		921		666
Less long-term liabilities		250		225
		671		441

Relevant rates of exchange are:

	HK$ to £1
1 January 20X7	9
Average for the year	10
31 December 20X7	11

Required:

(a) Prepare a set of consolidated accounts for Expansion plc and its subsidiary for the year ended 31 December 20X7 using the closing rate method of translation. Follow the provisions of SSAP 20 (*Accounting for Foreign Currency Translation*), and use the average rate of exchange for translation of the profit and loss account.

(b) Prepare a set of consolidated accounts for Expansion plc and its subsidiary for the year ended 31 December 20X7 using the temporal method of translation, following the provisions of SSAP 20.

References

1 'Data Briefing', *Accountancy*, February 1998, p. 26.
2 C. Nobes and R. Parker, *Comparative International Accounting*, (4th edition), Prentice Hall, 1995, p. 353.
3 SSAP 20, *Foreign Currency Translation*, ASC, 1983, para. 41.
4 C. Nobes and R. Parker, *op. cit.*, p. 353.
5 SSAP 20, para. 42.
6 SSAP 2, *Disclosure of Accounting Policies*, ASC, 1971, para. 14(d).
7 SSAP 20, paras 50 and 11.
8 SSAP 20, paras 65 and 10.
9 UITF Abstract 7, True and fair view override disclosures, ASB, 1992.
10 SSAP 20, para. 51.
11 C. Nobes and R. Parker, *op. cit.*, p. 367.
12 SSAP 20, para. 41.
13 SSAP 20, paras 2 and 17.
14 SSAP 20, para. 17.
15 SSAP 20, para. 21.
16 SSAP 20, para. 23.
17 SSAP 20, para. 20.
18 UITF Abstract 9, *Accounting for Operations in Hyper-inflationary Economies*, ASB, June 1993.
19 Euro Checklist, *ACCA Practice Society Fact Sheet 15*, 1998.
20 *Checklist on Introduction of Euro*, FEE, 1998, available from Website http://euro.fee.be.
21 UITF 21, *Accounting Issues Arising from the Proposed Introduction of the Euro*, ASB, 1998.

PART 5

Interpretation

CHAPTER 23

Earnings per share

23.1   Introduction

In this chapter we consider

- why the earnings per share figure is important
- how it is used by shareholders
- FRS 3 calculation of Basic Earnings per Share (BEPS)
- BEPS when there has been a bonus issue, share split, new issue and buyback of shares
- BEPS when there has been a rights issue
- Calculation of Diluted EPS
- FRS 14 procedure where there are several potential dilutions e.g. conversion rights and options
- EPS when conversion rights are exercised
- Institute of Investment Management and Research (IIMR) definition of an alternative EPS

23.2   Why is the earnings per share figure important?

One of the most widely publicised ratios for a public company is the price/earnings or PE ratio. The PE ratio is significant because, by combining it with a forecast of company earnings, analysts can decide whether the shares are currently over- or undervalued.[1]

The ratio is published daily in the financial press and is widely employed by those making investment decisions. The following is a typical extract from the *Risk Measurement Service*:[2]

Breweries, Pubs and Restaurants

Company	Price 31/3/98	PE ratio
Greenalls Group	453	12.6
J D Wetherspoon	340	39.3
Whitbread	1,125	19.6

The PE ratio is calculated by dividing the market price of a share by the earnings that the company generated for that share. Alternatively, the PE figure may be seen as a multiple of the earnings per share, where the multiple represents the number of years' earnings required to recoup the price paid for the share. For example, it would take a shareholder in J D Wetherspoon just under forty years to recoup her outlay if all earnings were to be distributed, whereas it would take a shareholder in Greenalls Group just over twelve years to recoup his outlay, and one in Whitbread just under twenty years.

23.2.1 What factors affect the PE ratio?

The PE ratio for a company will reflect investors' confidence and hopes about the international scene, the national economy and the industry sector, as well as about the current year's performance of the company as disclosed in its financial report. It is difficult to interpret a PE ratio in isolation without a certain amount of information about the company, its competitors and the industry within which it operates.

For example, a **high PE ratio** might reflect investor confidence in the existing management team: people are willing to pay a high multiple for expected earnings because of the underlying strength of the company. Conversely, it might also reflect lack of investor confidence in the existing management, but an anticipation of a take-over bid which will result in transfer of the company assets to another company with better prospects of achieving growth in earnings than has the existing team.

A **low PE ratio** might indicate a lack of confidence in the current management or a feeling that even a new management might find problems that are not easily surmounted. For example, there might be extremely high gearing, with little prospect of organic growth in earnings or new capital inputs from rights issues to reduce it.

These reasons for a difference in the PE ratios of companies, even though they are in the same industry, are market-based and not simply a function of earnings. However, the current earnings per share figure and the individual shareholder's expectation of future growth relative to that of other companies also have an impact on the share price.

23.2.2 How is the EPS figure calculated?

Because of the importance attached to the PE ratio, it is essential that there is a consistent approach to the calculation of the EPS figure. FRS 14 *Earnings per Share* was issued for this purpose.

The EPS figure is of major interest to shareholders not only because of its use in the PE ratio calculation, but also because it is used in the earnings yield percentage calculation. It is a more acceptable basis for comparing performance than figures such as dividend yield percentage because it is not affected by the distribution policy of the directors. The formula is:

$$\text{EPS} = \frac{\text{Earnings}}{\text{Number of ordinary shares}}$$

The standard defines two EPS figures for disclosure, namely,

● **Basic EPS** based on ordinary shares currently in issue; and
● **Diluted EPS** based on ordinary shares currently in issue *plus* potential ordinary shares.

Basic EPS is defined in FRS 14 as follows:

● Basic earnings per share is a measure of past performance, calculated by dividing the net profit or loss attributable to ordinary shareholders by the weighted average number of ordinary shares outstanding during the period.

– The net profit or loss attributable to ordinary shares should be the net profit or loss for the period after deducting dividends and other appropriations in respect of non-equity shares.[3]
– The weighted average number of ordinary shares should be adjusted for events, other than the conversion of potential ordinary shares, *that have changed the number of ordinary shares outstanding, without a corresponding change in resources.*[4]

Diluted EPS is defined as follows:

● For the purpose of calculating diluted earnings per share, the net profit attributable to ordinary shareholders and the weighted average number of shares outstanding should be *adjusted for the effects of all dilutive potential ordinary shares.*[5]

This means that **both** the earnings and the number of shares used *may* need to be adjusted from the amounts that appear in the profit and loss account and balance sheet.

23.3 The use to shareholders of the EPS

Shareholders use the reported EPS to estimate future growth which will affect the future share price. It is an important measure of growth over time. There are however limitations in its use as a performance measure and for inter-company comparison.

23.3.1 How does a shareholder estimate future growth in the EPS?

The current EPS figure allows a shareholder to assess the wealth-creating abilities of a company. It recognises that the effect of earnings is to add to the individual wealth of shareholders in two ways: first, by the payment of a dividend which transfers cash from the company's control to the shareholder; and, secondly, by retaining earnings in the company for reinvestment, so that there may be increased earnings in the future.

The important thing when attempting to arrive at an estimate is to review the profit and loss account of the current period and identify the earnings that can reasonably be expected to continue. In accounting terminology, you should identify the **maintainable post-tax earnings** that arise in the **ordinary course of business**.

Companies are required to make this easy for the shareholder by disclosing separately, by way of note, any exceptional items and by analysing the profit and loss on trading between discontinued, continuing and acquired activities.[6]

Shareholders can use this information to estimate for themselves the maintainable post-tax earnings, assuming that there is no change in the company's trading activities. This is in line with the ASB's view that companies should provide an information set from which each user can make an individual estimate or appraisal.

Clearly, in a dynamic business environment it is extremely unlikely that there will be no change in the current business activities. The shareholder needs to refer to any information on capital commitments which appear as a note to the accounts and also to the chairman's statement and any coverage in the financial press. This additional information is used to adjust the existing maintainable earnings figure.

23.3.2 Limitations of EPS as a performance measure

EPS is thought to have a significant impact on the market share price. However, there are limitations to its use as a performance measure.

The limitations affecting the use of EPS as an inter-period performance measure include:

● It is based on historical earnings. Management might have made decisions in the past to encourage current earnings growth at the expense of future growth e.g. by reducing the amount spent on capital investment and research and development. Growth in the EPS cannot be relied on as a predictor of the rate of growth in the future.

● EPS does not take inflation into account. Real growth might be materially different from the apparent growth.

The limitations affecting inter-company comparisons include:

● The earnings are affected by management's choice of accounting policies e.g. the choice of the depreciation method

● EPS is affected by the capital structure e.g. changes in number of shares by making bonus issues.

However, the **rate of growth** of EPS may be compared between different companies and over time within the same company.

23.4 Illustration of the Basic EPS calculation

Assume that Watts plc had post-tax profits for 20X1 of £1,250,000 and an issued share capital of £1,500,000 comprising 1,000,000 ordinary shares of 50p each and 1,000,000 £1 10% Preference shares. The basic EPS (BEPS) for 20X1 is calculated at 115p as follows:

	£000
Profit on ordinary activities after tax	1,250
Less Preference dividend	(100)
Profit for the period attributable to ordinary shareholders	1,150

$$\text{BEPS} = \text{£}1,150,000/1,000,000 \text{ shares} = \text{£}1.15$$

Note that it is the *number* of issued shares that is used in the calculation and *not the nominal value* of the shares. The market value of a share is not required for the BEPS calculation.

23.5 Adjusting the number of shares used in the Basic EPS calculation

The earnings per share is frequently used by shareholders and directors to demonstrate the growth in a company's performance over time. Care is required to ensure that the number of shares is stated consistently to avoid distortions arising from changes in the capital structure that have changed the number of shares outstanding without a corresponding change in resources during the whole or part of a year. Such changes occur with (a) bonus issues and share splits; (b) new issues and buybacks at full market price during the year and (c) bonus element of a rights issue

We will consider the appropriate treatment for each of these capital structure changes in order to ensure that EPS is comparable between accounting periods.

23.5.1 Bonus issues

A bonus issue, or capitalisation issue as it is also called, arises when a company capitalises reserves to give existing shareholders more shares. In effect, a simple transfer is made from reserves to issued share capital. In real terms, neither the shareholder nor the company is giving or receiving any immediate financial benefit. The process indicates that the reserves will not be available for distribution, but will remain invested in the physical assets of the company. There are, however, more shares.

Treatment in current year

In the Watts plc example, assume that the company increased its shares in issue in 20X1 by the issue of another 1 million shares and achieved identical earnings in 20X1 as in 20X0. The EPS reported for 20X1 would be immediately halved from 115p to 57.5p. Clearly, this does not provide a useful comparison of performance between the two years.

Restatement of previous year's BEPS

The solution is to restate the EPS for 20X0 that appears in the 20X1 accounts, using the number of shares in issue at 31.12.20X1 i.e. £1,150,000/2,000,000 shares = BEPS of 57.5p.

23.5.2 Share splits

When the market value of a share becomes high some companies decide to increase the number of shares held by each shareholder by changing the nominal value of each share. The effect is to reduce the market price per share but for each shareholder to hold the same total value. A share split would be treated in the same way as a bonus issue.

For example, if Watts plc split the 1,000,000 shares of 50p each into 2,000,000 shares of 25p each, the 20X1 BEPS would be calculated using 2,000,000 shares. It would seem that the BEPS had halved in 20X1. This is misleading and the 20X0 BEPS is therefore restated using 2,000,000 shares. The total market capitalisation of Watts plc would remain unchanged e.g. if, prior to the split, each share had a market value of £4 and the company had a total market capitalisation of £4,000,000, after the split each share would have a market price of £2 and the company market capitalisation would remain unchanged at £4,000,000.

23.5.3 New issue at full market value

Selling more shares to raise additional capital should generate additional earnings. In this situation we have a real change in the company's capital and there is no need to adjust any comparative figures. However, a problem arises in the year in which the issue took place. Unless the issue occurred on the first day of the financial year, the new funds would have been *available to generate profits* for only a part of the year. It would therefore be misleading to calculate the EPS figure by dividing the earnings generated during the year by the number of shares in issue at the end of the year. The method adopted to counter this is to use a time-weighted average for the number of shares.

For example, let us assume in the Watts example that the following information is available:

	No. of shares
Shares (50p nominal value) in issue at 1 January 20X1	1,000,000
Shares issued for cash at market price on 30 September 20X1	500,000

The time-weighted number of shares for EPS calculation at 31 December 20X1 will be:

No. of shares

Shares in issue for 9 months to date of issue

$(1,000,000) \times (9/12 \text{ months})$ 750,000

Shares in issue for 3 months from date of issue

$(1,500,000) \times (3/12 \text{ months})$ 375,000

Time-weighted shares for use in BEPS calculation   1,125,000

BEPS for 20X1 will be £1,150,000/1,125,000 shares = **£1.02**

23.5.4 Buybacks at market value

Companies are prompted to buy back their own shares when there is a fall in the stock market. The main arguments that companies advance for purchasing their own shares are:

● To reduce the cost of capital when equity costs more than debt.

● The shares are undervalued.

● To return surplus cash to shareholders.

● To increase the apparent rate of growth in BEPS.

Examples are found amongst the FTSE 100 companies e.g. in 1998 NatWest Bank purchased 175,000; Rio Tinto 2.965m; BTR 700,020 ordinary shares.[7]

The shares bought back by the company are included in the basic EPS calculation time apportioned from the beginning of the year to the date of buyback.

For example, let us assume in the Watts example that the following information is available:

	No. of shares
Shares (50p nominal value) in issue at 1 January 20X1	1,000,000
Shares bought back on 31 May 20X1	240,000
Profit attributable to ordinary shares	£1,150,000

The time-weighted number of shares for EPS calculation at 31 December 20X1 will be:

1.1.20X1	Shares in issue for 5 months to date of buyback		
		$1,000,000 \times 5/12$	416,667
31.5.20X1	Number of shares bought back by company	(240,000)	
31.12.20X1	Opening capital less shares bought back	$760,000 \times 7/12$	443,333
	Time-weighted shares for use in BEPS calculation		860,000

BEPS for 20X1 will be £1,150,000/860,000 shares = **£1.34**

Note that the effect of this buyback has been to increase the BEPS for 20X1 from £1.15 as calculated in para 11.4 above. This is a mechanism for management to lift the BEPS and achieve EPS growth.

23.6 Rights issues

A rights issue involves giving existing shareholders 'the right' to buy a set number of additional shares at a price below the fair value which is normally the current market price. A rights issue has two characteristics being both an issue for cash and, because the price is below fair value, a bonus issue. Consequently the rules for *both* a cash issue *and* a bonus issue need to be applied in calculating the weighted average number of shares for the basic EPS calculation.

The following four steps are required:

Step 1: Calculate the average price of shares before and after a rights issue to identify the amount of the bonus the company has granted.

Step 2: The weighted average number of shares is calculated for current year.

Step 3: The BEPS for current year is calculated.

Step 4: The previous year BEPS is adjusted for the bonus element of the rights issue.

Step 1: Calculate the average price of shares before and after a rights issue to identify the amount of the bonus the company has granted

Assume that Mr Radmand purchased two 50p shares at a market price of £4 each in Watts plc on 1 January 20X1 and that on 2 January 20X1 the company offered a 1:2 rights issue (i.e. one new share for every two shares held) at £3.25 per share.

If Mr Radmand had bought at the market price, the position would simply have been:

		£
2 shares at market price of £4 each on 1 January 20X1	=	8.00
1 share at market price of £4.00 per share on 2 January	=	4.00
Total cost of 3 shares as at 2 January		12.00
Average cost per share unchanged at		4.00

However, this did not happen. Mr Radmand only paid £3.25 for the new share. This meant that the total cost of 3 shares to him was:

		£
2 shares at market price of £4 each on 1 January 20X1	=	8.00
1 share at discounted price of £3.25 on 2 January 20X1	=	3.25
Total cost of 3 shares	=	11.25
Average cost per share (£11.25/3 shares)	=	3.75

The rights issue has had the effect of reducing the cost per share of each of the three shares held by Mr Radmand on 2 January 20X1 by (£4.00 − £3.75) **£0.25 per share**.

The accounting terms applied are:

● Average cost per share after the rights issue (£3.75) is : *the theoretical ex-rights value*.

● Amount by which the average cost of each share is reduced (£0.25) is : *the bonus element*.

In accounting terminology Step 1 is described as follows:

Step 1: The bonus element is ascertained by calculating the theoretical ex-rights value, i.e. the £0.25 is ascertained by calculating the £3.75 and deducting it from £4 pre-rights market price

Step 1: Theoretical ex-rights calculation

In accounting terminology, this means that existing shareholders get an element of bonus per share (£0.25) at the same time as the company receives additional capital (£3.25 per new share). The bonus element may be quantified by the calculation of a **theoretical ex-rights price (£3.75)**, which is compared with the last market price (£4.00) prior to the issue; the difference is a bonus. The theoretical ex-rights price is calculated as follows:

	£
2 shares at fair value of £4 each prior to rights issue	= 8.00
1 share at discounted rights issue price of £3.25 each	= 3.25
3 shares at fair value after issue (i.e. ex-rights)	= 11.25
The theoretical ex-rights price is £11.25/3 shares	= 3.75
The bonus element is fair value £4 less £3.75	= 0.25

Note that for the calculation of the number of shares and time-weighted number of shares for a bonus issue, share split and issue at full market price per share the market price per share is not relevant. The position for a rights issue is different and the market price becomes a relevant factor in calculating the number of bonus shares.

Step 2: The weighted average number of shares is calculated for current year

There is a formulaic approach illustrated in Table 23.1 which can be applied when calculating BEPS following a rights issue. However it is helpful to understand the underlying rationale which is explained as followed.

Table 23.1   Formula approach to calculating weighted average number of shares.

				No. of shares
Shares to date of rights issue:				
No. of shares	× Increase by bonus fraction	× Time adjustment		
1,000,000		× 9/12	=	750,000
Bonus:	((1,000,000 × 4/3.75) −1,000,000)	× 9/12	=	50,000
Shares from date of issue:				
1,500,000	×	× 3/12	=	375,000
Weighted average number of shares				1,175,000

Assume that Watts plc made a rights issue of 1 share for every 2 shares held on 1 January 20X1.

There would be no need to calculate a weighted average number of shares. The total used in the BEPS calculation would be as follows:

	No. of shares
Shares to date of rights issue:	
1,000,000 shares held for a full year	= 1,000,000
Shares from date of issue:	
500,000 shares held for full year	= 500,000
Total shares for BEPS calculation	1,500,000

However, if a rights issue is made part way through the year, a time apportionment is required. For example, if we assume that a rights issue is made on 30 September 20X1, the time-weighted number of shares is calculated as follows:

	No. of shares
Shares to date of rights issue:	
1,000,000 shares held for a full year	= 1,000,000
Shares from date of issue:	
500,000 shares held for 3 months (500,000 × 3/12)	= 125,000
Weighted average number of shares	1,125,000

Note, however, that the 1,125,000 has not taken account of the fact that the new shares had been issued at less than market price and that the company had effectively granted the existing shareholders a bonus. We saw above that when there has been a bonus issue the number of shares used in the BEPS is increased. We need, therefore, to calculate the number of bonus shares that would have been issued to achieve the reduction in market price from £4.00 to £3.75 per share. This is calculated as follows:

Total market capitalisation was 1,000,000 shares		
@ £4.00 per share	=	£4,000,000
Number of shares that would reduce the		
market price to £3.75	=	£4,000,000/£3.75
	=	1,066,667 shares
Number of shares prior to issue	=	1,000,000
Bonus shares deemed to be issued to existing shareholders	=	66,667
Bonus share for period of 9 months to date of issue		
(66,667/12 × 9)	=	**50,000**

The bonus shares for the 9 months are added to the existing shares and the time apportioned new shares as follows:

		No. of shares
Shares to date of rights issue:		
1,000,000 shares held for a full year	=	1,000,000
Shares from date of issue:		
500,000 shares held for 3 months (500,000 × 3/12)	=	125,000
Weighted average number of shares		1,125,000
Bonus share:		
66,667 shares held for 9 months (66,667/12 × 9)	=	50,000
		1,175,000

The same figure of 1,175,000 can be derived from the following approach using the relationship between the market price of £4.00 and the theoretical ex-rights price of £3.75 to calculate the number of bonus shares as in Table 23.1.

Step 3: Calculate BEPS for current year

BEPS for 20X1 is then calculated as £1,150,000 / 1,175,000 shares   =   **97.9p**

Step 4: Adjusting the previous year's BEPS for the bonus element of a rights issue

The 20X0 BEPS of £1.15 needs to be restated i.e. reduced to ensure comparability with 20X1.

In Step 2 above we calculated that the company had made a bonus issue of 66,667 shares to existing shareholders. In re-calculating the BEPS for 20X0 the shares should be increased by 66,667 to 1,066,667. The restated BEPS for 20X0 is as follows:

Earnings	/	restated number of shares		
£1,150,000	/	1,066,667	=	£1.078125

Assuming that the earnings for 20X0 and 20X1 were £1,150,000 in each year the 20X0 BEPS figures will be reported as follows:

As reported in the 20X0 accounts as at 31.12.20X0 =
£1,150,000/1,000,000 = £1.15
As restated in the 20X1 accounts as at 31.12.20X1 =
£1,150,000/1,066,667 = £1.08

The same result is obtained using the bonus element approach by reducing the 20X0 BEPS as follows by multiplying it by:

$$\frac{\text{Theoretical ex-rights fair value per share}}{\text{Fair value per share immediately before the exercise of rights}} = \frac{£3.75}{£4.00}$$

As restated in the 20X1 accounts as at 31.12.20X1 = £1.15 x (3.75/4.00) = £1.08

23.6.1 Would BEPS for current and previous year be the same if the company had made a separate full market price issue and a separate bonus issue?

This section is included to demonstrate that the BEPS is the same i.e. £1.078125 if we approach the calculation on the assumption that there was a Full Price Issue followed by a Bonus Issue. This will demonstrate that the BEPS is the same as that calculated using theoretical ex-rights. There are five steps as follows:

Step 1: Calculate the number of full value and bonus shares in the company's share capital

	No. of shares
Shares in issue *before* bonus	1,000,000
Rights issue at full market price	
(500,000 shares × £3.25 issue price / full market price of £4)	406,250
	1,406,250
Total number of bonus shares	93,750
Total shares	1,500,000

Step 2: Allocate the total bonus shares to the 1,000,000 original shares

(Note that the previous year will be restated using the proportion of original shares: original shares + bonus shares allocated to these original 1,000,000 shares)

Shares in issue before bonus		1,000,000
Bonus issue applicable to pre-rights:		
93,750 bonus shares × (1,000,000/1,406,250) =		
66,667 shares × 9/12months	= 50,000	
Bonus issue applicable to post-rights		
93,750 bonus shares × (1,000,000/1,406,250) =		
66,667 shares × 3/12months	= 16,667	
Total bonus shares allocated to existing 1,000,000 shares		66,667
Total original holding plus bonus shares allocated to that holding		1,066,667

Step 3: Time weight the rights issue and allocate bonus shares to rights shares

Rights issue at full market price
500,000 shares × (£3.25 issue price / full market price of £4)
= 406,250 × 3/12months   101,563
Bonus issue applicable to Rights issue:
    93,750 bonus shares × (406,250/1,406,250) = 27,083 shares × 3/12 months   6,770
Weighted average ordinary shares (includes shares from Steps 2 and 3)   1,175,000

Step 4: BEPS calculation for 20X1

Calculate the BEPS using the post-tax profit and weighted average ordinary shares, as follows:

$$\text{20X1 BEPS} \quad = \quad \frac{£1,150,000}{1,175,000} \quad = \quad 97.9\text{p}$$

Step 5: BEPS restated for 20X0

There were 93,750 bonus shares issued in 20X1. The 20X0 BEPS needs to be reduced, therefore, by:

the same proportion as applied to the 1,000,000 ordinary shares in 20X1 i.e.
1,000,000:1,066,667
20X0 BEPS = 20X0 BEPS × Bonus adjustment = Restated 20X0 BEPS
i.e. 20X0 = £1.15   × (1,000,000/1,066,667) = £1.078125

This approach illustrates the rationale for the time-weighted average and the restatement of the previous year's BEPS. The adjustment using the theoretical ex-rights approach produces the same result and is simpler to apply but the rationale is not obvious.

23.7 Adjusting the earnings and number of shares used in the Diluted EPS calculation

We will consider briefly what dilution means and the circumstances which require the weighted average number of shares and the net profit attributable to ordinary shareholders used to calculate Basic EPS to be adjusted.

23.7.1 What is dilution?

In a modern corporate structure, a number of classes of person such as the holders of convertible bonds, the holders of convertible preference shares, members of share option schemes and share warrant holders may be entitled as at the date of the balance sheet to become equity shareholders at a future date.

If these people exercise their entitlements at a future date, the EPS would be reduced. In accounting terminology, the EPS will have been diluted. The effect on future share price could be significant. Assuming that the share price is a multiple of the EPS figure, any reduction in the figure could have serious implications for the existing shareholders; they need to be aware of the potential effect on the EPS figure of any changes in the way the capital of the company is or will be constituted. This is shown by calculating and disclosing both the basic and 'fully diluted EPS' figures.

FRS 14 therefore requires a Diluted EPS figure to be reported using as the denominator potential ordinary shares that are dilutive i.e. would decrease net profit per share or increase net loss from continuing operations.[8]

23.7.2 Circumstances in which the number of shares used for Basic EPS is increased

The holders of convertible bonds, the holders of convertible preference shares, members of share option schemes and the holders of share warrant will each be entitled to receive ordinary shares from the company at some future date. Such additional shares, referred to as potential ordinary shares, *may* need to be added to the Basic weighted average number *if they are dilutive*. It is important to note that if a company has potential ordinary shares they are not automatically included in the fully diluted EPS calculation. There is a test to apply to see if such shares actually are dilutive – this is discussed further below in section 11.8.

23.7.3 Circumstances in which the earnings used for Basic EPS is increased

The earnings are increased to take account of the post-tax effects of amounts recognised in the period relating to dilutive potential ordinary shares that will no longer be incurred on their conversion to ordinary shares e.g. the loan interest payable on convertible loans will no longer be a charge after conversion and earnings will be increased by the post-tax amount of such interest.

23.7.4 Procedure where there are share warrants and options

Where options, warrants or other arrangements exist which involve the issue of shares below their fair value i.e at a price lower than the average for the period then the impact is calculated by notionally splitting the potential issue into shares issued at fair value and shares issued at no value for no consideration.[9] Since shares issued at fair value are not dilutive that number is ignored but the number of shares at no value is employed to calculate the dilution. The calculation is illustrated for Watts plc:

Assume that Watts plc had at 31 December 20X1:

● an issued capital of 1,000,000 ordinary shares of 50p each nominal value;
● post-tax earnings for the year of £1,150,000;
● an average market price per share of £4; and
● share options in existence 500,000 shares issuable in 20X2 at £3.25 per share.

The computation of Basic and Diluted EPS is as follows:

	Per share	Earnings	Shares
Net profit for 20X1		£1,150,000	
Weighted average shares during 20X1			1,000,000
Basic EPS (£1,150,000/ 1,000,000)	*1.15*		
Number of shares under option			500,000
Number that would have been issued			
At fair value (500,000 × £3.25)/£4			(406,250)
Diluted EPS	*1.05*	*£1,150,000*	*1,093,750*

23.7.5 Procedure where there are convertible bonds or convertible preference shares

The post-tax profit should be adjusted[10] for

- any dividends on dilutive potential ordinary shares that have been deducted in arriving at the net profit attributable to ordinary shareholders;
- interest recognised in the period for the dilutive potential ordinary shares; and
- any other changes in income or expense that would result from the conversion of the dilutive potential ordinary shares e.g. the reduction of interest expense related to convertible bonds results in a higher post-tax profit.

23.7.6 Convertible preference shares calculation is illustrated for Watts plc

Assume that Watts plc had at 31 December 20X1:

- an issued capital of 1,000,000 ordinary shares of 50p each nominal value;
- post-tax earnings for the year of £1,150,000;
- convertible 8% preference shares of £1 each totalling £1,000,000;
- convertible at one ordinary share for every five convertible preference shares.

The computation of Basic and Diluted EPS for convertible bonds is as follows:

	Per share	Earnings	Shares
Post-tax net profit for 20X1 (after interest)		£1,150,000	
Weighted average shares during 20X1			1,000,000
Basic EPS (£1,150,000/1,000,000)	*£1.15*		
Number of shares resulting from conversion			200,000
Add back the preference dividend paid in 20X1		80,000	
Adjusted earnings and number of shares		1,230,000	1,200,000
Diluted EPS (£1,230,000/1,200,000)	*£1.025*		

23.7.7 Convertible bonds calculation is illustrated for Watts plc

Assume that Watts plc had at 31 December 20X1:

- an issued capital of 1,000,000 ordinary shares of 50p each nominal value;
- post-tax earnings after interest for the year of £1,150,000;
- convertible 10% loan of £1,000,000;
- an average market price per share of £4; and
- convertible loan is convertible into 250,000 ordinary shares of 50p each.

The computation of Basic and Diluted EPS for convertible bonds is as follows:

	Per share	Earnings	Shares
Post-tax net profit for 20X1 (after interest)		£1,150,000	
Weighted average shares during 20X1			1,000,000
Basic EPS (£1,150,000/1,000,000)	*£1.15*		
Number of shares resulting from conversion			250,000

Interest expense on convertible loan	100,000	
Deferred tax liability relating to interest expense –		
Assuming the firm's marginal tax rate is 40%	(40,000)	
Adjusted earnings and number of shares	1,210,000	1,250,000
Diluted EPS (£1,210,000/1,250,000) £0.97		

23.8 Procedure where there are several potential dilutions

Where there are several potential dilutions the calculation must be done in progressive stages starting with the most dilutive and ending with the least.[11] Any potential 'anti-dilutive' (i.e. potential issues that would increase earnings per share) are ignored.

Assume that Watts plc had at 31 December 20X1:

● an issued capital of 1,000,000 Ordinary shares of 50p each nominal value;

● post-tax earnings after interest for the year of £1,150,000;

● an average market price per share of £4; and

● share options in existence 500,000 shares
  – exercisable in year 20X2 at £3.25 per share

● convertible 10% loan of £1,000,000
  – convertible in year 20X2 into 250,000 ordinary shares of 50p each.

● convertible 8% preference shares of £1 each totalling £1,000,000
  – convertible in year 20X4 at 1 ordinary share for every **40** preference shares.

There are two steps in arriving at the Diluted EPS, namely:

Step 1: Determine the increase in earnings attributable to ordinary shareholders on conversion of potential ordinary shares;

Step 2: Determine the potential ordinary shares to include in the Diluted Earnings per Share.

Step 1: Determine the increase in earnings attributable to ordinary shareholders on conversion of potential ordinary shares

	Increase in earnings	Increase in number of ordinary shares	Earnings per incremental share
Options			
Increase in earnings			
Incremental shares issued			
for no consideration			
500,000 × (£4–3.25)/£4	nil	93,750	nil
Convertible preference shares			
Increase in net profit			
8% of £1,000,000	80,000		
Incremental shares			
1,000,000/40		25,000	3.20

10% convertible bond
Increase in net profit
£1,000,000 × 0.10 × (60%)   60,000
(assumes a marginal tax rate of 40%)
Incremental shares
1,000,000/4   250,000   0.24

Step 2: Determine the potential ordinary shares to include in the computation of diluted earnings per share

	Net profit attributable to continuing operations	*Ordinary shares*	*Per share*
As reported for BEPS	1,150,000	1,000,000	1.15
Options	—	93,750	
	1,150,000	1,093,750	1.05 dilutive
10% convertible bonds	60,000	250,000	
	1,210,000	1,343,750	0.90 dilutive
Convertible preference shares	80,000	25,000	
	1,290,000	1,368,750	0.94 antidilutive

Since the diluted earnings per share is increased when taking the convertible preference shares into account (from 94p to 90p), the convertible preference shares are antidilutive and are ignored in the calculation of diluted earnings per share. The lowest figure is selected and the Diluted EPS will, therefore, be disclosed as 90p. The following illustration is from the 1998 Accounts of the Sony Corporation.

Reconciliation of the differences between basic and diluted net income per share (EPS) for the year ended 31 March 1998:

	Yen (million) income	*Shares (000s) weighted average*	*Yen Dollars* *EPS*
Basic EPS			
Net income available to common stockholders	222,068	398,181	557.7 4.23
Effect of dilutive securities			
Warrants		51	
Convertible bonds	2,271	65,890	
Diluted EPS			
Net income for computation	224,339	464,122	Y483.4 $3.66

This shows that warrants currently carry no interest expense cost and will increase the shares when issued; that convertible bonds currently incur an interest expense of 2,271m yen that will no longer be paid on conversion and that both are dilutive.

23.9 Exercise of conversion rights during financial year

Shares actually issued will be in accordance with the terms of conversion and will be included in the Basic EPS calculation on a time apportioned basis from the date of conversion to the end of the financial year.

23.9.1 Calculation of Basic EPS assuming that convertible loan has been converted and options exercised during the financial year

This is illustrated for the calculation for the year 20X2 accounts of Watts plc as follows. Assume that Watts plc had at 31 December 20X2:

● an issued capital of 1,000,000 Ordinary shares of 50p each as at 1 January 20X2;

● convertible 10% loan of £1,000,000 **converted** on 1 April 20X2 into 250,000 ordinary shares of 50p each;

● share options for 500,000 ordinary shares of 50p each **exercised** on 1 August 20X2.

The weighted average number of shares for Basic EPS is calculated as follows:

1.1.20X2	Ordinary shares in issue	1,000,000	× 3/12	250,000
1.4.20X2	Issued on conversion of the 10% Loan	250,000		
		1,250,000	× 4/12	416,667
1.8.20X2	Issued on exercise of options	500,000		
		1,750,000	× 5/12	729,167
31.12.20X2 Weighted average number of shares				**1,395,834**

23.10 Disclosure requirements of FRS 14

The standard[12] requires the following disclosures:

● All listed companies should disclose the Basic and Diluted EPS figures, whether positive or negative, on the face of the profit and loss account for each class of ordinary share that has a different right to share in the profit for the period.

● The amounts used as the numerators in calculating basic and diluted earnings per share, and a reconciliation of those amounts to the net profit or loss for the period.

● The weighted average number of shares used as the denominator in calculating the basic and diluted earnings per share and a reconciliation of these denominators to each other.

23.11 Critique

The strategy of many companies is directed towards ensuring that the EPS figure is maintained or increased, with the financial markets applauding companies that achieve a growth in their EPS.

Management is aware of this concentrated focus and endeavour to produce a stable or growing EPS figure. This can be achieved in a number of ways, ranging from operational activities, such as increasing output or reducing costs, to accounting distortions such as bootstrapping, whereby companies with high PE ratios acquire companies with lower PE ratios.[13]

Until 1992 management had the flexibility to manipulate the earnings figure used in the BEPS calculation by the way in which it classified items in the profit and loss account e.g. omitting expenses and losses selectively from the earnings figure used.[14] The practice may be seen as unacceptable or as a rational response.[15] The ASB stamped this practice out by the issue of FRS 3 in 1992 which prescribed how the earnings figure should be calculated i.e. it took away from management their ability to choose which losses and gains to include. This avoids the element of subjectivity that remained after the revision of SSAP 6 in 1986.[16]

The issue of FRS 14 has been prompted by the different approach taken by the IASC to the calculation of Diluted EPS. The ASB approach illustrated in 11.7 above reflects IASC practice.

23.11.1 The future of EPS

Confidence in the use of EPS to assess performance has been shaken by financial failures such as Polly Peck, where profits of £161m were reported shortly before the company collapsed, and by profit restatements such as Daimler Benz, which reported a high profit in Germany in 1993 but a loss when the accounts were restated to comply with US GAAP following its admission to the New York Stock Exchange.

The ASB has a twofold approach. On the one hand, it is persuading users to treat the accounts as an information set and *not to rely on a single figure*;[17] and on the other, it is attempting to limit management capacity to manipulate the figures.

The response of investment advisers is to look for an alternative to EPS, such as future cash flows. However, although cash flows are an important factor in assessing share values, managers still perceive EPS as an important measure for comparing company performance with competitors.

23.12 Analysts' approach to calculating an alternative EPS figure

In 1993 the Institute of Investment Management and Research (IIMR)[18] published Statement of Investment Practice No. 1, entitled *The Definition of Headline Earnings*, in which it identified two purposes for producing an EPS figure:

● As a measure of the company's **maintainable earnings** capacity, suitable in particular for forecasts and for inter-year comparisons, and for use on a per share basis in the calculation of the price/earnings ratio.

● As a factual headline figure for historical earnings, which can be a benchmark figure for the **trading outcome for the year**.

The Institute recognised that the maintainable earnings figure required exceptional or non-continuing items to be eliminated, which meant that, in view of the judgement involved in adjusting the historic figures, the calculation of maintainable earnings figures could not be put on a standardised basis. It took the view that there was a need for an earnings figure, calculated on a standard basis, which could be used as an unambiguous reference point among users. The Institute accordingly defined a **headline earnings** figure for that purpose.

The ASB position is that it is not possible to distil the performance of a complex organisation into a single measure.[19] The Institute acknowledges that the headline figure is inferior to maintainable earnings as a basis for forecasts, and to the use of maintainable earnings in the calculation of PE ratios, but takes the view that the headline figure is justified by its practical usefulness. It believes it to be a reliable figure and therefore suitable for publication in objective contexts such as newspapers and statistical services.

23.12.1 Definition of IIMR headline figure

The Institute criteria for the headline figure are that it should be:

1 **A measure of the trading performance**, which means that it will:
  (a) *exclude* capital items such as profits/losses arising on the sale or revaluation of fixed assets; profits/losses arising on the sale or termination of a discontinued operation and amortisation charges for goodwill, because these are likely to have a different volatility from trading outcomes;
  (b) *exclude* provisions created for capital items such as profits/losses arising on the sale of fixed assets or on the sale or termination of a discontinued operation; and
  (c) *include* abnormal items with a clear note and profits/losses arising on operations discontinued during the year.

2 **Robust**, in that the result could be arrived at by anyone using the financial report produced in accordance with FRS 3.

3 **Factual**, in that it will not have been adjusted on the basis of subjective opinions as to whether a cost is likely to continue in the future.

The strength of the Institute's approach is that, by defining a headline figure, it is producing a core definition. Additional earnings, earnings per share and price/earnings ratio figures can be produced by individual analysts, refining the headline figure in the light of their own evaluation of the quality of earnings.

In accordance with FRS 3, para. 25, if an additional EPS is calculated at any other level than that set out on FRS 14, it should be presented on a consistent basis over time and reconciled to the amount required by the FRS.

An illustration of a reconciliation is set out in Statement of Investment Practice No. 1, appendix C, shown in Figure 11.1.

23.12.2 How are companies reacting to the ASB's permission to include an alternative EPS figure?

In 1994 Coopers & Lybrand surveyed the treatment of exceptional items and EPS based on the published accounts of 100 top UK companies.[20] The results showed the following frequency of reporting:

● Exceptional items credited or charged most frequently in arriving at the operating profit were:

Item	*No. of companies*
Reorganisation costs, e.g. redundancy	9
Restructuring costs	9
Provision for permanent diminution in value of property	6
Provision for business rationalisation	4

● Exceptional items credited or charged most frequently below the operating profit were:

Item	*No. of companies*
Profits or losses on sale or termination of an operation	59
Profits or losses on the disposal of fixed assets	46
Costs of fundamental reorganisation or restructuring	18

Figure 23.1 IIMR headline earnings: adjustments for 1993.

	Notes	Profits on ordinary activities £m	Tax £m	Minority interests £m	Profit £m
Per accounts	(i)	45	(14)	(2)	29
Adjustments					
Less: 1992 provision	(ii)	(10)	3	—	(7)
Exceptional items:					
Loss on disposal of discontinued operations	(iii)	17	(5)	—	12
Less: 1992 provision	(iv)	(20)	6	—	(14)
Provision for loss on operations to be discontinued	(v)	1	—	—	1
Profit on sale of properties	(vi)	(12)	3	1	(8)
Goodwill amortisation	(vii)	2	—	—	2
Total adjustments					
(per share 19p)	(viii)				(14)
IIMR headline earnings	(ix)	**23**	**(7)**	**(1)**	**£15**
IIMR headline earnings per share					**20p**

Notes:

(i)   Figures as shown in the published profit and loss account as 'profit on ordinary activities'.

(ii)   This adjustment is in respect of the provision made in the 1992 accounts in respect of loss on operations to be discontinued and relates only to the operating losses of the operations in the 1993 financial year up to the date of termination/sale (and not the direct costs of termination/sale).

(iii) As shown in the published profit and loss account.

(iv)   This adjustment is similar to that described in note (ii) above: in this case it relates to a provision made in the 1992 accounts in respect of the loss on disposal of operations discontinued in 1993.

(v)   This adjustment relates to the provision made in the 1993 financial year in respect of loss on an operation to be discontinued in the next financial year – 1994. This provision, when released in 1994, will be adjusted for in arriving at 1994 IIMR headline earnings.

(vi)   As shown in the published profit and loss account.

(vii) It is assumed that this charge to the profit and loss account is disclosed in the notes to the accounts.

(viii) It is assumed that both the associated tax credit or charge and the minority charge in respect of each adjustment are disclosed in the notes to the accounts as required by FRS 3.

(ix)   It is assumed that the review of the remaining exceptional items (i.e. those other than those disclosed on the face of the profit and loss account) does not necessitate any further adjustment to the headline earnings figure.

The survey then considered additional EPS figures. It found that 54 companies reported additional EPS figures, which varied from 62% lower to 278% higher than the reported FRS 3 figure. The basis of the most frequently used additional EPS figures was as follows:

Basis of additional EPS	No. of companies
IIMR headline EPS	16
Adjusted for exceptional items reported below operating profit	16
Adjusted for all exceptional items above and below operating profit	13

A number of other bases were used. Commenting on the choice of basis, the authors stated:

> This may result in stability for an individual company, but they certainly do not give rise to comparability across companies. To our surprise, only 16 of the 54 companies used the IIMR headline figures as their EPS. The remainder evidently preferred to tell their own story despite the analysts' announcement of the basis on which they will perform their analysis.

It was a widely held view that, prior to FRS 3, companies would disclose gains as exceptional and losses as extraordinary in order to show the highest EPS figure possible. The survey, therefore, also tested the hypothesis that companies would produce an alternative EPS figure where the alternative exceeded the FRS 3 figure. The outcome suggested that companies show additional EPS figures primarily to stabilise their earnings figures and not merely to enhance their reported performance.

Summary

While most analysts have welcomed the greater detail disclosed as a result of FRS 3, the new definition has been more controversial. The Association of Investment Analysts has expressed the view that EPS should be calculated to show the future maintainable earnings and has arrived at a formula designed to exclude the effects of unusual events and of activities discontinued during the period.

FRS 3 permits the inclusion of an EPS figure calculated in a different way, provided that there is a reconciliation of the two figures. The ASB's view remains that only the employment of the all-inclusive principle can produce an EPS figure capable of showing a true and fair view.

For many years the EPS figure was regarded as the key figure. It was widely believed that management performance could be assessed by the comparative rate of growth in this figure. This meant that the earnings available for distribution, which was the base for calculating the EPS, became significant. Management action was directed towards increasing this figure: sometimes by healthy organic growth; sometimes by buying-in earnings by acquisition; sometimes by cosmetic manipulation, e.g. structuring transactions so that all or part of the cost by-passed the profit and loss account; and other times by the selective exercise of judgement, e.g. underestimating provisions.

The regulators intervened to control management practice by defining as extraordinary the gains and losses that should be excluded from the earnings available for distribution. However, the definition proved impossible to enforce and companies were able to classify gains as exceptional, and so within the earnings available for distribution figure, and losses as extraordinary, and so outside that figure.

The ASB has tried to reduce the emphasis given to the EPS figure by presenting the financial statements as an information set for individual shareholder evaluation. It removed the distinction between exceptional and extraordinary items and required all realised gains and losses to being reflected in the EPS figure. It also required disclosure of the reasons for the exceptional items, so that shareholders could make their own assessment of the implication for future cash flows.

Shareholders are still perceived to be interested in an EPS figure based on maintainable earnings. The IIMR, in recognition of this, has produced a definition that shareholders might find more meaningful than the ASB figure. The ASB approach has accepted the publication of alternative figures, provided the ASB-defined figure is also produced and there is a clear reconciliation of the two figures.

The increasing globalisation of stock market transactions places an increasing level of importance on international comparison and, in consequence, is pushing the work of the International Accounting Standards Committee into greater prominence. EPS is considered a key indicator by analysts throughout the world and it thus becomes important to follow an international basis for its calculation. It is, perhaps, this consideration that led the ASB to adopt in FRS 14 virtually all of the IASC's proposals which also now coincide with US GAAP.

Review questions

1 Explain: (i) basic earnings per share; (ii) fully diluted earnings per share; (iii) potential ordinary shares; and (iv) limitation of EPS as a performance measure.

2 Why are issues at full market value treated differently from rights issues?

3 Directors are permitted to show their own EPS figure in addition to that calculated in accordance with FRS 14. In the 1999 Annual Report and Accounts of Associated British Ports Holdings plc, the directors report earnings per share – basic and earnings per share – underlying as follows:

	Underlying	Goodwill Amortisation	Exceptional items	Total 1999	1998
	£m	£m	£m	£m	£m
Profit on ordinary activities after tax attributable to shareholders	86.3	(3.8)	(76.9)	5.6	84.1
Dividends	(39.4)	—	—	(39.4)	(37.2)
Retained profit/(loss)	46.9	(3.8)	(76.9)	(33.8)	46.9
Earnings per share – basic	24.6	(1.1)	(21.9)	**1.6p**	22.4p
Earnings per share – underlying				**24.6p**	22.4p

Note 11 reconciliation of profit used for calculating the basic and underlying earnings per share:

	1999	1998
	£m	£m
Profit for year attributable to shareholders for calculating basic earnings per share	**5.6**	84.1
Amortisation of goodwill	3.8	2.0
Impairment of goodwill	60.6	—
Impairment of fixed assets	19.6	—

Profit on sale of fixed assets	(3.3)	(1.2)
Withdrawal from a discontinued business	—	(1.2)
Attributable tax	—	0.3
Profit for year attributable to shareholders for calculating the underlying earnings per share	**86.3**	84.0

The directors state that the underlying basis is a more appropriate basis for comparing performance between periods.

Discuss the relevance of the basic figure of 1.6p reported for 1999.

4   When disclosing EPS, how should a company deal with the issue of a separate class of equity shares which do not rank for any dividend in the current accounting period, but will do so in the future?

5   The following note appeared in the 1997 Accounts of Mercer International Inc

The EPS data is summarised as follows:

Income (loss)	1997	1996
Income (loss) from continuing operations	(32,623)	15,557
Effect of dilutive securities, interest on convertible debentures	—	11
	(32,623)	15,568

Shares	1997	1996
BEPS, weighted number of shares outstanding	14,994,826	13,829,056
Effect of dilutive securities:		
Convertible debentures	—	21,756
Warrants	—	33,900
Options	—	72,393
	14,994,826	13,957,105

For the year ended 31 December 1997 convertible debentures, warrants and options were not included in the computation of diluted EPS because they were antidilutive. Options to acquire 192,500 were outstanding at 31 December 1996, but were not included in the computation of diluted shares because the options' exercise price was greater than the average market price of the shares.

Explain

(a) why interest of 11 was added in 1996;

(b) why the BEPS shares were weighted;

(c) what is meant by antidilutive;

(d) why the difference in exercise price and market price meant that options were not included in 1996.

6   Would the following items justify the calculation of a separate EPS figure under FRS 3?

(a) A charge of £1,500m that appeared in the 1989 accounts of Lloyds Bank plc, described as additional provisions relating to exposure to countries experiencing payment difficulties.

(b) Costs of £14m that appeared in the 1990 accounts of Johnson Matthey plc, described as redundancy and other non-recurring costs.

(c) Costs of £62.1m that appeared in the 1990 accounts of Johnson Matthey plc, described as cost of rationalisation and withdrawal from business activities.

(d) The following items that appeared in the 1989 accounts of Grand Metropolitan plc:
   (i) Profit on sale of property   £80m
   (ii) Reorganisation costs   £35m
   (iii) Disposal and discontinuance of hotels   £659m

7 Income smoothing describes the management practice of maintaining a steady profit figure.

(a) Explain why managers might wish to smooth the earnings figure. Give three examples of how they might achieve this.

(b) It has been suggested that debt creditors are most at risk from income smoothing by the managers. Discuss why this should be so.

8 In connection with FRS 14 *Earnings per Share*:

(a) Define the profit used to calculate Basic and Diluted EPS.

(b) Explain the relationship between EPS and the price/earnings (P/E) ratio. Why may the P/E ratio be considered important as a stock market indicator?

Exercises
··················

An outline solution is provided in the appendix at the end of the text for exercises marked with an asterisk (*).

* Question 1

Alpha plc had an issued share capital of 2,000,000 ordinary shares at 1 January 20X1. The nominal value was 25p and the market value £1 per share. On 31 March 20X1 the company made a rights issue of 1 for 4 at a price of 80p per share. The post-tax earnings were £4.5m and £5m for 20X0 and 20X1 respectively.

Required:
 (i) Calculate the Basic Earnings per Share for 20X1
 (ii) Restate the Basic Earnings per Share for 20X0

* Question 2

Beta plc had the following changes during 20X1:

1 January	1,000,000 shares of 50p each
31 March	500,000 shares of 50p each issued at full market price of £5 per share
30 April	Bonus issue made of 1 for 2
31 August	1,000,000 shares of 50p each issued at full market price of £5.50 per share
31 October	Rights issue of 1 for 3. Rights price was £2.40 and Market value was £5.60 per share

Required:
Calculate the time-weighted average number of shares for the Basic Earnings per Share denominator. Note that adjustments will be required for time, the Bonus Issue and the bonus element of the Rights Issue.

* Question 3

The computation and publication of earnings per share (EPS) figures by listed companies are governed by FRS 14 *Earnings per Share* and FRS 3 *Reporting Financial Performance*.

Nottingham Industries plc
Profit and loss account for the year ended 31 March 20X6
(extract from draft unaudited accounts)

		£000
Profit on ordinary activities before taxation	(Note 2)	1,000
Tax on profit on ordinary activities	(Note 3)	(420)
Profit on ordinary activities after taxation		580
Dividends		(479)
Amount added to reserves for the financial year		101

Notes:

1 Called-up share capital of Nottingham Industries plc:

In issue at 1 April 20X5:

16,000,000 ordinary shares of 25p each
1,000,000 10% cumulative preference shares of £1 each

1 July 20X5: Bonus issue of ordinary shares, 1 for 5.
1 October 20X5: Market purchase of 500,000 of own ordinary shares at a price of £1.00 per share.

2 In the draft accounts for the year ended 31 March 20X6, 'profit on ordinary activities before taxation' is arrived at after charging or crediting the following items:
   (i) accelerated depreciation on fixed assets, £80,000;
   (ii) book gain on disposal of a major operation, £120,000.

3 Profit after tax included a write-back of deferred taxation (accounted for by the liability method) in consequence of a reduction in the rate of corporation tax from 45% in the financial year 20X4 to 40% in the financial year 20X5.

4 The following were charged:
   (i) Provision for bad debts arising on the failure of a major customer, £150,000. Other bad debts have been written off or provided for in the ordinary way.
   (ii) Provision for loss through expropriation of the business of an overseas subsidiary by a foreign government, £400,000.

5 In the published accounts for the year ended 31 March 19X5, basic EPS was shown as 2.2p; fully diluted EPS was the same figure.

Required:
(a) On the basis of the facts given, compute the Basic EPS figures for 20X6 and restate the Basic EPS figure for 20X5, stating your reasons for your treatment of items that may affect the amount of EPS in the current year.
(b) Compute the Fully Diluted Earnings per Share for 20X6 assuming that on 1 January 19X6 Executives of Nottingham Industries plc were granted options to take up a total of 200,000 unissued ordinary shares at a price of £1.00 per share: no options had been exercised at 31 March 20X6. The average fair value of the shares during the year was £1.10.
(c) Give your opinion as to the usefulness (to the user of financial statements) of the EPS figures that you have computed.

* **Question 4**

The following information relates to Simrin plc for the year ended 31 December 20X0:

	£
Turnover	700,000
Operating costs	476,000
Trading profit	224,000
Net interest payable	2,000
	222,000
Exceptional charges	77,000
	145,000
Tax on ordinary activities	66,000
Profit after tax	79,000
Dividends – ordinary	(15,000)
– preference	(9,000)
Profit retained for the year	55,000

Simrin plc had 100,000 ordinary shares of £1 each in issue throughout the year. Simrin plc has in issue warrants entitling the holders to subscribe for a total of 50,000 shares in the company. The warrants may be exercised after 31 December 20X5 at a price of £1.28 per share. The average fair value of shares was £1.1.

Required:

(a) Calculate the Basic EPS for Simrin plc for the year ended 31 December 20X0, in accordance with best accounting practice.

(b) Calculate the Fully Diluted EPS figure, to be disclosed in the statutory accounts of Simrin plc in respect of the year ended 31 December 20X0.

(c) Briefly comment on the need to disclose a fully diluted EPS figure and on the relevance of this figure to the shareholders.

(d) In the past, the single most important indicator of financial performance has been earnings per share. In what way has the profession attempted to destroy any reliance on a single figure to measure and predict a company's earnings, and how successful has this attempt been?

* Question 5

Gamma plc had an issued share capital at 1 April 20X0 of:

● £200,000 made up of 20p shares.

● 50,000 £1 convertible preference shares receiving a dividend of £2.5 per share
  – these shares were convertible in 20X6 on the basis of 1 ordinary share for 1 preference share.

There was also loan capital of:

● £250,000 10% convertible loans
  – the loan was convertible in 20X9 on basis of 500 shares for each £1,000 of loan;
  – the tax rate was 40%.

Earnings for the year ended 31 March 20X1 were £5,000,000 after tax.

Required:

(a) Calculate the Fully Diluted Earnings per Share for 20X1.

(b) Calculate the Fully Diluted Earnings per Share assuming that the Convertible Preference Shares were receiving a dividend of £6 per share instead of £2.50.

Question 6

Delta plc has share capital of £lm in shares of 25p each. At 31 May 20X1 shares had a market value of £1 each. On 1 June 20X1 the company makes a rights issue of 1 share for every 4 held at 60p per share. Its profits were £500,000 in 20X1 and £440,000 in 20X0. The year end is 30 November.

Required:

Calculate

(a) the theoretical ex-rights price

(b) the bonus issue factor

(c) the Basic Earnings per Share for 19X8

(d) the Basic Earnings per Share for 19X9.

Question 7

The following information is available for X plc for the year ended 31 May 19X7:

Net profit after tax and minority interest	£18,160,000
Ordinary shares of £1 (fully paid)	£40,000,000
Average fair value for year of ordinary shares	£1.50

1 Share options have been granted to directors giving them the right to subscribe for ordinary shares between 20X1 and 20X3 at £1.20 per share. The options outstanding at 31 May 19X7 were 2,000,000 in number.

2 The company has £20 million of 6% convertible loan stock in issue. The terms of conversion of the loan stock per £200 nominal value of loan stock at the date of issue (1 May 19X9) were

Conversion date	No. of shares
31 May 20X0	24
31 May 20X1	23
31 May 20X2	22

No loan stock has as yet been converted. The loan stock had been issued at a discount of 1%.

3 There are 1,600,000 convertible preference shares in issue. The cumulative dividend is 10p per share and each preference share can convert into two ordinary shares. The preference shares can be converted in 20X2.

4 Assume a corporation tax rate of 33% when calculating the effect on income of converting the convertible loan stock.

Required:

(a) Calculate the diluted EPS according to FRS 14.

(b) Discuss why there is a need to disclose diluted earnings per share.

References

1 J. Day, 'The use of annual reports by UK investment analysts', *Accounting Business Research*, Autumn 1986, pp. 295–307.

2 *Risk Measurement Service*, London Business School, April–June 1998, ISBN 0361-3344.

3 FRS 14, *Earnings per Share*, ASB, 1998 para. 10.

4 *Ibid.*, para. 21.

5   *Ibid.*, para. 27.
6   FRS 3, ASB, 1992, paras 13–17.
7   *Accountancy*, November 1998, p. 73.
8   FRS 14, *Earnings per Share*, ASB, 1998 para. 56.
9   *Ibid.*, para. 35.
10 *Ibid.*, para. 53.
11 *Ibid.*, para. 61.
12 *Ibid.*, para. 71.
13 B. Rees, *Financial Analysis*, Prentice Hall, 1990, pp 356–357.
14 A. Barnea, J. Ronen and S. Sadan, 'Classifactory smoothing of income with extraordinary items', *The Accounting Review*, 1976, vol. 51, pp. 110–122.
15 P. Lambert, 'Income smoothing as rational equilibrium behaviour', *Accounting Review*, 1984, vol. 59(4), pp. 604–618.
16 M. Greener, 'The accountant's extraordinary predicament', *Accountancy*, June 1988, pp. 95–96.
17 *The Structure of Financial Statements – Reporting of Financial Performance*, ASB, December 1991, FRED 1, preface para. iv.
18 Statement of Investment Practice No. 1, *The Definition of Headline Earnings*, IIMR, 1993.
19 FRS 3, *Reporting Financial Performance*, ASB, 1992, para. 52.
20 Coopers and Lybrand, *EPS and Exceptional Items*, 1994.

CHAPTER 24

Cash flow statements

24.1 Introduction

In this chapter we consider why funds flow statements came to be replaced by cash flow statements in recent years. We analyse the application of FRS 1 and the extent to which it gives users of financial statements more information about the solvency and liquidity of companies, and enables them to make comparisons between firms.

24.2 Development of cash flow statements

In 1975 SSAP 10 was issued, requiring companies to publish a funds flow statement with the annual accounts.[1] The funds flow statement explained the changes between the opening and closing balance sheet by classifying the changes in fixed assets and long-term capital under two headings:

- **source of funds**, comprising funds from operating and other sources such as sale of fixed assets and issue of shares and loans; and
- **application of funds**, comprising tax paid, dividends paid, fixed asset acquisitions and long-term capital repayments. The difference represented the net change in working capital.

In 1987 SFAS 95 *Statement of Cash Flows* was published in the USA.[2] It concluded that a cash flow statement should replace the funds flow statement, concentrating on **changes in cash** rather than **changes in working capital**. The cash flow statement should represent all of a company's cash receipts and cash payments during a period. There was also widespread support in the UK, e.g. Macdonald in 1988,[3] for the belief that **cash flow statements were more decision-useful** and that they should replace the funds flow statement.

In 1990 the ASC issued ED 54, which appeared to be based on SFAS 95.[4] It proposed that cash flow statements should replace funds flow statements in financial reporting. Guidelines were given about reporting cash flows, appropriate formats and minimum disclosure.

A report by the Institute Research Board, entitled *The Future Shape of Financial Reports*, recommended a number of reporting reforms.[5] One of the main areas for improvement was reporting a company's cash position. Professor Arnold wrote:

> little attention is paid to the reporting entity's cash or liquidity position. Cash is the lifeblood of every business entity. The report ... advocates that companies should provide a cash flow statement ... preferably using the direct method.[6]

An important issue is the relationship of cash flows to the existing financial statements. As the following quotation illustrates, cash flows are not a substitute for the profit and loss account:

> The emphasis on cash flows, and the emergence of the statement of cash flows as an important financial report, does not mean that operating cash flows are a substitute for, or are more important than, net income. In order to analyse financial statements correctly we need to consider **both** operating cash flows and net income.[7]

The overwhelming reason for replacing a funds flow statement with a cash flow statement was that the latter provides more relevant and useful information to users of financial statements. When used in conjunction with the accrual-adjusted data included in the profit and loss account and the balance sheet, cash flow information helps to assess liquidity, viability and financial flexibility. This view is held by Henderson and Maness, who stress the need to integrate different types of analysis to achieve an overall assessment of an organisation's financial health: 'cash flow analysis should be used in conjunction with traditional ratio analysis to get a clear picture of the financial position of a firm'.[8]

The financial viability and survival prospects of any organisation rest on the ability to generate net positive cash flows. Cash flows help to reduce an organisation's dependency on external funding, service existing debts and obligations, finance investments, and reward the investors with an acceptable dividend policy. The end-result is that, independent of reported profits, if an organisation is unable to generate sufficient cash, it will eventually fail.

Cash flow statements can also be used to evaluate any economic decisions related to the financial performance of an organisation. Decisions made on the basis of expected cash flows can be monitored and reviewed whenever additional cash flow information becomes available.

Finally, the quality of information contained in cash flow statements should be better than that contained in funds flow statements because it is more consistent and neutral. Cash flows can be reliably traced to when a transaction occurred, while funds flows are distorted by the accounting judgements inherent in accrual-adjusted data.[9]

The following extract from Heath and Rosenfield's article on solvency is a useful conclusion to our analysis of the benefits of cash flow statements:

> Solvency is a money or cash phenomenon. A solvent company is one with adequate cash to pay its debts; an insolvent company is one with inadequate cash ... Any information that provides insight into the amounts, timings and certainty of a company's future cash receipts and payments is useful in evaluating solvency. Statements of past cash receipts and payments are useful for the same basic reason that income statements are useful in evaluating profitability: both provide a basis for predicting future performance.[10]

24.3 Applying FRS I *Cash Flow Statements*

24.3.1 FRS I issued

FRS 1 was the first standard issued by the ASB. Its objective was to require companies to report on a standardised basis their cash generation and cash absorption for a period. Its principal feature was the analysis of cash flows under **five** standard headings of 'operating activities', 'returns on investments and servicing of finance', 'taxation', 'investing activities' and 'financing'.

The chairman of the ASB, David Tweedie, said: 'It is right that cash flow should be the subject of the Board's first standard. Recent experience has demonstrated all too clearly that adequate information on cash is an essential element of a company's financial statements.'[11] The ASB issued the following statement on publishing FRS 1 in 1991:

> The ASB's view is that a cash flow statement forms an essential element of the information required for accounts to give a true and fair view of the state of affairs of **large** companies at the end of the financial year, and of the profit or loss for the year. Accordingly, non-compliance with the standard may be ... taken into account by the Financial Reporting Review Panel or the court in any consideration of whether or not the accounts comply with the Companies Act.

24.3.2 FRS 1 reviewed and revised by ASB

In 1994 the ASB decided to review FRS 1 following the criticisms that had been made since its issue in 1991. Such a review of the standard after being in force for three years was in line with the ASB view that standards should be amended regularly in the light of experience in their operation and changes in circumstances.

We will consider briefly how three of the criticisms have been dealt with in the FRS 1 (Revised) issued in October 1996, namely, **method of presenting cash flows from operating activities, cash equivalents and reconciling operating profit in FRS 3 format to operating cash flows.**

Method of presenting cash flows from operating activities

FRS 1 permitted either the direct or indirect method of presentation to be used.

● The **direct** method reports cash inflows and outflows directly, starting with the major categories of gross cash receipts and payments. This means that cash flows such as receipts from customers and payments to suppliers are stated separately within the operating activities.

● The **indirect** method starts with the operating profit (before tax and extraordinary items) and then adjusts this figure for non-cash items such as depreciation and changes in working capital.

The two methods provide different types of information to the users. The indirect method applies changes in working capital to net income and FRS 1 para. 70 states.

> The principal advantage of the indirect method is that it highlights the differences between operating profit and net cash flow from operating activities. Many users of financial statements believe that such a reconciliation is essential to give an indication of the quality of the reporting entity's earnings. Some investors and creditors assess future cash flows by estimating future income and then allowing for accruals adjustments; thus information about past accruals adjustments may be useful to help estimate future adjustments.

The direct method demonstrates more of the qualities of a true cash flow statement because it provides more information about the sources and uses of cash. This information is not available elsewhere and helps in the estimation of future cash flows.

FRS 1 para 70 states

The principal advantage of the direct method is that it shows operating cash receipts and payments. Knowledge of the specific sources of cash receipts and the purposes for which cash payments were made in past periods may be useful in assessing future cash flows. However, the Board does not believe at present that in all cases the benefits to users of this information outweigh the costs of providing it and has not, therefore, required the information to be given. Nevertheless, in those circumstances **where the benefits to users ... outweigh the costs of providing it the Board encourages reporting entities to provide the relevant information.**

When are benefits to users likely to outweigh costs?

One such time is when the user is attempting to predict bankruptcy or future liquidation of the company. A research study looking at the cash flow differences between failed and non-failed companies[12] established that seven cash flow variables and suggested ratios captured statistically significant differences between failed and non-failed firms as much as five years prior to failure. The study further showed that the research findings supported the use of a direct cash flow statement and the authors commented that:

An indirect cash flow statement will not provide a number of the cash flow variables for which we found significant differences between bankrupt and non-bankrupt companies. Thus, using an indirect cash flow statement could lead to ignoring important information about creditworthiness.

The major deficiency therefore with the ASB approach is that few, if any, companies would elect to use the direct method if it was more likely than the indirect method to indicate that the company was at risk of failing!

Although the Gahlon research supports the direct method and, also, the Board proposal was criticised during the Exposure Draft stage on the basis that the availability of a choice between the direct and indirect methods made inter-company comparisons misleading and allowed companies to select the less informative indirect method, FRS 1 Revised continues to permit the choice on cost grounds and there is no guidance offered on 'when benefits to users are likely to outweigh costs'.

Cash equivalents

FRS 1 recognised that companies' cash management practices vary in the range of short- to medium-term deposits and instruments in their cash and near-cash portfolio. In 1991 it standardised the treatment of near-cash items by applying the following definition when determining whether items should be aggregated with cash in the cash flow statement. The definition stated 'Cash equivalents are short-term, highly liquid investments which are readily convertible into known amounts of cash without notice and which are within three months of maturity when acquired'. Near-cash items falling outside this definition were reported under the *Investment* heading.

There was criticism that this definition was not always appropriate. It is not, for example, commercially appropriate to deal with deposits over three months under the heading of 'investments' rather than as cash. The effect was to split the activities of corporate treasury operations between investing activities and increases/decreases in cash. If cash was put on deposit for more than three months it was shown as a cash outflow under *Investing*; if it was put on deposit for less than three months it was not shown as actually being a cash outflow. This made the evaluation of the movements on cash misleading.

FRS 1 Revised has taken account of this criticism by adding a new classification within the cash flow statement headed *Management of liquid resources*. FRS 1 Revised defines liquid resources as 'Current asset investments held as readily disposable stores of value. A readily disposable investment is one that:

(a) is disposable by the reporting entity without curtailing or disrupting its business; and is either:

(b) (i) readily convertible into known amounts of cash at or close to its carrying amount; or

(ii) traded in an active market.

Reconciling operating profit in FRS 3 format to operating cash flows

FRS 1 Revised takes account of the FRS 3 format in Example 2 of Appendix 1 with details of operating profits arising under Continuing and Discontinued operations as follows:

Reconciliation of operating profit to operating cash flows:

	£000	Continuing £000	Discontinued £000	Total £000
Operating profit		20,249	(1,616)	18,633
Depreciation charges		3,108	380	3,488
Share of profit of associate	(1,420)			
Dividend from associate	350			
		(1,070)		(1,070)
Cash flow relating to previous years' restructuring provision			(560)	(560)
Increase in stock		(11,193)	(87)	(11,280)
Increase in debtors		(3,754)	(20)	(3,774)
Increase in creditors		9,672	913	10,585
Net cash flow from continuing operations		17,012		
Net cash flow in respect of discontinued activities			(990)	
Net cash flow from operating activities				16,022

24.4 FRS 1 (Revised) format of cash flow statements

An illustration is provided below, Tyro Bruce, of the application of the FRS 1 Revised format.

24.4.1 The FRS 1 Revised format is classified under 9 headings as follows:

1 Reconciliation of operating profit to cash flows from operating activities

- Operating profit before interest and tax
  - Adjust for non-cash charges:
    + Depreciation charges for tangible assets and Amortisation charges for intangible assets
    + Loss on sale of fixed assets
    − Profit on sale of fixed assets

● **Adjust for changes in current assets and current liabilities:**
  – Stock increase
  – Debtor and prepayment increases
  – Creditor and accrual decreases (excluding tax and dividends which are dealt with separately)
  + Stock decrease
  + Debtor and prepayment decreases
  + Creditor and accrual increases (excluding tax and dividends which are dealt with separately)

Net cash inflow/(outflow) from operating activities (this subtotal is the sum of the above)

2 Returns on investments and servicing of finance

● Interest received/paid
● Interest element of finance lease rentals payments
● Preference dividends paid

3 Taxation

● Tax paid

4 Capital expenditure and financial investments

● Purchase of intangible assets, tangible assets and trade investments
● Proceeds from sale of intangible assets, tangible fixed assets and trade investments

5 Acquisitions and disposals Note: This section is relevant for group accounts

6 Equity dividends paid

● Cash paid to ordinary shareholders

7 Management of liquid resources

● Purchase of government securities, corporate bonds or placing of funds on short-term deposit
● Proceeds from sale of government securities, corporate bonds or cash withdrawn from short-term deposits

8 Financing

● Proceeds from issue of shares, short-term and long-term debt
● Payments to redeem shares, short-term and long-term debt
● Capital element of finance lease rental payments

9 Increase/(Decrease) in cash

[being a subtotal calculated as the sum of Sections 1 to 8 above]

24.4.2 Tyro Bruce accounts

The profit and loss account for the year ended 31 March 20X2 and balance sheets as at 31 March 20X1 and 20X2 (including the fixed asset schedule) for Tyro Bruce with explanatory notes to explain how each item is classified in the Cash Flow Statement are as follows:

Profit and Loss Account of Tyro Bruce for the year ended 31 March 20X2

How treated in cash flow statement

	£000		
Sales	6,000		
Cost of sales	4,000		
Gross profit	2,000		
Net operating expenses	(986)		
Operating profit before interest and tax	1,014		
Profit on sale of land	80		
Loss on sale of plant	(54)		
Profit before interest and tax	**1,040**	(1) Reconciliation statement starts here	**(+1,040)**
Interest payable	(40)	(2) Returns on investment and servicing of finance	(−40)
Profit before tax	1,000		
Tax	(400)	(3) Tax	(−400)
Profit after tax	600		

Balance sheets for 20X1 and 20X2   *How treated in cash flow statement*

	20X2 £000	20X1 £000	Change £000		
Intangible fixed assets					
R & D written off	360	840	480	(1) Reconciliation of operating profit	
Tangible fixed assets	4,596	4,136	460	(4) The figure of 460 is not used. Refer to fixed asset schedule for **Additions**	
Stock	2,400	1,600	800	(1) Reconciliation of operating profit	(−800)
Debtors	1,800	1,360	440	(1) Reconciliation of operating profit	(−440)
Government securities	30	—	30	(7) Management of liquid resources	(+30)
Cash	30	20	10	(9) Cash increase	(10)
Creditors	1,360	1,080	280	(1) Reconciliation of operating profit	(+280)
Taxation	340	380	40	(3) Taxation	(−40)
Dividends	—	140	140	(6) Equity dividends paid	(−140)
Overdraft	1,116	1,356	240	(9) Cash increase	(240)
	6,400	5,000			
Ordinary shares	2,000	1,600	400	(8) Financing	(+400)
7% Preference shares	2,000	2,000			no change
Share premium account	400	100	300	(8) Financing	(+300)
Revaluation reserve	400	200			non cash movement
Retained profits at 31.3.20X1	700	700			no change
Retained profit for year	600	—		(1) Reconciliation of profit uses profit before interest and tax	
10% Debentures 20X0 – 04	300	400	100	(8) Financing	(−100)
	6,400	5,000			

The non–cash items required for the Reconciliation are calculated as follows:

● Depreciation is given in Schedule of Fixed Assets

● R&D amortised obtained from Change in Balance Sheets: £840,000 – £360,000 = £480,000

● Profit on sale of land is an FRS 3 exceptional item in the profit and loss account: £80,000

● Loss on sale of plant is an FRS 3 exceptional item in the profit and loss account: £54,000

The fixed asset schedule for Tyro Bruce as at 31 March 20X2 is as follows:

	Land £000	Buildings £000	Plant £000	Vehicles £000	Total £000	How treated in cash flow statement
At cost 31.3.20X1	3,200	800	840	200	5,040	
Additions	800	200	120		1,120	(4) Capital expenditure
Revaluations	200				200	non-cash movement
	4,200	1,000	960	200	6,360	
Disposals	600	—	240	—	840	(4) Used to calculate proceeds
At cost/valuation 31.3.20X2	3,600	1,000	720	200	5,520	
Depreciation						
At 31.3.20X1		384	400	120	904	
P & L charge		20	144	40	204	(1) Reconciliation of operating
		404	544	160	1,108	profit
Disposals		—	184	—	184	(4) Used to calculate proceeds
At 31.3.20X2	3,600	404	360	160	924	
Net book value 20X1	3,200	416	440	80	4,136	
Net book value 20X2	3,600	596	360	40	4,596	

The sales proceeds from the sale of land and plant are calculated for the capital expenditure section as follows:

● Cost £600,000 in fixed asset schedule + profit on disposal £80,000 = £680,000 proceeds

● Cost £240,000 – £184,000 depreciation – loss on disposal £54,000 = £2,000 proceeds

Reconciliation of operating profit to operating cash flows

The reconciliation is required by way of Note when companies use the indirect method to support the £738,000 Net cash flow from operating activities appearing in the cash flow statement. It is calculated as follows:

	£000
Profit before interest and tax	**1,040**
Add back non-cash charges:	
Depreciation	204
R & D amortisation charge	480
Loss on sale of plant	54
Less non-cash creditors:	
Profit on sale of land	(80)
Changes in current assets:	
Less current asset increases	
Stock	(800)
Debtors	(440)
Add current liability increases	
Creditors	280
Net cash flow from operating activities	**738**

One criticism of FRS 1 was that it did not standardise on the use of the direct method. The 'operating activities' of the cash flow statement are presented differently under the direct method. Actual cash flows from customers and to suppliers are disclosed as follows:

	£000
Cssh received from customers (Working 1)	5,560
Casy payments to suppliers (Working 2)	4,822
Net cash inflow from operations	738

Working 1: Sales £6,000,000 – Debtors increase £440,000

Working 2: Cost of sales £4,000,000 – Creditors increase £280,000 + Stock increase £800,000 – Depreciation £204,000 – R & D £480,000 – Loss on sale of plant £54,000 + Profit on sale of land £80,000 + Selling and distribution expenses £600,000 + Administration costs £360,000

24.4.3 Tyro Bruce cash flow statement

The cash flow statement can now be prepared for Tyro Bruce for the year ended 31.3.20X2 (using indirect method)

		£000
1 Net cash inflow from operating activities (detail required as a Note)		738
2 Returns on investments and servicing of finance		
Interest [40 (P & L) there are no accruals in 20X1 or 20X2]		(40)
3 Taxation		
Tax paid [380 (20X1 accrual) + 400 (P & L) – 340 (20X2 accrual)]		(440)
4 Capital expenditure		
Fixed asset purchase	(1,120)	
Proceeds from sale of land and plant	682	
		(438)
5 Acquisitions and disposals		—
6 Equity dividends [140 (P & L) there are no accruals in 20X1 or 20X2]		(140)
		(320)
7 Management of liquid resources		
Government securities		(30)
8 Financing		
Issue of shares	700	
Repayment of debentures	(100)	600
9 Increase in cash		250

24.4.4 Additional notes required by FRS I Revised

A general criticism of FRS 1 was that it did not help to assess the solvency and liquidity of a company, as it did not show the changes in the company's **net debt** position. It was argued that it was necessary to consider changes not only in its cash flow position, but also in its debt position.

FRS 1 Revised requires a statement reconciling net cash flow to movement in net debt. This statement should include all cash flows in the main cash flow statement which affect the net debt position, with a note reconciling net debt at the beginning of the period to net debt at the end of the period. Hence it should include the changes in cash, debt and liquid resources, and also any changes in finance leases and translation differences. The notes for Tyro Bruce are as follows:

Note 2: Analyses of changes in net debt

	At 1.4.20X1 £000	Cash flows £000	Other changes £000	At 31.3.20X2 £000
Cash	20	10	—	30
Overdraft	(1,356)	240	—	(1,116)
Debts due after 1 year	(400)	100	—	(300)
Also Finance lease (if appropriate)				
Current asset investment	—	30	—	30
Total	(1,736)	380	—	(1,356)

Note 3: Reconciliation of net cash flow to movements in net debt

	£000
Increase in cash in period	250
Cash repurchase debentures	100
Cash used to increase liquid resources	30
Change in net debt	380
Net debt at 1 April 20X1	(1,736)
Net debt at 31 March 20X2	1,356

The reconciliation statement and note will help to assess the company's liquidity and financial adaptability.

24.5 Consolidated cash flow statements

A consolidated cash flow statement differs from that for a single company in two respects, namely, there are additional items and adjustments may be required to the actual amounts.

24.5.1 Additional items

Additional items appear in Sections 1, 2 and 5 of the Statement, as follows:

1 Cash flows from operating activities

- Operating profit before interest and tax
  Adjust for non-cash charges:
  Adjust for changes in current assets and current liabilities:
  Adjust for additional items if a consolidated cash flow statement:
  – Share of associate profit less dividend received by investor

2 Returns on investments and servicing of finance

● Interest paid and payable
  Minority interest – dividends paid
  [calculated as minority interest in opening consolidated balance sheet plus minority interest in consolidated profit and loss account less minority interest in closing consolidated balance sheet]

3 Acquisitions and disposals

● *Purchase of subsidiary, interest in associated/joint venture undertaking or of a business*
● *Proceeds from sale of subsidiary, interest in associated/joint venture undertaking or of a business*

24.5.2 Adjustments to amounts

Adjustments are required if the closing balance sheet items have been increased or reduced as a result of **non-cash movements**. Such movements occur (a) if there has been a purchase of a subsidiary to reflect the fact that the asset and liabilities from the new subsidiary have not necessarily resulted from cash flows; and (b) if there are exchange differences arising on consolidating foreign subsidiaries.

(a) Subsidiary acquired during year

For example, if in Tyro Bruce, a subsidiary had been acquired at the 31 March 20X2 on the following terms:

In consolidated cash flow the effect will be:

Net assets acquired:

	£000	
Working capital:		
Stock	10	(1) Reduce stock difference
Creditors	(12)	(1) Reduce creditor difference
Capital expenditure:		
Vehicles	20	(4) Reduces capital expenditure
Cash/Bank:		
Cash	5	(5) Inflow in Acquisitions section
Net assets acquired	23	

Consideration from Tyro Bruce:			
Shares	10		(8) Reduce share cash inflow
Premium	10		(8) Reduce share cash inflow
Cash	3		(5) Outflow in Acquisition section
		23	

The consolidated cash flow would be adjusted as follows:

The cash flow statement can now be prepared for Tyro Bruce for the year ended 31.3.20X2 using indirect method

			£000
1 Net cash inflow from operating activities **Note 1**			736
2 Returns on investments and servicing of finance interest			(40)
3 Taxation			
Tax paid			(440)
4 Capital expenditure			
Fixed asset purchase		(1,120)	
Less Vehicles brought in on acquisition		*20*	
		(1,100)	
Proceeds from sale of land and plant		682	
			(418)
5 Acquisitions and disposals			—
Cash flow arising from acquisition			
[Cash flow in £5,000 less cash flow out £3,000]			2
6 Equity dividends			(140)
			(300)
7 Management of liquid resources			
Government securities			(30)
8 Financing			
Issue of shares		700	
Less shares issued on acquisition not for cash		(20)	
		680	
Repayment of debentures		(100)	580
9 Increase in cash			250

Note 1: Reconciliation of operating profit to operating cash flows

			£000
Profit before interest and tax			1,040
Add back non-cash charges:			
Depreciation			204
R & D amortisation charge			480
Loss on sale of plant			54
Less non-cash credits:			
Profit on sale of land			(80)
Changes in current assets:			
Less current asset increases			
Stock		*(800)*	
Less stock brought in on acquisition		*10*	
		(790)	
			(790)
Debtors			*(440)*
Add current liability increases			
Creditors		*280*	
Less creditors brought in on acquisition		*12*	
		268	
			268
Net cash flow from operating activities			736

If there had been a disposal of a subsidiary, the same adjustments would have been required except that they would have been in the opposite direction, e.g. Capital Expenditure on vehicles would have been increased from £1,120,000 to £1,140,000.

(b) Exchange differences arising on consolidation

If the subsidiary's accounts have been translated using the net investment method whereby the closing rate has been used and the exchange differences taken to reserves, then the asset and liabilities in the consolidated balance sheet will contain **non-cash movements**. Let us assume that the non-cash differences that arose from exchange rate translation were the same amounts as those that arose on an acquisition of a subsidiary, namely:

Working capital:	*£000*	*Cash flow treatment*
Stock	10	**(1)** Reduce stock difference
Creditors	(12)	**(1)** Reduce creditor difference
Fixed assets:		
Vehicles	20	**(4)** Reduces capital expenditure
Cash/Bank:		
Cash	5	**(9)** Reduces cash
Exchange gain	23	

Section 1 Cash flow from operations would be the same as for the subsidiary acquired during the year, i.e. £736,000 (£738,000 – Creditor increase of £12,000 + Stock decrease of £10,000).

Section 4 Capital expenditure would be the same as for subsidiary acquired during the year, i.e. £418,000 (£438,000 – Fixed asset decrease of £20,000).

Section 9 Cash balance would be reduced by the exchange difference of £5,000, i.e. £245,000 (£250,000 – £5,000).

Note: The exchange gain of £23,000 would have been credited to reserves in Tyro Bruce.

24.6 Analysing a cash flow statement

The cash flow statement provides additional information on interest cover, working capital and fixed asset investment and financing cash flows.

24.6.1 Interest cover

Interest cover is normally defined as the number of times the profit before interest and tax covers the interest charge: in the Tyro Bruce example, £1,040,000/£40,000 = 26.1 times.

The position as disclosed in the cash flow statement is weaker. It is the number of times the net cash flow from operating activities covers the payment, i.e. £738,000/£40,000 = 18.45 times.

This does not allow us to assess the financing policy of the company, e.g. whether the capital was raised the optimum way. Nor does it allow us to assess whether the company would have done better to provide finance by improved control over its assets, e.g. working capital reduction.[13]

24.6.2 Impact of working capital movements on cash flows

From the Reconciliation on page 636 we can see that there has been an increase in working capital of £960,000. This is made up of:

	£000
Stock increase	800
Debtor increase	440
Creditor increase	(280)
	960

Using the information in the Reconciliation, we are able to calculate how much of the funds from operations are reinvested into working capital. This shows that the working capital increase is taking 56% of the funds flow from operations, i.e. £960,000/£1,698,000 × 100:

	£000
Profit before interest and tax	1,040
Non-cash items:	
Depreciation charged	204
Loss on sale of plant	54
R & D written off	480
Profit on sale of land	(80)
	1,698

We can see the cash implication, but not the reason for the working capital change or the likelihood of the cash flow movements recurring in future years.

To assess the underlying reasons for the change, we would need to extract additional ratios such as stock turnover. If the increase in the investment in stock is related to turnover, a similar increase could recur if the turnover is forecast to continue increasing. If it is due to poor stock control, it is less likely that the increase will recur: in fact, the opposite.

The same comments could be made in relation to the debtors and creditors. The cash flow statement indicates the cash extent of the change: additional ratios are required to allow us to evaluate the change.

24.6.3 Evaluating the investing activities cash flows

It is useful to consider how much of the expenditure is to replace existing fixed assets. One way is to relate the cash expenditure to the depreciation charge; this indicates that the cash expenditure is 549% greater than the depreciation charge calculated as follows: [(£1,120,000/£204,000) × 100]. This seems to indicate a possible increase in productive capacity. However, the cash flow does not itemise the expenditure and referring to the fixed asset schedule reveals that only £120,000 of the total of £1,120,000 was spent on plant.

There has been a criticism that it is not possible to assess how much of the investing activities cash outflow related to simply maintaining operations by replacing fixed assets that were worn out rather than related to increasing existing capacity with a potential for an increase in turnover and profits. The solution proposed was that investment that merely maintained should be shown as an operating cash flow and that the investing cash flow should be restricted to increasing capacity. The ASB doubted the reliability of such a distinction but there is a view[13] that such an analysis provides additional information, provided the breakdown between the two types of expenditure can be reliably ascertained.

24.6.4 Evaluating the financing cash flows

A comparison of the net cash outflow before financing with the cash inflow from financing indicates the extent to which the cash flow after investing has been utilised or financed, e.g. financing has contributed over 100% [(£600,000/£320,000) × 100] and there has been no reduction in cash.

Arranging cash flows into specific classes provides users with relevant and decision-useful information. This specific categorisation into operating, investing and financing activities allows users to draw conclusions about future cash flows. It would be difficult to make these conjectures using traditional accrual-based techniques.[14]

24.7 Critique of cash flow accounting

In this section we look at cash flow accounting from the viewpoint of users. We discuss the conflicting objectives of flexibility and uniformity, and comment on the two methods available under FRS 1.

24.7.1 Users

One of the main measures for evaluating the effectiveness of cash flow statements is the extent to which user needs are satisfied. Initial questions surrounding the replacement of funds flow statements with cash flow statements involved consideration of the following:

● For which user groups was the original SSAP 10 designed?

● Which user groups actually used funds flow statements and found the resultant information useful?

● Which user groups were consulted during the formulation of FRS 1?

● For which user groups was FRS 1 designed?

During this chapter we have identified the strengths and weaknesses of funds flow statements and cash flow statements. Funds flow statements did provide some useful information and were perceived as useful by users. Different user groups were able to extract different information from the statement; for instance:

● **Shareholders** could assess the stability of the company's dividend distribution policy by determining what proportion of net profit was accounted for by tax and dividends.

● **Creditors** could assess the company's ability to meet long-term obligations and maintain the working capital investment.

● **Lenders** could assess the company's reliance on either borrowings or share capital for financing investment and expansion projects.

Unfortunately, even though the funds flow statement satisfied some user needs, many areas could not be evaluated using it. Solomons explains this aspect of user needs:

> If ... the main concerns of the primary groups of users of general purpose financial reports are with the profitability and the viability of the enterprises in which they have an interest, that points to the need for financial statements that at least disclose:
> (a) the enterprise's capacity to generate income for its owners, employees, and lenders who are entitled to interest on their loans;
> (b) its present and probable future solvency.[15]

Solomons states that the link between profitability and viability is expressed by an enterprise's cash flows. The disclosure of this information is one of the arguments in favour of producing a cash flow statement.

24.7.2 Flexibility versus uniformity

One premise for the replacement of funds flow statements with cash flow statements is that SSAP 10 allowed too much flexibility in the presentation of funds flow information. This led to an increase in the variety of formats and a decrease in comparability between companies.

There appears to be an assumption that management, left to its own devices, will choose an accounting format for purely self-satisfying motives that will mislead the user. But perhaps the format of funds flow statements was properly left to the discretion of management. This discretion allowed management to decide which user groups the statement was aimed at, so that management could then select the most appropriate format to disclose and highlight the relevant information about recent activities. This might be more helpful than having the figures arrayed in a standard, uniform fashion.

On the assumption that too much flexibility was undesirable, FRS 1 applied stricter requirements to the format and presentation of cash flow statements. However, it still allowed companies to choose between the direct and indirect methods, and hence it could be argued that it failed to rectify the problem of lack of comparability between statements.

An important point is that, in its search for improved comparability, FRS 1 reduced the scope for innovation. It might be argued that standard-setters should not be reducing innovation, but that there should be a concerted effort to increase innovation and improve the information available to user groups. The acceptability of innovation is a fundamental issue in a climate that is becoming increasingly prescriptive under the influence of Europe.

24.7.3 Cash flows or funds flows

Our final consideration is the option of direct or indirect methods allowed in FRS 1. The direct method appears to be a genuine format for a cash flow statement, whereas the indirect method is a cross between a cash flow statement and a funds flow statement. Is it appropriate to continue to offer this hybrid format in FRS 1 Revised as a replacement for a funds flow statement?

Summary

The funds flow statements produced in accordance with SSAP 10 from 1975 to 1991 were criticised for not highlighting potential financial problems and for allowing too much choice to companies in how items were disclosed. FRS 1 defines more tightly the format and treatment of individual items within the cash flow statement. This leads to uniformity and greater comparability between companies.

In response to several criticisms, FRS 1 Revised has made a number of changes. These are based on the need to:

- Separate discretionary and non-discretionary cash flows. Dividends are discretionary payments and should be treated separately from items such as interest.
  FRS 1 Revised shows dividends as a separate heading after non-discretionary payments.

- Separate cash flows for expansion from cash flows for capital maintenance. FRS 1 did not differentiate and it was not always easy in practice to make such a separation.
  FRS 1 Revised shows cash flows arising from acquisitions and disposals of shares and from acquisitions and disposals of a business separately from fixed asset expenditure.

- Separate cash from near cash.
  FRS 1 Revised defines cash as cash in hand, cash at bank (receivable on demand) less bank overdraft (repayable on demand). It requires current asset investments that are readily disposable in an active market without significant effect on prices and without disrupting a company's business to be disclosed separately under a heading 'Management of liquid resources'. This category will include cash flows from the sale or purchase of liquid resources such as government securities, equities, debts and other instruments, which will help the user to understand the treasury activities of a company.

Review questions

1 The management of any enterprise may put considerable emphasis on the cash flow effects of its decisions and actions, monitoring these with the internal reporting system. Cash flow information is also relevant to those with external interests in the enterprise. Discuss the importance of cash flow information for both internal and external decisions. What internal and external user needs does cash flow reporting satisfy? Is the current cash flow information adequate for these purposes?

2 FRS 1 Cash Flow Statements preferred the direct method, but did not require it. Discuss possible reasons for allowing choice and the effectiveness of the ASB's encouragement to companies to use the direct method.

3 Explain the information that a user can obtain from a cash flow statement that cannot be obtained from the current or comparative balance sheets.

4 Explain the reasons for FRS 1 Revised increasing the number of sections in the cash flow statement.

5 'The traditional profit and loss statement in published accounts should be replaced (or at least supplemented) by a cash flow statement.'

(a) Explain what you understand by such a cash flow statement.

(b) Explain the basis on which the above view can be justified, and state any drawbacks of disclosing cash flow information.

6 Explain why the fixed assets acquired on the acquisition of a subsidiary during the year have the same effect on the consolidated cash flow statement as an exchange gain of equal amount resulting from the translation at closing rate.

Exercises
··················

An extract from the solution is provided in the appendix at the end of the text for exercises marked with an asterisk (*).

* Question 1

The draft balance sheets of Example plc as at 31 March 20X0 and 31 March 20X1 are as follows:

		20X1			20X0		
(£000)		Cost	Depn	NBV	Cost	Depn	NBV
Fixed assets		2,760	462	2,298	2,520	452	2,068
Current assets							
Stock			1,200			800	
Debtors			900			640	
Government securities			20			—	
Cash			10			80	
			2,130			1,520	
Current liabilities							
Creditors			500			540	
Taxation			170			190	
Dividends			—			—	
Overdraft			478			8	
			1,148			738	
Net current assets				982			782
				3,280			2,850
Ordinary share capital				1,400			1,300
Share premium account				400			200
Retained profits at 31 Mar 20X0				1,150			1,150
Profit for year				180			—
10% Debentures repayable 20X0–X4				150			200
				3,280			2,850

The profit and loss account of Example plc for the year ended 31 March 20X1 is as follows:

	£000	£000
Sales		3,000
Cost of sales		2,000
Gross profit		1,000
Selling and distribution expenses	300	
Administrative expenses	180	–480
		520
Interest payable		–20
Profit before tax		500
Tax		–200
Profit after tax		300
Dividend		–120
		180

Notes:

1 Fixed assets having a cost of £320,000 on which £92,000 of depreciation had been provided were sold during the year at a profit of £13,000.

2 The fixed asset schedule included the following:

Cost	£000	Depreciation	£000	Net book value	£000
At cost 31 Mar 20X0	2,520	At 31 Mar 20X0	452	At 31 Mar 20X0	2,068
Additions	560	P & L charge	102		
	3,080		554		
Disposals	320	Disposal	92		
At 31 Mar 20X1	2,760		462	At 31 Mar 20X1	2,298

Required:
A statement using the format of FRS I Revised on the Example plc data.

* **Question 2**

Shown below are the summarised final accounts of Martel plc for the last two financial years:

Balance sheet as at 31 December

| | 20X1 | | 20X0 | |
	£000	£000	£000	£000
Fixed assets				
Tangible				
Land and buildings	1,464		1,098	
Plant and machinery	520		194	
Motor vehicles	140		62	
		2,124		1,354
Current assets				
Stocks	504		330	
Trade debtors	264		132	
Government securities	40		—	
Bank	—		22	
	808		484	

	20X1		20X0	
	£000	£000	£000	£000
Creditors – less than one year				
Trade creditors	266		220	
Taxation	120		50	
Proposed dividend	72		40	
Bank overdraft	184		—	
	642		310	
Net current assets		166		174
Total assets less current liabilities		2,290		1,528
Creditors – more than one year				
9% Debentures		(432)		(350)
		1,858		1,178
Capital and reserves				
Ordinary shares of 50p each fully paid		900		800
Share premium account	120		70	
Revaluation reserve	360		—	
Gerneral reserve	100		50	
Retained profit	378		258	
		958		378
		1,858		1,178

*Summarised profit and loss account for the
year ending 31 December*

	20X1	20X0
	£000	£000
Operating profit	479	215
Interest paid	52	30
Profit before taxation	427	185
Corporation tax	149	65
Profit after taxation	278	120
Less: Dividends – interim	36	30
– proposed	72	40
	170	50
Less: Transfer to general reserve	50	—
Retained profit	120	50

Additional information:

1 The movement in fixed assets during the year ended 31 December 20X1 was as follows:

	Land and buildings £000	Plant, etc. £000	Motor vehicles £000
Cost at 1 January 20X1	3,309	470	231
Revaluation	360	—	—
Additions	81	470	163
Disposals	—	(60)	—
Cost at 31 December 20X1	3,750	880	394
Depreciation at 1 January 20X1	2,211	276	169
Disposals	—	(48)	—
Added for year	75	132	85
Depreciation at 31 December 20X1	2,286	360	254

The plant and machinery disposed of during the year was sold for £20,000.

2 During 20X1, a rights issue was made of one new ordinary share for every eight held at a price of £1.50.

Required:

(a) Prepare a cash flow statement for the year ended 31 December 20X1, in accordance with FRS 1.

(b) Prepare a report on the liquidity position of Mantel plc for a shareholder who is concerned about the lack of liquid resources in the company.

Question 3

The following financial statements relate to Blue Ting plc for the year ended 31 May 20X5.

Profit and loss account for the year ended 31 May 20X5

	£m	£m
Turnover		335
Cost of sales		(177)
Gross profit		158
Distribution costs	(31)	
Administrative expenses	(27)	(58)
Operating profit		100
Interest payable	(7)	
Interest receivable	3	(4)
Profit before tax		96
Taxation		(22)
Profit for the financial year		74
Dividends		(12)
Retained profit for financial year		62

Balance sheets at 31 May

	20X5		20X4	
	£m	£m	£m	£m
Tangible fixed assets		272		196
Intangible fixed assets				
(development expenditure)		3		4
		275		200
Current assets				
Stock	140		155	
Debtors	130		110	
Cash and liquid resources	102		23	
	372		288	
Creditors: Amounts falling due				
within one year	(249)		(172)	
Net current assets		123		116
Total assets less current liabilities		398		316
Creditors: Amounts falling due				
after more than one year		(80)		(90)
		318		226
Capital and reserves				
Ordinary share capital		120		100
Share premium account		45		35
Capital redemption reserve		12		—
Profit and loss account		141		91
		318		226

The following information relates to the financial statements of Blue Ting plc

(1) Ordinary share capital   £m

£1 Shares fully paid at 1.6.X4	100
Issued during year	10
Purchase of own shares	(12)
Shares converted	22
	120

(2) Reserves

	Share premium account	Capital redemption reserve	Profit and loss account
	£m	£m	£m
At 1.6.X4	35		91
Premium on issue			
(net of issue costs of £1m)	3		
Premium on conversion of debentures	7		
Transfer to CRR		12	(12)
Profit for period			62
	45	12	141

(3) Creditors: Amounts falling due after more than one year

	20X5 £m	20X4 £m
Obligations under finance leases	49	30
6% Debentures 20X5–2011	31	60
	80	90

£29m of 6% Debentures 20X5–2011 were converted into £22m of ordinary shares during the year and interest paid in the year amounted to £2m.

(4) Creditors: Amounts falling due within one year

	20X5 £m	20X4 £m
Bank overdraft	8	20
Obligations under finance leases	5	3
Trade creditors	220	131
Taxation	16	10
Dividends	—	8
	249	172

(5) Tangible fixed assets

	£m
Carrying value at 1.6.X4	196
Additions – finance leases	28
– purchases at cost	104
Disposals at carrying value	(19)
Depreciation for the year	(37)
Carrying value at 31.5.X5	272

The fixed assets disposed of realised £21m.

(6) Cash and liquid resources

	20X5 £m	20X4 £m
Treasury Stock 8.5% 20X9	60	—
Treasury Stock 12.75% 20X9 (June)	20	20
Loan notes repayable on demand	15	—
Cash at bank and in hand	7	3
	102	23

(Notes that all of the interest due on the Treasury Stock for the year ending 31.5.X5 has been received and there was no interest due on 31.5.X4.)

(7) Interest payable

	20X5 £m
Bank overdraft	2
Finance charges payable under finance leases	3
Debentures not wholly repayable within five years	2
	7

(8) Obligations under finance leases

	20X5	20X4
	£m	£m
Amounts payable within one year	6	4
Within two to five years	55	33
	61	37
Less finance charges allocated to future periods	(7)	(4)
	54	33

Interest paid on finance leases in the year to 31 May 20X5 amounted to £3m.

Required:
(a) Prepare a cash flow statement for Blue Ting plc for the year ended 31 May 20X5 in compliance with FRS 1 (Revised) *Cash Flow Statements*. Students should show as a note to the cash flow statement a reconciliation of operating profit to net cash inflow from operating activities.
(b) Discuss the principal advantages and disadvantages of publishing forecast cash flow statements for the next accounting period.

(ACCA)

Question 4

Carver plc is a listed company incorporated in 1958 to produce models carved from wood. In 1975 it acquired a 100% interest in a wood importing company, Olio Ltd; in 1989 it acquired a 40% interest in a competitor, Multi-products Ltd; and on 1 October 1993 it acquired a 75% interest in Good Display Ltd. It is planning to make a number of additional acquisitions during the next three years.

The draft consolidated accounts for the Carver Group are as follows:

Draft consolidated profit and loss account for the year ended 30 September 1994

	£000	£000
Operating profit		1,485
Share of profit of associated undertakings		495
Income from fixed asset investment		200
Interest payable		(150)
Profit on ordinary activities before taxation		2,030
Tax on profit on ordinary activities		
Corporation tax	391	
Deferred taxation	104	
Taxation attributable to income of associated undertakings	145	
Tax attributable to franked investment income	45	
		(685)
Profit on ordinary activities after taxation		1,345
Minority interests		(100)
Profit for the financial year		1,245
Dividends paid and proposed		(400)
Retained profit for the year		845

Draft consolidated balance sheet as at 30 September

	1993 £000	1993 £000	1994 £000	1994 £000
Fixed assets				
Tangible assets				
Buildings at net book value		2,200		2,075
Machinery				
Cost	1,400		3,000	
Aggregate depreciation	(1,100)		(1,200)	
Net book value		300		1,800
		2,500		3,875
Investments in associated undertaking		1,000		1,100
Fixed asset investments		410		410
Current assets				
Stocks		1,000		1,975
Trade debtors		1,275		1,850
Cash		1,820		4,515
		4,095		8,340
Creditors: Amounts falling due within one year				
Trade creditors		280		500
Obligations under finance leases		200		240
Corporation tax		150		375
ACT		67		87
Dividends		200		300
Accrued interest and finance charges		30		40
		927		1,542
Net current assets		3,168		6,798
Total assets less current liabilities		7,078		12,183
Creditors: Amounts falling due after more than one year				
Obligations under finance leases		170		710
Loans		500		1,460
Provisions for liabilities				
Deferred taxation		13		30
Net assets		6,395		9,983
Capital and reserves				
Called up share capital in 25p shares		2,000		3,940
Share premium account		2,095		2,883
Profit and loss account		2,300		3,045
Total shareholders' equity		6,395		9,868
Minority interest		—		115
Net assets		6,395		9,983

Note 1: There had been no acquisitions or disposals of buildings during the year.
Machinery costing £500,000 was sold for £500,000 resulting in a profit of £100,000. New machinery was acquired in 1994 including additions of £850,000 acquired under finance leases.

Note 2: Information relating to the acquisition of Good Display Ltd.

	£000
Machinery	165
Stocks	32
Trade debtors	28
Cash	112
Less: Trade creditors	(68)
Corporation tax	(17)
	252
Less: Minority interest	(63)
	189
Goodwill	100
	289

	£000
880,000 shares issued as part consideration	275
Balance of consideration paid in cash	14
	289

It is group policy to write off goodwill to reserves.

Note 3: Loans were issued at a discount in 1994 and the carrying amount of the loans at 30 September 1994 included £40,000 representing the finance cost attributable to the discount and allocated in respect of the current reporting period.

Required:
Prepare a consolidated cash flow statement for the Carver Group for the year ended 30 September 1994.

(ACCA)

References
1 SSAP 10, *Statements of Source and Application of Funds*, July 1975.
2 SFAS 95, *Statement of Cash Flows*, FASB, November 1987.
3 N. MacDonald, 'Funds flow reporting', in L.C.L. Skerrat and D.J. Tonkin (eds), *Financial Reporting 1987–88: A Survey of UK Reporting Practice*, ICAEW, 1988.
4 ED 54, *Cash Flow Statements*, ASC, July 1990.
5 J. Arnold *et al.*, *The Future Shape of Financial Reports*, ICAEW and ICAS, 1991.
6 J. Arnold, 'The future shape of financial reports', *Accountancy*, May 1991, p. 26.
7 G.H. Sorter, M.J. Ingberman and H.M. Maximon, *Financial Accounting: An Events and Cash Flow Approach*, McGraw-Hill, 1990.
8 J.W. Henderson and T.S. Maness, *The Financial Analyst's Deskbook*, Van Nostrand Reinhold, 1989, p. 12.
9 J. Crichton, 'Cash flow statements – what are the choices?' *Accountancy*, October 1990, p. 30.
10 L.J. Heath and P. Rosenfield, 'Solvency: the forgotten half of financial reporting', in R. Bloom and P.T. Elgers (eds), *Accounting Theory and Practice*, Harcourt Brace Jovanovich, 1987, p. 586.

11   ASB Press Notice 6, 26 September 1991.

12   J.M. Gahlon and R.L. Vigeland, 'Early warning signs of bankruptcy using cash flow analysis', *Journal of Commercial Lending*, December 1988, pp. 4–15.

13   G. Holmes and A. Sugden, *Interpreting Company Reports and Accounts* (5th edition), Woodhead Faulkner, 1995, p. 134.

14   J.W. Henderson and T.S. Maness, *op. cit.*, p. 72.

15   D. Solomons, *Guidelines for Financial Reporting Standards*, ICAEW, 1989.

CHAPTER 25

Review of financial ratio analysis

Introduction

In this chapter we consider the following:

- Accounting ratios and ratio analysis
- Six key ratios
- Pyramid of ratios
- Other important ratios
- Application of pyramid of ratios to J D Wetherspoon
- Segmental analysis
- Interfirm comparisons and industry averages
- Interfirm comparisons: J D Wetherspoon and the independent public houses and bars sector
- World Wide Web (WWW) pages
- Non-financial ratios
- Interpretation problems when using consolidated financial statements

This chapter reviews the use of financial ratio analysis for the interpretation of a company's financial statements. The techniques that we discuss are fundamental to user appraisal of financial statements and should be used in conjunction with any alternative interpretative techniques available.

The key to understanding and interpreting financial statements is an extremely inquisitive and enquiring frame of mind. When examining a set of accounts, we should try to understand exactly what the figures mean.

Some issues will be evident from a cursory look at the accounts. For example, an initial glance might reveal a company that has made losses in the past two years; that has a declining sales turnover, a large overdraft and a greatly increased creditor figure. This would clearly raise questions about, for example, the increase in creditors. The initial look is a prelude to a more systematic review and is helpful in quickly putting the accounts into context.

Following the overview, financial ratios become important. One of the main strengths of financial ratios is that they help to direct the user's focus of attention. They identify and highlight areas of good and bad performance, and areas of significant change. In each instance, the user should attempt to explain exactly why the accounts reveal this behaviour.

Before we embark on a full investigation of financial ratios, a word of warning. Ian Griffiths has written a book on creative accounting which questions the reliability of financial statements: 'Every company in the country is fiddling its profits. Every set of published accounts is based on books which have been gently cooked or completely roasted ... it is the biggest con trick since the Trojan Horse.'[1]

We should take heed of these reservations when we undertake any analytical interpretations. They should make us even more open-minded and investigative when confronted by a set of financial statements:

> Whether the differences in accounting treatment and presentation are real or imagined, it is clear that there is scope for tremendous variation in reported figures ... perhaps the best safeguard is to look upon the annual accounts with a more cynical and jaundiced eye. The myth that the financial statements are an irrefutable and accurate reflection of the company's trading performance for the year must be exploded once and for all. The accounts are little more than an indication of the broad trend.

25.2 Accounting ratios and ratio analysis

Accounting ratios identify irregularities, anomalies and surprises that require further investigation to ascertain the current and future financial standing of a company. This sounds very useful, but what are ratios and how can we use them?

25.2.1 What are ratios?

Ratios describe the relationship between different items in the financial statements. Obviously, we could calculate hundreds of ratios from a set of financial statements; the expertise lies in knowing which ratios provide useful information. The relative usefulness of each ratio depends on what aspects of a company's business affairs are being investigated. Some of the most important and frequently used ratios are outlined in section 25.3.

25.2.2 How can we use ratios?

An important lesson about ratios is that, if they are applied incorrectly, they may be completely useless or, perhaps even worse, misleading. Alternatively, if they are used correctly, they are a powerful tool for understanding and interpreting company accounts. Some basic rules for financial ratio analysis are as follows.

Compare like with like

The relative performance of a company can be gauged in a number of different terms by comparing that company's financial ratios with:

● financial ratios for a preceding period;
● budgeted financial ratios for the current period;
● financial ratios for other profit centres within the company;
● financial ratios for other companies within the same industrial sector.

In each case, comparison is possible only if an identical basis of compilation is employed. There must be conformity and uniformity in the preparation of accounts to ensure a comparison of like with like. In addition, if one is comparing companies in different countries, one needs to be aware of any differences in international accounting policies (see Chapter 27 'International Reporting and Interpretation').

Clear definition of the financial ratio

A full understanding of the precise implications of a given ratio is possible only if it is accompanied by a clear definition of its constituent parts. The user must be able to judge the accuracy and reliability of the underlying business operations before the reliability of the ratio can be assessed. In addition, the definitions of ratios may vary from source to source as concepts and terminology are not universally defined.[2]

Awareness of underlying trends

As a ratio compares two values, changes in either of these underlying values over time may be obscured in the final ratio figure. Let us take the example of Radmand plc:

	Net profit £	Capital employed £	Return on capital employed
20X1	100,000	1,000,000	10%
20X2	150,000	1,500,000	10%
20X3	225,000	2,250,000	10%

Although the return on capital employed (ROCE) remains a constant 10% over the years 20X1–20X3, no assumptions can be made about the underlying figures. As we can see, the net profit increased by 50% in both 20X2 and 20X3, and this trend is not ascertainable in the ROCE ratio. The user should be aware that a ratio is not saying anything about the trends of its individual components – only about the combined effect of both components.

25.3 Six key ratios

In our analysis we identify six key ratios and a number of subsidiary ratios. The key ratios are presented as a pyramid in Figure 25.1. The pyramid illustrates how the constituent parts of each ratio relate to a set of financial statements.

The six key ratios are divided into three categories, as follows:

Primary investment level ratios

1 Primary investment ratio (**operating return on equity**)

$$\frac{\text{Net profit before interest and tax}}{\text{Shareholders' funds}}$$

2 Primary financing ratio (**financial leverage multiplier**)

$$\frac{\text{Capital employed}}{\text{Shareholders' funds}}$$

Primary operative level ratios

3 Primary operating ratio (**return on capital employed**)

$$\frac{\text{Net profit before interest and tax}}{\text{Capital employed}}$$

Figure 25.1 Pyramid of key ratios.

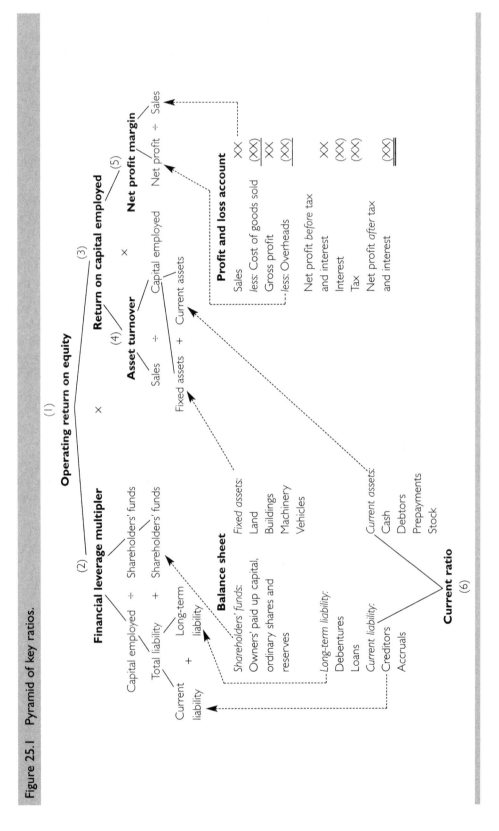

4 Primary utilisation ratio (**asset turnover**)

$$\frac{\text{Sales}}{\text{Capital employed}}$$

5 Primary efficiency ratio (**net profit margin**)

$$\frac{\text{Net profit before interest and tax}}{\text{Sales}}$$

Primary liquidity level ratios

6 Primary liquidity ratio (**current ratio**)

$$\frac{\text{Current assets}}{\text{Current liabilities}}$$

25.4 Description of the six key ratios

25.4.1 Primary investment level ratios

1 Primary investment ratio (operating return on equity)

The operating return on equity represents the net profit of a company as a percentage of the shareholders' funds (i.e. the total investment by the owners). This ratio is at the apex of the ratio pyramid, and it is the product of the financial leverage multiplier and the ROCE. Note that our 'operating return on equity' is defined differently to a more traditional 'return on equity' (Earnings/Shareholders' funds).

2 Primary financing ratio (financial leverage multiplier)

The financial leverage multiplier expresses how many times bigger the capital employed is than the shareholders' funds. This multiplier implies that assets funded by sources other than the owners will increase the profit or loss of the company relative to shareholders' funds.

25.4.2 Primary operative level ratios

3 Primary operating ratio (return on capital employed)

The ROCE is a fundamental measure of the profitability of a company. It is a popular indicator of management efficiency because it contrasts the net profit generated by the company with the total value of fixed and current assets, which are presumed to be under management control. Therefore, the ROCE demonstrates how well the management has utilised total assets.

ROCE is the product of the remaining two primary operative level ratios:

$$\text{ROCE} = \text{Asset turnover} \times \text{Net profit margin}$$

Many different factors impact on the ROCE figure, including asset valuation policies, depreciation policies, revaluation policies, pricing policies, the treatment of goodwill and the treatment of expenses. In particular, the accounting treatment of goodwill (prior to FRS 10) resulted in the vast majority of companies writing off goodwill against their reserves. For some acquisitive companies, the goodwill write-off was so substantial that their shareholders' funds became negative. For instance, in The GGT Group's 1997 annual report their shareholders' funds were –£98,688,000. This makes interpretation and comparisons more difficult.

4 Primary utilisation ratio (asset turnover)

The asset turnover is a measure of how much sales are generated by the capital asset base of a company. Although this ratio can act as a good guide to company performance, it can also be misleading. Its magnitude should therefore be evaluated in terms of its constituent parts.

If asset turnover increases, either the total value of sales is increasing, or the capital asset base is decreasing, or both. If it is because sales are increasing, this might signify improved performance. However, if it is because the capital asset base is reduced, this needs further investigation. For example, it could be caused by failure to maintain fixed assets, or a massive drop in stock levels.

5 Primary efficiency ratio (net profit margin)

Net profit margin is another widely used ratio in the assessment of company performance and in comparisons with other companies.

Profit margin depends on the type of industry a company is operating within (e.g. high-volume/low-margin), the company pricing policies, the sales volumes and cost handling. A higher margin generally suggests good performance, but the profit margin should not be taken at face value. When analysing profit margin we should ask questions such as: why is the profit margin higher than average; or why it is lower than it was last year; or is the company management setting profit margin strategically?

25.4.3 Primary liquidity level ratios

6 Primary liquidity ratio (current ratio)

The current ratio is a short-term measure of a company's liquidity position. This ratio (which should be appraised in conjunction with the acid test ratio) compares current assets with current liabilities. In cases where the value is greater than unity, the current asset value exceeds the value of current liabilities. It is often claimed that the current ratio should be greater than 2, but the recommended current ratio depends (as always) on the industry sector. Moreover, the current ratio should be analysed in terms of its constituent parts to test the quality of the value. We should ask: what part of current assets is cash, debtors or stock; what is the likelihood of debtors defaulting; what is the condition of the stock; and what are the timings of all the current liabilities?

25.5 Description of subsidiary ratios

25.5.1 Gearing ratios

$$\text{Gearing ratio} = \frac{\text{Total liability} - \text{Current liability}}{\text{Capital employed}}$$

The gearing ratio represents the proportion of capital employed which is accounted for by long-term fixed interest debt. The gearing structure of a company refers to the amount of borrowings compared with the amount of shareholders' funds. A company with high gearing is predominantly financed by debt, whereas a company with low gearing relies on equity finance. Different user groups prefer different gearing structures. Creditors and shareholders will be influenced by gearing as it affects factors such as annual interest payments and earnings per share.

This particular definition of gearing concentrates on long-term debt financing. An alternative measure might be Total Liabilities/Capital Employed, which includes short-term financing as well as long-term financing. This might be more pertinent because some companies rely on high levels of overdraft. As a further refinement one might dis-aggregate current liabilities into interest-bearing finance (overdrafts; short-term loans) and more indirect finance (trade creditors; tax payable; dividends payable).

$$\text{Shareholders' ratio} = \frac{\text{Shareholders' funds}}{\text{Capital employed}}$$

This represents the proportion of capital employed that is made up by shareholders' funds.

$$\text{Interest cover} = \frac{\text{Net profit before interest and tax}}{\text{Interest}}$$

Most companies are committed to paying a certain amount of interest charges. This ratio describes how many times greater the profit is than the interest charges. It gives creditors an indication of how secure these repayments are. An alternative measure is to compare the actual cash flow (rather than profit) to interest payments to give an indication of the availability of cash to cover interest charges.

25.5.2 Liquidity ratios

$$\text{Acid test ratio} = \frac{\text{Current assets} - \text{Stock}}{\text{Current liabilities}}$$

The acid test or quick ratio indicates the company's ability to repay immediate commitments using cash or near-cash. It excludes the value of stock in order to show the immediate solvency of the company.

25.5.3 Asset utilisation ratios

The asset turnover ratio can be subdivided into more specific component parts, so that each element of fixed and current assets can be analysed separately. The asset turnover ratio measures the amount of sales generated by the capital employed as a whole, whereas individual asset utilisation ratios compare total sales with the selected asset under management control. The breakdown of the asset turnover ratio is illustrated in Figure 25.2.

The fixed asset, tangible, property and plant utilisation ratios are measures of efficiency. They all indicate the sales volume produced by the available fixed assets. Although an improvement in these ratios will also improve the ROCE, it must be remembered that the depreciation policies and historical cost valuation of fixed assets will cause a distortion.

Three utilisation (or turnover) ratios that are particularly informative for understanding and interpreting financial statements are stock turnover, debtor turnover and creditor turnover. Stock turnover can be calculated as:

$$\text{Stock turnover} = \frac{\text{Sales}}{\text{Stock}} \quad \text{or} \quad \frac{\text{Cost of sales}}{\text{Average stock}} \quad \text{or more usually} \quad \frac{\text{Cost of sales}}{\text{Closing stock}}$$

Figure 25.2 Asset turnover ratio.

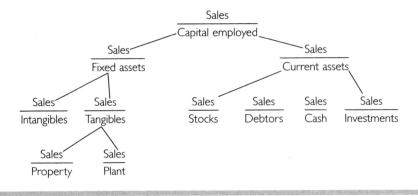

Stock control involves careful planning and management. A company must avoid tying up too much capital in stock, yet the stock levels must always be sufficient to meet customer demand and maintain continuous production. Any changes in this ratio must be investigated to determine exactly why stock turnover is fluctuating – it could be due to changing sales volumes; different stock valuation policies; or obsolete stock. The average stock holding period (in days) can be calculated as:

$$\frac{\text{Closing stock}}{\text{Cost of sales}} \times 365$$

The debtor ratio (usually trade debtors) is usually expressed in terms of the debtor collection period (in days):

$$\frac{\text{Debtors}}{\text{Sales}} \times 365$$

This ratio can be used to evaluate credit control and how quickly the company receives cash. Changes in the debtor collection period might be misleading, so the root cause must be ascertained. A falling debt collection period might mean that the company is successfully reducing bad debts and eliminating poor risks; or the liquidity position might be so poor that the company is extending discounts and incentives to customers who pay early (or on time). An increasing debt collection period might mean that the company has poor credit control and is besieged with bad debts; or that it has a strategy for attracting new customers.

The creditors turnover ratio (usually trade creditors) is calculated as:

$$\text{Creditors turnover} = \frac{\text{Sales}}{\text{Creditors}} \quad \text{or more usually} \quad \frac{\text{Cost of sales}}{\text{Creditors}}$$

It is usually expressed in terms of the creditor payment period (in days):

$$\frac{\text{Creditors}}{\text{Sales}} \times 365 \text{ or more usually} \quad \frac{\text{Creditors}}{\text{Cost of Sales}} \times 365$$

This ratio indicates the credit facilities extended to a company by its suppliers. Any changes in the payment period might be due to suppliers altering credit terms (either more or less generous), the company trying to gain maximum credit facilities, or the company utilising early payment incentives.

25.5.4 Investment ratios

Investment ratios are of great interest to investors. Earnings per share (EPS) indicates the amount of profit after tax, interest and preference shares earned for each ordinary share. The price/earnings ratio (PE ratio) is a measure of market confidence in the shares of a company. Dividend cover compares net profit with dividends to show how many times over the dividends could be paid and how safe this annual yield is. Dividend yield expresses dividends as a proportion of the market value of total shares.

25.5.5 Profitability ratios

Profitability ratios allow a more specific analysis of profit margin, e.g. expressing individual expenses as a proportion of sales or cost of sales. These ratios will identify any irregularities or changes in specific expenses from year to year.

A list of the subsidiary ratios is set out in Figure 25.3.

Figure 25.3 Subsidiary ratios.

Gearing ratios

$$\text{Gearing ratio} = \frac{\text{Total liability} - \text{Current liability}}{\text{Capital employed}}$$

$$\text{Shareholders' ratio} = \frac{\text{Shareholders' funds}}{\text{Capital employed}}$$

$$\text{Interest cover} = \frac{\text{Net profit before interest and tax}}{\text{Interest}}$$

Liquidity ratios

$$(6)\ \text{Current ratio} = \frac{\text{Current assets}}{\text{Current liabilities}}$$

$$\text{Acid test ratio} = \frac{\text{Current assets} - \text{Stock}}{\text{Current liabilities}}$$

Investment ratios

Earnings per share =

$$\frac{\text{Net profit after tax} - \text{Preference dividends}}{\text{Number of ordinary shares}}$$

$$\text{Price/earnings ratio} = \frac{\text{Share price}}{\text{Earnings per share}}$$

Dividend cover (ordinary shares) =

$$\frac{\text{Net profit after tax} - \text{Preference dividends}}{\text{Dividends on ordinary shares}}$$

$$\text{Dividend yield} = \frac{\text{Dividend on ordinary shares}}{\text{Market value of ordinary shares}}$$

Asset utilisation ratios (turnover ratios)

$$\frac{\text{Sales}}{\text{Fixed assets}}$$

$$\frac{\text{Sales}}{\text{Current assets}}$$

$$\frac{\text{Sales}}{\text{Working capital}}$$

$$\frac{\text{Cost of sales}}{\text{Stock}}$$

$$\frac{\text{Sales}}{\text{Debtors}}$$

$$\frac{\text{Cost of sales}^{a}}{\text{Trade creditors}}$$

[a]Ideally cost of materials used should be used.

Profitability ratios

$$\frac{\text{Gross profit}}{\text{Sales}}$$

$$\frac{\text{Cost of sales}}{\text{Sales}}$$

$$\frac{\text{Total overheads}}{\text{Sales}}$$

$$\frac{\text{Cost of materials}}{\text{Cost of sales}}$$

$$\frac{\text{Cost of labour}}{\text{Cost of sales}}$$

25.6 Application of pyramid of ratios to J D Wetherspoon plc

To illustrate financial ratio analysis and trend analysis we are using the accounts of J D Wetherspoon plc.[3] The company's principal activities are the development and management of public houses.[4] J D Wetherspoon's profit and loss account and balance sheet are reproduced in Figure 25.4. The 1998 and 1999 Accounts for J D Wetherspoon are set out in Question 10 (see also http://www.wetherspoon.co.uk).

Figure 25.4 Wetherspoon (JD) Consolidated profit and loss account for the year ended 31 July 1997.

	1997	1996
	£000	£000
Turnover from continuing operations	139,444	100,480
Cost of sales	(106,972)	(76,001)
Gross profit	32,472	24,479
Administrative expenses	(9,533)	(7,476)
Operating profit	22,939	17,003
Net interest payable	(5,373)	(3,898)
Profit on ordinary activities before tax	17,566	13,105
Tax on profit on ordinary activities	(770)	(564)
Profit on ordinary activities after tax	16,796	12,541
Dividends	(3,894)	(3,417)
Retained profit for the year	12,902	9,124

Wetherspoon (JD)
Group balance sheet at 31 July 1997

	1997	1996
	£000	£000
Fixed assets		
Tangible assets	244,513	182,123
	244,513	182,123
Current assets		
Stocks	2,215	1,167
Debtors	3,026	1,544
Cash	7,196	14,801
	12,437	17,512
Creditors due within one year	(34,998)	(24,450)
Net current liabilities	(22,561)	(6,938)
Total assets less current liabilities	221,952	175,185
Creditors due after one year	(97,289)	(67,077)
	124,663	108,108
Capital and reserves		
Called up share capital	3,898	3,866
Share premium account	59,676	57,728
Revaluation reserve	22,023	20,350
Profit and loss account	39,066	26,164
Equity shareholders' funds	124,663	108,108

Calculation of the six key ratios

1 Operating return on equity

$$1997 \quad \frac{22{,}939}{124{,}663} = 18.40\% \qquad 1996 \quad \frac{17{,}003}{108{,}108} = 15.73\%$$

2 Financial leverage multiplier

$$1997 \quad \frac{256{,}950}{124{,}663} = 2.06 \text{ times} \qquad 1996 \quad \frac{199{,}635}{108{,}108} = 1.85 \text{ times}$$

3 Return on capital employed

$$1997 \quad \frac{22{,}939}{256{,}950} = 8.93\% \qquad 1996 \quad \frac{17{,}003}{199{,}635} = 8.52\%$$

4 Asset turnover

$$1997 \quad \frac{139{,}444}{256{,}950} = 0.54 \text{ times} \qquad 1996 \quad \frac{100{,}480}{199{,}635} = 0.50 \text{ times}$$

5 Net profit margin

$$1997 \quad \frac{22{,}939}{139{,}444} = 16.45\% \qquad 1996 \quad \frac{17{,}003}{100{,}480} = 16.92\%$$

6 Current ratio

$$1997 \quad \frac{12{,}437}{34{,}998} = 0.36 : 1 \qquad 1996 \quad \frac{17{,}512}{24{,}450} = 0.72 : 1$$

Figure 25.5 Pyramid of ratios.

1997

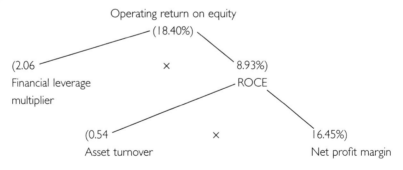

1996

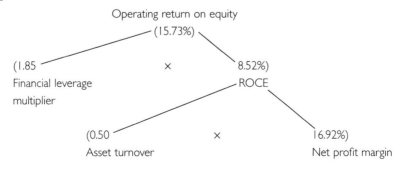

Five of these key ratios are shown in the pyramid structure of Figure 25.5 (allowing for rounding).

25.6.1   Interpretation of J D Wetherspoon plc's accounts

Using the pyramid structure to analyse JD Wetherspoon in 1997 and 1996 we can iden-tify a number of areas of the business in which further investigations should be carried out. To begin with, the operating return on equity has improved from 15.73% to 18.40%. Disaggregating this ratio we can see that the improvement is due to both an increase in the financial leverage multiplier (1.85 to 2.06) and an increase in the ROCE (8.52% to 8.93%).

The increase in the financial leverage multiplier means that there has been an increased proportion of total liabilities within the capital employed figure. Looking at the balance sheet, it is evident that long-term loans have risen by nearly £30 million (from £67,077,000 to £97,289,000). For interest, the cash flow statement (not reproduced here) shows that the company has received £30 million of 'advances under secured bank loans' (in the Financing section) primarily to finance the 'investment in new pubs and pub extensions' of £63,010,000 (in the Capital expenditure section).

The increase in the ROCE is driven by an improved asset turnover (from 0.5 to 0.54), despite a drop in the net margin (16.92% to 16.45%). The improved asset turnover means that each £ of capital employed (or total assets) produces a higher level of sales. If the decline in net margin is investigated further it is evident that the main cause has been a decline in the gross margin (gross profit/sales) from 24.36% to 23.29%. The declining gross margin might be due to a decline in sales prices or higher cost of sales (which, according to the Wetherspoon annual report, include distribution costs and all pub operating costs).

Some other considerations become apparent when evaluating the accounts in general. First of all, consider the profit and loss account:

● The tax charge in both years is extremely low. For instance, in 1997 the tax is 4.4% of profit before tax. The explanation for this is that the company has utilised unused tax allowances brought forward and high capital allowances generated in the year.

● The company distributed only 23.2% of the after-tax profits in the form of dividends. The explanation for this, in the Finance Director's report, is that the company 'wishes to preserve cash for future expansion'.

● There are no exceptional items to consider.

Second, consider the balance sheet:

● The cash balance has fallen by over £7 million. The cash flow statement shows that this has been used to part-finance expansion.

● The current liabilities are much higher than the current assets, generating a net current liability. This is illustrated by the current ratio (0.36 in 1997 and 0.72 in 1996). One would need to compare this with the industry average (note that the current ratio for brewers is quite low) and determine whether this drop in current ratio is deliberate policy or needs attention. The notes to the accounts (not reproduced here) show that trade creditors have doubled from £9.4m to £18.4m.

● There is a revaluation reserve of £22,023,000 (17.7% of shareholders' funds). One would need to consider the impact of this figure on some of the ratios, especially when comparing with other brewers.

25.7 Segmental analysis

In this section we review the reasons for and importance of segmental accounting in the analysis of financial statements.

Reasons for segmental accounting

Segmental information is provided on a consistent basis that allows it to be comparable over time so as to assist the users to:

● appreciate more thoroughly the results and financial position by permitting a better understanding of past performance and thus a better assessment of future prospects;

● be aware of the impact that changes in significant components of a business may have on the business as a whole.

Importance of segmental accounting

Segmental information makes the user aware of the balance between the different operations and thus able to assess:

● the quality of the company's reported earnings;

● the specific risks to which the company is subject;

● the areas where long-term growth may be expected.

Constraints on comparison between companies

Segmental analysis is intrinsically subjective. This means that there are likely to be major differences in the way segments are determined, and because costs, for example, may be allocated differently by companies in the same industry it is difficult to make inter-company comparisons at the segment level and the user still has to take a great deal of responsibility for the interpretation of that information.[13]

We also consider the rules applicable to segmental accounting, provide an extract from a set of accounts to illustrate what information might be disclosed, and evaluate the information provided in The Greenalls Group accounts (see 25.7.2).

25.7.1 Segmental accounting

Although the Companies Act 1967 introduced some requirements for the disclosure of segmental information, an accounting standard on the topic was not issued until June 1990.[5] The objective of segmental reporting is to assist users of accounts in evaluating the different business segments and geographical regions of a group and how they affect its overall results.[6] SSAP 25 *Segmental Reporting* sets out how these different segments should be defined and the information that should be disclosed.

SSAP 25 gives guidance on the factors that directors should take into account when defining segments, e.g. the nature of the products or services, and how the group's activities are organised. These factors help to determine whether a segment is distinguishable. However, it must also be a significant segment to require disclosure: a significance test will measure if any of the turnover, results (profit or loss) or net assets accounts for more than 10% of the group's total. SSAP 25 also states that turnover, results (profit or loss before tax, minority interests and extraordinary items) and net assets (not defined in the standard) should be disclosed for both business and geographic segments.

Despite the existence of SSAP 25, there are many concerns about the extent of segmental disclosure and its limitations must be recognised.[7] A great deal of discretion is imparted to the directors concerning the **definition of each segment**. However, 'the factors which provide guidance in determining an industry segment are often the factors which lead a company's management to organise its enterprise into divisions, branches or subsidiaries'.[8] There is discretion concerning the **allocation of common costs** to segments on a reasonable basis. There is flexibility in the **definition of some of the items** to be disclosed (particularly net assets). Finally, there is a get-out clause. Where the directors consider the disclosure of information to be seriously prejudicial to the interests of their group, they do not have to disclose it (as long as the accounts report this non-disclosure).

The revised version of IAS 14[9] requires a much greater disclosure of information than both the original IAS 14[10] and SSAP 25. In particular, separate disclosure of both segment assets and segment liabilities are required (as opposed to net assets for SSAP 25) and the basis of inter-segment pricing. In the UK, ED 45[11] proposed that the basis of inter-segment pricing (transfer pricing[12]) should be disclosed, but this particular proposal was not implemented in SSAP 25.

25.7.2 Segmental accounting – extract from a set of accounts

Where a segment can be distinguished, it is significant and the 'seriously prejudicial' clause is not invoked, one would expect to see disclosure of turnover, results and net assets for both business segments and geographical segments. However, a business may have only one business segment or operate in only one geographical region. Also, not all groups disclose net asset information, e.g. Leicester City Plc state in the 1999 Accounts: 'In the opinion of the Directors, it is not possible to analyse the assets between the businesses due to the shared nature of many of the assets'.

The following extract shows a summarised segmental report from the Bass plc 1999 Accounts of their Business Segment and Geographical Segment (turnover by origin):

	External turnover £m	Operating profit £m	Non-operating exceptionals £m	Profit on ordinary activities before int £m
Bass Hotels & Resorts	1,162	321	(107)	214
Bass Leisure Retail	1,428	298	—	298
Bass Brewers	1,576	160	(7)	153
Britvic Drinks	507	44	—	44
Other activities	13	1	2	3
	4,686	824	(112)	712
United Kingdom	3,564	556	3	559
Rest of Europe, Middle East and Africa	496	71	(6)	65
United States	482	170	(110)	60
Rest of Americas	86	17	1	18
Asia Pacific	58	10	—	10
	4,686	824	(112)	712

Assets	£m
UK	5,328
Rest of Europe, Middle East and Africa	1,076
United States	1,144
Rest of Americas	85
Asia Pacific	107
	7,740

The segmental information provides a rough idea about how a group is performing in its main business segments and geographical regions. Bearing in mind the initial discussions on segmental accounting, a number of general observations can be made. Bass has significant interests in hotels, leisure retailing and branded drinks. Although most of Bass business is UK-based, there are high levels of sales in the United States and the Rest of Europe, the Middle East and Africa.

To get a feel for the profitability of the different business segments and markets, it is possible to calculate profit margins (based on operating profit/external sales as disclosed in the above note). For instance the profit margin for the hotel segment is 27.6% compared to 10.2% for Bass Brewers. In addition, the profit margin for the UK is 15.6% compared to 35.3% for the US. This illustrates just how important it is to understand what different business segments are part of a group and which different markets the company is operating in. Furthermore, is the group changing its direction from one year to the next? The profit margin on the hotel segment might indicate that the company would make acquisitions to strengthen this area. The 1998 Accounts showed that this happened with the acquisition of Inter-Continental Hotels for £1,765 million. Is the group a conglomerate operating in numerous different business segments? What are the group's core competencies? Have there been any acquisitions during the year? Have there been any divestments? In relation to Bass, the 1998 Operating and Financial Review stated that there had been a switch in its focus from one of maximising Group benefits through operating tied beer outlets to one of being a leisure retailer.

The 1999 Review stated that the Group made significant progress during 1999, capitalising on the strategic activity undertaken in 1998 which saw the acquisition of the Inter-Continental Hotel (ICH) business, the disposal of the leased pub operation and the leisure businesses and the return of over £800m of capital to shareholders.

With regard to the Bass Hotels & Resorts segment of the business, the OFR states: 'As an indicator of future expansion, at 30 September 1999, BHR had approved franchise applications for 571 hotels (1998 – 575) with approximately 58,000 rooms, though the hotels had yet to enter the system...'

25.8 Interfirm comparisons and industry averages

Financial ratios are a convenient way of assessing the current financial health and performance of a company relative to similar companies in the same industrial sector. This enables a company to be judged directly against its competitors, rather than merely against its own previous performance. Provided that each company uses exactly the same bases in calculation ratios, interfirm comparisons provide a more controlled and objective means of evaluation. Every company is subject to identical economic and market conditions in the given review period, allowing a much truer comparison than a single company's fluctuating results over several years.

Interfirm comparisons are ideal for identifying the strengths and weaknesses of a company relative to its industrial sector. These comparisons can be analysed by both internal users (management can take the necessary actions to maintain strengths and rectify weaknesses) and external users (lenders, creditors, investors, etc.). There are numerous sources of interfirm information, but the organisations providing it can be divided into those which gather their data from external published accounts and those which collect the data directly from the surveyed companies on a strictly confidential basis.

25.8.1 Data collected from external published accounts

Organisations that prepare interfirm comparisons from external published accounts face all the limitations associated with company accounts. These limitations include the following:

● The comparative ratios that can be included in an interfirm comparison are limited to the information content of a set of published accounts. The inadequacies of compulsory disclosure restrict the amount of useful information and make it impossible to prepare every desirable ratio.

● There is insufficient standardisation in the preparation of published accounts. This is particularly relevant to ratio analysis because comparisons are meaningful only if the ratios are calculated from financial data that have been prepared on the same basis.

● The timeliness of any interfirm comparison is dependent on the timeliness of published accounts. As published accounts are not usually available immediately after a financial year-end, there will be a time lag in the publication of interfirm comparison information.

Although these drawbacks affect the reliability and completeness of survey results, such agencies have several advantages:

● The scope of an interfirm comparison is extremely wide as it can include an analysis of any firm that produces published accounts.

● The quality of ratio analysis is improved because survey organisations attempt to standardise the bases of every ratio in the survey. This increases the uniformity and comparability of the ratio information.

● The survey information is easy to access and available at a relatively low cost.

What organisations provide interfirm comparisons prepared from external published accounts?

Useful sources for interfirm ratio comparisons include *Company REFS*,[14] *Handbook of Market Leaders*,[15] Dun & Bradstreet's *Key Business Ratios: The Guide to British Business Performance*,[16] *'The Company Guide'*[17] and the online and CD-ROM computer services, including Datastream, Company Analysis, OneSource,[18] Fame and Extel Financial Workstation. In addition, the World Wide Web (WWW) provides an excellent source for corporate information.

25.8.2 Data collected direct from member companies of the private interfirm comparison scheme

These interfirm comparisons are prepared on a confidential basis and the analysed information is usually available only to the participating companies.

The advantages of private schemes are that interfirm comparisons consist of a comprehensive analysis of every firm in the scheme, and a higher degree of reliability can be attached to their findings than if external published accounts alone were used.

The drawbacks of private schemes are as follows:

● There are onerous requirements concerning the quality of information that companies contribute to private schemes. All information must comply with strict uniformity requirements.

● The cost of these schemes is relatively high.

The advantages of private schemes are that interfirm comparisons consist of a comprehensive analysis of every firm in the scheme, and a higher degree of reliability can be attached to their findings than if external published accounts alone were used.

What organisations provide private schemes?

Numerous organisations coordinate private interfirm comparison schemes for the majority of different trade groups and industrial sectors. One of the best known is the Centre for Interfirm Comparison, which was founded by the British Institute of Management.

25.9 Interfirm comparisons: J D Wetherspoon and the brewing industry

The necessity for comparing like with like has been stressed throughout this chapter. For true comparisons, we must ensure not only that the bases of ratios are identical, but that one company is compared only with companies in the same industrial sector. If it is compared with a company in a different industrial sector, the results might be interesting, but they might not be suitable for any decision-useful analysis.

25.9.1 Brewing industry results – FAME (Financial Analysis Made Easy)

FAME (November 1999) provides the following information on the top 10 public house chains in the UK by turnover. The 10 companies listed below are selected on the basis of an industry code (SIC Code 5540 – primary description 'bars'). The list illustrates the number of employees, turnover (£000) and profit margin. In addition, the lower quartile, median and upper quartile values of each of these measures are shown. We can see that J D Wetherspoon has a turnover of £188,515,000 in 1998 making it the fifth highest, although the top four groups are substantially larger. However, its profit margin, 10.7%, is broadly in line with the median of the top 10 companies.

Top 10 Public House Chains in the UK
Selected by SIC code and ranked by turnover

Company name	Trade description	Primary SIC 92 Code	Primary SIC 92 Code description	Latest number of employees	Turnover £000	Profit margin (%) last year
Allied Domecq (Holdings) Plc	The production, marketing and sale of spirits and wine, the operation of public houses and franchising.	5540	Bars	49,709	4,308,000	10.56
Punch Retail Limited	Retailing of beers and other drink and food through licensed and off-licensed premises.	5540	Bars	36,571	1,599,000	7.65

Company name	Trade description	Primary SIC 92 Code	Primary SIC 92 Code description	Latest number of employees	Turnover GBP	Profit margin (%) last year
Bass Taverns Limited	Leisure retailing through the ownership and management of public houses.	5540	Bars	45,755	1,294,000	10.12
The Greenalls Group Plc	The operation of public houses, hotels, restaurants and off-licences.	5540	Bars	14,153	983,432	16.09
J D Wetherspoon Plc	The develpment and management of public houses.	5540	Bars	5,538	188,315	10.7
John Marston's Taverners Limited	Licensed retailer.	5540	Bars	59	88,541	10.97
Mansfield Inns Limited	The principal activities of the company during the period have been food and drinks retailing.	5540	Bars	3,894	84,551	12.96
Punch Taverns Limited	The management and operation of public houses.	5540	Bars	119	66,076	8.84
Old English Inns Plc	The ownership and management of character freehouses.	5540	Bars	2,117	63,252	11.5
Pubmaster Limited	Management of public houses.	5540	Bars	165	58,430	9.73
	Lower quartile			653	70,695	9.8
	Median			4,716	138,528	10.6
	Upper quartile			30,967	1,216,358	11.4

Source: FAME November 1999

Of course, when using any published inter-company comparison data, it is essential to understand how the ratios are calculated. Each publication defines key terms, how ratios are computed and the methodologies used. The principal activities of the companies are similar, e.g. Bass Taverns Ltd: leisure retailing through the ownership and management of public houses; J D Wetherspoon: development and management of public houses. However, Allied Domecq is slightly wider, with 'the production, marketing and sale of spirits and wine, the operation of public houses and franchising'.

As stressed before, ratio definitions are not 'set in stone'. Different publications and inter-company comparison schemes will use different definitions of seemingly identical ratios. For instance, when using FAME's profit margin, we would need to ascertain what measure of profit is used (e.g. is other income and/or interest received included?).

25.9.2 Independent public houses and bars – OneSource

OneSource is a service available on the WWW. It provides plenty of useful industry information including a 'Peer Listing – 9 closest companies by sales anywhere in the UK in the same primary SIC code' and an analysis of selected ratios for 55402 – Independent public houses and bars. The extracts included in this section for J D Wetherspoon's are from their 1999 Accounts.

Peer Listing Extract – 9 closest companies by sales anywhere in the UK in the same primary SIC code:

Company	Sales ($£000$)	Pre-tax profit ($£000$)	Number of employees	Total assets ($£000$)
Greene King plc	292,600	46,700	6,536	550,000
Wolverhampton & Dudley Breweries (Trading) Ltd	285,710	9,187	10,369	174,848
Wolverhampton & Dudley Breweries Public Co Ltd	285,700	44,200	10,369	620,900
Greene King Brewing & Retailing Ltd	282,945	21,921	6,431	275,660
Wetherspoon, JD plc	269,699	48,002	8,314	453,884
Marston Thompson & Evershed Ltd	212,400	30,300	6,624	400,500
Mansfield Brewery plc	175,890	18,438	4,450	321,976
Yates Bros Wine Lodges plc	120,281	14,126	3,253	175,907
Yates Wine Lodges Ltd	95,746	8,011	2,752	22,704
Mansfield Inns Ltd	84,551	10,959	3,894	19,675

55402 – Independent public houses and bars extract

	Wetherspoon	25th percentile	50th percentile	75th percentile	90th percentile	Number of companies
Turnover ($£000$)	269,699	1,811	4,328	16,888	63,252	148
Pre-tax profit	48,002	0	187	1,957	8,011	154
Pre-tax profit margin	17.80	0.00	6.17	12.71	20.23	146

25.10 World Wide Web (WWW) pages for company information[19, 20]

The WWW offers enormous opportunities to access company information and selected accounting information. A number of sources include:

CORPORATE REPORTS	http://www.corpreports.co.uk/
Companies' annual reports on line	http://www.carol.co.uk
BIZ/ED	http://bized.ac.uk
COMPANY REFS (demo)	http://www.companyrefs.com
Hemmington Scott	http://www.hemscott.com
Financial Reporting Council	http://www.frc.org.uk
Accounting Standards Board	http://www.asb.org.uk
The Financial Reporting Review Panel	http://www.frrp.org.uk

Some good link pages (for other accounting sites) include:

ICAEW	http://www.icaew.co.uk
IASC	http://www.iasc.org.uk
British Accounting Association	http://www.shef.ac.uk/~baa
European Accounting Association	http://www.bham.ac.uk/EAA/

Accounting Firms :

Arthur Andersen	http://www.arthurandersen.com
Deloitte & Touche	http://www.deloitte.co.uk

Ernst & Young http://www.ernsty.co.uk

KPMG http://www.kpmg.com

Price Waterhouse Coopers http://www.pwcglobal.com

25.11 Non-financial ratios

As well as some of the more traditional financial statistics, each industry will have important operational statistics which provide some clues to the direction a company is moving and its performance in its area of expertise. For instance, BT provides information which charts the changes in technology (from the BT Annual Report and Accounts 1999):

BT Cellnet	1995	1996	1997	1998	1999
Digital GSM ('000)	34	353	1,125	2,303	4,163
Analogue ('000)	1,700	2,036	1,573	774	359
% growth over previous year	70.2	37.8	12.9	14.0	47.0

Optical fibre					
Kilometres in the network ('000)	1995	1996	1997	1998	1999
Fibre	2,782	3,043	3,302	3,591	4,058

25.12 Interpretation of problems when using consolidated financial statements

Certain limitations need to be recognised when analysing a consolidated balance sheet, making inter-company comparisons and forming a judgement on distributable profits based on the consolidated profit and loss account. These are as follows:

● The consolidated balance sheet aggregates the assets and liabilities of the parent company and its subsidiaries. The current and liquidity ratios that are extracted to indicate to creditors the security of their credit and the likelihood of the debt being settled will be valid only if all creditors have equal rights to claim against the aggregated assets. This may be the case if there are cross-guarantees from each company, but it is more likely that the creditors will need to seek payment from the individual group company to which it allowed the credit. One needs to be aware that the consolidated accounts are prepared for the shareholders of the parent company and that they may be irrelevant to the needs of creditors. This is not a criticism of consolidation, merely a recognition of the purpose for which they are relevant.

● Inter-company comparisons may be invalidated if groups follow different accounting policies in relation to the choice of consolidation process. For example, one group might organise a combination to fall within the criteria for treatment as a merger, without goodwill and using book values for the aggregation; another group might organise the combination to be treated as an acquisition, with goodwill arising on consolidation and fair values used for the aggregation.

● The consolidated profit and loss account does not give a true picture of the profits immediately available for distribution by the holding company to its shareholders. It shows the group profit that could become available for distribution if the holding company were to exercise its influence and control, and require all its subsidiary companies and associated companies to declare a dividend of 100% of their profits for the year. Legally, it is possible for the company to exercise its voting power to achieve the passing up to it of the subsidiary companies' profits – although commercially this is highly unlikely. The position of the associated companies is less clear: the holding company only has influence and does not have the voting power to guarantee that the profit disclosed in the consolidated profit and loss account is translated into dividends for the holding company shareholders.

Summary

Financial ratio analysis is integral to the assessment and improvement of company performance. Financial ratios help to direct attention to the areas of the business that need additional analysis. In particular, they provide some measure of the profitability and cash position of a company.

Financial ratios can be compared against preceding period's ratios, budgeted ratios for the current period, ratios of other companies in the same industry and the industry sector averages. This comparison is meaningful and decision-useful only when like is compared with like. Users of financial ratios must ensure that the composition of ratios is clearly defined and agreed.

Unfortunately, many of the problems that arise are not simply problems of different definitions for ratios, but far more fundamental. They result from the lack of uniformity and comparability of published financial statements.

Ratios are useful only if they are used properly. They are a starting point for further investigations and should be used in conjunction with other sources of information and other analytical techniques. Financial reports are only one of many sources of information available about an enterprise; others include international, national and industrial statistics and projections, trade association reports, market and consumer surveys, and reports prepared by professional analysts.

In Chapter 26 we consider some additional techniques that complement the pyramid approach to ratio analysis.

Review questions

1   Explain how the reader of an annual report prepared for a group might become aware if any subsidiary or associated company was experiencing:

   (a) solvency problems;

   (b) profitability problems.[21]

2   Using the segmental analysis from the Bass plc 1999 accounts on page 680, discuss the following:

   (a) Explain the value of the segmental analysis to an existing shareholder, a potential shareholder and a creditor of the company.

   (b) Which is the most profitable business segment?

   (c) What further segmental information would it be useful for a shareholder to receive in the Operating and Financial Review?

   (d) How subjective are the figures for turnover and profit ?

   (e) How useful do you consider the separate disclosure of business and geographic segment information?

3   'The problems of using ratio analysis on a set of published accounts exceed the benefits to be gained.' Discuss.

4 (a) Explain the uses and limitations of ratio analysis when used to interpret the published financial accounts of a company.

(b) State and express two ratios that can be used to analyse each of the following:
  (i) profitability;
  (ii) liquidity;
  (iii) management control.

(c) Explain briefly points which are important when using ratios to interpret accounts under each of the headings in (b) above.

5 (a) Describe the current requirements for the disclosure of segmental information in the annual report.

(b) Discuss the advantages and disadvantages to the users and preparers of annual reports of disclosing segmental data classified by (i) industry groupings, (ii) legal entities within the group structure.

(c) Discuss the importance of the disclosure of exceptional items to the users of the annual report in addition to the operating profit.

6 'Unregulated segmental reporting is commercially dangerous to companies making disclosures.'[22] Discuss.

Exercises

An outline solution is provided in the appendix at the end of the text for exercises marked with an asterisk (*).

Question 1

Saddam Ltd is considering the possibility of diversifying its operations and has identified three firms in the same industrial sector as potential take-over targets. The following information in respect of the companies has been extracted from their most recent financial statements.

	Ali Ltd	Baba Ltd	Camel Ltd
ROCE before tax %	22.1	23.7	25.0
Net profit %	12.0	12.5	3.75
Asset turnover ratio	1.45	1.16	3.73
Gross profit %	20.0	25.0	10.0
Sales/fixed assets	4.8	2.2	11.6
Sales/current assets	2.1	5.2	5.5
Current ratio	3.75	1.4	1.5
Acid test ratio	2.25	0.4	0.9
Average number of weeks debtors outstanding	5.6	6.0	4.8
Average number of weeks' stock held	12.0	19.2	4.0
Ordinary dividend %	10.0	15.0	30.0
Dividend cover	4.3	5.0	1.0

Required:

(a) Prepare a report for the directors of Saddam Ltd, assessing the performance of the three companies from the information provided and identifying areas which you consider require further investigation before a final decision is made.

(b) Discuss briefly why a firm's balance sheet is unlikely to show the true market value of the business.

* Question 2

The major shareholder/director of Esrever Ltd has obtained average data for the industry as a whole. He wishes to see what the forecast results and position of Esrever Ltd would be if in the ensuing year its performance were to coincide with the industry averages.

At 1 July 20X9, actual figures for Esrever Ltd included:

	£
Land and buildings (at written-down value)	132,000
Fixtures, fittings and equipment (at written-down value)	96,750
Stock	22,040
12% loan (repayable in 20X5)	50,000
Ordinary share capital (50p shares)	100,000

For the year ended 30 June 20X0 the following forecast information is available:

1 Depreciation of fixed assets (on reducing balance)

Land and buildings	2%
Fixtures, fittings and equipment	20%

2 Net current assets will be financed by a bank overdraft to the extent necessary.

3 At 30 June 20X0 total assets minus current liabilities will be £231,808.

4 Profit after tax for the year will be 23.32% of gross profit and 11.16% of total assets minus all external liabilities, both long-term and short-term.

5 Corporation tax will be an effective rate of 20% of profit before tax.

6 Cost of sales will be 68% of turnover (excluding VAT).

7 Closing stock will represent 61.9 days' average cost of sales (excluding VAT).

8 Any difference between total expenses and the aggregate of expenses ascertained from this given information will represent credit purchases and other credit expenses, in each case excluding VAT input tax.

9 A dividend of 2.5p per share will be proposed.

10 The collection period for the VAT-exclusive amount of trade debtors will be an average of 42.6 days of the annual turnover. All the company's supplies are subject to VAT output tax at 15%.

11 The payment period for the VAT-exclusive amount of trade creditors (purchases and other credit expenses) will be an average of 29.7 days. All these items are subject to (reclaimable) VAT input tax at 15%.

12 Creditors, other than trade creditors, will comprise corporation tax due, proposed dividends and VAT payable equal to one-quarter of the net amount due for the year.

13 Calculations are based on a year of 365 days.

Required:
Construct a forecast profit and loss account for Esrever Ltd for the year ended 30 June 20X0 and a forecast balance sheet at that date in as much detail as possible. (All calculations should be made to the nearest £1.)

* **Question 3**

Amalgamated Engineering plc makes specialised machinery for several industries. In recent years, the company has faced severe competition from overseas businesses, and its sales volume has hardly changed since 1983. The company has recently applied for an increase in its bank overdraft limit from £750,000 to £1,500,000. The bank manager has asked you, as the bank's credit analyst, to look at the company's application.

You have the following information:

(i) Balance sheets as at 31 December 20X5 and 20X6:

	20X5		20X6	
	£000	£000	£000	£000
Tangible fixed assets				
Freehold land and buildings, at cost		1,800		1,800
Plant and equipment, at net value		3,150		3,300
		4,950		5,100
Current assets				
Stock and work in progress	1,125		1,500	
Trade debtors	825		1,125	
Short-term investments	300		—	
	2,250		2,625	
Current liabilities				
Bank overdraft	225		675	
Trade creditors	300		375	
Taxation payable	375		300	
Dividends payable	225		225	
	1,125		1,575	
Net current assets		1,125		1,050
		6,075		6,150
Long-term liability				
8% Debentures, 20X9		1,500		1,500
		4,575		4,650
Capital and reserves				
Ordinary shares of £1 each		2,250		2,250
Share premium account		750		750
Profit and loss account		1,575		1,650
		4,575		4,650

(ii) Profit and loss accounts for the years ended 31 December 20X5 and 20X6:

	20X5		20X6	
	£000	£000	£000	£000
Turnover		6,300		6,600
Cost of sales: materials	1,500		1,575	
: labour	2,160		2,280	
: production				
: overheads	750		825	
		4,410		4,680
		1,890		1,920
Administrative expenses		1,020		1,125
Operating profit		870		795
Investment income		15		—
		885		795
Interest payable: debentures	120		120	
: bank overdraft	15		75	
		135		195
Profit before taxation		750		600
Taxation		375		300
Profit attributable to shareholders		375		300
Dividends		225		225
Retained earnings for year		150		75

You are also provided with the following information:

(iii) The general price level rose on average by 10% between 20X5 and 20X6. Average wages also rose by 10% during this period.

(iv) The debenture stock is secured by a fixed charge over the freehold land and buildings, which have recently been valued at £3,000,000. The bank overdraft is unsecured.

(v) Additions to plant and equipment in 20X6 amounted to £450,000: depreciation provided in that year was £300,000.

Required:
(a) Prepare a cash flow statement for the year ended 31 December 20X6.
(b) Calculate appropriate ratios to use as a basis for a report to the bank manager.
(c) Draft the outline of a report for the bank manager, highlighting key areas you feel should be the subject of further investigation. Mention any additional information you need, and where appropriate refer to the limitations of conventional historic cost accounts.

Question 4

Sally Gorden seeks your assistance to decide whether she should invest in Ruby plc or Sapphire plc. Both companies are quoted on the London Stock Exchange. Their shares were listed on 20 June 20X4 as Ruby 475 and Sapphire 480.

The performance of these two companies during the year ended 30 June 20X4 is summarised as follows:

	Ruby plc £000	Sapphire plc £000
Operating profit	588	445
Interest and similar charges	(144)	(60)
	444	385
Taxation	(164)	(145)
Profit after taxation	280	240
Interim dividend paid	(30)	(40)
Preference dividend proposed	(90)	—
Ordinary dividend proposed	(60)	(120)
Retained profit for the year	100	80

The companies have been financed on 30 June 20X4 as follows:

	Ruby plc £000	Sapphire plc £000
Ordinary shares of 50p each	1,000	1,500
15% Preference shares of £1 each	600	—
Share premium account	60	—
Profit and loss account balance	250	450
17% Debentures	800	—
12% Debentures	—	500
	2,710	2,450

On 1 October 20X3 Ruby plc issued 500,000 ordinary shares of 50p each at a premium of 20%. On 1 April 20X4 Sapphire plc made a 1 for 2 bonus issue. Apart from these, there has been no change in the issued capital of either company during the year.

Required:
(a) Calculate the earnings per share (EPS) of each company.
(b) Determine the price/earnings ratio (PE) of each company.
(c) Based on the PE ratio alone, which company's shares would you recommend to Sally?
(d) On the basis of appropriate accounting ratios (which should be calculated), identify three other matters Sally should take account of before she makes her choice.

Question 5

Innovations plc is preparing a segmental report to include with its financial accounts prepared for the year ended 30 June 20X9.

The relevant information given below is based on the consolidated figures of Innovations plc and its subsidiaries. Associate company information is not shown.

	20X9 £000	20X8 £000
Sales to customer outside the group by the Fruit Growing Division	12,150	13,500
Sales to customer outside the group by the UK companies	27,000	24,300
Sales not derived from Fruit Growing, Canning or Bureau activities	2,700	1,350
Sales made to customers outside the group by the Canning Division	17,550	13,095
Assets used by the US companies	32,400	24,300
Assets not able to be allocated to Fruit Growing, Canning or Bureau Activities	13,500	11,003
Assets used by Fruit Growing Division	33,750	32,400
Sales by the Canning Division to other group members	2,970	3,105
Assets used by the Bureau service	18,765	17,563
Assets used by the UK companies	43,200	40,500
Sales by the Fruit Growing Division to other group members	1,485	1,688
Sales not allocated to the UK, USA or other areas	2,700	1,350
Sales made by group to other areas of the world	1,350	1,215
Expenses not allocated to UK, USA or other areas	4,590	3,834
Sales to customers outside the group by US companies	6,750	5,130
Expenses not allocated to Fruit Growing, Canning or Bureau service	5,130	4,104
Sales by US companies to group members	2,160	1,215
Sales to customers outside the group for Bureau service	5,400	4,050
Sales made by UK companies to other group members	2,700	1,890
Assets used by Canning Division	40,500	33,750
Assets used by group in other areas	18,360	19,683
Assets not allocated to UK, USA or other areas	12,555	10,233
Segmental net operating profit by industry		
Fruit growing	2,565	3,375
Canning	4,725	3,600
Bureau	412	540
Consolidated segmental net operating profit	7,695	6,750
Segmental net operating profit by geographical area		
UK	5,130	4,590
USA	2,430	1,890
Other areas	270	405
Consolidated segmental net operating profit by geographical area	7,155	6,480

Required:
(a) Briefly state:
  (i) the case for segmental reporting;
  (ii) the case against segmental reporting.
(b) Draft an industry and geographical segmental report for inclusion in the annual report to give the maximum information to the shareholders.

(c) Segmental reports are designed to provide the reader with the means to identify trends more clearly. Discuss four items, illustrating with the Innovations plc information, where you consider that there is a need for further information to assist the reader to interpret the segmental data.

Question 6

Filios Products plc brews beers, owns and manages pubs and hotels, manufactures and supplies alcoholic and soft drinks, and is a supplier and operator of amusement machines and other leisure facilities.

The accounts for 1997 contain the following information:

Balance Sheet of Filios Products

	£m
Fixed assets at book value	1,663
Current assets	
Stocks and debtors	381
Bank balance	128
	509
Less: Creditors falling due within one year	193
Net current assets	316
Total assets less current liabilities	1,979
Less: 10% debentures	140
	1,839
Capital and reserves	
Share capital	800
Retained profit	1,039
	1,839

Profit and Loss Account of Filios Products

	£m	£m
Turnover		1,028
Less: Cost of sales	684	
Administration expenses	110	
Distribution costs	101	
Interest charged	14	909
Net profit		119

The following breakdown is provided of the company's results into three divisions and head office:

	Beer and pub operations	*Hotel business*	*Other drinks & leisure*	*Head office*
	£m	£m	£m	£m
Turnover	508	152	368	—
Cost of sales	316	81	287	—
Administration expenses	43	14	38	15

Distribution costs	64	12	25	—
Interest charged	10	—	—	4
Fixed assets at book value	890	332	364	77
Stocks and debtors	230	84	67	—
Bank balance	73	15	28	12
Creditors	66	40	56	31
10% debentures	100	—	—	40

The following information is obtained for competitor companies: Dean, which brews beer and manages pubs; and Clarke, which is in the hotel business:

	Dean	Clarke
	£m	£m
Turnover	600	150
Operating profit	80	60
Net assets	1,300	300

Required:

(a) Outline the nature of segmental reports and explain the reason for presenting such information in the published accounts.

(b) Prepare a segmental statement for Filios Products plc for 1997 complying, so far as the information permits, with the provisions of SSAP 25 entitled 'Segmental Reporting', so as to show for each segment and the business as a whole:
– turnover;
– profit;
– net assets.

(c) (i) Examine the relative performance of the operating divisions of Filios Products; and

(ii) Compare the performance of the operating divisions of Filios Products, where appropriate, with that of the competitor companies.

The examination and comparison should be based on the following accounting ratios:
– operating profit percentage;
– net asset turnover;
– return on net assets.

(The Chartered Institute of Bankers)

Question 7

The Housing Department of Chaldon District Council has invited tenders for re-roofing 80 houses on an estate. Chaldon Direct Services (CDS) is one of the Council's direct services organisations and it has submitted a tender for this contract, as have several contractors from the private sector.

The Council has been able to narrow the choice of contractor to the four tenderers who have submitted the lowest bids, as follows:

	£
Nutfield & Sons	398,600
Chaldon Direct Services	401,850
Tandridge Tilers Ltd	402,300
Redhill Roofing Contractors plc	406,500

The tender evaluation process requires that the three private tenderers be appraised on the basis of financial soundness and quality of work. These tenderers were required to provide their latest final accounts (year ended 31 March 20X4) for this appraisal; details are as follows:

	Nutfield & Sons	Tandridge Tilers Ltd	Redhill Roofing Contractors plc
Profit and loss account for year ended 31 March 20X4			
	£	£	£
Turnover	611,600	1,741,200	3,080,400
Direct costs	(410,000)	(1,190,600)	(1,734,800)
Other operating costs	(165,000)	(211,800)	(811,200)
Interest	—	(85,000)	(96,000)
Net profit before taxation	36,600	253,800	438,400
Balance sheet as at 31 March 20X4			
	£	£	£
Fixed assets (net book value)	55,400	1,542,400	2,906,800
Stocks and work in progress	26,700	149,000	449,200
Debtors	69,300	130,800	240,600
Bank	(11,000)	10,400	(6,200)
Creditors	(92,600)	(140,600)	(279,600)
Proposed dividend	—	(91,800)	(70,000)
Loan	—	(800,000)	(1,200,000)
	47,800	800,200	2,040,800
Capital	47,800	—	—
Ordinary shares @ £1 each	—	250,000	1,000,000
Reserves	—	550,200	1,040,800
	47,800	800,200	2,040,800

Nutfield and Sons employ a workforce of six operatives and have been used by the Council for four small maintenance contracts worth between £60,000 and £75,000 which they have completed to an appropriate standard. Tandridge Tilers Ltd have been employed by the Council on a contract for the replacement of flat roofs on block of flats, but there have been numerous complaints about the standard of the work. Redhill Roofing Contractors plc is a company which has not been employed by the Council in the past and, as much of its work has been carried out elsewhere, its quality of work is not known.

CDS has been suffering from the effects of increasing competition in recent years and achieved a return on capital employed of only 3.5% in the previous financial year. CDS's manager has successfully renegotiated more beneficial service level agreements with the Council's central support departments with effect from 1 April 20X4. CDS has also reviewed its fixed asset base which has resulted in the disposal of a depot which was surplus to requirements and in the rationalisation of vehicles and plant. The consequence of this is that CDS's average capital employed for 20X4/X5 is likely to be some 15% lower than in 20X3/X4.

A further analysis of the tender bids is provided below:

	Nutfield & Sons £	Chaldon Direct Services £	Tandridge Tilers Ltd £	Redhill Roofing Contractors plc £
Labour	234,000	251,400	303,600	230,400
Materials	140,000	100,000	80,000	140,000
Overheads (including profit)	24,600	50,450	18,700	36,100

The Council's Client Services Committee can reject tenders on financial and/or quality grounds. However, each tender has to be appraised on these criteria and reasons for acceptance or rejection must be justified in the appraisal process.

Required:
In your capacity as accountant responsible for reporting to the Client Services Committee, draft a report to the Committee evaluating the tender bids and recommending to whom the contract should be awarded.

(CIPFA)

Question 8

Chelsea plc has embarked on a programme of growth through acquisitions and has identified Kensington Ltd and Wimbledon Ltd as companies in the same industrial sector, as potential targets. Using recent financial statements of both Kensington and Wimbledon and further information obtained from a trade association, Chelsea plc has managed to build up the following comparability table:

	Kensington	Wimbledon	Industrial average
Profitability ratios			
ROCE before tax %	22	28	20
Return on Equity %	18	22	15
Net profit margin %	11	5	7
Gross profit ratio %	25	12	20
Activity ratios			
Total assets turnover = times	1.5	4.0	2.5
Fixed asset turnover = times	2.3	12.0	5.1
Debtor collection period in weeks	8.0	5.1	6.5
Stockholding period in weeks	21.0	4.0	13.0
Liquidity ratios			
Current ratio	1.8	1.7	2.8
Acid test	0.5	0.9	1.3
Debt/Equity ratio %	80.0	20.0	65.0

Required:
(a) Prepare a performance report for the two companies for consideration by the directors of Chelsea plc indicating which of the two companies you consider to be a better acquisition.
(b) Indicate what further information is needed before a final decision can be made.

Question 9

'The consolidation of financial statements hides rather than provides information.'

Required:
Discuss the above statement.

Question 10

Required:
Analyse the 1999 Accounts of J D Wetherspoon below:

JD Wetherspoon consolidated profit and loss account for the year ended 1 August 1999

	1999			*1998*		
	Before exceptional items	*exceptional items*	*After exceptional items*	*Before exceptional items*	*exceptional items*	*After exceptional items*
	£000	*£000*	*£000*	*£000*	*£000*	*£000*
Turnover from continuing operations	269,699		269,699	188,515		188,515
Cost of sales	–219,035	0	–219,035	–149,317	0	–149,317
Gross profit	50,664	0	50,664	39,198	0	39,198
Administrative expenses	–14,438	–837	–15,275	–10,831	0	–10,831
Operating profit	36,226	–837	35,389	28,367	0	28,367
Profit on disposal of tangible fixed assets	0	22,625	22,625	0	14,968	14,968
Net interest payable	–10,012	0	–10,012	–8,202	0	–8,202
Profit on ordinary activities before tax	26,214	21,788	48,002	20,165	14,968	35,133
Tax on profit on ordinary activities	–751	0	–751	–726	0	–726
Profit on ordinary activities after tax	25,463	21,788	47,251	19,439	14,968	34,407
Dividends	–4,809	0	–4,809	–4,321	0	–4,321
Retained profit for the year	20,654	21,788	42,442	15,118	14,968	30,086

JD Weatherspoon balance sheet as at 1 August 1999

	1999	*1998*
	£000	*£000*
Fixed assets		
Tangible assets	370,148	334,695
	370,148	334,695
Current assets		
Investments	253	286
Stock	3,845	3,195
Debtors due within 1 year	11,472	11,385
Debtors due after more than 1 year	5,588	0
Cash	62,578	12,750
	83,736	27,616

	1999 £000	1998 £000
Creditors due within 1 year	−67,296	−62,564
Net current assets/(liabilities)	16,440	−34,948
Total assets less current liabilities	386,588	299,747
Creditors due after 1 year	−180,592	−140,555
Total net assets	205,996	159,192
Capital and reserves		
Called-up share capital	3,962	3,931
Share premium account	65,463	62,000
Revaluation reserve	25,166	22,843
Profit and loss account	111,405	70,418
Equity shareholders' funds	205,996	159,192

References

1 I. Griffiths, *Creative Accounting*, Sidgwick & Jackson, 1986.

2 M. Stead, *How to Use Company Accounts for Successful Investment Decisions*, FT Pitman Publishing, 1995, pp. 134–136.

3 'Brought to account: Richard Pennycook, Finance Director, J D Wetherspoon', *Accountancy*, July 1996, p. 58.

4 N. Cope, 'Bitter battles in the beer business', *Accountancy*, May 1993, p. 32.

5 SSAP 25, *Segmental Reporting*, ASC, June 1990.

6 S. Hussain, 'What do segmental definitions tell us?', *Accountancy*, June 1996, p. 103.

7 C. Emmanuel and N. Garrod, 'Segmental reporting in the UK – how does SSAP 25 stand up to international comparison?', *European Accounting Review*, Vol. 3, no. 3, 1994, pp. 547–562.

8 M. Davies, R. Patterson and A. Wilson, *UK GAAP*, Ernst & Young, (5th edition), 1997, p. 1079.

9 IAS 14 (revised), *Reporting Financial Information by Segment*, IASC, July 1997.

10 IAS 14, *Reporting Financial Information by Segment*, IASC, 1981.

11 ED 45, *Segmental Reporting*, ASC, November 1988.

12 C.R. Emmanuel and M. Mehafdi, *Transfer Pricing*, The Chartered Institute of Management Accountants and Academic Press, London, 1994.

13 D. Chopping, R. Carroll and R. Skerratt, *Applying GAAP*, ICAEW, 1999/2000, p. 100.

14 *Company REFS – Really Essential Statistics*: Tables Volume devised by Jim Slater, Hemmington Scott Publication.

15 *Handbook of Market Leaders*, Extel Financial Ltd.

16 *Key Business Ratios: The Guide to British Business Performance*, Dun & Bradstreet Ltd.

17 *The Company Guide*, Hemmington Scott Publishing.

18 http://www.onesource.co.uk.

19 L. Meall and T. Reardon, 'Surfing for Beginners', *Accountancy*, January 1998, pp. 63–67.

20 A.M. Lymer, A. Sangster and A.A. Baldwin, 'Using the World Wide Web in accounting research: a huge step forward or a new constraint?', *British Accounting Review*, 29, pp. 395–407.

21 P. Anderson, 'Are you ready for ratio analysis?', *Accountancy*, September 1996, p. 92.

22 G. J. Kelly, 'Unregulated segment reporting: Australian evidence', *British Accounting Review*, 26(3), 1994, p. 217.

CHAPTER 26

Trend analysis and multivariate analysis

26.1 Introduction

In the preceding chapter we introduced ratio analysis as a means for interpreting financial statements. In this chapter we present further techniques that can be used in conjunction with ratio analysis. The main similarity between these techniques is their purpose: each technique acts as a focus for more detailed investigation. By various means, they can be applied to a set of financial statements to identify areas of interest and concern. If the initial investigation throws up unexpected and unexplained results, the root cause should then be ascertained by more rigorous investigation.

In this chapter we consider the following:

● Horizontal analysis between two periods
● Trend analysis over a series of periods
● Historical summaries
● Vertical analysis – common size statements
● Multivariate analysis – Z-scores
● A-scores
● Balanced scorecards
● Valuing shares of an unquoted company – quantitative process
● Valuing shares of an unquoted company – qualitative process
● Shareholder value analysis
● Financial reporting and risk
● Financial instruments

We will illustrate the techniques using the accounts of J D Wetherspoon plc, which were used in the preceding chapter to demonstrate ratio analysis.

26.2 Horizontal analysis between two periods

The mechanics of horizontal analysis between two periods are very simple. The percentage change (positive or negative) for each item in the financial statements between two periods needs to be calculated. Usually, the percentage changes are calculated for all balance sheet items and profit and loss items over two successive years.

Although the calculations are straightforward, the skill rests with their interpretation. What do the percentages mean? Which changes are significant and warrant detailed analysis? Which changes require an explanation so that we can determine whether or not we need to implement rectifying measures?

The percentage changes between J D Wetherspoon plc's 1996 and 1997 consolidated profit and loss accounts are calculated below.

	% change	1997 £000	1996 £000
Turnover from continuing operations	38.8%	139,444	100,480
Cost of sales	40.8%	(106,972)	(76,001)
Gross profit	32.7%	32,472	24,479
Administrative expenses	27.5%	(9,533)	(7,476)
Operating profit	34.9%	22,939	17,003
Net interest payable	37.8%	(5,373)	(3,898)
Profit on ordinary activities before tax	34.0%	17,566	13,105
Tax on profit on ordinary activities	36.5%	(770)	(564)
Profit on ordinary activities after tax	33.9%	16,796	12,541
Dividends	14.0%	(3,894)	(3,417)
Retained profit for the year	41.4%	12,902	9,124

The profile of the profit and loss accounts for both years is very similar. The turnover has increased by 38.8%, but most of the other items have also increased by around 30–40%. The obvious exception to this is the low growth in dividends (14%), which is consistent with the company's expansion plans, and the subsequent increase in retained profit (41.4%) (see also Question 8).

26.3 Trend analysis over a series of periods

Trend analysis is used to analyse company accounts over a series of years. It is usually applied to five-year or ten-year summaries supplied in company accounts. The main advantage of this technique is that it gives a very quick rough guide to specific trends in individual items in the financial statements. The main disadvantage is that the figures may ignore the effects of inflation and not represent company performance in real terms. An easy way to take some account of inflation is to use the retail price index (RPI) as a proxy for inflation and adjust calculated trends for the trend in RPI.

The two forms of trend analysis considered here are percentage changes and index numbers.

Percentage changes illustrate the change each year and show the exact trend in percentage changes. For instance, Jacklin Cripes plc records the following profits in the five-year record:

	20X1 £000	20X2 £000	20X3 £000	20X4 £000	20X5 £000
Net profit	150	195	249	309	375
% change		+30.0%	+27.7%	+24.1%	+21.4%

The percentage changes show that the net profit for Jacklin Cripes plc has increased every year between 20X1 and 20X5. However, the rate of increase in net profit has decreased. The increase is 30% in 20X2, but only 21.4% in 20X5.

Index numbers give a good indication of how the results over a series of years compare with each other, and the general direction of the trend. To calculate index numbers, year 1 in the series is set to 100 and the other years are scaled down to correspond to the index number. To demonstrate this, consider Jacklin Cripes plc:

	20X1	20X2	20X3	20X4	20X5
	£000	£000	£000	£000	£000
Net profit	150	195	249	309	375
Index number	100	130	166	206	250

where index (20X2) = 195/150 × 100 = 130
where index (20X3) = 249/150 × 100 = 166
where index (20X4) = 309/150 × 100 = 206
where index (20X5) = 375/150 × 100 = 250

The index numbers show that net profit increases every year over this period.

Now consider the trends in the five-year record for J D Wetherspoon plc (Figure 26.1). Both the percentage changes and the index numbers show that J D Wetherspoon's turnover, operating profit and retained profit have increased significantly each year from 1993 to 1997. See Question 8 for J D Wetherspoon's five year record from 1995 to 1999.

26.4 Historical summaries

The Companies Act 1985 does not require a company to include a historical summary in its annual report. However, following a comment by the chairman of the Stock Exchange, the practice has arisen for companies to include a five-year historical summary.

Figure 26.1   J D Wetherspoon's Five Year Record.

	1993	1994	1995	1996	1997
	£000	£000	£000	£000	£000
Turnover	30,800	46,600	68,536	100,480	139,444
Operating profit	6,115	8,787	12,232	17,003	22,939
Retained profit	2,176	3,680	6,031	9,124	12,902
a) *Percentage changes*	*1993*	*1994*	*1995*	*1996*	*1997*
Turnover		+51.3%	+47.1%	+46.6%	+38.8%
Operating profit		+43.7%	+39.2%	+39.0%	+34.9%
Retained profit		+69.1%	+63.9%	+51.3%	+41.4%
b) *Index number*	*1993*	*1994*	*1995*	*1996*	*1997*
Turnover	100	151	222	326	452
Operating profit	100	144	200	278	375
Retained profit	100	169	277	419	593

There is no accounting standard relating to such summaries, but there may well be circumstances where the reported figures need to be adjusted to make the series comparable: for example, a change in accounting policy; a change in the composition of the group; bonus issues, rights issues and share splits. In the ASC handbook *Accounting for the Effects of Changing Prices*, it was recommended that companies which publish historical summaries should restate certain figures such as turnover, earnings and dividends in units of current purchasing power.[1]

Historical summaries should assist shareholders to answer such questions as: Is growth being achieved in excess of the rate of inflation? Is the growth in all segments of the business? What is the dividend cover over the past five years? Is the change in turnover and profitability constant or fluctuating?

Given the usefulness of the historical summaries, this is an area that requires a standard approach of the kind provided by SSAP 25 for segmental reporting. Without such a standard, the information may be unavailable or partially presented, e.g. it may disclose profit and loss data, but no balance sheet data to assess the rate of change in assets and rates of return.

26.5 Vertical analysis – common size statements

Vertical analysis concentrates solely on one year's financial statements, rather than comparing a number of years. Common size statements express all items in each financial statement as a percentage of a selected figure. For instance, all items in the profit and loss account can be expressed in terms of turnover; and all items in the balance sheet can be expressed in terms of capital employed or total shareholders' funds.

The advantages of vertical analysis are as follows:

● Common size statements allow comparisons between companies of different sizes. However, like ratio analysis, particular care should be taken to ensure the comparison of like companies with like.

● The balance sheet will identify changes in financial structure relative to the total capital employed or total shareholders' funds. The profit and loss account will identify changes in expenses relative to turnover.

● As all figures are expressed as annual percentages, this will redress many of the distortions of inflation. However, different financial statement items might be affected by different specific rates of inflation.

The disadvantages are as follows:

● Accounting policies might distort changes in financial structure and expenditure.

● Common size statements eliminate the concept of different-sized companies so that comparison is possible. However, the actual size of a company determines the specific risks to which the company is subject.

To illustrate common size statements, the 1997 balance sheet and profit and loss accounts for J D Wetherspoon plc are analysed below. The balance sheet expresses all items in terms of shareholders' funds, while the profit and loss account expresses all items in terms of turnover.

Wetherspoon (JD)
Consolidated profit and loss account for the year ended 31 July 1997

	1997 £000	Calculations	%
Turnover from continuing operations	139,444	139,444/139,444	100
Cost of sales	(106,972)	(106,972)/139,444	(76.7)
Gross profit	32,472	32,472/139,444	23.3
Administrative expenses	(9,533)	(9,533)/139,444	(6.8)
Operating profit	22,939	22,939/139,444	16.5
Net interest payable	(5,373)	(5,373)/139,444	(3.9)
Profit on ordinary activities before tax	17,566	17,566/139,444	12.6
Tax on profit on ordinary activities	(770)	(770)/139,444	(0.6)
Profit on ordinary activities after tax	16,796	16,796/139,444	12.0
Dividends	(3,894)	(3,894)/139,444	(2.8)
Retained profit for the year	12,902	12,902/139,444	9.2

Balance sheet at 31 July 1997

	1997 £000	Calculations	%
Fixed assets			
Tangible assets	244,513	244,513/124,663	196.1
	244,513	244,513/124,663	196.1
Current assets			
Stocks	2,215	2,215/124,663	1.8
Debtors	3,026	3,026/124,663	2.4
Cash	7,196	7,196/124,663	5.8
	12,437	12,437/124,663	10.0
Creditors due within one year	(34,998)	(34,998)/124,663	(28.1)
Net current liabilities	(22,561)	(22,561)/124,663	(18.1)
Total assets less current liabilities	221,952	221,952/124,663	(178.0)
Creditors due after one year	(97,289)	(97,289)/124,663	(78.0)
	124,663	124,663/124,663	100
Capital and reserves			
Called up share capital	3,898	3,898/124,663	3.1
Share premium account	59,676	59,676/124,663	47.9
Revaluation reserve	22,023	22,023/124,663	17.7
Profit and loss account	39,066	39,066/124,663	31.3
Equity shareholders' funds	124,663	124,663/124,663	100

Another strength of common size statements is to identify their trends over time. In effect, this applies horizontal analysis to vertical analysis, analysing the changes in financial structure and cost structure over time. To examine the technique, we compare the 1996 and 1997 common size statements for J D Wetherspoon's profit and loss account.

	1997	1996
	%	%
Turnover from continuing operations	100	100
Cost of sales	(76.7)	(75.6)
Gross profit	23.3	24.4
Administrative expenses	(6.8)	(7.4)
Operating profit	16.5	16.9
Net interest payable	(3.9)	(3.9)
Profit on ordinary activities before tax	12.6	13.0
Tax on profit on ordinary activities	(0.6)	(0.5)
Profit on ordinary activities after tax	12.0	12.5
Dividends	(2.8)	(3.4)
Retained profit for the year	9.2	9.1

What are the main questions which arise from these two common size statements? Some of the issues were identified also in the previous chapter using other analytical methods. All the ratios are expressed as a proportion of sales:

● The gross profit and operating profit in 1997 have decreased. However, the administrative expenses have improved from 7.4% to 6.8%.

● The dividend distribution has decreased.

● The retained profit is very similar for 1996 and 1997.

26.6 Multivariate analysis – Z-scores

In the preceding chapter we extolled the virtues of ratio analysis for the interpretation of financial statements. However, ratio analysis is an excellent indicator only when applied properly. Unfortunately, a number of limitations impede its proper application. How do we know which ratios to select for the analysis of company accounts? Which ratios can be combined to produce an informative end-result? How should individual ratios be ranked to give the user an overall picture of company performance? How reliable are all the ratios – can users place more reliance on some ratios than others?

Z-score analysis can be employed to overcome some of the limitations of traditional ratio analysis. It evaluates corporate stability and, more importantly, predicts potential instances of corporate failure. All the forecasts and predictions are based on publicly available financial statements.[2] The aim is to identify potential failures so that 'the appropriate action to reverse the process [of failure] can be taken before it is too late'.[3]

26.6.1 What are Z-scores?

Inman describes what Z-scores are designed for:

> Z-scores attempt to replace various independent and often unreliable and misleading historical ratios and subjective rule-of-thumb tests with scientifically analysed ratios which can reliably predict future events by identifying bench marks above which 'all's well' and below which there is imminent danger.[4]

Z-scores provide a single-value score to describe the combination of a number of key characteristics of a company. Some of the most important predictive ratios are weighted according to perceived importance and then summed to give the single Z-score. This is then evaluated against the identified benchmark.

The two best known Z-scores are: Altman's Z-score and Taffler's Z-score.

Altman's Z-score

The original Z-score equation was devised by Professor Altman in 1968 and developed further in 1977.[5] The original equation is:

$$Z = 0.012X_1 + 0.014X_2 + 0.033X_3 + 0.006X_4 + 0.999X_5$$

where

X_1 = Working capital/Total assets
X_2 = Retained earnings/Total assets
X_3 = Earnings before interest and tax/Total assets
X_4 = Market capitalisation/Book value of debt
X_5 = Sales/Total assets

Altman identified two benchmarks. Companies scoring over 3.0 are unlikely to fail and should be considered safe, while companies scoring under 1.8 are very likely to fail. The value of 3.0 has since been revised down to 2.7.[6] Z-scores between 2.7 and 1.8 fall into the grey area. The 1968 work is claimed to be able to distinguish between successes and failures up to two or three years before the event. The 1977 work claims an improved prediction period of up to five years before the event.

Taffler's Z-score

The exact definition of Taffler's Z-score[7,8] is unpublished, but the following components form the equation:

$$Z = c_0 + c_1X_1 + c_2X_2 + c_3X_3 + c_4X_4$$

where

X_1 = Profit before tax/Current assets (53%)
X_2 = Current assets/Current liabilities (13%)
X_3 = Current liabilities/Total assets (18%)
X_4 = No credit interval = Length of time which the company can continue to finance its operations using its own assets with no revenue inflow (16%)

c_0 to c_4 are the coefficients, and the percentages in brackets represent the ratios' contributions to the power of the model.

The benchmark used to detect success or failure is 0.2.[9] Companies scoring above 0.2 are unlikely to fail, while companies scoring less than 0.2 demonstrate the same symptoms as companies that have failed in the past.

PAS-score: performance analysis score

Taffler adapted the Z-score technique to develop the PAS-score. The PAS-score evaluates company performance relative to other companies in the industry and incorporates changes in the economy.

The PAS-score ranks all company Z-scores in percentile terms, measuring relative performance on a scale of 0 to 100. A PAS-score of X means that $100 - X\%$ of the companies have scored higher Z-scores. So, a PAS-score of 80 means that only 20% of the companies in the comparison have achieved higher Z-scores.

The PAS-score details the relative performance trend of a company over time. Any downward trends should be investigated immediately and the management should take appropriate action. For other danger signals see Holmes and Dunham.[10]

26.7 A-scores

A-scores concentrate on non-financial signs of failure.[11] This method sets out to quantify different judgmental factors. The whole basis of the analysis is that financial difficulties are the direct result of management defects and errors which have existed in the company for many years.

A-scores assume that many company failures can be explained by similar factors. Company failure can be broken down into a three-stage sequence of events:

1 **Defects**. Specific defects exist in company top management. Typically, these defects centre on management structure; decision-making and ability; accounting systems; and failure to respond to change.

2 **Mistakes**. Management will make mistakes that can be attributed to the company defects. The three mistakes that lead to company failure are very high leverage; overtrading; and the failure of the company's main project.

3 **Symptoms**. Finally, symptoms of failure will start to arise. These are directly attributable to preceding management mistakes. Typical symptoms are financial signs (e.g. poor ratios, poor Z-scores); creative accounting (management might attempt to 'disguise' signs of failure in the accounts); non-financial signs (e.g. investment decisions delayed; market share drops); and terminal signs (when the financial collapse of the company is imminent).

To calculate a company A-score, different scores are allocated to each defect, mistake and symptom according to their importance. Then this score is compared with the benchmark values. If companies achieve an overall score of over 25, or a defect score of over 10, or a mistakes score of over 15, then the company is demonstrating typical signs leading up to failure. Generally, companies not at risk will score below 18, and companies which are at risk will score well over 25.

Consider our A-score assessment of DNB Computer Systems plc:

Defects:	Weak finance director	2	
	Poor management depth	1	
	No cash flow plans	3	
	No costing system	3	
			9
Mistakes:	Main project failure	15	
			15
Symptoms:	Financial signs	4	
			4
	Total A-score:		28

According to our benchmarks, DNB Computer Systems plc is at risk of failure because the mistakes score is 15 and the overall A-score is 28. Therefore, there is some cause for concern. Why did the main project fail? To which of the symptoms was it due?

26.8 Balanced scorecards

Move away from a single performance measure

We saw in Chapter 23 that the ASB wished to move away from the EPS figure as *the* single performance measure. It did this through the FRS 3 *Reporting Financial Performance* disclosures and the *Operating and Financial Review* (OFR) document. Similarly, business is moving away from relying simply on traditional financial measures, such as the return on capital and earnings per share. These can encourage companies to achieve short-term financial results, while damaging employee morale and customer service to the extent of causing long-term damage to the organisation's profitability.[12]

Move towards different perspectives

Four perspectives are seen to affect the long-term economic value of a company.

1 **Financial perspective.** This includes consideration of factors such as the return on capital employed, cash flows, project profitability and the setting of realistic targets. For example, was the company aiming to maximise its return on capital employed or maintain a steady rate of improvement?

2 **Customer perspective.** This requires the company to set specific goals, besides price, that are important to the customer, e.g. quality, performance and service. For example, was the customer interested in the lowest price or in obtaining a regular, guaranteed supply at a reasonable price?

3 **Internal business perspective.** This includes consideration of factors such as tender success rate. For example, was the presentation and preparation effective?

4 **Innovation and learning perspective.** This includes the generation of new business from innovation, and staff attitudes and morale.

The balanced scorecard approach requires a company to focus both on hard financial targets and on important soft or non-financial factors that affect long-term profitability, and to understand the links between the different perspectives. For example, reducing staff numbers might produce an immediate improvement in the short-term financial performance as measured by ROCE and EPS, but could so adversely affect customer satisfaction and staff morale that it has a long-term adverse effect.

According to Kaplan and Norton,[13] the balanced scorecard allows managers to look at the business from four important perspectives. It provides answers to four basic questions:

● How do customers see us? (customer perspective)

● What must we excel at? (internal perspective)

● Can we continue to improve and create value? (innovation and learning perspective)

● How do we look to shareholders? (financial perspective).

There is nothing particularly new in the perspectives. Customers and staff are invariably referred to by the chairman in the annual report as important contributors to the company's success. The difference that the balanced scorecard approach makes is to raise awareness that the perspectives are interdependent and that management performance can be appraised on more than just the bottom line. Of course, the bottom line needs to be healthy for a company to be successful, but it does not exist in isolation; other important factors affect long-term health.

26.9 Valuing shares of an unquoted company – quantitative process

The valuation of shares brings together a number of different financial accounting procedures that we have covered in previous chapters. The assumptions may be highly subjective, but there is a standard approach. This involves the following:

● Estimate the maintainable income flow based on earnings defined in accordance with the IIMR Guidelines, as described in Chapter 11. Normally the profits of the past five years are used, adjusted for any known or expected future changes.

● Estimate an appropriate dividend yield, as described in Chapter 25, if valuing a minority holding; or an appropriate earnings yield if valuing a majority holding.

● Make a decision on any adjustment to the required yields. For example, the shares in the unquoted company might not be as marketable as those in the comparative quoted companies and the required yield would therefore be increased to reflect this lack of marketability; or the balance sheet might not be as strong with lower current/acid test ratios or higher gearing, which would also lead to an increase in the required yield.

● Calculate the economic capital value, as described in Chapter 3, by applying the required yield to the income flow.

● Compare the resulting value with the net realisable value (NRV), as described in Chapter 4, when deciding what action to take based on the economic value.

EXAMPLE ● The Doughnut Ltd is an unlisted company engaged in the baking of doughnuts. The balance sheet of The Doughnut Ltd as at 31 December 20X4 showed:

	£000	£000
Freehold land		100
Fixed assets at cost	240	
Accumulated depreciation	40	
		200
Current assets	80	
Current liabilities	(60)	
		20
		320
Share capital in £1 shares		300
Profit and loss account		20
		320
Estimated net realisable values:		
Freehold land		310
Fixed assets		160
Current assets		70

It achieved the following profit after tax (adjusted to reflect maintainable earnings) for the past five years ended 31 December:

	20X0	20X1	20X2	20X3	20X4
Maintainable earnings (£000)	36	40	46	38	42
Dividend payout history: Dividends	10%	10%	12%	12%	12%

Current yields for comparative quoted companies as at 31 December 20X4:

	Earnings yield %	Dividend yield %
Ace Bakers plc	14	8
Busi-Bake plc	10	8
Hard-to-beat plc	13	8

You are required to value a holding of 250,000 shares for a shareholder, Mr Quick, who makes a practice of buying shares for sale within three years.

Now, the 250,000 shares represent an 83% holding. This is a majority holding and the steps to value it are as follows:

1 Calculate average maintainable earnings (in £000):

$$\frac{36,000 + 40,000 + 46,000 + 38,000 + 42,000}{5} = £40,000$$

2 Estimate an appropriate earnings yield:

$$\frac{14\% + 10\% + 13\%}{3} = 12.3\%$$

3 Adjust the rate for lack of marketability by, say, 3% and for the lower current ratio by, say, 2%. Both these adjustments are subjective and would be a matter of negotiation between the parties.

		%
Require yield	=	12.3
Lack of marketability weighting	=	3
Balance sheet weakness	=	2
Required earnings yield		17.3

The adjustments depend on the actual circumstances. For instance, if Mr Quick were intending to hold the shares as a long-term investment, there might be no need to increase the required return for lack of marketability.

4 Calculate share value:

$$(£40,000 \times 100/17.3)/300,000 = 77p$$

5 Compare with the net realisable values on the basis that the company were to be liquidated:

		£
Net realisable values = 70,000 + 160,000 + 310,000	=	540,000
Less: Current liabilities		60,000
		480,000
Net asset value per share = £480,000/300,000	=	£1.60

The comparison indicates that, on the information we have been given, Mr Quick should acquire the shares and dispose of the assets and liquidate the company to make an immediate capital gain of 83p per share.

Let us extend our illustration by assuming that it is intended to replace the fixed assets at a cost of £20,000 per year out of retained earnings, whether Mr Quick or Mr Longfellow acquires the shares. Advise Mr Small, who has £10,000 to invest, how many shares he would be able to acquire in The Doughnut Ltd.

There are two significant changes: the cash available for distribution as dividends will be reduced by £20,000 per year, which is used to replace fixed assets; and Mr Small is acquiring only a minority holding, which means that the appropriate valuation method is the **dividend yield** rather than the **earnings yield**.

The share value will be calculated as follows:

1 Estimate income flow:

	£
Maintainable earnings	40,000
Less: Fixed asset investment	20,000
Cash available for distribution	20,000

Note that we are here calculating not distributable profits, but the available cash flow.

2 Required dividend yield:

	%
Average dividend yield	8
Lack of negotiability, say	2
Financial risk, say	1.5
	11.5

3 Share value:

$$\frac{£20,000}{300,000} \times \frac{100}{11.5} = 58p$$

At this price it would be possible for Mr Small to acquire (£10,000/58p) = 17,241 shares.

26.10 Valuing shares of an unquoted company – qualitative process

In the section above we illustrated how to value shares using the capitalisation of earnings and capitalisation of dividends methods. However, share valuation is an extremely subjective exercise: for example, when Rhône-Poulenc Rorer made a bid for Fisons in 1995 the share price moved from 193p per share to 265p, with the analysts expecting the final bid price to be between 270p and 300p. The values we have calculated for The Doughnut Ltd shares could therefore be subject to material revision in the light of other relevant factors.

A company's future cash flows may be affected by a number of factors. These may occur as a result of action within the company (e.g. management change, revenue investment) or as a result of external events (e.g. change in the rate of inflation, change in competitive pressures).

● **Management change** often heralds a significant change in a company's share price. For example, the new chief executive of Fisons made significant changes to Fisons in 1994/5 by reducing the business to its valuable core, which then saw the share price move from 103p to 193p.

● **Revenue investment** refers to discretionary revenue expenditure, such as charges to the profit and loss account for research and development, training, advertising and major maintenance and refurbishment. The ASB in its exposure draft for FRS 3 *Reporting Financial Performance* had proposed to disclose this information in the profit and loss account. The proposal did not find support at the exposure stage and it is suggested that such information should instead be disclosed in the operating and financial review, which was discussed in Chapter 8.

● **Changes in the rate of inflation** can affect the required yield. If, for example, it is expected that inflation will fall, this might mean that past percentage yields will be higher than the percentage yield that is likely to be available in the future.

● **Change in competitive pressures** can affect future sales. For example, increased foreign competition could mean that past maintainable earnings are not achievable in the future and the historic average level might need to be reduced.

These are a few of the internal and external factors that can affect the valuation of a share. The factors that are relevant to a particular company may be industry-wide (e.g. change in rate of inflation), sector-wide (e.g. change in competitive pressure) or company-specific (e.g. loss of key managers or employees). They may not be immediately apparent from an appraisal of financial statements alone: for example, the application and success of the balanced scorecard approach might not be immediately apparent without discussions with all of the stakeholders. The valuer will need to carry out detailed enquiries in order both to identify which factors are relevant and to evaluate their impact on the share price.

If the company supports the acquisition of the shares, the valuer will be able to gain access to relevant internal information. For example, details of research and development expenditure may be available analysed by type of technology involved, by product line, by project and by location, and distinguishing internal from externally acquired R&D.

If the acquisition is being considered without the company's knowledge or support, the valuer will rely more heavily on information gained from public sources: for example, statutory disclosures such as the annual accounts, voluntary disclosures such as the OFR, and industry information such as trade journals. Information on areas such as R&D may be provided in the OFR, but probably in an aggregated form, constrained by management concerns about use by potential competitors.[14]

26.11 Shareholder value analysis (SVA)

Rappaport[15] identified a number of reasons why there has been a growing interest in shareholder value analysis:

● a belief that take-overs are based on undervalued assets;

● a belief that accounting measures (e.g. EPS) are unrelated to share value;

● wider reporting of returns to shareholders;

● wider adoption and endorsement;

● the linkage of executive rewards to shareholders' returns.

Copeland *et al.*[16] argued that 'managers at both business-unit and corporate levels need to broaden their conceptions of strategy; they need to manage value'. Mills[17, 18] explained that 'the pursuit of such an approach involves moving the focus of attention away from simply looking at short-term profits to a longer-term view of value creation'.

Essentially, SVA discounts forecasted cash flows, factors in a terminal value for the period beyond the forecast period, and adjusts for the value of debt. Rappaport proposed a seven value-driver approach (which was adopted by Mills *et al.*[19]) based on:

● Sales growth

● Operating margin

● Fixed capital investment

● Working capital investment

● Cash taxes

● Planning period

● Cost of capital

There are several other variations for determining wealth. Two of these measures[20] are:

Market Value Added (MVA) – the difference between total market value and invested capital (i.e. the difference between what investors can take out of a business and what they put in).

Economic Value Added (EVA) – this is the wealth a company creates each year as measured by net income from operations less the cost of capital needed to generate that income. Essentially, MVA is the valuation of all future annual EVAs.

The strength of the MVA/EVA framework is that it 'improves a company's focus on the maximisation of shareholder value ... discourages new investments that are likely to earn inadequate rates of return while encouraging periodic culling of existing assets'.[21]

26.12 Financial reporting of risk

The ICAEW has proposed that listed companies should be at the forefront of improved risk reporting in financial statements. In a recent discussion paper,[22] the ICAEW attempt to encourage the inclusion of better quality information on business risks so that users of accounts have a better understanding of the risks underlying a business's activity. With specific reference to ratio analysis, the discussion paper argues that 'the preparation of a statement of business risk should help preparers and users to focus on the ratios that are most relevant to the particular business risks that are most relevant to individual companies' (para. 6.16).

The summary of the main thrust of the discussion paper is as follows:

Why increase risk reporting in annual reports?

'Enhanced information about what companies do to assess and manage key business risks of all types will:

● provide practical forward-looking information;

● reduce the cost of capital;

● encourage better risk management;

● help ensure the equal treatment of all investors; and

● improve accountability for stewardship, investor protection and the usefulness of financial reporting.'

What should a statement of business risk include?

● Identification: a company should identify and prioritise its key risks;

● Risk management: a company should describe the actions it has taken to manage each of the identified risks;

● Measurement: the company should identify how each risk is measured.

What should preparers consider when preparing the statement of business risk?

Preparers need to ensure that the information satisfies a range of qualitative characteristics (e.g. relevant, reliable); is forward-looking; is suitable for users; is clear with respect to time-scales; and is not too commercially sensitive.

At present, there are a number of accounting standards which ensure that a certain element of risk-related information is reported in the financial statements. These standards include:

SSAP 25   *Segmental Reporting*
FRS 4   *Capital Instruments*
FRS 5   *Reporting the Substance of Transactions*
FRS 8   *Related Party Disclosures*
FRS 12   *Provisions, Contingent Liabilities and Contingent Assets*
FRS 13   *Derivatives and other Financial Instruments: Disclosure*

Derivatives and financial instruments is the area of financial reporting for business risk which we concentrate on in this chapter.

26.12.1   Financial instruments: an introduction

In July 1993, an international association of bankers and former government officials published a document which called for improved disclosure in financial statements of transactions involving derivatives and other financial instruments.[23] However, it took three years for the ASB to issue a discussion paper on financial instruments in July 1996[24] and a further two years to issue FRS 13, the standard on disclosure. At the time of the discussion paper's release, Sandra Thompson, a project director at the ASB, summed up the importance of financial instruments:

> Derivatives. The word can strike fear into finance directors, auditors and shareholders alike. Companies increasingly use derivatives and financial instruments to manage risk. But, improperly used, such instruments can turn into dangerous gambles, giving rise to spectacular losses. While much has been written about the use of financial instruments, there is relatively little guidance on their accounting.[25]

The main problem is that for a relatively small outlay financial instruments can transform the risk profile of a company. In particular, some organisations which have been exposed to huge risks have suffered the consequences of their dealings in financial instruments. These well publicised losses highlighted the fact that existing accounting practice did not provide an adequate framework for reporting the risk associated with financial instruments. For instance, some derivatives cost nothing and their book value is nil under a historical cost system. Similarly, the gains or losses on a derivative might not be realised, and hence reported, until it is sold. Consequently, how can shareholders assess the riskiness of an investment if they are unaware of the existence and/or the implications of an organisation's transactions involving financial instruments?

26.12.2 Financial instruments: current position

Most of the major standard-setters have tackled the accounting treatment of financial instruments in two stages. First, the issue of disclosure is considered. What information should companies disclose in their accounts and where should this information be shown? Disclosure has been addressed by both the IASC and the ASB. The IASC published IAS 32[26] in 1995 and the ASB published FRS 13[27] in 1998. In addition, the USA, Australia, Canada and New Zealand have all issued disclosure standards. Secondly, the more difficult issue of recognition and measurement needs to be considered.[28] What financial instruments should be recognised in the financial statements and how should they be measured (both initially and subsequently)? The IASC approved IAS 39,[29] its recognition and measurement standard, in late 1998. The ASB's longer term objective, after implementing a disclosure FRS, will be to introduce a recognition and measurement standard.

A Financial Instruments Joint Working Group of standard setters (IASC plus nine national standard setters) is developing proposals for a harmonised approach to accounting for financial instruments. The intention is that these developments will replace standards such as IASC 39. In the UK, the ASB's progress in issuing a recognition and measurement standard awaits the results of the Joint Working Group and therefore it is unlikely that such a standard will be issued in the UK before 2002.

26.12.3 Financial instruments: FRS 13

FRS 13 applies to all companies whose own capital instruments (basically shares or debt) are listed, all banks and similar institutions (at present insurance companies are excluded from FRS 13). The definition of a financial instrument broadly covers all monetary assets and liabilities. 'Financial instruments ... capture non-derivatives (such as loans, bonds, finance leases, liquid resources and most other debtors and creditors) and derivatives. In essence, financial instruments are cash and all rights to cash receipts or obligations to make cash payments.'[30]

The disclosure requirements are divided into two categories: narrative and numerical. With regard to these disclosures, the ASB states that it has 'sought to reduce the disclosures to what it believes is essential to provide a broad overview of the entity's financial instruments and its risk position, focusing on those instruments that are of greatest significance'.

Narrative disclosures

This information can be disclosed in either the accounts or the accompanying statements (e.g. the operating and financial review). The required disclosures include:

● major financial risks faced by the business;

● main policies adopted for managing those risks;

● objectives, policies and strategies for holding/issuing derivatives and other financial instruments.

Numerical disclosures

This information should be disclosed in the notes to the accounts. The required disclosures include numerical disclosure about:

● interst rate risk

- currency risk
- liquidity risk
- fair values
- financial instruments used for trading purposes
- financial instruments used for hedging
- certain commodity contracts.

Encouraged disclosures include:

- quantification of the possibility that market price changes might affect the value of financial instruments held (referred to as 'market price risk').

FRS 13 favours a high degree of aggregation for this information.

26.12.4 Financial instruments: accounting treatment in practice

Appendix III of FRS 13 provides illustrations of the required disclosures and Appendix IV gives guidance on procedures for estimating fair values. In this section, we include an extract from The BOC Group on the way in which financial instruments are accounted for.

The BOC Group
Report and Accounts 1999

Financial instruments

The Group uses financial instruments, including interest rate and currency swaps, to raise finance for its operations and to manage the risks arising from those operations. All transactions are undertaken only to manage interest and currency risk associated with the Group's underlying business activities and the financing of those activities. The Group does not undertake any trading activity in financial instruments.

- **Foreign exchange transaction exposures** The Group generally hedges actual and forecast foreign exchange exposures up to two years ahead. Forward contracts are used to hedge the forecast exposure and any gains or losses resulting from changes in exchange rates on contracts designated as hedges of foreign exchange are deferred until the financial period in which they are realised. If the contract ceases to be a hedge, any subsequent gains and losses are recognised through the profit and loss account.

- **Balance sheet translation exposures** A large proportion of the Group's net assets are denominated in currencies other than sterling. Where practicable and cost effective the Group hedges these balance sheet translation exposures by borrowing in relevant currencies and markets and by the use of currency swaps. Currency swaps are used only as balance sheet hedging instruments and the Group does not hedge the currency translation of its profit and loss account. Exchange gains and losses arising on the notional principal of these currency swaps during their life and at termination or maturity are dealt with as a movement on reserves. If the swap ceases to be a hedge of the underlying transaction, any subsequent gains or losses are recognised in the profit and loss account.

- **Interest rate exposures** The Group hedges its exposure to movements in interest rates associated with its borrowings primarily by means of interest rate swaps and forward rate agreements. Interest payments and receipts on these agreements are included with net interest payable. They are not revalued to fair value or shown in the Group balance sheet at the balance sheet date.

Summary

This chapter has introduced a number of additional analytical techniques to complement ratio analysis. These techniques include horizontal analysis, vertical analysis, Z-scores, A-scores and balanced scorecards. In addition, this chapter has described how to value unquoted shares and introduced the concept of shareholder value analysis. Finally, the ICAEW has published a discussion paper on the financial reporting of risk. We consider one aspect of the financial reporting of risk, namely financial instruments. Business risk reporting is an area which will become increasingly important and prominent.

The prime purpose of each analytical method in the first half of the chapter is to identify potential financial problem areas. Once these have been identified, thorough investigations should be carried out to determine the cause of each irregularity. Management should then take the necessary actions to correct these irregularities and deficiencies.

All users of financial statements (both internal and external users) should be prepared to utilise any or all of the interpretative techniques suggested in this chapter and the preceding one. These techniques help to evaluate the financial health and performance of a company. Users should approach these financial indicators with real curiosity – any unexplained or unanswered questions arising from this analysis should form the basis of a more detailed examination of the company accounts.

Review questions

1 As well as the balance sheet, profit and loss account and cash flow statement, a company's annual report and accounts contain other useful information.

Discuss the interpretative importance of the report of the directors, the chairman's statement, group structure information, employee statistics, geographical and activity breakdowns, and other supplementary information.

How useful and reliable is this additional information in the assessment of financial performance and the interpretation of financial statements?

2 Discuss Z-score analysis with particular reference to Altman's Z-score and Taffler's Z-score. In particular:

(i) What are the benefits of Z-score analysis?

(ii) What criticisms can be levelled at Z-score analysis?

3 Robertson identifies four main elements which cause changes in the financial health of a company: trading stability; declining profits; declining working capital; increase in borrowings.[31]

Robertson's Z-score is represented by:

$$Z = 3.0X_1 + 3.0X_2 + 0.6X_3 + 0.3X_4 + 0.3X_5$$

where

X_1 = (Sales – Total assets)/Sales
X_2 = Profit before tax/Total assets
X_3 = (Current assets – Total debt)/Current liabilities
X_4 = (Equity – Total borrowing)/Total debt
X_5 = (Liquid assets – Bank overdraft)/Creditors

Interpretation of the Z-score concentrates on rate of change from one period to the next. If the score falls by 40% or more in any one year, immediate investigations must be made to identify and rectify the cause of the decrease in Z-score. If the score falls by 40% or more for two years running, the company is unlikely to survive.

Compare and contrast Robertson's Z-score with:

(i) Altman's Z-score;

(ii) Taffler's Z-score and PAS-score.

4 The Datastream Multivariate Model uses a classification model developed by Marais[32] based on a sample of 100 UK companies consisting of 50 failed and 50 non-failed companies and using four variables:

X_1 measures profitability
X_2 measures liquidity
X_3 measures gearing
X_4 measures stock turnover

The Altman model is described in the text (section 26.6.1). Research by Letza[33] looked at the accuracy of these two models, with the following results:

Ex-ante classification accuracy	Altman		Datastream	
Years prior to event	1	3	1	3
Correct classification				
Survivor	108	109	112	113
Failure	2	3	2	2
Incorrect classification				
Wrongly predicting failure	29	28	25	24
Wrongly predicting survival	1	0	1	1
Total	140	140	140	140

Discuss the effectiveness of these two predictive models for financial analysts and consider what other variables could be incorporated into each of the models that might make the predictions more accurate.

5 The details given below are a summary of the balance sheets of six public companies engaged in different industries:

	A %	B %	C %	D %	E %	F %
Land and buildings	10	2	26	24	57	5
Other fixed assets	17	1	34		13	73
Stocks and work in progress	44		22	55	16	1
Trade debtors	6	77	15	4	1	13
Other debtors	11			8	2	5
Cash and investments	12	20	3	9	11	3
	100	100	100	100	100	100

Capital and reserves	37	5	62	58	55	50
Creditors: over one year	12	5	4	13	6	25
Creditors: under one year						
Trade	32	85	34	14	24	6
Other	16	5		14	15	11
Bank overdraft	3			1		8
Total capital employed	100	100	100	100	100	100

The activities of each company are as follows:

1 Operator of a chain of retail supermarkets.

2 Sea ferry operator.

3 Property investor and house builder. Apart from supplying managers, including site management, for the house building side of its operations, this company completely subcontracts all building work.

4 A vertically integrated company in the food industry which owns farms, flour mills, bakeries and retail outlets.

5 Commercial bank with a network of branches.

6 Contractor in the civil engineering industry.

Note: No company employs off-balance-sheet financing such as leasing.

(a) State which of the above activities relate to which set of balance sheet details, giving a brief summary of your reasoning in each case.

(b) What do you consider to be the major limitations of ratio analysis as a means of interpreting accounting information?

6 It has been suggested that 'growth in profits which occurred in the 1960s was the result of accounting sleight of hand rather than genuine economic growth'. Consider how 'accounting sleight of hand' can be used to report increased profits and discuss what measures can be taken to mitigate against the possibility of this happening.

7 Discuss the main features/perspectives of the 'Balanced Scorecard'.

8 Unilever 1999 Annual Review stated:

Total Shareholder Return (TSR) is a concept used to compare the performance of different companies' stocks and shares over time. It combines share price appreciation and dividends paid to show the total return to the shareholder. The absolute size of the TSR will vary with stock markets, but the relative position is a reflection of the market perception of overall performance. The Company calculates the TSR over a three year rolling period…. Unilever has set itself a TSR target in the top third of a reference group of 21 … companies.

Discuss (a) why a three year rolling period has been chosen, and (b) the criteria you consider appropriate for selecting the reference group of companies.

Exercises

An extract from the solution is provided in the appendix at the end of the text for exercises marked with an asterisk (*).

Question 1

The following five-year summary relates to Wandafood Products plc and is based on financial statements prepared under the historic cost convention:

Financial ratios

Profitability

			20X9	20X8	20X7	20X6	20X5
Margin	$\dfrac{\text{Trading profit}}{\text{Sales}}$ %		7.8	7.5	7.0	7.2	7.3
Return on assets	$\dfrac{\text{Trading profit}}{\text{Net operating assets}}$ %		16.3	17.6	16.2	18.2	18.3

Interest and dividend cover

			20X9	20X8	20X7	20X6	20X5
Interest cover	$\dfrac{\text{Trading profit}}{\text{Net finance charges}}$ times		2.9	4.8	5.1	6.5	3.6
Dividend cover	$\dfrac{\text{Earnings per ordinary share}}{\text{Dividend per ordinary share}}$ times		2.7	2.6	2.1	25	3.1

Debt to equity ratios

			20X9	20X8	20X7	20X6	20X5
	$\dfrac{\text{Net borrowings}}{\text{Shareholders' funds}}$ %		65.9	61.3	48.3	10.8	36.5
	$\dfrac{\text{Net borrowings}}{\text{Shareholders' funds plus minority interests}}$ %		59.3	55.5	44.0	10.1	33.9

Liquidity ratios

			20X9	20X8	20X7	20X6	20X5
Quick ratio	$\dfrac{\text{Current assets less stock}}{\text{Current liabilities}}$ %		74.3	73.3	78.8	113.8	93.4
Current ratio	$\dfrac{\text{Current assets}}{\text{Current liabilities}}$ %		133.6	130.3	142.2	178.9	174.7

Asset ratios

			20X9	20X8	20X7	20X6	20X5
Operating asset turnover	$\dfrac{\text{Sales}}{\text{Net operating assets}}$ times		2.1	2.4	2.3	2.5	2.5
Working capital turnover	$\dfrac{\text{Sales}}{\text{Working capital}}$ times		8.6	8.0	7.0	7.4	6.2

Per share

		20X9	20X8	20X7	20X6	20X5
Earnings per share	– pre-tax basis ....p	23.62	21.25	17.96	17.72	15.06
	– net basis ....p	15.65	13.60	10.98	11.32	12.18
Dividends per share	....p	5.90	5.40	4.90	4.60	4.10
Net assets per share	....p	102.1	89.22	85.95	85.79	78.11

Net operating assets include tangible fixed assets, stock, debtors and creditors. They exclude borrowings, taxation and dividends.

Required:
Prepare a report on the company, clearly interpreting and evaluating the information given. Include comments on possible effects of price changes which may limit the quality of the report.

(ACCA, June 1990)

Question 2

Morrison and McLaren Limited produces dairy products, and has seasonal working capital requirements. These have been financed mainly by bank loans and overdraft facilities, now totalling £120,000. A limit on dairy product prices, and a new contract with the unions which increased wages, caused a fall in the company's profit during the second half of 20X8 and most of 20X9. Sales increased over both these years due to an aggressive marketing strategy.

In early 20X0 the company's bank manager became aware of the deteriorating financial position of the company by studying a ratio analysis from the bank's computer system. This showed that certain key ratios, taken from the quarterly management accounts, were falling below the average for the industry, and were moving downwards. The manager sent a copy of the analysis to the company's managing director, together with a letter expressing his concern, although none of the ratios had fallen below the level specified in the loan agreement.

Three months later, the next analysis showed that the current ratio had fallen below 2.0, the limit specified in the agreement. Legally, the bank could call in a receiver if the loan was not repaid in full within one month.

The bank manager again forwarded the analysis to the managing director. However, this time the accompanying letter said that the bank would insist on immediate repayment of the loan unless the company could show how the financial position could be improved.

The managing director said that the present level of sales could not be continued without spending £50,000 on extra plant and machinery in July 20X0. This would need an increase in the loan and overdrafts from £120,000 to £170,000.

It is now July 20X0. The accounts for the year ended 31 December 20X9 are as follows:

Morrison and McLaren Limited balance sheets at 31 December				
	20X9	*20X8*	*20X7*	*20X6*
	£000	*£000*	*£000*	*£000*
Tangible fixed assets				
Land and buildings	51	54	20	26
Plant and machinery	43	49	63	74
Fixtures and fittings	2	3	12	20
	96	106	95	120
Current assets				
Stocks	344	213	128	85
Debtors	162	116	102	68
Cash at bank	8	12	26	17
	514	341	256	170

Creditors: amounts falling due within one year

Trade creditors	175	105	80	62
Bank overdraft	59	13	—	—
	234	118	80	62
Net current assets	280	223	176	108

Total assets

Less: Current liabilities	376	329	271	228

Creditors: amounts falling due after more than one year

Bank loan	60	30	—	—
	316	299	271	228

Capital and reserves

Called-up share capital	85	85	85	85
Profit and loss account	163	146	118	75
Other reserves	68	68	68	68
	316	299	271	228

Morrison and McLaren Limited profit and loss accounts for the years ended 31 December

	20X9 £000	20X8 £000	20X7 £000
Turnover	1,190	1,147	1,105
Cost of sales	952	918	884
Gross profit	238	229	221
Distribution costs	14	13	11
Administration expenses	178	156	125
Operating profit	46	60	85
Interest payable	12	3	—
Profit on ordinary activities before taxation	34	57	85
Tax on profit on ordinary activities	17	29	42
Profit retained	17	28	43
Note: depreciation	51	43	34

Required:

I Calculate the key ratios for the company and compare the trends in the ratios to the industry averages. For 20X7–20X9 the industry averages were:

Gearing (debt : equity)	0.5
Quick ratio	1.0
Current ratio	2.5
Stock turnover	6 times*
Debtor asset turnover	33
Fixed asset turnover	13 times
Total asset turnover	2.6 times*
Return on total assets	9.0%
Profit margin on sales	3.5%

* Based on year-end balance sheet figures

2 **What strengths and weaknesses are revealed by these ratios?**
3 **What sources of internal funds would be available to pay off the bank loan? If the bank granted the additional loan, could the company pay the loan off by 31 December 20X0?**
4 **Do you think that the bank should grant the additional loan?**
5 **What particular factors affect this company in this industry?**

* ## Question 3

Liz Collier runs a small delicatessen. Her profits in recent years have remained steady at around £21,000 per annum. This type of business generally earns a uniform rate of net profit on sales of 20%.

Recently, Liz has found that this level of profitability is insufficient to enable her to maintain her desired lifestyle. She is considering three options to improve her profitability.

Option 1 Liz will borrow £10,000 from her bank at an interest rate of 10% per annum, payable at the end of each financial year. The whole capital sum will be repaid to the bank at the end of the second year. The money will be used to hire the services of a marketing agency for two years. It is anticipated that turnover will increase by 40% as a result of the additional advertising.

Option 2 Liz will form a partnership with Joan Mercer, who also runs a local delicatessen. Joan's net profits have remained at £12,000 per annum since she started in business five years ago. The sales of each shop in the combined business are expected to increase by 20% in the first year and then remain steady. The costs of the amalgamation will amount to £6,870, which will be written off in the first year. The partnership agreement will allow each partner a partnership salary of 2% of the revised turnover of their own shop. Remaining profits will be shared in the ratio of Liz 3/5, Joan 2/5.

Option 3 Liz will reduce her present sales by 80% and take up a franchise to sell Nickson's Munchy Sausage. The franchise will cost £80,000. This amount will be borrowed from her bank. The annual interest rate will be 10% flat rate based on the amount borrowed. Sales of Munchy Sausage yield a net profit to sales percentage of 30%. Sales are expected to be £50,000 in the first year, but should increase annually at a rate of 15% for the following three years then remain constant.

Required:
(a) **Prepare a financial statement for Liz comparing the results of each option for each of the next two years.**
(b) **Advise Liz which option may be the best to choose.**
(c) **Discuss any other factors that Liz should consider under each of the options.**

Question 4

Background information

The directors of Chekani plc, a large listed company, are engaged in a policy of expansion. Accordingly, they have approached the directors of Meela Ltd, an unlisted company of substantial size, in connection with a proposed purchase of Meela Ltd.

The directors of Meela Ltd have indicated that the shareholders of Meela Ltd would prefer the form of consideration for the purchase of their shares to be in cash and you are informed that this is acceptable to the prospective purchasing company, Chekani plc.

The directors of Meela Ltd have now been asked to state the price at which the shareholders of Meela Ltd would be prepared to sell their shares to Chekani plc. As a member of a firm of independent accountants, you have been engaged as a consultant to advise the directors of Meela Ltd in this regard.

In order that you may be able to do so, the following details, extracted from the most recent financial statements of Meela, have been made available to you.

Meela Ltd accounts for year ended 30 June 20X4

Balance sheet extracts as at 30 June 20X4:

	£000
Purchased goodwill unamortised	15,000
Freehold property	30,000
Plant and machinery	60,000
Investments	15,000
Net current assets	12,000
10% Debentures 20X9	(30,000)
Ordinary shares of £1 each, (cumulative)	(40,000)
7% preference shares of £1 each, (cumulative)	(12,000)
Share premium account	(20,000)
Profit and loss account	(30,000)

Meela Ltd disclosed a contingent liability of £3.0m in the notes to the Balance Sheet.

(Amounts in brackets indicate credit balances)

Profit and loss account extracts for the year ended 30 June 20X4:

	£000
Profit before interest payments and taxation and exceptional items	21,000
Exceptional items	1,500
Interest	(3,000)
Taxation	(6,000)
Dividends paid – Preference	(840)
– Ordinary	(3,000)
Retained profit for the year	9,660

(Amounts in brackets indicate a charge or appropriation to profits)

The following information is also supplied:

(i) Profit before interest and tax for the year ended 30 June 20X3 was £24.2m and for the year ended 30 June 20X2 it was £30.3m.

(ii) Assume Corporation Tax at 30%.

(iii) Exceptional items in 20X4 relate to the profit on disposal of an investment in a related company. The related company contributed to profit before interest as follows:

To 30 June 20X4	£0
To 30 June 20X3	£200,000
To 30 June 20X2	£300,000

(iv) The preference share capital can be sold independently, and a buyer has already been found. The agreed purchase price is 90 pence per share.

(v) Chekani plc has agreed to purchase the debentures of Meela Ltd at a price of £110 for each £100 debenture.

(vi) The current rental value of the freehold property is £4.5m per annum and a buyer is available on the basis of achieving an 8% return on their investment.

(vii) The investments of Meela Ltd have a current market value of £22.5m.

(viii) Meela Ltd is engaged in operations substantially different from those of Chekani plc. The most recent financial data relating to two listed companies that are engaged in operations similar to those of Meela Ltd are:

	NV per share	Market price per share	P/E	Net dividend per share	Cover	Yield
Ranpar plc	£1	£3.06	11.3	12 pence	2.6	4.9
Menner plc	50p	£1.22	8.2	4 pence	3.8	4.1

Required:
Write a report, of approximately 2000 words, to the directors of Meela Ltd, covering the following:
(a) Advise them of the alternative methods used for valuing unquoted shares and explain some of the issues involved in the choice of method.
(b) Explain the alternative valuations that could be placed on the ordinary shares of Meela Ltd.
(c) Recommend an appropriate strategy for the Board of Meela Ltd to adopt in their negotiations with Chekani plc.
Include, as appendices to your report, supporting schedules showing how the valuations were calculated.

* Question 5

A budget is being prepared at Noriega plc, a 'leisure' group selling equipment for overstressed executives. The summarised balance sheet as at 30 June 20X5 is as follows:

	£		£
Share capital (£1 ordinary shares)	600,000	Fixed assets	480,000
Retained earnings	138,000	Investments	100,000
Trade creditors	80,000	Stock	120,000
Corporation tax payable	72,000	Debtors	60,000
		Cash at bank	130,000
	890,000		890,000

Actual and projected sales are:

		£
20X5	1st quarter (actual)	125,000
20X5	2nd quarter (actual)	300,000
20X5	3rd quarter (estimated)	200,000
20X5	4th quarter (estimated)	230,000
20X6	1st quarter (estimated)	220,000

Past experience indicates that 80% of sales will be collected during the quarter in which sales take place and 20% will be collected in the following quarter.

Gross profit is on average 60% of sales.

There is a recommended base level of stock of £40,000 and the company policy is to equate each quarter's purchases to the projected sales for the following quarter. Payment is made in the quarter of purchase. (The £80,000 due to creditors will be paid off in the third quarter.)

Selling and administration costs are estimated at £36,000 plus 5% of the sales value for each quarter and paid as incurred.

Taxation is 33% of net profit. Taxation due on 30 June 20X5 will be paid in the fourth quarter of 20X5.

Investment income of £7,500 net is expected in the fourth quarter of 20X5. The income is interest.

An interim dividend of 5% on ordinary shares will be declared in the third quarter and paid in the fourth quarter of 20X5.

Required:
(i) **Prepare a single budgeted profit and loss account for the period of the third and fourth quarters of 20X5 and a budgeted balance sheet as at 31 December 20X5. (You will need to prepare a purchases budget, a debtors forecast and a cash flow forecast.)**
(ii) **Give any advice, based on the above, which might help Noriega plc.**
(Any assumptions made should be stated.)

Question 6

R. Johnson inherited 810,000 £1 ordinary shares in Johnson Products Ltd on the death of his uncle in 20X5. His uncle had been the founder of the company and managing director until his death. The remainder of the issued shares were held in small lots by employees and friends, with no one holding more than 4%.

R. Johnson is planning to emigrate and is considering disposing of his shareholding. He has had approaches from three parties, who are:

1 A competitor – Sonar Products Ltd. Sonar Products Ltd considers that Johnson Products Ltd would complement their own business and they are interested in acquiring all of the 810,000 shares. Sonar Products Ltd currently achieve a post-tax return of 12.5% on capital employed.

2 Senior employees. Twenty employees are interested in making a management buy-out with each acquiring 40,500 shares from R. Johnson. They have obtained financial backing, in principle, from the company's bankers.

3 A financial conglomerate – Divest plc. Divest plc is a company that has extensive experience of acquiring control of a company and breaking it up to show a profit on the transaction. It is their policy to seek a pre-tax return of 20% from such an exercise.

The company has prepared draft accounts for the year ended 30 April 20X9. The following information is available.

(a) Past earnings and distributions:

Year ended 30 April	Profit/(Loss) after tax	Gross dividends declared
£	%	
19X5	79,400	6
19X6	(27,600)	—
19X7	56,500	4
19X8	88,300	5
19X9	97,200	6

(b) Balance sheet of Johnson Products Ltd as at 30 April 20X9:

	£000	£000
Fixed assets		
Land at cost		376
Premises at cost	724	
Aggregate depreciation	216	
		508
Equipment at cost	649	
Aggregate depreciation	353	
		296
Current assets		
Stock	141	
Debtors	278	
Cash at bank	70	
	489	
Creditors due within one year	(335)	
Net current assets		154
Non-current liabilities		(158)
		1,176
Represented by:		
£1 Ordinary shares		1,080
Profit and loss account		96
		1,176

(c) Information on the nearest comparable listed companies in the same industry:

Company	Profit after tax for 20X9 £000	Retention %	Gross dividend yield %
Eastron plc	280	25	15
Westron plc	168	16	10.5
Northron plc	243	20	13.4

Profit after tax in each of the companies has been growing by approximately 8% per annum for the past five years.

(d) The following is an estimate of the net realisable values of Johnson Products Ltd's assets as at 30 April 20X9:

	£000
Land	480
Premises	630
Equipment	150
Debtors	168
Stock	98

Required:
(a) As accountant for R. Johnson, advise him of the amount that could be offered for his shareholding with a reasonable chance of being acceptable to the seller, based on the information given in the question, by each of the following:

     (i) **Sonar Products Ltd;**

    (ii) **the 20 employees;**

   (iii) **Divest plc.**

(b) **As accountant for Sonar Products Ltd, estimate the maximum amount that could be offered by Sonar Products Ltd for the shares held by R. Johnson.**

(c) **As accountant for Sonar Products Ltd, state the principal matters you would consider in determining the future maintainable earnings of Johnson Products Ltd and explain their relevance.**

(ACCA)

Question 7

Discuss the following issues with regard to financial reporting for risk:

(a) **How can a company identify and prioritise its key risks?**

(b) **What actions can a company take to manage the risks identified in (a)?**

(c) **How can a company measure risk?**

References

1 *Accounting for the Effects of Changing Prices: A Handbook*, ASC, 1986.

2 C. Pratten, *Company Failure*, Financial Reporting and Auditing Group, ICAEW, 1991, pp. 43–45.

3 R.J. Taffler, 'Forecasting company failure in the UK using discriminant analysis and financial ratio data', *Journal of the Royal Statistical Society*, Series A, Vol. 145, part 3, 1982, pp. 342–358.

4 M.L. Inman, 'Altman's Z-formula prediction', *Management Accounting*, November 1982, pp. 37–39.

5 E.I. Altman, 'Financial ratios, discriminant analysis and the prediction of corporate bankruptcy', *Journal of Finance*, Vol. 23(4), 1968, pp. 589–609.

6 M.L. Inman, 'Z-scores and the going concern review', *ACCA Students' Newsletter*, August 1991, pp. 8–13.

7 R.J. Taffler, *op. cit.*

8 R.J. Taffler, 'Z-scores: an approach to the recession', *Accountancy*, July 1991, pp. 95–97.

9 M.L. Inman, 1991, *op. cit.*

10 G. Holmes and R. Dunham, *Beyond the Balance Sheet*, Woodhead Faulkner, 1994.

11 J. Argenti, 'Predicting corporate failure', *Accountants Digest*, No. 138, Summer 1983, pp. 18–21.

12 R. Newing, 'Benefits of a balanced scorecard', *Accountancy*, November 1994, pp. 52–53.

13 R.S. Kaplan and D.P. Norton, 'The balanced scorecard – measures that drive performance', *Harvard Business Review*, January–February 1992, pp. 71–79.

14 W.A. Nixon and C.J. McNair, 'A measure of R&D', *Accountancy*, October 1994, p. 138.

15 A. Rappaport, *Creating Shareholder Value: The new standard for business performance*, The Free Press, 1986.

16 T. Copeland, T. Koller and J. Murrin, *Valuation: Measuring and Managing the Value of Companies*, John Wiley and Sons, New York, 1990.

17 R.W. Mills, 'Shareholder value analysis', *Management Accounting*, February 1998, pp. 39–40.

18 R.W. Mills *et al.*, *The Use of Shareholder Value Analysis in Acquisition and Divestment Decisions by Large UK Companies*, CIMA, 1997.

19 R.W. Mills, J. Robertson and T. Ward, 'Strategic value analysis: Trying to run before you can walk', *Management Accounting*, November 1992, pp. 48–49.

20 'America's best wealth creators', *Forbes*, 28 November 1994, pp. 77–91.

21 J. Stern, 'Management: its mission and its measure', *Director*, October 1994, pp. 42–44.

22 ICAEW, *Financial Reporting of Risk*, Discussion Paper, 1998.

23 Group of Thirty (G30), 'Derivatives: Practices and Principles', July 1993, Washington.

24 Discussion Paper, *Derivatives and other Financial Instrument*, ASB, July 1996.

25 S. Thompson, 'Playing a different tune on financial instruments', *Accountancy*, September 1996, p. 97.

26 IAS 32, *Financial Instruments: Disclosure and Presentation*, IASC, 1995.

27 FRS 13, *Derivatives and Other Financial Instruments: Disclosure*, ASB, September 1998.

28 M. Scicluna 'US pressure warps derivative accounting', *Accountancy*, November 1997, p. 85.

29 IAS 39, *Financial Instruments: Recognition and Measurement*, February 1999.

30 N. Dealy, 'Deriving sense from financial instruments', *Accountancy*, June 1997, p. 93.

31 J. Robertson, 'Company failure – measuring changes in financial health through ratio analysis', *Management Accounting*, November 1983.

32 D.A. Marais, *A Method of Quantifying Companies' Relative Financial Strength*, Bank of England Discussion Paper No. 4, 1979.

33 S.R. Letza, 'Issues in assessing MDA models of corporate failure: a supporting research note', *British Accounting Review*, Vol. 26(3), 1994, p. 281.

CHAPTER 27

International reporting and interpretation

27.1 Introduction

There has been a globalisation of world capital markets. This has provided an additional opportunity for lucrative investment across national boundaries. For example, the all share indices in the following markets rose as follows:[1]

	Stockmarket index 12 January 2000	% change on 31 December 1998 in local currency
UK (FTSE 100)	6,532.8	+11.7%
US (DJIA)	11,551.0	+25.8%
France (SBF 250)	3,608.7	+44.3%
Germany (Xetra DAX)	6,912.8	+38.1%
Sweden (Affärsvärlden Gen)	5,443.3	+64.2%
China	1,528.4	+25.3%
Greece	5,187.3	+89.5%
Russia	189.2	+328.4%
Japan (Nikkei 250)	18,677.4	+34.9%

Private investors may therefore seek to benefit from variations in growth rates by simply buying shares listed on the overseas stock exchanges.

Corporate investors have an additional strategy open to them in that they can set up trading branches or subsidiaries abroad and carry on business in the other countries. Such investment opportunities have increased with the changes that we have seen in political regimes that have resulted in the emerging markets of Eastern Europe, Asia and the Far East. At the same time actual management of the branches and subsidiaries has been made easier by the improvements in world travel and communications.

Financial reports are required from the foreign investees by both the private and corporate investors in order to assess performance and make buy, hold and sell decisions. However, just as there are national cultural differences, there are also financial reporting differences within countries. In order to assist the reader to understand some of the issues pertinent to interpreting international financial statements, in this chapter we consider the following:

● National differences generate different accounting systems

● Reasons for differences in financial reporting

● Classification of national accounting systems

● Attempts to reduce national differences
● International analysis of financial statements
● Country studies

27.2 National differences generate different accounting systems

We are all familiar with national differences that have become almost stereotypes. Consider the French, for example, who are described as:

> ... proud, patriotic, sardonic people driven by a clear sense of their own greatness ... social interactions are profoundly affected by social stereotypes ... status depends to a great degree on family origins ... outward signs of social status are the individual's level of education, a tasteful house or flat, and knowledge of literature and fine arts. But the all important structure within which the system operates depends on each individual's family origins.[2]

It is natural that such strongly felt influences such as family origin should be reflected in the way business is structured. This can be seen in the extent of family firms in France with a large proportion of all businesses family owned, run, or dominated through major shareholdings and in the strongly autocratic style of management.

On the other hand, it is pointed out that:

> maximising profitability is not always the German's first priority. As in the case of many other Europeans, Germans often feel that the firm has a responsibility to society and the environment.[3]

27.2.1 How do national differences affect financial reporting?

The French business structure indicates that the owners are also frequently the managers. This is different from the UK where there is separation of ownership and management. Consequently, in France, there is far less need for regulations to ensure that financial reports present a true and fair view; the emphasis is not so much on attempting to compensate for potential conflicts of interest between owners and managers as ensuring that the financial reports are accurate.

However, this is only one aspect. There are many other differences in economic and cultural conditions, which have led to an array of different financial reporting practices around the world. An understanding of this improves the awareness of potential misinterpretation when appraising financial statements prepared in non-UK countries. It is useful to appreciate the reasons for these variations in order to improve understanding of the business activities represented by the accounts.

27.3 Reasons for differences in financial reporting

A number of attempts have been made to identify reasons for differences in financial reporting.[4] The issue is far from clear but most writers agree that the following are among the main factors influencing the development of financial reporting:

● the character of the national legal system;
● the way in which industry is financed;

● the relationship of the tax and reporting systems;

● the influence and status of the accounting profession;

● the extent to which accounting theory is developed;

● accidents of history;

● language.

We will consider the effect of each of these.

27.3.1 The character of the national legal system

There are two major legal systems namely, that based on common law and that based on Roman law. It is important to recognise this because the legal systems influence the way in which behaviour in a country, including accounting and financial reporting, is regulated.

Countries with a legal system based on common law include England and Wales, Ireland, United States, Australia, Canada and New Zealand. These countries rely on the application of equity to specific cases rather than a set of detailed rules to be applied in all cases. The effect in the UK, as far as financial reporting was concerned, was that there was limited legislation regulating the form and content of financial statements until the government was required to implement the EC Fourth Directive. The Directive was implemented in the UK by the passing of the Companies Act 1981 and this can be seen as a watershed because it was the first time that the layout of company accounts had been prescribed by statute in England and Wales.

English common law heritage was accommodated within the legislation by the provision that the detailed regulations of the Act need not be applied if, in the judgement of the directors, strict adherence to the Act would result in financial statements that did not present a true and fair view.

Countries with a legal system based on Roman law include France, Germany and Japan. These countries rely on the codification of detailed rules, which are often included within their companies act legislation. The result is that there is less flexibility in the preparation of financial reports in those countries. They are less inclined to look to fine distinctions to justify different reporting treatments which are inherent in the common law approach.

However, it is not just that common law countries have fewer codified laws than Roman law countries. There is a fundamental difference in the way in which the reporting of commercial transactions is approached. In the common law countries there is an established practice of creative compliance. By this we mean that the spirit of the law is elusive[5] and management is more inclined to act with creative compliance in order to escape effective legal control. By creative compliance we mean that management complies with the form of the regulation but in a way that might be against its spirit, e.g. structuring leasing agreements in the most acceptable way for financial reporting purposes.

27.3.2 The way in which industry is financed

Accountancy is the art of communicating relevant financial information about a business entity to users. One of the considerations to take into account when deciding what is relevant is the way in which the business has been financed, e.g. the information needs of equity investors will be different from those of loan creditors. This is one factor responsible for international financial reporting differences because the predominant provider of capital is different in different countries.[6] Figure 27.1 makes a simple comparison between

Figure 27.1 Domestic equity market capitalisation/ gross domestic product.

	Market capitalisation/GDP (%)	
	1994	1998
Germany	22	49
France	33	65
UK	116	170
Sweden	64	125
USA	73	158

domestic equity market capitalisation and Gross Domestic Product (GDP).[7] The higher the ratio, the greater the importance of the equity market compared with loan finance.

We see that in the UK, the US and Sweden, companies rely more heavily on individual investors to provide finance than in France or Germany. An active stock exchange has developed to allow shareholders to liquidate their investments and a system of financial reporting has evolved to satisfy a stewardship need where prudence and conservatism predominate and a capital market need for fair information[8] which allows interested parties to deal on an equal footing where the accruals concept and the doctrine of substance over form predominate. It is important to note that equity has gained importance in all the countries in Table 27.1. This can be an important factor in the development of accounting.

In Germany, as well as equity investment having a lower profile, there is also a significant difference in the way in which shares are registered and transferred. In the UK individual shareholders are entered onto the company's Register of Members. In Germany many shares are bearer shares which means that they are not registered in the individual investor's name but are deposited with a bank that has the authority to exercise a proxy. It could perhaps appear at first glance that the banks have undue influence but they state that, in the case of proxy votes, shareholders are at liberty to cast their votes as they see fit and not to follow the recommendations of the bank.[9] In addition to their control over proxy votes, the big three German banks, The Deutsche Bank, the Dresdner Bank and the Commerzbank, also have significant direct equity holdings, e.g. in 1992 the Deutsche Bank had a direct holding of 28% in Daimler-Benz.[10]

There was an investigation carried out in the 1970s by the Gessler Commission into the ties between the Big Three and large West German manufacturing companies. The Commission established that the banks' power lay in the combination of the proxy votes, the tradition of the house bank which kept a company linked to one principal lender, the size of the banks' direct equity holdings and their representation on company supervisory boards.[11]

In practice, therefore, the banks are effectively both principal lenders and shareholders in Germany. As principal lenders they receive internal information such as cash flow forecasts which, as a result, is also available to them in their role as nominee shareholders. We are not concerned here with questions such as conflict of interest and criticisms that the banks are able to exert undue influence. Our interest is purely in the financial reporting implications which are that the banks have sufficient power to obtain all of the information they require without reliance on the annual accounts. Published disclosures are far less relevant than in the UK.

During the 1990s there has been a growth in the UK and US of institutional investors such as pension funds which form an ever increasing proportion of registered shareholders. In theory, the information needs of these institutional investors should be the same as of individual investors. However, in practice, they might be in a position to obtain information by direct access to management and the directors. One effect of this might be that they will become less interested in seeking disclosures in the financial statements – they will have already picked up the significant information at an informal level.

27.3.3 The relationship of the tax and reporting systems

In the UK separate rules have evolved for computing profit for tax and computing profit for financial reporting purposes. The legislation for tax purposes tends to be more prescriptive, e.g. there is a defined rate for capital allowances on fixed assets which means that the reduction in value of fixed assets for tax purposes is decided by the government. The financial reporting environment is less prescriptive but this is compensated for by requiring greater disclosure. For example, there is no defined rate for depreciating fixed assets but there is a requirement for companies to state their depreciation accounting policy. Similar systems have evolved in the US and the Netherlands.

However, certain countries give primacy to taxation rules and will only allow expenditure for tax purposes if it is given the same treatment in the financial accounts. In France and Germany the tax rules effectively become the accounting rules.

This can lead to difficulties of interpretation, particularly when capital allowances, i.e. depreciation for tax purposes, are changed to secure public policy objectives such as encouraging investment in fixed assets by permitting accelerated write-off when assessing taxable profits. In fact, the depreciation charge against profit would be said by a UK accountant not to be fair, even though it could certainly be legal or correct.[12]

Depreciation has been discussed to illustrate the possibility of misinterpretation because of the different status and effect of tax rules on annual accounts. Other items that require careful consideration include stock valuations, bad debt provisions, development expenditure and revaluation of fixed assets. There might also be public policy arrangements that are unique to a single country, e.g. the availability of transfers to reserves to reduce taxable profit as occurs in Sweden.[13]

27.3.4 The influence and status of the accounting profession

The development of a capital market in the UK for dealing in shares created a need for reliable, relevant and timely financial information. Legislation was introduced requiring companies to prepare annual accounts and have them audited. This resulted in the growth of an established and respected accounting profession able to produce relevant reports and attest to their reliability by performing an audit.

In turn, the existence of a strong profession had an impact on the development of UK accounting regulations. It is the profession that has been responsible for the promulgation of accounting standards and recommendations. This pattern is seen in other countries, e.g. US, Australia, Canada, Netherlands.

In countries where there has not been the same need to provide market sensitive information, e.g. in Eastern Europe in the 1980s, accountants have been seen purely as bookkeepers and have been accorded a low status. This explains the lack of expertise among financial accountants. There was also a lack of demand for financial management skills because production targets were set centrally without the emphasis for maximising the use of scarce resources at the business entity level. The attributes that are valued in a market economy such as the exercise of judgement and the determination of relevant information were not required. This position is rapidly changing and there will be a growth in the training, professionalism and contribution for both financial and management accountants as these economies become market economies.

27.3.5   The extent to which accounting theory is developed

Accounting theory can influence accounting practice. Theory can be developed at both an academic and professional level but for it to take root it must be accepted by the profession. For example, we saw in Chapter 5 the attempts in the UK to introduce a form of current value accounting. The theories such as current purchasing power and current cost accounting first surfaced in the UK in the academic world and there were many practising accountants who regarded them then, and still regard them now, as academic.

In the Netherlands, professional accountants receive an academic accountancy training as well as the vocational accountancy training which is typical in the UK. Perhaps as a result of that there is less reluctance on the part of the profession to view academics as isolated from the real world. This might go some way to explaining why it was in the Netherlands that we saw general acceptance by the profession for the idea that for information to be relevant it needed to be based on current value accounting. Largely as a result of pressure from the Netherlands, the Fourth Directive contained provisions which allowed member states to introduce inflation accounting systems.[14]

In an earlier chapter, we discussed the search for a conceptual framework for financial reporting in the UK. Similar attempts have been made to formulate a conceptual framework in countries such as the US, Canada and Australia[15] and the International Standards Committee has also contributed to this field. One of the results has been the closer collaboration between the regulatory bodies which might assist in reducing differences in the longer term.

27.3.6   Accidents of history

The development of accounting systems is often allied to the political history of a country. Scandals surrounding company failures, notably in the US in the 1920s and 1930s and in the UK in the 1960s and 1980s had a marked impact on financial reporting in those countries. In the US the Securities and Exchange Commission was established to control listed companies, with responsibility to ensure adequate disclosure in annual accounts. Ever increasing control over the form and content of financial statements through improvements in the accounting standard setting process has evolved from the difficulties in the UK.

International boundaries have also been crossed in the evolution of accounting. In some instances it has been a question of pooling of resources to avoid repeating work already carried out elsewhere, e.g. the Norwegians studied the report of the Dearing Committee in the UK before setting up their new accounting standard setting system.[16] Other changes in nations' accounting practices have been a result of external pressure, e.g. Spain's membership of the European Community led to radical changes in accounting,[17] while the Germans influenced accounting in the countries they occupied during the Second World War.[18] Such accidents of history have changed the course of accounting and reduced the clarity of distinctions between countries.

27.3.7 Language

Language has often played an important role in the development of different methods of accounting for similar items. Certain nationalities are notorious for speaking only their own language, which has prevented them from benefiting from the wisdom of other nations. There is also the difficulty of translating concepts as well as phrases, where one country has influenced another.

27.4 Classification of national accounting systems

A number of attempts have been made to classify national accounting systems in much the same way that biologists attempt to classify flora and fauna.[19] However, as can be seen from the reasons for different systems described above, national differences are far from straightforward. Any classifications need to be constantly updated as accounting is such a dynamic activity. There are constant changes as a result of events taking place both within and beyond the accounting profession. Such classifications are therefore useful in gaining a greater understanding of particular features of accounting in a country, but do need to be treated with a degree of caution.

27.5 Attempts to reduce national differences

Given the increasing numbers of transnational users of accounts, many attempts have been made to reduce the differences between reports prepared in different countries. There are, in essence, two approaches: standardisation and harmonisation.[20] These terms have become technical terms in the study of international accounting. Standardisation advocates the setting out of rules for accounting for similar items in all countries. Harmonisation is less radical in that it allows for some different national approaches but provides a common framework so that major issues will be dealt with in similar ways across national borders.

Attempts have been made to standardise or at least harmonise financial reporting to satisfy the needs of a number of different groups. The main emphasis of this chapter is on users of accounts who are seeking to assess a company's past or potential investment performance. However, government agencies, such as tax and customs authorities also have an interest in greater compatibility of information between countries. International accountancy firms deal with large numbers of multi-national clients, whose accounts frequently need to be adjusted to common accounting principles before consolidations can be prepared. A reduction in national accounting differences would reduce the training costs of these firms and increase staff mobility (however it would ultimately limit the fees they could charge!).

A number of international bodies are involved in the processes of harmonisation or standardisation. These have included organisations, which may not immediately be associated with accounting, such as the United Nations and the Organisation for Economic Co-operation and Development (OECD). However, the most influential have probably been the International Accounting Standards Committee and the European Community. Their contribution is summarised below.

27.5.1 The International Accounting Standards Committee

The International Accounting Standards Committee (IASC) was established in 1973 by the professional accounting bodies of Australia, Canada, France, Germany, Japan, Mexico, the Netherlands, the UK and Ireland and the USA. It is now associated with the International Federation of Accountants (IFAC). The objectives of the IASC are:

(a) to formulate and publish in the public interest accounting standards to be observed in the presentation of financial statements and to promote their world-wide acceptance and observance;

(b) to work generally for the improvement and harmonisation of regulations, accounting standards and procedures relating to the presentation of financial statements.[21]

The IASC now has member bodies in over 100 countries, representing accountants in industry and commerce, public practice, academic institutions and government. The structure of the IASC is about to be altered to give an improved balance between geographical representation, technical competence and independence.[22] International Accounting Standards currently in effect are shown in Figure 27.2. The IASC has also issued a *Framework for the Preparation and Presentation of Financial Statements*.[23] This will assist in the development of future accounting standards and improve harmonisation by providing a basis for reducing the number of accounting treatments permitted by IASs. Professional accountancy bodies have prepared and published translations of IASs, making them available to a wide audience and the IASC itself has set up a mechanism to issue interpretation of the standards.

Figure 27.2 International Accounting Standards.

International Accounting Standards (effective date)	Corresponding UK Standards	Principal requirements of IAS where different from UK Standard
IAS 1 Presentation of Financial Statements (1/7/98 replaces IAS 1 Disclosure of Accounting Policies)	SSAP 2, FRS 3	
IAS 2 Inventories (1/1/76, revised in 1993)	SSAP 9	
IAS 7 Cash Flow Statements (1/1/79 revised in 1992)	FRS 1	Concentrates on 'cash and cash equivalents' rather than cash. Does not require a reconciliation to movement in net debt. Permits direct and indirect methods and does not require reconciliation to operating profit. No separate headings for returns on investments and servicing of finance, taxation, capital expenditure and financial investments, acquisitions and disposals and equity dividends paid.
IAS 8 Net Profit or Loss for the Period, Fundamental Errors and Changes in Accounting Policies (1/1/79 revised in 1993; paragraphs 19–22 superseded by IAS 35)	FRS 3	Definition of extraordinary items is less rigorous, but they will arise only on rare occasions.

Figure 27.2 (cont.)

International Accounting Standards (effective date)	Corresponding UK Standards	Principal requirements of IAS where different from UK Standard
IAS 10 Contingencies and Events Occurring After the Balance Sheet Date (1/1/80, revised 1999; IAS 37 supersedes those parts of IAS 10 that deal with contingencies, effective 1/7/1999)	SSAP 17, FRS 11	Disclosure of tax implications of contingencies not required.
IAS 11 Construction Contracts (1/1/80 revised in 1993)	SSAP 9	
IAS 12 Income Taxes (1/1/98 replaces IAS 12 Accounting for Taxes on Income)	FRS 16	Separate presentation of current tax on face of balance sheet. Disclosure of tax expense relating to discontinued operations.
IIAS 14 Segment Reporting (1/7/98 replaces Reporting Financial Information by Segment)	SSAP 25	No exemption from disclosure on grounds that it would be damaging to the company. Requires segmental capital expenditure, depreciation, details of associates and assets and liabilities in addition to that required by SSAP 25.
IAS 15 Information Reflecting the Effects of Changing Prices (1/1/83)		Standard is not mandatory, but requires: – depreciation adjustment; – cost of sales adjustment; – monetary items adjustment; – overall effects of above and other adjustments.
IAS 16 Property, Plant and Equipment (1/1/83, revised in 1993 and by IAS 36 in 1998)	FRS 15	Where revaluations are used, this must be to 'fair value' which is broader than FRS 15's 'value to the business model'. Revaluation gains and losses may be recognised through the statement of total recognised gains and losses. Additional disclosures required regarding pledges of assets, assets under construction, commitments to acquire assets, measurement bases and revaluation surpluses (these are mostly required under the Companies Act 1985 in the UK but are not specifically mentioned in FRS 15).
IAS 17 Accounting for Leases (1/1/84 revised 1997 effective 1/1/99)	SSAP 21, FRS 5	
IAS 18 Revenue (1/1/84 revised in 1993)	Draft Statement of Principles	Greater disclosure of revenue recognition policies and amounts.

Figure 27.2 (cont.)

International Accounting Standards (effective date)	Corresponding UK Standards	Principal requirements of IAS where different from UK Standard
IAS 19 Employee Benefits (1/1/85 revised in 1993 and 1998 effective 1/1/99)	SSAP 24	Actuarial gains and losses may be taken to P&L immediately or amortised over a period up to the average remaining work life of employees
IAS 20 Accounting for Government Grants and Disclosure of Government Assistance (1/1/84)	SSAP 4	Deduction of grant is permitted in arriving at carrying amount of the asset.
IAS 21 The Effects of Changes in Foreign Exchange Rates (1/1/85 revised in 1993)	SSAP 20, FRS 3	Income and expenses of foreign enterprises are to be translated at the rate ruling on the date of the transaction (or an average rate). Disclosure required of amount of exchange differences taken to P&L. Disclosure required of impact of changes from/to temporal and closing rate methods and vice versa.
IAS 22 Business Combinations (1/1/85 revised in 1993 and 1996 and by IAS 36 in 1998)	FRS 6, FRS 7, FRS 10	Positive goodwill is to be capitalised and is normally amortised over a maximum period of five years unless a longer period (which cannot exceed twenty years) can be justified. Requirements relating to contingent consideration less prescriptive than FRS 7. Disclosures for mergers not as onerous as FRS 6.
IAS 23 Borrowing Costs (1/1/86 revised in 1993)	FRS 15	Capitalisation is an allowed alternative treatment similar to the strict application of the Companies Act 1985.
IAS 24 Related Party Disclosures (1/1/86)	FRS 8	Disclosures generally less rigorous than FRS 8, e.g. do not need to give names of related parties or amounts of transactions.
IAS 25 Accounting for Investments (1/1/87, portions relating to investments in financial assets are superseded by IAS 39)	SSAP 19	Investment properties must be depreciated in accordance with IAS 16. Long-term investments may be revalued or stated at cost.
IAS 26 Accounting and Reporting by Retirement Benefit Plans (1/1/88)		
IAS 27 Consolidated Financial Statements and Accounting for Investments in Subsidiaries (1/1/90 amended by IAS 39)	FRS 2	

Figure 27.2 (cont.)

International Accounting Standards (effective date)	Corresponding UK Standards	Principal requirements of IAS where different from UK Standard
IAS 28 Accounting for Investments in Associates (1/1/90)	FRS 9	Emphasis in definition of associate in IAS 28 requires investor to have the potential to participate in the financial and operating policy decisions, whereas FRS 9 definition requires investor to participate and exert significant influence. When investments are shown at cost, dividends made from post-acquisition projects are treated as a reduction in the cost of the investment in the associate. In the entity accounts, the associate can be accounted for using equity method, cost or revalued amounts.
IAS 29 Financial Reporting in Hyperinflationary Economies (1/1/90)		Hyperinflation is where (amongst other things) cumulative inflation over three years exceeds 100%. Financial statements must be presented in a measuring unit current at the balance sheet date.
IAS 30 Disclosures in the Financial Statements of Banks and Similar Financial Institutions (1/1/91 amended by IAS 39)		
IAS 31 Financial Reporting of Interests in Joint Ventures (1/1/92 amended by IAS 36 and IAS 39 in 1998)	FRS 9	Broader definition of types of operation which may be joint venture. Proportional consolidation is the preferred method, with equity accounting a permitted alternative.
IAS 32 Financial Instruments: Disclosure and Presentation (1/1/96 revised by IAS 39)	FRS 13 FRS 4 FRS 5	'Split accounting' required for hybrid instruments, e.g. proceeds of issue of convertible bond must be split between the financial liability and equity instrument. Additional specific disclosures about credit risk and hedging.
IAS 33 Earnings per Share (1/1/98)	FRS 14	IAS provides less specific guidance than FRS 14.
IAS 34 Interim Financial Reporting (1/1/99)	–	There is no FRS but IAS is similar to voluntary disclosure in UK.
IAS 35 Discontinuing Operations (1/1/99)	FRS 3	–

Figure 27.2 (cont.)

International Accounting Standards (effective date)	Corresponding UK Standards	Principal requirements of IAS where different from UK Standard
IAS 36 Impairment of Assets (1/7/99)	FRS 11	Impairment caused by consumption of economic benefits need only be recognised in the profit and loss account to the extent that the loss exceeds the balance on the revaluation reserve relating to the assets in question.
IAS 37 Provisions, Contingent Liabilities and Contingent Assets (1/7/99)	FRS 12	–
IAS 38 Intangible Assets (1/7/99)	FRS 10	Internally generated intangible assets should be capitalised if certain strict criteria are met.
IAS 39 Financial Instruments: Recognition and Measurement (1/1/2001)	FRS 13	

International Accounting Standards (IASs) may be applied in one of the following ways:

● An IAS may be adopted as a national accounting standard. This can be useful where there are limited resources and an 'off the peg' solution is required. This is the practice in countries such as Botswana, Cyprus, Malaysia and Zimbabwe. The disadvantage is that the standard may not meet specific local needs, due to the influence of the larger industrialised nations on the IASC.

● An IAS may be used as a national requirement but adapted for local purposes. This approach is used in Fiji, Lesotho and Singapore for example.

● National requirements may be derived independently, but adapted to conform with IASs. This is the procedure in the UK, although recently the programmes of the IASC and ASB have converged. Indeed, IAS 37 and FRS 12 were developed jointly.

The large number of members of the IASC has meant that it has been difficult to achieve a consensus on many of the issues that the Committee has addressed. Consequently, many IASs initially permitted a range of treatments. Whilst this was an improvement on not having a standard at all, it was still far from ideal. In response to this criticism, the IASC began its comparability/improvements project in 1987, which resulted in the revision of ten standards.

The IASC and IOSCO have been co-operating on the accounting problems of multi-national companies involved in foreign listings since 1987.[24] In July 1995 it was agreed that if the IASC were to produce a set of core standards which were acceptable to the technical committee of IOSCO, any company would be able to use IAS financial statements to obtain listings of its securities on any foreign stock exchange. This would be particularly useful for companies seeking listing on the US stock exchange, which currently requires companies to present financial statements in accordance with US GAAP or reconcile domestic accounts to US GAAP. The ramifications of this for preparers and users of financial statements of multinational companies are tremendous:

considerable time and effort would be saved. The IASC completed its core standards in December 1998. However, before full advantage can be taken of global accounting standards, the following must happen:

1 *IOSCO technical committee must endorse the standards*
As the committee is made up of representatives from different countries, there is a risk that members could raise objections as a result of their accounting background, e.g. some IASs may be seen to be too much at variance with US GAAP.

2 *Individual securities regulators must implement the IOSCO endorsement in their national rules to allow foreign issuers to present IAS financial statements without modification.*
In Europe there is already mutual recognition of financial statements prepared in other member states, so it would seem a simple step to recognise IAS statements. Indeed, certain countries (e.g. France and Germany) have already implemented legislation permitting the preparation of consolidated financial statements in accordance with IASs under certain conditions. Once standards are endorsed by IOSCO, it seems natural that national regulators would follow. Nevertheless, certain regulators may prove more difficult to convince. It has been suggested that the SEC in the US could take several years to complete its assessment of IASs and the outcome should not be regarded as a foregone conclusion.[25]

Domestic companies would continue to use national accounting standards, but eventually it seems likely that national requirements would move closer to IASs, thus reducing differences further. However, before true comparability could be achieved, a more effective mechanism is necessary to ensure consistent application of IASs. Surveys of companies purporting to follow IASs[26] have demonstrated that many companies disclose exceptions from full compliance. While IAS 1 (revised) will ban this practice (i.e. companies will be required to follow all IASs if they wish to claim their financial statements comply with IASs), it is difficult to see how it can be enforced.

27.5.2 The European Union[27]

The Treaty of Rome was signed in 1957 to establish a European Economic Community. The objectives of the Community were set out in article 2 of the Treaty:

> The Community shall have as its task, by establishing a common market and progressively approximating the economic policies of member states, to promote throughout the Community a harmonious development of economic activities, a continuous and balanced expansion, an increase in stability, an accelerated raising of the standard of living and closer relations between the States belonging to it.

In order to achieve these objectives, the Treaty set out specific provisions for the free movement of goods, services, people and capital. The single European currency will remove yet another barrier to trade and will link the economies of members more closely.

It was envisaged that the Treaty would be supported by action in other spheres developing common legislation where necessary. The harmonisation of company law across the Community has been part of this process. To date, the most important EC Directives adopted in respect of Financial Reporting are the Fourth (company accounts), Seventh (consolidated accounts) and Eighth (auditing). The Fifth Directive (corporate governance) is yet to be adopted by member states and the draft Tenth Directive (international mergers) is still under debate.

Member states are required to incorporate these Directives into their national legislations within an agreed time scale. This has succeeded in achieving greater comparability between financial statements prepared in different member states, although a number of cultural differences remain. The Directives have also had an impact on financial reporting in countries seeking membership or involved in trade with existing members of the EU (e.g. Norway has implemented the Directives as a condition of membership of the European Economic area and Latvia has based its new accounting legislation on the Danish implementation of the Directives).

Although they have had a major impact on accounting in some countries, e.g. Greece and Spain, the Directives still only provide a framework for financial reporting and provide a range of options. This has to be supported by national legislation or accounting standards to provide the detailed regulation that leads to comparability within countries. These national practices can then counteract the harmonisation efforts. An obvious solution would be to have a European Accounting Standards Board. However, the practicalities of setting up such an organisation and reaching agreement on accounting issues within a reasonable time have meant that such a board has not been established. At the end of 1995, it was decided that the European Union could play a more active role in the IASC with a view to using IASs to support the Directives. As a first step, the Contact Committee on the Accounting Directives prepared a report entitled *An examination of the conformity between the international accounting standards and the European accounting Directives* in 1996. This established that there were few major differences between the IASs and the Directives.

27.5.3 The future

A number of suggestions have been made as to how greater comparability can be achieved between financial statements prepared in different countries at minimal cost to the companies involved. As most international analysis of financial statements involves the accounts of groups, whereas tax calculations are based on the accounts of individual companies, one solution would be to have international harmonisation or even standardisation of group accounts, but national rules for company accounts. Another answer could be for more countries to establish mutual recognition. A certain amount of harmonisation would be necessary before this could take place, but further harmonisation would undoubtedly follow afterwards.[28]

However, perhaps a word of caution should be introduced. Although business is becoming increasingly international, it is still based in individual countries. Users of financial statements should not allow harmonised annual reports to obscure cultural differences which may be inherent in the management of the business.

It seems that we are now reaching a crucial time for policy makers in directing the future of international reporting. In addition to the developments with IASs discussed above, a paper was recently put to the Financial Services Policy Group on the way ahead for EU accounting policy.[29] It set out three options to support the development of comparable financial information crucial to support the pan-European market:

1 Withdraw the Directives and allow market forces to prevail. The disadvantage with this is that financial reporting in companies that do not use the capital markets could become less comparable.

2 Withdraw the Directives and require compliance with IASs. This could be costly, particularly for smaller companies, due to the more onerous disclosure requirements of IASs.

3 Require compliance with IASs by companies whose shares or debt instruments are publicly traded and keep the Directives in place for all other companies. This is

thought to be the preferred option of the Commission, although it is not clear whether listed companies would be expected to comply with both IASs and the Directives. This could become increasingly difficult as IASs evolve to meet the changing needs of the business environment.

The review of company law in the UK is giving serious consideration to what it refers to as the 'European Dimension' and the 'Comparative Dimension'. Views are being sought as to whether the UK should allow the use of IASs.[30] In the US, the Financial Accounting Standards Board (FASB) has set out a vision for the future[31] which includes an International Standard Setter (ISS) whose standards are recognised or endorsed by each national standard-setter and any other relevant regulators for cross-border capital raising purposes. The ISS would be an international organisation independent of national standard-setters, although national standard setters would participate in the process. The quality of the standards would be ensured by being based on a conceptual framework and being supplied with adequate resources. It could be argued that this is not so very different from what is being suggested by the IASC.

27.5.4 Economic consequences of accounting differences

While the debate continues about the future regulatory framework, businesses and employees are facing the economic consequences of different accounting practices. Following the acquisition of British car maker, Rover in 1994 by German company, BMW, performance has been measured in accordance with the generally more conservative German accounting principles. This information has been used for making management decisions. The publication of the £620m loss for 1998 led to a wave of speculation about possible closure of production plants with consequent redundancies. However, it has been pointed out that results under UK accounting rules (which were published later) would not have been quite so dramatic. Figure 27.3 shows a comparison of the company's results under British and German rules. Following the takeover of Rover by Phoenix in 2000, Rover will report using UK accounting standards which could significantly cut the losses that would have been reported under German accounting standards if Rover had remained as part of BMW.

Nevertheless the danger of making assumptions about a particular country's measurement rules was highlighted in 1993 when Daimler Benz became the first German company to be listed on the New York Stock Exchange. Figure 27.4 summarises the company's results under German and US rules. In the year of listing (1993) there was a large difference between the two sets of figures, which created the impression that US and German accounting principles were very different and that US rules were more prudent. With hindsight, it is easy to see that 1993 was atypical and most of the differences

Figure 27.3 Rover results under UK and German rules.[32]

	Rover results using UK rules £m	Rover results using German rules £m
1994	279	unpublished
1995	(51)	(163)
1996	(100)	(109)
1997	19	(91)
1998	(571)	(620)

Figure 27.4 Daimler Benz results under US and German rules.[33]		
	Daimler Benz results using German rules DM m	*Daimler Benz results using US rules* DM m
1990	1,795	884
1991	1,942	1,886
1992	1,451	1,350
1993	615	(1,839)
1994	895	1,052
1995	(5,734)	(5,729)

could be attributed to permitted treatments of provisions which vary between the two countries. However the financial markets did not have the benefit of hindsight and responded to the information available at the time.

27.6 International analysis of financial statements

From the examples in 27.5.4 it can be seen that in spite of the best efforts of the bodies described in 27.5, there are still a number of difficulties which the financial analyst faces when approaching the accounts of multinational enterprises or enterprises based in another country. Analysts tend to concentrate on the primary financial statements,[34] but do they provide sufficient background information for adequate understanding? Areas where particular caution should be exercised when dealing with international financial statements are set out below.

27.6.1 Language

Language may present a difficulty for the analysis of accounts. Differences in language may be apparent when, for example, an Italian is using accounts prepared in Canada, as there is clearly a different language. However, there may also be difficulties for an English user of American financial statements, because usage of the language may be different (e.g. in the US 'notes' are what would be called 'bills' in the UK and vice versa). Translations of accounting terms create difficulties because not only the words but their meanings must be conveyed. The requirement of the EC Fourth Directive for annual accounts to give a 'true and fair view' has generated a wealth of research into the degree of success with which this Anglo-Saxon concept has been translated into the other language versions of the Directive and the corresponding national legislations.[35] Briefly, the understanding of the 'true and fair' term has been described as being virtually synonymous with Generally Accepted Accounting Practice (GAAP). It is therefore heavily influenced by prior accounting traditions, so countries with a history of applying accounting plans will consider accounts prepared in accordance with the rules give a true and fair view. However, this is to ignore the English understanding of the term as some kind of higher ideal, which can be appealed to in order to devise an appropriate accounting treatment for new situations.

Certain companies operating in countries with a minority language but with significant overseas investors have taken to publishing English language versions of their annual accounts. This is particularly common in Scandinavia, but an increasing number of German and Japanese companies are adopting this practice.

27.6.2 Format and extent of disclosure

Information may be presented in an unfamiliar format. UK users have become accustomed to standard formats for the presentation of financial statements. However, these formats are not as prescriptive as those applied in countries dominated by accounting plans, such as France and Spain. The application of judgement in presenting information has been important in Anglo-Saxon countries, whereas continental Europeans are more concerned with the application of rules. Balance sheets in the US present assets and liabilities in a different order from the UK, but there is consistent presentation. Developing countries may have very little standardisation of formats, so it may be quite difficult to locate a particular item in a set of Chinese accounts for example.

27.6.3 Currency

Financial statements usually use the currency of the country of domicile. Dealing with financial statements denominated in an unfamiliar currency can make it difficult to assess the true size of the entity or the volume of transactions. Some companies have responded to this by publishing 'convenience' accounts, showing amounts in, for example, US Dollars. Since The Companies Act 1985 (Accounts of Small and Medium-Sized Enterprises and Publication of Accounts in ECUs) Regulations 1992, UK companies have been permitted to file their annual financial statements in European Currency Units. This is discussed further in 27.6.10.

The second pitfall associated with currency is the translation of transactions within a company denominated in a variety of currencies. Further complications arise in consolidating companies whose accounts have been prepared using more than one currency. The UK treatment is laid down by SSAP 20, but there is more than one permitted method and companies based in other countries may take yet another approach.

When a parent acquires a foreign subsidiary it is necessary to translate the items in the subsidiary company's accounts, i.e. convert the foreign currency into sterling, in order to aggregate the parent and subsidiary figures. The actual conversion is a purely mechanical exercise, e.g. if the item is stated at 8,000 francs and the exchange rate is 8 francs to the pound then clearly the sterling equivalent is £1,000. However there are differences of opinion as to the choice of the appropriate date in selecting the rate to be used.

The appropriate date might be considered to be either:

(a) the date upon which the transaction was recorded in the foreign currency; or

(b) the accounting reference date.

If the date upon which the transaction was recorded in the foreign currency is chosen and applied to all items in the balance sheet, we describe this as the temporal method.

If the accounting reference date is chosen and applied to all items in the balance sheet, we describe this as the closing rate method. This has been explained more fully in Chapter 23 Foreign currency translation.

However, there have been other approaches under which items in the same balance sheet have been treated differently, i.e. some translated using the rate applicable to the date of the transaction and some using the rate applicable at the end of the current financial year. The two major methods have been the Current/Non-current (CNC) method and the Monetary/Non-monetary (MNM) method.

The application of the four methods is illustrated in Figures 27.5 and 27.6:[36]

Figure 27.5 Translation rates for balance sheet items under historical cost.

	Closing rate	CNC	MNM	Temporal
Fixed assets and long-term investments: cost	C	H	H	H
Stocks and short-term investments: cost	C	C	H	H
Stocks and short-term investments: market	C	C	H*	C
Debtors	C	C	C	C
Cash	C	C	C	C
Long-term debt	C	H	C	C
Current liabilities	C	C	C	C

C = closing rate

H = historical rate

*Some variants of MNM translate current items held at NRV using the closing rate

Figure 27.6 Example of translation.

Foreign HC balances in Picos	Balances	Closing rate £	CNC £	MNM £	Temporal £
10,000	Fixed assets	5,000	2,500	2,500	2,500
3,000	Stock (cost)	1,500	1,500	1,000	1,000
2,000	Stock (NRV)	1,000	1,000	667	1,000
3,000	Debtors	1,500	1,500	1,500	1,500
1,000	Cash	500	500	500	500
19,000	Total assets	9,500	7,000	6,167	6,500
12,000	Equity	6,000	4,500	2,667	3,000
4,000	Loans	2,000	1,000	2,000	2,000
3,000	Creditors	1,500	1,500	1,500	1,500
19,000	Total capital	9,500	7,000	6,167	6,500

Historical rate for fixed assets and loans: 4 picos = £1

Historical rates for stocks: 3 picos = £1

Closing rate: 2 picos = £1

27.6.4 Valuation and profit measurement

The value at which items appear in financial statements will vary, depending on the regime under which they are reported. An example of this would be fixed assets, which may be shown at current market value in the UK. They may be revalued at certain dates according to official indices in France and they must always be shown at historical cost in Japan. It is possible to make some generalisations about approaches to valuation, so the Japanese seem to be more conservative than the British. However, there are still surprises: the US is seen to be extremely prudent, yet accounts do not include an accrual for proposed dividends.

Figure 27.7 A comparative analysis of profit measurement behaviour (percentage of companies falling into classes I, II and III).

	France	West Germany	UK
	%	%	%
I Pessimistic	77	75	14
II Neutral	8	8	28
III Optimistic	15	17	58

There is some interest in using a form of current cost accounting (CCA) in countries where there is high inflation, such as in South America, which can necessitate adjustments by outside users. A full understanding of measurement rules is therefore required before jumping to conclusions about apparently unsatisfactory performance indicators.

Gray[37] identified that there was a tendency to be more pessimistic in measuring profit in certain countries. At the time of his study, he concluded that financial statements prepared in the UK were more optimistic than those prepared in France or Germany. The results of his study are summarised in Figure 27.7.

27.6.5 Taxation

The development of taxation rules and their effect on financial statements have been mentioned above. Caution should therefore be exercised when considering the treatment of fixed assets, stock and bad debts. The presentation of tax itself is also an area of variation, particularly provisions (full or partial) for deferred tax.

27.6.6 Groups

The company law harmonisation programme in Europe has improved the comparability of group accounts within the EU, but there are many variations across the world. These may derive simply from consolidation or non-consolidation of a 'subsidiary', because the definition of a subsidiary varies. Where figures are consolidated, there are potential variations in the choice of method, e.g. acquisition, equity or merger method, and in the application of the selected method, for example, the treatment of goodwill in acquisition accounting can range from immediate write-off to amortisation over forty years. There may also be different accounting policies applied in the group accounts from in the individual accounts, e.g. in France. Once again, a detailed study of the notes to the accounts will be necessary to ensure accurate interpretation.

27.6.7 Transfer pricing

Multinational enterprises take advantage of the different tax systems of the countries in which they operate. Careful organisation of production and selling divisions and the prices charged between the divisions can ensure that most profits are earned in the country with the lowest effective rate of tax. This can lead to somewhat misleading information if the accounts of a single division are considered in isolation. It is therefore important to ensure that any analysis is based on the financial statements of the enterprise as a whole.

27.6.8 Extraordinary items

The issue of extraordinary items in the UK has been 'resolved' relatively recently by their virtual abolition with FRS 3. However, accountants world wide have made efforts to focus analysts' attention on 'the good news'. This is another area where international users must ensure that any decisions are based on full information, that may be published in an imaginative form, if at all.

27.6.9 Financial instruments

The variety of financial instruments that are available to companies has added greater complexity to the presentation of financial statements. It would seem that some of these instruments have been designed to obscure the source of finance. While national and international accounting standard-setters are doing their best to keep pace with the financial markets, this is an area that is causing some significant national differences.

27.6.10 Multiple reporting

To assist users, or to comply with the requirements of foreign stock exchanges, some companies present financial statements in more than one currency, in more than one format or in accordance with more than one accounting convention. Some examples of this are shown in Figure 27.8 for Eybl International AG (Austria's largest textile company) and Glaxo Wellcome plc (UK pharmaceuticals company).

Restating figures in another currency may present information so that it is more familiar, but, of course, there is no effect on financial ratios, as all figures have been adjusted by the same factor. This can be seen from the Eybl accounts presented in Austrian Schillings and Euros. The difficulty of finding information presented in a different format was addressed by Glaxo Wellcome, which also presented its UK financial statements in the US format. This has not been reproduced in Figure 27.8, as there are no amendments to individual figures. Presenting financial statements in accordance with another accounting convention will result in amendments to figures. The differences

Figure 27.8 Examples of multiple reporting in financial statements for the year ended 31 December 1998.

Company	Eybl	Eybl	Eybl	Glaxo Wellcome	Glaxo Wellcome
Accounting convention	Austrian	Austrian	IAS	UK	US
Currency	ATS m	€ m	ATS m	£m	£m
Shareholders' equity	631	46	628	2,702	8,112
Income attributable to ordinary shareholders	128	9	119	1,836	1,015
Return on shareholders' equity	20%	20%	19%	68%	13%
Earnings per share	ATS 54	€ 4	ATS 50	51.1p	28.2p

between Eybl's financial statements prepared in accordance with Austrian regulations and IASs are not substantial. This is perhaps unsurprising given that Austrian regulations have implemented the European Directives and IASs are generally in line with the European Directives. The differences between Glaxo Wellcome's financial statements prepared in accordance with UK and US practice are far more significant. The financial statements provide a full reconciliation of the profit under UK GAAP to net income under US GAAP and between shareholders' equity under each convention. The largest reconciling items relate to goodwill, intangible fixed assets and deferred tax. These differences will gradually disappear as FRS 10 takes effect and the treatment of deferred tax in the UK falls in line with international practice.

27.6.11 Surveys of accounting practice

The variety of accounting treatments that are possible in the areas described above may seem confusing to a potential analyst. However, it is possible to quickly ascertain the most likely policies in particular countries by reference to published surveys of accounting practice. Some surveys may concentrate on a particular country (e.g. the annual ICAEW surveys in the UK) while others may be international (e.g. those produced periodically by Price Waterhouse). They may provide details on areas which are topical (e.g. *Fédération des Experts Comptables Européens* published a survey in 1993 on Seventh Directive options and their implementation) or may attempt to be more comprehensive (e.g. Price Waterhouse). The surveys do provide useful background information, but do have limitations insofar as they have been prepared for a specific purpose (which may not match the analyst's) and they may contain data that could be misleading or even incorrect. There is therefore no substitute for performing your own analysis that satisfies your objectives.

27.7 Country studies

The differences and similarities between financial statements prepared in different countries are now investigated more closely by looking at three countries in greater detail.

27.7.1 United States

Given the historical links between the UK and the US, it is unsurprising that the two systems of financial reporting have much in common. However, there are more rules in the US than in the UK (or perhaps even than anywhere in the world) which has resulted in greater standardisation and disclosure of information.

Legal

There is no direct equivalent of the UK Companies Acts in the US. The main federal regulation of trade in shares comprises the Securities Act 1933 and the Securities Exchange Act 1934. Neither of these includes any detailed provisions for the form and content of financial statements. The Securities and Exchange Commission (SEC) was born out of this legislation. This body is responsible for requiring the publication of financial information for the benefit of shareholders. It has the power to dictate the form and content of these reports. The largest companies whose shares are listed must register with the SEC and comply with its regulations. However, the majority of companies fall outside of its jurisdiction, although shareholders or lenders may require publication of equivalent information and a full audit. Individual states have the power to introduce their own legislation to control businesses and even set taxes. They are also responsible for conferring the right to practise as a public accountant.

Standard-setting body

The Financial Accounting Standards Board (FASB) is responsible for setting accounting standards in the US. Its independence is ensured by limiting the voluntary contributions to its funding from the various public accounting firms, industry and other interested parties. FASB issues the following documents:

● Statements of Financial Accounting Standards – deal with specific issues
● Statements of Concepts – give general information
● Interpretations – clarify existing standards

A subcommittee of FASB is the Emerging Issues Task Force which provided the inspiration for the UK Urgent Issues Task Force. The SEC recognises the authority of FASB's pronouncements, thus ensuring compliance by the largest companies.

Financial statements

The main financial statements are:

● Balance sheet
● Income statement
● Statement of cash flows

Treatment of specific items

Historical cost accounting predominates and transactions are not recognised in the financial statements until an arm's-length transaction has taken place. All fixed assets are therefore disclosed at historical cost and are depreciated over their anticipated useful life (there are no exceptions for investment properties). The straight-line method of depreciation is the most common although other methods are permitted. Leasing of assets is well established in the USA and leases are accounted for in a similar manner to in the UK.

Stocks (known as 'inventories') are valued at the lower of cost and market value (usually replacement cost). The most noticeable difference between the US and the UK is that the LIFO method of stock valuation is permitted in the US. This can be confusing when dealing with the accounts of long established companies as the balance sheet stock figure could be based on very old prices. However, it is argued that the income statement is more realistic as the cost of sales figure reflects the most recent prices.

Research and development expenditure must be written off as soon as it is incurred, unless a tangible asset is created. This is more conservative than SSAP 13, which allows certain expenditure to be carried forward. However, the cost of developing computer software products in the US may be capitalised at the lower of cost and net realisable value.

Another significant difference between financial statements prepared in the UK and the US is the treatment of deferred tax. The US take the more conservative 'full provision' approach, compared with the UK's partial provision.

Both acquisition and merger methods of accounting for business combinations are permitted, with restriction of merger accounting to circumstances involving a pooling of interests in exchange for equity shares. Any goodwill on acquisition may be capitalised and written off over a period not exceeding forty years. This means that in practice, most groups amortise goodwill over forty years. FASB has reduced the amortisation period for goodwill from forty to twenty years and has discontinued the pooling of interests method from 1 January 2000.[38]

Audit

All companies are required to have an annual audit if they are registered with the SEC or shareholders or lenders require it. The report of the independent auditor explains the basis of his opinion before expressing an opinion on whether the financial statements present fairly the results and changes in financial position in conformity with generally accepted accounting principles. This emphasises the importance of regulations over subjective application of broader concepts.

Effect of differences between UK and US accounting principles

As international, US and other national standards converge, the effect on net income and shareholders' equity of differences should also converge. However, at present there can be significant differences in the reported results and financial position. For example, the ICI 1999 Annual Report and Accounts disclosed the following:

	1999 £m	1998 £m	1997 £m
Net income after exceptional items – UK GAAP	252	83	369
Adjustments to conform with US GAAP	(199)	(127)	(228)
Net income (loss) – US GAAP	53	(44)	141
Shareholders' equity – UK GAAP	244	149	146
Adjustments to conform with US GAAP	3,129	3,408	3,952
Shareholders' equity – US GAAP	3,373	3,557	4,098

With the UK shareholders' equity in 1999 being only 7% of the US figure, and the UK profit in 1998 being reported as a US loss, it is extremely difficult to conceive that we are discussing the same company.

27.7.2 France

France has a well developed system of financial reporting which is highly regulated and legalistic in nature. It is used here as one example of accounting in mainland Europe. There are similarities with France in Spain and Greece. France is also an example of a country where variations in practice have developed between entity and group accounts.

Legal

The most important legislation is the 1982 General Accounting Plan which was developed from earlier accounting plans and incorporated the requirements of the EC Fourth Directive. The 1986 addition regarding consolidated accounts implemented the Seventh Directive. The plan was reviewed in 1997–8 and approved in 1999 with amendments intended to make it more accessible to users.[39] The idea behind the accounting plan is that control can be exercised because there is a uniform accounting system for all businesses. In essence the code comprises:[40]

● a statement of general accounting principles;
● arrangements for the organisation of accounting;
● rules for valuation and measurement of operating results;
● a standardised chart of accounts;
● instructions and guidelines for usage of accounts within the chart;
● standard format financial statements and notes to the accounts.

The Ministry of Finance has responsibility for accounting matters.

There are clearly advantages of standardisation, but the use of standard rates of depreciation and the application of rigid rules can make it difficult to reflect the economic substance of a business.

Standard-setting body

Given the prescriptive nature of the Accounting Plan, there is little need for accounting standards as such. However, the *Conseil National de la Comptabilité* (National Accounting Council) which is responsible for the development of the Plan, publishes descriptions of its work and interpretations of the Plan. The Council also invites comment. In 1996 the *Comité d'Urgence* (Urgent Issues Committee) was established to deal with any issue of interpretation or application of a standard requiring an urgent ruling. Part of the 1998 reform included the establishment of the *Comité de Réglementation Comptable* (CRC – Accounting Regulation Committee) providing regulatory authority to accounting standards. Regulation has also been provided by the *Commission des Operations de Bourse* (COB – National Securities Commission) since 1967.

Financial statements

The financial statements comprise

● Balance sheet
● Profit and loss account
● Notes
● Management Report

In accordance with the EC Fourth Directive, the overriding principle is the true and fair view, translated as the *image fidèle* (faithful image). There is also extensive reporting of employee information in the nature of Social Reporting which is more highly developed than in many other countries.

Treatment of specific items

Tangible fixed assets are generally shown at historical cost less depreciation. Revaluations have been permitted by tax law at certain dates: advantage has been taken of this facility insofar as it would not jeopardise the company's tax position. Leases may be capitalised in consolidated accounts in accordance with IAS 17, but French law does not provide a satisfactory definition of a finance lease. Consequently, in most accounts, all leases are treated as operating leases.

Stocks are valued at the lower of cost and market value (net realisable value or replacement cost). In general, cost is based on a weighted average calculation although FIFO is permitted. LIFO may only be used in consolidated accounts.

The attitude towards research and development expenditure is similar to that in the UK insofar as costs may be carried forward provided they can be identified and they relate to a specific project which is expected to be profitable. However, they must be written off within five years and dividends may not be paid out until they are written off, unless there are sufficient reserves to cover the carrying value of research and development.

Despite the close relationship between tax and financial accounting profit calculations, deferred tax liabilities do arise. It is unusual for deferred tax to be provided in the accounts of a single company, but partial or full provision may be made in consolidated financial statements.

Consolidated accounts must be prepared in accordance with the provisions of the EC Seventh Directive. Treatment of goodwill varies from immediate write-off to perpetual asset. Most companies write off goodwill over a period of twenty to forty years.[41]

Audit

The Ministry of Justice deals with auditing. Apart from proprietary limited liability companies below a defined size, annual accounts of commercial enterprises are subject to audit. All limited companies and co-partnerships must have their accounts audited by a *commissaire aux comptes* (accounting commissioner). Larger and listed companies must appoint two *commissaires aux comptes*, neither of whom must have been responsible for the preparation of the annual accounts.

27.7.3 Germany

Germany is the second continental European country to be considered. Although, like France, accounting is legalistic in nature, it has developed in somewhat different ways. As mentioned in 27.3.2, business in Germany has traditionally been financed by the banks, which has led to a limited need for financial reporting to outsiders. German accounting plans influenced those developed in France, but in Germany they have developed as industry specific or company specific charts of accounts, rather than a national plan.

Legal

Until 1985 the only real source of accounting regulation was the *Aktiengesellschaft* 1965 (AktG – Stock Corporation Law). Further regulations were introduced with the implementation of the Fourth, Seventh and Eighth Directives in 1985. Accounting rules were codified in the third book of the *Handelsgesetzbuch* (HGB – Commercial Code). The relationship between commercial accounts and tax accounts is very close in Germany, which means that tax legislation is also important. Accounting policies may be chosen to minimise tax liabilities, rather than necessarily presenting a closer picture of economic reality.

Standard-setting body

Because of the importance of statute, there has been no need for a standard-setting body, in the sense that they exist in the UK or US. Nevertheless, in March 1998, the German parliament adopted a new law which introduced requirements for the establishment of a national standard-setting body. This private sector body, *Deutsches Rechnungslegungsstandards Committee* (German Accounting Standards Committee) should provide recommendations on the principles of group accounting and represent Germany in international committees.[42] So far, the committee has issued a number of draft accounting standards and discussion papers on issues not specifically covered by statute and likely to be of interest to larger listed companies, e.g. cash flow statements and comparisons between IASs, EU Directives and German practice.[43]

Financial statements

The financial statements comprise

● Balance sheet
● Profit and loss account
● Notes
● Management Report.

In accordance with the EC Fourth Directive, financial statements must give a true and fair view. However, the Germans do not accept that the principle can be overriding: additional information may be necessary in the notes to provide a true and fair view, but departure from specific statutory provisions can never result in a true and fair view.[44]

Treatment of specific items

Consolidated financial statements have gained importance in recent years and they have been recognised as being of particular benefit to international users. It is perhaps for this reason, that some large German multinationals have been in the habit of preparing group accounts which follow or refer to IASs. This was legitimated by a change in statute in 1998 permitting companies to follow IASs or US GAAP in the group accounts provided they still comply with the EC Directives, they approximate to the German statutory provisions and appropriate explanations are provided.

Fixed assets are shown at historical cost less depreciation. The only form of revaluations which are seen involve writing back a previous write down. Because of the tax consequences of such revaluations, they are extremely rare. Finance leases are capitalised, which is a rare example of 'substance over form' being applied in German accounts. A consequence of this treatment is the recognition of the full liability for the lease which could be regarded as typically German with its emphasis on prudence.

Stocks are valued at the lower of cost and market value. FIFO, LIFO and average cost are all permitted. Stocks may also be written down to account for decreases in value that may occur in the near future. Only the completed contract method is permitted for long-term work in progress.

In addition to accruals for more or less certain expenses such as taxation and pensions, it is also common to accrue for possible liabilities such as repairs and maintenance. The discretion which is available in the calculation of provisions provides scope to 'smooth' income between one period and another.

Although there may be some differences between the financial accounts and the figures used for computing the tax liability, deferred tax does not play an important role in German reports.[45]

To protect creditors, there are strict regulations about the calculation of distributable profit. Part of this involves the requirement to build up a legal reserve in the balance sheet through an appropriation of profit each year until the reserve reaches a predetermined level.

Audit

Large companies must have their accounts audited by a member of the elite Chamber of Auditors (a *Wirtschaftsprüfer*, or *WP*) while medium sized companies may use a certified accountant (a *vereidigte Buchprüfer*, or *vBP*). The auditor prepares a long form report to members of the supervisory report. Because of the potentially sensitive nature of the full report, only the auditor's opinion on the financial statements is published with the financial statements. The opinion indicates whether the financial statements comply with the law and give a true and fair view. In addition, the auditor comments on whether the management report is in agreement with the financial statements.

27.7.4 Sweden

Accounting in Sweden has some similarities with Germany, but there are also some peculiarly Scandinavian traits. The relatively high proportion of multi-national corporations compared with its population in Sweden[46] has led to greater consideration of outsiders as potential users of financial reports. This has resulted in extensive disclosure to explain the basis of preparation of accounts and differences from other accounting conventions.

Legal

There is a long history of regulations governing book-keeping and financial reporting in Sweden and there were attempts to harmonise accounting legislation with the other Nordic countries (Denmark, Finland, Iceland and Norway) as early as the 1930s. Tangible evidence of this harmonisation effort came in similar companies acts which were implemented in each of the five countries in the 1970s. Sweden joined the European Union in 1995 following a referendum with a marginal 52% of voters in favour of membership. The accounting Directives were implemented in the Financial Statements Act 1995 (*Årsredovisningslag, ÅRL*) which supports the 1976 Accounting Act (*Bokföringslag*). Like Germany, Sweden has decided that the true and fair view cannot override the law, although it has been suggested that the principle could be used to justify departures from standards and guidelines.[47] Sweden has also retained its requirement that financial statements should be prepared in accordance with 'Good Accounting Practice' (*god redovisningssed*).

Standard-setting bodies

Sweden has a plethora of bodies which have provided and, in some cases, continue to provide guidance on accounting and financial reporting matters. The output of these bodies is generally referred to as 'standards' although direct translation of the Swedish would be 'guidelines' or 'recommendations'. The governmental body, *Bokföringsnämnden* (BFN) deals with accounting (as opposed to reporting) issues, dealing with documentation and providing specific answers to more limited accounting issues and has a general overview. The professional body, *Föreningen Auktoriserade Revisorer* (FAR) issued pronouncements until the end of the 1980s. The Accounting Council (*Redovisningsrådet*, RR) took over standard-setting in 1991 and is gradually replacing FAR's standards. A body equivalent to the UK's Urgent Issues Task Force was set up in 1995 to deal with matters requiring prompt actions or interpretations.

Financial statements

The financial statements comprise

● Balance sheet
● Profit and loss account
● Cash flow statement
● Notes
● Management Report

Swedish companies must use the horizontal format balance sheet and the vertical profit and loss account (although expenditure may be shown by nature or by function) from the 4th Directive's formats. A special feature of Swedish financial statements is the inclusion of an additional category, 'untaxed reserves' in the balance sheet, between equity and provisions. As in Germany, there is a close relationship between the financial accounts and the tax accounts. The disclosure of untaxed reserves is intended to help users understand items such as undervaluation of fixed assets or stocks which have been made to achieve tax benefits. Untaxed reserves are partly equity and partly deferred tax.[48]

With a view to informing investors, the group accounts (which are not affected by tax considerations) may use principles that are different from the entity's accounts. This is permitted by law. Swedish companies are keen to point out compliance with IASs. It is common to include a sentence along the lines of 'the financial statements comply with IASs in all material respects'. However, this is somewhat misleading, as Swedish companies do not comply with IAS 1 and follow all relevant IASs. Standards with oner-ous disclosure requirements, e.g. employee benefits, or those that would not comply with the Directives, are not followed. As mentioned above, this form of disclosure and prac-tice will not be permitted in future.

Treatment of specific items

Fixed assets are generally shown at historical cost less depreciation, but revaluation is permitted where the difference is permanent and material. Most leases were treated as operating leases but the RR's standard, which was effective from 1 January 1997, requires capitalisation of finance leases with provision for the leasing liability.

Stocks are valued at the lower of cost and net realisable value and LIFO is expressly prohibited. Tax deductible obsolescence provisions are permitted. Long-term work in progress is usually valued using the completed contract method, although percentage completion may be used.

Research and development can be capitalised and written off over a period that does not normally exceed five years. This is a provision of the ÅRL and does not include the detailed conditions of the UK standard, although there is further guidance in the Swedish accounting standards.

Group accounts must be prepared in accordance with the seventh Directive. Merger accounting is extremely rare. Goodwill should be capitalised and written off over up to five years, unless a longer period can be justified (but this cannot be more than 20 years).

As indicated above, different principles may be applied in the group accounts, which are independent of tax, so this leads to provisions for deferred tax in certain consolidated financial statements.

Audit

All companies are required to have their financial statements audited, but smaller com-panies may use the services of an auditor registered with a second tier body. In addition to expressing an opinion on compliance with statute, the audit report must indicate whether the directors have discharged their responsibilities and provide guidance on the board's suggestion on the use of profit.

27.7.4   Malaysia

Malaysia is a member of the British Commonwealth, the Association of South East Asian Nations (ASEAN) and the Organisation of Islamic Countries. Companies in Malaysia tend to be large compared with those operating in other countries in the immediate vicin-ity. Malaysia is a rapidly developing country that used to adopt IASs as a national requirement with relatively little local involvement. However, difficulties in interpreting Malaysian accounts used to arise due to lack of compliance with these standards.[49] The development of a regulatory structure for accounting has not been without tensions.[50]

Legal

As a result of its colonial history, the legal system in Malaysia has been strongly influ-enced by the British. The legal requirements for annual accounts are set out in the Companies Act 1965 as revised in 1985.

Standard-setting body

There are a number of sources of professional accounting regulation in Malaysia:

● IASC – certain specific IASs have been adopted by the Malaysian Association of Certified Public Accountants (MACPA), which was also responsible for
  – Malaysian Accounting Standards (MASs) (approved accounting standards);
  – Technical Bulletins (opinions on best practice);
  – Statements (more opinions on best practice).

The Financial Reporting Act (1997) established the Malaysian Accounting Standards Board (MASB) as the sole authority to develop and issue accounting standards. This body has adopted the existing standards which will continue to be called either International Accounting Standards or Malaysian Accounting Standards according to their origin.[51]

Whilst the use of IASs is convenient and they are broadly in line with the regulation of the business environment which has been influenced by the country's colonial past, it has been argued that they may not be the most appropriate form of regulation.[52] However, the MASs provide a structure within which standards could be tailored to meet local requirements. The MASB's standards are gradually taking over: by January 2000, there were thirteen approved accounting standards and a discussion paper for a conceptual framework.[53]

Financial statements

The financial statements comprise:

● Balance sheet
● Profit and loss account
● Cash flow statement
● Notes

The overriding principle is the true and fair view. The director responsible for the company's financial management must provide a statutory declaration on the correctness of the financial statements.

Treatment of specific items

Fixed assets are stated at historical cost as amended by the revaluation of land and buildings less depreciation. Unfortunately disclosure of the date and basis of any revaluation may be lacking. Leasing is a relatively rare phenomenon in Malaysia, so both capital and revenue treatments may be found.

Stocks are stated at the lower of cost and net realisable value. FIFO and weighted average are the most common methods of valuation although LIFO and base cost are permitted.

Research and development is not a major item of expenditure, but where it is incurred the cost is usually capitalised and amortised over a number of years.

Deferred tax should be provided by the partial or full provision method. Practice generally accords with theory on this item.

Group accounts, where necessary, usually fall within the requirements for the acquisition method of accounting. Goodwill is most commonly retained on the balance sheet indefinitely. Non-consolidation of subsidiaries is usually on grounds of dissimilar activities: they would then be brought in under the equity method.

Audit

All companies are subject to audit, regardless of size. The auditor must be approved by the Minister of Finance, which will usually require him to be a member of the Malaysian Institute of Accountants (MIA) and have his principal or only residence in Malaysia.

Membership of the MIA is usually obtained through membership of another accounting body, principally MACPA. Difficulties have arisen in the past due to the variety of backgrounds of professional accountants and steps are being taken by MIA and MACPA to remedy this situation. Partners of firms of public accountants must be registered with the Registrar of Companies. Their registration number must then be quoted on all audit reports. Public accountants are permitted to provide other accountancy services in addition to statutory audits.

Summary

The expansion in the number of multinational enterprises and transnational investments has led to a demand for a greater understanding of financial statements prepared in a range of countries. The study of international accounting has developed from being purely descriptive to being more analytical. In spite of a number of attempts to improve comparability of accounts, there remain a number of international differences. The way forward for analysts would seem to be continued pressure for harmonisation along with increased education. A full interpretation of financial statements can only be made in the context of the financial and cultural environment in which a business operates. This chapter has given an indication of the diversity of accounting around the world and opportunities for further study.

Review questions

1 How does the regulatory framework for financial reporting in the UK differ from that in the USA? Which is better for particular interest groups and why?

2 'Standardisation is the only way forward for European financial reporting.' Discuss this statement in the light of efforts which have already been made in the harmonisation of company law.

3 Suggest criteria which could be used to classify systems of financial reporting employed in different countries. What difficulties are there in performing an exercise of this nature?

4 Identify the main problems which an analyst would face when dealing with financial statements prepared in another country.

5 CIC plc is a multinational chemical company that is registered in the Republic of Ireland and quoted on the Dublin Stock Exchange. The company is a member of an inter-company comparison scheme for companies that operate in the Republic of Ireland and it receives an annual comparison report including information such as returns on capital employed, returns on investment, asset utilisation and liquidity. The information relates to CIC plc and 32 other chemical companies that operate in the Republic of Ireland market. However, the directors are not finding the report as useful as they wished because CIC plc has over 90% of the Republic of Ireland market and the other 32 companies are Republic of Ireland registered marketing subsidiaries of major multinational companies which are based in other countries such as the US, France, Germany, Italy, Japan and South America.

   CIC plc has requested the accountant to produce an internal comparison report based on the annual reports of the other multinational companies rather than on the financial statements of the marketing subsidiaries and also to advise it of any problems that may arise in extracting and interpreting ratios from the consolidated financial statements of foreign multinational competitors.

   (a) Explain the problems that may arise in:
       (i) collecting the relevant data;

(ii) interpreting the data when they have been prepared to satisfy different disclosure requirements;

(iii) interpreting the data when there may be differing attitudes to financing and risk;

(iv) interpreting the data when there may be differing user requirements.

(b) Discuss the extent to which you consider that the harmonisation of accounting disclosure requirements will reduce the problems.

6 There was an expectation that IASs would be adopted by countries that did not have their own standards. We have seen that in Malaysia the adoption of IASs has been followed by the issue of national accounting standards. Discuss why this is happening and the implication for worldwide harmonisation.

Exercises

Question 1

Compare the treatment of tangible and intangible fixed assets in accounts prepared in the UK, North America, Europe and Asia. You may wish to focus your answer on specific countries in these continents.

Question 2

Discuss the degree of conservatism apparent in financial statements prepared in North America, Europe and Asia. How does this manifest itself in the treatment of research and development expenditure?

Question 3

Comment on the following audit report issued to shareholders of BMW AG. Discuss the similarities and differences between it and a standard UK audit report. Evaluate the impact that these similarities and differences have for users of the accounts of multinational enterprises. Consider whether the opinion should be qualified with respect to the accounting policy for certain joint ventures.

> BMW Annual Report 1998
> **Auditors' note of confirmation**
>
> The Consolidated Financial Statements, which we have audited in accordance with professional standards, comply with the German legal provisions. The Consolidated Financial Statements present, in compliance with required accounting principles, a true and fair view of the Group's assets, liabilities, financial position and net income. The Business Review of the Group is consistent with the Consolidated Financial Statements.
>
> Munich, March 4 1999
> **KPMG Deutsche Treuhand-Gesellschaft**
> Aktiengesellschaft
> Wirtschaftsprüfungsgesellschaft
> (Auditors)
>
> Dr. Hoyos   Große-Brauckmann
> Auditor   Auditor

Question 4

The following table summarises mean differences in aggregate financial ratios between the US and Japan.[48]

| | | All manufacturing companies | | |
		US	Japan	% Difference
Current ratio	Current assets / Current liabilities	1.9:1	1.1:1	40%
Inventory Turnover	cost of goods sold / average inventory	6.8 times	5.0 times	26%
Average collection period	average receivables / sales per day	43 days	86 days	(102%)
Debt ratio	total debt / total assets	47%	84%	(77%)
Times interest earned	earnings before interest and tax / interest charges	6.5 times	1.6 times	75%
Profit margin	net profits / sales	5.4%	1.3%	74%
Return on total assets	earnings before interest and tax / average total assets	7.4%	1.2%	84%
Return on net worth	net profit / average net worth	13.9%	7.1%	49%

Required:
State what further information you would require in order to be able to make a comparative evaluation of the US/Japanese performance.

Question 5

The table below[54] summarises the UK GAAP/US GAAP reconciliations of net income and equity for fifteen of the UK's largest companies.

	Reconciliation of net income from UK GAAP to US GAAP							
	Net income (UK GAAP)	Goodwill intangibles	Borrowing costs	Deferred taxes	Pension costs	Restructuring costs, etc.	Other	Net income (US GAAP)
BP	2,552	—	—	(260)	—	—	46	2,338
BT	1,986	(36)	(22)	14	18	—	(154)	1,806
Cable and Wireless	607	(17)	2	(24)	(7)	(21)	6	546
Cadbury Schweppes	340	(88)	—	—	(2)	(6)	3	247
Glaxo Wellcome	1,997	(1,028)	—	—	—	—	10	979
Grand Metropolitan	345	(155)	—	83	(8)	(89)	14	190
Hanson	1,419	(150)	—	103	43	—	(3,320)	(1,905)
National Power	608	—	23	(17)	—	—	(5)	609
Powergen	519	(1)	15	(93)	7	—	(10)	437
Reed Elsevier	604	(107)	—	(27)	18	—	5	493
Reuters	491	(49)	—	5	—	—	(7)	440
SmithKline Beecham	1,035	(187)	—	21	—	(104)	35	800
Unilever	1,610	(221)	6	50	(2)	(76)	—	1,367
Vodafone	310	(19)	—	4	—	—	(1)	294
Zeneca	643	(34)	(5)	(6)	(15)	(14)	15	584

	Equity (UK GAAP)	Goodwill intangibles	Borrowing costs	Deferred taxes	Pensions, etc.	Restructuring costs, etc.	Revalu- ations	Proposed dividends	Other	Equity (US GAAP)
					Reconciliation of equity from UK GAAP to US GAAP					
BP	12,795	—	—	(2,217)	71	—	—	—	1,014	11,663
BT	12,678	2,370	366	(1,802)	(1,308)	—	—	715	(9)	13,010
Cable and Wireless	3,259	962	202	(896)	(21)	5	—	154	150	3,815
Cadbury Schweppes	1,287	1,236	35	(98)	(43)	—	(76)	118	26	2,485
Glaxo Wellcome	1,225	6,209	—	(273)	—	—	—	673	319	8,153
Grand Metropolitan	3,211	3,420	—	(1,091)	(132)	22	(88)	211	(404)	5,149
Hanson	2,535	3,204	—	(732)	172	—	(165)	—	202	5,216
National Power	2,666	—	276	(772)	38	—	—	200	51	2,459
Powergen	2,252	16	51	(456)	5	—	—	106	30	2,004
Reed Elsevier	2,071	952	—	(191)	(9)	—	—	235	17	3,075
Reuters	1,260	216	—	(13)	—	—	—	145	(47)	1,561
SmithKline Beecham	1,369	3,363	—	(39)	(59)	79	(56)	160	(82)	4,735
Unilever	5,181	4,904	440	(707)	171	140	—	465	—	10,594
Vodafone	1,022	232	—	(79)	(2)	—	—	62	6	1,241
Zeneca	2,034	600	101	(45)	(151)	—	—	214	12	2,765

What do these reconciliations tell you about differences between accounting principles generally accepted in the UK and the US?

What would be the impact on such reconciliations of the ASB's change in the treatment of goodwill?

If IOSCO endorses the IASC's core standards and these were accepted by stock exchanges for cross border listings, UK companies would be able to present their accounts in accordance with IASs. What would a reconciliation of UK GAAP to IASs look like for the fifteen UK companies?

Question 6

Below are extracts from the financial statements of Electrolux, the Swedish based manufacturer of appliances. The company reconciles its financial statements prepared in accordance with Swedish regulations to US generally accepted accounting principles.

● Compare the two balance sheets on a line by line basis, to identify areas of difference.

● Compare your notes with the company's explanation of major differences between Swedish and US GAAP.

● Are there any areas which you have identified which are not adequately explained by the company's note?

● Which of the two sets of accounting principles gives the fairest representation of the economic position of the company?

● Which of the two sets of accounting principles gives the most prudent representation of the economic position of the company?

● Discuss reasons for Electrolux choosing to present its accounts according to two sets of principles. Your discussion should include the following areas: Stock exchange listings; Users of financial statements; Size of country of domicile; Size of company; Industry in which the company operates; Accounting theory.

Balance sheet (SEKm) – Electrolux Annual Report 1998

The table below summarises the consolidated balance sheets prepared in accordance with the Swedish accounting principles and US GAAP.

	According to Swedish principles		According to US GAAP	
	1998	1997	**1998**	1997
Intangible assets	**3,327**	3,517	**2,366**	2,546
Tangible assets	**21,959**	22,519	**21,913**	22,442
Financial assets	**2,599**	1,744	**2,779**	1,876
Current assets	**55,404**	51,860	**58,642**	55,710
Total assets	**83,289**	79,640	**85,700**	82,574
Equity	**24,480**	20,565	**24,018**	20,332
Minority interests	**953**	913	**953**	913
Provisions for pensions and similar commitments	**4,298**	6,247	**4,518**	6,461
Other provisions	**4,026**	4,656	**3,371**	3,685
Financial liabilities	**29,070**	28,479	**32,378**	32,403
Operating liabilities	**20,462**	18,780	**20,462**	18,780
Total liabilities and equity	**83,289**	79,640	**85,700**	82,574

Note 25. Consolidated financial statements according to US GAAP

The consolidated accounts have been prepared in accordance with Swedish accounting standards, which differ in certain significant respects from American accounting principles (US GAAP). The most important differences are described below:

Adjustment for acquisitions

In accordance with Swedish accounting principles, the tax benefit arising from application of tax-loss carry-forwards in acquired companies is deducted by the Group from the current year's tax costs. According to US GAAP, this tax benefit should be booked as a retroactive adjustment of the value of acquired intangible assets.

Pensions

According to the American recommendations for pensions known as FAS 87 (Employers' Accounting for Pensions), computation of the projected benefit obligation and pension costs for the year must take account of assumptions regarding such factors as future salary increases and inflation which in some aspects differ from the actuarial assumptions used for the pension plans within Electrolux.

Securities

According to Swedish accounting principles, holdings of debt and equity securities should be reported according to the lowest-value principle. According to FAS 115 (Accounting for Certain Investments in Debt and Equity Securities), these holdings should be classified with respect to intention, i.e. if they are to be traded, if they are to be retained until maturity, or if they are in an intermediate category. Valuation and reporting of income differ according to the classification of the securities. For Electrolux, this means that certain securities must be reported at market value in the balance sheet, while the difference between market and acquisition value must be taken directly to equity, according to US GAAP. In connection with the sale of these securities, the change in value previously reported directly against equity is reported in the income statement.

Deferred taxes

Taxation and financial reporting are affected during different periods by certain items. Electrolux reports deferred taxes on the most important timing differences, which refer mainly to untaxed reserves, with due consideration in certain cases for the future fiscal effects of tax-loss carry-forwards. US-GAAP requires reporting of fiscal effects for all significant differences and tax-loss carry-forwards, with the proviso that deferred tax assets may be reported only if it is probable that the tax benefit will be utilized.

Timing differences

According to Swedish accounting principles, provisions for costs referring to a shutdown are booked when the decision is made to shut down the plant. US GAAP rules require meeting additional criteria before provisions can be made for severance pay and other costs related to shutdowns. Therefore, compliance with US GAAP requires that provisions for these and similar costs be made at a later date.

Distribution of Gränges

In accordance with the decision by the Annual General Meeting in April 1997, all shares in Gränges AB were distributed to Electrolux shareholders on May 20, 1997. In accordance with Swedish accounting principles, Gränges has been removed from the Group's financial statements for 1997.

According to the US GAAP, Gränges should be included in the Group's balance sheet and income statement up to the date that the decision to distribute the shares was made, and should be reported in the income statement as a divested operation.

Comprehensive income

According to FAS 130 (Reporting Comprehensive Income), the financial statements should include an income concept 'Comprehensive income' which, in addition to net income for the year according to the income statement, should include other items affecting equity. Comprehensive income includes all changes in equity except capital transactions with the owners. Examples of items that should be included are translation differences, certain changes in provisions for pensions that according to US GAAP are charged directly to equity and changed values during the holding of securities where the profit/loss is not shown in the income statement before disposal. The accounting standard is mandatory for Electrolux as from 1998.

References

1 *The Economist*, 2 January 1999, p. 97.
2 R.T. Moran, *Cultural Guide to doing Business in Europe* (2nd edition), Butterworth-Heinemann Ltd, 1992, p. 51.
3 *Ibid.*, p. 60.
4 C. Nobes and R. Parker, *Comparative International Accounting* (5th edition), Prentice Hall International, 1998, pp. 13–29.
5 J. Freedman, and M. Power, *Law and Accountancy – Conflict and Cooperation in the 1990s*, Paul Chapman Publishing Ltd, 1992, p. 105.
6 For more detailed discussion see C. Nobes, 'Corporate financing and its effects on European accounting differences,' Reading University discussion paper, 1996.
7 Source: BZW Securities Ltd.
8 C. Nobes, *Towards 1992*, Butterworths, 1989, p. 15.
9 C. Randlesome, *Business Cultures in Europe* (2nd edition), Heinemann Professional Publishing, 1993, p. 27.
10 J.D. Daniels and L.H. Radebaugh, *International Business* (8th edition), Addison-Wesley, 1998, p. 818.

11   C. Randlesome, *op cit.*, p. 25.

12   C. Nobes, *Towards 1992*, Butterworths, 1989, p. 8.

13   T. Cooke, *An Empirical Study of Financial Disclosure by Swedish Companies*, Garland, 1989, pp. 112–113.

14   C. Nobes and R. Parker, *op cit.*, p. 66.

15   S.P. Agrawal, P.H. Jensen, A.L. Meader and K. Sellers, 'An international comparison of conceptual frameworks of accounting', *The International Journal of Accounting*, Vol. 24, 1989, pp. 237–249.

16   *Accountancy*, June 1989, p. 10.

17   See, for example, B. Chauveau, 'The Spanish *Plan General de Contabilidad*: Agent of development and innovation?' *European Accounting Review*, Vol. 4, no. 1, 1995, pp. 125–138.

18   See, for example, P.E.M. Standish, 'Origins of the *Plan Comptable Général*: a study in cultural intrusion and reaction', *Accounting and Business Research*, Vol. 20, no. 80, 1990, pp. 337–351.

19   C. Nobes and R. Parker, *op cit.*, pp. 46–62.

20   *Ibid.*, p. 66.

21   International Accounting Standards Committee, *International Accounting Standards*, Burgess Science Press, 1994, p. 7.

22   For further details, see *Accountancy*, International Edition, December 1999, p. 5.

23   International Accounting Standards Committee, *op. cit.*, p. 29.

24   For further details see D. Cairns (1997) 'The future of the IASC and the implications for UK companies' in ICAEW, *Financial reporting today – current and emerging issues*, Accountancy Books, 1998, pp. 115–152.

25   *Accountancy*, International Edition, January 1999, p. 9.

26   See, for example, D. Cairns, *Financial Times International Accounting Standards Survey 1999*, FT Business, 1999.

27   The European Economic Community established by the Treaty of Rome in 1957 became known as the European Community in 1985 and the European Union in November 1993 following the Maastricht Treaty.

28   S.J. Key (1989) cited in P. Thorell and G. Whittington (1994), 'The harmonisation of accounting within the EU. Problems, perspectives and strategies', *The European Accounting Review*, 3:2, p. 226.

29   *Accountancy*, International Edition, March 1999, p. 5.

30   See *Modern Company Law for a Competitive Economy: The Strategic Framework.*
A consultation document from the Company Law Review Steering Group, February 1999, Department of Trade and Industry.

31   Financial Accounting Standards Board (1998) *International Accounting Standard Setting: A Vision for the Future*, report of the FASB.

32   C. Quick and D. Wild, 'Rover trouble was avoidable', *Accountancy Age*, 18 February 1999, p. 7.

33   Source: Daimler Benz, Form 20-F 1995; L.H. Radebaugh, G. Gebhardt and S.J. Gray, 'Foreign stock exchange listings: A case study of Daimler Benz', *Journal of International Financial Management and Accounting*, 1995, 6(2), pp. 158–92.

34   See L.S. Chang, K.S. Most and C.W. Brian, 'The utility of annual reports: an international study', *Journal of International Business Studies*, Spring/Summer 1983, pp. 63–84.

35   See for example *The European Accounting Review*, Vol. 2, No. 1, May 1993, which devoted a whole section to the issue.

36   C. W. Nobes, 'A review of the translation debate' in S.J. Gray (ed.), *International Accounting and Transnational Decision*, Butterworths, 1983, p. 216.

37   S.J. Gray, 'The impact of international accounting differences from a security analysis perspective', *Journal of Accounting Research*, Spring 1980, pp. 64–76.

38   For further discussion, see *Accountancy*, International Edition, July 1999, p. 62.

39   For further details, see P. Standish, *Developments in French Accounting and Auditing 1998*, Export Comptable Média, 1999.

40 P. Standish, *ibid.*, p. 16.

41 See survey reported in P. Standish, *op cit.*, p. 214.

42 *Accountancy*, International Edition, May 1998, pp. 71–72.

43 See, for example, *Accountancy*, International Edition, September 1999, pp. 56–57; November 1999, p. 71; December 1999, p. 54.

44 For further discussion see D. Ordelheide, 'True and fair view: a European and German perspective. A commentary on "A European true and fair view?" by David Alexander', *European Accounting Review*, 2:1, 1993, pp. 81–90; D. Ordelheide 'True and fair view. A European and German perspective II', *European Accounting Review*, 3:5 1996, pp. 495–506.

45 See for example G. Seckler in D. Alexander and S. Archer, *European Accounting Guide*, (2nd edition) Harcourt Brace, Jovanovich 1995.

46 T.E. Cooke, 'Disclosure in the corporate annual reports of Swedish companies', *Accounting and Business Research*, 19: 74, 1989, pp. 113–124.

47 KPMG, *Accounting Principles: Significant Differences Between Sweden And The US*, KPMG, 1997, p. 1.

48 For a more detailed explanation of untaxed reserves, see K. Artsberg (1998) in P. Walton, A. Haller and B. Raffournier, *International Accounting*, Thompson Business Press, 1998, pp. 288–290.

49 J.S.W. Tay, 'Malaysia', in T.E. Cooke and R.H. Parker (eds), *Financial Reporting in the West Pacific Rim*, London: Routledge 1994.

50 See S. D. Susela, '"Interests" and accounting standard setting in Malaysia', *Accounting, Auditing and Accountability Journal* Vol. 12, No. 3, 1999, pp. 358–387.

51 *Accountancy*, International Edition, February 1998, pp. 81–82.

52 C. Nobes and R. Parker, *op cit.*, p. 130.

53 www.mash.org.my/About_MASB/about_mash.html

54 D. Cairns (1997) in ICAEW, *Financial Reporting Today – current and emerging issues*, Accountancy Books, 1998 edition.

PART **6**

Accountability

CHAPTER 28

Accountability of directors and auditors

28.1 Introduction

In this chapter we consider:

A – **Corporate governance – directors**
- corporate governance pre-Cadbury
- the Cadbury Report
- the Greenbury Report
- the Hampel report
- the Combined Code
- directors' remuneration
- relations with shareholders
- institutional investors
- the Myners Report

B – **Corporate governance – auditors**
- accountability and audit
- assessing quality of management performance
- the way forward
- role of the Auditor

A – CORPORATE GOVERNANCE – DIRECTORS

28.2 Corporate governance pre Cadbury

Private shareholders were powerless

The directors of quoted companies were aware that private shareholders were powerless because there were a large number of individuals with relatively very small holdings who could be safely ignored. In theory, shareholders are deemed to exercise control over the directors by attending the annual general meeting and voting to approve the accounts, to approve the dividend, to approve the directors' salaries and to approve the appointment of auditors. In practice, the situation is totally different. Only 500 shareholders might turn up for the AGM out of a total of 50,000, and then only to enjoy the buffet. The majority give the directors a proxy to vote as they wish. The reality was that directors became entrenched and the approval of any recommendation they put forward was invariably a formality. They were able to be displaced only if there was a take-over and, even then, they might have entered into contracts which ensured that they received an attractive golden handshake. Not all directors were impervious to the wishes of the shareholders, but they could be if they so wished.

There was a polite fiction that companies were controlled by or accountable to their shareholders, but there was little evidence that any control actually existed. The directors had almost unbridled power. They decided on the persons to be nominated as directors; they decided on the choice of non-executive directors; they selected from their fellow directors the audit committee and the remuneration committee (if indeed either committee existed) they decided whether to disclose 'sensitive issues', such as the number of times the company had been prosecuted for breaches of environmental regulations.

Institutional investors received private briefings to obtain comparative advantage

The directors were aware of the power that institutional investment organisations, 50 of which control half of the stock market, could exercise. They were also aware that institutional investors did not see their role primarily as getting involved in corporate governance.

A shareholder who became involved in corporate governance benefited all the other shareholders as well, whereas institutions were looking to gain a comparative advantage. One leading firm of chartered accountants commented that it saw little prospect of a significant change of attitude by institutions while they were able to receive private briefings from companies on their performance. This practice continued in 1997 (see *Accountancy*, June 1997, p. 77).

Fund managers might have a little more influence, but even that was doubtful unless the directors required their active support. As mentioned in *Making Corporate Reports Valuable*,[1] some of the information that management has but does not normally communicate only comes out into the open when management wants something. For example, if managements wanted additional capital, or to defend or promote a take-over, or to maintain the company's share price, then disclosures might be made that would not otherwise become public.

Domination of the boardroom

There was evidence that in some companies there was a single person who acted as both Chairman and Chief Executive Officer, or a small group of directors, who dominated the board. There was no counter-balance from strong executive or non-executive directors.

Non-executive directors seen as lacking independence

It was the existing directors who decided who would join them on the board, whether as executive or non-executive directors. Non-executive directors were perceived to lack independence and did not act as a counter-balance on the board. The chairman of Thames Water has commented in the press[2] that Thames Water's board of nine directors comprised a majority of non-executive directors selected through a professional agency, not simply to avoid accusations about the 'old boys' network', but also to obtain the best talent available. This was excellent practice, but it highlighted the difference between Thames Water and many other boardrooms. For example, other press comment has been more critical:

> the Manchester Business School believes it is time to end the charmed circle in Britain's boardrooms in which directors swap seats in a non-executive merry-go-round, rewarding each other with better salaries.[3]

Directors remuneration was excessive

Shareholders had no direct way of knowing whether the directors were putting the welfare of the shareholders first, or whether they were pursuing personal goals such as maximising their salaries and bonuses.

Directors had virtually unlimited powers to extract ever increasing remuneration, often in the guise of salary comparability studies with a built-in tendency to match increases in other companies regardless of value for money, even when the company was performing badly

Even the authorities were concerned because the problem was so visible. The following press extract indicated the worries of the Stock Exchange and the Bank of England about the high remuneration of directors:

> The Bank of England and stock exchange are today lending their support to a strict code on how directors' remuneration should be set ... the organisation for the promotion of non-executive directors has produced draft guidelines ... the central element of the advice is that salaries and benefits should be set by 'remuneration committees' consisting exclusively of non-executive directors ... the processes by which benefits are set should be made public and those who make the decisions should have no 'direct interest' in the results ... the remuneration committees should ensure company executives receive fair reward with due regard to the interests of shareholders, employees and the commercial and financial health of the company.[4]

A compromise had been suggested in which the directors restrained their demands at a level below that at which shareholders would lose tolerance and replace them, and the shareholders suffered the cost of auditing the sensitive areas where conflict of interest might arise.[5] This is why directors' emoluments, pensions and compensation for loss of office are required to be disclosed by the Companies Act 1985,[6] together with disclosure of interests in contracts and options to subscribe for shares; it is also why these disclosures are audited.

These were rather negative tests and compromises, and there was evidence that current disclosures were not effective. This was illustrated by press comment relating to the position in the USA:

> The Securities and Exchange Commission is seeking to force companies to spell out clearly to shareholders just how much top executives are being paid ... the SEC is proposing to make companies use a specific method for valuing stock options granted to senior corporate officials ... among executives whose stock options have attracted attention are Steven Ross and N J Nichola, co-chief executives of Time Warner who together made $99.6 million in 1990 ... One Democratic proposal would open the pay-setting process to shareholders rather than just board members and hand picked compensation advisers.[7]

It was suggested that the annual report should contain a statement of corporate objectives.[8] However, it is debatable whether such a process gives shareholders any real control over directors' actions and behaviour. The level of directors' remuneration was, and is, not an accounting problem, but a problem of company governance. It cannot be resolved by issuing an accounting standard; it needed effort at a political level and there is little evidence of any determination to introduce regulatory controls. In the meantime the system tolerates increases even where there is poor performance.

Other stakeholders' interests had low priority

It has been a generally accepted theoretical view that the directors of a company should maximise profits for the benefit of the shareholders. Social and environmental issues had a low priority.

Directors' duty of care

A director has a duty of care, but it is often not realised that there are limits to this duty. Some of the limits are set out in J. Romer's comments in 'Re City Equitable Fire Insurance Co. Ltd':

1 a director need not exhibit in the performance of his duties a greater degree of skill than may be reasonably expected from a person of his knowledge and experience ... they are not liable for errors of judgement.

2 a director is not bound to give continuous attention to the affairs of his company. His duties are of an intermittent nature to be performed at periodical board meetings.[9]

Given that this decision was made in 1925, it could well be that a higher standard would now be required. The implication for the shareholders was that they should themselves exercise care in the appointment of the directors. They should only appoint directors who are unlikely to make errors of judgement.

However, shareholders are not in a position to make an informed decision. They do not always receive sufficient information about the directors and managers to whom they entrust their capital. It has been suggested that shareholders need further information to be able to assess the experience and background of company directors and officials, including details of other past and present directorships or official positions.[10]

The Law Commission has produced a draft statement of directors' duties[11] which sets out a summary of the main duties of a director to his company. These duties are:

● Loyalty – to act in good faith in the interests of the company.

● Obedience – to act lawfully and in accordance with the articles and memorandum of association.

● No secret profits – not to use the company's property, information or opportunities for his own or anyone else's benefit unless allowed by the company's constitution or he has disclosed it at the Annual General Meeting and the company has consented to it.

● Independence – not to agree to restrict his power to exercise independent judgement unless the outcome is for the benefit of the company.

● Conflict of interest – to account to the company for any benefit he receives unless it is within the company's constitution or approved by the company.

● Care, skill and diligence – to exercise the care, skill and diligence that a reasonable person would have exercised, having:
  ● the knowledge and experience that may be reasonably expected; and
  ● the knowledge and experience which the director has.

● Interests of employees and shareholders – to have regard to the interests of both.

● Fairness – to act fairly as between different members.

Directors were unaccountable

Private shareholders were powerless. Institutional investors received private briefings and did not see their role to be one of policing good corporate governance. Regulators were mainly concerned with the operation of the capital market 'as a whole' and did not provide or encourage active participation in the governance of a company by anyone other than the directors. As far, therefore, as the individual company was concerned, the shareholders exercised no control, the employees certainly exercised no control and even the regulators themselves appeared to exercise ineffective control. This is illustrated by the need for an inquiry by Lord Justice Bingham into the supervision of the collapsed Bank of Credit and Commercial International by the Bank of England and the Treasury.

The lack of accountability had unacceptable results. These ranged from catastrophic results e.g. company pension funds misappropriated on a massive scale, banks failing through misappropriation of funds or lack of adequate control to prevent staff incurring crippling losses to what amounts to a failure of the duty of trust whereby directors extracted unfair salaries, pensions, bonuses and share options.

There was unease about the fairness of the remuneration that directors awarded themselves. The process was not transparent even where remuneration committees determined the package. Such committees gave little evidence that they used valid performance criteria for salary, bonuses or share options. For example, a study carried out by Arthur Andersen[12] found no significant correlation between bonuses and company performance measured by the shareholder return. Another report prepared by KPMG Peat Marwick[13] showed that two-thirds of listed companies operated executive share option schemes that were not linked to targets, so that about £7 billion of the £10.5 billion that public quoted shares allocated to such schemes were not connected to company performance. Rewards were more likely to depend on stock market cycles than on executive performance: managers did well out of a strong stock market even though their company results and share price performance were relatively poor. Remuneration packages were so complex that the shareholders were unable to identify their total value, and companies were resistant to greater transparency.

Clearly this lack of accountability had become too visible to be allowed to continue unchecked and the Committee on the Financial Aspects of Corporate Governance (Cadbury Committee) was appointed and reported in December 1992, followed by the Greenbury Report in 1995, the Hampel report in January 1998 and the Combined Code in June 1998. We will consider each of these reports.

28.3 The Cadbury Report[14]

The Cadbury Committee was set up by the Financial Reporting Council, the London Stock Exchange and the accountancy profession in 1991 under the chairmanship of Sir Adrian Cadbury. The London Stock Exchange adopted as part of its Listing Rules a statement in the annual report as to whether the company had complied with the Code or not.

The Cadbury Report produced a *voluntary* Code of Best Practice. The points it made were as follows:

The board

1.1 The board should meet regularly, retain full and effective control over the company and monitor the executive management.

1.2 There should be a clearly accepted division of responsibilities at the head of a company, which will ensure a balance of power and authority, such that no one individual has unfettered powers of decision. Where the chairman is also the chief executive, it is essential that there should be a strong and independent element on the board, with a recognised senior member.

1.3 The board should include non-executive directors of sufficient calibre and number for their views to carry significant weight in the board's decisions.

1.4 The board should have a formal schedule of matters specifically reserved to it for decision to ensure that the direction and control of the company is firmly in its hands.

1.5 There should be an agreed procedure for directors in the furtherance of their duties to take independent professional advice if necessary, at the company's expense.

1.6 All directors should have access to the advice and services of the company secretary, who is responsible to the board for ensuring that board procedures are followed and that applicable rules and regulations are complied with. Any question of the removal of the company secretary should be a matter for the board as a whole.

Non-executive directors

2.1 Non-executive directors should bring an independent judgement to bear on issues of strategy, performance and resources, including key appointments and standards of conduct.

2.2 The majority should be independent of management and free from any business or other relationship that could materially interfere with the exercise of their independent judgement, apart from their fees and shareholdings. Their fees should reflect the time which they commit to the company.

2.3 Non-executive directors should be appointed for specified terms and reappointment should not be automatic.

2.4 Non-executive directors should be selected through a formal process and both the process and their appointment should be a matter for the board as a whole.

Executive directors

3.1 Directors' service contracts should not exceed three years without shareholders' approval.

3.2 There should be full and clear disclosure of directors' total emoluments and those of the chairman and the highest-paid UK director, including pension contributions and stock options. Separate figures should be given for salary and performance related elements and the basis on which performance is measured should be explained.

3.3 Executive directors' pay should be subject to the recommendations of a remuneration committee made up wholly or mainly of non-executive directors.

Reporting and controls

4.1 It is the board's duty to present a balanced and understandable assessment of the company.

4.2 The board should ensure that an objective and professional relationship is maintained with the auditors.

4.3 The board should establish an audit committee of at least three non-executive directors with written terms of reference which deal clearly with its authority and duties.

4.4 The directors should explain their responsibility for preparing the accounts next to a statement by the auditors about their reporting responsibilities.

4.5 The directors should report on the effectiveness of the company's system of internal control.

28.4 The Greenbury Report[15]

In July 1995 the Greenbury Committee issued a four-part code on directors' remuneration and covering good practice in relation to the following:

● **The remuneration committee**. The board should set up remuneration committees of non-executive directors to determine the company's policy on executive remuneration and specific remuneration packages for each of the executive directors, including pension rights and compensation payments.

● **Disclosure**. The remuneration committee should report to the shareholders each year the company's policy on executive directors' remuneration, including levels, comparative groups of companies, individual components (e.g. basic salary, benefits in kind, annual bonuses and long-term incentive schemes including share options), performance criteria and measurement, pension provision, contracts of service and compensation commitments on early termination.

● **Remuneration policy**. Remuneration committees must provide the packages needed to attract, retain and motivate directors of the quality required, but avoiding paying more than is necessary.

● **Service contracts**. Remuneration committees should consider what compensation commitments their directors' contracts of service would entail in the event of early termination, particularly for unsatisfactory performance, with a strong case for setting contract periods at one year or less.

Two of the most controversial recommendations – issuing options at discounts and pension entitlements – were initially resisted by a number of companies maintaining that they were unable to value these benefits. However, the existence of the code was yet another step exerting pressure on companies to give more information to the shareholders. The Greenbury Report was followed by the Committee on Corporate Governance: Final Report (Hampel Report).

28.5 The Hampel Report[16]

In January 1998 the Hampel Report was produced which was defined by the chairman as a 'fine tuning exercise' of the Cadbury and Greenbury Reports. The main provisions are:

● Chairman and Chief Executive should be separate roles. This was stronger than the Cadbury recommendation that where the chairman is also the chief executive, it is essential that there should be a strong and independent element on the board, with a recognised senior member.

● Directors should be on contracts lasting one year or less. This was more restrictive than the Cadbury recommendation that directors' service contracts should not exceed three years without shareholders' approval.

● Remuneration committee should be made up of independent non-executive directors. This was more restrictive than the Cadbury recommendation that executive directors' pay should be subject to the recommendations of a remuneration committee made up wholly **or mainly of non-executive directors**.

● Non-executive directors may be paid in company shares although this is not recommended. This view is more restrictive than the existing Cadbury recommendation that accepts non-executive directors **holding shares** but is **against** them **holding share options** that means they are tied to the company performance. The Hampel view appeared more logical. It was difficult to see why independence was not compromised by holding shares whilst it was by holding share options – if anything the pressure on the non-executive director was even greater if he or she actually had an existing shareholding to protect rather than a speculative gain.

● A senior non-executive director should be nominated to deal with shareholders' concerns. Hampel has expressed the view that, if directors pay themselves too much or do not invest enough in the company, it was the power wielded by the shareholders rather than books of corporate governance rules that really counted. However, it is difficult to see how a busy non-executive director, often with extensive commitments elsewhere, will be in a position to respond to other than limited requests for information or action.

● Directors should be trained.

The Hampel Report was followed by the Combined Code.

28.6 The Combined Code[17]

The Combined Code is described in the Preamble to the Code as 'a consolidation of the work of the three committees, not a new departure'.

It made clear that companies should be ready to explain their governance policies, including any circumstances, justifying departure from best practice and that those concerned with the evaluation of governance should do so with common sense and with due regard to companies individual circumstances.

The Code proposes principles and code provisions under five headings:

(a) directors

(b) directors' remuneration

(c) relations with shareholders

(d) accountability and audit

(e) institutional shareholders

We considered directors in Chapter 6. We will now consider headings (b), (c) and (e).

28.7 Directors' remuneration

The proposals are as in previous reports i.e.

● companies should establish a formal and transparent procedure for developing policy;

● companies should pay enough to attract suitable directors;

- companies should pay no more than enough;
- part of the remuneration should be linked to individual and corporate performance;
- policy and remuneration of each director should be disclosed in the Annual Report.

28.7.1 Where do accountants feature in setting directors' remuneration?

The equity of the remuneration is not normally seen as an accounting matter, but accountants should ensure transparent disclosure of the performance criteria and of the payments.

28.7.2 Performance criteria

Directors are expected to produce increases in the share price and dividends. Traditional measures have been largely based on growth in earnings per share (EPS), which has encouraged companies to seek to increase short-term earnings at the expense of long-term earnings, e.g. by cutting back capital programmes. Even worse, concentrating on growth in earnings per share can result in a reduction in shareholder value, e.g. by companies borrowing and investing in projects that produce a return in excess of the interest charge, but less than the return expected by equity investors.

28.7.3 What alternatives are there?

This is not the place to discuss performance-related pay in detail. However, it is interesting to identify the suggested criteria because they could have an impact on the financial information that has to be disclosed in the annual accounts. Suggested criteria include the following:

- **Relative share price increase**, i.e. using market comparisons. Grand Met has revised its scheme so that, before executives gain any benefit from their share options, Grand Met's share price must outperform the FT All-Share Index over a three-year period, i.e. the scheme focuses management on value creation.[18] If this policy is adopted, it would be helpful for the annual accounts to contain details of share price and index movements. Comparative share price schemes should also, in the opinion of the Association of British Insurers, be conditional on a secondary performance criterion, validating sustained and significant improvement in underlying financial performance over the same period.

- **Indicators related to business drivers**, i.e. using internal data. Schemes would need to identify business drivers appropriate to each company, such as customer satisfaction or process times. If this policy is adopted, it would be helpful for the annual accounts to contain details in the business review section of the nature of the drivers and how well they have been achieved. The 1997 Allied Colloids Annual Report explains the company's Remuneration Policy as:

  (i) Basic salary
      Basic salaries and benefits are determined after an annual review of performance. The Remuneration Committee also takes into account external information on remuneration for similar positions in comparable companies. Any increases reflect both individual and business performance.

  (ii) Performance related bonuses
      Senior management participate in a performance related bonus scheme which can pay up to 40% of salary as an annual bonus. The amount of the bonus

is determined by achievement of performance targets set by the Committee, in respect of growth in sales, gross profit, profit before interest and tax, cash flow and return on shareholders' funds. The targets set are demanding and are intended to reward substantial improvements in performance. The scheme will pay a bonus of 9% in respect of the year ended 31 March 1997.

The problem for the shareholder is 'How is this to be interpreted?' It could be argued that the directors only achieved 23% of the improvement that was being sought – in which case, why is there any bonus being paid?

● **Indicators based on factors such as size and complexity.** Schemes would need to take account of factors such as market capitalisation, turnover, number of employees, breadth of product and markets, risk, regulatory and competitive environment, and rates of change experienced by the organisation. This information could again be disclosed in the business review section of the annual report.

The indications are that there will be a growth in the number of firms offering schemes. However, regulators will need to keep a close eye on the position to avoid schemes creeping in that avoid the existing disclosure requirements. For example, there has been a growth in long-term incentive plans, under which free shares are offered in the future if the executive remains with the company and achieves a certain performance level. This is a perfectly healthy development that retains staff, but such schemes fall outside the definition of a share option plan and allow companies to avoid disclosure.

One of the problems is the innovative nature of the remuneration packages that companies might adopt and the fact that there is no uniquely correct scheme. The Association of British Insurers, in its publication *Share Option and Profit Sharing Incentive Schemes* (February 1995), commented on this very point:

> There is growing acceptance that the benefit arising from the exercise of options should be linked to the underlying financial performance of the company.
>
> Initially, attention focused on performance criteria showing real growth in normalised earnings; however, a number of other criteria have subsequently emerged. The circumstances of each individual company will vary and there is a reluctance, therefore, on the part of institutional investors to indicate a general preference for any particular measurement. On the other hand, a considerable number of companies have stated that they welcome indications of the sort of formulae that are considered to be acceptable ... It is felt that remuneration committees should have discretion to select the formula which is felt to be most appropriate to the circumstances of the company in question. Nevertheless ... it is important that whatever criterion is chosen ... the formula should be supported by, or give clear evidence of, sustained improvement in the underlying financial performance of the group in question.[19]

28.7.4 Requiring adequate disclosure

There is a need for greater disclosure because, in addition to their salaries, directors have been rewarded with bonuses and share options which were not disclosed in the annual accounts in a form that was readily understandable.

In the UK, this prompted the ASB[20] in 1994 to issue a UITF Abstract *Disclosure of Directors' Share Options*, recommending disclosure of information about option prices and market prices. In the USA, the SEC had already addressed the issue by requiring a precise description of salary, bonuses and share options for the five most highly paid executives, identified by name; and requiring the options to be valued and the information to be presented in a standardised format.

28.7.5 Why should disclosure be required?

In the USA, the disclosure approach has indicated that the very fact of disclosure exerted a moderating influence on the levels of executive reward.[21] It might be argued that financial reporting should not concern itself with the level of an individual executive's remuneration. However, there is a statutory duty to report on directors' remuneration and, under the *Statement of Principles*, a requirement that the information should be reliable. This is an excellent example of where the *Statement of Principles* can assist the financial reporting process. Details about the remuneration package need to be relevant and reliable.

28.7.6 Relevance implication

For information to be relevant, it needs to be predictive. Given that the major purpose of the motivational aspects of the package is to guide the directors towards maximising a defined attribute, e.g. EPS, it is vital to be aware of this when assessing the future performance of the company. If the scheme succeeds, the defined attributes will be the ones that the directors concentrate on. The financial statements should make the shareholder aware of the aim and in subsequent periods provide confirmation as to the level of achievement.

28.7.7 Reliability implication

The *Statement of Principles* states that for information to be reliable it needs to be a valid description and measure, to be complete and to convey the substance of the transaction in an understandable fashion with due regard for the user's abilities. This has not yet been achieved with directors' remuneration and the ASB approach of substance over form could well be followed.

28.7.8 Evaluation of current practice

Following the Greenbury Committee in 1995, Remuneration Committees now make their own reports to shareholders. The accounts have clearer messages concerning basic salary, constituents of the bonus calculation (although no information that allows the shareholder to assess targets or achievement of targets), long-term incentive plans, share options and pension contributions.

This would seem to indicate that all is well. However, this is certainly not the view presented in an article in *Management Today*.[22] This makes positive reference to the effect of Cadbury, Greenbury and Hampel in forcing companies to adopt long-term incentive plans linked to future performance over a three- to five-year period which, on the surface, appears to be a far more effective way of aligning the interests of executives with those of their investors and their workers; it also recognises that some companies are introducing more stringent performance criteria e.g. the Whitbread requirement that, unless over a three-year period it improves its minimum total shareholder ranking from 75th to 60th out of the FTSE 100, executives participating in the scheme will not be entitled to any shares. There is a note of caution, however, in that 40% of FTSE 100 companies are still paying above average rewards for poor performing executives and more challenging objectives should be found that support shareholder value creation.

The search to tailor remuneration packages will continue and may see a move away from measures such as share price movements which are often a reflection of market movements rather than executive performance. An interesting suggestion was made by Robert Heller in *Management Today*, July 1997,[23] that, if the true top task is to provide successful medium and long-term strategic direction, and to ensure its implementation, then this should loom largest in determining rewards, and never mind the short-term price of shares. This could be implemented by the use of techniques such as the balanced scorecard with its combination of financial measures and non-financial measures.

The Code itself sets out Provisions to act as warnings to the Remuneration Committee e.g. 'comparisons with other companies should be used with caution, in view of the risk that they can result in an upward ratchet of remuneration levels with no corresponding improvement in performance' and 'avoid paying more than is necessary' and 'options should not be exercisable in under three years' and 'total rewards potentially available should not be excessive' and 'incentive schemes should be subject to challenging performance criteria'.

However, in The Combined Code there is recognition that the achievement of a fair remuneration policy has not been completed and it states in its preamble: 'We wish to make it clear in our report that it is still too soon to assess definitively the results of the Cadbury and, more especially, the Greenbury codes'.

28.7.9 How well do executives' rewards correlate with performance?

A comparison[24] of the top FTSE 100 performers with those at the bottom showed that the presence or otherwise of long-term incentive plans (LTIPs) made very little difference to an executive's performance. The comparison showed the following information for the Chief Executive Officers (CEOs):

Footsie leaders

Company	Salary(£)	Bonus(£)	LTIP(£)	Total(£)
Misys	285,717	329,287	193,228	808,232
Stagecoach	372,000	250,000	80,069	630,069
Legal & General	440,000	400,000	361,215	1,201,215
Vodaphone	587,000	0	3,246,985	3,833,985
Lloyds TSB	475,000	199,000	940,797	1,614,797

Footsie laggards

Hanson	310,000	155,000	544,223	1,009,223
Rio Tinto	669,000	144,000	1,179,548	1,992,548
EMI Group	543,300	105,500	361,600	1,010,400
Allied Domecq	460,000	165,000	732,065	1,357,065
Reuters	522,000	255,000	815,938	1,592,938

28.8 Relations with shareholders

There is simply a proposal that companies to enter into dialogue with institutional shareholders and for chairmen of the remuneration, audit and nomination committees to be available to answer questions at the AGM.

28.9 Institutional investors

There are three principles, namely that institutional shareholders:

● have a responsibility to make considered use of their votes,

● should be ready to enter into dialogue with companies,

● should give due weight to all factors drawn to their attention when evaluating companies' governance arrangements.

For greater detail, we need to refer to the governance documents produced by the various institutional investor organisations e.g. the Association of British Insurers and National Association of Pension Funds.

28.9.1 Association of British Insurers (ABI)

The ABI[25] has published a Statement of Voting Policy and Corporate Governance Good which sets out that ABI members' overall objective is, and must be, to achieve on behalf of those for whom they act a competitive return on the funds invested and that the exercise of their voting policy will be in support of the proper management of companies and directed towards the enhancement of long-term shareholder value and the wider economic benefits which this should engender.

The Statement includes the following points:

● ABI members fully support the principles of the Cadbury, Greenbury and Hampel committees.

● The exercise of voting rights is inseparable from the investment management function and the objective of maximisation of long-term shareholder value.

● It is considered important to support boards by a positive use of their voting rights unless they have good reason for doing otherwise so that it would be a matter of concern for the board if that support was not forthcoming.

● If considering voting against a proposal it is important to make representations to the board in time for consultation and satisfactory resolution.

● Voting decisions by ABI members will reflect the Association's guidance notes e.g. on share incentive schemes and policy statements e.g. roles of Chairman and Chief Executive should not normally be combined.

● Structured dialogue is encouraged to better understand management's objectives, the problems confronting management and the quality of management whilst at the same time making clear the expectations and requirements of shareholders.

● Institutional investors will not wish to receive price sensitive information and, if they do, there would be a requirement that they suspend their ability to deal in the shares.

● They are concerned to ensure the appointment of a core of non-executives of sufficient number and of appropriate calibre, experience and independence to identify where there may be undue concentrations of decision-making power not formally constrained by appropriate checks and balances.

● On directors' remuneration, institutional investors support the key recommendations of the Greenbury Committee.

28.10 The Myners Report

Developing a Winning Partnership is a report of a joint City/industry working group estab-lished under the chairmanship of Paul Myners. The report considered how companies and institutional investors are working together.

The report recognises that there has been a perceived antagonism between companies and institutional investors. Institutional investors have been accused of short-termism which has discouraged investment. Companies need supportive long-term shareholders to encourage them to invest for the future. There is an urgent need for a long-term working relationship to be developed.

What is meant by short-termism?

Short-termism of investors has been blamed for the UK's lack of investment. It is evi-denced by the churning of shares, driven in part by the buy and sell recommendations of stockbrokers' analysts, the ready acceptance of hostile take-overs, and unreasonable demands for early earnings growth and increasing dividends. However, the National Association of Pension Funds has estimated that the average holding period for a share in a pension fund portfolio is over eight years.

There is also, of course, the short-termism of management evidenced by excessive management remuneration and share option schemes which are not in the best interest of the shareholders.

The Combined Code refers to 'dialogue'. This implies a two-way commitment from both the institutional investors and the company managers.

Institutional investors

Institutional investors want company managers to articulate more clearly their long-term corporate objectives and financial policies, of which dividend policy is an important part, and to emphasise in the discussion their vision for the company and the corporate val-ues. They want managers to be consistent in their communication with investors and the press, and to be open about bad news as well as good.

Company managers

Whilst many companies are spending more time and effort in investor relations the report comments:

> They recognise the benefit of more constructive dialogue with their shareholders, which leads to better understanding. What company managers want now is greater value from the time and effort they are putting in to investor relations. They want more openness from investors, candour about objectives and expectations, and a professional approach to the relationship. They justifiably expect better shareholder preparation for meetings, better sector and industry knowledge and better use of time in meetings'.

Constraints on dialogue

The report identified that as regards the companies:

● Many company managers are not confident that their messages will be listened to and fear that information given to investors beyond the minimum required will be used against them.

- Many companies are reluctant to give details of investment plans fearing that:
  - explicit forecasting is a hostage to fortune;
  - investors will use the plans against them;
  - plans were too commercially sensitive.

  The report identified that as regards the investors:

- Most fund managers are ambivalent about the responsibilities of ownership where these have been delegated by beneficial owners.

- There is a difficulty in determining the boundaries of legitimate involvement.

How will constraints on dialogue be removed?

The report comments that there was frequently a lack of confidence between company managers and investors but that open and informed dialogue can overcome this lack of trust. It is important also to see the company manager/institutional investor relationship in the context of the growing pressure for more transparency as seen with the corporate governance developments discussed above and the social and environmental reporting and business ethics discussed in the following two chapters.

B – CORPORATE GOVERNANCE – AUDITORS

28.11 Accountability and audit

Principle D2 of the Combined Code states that 'The board should **maintain a** *sound* **system of internal control** to safeguard shareholders' investment and the company's assets'.

Provision D2.1 states that 'The directors should, at least annually, conduct a *review* **of the effectiveness of internal controls**'.

An Internal Control Working Party formed by the ICAEW and chaired by Nigel Turnbull, the Finance Director of Rank Group plc, produced a Consultation Draft (The Turnbull Report) in April 1999 entitled 'Internal Control – Guidance for Directors of Listed Companies Incorporated in the UK' which effectively provided guidance on applying Principle D2 and D2.1. In September 1999, the ICAEW issued *Internal Control: Guidance for Directors on the Combined Code*.

28.11.1 A *sound* system of Internal Control as set out in Turnbull Report

It is recognised that directors set companies objectives in order to maximise profits and enhance the value of the shareholders' investment as a reward for risk taking, whilst safeguarding the company's assets. The purpose of Internal Control is, therefore, to help manage and control rather than eliminate risk e.g. it cannot provide protection against a company failing to meet its business objectives nor against all material errors, losses, fraud or breaches of laws or regulations. It has constraints such as cost-benefit assessment of particular controls, human fallibility and the risk of unforeseeable occurrences.

By 'sound' is meant that there is **reasonable assurance** that a company will not be prevented from achieving its objectives by **reasonably foreseeable occurrences** and that it will be able to respond effectively to significant business, operational, financial, compliance and other foreseeable risks.

It is important to recognise that internal control is not simply internal **financial** controls such as:

- procedures to ensure complete and accurate accounting for transactions.
- appropriate authorisation limits for transactions that reasonably limit the company's exposures.
- procedures to ensure the reliability of data processing and the integrity of the information generated.
- controls such as physical controls and segregation of duties that limit exposure to loss of assets or records.
- checks to provide effective supervision e.g. surprise site visits.

It also embraces matters such as:

- ensuring an appropriate organisation structure is in place within which business can be planned, controlled and monitored.
- written codes of conduct setting out agreed standards of business behaviour.
- a commitment by directors, management and employees to competence.
- identification of the key business, operational and compliance risks as well as financial risks e.g. risks associated with market, technology and business ethics.
- consideration of the likelihood of those risks crystallising and their likely impact.

Reviewing the effectiveness of internal control is the responsibility of the board of directors. It may delegate to its committees e.g. audit committee, safety and environmental issues committee but it remains responsible as a board for forming its own view on the adequacy of the review.

Examples of the application of the Turnbull recommendations and the ICAEW guidance

The Leicester City plc 1999 Annual Reports and Accounts ended before the guidance was issued and these state in the Statement of Corporate Governance:

Turnbull Report
The Directors are aware of the recently published recommendations of the Turnbull Committee and will be developing and introducing procedures recommended by the Turnbull committee during the year ending 31 July 2000.

The Associated British Ports Holdings plc ended after the guidance was issued and these state in the Corporate Governance Statement:

Combined code compliance
In September 1999 the Institute of Chartered Accountants in England and Wales issued 'Internal Control: Guidance for Directors on the Combined Code'; The Turnbull Report. This guidance was issued with the support and endorsement of the London Stock Exchange, and provides guidance to permit compliance with principle D2 of the Combined Code annexed to the London Stock Exchange listing rules. The directors confirm that the Company has established the procedures necessary to implement the guidance. For the year ended 31 December 1999 a statement is provided on Internal Financial Controls within the Report of the Directors on page 24 in accordance with existing guidance: 'Internal Control and Financial reporting'.

Page 24 of the Report of the Directors states:

Internal financial controls
The responsibility for the Group's system of internal financial control rests with the directors of the Company. The system is designed to ensure the maintenance of

proper accounting records and the reliability of the financial information used within the business for publication; but, while the system is subject to regular review and updating, it can provide reasonable, but not absolute, assurance against material mis-statement or loss.

The directors, through the Audit Committee, have conducted a review of the effectiveness of the system of internal financial control for the period covered by the accounts.

The directors then proceed to list the key elements of internal control. These include:

● A comprehensive budgeting system culminating in an annual budget approved by the Board:
    ● monthly actuals are compared with budget
    ● forecasts are revised regularly
    ● cash flow and borrowing requirements are reviewed regularly
    ● 5 year projected profit and cash flow forecasts are reviewed annually.
● Clearly defined capital expenditure systems.
● Clearly defined reporting lines and authorisation procedures.
● An Internal Audit Department that has a programme of regular reviews which give priority to areas of greatest risk; control weaknesses are reported so that corrective action can be taken.
● Internal and external audit procedures are complemented by a formal system for the measurement and assessment of risk areas.

Need to balance risks

Directors need to balance the effectiveness of internal control with the generation of profit e.g. the Stakis 1997 Annual Report states

The Board has reviewed the effectiveness of the Group's internal control systems generally, and specifically those relating to the main controllable risks. In reviewing this system, the need to avoid unreasonably constraining the Group's ability to make profits was taken into account. Certain risks are thus accepted and managed. Although unavoidably vulnerable to being circumvented or overridden, the Group's system of internal control is designed to provide reasonable, but not absolute, assurance against material mis-statement or loss.

Auditors also prepare a review report on corporate governance matters. The objective of the review report is to draw attention to non-compliance with the Code and does not mean there has been any additional audit work to express an opinion as to the effectiveness of the internal financial control, e.g. Tesco's 1999 Review Report by the Auditors on Corporate Governance Matters states:

We review whether the statement on pages 9 to 11 reflects the company's compliance with those provisions of the Combined Code specified for our review by the London Stock Exchange, and we report if it does not. We are not required to form an opinion on the effectiveness of the company's corporate governance procedures or its internal controls.

The approach taken by the auditors recognises that, as described in the Stakis Annual Report, the objective is not simply absolute assurance against mis-statement or loss – the degree of risk that is accepted is a commercial decision for the board. The auditors are not qualified to assess the acceptability of the level of risk. The audit stance was supported in the Hampel Report, para. 52, where the view was that the auditors should report privately to the directors on internal control matters. Directors could then take account of such a report in appraising the level and acceptability of risks.

There is also the view expressed by G. Archer in *The Times* of 6 January 1994 that it is impossible to report weaknesses in internal control publicly in a manner that is intelligible and useful and to convey the right message about a complex system of internal controls where few issues, if any, are black and white. The argument continues that the way forward is for the auditor to report to the Audit Committee and that it is for that committee to take appropriate action through the board.

In addition to safeguarding assets in dealings with third parties, there is also a need to safeguard the assets from misuse by the directors. Shareholders therefore need to be made aware of any material transactions that their company has with companies that are related in any way to the directors or senior managers.

This is particularly the case when directors use companies incorporated in other countries whose disclosure requirements are less stringent than those in the UK. For example, press comment has stated that:

> Price Waterhouse is believed to have prepared a second wide-ranging report on Maxwell Communication Corporation, where the firm was appointed as administrator last month. A preliminary examination revealed that six Liechtenstein companies – Corry, Kiara, Allandra, Jungo, Baccano and Akim – were part of an alleged £300 million MCC share support scam.[26]

It is a relief that the administrator is able to unravel the facts, but why do the regulators tolerate a situation where overseas companies can be used to conceal what is happening? There is nothing new about the use of overseas companies to conceal the true nature of transactions. Presumably, the regulators believe that, on balance, their use makes the UK attractive to international capital. However, the individual shareholders should be aware that this is how the regulators think, and not fondly imagine that the protection of individual shareholders in individual companies is of paramount concern to them. Shareholders need to press for confirmation from the auditors that such devices are not being used. It should not take a catastrophe for basic facts to be disclosed about how a company is conducting its affairs to the detriment of its shareholders.

28.11.2 Providing reliable information that presents a true and fair view of the company's affairs and does not misrepresent the position

Reliable information depends on the company having adequate accounting systems, so that all transactions are recorded, classified and included under their appropriate headings in the profit and loss account and balance sheet.

The annual report now includes a statement of directors' responsibilities e.g. Orange plc Annual Report states:

> Company law requires the Directors to prepare financial statements which *give a true and fair view* of the state of affairs of the Company and the Group and of the profit or loss and cash flows of the Group for that period. In preparing these financial statements, the directors are required to:
>
> ● select *suitable* accounting policies and then apply them *consistently*;
>
> ● make *judgements* and estimates that are *reasonable* and *prudent*;
>
> ● state whether applicable accounting standards have been *followed*, subject to any material *departures disclosed* and explained in the financial statements;

● prepare the financial statements on the *going concern* basis unless it is inappropriate to presume that the Group will continue in existence.

The directors are responsible for keeping *proper accounting records* which disclose with reasonable accuracy at any time the financial position of the Company and to enable them to ensure that the financial statements *comply* with the Companies Act 1985. They are also responsible for *safeguarding* the assets of the Group and hence for taking *reasonable steps* for the prevention of fraud and other irregularities.

The auditors are not responsible for the preparation of the financial statements. It is the auditors' responsibility to form an independent opinion, based on their audit, and report to the shareholders. Part of the work undertaken to form an opinion is to test that the accounting system is adequate. By 'adequate' we mean that transactions are sampled to test that they are:

● **authorised** by an appropriate person (e.g. capital expenditure in excess of £1m may require board approval);

● **accurate** (e.g. copy sales invoices contain accurate information on the items sold, their price, the discount allowed, the calculation of the net amount due, the name and address of the debtor, and the account to be credited); and

● **complete** (e.g. no copy sales invoices are mislaid with the effect that the company does not receive cash due to it and that the sales are understated by the amount of the invoice).

28.11.3 Auditor has to rely on persuasive evidence

Some shareholders mistakenly believe that the audit opinion is based on conclusive evidence rather than persuasive evidence. A study by Arthur Andersen in 1974 indicated that a substantial minority (37%) erroneously thought that the auditor determines the accuracy of financial statements by going through all financial records.[27]

In practice, disclosure of lack of trustworthiness appears to surface only when it is impossible to conceal it from the shareholders. For example, the massive pension fund losses at Maxwell Communication Corporation and Mirror Group Newspapers became public knowledge only following the death of Robert Maxwell.

28.12 Assessing quality of management performance

Shareholders also sometimes mistakenly believe that the auditor reviews the **performance** of the management. This is not the case and is unlikely to become the case.[28] It has been suggested that the role of the independent assessor should not extend to forming an opinion on the efficiency of management. As a result, inefficient managements have been able to operate for many years to the detriment of the entities for which they are responsible.

28.12.1 How does a shareholder assess the quality of performance?

Shareholders may base their assessment on the trend in earnings over time or on the trend in the share price over time. Management is aware of this and may take steps to show steady and increasing prosperity to the outside world.[29] There may be temptation to use existing accounting conventions to this end. For example, treating a business combination under merger accounting rather than acquisition accounting will show an improved profit trend not only in the current year, as all of the year's profits of the acquired company are brought into the profit and loss account, but also in future years because there will be no charge for the amortisation of goodwill. Such steps are generally referred to as 'creative accounting'.

Creative accounting

This term implies that management has reported transactions in a way that satisfies management rather than shareholder objectives. There are pressures on management to show a rising profit trend and a strong balance sheet. Consequently, it may resort to income smoothing to produce the profit figure it wants, and devices such as off balance sheet financing to exclude liabilities from the balance sheet.

There has been gradual progress by standard setters to make such devices transparent. However, we cannot overlook the pressure on executives to achieve ever-increasing earnings per share, which can encourage creative accounting. For example, the comment has been made[29] following the better than expected profit figures from American companies that the stock market obsession with executives has resulted in a growing number of high-grade managers coming to the view that it is okay to manipulate earnings to satisfy what they see as Wall Street's desires, and it is estimated that write-downs and special charges reported by leading US companies in 1998 totalled $70 billion.

Income smoothing

Income smoothing may arise from:

● A change in accounting policy e.g. depreciation policy using reducing balance rather than straight-line (an accounting policy should only be changed if the new policy is preferable to the policy it replaces because it gives a fairer representation of the results and financial position).

● A change in classification e.g. a current asset such as an unsold trading asset being re-classified as a fixed asset to avoid a charge to the profit and loss account if net realisable value is lower than cost (UITF abstract 5: transfer from current assets to fixed assets requires the asset to be transferred at the net realisable value (if lower than cost) at the date of the management intent and this cannot be backdated. This prevents a retrospective change at cost being put into effect after a loss in value has become apparent).

● A change in the assumptions (e.g. increasing the life of an asset for depreciation purposes) (this would be considered by the auditor as part of normal audit work. However, assumptions are frequently a result of **directors' attitudes**. For example, if the directors have obtained a shareholding as a result of a management buy-out and are preparing the company for sale to realise their investment, they will take an optimistic view e.g. in assessing stock obsolescence provisions; if, on the other hand, they are preparing to make an offer for a MBO then they will take a pessimistic view to reduce results and asset values to the minimum. It is extremely difficult for auditors or other shareholders to be aware of the effect or extent of these assumptions. However, the ASB has, with FRS 12 *Provisions, Contingent Liabilities and Contingent Assets*, made it more difficult for companies to use provisions to smooth income).

● A change in the timing of capital expenditure e.g. delaying capital expenditure so that depreciation does not arise on newly acquired fixed assets (this remains within the control of the directors and would not be commented on by the auditors).

Off-balance-sheet financing

Off-balance-sheet finance arises when companies organise their borrowings so that they do not appear on the balance sheet: for example, arranging leases so that they fall outside the definition of a finance lease. The liability to make operating lease payments in future years is disclosed as a note, but it is not included in the balance sheet, and gearing ratios are consequently improved. (The treatment of operating leases is under review and it could well be that they will be required to appear on the balance sheet under proposals being considered by the IASC.)

28.12.2 How is a shareholder to know whether creative accounting has been taking place?

Virtually every revenue and expense item in the profit and loss account, and asset and liability in the balance sheet, involves the exercise of judgement. We have seen that there is judgement in determining when to recognise income (e.g. at what point does one take profit on a long-term contract?). There is judgement in determining expenses (e.g. is an item research or development expenditure?). There is judgement in determining assets (e.g. what overheads are to be included in the stock valuation?). There is judgement in determining liabilities (e.g. is a lease a finance or an operating lease?).

There is little prospect of a shareholder or, indeed, any user of the accounts being able to ascertain or assess the significance of the decisions being made. Information is not provided in a form that allows the shareholder to determine the effect of changes in the way the management is exercising its judgement.

The financial press has a natural interest in creative accounting, but it is restricted by the information that is provided. Consequently, attention is directed at the items that are disclosed, such as goodwill and the treatment of merger provisions. These can have an immense impact on the financial statements, but they are only part of the problem. For example, the information provided does not allow comment on the valuation of long-term contracts, which might be a far more fertile source of creative accounting.

28.12.3 Can the shareholder rely on the auditor to highlight creative accounting?

The auditor has an obligation to report to the shareholders. The practice in the UK was for the report to be on an exception basis: in other words, no news is good news. A typical report reads as follows:

> We have audited the financial statements in accordance with Auditing Standards. In our opinion the statements give a true and fair view of the state of affairs of the company and of the profit and source and application of funds for the year and have been properly prepared in accordance with the Companies Act 1985.

Unfortunately, the brevity of this report does not assist us in understanding what the auditor has actually done. For example, how many shareholders would have the faintest idea of the content or purpose of the auditing standards and guidelines?

This approach to audit reporting encouraged a belief that the level of audit checking was higher than it really was. It had long been suggested that the audit report should be fuller to allow the shareholders to form their own view of the degree of accountability that had been achieved, and that the report should contain additional information such as the following:[30]

● Identify for whom the audit report is written.

● Explain that the financial statements are prepared by the directors and that the main purpose of the audit is to provide an independent opinion on the reliability of those financial statements.

● Identify the financial statements to which the audit report relates and explain the extent of any auditor responsibility for information in the audit report but outside the financial statements.

● Explain the limits of the auditors' responsibility for detecting fraud and irregularity.

● Give an indication of the fact that the evidence available to support any audit opinion is persuasive rather than conclusive.

● Describe the audit work performed on the financial statements and in particular the role of internal control.

● Positively state all audit opinions.

● As regards the true and fair view opinions, indicate the basis on which the true and fair view is judged.

● Make clear that the true and fair view opinions relate to the financial statements as a whole rather than to individual figures within those financial statements.

● Clearly explain the nature of, reasons for and effect of any qualified audit opinion.

By making a fuller report the auditor will be able to dispel the misplaced belief that:[31]

● The auditor checks each transaction.

● The auditor judges the wisdom and legality of each transaction.

● The auditor certifies the accounts for the purpose of investment decisions.

● The auditor certifies the accounts as being correct.

● The auditor agrees that a company's results can be shown as a single number.

The authors suspect that the appearance of the auditor's name in relation to the financial information implies to the shareholders that the information is all right. They go on to say that 'If true, this is not a healthy state of affairs.'

The changes are discussed further in section 28.12.

The Auditing Practices Board issued SAS 600 Auditors' Reports on Financial Statements in May 1993 to address some of the points raised above. SAS 600[32] sets out the basic elements of the auditors' report, specifying that auditors' reports should include the following matters:

(a) a title identifying the person or persons to whom the report is addressed;

(b) an introductory paragraph identifying the financial statements audited;

(c) separate sections, appropriately headed, dealing with
   (i) respective responsibilities of directors and auditors,
   (ii) the basis of the auditors' opinion,
   (iii) the auditors' opinion on the financial statements;

(d) the signature of the auditor;

(e) the date of the auditors' report.

SAS 600[33] requires auditors to explain the basis of their opinion in their report by including:

(a) a statement as to their compliance or otherwise with Auditing Standards, together with the reasons for any departure therefrom;

(b) a statement that the audit process includes
   (i) examining, on a test basis, evidence relevant to the amounts and disclosures in the financial statements,
   (ii) assessing the significant estimates and judgements made by the directors,
   (iii) considering whether accounting policies are appropriate to the reporting entity's circumstances, consistently applied and adequately disclosed;
(c) a statement that they planned and performed the audit so as to obtain reasonable assurance that the financial statements are free from material mis-statement, whether caused by fraud or other irregularity or error, and that they have evaluated the overall presentation of the financial statements.

28.12.4 Why is it not healthy to assume that everything is all right if the auditors have signed their audit report?

The auditor merely indicates reasonable confidence that no material mis-statement (e.g. significant fraud or error) exists in the financial statements. But the auditor has only tested and sampled the transactions and cannot possibly certify that there has been no fraud or error. This is particularly true if the fraud or error arises from senior staff.

However, they do not specify clearly in their audit report the significance of 'material mis-statement'. For example, if the auditor interpreted material as being 10% of pre-tax profits then taking Tesco 1999 accounts as an example, it would seem that errors of up to £84m would not be material. This is not immediately obvious to any user of the accounts.

It is unfortunate that for all of the Code requirements on internal financial controls and the Auditing Practices Board's Statements of Auditing Standards there is no indication of the range of error attaching to any figure or whether it is cumulative. Taking the Tesco 1999 accounts as an example, if stock misappropriations of £67m (on a total in the balance sheet of £667m) were not material in 1999 are we to assume that a similar misappropriation could have occurred in each year? If so, over 10 years the presumption would be that the misappropriations totalled £667m, i.e. equivalent to the total 1999 stock of the company! This is assuming, because the auditors have not disclosed it, that the acceptable figure is 10% of the stock value – if it were, instead, 10% of pre-tax profits then a cumulative loss of stock totalling £667m would have been achieved (if that is the right word!) in just over 8 years. Looking at it from a shareholder's point of view, the company could have actually paid a dividend that was 30% higher, every year.

28.13 Role of the auditor

The integrity of financial reporting and business conduct is fundamental to confidence in capital markets and to the stakeholder. Confidence in the capital market requires quality governance and a robust independent audit process.

The regulators' view is that audit is about **governance**;[34] it is about upholding the integrity of financial reporting and business conduct; it is about seeking the truth. It is not about stifling companies, but about constructively **adding value** to confidence in those companies and recognising that the provision of financial information is itself an economic service.

The auditor is independent, able to be objective at the same time as being close enough to the company to gain the necessary information; someone respected for objectivity, robustness, scepticism, fairness and, above all, integrity and broad business knowledge. The reference to scepticism is an interesting one to explore.

28.13.1 Scepticism by the auditor

This has actually been written into the rules issued by the International Auditing Practices Committee, with a requirement that an auditor 'should plan and perform the audit with an attitude of *professional scepticism*, recognising that circumstances may exist which may cause financial statements to be materially misstated'.[35]

Given the failure of companies such as BCCI and evidence that auditors do not appear to be qualifying their audit reports in the years immediately prior to them failing, this seems a reasonable attitude for the auditors to be expected to take. However, in the UK there was felt to be a problem in how exactly they would demonstrate compliance with such a requirement. Hence the APB in the UK has not followed the IAPC and instead relies on specific operational requirements that can be monitored. For example, there is a requirement that, in planning the audit, auditors record an assessment of the business risk and the evidence necessary to satisfy themselves that the accounts have not been mis-stated as a consequence of this risk. A company might be extremely short of liquid funds, which could tempt it towards reclassifying current liabilities as long term in order to improve the current ratios.

28.13.2 The APB

The APB was established in 1991 to advance standards of auditing. Its membership includes practising auditors and others from the business, academic, public sector and legal world. It is committed to establishing high standards in auditing, meeting the developing needs of users and ensuring public confidence in the auditing process.

How confident are the shareholders in the auditor or audit firm?

There are two types of expectation gap:

● A communication gap. Shareholders might have unreasonable expectations of the audit process, e.g. that all transactions are checked and that the audit means the company is being managed efficiently.
● A performance gap. Shareholders might have reasonable expectations, but the auditors fail to perform adequately, e.g. by failing to verify bad debt provisions which are material to the reported profit for the year.

Recognising that there was an expectation gap, the APB set up the McFarlane Committee, which produced its report *The Future Development of Auditing*[36] in 1992.

The Future Development of Auditing

This report redefined the purpose of an audit as being to provide an **independent opinion**, to those with an interest in a company, that they have received from those responsible for its direction and management an adequate account of:

● the proper conduct of the company's affairs, i.e. to require reporting on internal controls and fraud;
● the company's financial performance and position, i.e. the existing role of stewardship reporting;
● future risks attaching to the company, i.e. to require reporting on factors that would question the assumption of going concern for a defined period, say for one year.

It also suggested ways of enhancing the auditor's independence, e.g. by the formation of audit committees as recommended by the Cadbury Report.

There was a mixed response to the McFarlane Report, based mainly on the proposed extension of the auditor's role to include reporting on proper conduct and future risk. In 1994, the APB issued the *Audit Agenda*,[37] taking account of responses to the McFarlane Report.

Audit Agenda

Among its proposals, the *Audit Agenda* recognised that there are obligations to more than the primary users, i.e. the shareholders. Although, legally, the auditors are accountable only to the shareholders, the *Audit Agenda* proposed that the APB should undertake research jointly with the ASB into developing a framework for reporting and giving assurance to secondary and tertiary users.

Secondary users include lenders, other creditors, employees and others with a direct economic interest in the entity which falls short of ownership; tertiary users include potential investors and their advisers, brokers, underwriters, lawyers, tax authorities and members of the public, and other users of published reports. Such a major change would need to be accompanied by changes to limit auditors' liability.

Audit Agenda – brief comment on meeting expectations

The Audit Agenda used the Institute of Chartered Accountants in Scotland's publication[38] *Auditing into the Twenty-first Century* to identify the public nature of expectations ('Public' below) and the *Audit Agenda* view of what could be reasonably expected ('Agenda') as follows:

Public
Financial statements are right.

Agenda

● Total accuracy is impractical, if not impossible.

● Right means true and fair.

● Auditors should consider all textual information in the accounts and confirm that it is consistent with the financial data and not misleading.

Public
The company will not fail.

Agenda

● This is a dream assurance that readers will always wish for, but which in a market economy is not achievable in the absolute by directors or auditors.

● In a market where profit is a reward for taking risks, shareholders and other stakeholders need to accept that some companies will fail.

● Directors should explain their confidence as to the going concern nature of the company at the year-end and indicate the risks when at the margin.

● Auditors should take an active approach to assessing going concern, i.e. review the steps taken by the directors when they made their assessment and consider a longer period than in the past.

Public
The company is competently managed.

Agenda

● It is not practical for auditors' comments made to the board to be published.

- The quality of such comments will depend on the quality and experience of the auditor. This will no doubt become a factor in choosing auditors.

Public

The company is and will be run in accordance with the law.

Agenda

Auditors must report illegal running in accordance with actions to the board. If no action is taken, auditors must consider whether the public interest is involved.

Public

The company is free of fraud.

Agenda

- Fifty per cent of the public feel that it is the auditor's duty to detect fraud.
- The profession's view is that it is the directors' duty to prevent fraud and to have systems in place to minimise fraud.
- Directors should consider commissioning a periodic forensic audit to assist directors and the audit committee.
- The profession's view is that the auditor should review and report to the directors on the operation of such systems.

Public

The company adopts a responsible attitude to environmental and social issues.

Agenda

- Assessing environmental impact can require complex scientific and analytical skills in areas well outside those of financial reporting.
- It is not practicable to look solely to those trained in financial auditing to provide assurance on all aspects of environmental issues, e.g. levels of emission of dangerous chemicals.
- Auditors should form judgements as to whether particular environmental issues could materially affect a company's financial statements. This means that they should ensure that they have access to appropriate expert advice in non-financial areas, so that they can properly assess the directors' assertions about a company's financial position.

Public

The company's annual report can be relied on by all its stakeholders and has been subject to audit scrutiny.

Agenda

- Auditors only owe a duty of care which can be relied on by all parties to whom they are required to report. Other stakeholders should contract separately if they require their own assurance from the auditors.
- Accounts prepared for primary users can be useful to all stakeholders, particularly the narrative aspects.
- Narrative aspects should be checked by auditors to ensure consistency with the financial data.

Public

The company's auditors are independent and professionally qualified.

Agenda

● Auditors can never be totally independent because they are dependent on directors and staff for information.

● Public perception is that the relationship between management and auditors is too comfortable.

● Audit committees should assist in removing this perception of cosiness.

APB and the communication gap

We have seen that the APB has issued the McFarlane Report and the *Audit Agenda* to address the communication gap. The effect of the search for greater understanding by the shareholders of the auditor's role is illustrated by the change that has taken place in the audit report, which has become much fuller and clearer.

APB and the performance gap

The APB issues Statements of Auditing Standards (SASs) with which auditors are required to comply. Whereas the *Audit Agenda* was indicative, the SASs are mandatory. They cover a range of audit functions, as can be seen from the following list:

● Responsibility, e.g. SASs 100 and 110 *Fraud and Error*.

● Planning an audit, e.g. SAS 210 *Knowledge of the Business*.

● Accounting systems and internal control, e.g. SAS 300 *Accounting and Internal Control Systems and Audit Risk Assessments*.

● Evidence, e.g. SAS 410 *Analytical Procedures*.

● Reporting, e.g. SAS 610 *Reports to Directors or Management*.

For the purposes of this text, SAS 100 is relevant. It sets out for the auditor the objective and general principles governing an audit of financial statements. An awareness of these principles will assist the user to evaluate the audit report.

Provisions of SAS 100

The statement says that the objective of an audit is to enable the auditor to give an opinion on the financial statements taken as a whole and thereby to provide reasonable assurance that the financial statements give a true and fair view and have been prepared in accordance with relevant accounting or other requirements.[39]

It also recognises that financial statements cannot be absolutely accurate by providing that:

> A degree of imprecision is inevitable in the preparation of all but the simplest of financial statements because of inherent uncertainty and the need to use judgement in making accounting estimates and selecting appropriate accounting policies; and that financial statements can accordingly be prepared in different ways and yet still be true and fair.[40]

An example would be the amount of profit recognised by different companies on long-term contracts which had identical terms and were at an identical stage of completion.

The statement also recognises that the auditor cannot guarantee the future viability of the company, or the efficiency and effectiveness of its management.[41]

From the above explanation of the *Audit Agenda* and the Statements of Auditing Standards, it is clear that auditors are expressing an opinion, based on testing, that they are reasonably confident that there are no material mis-statements in the financial statements. The opinion is based only on a sample of the transactions and auditors cannot certify that there has been no fraud or error. This is particularly true if the fraud or error arises from collusion between senior executives.

APB's ongoing programme of reviewing auditing standards

An Exposure Draft SAS 240 Quality Control for Audit Work

The APB view[42] is that the independent audit function is an important aspect of good corporate governance necessary for the maintenance of confidence in the operation of business and capital markets and that quality control is of paramount importance to the independent audit function.

The Exposure Draft has taken an interesting approach by considering enablers and results. The enablers are:

● the audit firms who should plan to have sufficient audit partners and audit staff with the relevant competencies;
● the audit partners who are responsible for ensuring that:
  ● the audit work is directed, supervised and reviewed to obtain reasonable assurance that the work has been performed competently
  ● there are adequate arrangements in place to safeguard their objectivity and the firm's independence;
● the audit staff;
● the senior audit partner or suitably qualified external consultant to monitor the quality of audits.

The results are:

● client satisfaction;
● management satisfaction;
● employee satisfaction.

The APB view[43] is that there is benefit in discussing audit performance with these parties but that management satisfaction does not signify that an audit has been performed in accordance with auditing standards.

The importance of independence

Audit independence can be jeopardised in a number of ways,[44] including:

● economic dependence of the firm on a single client whether for audit or non-audit fees;
● financial interest in the client by a partner or staff;
● close relationship between auditor(s) and a senior manager of a client company.

Where independence has been jeopardised, there is the potential risk that confidential information might be used inappropriately, the financial results misrepresented or not challenged, or misappropriations concealed.

In the US, the Securities Exchange Commission has detailed rules which ban partners, senior staff and close associates from holding financial interests in clients. In the UK, the view taken by the regulator is rather different in that while close connection is recognised as a threat, the approach is to declare the interest and demonstrate that procedures are in place to ensure objectivity and independence.

Quality control is designed to ensure that the audit work is carried out in a competent fashion and also that the firm is independent. This is addressed in SAS 240 with the requirement for the Audit Partner to ensure that there are adequate arrangements in place to safeguard their objectivity and the firm's independence.

28.14 The way forward

Shareholders have entrusted their money to the control of other people. They are entitled to a base level of protection by statutory and professional regulation.

28.14.1 Base level of protection

By this we mean that shareholders are entitled to assume that:

● statute will prescribe that people who are clearly untrustworthy or incompetent should not be eligible to become directors;

● a company should operate physical and accounting system controls to safeguard the assets;

● a company should operate an accounting system that will allow financial reports to be produced that satisfy the statutory and professional guidelines;

● an independent assessment should be made each year to confirm that an effective system is in operation;

● there is reasonable certainty that the financial statements give a true and fair view of the company's state of affairs and results for the year.

The base level of protection will not, however, provide shareholders with the means to satisfy themselves on all aspects of commonality of interest, exercising due care, trustworthiness and quality of performance. They require additional information if management is to be more fully accountable to the proprietors.

The current process is misunderstood and the current information is inadequate. Statutory regulations will tend towards the minimum required to maintain sufficient confidence for the capital markets to operate. Anything beyond this base level is a matter for the shareholders. It is the responsibility of the shareholders to create pressure for a reporting process that will make management more accountable to them.

28.14.2 What information should shareholders be seeking?

We comment briefly on commonality of interest, exercising due care, trustworthiness and quality of performance.

Commonality of interest

● Shareholders need to be aware of the corporate objectives of the company. They should require their directors to formulate and publish such objectives. The corporate objectives should cover both economic and social factors.

● Shareholders need to be able to assess how successful the management has been in achieving these objectives. They should require the directors to report annually on their performance.

● Shareholders need to be aware of the way in which directors' remuneration is being determined.

Exercising due care

● Shareholders need to be able to assess the abilities of the directors before appointing them to office. At present, however, appointments are controlled by the existing board.

● Shareholders need to be aware of any possible conflict of interest if the company has dealings with other organisations in which a director or senior manager has an interest. This is particularly the case if the directors have taken deliberate steps to operate through private family companies registered in countries that restrict the amount of information that a company is required to file. If the statutory system permits this to happen, shareholders should exert pressure for the statute to be amended to forbid dealings with related companies where they are prevented from ascertaining what is happening.

Trustworthiness

● Shareholders need to be aware of the audit work that has actually been carried out: for example, that the opinion expressed on the sales recorded in the profit and loss account may be based on a review of the system of internal control and the sampling of copy invoices that might represent less than one day's sales.

● There is a credibility gap, with shareholders expecting far more than the auditor is able to deliver. It is encumbent on both parties to take steps to bridge the gap. Shareholders need to educate themselves as to what they can reasonably expect. Auditors need to inform the shareholders of the work they have actually undertaken.

● Shareholders need to be aware of any possible question about the independence of the auditors. This is a particularly difficult area because the audit partner traditionally establishes close links with the directors and senior staff over many years, and there is the risk of audit judgement being, or appearing to be, influenced by the relationship.

Quality of performance

Statutory audit does not look at how well management has performed. It concerns itself with testing, in order to form an opinion as to whether there is reasonable confidence that the financial statements give a true and fair view of the financial position and profit.

● Shareholders cannot rely on the auditor to assess management performance.

● Shareholders need to be aware of how successful the management has been in achieving its strategic plan and budgets. This presupposes that the shareholders will receive future-based information. Unfortunately, such information would give the shareholders the means to hold management accountable. Consequently, there is little hope that managers will volunteer it, unless specific circumstances threaten their tenure of office, e.g. a threatened takeover bid.

Quality of performance is reflected in the extent to which there has been a change in the financial wealth of the company. The present reporting system based on the historical cost convention is unable to provide this information. This means that even if the directors and shareholders have a common interest, the directors exercise due care, and the auditors confirm that the assets have been protected and the profit realised, the shareholders still cannot assess the quality of performance because the financial statements do not portray economic reality.

We need to understand the concepts and conventions upon which current financial statements are based. This chapter has attempted to provide such understanding, together with a critical awareness of the areas of dispute in the application of such concepts and conventions.

We also need to understand that financial reporting is evolving. There are clear signs that it will gradually move from the historical cost convention to a value system such as net realisable value or current replacement cost, which were discussed in Chapters 3 and 4.

Summary

The creation of limited liability companies heralded a separation of ownership and management. The division between the two has become infinitely greater with the rise of financial institutions such as pension funds, which collect funds that they then invest on behalf of their members.

Directors became virtually unaccountable and, provided performance was not absolutely dreadful, were free to pursue personal rather than shareholder objectives.

Reports emanating from the Committee on the Financial Aspects of Corporate Governance have sought to encourage companies to follow good governance in relation to the board, directors' remuneration, relations with shareholders, accountability and audit, and institutional investors.

Fund managers have been encouraged by the Combined Code to enter into a dialogue with companies and evaluate their governance arrangements. Organisations such as the Association of British Insurers and the National Association of Pension Funds have responded positively formulating policies and guidance on governance issues for their members.

It is hoped that the proposals in the Combined Code will provide effective constraints on their business decisions (unless they are grossly ineffectual) and on their remuneration and make directors more accountable. However, as the Combined Code stated, it is still too soon as we enter the 21st century to assess definitively the results of the Cadbury and, more essentially, the Greenbury Codes.

Auditing has made strenuous efforts to ensure quality assurance. However, no quality assurance measures appear to be even contemplated for company directors: training has been proposed by the Hampel Committee but no minimum experience or qualifications are required; there is no job specification; no clear financial and non-financial targets are set; no financial forecasts are published. Why should shareholders settle for less?

Review questions

1 The Association of British Insurers held the view that options should be exercised only if the company's earnings per share growth exceeded that of the retail price index. The National Association of Pension Funds preferred the criterion to be a company's outperformance of the FTA All-Share Index.

(a) Discuss the reasons for the differences in approach.

(b) Discuss the implication of each approach to the financial reporting regulators and the auditors.

2 'Management will become accountable only when shareholders receive information on corporate strategy, future-based plans and budgets, and actual results with explanations of variances.' Discuss.

3 (i) Discuss the extent to which directors should be accountable to: (a) shareholders; (b) employees; (c) suppliers; (d) customers; (e) the government; (f) the public.

(ii) Research[45] suggests that companies whose managers own a significant proportion of the voting share capital tend to violate the Cadbury recommendations on board composition far more frequently than other companies. Discuss the advantages and disadvantages of enforcing greater compliance.

4 A number of creative accounting techniques have been identified. These include the following:

● Excessive write down of assets on acquisition.
● Profits on disposal included in trading profit.
● Depreciation policy.
● Brand accounting.
● Capitalisation of interest.
● Off-balance-sheet debt.

(a) Explain in each case how a company is able to use the technique to improve its financial reports, i.e. profit and loss account, balance sheet or sensitive ratios.

(b) Explain in each case whether there has been an arm's-length transaction.

(c) Explain in each case the current statutory or mandatory provisions relating to the item.

(d) Discuss whether this implies that investors are not given adequate information because:
(i) the ASB standard setting programme is defective;
(ii) audit procedures and reporting are defective.

(e) Discuss which of the techniques is currently operative.

5 The Chartered Institute of Management Accountants (CIMA) has warned that linking directors' pay to EPS or return on assets is open to abuse, since these are not the objective measures they might appear.[46] Discuss:

(a) Can shareholders rely on the ASB to prevent abuse?

(b) Identify five ways in which the directors might manipulate the EPS and return on assets without breaching existing standards.

6 It has been suggested that 'changes in market capitalisation from period to period should be the subject of comment [and] it would be sensible for investors to be guided on the nature of the market capitalisation figure and to be given an indication of share price trends'.[47] Discuss the advantages and disadvantages of such disclosure in relation to corporate governance.

7 Philip Ashton, chairman of the APB's internal control working party, warned against the creation of further expectation gaps: 'Users should fully understand the likely costs and inherent limitations of reports by auditors on the effectiveness of internal financial controls ... cost for auditors could spiral out of control if litigation fever were to set in and investors attempted to use auditors' internal control opinions as a guarantee of the company's reliability.'[48]

Discuss the inherent limitations referred to and whether it is unreasonable for investors to expect auditors to make them aware of the risk if directors have not instigated effective internal controls on cost/benefit grounds.

8 (a) The Companies Act 1985 (Disclosure of Remuneration for Non-audit Work) Regulations SI No 1991/2181 requires companies[49] to disclose all payments made to their auditors. Discuss the additional information that would be required in order to make the disclosure of the non-audit fees meaningful.

(b) The Combined Code provides that the audit committee should keep the nature and extent of non-audit services provided by the auditor under review, seeking to balance the maintenance of objectivity and value for money. Discuss criteria that could be applied in seeking to establish this balance.

9 In the modern commercial world, auditors provide numerous other services to complement their audit work. These services include the following:

(a) Accountancy and book-keeping assistance, e.g. in the maintenance of ledgers and in the preparation of monthly and annual accounts.

(b) Secretarial help, e.g. ensuring that the company has complied with the Companies Act in the maintenance of shareholder registers and in the completion of annual returns to Companies House.

(c) Consultancy services, e.g. advice on the design of information systems and organisational structures, advice on the choice of computer equipment and software packages, and advice on the recruitment of new executives.

(d) Investigation work, e.g. appraisals of companies that might be taken over.

(e) Receivership work, e.g. when the firm assumes the role of receiver or liquidator on behalf of an audit client.

(f) Taxation work, e.g. tax planning advice and preparation of tax returns to the Inland Revenue for both the company and the company's senior management.

Discuss:

(i) Whether any of these activities is unacceptable as a separate activity because it might weaken an auditor's independence.

(ii) The advantages and disadvantages to the shareholders of the audit firm providing this range of service.

10 The audit fee disclosed for Cable & Wireless plc was £1.7 million in its 1997 accounts.

(a) Discuss how many man-days of audit time you think would be reasonable to audit an industrial company where:

(i) the sales were £7,002 million;

(ii) the fixed assets were £6,442 million;

(iii) the current assets were £3,225 million; and

(iv) there were 37,448 staff in Hong Kong, the UK, continental Europe, North America, Caribbean and the rest of the world.

(b) Discuss the suggestion that audit fees are inadequate.

References
....

1 ICAS, *Making Corporate Reports Valuable*, Kogan Page, 1988, p. 19.
2 *Observer*, 19 January 1992.
3 *Guardian*, 22 January 1992.
4 *Independent*, 13 January 1992.
5 M. Sherer and D. Kent, *Auditing and Accountability*, Pitman, 1983, p. 3.
6 Companies Act 1985, Schedule 6.
7 *Guardian*, 22 January 1992.
8 ICAS, *Making Corporate Reports Valuable*, p. 43.
9 S.W. Mayson, D. French and C. Ryan, *A Practical Approach to Company Law*, Financial Training Publications Ltd, 1987, p. 364.

10 ICAS, *Making Corporate Reports Valuable*, p. 53.
11 *Company Directors: Regulating Conflicts of Interest and Formulating a Statement of Duties*, Law Commission No 153; Scot Law Com No 105, 1998.
12 *The Times*, 30 March 1995.
13 *Accountancy*, May 1994, p. 35.
14 *Report of the Committee on the Financial Aspects of Corporate Governance, (Cadbury Committee Report)*, December 1992, Gee Publishing.
15 *Directors' Remuneration: Report of a Study Group Chaired by Sir Richard Greenbury (Greenbury Committee Report)*, July 1995, Gee Publishing.
16 *Committee on Corporate Governance: Final Report (Hampel Committee Report)*, January 1998, Gee Publishing.
17 *Committee on Corporate Governance: The Combined Code*, June 1998, Gee Publishing.
18 *Accountancy*, September 1995.
19 ABI, *Share Option and Profit Sharing Incentive Schemes*, February 1995.
20 UITF Abstract, *Disclosure of Directors' Share Options*, ASB, 1994.
21 *The Times*, 30 March 1995.
22 M. Pagano, *Management Today*, January 1998, pp. 70–72.
23 Robert Heller, *Management Today*, July 1997.
24 'What is the incentive', *Management Today*, July 1999, p. 46.
25 ABI, *Statement of Voting Policy and Corporate Governance Good*, 1998.
26 *Observer*, 19 January 1992.
27 D. Kent, M. Sherer and S. Turley (eds), *Current Issues in Auditing*, Harper & Row, 1985, p. 143.
28 ICAS, *Making Corporate Reports Valuable*, p. 32.
29 A. Hilton, *Management Today*, July 1999, p. 51.
30 D. Kent, M. Sherer and S. Turley (eds), *op. cit.*, p. 135.
31 ICAS, *Making Corporate Reports Valuable*, p. 41.
32 SAS 600, *Auditors Report on Financial Statements*, APB, 1993, para. 14.
33 *Ibid.*, para. 24.
34 *Audit Agenda*, APB, Accountancy Books, 1994, Foreword.
35 International Auditing Practices Committee, ISA 200, 1995.
36 *The Future Development of Auditing*, McFarlane Committee, APB, 1992.
37 APB, *Audit Agenda*, *op. cit.*
38 ICAS, *Making Corporate Reports Valuable*, p. 103.
39 APB, SAS 100, *Objectives and General Principles Governing an Audit of Financial Statements*, March 1995, para. 1.
40 *Ibid.*, para. 4.
41 *Ibid.*, para. 5.
42 APB, SAS 240, *Quality Control for Audit Work*, January 2000, para. 1.
43 *Ibid.*, para. 4.
44 S. Fearnley and R. Brandt, 'When the rules don't quite fit', *Accountancy*, March 2000, p. 63.
45 K. Peasnell, P. Pope and S. Young, *Accountancy*, July 1998, p. 115.
46 *Guardian*, 23 July 1991, p. 13.
47 ICAS, *Making Corporate Reports Valuable*, p. 103.
48 *Accountancy Age*, 13 April 1995.
49 The Companies Act 1985 (Disclosure of Remuneration for Non-audit Work) Regulations SI No 1991/2181.

Social and environmental reporting

29.1 Introduction

In this chapter we consider the following:

- Accountants' role in a capitalist industrial society
- Concept of social accounting
- Background to social accounting
- Process of social accounting
- Future of social accounting
- Environmental accounting

29.2 Accountants' role in a capitalist industrial society

In a capitalist, industrial society, production requires the raising and efficient use of capital largely through joint stock companies. These operate within a legal framework which grants them limited liability subject to certain obligations. The obligations include **capital maintenance provisions** to protect creditors, e.g. restriction on distributable profits, and **disclosure provisions** to protect shareholders, e.g. the publication of annual reports.

The state issues statutes to ensure there is effective control of the capital market; the degree of intervention depends on the party in power. Accountants issue standards to ensure there is reliable information to the owners to support an orderly capital market. Both the state and the accountancy profession have directed their major efforts towards servicing the needs of capital. This has influenced the nature of the legislation, e.g. removing obligations that are perceived to make a company uncompetitive, and the nature of the accounting standards, e.g. concentrating on earnings and monetary values.

However, production and distribution involve complex social relationships between private ownership of property and wage labour[1] and other stakeholders. This raises the question of the role of accountants. Should their primary concern be to serve the interests of the shareholders, or the interests of management, or to focus on equity issues and social welfare?[2]

Prior to the ASB, the profession identified with management and, willingly or unwillingly, it appeared to allow information to be reported to suit management. If management was unhappy with a standard, e.g. SSAP 11 and SSAP 16, it was able to frustrate its implementation. Often, reported results bore little resemblance to the commercial substance of the underlying transactions.

The ASB has concentrated on making reports congruent with commercial reality; it sees financial information as being an economic commodity in its own right. It has developed a conceptual framework for financial reporting to underpin its reporting standards; assets, liabilities, income and expense have been defined with criteria for their recognition which include the ability to state them in monetary terms.

The ASB has not produced mandatory requirements for narrative or qualitative disclosures – the *Operating and Financial Review* (OFR) is voluntary. However, the proposal for the publication of an OFR is an important shift: it is recognition that there is a need for narrative disclosure, even where this is not capable of audit verification.

Why is the qualitative information voluntary?

It is voluntary in recognition of the fact that market and political pressures exist; that each company balances the perceived costs, e.g. competitive disadvantage, and the perceived benefits of voluntary disclosure,[3] e.g. improved investor appeal in determining the extent of its voluntary disclosures.

Companies have traditionally been ranked according to various criteria, e.g. their ability to maximise their shareholders' wealth or return on capital employed or EPS growth rates. However, there is a philosophical view that holds that a company:

> possesses a role in society because society finds it useful that it should do so ... cannot expect to find itself fully acceptable to society if it single-mindedly pursues its major objective without regard for the range of consequences of its actions.[4]

This means that a company is permitted to seek its private objectives subject to legal, social and ethical boundaries. This takes accounting beyond the traditional framework of reporting monetary transactions that are of interest primarily to the shareholders. It takes it into a realm where there is, at present, no obvious paymaster.

29.3 Concept of social accounting

This is a difficult place to start because there are so many definitions of social accounting[5] – the main points are that it includes non-financial as well as financial information and addresses the needs of stakeholders other than the shareholders. Stakeholders can be broken down into three categories:

- **internal stakeholders** – managers and workers;
- **external stakeholders** – shareholders, creditors, banks and debtors;
- **related stakeholders** – society as represented by national and local government and the increasing role of pressure groups such as Amnesty International and Greenpeace.

We have identified certain elements that we consider essential components of social accounting. These are:

- Reporting at corporate level
- Accountability
- Ease of understanding
- Comprehensive coverage of all areas of interest
- An independent, unbiased review process.

29.3.1   Reporting at corporate level

Prior to 1975, social accounting was viewed as being in the domain of the **economist** and concerned with national income and related issues. In 1975, *The Corporate Report* gave a different definition:

> the reporting of those costs and benefits, which may or may not be quantifiable in money terms, arising from economic activities and subsequently borne or received by the community at large or particular groups not holding a direct relationship with the reporting entity.[6]

This is probably the best working definition of the topic and it establishes the first element of the social accounting concept, namely **reporting at a corporate level** and interpreting corporate in its widest sense as including all organisations of economic significance regardless of the type of organisation or the nature of ownership.

29.3.2   Accountability

The effect of the redefinition by *The Corporate Report* was to introduce the second element of our social accounting concept: accountability. The national income view was only of interest to economists and could not be related to individual company performance – *The Corporate Report* changed that. Social accounting moved into the accountants' domain and it should be the aim of accountants to learn how accountability might be achieved and to define a model against which to judge their own efforts and the efforts of others.[7]

What to report?

One problem is the selection of areas of social concern – those areas on which all companies should report unless good reason exists not to do so. Perhaps accountants could assist by identifying areas that are significant, possibly on an industry basis.

What measures to use?

Another concern is to establish measurement principles and techniques. Financial measure might not be the most appropriate and the experience that management accountants have in the determination of relevant information could be useful. For example, how are cost savings arising from better scheduling of deliveries best reported? Should they be expressed in terms of improvement in EPS, or would it be more relevant to express them on the basis of the reduction achieved in the total distance covered to service regular customers?

What if there are no quantitative data?

This could be a problem. Verbal descriptions appear less precise than quantitative data and therefore more open to bias – they appear less credible. The problem has not been resolved and the question still remains: how is it best to provide neutral qualitative information and, if it is impossible to achieve neutrality, how is it best to balance the story that is being told? Would another perspective help?

29.3.3   Ease of understanding

The national income presented a picture that was largely only comprehensible to specialist economists. *The Corporate Report* envisaged a very different audience that had no special qualifications. This set our third element, which was that social accounting should provide information to all interested parties in a form that was understandable at all levels of recipient. The accountancy profession and the regulators have already experienced the difficulty with annual reports being produced that are understood by few and misinterpreted by many. Social accounting must not go down that elitist route.

29.3.4 Comprehensive coverage

The annual report is concerned mainly with monetary amounts or clarifying monetary issues. Despite the ASB identifying employees and the public within the user groups,[8] no standards have been issued that deal specifically with reporting to employees or the public.

Instead, the ASB prefers to assume that financial statements that meet the needs of investors will meet most of the needs of other users.[9] For all practical purposes, it disassociates itself from the needs of non-investor users by assuming that there will be more specific information that they may obtain in their dealings with the enterprise.[10]

The information needs of different categories, e.g. employees and the public, need not be identical. The provision of information of particular interest to the public has been referred to as **public interest accounting**,[11] but there is a danger that, whilst valid as an approach, it could act as a constraint on matters that might be of legitimate interest to the employee user group. For example, safety issues at a particular location might be of little interest to the public at large but of immense concern to an employee exposed to work-related radiation or asbestos. The term 'social accounting' as defined by *The Corporate Report* is seen as embracing all interests, even those of a small group.

Equally, the information needs within a category, say employees, can differ according to the level of the employees. One study identified that different levels of employee ranked the information provided about the employer differently, e.g. lower-level employees rated safety information highest, whereas higher-level employees rated organisation information highest.[12] There were also differences in opinion about the need for additional information, with the majority of lower-level but minority of higher-level employees agreeing that the social report should also contain information on corporate environmental effects.[13]

The need for social accounting to cope with both intergroup and intragroup differences was also identified in a Swedish study.[14]

29.3.5 Independent review

The degree of credibility accorded a particular piece of information is influenced by factors such as whether it is historical data or deals with the future; whether appropriate techniques exist for obtaining it; whether its source causes particular concern about deliberate or unintentional bias towards a company view; whether past experience has been that the information was reasonably complete and balanced; and, finally, the extent of independent verification.[15]

Given that social accounting is complex, technically underdeveloped, dealing with subjective areas or future events, reported on a selective basis within a report prepared by the management, it is understandable that its credibility will be called into question. Questions will be raised as to why particular items were included or omitted – after all, it is not that unusual for companies to want to hide unfavourable developments.

What form should a review take?

A review is unlikely to take the form of the audit that is carried out on the financial statements. Financial statements are now subject to a conceptual framework that gives guidance on identification, recognition and valuation within a transaction-based objective system. Social accounting does not have such a conceptual framework and it is subjective.

What sort of review is feasible?

Should there be an independent review of the appropriateness of the areas selected? On whether quantitative indicators are used where available? On whether the story that is told appears reasonable?

Is an independent review feasible if there is no conceptual framework for social accounting? Should there be a conceptual framework? Are a social accounting standards board and a social auditing practices board required?

Social audit

The idea of public interest has also produced another term, **social audit**, which attempts to cover some aspects of social accounting but is only a small part of the overall picture. The practical offshoot has been the so-called audits of public services, e.g. NHS, education and local government services. While of interest in themselves, are these activities social accounting?

● Do they pay undue emphasis to money as a measure of efficiency?

● Are they for the benefit of the user of the service or the paymaster?

● Is it a value-for-money exercise or a quality assessment?

● Is feedback obtained from the user and, if so, what action results?

● Is there any question as to their independence and freedom from political interference?

● Do they provide an independent, unbiased review process?

These matters are raised as questions rather than as statements because a social accounting conceptual framework does not exist.

29.4 Background to social accounting

A brief consideration of the history of social accounting in the UK could be helpful in putting the subject into context. *The Corporate Report* (1975) was the starting point for the whole issue. This was at a time when there was the general dissatisfaction with the quality of financial reporting which had resulted in the creation of a standard-setting regulatory body (Accounting Standards Steering Committee – ASSC) and additional statutory provisions, e.g. Companies Act provisions relating to directors.

The Corporate Report was a discussion paper issued by the ASSC which represented the first UK conceptual framework. Its approach was to identify users and their information needs. It identified seven groups of user, which included employees and the public, and their information needs. However, although it identified that there were common areas of interest among the seven groups, such as assessing liquidity and evaluating management performance, it concluded that a single set of general-purpose accounts would not satisfy each group – a different conclusion from that stated by the ASB in 1991, as discussed above.[16] The conclusions reached in *The Corporate Report* were influenced by the findings of a survey of the chairmen of the 300 largest UK listed companies. They indicated a trend towards acceptance of multiple responsibilities towards groups affected by corporate decision-making and their interest as stakeholders.[17]

The Corporate Report proposed that there should be additional reports to satisfy the needs of the other stakeholders. These included a statement of corporate objectives, a statement of future prospects, an employment report and a value added statement.

Statement of corporate objectives

Would this be the place for social accounting to start? Would this be the place for vested interests to be represented so that agreed objectives take account of the views of all stakeholders and not merely the management and, indirectly, the shareholders? At present, social accounting appears as a series of add-ons, e.g. a little on charity donations, a little on disabled recruitment policy. Corporate objectives or the mission statement are often seen as something to be handed down; could they assume a different role?

The employment report

The need for an employment report was founded on the belief that there is a trust relationship between employers and employees and an economic relationship between employment prospects and the welfare of the community. The intention was that such a report should contain statistical information relating to such matters as numbers, reasons for change, training time and costs, age and sex distribution, and health and safety.

Statement of future prospects

There has always been resistance to publishing information focusing on the future. The arguments raised against it have included competitive disadvantage and the possibility of misinterpretation because the data relate to the future and are therefore uncertain.

The report nevertheless considered it appropriate to publish information of future employment and capital investment levels that could have a direct impact on employees and the local community.

Value added reports

A value added report was intended to give a different focus from the profit and loss account with its emphasis on the bottom line earnings figure. It was intended to demonstrate the interdependence of profits and payments to employees, shareholders, the government and the company via inward investment. It reflected the mood picked up from the survey of chairmen that distributable profit could no longer be regarded as the sole or prime indicator of company performance.[18]

The value added statement became a well-known reporting mechanism to measure how effectively an organisation utilised its resources and added value to its raw materials to turn them into saleable goods. Figure 29.1 is an example of a value added statement.

Several advantages have been claimed for these reports, including improving employee attitudes by reflecting a broader view of companies' objectives and responsibilities.[19,20]

There have also been criticisms, e.g. they are merely a restatement of information that appears in the annual report; they only report data capable of being reported in monetary terms; and the individual elements of societal benefit are limited to the traditional ones of shareholders, employees and the government, with others such as society and the consumers ignored.

There was also criticism that there was no standard so that expenditures could be aggregated or calculated to disclose a misleading picture, e.g. the inclusion of PAYE tax and welfare payments made to the government in the employee classification so that wages were shown gross whereas distributions to shareholders were shown net of tax. The effect of both was to overstate the apparent employee share and understate the government and shareholders' share.[21]

In the years immediately following the report, companies published value added statements on a voluntary basis but their importance has declined. There was a move

Figure 29.1 Demo Group value added statement for the year ended 3 December 20X7.

	£000	%	20X6 %
Funds available			
Sales	50,000		
Less: Bought-in materials and services	20,000		
Value added	30,000		
Add: Investment income	2,000		
Total funds available for allocation	32,000	100.0	*100.0*
Applied in the following way			
To employees:			
Wages. pensions. other benefits	16,000	50.0	*45.0*
To governments:			
Corporate taxes	5,120	16.0	*5.0*
Local taxation	800	2.5	*2.3*
To providers of capital:			
Interest on loans	640	2.0	*2.4*
Dividends to minority shareholders	576	1.8	*1.1*
Dividends to parent company shareholders	2,304	7.2	*6.0*
Retained by the company and its subsidiaries:			
To pay for capital expenditure to replace			
existing assets, to expand working capital			
and for growth:			
Depreciation	3,200	10.0	*11.0*
Retained earnings	3,360	10.5	*17.2*
Total allocated funds	32,000	100.0	*100.0*

away from industrial democracy and the standard-setting regulators did not make it mandatory.

29.4.1 Why *The Corporate Report* was not implemented

The Corporate Report's proposals for additional reports have not been implemented. There are a number of views as to why this was so. There is a view that the business community, despite the results of the chairmen survey, were concerned about the possibility of their reporting responsibility being extended through the report's concept of public accountability and welcomed the release of the Sandilands Report on inflation accounting which overshadowed *The Corporate Report*. There is a view that *The Corporate Report* fell short of making a significant contribution 'by virtue of its failure to select the accounting models appropriate to the informational needs of the individual user groups which it had identified'.[22]

However, the most likely reason for it not being fully implemented was the change of government. The Labour government produced a Green Paper in 1976, *Aims and Scope of Company Reports*, which endorsed much of *The Corporate Report* concept. The reaction from the business community and the Stock Exchange was hostile to any move away from the traditional stewardship concept with its obligations only to shareholders. The CBI view was that other users could ask for information, but that was no reason for companies to be required to provide it.[23] In the event, there was a change of government and the Green Paper sank without trace.

The new government supported the view of Friedman, who wrote in 1962 that 'few trends could so ... undermine the very foundations of our free society as the acceptance by corporate officials of a social responsibility other than to make as much money ... as possible'.

Many responsible members of the business community pressed for change,[24] but the mid 1980s saw a decline in the commercial support for social accounting, as profit, dividends and growth superseded all other social goals in business. The movement continued but advocates were regarded at best as well-meaning radicals and at worst as dangerous politicised activists devoted to the destruction of the capitalist system.

By the early 1990s, interest was appearing in the commercial sector but from a free market rather than regulatory viewpoint. The thought was that socially responsible policies need not mean lower profits – in fact, quite the opposite. Given this change in perception, companies began to embrace social accounting concepts – suddenly accountants were able to make a contribution, e.g. evaluating the profit implication of providing crèche facilities for working mothers by the employer rather than the state. There was also a growth within society in general of a socially responsible point of view which even extended to share investment decisions with the marketing of ethically sound investments.

It is interesting at this point to refer to the **long wave theory** of economic change.[25] This theory is that there is a fifty-year repeating rise and fall of economic activity, called the long wave or **Kondratieff cycle**. The cycle comprises a decade of depression, thirty years of technical innovation and active capital investments and, finally, ten years of economic uncertainty while the growth forces of the past subside.

It could be important for those who wish to see social and environmental accounting developed to identify two things. First, the point at which we are on the cycle. If we are in decline, labour power will be weak but environmental/consumer power will be high as capital seeks a market for its products. If we are in the thirty-year period, then labour will be scarce and better able to exercise power and influence social accounting.

Secondly, the mindset of the political party in power must be ascertained. If the mindset of the political party coincides with that of the user group currently enjoying power, then significant change will be possible. The stakeholders identified by *The Corporate Report* will lack influence until the ruling political party enfranchises them.

Progress is being made on a number of fronts but it is fair to acknowledge that the full adoption of social accounting is many years away and, until the commercial sector embraces the ideals, little can happen. The regulators do not see it as their role to encourage social reporting, e.g. the ASB approach; the government is committed to voluntary disclosure as being the most appropriate way forward, i.e. progress will be market-driven. Since the 1970s, accountants have addressed the problems of identification, recognition, measurement and disclosure within financial reporting and the ASB is now producing conceptually sound standards. A similar need exists for accountants to contribute to the development of social accounting. In this regard, an encouraging development with the support of the accounting profession has been the formation of the Centre for Social and Environmental Accounting Research at Dundee University.

29.5 Process of social accounting

This is a difficult area to comment on because so little progress has been made in practice. However, a review of some of the possibilities will help in appreciating where a social accounting approach could produce benefits even now without great effort. These include employment; products and services; organisational ethos; employee reports; human asset accounting; and social accounting implications of structural change.

29.5.1 Employment

There are existing requirements to report certain information under the Companies Act 1985, e.g. employee statistics, directors' remuneration, employment of disabled staff, employee consultation.

Employee statistics

Statistics include the average weekly number of employees, an analysis of this total by categories determined by the directors, and staff costs analysed into wages, salaries, social security cost and other pension costs.[26] However, one can think of a number of additional issues that would be of interest, e.g. safety, ethnic issues, equal opportunities issues, future employment plans, training provision.

Directors' remuneration[27]

We have already seen with regard to directors' remuneration that disclosures that have satisfied the statutory requirements have not been adequate. Disclosures have not been easy to understand and companies have resisted pressure to make the remuneration package more transparent.

Employment of disabled staff

The annual report contains a description of the company policy for giving full and fair consideration to applications for employment by disabled persons, having regard to their particular aptitudes and ability.[28]

This is helpful in raising the company's profile but is there a better way of presenting relevant, timely information than the simple descriptive statements that are required in the annual report, e.g. 'It is company policy to give full and fair consideration to applications for employment by disabled persons, having regard to their particular aptitudes and ability?'

Employee consultation

The annual report contains a description of the action taken during the year systematically to provide employees with matters of concern to them as employees and consulting them in making decisions which are likely to affect their interests.[29]

This is helpful in raising the company's profile but does not provide sufficient information to allow the user to evaluate the extent and effectiveness of the consultation, especially in cases where the issue is commercially sensitive and will also affect the staff, e.g. a planned closure or transfer of productive or office facilities.

However, we are in an evolving situation and should be seeking the publication of more detailed supporting information – policy statements are a start but they are not sufficient in themselves. Accountants have a role in providing data and information that allow users to evaluate the policy statements.

29.5.2   Products and services

Social accounting could assist by making disclosures about the social effects of the production process, e.g. pollution and use of scarce resources, and the end-use of the product or service, e.g. the cases of Matrix Churchill and unfortunate role of Sheffield Forgemasters in the Supergun affair. These illustrate the dangers of unaccountable business and government practices and products. All organisations, including the government, need to become more transparent in their activities as evidenced, for example, by the appalling series of expenditure overruns in defence contracts.

When considering service delivery, accountants have made a contribution towards the evaluation of the efficiency of the service expressed in terms of its cost effectiveness but there has been less attention to the evaluation of the effectiveness of the service delivered. For example, there is a tension in education between, on the one hand, reducing the unit cost per student by cramming them into ever larger groups with minimal opportunity for individual interaction and, on the other, producing high-quality individuals who have enjoyed a rich fulfilling educational experience.

This raises the question of the expertise and skills that will be required for social accounting. The user of the term implies that the task will fall within the accountants' domain but it is not by any means restricted to that profession or exclusive. Other expert opinion will be necessary. For example, evaluating the effectiveness of the educational process might well require a psychologist's expertise rather than that of an accountant. The existence of multidisciplinary teams within the management consulting arms of the large accounting practices could provide the mix of manpower to produce reliable, relevant social accounting reports – once the commercial paymasters become converted.

29.5.3   Organisational ethos

Organisations do have a specific way of behaving and reacting, and society has a right to know and have explained to it the behaviour of the management of the organisation. Already we see management taking advice from psychologists and public relations (PR) firms on how best to present its social responsibility image. Much more is required than this. For example, what is the organisation's relationship with the local communities in which it operates around the world? We are aware that there is health and safety legislation in the UK, but what is the position in other parts of the world, particularly in the developing areas? Are there disparate safety and employment conditions? Are these conditions satisfactory from an ethical standpoint?

29.5.4   Employee reports

Employee reports are commonplace in many organisations but they do vary in content, style and usefulness. The objective is to communicate with employees, aid the development of a system of *esprit de corps* and improve morale.[30] However, the lack of perceived independence limits their use and they are primarily seen as PR documents for management. Suggestions to reduce perceived bias include forming a working committee of employees from all levels and encouraging trade union officials to contribute.[31]

Employee needs may vary. They are not a homogeneous group and different levels of employees will have different needs.[32] There is one common need at every level: job security, and many companies provide divisional and product line information.[33] It is not clear, however, the extent to which management would provide timely information on factors that threaten job security.

As with other social accounting reports there is a need for an independent review or audit.

29.5.5 Human asset accounting

The ASB Discussion Paper *Goodwill and Intangible Assets* (1995)[34] stated that although economic benefits are expected to arise, as from a portfolio of clients or a team of staff with certain expert skills, there may be insufficient control for an asset to exist, and that although there may be an expectation that the team of staff will continue to make its expert skills available, this cannot be guaranteed because of the lack of control over the team. This is a difficult problem because some companies, e.g. a software company, may have few tangible fixed assets and the real worth of the company lies in its employees' skills. Already the stock market values the human assets within the share price but the regulators have not yet created a definition that will allow the asset to appear on the balance sheet. However, the regulators have changed the definition of assets: assets were originally required to be owned by the organisation but this has been relaxed to controlled in order, initially, to catch leasing arrangements. The present position is anomalous. It is permissible to carry goodwill as an asset on the balance sheet subject to an impairment test which consists of net present value (NPV) calculation of the cash flows arising from the very skilled workforce that apparently cannot be recognised because they are not controlled. What is the difference between recognising the NPV of the cash flow arising from the skilled workforce as an asset labelled 'human assets: skilled employees' and recognising the NPV of exactly the same cash flow labelled as 'intangible assets: goodwill'? The 'human asset' label would appear to be far more descriptive and relevant. The users would be made aware of the fact that the worth of the company resided in the skilled staff and not in a nebulous intangible called goodwill. There has been research into possible methods for valuing human assets;[35] these include both cost-based methods, which reclassify amounts from expense to asset, and value-based methods, which discount future salaries or discount future earnings.

The assets might not currently satisfy the regulators' definition of an asset and the social accounting report might be an appropriate vehicle for disclosure.

29.5.6 Social accounting implications of structural change

Management accountants have a role in this area: they have the skills to produce relevant data for decision-making purposes. However, because they are employees they are constrained to produce information and reports in the format and with the focus specified by management.

For example, let us speculate on the decline of the British coal industry. Before privatisation there appeared to be a distinct ring-fenced political decision to reduce the size of the industry. Costs were produced to support the decision which resulted in thousands of miners losing their jobs. The reason given was that it was on cost grounds, and it is one of the powerful attributes of costs which are that they appear to be objective and irrefutable – their air of inevitability authenticates economic decisions.

However, care has to be taken as to how costs are defined and how it is determined which are relevant. In the case of the coal industry, costs were shifted, from British Coal to the state via social benefits. Should this aspect have been excluded from the decision process?

From an accountant's perspective, the accountants employed by the Coal Board and government could scarcely exercise the independent right to produce figures or formats that did not support their employer's position. Who, in such cases, can produce social

accounting reports with a different definition of relevance? Can the professional accounting bodies be expected to comment on the validity or relevance of the data supporting
the decision-making process? Perhaps this is an area where academic accountants can
function. If so, how are they to be financed?

The point being made is not one of political bias. It is to be expected that any decision-
making body, whether a commercial concern or government, would seek to present the facts
in a manner that supports its plans. The problem is how to encourage good citizenship
to thrive if there are no social accounting standards governing the reporting of events to
society.

29.6 Future of social accounting

The areas that fall within social accounting are both quantitative and qualitative, backward-
and forward-looking, and often significant only to small non-investor groups. The
conceptual framework developed by the ASB and its mandatory standards do not accommodate all of these aspects.

The regulators find auditors object to qualitative statements because they are not verifiable. They find management objects to forward-looking information because it exposes
the company to unacceptable competitive threats, and auditors object because it exposes
them to an increased risk of litigation. They find it difficult to take interests other than
those of the shareholders into account on the grounds that there is already information
overload.

The result is that issues which are of immense concern to certain users, such as the
risk of loss of employment, defective products, questionable destination for products and
unethical business practices, are not reported.

How is progress to be made? Is there a need for a different regulatory body, a social
accounting standards board? Is it realistic or indeed appropriate to expect a financial
reporting regulatory body consisting of accountants, auditors and management to change
its mindset? Who should undertake the research and development of standards of disclosure and measurement that social accounting requires? How should research and development of standards be financed?

The issues that would initially be included have been touched on above and, just as
the financial accounting environment evolves with new commercial practices and standards, social accounting would also evolve as more areas become reportable in response
to the expressed needs of interest groups.

Social Responsibility Audits (SRAs)

These are a growing trend in the USA to give public credibility to an organisation's claim
to be a 'socially responsible organisation'. It is being recognised that commercial success
can be a function of public approval just as much as a function of fiscal prudence and
efficiency.

It is therefore essential for the company's claim to be 'audited' as would any other
normal financial report.

Many US audit firms are specialising in such work and it is proving to be a crucial
part of an organisation's 'public face'.

The scope of a SRA is considerable and covers the following main areas:

● Community development – how does the organisation interact with the local and
  wider community?

- Diversity – how does the organisation deal with the diversity of customers, suppliers and employees? This is, of course, partially an examination of policies on ethnic groups, disabilities and gender issues.

- Environmental – how does the organisation interact with the environment with particular reference to regulation compliance?

- International relations – how does the organisation treat customers and workers overseas? Is the company dealing with 'dubious' enterprises?

- Marketplace practices – how does the organisation operate in the market? This is a question of marketing practices, customer care practices and financial practices.

- Fiscal responsibility – how is the organisation behaving in terms of its financial practices and taxation liabilities?

- Accounting, auditing, monitoring and reporting – how is the organisation behaving in respect of these practices in relation to the required regulations?

The audit team is somewhat different to normal in that it would include accountants, lawyers, engineers and behavioural scientific practitioners.

A development for the SRA is the valuation of key intangible assets, currently invisible on the balance sheet but of vital interest to stakeholders. The intangibles could include:

- Intellectual capital

- Customer/vendor loyalty

- Employee satisfaction

- Creative synergy (the entrepreneurial spark that invents and creates profitable activities)

- Community support.

As we move towards the 'learning organisation' it does become critical to be able to value these intangibles as they are crucial to the success of the organisation.

An example of a company doing such work is Vasin, Heyn and Company of California.

29.7 Environmental accounting

The whole issue of environmental accounting must be seen as a subset of the wider concept of social accounting. Its development has been a part of the growth in demand by interested parties for relevant information. The area of **green accounting** is probably more popular than pure social accounting because of the high profile of green issues in general. As with social accounting, environmental accounting is really a philosophy of reporting and accounting rather than a specific technique. However, certain key phrases such as 'sustainability' and 'pollution' keep appearing and a review of these could prove useful.

29.7.1 Sustainability

The concept of sustainability is predicated on the view that all resources are limited and cannot be easily replaced. Thus, the prudent organisation will attempt to minimise the use of these valuable scarce resources and replace them by the use of renewable resources. An interesting example appears in the 1993 annual report of Pearson, which states that:

One aspect of our company's environmental responsibilities is to keep their purchasing policies under review. Pearson's most significant purchase is paper. Our publishing companies between them buy some 180,000 tonnes of paper a year. Most of the paper comes from spruce, aspen and pine growing in Northern latitudes, with limited amounts of birch. Some comes from softwoods and eucalyptus growing in coastal regions of Brazil. Pearson makes certain that it buys paper only from responsibly managed forests and avoids paper bleached with chlorinated organic compounds where possible. Much has been said in recent years about the merits of recycled paper but its superiority over virgin paper is debatable. Recycled paper is unsuitable for some purposes and the recycling process itself consumes energy; it also creates toxic waste if the paper needs to be washed clean of inks. Managed forests on the other hand contain young healthy trees which consume carbon dioxide and give off oxygen.... Given the complexity of this subject and the lack of agreement among experts, Pearson is using its purchasing power to encourage good practice in the light of today's knowledge while keeping an open mind about future developments.

Why is this information reported in the annual accounts since the technical assessment falls outside an accountant's skill or expertise? One reason is that the government has indicated that investors can seek information about the environmental practices of companies they invest in and make their views known.[36] Another reason is the cost implications which have relevance to existing shareholders because they could affect future earnings and also to acquisitive companies who need to be aware of contingent liabilities.[37] These contingent liabilities can be enormous, and in the USA the potential cost of clearing up past industrially hazardous sites has been estimated at $675 billion. Even in relation to individual companies the scale of the contingency can be large, as in the Love Canal case. In this case a housing project was built at Love Canal in Upper New York State on a site that until the 1950s had been used by Hooker Chemicals Corporation for dumping chemical waste containing dioxin. Occidental, which had acquired Hooker Chemicals, was judged liable for the costs of clean-up of more than $260 million.[38]

29.7.2 Pollution

There is a growing amount of national legislation setting stringent environmental controls to reduce pollution and a large number of EU environmental proposals which will have substantial cost implications estimated at £15 billion for Britain.[39]

The 1994 annual report of Scottish Power discloses significant cost implications:

The company is committed to meeting or bettering increasingly stringent environmental controls for electricity generation and is developing new technologies and plant which can achieve significant benefits at realistic cost. At Longannet Power Station, more than £24 million is being invested in low NOx burners, which produce fewer nitrous oxides, and in renewing equipment to reduce dust from flue gases.... This process is expected to be environmentally superior and lower in cost than alternative technologies.

We can see, therefore, that sustainability and pollution issues both have serious implications for the balance sheet, e.g. under SSAP 18 *Contingent Liability* the potential liabilities arising in connection with the Hooker Chemicals acquisition would have been considered for treatment as a provision or contingent liability note with an eventual impact on the bottom line.

There are, of course, other environmental threats that can have serious financial implications for individual companies and investors need to be aware of the potential impact, e.g. Exxon was liable for costs of $850 million for the clean-up in 1989 after the Exxon Valdez oil tanker went aground.

29.7.3 What disclosure is required in the annual report?

There is a need to disclose the types of environmental issue relevant to the business and its industry. The importance of the information would clearly be expected to vary according to the industry in which the business operates, with the most obvious polluters such as the chemical, oil, steel, aircraft and motor industries having the most information of relevance to report and being most likely to do so on a voluntary basis.[40]

There is a need for the accounting policies' notes to include the policies for accounting for environmental protection measures, e.g. for recording liabilities and provisions, for setting up catastrophe reserves out of retained earnings and for disclosing contingent liabilities. The notes should also disclose, where material, the current and accumulated amounts of these items.[41]

The area will call for multidisciplinary teams and technical expertise to evaluate the extent of environmental liabilities. Environmental accounting is an area that people feel strongly about, e.g. the president of the ICAEW said in 1991: 'We chartered accountants must measure up to the environmental challenge if we are to fulfil our duty as a profession to promote the public interest'.[42] The subject is emotive and it was a natural comment to make. However, we have already commented at the beginning of the chapter that accountants are in a service industry role. This point is made by Roger Adams in 1994: 'As an accounting body first and foremost, ACCA cannot become deeply involved in non-accounting issues'.[43] This is a pertinent and timely comment because the subject is emotive and it is often difficult to separate accounting from good citizen considerations.

29.7.4 The accounting profession and environmental accounting

The professional bodies have been committed to making a contribution in the area, e.g. ACCA has commissioned and published research.[44,45,46] It has also set up the Environmental Reporting Award Scheme encouraging companies to experiment with ways of bringing details of their environmental performance to the attention of the City financial institutions.

The ICAEW environmental steering group has published a discussion paper aimed at ascertaining whether existing accounting principles are adequate for environmental issues and recommending additional guidance on the subject of impaired assets. The Institute supports the development of more uniform disclosures.[47]

Perhaps this will lead to the involvement of the ASB, but a survey by the *Fédération des Experts Comptables Européen* carried out in 1994 found that none of the accounting or auditing standard-setting bodies in any of the eighteen European countries surveyed was involved in developing standards that specifically address the environment.

The indications are, however, that there will be important implications for the accountancy profession arising from the issue of the Fifth Action Programme on the Environment, *Towards Sustainability*, which proposes a redefinition of accounting concepts, rules, conventions and methodology in order to ensure that the full cost of the consumption of goods and use of the environmental resources is reflected in market prices.

A comment by Hibbert makes a fitting close to the chapter:

The environmental challenge represents a golden opportunity for the profession to serve management, shareholders, governments and other stakeholders...

The ASB should set up a task force to address accounting for sustainable development ... The profession's raison d'être as the assurer of the integrity of financial information depends on it. Public trust demands it.[48]

This has been a brief introduction to an important topic that will increasingly impact on reported earnings and liabilities disclosed in the balance sheet. Readers are encouraged to refer to the reading list that follows this chapter to further their understanding.

29.8 Environmental auditing

This activity is often regarded as fundamental to the effective application of environmental policies within all organisations. It is a service that is often offered by external auditors for their clients and it is increasingly becoming a responsibility of internal auditors.

29.8.1 The aims of an environmental audit

There are four main aims, namely, to:

● assess risk;

● highlight good (and also poor) practices;

● increase environmental awareness throughout the organisation; and

● produce an **environmental situation report** to help with planning for the future.

29.8.2 The skills of an environmental auditor

The International Standards Organisation (ISO) has outlined certain attributes for the embryonic profession of Environmental Auditor which include both scientific skills and audit skills – the latter being the reason for the involvement of accountants in the process of environmental auditing.

29.8.3 The activities involved in an environmental audit

There are many activities commonly seen in practice. These can be grouped into those assessing the *current position* and those evaluating decisions affecting the *future*.

Assessing the current position

The assessment embraces physical, systems and staff appraisal.

● Physical appraisal is carried out by means of:
  – **site inspections**;
  – **scientific testing** to sample and test substances including air samples;
  – **off-site testing and inspections** to examine the organisation's impact on its immediate surroundings; after all, the company's responsibility does not stop at the boundary fence.

- Systems appraisal is carried out by means of:
  - **systems inspections** to review the stated systems of management and control in respect of environmental issues;
  - **operational reviews** to review actual practices when compared to the stated systems.
- Staff appraisal is carried out by means of:
  - **awareness tests for staff** to test, by questionnaire, the basic knowledge of all levels of staff of the systems and practices currently used by the organisation. This will highlight any areas of weakness.

Assessing the future

The assessment embraces planning and design processes and preparedness for emergencies.

- Planning and design appraisal is carried out by means of:
  - **review of planning procedures** to ensure that environmental factors are considered in the planning processes adopted by the organisation;
  - **design reviews** to examine the basic design processes of the organisation (if applicable) to ensure that environmental issues are addressed at the design stage so the organisation can avoid problems rather than have to solve them when they happen.
- Preparedness for emergencies is appraised by means of:
  - **review of emergency procedures** to assess the organisation's preparedness for specific, predictable emergencies;
  - **review of crisis plans** to review the organisation's general approach to crisis management with the audit covering such topics as the formation of **crisis management teams** and resource availability.

29.8.4 The environmental audit report

We can see from the above than an environmental audit may be wide-ranging in its scope and time consuming, particularly when auditing a major organisation. A typical report could include:

- Current practice
  - A comprehensive review and comment on current operational practices.
- List of action required
  - areas of **immediate concern** which the organisation needs to address as a matter of urgency;
  - areas for improvement over a set period of time.
- Qualitative assessment
  - A **statement of risk** as seen by the audit team based on an overview of the whole situation with a qualitative assessment of the level of environmental risk being faced by the organisation.
- An action plan
  - A **schedule of improvement** may also be produced which gives a timetable and series of stages for the organisation to follow in improving its environmental performance.
- Encouraging good practice
  - A positive statement of 'good practice' may be included. This has a dual value in that it is a motivational tool for management and an educational tool to foster staff awareness of what constitutes 'good practice'.

29.8.5 What is the status of an environmental audit report?

Legal position

There is no legal obligation to carry out an environmental audit or to inform outside parties of any critical findings when such an audit is carried out. The reports are usually regarded as 'confidential' even when carried out by external auditors who provide the service as an 'optional extra' which is offered to the organisation for an additional fee.

Public interest

There is a strong case for requiring both environmental audits and the publication of the resultant reports. Requiring reports to be put into the public domain would encourage transparency in the process and avoid accusations of secrecy. However, this 'public interest' argument has been heard before in accounting and has met with some resistance in the guise of commercial sensitivity.

Mandatory position

The lack of legal obligation could be regarded as a crucial weakness of the environmental audit process as there could be a major danger to the environment which remains 'secret' until after the crisis when it is then too late. The responsible organisation will of course inform all appropriate parties of any revealed risk but it would be foolhardy to assume that all organisations are responsible. The ASB has become involved with potential liability for the company in its consideration of *Provisions*. Whilst this is only viewing it from the viewpoint of the shareholder, it may well be the only pragmatic way forward at this point in time.

29.8.6 Accountants and the future of environmental auditing

Environmental auditing remains a topic to be formally addressed by the accounting profession. The profession's involvement with environmental issues is growing and the profession is finding itself at the centre of the verification and assessment process. It promises to be an exciting future which will require the application of existing skills and also the acquisition of new skills.

29.8.7 Experience in the USA

The increasing importance of environmental accounting can be seen in the USA by the work of the Untied States Environmental Protection Agency (EPA) and its Environmental Accounting Project (EAP) which has been operating since 1992.

In this large project the EPA attempts to identify the currently 'hidden' societal costs faced by organisations. These costs are those which an organisation incurs in its interaction with the environment and which in theory are totally avoidable. By identifying these costs, the organisation is motivated to address them and by implication make every attempt to reduce them, thus improving the environment.

The EPA has a very impressive website, which can be found at the following address: *http://www.epa.gov/opptinr/acctg/eaproject.htm*. Here the basic ideas and concepts governing the EPA's study of environmental accounting are set out.

The work of the EPA has also been of a more practical nature in helping organisations address environmental issues from an environmental viewpoint. A brief review of three such cases may help explain the proactive approach to environmental accounting, which goes beyond traditional reporting.

A. The Chrysler Corporation (a major vehicle manufacturer) was faced with a problem with the use of mercury switches in its electrical systems on vehicles. Mercury is dangerous to use and is very dangerous as a waste product when the vehicle is scrapped. The company had always resisted the use of non-mercury switches on pure cost terms.

However, during the EPA project, by looking at the environmental cost it was seen that non-mercury switches actually made an $0.11 per unit saving. The company on an annual basis would make an $18,000 annual saving on one plant alone by this component change.

B. Amoco Corporation (a major oil company) needed to identify the cost of complying with environmental protection regulations and used one of its refineries in Yorktown, Virginia, as an experimental site. From an analysis of the financial accounts it was found that environmental costs represented 21.9% of the non-crude cost of the product (crude oil being the major cost).

This figure was six times the level previously assumed to be the environmental cost of production. The realisation of the scale of the cost led to changes in managerial policies and practices.

C. Majestic Metals Inc. of Denver Colorado had a problem with pollution caused by its paint spraying machinery and practices. Through an environmental accounting exercise, the company decided to use high-volume, low-pressure (HVLP) sprayers and this reduced the cost of environmental damage (as shown by fines and rectification costs) by $40,000 per year. From a capital investment appraisal viewpoint the project gave a positive NPV over 8 years of $140,000, an internal rate of return (IRR) of 906% and a discounted payback of 0.12 years – an impressive range of results in any terms.

The EPA's website has many more cases showing the impact of an environmental accounting approach.

Summary

Social accounting is a viewpoint rather than a specific technique in the reporting structures of organisations. It follows the movement towards greater accountability and the developments in the UK such as the growth of consumerism and the Citizen's Charter. It represents a possible route to meet the needs of society for timely and relevant quantitative and qualitative information that might not have been verified in the sense in which the financial statements are audited, but would be credible. Individuals are accustomed to filtering information. They are not in their normal daily life presented with verified data and they are usually able to form an opinion if only they are given some information. The difficulty is that in the UK information is perceived as power – there is no Freedom of Information Act for example – and there has been a vested interest in preserving the status quo.

Developments such as the Citizen's Charter are encouraging because they are starting the process of accountability. There might be disagreement with the nature of the disclosure, e.g. ranking schools by examination results, but the important point is that there is disclosure – the process is being put into place. Accountants can play an important role in making certain that the disclosures also meet, as far as is practical, the qualitative characteristics of accounting information established by the ASB. This may be difficult to achieve in the short term until it becomes generally acknowledged that quantitative measures need supplementing with qualitative information.

Review questions

1 Discuss *The Corporate Report*'s relevance to modern business, identify changes that would improve current reporting practice and the conditions necessary for such changes to become mandatory.

2 (a) Explain the term 'stakeholders' in a corporate context.

(b) Social accounting recognises all *Corporate Report* users as stakeholders. Discuss.

3 Discuss the value added concept, giving examples, and ways to improve the statement.

4 Outline the arguments for and against a greater role for the audit function in social accounting.

5 (a) Human assets are incapable of being valued. Discuss.

(b) Football clubs have followed various policies in the way in which they include players within their accounts. For example, some clubs capitalise players, as shown by a 1992 Touche Ross survey:[49]

Club	Value £m	Basis	Which players
Tottenham Hotspur	9.8	Cost	Those purchased
Sheffield United	8.7	Manager's valuation	Whole squad
Portsmouth	7.0	Directors' valuation	Whole squad
Derby County	6.5	Cost	Those purchased

Other clubs disclose squad value in notes to the accounts or in the directors' report:

Manchester United	24.0	Independent valuation
Charlton Athletic	4.1	Directors' valuation
Millwall	11.0	Manager's valuation

Discuss arguments for and against capitalising players as assets. Explain the effect on the profit and loss account if players are not capitalised.

6 Formulate arguments to support a request by the employees of an organisation of your choice for an employee report. Prepare a list of the items that you would like to see.

7 (a) Examine the recent financial press to identify examples of a failure to meet information needs in respect of an area of public interest.

(b) Obtain a set of accounts from a public listed company and assess the success in meeting the needs of the traditional users. Repeat the process for non-traditional users and discuss how you could improve the situation (a) marginally, (b) significantly.

8 Discuss the impact of the following groups on the accounting profession:

(a) Environmental groups;

(b) Customers;

(c) Workforce;

(d) Ethical investors.

9 Nissan, the Japanese car company, decided that 'any environmentalism should pay for itself and for every penny you spend you must save a penny. You can spend as many pennies as you like as long as other environmental actions save an equal number.'[50] Discuss the significance of this for each of the stakeholders.

10 (a) Accounting should contribute to the protection of the environment. Discuss whether this is a proper role for accounting and outline ways in which it could.

    (b) Outline, with reasons, your ideas for an environmental report for a company of your choice.

    (c) Discuss the arguments against the adoption of environmental accounting.

11 (a) Obtain the annual reports of companies that claim to be environmentally aware and assess if these reports and accounts reflect the claim. The various oil, chemical and pharmaceutical companies are useful for this.

    (b) Look at your own organisation/institution, outline the possible environmental issues and discuss how these could or should be disclosed in the annual report.

The following references have been helpful for students carrying out assignments in the developing areas of Social and Environmental Reporting:

Accounting Advisory Forum, *Environmental Issues in Financial Reporting*, 1995, Accounting Advisory Forum (Brussels).

C. A. Adams, W. -Y. Hill and C. B. Roberts, 'Corporate social reporting practices in Western Europe: legitimating corporate behaviour?', *British Accounting Review*, 1998, Vol. 30(1), pp. 1–22.

C. C. Adams, A. Coutts and G. Harte, 'Corporate equal opportunities (non-) disclosure', *British Accounting Review*, 1995, Vol. 27(2), pp. 87–108.

F. K. Birkin, 'Environmental Management Accounting', *Management Accounting*, 1996, pp. 34–37.

F. Birkin and D. Woodward, 'Management accounting for sustainable development', *Management Accounting*, June 1997, pp. 24–26.

J. H. Blokdijk and F. Drieenhuizen, 'The environment and the audit profession – a Dutch research study', *The European Accounting Review*, December 1992, pp. 437–443.

R. L. Burritt and G. Lehman, 'The Body Shop wind farm – an analysis of accountability and ethics', *British Accounting Review*, 1995, Vol. 27(3), pp. 167–186.

J. Colllier, *The Corporate Environment*, Prentice Hall, 1995.

D. Dodds, J. A. Lesser and R. O. Zerbe, *Environmental Economics and Policy*, Addison Wesley, 1997.

R. Gray, J. Bebbington, D. Walters and M. Houldin (eds), *Accounting for the Environment*, Paul Chapman Publishing, 1993.

R. Gray, D. Owen and C. Adams, *Accounting and Accountability – Changes and Challenges in Corporate Social and Environmental Reporting*, Prentice Hall, 1996.

M. J. Jones, 'Accounting for Biodiversity', *British Accounting Review*, 1996, Vol. 28(4), pp. 281–304.

L. Lewis, C. Humphrey and D. Owen, 'Accounting and the Social: A Pedagogic Perspective', *British Accounting Review*, 1992, Vol. 24(3), pp. 219–234.

M. Lynn, '*A Note on Corporate Social Disclosure in Hong Kong*', *British Accounting Review*, 1992, Vol. 24, No. 2, pp. 105–110.

M. Matthews and M. H. B. Perera, *Accounting Theory and Development* (3rd edition), Thompson Business Press, 1996.

T. Mouck, 'Financial reporting, democracy and environmentalism: a critique of the commodification of information', *Critical Perspectives on Accounting*, 1995, Vol. 6(6), pp. 535–553.

M. K. Neimark, *The Hidden Dimensions of Annual Reports – Sixty Years of Social Conflict at General Motors*, Paul Chapman Publishing, 1993.

D. Owen (ed.), *Green Reporting – Accounting and the Challenge of the Nineties*, Thompson Business Press, 1992.

R. Roslender and J. R. Dyson, 'Accounting for the worth of employees: a new look at an old problem', *British Accounting Review*, 1992, Vol. 24(4), pp. 311–330.

D. Rubenstein, *Environmental Accounting for the Sustainable Corporation*, Westport, Quorum Books, 1994.

S. Schaltegger, K. Muller and H. Hindrichsen, *Corporate Environmental Reporting*, Wiley, 1996.

C. A. Tilt, 'Environmental policies of major companies: Australian evidence', *British Accounting Review*, 1997, Vol. 29(4), pp. 367–394.

T. Tinker and T. Puxy, *Policing Accounting Knowledge – The Market for Excuses Affair*, Paul Chapman Publishing, 1995.

G. Tower, 'A public accountability model of the accounting profession', *British Accounting Review*, 1992, Vol. 25(1), pp. 61–86.

Exercises
....

An extract from the solution is provided in the appendix at the end of the text for exercises marked with an asterisk (*).

* Question I

The following information relates to the Plus Factors Group plc for the years to 30 September 20X8 and 20X9:

	Notes	20X9 £000	20X8 £000
Associated company share of profit		10.9	10.7
Auditors' remuneration		12.2	11.9
Creditors for materials			
At beginning of year		1,109.1	987.2
At end of year		1,244.2	1,109.1
Debtors			
At beginning of year		1,422.0	1,305.0
At end of year		1,601.0	1,422.0
11% Debentures	1	500.0	600.0
Depreciation		113.7	98.4
Employee benefits paid		109.9	68.4
Hire of plant, machinery and vehicles	2	66.5	367.3
Materials paid for in year		3,622.9	2,971.4
Minority interest in profit of the year		167.2	144.1
Other overheads incurred		1,012.4	738.3
Pensions and pension contributions paid		319.8	222.2

Profit before taxation		1,437.4	1,156.4
Provision for corporation tax		464.7	527.9
Salaries and wages		1,763.8	1,863.0
Sales	3	9,905.6	8,694.1
Shares at nominal value			
Ordinary at 25p each fully paid	4	2,500.0	2,000.0
7% Preference at £1 each fully paid	4	500.0	200.0
Stocks of materials			
Beginning of year		804.1	689.7
End of year		837.8	804.1

Ordinary dividends were declared as follows:

    Interim   1.12 pence per share (20X8, 1.67p)
    Final   3.57 pence per share (20X8, 2.61p)
    Average number of employees was 196 (20X8, 201)

Notes:

1 £300,000 of debentures were redeemed at par on 31 March 20X9 and £200,000 new debentures at the same rate of interest were issued at 98 on the same date. The new debentures are due to be redeemed in 5 years time.

2 This is the amount for inclusion in the profit and loss account in accordance with SSAP 21.

3 All the groups' sales are subject to value added tax at 15% and the figures given include such tax. All other figures are exclusive of value added tax.

4 All shares have been in issue throughout the year.

The statement of value added is available for 20X8 and the 20X9 statement needs to be completed.

	Workings	£000	
Turnover	1	7,560.1	
Less: Bought-in materials and services	2	4,096.4	
Value added by group		3,463.7	
Share of profits of Associated company		10.7	
		3,474.4	
Applied in the following ways			
To pay employees	3	2,153.6	62.0%
To pay providers of capital	4	566.5	16.3%
To pay government		527.9	15.2%
To provide for maintenance and expansion of assets	5	226.4	6.50%
		3,474.4	100.0%
Workings			
1 *Turnover*			
Sales inclusive of VAT		8,694.1	
VAT at 15%		1,134.0	
		7,560.1	

2 *Bought-in materials and services*
  Cost of materials

Creditors at end of year	1,109.1
Add: Payments in year	2,971.4
	4,080.5
Less: Creditors at beginning of year	987.2
Materials purchased in year	3,093.3
Add: Opening stock	689.7
Less: Closing stock	(804.1)
Materials used	2,978.9
Add: Cost of bought-in services	
Auditors' remuneration	11.9
Hire of plant, machinery and vehicles	367.3
Other overheads	738.3
	4,096.4

3 *To pay employees*

Benefits paid	68.4
Pensions and pension contributions	222.2
Salaries and wages	1,863.0
	2,153.6

4 *To pay providers of capital*
  Debenture interest

11% of £600,000	66.0
Dividends	
Preference 20X8 7% of £200,000	14.0
Ordinary 20X8 8 million shares at 4.28p	342.4
Minority interest	144.1
	566.5

5 *To provide for maintenance and expansion of assets*

Profit before tax	1,156.4
Less: tax	(527.9)
: minority interest	(144.1)
: dividends	(356.4)
Retained profits	128.0
Depreciation	98.4
	226.4

Required:

(a) **Prepare a statement of value added for the year to 30 September 20X9. Include a percentage breakdown of the distribution of value added.**

(b) **Produce ratios related to employees' interests based on the statement in (a) and explain how they might be of use.**

(c) **Explain briefly what the difficulties are of measuring and reporting financial information in the form of a statement of value added.**

Question 2

David Mark is a sole trader who owns and operates supermarkets in each of three villages near Ousby. He has drafted his own accounts for the year ended 31 May 20X4 for each of the branches. They are as follows:

	Arton		*Blendale*		*Clifearn*	
	£	£	£	£	£	£
Sales		910,800		673,200		382,800
Cost of sales		633,100		504,900		287,100
Gross profit		277,700		168,300		95,700
Less: Expenses:						
David Mark's salary	10,560		10,560		10,560	
Other salaries and wages	143,220		97,020		78,540	
Rent			19,800			
Rates	8,920		5,780		2,865	
Advertising	2,640		2,640		2,640	
Delivery van expenses	5,280		5,280		5,280	
General expenses	11,220		3,300		1,188	
Telephone	2,640		1,980		1,584	
Wrapping materials	7,920		3,960		2,640	
Depreciation:						
Fixtures	8,220		4,260		2,940	
Vehicle	3,000	203,620	3,000	157,580	3,000	111,237
Net profit/(loss)		74,080		10,720		(15,537)

The figures for the year ended 31 May 20X4 follow the pattern of recent years. Because of this, David Mark is proposing to close the Clifearn supermarket immediately.

David Mark employs twelve full-time and twenty part-time staff. His recruitment policy is based on employing one extra part-time assistant for every £30,000 increase in branch sales. His staff deployment at the moment is as follows:

	Arton	Blendale	Clifearn
Full-time staff (including managers)	6	4	2
Part-time staff	8	6	6

Peter Gaskin, the manager of the Clifearn supermarket, asks David to give him another year to make the supermarket profitable. Peter has calculated that he must cover £125,500 expenses out of his gross profit in the year ended 31 May 20X5 in order to move into profitability. His calculations include extra staff costs and all other extra costs.

Additional information:

1 General advertising for the business as a whole is controlled by David Mark. This costs £3,960 per annum. Each manager spends a further £1,320 advertising his own supermarket locally.

2 The delivery vehicle is used for deliveries from the Arton supermarket only.

3 David Mark has a central telephone switchboard which costs £1,584 rental per annum. Each supermarket is charged for all calls actually made. For the year ended 31 May 20X4 these amounted to:

Arton	£2,112
Blendale	£1,452
Clifearn	£1,056

Required:

(a) A report addressed to David Mark advising him whether to close Clifearn supermarket. Your report should include a detailed financial statement based on the results for the year ended 31 May 20X4 relating to the Clifearn branch.

(b) Calculate the increased turnover and extra staff needed if Peter's suggestion is implemented.

(c) Comment on the social implications for the residents of Clifearn if (1) David Mark closes the supermarket, (2) Peter Gaskin's recommendation is undertaken.

* **Question 3**

(a) You are required to prepare a value added statement to be included in the corporate report of Hythe plc for the year ended 31 December 20X6, including the comparatives for 20X5, using the information given below:

	20X6 £000	20X5 £000
Fixed assets (net book value)	3,725	3,594
Debtors	870	769
Creditors	530	448
14% Debentures	1,200	1,080
6% Preference shares	400	400
Ordinary shares (£1 each)	3,200	3,200
Sales	5,124	4,604
Materials consumed	2,934	2,482
Wages	607	598
Depreciation	155	144
Fuel consumed	290	242
Hire of plant and machinery	41	38
Salaries	203	198
Auditors' remuneration	10	8
Corporation tax provision	402	393
Ordinary share dividend	9p	8p
Number of employees	40	42

(b) Although value added statements were recommended by *The Corporate Report*, as yet there is no accounting standard related to them. Explain what a value added statement is and provide reasons as to why you think it has not yet become mandatory to produce such a statement as a component of current financial statements either through a Financial Reporting Standard or company law.

Question 4

Gettry Doffit plc is an international company with worldwide turnover of £26 million. The activities of the company include the breaking down and disposal of noxious chemicals at a specialised plant in the remote Scottish countryside. During the preparation of the financial statements for the year ended 31 March 20X5, it was discovered that:

1 Quantities of chemicals for disposals on site at the year-end included:

      (A) Axylotl peroxide   40,000 gallons
      (B) Pterodactyl chlorate   35 tons

Chemical A is disposed of for an Italian company, which was invoiced for 170 million lire on 30 January 20X5, for payment in 120 days. It is estimated that the costs of disposal will not exceed £75,000. £60,000 of costs have been incurred at the year-end.

Chemical B is disposed of for a British company on a standard contract for 'cost of disposal plus 35%', one month after processing. At the year-end the chemical has been broken down into harmless by-products at a cost of £77,000. The by-products, which belong to Gettry Doffit plc, are worth £2,500.

2 To cover against exchange risks, the company entered into two forward contracts on 30 January 20X5:

      No. 03067   Sell L170 million at L1,950 = £1: 31 May 20X5
      No. 03068   Buy $70,000 at $1.60   = £1: 31 May 20X5

Actual sterling exchange rates were:

	L	$
30 January 20X5	1,900	1.70
31 March 20X5	2,000	1.38
30 April 20X5 (today)	2,100	1.80

The company often purchases a standard chemical used in processing from a North American company, and the dollars will be applied towards this purpose.

3 The company entered into a contract to import a specialised chemical used in the breaking down of magnesium perambulate from a Nigerian company which demanded the raising of an irrevocable letter of credit for £65,000 to cover 130 tons of the chemical. By 31 March 20X5 bills of lading for 60 tons had been received and paid for under the letter of credit. It now appears that the total needed for the requirements of Gettry Doffit plc for the foreseeable future is only 90 tons.

4 On 16 October 20X4 Gettry Doffit plc entered into a joint venture as partners with Dumpet Andrunn plc to process perfidious recalcitrant (PR) at the Gettry Doffit plc site using Dumpet Andrunn plc's technology. Unfortunately, a spillage at the site on 15 April 20X5 has led to claims being filed against the two companies for £12 million. A public inquiry has been set up, to assess the cause of the accident and to determine liability, which the finance director of Gettry Doffit plc fears will be, at the very least, £3 million.

Required:
Discuss how these matters should be reflected in the financial statements of Gettry Doffit plc as on and for the year ended 31 March 20X5.

Question 5

Examine the EPA's website and prepare one of the cases as a presentation to the group showing clearly how environmental accounting was used and the results of the exercise.
[http://www.epa.gov/opptintr/acctg/earesources.htm]

References

1   C. Lehman, *Accounting's Changing Roles in Social Conflict*, Markus Weiner Publishing, 1992, p. 64.
2   *Ibid.*, p. 17.
3   S.J. Gray and C.B. Roberts, *Voluntary Information Disclosure and the British Multinationals: Corporate Perceptions of Costs and Benefits, International Pressures for Accounting Change*, Prentice Hall, 1989, p. 117.
4   AICPA, *The Measurement of Corporate Social Performance*, 1977, p. 4.
5   M.R. Matthews and M.H.B. Perera, *Accounting Theory and Development*, Chapman and Hall, 1991, p. 350.
6   *The Corporate Report*, ASSC, 1975.
7   R. Gray, D. Owen and K. Maunders, *Corporate Social Reporting*, Prentice Hall, 1987, p. 75.
8   *Statement of Principles: The Objective of Financial Statements*, ASB, 1991, para. 9.
9   *Ibid.*, para. 10.
10 *Ibid.*, para. 11.
11 F. Okcabol and A. Tinker, 'The market for positive theory: deconstructing the theory for excuses', *Advances in Public Interest Accounting*, 1990, Vol. 3.
12 H. Sebreuder, 'Employees and the corporate social report: the Dutch case', in S.J. Gray (ed.), *International Accounting and Transnational Decisions*, Butterworth, 1983, p. 287.
13 *Ibid.*, p. 289.
14 *Ibid.*, p. 287.
15 AICPA, *op. cit.*, p. 243.
16 *Statement of Principles, op cit.*
17 R. Gray, D. Owen and K. Maunders, *op. cit.*, p. 44.
18 *Ibid.*
19 S.J. Gray and K.T. Maunders, *Value Added Reporting: Uses and Measurement*, ACCA, 1980.
20 B. Underwood and P.J. Taylor, *Accounting Theory and Policy Making*, Heinemann, 1985, p. 298.
21 *Ibid.*, p. 174.
22 M. Davies, R. Patterson and A. Wilson, *UK GAAP* (4th edition), Ernst & Young, 1994, p. 71.
23 R. Gray, D. Owen and K. Maunders, *op. cit.*, p. 48.
24 R.W. Perks and R.H. Gray, 'Corporate social reporting – an analysis of objectives', *British Accounting Review*, 1978, Vol. 10(2), pp. 43–59.
25 C. Lehman, *op. cit.*, p. 65.
26 Companies Act 1985, 4 Sec. 56.
27 Companies Act 1985, 6 Sch. Part I.
28 Companies Act 1985, 7 Sch. 9.
29 Companies Act 1985, 7 Sch. 11.
30 R. Hussey, *Who Reads Employee Reports?*, Touche Ross, 1979.
31 R. Gray, D. Owen and K. Maunders, *op. cit.*, p. 174.
32 H. Sebreuder, *op. cit.*
33 K.T. Maunders, 'Simplified and employee reports', in L.C.L. Skerratt (ed.), *Financial Reporting, 1981–82*, ICAEW, 1981, pp. 217–227.
34 *Goodwill and Intangible Assets*, ASB, 1995.
35 R. Gray, D. Owen and K. Maunders, *op. cit.*, pp. 161–167.
36 *This Common Inheritance*, Government White Paper, 1990.
37 KPMG Peat Marwick McLintock, *Environmental Considerations in Acquiring*, Corporate Finance Briefing, 17 May 1991.
38 M. Jones, 'The cost of cleaning up', *Certified Accountant*, May 1995, p. 47.
39 M. Campanale, 'Cost or opportunity', *Certified Accountant*, November 1991, p. 32.
40 D. Butler, C. Frost and R. Macve, *Environmental Reporting: Student Financial Reporting, 1991–92*, ICAEW, 1992, p. 60.

41 *Ibid.*, p. 62.
42 Sir Michael Lickiss, *Accountancy*, January 1991.
43 R. Adams, 'Accounting, the environment and the ACCA', *Certified Accountant*, August 1994, p. 56.
44 R. Gray, *The Greening of Accountancy: The Profession After Pearce*, ACCA Research Report 17, 1990.
45 C. Roberts, *International Trends in Social and Employee Reporting*, ACCA Occasional Research Paper No. 7, 1991.
46 R. Gray, *Accounting for the Environment*, Paul Chapman/ACCA, 1993.
47 ICAEW Environmental Steering Group, FRAG 12/95.
48 C. Hibbert, 'Green reporting: it's time the UK profession responded', *Accountancy*, October 1994, p. 98.
49 R. Bruce, *The Independent*, 25 October 1993, p. 29.
50 M. Brown, 'Greening the bottom line', *Management Today*, July 1995, p. 73.

CHAPTER 30

Ethics for accountants

30.1 Introduction

In this chapter we consider the following:

- The nature of business ethics
- The ethical code of business
- The background to business ethics
- The role of ethics in modern business
- The role of professional accounting ethics
- The role of the accountant as a guardian of business ethics

The issue of ethics is at the very centre of all societies. Every society, such as a nation, must operate according to some ethical guidelines, however idiosyncratic or singular they may seem to outsiders – without such guidelines the society would lapse into anarchy and eventual collapse. This also applies to sub-societies, e.g. a family, a group of friends or even a business organisation and in this chapter we introduce the student of accounting to the basics of ethics as they could be applied to business.

What do we mean by 'ethics'?

In any study a good starting point is the production of a working definition of the issue under consideration. The *Oxford English Dictionary* has one of the more accessible definitions of ethics, it states four possible views of ethics:

> Ethics can be defined as (i) the science of morals, (ii) moral principles, (iii) a philosophy **or (iv) a code**.

In this chapter we will adopt the fourth definition of ethics as **an ethical code**, i.e. we will concentrate on the bureaucratic view of how to operate ethics in practice. The other three views are more properly the domain of philosophers as they are really concerned with what ethics should be.

30.2 The nature of business ethics

Business ethics refers to the relationship of a business to three significant 'environments' or 'levels'. Each business seeks for a harmonisation (or even a compromise) between the three levels of ethics which are traditionally viewed as follows:

I The macro level

The macro ethical guidelines applied to a business in the national and international context are usually the result of political, cultural, legal and religious pressures.

2 The organisational level

The organisational ethical guidelines are the ethics specific to an organisation. In many texts they are referred to as 'corporate social responsibility'. The guidelines may be of long duration, e.g. the ethics of the original founders of the organisation (such as the Co-Operative Wholesale movement or the John Lewis Partnership) or short duration, e.g. the ethical beliefs of the current senior managers of the business and of the current trading partners in the industrial sector within which the organisation operates.

3 The individual level

Individual ethical guidelines or personal ethics refers to the ethics of each individual in the organisation. These are naturally the result of a much more varied set of influences or pressures. As an individual each of us 'enjoys' a series of ethical pressures or influences including the following:

● parents – the first and, according to many authors, the most crucial influence on our ethical guidelines;
● family – the *extended* family which is common in Eastern societies (aunts, uncles, grandparents and so on) can have a significant impact on personal ethics; the *nuclear* family which is more common in Western societies (just parent(s) and siblings) can be equally as important but more narrowly focused;
● social group – the ethics of our 'class' (either actual or aspirational) can be a major influence;
● peer group – the ethics of our 'equals' (again actual or aspirational) can be another major influence;
● religion – ethics based in religion are more important in some cultures, e.g. Islamic societies have some detailed ethics demanded of believers as well as major guidelines for business ethics. However, even in supposedly secular cultures, individuals are influenced by religious ethics;
● culture – this is also a very effective formulator of an individual's ethics;
● professional – when an individual becomes part of a professional body then s/he is subject to the ethics of the professional body.

How do professional ethics differ from those arising from parents and peers?

The essential difference is that the ethics handbook which governs the behaviour of all staff in an organisation are more likely to be formally codified. A code of behaviour may be written as a formal Statement of Professional Ethics or subsumed within the staff. The fact that the Code is formally specified means that it is capable of being policed with information systems in place to assist monitoring and enforcement.

Harmonisation

We have seen above that 'business' has a complex 'web' of relationships with various parties each operating with their own ethics guidelines. The task of the business is therefore to ensure effective operations whilst meeting the various ethical demands of all interested parties.

30.3 The ethical code of a business

There are two approaches to defining an ethical code, namely, the positive and normative approaches.

The rationale for the positivist approach

This places emphasis on the preparation of a formal, written ethical code for the guidance of all employees within an organisation. Such an approach is to be expected as, in all control models, it is considered to be essential to have a fixed, rigid standard against which to measure performance. Any ambiguities of performance measurement can lead to disputes and confusion. This is especially true with ethics as the term has a variety of meanings and constructs within the mind of each individual. It is, therefore, hardly surprising that a business tries to produce a 'hard copy' of ethics for the use of all interested parties.

There are many examples of ethical codes in practice and for further study reference can be made to the codes of the following organisations:

● Trusthouse Forte PLC – with its 'Company Philosophy' document.
● British Gas plc – with its 'Code of Conduct'.
● Royal Dutch Shell Group of Companies – with its 'Statement of General Business Principles'.
● BICC plc – with its 'Statement of Company Principles'.
● The Body Shop – which publish a considerable amount of information showing their belief in classic business ethics.

The limitations of the positivist approach

Key arguments against the positivist approach of written codes can be summarised as follows:

● **Status of the source**: the source, or who writes the code of ethics, can be a crucial question with the risk that ethical codes could be imposed on a business against the 'natural' beliefs of its employees. This is always a key danger in multinational companies where the management in the parent country may impose ethical beliefs on subsidiaries in other counties which are contrary to the cultural or religious beliefs of the host country.

● **Flexibility**: it is a well known axiom that rules once in place do tend to have an existence well beyond their appointed time and this could cause serious ethical problems. It is important that there are procedures in place determining how written codes may be changed to meet changing beliefs and customs.

● **Comprehensiveness**: it is questionable whether one written code can cover all the possible issues raised under ethics. It is a weakness of all codified rules that they tend to apply only to known or, at least, anticipated situations. As discussed under flexibility, procedures are required to cope with totally new and unexpected situations – ethical issues often fall into this category and new situations and potential conflicts are always arising which limits the effectiveness of a written code.

The rationale for the normative approach

The alternative approach is to adopt a more 'normative' ethical stance where a philosophy is developed for the business following a theoretical, religious or pragmatic approach as follows:

The theoretical approach

A business may take any one of the many theoretical stances on ethics. It is not the purpose of the chapter to go into detail but typically the business could adopt any philosophy including:

- **Utilitarianism,** as propounded by Jeremy Bentham (1748–1832) or John Stuart Mill (1806–1873), where individual happiness is balanced against the needs of society.

- **Deontological Philosophy,** as propounded by Immanuel Kant (1724–1804), revised by David Hare (b. 1919), which is a philosophy based upon perceived absolutes of 'right', 'wrong' and 'duty'.

- **Marxism and Post-Marxism,** based on the ideas of Karl Marx (1818–1883) and the post-marxists such as Herbert Marcuse (1898–1979), Roland Barthes (1915–1980) and Michel Foucault (1926–1984). Their views are of importance in multi-national situations and look at the imposition of ethics based upon economic power.

- **Post-Modernism,** put forward by those such as A.J. Ayer (1910–1989), Jean Francois Lyotard (b. 1924) and Jacques Derrida (b. 1930), has a particular resonance for business by offering an almost 'free market' approach to ethics.

- **Social Philosophy,** with the work of John Rawls (b. 1921) and Alasdair MacIntyr (b. 1929), who adopt a more community centred approach.

There are many theorists whose views can be explored for a deeper understanding of the approach.

The religious approach

This approach is applied when business ethics are formulated on some basic religious foundation, e.g. Judeo-Christian or Islamic or Hindu or Buddhist or Jainist.

The pragmatic approach

This is the approach where a business simply addresses each ethical problem as it arises and solves such problems by committee – the establishment of ethical committees is common place in many large organisations.

There are however difficulties with the approach which can be summarised as:

- Inefficiency: this is a very time consuming process and some issues are urgent and need a swift solution.

- Inconsistency: the approach can, over time, lead to inconsistencies and apparent changes of approach which can be embarrassing and confusing.

- Theoretical underpinning: there is the question of who is qualified to sit on such committees, which can be a major question for a business. In some hospitals in the USA philosophers are employed by hospitals to help medical staff address key ethical issues on a case by case basis. These philosophers however will operate from one of the theoretical standpoints highlighted above.

Thus the 'normative' approach, whilst being sound in concept, does raise enormous practical difficulties for business. This explains the reliance on a written code, which despite its drawbacks is at least accessible and in many ways 'reliable'.

30.4　The background to business ethics

A brief survey of the recent history of business ethics may prove useful at this point in our study.

The separatist view

In classical economic theory the business has only one purpose, as typified by the following précis of the ideas of Milton Friedman:

> Managers should single-mindedly pursue only one goal: the maximisation of profit for the benefit of shareholders. The invisible hand of the market then guarantees their actions contribute to social welfare in the best possible way.
>
> (Jeurissen 1995)

This view of ethics is often referred to as the 'separatist view' and assumes that the business will conform to some ethical standard because of the combined influence of the law (via governmental pressure) and the (almost magical) powers of 'market forces'. Thus it assumes that businesses will behave ethically because it makes sound business sense to do so!

The integration view

The alternative view proposed by Jeurissen in his Sankt Gallen lecture is known as the 'integration view'. This view recognises the impact of law and market forces but also gives the organisation a duty or responsibility to respond and reflect the views of the moral community within which it operates. In other words the business may well have a wider social responsibility with objectives broader than simply profit maximisation.

Thus society allows the business the freedom to operate on 'market lines' provided that the 'public' can rely upon the integrity of the management to operate for the wider benefit of society in the long term. It is the conditional nature of the freedom that makes business ethics important.

Promotion of business ethics

At an institute level, the Chair of the Institute of Business Ethics, Neville Cooper put the issue with remarkable clarity in 1987 when he said:

> Our conviction is that, essentially, industry and commerce are highly ethical undertakings. The ethical demands on us ... are to run them supremely efficiently, responsibly and with clear moral standards.[1]

At a corporate level, the Chairman of a major UK food company in referring to his company's code of ethics said:

> ... business ethics are not negotiable – a well founded reputation for scrupulous dealing is itself a priceless company asset and the most important single factor in our success is faithful adherence to our beliefs.

Management commitment to business ethics

This view of business ethics has its spiritual home in the development of codes of behaviour formulated in the United States since the 1960s and imported into Britain in the 1980s. Research carried out by the Institute of Business Ethics in 1987 in respect of the 300 largest UK companies did support this view, where the replies received did show ethics being taken seriously by senior management. Many ethical statements were shown to be published in the Annual Accounts and Report documents produced by these companies. This research supported other surveys especially that carried out by the journal *International Management* in 1982.

Well known failures to follow acceptable ethical practices

The importance of business ethics is also, sadly, reinforced by a series of high profile scandals caused by an obvious lack of business ethics. There are many examples including BCCI and the activities of the late Robert Maxwell with the Mirror Group of companies.

The issue of public confidence in business integrity is at the key of the continued acceptance of the freedom to operate within a market economy. It was as a result of such scandals that the Institute of Business Ethics was formed in 1987 to:

> ... clarify ethical issues in business, to propose positive solutions to problems and to establish common ground with people of goodwill of all faiths.

This, voluntary, organisation has been attempting to spread the issue of ethics and ethical behaviour across all business enterprises both nationally and internationally.

UK commitment to self-regulation

The self-regulation approach is a feature of the business culture of the UK. The work of the Cadbury Committee (1991, updated in 1992) helped the issue of corporate governance and managerial behaviour and the Greenbury Report (1995), which looked in detail at the issue of directors' remuneration packages, included an ethical view of such, again reflecting the usual UK approach. The Hampel Report (1998) reinforced the voluntary, self-regulatory nature of such views of business ethics.

Thus the issue of business ethics is seen to be a key feature of business success but ethics are (in the view of business) best 'enforced' on a voluntary basis.

30.5 The role of ethics in modern business

When considering the issues raised under business ethics a useful starting point is to examine the areas covered by the Ethical Codes published by the various organisations which indicate the key areas of concern.

I Conflicts of interest

These are always issues of concern as management must be concerned with the benefit of the organisation and they must not put personal gain ahead of the gain for the organisation. Where there is a possibility of conflict, the usual practice is for the manager (including directors) to declare an interest to their fellow managers who can then assess the actions of the manager in such a light. Ideally the manager should withdraw from taking decisions where s/he may gain personally, but this may not always be practical. The awarding of contracts, employment of relatives and share dealings are all areas of concern here.

Public perceptions

The manager needs to not only be behaving ethically but also to be **seen** to be behaving ethically. Recent issues in Parliament have highlighted the dangers of conflicts of interest and how even innocent conflicts can be seen to have a more sinister, ulterior motive. The whole issue of **insider dealing** has recently caused problems in respect of share options for directors and their actions in taking up the options at advantageous times.

2 Gifts

The practice of giving and receiving gifts in business has always been a very fine ethical question. Ideally gifts should not be seen as an inducement to promote business in a manner which is less than open and honest. However, gifts are often intended as a sign of goodwill and respect and have no other motive than this. The issue becomes even more cloudy when we consider corporate hospitality, e.g. are tickets for the Football World Cup given to potential customers a legitimate gift? An apparently innocent social event could be seen to have sinister overtones in the 'cold light of day'.

There is a normal, human need to show respect and the giving and receiving of gifts is a key part of this. Japan for example is an illustration of cultural ethical differences where gifts are commonplace in business. In most businesses the key factor is scale. Small, low value gifts are not perceived as a threat to ethical behaviour (diaries, low cost pens etc.) but high value gifts are not acceptable.

The issue also applies to the payment of 'bribes' to encourage business, totally unacceptable in the eyes of most managers but common practice in many countries and industries (e.g. the defence industry). Thus, ethically no bribes (however named) should be paid or received.

There is a growing concern over the use of gifts of cash, goods or services in relation to governmental officials. Such officials, by the very nature of their work, must be above reproach in respect of ethical behaviour. Unfortunately these officials are often very poorly paid and thus the temptation is great.

Commercial organisations must have very precise codes for dealing with governmental officials. This code must also cover the relationship with the official before, during and after the main business has been carried out. This is to prevent the temptation of payment paid later, even after the official has left government service, since the suspicion will always remain of unfair treatment.

3 Confidentiality

The business has secrets which could have commercial value if revealed, so the manager is required to maintain confidentiality. This does however raise itself a keen ethical point: what should the manager do if the organisation is carrying out an illegal or immoral act? In most codes of practice, published by organisations and professional bodies, secrecy must be maintained but there is, surely, a wider social element of the individuals duty to society? It is here that the concept of **whistle-blowing** starts to be a possible course of action. This involves the employee in informing an outside agency of the organisation's unacceptable behaviour. Most organisations would regard this as 'gross misconduct' and would dismiss the employee even though the employee was acting with the highest of motives.

Governments have seen the danger to individuals of this and have taken steps to prevent the victimisation of employees who whistleblow. The UK and USA governments are taking a lead in this approach. In the USA many organisations have **whistle-blowing hotlines** where employees can tell about unethical behaviour in confidence; in the UK there are professional organisations who provide this service to their members. An interesting approach to whistle-blowing can be seen in the work of the charity Public Concern at Work. They outline the process and protection offered to whistle-blowers on their website: *http://www.pcaw.demon.co.uk*.

4 Products and processes

It is becoming a recognised fact of business that society expects certain standards in respect of processes of production and products, and businesses could face severe censure if these standards are broken.

Processes

The environment is a major topic of concern so businesses have to be 'green' in their products and processes; this is very apparent in the oil industry.

Products

The product can also be an issue; for instance tobacco products cause major issues of concern for much of society. An additional example was the sale of 'alco-pops', the alcoholic drink in an apparent 'soft drink' form.

Selling practices

Selling practices can also cause concern as instanced by the concern voiced over the sale of baby milk substitute products in the Third World. Changes in marketing practices were demanded and were forthcoming because of ethical concerns.

5 Employment practices

The treatment of employees is also a major ethical concern for business; they need to be seen to be fair to their workers. This means looking, for example, at the status of women, ethnic minorities, older employees and disabled people within the workplace.

It also covers the employment of children, a very sensitive issue as evidenced by the recent court case of a major high street retailer taking legal action against a TV programme for suggesting they **knowingly** bought products from manufacturers overseas who employed child labour. Thus the ethics of an organisation in this area is a matter of interest to society.

Most business organisations of any size will take action to address these very real areas of societal concern within their formal, written, ethical code. It is here that the main ethical effort in business is concentrated.

30.6 The role of professional accounting ethics

Within the UK the various professional accounting bodies do provide their members with very detailed ethical guidelines. Accountants both in practice and in businesses are required to follow these guidelines in their normal patterns of work and can be punished individually for breaches of these professional codes of ethics. There are, however, two distinct approaches to ethics, one for the accountant in practice and another for those within business.

Accountants in practice

The accountant in practice has a considerable body of ethical support to work from, particularly if s/he is a member of one of the various Chartered Accountancy bodies.

These bodies (for England and Wales, Scotland and Ireland) publish guidelines covering key areas of accounting work and behaviour such as:

- their relationship with the client;
- the type of work they can do for the client;
- the way to safeguard independence;

- the standards of behaviour expected of accountants;
- the manner of dealing with conflicts of interest;
- the way in which they will behave in given situations such as take-overs, insolvencies and so on;
- the nature and type of advice they can give clients.

In April 1999 a new framework of non-statutory independent regulation for accountants was announced in response to the Government's Business Manifesto commitment to put in place a system of regulation that was transparent, effective and independent both of the profession and of other sectional interests. The framework built on the work carried out by a Working Group of the Consultative Committee of Accountancy Bodies (CCAB) chaired by Chris Swinson. The new framework ensures that the public interest activities of the six CCAB bodies (ACCA, CIMA, CIPFA, ICAEW, ICAI, ICAS) will be overseen by new bodies as follows:

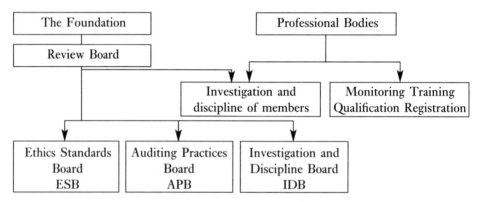

How will independence be achieved?

The intention is that matters of significant public interest should be dealt with by three separate new boards. There have been criticisms that their independence will be weakened because the funding is provided by the CCAB bodies. However, the Foundation will determine the amount of funding required and the CCAB bodies will not determine how the funds are applied; 60% of the members of each Board will be non-accountants; and the Review Board will have the authority to monitor the work of both the new Boards and the Professional Bodies. It will, of course, be important to appoint independent members of substantial experience to the Boards.

Will the new Framework be effective?

The Framework has taken a profession-wide approach to dealing with matters of public interest and is the result of detailed consultation between the Government, the Professional Bodies and members. The CCAB is committed to making it work and has established an Implementation Working Party to have detailed arrangements established by January 2000. In addition, individual CCAB bodies have begun taking proactive steps e.g. CIPFA has commenced a review of its Standards of Professional Practice, including the Standard on Ethics.

Accountants in business

The accountant working within business has a different set of problems due to the dual position as an employee and a professional accountant. There is a potential clash of issues where the interests of the business could be at odds with professional standards.

The various professional bodies approach things in different ways. For example, the ICAEW established the Industrial Members Advisory Committee on Ethics (IMACE) in the late 1970s to give specific advice to members with ethical problems in business. This is supported by a strong local support network as well as a national helpline for the guidance of accountants. At the moment IMACE is dealing with 200 to 300 problems per year but this is more a reflection of the numbers of chartered accountants in business than a reflection on the lack of ethical problems. A survey[2] carried out by the Board of Chartered Accountants in Business indicated that 11% of members had put their jobs on the line over ethical issues.

Type of ethical problems

The type of problem raised is a good indication of the ethical issues raised for accountants in business. They include:

● requests by employers to manipulate tax returns;
● requests to produce figures to mislead shareholders;
● requests in conceal information;
● requests to manipulate overhead absorption rates to extort more income from customers (an occurrence in the defence industries);
● requests to authorise and conceal bribes to buyers and agents, a common request in some exporting businesses;
● requests to produce misleading projected figures to obtain additional finance;
● requests to conceal improper expense claims put in by senior managers;
● requests to over- or undervalue assets;
● requests to misreport figures in respect of government grants;
● requests for information, which could lead to charges of 'insider dealing';
● requests to redefine bad debts as 'good' or vice versa.

These issues are also reflected by the other professional bodies, the Chartered Association of Certified Accountants (ACCA), the Chartered Institute of Management Accountants (CIMA) and the Chartered Institute of Public Finance and Accountancy (CIPFA). The last of these organisations has added problems in that there is an overt political dimension to many decisions taken as its members are working in Local Government and the concept of 'value for money' is becoming a key feature of their work. Cases in respect of local councils in Westminster and Doncaster have demonstrated the ethical difficulties encountered by CIPFAs in carrying out their duties within their very singular environment.

The accountant in business has this problem of dual ethical structures; they are professionals but they are also employees and on a surprising number of occasions there is a conflict between the two roles on ethical issues. The solution of this conflict causes many problems for the accountant who is left with only three possible solutions, namely:

1 Take some action by either informing a superior (letting them take some action) or by whistle-blowing to an outside agency such as the professional body, the police, the media or whatever. This may well cause the accountant some personal problems and is difficult if the superior is the 'guilty party'.

2 Resign on principle and leave the organisation with personal and professional ethics in tact but with a possibly damaged career.

3 Ignore the action and hope someone else notices the unethical behaviour and takes the appropriate action.

Each accountant has to face these choices at some time during their career and it is a test of character which choice is made. The choice itself may well be a function of the individual's own ethical background influenced by the factors mentioned earlier.

National and international regulation

It is likely that there will be an increase in formal regulation as the search for greater transparency and ethical business behaviour continues.

National regulation

Money Laundering

Auditors in the UK are required under APB Practice Note 12 *Money Laundering* to take the possibility of money laundering into account when carrying out their audit and to report to the appropriate authority if they become aware of suspected laundering. Certain businesses are identified as being more prone to money laundering e.g. import/export companies and cash businesses such as antiques, art dealers, auction houses, casinos and garages.

Whistle-blowing responsibilities

There is also a general requirement that where auditors become aware of suspected or actual non-compliance with law and regulation which gives rise to a statutory right or duty to report, they should report to an appropriate authority immediately e.g. where a company whose main activity is the development of a single property has not complied with planning regulations.

Breach of confidentiality

Auditors are protected from the risk of liability for breach of confidence provided that:

(a) disclosure is made in the public interest

(b) disclosure is made to a proper authority

(c) there is no malice motivating the disclosure.

International regulation

The OECD drew up a new anti-bribery convention making it a criminal offence for business executives to bribe foreign officials. The implication for accountants is that companies will have to ensure financial statements do not omit or falsify cases involving bribery and prohibit the establishment of off-the-books accounts for the purpose of bribing foreign public officials or of hiding the bribery. The convention has been ratified by major trading nations including the UK, US, Japan and Germany.

The recent events with the European Union Commission have highlighted the potential for ethical issues and the inevitability of whistle-blowing as being a logical step in the absence of an effective internal process for dealing with ethical issues. In this case, the whole Commission resigned due to the ethical malpractice of a few, brought to light by the public revelation of a 'whistle-blower' in the accounting function.

SEC investigations in the USA

In the early part of 2000, the US Stock Exchange Commission (SEC) was looking seriously at the 'big' accountancy firms and their ethical practices especially in two areas:

● The additional services offered to clients in terms of tax advice, management consultancy and general accounting support. In most companies the income from such work exceeds that of the traditional audit work. There is therefore a *de facto* clash of interests, which could lead to an audit report being influenced by commercial considerations.

● Members of staff in the audit firms need to declare a fiduciary interest in any firm they may audit and this requires detailed lists of employees' external interests to be maintained. Such lists are not readily available in most audit firms.

The SEC is threatening action if the audit firms do not produce and implement policies to address these issues as a matter of urgency.

30.7 The role of the accountant as guardian of business ethics

There is therefore an established need for business ethics but the question arises who can police the organisation for ethical breaches? This is a crucial question as any set of rules is only as effective as its enforcement mechanism allows it to be.

There needs to be some sort of 'ethical guardian' who can police the code of ethics within an organisation to bring out any unethical practices and ensure that corrective action is taken as appropriate.

There are 'ethics committees' in some organisations which act as a court to judge ethical breaches, but in themselves they are only part of the guardian function.

It is therefore a possible function of an accountant's role to be the guardian of ethics within a business because the following attributes are possessed by the accountant:

● skill – the accountant is trained in the establishment and management of control systems and ethics is simply another layer of control;
● stewardship – the accountant already acts as the steward of the shareholders' interests and the function is similar when discussing ethics;
● rule orientation – the accountant is a trained follower of rules and is accomplished at ensuring others obey stated rules and regulations;
● judgement – ethics requires the application of fine judgement, an attribute common in many accountants;
● professionalism – the accountant is one of the main professionals working within businesses and the attributes of a professional are essential to make judgements on ethical breaches.

The role of the accountant in practice

This could well prove to be a new area of responsibility for accountants in both practice and business and it is not without precedent. The work, for example, of the Audit Commission in the public sector is perhaps an indication of the future role of accountants in practice. The Commission does make judgements on the traditional accounting areas but it is also looking at other more subjective measures of performance within public sector organisations and perhaps this is a growth area, especially as the demand by society for more accountability in business becomes more powerful and politically impossible to ignore.

The role of the accountant in business

The accountant within business could also be seeing a growth in the ethical policing role as internal auditors take on the role of assessing the performance of managers as to their adherence to the ethical code of the organisation. This is already partially happening as conflicts of interest are often highlighted by internal audits and comments raised on managerial practices. This is after all a traditional role for accountants, ensuring that the various codes of practice of the organisation are followed. The level of adherence to an ethical code is but another assessment for the accountant to undertake.

Implications for training

If, as is likely, the accountant has a role in the future as 'ethical guardian', additional training will be necessary. This should be done at a very early stage, as in the USA, where accountants wishing to be Certified Public Accountants (CPAs) are required to pass formal exams on ethical practices and procedures before they are allowed the privilege of working in practice. Failure in these exams prevents the prospective accountant from practising in the business environment.

30.8 Growth of voluntary standards

Social, environmental and ethical reporting is at an early stage but it is receiving increasing attention from industry and commerce with the growing recognition that long-term shareholder value cannot be achieved without acknowledging responsibility to wider stakeholder groups.[4] There has already been stakeholder pressure for management to balance the interests of investors, employees, suppliers, customers and the public. Finally, industry, commerce and stakeholders are moving towards a common goal which is to provide innovative reports. However, this requires a commitment from the directors who are the ones who control the information and an acceptance of the fact that it is not appropriate to produce only favourable comments. This has now been recognised by some of our major companies, e.g. BT's 1999 Social Report.

The Institute of Social and Ethical Accountability was founded in 1996 as an international membership organisation, based in the UK. In November 1999 the institute launched a world first international processing standard, AA1000, enabling organisations to build quality into their existing and developing social and ethical management systems. The standard defines how companies should report on issues such as pollution and labour issues. Its objective is to encourage a collaborative approach, with inputs from stakeholders including interest and pressure groups. Two major concerns that have been voiced are:

● Companies should not see consultation with a wide range of stakeholders as an excuse to avoid their responsibility for dealing with adverse social and environmental effects.

● Credibility will only be achieved if there is an independent audit and there could be a risk of ineffectual auditing.

AA1000 addresses the latter point by setting out criteria for the social and ethical auditor, namely:

● Integrity

● Objectivity and independence

● Professional competence

● Professional behaviour exercising rigour, judgement and clear communication

● Confidentiality

● Due care to stakeholders.[5]

AA1000 will provide a consistent measure of performance and a uniform basis for reporting but the institute recognises that this is a dynamic field and plans to keep the standard under constant review. In this it resembles the ASB policy of revisiting FRSs when there has been experience and feedback from stakeholders and management.

Summary

In this chapter we have attempted to explain how business ethics has adopted the definition of ethics as **an ethical code** in order to have a mechanism that (a) makes the ethical expectations of the business clear to staff and other stakeholders and (b) allows performance to be monitored. Although ethics are often perceived as a qualitative or philosophical matter, there is a public expectation and demand for quantitative measures – after all, we live in the age of performance criteria and league tables!

Accountability requires that a report should be made to relevant parties if the monitoring provides evidence that there has been a breach of the code. The relevant party would depend on the nature of the breach, e.g. petty dishonesty by junior staff might be reported to the immediate line manager, fraud by senior managers reported to the audit committee and material misrepresentation of the profit reported to the shareholders.

The accountant is heavily involved with ethical issues as a member of society, as a member of a professional body with a formal code of ethics and as a member/employee of a business. The prevalence of the self-regulation ethos in the UK also supports directors delegating to the accountant responsibility for ethical policing.

Accountants' expertise in designing systems and measuring compliance leaves them in a strong position to undertake the monitoring of the ethical code and, as with all control systems, there will be a continuing need to balance costs and benefits. It would, for example, be uneconomic to require all staff to take a truth test to support every expense claim that was lodged!

It is interesting to note that the Auditing Practices Board is actively considering an approach to the government to provide auditors with greater powers in relation to fraud. Given that companies might be reluctant to increase the fees paid to auditors, there might well be a case for state funding for monitoring that is a form of ethical policing. One attraction of this might be that there would be pressure from the government to formulate an ethical code. It is a strength of the self-regulatory ethos that best practice trickles down but it can trickle mighty slowly!

Review questions

1 Outline **three** areas where ethics and ethical behaviour are of importance to business.

2 Discuss the role of the accounting profession in the issue of ethics.

3 How might a company develop a code of ethics for its own use?

4 Outline the advantages and disadvantages of a written code of ethics.

5 (a) Obtain an ethical statement from:
      (i) a commercial organisation;
      (ii) a charitable organisation.
   (b) Review each statement for content and style.
   (c) Compare each of the two statements and highlight any areas of difference which, in your view, reflect the different nature of the two organisations.

6 In each of the following scenarios outline the ethical problem and suggest ways in which the organisation may solve the problem and prevent its reoccurrence.
   (a) The use by a director's wife of his company car for shopping.
   (b) The inclusion of groceries bought for personal use on a director's company credit card.
   (c) The director is sent overseas on business with a business air ticket but he converts it to two economy class tickets and takes his wife with him.

(d) A director negotiates a contract for management consultancy services but it is later revealed that her husband is a director of the management consultancy company.

(e) The director of a company hires her son for some holiday work within the company but does not mention the fact to her fellow directors.

(f) You are the accountant to a small engineering company and you have been approached by the Chairman to authorise the payment of a fee to an overseas government employee in the hope that a large contract will be awarded.

(g) Your company has had some production problems which have resulted in some electrical goods being faulty (possibly dangerous) but all production is being despatched to customers regardless of condition.

(h) Your company is about to sign a contract with a repressive regime in South America for equipment which **could** have a military use. Your own government has given you no advice on this matter.

(i) Your company is in financial difficulties and a large contract has just been gained in partnership with an overseas supplier who employs children as young as seven years old on their production line. The children are the only wage earners for their families and there is no welfare available in the country where they live.

(j) You are the accountant in a large manufacturing company and you have been approached by the manufacturing director to prepare a capital investment proposal for a new production line. After your calculations the project meets **none** of the criteria necessary to allow the project to proceed but the director instructs you to change the financial forecast figures to ensure the proposal is approved.

(k) Review the last week's newspapers and select **three** examples of failures of business ethics and justify your choice of examples.

(l) At the year-end goods are despatched although not tested in order to improve the current year's sales figures. The management fully expect returns to be made but not within the period prior to the auditor signing the accounts.

7 Select one philosophical viewpoint of ethics and prepare a single A4 piece of paper with a set of notes summarising the viewpoint.

8 With your researches produced for question 7 discuss how this viewpoint may be applied to a **named** business of your choice to help develop appropriate ethics for this business.

9 Discuss the contention that the only purpose of business is the maximisation of profit for shareholders.

10 Discuss the following:

(a) Why an accountant should be involved with designing or monitoring ethical codes.

(b) What additional training this would require.

(b) How an accountant could become an effective 'guardian of business ethics'.

11 Confidentiality means than an accountant in business has a loyalty to the business which employs him/her which is greater than any commitment to a professional code of ethics. Discuss.

12 Lord Borrie QC has said[3] of the Public Interest Disclosure Bill that comes into force in 1999 that the new law would encourage people to recognise and identify with the wider public interest, not just their own private position and it will reassure them that if they act reasonably to protect the legitimate interest of others, the law will not stand idly by should they be vilified or victimised. Confidentiality should only be breached, however, if there is a statutory obligation to do so. Discuss.

References

1 Simon Webley, *Company Philosophies and Codes of Business Ethics*, Institute of Business Ethics (1988) (source 1 in the text).
2 Dispute Resolution, *Accountancy*, May 1998, p. 99.
3 Andrew Bolger, *Financial Times*, 2 July 1998, p. 10.
4 John Plender, *Financial Times*, 15 July 1999.
5 W. Raven, 'Social auditing', *Internal Auditor*, February 2000, p. 8.

Bibliography

Tom Burke and Julie Hill, *Ethics Environment and the Company*, Institute of Business Ethics, 1990.
T. Cannon, *Corporate Responsibilty. A Textbook on Business Ethics, Governance, Environment: Roles and Responsiblities*, Pitman, 1994.
Neville Cooper, *What's All This About Business Ethics*, Institute of Business Ethics, 1989.
J. Donaldson, *Key Issues in Business Ethics*, Academic Press, 1989.
Trevor Gambling and Rifaat Ahmed Abdel Karim, *Business and Accounting Ethics in Islam*, Mansell, 1991.
R.M. Green, *The Ethical Manager: A New Method for Business Ethics*, Macmillan, 1994.
B. Harvey (ed.), *Business Ethics: A European Approach*, Prentice Hall, 1994.
V. Henderson, *What's Ethical in Business?* McGraw Hill, 1992.
ICAEW, *Guide to Professional Ethics*, ICAEW Members Handbook, Vol. 1, 1996.
Institute of Business Ethics, *Take-overs – What Ethical Considerations Should Apply?* Institute of Business Ethics, 1990.
Institute of Applied Professional Ethics – http://www.cats.ohiou.edu/ethics.
International Business Ethics Institute – http://www.business-ethics.org.
H. van Luijk, *Business Ethics: The Field and its Importance*, Prentice Hall, 1994.
Jack Maurice, *Accounting Ethics*, Pitman Publishing, 1996.
Peter Pratley, *The Essence of Business Ethics*, Prentice Hall, 1995.
M. Velasquez, *Business Ethics, Concepts and Cases*, Prentice Hall, 1992.
Simon Webley, *Business Ethics and Company Codes*, Institute of Business Ethics, 1992.
Simon Webley, *Codes of Business Ethics*, Institute of Business Ethics, 1993.
Simon Webley, *Apply Codes of Business Ethics*, Institute of Business Ethics, 1995.
Simon Webley, *Codes of Ethics and International Business*, Institute of Business Ethics, 1997.

Outline solutions to selected exercises

Chapter 1

Question 1

(a) (i) (£000)	Jan	Feb	Mar	Apr	May	Jun
Cash balance c/f	17.55	(17.85)	(70.05)	(51.75)	(55.95)	(47.25)

(ii) Operating cash flow at 30 June 20X1   (143.55)

Question 2

(b) (£000)	Jan	Feb	Mar	Apr	May	Jun
Cash balance c/f	(28.80)	(26.40)	(18.10)	(12.10)	(7.70)	(0.80)

(c) Operating cash flow at 30 June 20X8   £29.20

Chapter 2

Question 1

(a) (£000)	Jan	Feb	Mar	Apr	May	Jun
Cash balance c/f	17.25	(17.25)	(69.75)	(74.25)	(63.75)	(4.65)

(b) Net profit	£47.90
Net capital employed	£263.90

Question 2

(b) (£000)	Jan	Feb	Mar	Apr	May	Jun
Cash balance c/f	85.90	67.50	87.15	104.95	119.55	142.30

(c) Net profit	£34.87
Net capital employed	£184.87

Question 4

(a) Sales = £138,040; Cost of sales = £77,720; Net loss = £1,360; Net capital employed = £7,840

Chapter 3

Question 2

Economic income: $Y_1 = £153$, $Y_2 = £168$, $Y_3 = £185$

Question 3

(a) (i) Accounting income = £36,700; (ii) Realisable income = £26,200; (iii) Economic income *ex ante* = £27,894; (iv) Economic income *ex post* = £35,000

Chapter 4

Question 1

	£
GPP net profit before loss on monetary items =	263,859
Loss on monetary items =	(142,003)
GPP net profit	121,856
RCA profit =	236,083
NRV operating gain =	241,800
Holding gain =	18,188
	259,988

Question 2

(i) Net profit = £13,052; Realised holding gains = £5,148; Unrealised holding gains = £43,802

Question 3

(i) Net profit = £16,532; Gains = £1,135; Losses = £704

Chapter 5

Question 1 Income statements and balance sheets show:

(i) Historical profit = £3,800; Total assets £13,800

(ii) *CPP*: Monetary gains = £11,200; Monetary losses = £(6,000); Net income = £10,720; Total assets £23,520

(iii) *Replacement cost*: Realised holding gains = £3,200 (Fixed assets £1,200 + Stock £2,000); Unrealised holding gains = £6,900 (Fixed assets £4,800 + Stock £2,100); Net income = £10,700; Total assets £20,700

(iv) *Continuous contemporary accounting*: Operating income = £5,000; Price variation adjustments = £(1,900); Capital maintenance £(2,800); Net income = £300; Total assets £13,100

Question 2 (£000)

(a) (i) Cost of goods sold = £39,162; (ii) Stock = £11,735; (iii) Depreciation charge = £10,083 or £10,614; (iv) Equipment = £49,822

Question 3

(a) MWCA = £6,190

Chapter 7

Question 1

(a) Turnover = £200; Charge for goods sold = £64; Wealth created by operations = £97

(b) Realisable increase in net assets = £157

Chapter 8

Question 1 (£000)

(a) Gross profit = £5,724; Profit before tax = £2,795; Profit for year = £2,233; Retained profit = £1,871

(b) Trading profit = £2,820; Profit on ordinary activities before tax = £2,795; Amount to reserves = £1,871

Question 2 (£000)

(a) Profit before tax = £14,243; Profit for year = £9,059; Retained profit = £7,985

Chapter 9

Question 1 (£000)

(a) Gross profit = £12,000; Operating profit – continuing operations = £6,710, discontinued operations = £210; Profit after tax = £4,970

Question 2 (£000)

(a) Gross profit = £1,902.9; Profit after tax = £447

(b) Net capital employed = £1,938; Net current assets = £285

Chapter 10

Question 1

(a) Distributable profit for private company A = £95,000

(b) Distributable profit for public company A = £95,000

Question 3

(b) Alpha plc maximum distribution = £2,844,000; Beta plc = £200,000; Gamma plc = (£2,800,000)

Chapter 11

Question 3

(ii) Sundry assets = £32,170,000; Cash = £6,185,000; Share capital = £18,900,000; CRR = £500,000; Share premium = £4,380,000; Retained profits = £1,755,000; Debentures = £2,400,000; Creditors = £10,420,000

Question 5

(a) *Balance sheet as at 31 Dec 20X1*: Ordinary shares = £1,005,000; CRR = £80,000; Reserves = (£380,000); Debentures = £400,000; Creditors = £400,000

Chapter 12

Question 1

Finance charge for year 1 = £284,375; Carrying value in balance sheet = £2,309,375

Question 2

Finance charge for year 1 = £58,900; Balance sheet = £958,900

Chapter 13

Question 2

(a) (i) Deferred tax provision – *deferral method*
19X1 = £487.50; 19X2 = £819.53; 19X3 = £834.18; 19X4 = £619.73; 19X5 = £233.89

(ii) Deferred tax provision – *liability method*
19X1 = £487.50; 19X2 = £800.78; 19X3 = £815.43; 19X4 = £586.36; 19X5 = £182.52

Chapter 14

Question 3

(a) £11,700

Question 4

The solution for Years 1 and 2:

(a) Year 1 Depreciation = £5,914.43; Income from secondary assets = £0; Interest = £3,000;
Net profit = £22,085.57

Year 2 Income from secondary assets = £437.16; Interest = £2,562.84

Chapter 15

Question 1

(a) Fixed asset = £306,250; Liability = £310,000; Interest = £52,500; Depreciation = £43,750

Question 2

(b) Depreciation 20X8 = £2,000; Finance charges 20X8 = £1,200; Liability 31 Mar 20X8 = £12,200

Chapter 16

Question 3

(i) *Balance c/f*: R&D costs account = £500,000; Laboratory account cost = £500,000;
Depreciation = £45,000; Equipment cost = £225,000; Depreciation = £70,000

Question 6

(a) Net capital employed = £3,082,000; Minority interest = £240,000; Net current assets = £2,600,000; Fixed assets = £780,000; Intangible assets = £42,000

Chapter 17

Question 2

(i) *Cost of goods sold*: FIFO = £2,648, LIFO = £2,626, Weighted average = £2,638

Question 3

Raw materials = £14,000; Finished units = £35,000; Semi-finished units = £10,000

Chapter 18
....

Question 2

Long-term contracts = £214,000. Amounts recoverable on long-term contracts = £108,000; Payments on account = £165,000; Provision for foreseeable losses = £45,000

Question 3

(b) Stock = £3,000; Long-term contracts = £14,900; Amount recoverable on long-term contract £30,000

Chapter 19
....

Question 1

Parent company accounts: Investment in subsidiary = £10,800

Question 2

Group accounts: Capital and reserves = £61,200

Question 3

Parent company accounts: Investment in subsidiary = £16,200; Group accounts: Capital and reserves = £61,200

Question 4

Group accounts: Negative goodwill = (£4,800)

Question 6

Share capital = £21.6m; Retained profit = £65.0m; Share premium = £22.4m; Fixed assets = £89.4m; Current assets = £38.8m; Current liabilities = £26.2m; Goodwill = £7.0m

Question 7

Share capital = 21.6m; Retained profit = £72.0m; Capital reserve = £8.4m; Fixed assets = £89.4m; Current assets = £38.8m; Current liabilities = £26.2m

Question 8

(a) Merger basis capital employed = £19m; (b) Acquisition basis capital employed = £23m

Question 9

(b) Share capital = £415,000; Consolidated reserves = £109,200; Cost of control = £78,600; Minority interest = £20,800

Chapter 20
....

Question 3

Capital and reserves = £192,600; Minority interest = £28,750; Total capital employed = £271,350

Question 5

(a) *Consolidated balance sheet* (£000): Fixed assets (net) = £4,364; Stock = £840; Debtors = £1,230; Bank = £160; Creditors = £816; Dividend = £36; Bank overdraft = £200; Share capital = £3,000; Unrealised reserves = £170; general reserve = £960; Profit and loss account = £912; Minority interest = £500

Chapter 21
·····················

Question 2

(a) Profit after tax = £230,000; Retained profit = £130,000; Share capital and reserves = £840,000

Question 3

(a) Profit after tax = £234,000; Retained profit = £124,000; Share capital and reserves = £880,000

Question 4

(a) Retained profit = £130,000; Balance c/f = £185,000; Capital reserve = £20,000

Question 5

(a) Retained profit = £124,000; Balance c/f = £178,000; Goodwill = £24,000

Question 6

(a) Gross profit = £488,000; Net profit before tax = £195,000; Minority interest = £13,600; Balance c/f = £141,800

Fixed assets = £417,600; Net current assets = £198,060; Share capital = £180,000; Capital reserve = £234,000; Capital reserve on consolidation = £5,820; Profit and loss account = £141,800; Minority = £54,040

Chapter 22
·····················

Question 2

Exchange gains: Creditors = £24,000; Debtors = £200 gain on DM; Loan = £18,300; Exchange losses: Debtors = £360 on KR; Cost of sales = £400

Question 3

Exchange gains = £474,916

Question 5

(b) Exchange losses: Temporal method = £45,000; Closing rate method = £608,000

Chapter 23
·····················

Question 1

(a) (i)   BEPS for 20X1 = £2.29
          BEPS for 20X0 = £2.16 (restated)

Question 2

(a) 2,885,416 shares

Question 3

(a) Basic EPS for 20X6 = 2.53p; Basic EPS for 20X5 = 1.83p; (b) Fully diluted EPS = 2.53p

Question 4

(a) Basic EPS = 70p (b) Diluted EPS = 66.15p

Question 5

(a) Diluted EPS = £4.37

(b) Diluted EPS = £4.48

Chapter 24
....

Question 1

Net cash flow from operations = (£91,000); Returns on investments = (£20,000); Tax = (£220,000); Capital expenditure = (£319,000); Equity dividends = (£120,000); Management of liquid resources = (£20,000); Financing = £250,000

Question 2

(a) Net cash flow from operations = £503,000; Returns on investment = (£52,000); Tax = (£79,000); Capital expenditure = (£694,000); Equity dividends = (£76,000); Management of liquid resources = (£40,000); Financing = £232,000

Chapter 25
....

Question 2

Turnover = £271,897; Cost of goods sold = £184,890; Profit before tax = £25,362; Retained profit = £15,290; Fixed assets = £206,760; Net current assets = £25,048; Net capital employed = £181,808

Question 3

(a) Net cash flow from operating = £495,000; Servicing finance = £195,000; Taxation = £375,000; Capital expenditure = (£150,000); Dividend paid = £225,000

Chapter 26
....

Question 3

(a) Option 1: Profit Year 1 = £28,400; Year 2 = £28,400; Option 2: Profit Year 1 = £19,782; Profit Year 2 = £23,904; Option 3: Profit Year 1 = £23,800; Profit Year 2 = £26,050

Question 5

(i) Profit before tax = £174,500; retained earnings for year = £87,715

Chapter 29

Question 1

(a)

	20X9 £000
Employees	2,193.5
Providers of capital	735.7
Government	464.7
Asset maintenance	415.2

Question 3

(a)

	20X5 £000
Employees	796
Providers of capital	431
Government	393
Asset maintenance	214

INDEX
··············